AMERICAN INDIAN LANGUAGES

OXFORD STUDIES IN ANTHROPOLOGICAL LINGUISTICS
William Bright, General Editor

AMERICAN INDIAN LANGUAGES

The Historical Linguistics of Native America

Lyle Campbell

New York   Oxford
OXFORD UNIVERSITY PRESS
1997

Oxford University Press

Oxford   New York
Athens   Auckland   Bangkok   Bogota   Bombay   Buenos Aires
Calcutta   Cape Town   Dar es Salaam   Delhi   Florence   Hong Kong
Istanbul   Karachi   Kuala Lumpur   Madras   Madrid   Melbourne
Mexico City   Nairobi   Paris   Singapore   Taipei   Tokyo   Toronto   Warsaw

and associated companies in
Berlin   Ibadan

Published by Oxford University Press, Inc.
198 Madison Avenue, New York, New York 10016

Library of Congress Cataloging-in-Publication Data
Campbell, Lyle.
American Indian languages : the historical linguistics of Native America / Lyle Campbell.
p.   cm.—(Oxford studies in anthropological linguistics : 4)
Includes bibliographical references and index.
ISBN 0-19-509427-1
1. Indians—Languages. 2. Languages—America—Classification.
3. Languages—America—History. 4. Anthropological linguistics—America. I. Title. II. Series.
PM108.C36   1997
497'.012—dc20   95-31905

3 5 7 9 8 6 4 2

Printed in the United States of America
on acid-free paper

For Susan

PREFACE

This book is intended as a general survey of what is known about the history of Native American languages. I hope that it will resolve certain outstanding issues, contribute generally to understanding of the history of Native American languages, and stimulate further research. True to tradition in Native American linguistics and due to the dynamic nature of research in this field, this book should by no means be taken as a static statement of "That's how it is"; rather it is intended as a working model, representative of a changing and progressing enterprise. Since this is an enormous field, encompassing by some counts more than one-quarter of the world's languages, clearly no individual (even with abundant help from friends and colleagues) could hope to provide a complete, up-to-date, and unflawed treatment of the historical linguistics of Native American languages. Moreover, research in this field has involved certain highly publicized controversies in recent years, which are best taken as indicative of unresolved historical questions and as proof that the field is developing, in some areas at a rapid pace, making it a moving target—exciting, but hard to hit squarely in every detail in a broad survey of this sort. For that reason, perhaps, a warning (or even an apology) is in order here: Readers should be aware of possible omissions or inaccuracies that specialists may find. The vastness of the topic and the limitations of the available information make it almost certain that some such infelicities will be found in this book. Still, I hope these will be few. I have consciously chosen to attempt broader coverage, despite the attendant risks.

Lest this warning leave the wrong impression, let me hasten to add that I believe the coverage in this book is probably as generally representative and as accurate as can be hoped for, given current circumstances, and that the inevitable errors will be minimal in relation to the book's overall contribution as a reasonably detailed survey, and as an updating of this large field.

As advances are made in the field, some of the tentative, incomplete, and inaccurate aspects of this book will likely be completed and improved. The present state of Native American historical linguistic knowledge, the presentation of which is the major goal of this book, is exciting, and future research, some of which this book may help to foster, promises abundant and significant advances that are perhaps at present barely imaginable.

Christchurch, New Zealand   L.C.
July 1995

ACKNOWLEDGMENTS

I have received helpful comments, information, and input and feedback from many individuals in writing this book, and I wish to express my gratitude to them. The list includes Willem Adelaar, Peter Bakker, M. Lionel Bender, Cathy Bereznak, Karen Booker, William Bright, Catherine Callaghan, Rodolfo Cerrón-Palomino, Ives Goddard, Victor Golla, Kenneth Hale, Hans Hock, Jaan Ingle, William Jacobsen Jr., Terrence Kaufman, M. Dale Kinkade, Margaret Langdon, Roger Lass, Osahito Miyaoka, Elena Najlis, William Poser, Robert Rankin, and Richard Rhodes. Some of these friends and colleagues were extremely generous with their time and information, and all were very helpful in one way or another. None of these individuals should, however, be held responsible for any misuse I have made of their information or for claims I have made in this book with which they may not wish to be associated.

I am also thankful to Mary Lee Eggart of Louisiana State University, and to Michele Rogan and Lee Leonard, cartographers at the University of Canterbury, who produced the maps in this volume, for their expertise and for their patience in this difficult process; and to the Department of Geography and Anthropology at Louisiana State University for its support of the map production. Thanks are due as well to Megan Melançon for checking the French translations and to Heidi Quinn for help in preparation of the index. I thank the College of Arts and Sciences of Louisiana State University for a Faculty Research Award, which gave me one semester free from teaching obligations to work on this book. Although no other financial support was directly received for this project, several National Science Foundation grants I received over the years for work on various aspects of Native American languages afforded me experience and background important to the making of this book.

Ives Goddard's chapter, "The Classification of the Native Languages of North America" (in press), is cited with permission from the *Handbook of North American Indians,* published by the Smithsonian Institution. M. Dale Kinkade's chapter, "Languages" (in press), to appear in volume 12: *Plateau,* of the *Handbook of North American Indians,* is also cited with permission.

CONTENTS

MAPS

PHONETIC SYMBOLS

	Bilabial	Dental	Palatalized	Alveolar	Retroflex (apical)	Alveolar sibilants	Alveopalatal
Plain stops and affricates	p	ṭ	tʸ	t	ṭ	c	č
Glottalized (ejective) stops and affricates	p'	ṭ'		t'	ṭ'	c'	č'
Labialized glottalized stops							
Aspirated stops and affricates	pʰ			tʰ		cʰ	čʰ
Labialized aspirated stops							
Implosive stops	b'						
Labialized stops and affricates							čʷ
Voiced stops and affricates	b		dʸ	d		dz	ǰ
Voiced labialized stops							
Non-strident affricates	pf	tθ		tl			
Voiceless glottalized lateral affricate				tl'			
Voiced lateral affricate				dl			
Voiceless (plain) fricatives	f	θ			ṣ	s	š
Voiceless bilabial and labialized fricatives	φ						
Voiceless glottalized fricatives	f'					s'	š'
Voiced fricatives	v	ð				z	ž
Voiced glottalized velar fricatives							
Voiced bilabial and labialized fricatives	β						
Voiced lateral approximant				l			
Voiceless lateral approximant				ł			
Glottalized lateral resonant				l'			
Voiced alveolar approximant				r			
Glottalized alveolar approximant				r̉			
Voiced alveolar flap (tap)				ř			
Voiced alveolar trill				r̄			
Voiced nasals	m			n	ṇ		ñ
Labialized nasals							
Glottalized nasals	m̉			n̉			
Glottalized labialized nasals							
Voiceless nasals	M			N			
Glides (semivowels)	w						
Glottalized glides (semivowels)	ẘ						
Voiceless glides (semivowels)	W						
Nasalised glides (semivowels)	w̃						
High tense vowels							
High lax vowels							
Mid tense vowels							
Mid lax vowels							
Low vowels							

V·, V: vowel length
Ṽ, V̨   vowel nasalization, nasalized vowel
Cʰ   aspirated consonant
C'   glottalized (ejective) consonant
Cʷ   labialized consonant
Cʸ   palatalized consonant
Ç   retroflexed consonant
C̦   fronted consonant
b'   voiced imploded labial stop (in Mayan languages)

tl   voiceless alveolar lateral affricate
tl'   voiceless glottalized alveolar lateral affricate
c   voiceless alveolar affricate
dz   voiced alveolar affricate
q   voiceless uvular stop
G   voiced uvular stop
θ   voiceless interdental fricative
ð   voiced interdental fricative
X   voiceless uvular fricative
ŋ   voiced velar nasal

Retroflex (laminal)	Palatal (fronted velar)	Velar	Uvular	Glottal	Pharyngeal	Front unrounded vowels	Front rounded vowels	Central vowels	Back vowels
č	ḵ	k	q	ʔ	ʕ				
č'	ḵ'	k'	q'		ʕ'				
		kʷ'	qʷ'						
		kʰ	qʰ						
		kʷʰ							
		kʷ	qʷ						
	g̱	g	G						
		gʷ	Gʷ						
ṣ	x̣	x	X	h	ḥ				
		xʷ	Xʷ						
		x'							
	γ̱	γ	γ						
		(γ')	γ'						
		γʷ	γ̣ʷ						
		ŋ							
		ŋʷ							
		ŋ̣							
		ŋ̣ʷ							
	y								
	ỵ								
	Y								
	ỹ								
						i	ü	ɨ	u
						ɪ			ʋ
						e	ö	ə	o
						ɛ			ɔ
						æ			a

ñ   voiced alveopalatal nasal, voiced palatalized nasal
ř   voiced alveolar flap
r̃   voiced alveolar trill
ṣ   voiceless alveolar (apical) retroflexed fricative
š   voiceless alveopalatal retroflexed fricative
č   voiceless alveopalatal retroflexed affricate
φ   voiceless bilabial fricative

b = β   voiced bilabial fricative
tʳ = ṭ   voiceless retroflexed (post-) alveolar stop
ḥ   voiceless pharyngeal fricative
ʕ   voiced pharyngeal fricative
ʕ'   glottalized pharyngeal fricative
ł   voiceless lateral
M, N   voiceless nasals
w̃, ỹ   nasalized glides

NOTE ON THE CLASSIFICATION LISTS AND THE MAPS

In the lists in Chapters 4–6, which present the classification of languages in the various language families, the degree of relatedness among groups within these families is indicated by successive indentations for closer relationships. That is, the names of larger, more inclusive units (subgroups) appear nearer the left margin, while the names of subordinate members within higher-level groups appear indented under these more inclusive groups' names. In some instances there are several layers of such indentations, indicative of several degrees of linguistic relationship. Information concerning where the language is (or was) spoken is presented in italics; alternative names for each language are given in parentheses, and names of frequently recognized dialects are also shown in parentheses with an indication that these are dialects. The status of languages is shown in the following ways: a language that is extinct is indicated by a dagger (†) before its name; a language with 10 or fewer speakers is indicated by the word "moribund" in square brackets; a language with fewer than 100 but more than 10 speakers is indicated by the word "obsolescent" in square brackets.

The numbers in parentheses before each language family heading in Chapters 4–6 are merely a counting device for easy reference; these numbers do not correspond to the numbers of the languages on the maps. There are 58 distinct genetic units in North America (Chapter 4), 18 in Middle America (Chapter 5), and 118 in South America (Chapter 6). The numbers of the groups discussed in Chapters 4 and 5 are mine. The numbers of the groups discussed in Chapter 6 are those used in Kaufman 1990a, included here for ease of cross-reference and comparison; they are sometimes grouped together out of numerical sequence following Kaufman's 1994 order of presentation.

The maps referred to in Chapters 4–6 are found just after Chapter 9, in a section that precedes the notes at the back of the book. The maps have been redrawn based on several sources but reflect the groupings discussed in this volume.

AMERICAN INDIAN LANGUAGES

1

INTRODUCTION

In the beginning all the World was *America.*
John Locke, *II Civil Government,* chap. V, 49

What foles [fools] do fable,
 take thou no hede [heed] at all,
For what they know not
 they cal [call] phantastical.
Richard Eden, *The First Three English Books on
America* (Arber 1885)

NATIVE AMERICAN LANGUAGES ARE
spoken from Siberia to Greenland and from the
Arctic to Tierra del Fuego; they include the
southernmost language of the world (Yagan
[alias Yámana]) and some of the northernmost
languages (Eskimoan). They number into the
hundreds (or, better said, into the low thousands). Yet what do we really know about them
and their history? Where did they come from?
To what extent are they related to one another?
What does their study reveal about the past of
their speakers and about the American Indian
languages themselves? These and related matters
are the concerns of this book. In 1954 Morris
Swadesh counseled:

> At times some scholars despair of solving the
> difficult problems of remote prehistory and confine
> themselves to details of historical phonology or to
> the compilation of descriptive materials. . . . Lit-
> tle could be accomplished without the painstaking
> detailed concentration on small component prob-

lems, but it is also well from time to time to
reexamine the broad questions in light of accumulated data and understanding, so that we may be
better guided in our work. (1954b:306)

The aim of this book is to follow Swadesh's
advice and attempt to take stock of what is
known currently about the history of Native
American languages. In particular, it has often
been lamented of late that there is no recent
overview of the field or general assessment of
the state of American Indian historical linguistics
(see Adelaar 1989:254, Liedtke 1991:38). This
book is an attempt to fill that gap. The need for
such a work is clear, given that there is not even
a consensus on how many Native American
languages there are; estimates from respected
linguists have ranged from as few as 400 to
more than 2,500, with *The Ethnologue*'s 938
languages a comfortable, if somewhat generous, figure for still-spoken languages (Grimes

1988:740).[1] It is often assumed that masses of these languages have disappeared without a trace (see Lamb 1959), and indeed many have become extinct since European contact; many more are currently obsolescent and will certainly cease to be spoken in the near future. When it comes to the number of independent genetic units (language families and isolates[2]) the dispute is extremely intense; estimates range from one to nearly 200 (see Chapter 2).[3] The methods for classifying these languages are hotly debated, and even the standard methods employed throughout the history of historical linguistics have frequently been misinterpreted (see Chapters 2 and 7).

The typological structure of American Indian languages has been an important factor in the history of their classification; however, opinion has varied from assumptions that there is only one unified structural type, shared by all American languages, which unites them typologically and genetically (including Eskimo-Aleut, so-called Na-Dene, and in some extreme cases even the so-called Paleo-Siberian languages of northeast Asia; see Chapter 2), to opinions that there is greater typological diversity in the Americas than in the rest of the world combined (see Ibarra Grasso 1958:12, McQuown 1955:501). For example, Sapir and Swadesh felt that "it is safe to say that any grammatical category to be found elsewhere in the world is sure to have a near analog somewhere in the native languages of the new world" (1946:110). The number of migrations which brought languages to the New World and the dates when they took place, although not solely linguistic matters, are also sharply disputed at present. My goals in this book are (1) to present what is known about the history and classification of Native American languages, (2) to put into perspective some of the gaps in knowledge and the disagreements just mentioned, and (3) hopefully to resolve some issues and to contribute towards greater understanding of others.

Chapter 2 is a survey of the history of American Indian historical linguistic study, with special attention to the claims of the past and the methods that have been employed. Although some important aspects of this history have been misunderstood and hence misrepresented, it is seen here that the historical linguistic study of

Native American languages was usually up to date with the linguistic methods and theories of the day and not infrequently contributed significantly to them. The origin of Native American languages is the subject of Chapter 3. I attempt to clarify a number of misconceptions concerning the role of linguistics in the investigation of the origin (or origins) of languages in the Western Hemisphere. Chapter 4 is a historical linguistic survey of the noncontroversial North American language families and isolates; Chapter 5 surveys the families and isolates of Middle America, and Chapter 6 focuses on South American linguistic units.

The methods employed in the investigation of distant genetic relationships are reviewed and assessed in Chapter 7; this review resolves several currently outstanding issues concerning methods for the study of remote linguistic relationships. In Chapter 8 I apply the methods and criteria advocated in Chapter 7 to the evaluation of most of the main proposals of distant genetic relationships that have received attention in the linguistic literature. On the basis of the reevaluation of the evidence undertaken here, I recommend that several of these porposals be abandoned forever; the evidence for others is quite strong and these proposals should be considered probable or highly plausible. In some cases, however, the evidence proves inconclusive, meaning these proposals are to be neither embraced nor abandoned but require further investigation.

Chapter 9 surveys areal linguistics and the linguistic areas of the Americas as understood at present. A linguistic area involves the diffusion (or convergence) of structural traits across language boundaries. It is essential to understand linguistic areas if we are to comprehend the linguistic history of the Americas. In particular it is imperative to determine, where possible, whether shared traits are due to diffusion within a particular linguistic area or traceable to a genetic relationship (inheritance from a common ancestor).

The maps in this book represent the geographical picture of Native American languages at roughly the time of first European contact. However, because some groups were contacted much earlier than others, it is difficult to present a chronologically cohesive map in some instances. The blank spaces on some maps (for example, some maps for areas of South America) indicate areas of uncertainty; it is not known what language was spoken there at the time of contact.

In the remainder of this chapter, I attempt to dispose of a few misunderstandings concerning Native American languages and their history and to provide background information that is not taken up specifically in the subsequent chapters. I call attention to some general matters that often are not recognized or are forgotten in general discussions of these languages; it is hoped that this will contribute to a greater appreciation of these languages and of their history and geographical distribution. I touch on such matters as fakes and misrepresentations, misnomers, and pidgins and trade languages. In sum, I attempt to clear away the nomenclatural debris and certain misconceptions from the linguistic landscape that play no direct role in classification of the tongues of the Western Hemisphere; I also mention some of the particularly important contributions these languages have made to languages in the rest of the world.

What's in a Name?

The study of American Indian languages is complicated at times because there may be a variety of names by which a single language is (or was) known. For example, Hidatsa (a Siouan language) has also been called Minitari and Gros Ventre; Nahuatl (of Mexico) is also known as Aztec, Mejicano (Mexicano), and Nahua; Fulnió (of Brazil) is also called Fórnio, Carnijó, and Iaté (Yathé). The reverse problem is the application of a single name (or very similar names) to more than one language. For example, the name Gros Ventre has been applied to both Hidatsa (Siouan) and to Atsina (an Algonquian language) —a source of considerable potential confusion. "Montagnais" has been applied both to Chipewyan (Athabaskan) and to Cree-Montagnais (Algonquian) speakers in Canada, though linguists now restrict the reference to the Algonquian group (see Krauss and Golla 1981:80). In Mexico and Central America there are a number of languages called "Chontal" (Chontal of Tabasco [Mayan] and Chontal of Oaxaca [also called Tequistlatecan]), and several called "Popoloca,"

"Popoluca," "Pupuluca" (such as Popoloca [Otomanguean]; Sierra Popoluca, Sayula Popoluca, Oluta Popoluca [Mixe-Zoquean]; Pupuluca of Conguaco [affinity unknown]), and others. These names stem respectively from the Nahuatl terms čontal- 'foreigner' and popoloka 'to babble, speak unintelligibly, speak language badly' (see Brinton 1892; see also Chapter 5). J. Alden Mason's description of such problems of nomenclature with regard to South American languages is quite to the point:

> The situation is further complicated by the fact that, in a large number of instances, the same or a very similar name was applied by colonists to several groups of very different linguistic affinities. This may be a descriptive name of European derivation, such as [Spanish] *Orejón* "Big Ears"; [Spanish] *Patagón* "Big Feet"; [Portuguese] *Coronado* "Crowned" or "Tonsured"; [Portuguese] *Barbados* "Bearded"; [Spanish] *Lengua* "Tongue [, Language]." Or it may be an Indian word applied to several different groups in the same way that the *Maya Lacandón* of Chiapas are locally called *"Caribs,"* and the rustic natives of Puerto Rico and Cuba *"Gíbaros"* [cf. Jívaro] and *"Goajiros"* [cf. Guajiro], respectively. Thus, *"Tapuya,"* the *Tupí* word for "enemy," was applied by them to almost all non-*Tupí* groups, *"Botocudo"* to wearers of large lip-plugs, etc. Among other names applied to groups of different languages, sometimes with slight variations, are *Apiacá, Arará, Caripuna, Chavanté, Guaná, Guayaná, Canamarí, Carayá, Catawishi, Catukina, Cuniba, Jívaro, Macú, Tapieté,* not to mention such easily confused names as *Tucano, Tacana* and *Ticuna.* Many mistakes have been made due to confusion of such names. (1950:163)

While this profusion of overlapping names can be confusing to the uninitiated, it means only that one must make certain which language is being referred to by such names in any given instance. Often Native American groups have no particular name for their language other than something equivalent to "our language," "the language," or "the true speech." The names by which they are now commonly known to outsiders or referred to in the professional literature were often given to them by neighboring groups, even by enemies; some of these names seem positive, others often seem negative, in Western perceptions. For example, Cuicatec (an Otomanguean language of Mexico) is from Nahuatl $k^w i \cdot ka$- 'song' + -te·ka- 'people of' (like English '-ite'), presumably reflecting the tonal contrasts that are characteristic of this language; however, Cuitlatec (an isolate in Mexico) has the Nahuatl etymology $k^w itla$- 'excrement, feces' + -te·ka- '-ite', presumably an unflattering appellation. Sometimes the result of this imposition of foreign names has been that languages became known by names that contain sounds absent from the languages themselves; for example, Nitinat and Makah (Nootkan languages) have no primary nasals, though the names by which they are known do. In Central America, several language communities have simply come to be known in Spanish (the politically dominant language of the region) by whatever names non-Indians apply to them. Tektiteko (Teco, Mayan) speakers were told by schoolteachers and missionaries that they spoke Cakchiquel (Kaqchikel); that is, it was recognized that they did not speak the Mam (a related Mayan language) found in the region, and so arbitrarily someone decided to call it Cakchiquel (Kaqchikel), though true Kaqchikel (a Mayan language from a different subgroup) is spoken rather far from the Tektiteko area. Locals commonly called Cacaopera (Misumalpan) of El Salvador "Lenca," though Lenca is an unrelated language that was spoken nearby. Instances of this sort can lead to errors of classification. To take one example, the fact that Chipaya was misleadingly called "Puquina" (an unrelated and totally distinct language, once culturally important but now extinct in the Andes) has lead to serious errors in proposed linguistic classifications (see Chapters 6 and 7).

Another source of confusion, and sometimes of hard feelings, which is the reverse of that just mentioned, is that in a growing number of Native American groups, the preferred self-designations, or "native" names, differ from those ingrained in the popular and professional literature. For example, the language that was traditionally termed Papago (and Pima) is now generally called O'odham by its speakers and by those involved with the language. A few other of the many examples of the differences between older, entrenched names and the more recently preferred "native" ethnonyms include "Navajo" (as well as other Athabaskan languages) and "Diné" (with various modifiers);

"Costanoan" and "Ohlone"; "Karok" and "Karuk"; "Kwakiutl" and "Kwak'wala"; "Yuma" and "Quechan"; "Tarascan" and "Phorhépecha"; "Ocuilteco" and "Tlahuica"; and "Mapuche/Araucanian" and "Mapudungu." This conflict poses a problem. On the one hand, the desire to promote the interests of the native groups involved and to respect their wishes (and sensitivities) calls for the use of the recent "native" names. On the other hand, the traditional names are so entrenched in the literature that it is virtually impossible to avoid using them, if current work is to be related to past research in these areas. My compromise in this book is to utilize both the newer self-designations and the better known, more traditional names when I am aware of them, though often with a predominance of reference to the latter. This may not be an entirely satisfactory result, but it comes from my own ignorance about what is currently preferred and of how established some of the more recent names may have become. No disrespect to any group is intended.

There are also several instances in the literature of mistaken linguistic identifications that complicated earlier classifications and only later were discovered and corrected. For example, some early classifications were based on older Spanish documents or on early explorer and military reports in western North America. Such reports asserted that Seri (an isolate) and Yaqui (Uto-Aztecan) were identical, that the Yuma (Quechan, Yuman) spoke Pima (Uto-Aztecan), and that Comanche (Uto-Aztecan) and Kiowa (Kiowa-Tanoan) were the same language (Gursky 1966a:404).

Another matter that bears mentioning is the spellings with which names have been represented. It is not uncommon, particularly in Latin America, for language names to appear in more than one, and sometimes several, spellings. A number of language names are known in versions that reflect both Spanish and Portuguese orthographic conventions, and also there is a tradition among linguists concerning how to write them, as in examples such as Shoco/Xokó, Capanahua/Kapanawa, and Ye/Je/Ge (see Chapter 6 for details). Terrence Kaufman (1990a, 1994), in attempting to eliminate such variation and the confusion that comes with it, has followed a spelling convention that roughly trans-

literates both the Spanish and Portuguese orthographic representations of names to a uniform
English system which is loosely based on renditions of the phonetics into a practical English
orthography. However, Kaufman's spellings,
which constitute yet another version, have not
been followed by linguists, who opt for the more
conventionally known versions of the names
(see Chapter 6). For the names of Mayan languages spoken in Guatemala, native Mayan linguists have chosen renditions of the names of
the languages that reflect Kaufman's orthography for Mayan languages and that also underlie
the system he uses in his 1990a and 1994 publications (for example, K'iche' rather than Quiché,
Kaqchikel instead of Cakchiquel, and so on).
Since these new spellings are preferred by native
Mayan groups and have been given official status in Guatemala, I use them here (but retain the
more conventional versions for non-Guatemalan
Mayan languages (such as Huastec, not Wasteko,
spoken in Mexico).

The cases mentioned in this section illustrate
some of the difficulties that are encountered with
respect to the vast number of names of Native
American languages. In this book, an attempt is
made to provide clear road signs through the
tangles in this nomenclatural underbrush.

Terminology

In addition to language names, the terms linguists use to designate levels of relationship
within their classifications can be confusing,
since they are not always used consistently and
there is often controversy concerning the validity
of the units that some labels are intended to
identify. It is important to clarify this terminology and to specify how such terms are used in
this book at the outset. We need clear terminology for a range of entities, each more inclusive than the level below it—something akin
to, but clearer than, Rasmus Rask's dialect-
language-branch-stock-class-race hierarchy
(Benediktsson 1980:22) and more utilitarian
than Sydney Lamb's (1959:41) too finely segmented phylum-class-order-stock-family-genus-
language-dialect ranking. I employ the following
terms.

Dialect here means only a variety (regional

or social) of a language, mutually intelligible
(however difficult this concept may be to define
or apply in practice) with other dialects/varieties
of the same language; it does not mean here, as
it does in the usage of some historical linguists
(especially in the past), a daughter language in
a language family.[4] *Language* means any distinct
linguistic entity that is mutually unintelligible
with other languages. A (language) *family* is a
group of genetically related languages, ones that
share a linguistic kinship by virtue of having
developed from a common earlier ancestor. In
this book, linguistic families are normally designated with the suffix *-an* (Algonqui*an*, Uto-
Azte*can*). In addition, I use the term *genetic unit,*
less commonly encountered in the literature, to
designate independent (or otherwise not known
to be related) families and isolates. However,
language families can be of different magnitudes—that is, they can have different time
depths, with some larger-scale families including
smaller-scale families as their members or
branches. Unfortunately, a number of confusing
terms have been put forward in attempts to
distinguish more inclusive from less inclusive
family groupings. The term *subgroup* (or *subfamily, branch*) means a group of languages
within a well-defined language family that are
more closely related to each other than to other
languages of that family—that is, they constitute
a branch of that family. As a proto language (for
example, Proto-Indo-European) diversifies, it
develops daughter languages (for example, Germanic, Celtic); if a daughter (for example, Proto-
Germanic) then subsequently splits up and develops daughter languages of its own (such as
English, German), then the descendants (English, German) of that daughter language (Proto-
Germanic) constitute members of a subgroup
(Germanic languages), and the original daughter
language (Proto-Germanic) becomes, in effect,
an intermediate proto language, a descendant
of the original proto language (Proto-Indo-
European), but with daughters of its own (for
example, English, German).

Terms that have been used for postulated but
unproven higher order, more inclusive families
(proposed distant genetic relationships) include
"stock," "phylum," and the compounding element "macro-" (as in macro-family, macro-
stock, and macro-phylum). These terms have

proven confusing and controversial, as might be expected when proposed names for entities that are not fully agreed to exist are at stake. *Stock* is ambiguous in that in older usage it was equivalent to "language family" (a direct transfer of the common German linguistic term *Stamm* [or *Sprachstamm*]); however, the term has often been used in America in the sense of a postulated but unconfirmed larger long-range grouping that would include more than one established language family or genetic unit. If the larger grouping were confirmed, it would simply become a language family, and the families that were its constituents would become subgroups of the more inclusive family. "Stock" has sometimes been employed in the literature to mean more inclusive, larger-scale families; in this book, however, when established families of different degrees of magnitude need to be distinguished, I speak of smaller-scale families (or subgroups) and larger-scale families. The terms *phylum* and *macro-* have also been used in this sense of large-scale or long-range proposed but unestablished families. To avoid confusion and controversy, I do not use these terms. The term *family* is both sufficient and noncontroversial. Since the entities called "stock," "phylum," and "macro-" would be bona fide language families if they were established and will not be families if the proposals concerning them fail to hold up, I refer to them simply as "proposed distant genetic relationship," "postulated family," "hypothesized remote affinity," and the like.

Voegelin (1942) and Voegelin and Voegelin (1965, 1985) argued that the methods used in American Indian historical linguistics (particularly by Sapir) for "family" linguistics differed from those used for "phylum" linguistics. However, Campbell and Mithun (1979b:46–50) insisted that the question of distinct methods comes up only in the case of preliminary proposals framed as hypotheses for further testing (where a variety of considerations often were at play—typological notions in particular), but that there was general agreement on what methods and evidence would be required to establish a family relationship. I agree with Alfred L. Kroeber:

> It has been suggested to me that while there is probably some underlying truth in most of the recent mergings of stocks, the kind of relationship involved may be of a different sort from what has heretofore been regarded as the relationship binding together the members of a linguistic family. I wish to express my absolute opposition to this attitude. . . . I recognize only one criterion of relationship: reasonably demonstrable genetic unity. Either two languages can be seen to have been originally one, or they cannot be seen to have been one. The evidence may be of such kind and quantity as to leave us in doubt for a time; but there can be no such thing as half-relationship. (1915:289)

(For more discussion and examples, see Lamb 1959; Liedtke 1991:44–5; Voegelin 1942; Voegelin and Voegelin 1965, 1985; and Whorf and Trager 1937. See also Chapters 2 and 7.)

Written History: Philology in Native America

One rather serious misconception concerning Native American languages is that they, unlike European tongues, have no tradition of older written texts on which a study of their history might be based. In some sense, of course, this is true, since some American tongues have scarcely any written attestations, even to this day. However, the usual assertion, the wholesale denial of written records for Native American languages, misleadingly dismisses the rather extensive philological work that exists on the extant written texts of a considerable number of the languages.[5] As Ives Goddard explains, there has been a bias against philology in American Indian linguistics; "documents and documentation are rarely accorded the attention that they receive in the traditional study of Old World languages," principally because of the emphasis that has been placed on fieldwork and the tradition that "the investigator has to rely so heavily on the data he himself collects" (1973:728). This bias, reflecting Franz Boas's approach to linguistic and anthropological research, was expressed by Truman Michelson in 1912: "It is simply a waste of time to unravel the vagaries of the orthography of the older writers in the case of dialects existing today" (cited by Goddard 1973:728). The characterization of American Indian linguistics must be revised to include philology as an important component of historical linguistics in the New World.

Another common misconception is that the existing texts are mostly from English or Spanish language sources. For that reason it is worth mentioning that philological work on Native American tongues has had to deal not only with the native languages themselves, but with colonial materials containing attestations of Native American languages which are written in Danish, Dutch, English, French, German, Italian, Latin, Portuguese, Russian, Spanish, and Swedish. For example, older sources on Eskimoan languages are written in Danish, English, French, German, and Russian; old Cariban language sources are written in English, Dutch, French, German, Latin, Portuguese, and Spanish. Algonquian and Iroquoian materials are found in Dutch, English, French, German, Latin, and Swedish (Campanius 1696, for example). One of the best known early sources on Nootka (spoken on Vancouver Island, British Columbia) is Moziño Suárez de Figueroa's (1793) account written in Spanish (see Carreno 1913). Even Basque gets into the picture (see the appendix to this chapter and Chapter 2). Some of these studies include linguistic forms and information on Native Americans left by such historically prominent figures as Richard Burton, Jacques Cartier, Catherine the Great, Christopher Columbus, (Captain) James Cook,[6] Francisco Vázquez de Coronado, Hernán Cortes, John Eliot, Martin Frobisher, Albert Gallatin (secretary of the Treasury under Presidents Jefferson and Madison), Alexander von Humboldt, Wilhelm von Humboldt, Thomas Jefferson, Bartolomé de Las Casas, René Robert Cavelier de La Salle, Meriwether Lewis and William Clark, Bernardino de Sahagún, El Inca Garcilaso de la Vega, Álvar Núñez Cabeza de Vaca, and Roger Williams. It is not the purpose of this book to survey the philological studies of Native American languages; suffice it to say that there are many and that they cover languages from all regions of the two American continents. (For a sample of such work, see Campbell 1990b, Goddard 1973, Haas 1969d, and Hymes 1965.)

Native American Writing Systems

It should not be overlooked, though often this is ignored, that a number of Native American languages have their own writing systems, some of which should be mentioned here. The *syllabaries* include the Cherokee syllabary (developed by Sequoya[7]), "Cree syllabics" (developed in the late 1830s by Methodist missionary James Evans and used by Cree and Ojibwa in northwestern Ontario), the Chipewyan syllabary (based on the Cree syllabary), the Eskimo syllabary of the central and eastern Canadian Arctic (also based on the Cree syllabary), the Western Great Lakes syllabary (sometimes called the Fox syllabary, but used also by Potawatomi and some Ojibwas, as well as by Sauk, Fox, and Kickapoo; the Winnebago borrowed a version of it from the Fox), and Micmac (there was also a hieroglyphic writing system for Micmac).[8] These developed after European contact, some as a result of the direct efforts of European missionaries (for example, the cases of the invention of Micmac writing and the missionary E. J. Peck's adaptation of the Cree syllabary for Inuktitut), and others through stimulus diffusion, inspired by the idea of European writing (for example, Sequoya's Cherokee syllabary). Father Jean-Marie Le Jeune adapted the French Duployer shorthand in the last decade of the nineteenth century for writing native languages in British Columbia. Manuals, primers, vocabularies, and similar works were printed in Shuswap, Okanagan, Thompson, and Lillooet; "there were still elderly Shuswap people in the 1980s and 1990s who could read this material" (Kinkade et al. in press). A Greek-based orthography was even used by some to represent Creek (see Sturtevant 1994:141), in the belief that Greek orthography was better suited to represent certain sounds (for example, long vowels): "various letters [sounds of Creek] cannot be pronounced except in the Greek language" (quoted in Sturtevant 1994:140). There is certainly potential for confusion about names in this Creek-Greek connection. The Mesoamerican *hieroglyphic* systems are pre-Columbian in origin and include Aztec (see Dibble 1966, Prem 1979), Mixtec (Ñuiñe, Puebla-Mixteca), Zapotec, Epi-Olmec (see Justeson and Kaufman 1993), and Mayan hieroglyphics (see Justeson and Campbell 1979, Houston 1989). The investigation of Mayan hieroglyphic writing is currently a very active area of scholarship, and great strides have been made in reading the glyphic texts.

Native American Pidgins and Trade Jargons

It is well known that such American Indian trade languages as Chinook Jargon and Mobilian Jargon exist. Still, many would be surprised to realize the number of other such contact languages and related linguistic entities that are attested in the New World. Since their origins and histories are different from those of other languages with normal transmission (Thomason and Kaufman 1988), they are not normally considered in surveys of American Indian languages which usually emphasize genetic classification. For that reason, they are not considered in detail here. The contact languages and "mixed" systems involving native languages of the Americas of which I am aware are listed and briefly described in the appendix to this chapter. .

Sign Language

The Plains sign language used for intertribal communication may be familiar to many from popular accounts. Not all Plains tribes were equally proficient in its use. In the southern plains, the Kiowas were known to be excellent sign talkers; in the northern plains, the Crows were credited with disseminating sign language to others, including the tribes of the Plateau linguistic area. There was variation from tribe to tribe, with some using distinct signs (Hollow and Parks 1980:83). The sign language as a whole became the lingua franca of the Great Plains, and it spread from there as far as British Columbia, Alberta, Saskatchewan, and Manitoba. A limited use of the sign language among some groups persists even today.

Many scholars believe that North American Indian sign language was already in use before European contact (Taylor 1978:224–6), and the Kiowas are credited with its invention by other Plains Indian groups. Samarin (1987), however, has argued against the existence of Plains Indian sign language before contact with Europeans. Wurtzburg and Campbell (1995) present a number of early historical reports and attestations as evidence of the precontact existence of sign language in the Louisiana-Texas-northern Mexico area; this appears to be the ancestor of Plains sign language. As Schuetz points out, "the universality of the sign language was noted by every European who came in contact with natives of northeastern Mexico and Texas" (1987:259; see Goddard 1979b:356). Not only does it seem safe to conclude that sign language was in use among Native American groups of the Gulf Coast region prior to contact with Europeans, but also there is good reason to accept the thesis that the well-known Plains sign language owes its origin to diffusion from the Gulf Coast (Goddard 1979b:356, Taylor 1978:225). The attestations of sign language in the Gulf Coast region are earlier than those in the Plains area, and this "accords well with the known northward spread of sign use" (Taylor 1978:225).

Similar gesture systems are reported in association with deaf communication in Central America among the K'iche' and Kaqchikel of Guatemala and in South America among the Urubu, a Tupí-Guaraní language of Maranhão, Brazil, among others.

Vocabulary Contributions

Native American languages have borrowed many words from a number of European languages: from Russian (Oswalt 1958, Bright 1960, Jacobson 1984, Bergsland 1986[9]); from Spanish (called hispanisms), seen in Indian languages of California and the Southwest (Bright 1960, Kroskrity 1993:67–71, Shipley 1962) and in Mexican and Central American Indian languages (see Boas 1930; Bright 1979; Campbell 1976d, 1991a; Canfield 1934; Clark 1977; Karttunen and Lockhart 1976), and in South American languages (Morínigo 1931, Muñoz 1993, Nordenskiöld 1922; see Mejías 1980); from Dutch (Goddard 1974a, Swiggers 1985); from French (Cuoq 1886, Bloomfield 1962:23); from Swedish (Goddard 1974a); and from English (many examples; see Bright 1960). There are even a few Basque loans in Micmac and in some other languages of Canada's Maritime Provinces, as a result of early contact with fishing vessels (Bakker 1987, 1989a, 1989b). But American tongues also contributed much to the vocabularies of these European languages—in particular, terms for plants, animals, and native culture items, as well as place names. For example, *Mississippi* is usually said to be from Ojibwa *mišši-* 'big' + *-si·pi* 'river'; it was introduced by Marquette, who learned the word from the Illinois. *Alaska* is from the Aleut word for the Alaska Peninsula, *alakhskhakh; Connecticut* is from a Mohegan form meaning 'long river'; and *Minnesota* comes from the Dakota *mnisota* 'cloudy water'. *Nebraska* is from the Omaha name for the Platte River, *nibdhathka* 'flat river'; the name *Oklahoma* was coined as a substitute for Indian Territory by Choctaw chief Allen Wright, based on *okla* 'people, tribe, nation' + *homa-* 'red' as an attempted translation of 'Indian Territory'. *Tennessee* comes from the Cherokee *tanasi,* their name for the Little Tennessee River (Chafe 1974:153). *Mexico* and *Guatemala* are from Nahuatl (Aztec),[10] *Nicaragua* from Nicarao (a form of Nahua). English has abundant loanwords from a number of Native American languages. Some examples are:

Algonquian: caribou, chipmunk, hickory, hominy, Manitou, moccasin, moose, mugwump, opossum, papoose, pemmican, persimmon, powwow, raccoon, sachem, skunk, squash (Massachuset *askootasquash*), squaw (Massachuset *squa*), tammany, terrapin, toboggan, tomahawk (Virginian Algonquian *tamahaac*), totem, wickiup

Cahuilla: chuck(a)walla (lizard) (see Bright 1973:717)

Cariban: cannibal(?), cayman/caiman(?), pirogue

Chinook Jargon: cayuse (ultimately European), klootchman, muckamuck, potlatch, skookum, wawa

Costanoan: abalone

Dakota (Siouan): tipi (tepee)

Eskimo: igloo, kayak, muckluck

Guaraní: petunia

Nahuatl: atlatl, avocado, cacao, cocoa, chayote, chicle, chile/chili, chinampa, chocolate, copal (incense), coyote, milpa (cornfield), jalapeño, metate, ocelot, peyote, tamale, tomato, zapote, and many more

Navajo: hogan

Quechua: alpaca, coca, condor, guanaco, guano, jerky (jerked beef), llama, pampa, puma, quinine, vicuña, and several others

Salishan: coho (salmon), sasquatch, sockeye (salmon)[11]

Taino and other Arawakan: agouti, anotto, barbecue, batata/potato, bixa, cacique (chief), canoe, Carib/cannibal(?), cassava (manioc), cay, coli-

bri (hummingbird), guava, hammock, hurricane, iguana, macaw(?), maize, mammee, manatee, mangrove (cf. Spanish *mangle*), papaya, pawpaw, savanna(h), tafia(?), tobacco(?)

Tupian: cashew, cayenne(?), jaguar, manioc, tapioca, tapir, toucan

Many of these Nahuatl, Quechua, Taino, and Tupian terms were borrowed first into Spanish, with some borrowed into French, and these languages were the intermediaries from which English borrowed them (Chafe 1974, Migliazza and Campbell 1988:146–7, Taylor 1957). There is an extensive literature on American Indian language loanwords in Spanish. (A few examples are Bright 1993, Campbell 1991a, Canfield 1934, Friederici 1947, Mejías 1980, Suárez 1945, and Zamora 1982. On the topic in general, see Cutler 1994.)

More important, Native American languages have borrowed from one another, in some areas rather extensively (see Bright 1973). Such borrowed words can be extremely important for detecting aspects of the cultural history of the speakers of those languages, since they often provide information about past geography, contacts, kinds of interactions, ethnic identity, and other matters. One of the many loans is the term for 'buffalo', which has been widely borrowed among the languages of the southeastern United States: Choctaw *yaniš,* Alabama-Koasati *yanasa,* Hitchiti *yanas-i,* and Creek *yanása* (Muskogean); Cherokee (Iroquoian) *yahnsã;* Natchez *yanasah;* Tunica *yániši;* Biloxi *yinisa'/yanasa'/yunisa',* Catawba *yunnaus/yanas* (Siouan); compare also Santee *wana'sa* 'to hunt buffalo', Ponka *wana'se* 'to hunt buffalo' (Siouan) (Haas 1951:78, 1969d:81–2, Taylor 1976). Terms for 'cedar' are also diffused among several of the languages in the southeastern United States; in the case of Creek *acína* and Cherokee *atsina,* the direction of borrowing is not clear, though Hitchiti *acin-i* is probably one of many loans from Creek to Hitchiti. The *čuwahla* 'cedar' of Choctaw, Alabama, and Koasati may reflect the Proto-Muskogean form; Biloxi (Siouan) *čuwahna,* however, is borrowed from Muskogean (since Muskogean languages have both *l* and *n,* but Biloxi has only *n*) (Haas 1969d:81). Words for 'bean' are found widely borrowed, particularly in languages of the southwestern United States and western Mexico: Mandan *ó·mįnįe,*

Lakota *omníčka,* Kansa *hǫbrlịge;* Hopi *móri,* Southern Paiute *muutii-,* Papago *muuñ,* Tarahumara *muní,* Varihio *muʔuní, muuní,* Mayo *muúni,* Cora *muhúme,* Huichol *muumee;* Proto-Chiapanec-Mangue **(nu-)mu,* Tlapanec *ni¹-ma²* 'bean plant', Mazatec *yu⁴hmã²,* Proto-Popolocan **hmaʔ³,* Proto-Mazatec **na⁴hma¹,* Ixcatec *hma²;* and a form approximating *marík* among Yuman languages.

Loanwords in the native languages of Mesoamerica have been investigated in more detail than those in North American or South American languages (for a few examples, see Campbell 1972b, 1976c, 1977, 1978a, 1978c; Campbell and Kaufman 1976; Campbell et al. 1986; Justeson et al. 1985; Kaufman 1976; Thompson 1943; Whorf 1943). The patterns of borrowing among native languages of Mesoamerica also reveal much about culture history. The Mixe-Zoquean languages, for example, have contributed many early loanwords to the vocabulary of most other Mesoamerican languages. These loans are seen as evidence for the identification of the Olmecs (ca. 1200–400 B.C., who were responsible for the first highly successful civilization of the region) as speakers of Mixe-Zoquean languages (Campbell and Kaufman 1976; see Chapter 5). Similarly, the Mayan languages have contributed a number of borrowed words to the languages of their neighbors. For example, most Xincan agricultural terms are loanwords from Mayan, leading to the inference that Xincan speakers were probably not agriculturalists before their contact with Mayan speakers. The languages of the Maya Lowlands also borrowed much from one another and contributed significantly to other Mayan languages and to their non-Mayan neighbors, reflecting the fact that Cholan and Yucatecan speakers were the bearers of Classic Maya culture (Justeson et al. 1985). Nahua loanwords are found in languages throughout Middle America, as a result of the cultural impact of the Toltecs and later the Aztecs, both of whom spoke Nahua. Totonacan speakers also apparently had considerable cultural influence, judging from the Totonacan words borrowed by other languages. One revealing example is *pusik'al* 'heart, soul', borrowed by lowland Mayan languages—cf. Totonac *pu-* 'locative prefix' + *sikuʔlan* 'holy'; the Mayan form is a single

morpheme, though native Mayan morphemes are typically monosyllabic (Justeson et al. 1985:26). It has been hypothesized that Totonacan speakers were the builders of Teotihuacan (200 B.C.–A.D. 650), the most influential Mesoamerican city, and such examples are taken as evidence supporting this hypothesis (Justeson et al. 1985).

Some loans among Mesoamerican languages (and their neighbors) are rather widespread, as, for example, 'cacao' is: Proto-Mixe-Zoquean **kakawa;* pan-Mayan *kakaw* (or something similar; the native Mayan form is **pe:q*); Nahua *kakawa-;* Jicaque *kʰwa;* Tarascan *khékua* 'chocolate'; Lenca *kaw;* Paya *kaku,* Guatuso *kaxu.* Another widespread loan involves borrowings for 'turkey': Proto-Zoquean **tuʔnuk;* Mixtec *čũún* 'chickens', Proto-Chinantec **tuL,* San Juan Copala Trique *doʔlo³, doʔloh²l* 'chicken'; Totonac *taʔhnaʔ;* Chuj, Jakalteko, Motozintlec *tunuk',* Tzeltal, Tzotzil *tuluk'* (the native Mayan etymon is **ʔak'*); Jicaque *tolɨ;* Tequistlatec *-dulu* /tulu/; Huave *tel* 'female turkey', Proto-Huave **tɨll* 'turkey'; Proto-Nahua *to:tol-* 'turkey', Nahuatl *to:tol-* 'chicken', Pochutec *tutul* 'turkey'; Seri *tóo.*

In South America the most obvious examples of native borrowings are found in the Andes. Varieties of Quechua and Aymara have borrowed extensively from one another (see Chapter 8; also Adelaar 1987). Many languages of the Andes and the eastern foothills and beyond have also borrowed rather extensively from Quechua, and to a lesser extent from Aymara. For example, Quechua cultural influence has been considerable on Mapudungu (Araucanian, in Chile), which has borrowed, among other things, the terms for 'hundred' and 'thousand' (see Díaz-Fernández 1993). Amuesha has borrowed extensively from Quechua, but also from Panoan languages. Other languages with Quechua loans include Uru and Chipaya, Tacana, Leco (Lapalapa), Mosetén, and Aguaruna. Cavineño has a number of Aymara loans. To give just one example, Quechuan *atawalʸpa* or *walʸpa,* the terms for 'hen' and 'chicken' (Hamp 1964), were widely borrowed, after the arrival of the Spanish, in languages in adjoining regions of South America, for example: Mapudungu *ačawalʸ,* Mosetén *ataua, atavua,* Chama *waipa, waʔipa,*

Reyesano *walípa,* Tacana *warípa,* Huitoto-Ocaina *áʔtaβa,* Aguaruna *atáš,* Campa *atawa, tawalpa,* Jívaro *atáš,* Paez *atalloy,* Záparo *ata-wari,* Cayapa *wálʸapa,* Esmeralda *walʸpa,* Yuracare *talipa* (Carpenter 1985, Nordenskiöld 1922). In lowland South America, a number of loans have been identified between Tupí-Guaraní and some Cariban languages of the northern Amazonian area, and Língua Geral has contributed several loans to many of these same Cariban languages (Rodrigues 1985a:389–92). A few of these that might be recognized from broader borrowing also into European languages are Tupinambá *kwati,* Galibí *kuasi* 'coatimundi'; Tupinambá *nanã;* Galibí (and others) *nana* 'pineapple' (cf. *ananas* for 'pineapple' in several European languages); and Tupinambá *piRãy,* Galibí *pirai* 'piranha'. Yanomaman has borrowed from Cariban languages (for example, Pemón); Resígaro has borrowed much from Witotoan. Cariña (Carib, Galibí—a Cariban language) and Lokono (Arawakan) in the Antilles and northern South America share many loanwords, while Cariña and Tupí (unrelated languages) also share many lexical items, apparently as a result of diffusion (Taylor 1977a:4). Lexical borrowings in other areas of South America deserve more attention (see Carpenter 1985, Girard 1971b, Payne 1991).

Fakes and Mistaken Languages

Discussion of the classification of American Indian languages would not be complete without mention of the fakes, hoaxes, and mistaken identities that are part of the history of the field, but which are now safely rejected. I mention those that are better known.

Taensa

The most celebrated instance of a faked language in the history of American Indian linguistics is the "curious hoax of the Taensa language" (Brinton 1890a:452). The hoax was perpetrated in the 1880s by two French seminary students, Parisot and Djouy, who created a grammar and other materials said to be on Taensa, an otherwise undocumented language of Louisiana. The

"language" was vehemently disputed by the leading Americanists of the time; it was defended as authentic by Lucien Adam, Albert S. Gatschet, and others (see Chapter 2), and was first successfully debunked by Daniel Brinton in 1890. In his review of the Southeast, John Swanton (1946:239) determined that the language of the group known as the Taensa Indians was essentially the same as Natchez. (See Auroux 1984 for details; see also Parisot 1880, 1882; Hautmonté, Parisot, and Adam 1882; Adam 1885; and Brinton 1890a.)

Aguacatec II

Aguacatec II (supposedly of Aguacatán, central Guatemala) was made up by the maid of Otto Stoll (1958[1884]:244). Stoll mentioned 300 words she produced, but he presented only 68 of them, saying the others were too suspicious (of course, many of the 68 are also highly suspicious). Consequently, only Stoll has found anything remotely similar to Aguacatec II. Aguacatán is the center of Awakateko (Aguacatec), a Mayan language of the Mamean subgroup. There are no non-Mayan languages near this part of Guatemala and since the most probable location for the Proto-Mayan homeland is in this area, it is highly unlikely that there have ever been any non-Mayan languages in this region, at least not in the last several thousand years (see Kaufman 1976).

Pupuluca of Conguaco

Colonial sources report Pupuluca was spoken in Conguaco and in nearby towns near the Guatemalan Pacific Coast. But Pupuluca (Popoloca, Populuca, Popoluca) is a common designation for a number of languages from Nicaragua to Mexico, coming from Nahua *popoloka* 'to babble, speak unintelligibly'. Stoll (1958[1884]:31–4) found among C. Hermann Berendt's manuscripts one bearing the language name of Popoluca, and Stoll assumed it was from Conguaco. The Popoluca of the manuscript, however, was from Oluta, of Veracruz—a Mixe language, which explains why Stoll was able correctly to relate the language of the manuscript to the Mixe of Oaxaca. To this day we do not know what the Pupuluca of Conguaco was, and no native document, place name, surname, or any linguistic material attributable to it has yet been discovered—but we know it was not Oluta Popoluca, the language of Berendt's manuscript that Stoll mistakenly assumed to be from Conguaco. The best bet, based on geography, is that Conguaco Pupuluca was a variety of Xinca, but that is far from certain (Kaufman 1974a, Campbell 1979).

Tapachultec II

Tapachultec (in Chiapas, Mexico, near the Guatemalan border) belongs to the Mixean branch of the Mixe-Zoquean family (Kaufman 1964d). Karl Sapper (1912), the discoverer of the Tapachultec language, was convinced by his data that it belonged to the Mixe-Zoquean family. Unfortunately, however, he lost his field notes. He attempted to obtain new data through correspondence with A. Ricke, German vice consul in Tapachula. The forms sent by Ricke (obtained from mestizos) so surprised Sapper because of their difference from what he had collected earlier (and lost) that he believed Tapachula to have two distinct languages. Walter Lehmann (1920), a student of Sapper's, found that in reality only one language was spoken in Tapachula, but he followed his teacher in speaking of two, separating the Tapachultec vocabulary into two segments. The forms for which he could discover equivalences in other Mixe-Zoquean languages he called Tapachultec I; Tapachultec II was the portion of the Tapachultec vocabulary for which he could not find counterparts elsewhere in Mixe-Zoquean. Thus, there never were two distinct Tapachultec languages, only one.

Subinhá

Catherine the Great's project of collecting samples of all the world's languages received lists from the Audience of Guatemala in 1788–1789, including one entitled "Subinhá," said to be from Socoltenango, Chiapas. Though Subinhá was thought to be a separate Mayan language, examination of numerals shows every other word in fact to be Tzeltal alternating with Tojolabal (Tzeltal for even numbers, Tojolabal for odd) (Kaufman 1974a). In my fieldwork in 1980, I found only Tzeltal spoken in Socoltenango (Campbell 1988b).

"Aksanas"

Daniel Hammerly Dupuy (1952; also 1947a, 1947b) thought he had discovered a group of "Kaueskar" who spoke a language called "Aksanas," which he believed was different from Alakaluf (Kaweskar). The "discovery" of this allegedly different language came about as a result of Dupuy's comparison of fifty words from a 1698 vocabulary by the French pirate Jean de la Guilbaudière with one Dupuy himself had taken down—he judged the two vocabularies to be different. This mistaken identity is clarified by Christos Clairis:

> It is sufficient to examine just the first word of this comparative list in order to get an idea of the inevitable errors of this type of "method." Taking the word "water" for which la Guilbaudière noted *arret* [*sic*], Hammerly listed *čafalai*. Here one is dealing with an error made by la Guilbaudière. He showed the Qawasqar [Alakaluf] a bucket of water so as to obtain the equivalent in their language and did not notice that their response was to the receptacle and not to the contents. Thus, *aret* means "container of liquid." (1985:756)

Čestmír Loukotka unfortunately accepted Hammerly Dupuy's judgment and listed Aksanas as a language isolate distinct from Alakaluf (Kaweskar) in his classification of South American languages (Clairis 1985:757), and the "Aksanas" error seems not to have been corrected in the latest classifications of South American languages (see for example Kaufman 1994:67).

Membreño, Corobisi, and Other Non-Languages

Joseph H. Greenberg (1987) has entered some language names into the literature that are not languages at all. Membreño, which Greenberg (1987:194, 293, 382, 425) classified as a Lencan language, is actually the name of a person, a reference (Alberto Membreño 1897) which contains several Lenca word lists from different Honduran towns. In several instances, Greenberg gave the names of towns where a certain language was spoken as names of distinct languages (1987:382 and elsewhere): for example, there are not six Lencan languages; there are only two, though Greenberg gives as languages such town names as Guajiquero [sic, Guajiquiro], Intibucat [sic, Intibucá], Opatoro, and Similatón. Papantla is not a separate Totonacan language but a town where Totonac is spoken (Greenberg 1987:380); Chiripo and Estrella, presented as Talamancan languages (Greenberg 1987:382) are names of towns where Cabécar is spoken. "Viceyta" (given by Greenberg 1987 as also Talamancan) is a colonial name which referred to both Bribri and Cabécar, and certainly not to a third independent language. Moreover, Terraba, Tiribí, and Tirub are also not separate languages but rather refer to Tiribí. The christianized Tiribí brought by the Spanish from Panama to Costa Rica after 1700 are called Terraba; Tirub is merely the native version of the name of Tiribí that some scholars prefer to use (see Greenberg 1987:382).

Corobisi is a language name found in Spanish sources from the sixteenth and early seventeenth centuries, but no word of this language is known to have been recorded and preserved, and therefore its colonial referent is unknown. Eduard Conzemius (1930) nevertheless equated a word list from Upala with the Corobisi language, though Upala is not in the area attributed to the Corobisi in colonial reports (but it is near it). This word list turned out to be Rama, but whether the colonial Corobisi may have been associated somehow with Rama remains unknown. In any case, the Corobisi of Conzemius and Rama are not distinct languages, though Greenberg (1987:111) grouped his version of Corobisi with Guatuso, Cabécar, and Rama on the basis of a single cited "Corobisi" form (see Campbell 1988b:610).[12]

Fortunately, progress has been made in sorting out the nonexistent and the misidentified languages so that the work of classifying the native tongues of the Americas can go forward without this sort of complication.

Native American Languages and Linguistic Theory

In the history of linguistics, data from American Indian languages have been important to a number of theoretical issues (see Chapter 2); these languages have contributed to linguistic theory in several ways. To mention just one example, in word order universals it is now known that VOS, OSV, and OVS type languages exist (where V = verb, O = object, S = subject), all attested in the Americas, although Greenberg's (1966[1963]) important original research on word order universals suggested that these basic orders were impossible since they did not occur in his sample of languages. Both OVS and OSV are scarcely known outside Amazonia; hence understanding the potential word order arrangements in the world's languages depends crucially on data from these American tongues (Derbyshire 1977, 1981, 1985, 1986, 1987).

Some particular languages have had a special impact in the theoretical literature in linguistics theory. Eskimoan and Mayan languages have been influential in treatments of ergativity; Algonquian has had an impact on interpretations of animacy hierarchies and discourse analysis, and Yokuts and Klamath have influenced phonological theory. Some "small languages" have had a large impact on theoretical discussions— far greater than might be expected given their geographical remoteness, small number of speakers, and the few scholars who have studied them firsthand. This is often because some description of the language has become well known. For example, there is a veritable cottage industry in theoretical phonological restatements and reworkings of Stanley Newman's (1944) description of Yawelmani Yokuts, and there is a large secondary bibliography that relies on Edward Sapir's (1930) Southern Paiute, Leonard Bloomfield's (1962) Menominee, M. A. R. Barker's (1963, 1964) Klamath, Mary R. Haas's (1946, 1950, 1953) Tunica, and Harry Hoijer's (1946b, 1949, 1972) Tonkawa. It is encouraging that good descriptive work has been recognized and found useful, though there have often been problems. Concerning treatments of Menominee based on Bloomfield's work, Kenneth Miner says that "I have yet to see one treatment that does not seriously misrepresent the facts of the language" (1979:75; see Hockett [1973] for similar opinions about some treatments of Yokuts). Still, it is safe to say that Native American languages have had, and will continue to have, an impact on matters of linguistic theory. They have played a significant role in recent discussions of word order, noun-incorporation, animacy hierarchies, switch reference, evidentials, non-configurationality, optimality, release features, feature geometry, and areal linguistics, to mention but a few.

The Future: Language Endangerment

The future confronting Native American languages is an alarming one of massive extinction. Michael Krauss finds that of the 187 languages still spoken in the United States and Canada, 149 "are no longer being learned by children" (1992:5). In California, the region of greatest linguistic diversity in North America, of the approximately 100 languages encountered in 1800, only 50 still have speakers, but today "there is not a *single* California Indian language that is being learned by children as the primary languages of the household" (Hinton 1994:21; see Krauss 1992). Michael Foster finds that of Canada's 53 remaining native languages, only 3 (Cree, Ojibwa, and Inuktitut) have good prospects of survival (1982:12). This means that 80% of the remaining North American languages and *all* of the California Indian tongues will become extinct with the passing of this generation.[13] The imminent danger of extensive language extinction is no less serious in Middle and South America (for some examples, see Campbell and Muntzel 1989). The magnitude of the threat faced by endangered and doomed languages becomes clear when compared with that faced by endangered biological species. Of 4,400 mammals, 326 (7%) are on the endangered list; about 3% of the birds are on the list. The problem of endangered languages is just as serious, but the percentage facing extinction is much higher (Krauss 1992). Whereas endangered species have the resources and attention of numerous national and international organizations such as the World Wildlife Fund and Greenpeace, endangered languages have almost none. Resources must be created to address this truly serious problem.

Undocumented, the death of any of these languages represents an irretrievable loss to science and constitutes the loss of a portion of our own humanity. The loss of a language means

forfeiture of its contribution to the understanding of human language in general and what this teaches us about human cognition. To take a hypothetical but all too plausible example, suppose that in the current rapid extinction of Brazilian languages (and those in Amazonia generally), all languages which exhibit OSV and OVS basic word order were to disappear before they could be analyzed and described. Since these word orders are unknown elsewhere in the world, linguistic theorists would undoubtedly presume these orders to be universally absent from human languages, and they would draw conclusions about language in general and about human cognitive makeup based on this set of circumstances. Clearly, then, for scientific reasons it is important to document as fully as possible these languages while they are still spoken. However, the loss of a language also represents loss of human intellectual heritage, of all that could have been learned through that language about linguistic history, human values, cultural and verbal art, oral literature, and that particular society's way of organizing and coping with its physical and ideological world. Moreover, if linguists fail to provide descriptive materials for the now endangered languages, revitalization efforts will be doomed and members of the society (and other persons) subsequently will have no possible means by which to appreciate their otherwise lost linguistic and cultural heritage (see Campbell 1994a for more detail).

For the immediate interests of this book, with its focus on the historical linguistics of Native American languages, the loss of otherwise undocumented languages leaves large gaps in linguistic history, a loss of crucial information that can never be recovered later. Moreover, it is not merely the death of individual languages (much too serious in its own right) which will hamper historical research; in the Americas many whole language families are on the verge of extinction, and some have already been completely lost (see Gursky 1966a:402). This puts in high relief the urgency of descriptive work in our study area. As these languages become extinct, historical linguistic research on American Indian linguistics will of necessity become increasingly philological in nature, depending on the written documentation that remains, however fragmentary that may be. For the historical interests in focus here, good descriptive and analytical work is a necessary prerequisite for historical linguistic investigation.

Concern about language endangerment increases the need for reliable statistics on the number of speakers of each language. However, in the Americas dependable information on numbers of speakers is not always available; in particular, the estimates for some South American languages are quite rough, and often are not consistent from one source to the next. Rather than attempt to report numbers of speakers for each language in this book, I have attempted only to identify (in Chapters 4, 5, and 6), insofar as the information is available, languages with fewer than 10 speakers, which I label "moribund"; languages with 100 or fewer speakers (but more than 10), which I term "obsolescent"; and languages with more than 100 speakers, which are given no special designation.[14]

Summary

In this chapter I have attempted to eliminate some misconceptions and to clarify some matters of nomenclature. I have touched on topics that are not to taken up in detail elsewhere in the book but are nevertheless important. Subsequent chapters present an overview and an assessment of Native American historical linguistics.

APPENDIX
Native American Pidgins and Trade Languages

The pidgins, trade languages, and "mixed" systems involving Native American languages are rarely included in general surveys of Native American linguistics; such overviews are usually concerned primarily with genetic classification, and pidgin and trade languages fall outside those considerations. The languages of which I am aware are briefly described here. It is important to keep their existence in mind, since they, too, have interesting histories, and they deserve more study than they have received, for little is known about many of them. The languages are presented in roughly geographical order from north to south (and, where relevant, from west to east).[1]

Eskimo Trade Jargon

Stefánsson reported two trade jargons used by Eskimos in dealing with whites and Indians. Both are based on Eskimo grammar and lexicon. He referred to a "ships' jargon" on Herschel Island:

> At Herschel island, indeed, practically all forms of the jargon exist side-by-side, for here gather whalers who have picked it up in Kotzebue Sound, at Point Hope, Point Barrow, and at other places— and one or two who have it from near Marble island on the Atlantic ocean side. . . . As to pronunciation, much depends too on the individual white man.

He also reported the other Eskimo trade jargon, saying:

> Among the Mackenzie River Eskimo there is, beside the ships' jargon, a more highly developed one used in dealing with Athabasca Indians around Fort Arctic, Red River, and Fort Macpherson. . . . It has probably more than twice as extensive a vocabulary as the ships' variety and is so different from it that some white men who know the ships' jargon have employed as interpreters Loucheux Indians under the impression that the Indians spoke real Eskimo. (1909:218–9)

He suggested that the latter jargon has its origin in contacts among native peoples:

> Although the Loucheux employ their jargon at present largely in dealing with the Mackenzie Eskimo, the form of their jargon words shows pretty plainly that it (the jargon) must have been developed in contact with inland Eskimo or those from near Point Barrow. This is rendered probable, too, through our knowing that from remote times there was a trading rendezvous at Barter Island where met not only Eskimo from east, west, and inland, but also one or more groups of Indians. (1909:219; see also Schuhmacher 1977, Drechsel 1981)

Mednyj Aleut (Copper Island Aleut)

The Aleut spoken on Mednyj (Mendiy) or Copper Island (one of the two Commander Islands) is a mixed Aleut-Russian language. Only ten or twelve speakers remain. The population was made up of a small group of Russians who settled there for seal hunting, Aleuts who were first moved there in 1826 by the Russian-American Company (they were brought from other islands of the Aleutian chain), and children of Russian men and Aleut women. Most of the vocabulary and grammar of Mednyj Aleut are clearly Aleut, but virtually the entire finite verb morphology is Russian. The syntax reflects both Russian and Aleut, though Russian features predominate, with considerable variation. (See Golovko 1994, Menovščikov 1968, 1969,

Thomason and Kaufman 1988:18, 20, 233–8; Comrie 1989.)

Chinook Jargon

Chinook Jargon is probably the best known of the native pidgins and contact languages spoken in the New World. It was widely spoken (and it is claimed that some individuals still know it to some degree) among native groups and non-Indians alike through-out the Northwest Coast area. During the first half of the nineteenth century, it was used along the Colum-bia River and in the nearby coastal region; in the latter half of that century it reached its fullest distribu-tion—from southern Alaska and British Columbia to the northern California coast, and west to the Rocky Mountains, in use among speakers of one hundred or more mutually unintelligible languages (Jacobs 1932:27, Thomason 1983:820). Its history is contro-versial. Some scholars argue that its origin postdates contact with Europeans (Samarin 1986, 1987; Sil-verstein 1972), but most believe that it has a precon-tact origin (Hymes 1980, Powell 1990a, Thomason 1983, Gibbs 1863a, Hale 1890a, Lionnet 1853). Sarah Thomason presents cogent historical and linguistic arguments for a precontact origin without the neces-sity of European linguistic input (though unfortu-nately, there is no direct documentation from this period); however, William Samarin (1986) disputes her interpretation. (See also Jacobs 1932, Kaufman 1971, Drechsel 1981.)

Most of the native languages of this region also contain loans from Chinook Jargon. One that is partic-ularly widespread is Chinook Jargon *poston* 'white man', based on English *Boston,* since early represen-tatives of the fur trade were from Boston; *kinčočman* is a competing term for 'white man', from English 'King George man'—a reference to those of the British Northwest (see Powell 1990a).[2]

Broken Slavey (Slavey Jargon)

An Athabaskan-based "Broken Slavé" (Slavey) jargon has been reported, although very little is known about it. Dall described it as follows: "The usual mode of communication between the whites and Indians in this locality [Yukon Territory] is a jargon somewhat like Chinook, known by the name of "Broken Slavé." The basis of this jargon, which includes many modi-fied French and English words, is the dialect of Liard River" (1870:106). Peter Bakker (in press, a; Bakker and Grant, in press) also cites a few references to

this "jargon" by nineteenth-century travelers. Émile Petitot (1889:292–3) said the Jargon is comprised of Slavey (Athabaskan), French, and Cree (Algonquian) elements, and he presented a small sample (cited in Bakker and Grant, in press).

Loucheux Jargon

Petitot distinguished between Broken Slavey (Slavey Jargon) and "Jargon Loucheux" (1889:292–5), al-though he was the only one to do so. He reported that the Loucheux Jargon was used on the Yukon River and among the Gwich'in (Dindjié) of Peel River, and that it contained vocabulary elements from French, English, Chipewyan, Slavey, and Gwich'in, as well as some Cree. Broken Slavey was used on the MacKenzie River; Petitot's small sample is all that is known of it (Bakker and Grant, in press).

Michif (French Cree, Métis, Metchif)

Michif is a mixed language in which most nouns (approximately 90%) and most adjectives (together with their morphology and syntax) are French in origin, whereas almost all the verbs (and their associ-ated morphology and syntax) are from Plains Cree. Essentially, the noun phrases constitute a French sys-tem, including even the phonology; the verb phrases (and a few other grammatical bits) are entirely Cree (for details, see Bakker 1994). Michif is spoken by fewer than 1,000 Métis on the Turtle Mountain reser-vation in North Dakota, and by many more of them in the area extending from Turtle Mountain, near the border between North Dakota and Manitoba, north-ward to Manitoba; there are also some speakers in Saskatchewan and Montana. Ethnically, the Michif speakers are identified as Métis (descendants of French-speaking fur traders and Algonquian women), but most of the thousands of Métis are not Michif speakers (rather they speak varieties of Cree, Ojibwa, French, and English). (See Rhodes 1977, 1982; Smith 1994; Bakker, in press c.)[3]

"Broken Oghibbeway" (Broken Ojibwa)

An Ojibwa pidgin is reported by John Nichols (1992). It was apparently used by both Europeans and Native Americans inhabiting the western Great Lakes region in the early nineteenth century and was recognized by Ojibwa speakers as being something deviant.

Basque-Algonquian Pidgin

Bakker cites French sources that speak of a *lingua franca (langue franque)* "composed of Basque and two different languages of the Indians" that was established "when the Basques first started fishing for cod and whales in the Gulf of Saint Lawrence . . . [where] they traded with them [the Indians of this area], especially with the nation called Eskimos [Micmacs]" (1989a:259). It has also been called the Micmac-Basque Pidgin, as well as Souriquois (Smith 1994); a Pidgin Basque-Montagnais (called Montagnais Pidgin Basque in Smith [1994]) has also been mentioned, and may be associated with it. If it is accurately identified, this Basque-Algonquian Pidgin is perhaps the oldest pidgin attested in North America, thought to have been spoken ca. 1540–1640 (Bakker 1987, 1989a, 1989b).

American Indian Pidgin English

Ives Goddard (1977) demonstrates many Algonquian forms in the attestations of American Indian Pidgin English, used in New England along with Pidgin Massachusett (Goddard 1977, 1978b; Leechman and Hall 1955; M. R. Miller 1967).

Delaware Jargon

The Delaware-based Traders' Jargon, a pidgin, was used in interchanges between Delaware River whites and Indians in the seventeenth century. It is attested in several sources, but the total extant material is still quite limited. Perhaps best known is "the Indian Interpreter," a list of 261 words and phrases "in the English of the period and in a mixed dialect of the New Jersey Delaware language" (Prince 1912:508). Almost all of its lexical items are from Delaware (Algonquian). Its grammar is simplified as is typical of pidgins, but exhibits no European influence, and some of its features are at odds with the Dutch, English, and Swedish then spoken in the area; for example, OV (object-verb) basic word order and a native Delaware-based negative construction (Goddard 1977, Prince 1912, Thomason 1980b).

This may be only part of a bigger picture. Ives Goddard (personal communication) finds evidence that there was a pidgin Algonquian used all along the East Coast, attested for Virginia, Delaware and New York, southwestern Connecticut, and, indirectly, for Massachusetts.[4]

Pidgin Massachusett

Little is known of Pidgin Massachusett aside from its existence. It may have connections with Delaware Jargon or with the broader pidgin Algonquian referred to above (Goddard 1977:41).

Jargonized Powhatan

Jargonized Powhatan was reported by Captain John Smith. Next to nothing is known of it (Goddard 1977:41).

Lingua Franca Creek

There is hardly any documentation on what Drechsel (1983a) has called Lingua Franca Creek, but historical sources suggest its existence. It was based on Eastern Muskogean languages—Creek in particular. The question is whether normal Creek was used as a second language (as it appears to have been, at least in some instances), or whether some reduced, pidginized language based on Creek developed as a contact language for use among the speakers of different languages in the Creek Confederacy. If such a contact language existed, it is now long extinct. Drechsel (1984:177, 1987:27) suggests that it might legitimately be considered simply an Eastern Muskogean variety of Mobilian Jargon. He believes it was converted into Seminole Pidgin English as a result of relexification in the eighteenth century and eventually was converted to Afro-Seminole Creole (Drechsel 1983a, 1984:171; cf. Crawford 1978:6–7). What Drechsel calls Seminole Jargon was Creek-based jargon used among the Seminole Indians (former Creek separatists and "runaways," and their black associates). He believes that it was "a true contact language with its own grammatical rules, however variable" (1983a:394), that ultimately developed into Seminole Creole English. There is some controversy concerning these interpretations.

Lingua Franca Apalachee

A contact language based on Apalachee (Eastern Muskogean) is sometimes cited in historical, anthropological, and linguistic sources dealing with the southeastern United States, but it is long extinct and poorly attested. According to early colonial sources, it was a mixture of Spanish and Alabama (Alibama).

Fox suggests it might have influenced Mobilian Jargon (see below), accounting for some of the Spanish words found there (1980:607; see also Drechsel 1984:177, 178).

Mobilian Jargon

Mobilian Jargon (Mobilian Trade Jargon, sometimes called the Chickasaw-Choctaw Trade Language) is a pidgin apparently based on some Western Muskogean language in use as a trade language in the lower Mississippi Valley and along the Gulf coast. It was utilized by speakers of Choctaw, Chickasaw, Houma, Apalachee, Alabama, and Koasati (all Muskogean languages); Atakapa, Chitimacha, Natchez, and Tunica (isolates); Ofo and Biloxi (Siouan); Caddo and Natchitoches (Caddoan)—and possibly by Algonquian groups of southern Illinois, as well as speakers of English, French, German, and Spanish. It was spoken as recently as the 1950s by the Koasatis and their neighbors in southwestern Louisiana (Drechsel 1983b:168, 1984, 1993).

There is a variance of opinion as to whether Mobilian Jargon originated before European contact or not. James Crawford (1978:16–29) contended that Mobilian Jargon was first used in the eighteenth century and spread with the establishment of Louisiana as a French colony. However, Drechsel cites ethnohistorical sources, as well as structural and sociolinguistic considerations, to argue, as had Gatschet and Swanton before him, that it had a prehistoric origin, though Europeans "likely contributed to its diffusion later in the historic periods of greater Louisiana" (1984:172; cf. 1993; also Munro 1984:446).

There is also some controversy concerning the lexical sources of Mobilian Jargon. Munro (1984) maintains that the assumed predominance of Chickasaw forms is incorrect (see Crawford 1978:79–80), and that the major source is probably some other Western Muskogean language, perhaps Choctaw. Crawford came to believe that the source of most of the Mobilian Jargon vocabulary was "most likely a now-extinct Western Muskogean language, perhaps that of the Bayougoula, Houma, or Mobile tribes" (reported in Munro 1984:449–50). Drechsel (1987) disputes Munro's view and asserts that there were in fact numerous meanings with variant forms, some of which are derived directly from Chickasaw sources. He points out that most of the surviving attestations of Mobilian Jargon were recorded in Louisiana, where Choctaw has survived but where the Chickasaw never settled. Thus Drechsel suspects a bias in the corpus in favor of Choctaw-like forms, which would make

the forms that are clearly of Chickasaw origin even more important indicators of the jargon's origins. He concludes that since apparently "Chickasaw has not had any impact on MJ [Mobilian Jargon] during its recent history of the past 150 years or so . . . words of unquestionable Chickasaw origin in modern recordings of MJ would assume the special status of survivals" (1987:26). Crawford points out that a few words of Algonquian origin are sometimes associated with Mobilian Jargon, though for the most part they are attested either only in early French sources or later in Louisiana French, but not directly in Mobilian Jargon itself (1978:63–75): "The numerous occurrences of Algonquian words in the accounts of Frenchmen who wrote about the Indians of Louisiana cannot be interpreted to mean that the writers employed the words as a result of having heard them in the speech of the Louisiana Indians" (1978:74–5). The jargon also contains a few words from Spanish, French, and English, though usually borrowed not directly from these languages themselves but from some other Indian language intermediary which had previously borrowed the forms—'cow' and 'rice' from Spanish; 'coffee' and 'Indian' from French; 'cat', 'oak', and 'turkey' from English; and 'money' from Algonquian (Crawford 1978:76–7; Drechsel 1979, 1983a, 1983b, 1984, 1987; Munro 1984).

Güegüence-Nicarao

The language of the Güegüence dance drama (text appears in Brinton 1883) is sometimes thought to be a kind of creole, though it is difficult to determine from the scant material available what its true status was. As represented in the text, the language is mostly Spanish with some Nicarao words and phrases interspersed here and there. Nicarao is a variety of Nahua (Uto-Aztecan) once spoken in Nicaragua. The Güegüence drama was performed by people who clearly identified themselves ethnically as Indians and set themselves apart from Nicaraguans having European background, though linguistically they seem to have assimilated extensively to Spanish. The claim of language mixture in this case should be examined and the true composition of the language of the text determined. There seems to be a fairly clear distinction between the Spanish of the text and the interspersed Nicarao portions, with no real evidence of a mixed linguistic system as has been reported for other languages in the literature (for example, Callahuaya, Mednyj Aleut, and Media Lengua Quechua as described in this Appendix).[5]

Carib Pidgin or Ndjuka-Amerindian Pidgin (Ndjuka-Trio)

De Goeje (1906, 1908, 1946) observed a pidgin spoken by the Wayana and Trio (Tirió) Indians of southeastern Surinam in their dealings with the Ndjuka- or Djuka-speaking Bush Negroes (members of the Boni [African] tribe of Surinam and French Guiana, also called Ndjuka Maroons). Wayana and Trio are both Cariban languages (see Chapter 6). Nimuendajú (1926:112–3, 124, 140–3) reported this pidgin also in Brazilian territory, used there by the Palikur. Huttar (1982:1) found the language still in use in the 1970s and essentially unchanged from that recorded by de Goeje (see also Bakker 1987:20–1, Smith 1995). Taylor and Hoff (1980) claimed that a pidginized Cariña (or Galibí [Cariban]) has been in use for centuries on the mainland of South America (though it is sometimes said now to be extinct) (see also Hoff 1994). De Goeje (1908:215) reported that this pidgin trade language consisted mostly of words borrowed from Trio or from "Negro English," and that words of "Carib" [Cariña, Galibí] origin found in it were introduced by the Bush Negroes, whose English-based language also contains them (see Huttar 1982:1). The pidgin word order is SOV, unlike the SVO of Ndjuka and like the SOV of many Cariban languages.

Carib Pidgin-Arawak Mixed Language

Taylor and Hoff (1980) argue that a mixed language involving Carib Pidgin and Arawak is the ancestor of the Island Carib men's language, basically an Arawakan language with a special men's jargon based on Carib lexical items. Most of what is known about this language is based on forms presented in Raymond Breton's (1665, 1667) works on the Island Carib of Dominica and Saint Vincent (where the language is now extinct) which he designated as 'language of men' and 'language of women.' "A few remnants of the male register" (Hoff 1994:161) are also preserved in Garifuna (Black Carib) of Central America, whose speakers are descendants of Island Caribs who were deported from Saint Vincent in 1797 (see Chapters 4 and 5), though most to the men's language is now lost. The Cariban elements of the male jargon are limited to lexical items and one postposition, while the grammatical morphemes of both male and female styles are all of Arawakan origin. Hoff (1994) supports the argument that the Cariban elements in the men's jargon are from the Carib Pidgin and not directly from the mainland Carib language itself. This argument is based on the observation that, in both the

Carib Pidgin of Cayenne and the Island Carib men's jargon, the markers of transitive and intransitive verbal subclasses are derived historically from frozen personal pronominal prefixes. He speculates that this may have come about in the following way. In the wars against the Arawak inhabitants of the Lesser Antilles, able-bodied native men were killed off and Carib men took their place, resulting in a mixed society consisting of Iñeri- [Arawak-]speaking women and children and Mainland Carib–speaking men, who used Pidgin Carib to bridge the language gap between them. Children born of these unions learned their mothers' Arawakan language; the men's Carib failed to be imposed as a community language, but Pidgin Carib continued to be used because these people continued to identify themselves ethnically as Caribs and maintained political and trading relations with Mainland Caribs. Hence, the Pidgin Carib was retained for these functions and became the men's jargon.

Media Lengua and Catalangu

There are a number of languages in Ecuador which involve Quechua-Spanish mixture: the Media Lengua spoken around Salcedo (Cotopaxi province), the Media Lengua of the Saraguro area (Loja Province), and the Catalangu spoken around Cañar. Muysken defines *Media Lengua* (Spanish for 'half language'), and its varieties, as essentially "a form of Quechua with a vocabulary almost completely derived from Spanish, but which to a large extent preserves the syntactic and semantic structures of Quechua" (1980:75). He emphasizes that "*all* Quechua words, including all core vocabulary, have been replaced" by Spanish (1994b:203). Catalangu is also such a mixed language but is "much closer to Spanish than Media Lengua" (Muysken 1980:78). (For a discussion of the similarities and differences among these mixed language varieties, see Muysken 1980). Nevertheless, there has been considerable Spanish impact on the syntax of at least the Media Lengua of Cotopaxi, including the introduction of prepositions, conjunctions, complementizers, word order changes, and the subordinator *-ndu* (derived from Spanish participles in *-Vndo*). Muysken (1994b) speculates that Media Lengua probably originated with acculturated Indians who did not identify completely with either rural Quechua culture or Spanish culture, and Media Lengua served the role of ethnic self-identification. It did not begin as a trade or contact language. (See also Muysken 1981; Smith 1994.)

Callahuaya (Machaj-Juyai, Kallawaya)

Callahuaya is a mixed language (or jargon) based predominantly on lexical items from Puquina (an extinct languages of the Central Andes) with Quechua morphology. It is used only for special purposes, for curing ceremonies by male curers from Charazani and a few villages in the provinces of Muñecas and Bautista Saavedra, Department of La Paz, Bolivia, who travel widely throughout this part of South America to practice their profession. These Callahuaya curers also speak Quechua, Aymara, and Spanish. Stark (1972b) found in the Swadesh 200-word list that 70% of Callahuaya vocabulary was from Puquina, 14% from Quechua, 14% from Aymara, and 2% from Uru-Chipaya. Muysken (1994a) reports that some Callahuaya words are from Tacana. The morphology, however, is almost wholly identical to that of Cuzco Quechua; a few examples are: 'accusative' -ta (Callahuaya usi-ta, Quechua wasi-ta 'house'), 'imperative' -y (Callahuaya tahra-y, Quechua lʸank'a-y 'work!'), 'plural' -kuna (Callahuaya simi-kuna, Quechua ñan-kuna 'roads'). The possessive pronominal paradigm is identical in the two languages (-y 'my', -yki 'your', -n 'his/her/its', -n-čiš 'our [inclusive], -y-ku 'our [exclusive]'). The locative/case system is identical (-man 'to', -manta 'from'; -pi 'in', -wan 'with'; -rayku 'because of'). The Callahuaya verbal morphology is entirely from Quechua (e.g., -či 'causative', -na 'reciprocal', -ku 'reflexive', -mu 'directional hither', -rqa 'past', -sqa 'narrative past'). Muysken (1994b) finds a vowel-length distinction in words of Puquina origin (not found in the Quechua of the region), as well as aspirated and glottalized stops in words from both Quechua and Puquina (though Puquina had no such contrasts). (See Büttner 1983: 23, Muysken 1994b, Oblitas Poblete 1968, Stark 1972b.)

Nheengatú or Lingua Geral Amazônica ("Lingua Boa," Lingua Brasílica, Lingua Geral do Norte)

Technically, Nheengatú is neither a pidgin nor a mixed language but a simplified version of Tupinambá that developed as a lingua franca for interethnic communication in northern Brazil.[6] Tupinambá (a Tupian language) was spoken by many people over a considerable distance in Maranhão and Pará along the northern Brazilian coast, where Portuguese colonizers arrived nearly a hundred years after they had in São Paulo.

It came to be used widely among the Portuguese colonial population during the seventeenth century and gave rise to Lingua Geral or Nheengatú. This was the language spoken in the missions and by the colonizers who pushed into the Amazon interior to form settlements and towns in the Amazon basin in the seventeenth and eighteenth centuries. It came to be used also by slaves (including those of African origin) and various Indian groups, and was the language of administration and missionization until the nineteenth century. It spread throughout the whole of the Amazon basin, reaching the border of Peru in the west, penetrating Colombia on the Rio Vaupés in the northeast, and reaching Venezuela along the Rio Negro (where it is called Yeral). It is still spoken fairly extensively along the Rio Negro and elsewhere in pockets in the Amazon region.

The Nheengatú spoken today is different from both Tupinambá and the Lingua Geral recorded in the eighteenth century, for it has undergone several structural simplifications. For example, it reduced the system of demonstratives from one containing contrasts of visible/invisible and 'this'/'that'/'that yonder' to a system with only two forms, 'this' and 'that'. The personal pronouns were reduced from various plural forms for 'inclusive' and 'exclusive' to only one. It gave up its five moods, 'indicative, imperative, gerund, circumstantial, and subjunctive', for a single form corresponding to the old 'indicative', and it lost its system of six cases (though some words still have a separate locative form). It developed subordinate clause structures that are more similar in form to Portuguese. (See Bessa Freire 1983, Moore, Facundes, and Pires 1994, Rodrigues 1986:99–109, Sorensen 1985:146–7, Taylor 1985.)

Lingua Geral do Sul or Lingua Geral Paulista (Tupí Austral)

The other Lingua Geral of Brazil is less well known than Nheengatú (Lingua Geral Amazônica). Lingua Geral do Sul was originally the language of the Tupí of São Vicente and the upper Tietê River, which differs from Tupinambá. It was the language spoken in the seventeenth century by those of São Paulo who went to explore the states of Minas Gerais, Groiás, and Mato Grosso, as well as southern Brazil. As the language of these settlers and adventurers, this Lingua geral penetrated far to the interior. It was the dominant language in São Paulo in the seventeenth century but was displaced by Portuguese in the eighteenth century (Rodrigues 1986:102).

Other Pidgin and Trade Languages

Bakker, in his study of the historical and linguistic
information concerning early language use in northeastern Canada, reports evidence of the existence of
Labrador Eskimo Pidgin (called Labrador Inuit Pidgin
French by Smith [1994]); this was commented on in
a few reports from the late seventeenth and the eighteenth centuries and was involved in trade among
speakers of Basque, Breton, and Inuit in the Strait of
Belle Isle (Bakker 1987, 1989a, 1989b, in press b;
Bakker and Grant, in press). Hudson Strait Pidgin
Eskimo was "a rudimentary Eskimo pidgin" spoken
between 1750 and 1850, which also contained Cree
words (Bakker and Grant, in press). A Nootka Jargon
is reported; it was a pidgin Nootka spoken on the
Northwest Coast in the late eighteenth and early
nineteenth centuries that was later replaced by Chinook Jargon. Chinook Jargon incorporated a number
of Nootka vocabulary items from Nootka Jargon (see
especially Bakker and Grant, in press). Ocaneechi
(Occaneechee) is an extinct language, often assumed
to be related to Catawban (Siouan-Catawban) and
about which very little is known. It was used as a
lingua franca by a number of Native American groups
in Virginia and the Carolinas in early colonial times.
The extent to which it was pidginized for this purpose
is not known, but some scholars have asserted that it
was a pidgin language (see Chapter 4). Trader Navajo
could be added to this list, but it is apparently spoken
only by non-Navajo traders, not by Navajos themselves (see Werner 1963). Yopará is a variety of
Guaraní, generally held in low esteem, said to be
either excessively mixed with Spanish or a hybrid of
Guaraní and Spanish. It is spoken in Asunción and in
Corrientes Province in Paraguay, and by Paraguayan
immigrants in Buenos Aires (Muñoz 1993). Drechsel
refers to an "Afro-Seminole Creole" (1981:112,
1983a:394, citing Ian Hancock) spoken by people of
African and Seminole descent in communities along
the Texas-Mexico border and perhaps also in Oklahoma. Afro-Seminole Creole is called "Seminole" but
it is an English-based Creole—in fact it is a variety
of Gullah that includes only a few words from an
unidentified Native American language (Hancock
1980). Since this turns out to be but a variety of
Gullah, Drechsel's speculations about possible relexification from a former Muskogean base (mentioned
above) can apparently now be discarded (Hancock
1980; Peter Bakker, personal communication).

Other Pidgins and trade languages referred to by
Smith (1995), about which I have no additional information, include Haida Jargon (based on Haida, it was
used by speakers of English, Haida, Coast Tsimshian,
and Heiltsuk on Queen Charlotte Islands in the

1830s); Kutenai Jargon (based on Kutenai and used
in communication between Europeans and Kutenai
speakers in the nineteenth century); and an unnamed
Guajiro-Spanish mixed language (that is replacing
Guajiro in parts of Colombia and Venezuela). Muysken (1980:69–70) mentions numerous references to
Spanish-based pidgins among Native Americans of
the upper Amazon region; he cites examples from
different sources, some involving Jívaro and Záparo
speakers. However, he finds that it is unclear whether
the features he points out are conventionalized and
thus represent a real pidgin or not.

Sources indicate that several native languages
were used also as lingua francas in wider areas, for
example, Tuscarora, 'Savannah' ('Savannock, Sao-
nock', Drechsel 1983a:389–90), Catawba, Occaneechee (Ocaneechi), and Creek (Crawford 1978:5–
7). They include the various 'lenguas generales' of
Latin America (Nahuatl, Quechua, Tupí, and Guaraní), which played important roles in Spanish and
Portuguese colonial administration; some of them
had been in widespread use as lingua francas before
European contact (see Heath 1972, Mannheim 1991).
Plains sign language served this function in the Plains
culture area and beyond (see Wurtzburg and Campbell
1995).[7]

These Native American pidgins, creoles, trade languages, and mixed languages deserve much more
attention.

Notes to Appendix

1. I especially thank Peter Bakker for much helpful feedback on the subject matter of this appendix;
he sent much useful information and commentary, as
well as many bibliographic references, and various
articles to which I otherwise would not have had
access.

2. Ives Goddard points out (personal communication) that Hale (1846) presented a rather persuasive
account of a post-contact origin for Chinook Jargon.
When Hale was in the Northwest Coast area in 1842,
he found that the process of developing the pidgin
had taken place within living memory; his later view
seems to have been influenced by Gibbs. Silverstein,
in effect, holds that Chinook Jargon is a jargon, a
vocabulary with no identifiable grammar of its own;
rather it is mapped onto the grammatical structure of
the first language of the particular speaker. He refers
to "the systematic non-appearance in [Chinook] Jargon of anything not relatable to both Chinook and
English" (1972:616). This implies European input,
points to a post-contact origin, and denies that Chinook Jargon is a true pidgin. Thomason (1983) shows
this conclusion to be in error. There is a great deal in

both the phonology (for example, glottalized consonants) and grammar (for example, sentence-initial
negative marker) of Chinook Jargon that is quite at
odds with English or French structure and her arguments demonstate that Chinook Jargon is a true pidgin.
I am persuaded by Thomason's arguments, but perhaps
the matter deserves more intensive investigation.

3. There may be other cases of other languages
which are similar to Michif that merit study. For
example, Attikamek and Montagnais reportedly exhibit similarities; these two Algonquian languages,
closely related to Cree, also utilize French noun
phrases heavily in otherwise native discourse (see
Bakker 1994).

4. De Laet (1633:75) gave some fifty words and
a few numerals in a language which he called "Sanki-
kan(orum)", from Virginia, which Ives Goddard has
identified as being "Unami, but probably actually
Pidgin Delaware in its nascent state" (personal communication).

5. Often some material from a language which is
in the process of dying can function emblematically,
that is, as a "boundary marker" or a symbol of
identification to signal in-group identity, solidarity,
and intimacy, and to distinguish outsiders. It is possible that the Nicarao in the text had this function—a
reinforcer of ethnic identity for a group whose language was in the process of being replaced by dominant Spanish at the time (Campbell 1994a).

6. *Lingua geral* 'general or common language'
was a Portuguese term used in colonial times to refer
to the native language most commonly spoken in
various regions. Thus the Spanish term *lengua general*
in Paraguay was for Guaraní and in Peru it was
for Quechua. That is, the term is ambiguous and
is sometimes applied to languages other than the
Nheengatú that is descended from Tupinambá.

7. Bakker and Grant (in press) also report the
use of an independent sign language in the Plateau
area.

2

The History of American Indian (Historical) Linguistics

> I fear great evil from vast opposition in opinion on all subjects of classification.
>
> Charles Darwin, 1838 (pencil notes, quoted in Bowlby 1990:225)

IN 1925 EDWARD SAPIR THOUGHT that "the real problems of American Indian linguistics have hardly been stated, let alone studied" (1925a:527). Vastly more information is available now, especially descriptive material on many of the languages, and much excellent historical linguistic work involving various Native American language groups has been completed, though many controversies still attend the historical study of these languages. Therefore, if Sapir could update his statement today, he might well rephrase it as: Many of the problems in American Indian linguistics have already been solved, but disagreements remain. My goal in this chapter is to present an overview of the history of the historical linguistic study of Native American languages.

One purpose of this chapter is to determine what has been established concerning Native American historical linguistics and to distinguish this from past ideas that have proven incorrect and should therefore now be abandoned. Another goal is to correct some common misconceptions about this history and to show the important contribution that the study of these languages has made to the development of linguistic thinking in general. This survey emphasizes genetic classification, the historical linguistic methods employed, and the themes which recur throughout this history. The plot of the story, to the extent that there is one, is developed chronologically and concentrates on the role played by individuals in the development of thought in this field. Many quotations are included to permit these persons to speak for themselves.[1] Those who have played major roles, such as Peter Duponceau, Daniel Brinton, John Wesley Powell, Franz Boas, and Edward Sapir, are given considerable space to explain their impact on such important general matters as methods for investigating linguistic relationships, theoretical views concerning the nature of language which influenced how they and their followers viewed language relationships and linguistic change, and their specific contributions to the classification of Native American languages. Some topics are so important to the story line that the chronological flow is occasionally interrupted in order to devote the attention they warrant to them. In particular, there are sections on sound change and on classifications in South America. This means that some important recurrent themes are not explicated in a single location in the narrative but are revealed as the history of individuals' contributions unfolds. Such topics include the relative weights given to lexical and grammatical evidence for genetic relationship, conflicts in the interpretation of similarities as being shared as a result of either inheritance from a common ancestor or diffusion, and allegiances to "psychological" or "comparative/historical" outlooks. Some of the characters in this drama play only bit parts, but they are necessary to the story because issues associated with them have been given such prominence in recent discussions that they cannot be left in the wings. For example, the seriousness of the recent claim that sound correspondences played no role in American Indian linguistic history brings on stage some individuals who might otherwise have been left out. And the claim that American Indian linguistics was largely independent of European linguistic thought has focused attention on Europeans, Americans trained in Europe, and American impact on European linguistic thinking.

Two important topics occur throughout this history. The first is *issues of methodology,* and in particular the roles of grammar, sound correspondences, and (basic) vocabulary in evidence for genetic relationship (see Haas 1969b, Hymes 1959). It should be noted here at the outset that, throughout the history of linguistics (in Europe and in America), the criteria for establishing genetic relationships employed, both in pronouncements about method and in actual practice, consistently included grammatical evidence, sound correspondences, and agreements in basic vocabulary. It will be helpful to keep in mind Henry Hoenigswald's summary of the points on which seventeenth- and eighteenth-century linguistic scholars agreed:

First, . . . there was "the concept of a no longer spoken parent language which in turn produced the major linguistic groups of Asia and Europe". Then there was . . . "a concept of the development of languages into dialects and of dialects into new independent languages". Third came "certain minimum standards for determining what words are borrowed and what words are ancestral in a language", and, fourth, "an insistence that not a few random items, but a large number of words from the basic vocabulary should form the basis of comparison" . . . fifth, the doctrine that "grammar" is even more important than words; sixth, the idea that for an etymology to be valid the differences in sound—or in "letters"—must recur, under a principle sometimes referred to as "analogia". (1990:119–20, quoting from Metcalf's [1974:251] similar summary)

The second recurrent theme involves *philosophical-psychological(-typological-evolutionary) outlooks* concerning the nature and evolution of language in general. There were two partially overlapping, somewhat conflicting theoretical lines of (historical) linguistic thought, addressed by Sapir (1921b) and Bloomfield (1933) but largely forgotten by the current generation of linguists. These have to do with the frequent nineteenth-century clash between linguistics as a *Naturwissenschaft* and as a *Geisteswissenschaft,* usually discussed, if at all, in association with August Schleicher (1861–1862) and his more or less successful attempt to place linguistics in the natural (hard, physical) sciences while denying any value to viewing it as a branch of the humanities or of the more spiritual/mental/"sentimental" intellectual orientations.[2] Bloomfield recited the received opinion, that there was a "mainstream" in nineteenth-century study represented by the Neogrammarians and their followers and another "small . . . current," the psychological-typological-evolutionary orientation represented by the Humboldt-Steinthal-Wundt tradition (1933:17–18). The theoretical framework of Peter Stephen Duponceau, John Pickering, Wilhelm von Humboldt, and on to Brinton and Powell was one in which language, race, nation, and culture were often not clearly separated,[3] where folk (or national) psychology (coupled with the stage of social evolution assumed to have been attained—often called "progress") was thought to determine a language's typology. This was the sort of macro-level linguistic history later eschewed by Sapir,

Kroeber, and others as too psychological; they concentrated on the more immediate history proffered by comparative linguistics (that which became the "mainstream").

The different orientations were already clear to Duponceau (see below), who referred to them as the "etymologic" (that is, genetic or historical-comparative) and "ideologic" (that is, structural-psychological-typological) divisions of philology (see Robins 1987:437–8, Andresen 1990: 102, 110). Duponceau's terms are utilized on occasion in this chapter. Some aspects of the more remote "ideologic" (psychological-typological-evolutionary) approach and of the more concrete comparative-historical ("etymologic") approaches endured into the twentieth century, although the former was played down (by Bloomfield, for example) in the official histories written mostly by Neogrammarians (such as the well known one by Holger Pedersen (1962[1931], 1983[1916]); hence its impact is often not well understood by current generations of linguists (see Darnell 1988:1226, 1971a:74; Hymes 1963:73). Stocking confirmed that various "ideologic" psychological-typological-evolutionary assumptions are shared by virtually all nineteenth-century theorists of American Indian linguistics, "whether in a systematic, a random or even a self-contradictory way" (1974:467).

American Indian linguistics is not, as many have been believed, merely a Johnny-come-lately stepchild of American anthropology, but rather has an independent history of its own. It both contributed to theoretical and methodological developments in linguistics and generally was up to date with and benefited directly from contemporary linguistic thinking. My interpretation of the historical record is that European and other developments in linguistics were generally heeded in the study of Native American languages.

However, according to another line of thinking, which I believe to be mistaken, developments in America were somehow distinct. For example, Kroeber's view was that Indo-Europeanist methods were too philosophical-typological, too concerned with "inner form" (see the discussion of von Humboldt that follows), whereas the Americanists' methods reflected the practical ethnological expediency of classifying native groups, of "forc[ing] order out of this chaos" (Kroeber 1913:370). Moreover, "the European methods of discussing and establishing linguistic relationship are based on theoretical assumptions of philologists; the American methods were worked out by ethnologists for practical ethnological rather than philological purposes. . . . With a few noteworthy exceptions, philology as an abstract science has found little serious following in the New World" (1913:389–90). In her overview of forerunners to the Powell (1891a) classification (which is discussed in detail later in this chapter), Regna Darnell repeats this viewpoint unquestioningly.[4] This view is puzzling, given the number of European specialists in American Indian linguistics working both in Europe and in America, the number of Americans with European training, and the frequent mutual influence of European linguistics and the study of Native American languages on one another.[5]

Greenberg's view of American Indian linguistic history is similar, but seemingly less generous: "There exists among American Indianists and in general in linguistics no coherent theory regarding the genetic classification of languages" (in press). The historical record shows clearly that this is not true—neither of American Indian linguistics nor of linguistics in general (see Poser and Campbell 1992). As discussed in this chapter, the methods employed in research on the classification of native languages in the Americas, not surprisingly, were the same as those employed in Europe and elsewhere to establish family relationships and to work out their linguistic history. It will be more surprising to many to learn that, as a closer reading of history reveals, American Indian linguistic studies were consistently in tune with developments in European linguistics and Indo-European studies, and frequently contributed significantly to methodological and theoretical linguistic discussions in Europe, as well as in America.[6]

Early scholarship on Native American languages was shaped by the social and philosophical issues of the day. The enormous linguistic diversity in the Americas aroused a desire for classification, to bring the vast number of distinct languages into manageable genetic categories. As Duponceau put it: "We are arrested in the outset by the unnumbered languages and dialects. . . . But philology comprehends them all, it obliges us to class and compare them with each other" (1830[1816]:74). An earnest interest in the origin of American Indian languages (see Chapter 3) was frequently linked with a desire to establish relationships between New World languages and particular Old World tongues. Often, the acceptance of a Mosaic chronology (usually Bishop Usher's version) and other biblical interpretations (for example, Hebrew as the original language,[7] or the dispersal of distinct languages throughout the world at the Tower of Babel; see Borst 1959) significantly influenced (and limited) views concerning the linguistic past of the Americas and how linguistic diversity found there might have come about.[8]

The remarkable case of Jonathan Edwards will help us put the study of American Indian historical linguistics in perspective with regard to contemporary developments in European linguistics.

The Origin of Comparative Linguistics and American Indian Languages

Before Sir William Jones's third discourse (published in 1798), which contains the famous "philologer" passage—often erroneously cited as the beginning of comparative linguistics and Indo-European studies (see Poser and Campbell 1992)—Jonathan Edwards Jr. ([1745–1826), a native speaker of "Muhhekaneww," or Mohegan, reported to the Connecticut Society of Arts and Sciences (in Edwards 1788[1787]) on the genetic relationship among the Algonquian languages:

> This language [language family] is spoken by all the Indians throughout New England. Every tribe, as that of Stockbridge, that of Farmington, that of New London, &c. has a different dialect [different language]; but the language is radically the same [all are members of the same family]. Mr. [John] Eliot's [1663] translation of the Bible is in a particular dialect [Natick or Massachusetts] of this language. The dialect followed in these observations is that of Stockbridge [Mohegan]. This language [the Algonquian family] appears to be much more extensive than any other language in North America. The languages of the Delawares in Pennsylvania, of the Penobscots bordering on Nova

Scotia, of the Indians of St Francis in Canada [Abnaki ?], of the Shawanese [Shawnee] on the Ohio, and of the Chippewaus [Ojibwa] at the westward end of Lake Huron, are all radically the same with the Mohegan [Edwards determined that these were related through his own observations of these languages]. The same is said concerning the languages of the Ottowaus [Ottawa], Nanticooks [Nanticoke], Munsees, Menomonees, Messisaugas, Saukies [Sauk], Ottagaumies [Fox], Killistinoes [Cree], Nipegons [Winnebago], Algonkins, Winnebagoes [Winnebago, a Siouan language; Edwards's mistake is explained by the fact that they also spoke Ojibwa as a trading language—see Pickering's note in Edwards 1788:55, 71–3], &c. That the languages of the several tribes in New England, of the Delawares, and of Mr. Eliot's Bible, are radically the same [belong to the same family] with the Mohegan, I assert from my own knowledge.[9] (1788:8)

To show the genetic relationship, that is, "to illustrate the analogy between the *Mohegan,* the *Shawanee* [Shawnee], and the *Chippewau* [Ojibwa] languages," Edwards "exhibit[ed] a short list of words of those three languages" (Edwards 1788:9). Actual linguistic evidence—real data—was something that William Jones's discourses lacked.[10] Edwards concluded from "some 60 vocabulary items, phrases, and grammatical features" (Koerner 1986:ii), which he presented, that these languages are "radically the same [are from the same family]," though he was also fully aware of their differences: "It is not to be supposed, that the like coincidence is extended to all the words of those languages. Very many words are totally different. Still the analogy is such as is sufficient to show, that they are mere dialects [sisters] of the same original language [family]" (1788:11; see also Andresen 1990:45, Wolfart 1982:403, Koerner 1986:iii, Edgerton 1943:27). Moreover, Edwards concluded that "Mohauk [Mohawk, Iroquoian], which is the language of the Six Nations, is entirely different from that of the Mohegans [Algonquian]" (1788:11). He supported this observation with the comparison of a word list of Mohawk with Mohegan, similar to those he used to compare Shawnee and Ojibwa, and with a comparison of the Lord's Prayer in the two languages. Therefore, it cannot be suggested that Edwards was given to viewing Indian languages as being related, since he clearly distinguished between the Algonquian and Iroquoian families.

Edwards's observations deserve more attention than they have received in histories of linguistics, though they did not go unnoticed—his work was republished in several editions (see Benfey 1869:263). Thus in a sense, comparative linguistics involving American Indian languages has a beginning as early as, and a pedigree as respectable as, those of the better known Indo-European family.[11]

Spanish Colonial Contributions

The investigation of Native American languages started almost immediately following the discoveries of the earliest European explorers and colonizers (see Ibarra Grasso 1958:7, Wissler 1942: 190). Although it is overlooked in many discussions of the history of linguistics, the Spanish colonial period left an extremely rich linguistic legacy of descriptive resources, but also of several historical findings. For example, Bernard Pottier (1983:21) counts 109 works on native languages in Mexico alone between 1524 and 1572, and Sylvain Auroux reports:

> At the beginning of the 19th century [the Spanish production of the works of Amerindian languages] . . . greatly surpasses seven hundred original titles, more than two hundred of which date from the 16th century alone, with almost three hundred for the 17th, and about two hundred from the 18th century. If one refers to the different languages studied, one can present the following estimation: At the end of the 16th century, the Spanish patrimony weighs on thirty-three languages; at the end of the 17th, eighty-four languages. (1990:219)

A number of the American Indian languages to which Auroux refers have abundant written attestations which predate the earliest significant texts for several European languages (for example, for Latvian, 1531; for Finnish, 1543). Linguistic materials were produced shortly after the Spanish arrival in America, written in Indian languages using Spanish orthography. These include dictionaries and grammars (as well as abundant religious texts, land claims, and native histories) representing Aymara, Chiapanec, Chibcha (Muisca), Guarani, Matlatzinca, Mapudungu (Araucanian), Mixtec, Nahuatl, Otomí,

Lower Pima, Quechua, Tarahumara, Tarascan, Timucua, Tupí, Zapotec, Zoque, and several of the Mayan languages. The first grammars of American Indian languages were essentially contemporaneous with the first for nonclassical languages of Europe (that is, not Latin and Greek); for example, there are early grammars for the Mayan languages Kaqchikel (1550), K'iche' (1550), Q'eqchi' (1554), Huastec (1560), Tzeltal (1560, 1571), Mam (1644), Poqomchi' (1648), Yucatec Maya (1684), Choltí (1685), and Tzotzil (1688) (see Campbell et al. 1978 for references). With regard to the South American languages, there are grammars and dictionaries of Aymara (1603, 1616), Carib (Cariña, Galibí [Cariban], 1680, 1683), Cumanagoto (Cumaná [Cariban], 1687), Guaraní (1639, 1640, 1724), Huarpe (1607), Mapuche (Mapudungu, 1607), Quechua (1560, 1586, 1603, 1604, 1607, 1608, 1614, 1633, 1648, 1691), Tupí (1595, 1621, 1681, 1687), and Yunga (1644), to mention a few (see Migliazza and Campbell 1988:168, Pottier 1983:28–30). These can be compared with the earliest grammars for German (1573), Dutch (1584), English (1586), Danish (1688), Russian (1696), and Swedish (1696) (Rowe 1974). Rowe (1974:372) counted twenty-two languages for which grammars had been written by the end of the sixteenth century. Nebrija's Spanish grammar (1492) was the first grammar of a European language, other than Latin or Greek. Of these grammars, six were of American Indian languages. Rowe counted forty-one languages with grammars by the end of the seventeenth century, of which fifteen were of American Indian languages (see also McQuown 1967, Campbell 1990b).

Christopher Columbus

Columbus had only a peripheral interest in the Native American languages he encountered; nevertheless, the earliest observations of American Indian languages are his, and some of them are useful to scholars of linguistic history. They represent the beginning of the Spanish legacy to American Indian linguistics. Columbus's early voyages yielded observations on language similarities and differences, produced loans into Spanish (many of which later found their way to other European languages), and recorded some native vocabulary from now extinct Taino (Arawakan/Maipurean). Some of the *indigenismos* (loans from Native American languages) from Taino that were first attested in Spanish in Columbus's writings include *canoa* 'canoe', *cacique* 'chief', *aje* 'cassava' (bread)?, *caçabi* (*cazabi;* later Spanish *cazabe, casabe*) 'cassava' (manioc bread), *ají* 'chili pepper' (see Cummins 1992, Mejías 1980:127). Some other native words (mostly from Taino) recorded in the account of Columbus's first voyage are *nucay* (⟨nuçay⟩?), *nozay* 'gold' (on San Salvador); *caona* 'gold' (on Hispaniola); *tuob* 'gold' (from Ciguayo [Arawakan]); *nitayno, nitaino* (the "word for their dignitaries"—Cummins 1992:152); and *turey* 'sky'. Columbus talked about "the Caniba people, whom they call 'Caribs'," seemingly suggesting that he perceived the phonetic correspondence between the *n* of one group and the *r* of the other and understood something of linguistic change, as when he said:

> In the islands we discovered earlier there was great fear of Carib, which was called *Caniba* in some of them, but is called *Carib* in Española [Hispaniola]. These Carib people must be fearless, for they go all over these islands and eat anyone they capture. I understand a few words, which enable me to acquire more information, and the Indians I have on board understand more, but the language has changed now because of the distance between the islands. (Cummins 1992:170)

Francisco Ximénez

Several of the early Spanish priests left observations of family relationships among various Mayan languages, Quechua, and other languages they worked with. Ximénez (1667–1730[?]), a Dominican missionary, had a clear understanding of the family relationship among Mayan languages and of the nature of linguistic diversification:

> All the languages of this Kingdom of Guatemala, from the languages Tzotzil, Zendal [Tzeltal], Chañabal [Tojolabal], Coxoh, Mame [Mam], Lacandon, Peten [Itzá], Q'aq'chiquel [Kaqchikel/Cakchiquel], Q'aq'chi [Q'eqchi'/Kekchí], Poq'omchi [Poqomchi'/Pokomchí], to many other languages, which are spoken in diverse places, were all a single one, and in different provinces and towns they corrupted them in different ways; but the

roots of the verbs and nouns, for the most part, are still the same; and it is no miracle, since we see it in our own Castilian language—the languages of Europe being daughters of Latin, which the Italians have corrupted in one way, the French in another, and the Spanish in another; and even these different ways according to the different provinces, as one may see among the Galicians, the Montañese, and Portuguese, and even among the Castilians there may be differences according to the different cities and places. (ca. 1702:1; translation from Fox 1978:4)

Filippo Salvatore Gilij

Gilij (1721–1789) is celebrated in historical surveys of South American linguistics. Born in Legogne (Umbria), Italy, he entered the Jesuit Order and in 1741 was sent to Nueva Granada (as this administrative region of northern South America was then called). From 1748 until the expulsion of the Jesuits in 1767, he lived in central Venezuela, on the Orinoco River. He traveled widely and became familiar with several of the languages; he spoke Tamanaco (Mapoyo-Yavarana [Cariban], now extinct) well (Del Rey Fajardo 1971, 1:178). His linguistic insights were remarkable, for they were seemingly far ahead of his time.[12] He discussed such matters as loanwords among Indian languages (1965[1782]:133, 175, 186, 235, 236, 275), *indigenismos* (loans from Indian languages into Spanish and other European languages; pp. 186, 191–2), the origin of Native American languages, language extinction (p. 171), word order patterns among languages (pp. 273–4), sound change, sound correspondences, and several language families. He understood that accidental similarities accounted for many of the lexical similarities between American Indian and European languages, and that the *papa* (*abba, babbá*) 'father' and *mamma* 'mother' similarities "común a muchas naciones" [common to many peoples] did not have to do with genetic affinity; rather, "I too, with others, believe it [*mamma*] to be adopted by the mothers due to the ease which children have for pronouncing it"[13] (pp. 133–4; see Jakobson 1960; also Chapter 7). He reported also some of what linguists today would call areal-typological traits shared by the languages of the Orinoco area. For example, he observed that the words of all the languages except Guamo (isolate) always end in a vowel, even in those languages which are not genetically related, and that all except Guamo lack *f*. Gilij explained that the Guamos were living on the Orinoco but came from the region of the upper Apure River and share their linguistic features with the Situfos (Situfa, Cituja; Loukotka 1968:242), Jirares (Betoi), and others of that area and of the Casanare River area (pp. 136–7). He also cited what is apparently an "evidential" particle shared by Tamanaco (Cariban) and Maipure (Maipurean/Arawakan). Perhaps most surprising, Gilij recognized sound correspondences among several Cariban languages:

> Letters [sounds] together form syllables. The syllables *sa, se, si,* etc., very frequent in Carib [probably Cariña], are never found in its daughter language Tamanaco, and everything that is expressed in Carib as *sa,* etc., the Tamanacos say with *ča.* For example, the bowl that the Caribs call *saréra* the Tamanacos call *čaréra.* Pareca is also a dialect [sister] of the Carib language. But these Indians, unlike the Tamanacos and Caribs, say softly in the French fashion, *šarera.*[14] (p. 137)

Gilij reported a *correspondencia* among three Arawakan (Maipurean) languages—Maipure, Güipunave, and Cávere (Cabre, Cabere [Maipurean]; Loukotka 1968:130): "en la lengua de los maipures y en sus dialectos veo una coherencia mayor" [in the language of the Maipures and in their dialects (sister languages) I see greater coherence]. He cited the following examples:

	Maipure	Güipunave	Cávere
tobacco	yema	dema	shema
hill, bush [monte]	yapa	dapa	shapa

Also, he compared what he called the "rude, guttural" pronunciation of Avane with the "gentle, beautiful" pronunciation of Maipure, citing forms that exhibit the correspondence of Maipure medial *y* with Avane (Avani, Abane [Maipurean]; Loukotka 1968: 130) *x,* and *t* with *x,* as in:

	Maipure	Avane
I	nuya	nuxa
I go	nutacáu	nuxacáu
women	tiniokí	inioxí
axe	yavatí	yavaxí
tiger [jaguar?]	quatikí	quaxixí

Although he did not state them specifically, since he was speaking here of pronunciation, it seems safe to conclude that Gilij recognized these sound correspondences (p. 173).[15] He apparently had a good sense of how languages diversify, for he referred frequently to the differences among the Italian dialects (for example, Genoese, Napolitano, Tuscan, Venetian—essentially mutually unintelligible languages) and among Romance languages, such as Italian, French, and Spanish (p. 234).

Gilij also repeatedly referred to the large number of languages in the Orinoco area ("que parecían al principio infinitas" [that in the beginning seemed infinite], p. 175), but found that they belong to only nine *lenguas matrices* 'mother languages, language families'. He was the first to recognize the Cariban and Maipurean (Arawakan) families, as well as others. In recognizing nine, he also allowed for the possibility that some of these languages would have additional relatives in the Marañon, in Brazil, or somewhere else not yet known at that time. His nine families ("matrices") were:

1. Caribe (Cariban): Tamanaco, Pareca (Loukotka 1968:213), Uokeári (Wökiare, Uaiquire; Loukotka 1968:213), Uaracá-Pachilí, Uara-Múcuru (women only), Payuro (Payure; Loukotka 1968:150), Kikirípa (Quiriquiripa; Loukotka 1968:210), Mapoye (cf. Mapoyo-Yavarana), Oye, Akerecoto, Avaricoto (Aguaricoto; Loukotka 1968:210), Pariacoto (Pariagoto; Loukotka 1968:215), Cumanacoto (Cumaná), Guanero (Loukotka 1968:241), Guaikíri (Guaquiri; Loukotka 1968:213), Palenco (Patagora, Palenque), Maquiritare (Makiritare), Areveriana (Loukotka 1968:212), Caribe (Cariña, Galibí)
2. Sáliva (Sálivan): Ature (cf. Piaroa-Maco), Piaroa, Quaqua (Loukotka 1968:213), Sáliva
3. Maipure (Maipurean, Arawakan): Avane (Abane, Avani), Mepure (Loukotka 1968:229), Cávere (Cabere, Cabre), Parene (Yavitero), Güipunave, Kirrupa, Maipure (He also included "many other languages [lenguajes] hidden in the high Orinoco, the Río Negro, and the Marañon. . . . It is certain that Achagua is a dialect [sister] of Maipure."
4. Otomaca and Taparíta (Otomacoan)
5. Guama and Quaquáro (cf. Guamo)
6. Guahiba, "which is not dissimilar from Chiricoa" (Guajiban; see Loukotka 1968:148)

7. Yaruro
8. Guaraúno (Warao)
9. Aruáco (Arhuaco, cf. Ika, Bíntucua)

Gilij also reported Father Gumilla's opinion that the many languages of the Casanare River region were reducible to two *matrices,* Betoye (Betoi) and Jirara (considered by Kaufman 1994 to be two varieties of Betoi; see Chapter 6).

Gilij's insights are similar to those of Edwards in that both predate William Jones's famous third discourse (Jones 1798), and both men present actual evidence (which Jones did not) (see Durbin 1985[1977]:330). However, Gilij is like Hervás y Panduro, and unlike many of his contemporaries and predecessors, in that he seems not to have had the notion of a parent language that is no longer spoken (Hoenigswald 1990:119–20); he viewed Carib (Cariña) as the mother language *(lingua matriz)* of the other Cariban languages that he knew about (see Durbin 1985[1977]:330).

Lorenzo Hervás y Panduro

Hervás y Panduro (1735–1809), born in Horcajo, Spain, entered the Jesuit Order in 1749 and resided as a missionary in Mexico until the order was expelled in 1767. Returning with the order to Rome, he prepared a catalogue of the world's languages (1784–1787, 1800–1805) that contained many vocabularies and much information on American languages which he had solicited from his missionary colleagues (Del Rey Fajardo 1971, 1:190). Hervás y Panduro established several *lenguas matrices,* and he wrote at length about the three criteria (basic vocabulary, corresponding sounds, and grammatical evidence) that he and others used for determining family relationship among languages:

> The method and the means that I have kept in view . . . consist principally of the observation of the words of their respective languages, and principally their grammatical devices. This device has been in my observation the principal means which has proved valid for determining the affinity or difference of the known languages and to reduce them to determined classes.
>
> The careful observation of the different respective pronunciations of the rest of the nations of the world would be sufficient to distinguish them and to classify them.[16] (1800:22–23)

Although he was astute in his awareness of methods, he applied his methods haphazardly; his view of language families and linguistic change was rather imprecise. Like Gilij, Hervás y Panduro never grasped that the *lengua matriz,* the original language (akin to a "proto language" from which others descend), would not survive alongside its daughters (see Hoenigswald 1990: 119–20, Metcalf 1974:251). Nevertheless, he did correctly identify several American Indian language families using these methods, though he usually presented no evidence for his classifications, and occasionally he classified a language erroneously. Sometimes he relied also on geographical and cultural (nonlinguistic) evidence (as did Sir William Jones) rather than on the three linguistic criteria about which he wrote so much. Examples of his family classifications include the Northern Iroquoian languages: "The five nations Iroquois use five dialects of the Huron language, almost as different among themselves as the French, Spanish and Italian languages are" (1800:376).[17] He determined that several Mayan languages were genetically related: "The languages *Maya* [Yucatec Maya], *Cakchi* [Q'eqchi'], *Poconchi* [Poqomchi'], *Cakchiquil* [Kaqchikel] and *Pocoman* [Poqomam] are related."[18] He added, however, that "quizá la *maya* sea la matriz" (perhaps Maya [Yucatec] is the mother tongue) (p. 304). His evidence for this family included number words, many other words, and "not a little of their grammatical structure" (p. 304). He even did firsthand elicitation work with Domingo Tot Baraona, a Q'eqchi' (Kekchí) speaker who also knew Poqomam (two Mayan languages) and who had been taken to Rome. Hervás also correctly related Otomí, Mazahua, and "Chichimec" (Otomanguean languages; p. 309), and he gave four other family groups: (1) Tupí, Guaraní, Homagua (Omagua-Campeva), and "Brasile volgare" (Tupí-Guaraní family); (2) Guaicurú (Caduveo), Abipon, and Mocobí (Guaykuruan family); (3) Lule and Vilela (Lule-Vilelan proposal); and (4) Maipure and Moxa (Moxo) (Maipurean family) (see Migliazza and Campbell 1988:167). He named twenty-five *dialectos caribes* of the Cariban family, based largely on information from Gilij and listed twenty-seven *dialectos algonquinos* (pp. 204–5, 380).[19]

Hervás y Panduro represents the culmination

of Spanish colonial linguistics but, judging by the frequency with which he was cited, he was considered important in European linguistics.

French Colonial Contributions

There was also an important French colonial linguistic tradition in the New World that provided early grammars and dictionaries, and various religious texts, on some Iroquoian, Algonquian, and Athabaskan languages, and on Cariban languages of the Antilles, though it was less involved with historical linguistic aspects of these languages (for details, see Hanzeli 1969, Breton 1665, 1667, Pelleprat 1655).[20] Other French contributions are mentioned throughout the remainder of this chapter. I now turn to a more chronologically ordered consideration of the roles of individuals, ideas, and events in the development of American Indian historical linguistics.

Development of American Indian Historical Linguistics

Roger Williams

In North America, Williams's (1603–1683) work on the Algonquian languages of New England is considered an important early contribution to American Indian linguistics; *A Key into the Language of America* (1643) was very influential.[21] Of special interest is his discovery of what is in effect an Algonquian sound correspondence involving *n, l, r,* and *y* in several of the New England Algonquian languages (1643; Haas 1967b:817). John Eliot (1604–1690), another famous New England pioneer, observed the same correspondence (except for *y*): "We in *Massachusetts* pronounce N; the *Nipmuck* Indians pronounce L; and the *Northern* Indians pronounce R" (1966; quoted in Haas 1967b:817; see also Pickering 1833). The same correspondence set was observed again later by Pickering and Duponceau, and was confirmed much later in Algonquian linguistic studies (Haas 1967b: 817). This is significant, given the erroneous claim that sound change played no role in American Indian linguistics (see the section of sound correspondences later in this chapter).

Benjamin Smith Barton

Barton (1766–1815), a University of Pennsylvania professor of botany and natural history, collected vocabularies of American Indian (and other) languages and attempted to show that Native American languages were connected with tongues of Asia (see Darnell 1992:69).[22] Based on comparative word lists, Barton "show[ed], that the language of the Cheerake [Cherokee] is not radically different from [that is, belongs to the same family as] that of the Six-Nations [Northern Iroquoian languages]" (1797:xlv). Though Barton discovered it, the Cherokee affinity with other Iroquoian languages was conclusively demonstrated only much later by Horatio Hale (1883) (see below).

Alexander von Humboldt employed Barton's data in a sort of "mass comparison," but he arrived at generally erroneous conclusions (1811, 1:101–2). He had compared Barton's vocabularies and found "a few word similarities between the languages of Tartary and those of the New World" (Greene 1960:514; Barton himself had given a list of fifty-four such similarities), and three years later, citing data from both Barton and Vater, he concluded:

> Investigations made with the most scrupulous exactness, in following a method which had not hitherto been used in the study of etymologies, have proved, that there are a few words that are common in the vocabularies of the two continents. In eighty three American languages, examined by Messrs. Barton and Vater, one hundred and seventy words have been found, the roots of which appear to be the same; and it is easy to perceive that this analogy is not accidental. . . . Of these one hundred and seventy words, which have this connexion with each other, three fifths resemble the Mantchou, the Tongouse, the Mongul, and the Samoyede; and two fifths the Celtic and Tschoud, the Biscayan, the Coptic, and the Congo languages. These words have been found by comparing the whole of the American languages with the whole of those of the Old World. (Alexander von Humboldt 1814:19–20)

Once again, as in many other instances, superficial lexical similarities in mass comparisons led to erroneous conclusions. However, Alexander von Humboldt's program was much like that of William Jones, Hervás y Panduro, and others, for its primary interest was human history rather than language per se. Thus, although for Alexander von Humboldt the linguistic evidence may have been deficient, "there was plenty of evidence in the monuments, the hieroglyphics, the cosmogonies, and the institutions of the peoples of America and Asia to establish the probability of an ancient communication between them" (Greene 1960:514).

John Gottlieb Ernestus Heckewelder

As a Moravian missionary, Heckewelder (1743–1823) spent many years among the Delaware (and also traveled extensively among other native groups of eastern North America).[23] His writings have been very influential. For example, his *History, Manners, and Customs of the Indian Nations, Who Once Inhabited Pennsylvania and the Neighboring States* (1876[1819]) is believed to have been a major inspiration and source for the classic works of James Fenimore Cooper (1789–1851), which romanticized Native Americans as a dying race. Andresen (1990:93) reports that it was Pickering's (1819) review of Heckewalder's book that prompted Wilhem von Humboldt to correspond with Pickering about American Indian languages, a correspondence that was to have a major impact on general linguistic thinking (see Edgerton 1943, Müller-Vollmer 1974).

Heckewelder considered evidence in North America for different "principal languages, branching out . . . into various dialects, but all derived from one or the other of the . . . mother languages." Concerning Iroquoian languages in particular, he reported:

> This language in various dialects is spoken by the Mengwe or Six Nations, the Wyandots or Hurons, the Naudowessies, the Assinipoetuk, . . . All these languages, however they may be called in a general sense, are dialects of the same mother tongue, and have considerable affinity with each other. . . . It is sufficient to compare the vocabularies that we have . . . to see the great similitude that subsists between them. (1876[1819]:119–20)

Much of Duponceau's inspiration and a large portion of his early information on American Indian languages came from Heckewelder's writings and from correspondence with him (a sizeable amount of which was published as an appendix in Heckewelder 1876[1819]). (See the detailed duscussion of Duponceau's role later in this section.) Both men argued against certain prevalent European misconceptions about the structure and nature of Native American tongues. A particular goal of Heckewelder's (shared by Duponceau) was "to satisfy the world that the languages of the Indians are not so poor, so devoid of variety of expression, so inadequate to the communication even of abstract ideas, or in a word so *barbarous,* as has been generally imagined" (Heckewelder 1876[1819]:125; quoted in Andresen 1990:95). In particular, Heckewelder made the grammar of Delaware compiled by David Zeisberger (1721–1808), whose assistant Heckewelder had been, available to Duponceau. Duponceau's translation of it from German (commissioned by the American Philosophical Society) involved him deeply in the structure of the language. In their extensive correspondence (about 300 letters), Heckewelder provided insightful answers to Duponceau's many questions (Duponceau 1838: 66). Duponceau attributes to this translation task the rekindling of his "ancienne ardeur pour les études philologiques" (1838:65). Heckewelder, like Duponceau, was extremely well read in the linguistics of the time; he cited Maupertuis, Adam Smith, Rudiger, Turgot, Volney, and Vater, among others (see Andresen 1990:95).

Thomas Jefferson

Jefferson (1743–1826), third president of the United States (1801–1809) and third president of the American Philosophical Society, was a true intellectual with an abiding interest in Native Americans and American Indian languages. His efforts launched interests and raised fundamental questions which have endured in the history of American Indian linguistics. He was concerned with the origin of Native Americans (see Chapter 3) and believed that language would provide "the best proof of the affinity of nations which ever can be referred to" (quoted in Hinsley 1981:23). Jefferson collected vocabularies of many different Indian languages, and this sort of vocabulary collection would remain central to American Indian linguistic study until Powell's (1891a) famous classification (see below).[24] Jefferson also recognized the importance of basic vocabulary and of grammar for determining "the affinities of nations" (Darnell 1992:69):

> Were vocabularies formed of all the languages spoken in North and South America, preserving their appellations of the most common objects of nature, of those which must be present to every nation barbarous or civilised, with the inflections of their nouns and verbs, their principles of regimen and concord, and these deposited in all the libraries, it would furnish opportunities to those skilled in the languages of the old world to compare them with these, now, or at any future time, and hence to construct the best evidence of the derivation of this part of the human race. (Jefferson 1984:227)

Jefferson's opinion on the age of American Indians and of their languages in this hemisphere sounds remarkably like what is heard in current debates. His conclusions concerning the number of language families and their relationships seems very astute for his time:

> Arranging them [the tongues spoken in America] under the radical ones [different language familes] to which they may be palpably traced and doing the same by those of the red men of Asia, there will be found probably twenty in America, for one in Asia, of those radical languages [different language families], so called because if they were ever the same they have lost all resemblance to one another. A separation into dialects may be the work of a few ages only, but for two dialects to recede from one another till they have lost all vestiges of their common origin, must require an immense course of time; perhaps not less than many people give to the age of the earth. A greater number of those radical changes of language having taken place among the red men of America, proves them of greater antiquity than those of Asia. (1984:227)

Jefferson's sentiment about the age of American languages and his belief that the length of time required for their diversification was not much less than that of the age of the earth would be repeated frequently by later scholars (for example, Gallatin 1836:6, 142). Jefferson's opinion concerning the origin of Native Americans, however, is not so current-sounding, since he favored their passage to America from Norway across Iceland and Greenland (see Chapter 3).

In a letter to Pickering dated February 20, 1825, Jefferson again revealed his erudition in matters concerning Indian language origins and the debated aspects of their structure:

> I thank you for the copy of your Cherokee Grammar. . . . We generally learn languages for the benefit of reading the books written in them; but here our reward must be the addition made to the philosophy of language. In this point of view, analysis of the Cherokee adds valuable matter for reflection, and strengthens our desire to see more of these languages as scientifically elucidated. Their grammatical devices for the modifying their words by a syllable prefixed or inserted in the middle or added to its end, with other combinations so different from ours, prove that if man came from one stock, his languages did not. *A late grammarian has said that all words were originally monosyllables. The Indian languages disprove this. . . . I am persuaded that among the tribes on our two continents a great number of languages, radically different* [that is, different families], *will be found. It will be curious to consider how so many so radically different have been preserved* by such small tribes in coterminous settlements of moderate extent. (Emphasis added; printed in Pickering 1887:335–6)

Johann Severin Vater

Vater (1771–1826) was a linguist, an orientalist, and a theologian; he was engaged also in early America Indian comparative linguistics (Vater 1810; also Adelung and Vater 1816).[25] He was in contact with many of the linguistic intellectuals of his day, including Dobrovský, Thomas Jefferson, Kopitar, and of course Adelung. Vater and Wilhelm von Humboldt were frequently in correspondence, and they used each other's writings and material (Winter and Lemke 1984). Vater criticized Barton (1797) for limiting his comparisons to vocabulary, recommending that the key to linguistic affinity be extended to include structure as well (Greene 1960:515). Adelung and Vater, in volume 3 of their 1816 work (written mostly by Vater), recognized the genetic relationship among several Mayan languages, including Huastec as a member of the Mayan family for the first time (1816:5–6, 14–15, 106; also Vater 1810, Fox 1978:6). Vater presented a list of seventeen mostly correct cognates shared by Poqomchi', Yucatec Maya, and Huastec, though he mistakenly also saw *einiger Massen* [some] similarities between these and Otomí (an Otomanguean language) (see also Adelung and Vater 1816:22–3 for Mayan structural comparisons). Vater also presented a list of thirty cognates (most of which were correct) shared by Mexikanisch (Nahuatl), Cora, and Tarahumara, and also cited structural similarities (pp. 87–8).

Rasmus Kristian Rask

Rask (1787–1832), the Dane who was influential in Indo-European studies (who formulated what later became known as Grimm's law), applied the same sophisticated methods he had employed with the Indo-European languages to Aleut and Eskimo. He presented "grammatical proof," but also lexical comparisons and some phonetic parallels, in support of a genetic relationship between the two (Thalbitzer 1922).[26] That is, the same methods applied to Indo-European were also applied to Native American tongues in some of the earliest comparative linguistic studies.

Interestingly, Rask criticized some of the "ideologic" evolutionary notions associated with the language typologies of his day, which were based on findings in Native American languages. Already in 1806–1807 (before the famous typological statements of Schlegel, Bopp, and others, see Poser and Campbell 1992), Rask contrasted the Dutch Creole of the Danish West Indies, which lacked inflections, with Eskimo (Inuit) of Greenland, which was highly inflected. He observed that although the Creole represented (in his view) the last stage of evolution from Greek to Gothic to the modern language, it had the character attributed to the most primitive stage of language (according to the evolutionary typology of the day). Conversely, Eskimo had a highly complicated system of derivation and inflection, said to represent an advanced type of language, in spite of the assumed 'primitiveness' of Eskimo culture (Diderichsen 1974:295). The full impact of the "ideologic" evolutionary views against which Rask spoke will become apparent below.

Peter Stephen (Pierre Etienne) Duponceau

Duponceau (1760–1844) was elected corresponding secretary of the Historical and Literary Committee of the American Philosophical Society, which had as its principal goal the collection of historical documents and of manuscripts on Indian languages. Duponceau brought Heckewelder, who provided at least twenty-four manuscripts, into the committee. Duponceau's report to the committee on the structure of Indian languages (1819b) earned him a reputation as a learned philologist and resulted in his election to the French Institute's Academy of Inscriptions. His erudition was well known; he was said to have studied twenty-seven languages (Belyj 1975; Wissler 1942:191, 193).[27]

Duponceau's work with American Indian languages had a significant impact on general linguistic thinking in Europe, particularly on Humboldt (discussed later in this chapter). As his friend John Pickering said, Duponceau was "honorably recognized in Europe, by the voice of all Germany [Wilhem von Humboldt], and by the award of the [Volney] prize [in 1835] of the French Institute, for his *Mémoire* [Duponceau 1838, an expanded French-language version of his earlier report (1819b) to the committee]" (quoted in Andresen 1990:98). In Wissler's opinion, the award of the Volney prize to Duponceau "certified [him as] one of the few great linguists of the world" (1942:193). Moreover, that the announced question to be answered by contestants in the competition for the Volney prize should be on the structure and origin of languages of America, and that Duponceau should receive it, shows the strong international (or at least French) interest in questions of American Indian historical linguistics at the time. It is also shown by the 1831 award of the *médaille d'or* by the French Institute to Henry Rowe Schoolcraft (1793–1864) for his articles on Algonquian, which Duponceau had translated into French (Andresen 1984:110, 1990:70). Schoolcraft had considerable experience among Native Americans (mostly Algonquian groups) and wrote extensively on their languages and culture. In this way he became very influential in matters concerning political policy toward the Indians and in scholarly circles with interests in Indian ethnology and linguistics. Echoing Jefferson, Schoolcraft wrote in his diary in 1823 that "philology is one of the keys of knowledge. . . . I am inclined to think that more true light is destined to be thrown on the history of the Indians by a study of their languages than of their traditions, or any other features" (1851[1975]:176; quoted in Hinsley 1981:23). Schoolcraft's four main language families (much like Duponceau's, see below) were Algic, Ostic (Iroquoian), Abanic (mostly Siouan), and Tsallakee (Cherokee, Catawba, Muskogee, Choctaw).

Duponceau was in step with the linguistic scholarship of his day and could speak of "the astonishing progress which the comparative science of languages has made within the last thirty years" (1830:65), citing the work of Barton, Balbi, Court de Gébelin, De Brosses, Hervás y Panduro, Humboldt, Jefferson, Klaproth, de Maupertuis, Pallas, Relandus, Rousseau, Adam Smith, Vater, and the Port-Royal grammarians, as well as Gallatin's (1836) classification of American languages. Duponceau presented his own assessment of the status of linguistics at that time, revealing his views of its goals, which for him had both a philosophical and a historical orientation—the study of modes of human thought and the study of "the origin and progress" in language (1830:69).

As mentioned previously, the theoretical framework of scholars from Duponceau to Powell was one in which folk (or national) psychology (usually coupled with the stage of social evolution attained) was thought to determine language typology. Duponceau, like many other scholars of his day (Schlegel, Bopp, Humboldt, and later Schleicher), was thus involved with language typology.[28] It was Duponceau who first defined "polysynthesis" (essentially concerned with long words, each composed of many morphemes[29]) and applied it to a description of the structure of Native American languages (1819a:399–402, 430): "The general character of the American languages is that they unite a large number of ideas under the form of a single word, what American philologists call *polysynthetic languages*. This name fits all of them (or at least those that we are familiar with), from Greenland to Chile, without our being able to discover a single exception, with the result

that we believe ourselves to be right in presuming that none exists" (1838:89).[30]

Duponceau's view of the character of American Indian languages was first presented in his report to the committee (1819b), though it was discussed earlier in correspondence with Heckewelder (Duponceau 1819a, Heckewelder 1876[1819]):

> While the languages of Asia occupy the attention of the philologists of Europe, light from this quarter is expected to be shed on those of our own continent. This Society [American Philosophical Society] was the first to discover and make known to the world the remarkable character which pervades, as far as they are yet known, the aboriginal languages of America, from Greenland to Cape Horn. . . . [T]he astonishing variety of forms of human speech that exists in the eastern hemisphere is not to be found in the western. Here we find no monosyllabic language like the Chinese, and its cognate idioms; no analytical languages like those of the north of Europe, with their numerous expletive and auxiliary monosyllables; . . . [A] uniform system, with such differences only as constitute varieties in natural objects, seems to pervade them all, and this *genus* of human languages has been called *polysynthetic,* from the numerous combinations of ideas which it presents in the form of words. (1830:76–7)[31]

The refrain of "a wonderful organization," "distinct from the languages of all the known world," and "a uniformity of grammar from Greenland to Cape Horn" was to be repeated over and over in the subsequent history of American Indian historical linguistics.[32] The following is an influential and often cited passage from Duponceau's 1838 *Mémoire* that summarizes his main conclusions:

> This report presents as results the following facts:
> First, that the American languages, in general, are rich in words and grammatical forms, and that in their complex structure is found the greatest order and the most regular method;
> Second, that these complicated forms, to which I have given the name of *polysynthetic,* appear to exist in all these languages, from Greenland to Cape Horn;
> Third, that these same forms appear to differ essentially from those of the old and modern languages of the other hemisphere.[33] (1838:66–7)

It is interesting to juxtapose this view, which at the time was held generally by scholars, with that of Edward Sapir and Morris Swadesh, which is the very opposite in sentiment and which is almost universally held today:

> It is safe to say that any grammatical category to be found elsewhere in the world is sure to have a near analog somewhere in the native languages of the new world. And surely there are no exclusively American traits that are not to be found anywhere else. (1946:110).

Humboldt, influenced by his extensive correspondence with Duponceau, adopted the notion of "polysynthesis," and through Humboldt, Duponceau and this concept became well known to European linguistic scholars.[34]

Duponceau thought his 1838 work to be principally about Algonquian languages (rather than about American Indian languages generally; his title, in fact, shows this: *Mémoire sur le caractère grammatical des langues de l'Amérique du nord, connues sous le noms de Lenni-Lénapé, Mohégan et Chippéway;* 1838:75), and he thought these had something to tell us about languages in general:

> You have heard, I presume, that the French Institute have awarded me a medal of twelve hundred francs for a Memoir on the Algonkin family of languages. It was written in great haste; I had only five months for it, therefore I had no idea of publishing it; I did not even keep a complete copy of it. I have written a Preface for my French Memoir, in which *I recommend the study of languages, with a view to discovering the original formation of human language, and the various modes which different nations have adopted to attain that object.* That is the sense in which I have written the Memoir in question; *it is, in fact, an inquiry, through the Algonkin idioms, into the origin of language.* (Emphasis added; letter from Duponceau to Pickering, September 30, 1835; Pickering 1887:425)

In sum, Duponceau assumed that American Indian languages exhibit a uniform grammatical structure and underlying plan of thought. However, because he was reacting to erroneous European opinions concerning the structure of American languages, he avoided the negative associations of the typology with lower stages of human social evolution so common in subsequent views: "I do not, therefore, see as yet, that there is a necessary connexion between the greater or lesser degree of civilisation of a people, and the organization of their language" (Heckewelder 1876[1819]:378–9; quoted in Andresen 1990:97).

As mentioned earlier, Duponceau divided philology into "etymology" and "ideology"—which correspond to the historical-comparative and psychological-typological orientations that recur throughout the history of American Indian linguistics and, indeed, the history of linguistics in general. Phonology was his third division (Aarsleff 1988:lxiv). Etymology to Duponceau was "the mainly historical comparison of word forms, by which the affinities of languages may be established"; genetic classification belongs to this subdivision. Ideology encompassed "the various forms, structures, and systems of languages and the means whereby they differently group and expound the ideas of the human mind." In his view, typology and its psychological implications belonged to this subfield (Robins 1987:437–8; cited in Andresen 1990:102).[35]

Although he is better known for his statements concerning typology (his "ideologic" division), Duponceau also engaged in historical-comparative work (his "etymologic" division). He classified "the various Indian dialects on the Northern Atlantic side of America" (from Pickering, quoted by Haas 1978[1969b]:133) into four genetic families; three were accurate (Karalit or Esquimo-Greenlandic, Iroquois, and Lenni-Lenápe [Algonquian]), but his Floridian or Southern stock, often mistakenly equated with Muskogean, was "a sort of wastebasket category" (Haas 1969b:242). Duponceau's historical linguistic method included compared vocabulary, as seen, for example, in his Appendix B, called "Vocabulaire comparatif et raisonné des langues de la famille algonquine," in his 1838 *Mémoire,* in which he used forty-five basic glosses and cited forms from thirty Algonquian languages and dialects (1838:271–411).[36] He noted that "le ressemblance, dans le plus grand nombre, démontre une origine commune" [the resemblance, for the most part, shows a common origin] among these Algonquian languages, but at the same time demonstrates their marked difference from Iroquoian languages (Haas 1978[1969b]:132). Duponceau also correctly identified Osage as a Siouan language (Wissler 1942:193). Duponceau's legacy to American Indian linguistics is considerable.

In this context, it is relevant to mention the attempt of Francis Lieber (1800–1872) to improve Duponceau's terminology; he coined the term "holophrasis," meaning "words . . . which express a complex of ideas" or "words which express the whole thing or idea, undivided, unanalyzed" (1880[1837]:518). For Lieber, holophrasis had to do with the meaning of words (the expression of a complex of ideas in a single form); polysynthesis (as well as synthesis, parathesis, and inflection) was "the means used to arrive at the expression of a complex or a series of ideas" (1880[1837]:520). Though Lieber himself was concerned with languages in general, particularly with "classic" European tongues, and only tangentially with American Indian languages, the term "holophrasis" was often employed in later works on Native American languages, but the sense given to it by others was frequently not that of Lieber's original designation. This term appears in several passages cited later in this volume; it was, for example, a term preferred by Powell, and some scholars used it interchangeably with "polysynthesis." Likewise, the "plan of thought of the American languages" attributed to Lieber was included in Schoolcraft (1860), who expounded on "holophrasis."

John Pickering

Pickering's (1777–1846) special attention was drawn to Iroquoian, and to Cherokee in particular.[37] His introduction to John Eliot's grammar (1666), which he had edited (see Pickering 1822), received considerable attention, since it presented a "bird's-eye view of Indian languages generally" (Duponceau to Pickering, September 26, 1821; M. Pickering 1887:313) as the backdrop for considering this particular Algonquian language. His article on Indian languages in the *Encyclopedia Americana* (Pickering 1830–1831) was quite influential, particularly among European scholars after it was translated into German and published in 1834. Andresen considers this article (which drew many of its examples from Cherokee) to be a "state of the art" overview of American Indian linguistics at that time

(1990:109).[38] In it, Pickering spoke of thirty-four "stocks" for the languages of North America (see also Liedtke 1991:23).

As Pickering's correspondence shows (Müller-Vollmer 1974, M. Pickering 1887), there was extensive contact among scholars of the period working in both America and Europe, and American scholarship had a considerable impact on European thinking. Pickering and Duponceau were particularly close and exchanged letters frequently for more than twenty-five years; they also corresponded with Vater, Thomas Jefferson, Gallatin, Horatio Hale, and Lepsius, and they both had a long correspondence with Humboldt (Edgerton 1943, Müller-Vollmer 1974). These letters reveal their awareness of the work of most of the European luminaries of the time. Pickering's view is expressed clearly in a letter he sent to Professor Schmidt of St. Petersburg, dated October 1, 1834:

> The extensive researches which you have made into the Oriental languages will enable you to decide whether there is any clear and unequivocal *affinity, either etymological or grammatical, between the languages of the Old and New Continents.* At present our American philologists do not discover such affinity; and although among the American stocks *some appear to be etymologically as different as Mongol and German,* for example, yet *they all have a strong resemblance among themselves grammatically* and in some of those particulars in which they differ from the languages of the eastern continent; as, for example, in the classification of substantives, which are divided, not into the usual classes of masculine and feminine, but of animate and inanimate objects,—and so in other particulars. (Emphasis added; M. Pickering 1887:410)

Like others of his time, he did not clearly distinguish between "language," "nation," and "race," but Pickering had a clear insight into the value of language for prehistory:

> By means of languages, too, we ascertain the affinities of nations, however remote from each other. . . . In short, the affinities of different people of the globe, and their migrations in ages prior to authentic history, can be traced only by means of language; and among the problems which are ultimately to be solved by these investigations, is one of the highest interest to Americans—that of

the affinity between the original nations of this continent and those of the old world; in other words, the source of the aboriginal population of America. (Letter of July 13, 1836, to Jeremiah Reynolds, cited in Mackert 1994:3)

In brief, Pickering sought both grammatical and lexical evidence, thought that the American languages probably came from Asia, supported Duponceau's notion of shared grammatical traits, and believed linguistics to be of great value for resolving questions of prehistory. Moreover, he recognized the value of sound correspondences for attempts to establish genetic relationships among languages (see below). Pickering (1833, cited by Haas 1967b:817) also rediscovered the sound correspondences first pointed out by Williams and by Eliot (which are discussed later in this chapter). Finally, Pickering was instrumental in providing instructions for Horatio Hale, just as Hale later instructed Boas (see below).

Friedrich Wilhelm Christian Karl Ferdinand von Humboldt

Wilhelm von Humboldt (1767–1835), probably the most influential linguistic thinker of his time, was thoroughly fascinated by Native American languages.[39] He entered into an exchange of letters with North American scholars which Aarsleff calls "the most fruitful linguistic correspondence of his life" (1988:xi). In an early letter to Pickering dated February 24, 1821, Humboldt detailed the nature of his interest in American Indian languages in a clear exposition of his overall outlook, which indicates the importance of these languages for linguistic study in general:

> I have for a long time employed myself in researches concerning the American languages; I have collected by the assistance of my brother [Alexander von Humboldt, the famous geographer] (whose travels will have been known to you), as well as by my own exertions while I was Minister of the King at Rome, where I had an opportunity of consulting some of the ex-Jesuits, a very considerable quantity of materials; and I wish to form a work as complete and as detailed as possible upon the languages of the New Continent. These languages, as you, sir, and Mr. Heckewelder have so well shown, exhibit peculiarities so striking, natural beauties so surprising, and such a

richness in forms (which, indeed, would be embarrassing if it were not for a strict analogy, which comes in aid of memory) that it is impossible to apply one's self to the study of language in general without feeling the want of investigating these languages in particular. It seems to me particularly necessary to endeavor to determine in the surest manner whether the peculiarities of which I have just spoken are common to all the American languages, or whether they only belong to some of them; and next, whether they appertain to a certain train of thought and intellectual individuality altogether peculiar to the American nations, or rather, whether that which distinguishes them proceeds from the social state, from the degree of civilization in which those people happen to be who speak them. This last idea has often struck me; it has seemed to me sometimes that the character of the American languages is perhaps that through which all languages in their origin must at some time have passed, and from which they have departed only by undergoing changes and revolutions with which unfortunately we are too imperfectly acquainted. I have endeavored to investigate some European languages which seem to have been preserved in their original purity, such as the Basque language; and I have, in fact, found there several of these same peculiarities,—without, however, in consequence of that being able to join in opinion with Mr. Vater, who would fain establish a real affinity between that language and those of the New Continent. On the other hand, it might be equally possible that the people of America, however great the difference may be among yourselves, might by reason of their separation from the other parts of the world, have adopted an analogy of language and a different intellectual character which might have been impressed naturally on their languages. I have endeavored to lay before you, sir, the problem which I am particularly anxious to solve. (Quoted in M. Pickering 1887:301–2)

In his work on the origin of grammatical forms, Humboldt (1822) chose most of his examples from Native American languages (see Brinton 1890[1885d]:331). He was thoroughly committed to the view that American Indian languages derive from northeast Asia: "I have selected the American languages as the special subject of my investigations. They have the closest relationship of any with the tongues of north-eastern Asia" (from a letter written to Alexander von Rennenkampff in St. Petersburg in 1812; quoted in Brinton 1890[1885d]:330).

Although Humboldt's methodology concerning language genealogy was complex, it included the criteria that have been accepted throughout the history of linguistics (basic vocabulary, sound correspondences, and grammatical agreements; see Chapter 7), but with an emphasis on morphosyntax. Morpurgo Davies reports it as follows:

> In an Essay which was read to the Asiatic Society in 1828 (but published in 1830), and in an outstanding explanation of the aims and methods of comparative linguistics, Humboldt . . . argued that even the *fundamental vocabulary* cannot be guaranteed against the intrusion of foreign elements, *warned against any comparison based exclusively on lexicon,* and finally maintained that *"if two languages . . . exhibit grammatical forms which are identical in arrangement, and have a close analogy* [correspondence] *in their sounds, we have an incontestable proof that these two languages belong to the same family."* (Emphasis added; 1975:627–8)

Humboldt (1822, 1836) emphasized typology and aspects of universal grammar, and he dealt with the relationship between genetic and typological classification. His typology grouped languages as isolating, agglutinative ("mechanical affixing"), and flexional (that is, August Schlegel's three types), as well as "incorporating" *(einverleibende),* a fourth type which Humboldt added, which he found exhibited by most American Indian languages, Basque, and Malaysian languages. The relationship between "incorporating" languages and "polysynthetic" languages may not be clear, though many scholars subsequently assumed them to refer to the same thing.[40]

Humboldt distinguished three aspects of "comparative grammar," and his approach to genetic affinity helps to explain the welding of "ideologic" (philosophical-psychological-typological-evolutionary) concerns with the more lexically based comparative-historical considerations better known to linguists today. Robins explains this process as:

> comparison of the semantic content of grammatical classes and categories (e.g., whether the verbs of a language have a passive voice), the means whereby grammatical distinctions are maintained (e.g., affixes, vowel alternations, etc.), and the actual inflectional morphs themselves . . . and it

was this last that carried the greatest weight in historical affiliation. This clarifies Friedrich Schlegel's . . . reference to "die innere Struktur der Sprachen oder die vergleichende Grammatik" [the inner structure of the languages or the comparative grammar] (1808:28). But it was still comparative grammar, the comparison of inflectional morphs, rather than general lexical etymologies, that constituted the key, in Humboldt's eyes, to genetic relations. (1990:97; see also Hoenigswald 1990:127)

Humboldt's typology was fundamental to his philosophy of language and reflected German Romanticism; the types were interpreted as outward symptoms of the "inner form" of language (a concept which Humboldt shared with, among others, Herder, Goethe, Adelung, and Friedrich Schlegel), which itself was an expression of the "spirit" *(Volksgeist)* of the speakers and the "genius" of the language and nation (see also Drechsel 1988:233). However, Humboldt's writing was notorious even among his friends in his own day for "lack[ing] form, [getting] stuck in too many details, laps[ing] into excursions, and mov[ing] on a level that was too high and abstract" (Aarsleff 1988:xv). This is equally true of his writing on "inner form." As Aarsleff puts it:

> Humboldt's writings abound in terms and phrases that have gained currency and become cited as if we know what they mean, though in their contexts they are neither made clear nor consistently used. A good example is the term "inner form," . . . but what it means is never revealed by way of explanation or example, let alone definition, which is a device he seems to have spurned. It is generally believed that "inner form" is a central concept in Humboldt's thought, but for a hundred years all discussion has failed to converge on any accepted meaning. (1988:xvi)

Perhaps the clearest statement in Humboldt's own words, which reveals how the different ingredients are interconnected in his overall approach, is found in an 1830 letter to his friend F. G. Welcker:

> My aim is much simpler and also more esoteric, namely a study that treats the faculty of speech in its inward aspects, as a human faculty, and which uses its effects, languages, only as sources of knowledge and examples in developing the argument. I wish to show that what makes any particu-

lar language what it is, is its grammatical structure and to explain how the grammatical structure in all its diversities still can only follow certain methods that will be listed one by one, so that by the study of each language, it can be shown which methods are dominant or mixed in it. Now, in these methods themselves I consider of course the influence of each on the mind and feeling, and their explanation in terms of the causes of the origins of the languages, in so far as this is possible. Thus I connect the study of language with the philosophical survey of humanity's capacity for formation [*Bildung*] and with history. (Quoted in Aarsleff 1988:xiv)

Humboldt maintained that the recovery of the 'different possibilities of historical connection among languages' involved generalizations concerning the role of grammatical type, words, and affixes (Hoenigswald 1974:350). For him, "the science of languages is the history of progress and evolution of the human mind" (quoted in Aarsleff 1988:lxv), a sentence used also by Duponceau. Humboldt explained that "the *comparative study of languages* . . . loses all higher interest if it does not cleave to the point at which language is connected with the shaping of the *nation's mental power*" (1988[1836]:21).

Humboldt's outlook had an exceptional impact on American Indian linguistics in its subsequent history, particularly in "ideologic" discussions. It is worth repeating, however, that American linguistic research also had a strong impact on Humboldt.

Albert Gallatin and the First Overall Classification

Gallatin (1761–1849), born in Switzerland, was the secretary of the Treasury under President Jefferson and was the cofounder (in 1842) and first president of the American Ethnological Society. He "succeeded in ascertaining 32 distinct families in and north of the United States" (Gallatin 1848:xcviii), and his classification was quite influential until Powell's (1891a) superseded it. His first classification was made in 1823 at the request of Alexander von Humboldt and was quoted in Balbi's (1826) introduction. The Antiquarian Society asked him for a copy; however, he had not kept one but had collected much new material. Consequently, he produced

a new classification in 1836 dealing mostly with languages of eastern North America; this version was later revised in 1848 and again in 1854, incorporating Hale's information on languages of the Northwest Coast (examined later in this chapter). The 1836 "synopsis" surveyed eighty-one "tribes" divided into twenty-eight families (with Woccon added as a twenty-ninth in a footnote; Gallatin 1836:3). He found that

> [most of] the territory contained in the United States and in British and Russian America is or was occupied by only eight great families, each speaking a distinct language, subdivided, in most instances, into a number of languages and dialects belonging to the same stock. These are Eskimaux, the Athapascas (or Cheppeyans), the Black Feet, the Sioux, the Algonkin-Lenape, the Iroquois, the Cherokee, and the Mobilian or Chahta-Muskhog [Choctaw-Muskogee]. (1836:3)

To Algonquian he correctly added, for the first time, Cheyenne, Blackfoot, and Arapaho (including Atsina) (Haas 1967b:820).

Gallatin's methods relied heavily on vocabulary, but also on "much grammar" (1848: xcviii).[41] His procedures, as he describes them, reflect Duponceau's influence:

> The only object I had . . . was to ascertain by their vocabularies alone, the different languages of the Indians within the United States; and amongst these, to discover the affinities sufficient to distinguish those belonging to the same family. . . .
>
> The word "family" must, in the Indian languages, be taken in its most enlarged sense. Those have been considered as belonging to the same family which had affinities similar to those found amongst the various European languages, designated by the generic term, "Indo-European". But . . . this has been done without any reference to their grammar or structure; for it will be seen . . . that, however entirely differing in their words, the most striking uniformity in their grammatical forms and structure, appears to exist in all the American languages, from Greenland to Cape Horn, which have been examined. (1836:cxix)

Gallatin was careful to specify what he meant by "family" relationship:

> The expression "family," applied to the Indian languages, has been taken in its most extensive sense, and as embracing all those which contained a number of similar primitive words, sufficient to show that they must, at some remote epoch, have

had a common origin. . . . It is . . . used . . . in the same way as we consider the Slavonic, the Teutonic, the Latin and Greek, the Sanscrit, and, as I am informed, the ancient Persian, as retaining in their vocabularies conclusive proofs of their having originally sprung from the same stock. (1836:4; also 1836:cxix)

His overall outlook was, in spite of his seemingly clear understanding of methods for establishing family relationships, very Duponceauian (and Jeffersonian):

> Amidst that great diversity of American languages, considered only in reference to their vocabularies, the similarity of their structure and grammatical forms has been observed and pointed out by the American philologists. . . . The native inhabitants of America from the Arctic Ocean to Cape Horn, have, as far as they have been investigated, a distinct character common to all, and apparently differing from any of those of the other continent. . . .
>
> Whilst the unity of structure and of grammatical forms proves a common origin, it may be inferred from this, combined with the great diversity and entire difference in the words of the several languages of America, that this continent received its first inhabitants at a very remote epoch, probably not much posterior to that of the dispersion of mankind. (1836:5–6, 142)

Gallatin had accepted Duponceau's polysynthesis and the notion of a commonly shared structure of American Indian languages which was taken as indicative of a common origin. However, since other languages, such as Basque (as shown in Humboldt's work), also exhibited this feature thought to be characteristic of American languages, the possibility of linguistic connections across the oceans was for Gallatin an open question (Hinsley 1981:24).

Andresen attributes to Gallatin the introduction of "the first signs of an evolutionary optic into American Indian studies" (1990:110). My own suspicion is that Gallatin's views were neither more nor less evolutionary than those of most Europeans and Americans who had previously written on American Indian languages— the ethnocentricism and assumptions about lesser stages of development are discernible in the earliest of European reports on Native Americans. Certainly the concept of social evo-

lution correlated with language type was already well known in Rask's time. It is only later, and perhaps gradually, that this notion was codified in linguistic and anthropological theories.

The impact of Gallatin's work is seen in Powell's report that Gallatin was his starting point:

> As Linnaeus is to be regarded as the founder of biologic classification, so Gallatin may be considered the founder of systematic philology relating to the North American Indians. . . . He so thoroughly introduced comparative methods, and . . . he circumscribed the boundaries of many families, so that a large part of his work remains and is still to be considered sound. There is no safe resting place anterior to Gallatin, because no scholar prior to his time had properly adopted comparative methods of research, and because no scholar was privileged to work with so large a body of material. . . . Gallatin's work has therefore been taken as the starting point, back of which we may not go in the historic consideration of the systematic philology of North America. (1966[1891b]:85; see also Powell 1891a:418, Goddard 1914:560)

For Gallatin's (1836:305–6) classification, see the appendix to this chapter.

Horatio Hale

Hale (1817–1896) first undertook "ethnological" and linguistic research on Native Americans in 1834 and printed the results himself for distribution among his friends. "When I was a youth of seventeen, in my second year at Harvard," Hale explained, he "took down some words" of the language of Indians from Maine who came to Cambridge and camped near the college grounds (quoted in Gruber 1967:9). He argued philologically that the Wlastukweek Indians were an offshoot of the Micmacs rather than the Penobscots (Mackert 1994:11). Though Hale graduated in law, upon Pickering's recommendation he was accepted as the youngest member of the scientific corps of the Wilkes expedition to explore the South Pacific, charged with collecting data relating to "ethnology and philology" (Mackert 1994:1–6, 7; Tyler 1968:39). Pickering and Duponceau were both important in defining the role of the expedition's philologist and ethnographer, and they gave Hale extensive instructions to follow in his investigations (Mackert

1994). For example, Duponceau advocated the word list that Gallatin (1836) used, as well as "conjugation of some verbs, and some sentences of the most common use" (see Mackert 1994:5). The expedition stopped in the Oregon Territory in 1841, and Hale investigated many of the languages there. (His results were published in the expedition's report of 1846.) As Mackert (1994:1) tells us, "Hale's report constitutes a monument to the achievements of early American linguistics and was considered as containing "the greatest mass of philological data ever accumulated by a single inquirer" (Latham 1850, quoted in an 1881 letter from Hale to Powell, in Gruber 1967:37)."[42] Hale's findings formed the basis of Gallatin's (1848) classification of these languages. Hale took a comparative philological approach in order to attempt to reconstruct the history and migrations of Native American groups.

After publication of the expedition's report, Hale was not heard from by scholars for approximately thirty years. He moved to Clinton, Ontario, to manage properties his wife had inherited there. But later his correspondence with Lewis Henry Morgan (discussed later in this chapter) and his reading of Morgan's work appear to have prompted Hale to return to intellectual pursuits in the late 1870s and to undertake extensive research on Northern Iroquoian groups.

A comparison of his early work and his later work reveals that the methods Hale used to establish family relationships do not seem to have changed. In the early work he did not consider similarities in vocabulary to be sufficient: "More attention was given to grammatical peculiarities of this extensive family of languages [his Tsihali-Selish—that is, Salishan], than to those of any other, and the result was to place the affinities which prevail between them in a much clearer light than could have been effected by the mere comparison of words" (1846:536; see Mackert 1994:17). In his later work he demonstrated definitively that Cherokee was an Iroquoian language.[43] Here Hale again gave more value to grammatical evidence:

> The similarity of the two tongues [Cherokee and other "Huron-Iroquois" languages], apparent enough in many of their words, is *most strikingly shown,* as might be expected *in their grammatical structure,* and especially in the affixed pronouns, which in both languages play so important a part.
>
> When the languages of the two nations or tribes show a close resemblance in *grammar and vocabulary,* we may at once infer a common descent. (Emphasis added; Hale 1883:26, 19; cited in Haas 1978[1969b]:146)

However, he also required evidence from both grammar and vocabulary. He discovered and successfully demonstrated, utilizing the same methods he had used earlier, that Tutelo, which had formerly been grouped with Iroquoian (the Tutelo had joined the Iroquois at Five Nations), belonged to the Siouan family. Concerning his methods, Hale reported: "A vocabulary which I took down from his [a Tutelo speaker's] lips showed beyond question that his people belonged to the Dakotan [Siouan] stock. [I] compare[d] it, not merely in its phonology and its vocabulary, but also in its grammatical structure, with the Dakotan languages spoken west of the Mississippi" (1884:13; see Haas 1969b:248).[44]

Hale was literally a bridge between the earlier Duponceau and Pickering and the later Powell and (especially) Boas. The British Association for the Advancement of Science appointed Hale to a committee of Canadian and British scholars, chaired by Edward Tylor (1832–1917), whose purpose was the anthropological investigation of the Northwest Coast. Franz Boas was enlisted to do their fieldwork and Hale supervised his research for six years. Hale's instructions to Boas concerning field research were extensive, and often annoying to Boas (Gruber 1967, Stocking 1974), but they also reveal Hale's views in general and his criteria for establishing genetic relationships, as well as the impact he had on Boas's thinking (the extent of which is a subject of dispute; see Gruber 1967 and Stocking 1974). Instructions dated April 30, 1888, included the following advice:

> A comparative vocabulary will, of course, be important. I think it should contain all the words comprised in the list of Gallatin (which had been followed by myself in Oregon, and by Powell in California) with as many more from Major Powell's list in his "Introduction to the Study of the Indian Languages," as you think proper. . . . It would be desirable that, if possible, a minute outline of the grammar of *one language* belonging

to *each linguistic stock* should be given—somewhat after the style of those contained in F. Müller's "Grundriss der Sprachwissenschaft." I do not think it would be advisable, in this Report, to go very deeply into the peculiarities of different languages belonging to the same linguistic stock. A brief notice of the points of difference will be sufficient. (Quoted in Gruber 1967:27)[45]

And again on April 21 and April 22, 1888, he told Boas:

The main point is to ascertain the *total number and the grammatical characteristics of the distinct stocks in the whole Province.* The question of whether two linguistic groups are not distinct stocks is of great importance. In some cases, it can only be decided by a resort to the grammar of the languages. . . . You say—"It is likely that the Haida are allied to the Tlinget." I can find no resemblance in the vocabularies, except in the word for *elk,* which is evidently borrowed. It will be well to be cautious in suggesting such relationships, unless there is clear grammatical evidence to confirm the suggestions. . . .

A brief sketch of the grammar of each stock is most desirable. If in some instances you can do no more, you might at least manage to get the plural forms of nouns, the personal and the possessive pronouns (the latter more particularly as attached to nouns) and a few of the most common verb-inflections. With these data, the kinship of the languages can always be determined. (Quoted in Gruber 1967:28)[46]

Also in 1888, Hale presented a paper at the International Congress of Americanists in which he capitalized on his experiences with the languages of the South Pacific (acquired on the Wilkes expedition) and the Americas and publicly affirmed the principles he had advocated to Boas.

George Gibbs

Gibbs (1815–1873) was the chief linguistic adviser to the Smithsonian Institution during the 1860s—the first linguistically oriented scholar employed by the Smithsonian. The questionnaire he prepared (with the help of William Dwight Whitney) served as the basis for vocabulary collection for several years until it was expanded into Powell's (1877) instructions for work in this area. Gibbs studied law at Harvard (he

graduated in 1838), but spent twelve years (1848–1860) in Oregon and Washington as a government official, surveyor, geologist, miner, rancher, and adventurer. In the 1850s he collected word lists and tales from Indians of the Northwest, enlisting the help of army officers and doctors active in southwestern Oregon (Kinkade 1990:99). He later expanded his study by obtaining information on the languages of Alaska through correspondence with the Russian governor. His plan was a "complete collection of all languages west of the Rocky Mountains" (quoted in Hinsley 1981:52), with the goal of tracing migration routes and determining the geographical origins of the natives of America. He came to believe in a "theory of a westward movement from the Great Plains along the Columbia and Fraser river valleys to the Pacific" and thought the buffalo country was the "nursery" of the "countless hordes who have gradually pushed themselves southward and westward," though he assumed an Asiatic origin (Hinsley 1981:52).

Gibbs planned to establish an ethnological map of the area west of the Rockies, showing the migration routes he supposed, and to publish the more than fifty vocabularies he had collected, together with the historical connections they suggested (Hinsley 1981:53). His research agenda became that of the Bureau of American Ethnology (which Gibbs, along with Gallatin, helped to found) (Darnell 1971a:76). The aims of his much-delayed map project were ultimately realized in Powell's (1891a) linguistic map of North America. In 1870, Gibbs had 100 vocabularies and recommended that the Smithsonian Institution undertake an ambitious project encompassing all the North American languages to include not only these unpublished materials but also earlier vocabularies (Hinsley 1981:54). The caution urged by Dwight Whitney and J. Hammond Trumbull (discussed later in this chapter) caused the project as Gibbs proposed it to be delayed, and ultimately Powell was to achieve this goal. The manuscript collection of the Smithsonian Institution (founded in 1846) came to include 670 vocabularies which were given to Powell in 1877 when he became director of the Geological Survey of the Rocky Mountain Region, and they later were transferred to the Bureau of American Ethnology, which Powell founded in 1879 (see Gibbs 1853, 1863b, 1877).

Robert Gordon Latham

Latham (1812–1888) was a well-known British philologist (though also a practicing physician) who wrote on a variety of linguistic and ethnographic topics (see Latham 1860a). His *Elements of Comparative Philology* (1862) includes a classification of all the world's languages. He presented his 1856 study of American Indian languages as a supplement to Gallatin's *Archaeologia Americana* (1836), incorporating data collected by Hale on the Wilkes expedition. Latham, however, also made proposals of his own concerning the linguistic classification. He grouped Beothuk with "Algonkin" languages, and he proposed what may be considered an early version of the Macro-Siouan hypothesis (see Chapter 8) with his "class which . . . may eventually include" Iroquois, Sioux, "Catawba, Woccoon [*sic*], Cherokee, Choctah, and (perhaps) Caddo groups,—perhaps also Pawni and its ally the Riccaree [Arikara]" (1856:58). Gallatin had grouped Chemmesyan (Tsimshian), Billechula (Bella Coola, Salishan), and Hailtsa in his "Naas" group; Latham separated them but did not "absolutely deny the validity of the *Naas* family" (1856:73). He grouped Sahaptin and Waiilatpu (including Cayús [Cayuse] and Molelé [Molala]), which Gallatin had separated, and he recognized several Uto-Aztecan connections, grouping Utah (Ute), Shoshoni (or Snake), Wihinast (a Northern Paiute dialect), and Cumanch (Comanche), noting considerable vocabulary "coincidences" with Moqui (Hopi) (Latham 1856:97, 99, 102). Latham connected Caddo and Wichita (presenting seventeen probable cognates) (1856:104–5) but got some things clearly wrong; for example, earlier he had insisted that "the Athabaskan languages are undoubtedly Eskimo. . . . And the Kolooch [Tlingit] are equally Eskimo with the Athabaskan" (1860a[1844]:259), though he corrected this error in later writings.

It is not clear, however, that Latham understood his groupings to represent genetic or family units in the usual sense, as did Gallatin. He at times counted numbers of similar words in compared vocabulary lists, reporting "affinities" (of varying magnitudes) for the same language with various language groups, depending on the number of perceived similarities in the lists. For example, of Blackfoot he reported that "its affinities are miscellaneous; more however with the Algonkin tongues than with those of the other recognized groups" (1845:34). This statement was followed by approximately three pages of lexical comparisons involving some Algonquian languages, as well as some Iroquoian, Siouan, Eskimo, Salish, and others (1845:34–8); he later referred to these data as "showing the Blackfoot to be Algonkin" (1856:61). He said that Caddo "has affinities with the Mohawk, Seneca, and the Iroquois tongues in general, and . . . it has words common to the Muskoge, the Catawba, the Pawnee, and the Cherokee languages" (1845:44). Latham's 1856 classification is compared with other major classifications in the appendix to this chapter.

Latham's method was simply a rough comparison of vocabulary lists for "coincidences," much like that employed later by Powell, though it is suggestive also of Boas's areal-typological approach (see below) in that Latham contrasted languages of a region with their neighbors:

> If we compare Athabaskan with the tongues in its neighbourhood, we shall find that it is broadly and definitely separated from them. . . .
>
> The Kutani [Kutenai], then, differs notably from the tongues with which it is in geographical contact; though, like all the languages of America, it has numerous miscellaneous affinities. In respect to its phonesis it agrees with the North Oregon languages. (1856:69, 71)

Latham recognized one important methodological principle: that the matching of short forms may be due to chance and therefore such similarities are not necessarily inherited (see Chapter 7). Therefore, in response to those who had argued that there were Chinese affinities with Otomí based on Otomí's assumed more "monosyllabic" structure, and after having noted Otomí-Mayan similarities, Latham cautioned that "*some* difference in favour of the Otomi is to be expected, inasmuch as two languages with short or monosyllabic words will, from the very fact of the shortness and simplicity of their constituent elements, have more words alike

than two polysyllabic forms of speech"
(1856:95). However, as was typical of scholars
at that time, Latham adhered to the Duponceau
doctrine that the Native American languages
have a unified structure and hence a single, all-
encompassing family relationship. In general,
with respect to determining family membership,
Latham was not enthusiastic about any of the
traditional criteria and utilized mostly vocabulary:

> As a general rule, however, neither the phonesis
> of a language, nor the stage of development [mor-
> phological typology], are of much value in the
> question of relationship—at any rate, they are not
> of primary importance. Neither is the character of
> the grammatical structure. Of two nations closely
> allied the one may prefer prefixes to postfixes,
> whilst the other uses the postfix rather than the
> prefix; or, again, two languages may agree in
> preferring prefixes which agree in little else. In
> the way of generalizing the phonetic and ideologic
> character of large groups of languages much good
> work has been done. For the investigator, however,
> of affinities a great deal of it is out of place. It is
> only to a certain, though, doubtless, to a consider-
> able, degree that languages genealogically allied
> are also in the same stage of development. This
> means that no single character is worth much.
> (1862:709)

Latham also engaged in linguistic prehistory[47] to some degree, postulating linguistic
homelands and reconstructing migrations based
on distributions of related languages. For example, he inferred from geographical distributions
that the "Paduca" (several Numic or Northern
Uto-Aztecan languages) of South Oregon and
Utah were still "in situ," whereas those of New
Mexico, Arizona, Texas, "New Leon," and elsewhere were "intrusive" (1856:106). Later Gibbs,
Hale, Sapir, and others studying Native American languages would apply similar concepts
(though more rigorously) to the reconstruction
of culture history (treated later in this chapter).

William Dwight Whitney

Whitney (1827–1894) did no work specifically
dealing with American Indian linguistic classification (though his two textbooks on linguistics
present many American Indian examples [An-

dresen 1990:176]); however, given his position
as the most prominent linguist in America at the
time (Silverstein 1971:xii), his pronouncements
in this area were very influential in American
Indian linguistics and he worked closely with
key persons who were directly involved in the
classification, such as Gibbs, Trumbull, and
Powell (see below).[48] For example, Whitney's
"Lectures on the principles of linguistic science"
were first delivered at the Smithsonian Institution and were summarized (twenty-two pages)
in the 1863 annual report (which actually appeared in March 1864); these are the basis of
Whitney's *Language and the Study of Language*
(1867), the first American textbook in linguistics
(Edgerton 1943:25, Hinsley 1981:47). Whitney
assisted Gibbs in preparing his linguistic ques-
tionnaires, which played an important role in
Powell's classification (Hinsley 1981:47–8).
Whitney also worked with other Smithsonian
personnel, especially Gibbs, toward establishing
a phonetic alphabet for Native American languages. Powell also acknowledged having asked
Whitney "for assistance in devising an alphabet"
for his questionnaire (1880:vi).

Whitney's approach to method was solid,
based on all three of the principal criteria for
genetic relationship—vocabulary, sound correspondences, and grammatical evidence (see
Chapter 7)—and the standard application of the
comparative method. For example, concerning
more remote relationships among American Indian language families, he advocated the following:

> Sound method . . . requires that we study each
> dialect, group, branch, and family by itself, before
> we venture to examine and pronounce upon its
> more distant connections. What we have to do at
> present, then, is simply to learn all that we possibly
> can of the Indian languages themselves; to settle
> their internal relations, elicit their laws of growth,
> reconstruct their older forms, and ascend toward
> their original conditions as far as the material
> within our reach, and the state in which it is
> presented, will allow. (1867:351)

Nevertheless, Whitney's view of American Indian language classification, which was very
influential at the time, reflected the entrenched
version of Duponceau's claims and the evolutionism of the day:

It will be clearly seen that the comprehensive comparative study of American languages is beset with very great difficulties.

Yet it is the confident opinion of linguistic scholars that a fundamental unity lies at the base of all these infinitely varying forms of speech; that they may be, and probably are, all descended from a single parent language. For whatever their differences of material, there is a single type or plan upon which their forms are developed and their constructions made, from the Arctic Ocean to Cape Horn; and one sufficiently peculiar and distinctive to constitute a genuine indication of relationship. This type is called the incorporative or polysynthetic. It tends to the excessive and abnormal [sic] agglomeration of distinct significant elements in its words; whereby, on the one hand, cumbrous compounds are formed as the names of objects, and a character of tedious and time-wasting polysyllablism is given to the languages . . . and, on the other hand, and what is of yet more importance, an unwieldy aggregation, verbal or quasi-verbal, is substituted for the phrase or sentence. (1867:348)[49]

It is interesting that Whitney recognized that "the incorporative type is not wholly peculiar to the languages of our continent" (he cited Hungarian and Basque) and noted that it "is found, too, in considerably varying degree and style of development in the different branches of the American family." Nevertheless, he concluded that "its general effect is still such that the linguist is able to claim that the languages to which it belongs are, in virtue of their structure, akin with one another, and distinguished from all other known tongues" (1867:349). Like many before him, Whitney could claim a genetic unity for the American tongues based on the assumed shared structural property of incorporation or polysynthesis, in spite of his awareness of the marked distinctness among these languages in their lexical properties: "It has been claimed that there are not less than a hundred languages or groups upon the continent, between whose words are discoverable no correspondences which might not be sufficiently explained as the result of accident" (1867:350). He listed "a few of the most important groups" of Native American language families, largely following Gibbs and Gallatin, mentioning "Eskimo dialects (nearly allied with Greenlandish), the Athapaskan group, the numerous dialects of the Algonquin or Delaware stock, the Florida group (comprised of Creek, Choctaw, and Cherokee), the Sioux branch, and the sub-family which includes Shoshonee and Comanche" (1867:350).

J[ames] Hammond Trumbull

Trumbull (1821–1897), an independent scholar born in Stonington, Connecticut, assessed the methods that had previously been employed in American Indian linguistic classification. He struggled with the role of vocabulary, for he favored grammatical evidence as the basis for classification:

Forty or fifty years ago, when Mr. Gallatin [1836] undertook his great work of classifying the North American languages, the advantages to be secured by the adoption of a *standard* vocabulary were obvious. Twenty years afterwards, there was still good reason for employing the same vocabulary (with some unimportant changes introduced by Mr. Hale). . . . These works [Gallatin 1836, Hale 1846] opened a way to the intelligent study and discussion of what had previously been a chaotic mass of materials. . . . His [Gallatin's] method was well adapted to the end he had in view,—*to determine the more obvious groupings of American languages* and dialects. *The standard vocabulary continues to be useful to inexperienced collectors and as a guide in provisional classification.* Next to the satisfaction of learning a new language is that of learning something about it—of ascertaining by means of a comparative vocabulary that it is or is not like some other language which we know, at least by name, and that the two belong or do not belong to the same 'stock,' 'family,' 'class' or 'group,'—terms which are used with very uncertain apprehension of their meaning, when applied to North American tongues.

Duly recognizing the past and present usefulness of these vocabularies as stepping-stones to knowledge, we must at the same time be careful not to estimate their value too highly,—*remembering that the real work of the linguistic scholar begins where the provisional labors of the word-collector end.* Such lists of words give no insight to *grammatical structure,* contribute little or nothing to analysis, and even *with respect to the relationship of languages, they enable us to determine only the nearest and most obvious.* Professor Whitney has shown us "upon how narrow and imperfect a basis those comparative philologists build who are content with a facile setting side by side of words; whose materials are simple vocabularies, longer or shorter, of terms representing common ideas," and that "*surface collation without genetic analysis, as far-reaching as the attainable evidence allows, is but a travesty of the methods of comparative philology*" ([Whitney 1867]:246–7).

The suggestions I shall offer have to some extent been anticipated by the drift of the foregoing remarks. The first is—That a constant aim of the student of any of the American languages should be *the resolution of synthesis by analysis.* What the Indian has so skillfully put together—"agglutinated" or "incorporated"—must be carefully taken to pieces, and the materials of the structure be examined separately. (Emphasis added; Trumbull 1869–1870:56–9,64)

In short, Trumbull questioned the earlier typological classifications and advocated the comparative method (Hoijer 1973:662). He did, nevertheless, echo Duponceau with his statement that "the uniformity in plan of thought and verbal structure [of American Indian languages] . . . establishes something like a family likeness among them all" (1876:1155). However, he disagreed with Duponceau's typological perspective in that he recognized the historical implications of the fact that American languages are not the only polysynthetic tongues:

It has been discovered not only that American tongues differ among themselves in some of the features which formerly were regarded as distinctive of the class, but that no one of these features is, in kind if not in degree, peculiarly American. No morphological classification which has yet been proposed provides a place for American languages exclusively, nor in fact can their separation as a class be established by morphological characteristics or external peculiarities of structure. (1876:1157)

It is significant that Trumbull, unlike many scholars in America before him, urged the use of the comparative method in conjunction with more detailed grammatical descriptions, rather than vocabulary collection as an end in itself.

Trumbull's article (1869–1870) on methods so impressed Powell that he reproduced a large portion of it in his *Introduction to the Study of American Indian Languages* (1880:59–69). It prompted Powell to begin to consider the importance of grammar, in addition to his bias for lexical evidence alone, though to be used more

for determining internal subgrouping than for establishing family membership (see the discussion of Powell later in this chapter).

Mexican Contributions

Manuel Orozco y Berra

The treatise on Mexican Indian languages (1864), written by Orozco y Berra (1816–1881), although methodologically rather backward, had considerable influence because it provided a geographical overview and classification of the many Mexican languages that were mostly unknown to European and North American scholars at the time. While he presented little actual evidence for his classifications, he nevertheless professed to rely on grammatical structure and the comparison of *palabras primitivas* (roots) (1864:3, 26). However, he also classified several languages on the basis of geographical and cultural (that is, nonlinguistic) evidence, and not infrequently these conclusions proved misleading (see Chapter 7). For example, with regard to Ocuilteco and Matlatzinca (in fact, two closely related Otomanguean languages), he opined: "[Their] being neighbors in the same area and bearing the same customs induce us to think that there is a kinship between the two peoples and their languages; if this opinion seems daring, one needs only to reject it" (1864:31).[50] In the same way, he grouped together the so-called Coahuiltecan languages, mostly on the basis of geographical rather than linguistic considerations. This unsubstantiated grouping was to have a resounding impact on subsequent classifications (see below, Chapters 4 and 8). Orozco y Berra was not too specific about which languages he actually thought belonged in his Coahuiltecan group, saying only that several bands in the area used the unnamed language of Bartolomé García's (1760) bilingual confessional (see Troike 1963, 1967), which Orozco y Berra called *Coahuilteco:* "All the tribes which were found to the east of the missions of Parras and to the north of Saltillo, until one arrives at the Rio Grande should be referred to this family; not forgetting that if all these spoke Coahuilteco, in many some differences were noted" (1864:309).[51] Several of the "language" names associated with the later Coahuiltecan classifications were not even mentioned in Orozco y Berra's account (Powell 1891a; Brinton 1891; and Sapir 1920, 1929a—see Chapter 8).

Francisco Pimentel

Orozco y Berra was aware of the forthcoming work of Pimentel (1823–1893), but he had nothing of Pimentel's linguistic sophistication (though Orozco y Berra's work is geographically and historically very learned). Pimentel's work on linguistic classification in Mexico, unlike that of Orozco y Berra, was as up to date as that of any of his North American contemporaries. The second edition of Pimentel (1874)[52] had considerable influence on subsequent opinion concerning the classification of native languages in Mexico and Mesoamerica generally, and his work was heeded by Powell (1891a) and other scholars in North America. Pimentel claimed to be "the first to present a scientific classification of Mexican Indian languages based on comparative philology"[53] (1874, 1:xi). He proposed several families that were accurate (as well as a few that were not so accurate), including Uto-Aztecan (which he called "Mexicano-Ópata," with nine subgroup members); Costeño (Costanoan, of California) with Mutsun; Mixe with Zoque; Mixtec, Zapoteco, "así como la noticia de diversas lenguas pertenecientes á la misma familia" [as well as the announcement of several other languages which belong to the same family]. That is, Pimentel was relatively successful in his attempts to establish family relationships. Interestingly, his methods were those standard in European linguistic studies; in particular, he emphasized grammatical evidence but also utilized basic vocabulary:

> With respect to the principles upon which I base my classifications, the method that I follow and the conclusions which I deduce, I will say two words.
> It is known that linguists are divided into two schools concerning the means of classification; some seek the affinity of languages in their words and others in the grammar. I believe that the grammar is the most consistent, the most stable in a language, where its original character should be sought, while the dictionary changes with greater facility, it is corrupted more rapidly: a single

example will serve to confirm this. The Spanish during eight centuries did not adopt any essential element of the grammar from the Arabic language, while they did take a multitude of words from that language. Nevertheless, it is not for this reason that I declare myself exclusively in favor of grammatical comparisons: I have observed that in spite of how much the dictionary of a people may change, there remain at least some of the words that are called *primitive,* that is, names for body parts, kinship, more notable natural phenomena, numeral adjectives, more frequent verbs, etc.: these kinds of words are considered essential to all people in society, regardless of how imperfect they may be.
> Having supposed this, I will say that my system consists of comparing these so-called *primitive* words, and at the same time the grammar, its general system, as well as the principal forms, especially the verb. (1874, 1:xiii–xiv)[54]

Moreover, although Pimentel favored grammatical evidence, he rejected the generally held notion of the time, maintained by most scholars since Duponceau, that all American Indian languages share the same morphological type—polysynthesis: "Until now it has been customary to consider all the American languages as formed in the same mold; I show that in Mexico there exist four [different] types of languages from the morphological point of view" (1874, 1:xi).[55] (See Garza Cuarón 1990 for more information on Pimentel's role in Mexican linguistics and on the Europeans who influenced him.) Pimentel's work, along with that of Orozco y Berra, constitutes the foundation of linguistic classification in Mexico and Mesoamerica.

Lucien Adam: French Leader

Adam (1833–1918) was an extremely well-known and prolific French Americanist—the most cited French linguist at the close of the nineteenth century (Auroux 1984:169). Though many of his works are less than inspiring today, he has been credited by some with having given American Indian linguistics its scientific orientation (see Ortega Ricaurte 1978:124, Auroux 1984:170). Adam relied on both basic vocabulary and grammatical evidence (and occasionally on something akin to sound correspondences) for genetic classification:

It is universally admitted that simple lexicological agreements are not at all sufficient for scientifically establishing the original kinship of two or more languages, and that the comparisons of words which satisfied the etymologists of the old school will not have the same value that being corroborated by grammatical agreements has.[56] (1890:489)

Adam (1878) compared a list of 150 words along with grammatical features in the various languages he examined. He concluded that Cree, Algonkin, and Chippeway (Ojibwa), three Algonquian languages, are related on the basis of vocabulary and pronouns, both personal and demonstrative. He reached the same conclusion with regard to Dakota and Hidatsa (Siouan languages). He also presented several grammatical features uniting K'iche' and Yucatec Maya (Mayan languages).

Like Pimentel, Adam (1878) was one of the few who argued against polysynthesis (and against Brinton's "holophrasism," a term taken from Lieber [1837]) as a unique and therefore defining feature of American Indian languages (a notion that had been maintained by most other scholars since Duponceau): "I am authorized to conclude that this proposition, which has become almost a sort of cliché, must be held to be absolutely false; that if the American languages differ lexically among themselves, they have nevertheless in common a single and the same grammar" (1878:242; cited in Brinton 1890[1885c:356]).[57] Consequently, Adam, unlike Brinton and other followers of Duponceau, never accepted the proposition that all Native American languages should be considered genetically related (see Auroux 1984:161).

This debate between Brinton and Adam shows clearly, among other things, that American Indian linguistic study was international in character, and that fundamental issues of general linguistic theory involved Native American languages in an intimate way (cf. Andresen 1984:118). The collaboration of Gatschet in America with Adam and de la Grasserie in France (see below) further demonstrates this point.

Adam's (1893) work on Cariban languages, a significant contribution to the study of that language family, reveals his method. He presented a list of 329 words, as well as some comparative grammar, for more than thirty Cari-

ban languages (see Durbin 1985[1977]:331). His conclusions were based mostly on visual inspection rather than a rigorous application of the comparative method, which was well understood by this time. Still, he employed grammatical evidence effectively. To cite one example, Court de Gébelin had assigned to Island Carib (Galibí)—an Arawakan language, in spite of its name (see Chapter 6)—a Cariban genetic affiliation based on a comparison of vocabulary, but Adam (1879), through a morphological-syntactic comparison of the verbal systems, was able to show that Island Carib is actually an Arawakan (Maipurean) language (Auroux and Boes 1981:35).

Although Adam did not emphasize sound correspondences, he did, on occasion, utilize a related notion, which he called *permutations* (correspondences, though he did not consider them to be the basis of regular laws of phonetic change). In his book on Cariban languages (1893), he cited cognates and recognized in them the correspondence set/permutations: Caribiri (Caribisi?; see Loukotka 1968:199), Ouyana (Wayana), Aparais/Apalais (Apalaí), Yaomais (Yao?), Crichana *p* : Macusis (Makuxí) *b* : Maquiritarices (Makiritare) *h* : Bakaïri (Bakairí) *kx* (see Auroux 1984:167). (For some of his other comparative works on American Indian languages, see Adam 1896, 1897, and 1899.)

Sound Correspondences

During the nineteenth century, both before and after the Neogrammarian emphasis on the exceptionlessness of sound change, many scholars employed sound correspondences as evidence of genetic relationship (see Poser and Campbell 1992). Not surprisingly, a number of American Indian linguists also utilized this criterion (as previously discussed in this chapter). Since sound correspondences are an important source of evidence for establishing linguistic relationships (see Chapter 7), the instances of its usage discussed in this section demonstrate that this criterion has played an important role in American Indian linguistics, particularly during the last third of the nineteenth century and the early twentieth century, just as it did in Indo-European studies.[58]

John Pickering (1777–1846) reported anew the Algonquian sound correspondences discovered by Roger Williams and John Eliot (mentioned earlier in this chapter), of which he observed:

> An attention to these established differences [correspondences] is indispensable to a just comparison of the various dialects [languages], and the useful application of such comparisons [is indispensable] to the purposes of philology; and it will enable us to detect affinities, where at first view there may be little or no appearance of any resemblance. (1833; quoted in Haas 1967b:817)

As Haas pointed out, Pickering made it clear that he could extend Williams's and Eliot's "substitutions" to other Algonquian languages and that this helped him to identify cognates:

> The letter [sound] R . . . is a characteristic of the Abnaki dialect; as, for instance in the words *arem8s* [aremos], a dog, in the Delaware, L is used, and they would accordingly say, *n'dalemous,* my dog; the *n* being the inseparable personal pronoun, here signifying *my*. In Abnaki, *mirar8* [miraro] is the *tongue;* and in the Massachusetts dialect,— which takes N instead of R,—the same word becomes meenan [minan]. . . . The numeral *five,* which in Abnaki is *barenesk8* [bareneskw], in the Delaware is *palenach* [palenax] . . . though at first view their resemblance is not obvious. (1833; quoted in Haas 1967b:817)

Charles Felix Hyacinthe, Le Comte de Charencey

Charencey (1832–1916) used sound correspondences to classify and subgroup the languages of Mesoamerica. For example, in his "Yucatecan subgroup" of Mayan languages "Maya [Yucatec], Tzeltal, and their dialects, as well as Huastec," he made use of such "characteristics" as "the absence of the letter [sound] *r*, generally replaced by *i* or *y* [both phonetically *y*]" (1870:35).[59] Charencey's 1872 and 1883 works include several Mayan correspondences sets and associated sound changes, several of which are quite similar to those reported later by Stoll.

Otto Stoll

Stoll (1849–1922), too, presented a number of sound correspondences and associated sound changes among Mayan languages.[60] His remarks reveal the role of sound correspondences in some American Indian linguistic work: "These changes follow *regular phonetic laws* and bear a strong affinity to the principle of 'Lautverschiebung' (Grimm's law), long ago known as an agent of most extensive application in the morphology of the Indo-Germanic languages." (emphasis added; 1885:257). He elaborated further: "When . . . it concerns . . . on which basis . . . I proposed the diversification of the Mayan family [Stoll 1884] . . . the following can here be mentioned. . . . One of the most striking differences between the individual groups of Mayan languages is the *regular sound shift* from one group to the other [several examples of which are given]" (emphasis added; 1912–1913:40).[61]

Raoul de la Grasserie

Grasserie (1839–1914) listed sound correspondences among the criteria he used for genetic relationship that argue against chance: "[It is] the regular modification of the same root letter [sound], in passing from some language to some other, following a true *Lautverschiebung* [sound shift], which dispels the hypothesis of chance. Now, these means of control can be applied with success to the seven [Panoan] languages which we group" (1890:438–9).[62] Grasserie observed several sound changes and discussed explicitly the matter of regularity (1890:443, 447).

Adrien Gabriel Morice

Morice (1859–1938) established sound correspondences among several of the Athabaskan languages and compared them explicitly to Indo-European in the regularity of their development, "pleading for application to Athabaskan of the principles developed in Indo-European comparative philology" (Krauss 1986:150). Morice's 1892 essay included a comparative vocabulary of 370 cognate stems, for each of which he attempted to reconstruct the Proto-Athabaskan root (or at least the initial consonant) (Krauss 1986:150).[63] His 1907 study presented cognates and sound correspondences among consonants which included also data from Navajo and Hupa; that is, it was representative of the major branches of Athabaskan. As Krauss points out, by insisting that "Athabaskan consonant systems develop with the same regularity demonstrated to apply to languages of 'civilization' such as Indo-European, Morice was able to interpret [correctly] the inadequate transcriptions" of others (1986:151).

Others

Other, more recent scholars who have used sound correspondences in historical linguistic work on Native American languages include the following, and others.

Julien Vinson instructs us that "within the same family, the comparisons of words are legitimate and conclusive, depending on their having operated *in conformity with the phonetic and derivational rules, without respect for which etymology is nothing more than a puerile art, unworthy of occupying the attention of true scholar*s (emphasis added; 1876[1875]:40).[64] Representative of **Max Uhle**'s thinking is "the specific word comparisons, however, here receive important support through the discovery of existing sound laws, which customarily until now we have done without in comparisons of South American languages. *The discovery of sound laws scientifically supports the supposition of deeper relationships among the peoples*" (emphasis added; 1890:473–4).[65] **Karl von den Steinen** (1855–1929), who worked mostly on the Bakairí (Cariban) language, also had historical interests in which he assumed the importance of *Lautgesetze* (sound laws): "Still all these changes [in the material cited] are only regular phonetic differentiations from the old, often still detectable forms of the Carib proto language" (1892:259).[66] His kinship with Neogrammarian thought is evident in his use of such terms as "exceptionless" and "everywhere" (Auroux 1984).

Christianus Cornelius Uhlenbeck (1866–1951)[67] (cited by De Jong 1966:261) and **Heymann Steinthal** (1823–1899) (see 1890:436) also were supporters of Neogrammarian regularity and applied the concepts in work on American Indian languages, as were Gatschet, Sapir, and Bloomfield (discussed later in this chapter). It is appropriate to close this section with a quotation from P. E. Goddard, which reveals that American Indian linguists were aware of the importance of sound correspondences in establishing genetic relationships: "Modern linguistic study is based on a belief in phonetic laws which produce uniform results under identical conditions. The one recognized method of establishing genetic relationship is to point out the uniform changes which in the course of time have caused the separation of a uniform linguistic area into dialects and related languages" (1920:271).[68]

Comparative Syntax

Not only were sound correspondences known and utilized in American Indian historical linguistic study, but also serious historical syntactic studies of some Native American languages appeared no later than those of Indo-European languages. Eduard Seler (1849–1922), perhaps the most renowned authority on Mesoamerican antiquities of his time, was trained in comparative linguistics; his dissertation (1887) was on comparative Mayan grammar.[69] This study of the historical morphology and syntax of Mayan languages was squarely within the Indo-Europeanist tradition, but it actually appeared before Delbrück's celebrated works (1888, 1893), which are commonly held to be the foundation of historical syntax in the Neogrammarian tradition (Harris and Campbell 1995). This is further proof that American Indian linguistic study was not a late, second-rate copy of Indo-Europeanist study, but was frequently at the center of the general linguistic concerns of the day.

Daniel Garrison Brinton

Brinton's (1837–1899) classification had lasting impact.[70] He competed with Powell to present the first comprehensive classification of Native American languages (Kroeber 1960:4, Andresen 1990:198; see below). Brinton alleged that he was not permitted access to the large collection of linguistic materials at Powell's Bureau of American Ethnology (discussed in detail later in this chapter), a matter that he lamented in his preface to *The American Race:* "I regret that I have not been able to avail myself of the unpublished material in the Bureau of Ethnology in Washington; but access to this was denied me except under the condition that I should not use in any published work the information thus obtained; a proviso scarcely so liberal as I had expected" (1891:xii).[71] Consequently, Powell's classification (1891a), which was limited to North American languages, was far superior to Brinton's classification (1891) for North America, although Brinton's remained influential in subsequent considerations of Central American and particularly South American languages (Chapter 6). This notwithstanding, Brinton's classification did contain some North American proposals which proved to be influential long after the publication of Powell's work (1891a).

A major contribution of Brinton, it might be said, is that his competition with Powell apparently prodded Powell to hasten completion and publication of the Bureau of American Ethnology classification at a time when Powell was having strong doubts, based on a belief of his that had been developing for the past few years, that Indian languages often reflected extensive mixture and borrowing, thus making it difficult to distinguish genetic relationship from diffusion. Kroeber described the competition and its context as follows:

> There was some conscious competition between Powell's classification and D. G. Brinton, whose American Race appeared in 1891. It was a publisher's book, and a work of quite a different sort from Powell's monograph, although it did group many languages. Brinton was a bookish scholar playing a lone hand in Philadelphia, Professor of Linguistics and Archaeology at the University of Pennsylvania, though with almost no students. His wider generalizations have gone the way of Powell's and McGee's, but he was at home with languages, literatures, histories, calendars and rituals, and his concrete work was excellent for his time. He gave only tiny samples of evidence on linguistic relationship, insufficient to be sure; but then Powell wisely published none. Brinton's book covered North and South America. He was less ultra-conservative as to genetic kinship than Powell and Henshaw, and, having a feel for language,

> he affirmed some unions that have stood. . . . He had something of Sapir's flair for fruitful hunches as to connections, though he cut less deeply and ranged less widely. He has almost dropped out of modern linguistic and ethnographic awareness; unduly so perhaps. (1960:4–5)

Hodge and Merriam (1931:100) also concluded that Powell's final result was "expedited by the approaching appearance of Brinton's The American Race."

An interpretation frequently repeated in the literature is the belief that Brinton (1891) actually won in the race to publish the first definitive overall classification of Indian languages, since Powell 1891a, it is asserted, actually appeared in 1892 (Sturtevant 1959:196). However, scholars in this area have frequently lost sight of the fact that Powell 1891b was published in the February 6, 1891, issue of *Science,* before Brinton's book appeared later that year. This article contains a list of the fifty-eight families treated more fully in Powell 1891a.[72]

In his statement of methods, Brinton stressed grammatical evidence and utilized the same criteria as those found in Indo-European studies, but in practice he often relied on lexical evidence alone. Concerning his procedures, he explained:

> Wherever the material permitted it, I have ranked the grammatic structure of a language superior to its lexical elements in deciding upon relationship. In this I follow the precepts and example of students in the Aryan and Semitic stocks, although the methods have been rejected by some who have written on American tongues. As for myself, I am abidingly convinced that the morphology [overall structure] of any language whatever is its most permanent and characteristic feature. (1885a:17)

> A proper comparison of languages and dialects includes not merely the vocabulary, but the grammatical forms and the phonetic variations which the vocal elements undergo in passing from one form of speech to another. In some respects, the morphology is more indicative of relationship than the lexicon of tongues; and it is in these grammatical aspects that we are peculiarly poorly off when we approach American dialects. Yet it is also likely that the tendency of late years has been to underestimate the significance of merely lexical analogies. The vocabulary, after all, must be our main stand-by in such an undertaking. (1891:344)

The fact that Powell rejected Brinton's grouping of Uto-Aztecan languages because he did not accept Brinton's grammatical evidence emphasizes the sharp contrast between these two approaches. But Sapir (1913–1919[1915]), utilizing strictly traditional Indo-Europeanist methods of vocabulary, sound correspondences, and morphological matchings, demonstrated the validity of the once controversial family relationship to the satisfaction of all.

Brinton was not always consistent in the application of his methods, however. For example, he treated Aymara and Quechua as distinct (still a controversial classification; see Chapter 8) because only one-quarter of the vocabulary was shared, in spite of shared grammatical properties, and in spite of his stated preference for morphological criteria for establishing genetic relationships (Darnell 1988:146).

In spite of his apparent understanding of methods for establishing family relationship, Brinton took pains to align himself closely with Humboldt's "philosophic scheme of the nature and growth of languages"—that is, with the "inner form" of Humboldt and others (discussed earlier in this chapter) and with Duponceau's typological outlook (Brinton 1890[1885d]:329, 1890b:36, 1890[1885c]:351–62). Brinton was eager to promote Humboldt in the United States; in 1885 he translated Humboldt's (1822) essay on the structure of the verb in American Indian languages (Brinton 1885d). He repeated and advocated the Duponceau claim of an overall grammatical unity transcending lexical diversity among the American Indian languages:

> Here the red race offers a striking phenomenon. There is no other trait that binds together its scattered clans, and brands them as members of one great family, so unmistakably as this of language. From the Frozen Ocean to the Land of Fire, without a single exception, the native dialects, though varying infinitely in words, are marked by a peculiarity in construction which is found nowhere else on the globe and which is so foreign to the genius of *our* tongue that it is no easy matter to explain it. (1868:6–7; cf. Darnell 1988:131)

> The opinion of Duponceau and Humboldt, therefore, that these processes [incorporation and polysynthesis] belong to the ground-plan of American

languages, and are their leading characteristics, must still be regarded as a correct generalization. (1890[1885c]:389; see also Brinton 1890b:37)[73]

He specifically assailed Powell for not stressing this perspective sufficiently:

> How the author of that work [Powell 1880], J. W. Powell, Director of the Bureau [of American Ethnology], could have written a treatise on the study of American languages and not have a word to say about these doctrines [of Duponceau, Humboldt, and Steinthal], the most salient and characteristic features of the group, is to me as inexplicable as it is extraordinary. He certainly could not have supposed that Duponceau's theory was completely dead and laid to rest, for Steinthal, the most eminent philosophic linguist of the age, still teaches in Berlin, and teaches what I have already quoted from him about these traits [incorporation and polysynthesis]. What is more, Major Powell does not even refer to this structural plan, nor include it in what he terms the "grammatic processes" which he explains. This is indeed the play of "Hamlet" with the part of Hamlet omitted. (1890[1885c]:358)

Clearly, Brinton professed what later students of American Indian linguistics would call the psychological(-typological) orientation (Duponceau's "ideology"), with greater concern for cognitive development (as it was assumed to be then) than for historical events. However, as Stocking (1974:467) pointed out, Brinton was inconsistent in this regard:

> Thus Brinton at times waxed ecstatic on the beauty of Indian tongues, and was inclined to argue on occasion that Aryan [Indo-European] inflection was no nearer linguistic perfections than Algonkin incorporation (1890[1885a]:323). But he was equally capable of viewing his morphological types in evolutionary terms, of arguing that the higher languages separated the "material" from the "formal" elements; that outside of incorporation, American languages had "no syntax, no inflections, no declension of nouns and adjectives." (1890[1885d]:336, 342–3)

Brinton's mixture of methods is seen in his response to various marginal hypotheses of relationships which attempted to join certain Asian and various American Indian languages. His approach involved a combination of standard comparative method, used for more recent language history, and the psychological-typological-evolutionary ("ideologic") approach to assumed language developments in the more distant past:

> What one of the works I have mentioned [that unite American Indian and Asian languages] respects those principles of phonetic variation, of systematic derivation, of the historical comparison of languages, of grammatic evolution, of morphologic development, which are as accurately known to-day as the laws of chemistry or electricity? Not one of them. And yet to attempt comparisons in disregard of these laws is as insensate as to start on an ocean voyage without a compass or an instrument of observation. The craft is lost as soon as it is out of sight of land. (1894a:151)

Although Brinton professed to employ different methods, his classification of Native American languages would appear to be much more liberal (and hence more speculative) than Powell's (1891a). But for North America the two classifications are remarkably similar; both include fifty-eight families, though not exactly the same ones.[74] Brinton coined the name Uto-Aztecan and combined three branches—Aztecan, Sonoran, and Shoshonean—in this family (see Chapter 4). Powell (1966[1891a]:216) considered but rejected this classification, which was later fully confirmed (Sapir 1913–1919[1915]) and is now universally accepted. Brinton also combined Tequistlatec (Chontal of Oaxaca), Seri, and Yuman, a grouping later accepted by Kroeber (1907) and Sapir (1917a, 1917c) and associated with the Hokan hypothesis. This hypothesis is still quite controversial, however, and the status of Seri and Tequistlatec is the subject of dispute (see Bright 1970, Turner 1967; see Chapter 7). Both Brinton and Powell followed Orozco y Berra (1864) in grouping the so-called Coahuiltecan languages together, although the evidence now contradicts such a proposed relationship (see Goddard 1979b; see also Chapter 7). Brinton also grouped Pawnee with Caddoan (accurately), and Natchez with Muskogean (still controversial). However, Washo was not included in his classification, and Catawba and Siouan were left as distinct (though they were joined in Powell's classification). Brinton considered the possibility of a Kiowa and Shoshonean relationship but found the evidence insufficient; in this regard he antici-

pated the Aztec-Tanoan hypothesis (see Chapter 8 for an evaluation). Unfortunately, some of the groupings in Brinton's classification were based more on geographical and cultural information than on linguistic evidence; he had categories called Pueblos, Northwest Coast, and California, each encompassing various genetic families (Darnell 1971a:92). The result was that Brinton's classification included about eighty genetic units for North America and "as many more for South America" (Brinton 1891:57). For Brinton's (1891) classification of North American languages, see the appendix to this chapter.

The Bureau of American Ethnology and John Wesley Powell

Powell (1834–1902) is one of the superluminaries of American Indian linguistics.[75] In 1870 he was put in charge of the U.S. Geographical and Geological Survey of the Rocky Mountain region, which was assigned to collect ethnographic and linguistic information on the region. When the Smithsonian Institution's Bureau of Ethnology (soon renamed Bureau of American Ethnology [BAE]) was founded in 1879, he was its founding director; its main mission was the classification of American Indian languages (Stegner 1962).[76]

Powell's (1891a) classification of the Indian languages north of Mexico, which included fifty-eight families (or "stocks"), became the baseline for subsequent work in the classification of Native American languages—"the cornerstone of the linguistic edifice in aboriginal North America" (Sapir 1917d:79). He drew heavily on the work of his predecessors (see Darnell 1971a:79–85), but in the end presented a very conservative classification.[77] Powell's exceptional staff included Jeremiah Curtin, John Napoleon Brinton Hewitt, James Owen Dorsey, Albert S. Gatschet, Henry W. Henshaw, James Mooney, and James Constantine Pilling.[78] (The important contributions to American Indian linguistics of some of these individuals are discussed later in this chapter.) They produced the comprehensive classification of the North American languages that had been the goal of researchers of Indian languages since Jefferson.

In spite of his impact on most subsequent

work, Powell's method was not very refined; it was a rather impressionistic inspection of rough word lists and vocabularies: "The evidence of cognation [that languages are derived from a common ancestral speech] is derived exclusively from the vocabulary" (1891a:11).

Powell's application of the comparative method amounted to arranging vocabularies in parallel columns under family headings with no further analysis and without indicating which forms were assumed to be cognates. "The difficult matter was to obtain the vocabularies; once these were in hand, simple juxtaposition was all that was required and this could have been done by almost anyone, and certainly was done in different instances by almost all the early staff of the Bureau" (Sturtevant 1959:197). "Essentially this method is that of setting side-by-side what may be alike, and deciding, on common-sense inspection made without preconceived bias, which groups emerge as alike and which segregate off as unalike" (Kroeber 1940a:464). Using such a procedure, Powell could detect only the most obvious relationships (as has frequently been pointed out).

Nevertheless, reliance on vocabulary as the primary criterion of genetic affiliation among American Indian languages was by no means universal at that time. There were even sharp differences of opinion among the members of Powell's BAE staff, who prepared the 1891 classification. For example, while Powell (geologist) and Henshaw (ornithologist) favored vocabulary, Gatschet (philologist) "was inclined to favor grammatical evidence" (Darnell 1971a:80) and sound correspondences, as had several other Americanist linguists.

For many languages, word lists and vocabularies were the only information available, but Powell preferred lexical evidence over grammatical evidence for other reasons. These reflected the fact that American Indian linguistic study had not yet fully shaken off the Duponceau tradition. Powell's reliance on vocabulary was, in fact, a reflection of the then prevalent psychological-typological-evolutionary ("ideologic") line of European and American thought of the day. Many, including Powell, believed that the grammar of a language was essentially an automatic consequence of the stage of social evolution (from savagery to barbarism to civili-

zation) that the language's speakers had attained: "The age of savagery is the age of sentence words; the age of barbarism the age of phrase words; the age of civilization the age of idea words" (Powell 1888:121). In such a view, grammar was not considered an appropriate indicator of genetic relationship; rather, it indicated only "social progress." In the following statement, Powell explains his method (with its reliance on vocabulary), his distrust of grammar, and his belief that language structure reflected a stage of social evolution:

> Languages are supposed to be cognate when fundamental similarities are discovered in their lexical elements. When the members of a family of languages are to be classed in subdivisions and the history of such languages investigated, grammatic characteristics become of primary importance. The words of a language change by the methods described, but the fundamental elements or roots are more enduring. Grammatic methods also change, perhaps even more rapidly than words, and the changes may go to such an extent that primitive methods are entirely lost, there being no radical grammatical elements to be preserved. Grammatic structure is but a phase or accident of growth, and not a primordial element of language. The roots of a language are its most permanent characteristic . . . the grammatic structure or plan of a language is forever changing, and in this respect the language may become entirely transformed. (1891a: 11; cf. Powell 1891b:73)

Powell had based the BAE's intellectual assumptions on the views on evolution held by Lewis Henry Morgan (1818–1881). Morgan's *Ancient Society* (1877) "was part of the theoretical equipment of the entire Bureau staff" (Darnell 1969:129).[79] Thus, the American Indians were to be understood as representing a single stage of human development (a stage of social, mental, and linguistic evolution; see Hinsley 1981:29); "a major effort of the Bureau under Powell was to place the American Indian within the evolutionary development of mankind as a whole" (Darnell 1969:130, in reference to the bureau's eleventh annual report for 1889–1890). Consequently, Powell's questionnaire, intended to guide field research on American Indian languages, included a series of questions prepared by Morgan (Powell 1880:69–74).

In this context, Powell's reaction to Boas's

difference of opinion with the Smithsonian's Otis T. Mason is instructive. Boas was opposed to Mason's desire to base the Smithsonian Institution's museum displays on an evolutionary classification (see Hinsley 1981:99). When Mason consulted Powell, who was a confirmed supporter of such evolutionary groupings, about this difference of opinion, Powell confessed inability to decide definitively between the two but defended Mason's assumptions on the basis of his belief that organization of the museum displays along tribal lines was "impossible because of the constant migrations, absorptions, and redivisions of the North American tribes through the historical period. Under modern conditions there were no stable, permanent tribal units to be represented" (Hinsley 1981:99). Though Mason never abandoned his developmental orientation, the publication of Powell's (1891a) linguistic map prompted him to adopt the principle of organizing museum displays along language family lines and later along culture area lines (Hinsley 1981:110). Indeed, many considered the primary value of Powell's linguistic classification to be its utility for ethnological classification, and such views were fairly persistent. For example, Frederick W. Hodge's *Handbook of American Indians North of Mexico* (1907) was the direct result of the BAE's synonymy project (see below), which was based on linguistic classification. Kroeber's *Handbook of the Indians of California* (1925) was arranged according to linguistic families and culture areas. Kroeber had referred to linguistic classification (and survey) as the "rapidest, most economical and most decisive of the several methods of anthropology" (Kroeber to Barrows, June 25, 1909; quoted in Darnell 1969:302). One of the earliest post-Powell overviews of American Indian linguistic classification was that presented by Alexander Francis Chamberlain, Boas's first Ph.D. student, in the 1903 edition of the *Encyclopedia Americana.* This was an article on American Indians in general, but it reveals the extent to which linguistic classification influenced general anthropological thinking at that time:

> Doubtless the results of careful somatological, sociological, and other investigations of the various tribes of American aborigines will furnish us

ultimately with diverse ways of classifying them. At present, however, the most serviceable classification is a linguistic one, the result of the labors of Major J. W. Powell and the Bureau of American Ethnology, supplemented by the work of Dr. D. G. Brinton. (Chamberlain 1903:3)

The history of the Powell classification tells us a great deal about the history of ideas concerning linguistics and anthropology in America as they related to the study of Native Americans. Powell believed that the first task toward a definitive classification of American Indian languages was to achieve a consensus on terminology, and he had his staff begin to put together a card catalog, called a "synonymy," in about 1873. However, Powell and Henry W. Henshaw (on whom Powell relied greatly; see below) came to believe that the synonymy was impossible without some prior classification of North American tribes into linguistic groups. Therefore, in 1885 Henshaw and Mooney "spent several weeks on the synonymy, combining the almost 2,500 tribal names into linguistic categories." The result was the *List of Linguistic Families of the Indian Tribes North of Mexico, with Provisional List of the Principal Tribal Names and Synonyms,* a fifty-five-page booklet printed by Powell at the BAE, which served to direct bureau research until the 1891 classification was completed (see Hinsley 1981:156–7). Between 1880 and 1885, Powell and Henshaw filled in the linguistic map of North America, on the basis of vocabularies already located at the BAE and materials obtained by the staff (especially by Dorsey and Gatschet) (Hinsley 1981:162). Henshaw and Mooney were listed as the authors of the 1885 classification (Hinsley 1981:156), which was "substantially the same as the better-known 1891 publication," but Powell "assumed major credit and responsibility" for the 1891 version (Hinsley 1981:162; Sturtevant 1959:196; see Powell 1891b; see also Darnell 1971a:79).[80]

Comparison of the 1885 and the 1891 versions indicates that the following changes were made. Catawba and Siouan were grouped, Kwakiutl and Nootka were combined into Wakashan (based on Boas's work), and Natchez and Taensa were grouped in Natchesan (after Brinton [1890a] had exposed the Taensa grammar hoax, see Chapter 1). Aleut was classified with Eskimo. Beothukan was considered to be distinct from Algonquian (based on the Gatschet 1885–1890 articles; Powell 1891a:133–40). Chimarikan was separated from Pomo, Karankawan from Attakapan, and Tunican from Caddoan (Darnell 1971a:80).

The 1891 classification was the culmination of a great deal of effort.[81] Given that it was a team effort, it is difficult to assign specific responsibility, though in general the work done by individuals at the BAE is known. Powell's closest associates were Pilling,[82] James Stevenson (who died in 1888), Garrick Mallery, and Henshaw. Dorsey and Gatschet, however, "never enjoyed the director's full esteem. . . . Gatschet in particular became the laboring work-horse and philologist clerk for Powell and Henshaw" (Hinsley 1981:162).

Henshaw, a naturalist and an ornithologist with chronically weak health, was Powell's central staff person;[83] he provided some insight into Powell's operating assumptions: "It was Major Powell's opinion that a biologic training was a prerequisite to a successful career in anthropology, and this opinion he held to the last" (quoted in Hinsley 1981:162). Kroeber's assessment of how the final classification was achieved is that it "was made for Powell, who was a geologist and an army major, by Henshaw the ornithologist when Powell found that he would never get his philologist-linguists like Gatschet, Hewitt, and Pilling to come through with the commitment of a classification."[84] (1953:369).

Contributions of Albert Samuel Gatschet

Dorsey and Gatschet, the real linguists on the BAE staff, did most of the fieldwork. Gatschet (1832–1907), born in Beatenberg, Switzerland, was the most astute historical linguist on Powell's staff.[85] His methods were much more sophisticated than those of Powell. With regard to the methods for testing linguistic affinity, Gatschet explained that such investigation "extends over the words or lexical part of the languages, and over their grammatical forms" and that "all these comparisons must be made under the guidance of the *phonetic laws* traceable in both idioms to be compared" (emphasis added; 1879–1880:161, cited in Haas 1978[1969b]:148). Gatschet practiced what he preached, for he employed sound correspon-

dences in his own research, referring to them as "the sound shifts in related [American Indian] languages among which the far-reaching laws of consonantal sounds of the Indo-European languages also hold" (1876:13)[86]; he presented examples from the Pueblo language families of the Wheeler Survey. Gatschet approved of the lexical and grammatical evidence in Hale's article on Huron-Cherokee-Iroquoian stock (1883) and supplied his own further evidence of that relationship, in which he utilized both vocabulary and "affinity in grammatical elements," asserting that "in investigations of this kind grammatic affinity is of greater weight, however, than resemblances of words" (1886:xlii; cited in Haas 1978[1969b]:147). In this light, it is easy to comprehend why Gatschet disagreed with Powell's emphasis on vocabulary. Gatschet understood the importance of grammatical evidence and sound correspondences (a view that was traditional in comparative linguistics), whereas Powell made no use of sound correspondences and was dedicated to the psychological-typological-evolutionary approach, which considered grammar as only a stage of social evolution.

Gatschet, like most of his predecessors and contemporaries, was strongly influenced by the doctrine of Duponceau and Humboldt, which overlay his solid understanding of historical linguistic techniques.[87] Echoing Duponceau, Gatschet asserted:

> For an Indian is not accustomed to think in terms coherent, or words disconnected from others, or of abstract ideas, but uses his words merely as integral parts of a whole sentence, or in connection with others. This is the true cause of the large incorporative power of the American tongues, which in many of them culminates in an extended polysynthetism, and embodies whole sentences in one single verbal form. (1877a:146)

And recalling the views of Humboldt, he observed:

> Thus every language on this globe is perfect, but perfect only for the purpose it is intended to fulfill; Indian thought runs in another, more concrete direction than ours, and therefore Indian speech is shaped very differently from Indogermanic models, which we, in our inherited and unjustified

pride, are prone to regard as the only models of linguistic perfection. (1877a:147)[88]

Gatschet's classification work has been largely forgotten, although he presented a major portion of his "synopsis" several times (1876, 1877a, 1882), based on a comparison of information from Gibbs, Latham, Bancroft, and Powers, with other data available to him. For details of Gatschet's classification, see the appendix to this chapter, which combines the different lists of the families he recognized to make a single classification (although there are minor differences in the classifications he presented, most of which concentrate on areas of the West).

As Andresen (1990:193) points out, Gatschet provided a link between American studies of native languages and studies of the French Americanists, Lucien Adam and Raoul de la Grasserie, with whom he collaborated.

Powell's Methods and Classification

In the course of his work on classification, which extended over twenty years, Powell changed his thinking about linguistic change and language relationships. He increasingly came to believe that borrowing and convergence seriously complicated the interpretation of the similarities on which his method of grouping had been based:

> This general conclusion has been reached: That borrowed materials exist in all the languages; and that some of these borrowed materials can be traced to original sources, while the larger part of such acquisitions can not be thus relegated to known families. In fact, it is believed that the existing languages, great in number though they are, give evidence of a more primitive condition, when a far greater number were spoken. When there are two or more languages of the same stock, it appears that this differentiation into diverse tongues is due mainly to the absorption of other material, and that thus the multiplication of dialects and languages of the same group furnishes evidence that at some prior time there existed other languages which are now lost except as they are partially preserved in the divergent elements of the group. The conclusion which has been reached, therefore, does not accord with the hypothesis upon which the investigation began, namely, that common elements would be discovered in all these languages, for the longer the study has proceeded the more clear it has been

made to appear that the grand process of linguistic development among the tribes of North America has been toward unification rather than multiplication, that is, that the multiplied languages of the same stock owe their origin very largely to absorbed languages that are lost.

> The opinion that the differentiation of languages within a single stock is mainly due to the absorption of materials from other stocks, often to the extinguishment of the latter, has grown from year to year as the investigation has proceeded. . . . In the presence of opinions that have slowly grown in this direction, the author is inclined to think that some of the groups herein recognized as families will ultimately be divided, as the common materials of such languages, when they are more thoroughly studied, will be seen to have been borrowed. (1966[1891a]:216–17)

In this regard, Powell shares views propounded earlier by Schleicher (1983[1863]:60, 69) and Whitney (1867).

Many scholars have commended Powell's classification of the fifty-eight families for its thoroughness, accuracy, and conservatism (1891a; see the appendix to this chapter). However, in several respects this judgment is ill-founded. The classification was thorough, but it also had gaps. For example, Eyak had been mentioned in Russian publications since 1781 (see Radloff 1858), but it was missed by Powell and was not rediscovered by American linguists until 1930 (De Laguna 1937, Birket-Smith and De Laguna 1938; see Chapter 4). Also, much more information is available now; many new languages within groups Powell established have been recognized, and several groupings previously recognized have had to be divided into more than one language. Thus, when Powell's list of languages is compared with later lists—for example, Voegelin's list (1941), Chafe's conservative list (1962), and Landar's checklists with many languages named (1973)—there is clearly an increase in the number of languages. Powell's accuracy also must be qualified. Although he generally grouped only the most obviously related languages, some of his groupings have not been sustained and have had to be separated in subsequent work:[89]

1. Yakonan was split into Yakonan (Alsea) and Siuslaw (Powell 1915; see Chapter 4).
2. Yuman was separated into Yuman and Seri;

Pericú and Waikuri (Guaicuri) were removed because of lack of information (Gatschet 1900b:558, Powell 1915).
3. Waiilatpuan was severed into Cayuse and Molala (Rigsby 1966, 1969; Voegelin and Voegelin 1977:287).
4. Coahuiltecan was found to be composed of several distinct groups (Goddard 1979b; see Chapters 4 and 8).

Also, in one sense, Powell was not so conservative. He provided no internal classification or subgrouping of his families (except for Siouan), and the languages of some of his family units are more distantly related than others. For example, Powell grouped Eskimoan and Aleutan, two rather distantly related groups. Also, Catawban is only distantly related to the Siouan languages (see Chapter 4).[90] However, Powell placed Catawba on the same level with his other Siouan languages. He considered but rejected Uto-Aztecan (Shoshonean-Piman-Aztecan) and Miwok-Costanoan (Powell 1966[1891a]:168–9, 216), both of which were proposed before and confirmed after Powell (1891a). Specifically concerning what we now know to be Uto-Aztecan, Powell said in his "concluding remarks":

> The evidence brought forward by Buschmann and others seems to be doubtful. A part is derived from jargon words, another part from adventitious similarities, while some facts seem to give warrant to the conclusion that they should be considered as one stock, but the author [Powell] prefers, under the present state of knowledge, to hold them apart and await further evidence, being inclined to the opinion that the peoples speaking these languages have borrowed some part of their vocabularies from one another. (1966[1891b]:216)

Had Powell been consistent in his conservatism, he could not have grouped together Eskimoan with Aleutan or Catawba with Siouan, while rejecting Uto-Aztecan and Miwok-Costanoan, not to mention the four erroneous groupings just mentioned that subsequently had to be separated. Powell (1891a:102–3) stated that his fifty-eight families were equally dissimilar (Darnell 1988:55). However, if they were in fact equally dissimilar, the classification would not include families representing widely different degrees of genetic affinity.

Although his famous classification is generally considered to be a benchmark, Powell said he did "not desire that this work shall be considered final, but rather as initiatory and tentative" (1966[1891a]:215; see also 1891b:71), and indeed efforts to reduce further the ultimate number of genetic units in the Americas came hard on its heels. Soon Powell's fifty-eight were reduced to fifty-five (in the only revision of Powell's 1891 classification published by the BAE; see Boas 1911a): Adaizan (Adai) was combined with Caddoan, Natchez with Muskhogean, and Shasta with Achomawi (Dixon 1905; cf. Boas 1974[1906]:186, 1911b:82–3). None of these recombinations is accepted uncritically today, however (see discussion in Chapters 4 and 8). Since "over 40 per cent of Powell's families were in fact 'language isolates'" (Elmendorf 1965:95), these isolates in particular became targets of later efforts to combine and classify the languages into more inclusive groupings. The growing "reductionist" activity generated considerable dispute concerning the methods deemed appropriate for establishing remote linguistic relationships (discussed later in this chapter).[91]

Franz Boas

Boas (1858–1942) is considered by many to be the founder of American linguistics and American anthropology.[92] He discussed the classification of American Indian languages in a number of publications (1911b, 1917, 1920, 1929), referring frequently to the familiar criteria—phonetics, vocabulary, and morphology / structure / inner form)—for establishing families. Early in his career, he favored grammar for determining genetic relationships or resolving "genealogical questions" (perhaps in echoes of Hale):

> As long, however, as the inner form [of compared languages] remains unchanged, our judgement [concerning genetic affinity] is determined, not by the provenance of the vocabulary, but by that of the form. (1982[1917]:202)

> At that time [1893] I was inclined to consider these similarities [striking morphological similari-

ties between neighboring stocks] as a proof of relationship of the same order as that of languages belonging, for instance, to the Indo-European family. (1920:367–8)

In his early work, Boas had connected Kwakiutl and Nootka (as Wakashan, which Powell [1891a] accepted, cf. Boas 1894). He also thought Haida and Tlingit to be related (1889[1888]; cf. Swanton 1908b, 1911a, 1911b; see Chapter 8):

> This similarity of structure [between Haida and Tlingit] becomes the more surprising if we take into consideration that not one of the neighboring languages shows any of the peculiarities enumerated here. The structural resemblance of the two languages and their contrast with the neighboring languages can be explained only by the assumption of a common origin. The number of words which may possibly be connected by etymology is small, and the similarities are doubtful [Boas presented a list of seventeen potential cognates]. Nevertheless, the structural resemblance must be considered final proof of a historical connection between the two languages. (1894:342)

This quotation also reveals his areal-typological leanings, which would later become important (discussed later in this chapter; see also Chapter 9). Since the evidence for a Haida-Tlingit relationship was mostly grammatical rather than lexical, however, Powell (1891a) held the hypothesis to be unproven. (Haida, Tlingit, and Athabascan were grouped in Sapir's Na-Dene proposal, which is still controversial; see Chapter 8). On the basis of the same reasoning, Boas proposed that Salish, Chimakuan, and Nootka were also related: "The southern group of languages, the Kwakiutl, the Salishan and Chemakum, which have hardly any connections of relationship, so far as their vocabulary is concerned, have a series of peculiar traits in common. . . . These similarities are so pronounced and so peculiar that they must have originated from a common source" (1894:343–4). In fact, Boas indicated that the major goal of his 1894 article was to stress the methodological point that structure is important in matters of genetic relationship:

> Our review has shown that the seven languages of this region which show, so far as we can prove

at present, no etymological relationships worth considering, may be classed in four groups:

1. The Tlingit and Haida.
2. Tsimshian.
3. The Kwakiutl, Salish and Chemakum.
4. The Chinook.

> The similarities of the languages belonging to each group, on the one hand, and on the other the differences between the groups, are so striking, that we must assume that some genetic connection exists between the languages of each group. . . . So far our knowledge of most of the languages of the Pacific Coast is confined to a meager list of vocabularies. Therefore the classification must be considered in its infancy. Etymologies of Indian languages, the histories of which we do not know, is a subject of the greatest difficulty, and must be based on investigations on the structure of the languages, if it shall not sink to the level of mere guessing. In the present state of linguistic science, a classification ought to take into account structure as well as vocabulary. The former will give us valuable clues where the comparison of mere words ceases to be helpful. It is with the desire to call attention to the importance of this method that the imperfect comparison between the languages of the North Pacific Coast has been presented. (1894:345–6)

His general concern, however, which he would express repeatedly later (1920, 1929), was the difficulty of distinguishing between borrowing and inheritance—between "diffusional cumulation" and "archaic residue," to use Swadesh's (1951) terms—as explanations for similarities among compared languages: "Languages may influence one another to such an extent, that, beyond a certain point, the genealogical question has no meaning" (Boas 1982[1917]:202):

> While I am not inclined to state categorically that the areas of distribution of phonetic phenomena, of morphological characteristics, and of groups based on similarities in vocabularies are absolutely distinct, I believe this question must be answered empirically before we can undertake to solve the general problem of the history of modern American languages. If it should prove true, as I believe it will, that all these different areas do not coincide, then the conclusion seems inevitable that the different languages must have exerted a far-reaching influence upon one another. If this point of view

is correct, then we have to ask ourselves in how far the phenomena of acculturation extend also over the domain of language. . . . [There is a] tendency of language to absorb so many foreign traits that we can no longer associate a language with one or the other of the contributing stocks. In other words, the whole theory of an "Ursprache" for every group of modern languages must be held in abeyance until we can prove that these languages go back to a single stock and that they have not originated, to a large extent, by the process of acculturation. (1982[1920]:215–6)

Eventually Boas came to be associated with an areal-typological approach in which he compared and contrasted the typological traits of languages in a particular geographical area to determine how they might have been reshaped as a result of mutual influence in that limited area. Darnell (1969:330, 338–9) has suggested that it was Boas's work with the diffusion of folklore elements among Northwest Coast groups that convinced him of the difficulty of distinguishing linguistic traits that are due to an original unity from those that are due to borrowing and caused him to misunderstand Sapir's methods. Indeed, if Boas's belief in "morphological hybridization" was based on the ease with which folktale motifs diffuse and merge, then it is not hard to understand why linguists, with some feel for the difficulty of altering the "morphological kernel" of a language significantly through diffusion and with an understanding of how systematic correspondences help to distinguish borrowed from inherited material, would align themselves with Sapir's linguistically better informed approach (see below). It seems clear that Boas did equate changes in linguistic phenomena with changes in other cultural traits and apparently did not understand how different the two can be. This is evidenced in his letter to Sapir dated September 18, 1920:

I think, however, that we are not sufficiently familiar with the phenomena of mutual influences of languages in primitive life to decide whether we are dealing with a gradual development of divergence or whether the whole linguistic phenomena ought not to be considered from the same point of view as any ethnic phenomena. . . . If there is disagreement, it seems to my mind certain that *the linguistic phenomena must be looked at in the same way as the cultural phenomena.* (Emphasis added; Darnell 1990:122)

Boas's thinking also came to be associated with a "psychological" orientation in linguistics and ethnology. Reflecting the influence of Humboldt and Duponceau, he referred to "larger unities . . . based rather more on 'similarity of the psychological foundations of languages than on phonetic similarity' " (Boas to Woodard, January 13, 1905, quoted by Stocking 1974:477; see also Darnell 1969:335). His views (and the gradual changes in them) are revealed in his conception of the *Handbook of American Indian Languages.* Boas's letters indicate that he had conceived of the *Handbook* as a "morphological classification" of American Indian languages; the languages included in the *Handbook* were chosen to represent as many "psychologically distinct types of language" as possible (letter from Boas to Kroeber, April 4, 1904; quoted in Darnell 1969:275). Thus, the goals of the *Handbook* were "morphological classification and psychological characterization" (Darnell 1969:274); to a lesser extent, it was intended to serve historical interests, as "a uniform series of outlines of Indian languages to be published in synoptic form for use in comparative studies by the philologists of the world" (33rd annual report, for 1911–1912, 1919:xxxiv; quoted in Darnell 1969:273). A common interpretation is that Boas's inclusion of Tlingit, Haida, and Athabaskan in the *Handbook* reflects his desire to obtain more information that might sustain the genetic relationships he had suggested; this also reflects his historical interests (Boas 1894; see Darnell 1969:274. On the Na-Dene controversy, see Chapter 8 and Sapir's views discussed later in this chapter). Nevertheless, in spite of his "ideologic" bent (psychological orientation), Boas was strongly opposed to the Duponceau-Brinton-Powell assumption that certain historical, typological, and psychological aspects were shared by all (or nearly all) Native American languages: "It is often assumed that there is one type of American languages, but even a superficial knowledge of representative dialects shows that much greater than their similarities are their differences, and that the psychological basis of morphology is not by any means the same in the fifty-five stocks that occur on our continent" (Boas 1906:644). As Darnell aptly put it, "his emphasis was on the diversity of linguistic structures and accompanying mental worlds to be found in North America" (1969: 276). Boas explained that "the psychological groupings . . . depend entirely upon the inner form of each language" (1911b:77). In sum, "the personal linguistic interest of Professor Boas is primarily psychological, but the historical and comparative aspects have not been neglected" (Goddard 1914:561).

Boas was strongly opposed to the evolutionary-typological views so prevalent in the past, but he did not abandon Humboldt's psychological orientation—to the contrary, the notion of "inner form" became the core of Boas's view of ethnology. (His psychological orientation would seem to place him among nineteenth-century thinkers with regard to these matters.) However, he succeeded in turning attention from the more wrongheaded aspects of the Duponceau-Humboldt "ideologic" psychological-typological-evolutionary approach. Although he did not cite its proponents by name, Boas opposed the Duponceauian typological-structural(-genetic) unity of American Indian languages and "holophrasis" (Lieber's nomenclatural contribution to Duponceau's notions) in particular: "The tendency of a language to express a complex idea by a single term has been styled 'holophrasis,' and it appears therefore that every language may be holophrastic from the point of view of another language. Holophrasis can hardly be taken as a fundamental characteristic of primitive languages" (1911b:26; cf. Andresen 1990:217).[93] Boas showed that the traditional typological-evolutionary views of grammar were inaccurate and ethnocentric (Stocking 1974:471). After Boas, with some help from Sapir and Kroeber, the view that morphological types were representative of stages of social evolution died out and has been largely forgotten by linguists.

Nevertheless, "the psychological goals . . . proved less tractable than Boas had envisioned" (Darnell 1969:275); thus "Boas never found a way to formalize the results of the psychological investigations. . . . Carried to its logical extreme, Boas' position meant that historical lin-

guistics, as traditionally understood, was impossible" (Darnell 1971b:248). Boas never fully grasped the criteria used by historical linguists to establish genetic relationships and criticized Sapir for his emphasis on "phonetics" (that is, on sound correspondences) (letter from Boas to Hodge, February 8, 1910, quoted in Darnell 1971b:238). But Sapir fully understood and applied the comparative method, for he believed that systematic correspondences would help distinguish genetically inherited features from similarities that are due to diffusion. For example, concerning his demonstration that Uto-Aztecan was valid (Sapir 1913–1919[1915]), Sapir commented that he thought he had, with his methods, put it "on bedrock" and that the way that quite dissimilar stems could be matched when phonetic laws were applied was "almost humorous" (Sapir to Kroeber, June 21, 1913; cited in Darnell 1969:369). In a letter to Boas, he expressed his misgivings concerning Boas's psychological ("ideologic") orientation at the expense of the more basic comparative method:

> The great psychological differences you find do not, I am afraid, frighten me quite as much as they seem to yourself. . . . I must confess I have always had a feeling that you entirely overdo psychological peculiarities in different languages as presenting insuperable obstacles to genetic theories, and that, on the other hand, you are not sufficiently impressed by the reality of the differentiating processes, phonetic and grammatical, that have so greatly operated in linguistic history all over the world. (Sapir to Boas, July 10, 1918, quoted in Darnell 1990:117–18)

Sapir wrote further about this in his *Science* article: "Our persistently, and rather fruitlessly, 'psychological' approach to the study of American languages has tended to dull our sense of underlying drift, of basic linguistic forms, and of lines of historical reconstruction" (Sapir 1921a:408).[94] His psychological orientation led Boas to compare some languages typologically whose shared similarities Sapir believed to be evidence of genetic relationship—for example, Iroquois (Iroquoian) and Pawnee (Caddoan) (contrast Boas 1911b and Sapir 1920; see also Darnell 1971b:248).

The discussion of Boas in this chapter has

concentrated on his views concerning historical and "mental" aspects of language; however, it should also be kept in mind that a major concern for Boas was to obtain information on Native American languages and cultures before they disappeared or were permanently altered. He instructed his students on the urgency of field-work, and indeed he contributed the last, and sometimes the only, significant data on a number of languages, such as Lower Chinook, Cathla-met, Chemakum, Pentlach, Pochutec, and Tset-saut (see Kinkade 1990:101). Boas's dedication to getting accurate information while it was still possible is related to his well-known linguistic relativity and his emphasis on avoiding general-ization. Faced with the many errors that earlier scholars had made, Boas believed it important to avoid preconceptions and to describe lan-guages and cultures in their own terms—on the basis of information "derived internally from an analysis of language itself rather than imposed from without" (Stocking 1974:470). Some of Boas's most important contributions involve the correction of misconceptions concerning lan-guage and culture. His students took this position to be not one of heuristics for the time—waiting for enough accurate information to become available on a variety of languages and cultures so that later it might be possible to generalize—but rather a matter of principle, hence the em-phasis on description and against generalization, against theorizing about language, in American structuralism until Chomsky's views reoriented the field toward universals, generalizing, and theory.

Later, Sapir's approach to the historical study of American Indian languages, with its emphasis on genetic relationships, won the following of most students of Native American languages, but Boas's areal-typological view was also im-portant to subsequent developments. For exam-ple, his conception of areal linguistic traits and diffusion was instrumental in the development of the notion of *Sprachbund* or linguistic area (particularly in the Prague School; see Jakobson 1944 and Chapter 9). It subsequently made its way back to America to become highly influen-tial in contemporary American Indian linguistic studies, largely through the influence of Eme-neau (1956), particularly on the several students of Native American languages at the University of California at Berkeley, where Emeneau taught, aided significantly by Mary Haas (1969d:82–97; 1976; see Campbell 1985a; also Chapter 9).

Roland B. Dixon, Albert Louis Kroeber, and Post-Powellian Reductionism

Dixon (1875–1934) and Kroeber (1876–1960) proposed some of the first and ultimately most influential consolidations in Powell's fifty-eight families.[95] They collaborated on their typologi-cal classification (Dixon and Kroeber 1903) be-fore they turned to the genetic proposals for which they became so well known. Although Dixon "did little more than contribute data" (Golla 1986:25), Kroeber included him as coau-thor in his subsequent statements on classifica-tion (Dixon and Kroeber 1913a, 1913b, 1919; Golla 1984:13). In 1905 Dixon combined the Shastan and Palaihnihan languages (Dixon 1905), based on word lists of about twenty items each. Later he added Chimariko to the group, calling them all Shastan (Dixon 1910; for current thinking on these consolidations, see Chapters 4 and 8); Kroeber (1910) grouped Miwok and Costanoan. Later, together they proposed many wholesale reductions that are still considered important today, though they are controversial (Dixon and Kroeber 1913a, 1913b, 1919).

In the beginning Dixon and Kroeber's pur-pose was not genetic classification at all, but rather Boas-type areal-typological comparison (as seen in Boas' work on the Northwest Coast; cf. Dixon and Kroeber 1903).[96] They compared sixteen of Powell's families located in California and classified them according to three structural-geographical types: Northwestern Californian (Yurok was typical), Central Californian (Maidu was typical), and Southwestern Californian (typified by Chumash). These were not to be considered genetic groupings: "The classifica-tion that has been attempted deals only with structural resemblances, not with definite genetic relationships; . . . we are establishing not fami-lies, but types of families. . . . The classifica-tion here proposed is really one of another order from that used by Powell, for structure and not lexical content is made the basis on which all comparisons are made." (Dixon and Kroeber 1903:2–3).

Even then, Kroeber was open to other interpretations. In a letter to Boas (April 24, 1903), he mentioned that "in comparing vocabularies recently I found an unexpectedly large number of words common to two or more languages"; he suspected that these similarities resulted from "extensive borrowing," though he added that "it is by no means impossible that many of the languages will turn out to be related" (quoted in Darnell 1971b:241). Dixon and Kroeber (1903), in spite of their typological goals, nevertheless even then suggested the grouping of Shastan with Palaihnihan and of Miwokan with Costanoan. Following Boas's areal linguistic orientation, Kroeber accepted the possibility that the lexical similarities and the morphological similarities might point in different directions (given the effects of diffusion), and, following Powell, such similarities could be observed without committing oneself necessarily to explaining them as being based on either genetic relationship or diffusion and convergence. Again in reflections of Boas's attitude, Kroeber wrote to Dixon (December 3, 1910) that borrowing had been "so strong that we shall have to go very slow in the future in uniting any further stocks" (quoted in Darnell 1969:344). Darnell (1971b:242–3) argues that it was only with reluctance that Dixon and Kroeber turned from the areal-typological orientation to genetic hypotheses:

After analysis of the collected information (comparison of two hundred stem words) had progressed beyond a certain point, it became apparent that the only satisfactory explanation of the resemblances between certain languages was genetic relationship. On the basis of these indications the grammatical information extant on the same languages was reexamined, and in every instance was found strongly confirmatory. Lexical and structural similarities coinciding and being found relatively abundant, true relationships have been accepted as established. (Dixon and Kroeber 1913b:225)

Darnell feels that "something had changed between 1903 and 1913 when genetic unity became an acceptable explanation for linguistic similarity"; she attributes the change to "Kroeber's almost constant contact with Edward Sapir during the intervening decade" (1971b:244).

Sapir spent the year 1907–1908 in Berkeley as a research associate in the department of anthropology, and clearly these scholars influenced each other greatly (see their correspondence in Golla 1984). However, both Dixon and Kroeber had already been engaged in the proposal of a number of genetic relationships that would unite some of Powell's distinct families (Dixon 1905, 1910; Kroeber 1904, 1907, 1910), about which Sapir initially expressed reservations (in Golla 1984:81, 87, 181). Therefore, although Darnell may be correct, it is also possible that their reorientation toward genetic explanations came about independently of Sapir.

Seemingly in reflections of Powell's methods, Dixon and Kroeber in their genetic proposals relied largely on lexical similarities (though Kroeber was aware also of the value of morphological evidence; see below). They had assembled vocabulary lists on large, unpublished sheets of butcher paper[97] (referred to and criticized by Frachtenberg, below):

About 225 English words were selected on which material was most likely to be accessible in reasonably accurate and comparable form, and the native equivalents in 67 dialects of the 21 stocks [in California] were entered in columns. . . . The purpose of this study was three-fold: first, to ascertain the nature and degree of borrowing between unrelated languages; second, to trace through these borrowings any former contacts or movements of language groups not now in contact; third, in the event of any relationship existing between languages then considered unrelated, to determine this fact. (1919:49)

Based on a superficial scanning of these vocabularies, Dixon and Kroeber (1913a, 1913b) announced that they had reduced Powell's twenty-two California stocks to twelve. The more inclusive stocks in their proposal were:

Penutian[98] (based on words for the number 'two', approximating *pen* in some of the languages and *uti* in Miwok-Costanoan): Wintun, Maidu, Yokuts, Miwok, Costanoan.

Hokan (based on words for 'two' in these languages, similar to *hok*): Karok, Shasta, Chimariko, Achomawi-Atsugewi, Pomo, Yana, Esselen, Yuman.

Iskoman (based on Chumashan words for 'two'): Chumash and Salinan. (Later they lumped this stock with Hokan.)

Ritwan (based on the Wiyot word for 'two'): Yurok and Wiyot. (Later, these two proved to be related to Algonquian; see Spir 1913.)

The actual lexical similarities upon which these classifications were based were extremely rough and few in number. Hokan, for example, was formed on the basis of only five presumed cognate sets ('eye', 'tongue', 'water', 'stone', 'sleep'), and Iskoman was based on twelve. That is, these "1913 statements stand more as a declaration of faith with the barest amount of demonstration" (Langdon 1974:29).

The Hokan and Penutian hypotheses proved attractive to other scholars, though today both are still undemonstrated and controversial (see Chapter 8). William Shipley, who worked for years trying to demonstrate the Penutian relationship, now declares Penutian dead—though not all contemporary scholars concur with this pronouncement. In regard to Dixon and Kroeber's lexical criterion, Shipley reports that "there are many resemblant forms" (1980:437) and that he and Harvey Pitkin accumulated more than three hundred (Pitkin and Shipley 1958), but they do not sustain the hypothesis: "This view [that the so-called Penutian subfamilies are genetically related] has been continuously taken as axiomatic, in the face of the stubborn failure of the relevant data to provide any basis for establishing convincing sound correspondences or credible reconstructions" (Shipley 1980:438).

The Penutian and Hokan hypotheses are methodologically revealing; they are based on methods essentially the same as those of Powell (see Chapter 7). Such proposals of relationship based only on perceived lexical similarities are just a starting point; it is still necessary to undertake detailed investigation, using more standard techniques, to determine whether the lexical similarities are the result of inheritance from a former common ancestor (genetic relationship) or are the result of other factors such as borrowing, accident, onomatopoeia, sound symbolism, and nursery words (see Chapter 7).[99] Since Dixon and Kroeber did not investigate the similarities further to eliminate alternative possible explanations, their proposals based primarily on lexical scanning remain unconfirmed.

However, Kroeber wrote an article on the topic of determining family relationships in which he showed that he was fully aware of the impact of Indo-Europeanist methodology and the differences of opinion, concerning the relative weights to be given grammar and vocabulary, as well as of the importance of "phonetic laws," in research on the genetic classification of American Indian languages. Nevertheless, he opted for lexical evidence as the strongest indicator of relationship:

> It has often been asserted that grammar, or internal structure or form, is of more weight in determining relationship than the words or material content of a language. In Europe, this has been the generally agreed dictum of philologists, and has usually been accepted outright from them by historians and ethnologists.

> If, then, questions of genetic unity are purely or mainly historical, it is clear that the evidence of genetic unity can not be primarily either structural or lexical, but will be strongest where facts of both kinds point in the same direction. Further, both lexical and grammatical evidence will usually point the same way. Where they differ, or where one alone is available, *preference must be given to vocabulary,* of course with *due regard to phonetic laws.* (Emphasis added; Kroeber 1913:389, 394)

Antoine Meillet[100] took Kroeber to task for his emphasis on vocabulary and his less than orthodox view of the role of grammar in establishing genetic relationships:

> When an eminent Americanist, Mr. Kroeber, in his article in *Anthropos,* VIII (1913), p. 389 ff., entitled *The Determination of Linguistic Relationship,* protested the use of general agreements in morphological structure to establish the genetic relationships of languages, he was entirely correct. Only it is not proper to conclude from that that genetic relationships should be established considering vocabulary instead of morphology. Correct as it is, Kroeber's criticism does not justify the procedure of certain Americanists, who base their claims of genetic relationship between such and such a language and some other purely on agreements in vocabulary. Grammatical agreements and only grammatical agreements furnish rigorous proof, but only on the condition that the phonological shape of the forms be used and that one establish that particular grammatical forms used in the languages under consideration go back to a common origin. Agreements in vocabulary are

never absolute proof, because one may never be certain that they cannot be explained as borrowings. (Meillet 1948[1914]:91, Rankin's 1992: 329 translation) [101]

Although Kroeber's own proposals of relationships among American Indian languages are remembered as based primarily on lexical evidence, in many of his pronouncements he favored a more standard approach:

> The truth is the middle one that what is needed to establish positive relationship between languages, is similarity both in grammar and in lexicon. . . . On the other hand, to unite them genetically when their words present no resemblance, merely because they seem to employ similar formal procedures, is probably always hazardous and unsound. But everyone must admit a common origin when both form and content are substantially alike. As long as similarity is established only in one respect, there is always the possibility that such resemblance may be due to influence or borrowing. (Kroeber, 1913:390)

Edward Sapir

Sapir (1884–1939) is by far the most respected of all American Indian linguistics scholars.[102] He is best known for proposals of distant genetic relationships among American Indian languages, though it is sometimes forgotten that he also set rigorous standards for proof of relationships (Darnell 1971b:253). His attempts to establish remote family connections won Sapir many followers, but they also drew strong criticism. The following comments by Sapir are to the point. They show that the same methods employed in the establishment of Indo-European and other families were the ones favored by Sapir, and following him, by most American Indian linguists:

> The methods developed by the Indo-Europeanists have been applied with marked success to other groups of languages. It is abundantly clear that they apply just as rigorously to the unwritten primitive languages of Africa and America as to the better known forms of speech of the more sophisticated peoples. . . . *The more we devote ourselves to the comparative study of the languages of a primitive linguistic stock, the more clearly we realize that phonetic law and analogical leveling are the only satisfactory key to the unravelling of the development of dialects and languages from a common base.* Professor Leonard Bloomfield's experiences with Central Algonkian and my own with Athabaskan leave nothing to be desired in this respect and are a complete answer to those who find it difficult to accept the large-scale regularity of the operation of all those unconscious linguistic forces which in their totality give us regular phonetic change and morphological readjustment on the basis of such change. It is not merely theoretically possible to predict the correctness of specific forms among unlettered peoples on the basis of such phonetic laws as have been worked out for them—such predictions are already on record in considerable number. *There can be no doubt that the methods first developed in the field of Indo-European linguistics are destined to play a consistently important role in the study of all other groups of languages,* and that *it is through them* and through their gradual extension *that we can hope to arrive at significant historical inferences as to the remoter relations between groups of languages that show few superficial signs of a common origin.* (Emphasis added; 1949[1929c]:160–1)

> Phonetic law is justly considered by the linguist by far the most important single factor that he has to deal with. *Inasmuch as all sound change in language tends to be regular, the linguist is not satisfied with random resemblances in languages that are suspected of being related but insists on working out as best he can the phonetic formulas which tie up related words. Until such formulas are discovered,* there may be some evidence for considering distinct languages related—for example, the general form of their grammar may seem to provide such evidence—but *the final demonstration can never be said to be given until comparable words can be shown to be but reflexes of one and the same prototype by the operation of dialectic phonetic laws.* (Emphasis added; 1949[1931]:74)

While Sapir's thinking undoubtedly evolved over the years, his method consistently relied on lexical, morphological, and phonological evidence for genetic relationships among languages (Goddard 1986). Thus, in 1912, in a letter to Kroeber, Sapir described the criteria he used in establishing Uto-Aztecan:

> I am expecting to read a paper entitled "Southern Paiute and Nahuatl, A study in Uto-Aztekan," at

the Cleveland meeting [annual meeting of the American Anthropological Association; see Sapir 1913–1919(1915)]. I believe I now have *enough phonetic, morphological, and lexical evidence* at my disposal to demonstrate the soundness of your claims [Kroeber 1907] beyond cavil. I have even unearthed *some morphological resemblances of detail which are so peculiar as to defy all interpretation on any assumption but that of genetic relationship.* (Emphasis added; letter dated December 23, 1912, in Golla 1984:71)

The Powell (1891a) classification had rejected Uto-Aztecan as not demonstrated (see Brinton 1891); Sapir (1913–1919[1915]) established its validity once and for all—a successful demonstration of a hypothesis of distant genetic relationship. In 1913 Sapir presented evidence relating Ritwan (Wiyot and Yurok of California) to Algonquian—a proposed distant genetic relationship that was quite controversial at the time but whose validity has subsequently been established to the satisfaction of all (see Chapter 4). He utilized the standard methods: "There is good *lexical, morphological, and phonological evidence* to genetically relate Algonkin [Algonquian] to Wiyot and Yurok" (emphasis added; 1913:646). Moreover, he stressed the importance of regular sound correspondences (1913:639). In 1915 Sapir presented his Na-Dene proposal, linking Athabaskan, Tlingit, and Haida (1915c; see Chapter 8). The Haida connection continues to be controversial, and some scholars still hesitate concerning the Tlingit-Athabaskan connection (see Chapter 8). Sapir utilized the same methods for this proposal as he had in his Algonquian-Yurok-Wiyot case (1990[1915a]: 557). The Na-Dene article (Sapir 1915c) is divided into three sections, corresponding to the three usual criteria for genetic relationships. In the section on "morphological features," Sapir discussed several traits and concluded: "It has become evident that the morphologies of Haida, Tlingit, and Athabaskan present numerous and significant points of comparison" (1915c:550). In the "comparative vocabulary" section, Sapir mentioned "over three hundred distinct Athabaskan stems and grammatical elements" (p. 551). In the "phonology" section he listed thirty of "the more important [sound] correspondences" (pp. 554–5).

In 1917 Sapir presented a large amount of lexical evidence in support of the Hokan hypothesis (1917a); it so impressed Dixon and Kroeber (1919:103–4) that "they considered themselves exonerated from the obligation to present further justification of their Hokan stock" (Langdon 1974:37). Three years later, Sapir grouped together Hokan and the so-called Coahuiltecan languages (see Chapter 8), including also Tonkawa and Karankawa, based on 120 lexical similarities unevenly spread throughout the languages (Sapir 1920). He readily admitted the shaky (or preliminary) nature of his findings: "A certain amount of groping in the dark cannot well be avoided in the pioneer stage of such an attempt as this" (1920:289). Sapir's article on Subtiaba (1925a) is considered by many scholars to be the major statement on Hokan, and more important, a clear statement dealing with Sapir's method of distant genetic hypotheses (see Chapter 7).

The most common criticism levied at Sapir's proposals has not concerned the kind of evidence or the methods he employed but rather whether the available evidence warranted the conclusions he reached. For example, Truman Michelson[103] favored morphological criteria for genetic relationships similar to those used by Sapir but strongly disagreed with the conclusions of Sapir's Ritwan-Algonquian article (1913). Michelson based this objection on the many Wiyot and Yurok morphological traits that "are thoroughly un-Algonquian" (1914:362), claiming also that some of the resemblances among morphological elements are erroneous or accidental and that some morphological elements of Wiyot and Yurok strongly resemble those of various non-Algonquian languages. He concluded that he had presented enough "to show the utter folly of haphazard comparisons unless we have a thorough knowledge of the morphological structure of the languages concerned" (1914:367). Thus Michelson, like Sapir, favored morphological evidence in considerations of proposals of genetic relationships.

Pliny Earle Goddard,[104] who was also a proponent of Indo-Europeanist methods, found some of Sapir's conclusions to be premature. In evaluating Sapir's Na-Dene hypothesis, he contended:

With this striking likeness in morphology [between Tlingit and Athabaskan], one would expect lexical similarity leading to the definite conclusion that the languages were originally one, or sprang from the same source. The comparisons made of the lexical content, however, do not justify this conclusion. The similarities are few. . . . The few nouns that are common are probably due to borrowing.

Modern linguistic study is based on a belief in phonetic laws which produce uniform results under identical condition. The one recognized method of establishing genetic relationship is to point out the uniform changes which in the course of time have caused the separation of a uniform linguistic area into dialects and related languages. This method of establishing genetic relationship has failed in several instances to produce a definite conviction that relationship really exists. . . . The question then presents itself whether we shall retain the old definition of a linguistic stock as a group of languages whose genetic relationship has been established by showing that they have diverged as a result of uniform phonetic change, or whether we shall form a new definition. (Goddard 1920:270–71)

Goddard (1920:271) held that Sapir's various correspondences were the result of "acculturating influence" (language contact, borrowing).

As Swadesh pointed out with regard to the famous disagreement between Sapir and Boas (see below), the two differed with respect to methods much less than is commonly thought:

The theoretical differences between Boas and Sapir on the subject of language history were not as great as is sometimes supposed. It is not by any means that the one believed in diffusion and the other did not. On the contrary both were keen students of diffusion both as a general cultural phenomenon and in its application to language. Nor must one imagine that Boas did not accept the concept of common origin of groups of languages. The question rather turned on the extent to which science can trace groups of languages back to such prototypes. Boas' notion is simply that deceptive cases can arise as a cumulative result of the diffusion process, so that in some instances he considered it impossible to be certain that a group of languages has or has not a common origin. Sapir, on the other hand, is convinced that a careful examination of the evidence will

definitely establish the prehistory of the supposedly ambiguous cases. (1951:5)

Boas's doubt, as Swadesh indicated, primarily concerned "distantly related languages," whereas Sapir held that in such cases it would be possible to distinguish a language's "morphological kernel" from "superficial additions" (1951:6).

As Hoijer explained, if we set aside Sapir's far-reaching and controversial six-stock proposal for North America (Sapir 1920, 1929a), we find that Sapir, by the application of Indo-Europeanist methods, was able to recognize several remote relationships now established or at least widely accepted, including Uto-Aztecan and Algonquian-Ritwan (1941:4).[105] Hoijer, a student of Sapir's, summarized Sapir's methods as follows:

The criteria whereby genetic relationships between two or more linguistic stocks may be established are of two types, phonetic and morphological. Identities and regular correspondences of sound feature are clearly the most important. Where such phonetic correspondences can be established between a greater portion of the phonemes of the languages under consideration, those languages can only be regarded as descendants from a single common ancestor. It must be remembered, however, that phonetic correspondences of this sort, particularly in the case of languages only remotely related, are difficult of formulation. The correspondences are rarely obvious; indeed, obvious resemblances in sound feature must be viewed with suspicion, since they may be either purely fortuitous (as, for example, in the case of English *day* and Latin *dies*) or the result of borrowing (e.g. English *dental,* Latin *dentālis*). (1941:5)

Hoijer also discussed Sapir's treatment of morphological evidence and of "submerged features" (see Chapter 7), and concluded:

It is evident from this brief survey of Sapir's work that he achieved his revisions of the Powell classification by the strict application of the comparative method to American Indian materials. Because these materials, in many cases, were fragmentary or otherwise unsatisfactory, his formulations lack completeness and, at least to some of his critics, validity. It is clear, however, that the ultimate verification (or disproof) of Sapir's hypotheses will come, not by a refinement or major change in the methods he employed, but when additional data on the languages concerned are made available. (1941:8)

Inheritance versus Diffusion: The Sapir-Boas Debate

Approaches to the study of American Indian historical linguistics gradually became polarized along methodological lines. Though initially they were quite similar, by 1920 the opinions of Sapir and Boas had diverged radically (as mentioned above). Sapir came to doubt that extensive morphological patterns could be borrowed and thus believed more fully in the possibility of distinguishing borrowed forms from inherited material, and in the ability to establish more remote genetic groupings.[106] Boas came to emphasize the difficulty of distinguishing between the effects of borrowing and the effects of inheritance, thus favoring areal linguistic research, believing that the establishment of linguistic families would normally be possible only for less distant relationships. This was the basis of the disagreement between Boas and Sapir. The difficulty of distinguishing between diffused and genetically inherited material is still the concern of scholars investigating possible distant genetic relationships (for example, Tovar and Faust discuss this problem in classifications of South American Indian languages [1976:240]). It is for this reason that areal linguistics is now so salient in most reliable work on proposals of remoter relationships involving Native American languages.

The Reductionist Frenzy

The opposition from Boas, Frachtenberg, Michelson, and Goddard concerned what in retrospect might appropriately be called the "reductionist frenzy" in which Sapir, Kroeber, and others were involved. Between 1905 and 1920, Dixon and Kroeber were eagerly combining Powell's California families into more inclusive groupings in attempts to reduce the ultimate number of distinct genetic units in North America; Sapir soon joined in, then others (see

Dixon and Kroeber 1913a, 1913b, 1919, Sapir 1913, 1913–1919[1915], 1915c, 1917a, 1920, 1925a; also Golla 1984). The result was an outburst of far-flung proposals of distant genetic relationship, offered initially as hunches, tentative preliminary hypotheses, for further investigation, with a minimum of supporting evidence.[107] The literature and personal correspondence dating to this time gives the impression of a school of reductionist sharks in a feeding frenzy preying on Powell's fifty-eight defenseless families:

The process of slaughter of linguistic families, upon which several of us seem to have embarked of late, is going on apace. . . . I now seriously believe that Wishosk [Wiyot] and Yurok are related to Algonkin. (Emphasis added; Sapir to Radin, July 20, 1913; in Golla 1984:113)

We seem at last to have got Powell's old fifty-eight families on the run, and the farther we can drive them into a heap, the more fun and profit. (Emphasis added; Kroeber to Sapir, June 20, 1913; in Golla 1984:106)

We might do something to relate Lutuami [Klamath-Modoc] definitely to one of our California families. The Hokan group in particular lends itself to the supposition of being widespread. . . . *I should be surprised if our Hokan group did not prove ultimately to be the nucleus of a very large stock.* (Emphasis added; Kroeber to Sapir, May 8, 1913; in Golla 1984:97)

I have just gone over Seri and Tequistlatec, and find that Brinton [1891] was absolutely right in considering them to be Yuman. They are therefore, Hokan, and *this family now stretches from Oaxaca to Oregon. I should not be surprised if it were to grow far north and east also, or we may discover new relatives in Mexico.* . . .
    I have just taken stock and find that the eighty-two families given in 1911 on the combined maps of the Handbook [Boas 1911a], and in the Thomas and Swanton article on Mexico [1911], have already shrunk to sixty-four. *I believe it will be a very few years only before we are positively down to half that number.* I very much wish you could take a few evenings off and dispose of Beothuk. . . . I expect that it will be ten years before the majority of our colleagues get over thinking of me as having suddenly developed a streak of

craziness in uniting families. (Emphasis added; Kroeber to Sapir, September 8, 1914; in Golla 1984:150)

I am pleased you think well of the wider Hokan group, and that we weight points much alike. I don't much care if there are obvious omissions and even a few errors in my Seri comparisons. The natural doubters will cavil anyhow. *Others will be convinced as to the fact of relationship, and if they want the "how", that is another story for later, or let them work it out themselves.* (Emphasis added; Kroeber to Sapir, March 30, 1915; in Golla 1984:178)

I have always thought Zuñi was Siouan, but don't think it will hold. I can find just as much evidence—and that mighty little—pointing to Hokan. It is not Uto-Aztecan or Athabascan or Algonkin. I have even tried Muskogean. *I know it is something.* (Emphasis added; Kroeber to Sapir, November 28, 1915; in Golla 1984:199)

Predictions were made . . . as to the number of families that would be generally recognized in ten years. The estimates ranged from 15 to 30. Surely anthropologists may begin to realize that in these matters a new order is upon them. (Kroeber 1915:288)

[Salish is] a stubborn and specialized group . . . but *it will, of course, link up somewhere.* (Emphasis added; Sapir to Kroeber, November 21, 1918; quoted in Darnell 1969:332)

It is clear that the orthodox "Powell" classification of American Indian languages, useful as it has proved itself to be, needs to be superseded by a more inclusive grouping. . . . The recognition of 50 to 60 genetically independent "stocks" north of Mexico alone is tantamount to a historical absurdity. (Sapir 1921a:408)

As Klar observed, "the desire to make sense of so much diversity appears to have been more important than rigorous comparison," and so "the main purpose behind advancing the classification so quickly was to put forth a framework which could be disputed or justified by further work" (1977:151–2).[108] Pinnow suggests as an additional motivation for this reductionist tendency two basic assumptions which are shared among researchers: (1) all (or most of) the American Indian languages ultimately have a common ancestor in spite of the exceptionally large differences among them today, and (2) their long isolation has produced considerable linguistic diversity among them (1964a:25; see also Liedtke 1991:26).[109]

Reactions to Reductionism: Frachtenberg and Radin

As might be expected, responses to the reductions were varied.

Leo J. Frachtenberg

Frachtenberg (1883–1930), a member of the BAE research staff from 1912 to 1917, contributed significantly to the field of Oregon linguistics.[110] For example, he presented evidence relating Takelma and Kalapuya, and relating these two to Chinookan (1918), which significantly influenced Sapir's proposal concerning Oregon Penutian. Frachtenberg also noted some structural and lexical similarities among Salish, Wakashan, and Chimakuan and proposed the name Mosan, based on forms approximating *mōs* or *bōs* 'four' that are found among these languages (1920:295; see Chapter 8 for evaluations of these proposals).

Concerning the reductionist activities after Powell, and especially those of Kroeber and Dixon, Frachtenberg, in the first volume of the *International Journal of American Linguistics,* reported: "The last ten years or so have witnessed an almost feverish activity in the field of American Indian linguistics, culminating in more or less successful attempts to reclassify and to reduce the seemingly too great number of linguistic stocks that are found on the American continent north of Mexico" (1918:175). He pointed out that a number of the proposals were not new (for example, Uto-Aztecan from Buschmann and Brinton; Haida-Tlingit-Athabaskan from Boas and Swanton; Siuslawan and Yakonan from Latham and Gatschet; Lutuamian, Waiilatpuan, and Sahaptin from Gatschet and Hewitt; Salish, Chimakuan, Wakashan from Boas) and that "the younger linguists merely tried to follow up and develop the deductions arrived at by their predecessors" (1918:176). However, even Frachtenberg, in spite of this seemingly favorable report about reductionist efforts, expressed reservations concerning Dixon and Kroeber's method of relying almost exclusively on short word lists. He also disagreed over the relative weights given lexical evidence and structural evidence:

> I still must refuse to accept them [Dixon and Kroeber's Hokan and Penutian] as final, as long as these vocabularies [Dixon and Kroeber's proposed cognate lists] are continued to be withheld from publication and until more morphological evidence is brought into play. Nothing is more dangerous and unsatisfactory in an investigation of this sort than to arrive at so-called final conclusions that are seemingly based solely upon lexicographical material. In the same way it would be wrong to deny the existence of a relationship between two languages merely because the evidence of the lexical material is negative. It is well to bear in mind that in trying to establish genetic relationships between languages that seem to be, at first sight, non-related, lexical and morphological evidence must be treated separately, and that morphological evidence must be accorded greater weight. (1918:177)

The methods that Frachtenberg preferred are revealed in his comments on Dixon and Kroeber's evidence for relating Wiyot to Yurok and Sapir's evidence for relating Uto-Aztecan and Na-Dene; he speaks of "lexical correspondences," "phonetic shifts," and "structural similarities" (that is, "morphology and structural correspondences") which are "too numerous and too regular to be accounted for as due to accident or to borrowing" (1918:178). These are the three sources of evidence that have been standard for establishing linguistic families since the inception of comparative linguistics.

Paul Radin

Radin (1883–1959) proposed relationships among Huave, Mixe-Zoque, and Mayan, which influenced later notions about "Mexican Penutian" and "Macro-Mayan" (1916, 1924; see Chapter 8).[111] He is perhaps best remembered for the study he published in 1919 in which he argued that all Native American languages are genetically related and belong to one large fam-

ily. He saw in his associates' work (that of Dixon, Kroeber, and Sapir) only twelve remaining independent groups and thus felt that his merging of them into one was "hardly so revolutionary" (1919:490; see also Darnell 1990:119). However, most of Radin's contemporaries shunned his attempt to unite all these languages. On June 10, 1919, Sapir wrote to Goddard (then editor of *American Anthropologist*) that he was "most disgusted" with Radin's paper, that it was "deplorably lacking in method" and "full of all kinds of ignorance besides" (letter cited in Darnell 1990:119).[112] Still, there were some expressions of positive support for Radin's general idea (for example, J. P. Harrington, manuscript in the Bureau of American Ethnology, quoted in Darnell 1969:325; and Morris Swadesh 1954b:308).

Frachtenberg's opposition to reductionist proposals has already been mentioned. Hewitt's response was also negative: "On late linguistic work in California, Mr. Hewitt carefully examined the methods and the evidence for relationships relating to the Yuman, the Serian, the Tequistlatecan, the Waicuran, the Shoshonean, the Lutuamian and the Waiilatpuan, claimed in recent publications by Doctor Radin and Dr. Kroeber. In no instance did he find that these authors had proved their case" (forty-first BAE Annual Report, for 1919–1920, 1928:8; quoted in Darnell 1969:95). Michelson's unfavorable stance toward the proposed reductions was based on methodological considerations: "The recent efforts to prove genetic connections on a large scale have been deplorable from a methodological point of view. Enthusiasts have cast all prudence to the winds" (1921:73). Still greater reductions were yet to come.

Sapir's Super-Six Classification

The apex of the reductionist frenzy no doubt occurred in 1921, when Sapir presented the first version of his six-group classification of the North American Indian languages (the six superstocks; see Sapir 1921a), which was essentially the same as the version in his famous *Encyclopaedia Britannica* article (Sapir 1929a), except that Lutuamian, Waiilatpuan, and Sahaptian were added to Penutian. This 1929 classification is presented in full in the appendix to this chapter.[113]

As has often been pointed out, this scheme was based largely on broad typological categories—traits of a "dynamic order" (Golla 1986: 17)—though Sapir believed (or hoped) that lexical and phonological evidence would gradually emerge to support his groupings. The traits he surveyed, on which the six-fold classification was based, included "stem-types, the degree to which morphological elements were 'welded' to one another, the presence of tone, the 'fundamental phonetic pattern,' and the order of elements" (Golla 1986:17). Sapir's goal, as described in a 1920 letter to Kroeber, was "to make a really exhaustive questionnaire on morphological and phonetic features for the languages in Mexico and N[orth] America . . . to see what are the distributions of such features as use of syntactic cases, classification of verbs into active and static, use of diminutives -tsi and -si, and so on" (cited in Golla 1984:347–8); in the same letter, he reported as his "present feeling" a version of the six stocks. This classification later "achieved academic immortality" (Golla 1986:18). In the encyclopedia article, he briefly presented the characteristic traits of each of his six stocks; for example, Hokan-Siouan languages were said to be "prevailingly agglutinative; tend to use prefixes rather than suffixes for the more formal elements, particularly the pronominal elements of the verb; distinguish active and static verbs, and make free use of compounding of stems and of nominal incorporation" (1929a:140). In his initial conception of it, Penutian was characterized by a pervasive disyllabic stem form with repeated vowel, and patterns of reduplication and ablaut, as well as lexical sets (Golla 1986:31). (See Chapter 7 for discussion of Sapir's grammatical criteria and the methodological basis of this classification.)

Sapir did not arrive at his super-six classification overnight; he based it on, and incorporated into it, the proposals of several predecessors (for example, Powell, Boas, Frachtenberg, Dixon, Kroeber, Harrington, and Swanton), as well as some of his own earlier work (see Liedtke 1991:31, Golla 1986). Moreover, in spite of the fact that this classification was widely accepted and often unquestioningly repeated, Sapir presented it as "suggestive but far from demonstrable in all its features at the present time" (1949[1929a]:172).[114] This tentativeness is expressed more explicitly in his report of his Hokan-Coahuiltecan work: "Such a scheme must not be taken too literally. It is offered merely as a first step toward defining the issue, and it goes without saying that the status of these languages may have to be entirely restated" (1925a:526). Sapir described this strategy of offering tentative proposals in a letter to Speck (October 2, 1924), in which he contrasted Boas's conservativeness with the approach he and like-minded individuals preferred: "The second type [of state of mind about classification] is more intuitive and, even when the evidence is not as full or theoretically unambiguous as it might be, *is prepared to throw out* [offer] *tentative suggestions and to test as it goes along*" (emphasis added; quoted in Darnell 1969:324). Later, Kroeber (1940b:7) presented his recollections of this period and of the "preliminariness" of the proposals. Concerning Sapir's technique for arriving at his large-scale classification, he reminds us:

> From one point of view such a procedure is nothing less than forecasting. From another, it amounts to a defining of problems which are worthy of attack because they hold out some hope of yielding positive productive results. The procedure has therefore a certain justification and value, provided it is understood for what it really is. . . . It is in no sense whatever a definable or controllable method of science or scholarship.
>
> The danger of the procedure is that its prophecies may be mistaken especially by non-linguists, for proved or probable findings. Tremendous havoc can be worked when archaeologists or ethnologists begin to built structures of inference on Sapir's brilliant but flimsy gossamer web of prophecies as if it were a solid foundation. (1940a:466)

Haas, a student of Sapir's, calls it correctly: "Although a number of Sapir's [1929a] proposed connections were considered by him to be *merely working hypotheses (no more and no less),* the various suggested relationships have been taken too seriously by some and perhaps not seriously enough by others" (emphasis added; 1954:57).

Unfortunately, Sapir's intention that the 1929 schema be considered only a hypothesis to guide the direction of future research and to be tested was soon forgotten. Sapir was considered a genius (see, for example, Hockett 1952); it was said that his hunches were better than others' proofs. He did have extensive hands-on linguistic experience, which was respected by his contemporaries; he did fieldwork on some seventeen Indian languages between 1905 and 1920, and on some forty languages from many different families during his entire career (see Darnell 1990:17–18). Publication of the classification in the *Encyclopaedia Britannica* had the effect of "canonizing" it.[115] Thereafter, many accepted the schema literally. Clearly, Sapir's contemporaries did not fully understand what Sapir had done (as Darnell [1969] has shown), but many were willing to accept the six-stock scheme just because it had come from Sapir. For example, even Kroeber remarked that the six-stock classification was "hopelessly beyond my depth" (Kroeber to Sapir, December 27, 1920; quoted in Darnell 1969:348). Later it came to be assumed that this classification had been established by legitimate linguistic methods, and thus it became entrenched in the literature. Kroeber spoke of "Sapir's Greek gift of his classification, which is proving something of a Pandora's box to the hastily optimistic" (1940a:469). Much of the work on the classification of American Indian languages done after Sapir either followed his tradition of seeking ever more inclusive groupings with fewer ultimate genetic units in the Americas or attempted to confirm or recombine portions of Sapir's 1929 classification. This work is evaluated in Chapter 8.

As Darnell points out, Sapir's classification with six groupings and Powell's with fifty-eight (later fifty-five) were often contrasted as the bold and the conservative extremes, respectively (1969:358, 1971a:71–2, 1971b:256), but subsequent researchers have largely forgotten that Sapir's (1929a) classification also contains, in addition to the six stocks, an intermediate schema with some twenty-one groups, which reflected earlier work by Dixon, Kroeber, Radin, Swanton, Harrington, and Frachtenberg, as well as his own: Eskimo-Aleut, Algonkin-Ritwan, Kutenay, Mosan (Wakashan-Salish), Haida, Continental Nadene, California Penutian, Ore-gon Penutian, Chinook, Tsimshian, Plateau Penutian, Mexican Penutian, Hokan-Coahuiltecan, Yuki, Keres, Tunican, Iroquois-Caddoan, Eastern Group (Siouan-Yuchi, Natchez-Muskogian, Timucua), Uto-Aztecan, Tanoan-Kiowa, and Zuñi. Several of these twenty-one groups include rather far-flung languages, and as seen in Chapters 4 and 8, some are at best still quite controversial.

It is fitting to end the discussion of Sapir's classification with his own conclusion, written in 1933, near the end of his career, in which, in spite of his by then well-known "super-six" classification, he reaffirms the large number of unrelated families in the Americas: "in aboriginal America the linguistic differentiation is extreme and a surprisingly large number of essentially unrelated linguistic families must be recognized" (Sapir 1949[1933]:22).[116] It is unfortunate that his later stance on the matter has been forgotten in later discussions of Sapir's classification.

Although Sapir's imprint on the study of American Indian languages, both descriptive and historical, would be hard to overestimate, he was also no stranger to "ideologic" thinking. His master's thesis was on Herder's *Ursprung der Sprache* (see Sapir 1907–1908); in his *Language* (1921b), Sapir dealt insightfully with the broad morphological typologies of the preceding century, but without the evolutionism that characterized the treatment of Humboldt, Brinton, Powell, and others. Sapir, trained in Germanic linguistics, fully understood the psychological Humboldtian tradition (as did Boas) and passed it along to his student Benjamin Whorf, in whose hands it was transformed into the Whorf (or Sapir-Whorf) hypothesis, a dominant and lasting theme in linguistic anthropology, though many today are unaware of its pedigree harking back to German Romanticism.

The magnitude of Sapir's legacy to Native American linguistics is perhaps inestimable. Some of his other contributions are mentioned below and in subsequent chapters of this book.

Leonard Bloomfield

Bloomfield's (1887–1949) *Language* (1933) is considered a milestone in linguistics, the foundation of American structuralism, but it is Bloomfield's historical research that has been most important to American Indianists.[117] The historical reconstruction in his sketch of Central Algonquian (Bloomfield 1946) is still considered a model of excellence in historical linguistic research; "it has formed a reliable basis for work in the field [of Algonquian historical linguistics] and will continue to do so" (Goddard 1987a:206). His demonstration, based on Algonquian material that sound change is regular also in unwritten and so-called exotic languages (Bloomfield 1925, 1928), and that the comparative method is thus fully applicable to such languages, is generally considered to be a major contribution to linguistic thought (discussed in greater detail later in this chapter).

The Museum Linguists

Anthropological museums predate university departments of anthropology and linguistics in the United States, and in the period before and immediately after the Powell classification of 1891, much of the research on American Indian languages was conducted by individuals associated with museums and with the Bureau of American Ethnology. Wissler calls the years from 1860 to 1900 the "museum period," followed by the "academic period" after 1900 (1942:190). As mentioned, Boas's debut in American scholarship was the publication of an article in *Science* in which he debated the principles of museum exhibition with Otis Mason (director of the Smithsonian's National Museum); ultimately, organization of exhibits along evolutionary lines (savagery to barbarism to civilization) was abandoned and a plan of exhibition was adopted that followed Powell's linguistic classification (Darnell 1969:178). After the establishment of university departments of anthropology and linguistics beginning in the 1920s, museums no longer sponsored linguistic research and thus did not offer positions for linguists (with the exception, today, of those at the Smithsonian Institution). Swanton, Harrington, Radin, Michelson, and Goddard are representative of this tradition.

John R. Swanton

Swanton (1873–1958) was fundamentally a cultural anthropologist, though he was also extensively involved in linguistics.[118] He proposed several genetic groupings, but most have been abandoned or remain controversial. Haas's assessment is not flattering: "Swanton was perhaps not too good a linguist, but he did want things tied up in neat packages. And he almost always classified languages on a geographical basis" (discussed in Elmendorf 1965:106). Swanton suggested that Haida, Tlingit, and Athabaskan perhaps belonged to the same genetic grouping (Swanton 1908b, 1911a:209, 1911b:164; mentioned in 1904 and 1905 in letters to Kroeber—see Golla 1986:27); Sapir's Na-Dene hypothesis follows this suggestion. Swanton (1915) also proposed Coahuiltecan, a grouping that included Cotoname, Tonkawa, Coahuilteco, Comecrudo, and Karankawa. (He also mentioned Karankawa resemblances with Atakapa.) This proposal influenced Sapir, and ultimately it became part of his Hokan-Coahuiltecan grouping (see Chapters 4 and 8). Swanton further proposed a grouping he called Tunican, which included Tunica, Chitimacha, and Atakapa; he also grouped Natchez and Muskogean, and eventually he proposed that this Tunican was related to (Natchez-) Muskogean (1919, 1924). These proposals also played roles in Sapir's broader Hokan-Siouan grouping and in Haas's Gulf proposal (see Chapter 8). Swanton's methods appear to have been similar to those of Powell—generally, the juxtaposition of lexically resemblant forms without argument or systematic correspondences—though Swanton juxtaposed structural features as well. However, the similarities did not have to be quite as obvious for Swanton as for Powell, for, as Swanton explained, "languages may be related although on first inspection they show few resemblances" (1924:47).

John Peabody Harrington

Harrington (1884–1961) had a profound interest in recording Indian languages, especially those of California (beginning at least as early as 1903), and he spent most of his life in uninterrupted field research on Native American languages.[119] He became a staff member at the

Smithsonian Institution's BAE in 1915 which continued until his retirement in 1954 (Golla 1984:72–3, 1991b). "His archival legacy is of unique importance" (Golla 1991b:337; cf. Mills 1988). His *Nachlass* is truly a linguistic treasure. He left extensive, accurate field notes—close to one million pages collected during his lifetime (Hinton 1994:195), which included "at least some data on over 125 separate languages of California and the Far West" (Golla 1991b:340). Several of these languages had already been assumed to be dead, but Harrington was able to find and work with some surviving speakers; many languages on which he worked have subsequently become extinct. Although his forte was fieldwork and descriptive data, he did propose a number of genetic relationships. For example, he literally announced genetic relationships between Chumash and Yuman (presenting no data or evidence) (1913) and between Washo and Chumashan (1917; see also Darnell 1971b:240); he connected Kiowa and Tanoan (1910b, 1928) and provided a subgrouping of Tanoan (1909, 1910b). He also did historical work on Athabaskan (1940, 1943b). His proposal that Quechua is Hokan (1943a), though unfortunate, has often been cited. He also left several unpublished manuscripts concerning various proposed alignments, including one entitled "Zuñi discovered to be Hokan" (written between 1944 and 1950; Mills and Brickfield 1986:34). Specialists in the field are in Harrington's debt for the sheer volume of descriptive material he has left, which is the basis for many ongoing historical investigations.

Other Classifications of North American Indian Languages

Several overall classifications of North American Indian languages also deserve mention, though they have had less influence on the development of the field.

Hermann Ludewig

Ludewig's listing (1858) was more a catalog of language/tribal names; however, in many entries he identified the family and often other relatives

within it, thus in effect forming a classification. For example, "Chippeway, Ojibway" is identified as a "principal dialect of the great Algonquin stock" (p. 41), Comanche is described as "belonging to the great Shoshonee or Snake family" (p. 51) and Dogrib as "belong[ing] to the Dtinne or Athapaskan stock" (p. 66). The Navajos are "a powerful tribe of the Apache family, related to the great Athapascan stock" (p. 132). The language of the Pokonchi "bears close affinity to the Maya" (p. 151). Quiche (K'iche') is "closely related to . . . Kachiquels [Kaqchikel, Cakchiquel] and Zutugils [Tz'utujil], and bears much resemblance to the Maya" (p. 157). Tarahumara is "related to the Mexican [Nahuatl]" (p. 181); Winnebagos are "Indians of the Sioux stock" (p. 200); and "the Aymara language bears a close resemblance to the Quichua" (p. 17).

Christianus Cornelius Uhlenbeck

Uhlenbeck's classification (1908) probably deserved more attention than it received, but it was thought (partly with some justification) to be too similar to that of Powell (1891a).

George L. Trager

Trager's classification (Trager and Harben 1958, also Trager 1945) was "a slight modification, for the languages north of Mexico, made by Benjamin Lee Whorf and Trager, of the Sapir [1929a] classification" and is said to have been worked out in 1936 (Trager and Harben 1958:3). It differed from Sapir's classification principally in that it (1) created a Macro-Penutian composed of Penutian (much as Sapir had it; see Chapter 8), Sahaptian, Azteco-Tanoan, Tunican, Mayoid (Mayan), and Totonac, (2) rearranged Sapir's Hokan-Siouan so that Esselen-Yuman, Siouan-Yuchi, and Natchez-Muskogean were considered independent stocks (with Tunican now included in Macro-Penutian); and (3) added Tarascan and Macro-Otomanguean (from south of the border), with Mayoid and Totonac also added to Macro-Penutian. Trager's classification seem to have had little influence, though versions of Penutian similar to his and Whorf's have often been cited.

Sydney Lamb

Lamb's classification (1959) consists of twenty-three major groupings, a sort of compromise between Sapir's boldness (just six) and Powell's conservatism (fifty-eight). They are: Eskimo-Aleut, Na-Dene (including the controversial Haida), Chinook-Tsimshian, Coos-Takelman (Coosan includes Yakonan and Siuslaw, and Takelman includes Kalapuya), Pen-Uti (Penutian, that is, Sapir's California Penutian), Klamath-Sahaptian (includes Molala), Yuki, Karok-Yuman (Hokan, includes Seri and Tequistlatec), Comecrudo-Karankawa (includes Cotoname-Comecrudo, Coahuilteco, Karankawa, and Tonkawa), Atakapa-Muskogean (Haas's Gulf plus Timucua), Algonkian-Ritwan, Kutenay, Spokane-Bellacoola (Salish), Chimakuan-Wakashan, Iroquois-Caddoan, Yuchi-Siouan, Keres, Zuni, Aztec-Tanoan, Tarascan, Subtiaba, Zapotec-Otomian (that is, Otomanguean without Amuzgo or Tlapanec-Subtiaba), and Totonac-Mayan (including Totonacan, "Mizoquean" [Mixe-Zoquean], Huave, and Mayan). **Heinz-Jürgen Pinnow**'s classification (1964a) follows Lamb's (1959) compromise very closely.

Karl-Heinz Gursky

Gursky's classification (1966a) is quite similar to Lamb's (as Gursky [p. 441] points out). Gursky's classification is extremely well informed and carefully reasoned for the time, but unfortunately was long delayed in press (it was actually submitted for publication before 1964), and, consequently, the consensus classification from the 1964 Indiana University conference on the Classification of American Indian languages (reported in Voegelin and Voegelin 1965, 1967) eclipsed it almost immediately. Gursky's classification and that of the 1964 conference are very similar, though Gursky seems to have left out a number of languages of the Southeast. The updating survey of **William W. Elmendorf** (1965) was also superseded almost immediately by the report of the 1964 conference. In his review of classification efforts since Powell, Elmendorf found that "despite the present dilapidated condition of two of Sapir's superstocks,

Mosan-Algonkian and Hokan-Siouan, his 35-year-old synthesis of North American Indian language relationships is still in reasonably good working order in the majority of its parts."

The 1964 Conference Classification

Representing the consensus of some thirty of the best-known specialists of the day (reported in Voegelin and Voegelin 1965), the 1964 Conference Classification was very influential, though much of it has been discarded or remains controversial today, such as (1) American Arctic-Paleosiberian Phylum (said to be composed of Eskimo-Aleut and Chuckchi-Kamchatkan); (2) Na-Dene (as per Sapir); (3) Macro-Algonquian phylum (including Algonquian, Yurok and Wiyot, and Haas's proposed Gulf languages: Muskogean, Natchez, Atakapa, Chitimacha, Tunica, and Tonkawa); (4) Macro-Siouan (includes Siouan, Catawba, Iroquoian, Caddoan, and Yuchi—but the evidence presented thus far does not support this grouping); (5) Hokan Phylum (mostly as defined by Sapir, but minus Siouan); (6) Penutian Phylum (similar to Sapir's version of Penutian, but with the inclusion of Mixe-Zoquean, Mayan, Chipaya-Uru, Totonacan, and Huave); and (7) Aztec-Tanoan. (Groups 3 and 4 represent a dismantling of parts of Sapir's Hokan-Siouan superstock and their redistribution among groupings proposed here. See Chapter 8 for discussion of these groupings.) With regard to the languages of South America, the 1964 report gives Greenberg's classification (1960[1956]) much credence. For example, it puts Misumalpan, Xinca, and Lenca in Macro-Chibchan, together with several other language families of South America, though there is no real justification for grouping any of them. Thus the 1964 report represents in some sense the culmination of the "inspectional" or "lumper" orientation to the classification of North American Indian languages (see Chapter 3), work done in the Sapir tradition, much of it by his students. The 1964 classification became ingrained as a result of its dissemination in widely available reference sources, such as Voegelin and Voegelin's widely utilized map (1966) and their volumes on languages of the world (1965, 1977), Bright's *Encyclopaedia Britannica* article

(1974a), and even Rood's contribution to the *International Encyclopedia of Linguistics* (1992a).

The 1964 consensus classification was the one most often followed until publication of the volume edited by Campbell and Mithun (1979a). This work represents a more conservative orientation toward long-range proposals, requiring that the evidence for formerly proposed but never substantiated hypotheses be assessed carefully. It is still considered by many to be the standard reference for the classification of North American and Mesoamerican languages (Rood 1992a:110).

Greenberg (1987; also 1960[1956]) classified all the languages of the Americas into three groups: Eskimo-Aleut, Na-Dene, and Amerind. This proposal has received much attention in the popular media and by scholars of disciplines outside of linguistics, but it has been rejected by the majority of specialists in the field (see Chapters 3, 7, and 8).

Classifications of South American Indian Langauges

This section is a brief discussion of the linguistic classifications of South American Indian languages as a whole, with particular emphasis on methods. (For a fuller discussion of specific families, see Chapter 6.)

Karl Friedrich Philipp von Martius

Martius (1794–1864), who is unknown to many Americanists today, made significant contributions to South American linguistic research. From 1832 to 1867, he wrote extensively on Brazilian ethnography and linguistics, but his writings also contain considerable discussion of American Indian language issues in general, particularly of their study in North America, where he followed closely the work of Gallatin and Schoolcraft, and indirectly accepted Duponceau's views. He reported Schoolcraft's four main families—Algic, Ostic (Iroquoian), Abanic (mostly Siouan), and Tsallakee (Cherokee, Catawba, Muskogee, Choctaw)—and sought to achieve a similar grasp of Brazil's linguistic complexity, insisting, along with Duponceau,

that, "these languages show great differences in pronunciation, [but] none in their inner construction"[120] (1867, 1:165). Martius's extensive collection of South American vocabularies (with more than 120 Indian groups represented), his classification of Tupian languages, and his map showing the linguistic classification of lowland South America (excellent for its time) were much cited (see Benfey 1869:785). His method was largely that of vocabulary juxtaposition (cf. Martius 1867, 2:xiv), since he believed (following Duponceau) that the languages of the Americas had a grammar that was mostly held in common: "They [lowland South American languages] have in common with the languages of North America the polysynthetic character, and their grammar apparently can be traced to a few general far-reaching rules"[121] (1867, 2:vi).

Daniel Brinton

Brinton's catalogue (1891) (discussed earlier in this chapter) is usually considered the first overall classification of South American languages. He attempted to evaluate the sources, and drew heavily from scholars before him (cf. Wilbert 1968).

Alexander Francis Chamberlain

Chamberlain's classification published in the *Encyclopedia Americana* (1903, 1913), was well-known, but it was simply a short catalogue of South American languages, with no indication of how it was established. The 1903 version listed fifty-seven families; the 1913 version listed eighty-three (and included a map modeled on Powell's for North America) (see Wilbert 1968:8).[122]

Paul Rivet

Until recently, Rivet (1876–1958) was considered to have done the "primary classificatory work on the vast majority of South American languages" (Rowe 1954:14).[123] His alphabetical catalogue included 77 language families and some 1,240 languages and dialects (Wilbert 1968:8). Aspects of Rivet's classification were followed by most subsequent classifiers of South American languages, in particular Loukotka

(1942, 1968), Mason (1950), and Greenberg (1960[1956], 1987).

Rivet had done work on the classification of the languages of Bolivia, Peru, Ecuador, Colombia, and western Brazil. He utilized reasonably extensive vocabularies where available and compared the specific language he wished to classify with whole families. However, the way in which Rivet undertook his comparisons makes his methods unreliable. This is why Rowe assessed Rivet's methods so harshly:

> If, for example, he [Rivet] finds a new language, which he thinks may be Arawak, he compares each word of its vocabulary with words of similar meaning in perhaps thirty languages that he has already classified as "Arawak." If he finds any similar form in any of the thirty languages, it is evidence of relationship, and the fact that the total number of similarities to any one "Arawak" language may be very small is lost in the comparative table. Rivet is looking for similarities rather than systematic sound correspondences, and he does no reconstructing. *One of the advantages of this method is that the more languages a linguist has put into a family, the easier it is to find cognates for new ones. Rivet has even succeeded in relating Tehuelche* [of Chile] *to the Australian languages.* (Emphasis added; 1954:15; see also Wilbert 1968:9)

Other aspects of Rivet's methods have also been criticized: "He [Rivet] cuts up the words with hyphens, not according to etymological principles but in whatever way is convenient for his comparisons. Another thing that I cannot accept is the way in which he compares words whose meanings are too far apart" (Nimuendajú and Guérios 1948:233–4; translated and quoted by Rowe 1954:15–16). In some cases, Rivet proposed classifications based on very little or even no linguistic data. He even went so far as to suggest indirectly that the distribution of various cultural traits that he considered characteristically Carib, such as ligatures worn on the arms and legs, may "enable us to classify additional languages in the Carib family" (1943; Rowe 1954:17; see Greenberg 1963 and Chapter 7 for a discussion of why nonlinguistic evidence is invalid for linguistic classification. For a discussion of some of Rivet's mistaken classifications, see Rowe 1954 and Adelaar 1989). The same criticisms are found in assessments of many other proposals of remote relationship that rely on superficial lexical similarities.

Rivet (1925a) had expressed the same doubts as his teacher Meillet about whether sound change in "exotic" languages is regular. For this, and for his attempts to relate South American and Australian languages (1925a, 1925b, 1926, 1957[1943]), he received further criticism.

Čestmír Loukotka

If Rivet's methods were unreliable, those of Loukotka (?–1966) were even worse. Loukotka, Rivet's student, did no firsthand fieldwork but assembled vocabularies from other sources. In several instances, he followed Rivet's proposals. He revised and reissued his classification four times, recognizing first 94 South American families (1935), then 114 families with 27 unclassified languages (1942), and finally 117 stocks (including language isolates)—with a registry of 1,492 languages in all (1968; see also Wilbert 1968:13, 15–17). Loukotka's method was shockingly outmoded. It was "the special method of a standardized word list" in which he attempted, wherever possible, to assemble a list of "forty-five typical words." Classification was based merely on visual scanning of these lexical items (Rowe 1954:15). However, irrespective of the question of the method's lack of virtue, Loukotka did not even apply it in a consistent manner: "*Loukotka has classified dozens of languages, and even five whole families, without a single word to go on. This can be done only by using procedures like Rivet's*" (emphasis added; Rowe 1954:17–18).

In a sense, Loukotka shared Powell's and Boas's concern about the difficulty of determining the extent to which diffusion and language mixture could be at play, since one of his goals was "to solve the difficult classificatory problem of mixed languages" (Wilbert 1968:11); however, his solution would hardly be considered convincing today. A mixed language (*Mischsprache*) for Loukotka was one in which the number of non-native vocabulary items in the forty-five-word list exceeded one-fifth of the total (Loukotka 1942:1), but his judgments concerning native and borrowed forms were very impressionistic (Wilbert 1968:13–14).

In spite of the shortcomings of Loukotka's

methods, Kaufman finds Loukotka's classification "practically error-free as far as genetic groupings are concerned" (1990a:37). Kaufman considered Loukotka's mistakes to be only the inclusion of names of languages for which no data exist; the occasional language assigned to the wrong genetic group, often claiming faulty subgrouping for recognized groups; and proposing groupings not supported by the evidence (in two instances: Loukotka's inclusions in Chibchan, following Rivet, and his joining of Guajiboan with Arawakan) (see Chapter 6).

J. Alden Mason

Mason's (1885–1967) classification of South American languages (1950) is still frequently cited in the linguistic and anthropological literature.[124] It was informative for its time and, at least in spirit, was methodologically more on target than most others. Nevertheless, Rowe criticized it heavily; he found the fact that it was cited so frequently "unfortunate, because Mason's work is in many respects less reliable than Loukotka's" (1954:18)—which, it should be recalled, was said to be less reliable than Rivet's, which was severely criticized). Mason was squarely in the Kroeber-Sapir tradition which sought to reduce the vast diversity among American Indian languages by proposing preliminary but undemonstrated hypotheses of more far-reaching families. For example, he described part of his proposed Macro-Tupí-Guaraní super-stock in the following terms: "It is not advanced with any claim to certainty or with any evidence of proof, but as the result of opinions, deductions, and intuitions of the several authorities and of the present writer. . . . As all these families are contiguous a genetic connection is not unreasonable" (1950:236; quoted in Rowe 1954:18). Mason's classification of South American languages was a general and uncritical compilation and consolidation,

> the unifying principle of which seems to have been a desire to cut down the number of independent families as much as possible. As a result, he proposes a series of super-stocks that go far beyond any evidence now available and are more inclusive even than Rivet's.

On the other hand, Mason was disposed to

apply strict methodological principles: [For distant genetic comparisons among languages] to carry conviction, laws of sound-shift must be deduced, obeyed by a large proportion of the cases in question, and a basic similarity in morphological and phonetic pattern must be shown. . . . One of the pitfalls to be avoided in linguistic comparison is that of borrowing. (Rowe 1954:18–19)

Unfortunately, Mason's classification of South American languages could not benefit much from his principles, since little historical linguistic research on South American languages had been conducted at that time (Mason 1950: 162). (For examples of Mason's classification errors and of languages classified without supporting data, see Rowe 1954.)

However, much research has been done since the 1950s, and the overall picture is much clearer now. Also, a number of other long-range general classifications have been proposed (Greenberg 1960[1956], 1987; Kaufman 1990a, 1994; Migliazza and Campbell 1988; Suárez 1974; Swadesh 1959; Tovar 1961; Tovar and Larrueca de Tovar 1984). Nevertheless, it is difficult to say that any of these broad classifications is methodologically more sound than any of the precursors. That is, the scholars responsible for some of them have had an adequate understanding of historical linguistic methods; however, in view of the sheer number of languages and groups to be dealt with, as well as the lack of information on many of them (and the conflicting information on others), these classifications appear to share with Mason's the characteristic that they are mostly based on a sifting and repetition of portions of the proposals made by those who covered the same terrain earlier (though they are occasionally improved in detail by the incorporation of newer information on a specific language family). On the whole, these classifications are still relatively speculative, lacking the application of the sorts of methods that some of the scholars involved would have preferred, had the situation been conducive. The classification of Kaufman, the most recent and best informed of these compilations, illustrates this point:

> It is based on the overall agreements in the classification of Loukotka 1968, Greenberg 1987 [cf.

Greenberg 1960], Suárez 1974, and Swadesh 1959 as to what genetic groups and isolates are found in SA [South America]. It is also based on an examination of the evidence found in Loukotka as well as many other (but by no means all) studies of language classification in SA. (1990a:31; see also 1994)

Kaufman's classification is the point of departure for the discussion of South American languages in Chapter 6.

TABLE 2-1 Correspondence Sets for Central Algonquian

	Fox	Ojibwa	Plains Cree	Menomini	Proto-Central-Algonquian
(1)	hk	šk	sk	čk	*čk
(2)	šk	šk	sk	sk	*šk
(3)	hk	hk	sk	hk	*xk
(4)	hk	hk	hk	hk	*hk
(5)	šk	šk	hk	hk	*çk

The Comparative Method and Contributions of American Indian Linguistics

An old but often repeated question is, can the comparative method be applied successfully to the study of unwritten languages?[125] "Unwritten" in this context is usually associated with so-called primitive or exotic languages, and thus the question has two corollaries: (1) Is change in unwritten/primitive/exotic languages fundamentally different from change in written languages? (2) Is sound change regular in unwritten/exotic languages (regular sound change being a cornerstone of the comparative method)? One of the more significant contributions of American Indian linguistics is that it has conclusively answered these questions: NO, change in unwritten and exotic languages is not different from that known to occur in Indo-European and other language families; YES, sound change in unwritten and so-called exotic languages is regular. It was work on American Indian languages which convinced the scholarly world once and for all that the comparative method is indeed applicable to exotic languages and that sound change is regular in these languages as it is in written languages.

Bloomfield (1925) resolved to disprove the assertion that reconstruction cannot be successful in the absence of written records of earlier stages of the language (Haas 1969d:22, Sapir 1931). His famous Algonquian proof showed (though this was not his primary intention) that written record not only can be overrated but also sometimes can actually be an obstacle to reconstruction. He employed mixed "written" and "unwritten" source materials from the Algonquian languages he compared. He relied in part on earlier written records from missionaries and traders, but he trusted what he considered to be scientific recordings—his own field records for Menomini and Cree, and the renditions of Fox and Ojibwa recorded by William Jones, a linguistically trained native speaker of Fox.[126]

Bloomfield's well-known proof of the applicability of the comparative method in the study of exotic languages (1925, 1928) was based on correspondence sets and reconstructions for Central Algonquian, which he had extracted from his written and unwritten sources (see table 2-1). He postulated the reconstruction of *çk for set (5) as being distinct from the others on the basis of scant evidence—a single reconstructible morpheme. But assuming that sound change is regular, the difference in this correspondence set (though it exhibits only sounds that occur in different combinations in the other sets) could not be plausibly explained in any other way. Later, the correctness of his decision to reconstruct something different for this set was confirmed when Swampy Cree was found to contain the correspondence htk in the morpheme upon which set (5) was based—a set that was distinct in Swampy Cree from the reflexes of the other four reconstructions.[127] Based on this result, Bloomfield concluded that "as an assumption . . . the postulate [of sound change without exception] yields, as a matter of mere routine, predictions which otherwise would be impossible. In other words, the statement that *phonemes change* (sound-changes have no exceptions) is a tested hypothesis: in so far as one may speak of such a thing, it is a proved truth" (1928: 100).

However, there is an object lesson of another sort concerning the value of written records in Jones's renditions of Ojibwa. Since in Fox there is no contrast between *sk* and *šk,* Jones (as a native speaker of Fox) failed to recognize and record this contrast in Ojibwa. Had Jones's recordings of Ojibwa (the source Bloomfield chose to rely on solely) not failed to represent this contrast, Swampy Cree would not have been the only extant witness to the distinctness of set (5): "The fuss and trouble behind my note in Language [Bloomfield 1928] would have been avoided if I had listened to O[jibwa], which plainly distinguishes sk (< PA çk) from šk (< PA šk); instead, I depended on printed records which failed to show the distinction" (Bloomfield 1946:88; see also Hockett 1970[1948]:500–1). The truth of the matter is that the written source materials (Jones's recordings on which Bloomfield chose to rely) were an obstacle to reliable reconstruction by the comparative method, and Bloomfield would have us think (in the passage just quoted) that it was the later accurately recorded field data, the usual tender of "unwritten" languages, that led to the correct solution. However, there is an irony in Bloomfield's distrust of the older written sources: in fact, older missionary sources on Ojibwa (Baraga 1878, 1879[1878], 1881[1880]; Cuoq 1886) did correctly distinguish /sk/ from /šk/. The obstacle to reliable reconstruction was Bloomfield's blind faith in modern written records.[128] Hereby hangs an important tale: written representations require interpretation. Comparative reconstruction which depends on written records can be no better than our ability to extract from them relevant interpretations of the phonology of the languages being studied (Hockett 1970[1948]:502).

Since the work of Sapir and Bloomfield, the assumption that sound change is regular has proved useful and valid in case after case in work on American Indian languages, as well as other "exotic" languages. It should not to be forgotten that the assumption was employed fruitfully in many earlier instances (see Campbell 1994b). As a result of work on American Indian languages, the linguistic world now no longer questions the application of the comparative method to so-called exotic languages.

Summary

In this chapter the history of American Indian historical linguistic study has been surveyed. I have attempted to present what has been established in earlier work on these languages and have sought to distinguish this from erroneous ideas of the past which should now be discarded. I have also attempted to correct some misconceptions concerning this history and to point out the important contributions that the study of Native American languages has made to the development of linguistic thinking in general. Clearly, American Indian linguistics is not a recent stepchild of American anthropology but rather has a full history of its own and in fact has played a leading role in the development of anthropology in the United States and elsewhere. More important, American Indian linguistics has contributed to theoretical and methodological developments in linguistics in general and was usually up to date with and benefited from contemporary developments in linguistic thinking.

The history of the classification of Native American languages—in particular, the methods employed to determine genetic relationships—has been the focus of this chapter. Although the methods and criteria used by individuals have varied, many scholars coincided in stressing the importance of grammatical or structural evidence, sound correspondences, and basic vocabulary as criteria for determining whether languages belong to the same family. American Indian languages were involved in some of the earliest applications of the comparative method (for example, the work of Jonathan Edwards, which was contemporaneous with that of Sir William Jones, but actually displayed greater linguistic acumen). In the philosophical debate concerning typological classifications, "inner form," the "ideologic" orientation to language, and the evolutionary orientation, it was the evidence from the study of Native American languages that made possible the correction of these misconceptions. The study of American Indian languages demonstrated once and for all that the comparative method is applicable to so-called exotic and unwritten languages and that sound change is regular in those languages. Native American languages were also involved in early investigations of comparative syntax. American

Indian linguistic study has so often been in the forefront of major linguistic developments that it is difficult to understand how the attitudes concerning its backwardness or marginality could ever have developed.

For a fuller discussion of the individual language families, see Chapters 4, 5, and 6, and for discussion of methods and evaluation of proposals concerning distant genetic relationships, see Chapters 7 and 8.

APPENDIX
Comparison of Major Classifications of North American Languages

The classifications compared are those of Daniel Brinton (1891), Campbell (in this book), Albert Gallatin (1836), Albert S. Gatschet (1876, 1877a, 1882), Robert Latham (1856), John Wesley Powell (1891a), and Edward Sapir (1929a). Note: = means that a language or group is classified as a member of another group. For example, Seri is considered independent by some scholars, but Powell groups it with Yuman; hence "= Yuman" is indicated for Powell's Seri.)

Campbell	Sapir	Powell	Brinton	Gatschet	Latham	Gallatin
Eskimo-Aleut	Eskimo-Aleut	Eskimauan	Eskimo[1]	Eskimo[2]	(Eskimo)	Eskimaux[3]
	Nadene					
Tlingit-Athabaskan	Continental Nadene					
Tlingit	Tlingit	Koluschan	Tlinkit/Koloschan	Koloshish/Thlinkit		Koulischen
Eyak-	Athabaskan	Athapascan	Athabascan (Tinné)	Tinné family	Athabaskan Group[4]	Athapasca
Athabaskan						Kinai[5]
				Tolewa[6]	Tahlewah	
Haida	Haida	Skittagetan	Haidah (Skittagetan)	Skittagits	Haidah Group[7]	Queen Charlotte's Island
	Algonkin-Wakashan					
	Mosan[8]					
Wakashan	Wakashan	Wakashan	Nutka/Wakashan	Wakash	Wakash	Wakash
			Kwakiootl/	Nootka with Makah		Straits of Fuca[9]
			Haeltzukian		Fitzhugh Sound/	Hailtsa
					Hailtsa[10]	
Chimakuan	Chimakuan	Chimakuan	Chimakuan			
Salish(an)	Salish	Salish	Salish	Selish	Atna Group[11]	Salish
				Kawitsch group[12]		Atnah[13]
				Billechoola[15]	Billechula	Salmon River[14]
						(Friendly Village)
Kutenai	Kootenay	Kitunahan	Kutenay/Kitunahan	Kitunaha/Kootenai	Kitunaha/Kutani	
Algic[16]	Algonkin-Ritwan					
Algonquian	Algonkin	Algonquian	Algonkin	Algonkin[17]	Algonkin Group[18]	Algonkin-Lenape
						Black Feet[19]
					Fall Indians[20]	Rapid/Fall Indians[21]
				Arrapaho		
Wiyot-Yurok	Ritwan	Wishoskan	Wishoskan	Wishosk		
		Weitspekan	Weitspekan/Rurok	Weits-pok/Eurok	Weitspek[22]	
Beothuk	Beothuk[23]	Beothuk	Beothuk		Beothuck[24]	
	Penutian					
	California Penutian					
Miwok-Costanoan	Miwok-Costanoan					
Miwokan		Moquelumnan	Moquelumnian/	Meewoc		Moquelumne Group
			Mutsun			
				Talatui[25]		
Costanoan		Costanoan	Costanoan	Mutsun[26]		Costano
Yokutsan	Yokuts	Mariposan	Mariposan/Yokuts	Yucut	Mariposa	
				Telamé[27]		
Maiduan	Maidu	Pujunan	Pujunan/Maidu	Meidoo/Pujuni[28]	Pujuni	
Wintuan	Wintun	Copehan	Copehan/Wintun	Wintoon	Copeh	

Campbell	Sapir	Powell	Brinton	Gatschet	Latham	Gallatin
	Oregon Penutian					
Takelman (=Takelma-Kalapuyan)	Takelma	Takilman	Takilman	Takilma		
	Coast Oregon Penutian					
Coosan	Coos	Kusan	Kusan	Kúsa[29]		
		Yakonan	Yakonan	Yakon, Yákona[30]	Jakon	
Siuslawan	Siuslaw	Siuslaw	Siuslaw	Sayúskla[31]		
Alsea	Yakonan	Alsea	Alsea			Jacon
Kalapuyan (=Takelma-Kalapuyan)	Kalapuya	Kalapooian	Kalapooian	Kalapuya	Kalapuya	
Chinookan	Chinook	Chinookan	Chinook(an)	Chinook[32]	Tshinuk/Chinuk	Chinook
Tsimshian	Tsimshian	Chimmesyan	Tshimsian/Chimmessyan	Chimmesyan	Chemmesyan	
	Plateau Penutian					
Sahaptian-Klamath-Molala	Sahaptian	Shahaptian	Sahaptin/Sahaptanian	Sahaptin	Sahaptin-Waiilatpu Sahaptin	
	Waiilatpuan	Wailatpuan	Wayilaptu	Wayilatpu	Waiilaptu	
Cayuse	Cayuse			Cayuse	Cayús	
Molala (=Sahapatian-Klamath-Molala)	Molala			Molele	Molelé	
Klamath-Modoc (=Sahaptian-Klamath-Molala)	Lutuami[33]	Lutuamian	Lutuamian/Modoc	Klamath	Lutuami[34]	
	Hokan-Siouan					
	Hokan-Coahuiltecan					
	Hokan					
	Northern Hokan					
Karuk	Karok	Quoratean	Quoratean/Ehnek	Cahrok	Ehnek	
Chimariko	Chimariko	Chimarikan	Chimarikan	Chimariko[35]		
Shasta	Shasta-Achomawi[36]	Sastean	Sastean/Shasta	Shasta	Shasti	
Palaihnihan[37]		Palaihnihan	Palaihnihan/Achomawi			
				Pit River[38]	Palaik	
Yana	Yana	Yanan	Yanan/Nozi			
Pomoan	Pomo	Kulanapan	Kulanapan/Pomo	Pomo[39]	Mendocino Group	
Washo	Washo	Washoan		Washo[40]		
	Esselen-Yuman					
Esselen	Esselen	Esselenian	Esselenian			
					Cochimi	
Yuman	Yuman	Yuman	Yuma stock	Yuma[41]	Yuma languages	
	Salinan-Seri					
Salinan	Salinan	Salinan	Salinan		Salinas Group[42]	
Chumashan	Chumash	Chumashan	Chumashan	Santa Barbara[43]	Santa Barbara Group	
Seri	Seri	(= Yuman)	(= Yuma stock)			
Tequistlatecan	Tequistlatecan		(= Yuma stock)			
Subtiaba-Tlapanec (=Otomanguean)	Subtiaba-Tlappanec					
	Coahuiltecan					
Tonkawa	Tonkawa	Tonkawan	Tonkaway	Tonkawa		
Coahuiteco	Coahuilteco					
	Coahuilteco proper	Coahuiltecan	Coahuiltecan stock			
Cotoname	Cotoname					
Comecrudo[44]	Comecrudo					
Karankawa	Karankawa	Karankawan	Carankaway			
Yukian	Yuki	Yukian	Yukian	Yuki with Wappo		
Keresan	Keres	Keresan	Kera stock	Queres, Kera	Acoma/Laguna	
	Tunican					
Tunica	Tunica-Atakapa	Tonikan	Tonica		Tunica[45]	
Atakapa		Attacapan	Atakapa	Attacapa	Attacapa[46]	Attacapa
Chitimacha	Chitimacha	Chitimachan	Chetimacha	Chetimacha		Chetimacha
	Iroquois-Caddoan					
Iroquoian	Iroquoian	Iroquoian	Iroquois	Huron-Irokesish Cherokee	Iroquois	Iroquois Cherokee
Caddoan	Caddoan	Caddoan	Pani stock (Pawnee/Caddo)	Caddo Group	Caddo[47]	Caddo
				Pawnee[48]	Pawni[49]	Pawnee

Continued

87

APPENDIX
Comparison of Major Classifications
of North American Languages (*Continued*)

Campbell	Sapir	Powell	Brinton	Gatschet	Latham	Gallatin
	Eastern Group					
	Siouan-Yuchi					
Siouan	Siouan	Siouan	Dakota stock	Dakota/Sioux[50]	Sioux[51]	Sioux
			Catawba[52]	Catawba		Catawba
						Woccon[53]
Yuchi	Yuchi	Uchean	Yuchi			Utchee
	Natchez-Muskogian					
Natchez	Natchez	Natchesan	Natchez	Natchez		Natches
Muskogean	Muskogian	Muskhogean	Chahta-Muskoki	Chocktaw[54]		Muskhugee
					Choktah[55]	Chahta
Timucuan	Timucua[56]	Timuquanan	Timucua			
Adai		Adaizan	Adaize	Adaize	Adaize (Adahi)	Adaize
	Aztec-Tanoan					
Uto-Aztecan	Uto-Aztekan		Uto-Aztecan stock			
(= Uto-Aztecan)	Nahuatl	(Nahuatl)	Nahuatlan			
(= Uto-Aztecan)	Pima	Piman	Sonoran	Pima[57]	Pima[58]	
(= Uto-Aztecan)		Shoshonean	Shoshonian	Shóshoni stock	Utah, etc.[59]	Shoshonee, Eu-taw, Cumanch
	Shoshonean					
					Moqui[60]	
					Capistrano Group[61]	
Kiowa-Tanoan	Tanoan-Kiowa					
	Tanoan	Tañoan	Tehua stock	Pueblo languages[62]	Taos, Picuri[63]	
					Jemez	
					Tesuque	
	Kiowa	Kiowan	Kioway	Kinawa/Kioway	(Kioway)[64]	
Zuni	Zuñi[65]	Zuñian	Zuñi stock	Zuñi	Zuni	

1. Eskimo and Aleut.
2. Includes Aleut.
3. Includes Aleut.
4. Latham (1856:67) equated Kinai with Loucheux, an Athabaskan language. He also identified Atna (at the mouth of the Copper River) and Ugalents as Athabaskan (1856:68), though Eyak is probably what was involved here.
5. Gallatin's Kinai is an Athabaskan language.
6. Tolowa, an Athabaskan language of Northern California.
7. "Spoken by the Skittegats, Massetts, Kumshahs, and Kyganie of Queen Charlotte's Islands and the Prince of Wales Archipelago" (Latham 1856:72).
8. Sapir also called this "Wakashan-Salish."
9. Gallatin's Straits of Fuca is Makah, a Nootkan (Wakashan) language.
10. Also named Hailtsa or Haeetsuk (Latham 1956:64).
11. Also called "Tsihaili-Selish," the group includes many of the known Salishan languages.
12. Includes "Aht" and "Squallyamish."
13. Gallatin's Atnah is Shuswap, a Salishan language.
14. This is Bella Coola, a Salishan language.
15. Bella Coola, Salishan.
16. Algic is also called Algonquian-Ritwan.
17. "Algonquin (with an East branch [Oststämme], North branch [Nordstämme], and a West branch [West-stämme], together comprising most of the Algonquian languages known today, including Blackfoot and Cheyenne)" (Gatschet 1876:29).
18. Latham connected "Shyenne" [Cheyenne], Blackfoot, and Arapaho with "Algonkin."
19. Blackfoot is an Algonquian language.
20. Latham (1856:62) included the Fall Indians (Atsina)—also called Gros-Ventre, but not to be confused with the Siouan Gros-Ventre (Hidatsa)—with Algonquian.
21. Atsina (Gros Ventre), now known to be Algonquian.
22. "Weyot and Wishosk are mere dialects of the same language" (Latham 1856:77).
23. Sapir gave Beothuk with a question mark to indicate uncertainty of inclusion in "Algonkin-Ritwan."
24. "Further investigation show[s] that, of the ordinary American languages, it [Beothuk] was Algonkin rather than aught else" (Latham 1856:58).
25. On the Sacramento River, a Miwokan variety.
26. Mutsun included Runsien or Rumsen, Eslenes, Costaño, Olamentke (spoken in the area around Bodega Bay), and Chocuyem; Gatschet (1877a:159) gave eleven supposed cognates shared by Mutsun and Chocuyem.
27. A variety of Yokuts, Southern Valley (Gatschet 1876:32).
28. Pujuni is listed in Gatschet 1876; Meidoo is given in Gotschet 1877a.
29. Added in Gatschet 1882:257.

30. Yakon, Yákona has Yakona (Siuslaw?) and Alseya (Alsea) as members.

31. Added in Gatschet 1882:257.

32. Chinook is said to cover several "dialects and tribes"; Gatschet lists Chinook Jargon separately.

33. Also called "Klamath-Modoc."

34. "The Lutuami, Shasti, and Palaik are thrown by Gallatin into three separate classes. . . . Nevertheless they cannot be very widely separated" (Latham 1856:74).

35. Added in Gatschet 1882:255.

36. Karok, Chimariko, and Shasta-Achomawi are grouped together as one branch of Northern Hokan.

37. Palaihnihan or Achomawi-Atsugewi.

38. Achomawi.

39. Gatschet said there are several "bands" of Pomo.

40. Added in Gatschet 1882:255.

41. With "seven dialects."

42. For Latham this is possibly a geographical grouping, although ambiguous. For example, it includes "Ruslen," said also to be connected with "Costano." He also includes in this group "Soledad," "Eslen," and "San Antonio and San Miguel forms of speech [Salinan]." (1856:85).

43. Santa Barbara (Chumashan) is given with "southern dialects": Santa Inez, Santa Barbara, Kasús (or Kash-wáh), and Santa Cruz Island; the "northern dialects" included San Luis Obispo and San Antonio. These were listed independently in Gatschet 1876 but combined in Gatschet 1877a.

44. Also given here as separate, unclassified languages (commonly called "Coahuiltecan") from the area are Aranama-Tamique, Solano, Mamulique, and Garza (see also Goddard 1979b).

45. Latham says that "the Tunicas speak the same language as the Choctahs [Choctaw, Muskogean]" (1856:101); thus he does not distinguish between Tunica and Muskogean.

46. Latham erroneously groups "Carancouas" (Karankawa[s]) with "Attacapa" and asserts that they are "dialects of the same language." (1856:101).

47. Latham (1856:104) assumes that "Witchita" (Wichita) is connected with "Caddo Proper." But he gives "Washita" as an independent language (1856:103); it was, in fact, "a small Caddo tribe" (Swanton 1946:204).

48. "Pawnee (with Wichita, Kichai or Keechi [Kitsai], Riccaree [Arikara], and Pawnee)" (Gatschet 1876:33).

49. "Pawni" is said to be "allied to the *Riccaree* [Arikara]" (Latham 1856:100).

50. Includes the Siouan languages that were known at that time.

51. Latham suggests that there may be "some higher class" which includes Iroquois, Sioux, "Catawba, Woccoon, Cherokee, Choctah and (perhaps) also the Pawni and its ally the Riccaree" (1856:58).

52. Catawba is clearly Siouan, albeit the most divergent member of that family.

53. Woccon is now generally assumed to be Catawban (Catawba-Siouan).

54. "Chocktaw (spoken by Choctaws and Chickasaws; includes related Muskokee [spoken by Creeks and Seminoles], Hitchitee, and Yamassee)" (Gatschet 1876:33).

55. Latham discusses "Choktah" but previously on the same page says that "the Tunicas speak the same language as the Choctahs" (1856:101).

56. Given by Sapir with a question mark to indicate uncertain inclusion in this group.

57. With Névome and Papago.

58. Latham explains that "the Pima group contains the Pima Proper, the Opata, and the Eudeve" (1856:92). He also lists independently, without indicating any relationship among them, the several other languages now known to be Uto-Aztecan—his Hiaqui (Yaqui), Tubar, Tarahumara, and Cora, as well as "Moqui" (Hopi).

59. Latham seems to have recognized some version of what later scholars called "Shoshonean" or "Numic." He said that the evidence was sufficient to show affinities among "Cumanch" (Comanche), "Shonshoni" or "Snake," and "tongues of the southern parts of Oregon" (1856:102). "The Utah [Ute] with its allied dialects is Paduca, i.e. a member of the class to which the Shoshoni, Wihinast, and Cumanch languages belong" (1856:97). Latham (1860b:389) calls this the "Shoshoni (Paduca) group" and adds "Chemehuevi" to it.

60. "Moqui [Hopi] . . . has, out of twenty-one words compared, eight coinciding with the Utah [Ute]" (Latham 1856:99).

61. This includes the southern California Uto-Aztecan languages, Gabrielino and Juaneño.

62. Gatschet calls these the Pueblo languages "im engern Sinne des Wortes [in the stricter sense of the word]" (1876:33), which he later named the Rio Grande Pueblo family (1882:258–9) (Tanoan) (which included "dialects" from Isleta, Jemes, Taos and the Tehua Pueblos in New Mexico (1876); Taos, Taño (Isleta, Sandía, Isleta del Paso), Tehua or Téwa (Tesuque), San Ildefonso, Nambe, San Juan, Santa Clara, Pojoaque, Los Luceros, Temes [*sic,* read Jemes], Old Pecos, and Piro (1882:259). I became aware of Gatschet's Tanoan classification and the fact that he was the first to recognize the grouping after reading Goddard (in press; cited with permission).

63. Latham's discussion of "Pueblo Indians" is not particularly clear. He lists six different "vocabularies," but adds that "the three that, in their outward signs, most strike the eye in tables, as agreeing with each other, are the Laguna, the Jemez, and the Tesuque" (1856:98).

64. "For the *Kioway* we want [lack] specimens [vocabulary lists]" (Latham 1956:100).

65. Sapir gives Zuñi with a question mark, meaning that its place in this classification is uncertain.

3

The Origin of American Indian Languages

These [American] "families" may either have had a remote common ancestry
or multiple unrelated origins; of the origin and early form of speech we
know nothing.

J. Alden Mason (1950:164)

THE EARLIEST PEOPLING OF THE Americas is the subject of a lively current debate.[1] At issue is what really took place and how we can find out about it. The classification of American Indian languages has played an important role in research on this topic. The purpose of this chapter is to consider the implications that the classification of these languages has for how and when the first people came to the New World. The "more than 400 years of humanistic, antiquarian, and—within the last century—scientific [including archaeological, linguistic, and human biological/genetic] scholarship have not definitely resolved the question of when [or how or how many] human groups first made their appearance in the New World" (Taylor 1991:101). To explore these implications, it is helpful to contrast the different proposed classifications, since the methodological shortcomings of some of them prevent them from providing any real historical insight (see Chapter 7). The conclusion reached in this chap-

ter is that the linguistic picture is compatible with a wide range of possible scenarios for the earliest peopling of the Americas, and unfortunately the current state of knowledge does not help to restrict these possibilities significantly. This being the case, caution is to be urged against accepting too readily any claims about early population or migrations based on the classification of American Indian languages.

Early Views of Origin

A brief review of some early views concerning the origins of Native Americans and of the Native American languages will help to put the current debate in context. Hugo Grotius (1552[1884]) argued that American Indians north of the Isthmus of Panama were descendants of Norsemen, who emigrated from Norway via Iceland and Greenland. Already in 1552 he was aware of and argued against what is the equivalent of the Bering Strait hypothesis—that the ancestors of Native Americans entered the New World through Alaska from northeastern Asia. He apparently associated the Bering Strait area with what he called Anianus, but said he knew not whether it was a strait or a bay.[2] If the first inhabitants of America had come from that quarter of Asia, he reasoned, they would have come with horses, but there were no horses in America when the Spanish arrived, which constituted evidence, to Grotius's thinking, against a northern Asian origin. Moreover, according to Grotius, inhabitants of that part of Asia were known to be non-sailors and therefore were unlikely to have crossed water. For these reasons, he preferred the possibility of a crossing from northern Europe.

The hypothesis that American Indians owe their origins in America to migration across an Arctic land mass was held at least as early as Joseph de Acosta (1590). An extreme theory regarding of the origin of native languages in the Americas is that of Antonio Vázquez de Espinosa (1630), who estimated the number of New World languages to be 50,000 but did not consider this high number to be inconsistent with the theory that the Indians had a common origin; he attributed their origin and the linguistic diversity to sin and the intervention of the Devil (see Huddleston 1967:88). This hypothesis reflected Gregorio García's 1607 theory, which blamed the linguistic diversity of the Americas on the Devil, who helped Indians invent new languages in order to impede christianization efforts (see Huddleston 1967:66).[3]

The Atlantis theory of the origin of Native American languages is also not recent; Francisco López de Gómara (1941[1552], 2:248–9) reasoned that Nahuatl *a*[·]*tl* 'water' reflected Nahuatl speakers' memories of their ancient watery homeland in *Atl*antis. Even some generally reputable scholars held astounding views concerning origin. For example, Hervás y Panduro (1800: 108–9, 396) (see Chapter 2) contended that South America was populated by migrations from Africa across the lost continent of Atlantis and that North America was populated by migrations from Europe across Iceland and Greenland. At the same time, he also pointed to native folk traditions, mostly from Mexico and Central America, of migrations from the north; conse-

quently, he fully accepted that many American *naciones* were of Asian descent and had crossed what might be considered the equivalent of the Bering Strait (called the *estrecho de Anian*) (Hervás y Panduro 1800:393–6). Adriaan Reeland [Relandus/Relander] (1676–1718), in *De linguis Americanis* (volume three of his *Dissertationes Miscellaneae,* 1706–1708), also held that Native Americans had an Asiatic origin, but that they came across a chain of islands from New Guinea to America (see Droixhe 1978:43). James Parsons (1767), who is considered by some to be the real discoverer of the Indo-European language family (though he, too, like Sir William Jones, had many predecessors in this regard; see Poser and Campbell 1992), asserted that North American Indian languages showed clear Japhetic characteristics, and Parsons's Japhetic also included many European languages.

Thomas Jefferson had a keen interest in the origin of American Indian languages, and his views have echoes to this day. He reported:

> [The] great question has arisen from whence came those aboriginals of America? Discoveries, long ago made, were sufficient to shew that a passage from Europe to America was always practicable, even to the imperfect navigation of ancient times. In going from Norway to Iceland, from Iceland to Groenland, from Groenland to Labrador, the first traject is the widest: and this having been practised from the earliest times of which we have any account of that part of the earth, it is not difficult to suppose that the subsequent trajects may have been sometimes passed. Again, the late discoveries of Captain Cook, coasting from Kamschatka to California, have proved that, if the two continents of Asia and America be separated at all, it is only by a narrow streight. So that from this side also, inhabitants may have passed into America: and the resemblance between the Indians of America and the Eastern inhabitants of Asia, would induce us to conjecture, that the former are the descendants of the latter, or the latter of the former: excepting indeed the Eskimaux, who, from the same circumstance of resemblance, and from identity of language, must be derived from the Groenlanders, and these probably from some of the northern parts of the old continent. A knowledge of their several languages would be the most certain evidence of their derivation which could be produced. In fact, it is the best proof of the

affinity of nations which ever can be referred to. (Notes on the State of Virginia, 1784; in Jefferson 1984:226–7)

Hinsley is of the opinion that in statements such as this, and more directly in posing the question, "from whence came those aboriginals of America?", Jefferson had expressed "the central historical question that impelled American anthropology until the Civil War" (1981:21). On the matter of the genetic diversity among American Indian languages, Jefferson wrote:

> I suppose the settlement of our continent is of the most remote antiquity. The similitude between its' [sic] inhabitants & those of Eastern parts of Asia renders it probable that ours are descended from them or they from ours. The latter is my opinion, founded on this single fact. Among the red inhabitants of Asia there are but a few languages radically [i.e., genetically] different, but among our Indians the number of languages is infinite which are so radically different as to exhibit at present no appearance of their having been derived from a common source. The time necessary for the generation of so many languages must be immense. (Letter to Ezra Stiles on September 1, 1786, from Paris, Jefferson 1984:865)

Wilhelm von Humboldt was thoroughly committed to the view that American Indian languages derive from northeast Asia (see, for example, the letter written to Alexander von Rennenkampff in 1812 in St. Petersburg; quoted in Brinton 1890[1885d]:330; see Chapter 2). Pickering was open to the same opinion (see his letter of 1834 to Schmidt in M. Pickering 1887:410).

Duponceau's view was more prudent and skeptical:

> The less enthusiastic scholars, Vater, in Europe, and Barton, in America, the first in favor of searching for, the second of proving the Asiatic origin of the aborigines of the New World (Mr. Jefferson, on the other hand, wanted it to be America which had populated Asia), tried to compare between them the diverse languages of the two continents, and their laborious research produced no fruit at all. How is it possible to find, in effect, numerous affinities among all these languages, while one finds none at all between two neighboring languages, Iroquois and Algonquin, even though they resemble each other almost entirely with respect to structure, which I prove in the following mem-

oir by a comparative vocabulary of these two languages, where, out of 250 words, one scarcely finds one or two which can be ascribed to the same origin. What will it be then if one compares Greenlandic with Peruvian, [and] Huron or Sioux with the language of Chile? As far as I am concerned, this research is child's play and can lead to no useful result for the goal that has been proposed with less extended views. (1838:23)[4]

In a similar vein, Albert Gallatin wrote about Asiatic origins, but further interpreted these within his understanding of biblical chronology (echoing Duponceau's assumption of grammatical unity among American tongues):

> The uniformity of character in the grammatical forms and structure of all the Indian languages of North America, which have been sufficiently investigated, indicates a common origin. The numerous distinct languages, if we attend only to the vocabularies between which every trace of affinity has disappeared, attest the antiquity of the American population. This may be easily accounted for, consistently with the opinion that the first inhabitants came from Asia, and with the Mosaic chronology. The much greater facility of communication, either across Behring's Straits, or from Kamschatka or Japan by the Aleutian Islands, would alone, if sustained by a similarity of the physical type of man, render the opinion of an Asiatic origin, not only probable, but almost certain.
>
> In comparing the vocabularies of twenty distinct American [languages], with those of as many Asiatic languages, accidental coincidences will necessarily occur. The similarity of the structure and grammatical forms of those of America indicates a common origin, and renders it probable that the great diversity of their vocabularies took place in America. Should that have been the case, it can hardly be hoped that any one American [language] will be found to have preserved in its words indisputable affinities with any one Asiatic language. (1836:142, 144)

Brinton (1890b:20–35), on the other hand, argued against the hypothesis that the ancestors of the Native Americans came across the Bering Strait and in favor of the view that the first Americans crossed the North Atlantic to reach the New World. Today it is in vogue in some circles to think in terms of three possible migrations to the Western Hemisphere from northeast

Asia, a view influenced by opinions of Edward Sapir and his followers, which has been asserted more recently by Joseph Greenberg. Earlier, following Duponceau and Brinton, it was common to assume that there was only one migration. The reasoning appears to have been somewhat circular, in part because race, nation, and language were often not distinguished (see Chapter 2). Thus, so this line of thought seems to have gone, if there was a unity of American languages from Greenland to Cape Horn (given the assumed structural unity exemplified by polysynthesis or holophrasis), then there was but one American race—hence the title of Brinton's *The American Race* (1891), in which he classified the languages of the Americas. This racial unity was taken as evidence of linguistic unity and hence of a single migration to the Americas (see Ibarra Grasso 1958:11). This notion of racial and linguistic unity has been maintained (or at least not totally rejected) by most researchers since then, although it is common to exclude Eskimo-Aleut (under the assumption that its speakers are racially different and the result of more recent population movements), and following Sapir also to exclude Athabaskan or Na-Dene, which Sapir thought to be related to Sino-Tibetan (see Chapter 8).[5] The popularity in nonlinguistic circles of this tripartite division notwithstanding, opinions concerning the origins of Native American languages at present differ widely and the topic is surrounded by controversy. These different views reflect different approaches to the classification of American Indian languages, and the different classifications which have been proposed have distinct implications for the origins of the languages. The different approaches and their implications are the subjects of the next two sections. (Methodological differences are discussed in Chapter 7.)

Approaches to Classification of American Indian Languages

It has become almost traditional to speak of two broadly contrasting approaches to the classification of American Indian languages—that of the "lumpers" and that of the "splitters." So-called lumpers seek to reduce the number of language families (or genetic units) in the Americas by proposing more inclusive, more remote relationships among the language groups. So-called splitters ask for explicit evidence for proposals of distant relationship, rejecting those proposals for which the evidence is not found to be compelling. Since no one today is totally opposed to remote relationships in general, I propose abandoning the labels "lumper" and "splitter" and substituting in their stead the "inspectional" approach and the "assessment" approach, respectively. These terms are intended as neutral labels.[6] These two different approaches incorporate different claims and interpretations concerning the origin of New World languages and the peopling of the Americas.

The inspectional approach is represented today principally by Greenberg (1987), who calls his method "multilateral (or mass) comparison"; Golla calls this "the inspectional route to genetic classification" (1988:434); Watkins calls it "etymology by inspection" (1990:293). The terms used by Golla and Watkins reflect the fact that Greenberg's method depends essentially on lexical similarities determined by visual inspection (see Chapter 7). The assessment approach, dubbed "the major alternative" by Greenberg (see Greenberg, Turner, and Zegura 1986:477; see also Lewin 1988:1632), employs standard techniques of historical linguistics to attempt to work out the linguistic history of the languages involved (see Chapter 7). By Greenberg's estimate (in Lewin 1988:1632), 80% to 90% of American Indianists support the assessment approach. (Greenberg considers Campbell and Mithun 1979a a major representative of this approach.)

While this dichotomy of approaches is current, lines of thought akin to those of the two opposing camps have existed since early work in the classification of American Indian languages. For example, the two were characterized by Sapir in a letter to Speck in 1924:

> At last analysis these controversies boil down to a recognition of two states of mind. One, conservative intellectualists, like Boas, . . . who refuse absolutely to consider far-reaching suggestions. . . . Hence, from an overanxious desire to be right, they generally succeed in being more hopelessly and fundamentally wrong, in the long run, than many more superficial minds who are not committed to "principles." . . . The second type

is more intuitive and, even when the evidence is not as full or theoretically unambiguous as it might be, is prepared to throw out [offer] tentative suggestions. . . . I have no hope whatever of ever getting Boas and Goddard to see through my eyes or to feel with my hunches. I take their opposition like the weather, which might generally be better but which will have to do. (Cited in Darnell 1990:114)[7]

Sapir had contrasted the two approaches in a letter to Lee Frachtenberg in 1917: "It is only a question of whether one prefers to be conservative as long as he respectably can, or has a bit more courage than the crowd and is willing to look ahead" (cited in Darnell 1990:117). Sapir's approach was indeed less conservative, but he recognized that detailed work would be required to confirm or deny the tentative suggestions (see Chapter 2).[8] Boas gave a telling description of how the two camps differed at that time:

> There are two lines of research represented in American linguistics; the one strongly *imaginative,* bent upon theoretical reconstruction. This is represented by Sapir. The other more *conservative,* interested in the same problems but trying to reach it [reconstruction] going back step by step; in other words, more conservative. This is represented by myself. Both should be represented. (Emphasis added; letter to Edward Armstrong, 1927, cited in Darnell 1990:279–80)

Kroeber spoke of "the simple frontal attack by inspection" and "the reconstructive method" (1940a:463–4); his dichotomy is not quite the same as the lumper-splitter distinction, though it is clearly related. Merritt Ruhlen (1994b:113) divides the two groups into "diffusionists" (including Michelson, P. E. Goddard, and Boas) and "geneticists" (represented most truly by Sapir). Most specialists in Native American languages do not consider Ruhlen's labels very apt. Harold Fleming (1987:206) speaks of the "safe little ventures" of the splitters; presumably this is his way of negatively characterizing the more conservative assessment approach, which does not favor "imaginative" research on distant genetic relationships if that means "intuition" unrestrained by the realities and constraints of the linguistic evidence itself. Campbell and Mithun (1979a) examined the history of the lumping and splitting traditions in American Indian linguistic studies and opted for neither; rather, they called

for assessment of the evidence and for the use of reliable methods in research on possible distant genetic relationships. Ruhlen (1987a:224), who also reviewed this history, referred to Campbell and Mithun (1979a) as representing the " 'consensus' view . . . that the New World contains dozens, if not hundreds, of independent families." Goddard and Campbell (1994) called the two approaches "word comparison" (the inspectional approach) and "standard historical linguistics" (the assessment approach) (see also Hymes 1959, Lamb 1959.)[9]

There have been many other statements characterizing these two opposite approaches (for example, Lewin 1988, Meltzer 1993b). However, there are important differences, even between Greenberg's approach and that of others who fit within the inspectional camp. As both Golla (1988:435) and Rankin (1992) have independently pointed out, the methods of Greenberg and Sapir are fundamentally different, in spite of their shared interest in large-scale consolidation of linguistic groups in the Americas (see. Chapters 2, 7, and 8). A basic fact on which all agree is that there is extensive linguistic diversity in the Americas.[10] Greenberg claims that the Americas were settled by three separate population movements, equated in his linguistic terms with Amerind, Na-Dene, and Aleut-Eskimo, in that order (Greenberg, Turner, and Zegura 1986:477; see also Greenberg and Ruhlen 1992 and Ruhlen 1994b:5, 212). But those who advocate the assessment approach count approximately 55 genetic units (families and isolates) in North America (see Chapter 4), 10 in Middle America (Chapter 4), and more than 80 in South America (Chapter 6)[11]—a total of approximately 150 distinct genetic units. It is important to keep in mind, however, that supporters of the assessment approach put little stock in these numbers, since it is anticipated (or at least hoped) that continued research will demonstrate additional legitimate connections, thus further reducing the total number of genetic units (a view that is frequently misrepresented by its detractors). Most of these supporters are sympathetic to the notion that many or perhaps all American Indian languages may be related, but assessment scholars believe that this cannot be demonstrated at present because of the great time depth and the inadequacy of linguistic methods to recover history after so much change has taken place (see also Kaufman 1990a:25–6). According to this view, it cannot be demonstrated that two American Indian languages—or any two languages, for that matter—are not related, but the burden of proof falls on those who claim that closer affinity exists among some groups than among others (Bright 1970, Goddard and Campbell 1994).

Implications of Linguistic Classification for Understanding the Original Population of the New World

The theme that language holds the key to the origin and history of American Indians is neither new nor uncommon (Bieder 1986:24–5; see also Barton 1797 and Schoolcraft 1851:114, 184, among others; see also Chapter 2). Sapir gave linguistics a prominent role in the study of the peopling of the Americas. In 1909 he said that the "best piece of evidence of great antiquity of man in America is linguistic diversification rather than archaeological" (Darnell 1990:31, 123). His view strongly influenced subsequent thinking (see, for example, Lewin 1988:1632).[12] However, Sapir's well-known opinion indicates how little we have advanced in our ability to relate linguistic classification to the issue of the original population of the Americas:

> If the apparently large number of linguistic stocks recognized in America be assumed to be due merely to such extreme divergence on the soil of America as to make the proof of an original unity of speech impossible, then we must allow a tremendous lapse of time for the development of such divergences, a lapse of time undoubtedly several times as great as the period that the more conservative archaeologists and palaeontologists are willing to allow as necessary for the interpretation of the earliest remains of man in America. We would then be driven to the alternative of assuming that the linguistic differentiation of aboriginal America developed only in small part (in its latest stages) in the new world, that the Asiatic (possibly also South Sea) immigrants who peopled the American continent were at the earliest period of occupation already differentiated into speakers of several genetically unrelated stocks. This would make it practically imperative to assume that the peopling of America was not a single historical

process but a series of movements of linguistically unrelated peoples, possibly from different directions and certainly at very different times. This view strikes me as intrinsically highly probable. At the latest arrivals in North America would probably have to be considered the Eskimo-Aleut and the Na-dene (Haida, Tlingit, and Athabaskan). (Sapir 1949[1916]:454–5)

As this citation shows, the tripartite classification of American Indian languages (that is, Eskimo-Aleut, Na-Dene, and all others) is not new; it reflects the opinion handed down since Sapir (see also Ruhlen 1987a:222–3, Lamb 1959:36, Goddard and Campbell 1994).[13] This three-group view has also diffused widely into the thinking of many nonlinguists on the matter (Bray 1986, Carlson 1983:96, and Williams et al. 1985 are just a few examples from just before the appearance of Greenberg's book [1987]). Greenberg's three groupings clearly continue the tradition established by Sapir. For example, Swadesh, a student of Sapir's, argued:

> Research seems to show that the great bulk of American languages form a single genetic phylum going far back in time . . . that the entire phylum developed out of a single speech community in America. . . . *Eskimo-Aleutian and Nadenean seem to stand apart, and may therefore represent later waves of migration;* they would then be no more closely related to the remaining American languages than other languages still in the Old World.
>
> Some of the languages may, however, be of more recent arrival and therefore capable of being related to the Old World by means of methodology already developed. These probably include Nadene, which is evidently related to Sinotibetan, and Eskaleutian, which may be related to Indoeuropean or Uraltaic or both. (Emphasis added; Swadesh 1954b:307; see also 1960c:896)

See also Greenberg's Eurasiatic proposal, which includes Eskimo-Aleut as a member (1987:viii, 331–5, 1991) and Lamb's (1959) Macro-American grouping, which includes all of Lamb's American groups except Eskimo-Aleut and Na-Dene (see Haas 1960:989, Pinnow 1964a:25–6, Migliazza and Campbell 1988:16).

Greenberg, of the inspectional camp, is committed to the Sapir tradition with its three independent migrations to the New World. He sees these as separated in time, one for each of his major linguistic groups: Amerind, Aleut-Eskimo, and Na-Dene. Some supporters of the assessment approach also are sympathetic to such a possibility (although they do not attribute its proposal to Greenberg). In contrast to the three-migrations view, the assessment approach is compatible with several possibilities for the peopling of the Americas. That is to say, there is so much that we do not know that a number of scenarios are plausible and few can be conclusively eliminated at present. It should be noted that those who have attempted to determine the number of migrations responsible for the early peopling of the New World do not even provide a consistent definition of what is meant by "migration." For example, Hrdlička's notion of "dribbles" of people entering the Americas might be more realistic (Meltzer 1989:481), but it would leave few or no migrations to be counted. Several questions should be addressed: Were the first "immigrants" to America part of a single or continuous movement, or did they come in multiple, discontinuous, "dribble-like" migrations, or in a few large but distinct crossings to the New World? Were the migrations/ movements gradual or rapid? Were there incentives to come to the New World (were people "pulled") or to leave the Old World (were they "pushed")? Or was sheer happenstance at play? Did different groups (if different groups were involved) influence one another, displace one another, repel or attract one another, in the new environment? Did they move short distances or long distances? (see Dillehay and Meltzer 1991:288–9). In this book I continue to speak of "migration" but intend the term to cover any sort of movement of peoples.

Some of the (not mutually exclusive) possibilities for the origin of New World languages are discussed in the following paragraphs (see Swadesh 1960b:151, Goddard and Campbell 1994).

1. A Single, One-Language Migration

Given the possibility that many or even all American Indian languages may ultimately be genetically related (although at present this cannot be demonstrated), it is possible that speakers of a single language may have entered the New World in a single movement and later diversi-fied, producing the many language groups that are documented in the Americas. This scenario is not favored by most linguists, though it was commonly believed during the nineteenth century that all North American languages were genetically related; opinions to this effect are expressed in the writings of Duponceau, Gallatin, Horatio Hale, Latham, Brinton, and others (see also Bieder 1986; especially Swadesh 1960b:183, 1963b:318; and Lamb 1959:47; nonlinguist supporters of this view in recent years include Laughlin 1986 and Rogers 1986, 1987). Sapir, too, spoke at times in ways suggestive of a common ancestry for all or most of the languages of the Americas (except his Na-Dene); he even presented a number of traits as "certain Proto-American possibilities" (1990a[n.d.]:84, 1990c[n.d.]:86). Sapir specified some of them in a letter to Kroeber (October 1920):

> If I were to commit myself still further, I would suggest that C [Algonkin-Wakashan] is a specialized polysynthetic offshoot of D [Penutian]; and that E [Uto-Aztekan; Tewa-Kiowa] is probably a Mischsprache formed of D [Penutian] and F [Hokan-Siouan]. B [Na-Dene] stands most aloof of all (aside, possibly, from Eskimo, though I feel Eskimo is closer to Algonkin-Wakashan than Na-Dene to any other group. . . . I do not feel that Na-Dene belongs to the other American languages. I feel it as a great intrusive band that has perhaps ruptured an old Eskimo-Wakashan-Algonkin continuity. (1990b[1920]:81–3)

Paul Radin's (1919) attempt to unite all the American languages in a single large family implies a single migration, an opinion that J. P. Harrington apparently shared: "[T]he thesis of Radin [1919] was in deep accord with my own experience, . . . help[ing] toward the oneness in origin of American languages" (from a BAE manuscript, quoted in Darnell 1969:325). It was clear to Kroeber in 1920 that the notion of a single ancestor for the Native American languages was quite common before that time. He wrote to Sapir that he believed it was Hokan that "the older students were unconsciously thinking of when they attempted formulations for the American languages in general" (letter of December 27, 1920, cited in Darnell 1969:350). Sapir in private correspondence seems essentially to take up the view that Kroeber attributed to the "older students." He wrote to Speck:

It is becoming fairly clear that *the* great stock of North America is Hokan-Yuchi-Siouan-Muskogean-Tunican-Coahuiltecan, probably with further affinities southward. Na-dene, Penutian (as extended by me), Algonquian-Yokuts-Wiyot, Wakashan-Salish-Chimakuan stand apparently apart but even now there are some suggestive connections, visible here and there. Getting down to brass tacks, how in Hell are you going to explain general American *n-* "I" except genetically? (Letter of August 1, 1918, quoted in Darnell 1969:352)

Writing to Lowie, he referred directly to the possibility that *all* were related: "I am now flirting with the idea of undertaking the little job of grouping *all* American languages . . . morphologically and genetically. I think it can be done, if one has method" (letter of September 9, 1920, quoted in Darnell 1969:353).[14] Haas (1960:989) also mentioned that developments were propelling opinion in this direction.

2. A Few Linguistically Distinct Migrations

A second possibility, favored by Sapir (1949[1916]:454–5), is the view that there were more than one, but very few, linguistically distinct migrations. An important question (raised already by Sapir) with respect to both this possibility and the previous one is: Could so much linguistic diversity develop in the time that elapsed since the single or the few proposed movements to the Americas? Here it is interesting to note Boas's opinion: "These [American languages] are so different among themselves that it seems doubtful whether the period of 10,000 years is sufficient for their differentiation. The assumption of many waves of immigrants who represented many types and many languages is an arbitrary solution of the dilemma" (1933:362–3). We should keep in mind the date of ca. 12,000 B.P. favored by many scholars, called the "received chronology" by Nichols (1990a; referred to as "the conceptual impasse" by Alsoszatai-Petheo 1986:15), for entry of humans to the New World. I do not take a strong stand on the date of earliest entry, but at present I am inclined to accept some version of the received chronology, or of what may be considered the newly emerging received opinion, of somewhere between 16,000 and 12,000

B.P. (in any case probably not much before 20,000 B.P.). Denis Stanford argues persuasively that "it's time to acknowledge that we do have a pre-Clovis culture in the New World" (Morell 1990:439), but Thomas Lynch argues equally convincingly that "there are no indisputable or completely convincing cases of pre-Clovis archaeological remains in South America" (1990: 27; see also Meltzer 1993a). In any event, linguistics will in all likelihood not contribute in any significant way to the determination of the earliest date; we know next to nothing about how much time is required to produce extensive linguistic diversity, particularly on a virgin continent—Nichols (1990a, 1992, in press) notwithstanding—and we do not even know the number of movements that brought different languages, the seeds of linguistic diversity, to the New World.

The date of first entry, although for other reasons very interesting, is essentially irrelevant to the question of how many linguistically distinct genetic units there are in the Americas. Clear proof of great time depth for human occupation in the New World would be pleasing to those who believe that there were few movements into the Western Hemisphere because it would allow for the development of the extensive linguistic diversity now found. Of course, with no idea of how many different languages were brought to the Americas and with very little knowledge of how long might be required in circumstances such as those encountered by the first Americans to develop the extant linguistic diversity, we can hardly insist on a great time depth, or on any current estimate of time depth for that matter. I agree with Dillehay and Meltzer that "we must realize that the stakes of great antiquity in the Americas are simply not all that high. It makes little difference whether the first Americans were here at 32,000 B.P. as opposed to 12,000 B.P." (1991:293; see also Meltzer 1993b:19). The fact of the matter for now is that the divergence and diversity among the languages is what we have to work with. When more is understood, perhaps with some luck we can draw a finer bead on the question of time depth. However, for now, whether shallower or deeper, the relatively unknown age of human occupation in the New World solves none of the outstanding linguistic issues before us.

3. Multiple Migrations

Another possibility is that several, perhaps many, migrations may have brought different (perhaps unrelated) languages, at different times. In a letter to Radin in 1913, Sapir attributes to Boas a view consistent with this possibility and contrasts this view with one he favors (see possibility 2): "For some mysterious reason he [Boas] simply does not like to think of an originally small number of linguistic stocks, which have each of them differentiated tremendously, but prefers, with Powell, to conceive of an almost unlimited number of distinct stocks, many of which, in the course of time, become extinct. To me the former alternative seems a historical necessity" (cited in Darnell 1990:113). Needless to say, Boas—as described here—is not postulating many migrations, but the "almost unlimited number of distinct stocks" is in accord with such a view, since otherwise there would have to be many migrations or at least many different "stocks" would have to have participated jointly in whatever migrations happened to have taken place. A variant of this view, currently maintained by many, holds open the possibility of fewer migrations, but with so much subsequent linguistic diversification and change that it is now unclear how the many extant families and isolates may be connected with one another, if they are related (see also Swadesh 1960b:151 and Mason 1950:164).

4. Multilingual Migrations

Another possibility is that there may have been a single migration in which more than one language was present, or a small number of such multiple-language migrations. Again, the question that remains is: What evidence is there of such migrations, given no clear evidence of linguistic connections with Old World languages?[15]

5. The Influx of Already Diversified but Related Languages

It is also possible that some linguistic differentiation may have already developed in northeast Asia before the migrations to the New World and some unknown number of already distinct but related languages (or groups) may have been brought to the Americas, either together or at different times. Such a scenario would extend the time depth for divergence among American languages beyond the date of the first human settlement of the New World. It is interesting that Sapir, in spite of other views he expressed, appears also to have held a view similar to one:

> I no longer believe nor, for that matter, have I ever definitely held that the differentiation of languages in America has taken place entirely on the American continent. On the contrary, I think that the most far-reaching differences of grouping had already taken place on the Asiatic continent, and I believe it goes almost without saying that America was peopled by a number of historically different waves. (From a 1921 letter to Lowie, cited in Darnell 1990:128; see also Goddard 1926, Mason 1950:164, Turner 1983:150–151, Weiss and Woolford 1986:493)

Two questions to keep in mind here are: How many migrations were there? What is the evidence for them? With respect to possibilities (3), (4), and (5), it should be noted that most specialists find no credible evidence of connections between New World and Old World languages.[16]

6. Extinction of Old World Linguistic Relatives

Still another variation on the theme is the possibility that one or more migrations arrived in the New World, but subsequently their Old World linguistic relatives became extinct. On this theory, Robert Austerlitz reported that "they [the languages] came in ready-made proto-families. In doing so, they depleted the Old World of a number of already existing proto-families which were transported in toto into the New World. . . . These proto-families left no stragglers in the Old World or left stragglers there who eventually perished there" (1980:2).

Nichols (in press) points out that available evidence "suggests that it is more typical for movements into new territory to produce distributions . . . where part of the group moves and part stays behind. Colonizations, in short, are probably more often spreads than emigrations."

According to this view, it is unlikely that migrations to the New World depleted the Old World of whole linguistically distinct genetic groups, although it is possible that the language(s) of relatives left behind ultimately became extinct, especially if they were spoken by small populations in the hostile environment of northeastern Asia (see also Jacobsen 1989:15).

Such "depletion" of Old World language families, some might think, explains the interesting and generally accepted fact that there is far more linguistic diversity in the Americas than in the Old World, in spite of the relatively recent peopling of the New World. Austerlitz (1980:2) counted a total of only 37 genetic units for all of continental Eurasia (19 well-established families and 18 isolates), compared with the approximately 150 genetic units in the Americas.

7. Other Bering Strait Options

There are several additional possibilities consistent with the Bering Strait theory. Meltzer mentions some of these:

> Coming to North America was not an event that was physically impossible except along circumscribed routes within narrow time windows. There was not one, but many possible routes open at many different times. . . . Even if we did know the precise timing of the Land Bridge . . . or the timing of the ice-free corridor, which we do not . . . , that would all be irrelevant if the earliest migrants had boats and traveled down the Pacific coast. (1989:474; see also Fladmark 1979, 1986)

8. Less Plausible Possibilities

There are, of course, also a number of less plausible, non-Bering conjectures for the arrival of people in the Americas. Some hypotheses include immigrants from Africa, Japan, China, India, Polynesia, and Australia, along with the lost tribes of Israel, Egyptians, Phoenicians, Greeks, Romans, Welsh, Irish, Vikings, and other Scandinavians. (Some specific hypotheses are mentioned in Chapter 8.)[17] I do not support any of these notions, but it should be remembered that there is really little difficulty in crossing the oceans—coconuts have done it and established a reproducing coconut population; adventurers in rowboats have done it. The only

trick seems to be to stay alive and afloat long enough to be carried by the ocean currents to the other side (see Riley et al. 1971). While such notions regarding movements to the New World are not incompatible with the classification system of the assessment approach (though most supporters of that approach are partial to a Bering Strait hypothesis of some form and hold other theories to be for the most part implausible, though not impossible), it would be necessary to demonstrate that such migrations had actually left an impact on the linguistic picture of the Americas. All evidence presented to date reveals no such impact.

9. Extremists' Claims

For the sake of completeness, some popular conjectures by the radical fringe should be mentioned but discounted, such as entry by peoples from Atlantis or Moo, or extraterrestrials. I particularly like Whitney's dismissal of these radical notions:

> The absurd theories which have been advanced and gravely defended by men of learning and acuteness respecting the origin of the Indian races are hardly worth even a passing reference. The culture of the more advanced communities has been irrefragably proved to be derived from Egypt, Phoenicia, India, and nearly every other anciently civilized country of the Old World: the whole history of migration of the tribes themselves has been traced in detail over Behring's Straits, through the islands of the Pacific, and across the Atlantic; they have been identified with the Canaanites, whom Joshua and the Israelites exterminated; and, worst of all, with the ten Israelitish tribes deported from their own country by the sovereigns of Mesopotamia! *When men sit down with minds crammed with scattering items of historical information, abounding in prejudices, and teeming fancies, to the solution of questions respecting whose conditions they know nothing, there is no folly which they are not prepared to commit.* (Emphasis added; 1901[1867]:352)

Alas, not even these extremist views are incompatible with what we currently know, based on the classification of American Indian languages. There are simply many linguistically distinct genetic units in the Americas, and the circumstances under which they came to exist and to reach their current locations are for the most part unknown.

Linguistics and American Prehistory

While the assessment approach is compatible with all these scenarios for the peopling of the Americas, its supporters expect future developments to narrow the range of possibilities. It is hoped that careful historical linguistic research will find more American Indian groups to be linked genetically to one another (especially in South America), while archaeological, human-biological, and other evidence may restrict the range further. Nevertheless, we must be prepared to accept the possibility that we may never know the full answer because of the amount of linguistic change that has taken place since the first movements to the Americas and the limitations of our methods (see also Goddard and Campbell 1994).[18]

Questionable Claims

Despite the present imperfect state of knowledge concerning American Indian linguistic classification and the early prehistory of humans in the Americas, some of the specific claims that have been made for linguistic and human-biological correlations relevant to the question of origins can be shown to be misleading (see Meltzer 1993b:97–103 for a general discussion).

For example, it has been suggested that the tripartite classification of Native American languages has external, nonlinguistic support. Greenberg asserts that his "linguistic classification shows an almost exact match with genetic classification by population biologists and with fossil teeth evidence" (1989:113). Greenberg, Turner, and Zegura have claimed that "the three lines of evidence [linguistic, dental, genetic] agree that the Americas were settled by three separate population movements" and that "the following historical inferences may be derived from [Greenberg's] classification: There were three migrations. . . . The oldest is probably Amerind . . . and shows greater internal differentiation. . . . Aleut-Eskimo is probably the most recent" (1986:477, 479; see also Ruhlen 1987a:221, 1994a; Greenberg and Ruhlen 1992).

But these claims are highly controversial and lack clear support. This is not entirely unexpected, since there is no deterministic connection between languages and gene pools. People can learn a new language, but they cannot learn new genes or teeth. Languages can become extinct in populations that survive genetically (language replacement and extinction have been frequent in the Americas; see Chapter 1). We simply cannot expect, let alone assume, a priori, that linguistic history correlates well with human biological history: "Languages, unlike genes, are not constrained to a reproductive cycle or preprogrammed for replication" (Blount 1990: 15; see Boas 1911:6–10 and Spuhler 1979, for proofs). Moreover, "expansion and extinction of languages are not the same as expansion and extinction of people. Clearly, prehistorians must be very careful about using geographic distributions of linguistic families as evidence for past movements of people" (Lamb 1964b:461). Attempts to correlate language classifications with human genetic information face grave difficulties. A single language can be spoken by a genetically diverse population (for example, whites, blacks, Native Americans, and Asians speak American English); a genetically homogeneous group may speak more than one language (many multilingual Indian communities speak English or Spanish and the native language, or speak more than one Native American language; see Sorensen 1967 for an interesting case of extensive multilingualism). That is, both multilingualism and language shift or loss are facts of linguistic life—genes neither cause these phenomena nor cater to them (see Goddard and Campbell 1994).

This being the case, it is not surprising that claims of linguistic-genetic correlations in support of the three-way classification of Native American languages have been heavily criticized by non-linguists. It will be instructive to consider some of these criticisms.

Teeth

Christy Turner has investigated teeth of people from around the world, checking for about two dozen secondary dental attributes. The Asian sample divides into two groups, Sundadont (older, strongly represented in Southeast Asia) and Sinodont (characteristic of northern Asia and all Native American populations). American Sinodonts differ somewhat from their Asian relatives, and Turner classified them into three groups: Eskimo-Aleut, Greater Northwest Coast (including Athabaskans of the Southwest), and all other Indians. Later, when Turner became aware of Greenberg's (1987) tripartite classification of Native American languages, he associated his three dental groupings with Greenberg's three linguistic groups, changing the names of the latter two to Na-Dene and Amerind, respectively (see Meltzer 1993b:89–90). There are many problems with these dental-linguistic correlations, however. The Na-Dene [formerly Turner's Greater Northwest Coast] dental cluster does not match Greenberg's "Na-Dene" linguistic group well. The Northwest Coast area has both few Na-Dene languages and many non-Na-Dene languages. Szathmary pointed out that "Turner's Greater Northwest Coast includes Kachemak, Kodiak and Alaska Peninsula samples that are likely Eskimoan. . . . Turner's 'Na-Dene' in fact includes representatives of what Greenberg calls 'Amerind' and 'Aleut-Eskimo'. . . . I [Szathmary] found that the Nootka . . . , Haida, Tlingit, and Northern Athapaskan, and South Alaskan Eskimos . . . did not cluster together" (1986:490). The Northwest Coast is notorious for intermarriage, slaving, linguistic and cultural diffusion, and multilingualism. For example, in 1839 Duff found that 10% of the population of the lower Fraser region were slaves, and figures from 1845 indicate that slaves then constituted 6% of the population of the whole Northwest Coast region (Amoss 1993:10–11). When the numbers of refugees from other villages and intermarriages (where in this region polygyny was correlated with wealth) are added to this, it becomes quite evident that the amount of genetic flow across linguistic and ethnic borders was not insignificant in the Northwest Coast culture area. Therefore, the Northwest Coast is precisely an area where we would not expect the extant linguistic diversity and human genetic traits to be correlated as a clear reflection of earlier history (particularly given the fact that a large number of different languages from several different language families are found in this area). Given this situation, it is no great surprise that Turner's Na-Dene dental cluster (né Greater

Northwest Coast group) turns out to be represented by members of all three of Greenberg's major linguistic groups, and that it does not correlate well with any one of them. Turner's Eskimo-Aleut and Amerind dental groups are least like each other (that is, fairly well defined); however, his Greater Northwest Coast (Na-Dene) group is "awkwardly perched between these well-defined extremes ["Amerind" and "Eskimo-Aleut"] . . . its dental traits betwixt the other two" (Meltzer 1993a:163; cf. Meltzer 1993b:90). While there is no doubt that, linguistically, Eskimo and Aleut belong together in the Eskimo-Aleut family, Aleut teeth match those of the Na-Dene group much more closely than they do those of the Eskimo groups, and "Na-Dene teeth from the Gulf of Alaska are closer dentally to Eskimo-Aleuts than they are to Athabaskans," who are the principal members of the presumed Na-Dene linguistic classification (Meltzer 1993b:100). These clear problems show that the proposed linguistic-dental correlations are not as strong as purported to be.

Since Turner's Greater Northwest Coast (also known as Na-Dene) dental cluster is not nearly so clearly defined nor so distinct from the other two as asserted, this may suggest the genetic and cultural diffusion and mixture for which the Northwest Coast is so well known (Meltzer 1993a:164). Turner's paleoindian teeth reveal greater similarity to Eskimo-Aleut, Na-Dene, and Amerind teeth when all are grouped together than they do to Amerind by itself, in spite of Turner's assumption that paleoindian teeth represent only Amerind (Meltzer 1993b:100). Laughlin interprets the lack of clearly defined groupings in the dental record as follows: "The dental evidence is displayed in a dendrogram that carries no hint of a triple division but rather is eloquent evidence of a single migration. Clearly dental evidence comprehends greater time depth than linguistic evidence. . . . Turner proves the Asiatic affinities of [all] Indians" (1986:490).

A final and telling problem with Turner's assumed correlations between tooth groups and Greenberg's linguistic classification is that the two were not established entirely independently and then later correlated: "Although he [Turner] originally sorted samples just by dental traits, in subsequent analyses Turner pooled additional tooth samples into 'regional sets' by dental similarity and 'known or presumed linguistic affiliation' (Meltzer 1993a:164, quoting Turner 1985). It is circular, then, to claim that tooth groups, determined in part by presumed linguistic categories, constitute support for the validity of those proposed linguistic groupings, since the correlation was built into the research design and was not established independently. "Such discrepancies led Szathmary to accuse Turner of merely interpreting his results in light of a pre-existing hypothesis he assumed to be true" (Meltzer 1993a:164).

Even though Greenberg and Turner agree, they also differ significantly. Both believed in three migrations from the Old World, but where Greenberg sees the sequence as first Amerind, followed by Na-Dene, with Eskimo-Aleut last, Turner sees in his dental evidence a different order, with Amerind first, Eskimo-Aleut second, and Na-Dene last (Meltzer 1993b:90).

Thus, the genetic-linguistic claims based on the dental evidence are far from conclusive on the basis of Turner's own data and interpretations.[19] Moreover, there is a serious methodological obstacle to this sort of research. If, as usually assumed, the various migrations to America proceeded in and through Alaska several thousand years ago, then the very coming and going of groups in this area during such a long period so long ago makes it difficult, perhaps impossible, to determine from the dental record found there the identity of the people who left their teeth behind, and for which present-day surviving groups—wherever they may now be located—they may be the ancestors (cf. Meltzer 1993b: 100). I agree with Meltzer's conclusion: "So goes the dental evidence, neither a direct record of migration nor tightly linked to identifiable groups, nor (so far at least) producing internally homogeneous groups" (1993b:101).

Other Genetic Arguments

Several other conflicting claims have been made concerning possible correlations of human biological studies with linguistic classifications, but the interpretation of this evidence is even less clear than that of the dental evidence. For example, Greenberg, Turner, and Zegura have claimed

support for a tripartite linguistic classification also based on DNA research. However, even they regard their human genetic data as "still without strong confirmation" and therefore "supplementary" (1986:487). Others have pointed to problems with this claim such as the following:

> Genetic evidence from modern North American populations is somewhat equivocal. . . . The picture that emerges from comparing various gene distributions across those populations is one of 'discordant variation' [Zegura 1987:11]—even within major groupings such as 'Amerind'. Genetic studies thus far cannot confirm conclusively how many major groupings there are of modern native North Americans, much less the presumed number of migrations. (Meltzer 1989:481; see also Zegura 1987:11)

> Interestingly, a chi-square test reveals no significant difference between right and wrong assignments [allocation of gene frequencies into language phyla] for these three groups [Greenberg's big three]. . . . The [genetic] differences between American populations are not large enough to postulate more than one migration. (Laughlin 1986:490)

> Isolation by distance among groups with a long history of habitation in a single local area can produce generally the same kind of [genetic] diversity as is observed, especially if a certain amount of population movement and expansion or contraction over long time periods occurs. Thus, even if there is a *general* three-way division of arctic peoples, this proves neither that they have a three-part phylogenetic relationship nor that any such relationship as exists is due to separate waves of immigration. (Weiss and Woolford 1986:492)

The mitochondrial DNA studies, which have received so much attention in the popular press, although ultimately probably far more valuable than linguistic evidence for tracing the origins of Native American populations, have been strongly contested and variously interpreted. For example, Douglas Wallace interpreted the results of his research on the Pima as reflecting only a few mitochondrial DNA lineages in Pima ancestry. In later examination of Yucatec Maya and Ticuna mitochondrial DNA, Wallace and his team found that three groups (these two, plus one from the Pima study) "showed high frequencies (but not the same high frequencies) of identical genetic variants, again bespeaking common ancestry" (Meltzer 1993b:93). Since these three groups fall within Greenberg's Amerind linguistic classification, Wallace's team assumed that their mitochondrial DNA represented Amerind and then compared these results with those of so-called Na-Dene populations to get at the issue of the number of original migrations to the New World. The results were not conclusive: "Their results confirm the genetic integrity of the Na-Dene, although they leave their affinity to Eskimo-Aleut unresolved" (Meltzer 1993b: 94). They also raised the possibility of other, separate migrations to the New World. Still, Wallace aligned himself with the tripartite linguistic classification, inconclusive though his results were.

Others, however, find evidence of much greater human genetic diversity in the Americas, suggestive of many more migrations or of a genetically much more diverse original population. Rebecca Cann argued that the mitochondrial DNA evidence indicates that American Indians descended from at least eleven lineages, perhaps thirty-three; this indicates that there were either several migrating groups or large migrating groups with many genetically unrelated females (Morell 1990:440). Ward and Pääbo, in their study of mitrochondrial DNA of the Nootka (Wakashan, of Vancouver Island), found, in spite of the small size of the population, at least twenty-eight separate lineages in four fairly well-defined clusters (Meltzer 1993b:101). They interpret this to mean that the substantial genetic diversity among the Nootka did not develop in the New World but in Asia before their arrival here, that the first Americans were genetically heterogeneous upon arrival, and therefore that the claim of three migrations to the New World is in question. William Hauswirth, who investigated the mitochondrial DNA of well-preserved 8,000-year-old individuals in Windover, Florida, also found considerable genetic variation (Meltzer 1993b:101, 102). In a study of the haplotype frequencies (in the immunoglobulin Gm system) Szathmary also found the three-migration model untenable; the Eskimo groups did "not form a distinct unit"; four sample Eskimo groups were "interspersed in a cluster that includes the Ojibwa and all Athapaskans except the Mescalero Apache." The other Es-

kimo groups were "scattered throughout the dendrogram"; the unit that included Pima, Papago, Zuni, Walapai, and Hopi (in the southwestern United States), and Cree (Canada) was the only cluster "that includes no Eskimos or Athapaskans" (1994:121). Thus, none of these clusters reflected an Eskimo-Aleut, Na-Dene, or Amerind grouping as would be expected according to the tripartite hypothesis.

In short, the dental and human genetic groupings that have been proposed are in dispute and are inconclusive. Even if we were generously to grant the possibility that some of these human genetic groupings might ultimately pan out, the correlations claimed between these groups and linguistic groups have been called into question. Therefore, at least for now, postulated migrations to the New World based on such linguistic-biological correlations are unwarranted.[20] Some of these claimed biological-linguistic correlations have proven inaccurate, and in any case a close correspondence is not to be expected, since human populations easily can and frequently do lose their language, shift to the language of others, or become multilingual; moreover, human genetic features easily flow across language borders by means of the cultural mechanisms of intermarriage, slavery, and various types of contact. A close genetic-linguistic correlation is probably more the exception than the rule in some culture areas of Native America (see Chapter 9).

For the sake of perspective, perhaps it should be kept in mind that almost from the beginning of linguistic and anthropological research on Native Americans, it has been assumed that there is great linguistic diversity but basic homogeneity in human biology in the Americas—recall Hrdlička's famous opinion that the American race was essentially a single unit. The trait lists of American Indian "racial" features (for example, shovel-shaped incisors, Mongoloid spot, predominantly type O blood) may have been superseded by a more sophisticated understanding of gene pools and genetic variation within and among populations, but the basic picture has not really changed: there continues to be a seeming mismatch between the linguistic diversity and the genetic commonality in the Americas (see Kroeber 1940a:461). Whatever ultimately turns out to be the best understanding of

genetic groupings of Native American populations (be it 1, 3, 4, 28, or 33 genetic lineages or
founder groups), the fact remains that at present
we are unable to reduce linguistic diversity to
less than approximately 150 separate genetic
units (families and isolates). These 150 or so
linguistic groups neither constitute legitimate
support for nor conflict with any of the various
biological groupings.

Archaeology could conceivably provide evidence concerning the number of original migrations and perhaps who the migrants' descendants
are—and archaeology certainly has played a
very visible role in the drama. However, the
current picture from archaeology is one of many
competing though inconclusive interpretations,
hypotheses, and claims, but nothing sufficiently
concrete for encouraging any linguistic correlations. (For a detailed discussion of the problems
involved, see Meltzer 1993b.)

More to the point, potential correlations with
nonlinguistic evidence (dental, human genetic,
and archaeological) are ultimately irrelevant to
issues of remote linguistic affinities, as required
by Meillet's principle, which Greenberg advocates (discussed in Chapter 7), which states that
nonlinguistic evidence is irrelevant and in fact
often misleading for determining whether languages are related. As indicated by Newman,
there is an irony in Greenberg's appeal to nonlinguistic evidence in support of his American
Indian linguistic classification, since Greenberg
(1957, 1963) demonstrated that external nonlinguistic evidence is irrelevant to linguistic classifications (see Newman 1991:454, 459).[21]

The Coastal Entry Theory

An early notion that still has some adherents is
the coastal entry hypothesis, which seeks to
explain the apparent anomaly in the distribution
of languages in North America—that eastern
North America is dominated by a small number
of language families, whereas there is extensive
linguistic diversity on the West Coast. Already
in 1797, Benjamin Smith Barton had articulated
this theory: "When the Europeans took possession of the countries of North-America, they
found the western parts of the continent much
more thickly settled than the eastern . . . [lead-

ing to the conclusion that] all the earlier visitors
of America . . . are of Asiatic origin" (1797:xcv,
quoted in Andresen 1990:62). Thus, as Sapir
(1990[1929a]:95) pointed out, of Powell's
(1891b) famous fifty-eight families for North
America north of Mexico, thirty-seven were in
territory whose waterways drained into the Pacific and twenty-two were located along the
Pacific coastline; only seven were located along
the Atlantic coastline (see also Chamberlain
1903:3). Jacobsen reports twenty-two in California, thirty-two along the Pacific strip, and forty-
one west of the Rockies (1989:2; see also Bright
1974a:208). As Sapir and Swadesh report, "We
may say, quite literally and safely, that in the
state of California alone there are greater and
more numerous linguistic extremes than can be
illustrated in all the length and breadth of Europe" (1946:103). Seven of the eleven language
families represented in Canada are found in
British Columbia, and the majority of Canada's
individual languages are also located here (Foster 1982:8). It is assumed that these immigrants
arrived first in the West and thus they had more
time to develop linguistic diversity as they
moved down the West Coast, while the East—
with much less linguistic diversity—was populated in much later movements, which did not
leave them enough time to develop as much
linguistic diversity as that found in the West.
(For modern versions of this theory, see Gruhn
1988, Jacobsen 1989, Rogers, Martin, and
Nicklas 1990; cf. also Fladmark 1979, 1986,
Rogers 1985.)

There are serious problems with this notion,
however (Goddard and Campbell 1994, Meltzer
1989). For example, the time depth for the language families of eastern North America is extremely shallow, not more than 5,000 years at
most (which is a generous estimate for Iroquoian; glottochronological estimates [admit-
tedly not to be trusted] for Algonquian give
ca. 3,000 B.P. and for Iroquoian ca. 4,000 B.P.
(Lounsbury 1978:334). Consequently, the distribution of these families can have little or nothing
to do with events connected with the earliest
entrance of the humans to the New World (at
least as long ago as ca. 12,000 B.P. according to
the received chronology); paleoindian occupation is documented in the lower Great Lakes

region from ca. 11,000 B.P. (L. Jackson 1990). Between 12,000 B.P. and 3,000 B.C., many languages could have been replaced or become extinct in this region. The correlation of even the attested language families of this region, which are recent and relatively accessible, with archaeological data has been notoriously difficult (see Foster 1990, Goddard and Campbell 1994). Meltzer considered additional problems:

> There are more native American languages along the Pacific Northwest and California coasts than in any other area of North America, which is said to imply "great time depth for human occupation" and thereby the corridor of entry (Gruhn 1988:84). The number of languages in any given region of North America, however, is hardly a function of time alone. There are a greater number of languages known from the Pacific Northwest and California primarily because it is one of the areas on the continent where indigenous populations weathered the deadly effects of European contact and disease and survived (though in an altered form) at least until the end of the nineteenth century when intensive linguistic fieldwork began in North America. . . . It is probably no more realistic to infer Pleistocene migration routes to North America by the number and distribution of modern language groups than it would be to infer Hernando de Soto's route by looking at the number and distribution of Spanish dialects in the Southeast today—and at least we know that de Soto spoke Spanish. (1989:475)

Without addressing this issue directly, Nichols also presents arguments against the view that the greater linguistic diversity of the West Coast reflects greater time depth. She argues that greater linguistic diversity is to be expected in general in coastal areas, since "the ocean offers year-round rich sources of protein" and therefore "seacoasts offer the possibility of economic self-sufficiency for a small group occupying a small territory (in press; see also Swadesh 1960b:146–7).

These considerations also call into question the theory of Rogers, Martin, and Nicklas (1990), which relates coastal entry to glaciation. There are several problems with their correlation of language distribution with Wisconsinan biogeographic zones. First, their geographic-linguistic correlations are based on undemonstrated proposals of distant family relationships for several language groups. Second, the linguistic differentiation of the language families is far more recent than the effects of the geographical and geological factors thought to determine it. A third problem (pointed out by Nichols in press) is that the areas with more linguistic diversification have been influenced more by the constant protein supply of oceans than by the presence or absence of glaciers. Fourth, contrary to the claims of Rogers, Martin, and Nicklas, biogeographic zones do not constitute strong linguistic barriers. Whether or not it is easier for languages to spread within a biogeographic zone than across zone boundaries, it is clear that American Indian language groups have frequently spread across different biogeographic zones with ease; for example: (1) Athabaskan in Alaska, Canada, Washington, Oregon, California, the Southwest, and northern Mexico; (2) Uto-Aztecan from Oregon to Panama; (3) Siouan from the Gulf Coast to the Canadian plains, and from the Carolinas to the Rocky Mountains; and (4) Algic from the California coast to the Atlantic, and from Labrador to Virginia, the Carolinas, and Georgia (today represented even in northern Mexico).

Summary

There is great linguistic diversity in the Americas. While some scholars disagree on how Native American languages should be classified, most believe that there are approximately 150 different language families in the Western Hemisphere which cannot at present be shown to be related to each other. In spite of this diversity, it is a common hope that future research will be able to demonstrate additional genetic relationships among some (perhaps even all) of these families, reducing the ultimate number of genetic units that must be recognized. However, the linguistic diversity which currently must be acknowledged means that on the basis of language classification, we are unable to eliminate any of the various proposals concerning the origin of humans in the New World or accounts of the arrival of the first humans in the Americas;

the linguistic picture can thus be rendered consistent with a large number of possible scenarios. Significantly, however, careful scrutiny of the various claims which attempt to correlate linguistic classifications with human biological and archaeological data relevant to early population movements to the Americas reveals that these claims are inconclusive and flawed. The possibility that linguistic classification will contribute much to an understanding of the early entry of humans to the New World is slight, barring unforeseen breakthroughs.

4

Languages of North America

The greatest diversity of opinion prevails with regard to the languages of America. Some scholars see nothing but diversity, others discover everywhere traces of uniformity.

Max Müller (1866–1899[1861]:451); quoted by Haas (1969d:99)

THE STUDY OF THE NATIVE LANguages of North America (north of Mexico) has dominated American Indian linguistics. As a consequence of its long and respectable history (see Chapter 2), the history of the individual families and isolates is reasonably well understood in most cases. Still, most of the proposals of more inclusive, higher-order groupings remain uncertain or controversial. Traditionally, treatments of North American Indian languages have stopped at the border between the United States and Mexico, almost as though some sharp linguistic boundary existed there. However, this geographical limit is not significant from a linguistic point of view, since several language families are represented on both sides of the border; some extend into Mexico and even into Central America. In this chapter, the history and classification of the languages of North America are surveyed; no heed is taken of the national boundary—families which extend into Mexico from the north are discussed here. Only well-established and generally uncontested families are treated, with the focus on their linguistic history as currently understood. Uncertain proposals of distant genetic relationships are discussed in Chapter 8.

With each of the languages presented in this chapter a general indication of the number of speakers is given: "extinct" languages are preceded by the symbol †; languages known to have fewer than 10 speakers are specified as "moribund"; languages with more than 10 but fewer than 100 speakers are labeled "obsolescent." Languages known to have more than 100 speakers have no special indication in the text; many of the languages in the last category are viable, but many others are endangered.[1] This convention for indicating relative numbers of speakers is also used for the languages of Middle America and South America, which are the subjects of Chapters 5 and 6. The geographical location where the language is (or was) spoken is also included. The order of presentation is roughly from north to south and from west to east; an attempt has been made (when not inconvenient because of geographical considerations or competing proposals) to place next to one another those genetic units which are sometimes hypothesized to be distantly related.

(1) **Eskimo-Aleut**
(MAP 1)

See the classification list. To provide some perspective, it should be pointed out that Eskimoan extends from northeast Asia across North America and into Greenland—that is, it is represented in both hemispheres and extends beyond North America on both sides. Moreover, Eskimo (Greenlandic) was the first Native American language to have contact with a European tongue, visited already in the tenth century by Norsemen. Eskimoan groups also had contact during the early European explorations and colonization of America—for example, with Martin Forbisher's voyage of exploration (1576). In this family of languages we find instances of Danish, Russian, French, and English loans.

Knut Bergsland discussed Eskimo-Aleut sound correspondences in detail and presented many cognates, though he did not explicitly reconstruct the Proto-Eskimo-Aleut sound system. The phonemic inventory of Proto-Eskimo consists of: /p, t, č, k, k^w, q, q^w, s, x, x^w, X, X^w, v, γ, γ^w, γ̣, γ̣^{w}, m, n, ŋ, ŋ^w, ř, y; i, i:, ə, a, a:, u, u:/ (1986; see also Krauss 1979, Woodbury 1984).

The relationship between Eskimo and Aleut was discovered by Rasmus Rask in 1819 (Thalbitzer 1922), was known to Latham (1850) and Buschmann (1856, 1858, 1859), and has subsequently been thoroughly confirmed (Bergsland 1951, 1958, Marsh and Swadesh 1951; see also Fortescue 1994). Although it is a somewhat remote connection—Anthony Woodbury refers to the "enormous gap between Eskimo and Aleut" (1984:62)—it was accepted by Powell (1891b).

Aleut has just two main dialects, Eastern Aleut and Western Aleut (which has two subdialects, Atkan and Attuan; a third, which is practically unknown, may have been spoken by those who occupied the Rat Islands before the twentieth century) (Woodbury 1984:49). Among the more important phonological innovations involving these Aleut dialects are the merger of Proto-Aleut *δ and *y to y in Attuan, the change in Atkan of *w and *W to m and M, respectively (shared independently by Sirenikski Yupik), and the Attuan shift of nasals to corresponding voiced fricatives before oral consonants in both dialects (except *n* before velar or uvular fricatives) (for example, Atkan *qaŋlaaX,* Attuan *qaɣlaaX* 'raven'; this change is also found independently in all of Inuit-Inupiaq (Eskimo) (Woodbury 1984:50).

The Inuit-Inupiaq branch of Eskimo is a continuum of several closely related dialects, extending north from Alaska's Norton Sound, across the Seward Peninsula, and east across Arctic Alaska and Canada to the coasts of Que-

---

Eskimo-Aleut

Aleut *Aleutian Islands*
    Western (Atkan [obsolescent]; Attuan [obsolescent])
    Eastern
Eskimo[2]
    Yupik (Yup'ik)[3]
        Naukanski [obsolescent]
        Sirenikski [moribund] *Sireniki Village, Siberia*
        Central Siberian Yupik (Chaplinski) *Chukchi Peninsula, St. Lawrence Island*
        Alaskan Yupik
            Pacific Yupik (*šuk/suk,* Sugpiaq, Sugcestun, Alutiiq)   (Dialects: Chugach, Koniag)
            Central Alaskan Yupik *southwestern Alaska* (Dialects: Yukon-Kuskokwim, Hooper Bay-
                Chevak, Nunivak [Čux], Norton Sound [Unaliq], General Central Yupik, Aglurmiut)
    Inuit-Inupiaq[4] *Alaska, Canada, Greenland*

Krauss 1979, Woodbury 1984.

bec, Labrador, and Greenland. Isoglosses define four dialect regions, Alaska, Western Canada, Eastern Canada, and Greenland—though there are also isoglosses which cut across these areas.

The Yupik branch comprises five languages, aboriginally located on the coast of the Chukchi Peninsula and from Norton Sound south to the Alaska Peninsula and east to Prince William Sound (Woodbury 1984:49). They constitute a chain in which neighboring languages (though they differ considerably among themselves) share common innovations, some of which are old. What has been referred to as Siberian Yupik (also called Asiatic Eskimo or Yuit; including Serinikski, Naukanski, and Central Siberian Yupik [or Chaplinski]) is not a formal subgroup within Yupik; when Central Siberian Yupik was the only known variety, it appeared that Yupik had originally split into an Alaskan branch and a Siberian branch. However, now that Naukanski and Sirenikski are better known, it is difficult to find common innovations that unite Asiatic Eskimo and distinguish it from the Alaskan branch; that is, Siberian Eskimo is apparently not a valid subgroup of the Yupik languages, and hence Yupik is listed with five independent languages which share no lower-level branching among themselves (Woodbury 1984:55). Woodbury reports that Yupik was probably spoken "around the whole Chukchi Peninsula" as late as the seventeenth century but lost ground to advancing Chukchi and is now spoken only in fragmented areas there (1984:51). Sirenikski was spoken only in Sireniki village and nearby Imtuk at the beginning of the twentieth century (it is now quite moribund), and Naukanski was spoken around East Cape until 1958 when its speakers were relocated a short distance down the coast.

A better case (though one that is still inconclusive) can be made for grouping Central Alaskan Yupik and Pacific Yupik into an Alaskan subgroup (Woodbury 1984:55–6). Central Alaskan Yupik has four principal dialects; a fifth was attested in the nineteenth century. These are Norton Sound (or Unaliq, the only dialect to share a border with Inuit-Inupiaq in historical times); Hooper Bay-Chevak (north of Nelson Island); Nunivak Central Yupik (spoken on Nunivak Island, it is the most divergent dialect, sometimes called *Čux*, its cognate with *yuk* 'per-

son' in most other varieties of Yupik); General Central Yupik (the most widespread), and the Aglurmiut, which was attested in the 1820s, in the region that includes the coast of Bristol Bay and the Alaska Peninsula (it had been forced there earlier from the area around Kuskokwim and Nelson Island). Pacific Yupik (also called *šuk/suk*, Sugpiaq, Sugcestun, and Alutiiq) is distinct from Central Alaskan Yupik. There are two varieties of the Koniag dialect:, Kodiak (on the islands of Kodiak and Afognak) and the Alaskan Peninsula subdialect (bordering on Aleut).

The split up between Eskimo and Aleut is estimated to have occurred about 4,000 years ago. The original homeland (Urheimat) of Proto-Eskimo-Aleut appears to have been in western coastal Alaska, perhaps in the Bristol Bay–Cook Inlet area; Greenlandic Eskimo is a relatively recent expansion (Krauss 1980:7, Woodbury 1984:62).

Claims that Eskimo-Aleut may be related to Uralic (or to the now mostly abandoned Ural-Altaic) or to Indo-European have not been demonstrated and the evidence presented thus far is dubious (Krauss 1973a, 1979; see Chapter 8). The proposal of a genetic relationship between Eskimo-Aleut and "Chukotan" (Chukchi-Koryak-Kamchadal) in northeast Asia is seen as promising by a few scholars with knowledge of the languages of the area, but little direct research has been undertaken and at present there is not sufficient documentation for the proposal to be embraced uncritically (see Krauss 1973a, Swadesh 1962, Voegelin and Voegelin 1967:575).

It has been commonly assumed that Eskimo-Aleut is very different from other Native American linguistic groups, reflecting some later migration across the Bering Strait. Already in the late nineteenth century, Brinton could say: "The Asiatic origin of the Eskimos has been a favorite subject with several recent writers. They are quite dissatisfied if they cannot at least lop these hyperboreans from the American stem, and graft them on some Asian stock" (1894a:146–7). It should not be forgotten, however, that Sapir and some of his followers, at least on some occasions, also thought that so-called Na-Dene was the odd stock out, representing a more recent intrusion which broke up an older unity that included Eskimo-Aleut and all the remaining

Native American languages (see Chapters 3 and 8).

(2) Eyak-Athabaskan
(MAP 2; see also MAPS 3, 5, 8, 25)

See the classification list. Members of the Athabaskan family extend a remarkable distance, from Alaska to Mexico.

Eyak very recently became extinct; it was spoken on the south coast of Alaska near the mouth of Copper River. It was known in Russian sources (Rezanov 1805, Radloff 1858), and discussed in European linguistics. For example, Alexander von Humboldt (1809–1814[1811], 4:347) considered it highly probable that Eyak was an isolate (Pinnow 1976:31). Adelung and Vater (1816) discussed similarities they saw between Eyak, Tlingit, and Tanaina (Athabaskan) but interpreted the vocabulary resemblances as the result of borrowing. Radloff (1858) thought that "Eyak might be genetically related to Athapaskan, but also that the considerable vocabulary Eyak shares with Tlingit probably indicates a genetic relationship," while Buschmann (1856) found "Eyak and Athapaskan related, but Tlingit separate" (both quoted in M. Krauss 1964:128). Radloff's findings were also discussed by Aurel Krause (1885). However, Eyak was essentially unknown in American sources until its rediscovery in 1930 by Frederica De Laguna (see De Laguna 1937, Birket-Smith and De Laguna 1938). Kaj Birket-Smith and Frederica De Laguna (1938:332–7) present a comprehensive summary of the many who earlier had discussed Eyak, but who often misidentified it. Powell and others were misled by opinions that Eyak was just a Tlingitized form of Eskimo[5] (Krauss 1964:128; see also Fleming 1987:191).

The relationship among the Athabaskan languages had been recognized and the family well defined since the mid-1800s. Excellent early historical linguistic work was done by Emile Petitot (1838–1916) and Adrien Gabriel Morice (1859–1938) (Krauss 1986:149; see Chapter 2). Athabaskan subgrouping, however, is still somewhat controversial, due in Krauss's opinion (1973b, 1979) primarily to the dialect mixture that resulted from much contact, particularly among Northern Athabaskan languages and dialects: "The most important differences among

Athabaskan languages are generally the result of areal diffusion of separate innovations from different points of origin" (Krauss and Golla 1981:68). Language boundaries in several cases are also not settled. All this makes it difficult to establish the family tree. There are eleven Athabaskan languages in Alaska. The Pacific Coast and Apachean subgroups are clear; the Pacific Coast subgroup is "more divergent from the [languages of the] North than is Apachean" (Krauss 1973b:919, see also Thompson and Kinkade 1990:30). Kwalhioqua (in southwestern Washington) and Tlatskanai (in northwestern Oregon) (together also called Lower Columbia Athabaskan) seem to have been not separate languages but a single language consisting of two dialects. Its subgrouping position within Athabaskan is not clear; it may not belong to the Pacific Coast subgroup, in spite of its location. Laurence Thompson and Dale Kinkade (1990:31) consider Kwalhioqua-Tlatskanai probably to be an offshoot of the British Columbia languages.

Michael Krauss (1973b:953) believes that Proto-Athabaskan and Proto-Eyak separated about 1500 B.C. This split must have been definitive, since there is little evidence of subsequent influence, and Eyak is no more closely related to its geographically nearest Northern Athabaskan relative, Ahtna, than it is to, say, Navajo in the Southwest (Krauss and Golla 1981:68). Proto-Athabaskan was unified until 500 B.C. or later (Krauss 1973b:953, 1980:11). The original homeland of Proto-Eyak-Athabaskans was apparently in the interior of eastern Alaska (perhaps including the Yukon and parts of British Columbia), the area of greatest linguistic differentiation being in the Northern Athabaskan territory. The distribution of Athabaskan indicates an interior origin; in Northern Athabaskan only the Tanaina significantly occupied a coastline, and the Eyak, while on the coast, had a land-based economy (in contrast to the maritime orientation of the Eskimo and Tlingit). Eskimo influence on the Athabaskan languages is lacking (except for Ingalik and Tanaina, immediate neighbors of Yupik), which suggests that their homeland was not near the Eskimo area. Michael Krauss and Victor Golla hypothesize that Athabaskan spread from this homeland westward into Alaska and southward along the inte-

Eyak-Athabaskan

†Eyak[6] *South Central Alaska*
Athabaskan[7]
    Northern Athabaskan
        Ahtna[8] (Nabesna)-*Alaska*
        Tanaina[9] *Alaska*
        Ingalik[10] [obsolescent] *Alaska*
        Holikachuk [moribund] *Alaska*
        Koyukon[11] *Alaska* (Dialects: Lower Koyukon [Nulato], Central Koyukon, Upper Koyukon)
        Kolchan (Upper Kuskokwim) *Alaska*
        Lower Tanana (Tanana) [obsolescent] *Alaska*
        Tanacross *Alaska*
        Upper Tanana *Alaska*
        Han[12] [obsolescent] *Alaska, Yukon*
        Kutchin (Loucheux)[13] *Canada, Alaska*
        Tuchone *Yukon*
        †Tsetsaut *British Columbia*
        Tahltan[14] [obsolescent] *British Columbia, Yukon* (Varieties: Kaska, Tagish)
        Sekani *British Columbia*
        Beaver *British Columbia, Alberta*
        Chipewyan[15] *Alberta, Saskatchewan, Manitoba, Northwest Territories*
        Slavey-Hare[16] *Northwest Territories, Alberta, British Columbia*
            Mountain
            Bearlake
            Hare
        Dogrib[17] *Northwest Territories*
        Babine (Northern Carrier) *British Columbia*
        Carrier[18] *British Columbia*
        Chilcotin[19] *British Columbia*
        †Nicola[20]
        Sarcee [obsolescent] *Alberta*
    †Kwalhioqua-Tlatskanai[21] *Oregon*
    Pacific Coast Athabaskan
        Oregon Athabaskan *Oregon*
            †Upper Umpqua
            Tolowa-Chetco (Smith River Athabaskan) [moribund] *California*
            †Tututni-†Chasta Costa-†Coquille[22]
            †Applegate-Galice
        California Athabaskan *California*
            Hupa(-Chilula-Whilkut)[23] [obsolescent]
            †Mattole(-Bear River)
            †Wailaki-Sinkyone(-Nongatl-Lassik)[24]
            †Cahto (Kato)
    Apachean
        Navajo[25] *Arizona, New Mexico, Utah*
        Apache[26]
            Jicarilla *New Mexico*
            Lipan [moribund] *Texas (now New Mexico)*
            Kiowa Apache (Oklahoma Apache, Plains Apache) [obsolescent] *Oklahoma*
            Western Apache (San Carlos, White River, Cibecu, Tonto [Northern and Southern]) *Arizona*
            Chiricahua [moribund] *Oklahoma, New Mexico*
            Mescalero *New Mexico*

Krauss and Golla 1981, Krauss 1979, Young 1983, Cook and Rice 1989.

rior mountains to central and southern British Columbia (1981:68; see also Kinkade 1991b: 152). Pacific Coast Athabaskan "may have arrived at its present location more than 1,000 years ago" (Krauss 1980:12). Krauss and Golla have also described the Athabaskan's linguistic diversification and expansion:

> The degree of differentiation among the more isolated languages indicates that these intermontane and coastal migrations [the general expansion from the Athabaskan homeland] took place for the most part before A.D. 500. At a subsequent period two other Athapaskan expansions occurred. One was eastward into the Mackenzie River drainage and beyond to Hudson Bay; the other was south along the eastern Rockies into the Southwest. These two later movements may have been connected. The Apachean languages of the Southwest appear to have their closest linguistic ties in the North with Sarcee, in Alberta, rather than with Chilcotin or the other languages of British Columbia; however, it is not likely that this is evidence for the Apacheans having moved southward through the High Plains, as some have suggested. The Sarcee in the North, like the Lipan and Kiowa-Apache in the Southwest, are known to have moved onto the Plains in the early historical period from a location much closer to the mountains. (1981:68)

The Apachean branch represents a relatively recent expansion into the Southwest. Many archaeologists believe Athabaskan arrived in the Southwest only in the early 1500s. An older idea (one still not entirely abandoned by students of this topic) is that the Southwest Athabaskan

arrived as early as A.D. 1000, which might explain, at least in part, the abandonment of many Pueblo sites in the twelfth and thirteenth centuries, although there is no clear archaeological evidence to support such a view (Gunnerson 1979:162). That the Apachean languages came from the north was first recognized by William W. Turner in 1852 (cited by Latham 1856:70, 1862) and confirmed by Sapir's (1936) famous linguistic proof of a northern origin (see also Morice 1907). Glottochronological calculations (rejected by most linguists) indicate that Proto-Apachean split from the Northern Athabaskan languages at about A.D. 1000 (Hoijer 1956; see also Young 1983:393–4). Apachean languages share a number of distinct innovations which demonstrate their status as a clear subgroup within the family. For example, in Apachean the Proto-Athabaskan labialized alveopalatal affricates ($č^w$, $ǰ^w$, etc.) merged with their plain counterparts ($č$, $ǰ$, etc.) (see Young 1983:394–6).

Athabaskan historical phonology, it should be pointed out, served to confirm the regularity of sound change in unwritten and so-called exotic languages and to demonstrate the applicability of the comparative method to such languages (Sapir 1931; see Chapter 2). As currently reconstructed, Proto-Athabaskan had the sound system shown in Table 4-1.

The lack of labials in the parent language and in most of the daughters is a striking feature. Proto-Athabaskan stems were normally of the canonical form $CV(C)$. All the consonants in Table 4-1 could occupy the position of the first C of roots, while the final C could include most

TABLE 4-1 Reconstructed Sound System in Proto-Athabaskan

Aspirated	t	tl	c	č	$č^w$	k̲	q	q^w	
Unaspirated	d	dl	dz	ǰ	$ǰ^w$	g̲	G	G^w	ʔ
Glottalized	t'	tl'	c'	č'	$č'^w$	k̲'	q'	q'^w	
Voiceless		ł	s	š	$š^w$	x̲	X	X^w	h
Voiced		l	z	ž	$ž^w$	γ̲	γ	$γ^w$	
	n			ỹ[ñ/ŋ]	w̃[m]				
				y	w			
Full vowels	i		u						
	e[æ]		a[ɔ]						
Reduced vowels	α	ə	υ						

Source: Krauss and Golla 1981:71, Krauss 1979, Cook and Rice 1989.

of these positions, though it appears that the aspirated/unaspirated contrast did not occur in this position. The vowels include the four "full" or long vowels (*i, *e, *a, *u) and the three "reduced" (or short) vowels (*ə, *ʋ, *α). The reduced vowels apparently could appear only in *CVC* syllables in Proto-Athabaskan stems (though *CV* syllable prefixes with reduced vowels, normally ə, could also occur); distributional limitations of this sort have led some scholars to question the status of *ə (Cook and Rice 1989:12–13). While many Athabaskan languages have tonal contrasts, Proto-Athabaskan lacked tone—a trait that can be shown to have developed from (Pre-)Proto-Athabaskan differences among *V, and *Vʔ (and *V:) (Krauss 1979; see also Cook and Rice 1989:7). Krauss and Golla (1981:69) represent *Vʔ as *V̓, a vowel with a "glottal constriction":

> In some languages this feature [glottal constriction] is lost; in others the constricted/nonconstricted contrast develops into a phonemic tone system, with constricted vowels becoming high-toned and nonconstricted vowels low-toned, or vice versa. Tone systems have developed in at least 14 Northern Athapaskan languages. In the remaining 9 tone has either never developed or it has developed and been lost (leaving vestiges in some). (Golla 1981:71)

There appears to be general agreement that Athabaskan tonogenesis is linked closely to the constricted vowels and that in Pre-Proto-Athabaskan, at least, these vowels derive from *Vʔ; there is still some disagreement about whether or not Proto-Athabaskan itself had constricted vowels, however (see Leer 1979:12–13; Cook and Rice 1989:9–11). Cook and Rice (1989:6–7), in their overview of Proto-Athabaskan phonology, do not include the labialized uvular series in the inventory, although Krauss and Golla (1981:71) and others do. Leer suggests that the labialized uvular series of Pre-Proto-Athabaskan "merged with the non-labialized uvular series, accompanied by a rounding of reduced stem vowels to *ʋ" (1979:15). There is agreement, however, that the Pre-Proto-Athabaskan labialized front velar series (*ḵʷ, etc.) changed to become the Proto-Athabaskan labialized alveopalatals (*čʷ,

etc.) (Cook and Rice 1989:5; see also Leer 1979:15).

Some of the more interesting sound changes that some of the languages have undergone include:

*ts > tl in Koyukon
*ts > kʷ in Bearlake (variant of Slavey-Hare) and in Dogrib
*ts > p in Mountain (variant of Slavey-Hare)
*ts > f in Hare
*ts > tθ in several (Holikachuk, Ingalik, Tanacross, Han, Tuchone, Slavey)
*čʷ > pf in Tsetsaut
*t > k in Yellowknife Chipewyan and in Kiowa Apache

Most of the other Athabaskan sound shifts are rather natural and unremarkable in comparison (Krauss and Golla 1981:72). Some scholars have disputed the reconstruction of *w̃ and *ỹ on typological grounds; for example, it has been protested that nasalized glides in a language without nasalized vowels goes against language universals. Some prefer *m instead of *w̃, since its reflex is *m in several of the languages. Similarly, for *ỹ some propose *ñ (Cook 1981), others suggest *ŋ (in the front velar series) (Krauss and Leer 1981). Incidentally, in some of these languages (for example, Tanacross, Han), the reflex of *n is nd (or ⁿd). There now appears to be full agreement that Proto-Athabaskan contained three nasal consonants—labial, dental, and one which was either palatal or velar (see Cook and Rice 1989:8).

Proto-Athabaskan contained nouns, verbs, particles, and postpositions. (Some scholars have contended that the postpositions are "local nouns" and therefore are not a separate category.) Nouns could bear possessive prefixes, while verbs were complex, potentially preceded by several inflectional and derivational prefixes. Traditionally, verb prefixes have been divided into two classes: conjunct (all those morphemes that were closer to the verb stem and more tightly bonded phonologically) and disjunct (also called preverbs or proclitics, they were farther from the verb stem).

Eyak-Athabaskan is often associated with the controversial Na-Dene distant genetic proposal.

(3) **Tlingit**
Canada, Alaska (MAP 3)

Tlingit is a single language spoken along the Alaska panhandle.[27] It has moderate dialect differences, with more dialect differentiation in the South than in the North, leading to the supposition that Tlingit expansion moved from south to north (Krauss and Golla 1981:67). The Tongass dialect is quite conservative and has preserved the internal stem contrasts of /Vh, V?, V:?, and V:/, whereas in the other dialects these have developed into tonal contrasts (Krauss 1979).

Tlingit is usually assumed to be related to Eyak-Athabaskan, which together are sometimes called Na-Dene. Sapir's (1915c) original Na-Dene proposal included also Haida (together with Tlingit and Athabaskan; Eyak had not yet been (re)discovered by American linguists), but Haida's relationship to the others is now denied or at least seriously questioned by most specialists (Krauss 1979, 1980:3; Krauss and Golla 1981:67; Lawrence and Leer 1977; Leer 1990, 1991; Levine 1979; see Greenberg 1987:321–30 and Pinnow 1985 for arguments in favor). Therefore, it seems best to avoid the potentially misleading term Na-Dene. (See Chapter 8 for an assessment of the Na-Dene hypothesis.) Tlingit, as Krauss and Golla see it, "bears a close resemblance to Athapaskan-Eyak in phonology and grammatical structure but shows little regular correspondence in vocabulary" and therefore "the nature of the relationship between Athabaskan-Eyak and Tlingit remains an open question" (1981:67). (For "provisional" Tlingit + Eyak-Athabaskan evidence, see Krauss and Leer 1981; see also Pinnow 1964b, 1966, 1976.)

The question of areal linguistics and borrowing has been prominent in considerations of Tlingit's history and possible genetic affiliations. Tlingit has been considered a member of the Northwest Coast linguistics area, and more recently of the Northern Northwest Coast area (Leer 1991, see Chapter 9); hence, some shared traits that earlier were thought to be possible evidence of genetic relationship must now be reassessed as possibly being diffused within these linguistic areas. The proposal that Tlingit is a mixed or hybrid language fits in this context of possible diffusion. This hypothesis is interesting, but difficult to evaluate. Krauss (1973b:

953–63) suggested that Tlingit may be a hybrid of Eyak-Athabaskan and some unrelated language (see also Krauss and Golla 1981:67). Leer (1990, 1991) also views Tlingit as hybridized—not the hybrid of Krauss, but rather as a hybridization or creolization of closely related varieties, of more than one variety of pre-Tlingit involved in the creation of Tlingit as it is known today. Such hybridization, Leer suggests, may explain such things as lexical doublets and variant phonological shapes, and why it is difficult in some cases to find clear sound correspondences for what seem to be cognates between Tlingit and Eyak-Athabaskan.

(4) **Haida**
British Columbia, Alaska (MAP 3)

See the classification list. Haida is spoken on Queen Charlotte Island, to the south of the Tlingit area. The two varieties of Haida are nearing extinction.[28] They are perhaps as different as Swedish and Danish or German and Dutch. Opinion differs concerning whether these two main dialects constitute distinct languages or are only divergent dialects of a single language. Haida has tones (Krauss 1979, Thompson and Kinkade 1990).

As just mentioned, Haida is often assumed to be related to Tlingit and Eyak-Athabaskan, as suggested by the Na-Dene hypothesis. Adelung and Vater (1816) held that Haida words did not reveal any relationship between Haida and the other languages of the area; both Radloff (1858) and Buschmann (1856, 1857) thought that Haida might be related to Tlingit, but that this could not be proven on the basis of the material available at the time (Krauss 1964:128). Haida was hypothesized as being related to (Eyak-)Athabaskan and Tlingit in Sapir's (1915b) Na-Dene super-stock, but the relationship of Haida to the other languages is seriously doubted by most scholars who have worked on it (Krauss 1979; Krauss and Golla 1981:67; Lawrence and Leer 1977; Leer 1990, 1991; Levine 1979), though Pinnow (1985, 1990) and

Haida

Masset
Skidegate [obsolescent]

Greenberg (1987:321–30) support the hypothesis (for details see Chapter 8). As Leer explains: "Most of the comparable lexical items [between Haida and Eyak-Athabaskan/Tlingit] could well be borrowings, and the residue is too small to be considered proof of genetic relationship. The grammatical resemblances could be attributed to areal-typological influence and a long—perhaps intermittent—history of Tlingit-Haida bilingualism" (1990:73). Indeed, several of the shared features have been postulated to have resulted from areal convergence (see the sections on the Northern Northwest Coast and Northwest Coast linguistic areas in Chapter 9; see also Leer 1991). For now, it is perhaps best to consider the genetic affiliation of Haida unknown (see Chapter 8).

(5) Tsimshian
British Columbia, Alaska (MAP 3)

See the classification list. The Tsimshian[29] varieties are closely related and there has been some debate as to whether these are separate languages or merely divergent dialects of the same language. Even when separate languages are assumed, there is debate over whether they constitute three languages or only two; in the latter view, Coast Tsimshian and Southern Tsimshian are assumed to be dialects of a single language (see Thompson and Kinkade 1990:33).

Tsimshian

Nass-Gitksan *Alaska* (Dialects: Nishga/Niska, Eastern Gitksan, Western Gitksan)
Coast Tsimshian
Southern Tsimshian (Klemtu) [moribund]

Many scholars associate Tsimshian with the Penutian hypothesis (following Sapir 1929a), but this has not been demonstrated (see Chapter 8).

(6) Wakashan[30]
(MAPS 3, 4)

See the classification list. The original homeland of the Wakashan family probably lies within its present area, mainly Vancouver Island, but also a considerable part of the mainland to the east and north. Many scholars have pointed out that maritime culture is strongly reflected in the specialized vocabulary and grammar of these languages—for example, the existence of suffixes in Kwakiutl and Nootka which designate activities located on the beach, rocks, and sea (Lincoln and Rath 1980, Kinkade et al. in press).

The relationship between Northern and Southern Wakashan was postulated by Boas (1889a[1888]) and was included in Powell (1966[1891a]:205). The Wakashan languages are members of the Northwest Coast linguistic area. Nitinat and Makah (but not Nootka) belong to a smaller linguistic (sub)area in which the languages of several different families lack primary nasals. Thus Nitinat and Makah have changed their original nasals to voiced stops (*m, *m̃ > b; *n, *ñ > d) because of areal pressure. Nitinat and Nootka have changed certain original uvulars to pharyngeals (*q', *qʷ' > ʕ; *X, *Xʷ > ḥ). Finally, the widely diffused sound change of *k > č affected the Wakashan languages, as well as several Salishan, Chimakuan, and other Northwest Coast languages (Sapir 1926, Jacobsen 1979b; see Chapter 9).

Proposals have attempted to link Wakashan

Wakashan

Northern Wakashan
  Kwakiutlan
    Kwakiutl (Kwak'wala) *British Columbia*
    Heiltsuk (Bella Bella)[31] *British Columbia* (Dialects: Haihai, Bella Bella, Oowekyala)[32]
    Haisla (Kitamat)[33] [obsolescent] *British Columbia*
Southern Wakashan
  Nootkan
    Nootka[34] *Vancouver Island*
    Nitinat (Nitinaht) [obsolescent] *Vancouver Island*
    Makah[35] [moribund] *Washington*

with Chimakuan and to combine both of these with Salishan in the broader Mosan grouping; this is discussed in Chapter 8.

(7) Chimakuan
(MAPS 3, 4)

See the classification list. The small Chimakuan family must have been located in the northern part of the Olympic peninsula of western Washington before the intrusion from the north of Makah (Nootkan) and Clallam (Straits Salish). Chemakum, now extinct, was located in the vicinity of Port Townsend; Quileute is found just south of Makah on the western coast of the Olympic peninsula.[36] The peninsula was apparently the homeland of Proto-Chimakuan; though Chimakuan speakers were attested in historical times in a discontinuous distribution (with Chemakum in the northeast corner and Quileute on the northwest coast of the peninsula), it seems that earlier these and perhaps other Chimakuan groups must have occupied a continuous territory as neighbors on the Olympic peninsula and perhaps elsewhere in northwestern Washington (Collins 1949, Kinkade 1991b:151).

The inventory of Proto-Chimakuan phonemes is: /p, t, c, č, k, k^w, q, q^w, p', t', tl', c', č', k', k$^{w'}$, q', q$^{w'}$, ł, s, š, x, x^w, X, X^w, l, l', m, n,m̓, n̓, w, y, h, ʔ,w̓, y̓; i, a, o/ (Powell 1993:454). The palatals *č, *č', and *š appear to have developed from earlier *k^w, *k$^{w'}$, and *x^w, respectively, before front vowels. Quileute nasals became voiced stops, just as in Nitinat and Makah (Nootkan) and in some other languages in this linguistic area (see Chapter 9).

Quileute and Makah (Nootkan) share a "remarkably homogeneous" culture, which, on the basis of Nootkan loans into Quileute, appears to have been adopted by Quileute speakers from Nootkan. However, several sources of linguistic evidence (place names, loanwords, diffused sound changes, and classification and geographical distribution) support the hypothesis that Chimakuan-speaking peoples originally con-

---

Chimakuan *Washington*

†Chemakum (Chimakum)
Quileute [very moribund]

---

trolled the northern end of the Olympic peninsula and only later were influenced by immigrant Makah (Nootkan) and Clallam (Salishan) on the peninsula (Kinkade and Powell 1976:94–9).

Some scholars have thought Wakashan and Chimakuan to be related (see Powell 1993)—part of so-called Mosan, which would also include Salishan. These languages show considerable structural similarity, but much of this may be due to diffusion within the Northwest Coast linguistic area. In any case, the proposed Mosan grouping currently has little support (Jacobsen 1979a) (for discussion, see Chapters 8 and 9).

(8) Salish(an)
(MAP 4)

See the classification list. Salishan is a large language family, with considerable diversification, extending southward from the coast and southern interior of British Columbia to the central coast of Oregon and eastward to northwestern Montana and northern Idaho.

The inventory of Proto-Salishan sounds, based on Thompson (1979:725), is: /(p), t, c, k, k^w, q, q^w, ʔ, (p'), t', c', tl', k', k$^{w'}$, q', q$^{w'}$, s, ł, x, x^w, X, X^w, h, (m), n, (r), l, (ŋ), ŋ^w, γ, γ^w, (m̓), n̓, (r̓), l', ŋ̓^{w}, ʔ', γ$^{w'}$, ʕ', w, y, w̓, y̓; i, a, ə, u/. Kuipers (1981) presents a very similar inventory, but there is some disagreement or uncertainty concerning the reconstruction of *r (of which Kuipers disapproves, but see Kinkade and Thompson 1974), the labials, and the labialized velars, with doubts remaining concerning the Coast Salish counterparts of the Interior Salish uvular resonants (γ, γ^w). It is now generally agreed that though the system includes *tl' (a glottalized lateral affricate), no plain counterpart *(tl)* existed. The sounds r and r̓ as distinct from l and l' are found only in some of the Southern Interior Salish languages, where their status is marginal; Kuipers is tempted to treat them "either as remnants or as innovations" (1981:324) but not as part of the proto sound system. A γ is found only in Lillooet, Thompson, Shuswap, and northern Okanagan, and is thus also marginal. The distribution of the pharyngeals, *ʕ and *ʕ', and *r is limited in that they occur only in roots, not in affixes, and *r cannot be the first consonant of roots. Kinkade (1993)

Salish(an)

Bella Coola *British Columbia* (Dialects: Bella Coola, Kimsquit, Talio)
Central Salish
    Comox-Sliammon[37] *Vancouver Island, British Columbia* (Dialects: [Island] Comox [very moribund]; Sliammon)
    †Pentlatch[38] *Vancouver Island*
    Sechelt[39][obsolescent] *British Columbia*
    Squamish[40] [obsolescent] *British Columbia*
    Halkomelem[41] *British Columbia* (Dialects: Cowichan, Musqueam, Chilliwack)
    †Nooksack[42] *Washington*
    Straits (Northern Straits) [obsolescent] *Washington, British Columbia* (Dialects: Saanich [moribund]; †Songish [Songhees], †Sooke, Lummi[43] [moribund]; Samish [moribund])
    Clallam[44] [moribund] *Vancouver Island, Washington*
    Lushootseed (Puget/Puget Sound Salish, Niskwalli)[45] [moribund] *Washington* (Dialects: Northern, Southern)
    †Twana[46] *Washington*
Tsamosan
    Quinault[47] [moribund] *Washington*
        Lower Chehalis[48] [moribund] *Washington*
        Upper Chehalis [very moribund] *Washington*
    Cowlitz[49] [extinct?] *Washington*
†Tillamook *Oregon* (Dialects: Tillamook, Siletz)
Interior Division
    Northern *British Columbia*
        Lillooet *British Columbia* (Dialects: Lillooet, Fountain)
        Thompson *British Columbia*
        Shuswap *British Columbia* (Dialects: Eastern, Western)
    Southern
        Columbian (Moses-Columbian) [obsolescent] *Washington* (Dialects: Wenatchee, Sinkayuse, Chelan)
        Okanagan *British Columbia* (Dialects: Northern Okanagan, Lakes, Colville, Nespelem-San Poil, Southern Okanagan, Methow)
        Kalispel *Idaho, Montana* (Dialects: Spokane, Kalispel, Flathead)
        Coeur d'Alene [obsolescent] *Idaho*

Kinkade 1991b; Thompson and Kinkade 1990:34–5; Thompson 1973, 1979.

presents good arguments that *ǝ should not be reconstructed in Proto-Salishan.

Proto-Salishan grammar appears to be reconstructible with several reduplication patterns, a gender category (feminine and nonfeminine), partly ergative person marking, an elaborate system of suffixation (which expressed the categories of aspect, transitivity, control, voice, person, and causation), "lexical" suffixes (derivational markers that refer to body parts, common objects in nature, or culturally salient objects), and a lack of clear contrast between noun and verb as distinct categories[50] (Thompson and Kinkade 1990:33, Kinkade et al. in press).

Of more than 140 reconstructed terms in Proto-Salishan for plants and animals, most of which occur throughout the area and thus are of less value in localizing the Urheimat, Kinkade has determined that some "two dozen represent species found only on the coast, and hence suggest a coastal, rather than an interior, homeland for the Salish." They are the terms for 'harbor seal', 'whale', 'cormorant', 'band-tailed pigeon', 'seagull' (two terms), 'flounder', 'perch', 'smelt' (two terms), 'barnacle', 'horse clam', 'littleneck clam', 'cockle', 'oyster', 'sea cucumber', 'sea urchin', 'red elderberry', 'bracken fern', 'bracken root', 'sword fern', 'wood fern', 'red huckleberry' (two terms), 'salal', 'salmonberry' (two terms), 'seaweed', 'red cedar', and 'yew' (Kinkade 1991b:143–4). Several of these strongly suggest a coastal origin, but not all are equally good as evidence. The terms for 'band-tailed pigeon', 'oyster', 'barnacle', 'sea urchin', and 'flounder' would be supportive, but "similar forms occur widely throughout the area in several non-Salishan languages and may in the long run turn out to be loanwords. . . . [Probably] 'sea cucumber' and 'seaweed' were borrowed from neighboring Wakashan languages." Proto-Salishan speakers, with their coastal homeland, "must also have had access to mountains, in particular the Cascade Mountains, because they had names for mountain goats and hoary marmots, both of which are found only at higher elevations" (Kinkade 1991b:147). On the basis of the distribution of 'bobcats' (not far up the Fraser River) and of 'porcupines' and 'lynx' (which did not extend past southern Puget Sound)—for which Proto-Salishan terms are reconstructible—the homeland can be further pinpointed as "extend[ing] from the Fraser River southward at least to the Skagit River and possibly as far south as the Stillaguamish or Skykomish rivers. . . . From west to east, their territory would have extended from the Strait of Georgia and Admiralty Inlet to the Cascade Mountains. An arm of the family probably extended up the Fraser River through the Fraser Canyon" (Kinkade 1991b:148).

Kinkade suspects that expansion from this homeland area would have been rapid, with little obstruction. While the Interior Salishan split may represent one of the earliest divisions within the Salishan family, expansion into the interior may have been one of the later movements by branches of the family. From a "homeland along the lower Fraser River, the most likely expansion of Salish into the Plateau would be along the Fraser and Thompson Rivers, then down the Okanogan and Columbia into eastern Washington" (Kinkade et al. in press). Interior Salishan languages are more homogeneous than the others, with "perhaps less structural diversity than is found among western Germanic languages" (Kinkade 1991b:148) and with "diversity . . . on the order of Slavic languages" (Kinkade et al. in press). Bella Coola, the most divergent and most northerly Salishan language, may have had an interior origin, as suggested by the fact that a majority of its terms for coastal species are borrowed from Wakashan and it shares uniquely some cognates with Interior Salishan languages

(Kinkade 1991b:149–50). Thus, it may have originated at the northern end of the Proto-Salishan homeland area, along the Fraser River, near the Chilcotin River which perhaps provided a route to the coast.

As mentioned earlier in this chapter, Sapir (1929a) proposed to connect Salish to Wakashan and Chimakuan in a stock called Mosan. Subsequent research has called this classification into question and it is now largely abandoned (though see Powell 1993). The similarities among these languages suggest areal diffusion. Some scholars have proposed a possible Salish-Kutenai connection. Although this is not implausible, no thorough study has been attempted (see Chapter 8; also Thompson 1979).

(9) Kutenai
British Columbia, Idaho, Montana (Dialects: Upper, Lower) (MAP 4; see also MAP 24)

Kutenai (or Kootenay)[51] is an isolate spoken along the border between the United States and Canada in British Columbia, Idaho, and Montana. The historical territory of the Kutenai was centered around the Kutenai River drainage system. It was on the northeastern edge of the Plateau culture area bordering the Plains linguistic area, between Interior Salishan and Blackfoot (Algonquian) (Kinkade et al. in press). Proposals of genetic relationship have attempted to link it with its neighbors, Salishan and Algonquian, and also with Wakashan and others,[52] but these are unsubstantiated (see Haas 1965; see also Chapter 8).

(10) Chinookan[53]
Oregon, Washington (MAPS 3 and 4)

Chinookan

†Lower Chinookan (Chinook proper)
Upper Chinookan [obsolescent]
    Cathlamet
    Multnomah
    Kiksht (Dialects: Clackamas; Wasco, Wishram)

Silverstein 1974, 1990; Thompson and Kinkade 1990.

See the classification list. Speakers of Chinookan languages lived on the Pacific Coast from Willapa Bay in Washington to Tillamook Bay in Oregon, on the Willamette and Clackmas Rivers, and along the Columbia River. The two branches of the family are quite distinct. Upper Chinookan includes the closely related languages Cathlamet, Multnomah, and Kiksht (with varieties called Clackamas, Cascades, Hood River, and Wasco-Wishram).[54]

The homeland of the Chinookan family may have been around the confluence of the Willamette River with the Columbia River, since the greatest area of diversification is here, from whence the languages spread down the Columbia to the ocean and upriver to just above The Dalles (Kinkade et al., in press). Thus, Chinookan has representatives in both the Northwest Coast and Plateau linguistic areas (see Chapter 9), and the different dialects and languages show differences indicative of their respective areas; for example, Lower Chinookan "aspects" reflect the Northwest Coast areal trait, while varieties of Upper Chinookan have shifted to patterns of "tense" from earlier "aspect" under the influence of neighboring Sahaptian languages in the Plateau linguistic area (Silverstein 1974; for other areal traits, see Chapter 9).

Chinookan is also often assigned to the broader proposed Penutian classification, though as an outlier (see Sapir 1929a); this proposed relationship remains undocumented (see Chapter 8).

(11) †Alsea(n)
Oregon (MAP 3)

See the classification list. Alsea is an isolate; there are two closely related varieties, Aslea and Yaquina, which may be dialects of a single language or closely related but distinct languages.[55] Powell (1891a) had grouped Alsea and Siuslaw in his "Yakonan," which later upon closer scrutiny had to be abandoned (see Chapter 2). Alsea is often associated with (Oregon) Penutian (see Sapir 1929a), though the evidence has not been convincing (see Hymes 1956 in favor, Kinkade 1978 against; see also Chapter 8). Kinkade reports that he finds no convincing evidence that Alsea might be related to either Salishan or other putative Penutian languages, but "if pressed, [he] would probably accept a relationship between Alsea and Siuslaw, and leave further relationship with Coos open, but go no further than that" (1978:6–7).

(12) †Siuslaw
Oregon (Dialects: Siuslaw, Lower Umpqua) (MAP 3)

Siuslaw's two dialects, Siuslaw and Lower Umpqua,[56] are both extinct; they were spoken in southern Oregon around present-day Florence, on the lower courses of the Umpqua and Siuslaw Rivers and the adjacent Pacific Coast. The often assumed classification of Siuslaw as Penutian (or, more specifically, as Oregon Penutian) (Sapir 1929a) is not at present substantiated (Thompson and Kinkade 1990; Zenk 1990c; see Chapter 8).

(13) Coosan
Oregon (MAP 3)

See the classification list. Coosan is a small family of two closely related languages that were spoken by inhabitants of the Coos Bay and Coos River area of Oregon: Hanis is probably extinct; Miluk (also called Lower Coquille), once spoken on the lower part of the Coquille River, is extinct.[57] In 1857, due to the Rogue River War, the U.S. government removed the Coos Indians to Port Umpqua. Later they moved to the mouth of the Siuslaw River.

Coosan is also often assumed to be Penutian, part of Sapir's (1929a) Oregon Penutian group, though without sufficient proof. This assumption requires further study (see Chapter 8).

---

†Alsea(n)

Alsea
Yaquina

Coosan

Hanis [extinct?]
†Miluk (Lower Coquille)

---

(14) **Takelman** (Takelma-Kalapuyan)
Oregon (MAP 3)

See the classification list. The Takelman hypothesis, which unites Kalapuyan and Takelma, now seems highly likely, if not fully demonstrated, and is supported by a number of specialists in the area (see also Swadesh 1956 and Shipley 1969; see Chapter 8). I take up the two (sub)families in turn.

The three Kalapuyan languages, closely related to one another, were spoken in the Willamette Valley of western Oregon. They are now extinct. The Proto-Kalapuyan sound system had the following segments: /p, t, c, k, k^w, ?, p^h, t^h, c^h, k^h, k^{wh}, h, p', t', c', k', $k^{w'}$, f, s, ɬ, l, m, n, w, y; i, e, a, o, u; vowel length/ (Berman 1990a; cf. Shipley 1970). Berman (1990b:30–31) does not reconstruct short *e for Proto-Kalapuyan, and short *o is uncertain, given the limited number of cognate sets which seem to suggest it.

Takelma[58] was spoken in Oregon along the middle portion of the Rogue River. Sapir (whose doctoral dissertation was on this language) initially thought Takelma was related to Coos, and later added to these Siuslaw, Alsea, and Kalapuya in the Oregon Penutian branch of his Penutian super-stock (cf. Sapir 1921b, 1929a; Sapir and Swadesh 1953). These proposals do not have significant support at present, but warrant further investigation.

(15) **Sahaptian**
(MAP 4; see also MAP 24)

See the classification list. Nez Perce and Sahaptin were spoken throughout the southern Plateau linguistic area; they were encountered from west of the Cascade divide in Washington State to the Bitterroot Mountains in Idaho, a distance of 375 miles (Kinkade et al. in press). Nez Perce extended from the Bitterroot Mountains on the east to the Blue Mountains on the west, where Idaho, Oregon, and Washington meet, and was centered on the Clearwater River drainage basin and the northwestern part of the Salmon River system. The Snake River was the boundary between the two main dialect groupings of Nez Perce, Upper (Eastern) and Lower (Western) (Kinkade et al. in press). Whereas Nez Perce is relatively homogeneous, Sahaptin has much internal diversity, with two main dialect divisions: Northern (consisting of Northwest and Northeast subdialects) and Southern (made up of the Columbia River cluster of dialects). The Northwest dialect group includes Klickitat, Yakima, Taitnapam (also known as Upper Cowlitz), and Upper Nisqually (Mishalpam). The Northeast group includes dialects named Wanapum, Tygh, Palouse (Palus), Wallawalla (Waluulapam), and Lower Snake (Chamnapam, Wauyukma, and Naxiyampam); these dialects were all strongly influenced by Nez Perce. The Columbia River dialect group includes Tygh Valley,

Takelman

†Takelma
†Kalapuyan[59]
    Northern Kalapuya (Tualatin-Yamhill) (Dialects: Yamhill, Tualatin [Atfalati, Tfalati])
    Central Kalapuya (Santiam) (Dialects: Santiam, Mary's River, several others)
    Southern Kalapuya (Yonkalla)

Berman 1990a.

Sahaptian

Nez Perce[60] *Oregon, Idaho, Washington* (Dialects: Upper, Lower)
Sahaptin[61] [obsolescent] *Oregon, Washington* (Dialects: Northern, Southern, Columbia River)

Tenino, Celilo (Wayampam), John Day, Rock Creek, and Umatilla.

Nez Perce and Sahaptin are fairly closely and obviously related; this was recognized already in 1805–1806 by Lewis and Clark, the first recorded non-Native American visitors in the area (Kinkade et al. in press). Because the Sahaptian languages occupy a fairly extensive territory across the Plateau culture area, it is suggested that their expansion is probably recent (see Kinkade 1991b:152). The Proto-Sahaptian vowels, whose analysis has been the subject of some controversy (Aoki 1966, Rigsby 1965a, Rigsby and Silverstein 1969), were: /i, e, a, ə, o, u/. The Proto-Sahaptian consonants were: /p, t, c, č, k, kʷ, q, qʷ, p', t', c', č', k', q', s, š, X, Xʷ, ɬ, tl', m, n, (N), w, y, h, ʔ/ (Kinkade et al. in press).

Sahaptian is often thought to be a principal member of the proposed Plateau Penutian (after Sapir 1929a; see also Berman 1996); this hypothesis has not been substantiated and appears to be mostly dismantled even among scholars who have faith that the Penutian hypothesis will ultimately be proven (see Chapter 8). However, there is considerable evidence that Sahaptian, Klamath, and Molala are related (see below).

(16) **Klamath-Modoc**
Oregon, California (Dialects: Klamath, Modoc)[62] (see MAP 24)

The Klamath lived on the high plateau of southeastern Oregon, around the lakes from which the Klamath River originates. The southern part of this basin was the Modoc territory, which extended across the lava beds toward Pit River. The northern part was Klamath territory; it lies against the Cascade Range (Kinkade et al. in press). The Klamath and Modoc dialects are "very close," perhaps no more divergent than dialects of American English (Kinkade et al. in press; cf. Barker 1963). Distant genetic proposals would have Klamath as part of Plateau Penutian (Sapir 1929a), but Plateau Penutian is at best disputed today. The evidence for a genetic relationship between Klamath, Sahaptian, and Molala is more credible (see Aoki 1963; DeLancey 1992; DeLancey, Genetti, and Rude

1988; Rude 1987; Berman 1996), and it appears that these are probably related (see Chapter 8).

(17) **†Molala** (Molale)
Oregon (see MAP 24)

Molala territory probably stretched from Oregon City to Douglas County along the Cascade Mountains. The area inhabited by the Northern Molala occupied the Molalla River drainage system and the southwestern tributaries of the Clackamas River; that of the Southern Molala (unattested linguistically) was located upon the upper Rogue River and upper part of the North and South Forks of the Umpqua River (Kinkade et al. in press). Hale (1846) had placed Cayuse and Molala together as the members of the Waiilatpu family; this grouping was accepted by Powell (1891a) as the Waiilatpuan stock and unfortunately remained unquestioned until Rigsby (1965b, 1966, 1969) disproved the assumed close relationship. Hale's decision to group them had apparently been based on nonlinguistic evidence (see Chapter 8 for further discussion). On the other hand, Berman (1996) has recently shown that it is highly likely that Molala is related to Klamath and Sahaptian.

(18) **†Cayuse**[63]
Oregon, Washington (MAP 4; see also MAP 24)

Cayuse is extinct and extremely poorly attested. Already in 1837 the famous missionary Marcus Whitman wrote that the Cayuse had intermarried so extensively with their Nez Perce neighbors that all spoke Nez Perce and the younger ones did not understand Cayuse at all; it was replaced by Nez Perce. In the early nineteenth century, Cayuse territories included the drainage systems of the Butter Creek, the upper Umatilla, the upper Walla Walla, the Touchet, the Tucannon, the upper Grand Ronde, the Burnt, and the Powder Rivers (Silverstein 1979a:680, Kinkade et al. in press). (See Chapter 8 for discussion of proposed relationships, and see especially Molala, above.)

(19) †Shasta (and †Konomihu?)
California (Map 5)

Shasta (Powell's Sastean) aboriginally inhabited the area that includes a part of the Rogue River in southern Oregon and the Scott Valley, Shasta Valley, and a portion of the Klamath River in northern California. Shirley Silver (1978b:211) includes within Shasta the groups known as Shasta, Okwanuchu, New River Shasta, and Konomihu, though she says that the specific nature of their linguistic relationship is still unknown. A group called the Kammatwa lived on the fringes of Shasta territory and reportedly spoke both Shasta and Karuk. Larsson (1987) has cleared up the confusion concerning "Konomihu": one variety recorded as Konomihu is a dialect of Shasta, though it probably should not be identified as Konomihu; the other form recorded as Konomihu is a distinct language. Little is known of the latter Konomihu, which was spoken in the region around the North and South forks of the Salmon River. Whether it belongs with Shastan or not is an open question. Shasta was on the verge of extinction in the mid-1970s; the Rogue River Indian wars (1850–1857) and the gold rush led to the tribe's disintegration. The New River Shasta were located on the east and south forks of the Salmon River above Cecilville. They were nearly exterminated by gold seekers and U.S. Army troops. Okwanuchu is very poorly known; it was spoken from the junction of the north fork of Salt Creek to the upper Sacramento River (Silver 1978b).

Shasta was classified as Hokan in the original Hokan proposal (Dixon and Kroeber 1913a, 1913b, 1919) and was part of Sapir's (1929a) Northern Hokan group; these are contested proposals (see Chapter 8).

(20) Karuk (Karok)
[moribund] *Northwest California* (Map 5)

Karuk (called Quoratean by Powell)[64] is spoken in northern California along the middle course of the Klamath River, and more recently in Scott Valley. The Karuk knew almost nothing of the existence of white men until the arrival of the gold miners in 1850 and 1851 shattered their existence. Karuk is an isolate with no known relatives, though it was placed in the original Hokan hypothesis of Dixon and Kroeber (1913a, 1913b) and is usually presented as a Hokan language; Hokan is a disputed classification (see Chapter 8). Culturally, Karuk speakers differ little from neighboring Yurok (Algic) and Hupa (Athabaskan), and the three together constitute a small culture area, part of the larger Northwestern California culture area (Bright 1957, 1978a).

(21) †Chimariko
Northwest California (Map 5)

Chimariko (formerly also called Chimalakwe)[65] is extinct; already in 1906, Dixon (1910) found only two speakers remaining. The entire territory of the Chimariko in historical times consisted only of a narrow canyon along a twenty-mile stretch of the Trinity River in northwestern California. The earliest European contact, with trappers of the fur companies, was in approximately 1820, but intensive contact came in the early 1850s, when the gold seekers overran the Trinity River area and threatened to disrupt the salmon supply, the primary Chimariko food source. Conflicts with the miners resulted in the near annihilation of the Chimariko in the 1860s. The few remaining Chimariko took refuge with the Hupa and Shasta Indians (Silver 1978a).

Chimariko has long been grouped in Hokan, but evidence so far has not been sufficient to determine any such broader affinities and it therefore for the present remains an isolate (see Chapter 8).

(22) Palaihnihan
Northeast California (Map 5)

See the classification list. Palaihnihan was Powell's name for the family which is composed of the two languages Achomawi and Atsugewi, based on the name "Palaihnih" used by Hale

Palaihnihan

Achomawi (Achumawi) [moribund]
Atsugewi [very moribund]

(1846), said to be from Klamath *p'laikni* 'mountaineers, uplanders'.[66] The Achomawi (also called Pit River Indians) lived aboriginally along the Pit River in northeastern California (Olmsted and Stewart 1978). The Atsugewi speakers occupied the northern slopes of Mount Lassen, along streams draining into the Pit River. The two Atsugewi dialect groups were Atsuge ('pine-tree people'), of the valleys north of Mount Lassen, and Apwaruge, spoken in the area to the east of the Atsuge, on the more barren plain. Atsugewi is now quite moribund (Garth 1978, Olmsted 1984).

An incomplete listing of the Proto-Palaihnihan consonant phonemes is: /p, t, k, q, ʔ, s, š, x, h, w, y, l, L, r, m, n, (N), (ŋ)/ (see Olmsted 1964:34–5, 62). Many details of Palaihnihan reconstruction are yet to be worked out; for example, Olmsted reconstructed sixty-four proto sounds and clusters, but several of them (not listed here) are exhibited by only a couple of cognate sets, suggesting that with more information they could be shown to derive from certain of the others. It is interesting, however, that there are solidly attested correspondences for a number of liquids and nasals: *l (Achomawi *l* / Atsugewi *l*), *r (l/r), *L (l/n), *N (n/r), and *n (n/n).

As for its prehistory, Olmsted (1964:1) calculates the split up of Proto-Palaihnihan into the two languages at about 3,500 to 4,000 years ago, based on glottochronology and archaeology. This is correlated with the archaeological sequence at the Lorenzen site, which suggests that Palaihnihan speakers have been in place for at least 3,300 years (Moratto 1984:558). The two languages may have borrowed significantly from one another, since there was considerable bilingualism among the Atsugewi, as well as frequent intermarriage (Olmsted 1964:1).

Palaihnihan's potential broader connections have received a fair amount of attention. Gatschet thought Palaihnihan and Shasta were related (reported in Powell 1966 [1891a]: 174), and this was taken up by Dixon (1905, 1907[1906]), who proposed his Shasta-Achomawi "stock." Dixon and Kroeber (1913a, 1913b) included this group, which they called Shastan, in their original Hokan proposal, and Sapir (1929a) formulated a Northern Hokan sub-group (called Kahi by Bright 1955) which included so-called Shastan, Chimariko, and Karuk. However, Olmsted's (1956, 1957, 1959, 1964) comparative work has convinced most scholars that the Palaihnihan languages bear no closer relationship to Shasta than to any of the other so-called Kahi or Northern Hokan languages. The Hokan hypothesis, which includes Palaihnihan, is quite controversial in general (see Chapter 8). For the present, the family is best considered not known to be related to any other.

(23) †Yana
North Central California (MAP 5)

See the classification list. The Yana territory was in north central California, stretching between the Feather and Pit Rivers. Like other Indians in the area, the Yana suffered heavily in the first twenty years of their contact with white people, beginning about 1850. The Yahi[67] band isolated itself and was not rediscovered until 1908 (in the vicinity of upper Mill Creek and Deer Creek Canyon). By 1911 all had perished but one, Ishi, the famous last unassimilated "wild" Indian, who came to live and work at the University of California Museum, then in San Francisco, until his death in 1916. The four Yana varieties were "clearly identifiable dialects, mutually intelligible within limits" (Sapir and Swadesh 1960:13). All four are extinct, though the language is more thoroughly documented than other now extinct Native American tongues (see Sapir 1910, 1922, 1923; Sapir and Swadesh 1960).

Yana distinguished between forms used by males and those used by females (although Yana has no grammatical gender). For example, the male form *yana* 'person' (from whence the name of the language) corresponds to the female *ya* 'person' (see Sapir 1949[1929b]:207). Yana is usually associated with the disputed Hokan hypothesis.

Yana

Northern
Central
Southern
    South
    Yahi

(24) **Pomoan** (Kulanapan)
[obsolescent] *North Central California* (MAP 5)

See the classification list. The seven Pomoan languages are mutually unintelligible, with internal divergence greater than that of Germanic languages (McLendon and Oswalt 1978).[68] They were formerly spoken between the Pacific Coast and the Sacramento Valley in northern California. The earliest linguistic material is from Gibbs (1853), and Powell's name for the family (Kulanapan stock) in based on one of Gibbs's vocabulary lists entitled Kulanapo. Only the Kashaya (their *k'ahšá:ya*) have a distinct name for themselves.

Although there is not full agreement among those who have reconstructed Pomoan phonology, one proposal for the Proto-Pomoan phonemic inventory is: /t, ṭ, (c), k, q, ʔ, b, d, pʰ, (tʰ), ṭʰ, kʰ, qʰ, (p'), t', ṭ', c', k', q', s, x, X, h, m, n, l, w, y; i, e, a, o, u; vowel length; two tones/ (see McLendon 1973:20–33, 53; Oswalt 1976a:14; Moshinsky 1976:57; see also Webb 1971). It should be mentioned that, while the correspondence sets upon which these phonological segments are based are generally clear, opinions concerning the best reconstruction for some of these sounds have varied. For example, for the correspondence set with *x* in Southeastern Pomo and *š* in the other languages, Oswalt (1976a) reconstructed **š* but McLendon reconstructed **x*; and the set with Southeastern *X,* Eastern Pomo *x,* and others *h* is reconstructed by McLendon as **X* (see McLendon 1973:18). The Proto-Pomoan velar series (**k, *kʰ, *k'*) has for the most part shifted to alveopalatal affricates (*č,*

čʰ, č') in all the languages except Eastern Pomo, which retains the velar reflexes; this led Oswalt (1976a) to reconstruct the alveopalatals for Proto-Pomoan, whereas McLendon (1973) and Moshinsky (1976) selected velars for the reconstruction. Correlated with this is the shift of the uvular series (**q, *qʰ, *q'*) to velars in most of the languages (with the exception of Eastern Pomo and partially in Kashaya). Proto-Pomoan had some sort of pitch-stress accent, which was probably predictable morphologically, though its exact nature is disputed (see McLendon 1973:34). McLendon (1973:52) also includes in her reconstruction **-nʸ* and **-lʸ*. Proto-Pomoan had verbal suffixes for imperative, durative, causative, singular, optative, plural active, reciprocal, reflexive, semelfactive, speculative, and sentence connectives, with a series of instrumental prefixes. Some of the languages have verbal subordinating suffixes which also indicate whether the subject of subordinate and main verbs is the same or different (that is, with switch-reference functions) (McLendon 1973).

The Proto-Pomoan homeland appears to have been around Clear Lake, in the foothill oak woodlands. The Late Borax Lake Pattern (Mendocino Aspect) in the archaeology of the area has been correlated with Proto-Pomoan, indicating that this group arrived approximately 5,000 years ago in the Clear Lake region, which was formerly occupied only by Yukian speakers. In about 500 B.C., Western Pomo expanded to the Russian River drainage. The reconstructed vocabulary affords no precise picture of the proto-culture, but the evidence suggests that the Proto-Pomoan speakers were hunters and gatherers, in a natural environment similar to that of most of its current speakers. They subsisted on seafood, game, nuts (and acorns), grains, berries, and tubers; hunted with bow and arrow; fished with nets and traps, and used baskets for gathering, storing, and cooking. They danced and sang for ritual reasons, played at least one musical instrument, and had beads (McLendon 1973:63–4, Moratto 1984:551–2, Whistler 1983–1984).

Pomoan may be related to Yuman (Langdon 1979). More broadly, it is one of the proposed members of the controversial Hokan classification (see Chapter 8).

Pomoan (Kulanapan)

Southeastern [moribund]
Eastern
†Northeastern
Western Branch
    Northern Pomo
    Southern Group
        Central Pomo
        Southern Pomo
        Kashaya (Southwestern Pomo)

McLendon and Oswalt 1978:275.

(25) **Washo** (Washoe)
[obsolescent] *East Central California, Western Nevada* (MAP 5; see also MAP 7)

Washo is an isolate, with no known relatives.[69] The Washo territory is on the California and Nevada state line, in the drainages of the Truckee and Carson Rivers, centering on Lake Tahoe. Washo is a Great Basin tribe, and as such is the only non-Numic (Uto-Aztecan) group in this culture and linguistic area. However, it also shares areal traits with neighboring California languages (Jacobsen 1986:109–11; see also Sherzer 1976:128, 164, 238–9, 246; see Chapter 9). As for Washo linguistic prehistory, based on geography, on apparent older loanwords from neighboring languages (Numic, Miwokan, and Maiduan), and on the uncertainty of any external genetic relationships, "one can only assume that Washoe has long been in approximately the same area in which it is now found" (Jacobsen 1986:107). It has been associated with the Hokan classification (a closer kinship to Chumash has sometimes been assumed), but even Kroeber admits that "the affiliation with other Hokan languages can not be close" (1953:369) and many others find the Hokan hypothesis so inconclusive and controversial as to be more a hindrance than a help (see especially Jacobsen 1986; see Chapter 8).

(26) †Esselen
California (MAP 5)

The Esselen[70] were a small group in the mountains of northern Monterey County, California. The Spanish took the Esselen into three missions—San Carlos (Carmel), Soledad (in the Salinas Valley), and San Antonio. They were the first California Indians to lose their traditional culture, in the early nineteenth century (Hester 1978a); already in 1833, Fray Felipe Arroyo de la Cuesta reported that there were very few Esselen speakers left. The language is extinct and poorly documented in spite of its ten sources dating from 1786 to 1936, all short or problematic (see Beeler 1977). In total, these records contain about 300 words and a few short phrases and sentences.

Shaul (1988) presented a number of "lookalikes" suggestive of borrowing between Esselen and Costanoan (which are geographic neighbors), with a few shared also with certain Miwokan languages. He interprets the pattern of borrowing as indicative of Costanoan spreading south along the coast and absorbing (or at least being in contact with) Esselen(-related) speech communities. Moratto reports that Esselen territory was greatly reduced by Costanoan expansion, and "archaeologically these developments are seen in the replacement of the older 'Sur Pattern' [Esselen?] by the 'Monterey Pattern' [Costanoan?] between circa 500 B.C. and A.D. 1" (1984:558).

Esselen has usually been placed with Hokan (for an example, see Webb 1980), but the data are so fragmentary as to defy classification.[71]

(27) †Salinan
California (MAP 5)

The Salinan language, now extinct, was spoken in parts of San Luis Obispo, Monterey, and perhaps also San Benito Counties in California, in territory extending from the ocean to the ridge of the Coast mountain range (Turner 1980:53). Salinan had two documented dialects from the missions of San Antonio de Padua (Antoniano) and San Miguel (Migueleño), both in Monterey County.[72] They were named Salinan by Latham (1856) because at least some of the speakers were located along the Salinas River.[73] Early records of San Antonio, a vocabulario and phrase book, were prepared by Fray Buenaventura Sitjar, founder of the mission. Fray Felipe Arroyo de la Cuesta also made a vocabulary in 1821 (see Turner 1980). Kroeber (1904), Harrington (field notes from 1922 and 1932–1933 in the National Anthropological Archives, Smithsonian Institution), and Jacobsen (notes and tapes from 1954 to 1958 on file in the Survey of California and Other Indian Languages, Linguistics Department, University of California, Berkeley) obtained material before the language's extinction, though Mason (1918) is the principal published linguistic study of the language (but see also Turner 1980).

Dixon and Kroeber had united Salinan with Chumash in their "Iskoman" grouping, which subsequently was placed in their larger Hokan proposal (1913a, 1913b, 1919). For the Iskoman proposal, they presented only twelve presumed cognates. Obviously, the Iskoman proposal could not be considered well founded (nor any possible connections with so-called Hokan languages) on the basis of evidence such as this. Kaufman (1988) eliminated Chumash from his version of the Hokan hypothesis, but he retained Salinan, thus further countering the Iskoman proposal (see Chapter 8).

(28) †Chumashan[74]
Southern California (MAP 5)

See the classification list. The Chumash were among the earliest Californian Indians encountered by Europeans; Juan Rodríguez Cabrillo had abundant and friendly contacts with them in 1542–1543 when he sailed in their territory, where he died. Spaniards regarded the Chumash as superior to other tribes of California. The Chumashan languages are now extinct; the last speaker of Barbareño died in 1965. These languages are attested in varying degrees, from quite well for Inezeño, Barbareño, and Ventureño through the linguistic fieldwork of Madison Beeler and John P. Harrington, to very poorly for Interior Chumash for which only a word list of about sixty items exists (see Klar 1977 for details). Chumashan languages were spoken in southern California—on the Santa Barbara Islands and adjacent coastal territory from just north of San Luis Obispo to approximately Malibu, and they extended inland as far as the San Joaquin Valley. Five of the six Chumash languages are named for the Franciscan missions established in their territory: Ventureño (which probably included Castac and apparently also Alliklik as dialects) for San Buenaventura; Barbareño (which included Emigdiano) for

Chumashan

†Obispeño (Northern Chumash)
†Central Chumash
    †Ventureño (with Alliklik)
    †Barbareño (with Emigdiano)
    †Inezeño (Ineseño)
    †Purisimeño (?)
†Island (Isleño)
    †Cruzeño, †Roseño

Klar 1977:38, Beeler 1970:14, Beeler and Klar 1977, Grant 1978:505, Shipley 1978:86.

Santa Barbara; Inezeño for Santa Inez (sometimes spelled Ines or Ynez); Purisimeño for La Purísima (or La Purísima Concepción); and Obispeño for San Luis Obispo. Cruzeño (or Cruceño) is named for Santa Cruz, the island where this group lived before being settled on the mainland around 1824 (Beeler and Klar 1977; Klar 1977:1); Roseño is named for Santa Rosa Island. Obispeño (Northern Chumash) is generally recognized as the most divergent variety of Chumash (Kroeber 1910, 1953; Langdon 1974; Klar 1977). Cruzeño and Roseño are often listed as distinct but are considered dialects of Island Chumash. It is uncertain whether Cuyama (Interior Chumash) constituted a distinct variety, since so little data on it exist (Grant 1978:505).

Klar (1977:32) reconstructed Proto-Chumash with the following phonemic inventory: /p, t, k, q, ?, p', t', k', q', S, (C), h, (S'), C', m, n, ṁ, ṅ, l, l', w, y, ẇ, ẏ; i, e, a, ɨ, o, u/. While Proto-Chumash must have had both *q and *x, Klar reconstructs only *q, since these were in alternation in the proto language, and the evidence, although not fully clear, suggests they were not two contrastive sounds. Klar's *S covers both the dental s and the alveopalatal š found in most dialects—the sibilant harmony of Chumashan makes the correspondences irregular. The Chumash sibilant harmony is regressive assimilation in which a final š causes all preceding s sounds in a word to change to š, and a final s causes preceding š sounds to be changed to s (Beeler 1970, Klar 1977:125–8). Klar has only one cognate set for *C/*C' (covering both dental c/ c', and alveopalatal č/č'), with glottalization in Inezeño and Ventureño, but no glottalization in Obispeño. She includes *S' tentatively, though there are no sets which demonstrate that it should be reconstructed for the proto language. The reconstruction of the sibilants is further complicated by the sound-symbolic alternations, which were significant throughout Chumashan (Klar 1977:129–33). For example, Harrington observed for Ventureño that "any part of speech can be diminutivized by changing its consonants as follows: s > č; c > č; š > č, sometimes c; č > c; l > n; x > q. . . . Although not frequent in the language, it permeates the whole structure and lexicology" (1974:8; also Klar 1977:130). Chumashan languages also have aspirated stops, affricates, and fricatives, and although aspiration probably existed in Proto-Chumashan, it is apparently secondary, having developed (sporadically and not fully predictably) in three sets of circumstances: (1) from gemination, when identical consonants come together over morpheme boundaries (for example, s + s > s^h, p + p > p^h); (2) from dissimilation, when stops come before another consonant (for example, kt > k^{h}t); and (3) from combination with *h* (for example, k + h > k^h) (Klar 1977:14, 128–9). Proto-Chumashan had vowel alternations of *e* with *o* and *i* with *u*. Central Chumashan languages had a productive system of vowel harmony where within stems a non-high vowel (vowels of the set *e, o, a*) could co-occur with no other vowel from this set, rather only with itself—that is, sequences had to be identical (for example, no **e . . . a* forms exist). The high vowels *i* and *u* could co-occur with one another or in combinations with vowels from the non-high set (*e, o, a*) (Klar 1977:122–3). However co-occurrence of **ɨ* with other vowels was not so free and had to be specified in individual instances. "This lack of patterning with other vowels in the system" has led Klar to regard this as "evidence for the external origin of the high central vowel [ɨ] in Chumash"—that is, as a result of diffusion within the linguistic area (1977:123; cf. pp. 30–31; see Chapter 9). Proto-Chumashan had VOS basic word order (1977:133–5) and a large class of particles, which differ significantly among the daughters, including instrumental noun prefixes.

Chumashan prehistory appears to be characterized by continuous occupation of their coastal region from at least as early as 2,000 years ago (Moratto 1984:558).

Chumash is also usually placed with the broader but contested Hokan proposal, though as previously mentioned, Kaufman (1988) eliminates Chumashan from his version of the Hokan hypothesis and some others who work with so-called Hokan languages are now following him in this.

(29) Cochimí-Yuman
(MAP 5; see also MAPS 6 and 8)

See the classification list. The Proto-Yuman area appears to have been the lower Colorado River. Yuman groups now occupy the southernmost part of California and the northern part of Baja California along the Colorado River, as well as part of Arizona and adjacent areas of Sonora, Mexico. Cochimí is extinct and poorly documented, but it is clearly related to Yuman (Mixco 1978).

Proto-Yuman consonants and vowels are: /p, t, (t̪), c, k^y, k, k^w, q, q^w, ʔ, s, ṣ, x, x^w, m, n, n^y, l, l^y, r, w, y; i, a, u; vowel length/ (Langdon and Munro 1980:126; cf. Wares 1968).Yuman is one of the largest families from among those which are often thought to belong to the proposed but controversial Hokan grouping. Although Yuman has not definitely been shown to be related to any other languages, Langdon (1979) presents evidence suggestive of a possible Pomoan-Yuman genetic affiliation.

Cochimí-Yuman

Yuman
    Pai Subgroup (Northern Yuman)
        Upland: Walapai-Havasupai-Yavapai[75]
        Paipai (Akwa'ala) *Baja California*
    River Subgroup (Central Yuman)
        Mojave (Mohave) [obsolescent]; Maricopa, Quechan (Yuma)[76] *Arizona, California*
    Delta-California Subgroup
        Cocopa *Arizona, California, Baja California*
        Diegueño: Iipay (Ipai, Mesa Grande) [obsolescent]; Tiipay (Tipai, Jamul),[77] Kumeyaay (Campo)
            [obsolescent] *California*
    Kiliwa [obsolescent] *Baja California*
†Cochimí *Baja California*

Mixco 1978, León-Portilla 1985; also Langdon and Munro 1980:122, Langdon 1990a.

(30) **Wintuan** (Wintun)
North Central California (Map 5)

See the classification list. Wintuan speakers occupied the west of the Sacramento Valley and the upper Trinity River drainage in northern California. Wintuan (Powell's Copehan stock) is also called Wintun in the literature, but some scholars intend Wintun to mean only Wintu and Nomlaki (North Wintun), and therefore Wintuan is adopted to avoid confusion (see Lapena 1978:324). The name is derived from Wintu *wint^{h}u·h* 'person'. The family has a time depth approximating that of the Romance languages (Pitkin 1984:2). Nomlaki is very closely related to Wintu and has two divisions, River and Hill.[78] Patwin (derived from their *patwin* 'people') was called Copéh by Gibbs (1853)—hence Powell's name for the family, Copehan; Patwin has also been called Southern Wintun. Wintu proper has a range of dialects: Hayfork, South Fork Trinity, Upper Trinity, Sacramento Valley, and McCloud. Well-known varieties of North Patwin are Hill Patwin (Kabalwen; Tebti, Cache Creek, Cortina) and River Patwin (Colusa, Grimes). South Patwin has Knight's Landing and Suisun variants (Whistler 1977, Kroeber 1953).

Proto-Wintuan's phonemic inventory is: /p, t, tl (or ł), k, q, p^h, t^h, č^h, k^h, q^h, p', t', tl', č', k', q', b, d, s, l, r, m, n, w, y, h, (ʔ); i, e, a, o, u; vowel length/ (Whistler 1977).

It is hypothesized that Proto-Wintuan was spoken in interior southwestern Oregon or northwestern California, perhaps along the upper Rogue River (the middle Klamath and southern Umpqua Rivers' drainages are also possibilities), and that "Wintuans almost certainly entered California from the north" (Moratto 1984:563, Whistler 1977:166). The Patwins first moved south, into Miwok territory, disrupting them. Archaeologically, this incursion coincides with the beginning of the Augustine Pattern in central California. Thus, Wintuan speakers probably brought to the region traits such as the bow and arrow, harpoons, flanged stone pipes, and pre-interment grave-pit burning (Moratto 1984:563, Whistler 1977).

Wintuan was considered to be one of the five branches of (California) Penutian when the hypothesis was first framed (together with Yokutsan, Maiduan, and Miwok-Costanoan) (see Chapter 8).

(31) **Maiduan**
[moribund] *South Central California* (Map 5)

See the classification list. The Maiduan languages (also called Maidun, Powell's Pujunan stock) were spoken in the area of the American and Feather river drainages in the northern Sierra Nevada of California, with Nisenan in the valley, Konkow in the foothills, and Maidu in the mountains. Another now extinct variety was spoken in the area of Chico, but whether it is a separate language or a dialect of Konkow is not clear. Maidu (from their self-designation, *maydɨ* 'person'), spoken in the high mountain meadows between Lassen Peak and the town of Quincy, reportedly had four dialects: American Valley, Indian Valley, Big Meadows, and Susanville. Konkow (apparently with a number of dialects) was spoken along the lower Feather River, in the surrounding hills, and in parts of Sacramento Valley. The Nisenan territory was the drainages of the Yuba, Bear, and American Rivers, and the lower Feather River. There were three dialects: Northern Hill, Southern Hill, and Valley. Nisenan, Konkow, and Maidu are very closely related but are mutually unintelligible (Riddell 1978, Wilson and Towne 1978).

Proto-Maiduan phonemes are: /p, t, k, ʔ, p', t', c', k', b, d, s, m, n, w, y, h; i, e, a, ɨ, o, u; vowel length; phonemic stress/. Nisenan has apparently undergone the vowel shift: i > e, e > a, a > o, u > ɨ (Ultan 1964:356–61).

As Kenneth Whistler points out, Maiduan

Wintuan

(North) Wintun
    Wintu [moribund]
    Nomlaki [very moribund]
Patwin [very moribund]
    North Patwin
    South Patwin

Maiduan

Nisenan[79] [very moribund]
Konkow [moribund]
Maidu [very moribund]

plant terms show borrowing and irregularities which are evidence of the group's recent arrival in California, probably from northwestern Nevada (reported in Moratto 1984:562).

Maiduan was one of the component families of the originally postulated Penutian hypothesis (see Chapter 8).

(32) **Miwok-Costanoan** (Utian)
Central California (MAP 5)

See the classification list. Latham (1856:82) had suggested a relationship between some Miwokan and Costanoan languages, and Gatschet (1877a: 159) had classified the two together under the name of Mutsun (see Powell 1877:535), but by 1891 Powell separated them, calling the Miwokan languages his Moquelumnan stock (from Latham 1856). Kroeber (1910) presented a few sets of similar forms shared by the two families and noted certain sound correspondences, but concluded that a genetic relationship was "far from certain" (Callaghan 1988b:55). The two groups are, Powell notwithstanding, demonstra-

---

Miwok-Costanoan (Utian)

Miwokan *Northern California*
    Eastern Miwok
        Sierra Miwok [obsolescent]
            Southern Sierra Miwok
            Central Sierra Miwok
            Northern Sierra Miwok
        Plains Miwok [extinct?]
        †Saclan (Bay Miwok)
    Western Miwok
        Coast Miwok [very moribund]
            Marin Miwok (Western)
            Bodega Miwok (Southern)
        Lake Miwok [very moribund]
†Costanoan *Northwest California*
    †Karkin *southern edge of Carquinez Strait*
    †Northern Costanoan
        †Ramaytush (San Francisco)
        †Chocheño (East Bay)
        †Tamyen (Santa Clara)
        †Awaswas (Santa Cruz)
        †Chalon (Soledad)
    †Southern Costanoan
        †Mutsun (San Juan Bautista)
        †Rumsen (Monterey/Carmel)

Callaghan 1988b, 1990b.

---

bly related; Callaghan began to show this in 1967 and has worked out many of the historical details of this family, which she called Utian (1967, 1982, 1988a, 1991c).

Miwokan has roughly the time depth of Germanic (Callaghan 1988b:53).[80] Lake Miwok is geographically isolated from the other Miwokan languages. It had frequent contact with Eastern Pomo, Southeastern Pomo, Foothills Patwin, and Wappo, which is reflected in loanwords. Coast Miwok was spoken from the Marin Peninsula to Bodega Bay (Marin and Sonoma Counties). Eastern Miwok languages were formerly found on the western slopes of the Sierra Nevada, extending inland from Ione to Stockton. Saclan, now extinct, was spoken in the eastern parts of Contra Costa County. Plains Miwok was spoken near the lower reaches of the Mokelumne and Cosumnes Rivers and on the Sacramento River. Sierra Miwok languages were spoken from the Fresno River to the Cosumnes River on the western slopes of the Sierra Nevada. Northern Sierra Miwok was spoken in the foothills and mountains of the Mokelumne and Calaveras River drainages. Central Sierra Miwok was in the foothill and mountain areas of the Stanislaus and Tuolumne River drainages. It had two dialects, West and East. Southern Sierra Miwok was spoken in the upper drainages of the Merced and Chowchilla Rivers. It also had two dialects: the Merced River dialect (which retained /š/ for Proto-Sierra Miwok */š/) and the Mariposa-Chowchilla dialect (with /h/ for */š/). According to lexicostatistic calculations (held to be unreliable by most linguists), the split between Western Miwok and Eastern Miwok occurred approximately 2,500 years ago, and Plains Miwok separated from Sierra Miwok languages 2,000 years ago; the breakup of Sierra Miwok occurred about 800 years ago (Callaghan 1978, Levy 1978b).

Proto-Miwokan had the following sounds in its phonemic inventory: /p, t, ṭ, č, k, s, š, l, m, n, w, y, h; i, e, a, ɨ, u; vowel length/ (see Callaghan 1972, 1988a).

The Costanoan languages were probably all extinct by 1935 (though Harrington left recordings for Mutsun, Rumsen, and Chocheño; Callaghan 1988a:54). The name of this family comes from Latham's (1856) designation "Costano" (see also Callaghan 1958:190).[81] Costanoan territory extended from Monterey to San Francisco, probably also with a pocket at the end of the Marin Peninsula, and south to Big Sur. Karkin was the northernmost of these languages, spoken on the southern edge of the Carquinez Strait, and constitutes a separate branch of Costanoan (Callaghan 1988a). Chocheño (Chochenyo or East Bay Costanoan) was spoken on the eastern shore of San Francisco Bay, between Richmond and Mission San José. Tamyen (Santa Clara Costanoan) was spoken in the lower Santa Clara Valley and around the south end of San Francisco Bay. Ramaytush (San Francisco Costanoan) was spoken in San Mateo and San Francisco Counties. Awaswas (Santa Cruz Costanoan) was spoken along the coast in Santa Cruz County. Mutsun was spoken in the Pajaro River drainage. Rumsen was spoken along the lower Carmel, Sur, and Salinas Rivers. Finally, Chalon (Soledad) was spoken on the Salinas River. There is some difference of opinion concerning the classification of Chalon; Beeler (1961; see also Okrand 1979) places it within Southern Costanoan as a third language, though Callaghan (1988b) classifies it with the Northern Costanoan branch. Costanoan internal diversity is about as great as that of Western Romance (breaking up about 1,500 years ago) (Levy 1978a); however, there has been "enough interinfluence with Northern Costanoan [and Southern Costanoan] to make the Costanoan family tree more like a 'Stammbusch' than a 'Stammbaum' " (Callaghan 1988a:451; cf. Callaghan 1990b:121).

Proto-Costanoan had the sounds /p, t, č, ṭ, k, kʷ, s, x, l, (r), m, n, w, y, ʔ/ (see Callaghan 1967, 1982:24). The Proto-Miwok-Costanoan (also called Proto-Utian) phonemic inventory included: /p, t, ṭ, c, č, k, kʷ, ʔ, s, š, ṣ, h, l, m, n, w, y; i, e, a, ɨ, o, u; vowel length/ (Callaghan 1967, 1982:24, 1988b). In Proto-Miwok-Costanoan, *š became Proto-Costanoan *h, Proto-Miwokan *ṣ̌. Proto-Miwok-Costanoan *ɨ changed to Proto-Costanoan *e word-finally and *e/*i non-finally. Proto-Miwok-Costanoan *kʷ is not attested as such but is reflected as k (alternating with w) in Southern Costanoan and as w in the other Costanoan languages and in the Miwokan languages.

Miwok-Costanoan (Utian) was the earliest of the so-called Penutian families to enter California, perhaps bringing with them mortar and pestle technology in about 2500 B.C. A homeland inland from the San Francisco Bay area, near Alameda, has been suggested on the basis of plant and animal names. Proto-Miwok-Costanoan speakers settled in the area of San Francisco Bay and appear to represent the Berkeley Pattern in the archaeological record. Moratto emphasizes the match of early Miwok-Costanoan radiation with the distribution of marshlands, finding "most Utian [Miwok-Costanoan] settlements before circa 200 B.C. were situated on the margins of the best wetland environments in the Delta, Napa Valley, and San Joaquin Valley, as well as on the San Francisco Bay shore and central coast" (1984:557; see also Whistler 1977:169). Miwok speakers spread east into the Delta and later across to the Sierras. Wintuan speakers later moved rapidly into central California and ancestral Patwin in its southward thrust disrupted Miwok territory, separating Eastern and Western Miwok groups, and pushing Saclan (Bay Miwok) south of the Delta, isolating Lake Miwok. The Houx Aspect of the Berkeley Pattern (ca. 2000 B.C.) probably represents ancestral Lake Miwok; Western Miwok speakers (represented by the Houx Aspect) appear to have replaced earlier Wappo speakers (represented by the St. Helena Aspect of the Augustine Pattern) in the Napa Valley soon after A.D. 500 (Whistler 1977, Shipley 1973; cf. Moratto 1984:533–4, 566). At the time of earliest European contact, Costanoan languages were spoken on the California coast from Contra Costa County on San Francisco Bay to northern Monterey County; because of early and vigorous Spanish mission activities in the area, little is known of the languages' real precontact distribution. While Miwokan and Costanoan are clearly related, the other families in the Penutian proposal, with which Miwok-Costanoan is usually associated, have not been demonstrated to be related genetically, though some scholars see promising signs for the future (see Chapter 8).

(33) Yokutsan[82]

[obsolescent] *South Central California* (MAP 5)

See the classification list. The Yokuts were divided into a large number of groups resembling small tribelets, and each had its dialect. Powell's

Yokutsan

Poso Creek (Palewyami)
General Yokuts
    Buena Vista (Tulamni, Hometwoli)
    Nim-Yokuts[83]
        Tule-Kaweah (Wikchamni, Yawdanchi)
        Northern Yokuts
            Kings River (Chukaymina, Michahay, Ayticha, Choynimni)
            Gashowu
            Valley Yokuts
                Far Northern Valley
                    Yachikumne (Chulamni)
                    bd-Yokuts[84] (Lower San Joaquin; Lakisamni, Tawalimni)
                Northern Valley
                    Noptinte
                    Chawchila
                    Merced?
                Northern Hill (Chukchansi; San Joaquin [Kechayi, Dumna])
            Southern Valley (Wechihit; Nutunutu, Tachi; Chunut; Wo'lasi, Choynok; Koyeti, Yawel-mani)

Whistler and Golla 1986:320–21.

name for the family was Mariposan. The Yokuts tribes lived in the southern San Joaquin Valley and adjacent areas. It is probable that the Yokuts entered California from the north, displacing Uto-Aztecan groups into the San Joaquin Valley, after speakers of Miwokan and Costanoan had spread in the San Francisco Bay area. The Yokuts appear to be associated with the Meganos Pattern archaeologically, which spread approximately 2,000 years ago, separating Costanoan and Miwokan territory (Whistler 1977; cf. Moratto 1984:554–6, 563).

Proto-Yokutsan phonemes are: /p, t, (c), (ṭ), k, ʔ, p', t', c', ṭ', k', pʰ, tʰ, cʰ, ṭʰ, kʰ, s, ṣ, x, m, n, ŋ, ṁ, ṅ, (ṇ̇), l, l', w, y, h, ẇ, ẏ; i, a, ɨ, o, u; vowel length/. (The segments in parentheses may have been marginal; it is difficult to compile convincing cognate sets for them.) In Proto-Yokutsan, plain stops and affricates in syllable-final position were apparently aspirated (Whistler and Golla 1986:334). This is reminiscent of the widespread phonetic tendency in languages of Mesoamerica to aspirate final stops, though aspiration is not a contrastive, distinctive feature of the sound system of these Mesoamerican languages on the whole (see Chapter 9).

Yokutsan is frequently classified as Penutian; Yokutsan, together with Wintun, Maiduan, Mi-

wokan, and Costanoan, constituted Kroeber and Dixon's (1913a, 1913b, 1919) originally proposed Penutian, the kernel to which Sapir and others later proposed many language groups as possible additional relatives (see Chapters 2 and 8). Today a prevailing attitude, even among some "Penutian" specialists, is that these languages have not successfully been shown to be related and that no faith should be put in the original Penutian hypothesis, and by implication, certainly not in the broader, more far-flung Penutian proposals (see Shipley 1980, Whistler 1977). However, evidence is also mounting that at least some of these languages share a broader family relationship, and most specialists do not discount entirely the possibility that the future will see more successful demonstrations of some genetic relationships among some of the languages associated with the Penutian hypothesis (see Berman 1983, 1989; Silverstein 1975, 1979a, 1979b; Whistler and Golla 1986). The evidence for the Penutian hypothesis is assessed in Chapter 8, where I reach the conclusion that the overall hypothesis is not presently well supported, though some smaller-scale proposals to group a few of these languages appear promising and that additional research should be undertaken.

(34) Yukian
North Central California (MAP 5)

See the classification list. Yukian has been a controversial classification in that Wappo, the most divergent language, is thought by some scholars not to be demonstrably related to the other Yukian languages (Hinton 1994:78; Sawyer 1980; Sawyer 1991:8–9, 76, 102–3). Sawyer views the evidence negatively: "Looking for cognate words between Yuki and Wappo does not produce a particularly impressive array. Mostly one finds very short sequences, root syllables presumably, in which either the initial and the medial vowels or an initial consonant, the medial vowel, and a final consonant match rather well. An example would be Yuki *k'ismik'* 'bathing, swimming' as compared with Wappo *c'ése?* 'swimming' " (1978:256). Nevertheless, Elmendorf's (1988) evidence demonstrates conclusively that these languages are related—and not that distantly, either. In light of the strength of his evidence, it is difficult to imagine that the relationship would ever have been doubted. The misgivings stem from Sawyer's seeing the assembled evidence as due to convergence, borrowing, or shared areal features (Sawyer 1991:76), though Elmendorf's (1981, 1988) evidence makes it clear that this can hardly account for the mass of evidence with extensive, solid sound correspondences sufficient to demonstrate the genetic relationship. For example, Sawyer argues that, if Wappo and Yuki were genetically related, they should have common terms for 'black', 'white', and 'red', judging from notions of color universals, but that these terms are "totally unrelated" in Wappo and Yuki, and this is evidence against their relatedness (1991:103). However, lack of genetic relationships can scarcely be based on negative evidence. By this logic, then Latin and English (two Indo-European languages), with *niger-black, albus-white,* and *ruber/rufus-red,* would cease to be related.

Yuki proper was spoken on the Middle Fork of the Eel River. Huchnom was spoken on South Eel River, and Coast Yuki was spoken on the Mendocino coast. The three are dialects (at least partially mutually intelligible) of what is usually called simply Yuki (Miller 1978). The Wappo lived at Alexander Valley just north of San Francisco. Wappo is now very near extinction.[86]

The sound systems of the Yukian languages are similar, though Wappo lacks the nasalized vowels and set of uvular consonants found in Yuki, and the Wappo affricates /c, c', and c^h/ do not appear in Yuki. Wappo had five dialects (Clear Lake, Russian River [Western], Northern, Central, and Southern), all mutually intelligible. Wappo has borrowed from all the languages that surround it—from Lake Miwok, Coast Miwok, Southern Pomo, Eastern Pomo, Southeastern Pomo, and Wintun dialects (Sawyer 1978:256–7).

The Yukians (including the Wappo) may be the only truly autochthonous people of northern California. The Yuki and the Wappo seem to have been separated (approximately 3,000 years ago; Elmendorf 1968) by the expansion of Pomoan speakers into their territory. Both Yuki-Wappo and Pomoan peoples occupied the area before the arrival of Wintuan speakers. Pre-Proto-Yukians are perhaps correlated with the Post Pattern archaeologically, dating to 9000 B.C. The Mendocino Complex (ca. 3000 B.C.), centered on Clear Lake, is associated with Core Yukian. The prehistory of the Wappo is more complex. They were perhaps initially separated from the main body of Yukian before 2000 B.C., by movements of the Pomo from Clear Lake to the Russian River drainage. The Napa Valley Wappo are represented by the St. Helena Aspect of the Augustine Pattern. The Wappo moved to Alexander Valley in the nineteenth century, after a war with the Southern Pomo (Whistler 1977, 1983–1984; Kroeber 1953; Moratto 1984:538).

The small Yukian family is generally considered not to have any demonstrated external relationship, though several proposals have been made. Alfred Kroeber (1906) pointed out structural similarities shared by Yuki and Yokuts (though he found no convincing lexical agreements suggestive of a genetic relationship).

Yukian

Wappo [moribund]?
Core Yukian
   †Yuki
   †Coast Yuki
   †Huchnom[85]

Both Penutian and Hokan kinships have been proposed. Dixon and Kroeber (1919) found Yukian lexical similarities to their proposed Hokan and Penutian languages in about equal numbers, but suggested that they were largely due to borrowing (since the lexical similarities between these languages and the non-Yukian languages with which they were compared were mostly independent in Yuki and Wappo—not found in both). Also, Kroeber (1959) mentioned some structural similarities suggestive of early Athabaskan influence on Yuki. Paul Radin (1919), in his controversial attempt to relate all the North American Indian languages, saw both scattered lexical resemblances and structural similarities between Yukian and Siouan, yet he concluded that Yukian may belong with Penutian. Sapir (1929a) put Yukian in his Hokan-Siouan group, though his reasoning is unknown. Swadesh (1954b) included Yukian in his Hokogian net (which included Hokan, Muskogean, and several other languages of the Gulf region), but he did not group it with its Californian "Hokan" neighbors but rather with Coahuiltecan and Chitimacha. William Shipley (1957) presented some Yukian lexical similarities with so-called California Penutian languages but left open the question of affinity. Elmendorf (1963) took up the possibility of the Siouan connection suggested by Radin and accommodated by Swadesh; however, his ninety-five sets of lexical similarities, although suggestive, fall far short of supporting a genetic relationship (connecting Yukian and Siouan neither directly with each other nor as members of some more inclusive classification) (see Chapter 8).

(35) Uto-Aztecan
(MAP 6; see also MAPS 5, 7, 8, 12, and 25)

See the classification list. Of Native American language families, Uto-Aztecan is one of the largest in terms of numbers of languages and speakers, and geographical extent (from Oregon to Panama). It is also is one of the oldest families that is clearly established without dispute. For example, glottochronology gives the breakup of Proto-Uto-Aztecan at about 5,000 years ago (though glottochronology is rejected by most linguists).

The following additional names—not listed in the classification list—which have been identified from colonial and other sources, are generally associated with groups thought to be extinct but nevertheless usually identified as Uto-Aztecan. These need much more research. The list presented here is far from exhaustive, and the tentative affinities and alternate names here are those given in the sources cited. The names from California are all thought to belong to Takic (though some scholars believe some may have an independent status); these are San Nicolas (Nicoleño); Giamina (Kroeber [1907:153] and Lamb [1964a:110] thought this might be a separate branch of Uto-Aztecan; its status as an independent branch of Northern Uto-Aztecan is uncertain [Miller 1983b:122]); and Vanyume (clearly Takic). Languages from Mexico and farther south are Acaxee (Aiage) (closely related to Tahue, in the Cahitan group, linked with Tebaca and Sabaibo); Amotomanco (Otomoaco) (affiliation uncertain, perhaps Uto-Aztecan);[87] Cazcan (sometimes equated with Zacateca; some associate it closely with Nahua, though Miller [1983a:331] refrains from classifying it other than geographically); Baciroa (closely connected to Tepahue in the Taracahitic group); Basopa; Batuc (an Ópata dialect?); Cahuimeto, Cahuameto (which perhaps belongs with Oguera and Nio); Chínipa (which is either close to Ocoroni or a local name for a variety of Guarijío; Chínipa is said to be mutually intelligible with Ocoroni—in any case, it is Tarahumaran); Coca; Colotlan (Pimic, closely related to Tepehuan or Teul and Tepecano); Comanito (close to Tahue; belongs to the Taracahitic group); Concho (Chinarra and Chizo were subdivisions of Concho; Toboso is also related; perhaps belongs to the Taracahitic group; see Troike 1988);[88] Conicari (close to Tepahue; probably belongs to the Taracahitic group); Eudeve (a division of Ópata, with dialects Heve [Egue] and Dohema); Guachichil (a variety of Huichol?); Guasave (with dialects Compopori, Ahome, Vacoregue, Achire; perhaps a Taracahitic language; given its speakers' maritime economy, it may not be Uto-Aztecan at all but is possibly linked with Seri [Miller 1983a:331]; the Guasave, Comopori, Vacorgue, and Ahome spoke the same language); Guazapar (Guasapar) (either a dialect of Tarahumara or grouped with Guarijío and Chínipa; perhaps Guazapar, Jova, Pachera, and Juhine are all Tara-

Uto-Aztecan

Northern Uto-Aztecan
    Numic (Plateau Shoshoni)
        Western
            Paviotso-Bannock-Snake (Northern Paiute) *Oregon, Idaho, Nevada*
            Monache (Mono) [obsolescent] *California*
        Central
            Shoshoni-Goshiute, Panamint [obsolescent] *Nevada, Utah, Wyoming;* Comanche [obsolescent] *Oklahoma*
        Southern
            Southern Paiute *Utah, Nevada, California, Arizona*
            Ute, Chemehuevi [obsolescent] *Utah, Colorado, California, Arizona*
            Kawaiisu [obsolescent] *California*
    Tübatulabal[89] (Kern River) [moribund] *California*
    Takic (Southern Californian Shoshoni)
        Serran: Serrano [moribund]; †Kitanemuk *California*
        Cahuilla [moribund?]; Cupeño [moribund] *California*
        Luiseño-Juaneño [obsolescent] *California*
        †Gabrielino-†Fernandeño *California*
    Hopi[90] *Arizona*
Southern Uto-Aztecan
    Pimic (Tepiman)
        Pima-Papago[91] (Upper Piman) *Arizona, Sonora*
        Pima Bajo (Lower Piman) (Névome) *Sonora*
        Northern Tepehuan, Southern Tepehuan *Sonora, Durango, Jalisco*
        †Tepecano *Jalisco*
    Taracahitic
        Tarahumaran
            Tarahumara *Chihuahua*
            Guarijío (Varihio) *Chihuahua, Sonora*
        Tubar [extinct?] *Chihuahua*
        Cahitan (Yaqui-Mayo-Cahita)[92] *Arizona, Sonora, Sinaloa*
        Opatan
            †Ópata *Sonora*
            †Eudeve (Heve, Dohema) *Sonora*
    Corachol-Aztecan
        Cora-Huichol
            Cora *Nayarit*
            Huichol *Nayarit, Jalisco*
        Nahuan (Aztecan, Nahua, Nahuatlan)
            †Pochutec *Oaxaca*
            Core Nahua
                Pipil[93] (Nahuate, Nawat) [obsolescent] *El Salvador* (extinct in Guatemala and Nicaragua)
                Nahuatl[94] (Mexicano, Aztec) *Mexico* (many dialects)

---

humara dialects); Guisca (Coisa [Nahua]); Hio (Taracahitic?); Huite (close to Ocoroni; some scholars say it is Taracahitic; Miller [1983a:330] lists it as "unclassified"); Irritila (a Lagunero band); Jova (Jobal, Ova) (some classify Jova as a Tarahumara dialect; most link it with Ópata; Miller says it is "probably Taracahitan" [1983a:329]); Jumano (Humano, Jumano, Jumana, Xumana, Chouman [French source], Zumana, Zuma, Suma, Yuma) (Suma may well be the same language; Jumano is possibly Uto-Aztecan; Troike 1988);[95] Lagunero (Irritila may be the same language; it is like Nahua and may be affiliated with Zacateco or with Huichol);

Macoyahui (presumed to be related to Cahita); Meztitlaneca (a Nahua dialect?); Mocorito (a Tahue language; a member of the Taracahitic group); Naarinuquia (Themurete?) (may not be Uto-Aztecan at all but related to Seri, given its speakers' maritime economy [Miller 1983a: 331]); Nacosura (Ópata dialect); Nio (nothing is known about this language; Miller [1983a: 330] lists it as unclassified; it is perhaps affiliated with Ocoroni); Ocoroni (with which Chínipa reportedly was mutually intelligible; it is said to be similar to Ópata; Huite and Nio are also perhaps close to Ocoroni; it belongs to the Taracahitic group); Oguera (Ohuera); Ópata (Teguima is another name; Eudeve is also said to be Opatan; Batuc and Nacosura are Ópata dialects; a member of the Taracahitic or Pimic group); Patarabuey (affiliation unknown; Troike 1988:237); Sayultec (Aztecan, maybe it is a Nahua dialect); Suma (same language as Jumano); Tahue (may include Comanito, Mocorito, Tubar(?), and Zoe; Tahue is definitely not Nahuan; perhaps it belongs to the Taracahitic group); Tanpachoa (affiliation unknown; it was once spoken along the Rio Grande; Troike 1988); Tecuexe (a "Mexican" [Nahua] colony?); Teco-Tecoxquin (Aztecan); Tecual (like Huichol);[96] Témori (Tarahumaran?); Tepahue (Macoyahui, Conicari, and Baciroa are said to be close to Tepahue; it is presumably a member of the Taracahitic group); Tepanec (Aztecan); Teul (Teul-Chichimeca) (Pimic, perhaps grouped with Tepecano?); Toboso (grouped with Concho); Topia (maybe this name should be identified with Xixime); Topiame (Taracahitic?); Totorame (grouped with Cora); Xixime (Jijime) (Hine and Hume are subdivisions; this has a problematic classification; its links with Acaxee are not certain; perhaps it belongs to the Taracahitic group; Miller [1983a:330] gives it as unclassified); Zacateco (often equated with Cazcan; perhaps a Huichol group; see Harvey 1972:300; Miller [1983a:331–2] raises doubts about the forms usually thought to be from this language, suggesting they may actually be directly from Huichol); and Zoe (probably affiliated with Comanito; Baimena was a subdivision; it is perhaps a member of the Taracahitic group, though Miller [1983a:330] lists it as unclassified). (See Beals 1932; Dávila Garibi 1935, 1942; Escalante Hernández 1963; Harvey 1972; Jaquith 1970; Jimé-nez Moreno 1943; Kroeber 1934; Lombardo 1702; Mason 1936; McQuown 1955; Mendizá-bal and Jiménez Moreno 1944; Miller 1983a; and Sauer 1934.)

Bright interpreted the scant information available on the linguistic history of the upper Santa Clara valley (in Southern California) as indicating that two languages were spoken there, and that Tataviam was "a language showing some Takic affinities" (1975:230). Bright's interpretation is reasonable, given that the few words Harrington identified in his notes as "Tatavyam" look more like Takic and less like Chumash. King and Blackburn believe that Tataviam is " 'the remnant, influenced by Takic, of a language family otherwise unknown in Southern California,' or, more likely, that it is Takic (but not, apparently, Serran or Cupan)" (1978:535, citing Bright 1975). Beeler and Klar argue that there was no Takic Tataviam, but rather that Tataviam is a misidentified variety of Chumash from the interior, which others called "Castec, Castac" (closely connected with Ventureño) (1977:301–3). The Tataviam identification would benefit from further research. The "Al-liklik" that Kroeber (1925:614) had identified as a Uto-Aztecan language in this same region also turns out, on closer inspection, to be Chumash, a form of Ventureño (Beeler and Klar 1977:296, 299).[97]

The similarities among Uto-Aztecan languages were recognized by Johann Carl Eduard Buschmann (1859), who, however, was equivocal on the issue of genetic relationship. He coined the term "Sonoran languages" and recognized their relationship, although he thought Nahua (Aztecan) was distinct and that many of the similarities were due to influence from Aztecan. Bancroft (1874–1876) gave the more northerly languages the name Shoshonean, and Gatschet (1879) and others accepted the family relationship of these languages with Aztecan. Brinton (1891) classified the languages together as a family and coined the name Uto-Aztecan, with an internal classification of three branches: Shoshonean, Sonoran, and Nahuatl/Nahuatlecan (Aztecan). This division, although controversial, continued to be upheld by many scholars. Powell (1891a) considered but rejected Uto-Aztecan, separating the Shoshonean and Sonoran languages (later called Piman).[98] Kroeber's (1907) work on "Shoshonean or the northern languages," however, supported aspects of the Uto-Aztecan family. His Shoshonean had four branches: Plateau (now called Numic, following Lamb 1958, based on Proto-Numic *nɨmɨ 'person, Indian'), Southern Californian (now called Takic [compare Proto-Takic *taka 'person'], following Miller 1961, 1964), Tübatulabal (Kern River), and Hopi. This classification has proven valid. Sapir (1913–1919[1915]) proved the relationship among the members of the Uto-Aztecan family to everyone's satisfaction in one of the first systematic demonstrations of the applicability of the comparative method to languages that do not have long traditions of writing (see Chapter 2). While many early scholars followed Brinton's traditional three-way division, later Kroeber (1934:6) abandoned Sonoran, asserting that the languages usually so classified were really independent branches. Benjamin Whorf (1935) argued for the same conclusion regarding the so-called Shoshonean languages—those often classified today as the Northern Uto-Aztecan languages—and many others agreed with this view. But Mason (1936) and Hale (1964) presented evidence in support of the traditional Sonoran group (see also Hale 1958–1959 and Voegelin, Voegelin, and Hale 1962). Miller (1983b, 1984), however, basing his conclusion on lexical evidence (and glottochronology) and relying to some extent on phonological evidence, supported Southern Uto-Aztecan (with traditional Sonoran and Aztecan merged into a larger unit), but he did not recognize Shoshonean or Northern Uto-Aztecan as a unit, but rather as four independent branches within the family. The evidence of shared innovations, primarily phonological, but with some grammatical evidence, supports the classification presented at the beginning of this section. It is favored in many respects by Heath 1977; Campbell and Langacker 1978; and Kaufman 1974a, 1974b, though with some variation in opinion with respect to the position of whether Aztecan is seen as merely one member of Southern Uto-Aztecan or as sharing a subgroup node with Cora-Huichol within Southern Uto-Aztecan (the view originally proposed by Sapir 1913–1919[1915]; see Hale 1958–1959; Lamb 1964a; Miller 1983a, 1984).

Uto-Aztecan subgrouping has been and continues to be controversial. Eight branches at the lower levels are generally recognized (Numic, Takic, Tübatulabal, Hopi, Pimic, Taracahitic, Cora-Huichol, and Aztecan). There is no agreement concerning higher-level groupings. Recent research supports an early branching of the family into two divisions, Northern (including Numic, Takic, Tübatulabal, and Hopi) and Southern (including Pimic, Taracahitic, Cora-Huichol, and Aztecan). Also, it now appears that Cora-Huichol and Aztecan are more closely related to each other than to others within the Southern division (see Campbell and Langacker 1978), though several scholars simply consider both Aztecan and Cora-Huichol to be equal in status to the other branches of Southern Uto-Aztecan (or Sonoran, depending on their classification). Gabrielino (or Gabrieleño-Fernandeño) is also extinct; it is clearly a Takic language, but it may have been either an independent branch within Takic or more closely aligned with Serrano. Still not universally accepted are the traditional groups of Shoshonean (including at least Numic [Plateau Shoshoni], Takic [Southern California Shoshoni], and sometimes all the Northern languages) and Sonoran (including Pimic, Taracahitic, and Cora-Huichol) (see Heath 1977).

The most commonly cited reconstruction of the Proto-Uto-Aztecan phonemic inventory is: /p, t, c, k, kʷ, ʔ, s, h, m, (n), (ŋ), (l), (r), w, y; i, a, ɨ, o, u; vowel length/ (see Kaufman 1981, Langacker 1977:22). The long-running controversy about whether the fifth vowel was *ɨ or *e has now been resolved in favor of *ɨ (Langacker 1970, Campbell and Langacker 1978). The segments in parentheses in this inventory of sounds are somewhat disputed; at issue is not necessarily their existence but rather how they should be reconstructed. For example, traditional reconstructions have *l and *n, but Kaufman (1981) has instead *n and *ŋ. This discrepancy can be better understood through considering the correspondence sets in Table 4-2.

The question is, which is better, the traditional reconstruction with *n and *l (assumed to shift in appropriate contexts to ŋ and n, respectively, in NUA), or Kaufman's reconstruction with *ŋ and *n (which change to n and l,

TABLE 4-2 Some Nasal Correspondence Sets in Uto-Aztecan

	Initial	Initial	Medial	Medial[a]	In suffixes
Northern Uto-Aztecan	n-	ŋ-	-ŋ-	-n-	n
Southern Uto-Aztecan	n-	n-	-n-	-l-	n
Traditional Proto-Uto-Aztecan	*n-	*ŋ-	*-ŋ-	*-l-	*n
Kaufman's Proto-Uto-Aztecan	*n-	*ŋ-	*-ŋ-	*-n-	*ŋ

a. It is sometimes thought that there is a correspondence between NUA medial -n- and -n- medially in Southern Uto-Aztecan, reconstructed by some scholars as *-n-. Kaufman, however, shows that there are few putative cognate sets involved and that the reflexes are in fact not regular but sporadic; on this ground he eliminates such a correspondence from consideration.

respectively, in the relevant environments in SUA)? Both reconstructions are plausible. The question concerning *r is whether it may be eliminated from the reconstruction as one reflex of *t (or perhaps of some other sound), since *r also occurs only medially. Thus far there have been no persuasive arguments for its elimination.

Traditionally, Uto-Aztecan is viewed as having three famous phonological processes: spirantization (lenition), nasalization, and gemination (hardening) (after Sapir 1913–1919). Kaufman (1981) has explained these. Spirantization is the normal process affecting obstruents between vowels; nasalizing stems merely reflect an earlier nasal segment (which appears on the surface only in limited circumstances and otherwise has undergone various sound changes in the different languages); gemination results from an original consonant cluster with *-hC-. These phonological processes are largely limited to Northern Uto-Aztecan. In Southern Uto-Aztecan, *hC, *nC, and plain *C show no distinct reflexes, except for Proto-Uto-Aztecan *p after a vowel, which is weakened to a fricative or glide (or lost) in these languages (consistent with spirantization/lenition in Northern Uto-Aztecan). In Proto-Uto-Aztecan, all three processes took place both across morpheme boundaries and morpheme-internally. Thus an obstruent is spirantized between vowels whether within a single morpheme or at the boundary where two morphemes come together. Word-final *-n and *-h are lost (except final n is preserved in Shoshone and Tübatulabal), but when morpheme-final before another morpheme beginning in a consonant, some Northern Uto-Aztecan languages preserve distinct reflexes of the resulting *nC and *hC clusters. In Northern

Uto-Aztecan, the *h in *hC contexts is reflected as h in Hopi and Comanche, and partially in Shoshone, Serrano, and Southern Paiute; in the other Northern Uto-Aztecan tongues, it is reflected as gemination of the C of *hC (where the C is an obstruent) or as a nonlenited obstruent (an obstruent not protected by *h would be lenited). (For details of the correspondences and various sound changes in the individual branches and languages, see Kaufman 1981.) This explanation of the three historical processes is an important contribution to Uto-Aztecan linguistics. (See also Campbell and Langacker 1978; Heath 1977; Langacker 1977; Miller 1967, 1983b, 1984; Hale 1958–1959, 1964; and Voegelin, Voegelin, and Hale 1962 for general information on Uto-Aztecan.)

The Proto-Uto-Aztecan homeland appears to have been in Arizona and northern Mexico, perhaps extending into southern California (Fowler 1983). From here, speakers spread to as far north as Oregon (Northern Paiute), east to the Great Plains (Comanche), and south as far as Panama (Nahua groups; see Fowler 1989). The Proto-Numic homeland was in southern California, near Death Valley (Fowler 1972). Miller (1983b:123) suggested that the homeland of the proposed Sonoran grouping (essentially Southern Uto-Aztecan) was in the foothill area between the Mayo and the Sinaloa Rivers. Proto-Uto-Aztecans (at ca. 3,000 B.C.) may have been responsible for the western versions of the Cochise Desert Culture of southern Arizona and New Mexico. The Mogollon culture and later Anasazi culture may have included speakers of Uto-Aztecan languages though scholars usually associate these cultures more directly with Tanoan speakers. Kayenta Anasazi is frequently identified with Hopi (Hale and Harris 1979:176–7).

The Uto-Aztecan family today is very often assumed to be related to Kiowa-Tanoan, in a distant genetic proposal called Aztec-Tanoan (Whorf and Trager 1937), and some linguists place this in an even broader proposed version of so-called (Macro-)Penutian. The Kiowa-Tanoan hypothesis is very shaky, however, and should not be accepted. (It is discussed in more detail in Chapter 8.)

(36) **Keresan**[99]
New Mexico (MAP 8)

See the classification list. Keresan is spoken in seven varieties (usually assumed to be dialects of a single language, but with significant divergence between the Western and Eastern groups) at seven Indian pueblos in New Mexico. Five are Eastern Keresan, spoken in the Rio Grande valley area: Cochiti, Santo Domingo, San Felipe, Santa Ana, and Zia. The other two, Acoma and Laguna, are Western Keresan, situated about 100 kilometers to the southwest. The greatest linguistic differences are those between Acoma and Cochiti, although Davis (1959) maintains that the time depth within Keresan does not exceed 500 years—very shallow indeed.

Reconstructed Proto-Keresan sounds are: /p, t, c, ç, t^y, k, ʔ, p^h, t^h, c^h, ç^h, č^h, k^h, p', t', c', ç', č', k', s, ṣ, š, h, (s'), ṣ', š', m, n, ṁ, ṅ, r, ṙ, w, y, ẇ, ẏ; i, e, a, ɨ, o, u; vowel length/ (see Miller and Davis 1963).

Keresan has no demonstrable relatives. Sapir (1929a) had placed it with Hokan-Siouan, his default stock for most unrelated leftovers. Swadesh (1967b) suggested a connection between Keres and Caddo (actually Wichita), and

Rood clarified many of the compared forms, suggesting tentatively that the evidence "should go a long way toward proof of a Keres-Wichita relationship" (1973). Greenberg (1987:163) accepts a part of Sapir's proposal, lumping Keresan, Siouan, Yuchi, Caddoan, and Iroquoian into what he calls Keresiouan, part of his more far-flung Almosan-Keresiouan—where Almosan comprises (as in Sapir 1929a) Algic (Algonquian-Ritwan), Kutenai, and so-called Mosan (which includes Chemakuan, Wakashan, and Salish). Needless to say, these groupings are at best controversial and have been rejected by specialists in the field (see Davis 1979, Hale and Harris 1979:173; see also Chapter 8).

(37) **Kiowa-Tanoan**
(MAP 8; see also MAP 25)

See the classification list. The Tanoan groups inhabit many of the southwestern pueblos. Northern Tiwa is spoken at the pueblos of Taos and Picurís; those living in the pueblos of Isleta and Sandia speak Southern Tiwa. Tewa (essentially a single language of mutually intelligible, though divergent dialects) is (or was) spoken at San Juan, Santa Clara, San Ildefonso, Nambe, Pojoaque, and Tesuque in New Mexico, and at Hano on the Hopi reservation in Arizona. Towa is spoken in the Jemez Pueblo (Harrington 1909). Extinct Piro is poorly attested; most scholars accept that the lexical evidence shows it more closely related to Tiwa (Harrington 1909;

Kiowa-Tanoan

Kiowa *Oklahoma*
Tanoan[100]
  Tiwa *New Mexico*
    Northern Tiwa
      Taos[101]
      Picurís [obsolescent]
    Southern Tiwa
      Isleta
      Sandia
    †Piro
  Tewa[102] *New Mexico*
    Hopi Tewa
    Santa Clara–San Juan
  Towa (Jemez)[103] *New Mexico*

Keresan

Western Keresan
  Acoma
  Laguna
Eastern Keresan
  Zia–Santa Ana
  San Felipe–Santo Domingo
  Cochiti

cf. Davis 1959), and though Leap (1971) argued that it is not a Tanoan language, the evidence is more than sufficient to demonstrate its relationship to this family. Although extinct Pecos is often placed with Towa, the scant Pecos material remembered by descendants of Pecos at Jemez is not sufficiently clear to demonstrate a Towa identity, but Pecos is clearly a Tanoan language (see Hale and Harris 1979:171).

The Proto-Kiowa-Tanoan consonants are: /p, t, c, k, k^w, ʔ, p', t', c', k', (k$^{w'}$), p^h, t^h, c^h, k^h, k^{wh}, b , d, dz, (g), g^w, m, n, s, w, y, h/ (Hale 1967, Watkins 1978).

The unity of the Tanoan languages was recognized in the Powell (1891a) classification, and the classification into three branches was made by Harrington (1910b). The linguistic connection between Kiowa and Tanoan was first proposed by Harrington (1910b, 1928); it was accepted by Sapir (1929a) and has been confirmed by Hale (1962, 1967), Miller (1959), and Trager and Trager (1959).[104] Most specialists have thought, based on lexical evidence, that Kiowa separated from Tanoan at some time in the distant past and that the Tanoan languages diversified more recently, but there are two other views on the subject. One groups Kiowa and Towa (Jemez) in a Kiowa-Towa branch opposed to a Tewa-Tiwa branch; the other holds that the family diversified into four equally distinct branches simultaneously (Davis 1979:400–2). Irvine Davis sees all of these subgroupings as compatible with the available data. Laurel Watkins concluded that "it is difficult to point to any constellation of features that might indicate a particularly long period of separation [of Kiowa] from Tanoan before the Tanoan languages split from each other" (1984:2). Paul Kroskrity reports that the common view of the subgrouping (Kiowa versus Tanoan) is not supported by the grammatical and other evidence and that "a radical adaptive shift toward a Plains orientation on the part of the Kiowa might have produced linguistic consequences which give an unwarranted impression of great divergence." He recommends that "we abandon the notion of Kiowa divergence," though he recognizes that "the definitive comparative work remains to be done" (1993:56–7).

The glottochronological time depths have been calculated to be approximately 3,000 years for the separation of Kiowa from Tanoan and 2,000 or 2,500 years for the breakup of Tanoan (Hale and Harris 1979:171). While this reflects the original view that Kiowa is more divergent, it should be kept in mind that glottochronology is at best a rough gauge, rejected by most linguists. The Tanoan people are generally regarded as having been located in the San Juan basin during Basket-Maker times (A.D. 1–700 in some areas; A.D. 1–900 in others). Towa is associated with the Gallina culture and earlier with the Los Pinos Phase in the upper San Juan River area at about A.D. 1. The Tiwa developed in situ in the Rio Grande valley and presumably split from ancestral Tanoans of the San Juan area (between A.D. 500 and 700 ?). There is disagreement about the prehistory of the Tewa. Most scholars believe Mogollon culture should be identified with Tanoan linguistically (perhaps including also some Uto-Aztecan groups). Later Anasazi culture is also associated with Tanoans (as well as with speakers of Keresan, Hopi, and perhaps Zuni) (Hale and Harris 1979). The Kiowa homeland was apparently in the northern plains before their move into western Oklahoma. In early historical times they were located near the headwaters of the Missouri and Yellowstone Rivers (Davis 1979).

Kiowa-Tanoan and Uto-Aztecan are very frequently assumed to be related in the larger grouping called Aztec-Tanoan, proposed by Whorf and Trager (1937). This proposal (considered more fully in Chapter 8) is widely cited and often repeated, but its validity is doubtful.

(38) **Zuni** (older Zuñi)
New Mexico (Map 8)

Zuni[105] is an isolate. Sapir (1929a) had placed it tentatively in his Aztec-Tanoan phylum, but there is no real evidence of a relationship among these languages. Similarly, several scholars have placed Zuni with some version of Penutian, but again the evidence, although perhaps suggestive, is insufficient to support such a hypothesis (see Swadesh 1954b, 1956, 1967a, 1967b; Newman 1964). The Keresan-Zuni proposal is also unsupported (see Chapter 8).

(39) **Siouan** (Siouan-Catawban)[106]
(MAP 9; see also MAPS 25, 26, and 27)

Siouan languages are or were spoken in central and southeastern North America (see classification list). Catawban is the most divergent, though Frank Siebert (1945) demonstrated it to be definitely related to Siouan. The Catawba-Siouan grouping is now generally considered to be fully demonstrated, though as recently as the Voegelin and Voegelin classification (1967:577), Catawba was considered an "isolate" within the Macro-Siouan phylum, together with the Siouan family (minus Catawban), Iroquoian, Caddoan, and Yuchi, though the Voegelins reported that "Catawba is so closely related to the Siouan family that it has from time to time been regarded as a constituent language within this family rather than a language isolate within the Macro-Siouan phylum" (Voegelin and Voegelin 1967:577). That Catawba is connected with Siouan was first suggested by Lewis H. Morgan

(1870:54). Chamberlain (1888:3) also proposed that Catawba was Siouan, on the basis of a word list of seven probable cognates and about ten possible cognates from Catawba matched with resemblant forms in various Siouan languages (Siebert 1945:100); later Gatschet (1900a) independently confirmed this finding. The conclusive demonstration of the relationship is usually attributed to Siebert (1945), which is based largely on morphological evidence; in the beginning it was difficult to find enough clear cognates to work out the sound correspondences (see Wolff 1950–1951 and Siebert 1945; see also Gursky 1966a:406). Sturtevant (1958:740) reports that an unpublished manuscript in the Bureau of American Ethnology archives reveals that Dorsey had compared 116 Catawba words with forms from fifteen Siouan languages, finding 56 as cognate, 52 noncognate, and 18 doubtful. Of the 56 that he had marked as cognates, he considered 23 to be particularly close in form and meaning, though he did not attempt to estab-

---

Siouan (Siouan-Catawban)

Catawban *North and South Carolina*
   †Catawba
   †Woccon
(Core) Siouan
   Mississippi Valley–Ohio Valley Siouan
      Southeastern Siouan (Ohio Valley Siouan)
         Ofo-Biloxi
            †Ofo *Mississippi*
            †Biloxi *Mississippi*
         †Tutelo (Saponi, Occaneechi?) *Virginia*
      Mississippi Valley Siouan
         Dakota *North and South Dakota, Canadian Reserves* (Dialects: Santee, Yankton, Teton, Assiniboin, Stoney, etc.)
         Dhegihan[107]
            Omaha-Ponca (Dialects: Ponca [obsolescent]; Omaha)
            Kansa-Osage (Dialects: †Kansa, Osage [obsolescent])
            †Quapaw
         Chiwere-Winnebago
            Chiwere (Dialects: Iowa [Ioway], Oto [Otoe]; Oto [moribund]; †Missouri [Missouria])
            Winnebago[108] *Wisconsin*
   Missouri River Siouan
      Crow *Montana*
      Hidatsa *North Dakota*
   Mandan [moribund] *North Dakota*

Rood 1979, 1992b; Rankin 1993, personal communication.
Hollow and Parks's (1980:76) classification is slightly different.

lish sound correspondences. In any case, Catawba is much more distantly related to the other languages of the family than these languages are among themselves—that is, this constitutes a large language family with a related outlier branch which is very different. Some scholars prefer to call the family Catawba-Siouan or Siouan-Catawban (see, for example, Booker, Hudson, and Rankin 1992; Rankin, personal communication). Booker et al. put it this way: "Catawban as a family is distantly related to Siouan, but it is a mistake in modern nomenclature to call Catawba 'Siouan'. (It would be like calling Oscan and Umbrian 'Romance' . . .)" (1992:410).

A number of different languages and dialects once spoken in the Carolina Piedmont Region are often grouped as Catawban, though the evidence is mostly inconclusive and opinions vary greatly concerning them (Booker, Hudson, and Rankin. 1992:410). Only Catawba (with two dialects, Catawba proper and Iswą) and Woccon are attested linguistically. Woccon is one of several extinct languages of Virginia and the Carolinas; it is more closely related to Catawba, known only from a vocabulary of 143 items published in Lawson (1709) (cf. Carter 1980, Sturtevant 1958).[109] During colonial times the Catawba, together with the Cherokee, were the most important Indians of the Carolinas, but after smallpox epidemics (for example, in 1759 nearly half of the Catawba died of the disease) they ceased to play a prominent role in history. Later they were scattered—some settled near the Choctaw Nation, in Oklahoma, and some settled among the Cherokee; others remained on a small reservation near Rock Hill, South Carolina, where they are still, although their language is extinct. Booker et al. suggest that "Catawba grammar and vocabulary show evidence of language mixture" and that Catawba "may, in fact, be the descendant of a creolized language." They find this not at all surprising "given the number of different groups that ultimately united with the Catawbas" (1992:410).

The Ofo were reportedly located in or near southern Ohio before the 1670s, though this is controversial; they were first encountered by Europeans on the east bank of the Mississippi River below the mouth of the Ohio River, in 1673. However, by 1690, they had retreated to the Yazoo River in Mississippi, near the Yazoo and Tunica tribes. Record of them was lost for the period between 1784 and 1908; in 1908 John R. Swanton found a single surviving Ofo speaker living among the Tunica in Louisiana, from whom he obtained the extant linguistic material (see Haas 1969e, Swanton 1946:165–6). When first encountered by French and Spanish explorers, the Biloxi were located on the lower Pascagoula River and Biloxi Bay in Mississippi. They subsequently lived in several locations in Louisiana; some were removed to Texas and Oklahoma (Swanton 1946:96–8). Both Ofo and Biloxi are now extinct. Voegelin (1939) demonstrated that the two languages are fairly closely related. Tutelo was found near Salem, Virginia, in 1671. From here the Tutelo moved eastward and northward, and in 1714 they were settled with other tribes at Fort Christiana and on the Meherrin River. After peace was made between the Iroquois and the Virginia tribes in 1722, the Tutelo moved northward and settled before 1744 at Shamokin, Pennsylvania, under Iroquois protection. In 1753 they were formally adopted into the League of the Iroquois. In 1771 they settled near Cayuga Lake in New York State. They moved with the Cayuga to Canada after the American Revolution (see Swanton 1946:199).

Crow and Hidatsa are closely related and form a group distinct from the other Siouan languages. The Crow (earlier often called Upsaroka) have always, as far as is known, been located near the Yellowstone River in Montana. Their reservation is on the Big Horn River, a tributary of the Yellowstone. The Hidatsa were often called Minitari and are still frequently called Gros Ventre (not to be confused with Algonquian Atsina, also called Gros Ventre). They have always (according to current knowledge) been located in North Dakota along the Missouri River. In 1845 they moved to their present location in the Fort Berthold area. In historic times the Mandan lived in roughly the same area of North Dakota as the Hidatsa, and today they too live on the Fort Berthold Reservation.[110]

The group frequently called Chiwere comprises Iowa, Oto, and Missouri. Whether Winnebago also belongs to the Chiwere group is a matter of dispute. Winnebago is most closely related to that group but is a separate language. At one time Winnebago was called Hochangara. The Winnebago once lived south of Green Bay, Wisconsin, and some remain there; others (after many moves) eventually settled on a reservation in northeastern Nebraska. The Iowa occupied various places in the present state of Iowa and neighboring states. In 1836 they were given a reservation in Nebraska and Kansas; some of them later settled in Oklahoma. The Oto were first located near the confluence of the Platte and Missouri Rivers. For a time they lived in parts of Nebraska and Kansas, but they moved to Oklahoma in the 1880s. The Missouri, now extinct, were once located on the Missouri River near the Grand River in the state of Missouri. They were badly defeated by Sauk and Fox Indians at the end of the eighteenth century and suffered in a war with the Osage early in the nineteenth century. Thereafter they lived with the Oto, with whom they later moved to Oklahoma.

At the time of the earliest European contact, the Dhegiha were in the central plains, though tradition locates them at an earlier time farther east, near the junction of the Wabash and Ohio Rivers. The Omaha and Ponca were on the Missouri River in northeastern Nebraska, the Kansa on the Kansas River in the present state of Kansas, the Osage on the Osage River in Missouri, and the Quapaw near the junction of the Arkansas and Mississippi Rivers. The Omaha still live in Nebraska, as do some of the Ponca, but most Ponca have been in Oklahoma since 1873. The Osage were located mainly in Kansas during most of the nineteenth century, but in the 1870s they were established on a reservation in Oklahoma. The Quapaw occupied places in Arkansas, Kansas, and Oklahoma, and lived briefly in northern Louisiana until 1867, when they were confined to a small area in northeastern Oklahoma.

Europeans first encountered Dakota in the general area of the upper Mississippi River. Dakota dialects are variously called Santee, Yankton, Yanktonai(s), Teton (also called Lakhota), Assiniboine, and Stoney (Rood 1979, Chafe 1973).

There were other Siouan languages in Virginia and the Carolinas at the time of first European contact, but we know practically nothing about them. They included Woccon (Catawban) and three languages that were genuinely Siouan but perhaps more closely related to Tutelo: Saponi, Occaneechee, and Moniton.[111]

Proto-Siouan phonemes are: /p, t, k, ?, pʰ, tʰ, kʰ, p', t', k', s, š, x, s', ṣ̌, x̣, w, r, y, h, W, R; i, e, a, o, u; į, ą, ų; vowel length; pitch accent generally, but not always, on second syllable/ (Rood 1979; Rankin personal communication). Siouanists hope to be able to merge *W with *w and *R with *r, and thus to be able to eliminate *W and *R from the inventory, though at present it is not possible to do this. In the past, the aspirated and glottalized stop series were often treated as clusters of stop + h and stop + ?, but because this is not consistent with their analysis in any extant Siouan language, these series are a truer reflection of the languages (Rood 1979:279; Robert Rankin, personal communication).

Rankin (1993) dates the earliest internal Core Siouan split at approximately 3000 B.P. (or 1000 B.C.) and the Catawban split from Siouan at probably 1,000 years earlier.

For a detailed evaluation of the proposed broader grouping of Siouan with Caddoan and Iroquoian, see Chapter 8.

(40) Caddoan
(MAP 25)

See the classification list. The Caddoan languages were spoken in the heart of the Great Plains, from South Dakota to northeastern Texas and eastward in Arkansas and northwestern Louisiana (Chafe 1979:213). Of the languages of the family, Caddo is the most divergent and

Caddoan

Caddo *Oklahoma*
Northern Caddoan
    Wichita [obsolescent] *Oklahoma*
    Kitsai-Proto-Pawnee
      †Kitsai *Oklahoma*
    Proto-Pawnee
      Arikara *North Dakota*
      Pawnee *Oklahoma* (Dialects: South Band, Skiri)

    Hollow and Parks 1980:77; cf. Chafe 1979; Taylor 1963a, 1963b.

structurally the most different. It has glottalized consonants and *m,* which are not found in the other languages. Arikara and Pawnee are closely related; Pawnee has two distinct but similar dialects: South Band and Skiri. Tawakaru and Weku are associated with Wichita, while Hainai is linked with Caddo (Taylor 1963b:113). While expressing little faith in the results of their glottochronological studies, Hollow and Parks (1980:80) present Park's results for Northern Caddoan in terms of millennia of separation: Arikara-Wichita, 2; Kitsai-Wichita, 1.95; Pawnee-Wichita, 1.9; Arikara-Kitsai, 1.2; Pawnee-Kitsai, 1.2; and Pawnee-Arikara, 0.3.

The Proto-Caddoan phonemic inventory is: /p, t, c, k, (kw), ?, s, h, r, n, w, y; i, a, u/ (Chafe 1979:218–19; cf. Taylor 1963a). (For information on Proto-Caddoan morphology, see Chafe 1979:226–32.)

Proposals of a kinship of Caddoan with other families have tended to involve Iroquoian and Siouan, as discussed in detail in Chapter 8. The general conclusion is that these hypotheses are not supported.

(41) †Adai (Adaize)

Adai[112] is extinct and very poorly documented (see Sibley 1832). It has often been placed with Caddoan in classifications (Swanton 1946:83–4; Taylor 1963a, 1963b), though the available data are so scant that accurate classification would seem to be impossible.[113] Adai was first discovered by Europeans near Robeline, Louisiana. There were Adai Indians at the Mission of San Francisco de las Tejas, the first mission in eastern Texas, founded in 1690. Reports indicate that by 1778 the tribe was almost extinct; they were last reported in 1805 in a small settlement on Lake Macdon (Swanton 1917).

(42) †Tonkawa
Texas (MAP 25)

The Tonkawa were first mentioned in 1719; the earliest data are from 1828 to 1829, but it is not known where they were recorded. In 1872 the tribe was at Fort Griffin, Texas. Many bands (for example, Yojuane, Mayeye, Ervipiame, and Méye) are associated with the Tonkawa, but their identifications, based on historical sources, are very tentative (Goddard 1979b:358–9, Hoijer 1933:ix–x, 1946b). Ives Goddard argues that extensive taboo replacement of names and of words similar to names of the dead resulted in much change in the vocabulary of Tonkawa between older and later attestations.

Proposals of genetic relationship would place Tonkawa variously in the Coahuiltecan and Algonquian-Gulf hypotheses, but these placements do not hold up under scrutiny (see Chapter 8). At present, Tonkawa is best considered unrelated to other families.

(43) †Karankawa (Clamcoches)
Texas (MAPS 2c and 25)

Groups collectively called the Karankawa lived on the Texas coast from Galveston Bay to Corpus Christi Bay; they were not a homogeneous group politically and perhaps not even culturally. The language has long been extinct. Information on these groups is limited, extremely so in some cases, and it comes from Spanish, French, and American explorers, castaways, missionaries, and soldiers who came into contact with them, including Álvar Núñez Cabeza de Vaca, Robert Cavelier de La Salle, and Jean Laffite (the buccaneer). The earliest Karankawa linguistic data (twenty-nine words) were provided in 1698 by Jean-Baptiste Talon, a survivor of La Salle's expedition who had been captured by "Clamcoëh" (Karankawa) Indians living near Matagorda Bay in Texas (Troike 1987). Curiously, the most extensive vocabulary was obtained by Gatschet from Alice W. Oliver, a white woman in Massachusetts who had spent her childhood on the Texas coast in the neighborhood of the last Karankawa speaking band. Gatschet also obtained a few Karankawa forms from two Tonkawa speakers who had learned some of the language. A list of 106 words was provided in 1720 by Jean Béranger, a French sea captain sent to explore the Gulf coast (see Villiers du Terrage and Rivet 1919), and another list was given by Jean Louis Berlandier in 1828 (see Goddard 1979b, Newcomb 1983).

Proposals of distant genetic relationship have frequently placed Karankawa with the so-called Coahuiltecan languages; this hypothesis does not hold up (see Goddard 1979b, Swanton 1940, Troike 1987). (See Chapter 8 for discussion of this and other proposals concerning Karan-kawa.)

(44) **Coahuilteco** (Pajalate)
Texas, northeast Mexico (MAP 12)

Coahuilteco was spoken in the area between the Guadalupe River east of San Antonio and the middle course of the lower Rio Grande near Laredo, principally in Texas, extending slightly into present-day Mexico. The name Coahuilteco, given by Orozco y Berra (1864:63), reflects the earlier extension of the Mexican state of Coahuila into what is now Texas. The language is also sometimes called Pajalate (the name of one of the bands who spoke it). Identification of who spoke Coahuilteco is a difficult matter. Southern Texas and northeastern Mexico had literally hundreds of small hunting and gathering groups or bands identified by various names in Spanish colonial reports: "For this region and various areas immediately adjacent to it scholars have encountered over 1,000 ethnic group names in documents that cover a period of approximately 350 years" (T. Campbell 1983:347). Since there is no linguistic information on most of them, it is extremely difficult to determine which spoke Coahuilteco and which spoke the various other languages of the region known to have existed then. "This inability to identify all the named Indian groups who originally spoke Coahuilteco has been a perennial stumbling-block in efforts to distinguish them from their neighbors" (T. Campbell 1983:343). Some of the many bands which appear to have been Coahuilteco-speaking were Pacoas, Tilijayas, Pausanes, Pacuaches, Mescales, Pampopas, Tacames, and Venados. Extant materials indicate different dialects for those of San Antonio, Rio Grande, and the Pajalates of the Purísima Concepción mission. (T. Campbell 1983; Goddard 1979b; Swadesh 1959, 1963a; Swanton 1940:5; Troike 1967:82). (For proposals of genetic relationship, see below.)

(45) **†Cotoname** (Carrizo de Camargo)[114]
northeast Mexico

Cotoname was spoken in the Rio Grande delta area and is known only from Berlandier's 104-word vocabulary, called "Carrizo de Camargo" (cf. Berlandier and Chowell 1828–1829), and

Gatschet's 1886 notes taken in part from a native speaker of Comecrudo (Swanton 1940:5, 118–21; Goddard 1979b:370).

(46) **†Aranama-Tamique** (Jaranames)
Texas

Aranama is known only from a two-word phrase given to Gatschet in 1884 by a Tonkawa speaker, who also provided some of Gatschet's Karankawa material. He called the language Hanáma or Hanáme; other Tonkawas called it ⟨Chaimamé⟩ (where ⟨Ch⟩ was said to represent Spanish ⟨j⟩, or, phonetically, [x]); other known variants of its names are Charinames, Xaranames, and Taranames. The Tamique spoke the same language; the Espíritu Santo de Zúñiga mission was founded for these two groups in 1754, in their territory on the lower Guadalupe River in Texas. The language remains unclassified genetically (Goddard 1979b:372–3).

(47) **†Solano**
northeast Mexico

A twenty-one-word vocabulary list of Solano was found at the end of the book of baptisms from the San Francisco Solano mission dated 1703–1708; it is presumed to be of the Indians of that mission. Goddard (1979b:372) reports that Bolton thought it represented the language of the "Terocodame band cluster," associated with the eighteenth-century missions opposite what is today Eagle Pass, Texas. Solano is also genetically unclassified (see Swanton 1915:34–5, 1940:54–5; Goddard 1979b:371–2).

(48) **Comecrudan**
northeast Mexico

Goddard (1979b) has presented evidence that Comecrudo, Mamulique, and Garza, three little-known or unknown languages of the lower Rio Grande area of northeast Mexico, belong to a single family, Comecrudan.

†**Comecrudo** (Mulato, Carrizo)[115] *Tamaulipas, Mexico* (MAP 12).   The remnants of the Comecrudo were at Las Prietas near Camargo, Tamaulipas when Gatschet obtained his vocabulary in 1886 (Swanton 1940:55–118). Berlandier col-

lected a 148-word Comecrudo vocabulary in 1829 near Reynosa, Tamaulipas, and called the language "Mulato." Adolf Uhde (1861:185–6) also obtained Comecrudo data but called the language "Carrizo," the language of the lower Rio Grande (see Goddard 1979b:369–70).

†**Mamulique** (Carrizo) *northeast Mexico.* Mamulique (Carrizo de Mamulique) is known only from a twenty-two-word list given by Berlandier. It was spoken near Mamulique, Nuevo Léon, between Salinas Victoria and Palo Blanco, south of Villaldama (Goddard 1979b:370–71).

†**Garza**[116] *Lower Rio Grande.* The only record of Garza is Berlandier's twenty-one-word vocabulary list. In 1828 speakers of this languge lived at Mier on the lower Rio Grande. In a 1748 manuscript they were called *Atanaguayacam* (in Comecrudo); in Cotoname they were called *Meack(n)an* or *Miákan* (Goddard 1979b:371).

Recognition of the Comecrudan family is important, since the former common assumption of a large Coahuiltecan group containing these and various other languages has now largely been abandoned (see Chapter 8).

Tonkawa, Karankawa, Coahuilteco, Cotoname, Aranama-Tamique, Solano, and Comecrudan were assumed to belong to some larger grouping, usually called Coahuiltecan. The Coahuiltecan hypothesis began with Orozco y Berra's map (1864) and continued through differing interpretations to the present. The minimum grouping has assumed a relationship between only Comecrudo and Cotoname; the most common version of the hypothesis places Coahuilteco with these two; the maximum grouping has included these three plus Tonkawa, Karankawa, Atakapa, and Maratino, with the assumption that Aranama and Solano were varieties of Coahuilteco. Sapir's (1929a) Hokan-Coahuiltecan stock is perhaps best known; he grouped Tonkawa and Karankawa with Coahuilteco, Comecrudo, and Cotoname, proposing a relationship between these collectively and Hokan within his broader Hokan-Siouan super stock.

Goddard's (1979b) reexamination, especially in light of the Berlandier materials, indicates that none of these hypotheses has linguistic support. Even the minimum grouping of Comecrudo and

Cotoname dissolves. The recently investigated Berlandier Cotoname material shows many differences between the two languages where Gatschet's information shows similarities. Though the traditional groupings must be set aside, the Comecrudan relationship, which includes Comecrudo, Garza, and Mamulique, is now recognized (Goddard 1979b; see T. Campbell 1983:343). Manaster Ramer (1996) recently has presented evidence suggestive of what he calls the Pakawan family, a grouping of Coahuilteco, Cotoname, Comecrudo, Garza, and Mamulique. This is evaluated in Chapter 8.

There was apparently considerable multilingualism in the area where these languages were spoken. As mentioned, one of Gatschet's Cotoname informants was a Comecrudo speaker; Tonkawa speakers provided Karankawa vocabularies and the only recorded phrase of Aranama; and Mamulique women were said not to speak "their native language." Coahuilteco was a lingua franca in the area around Monterrey (Troike 1967, Goddard 1979b); it was a second language at least for the Orejones, Pamaques, Alazapas, and Borrados. According to García (1760), all the young people of the Pihuiques, Sanipaos, and Manos de Perro spoke Coahuilteco, which suggests that it was a second language for these groups.

There was a fully developed sign language in the lower Rio Grande area, reported in 1688, 1740, 1805, and 1828. This may have been the ancestor of the Plains sign language of the nineteenth century. Its existence highlights the linguistic diversity in the area and the communication among unrelated languages (see Goddard l979b, Wurtzburg and Campbell 1995).

(49) †**Atakapan**
Louisiana, Texas (MAP 27)

See the classification list. Atakapa(n), now extinct, was spoken from Vermilion Bay and the lower course of Bayou Teche, in Louisiana, to

---

†Atakapan

Akokisa
Western Atakapa
Eastern Atakapa

Galveston Bay and the Trinity River, in Texas. *Atakapa* is a Choctaw name meaning 'people eater' (*hattak* 'person' + *apa* 'to eat') (cf. Booker 1980:7), a reference to the cannibalism that Gulf coast tribes practiced on their enemies. The early Spanish name for the Western group was Horcoquisa or Orcoquisac, which appears to be similar to Akokisa, the name applied to a Louisiana group that was a different dialect or perhaps a closely related language (where the *isa* or *isac* portion may be derived from Atakapa *išak* 'people') (Gatschet and Swanton 1932:1). The Béranger vocabulary of Akokisa, all that is known of this language, was incorporated into Gatschet and Swanton's Atakapa dictionary (1932). Atakapa and Akokisa "embraced four or five principal bands—on Vermilion Bayou, Mermentau, Calcasieu, the Sabine and Neches, and Trinity Rivers" (Gatschet and Swanton 1932:2). Swanton suggested that the Han of Núñez Cabeza de Vaca's account, found on the east end of Galveston Island in 1528, were probably Atakapan, where Han may be derived from the Atakapa word *añ* or *ã* (/aŋ/?) 'house' (Gatschet and Swanton 1932:2, Swanton 1946:85). Morris Swadesh (1946, also Kimball 1993) classified Atakapan as a family consisting of three languages—Akokisa, Western Atakapa, and Eastern Atakapa—perhaps based on Swanton's discussion of Eastern and Western groups of Atakapa bands (1946:93–4), which was apparently not a linguistic classification. Other scholars usually mention only two languages, with some question whether even they are actually distinct languages or are merely dialects. In any event, the Atakapan varieties are quite closely related.

Swanton (1915) noted that Karankawa (part of his proposed Coahuiltecan stock) resembled Atakapa; however, he later argued that Atakapa, Chitimacha, and Tunica were genetically related in a stock he called Tunican (Swanton 1919). Sapir (1920) included Atakapa in his Coahuiltecan family, but he later omitted Atakapa from Coahuiltecan and instead placed it with Tunica and Chitimacha (as in Swanton's Tunican) in a separate division of his Hokan-Siouan grouping (1929a). Swadesh (1946, 1947) accepted Swanton's Tunican but compared only Atakapa and Chitimacha because of the availability of infor-

mation on these two. Several other broader proposals also include Atakapa (for example, Haas's Gulf proposal), but all of these suggested broader affiliations remain doubtful (see Haas 1979, Swanton 1919, Gatschet and Swanton 1932, Troike 1963).

(50) †Chitimacha
Louisiana (MAP 27)

The Chitimacha were living along Bayou La Fourche and on the west side of the Mississippi River below present Baton Rouge in southern Louisiana when first encountered by the French in the late seventeenth century. Chitimacha is an isolate. The Washa and Chawasha groups, historically known but linguistically unattested, are generally assumed to have spoken Chitimacha or something closely related to it (Swanton 1917). Chitimacha has also been implicated in Tunican, Gulf, and other broader proposals (see Chapter 8), but most specialists today have abandoned these; some scholars hold out for the possibility of a relationship between Chitimacha and Atakapan (Swadesh 1946, 1947), but I find this also very doubtful based on the evidence presented so far (see Chapter 8).

(51) †Tunica
Louisiana (MAP 27)

The Tunica were found in 1682 along the Yazoo River, in Mississippi, where they were known for trading salt. In 1706, fearing attack from the Chickasaw and other Indians leagued with the English (who were engaged in procuring Indian slaves for British colonies), the Tunica moved to the mouth of the Red River in Louisiana, where it empties into the Mississippi. Some time between 1784 and 1803 they abandoned their homes on the Mississippi River and moved up the Red River to Marksville, Louisiana, where they remain. The language is extinct.

As mentioned, Swanton (1919) believed Tunica to be related to Chitimacha and Atakapa in his Tunican stock, and Sapir (1929a) incorporated Swanton's proposed Tunican languages in his Hokan-Siouan super-stock. Haas (1951, 1952, 1958b) grouped these and other southeastern languages in her "Gulf" classification. None of these proposals is upheld today (see Chapter 8); Tunica is an isolate (see Haas 1979, Swanton 1919).

(52) †Natchez
Louisiana, Mississippi (MAP 27)

The Natchez were a strong and important group that lived in scattered villages along St. Catherine's Creek, east of present-day Natchez, Mississippi. The early 1700s saw the French involved in several missionizing attempts and several Indian attacks, which culminated in 1731 with the surrender of about 400 Natchez who were sent to the West Indies as slaves; the others scattered throughout the lowlands of the Mississippi. Gradually, some withdrew among the Chickasaw, and others settled among the Upper Creeks. One band reached South Carolina and ultimately united with the Cherokee. The language became extinct in the 1930s.

Attempts to relate Natchez to other languages have been unpersuasive. Swanton (1924) believed it to be related to Muskogean, an opinion shared by Mary Haas (1956) and Kimball (1994). Sapir (1929a) included Natchez and Muskogean in the Eastern division of his Hokan-Siouan. Haas (1951, 1952, 1958b) combined Swanton's Natchez-Muskogean and Tunican (Tunica, Atakapa, Chitimacha) in her Gulf grouping. Today none of these proposals is accepted uncritically, and Natchez is considered an isolate with no known relatives, although the possibility of a connection with Muskogean deserves further study (see Haas 1979; Swanton 1917, 1919; Kimball 1994).

(53) Muskogean
(MAP 27)

There are competing classifications for Muskogean, and the issue of Muskogean subgrouping "will not be easily solved" (Booker 1988:384). Karen Booker and several others favor a scheme like that of Haas (1949, 1979). Booker (1988, 1993) discussed phonological innovations shared by Creek and Seminole, and others shared by Alabama-Koasati and Hitchiti-Mikasuki, which are supportive of Haas's (1949, 1979) view of the subgrouping; see the classification list.

Muskogean (according to Haas)
Western Muskogean *Mississippi, Oklahoma, Louisiana*
    Choctaw
    Chickasaw
Eastern Muskogean
    Central Muskogean
        Apalachee-Alabama-Koasati
            †Apalachee *Florida, Georgia*
            Alabama-Koasati
                Alabama *Texas*
                Koasati *Louisiana, Texas*
        Hitchiti-Mikasuki
            †Hitchiti
            Mikasuki *Florida*
    Creek-Seminole
        Creek *Eastern Oklahoma*
        Seminole[117] *Oklahoma, Florida*[118]

Booker 1988, 1993; see Haas 1949, 1979.

Munro doubts the validity of the Haas-Booker subgrouping: "It is not clear whether the Eastern languages—despite their great number of similar sound correspondences—actually share any innovations. . . . The sibilant correspondences are much more complex than Haas (1941) implies, and the confusion among the protosibilants may have arisen because of sound-symbolic alternations like those discussed by Rankin 1987 [1986a])" (Munro 1993:394; see also Munro 1987a:3). Munro's subgrouping of the family (similar to that of Swanton 1917, 1924)—the more controversial of the two competitors—is based on shared lexical and morphological traits (some of them retentions), and it accommodates the sound changes in which Proto-Muskogean *k^w became *p/k* in Creek-Seminole, but became *b* in the other languages (see below). In particular, Munro lists several of what she takes to be morphological innovations shared by Southwestern Muskogean languages, a subgroup not recognized in Haas's and Booker's classifications. She pays particular attention to pronominals (1993:395–6).[119] See the classification list.

Before considering some of the reasons for the disagreements concerning this subgrouping, it will be helpful to look at the phonemic inventory of Proto-Muskogean and some of the sound correspondences. The proto sounds are: /p, t, c,

Muskogean (according to Munro)

Northern
    Creek
    Seminole
Southern
    Hitchiti-Mikasuki
        Hitchiti
        Mikasuki
    Southwestern
        Apalachee-Alabama-Koasati-Western
            Apalachee
            Alabama-Koasati
                Alabama
                Koasati
            Western
                Choctaw
                Chickasaw

Munro 1993:397; cf. Munro 1987a:5,
Broadwell 1991:270, Martin 1994.

č, k, k^w, f [or x^w], θ, s, š, h [or x], l, ɬ, m, n, w, y; i, a, o; vowel length/ (Booker 1980:17, cf. Haas 1941). Some of the correspondence sets upon which these reconstructed sounds are based are:

*θ (or *N)	WM *n* : EM ɬ
*c	WM *s* : EM *č*
*s	WM *š* : EM *s*
*š	WM *š* : EM *č*
*k^w	Creek *k* : others *b*
	(Booker 1980:17)

Note: WM = Western Muskogean, EM = Eastern Muskogean.

Haas's most recent reconstruction for the sound in the first set was *N, based on an assumed correspondence of WM *n* and EM ɬ with Natchez N (voiceless *n*).

Concerning the subgrouping controversy, Haas is of the opinion that "the problem is in part genetic and in part areal or diffusional" (1979:306); she saw changes involving all the languages except Creek as diffused areally among her Eastern and Western languages. Booker also indicates (following Haas) that some of the sound changes just listed seem to crosscut subgrouping lines and may be the result of " 'areal' or 'diffusional' phenomena in which overlapping isoglosses cloud the genetic picture" (1988:384). Muskogean subgrouping is made

difficult by such areal diffusion. As T. Dale Nicklas puts it:

> The entire Muskogean area has the appearance of a former continuous dialect area, with isoglosses running in several directions, which has been broken up into discrete languages by the loss of intermediate dialects. It has been argued that there are two extreme types, Choctaw to the west and Creek to the east, with the other languages in the middle being influenced now from the east, now from the west. (1994:15–16)

Hitchiti-Mikasuki shows strong influence from Creek. As Booker shows, the reflexes of Proto-Muskogean *k^w are not as straightforward as had been thought; among its various reflexes are *k* initially and *p* intervocalically of Creek-Seminole, which correspond to *b* of the other languages. Her classification reflects well the facts that Choctaw-Chickasaw *š* corresponds to *č* in the other languages, and Choctaw-Chickasaw *n* corresponds to others' ɬ; she presents a number of other convincing shared innovations, all of which favor this classification (see Booker 1993:414).

Nicklas (1994:16) locates the Proto-Muskogean homeland in the middle Mississippi region, from whence there was an eastward movement to a new homeland in eastern Mississippi and western Alabama, with subsequent expansion of Choctaw to the west and south, and of Creek and Apalachee to the east and south. Most of the Muskogean groups were forced to move west of the Mississippi River during the great Indian removal of 1836–1840, many to Oklahoma. The Mikasuki/Seminole tribal names and language names do not match exactly, which is a source of confusion. Mikasuki speakers were found among the various southeastern tribes after their resettlement in Indian Territory (Oklahoma), but few, if any, are to be found there today. The majority of the "Seminoles" of Florida, however, do speak Mikasuki, and a small number of them speak Seminole (Florida Seminole, a dialect of Creek) (Karen Booker, personal communication). In the sixteenth century, the Alabama (Alibamu) were located near present-day Starkville, Mississippi, and were tributaries of the Chickasaw. Koasati was probably the northernmost Muskogean language; it was located in northern Alabama in the eighteenth century, but in the sixteenth century it was spoken as far north as eastern Tennessee (Booker, Hudson, and Rankin 1992:411). It moved into Louisiana in the 1700s and is now centered on the Coushatta Reservation at Elton, Louisiana, and the Alabama-Coushatta Reservation in southeastern Texas.

Choctaw and Chickasaw appear to be subvarieties of the same language, but are politically distinct, though some scholars consider them to be distinct languages—this is the minority view (cf. Munro 1987b, Martin 1994). Alabama (Alibamu) and Koasati were probably still mutually intelligible in the sixteenth century (Booker, Hudson, and Rankin 1992:411). The only data on Apalachee are from a letter written in Spanish and Apalachee to King Charles II of Spain in 1688. The language has long been extinct. The Apalachee tribe was first encountered by the Spanish in 1528 between the Aucilla and Apalachicola Rivers in Florida. Haas (1949) and Kimball (1987a) have determined that Apalachee belongs together with the Alabama-Koasati in a subdivision of Muskogean. Broadwell (1991) has argued that two extinct languages, Guale and Yamasee, both once spoken in South Carolina and Georgia, are previously undetected Muskogean languages, belonging to the Northern branch of the family. However, Sturtevant (1994) shows that the forms Broadwell cited are in fact from Creek and not from Yamasee or Guale. Since the language(s) of the Yamasee and Guale, groups known from early historical records, remain unattested, it is best at present to leave them unclassified.

Broader connections of Muskogean with other language groups of the Southeast have been proposed, but none is supported by solid evidence. Haas's (1951, 1952) Gulf classification is widely known, although she largely abandoned the proposal later (Haas, personal communication, cf. Haas 1979). (Munro [1994] defends the proposal, but her evidence is weak; see Chapter 8.) The proposed Gulf would have connected Muskogean and Natchez, on the one hand, with Tunica, Atakapa, and Chitimacha on the other (Haas 1979, Kimball 1994, Swanton 1917). The possible connection between Natchez

and Muskogean deserves investigation (Haas 1956, Kimball 1994) (see Chapter 8).

(54) †Timucua
Florida (MAP 27)

Timucua (extinct) was spoken in northern Florida, from around Tallahassee to St. John's River near Jacksonville, and southward to Cape Canaveral on the Atlantic and Tampa Bay on the Gulf of Mexico (Swanton 1946:190–91; cf. Granberry 1990). It is said to have had from six to eleven dialects; Granberry (1990:61) lists Timucua proper, Potano, Itafi, Yufera, Mocama, Tucururu, Agua Fresca, Agua Salada, Acuera, Oconi, and Tawasa. A short Tawasa vocabulary from 1797 exists; most of the other extant Timucua materials represent the Mocama and Potano dialects.[120] The best known material is from Fray Francisco Pareja (1614; Pareja's various works constitute more than 2,000 pages of Timucua text [Granberry 1990:61]).

Many broader relationships, all unsuccessful, have been proposed for Timucua. Adelung and Vater (1816:285) noted a resemblance to Illinois (an Algonquian language). Brinton (1859:12) at first had expected Timucua eventually to prove to be related to Cariban languagues. Sapir (1929a) placed Timucua tentatively in his Hokan-Siouan phylum, for no apparent reason. Swadesh (1964b:548) compared Timucua with Arawakan. Crawford (1988) presented twenty-three lexical and morphological similarities shared by Muskogean and Timucua; he viewed eight as probable borrowings and the rest as possible cognates. Granberry claimed to have found a connection with Warao (an unaffiliated language of Venezuela and Guyana), but he also sees "cognates" with "Proto-Arawak, Proto-Gulf, Proto-Muskogean, and late Muskogean" (1970:607, quoted in Crawford 1988:157). Later, Granberry claimed that Timucua was a "creolized system," which he thought was probably the "reason that attempts to find *the* source of Timucua linguistically have been fruitless. . . . The language has no single provenience" (1991:204). He believes the basic patterns of Timucua grammar have the closest similarities to Warao and to Cuna, but he presents as evidence of multiple lexical sources similarities in lexical items from Warao, Chibchan, Paezan, Arawakan, Tucanoan, and other (mostly Amazonian) languages; he opts for a "Chibchan-related ultimate origin for the language" (1991:235). This is in no way convincing, however. The creole hypothesis will require more than lists of typical inspectional resemblances involving a variety of languages (see Chapter 7). Greenberg (1987) places Timucua in his vast Chibchan-Paezan grouping. Connections have also been suggested with Cherokee (Iroquoian) and Siouan. All of these proposals are highly doubtful. Timucua at present has no demonstrated affiliations (see Crawford 1979).

(55) **Yuchi** [obsolescent]
Georgia, Oklahoma (MAP 27)

Yuchi is an isolate. In the sixteenth century the Yuchis appear to have been located west of the Appalachians in eastern Tennessee (Booker, Hudson, and Rankin 1992:411). The Yuchi moved from Georgia to their present location near Sapulpa, Oklahoma, during the great Indian removal of 1836–1840. There were approximately 500 Yuchi in 1972, but only about 35 of them spoke the language with any fluency (Crawford 1973:173). Many relationships have been proposed which would combine Yuchi with other languages, but none has any significant support. Sapir (1921a, 1929a) placed it in his Hokan-Siouan phylum, closer to Siouan (see also Haas 1964a). Elmendorf (1963) had tried to link Yuchi and Yukian (of California), part of a broader assumed Siouan connection, but his evidence is unconvincing. Crawford felt that it looked "promising that a genetic relationship can eventually be shown to exist between Yuchi and Siouan" (1973:173), but he also presented similarities shared by Yuchi, Tunica, and Atakapa (1979). These various proposals require further investigation (see Chapter 8).

(56) **Iroquoian**
(MAPS 10 and 26)

See the classification list. An Iroquoian language was probably the first Native American language recorded by Europeans in North America. What is known of Laurentian was taken down on Cartier's voyages (1534, 1535–1536, 1541–1542) near what is today the city of Quebec (see below). When Europeans first came to North America, Iroquoian peoples were found from Quebec to Georgia, and from the coasts of Virginia and Carolina to Ohio, Pennsylvania, and Ontario.

Chafe and Foster (1981) give a somewhat different picture of Northern Iroquoian: a branch consisting of Tuscarora and Cayuga split off from the others first, but these two separated quite early, and Cayuga later underwent change as a result of frequent contact with other languages, especially Seneca. Huron next split from the remaining languages, and the others later split into three branches—Seneca, Onondaga (which later was influenced by Seneca), and Oneida-Mohawk. Oneida and Mohawk were the last to separate.

The phonemes of Proto-Northern-Iroquoian were: /t, c, k, kʷ, s, n, r, w, y, h, ʔ; i, e, a, o; ę, ǫ/ (Mithun 1979:162). Full reconstructions of Proto-Iroquoian phonology have not been published, though it is possible to extract from Floyd Lounsbury's (1978) discussion the following probable inventory of Proto-Iroquoian sounds (the vowels here are less certain): /t, k, ʔ, s, h, r, n, w, y; i, e, a, o, u ə/. The family split up, according to Mithun (1981:4), about 4,000 years ago (see Lounsbury 1978:334). Cherokee is the most divergent branch. During the seventeenth century, the Cherokees inhabited the southern Appalachian region of Tennessee, North Carolina, Virginia, South Carolina, Georgia, and Alabama. In 1838–1839, they were forced to march to Oklahoma, but many hid in the North Carolina mountains until 1849, when they were allowed to settle on land bought there on their behalf. The Tuscaroras, at the time of first European contact, were in eastern North Carolina, but they moved northward in the eighteenth century and were adopted into the League of the Iroquois in about 1723. Nottaway (extinct and known only from word lists recorded early in the nineteenth century) and Tuscarora are closely related in a subbranch of Northern Iroquoian. Senecas were first encountered by Europeans between Seneca Lake and the Genesee River in New York State. During the seventeenth century, they moved toward Lake Erie, and after the American Revolution, some moved to the Six Nations Reserve. Cayugas were first encoun-

Iroquoian

Cherokee (Southern Iroquoian) *Oklahoma, North Carolina* (Dialects: Elati, Kituhwa, Otali)
Northern Iroquoian
    Tuscarora-Nottaway[121]
        Tuscarora [obsolescent] *New York, Ontario*
        †Nottaway-Meherrin[122] *Virginia, North Carolina*
    Five Nations–Huronian–Susquehannock
        Huronian[123] (Huron-Tionnotati)
            Huron-Petun
                †Petun (?)
                †Wyandot[124] *Ontario, Quebec, Oklahoma*
            †Neutral *north of Lake Erie (?)*
        †Laurentian *Quebec*
        Five Nations-Susquehannok
            Seneca *New York, Ontario*
            Cayuga[125] *Ontario, Oklahoma*
            Onondaga[126] [obsolescent] *New York, Ontario*
            †Susquehannock[127] *Pennsylvania*
            Mohawk-Oneida
                Mohawk[128] *Ontario, Quebec, New York*
                Oneida[129] *New York, Wisconsin, Ontario*
Plus: †Wenro (east of Lake Erie) and †Erie (southeast of Lake Erie), whose position in Iroquoian sub-
    grouping is uncertain.

Lounsbury 1978; Mithun 1979, 1981.

---

tered on the shores of Cayuga Lake in New York State; after the revolution, most of them moved to the Six Nations Reserve. Onondagas were in New York State when Europeans first arrived, and many still live there; after the revolution a number moved to Ontario. The original home of the Oneidas was south of Oneida Lake, in New York State. After the revolution, many went to the Six Nations Reserve in Ontario. In 1846 a group of Oneida left New York for Wisconsin, where their descendants still live. Mohawks were first encountered by Champlain in 1609 in the Mohawk River Valley. Around 1670 many migrated north, settling near Montreal. Most who stayed in the Mohawk Valley sided with the British during the American Revolution, and afterward were moved to the Six Nations Reserve.

Laurentian (also called St. Lawrence Iroquois, Kwedech, Hochelaagan, and Stadaconan) was first recorded when Jacques Cartier sailed into the Gaspé Bay in 1534; 58 words of the language are given in his account of the first voyage, and another 170 appear in a list appended to the account of the second voyage. In the interval between Cartier's last voyage (1542)

and Champlain's visit to this area (1603), the Laurentians vanished. The position of Laurentian within the Iroquoian family has not been settled because of the limited material available and the difficulty of interpreting the orthography. The issue of whether Cartier's Laurentian material represents a single Iroquoian language or was obtained from speakers of more than one Iroquoian language also remains unsettled (see Lounsbury 1978:335). Extinct Susquehannock (also called Andaste, Minqua, Conestoga) belongs with the Five Nations languages (Mohawk, Oneida, Onondaga, Seneca, and Cayuga). (See Mithun 1981 for details concerning this interesting language and its identification from historical records.)

As for a postulated Proto-Iroquoian homeland, Lounsbury (1978:336) proposes much of New York State, central and northwestern Pennsylvania, and perhaps northeastern Ohio as the Iroquoian "center of gravity" (from which the languages dispersed). Proto-Iroquoian culture as revealed in reconstructed lexical material has been investigated by Marianne Mithun (1984b). In the domain of hunting, little can be reconstructed for Proto-Iroquoian, but Proto-

Northern-Iroquoian contained two terms for 'bow' (one perhaps originally meant 'stick'), and terms for 'bowstring', 'arrow', 'arrow-feather', and 'arrowhead'. The total absence of reconstructible terms for corn cultivation or agriculture in Proto-Iroquoian suggests, but does not prove, that in Proto-Iroquoian times such concepts were not yet known. Corn, so important to Iroquoian culture, seems to have arrived relatively recently in the Northeast. However, 'bread' is reconstructible at least to Proto-Northern-Iroquoian and perhaps to Proto-Iroquoian. Mithun suggests that the set of words that are reconstructible to Proto-Northern-Iroquoian involving "aquatic subsistence" (for example, 'lake' or 'large river', 'row a boat', 'fishhook') indicates the probability that the Proto-Iroquoians lived near a large river or lake. As for material culture, Proto-Northern-Iroquoian and perhaps Proto-Iroquoian had 'leggings', Proto-Northern-Iroquoian 'shoe' or 'moccasin', 'basket', 'wooden trough', 'kettle' or 'pot', 'dish', 'bowl', and 'cradleboard', 'knife', and 'axe'.

(57) Algic (Algonquian-Ritwan)
(MAP 11; see also MAPS 5 and 26)

See the classification list. While it is customary to picture Native American language families as having occupied rather restricted geographical areas, Algic covers a remarkably large geographical expanse (as do Eskimo-Aleut, Athabaskan, and Uto-Aztecan), from the northern California coast in the west to the Atlantic seaboard in the east, and from Labrador and the subarctic in the north to northern Mexico (the Kickapoo) and South Carolina in the south.

The Proto-Algonquian phonemes are: /p, t, č, k, s, š, h, m, n, θ, r, w, y; i, a o; vowel length/ (Goddard 1979a, 1988, 1990a, 1994b). Traditionally, Algonquianists have followed Leonard Bloomfield's (1946) reconstruction for Proto-Central-Algonquian, which is considered reasonably representative of the Proto-Algonquian phonology in general. Recently, Goddard (1994b, 1994c) has shown that Bloomfield's *l is more accurately reconstructed as *r (r being the reflex which predominates in the earliest reconstructions of the daughter languages). Bloomfield's *$θ$ was more controver-

sial, and even he said that it may have been a voiceless l (that is, *$ɬ$) in the proto language. Only Arapaho-Atsina and Cree-Montagnais retain separate reflexes for the *$θ$/*r (or *l) contrast; the two are merged in all the other branches of Algonquian. Goddard also argues cogently that the famous *$çk$ which Bloomfield reconstructed for Proto-Algonquian (see Chapter 2) is more accurately reconstructed as *rk, and he also reinterpreted Bloomfield's *x in *xp and *xk clusters as *s (1994c:205).

The connection of Wiyot and Yurok in northern California (which together were formerly called Ritwan, after Dixon and Kroeber's [1913a] grouping of the two as one of their more remote Californian stocks) with Algonquian was first proposed by Sapir (1913)[130] and was quite controversial at that time (see Michelson 1914, 1915; Sapir 1915a, 1915b; see also Chapter 2), but the relationship has subsequently been demonstrated to the satisfaction of all (see Haas 1958a; Teeter 1964a; Goddard 1975, 1979a, 1990a). Before 1850 the Yurok lived on the coast of northern California and on the lower Klamath River. The Wiyot (earlier called Wishosk) lived in the Humboldt Bay area, in the redwood belt; the last fully fluent speaker died in 1962 (Teeter 1964b). Many scholars have commented that although Wiyot and Yurok are neighbors in northern California, they seem not to have a closer relationship with each other than either has with Algonquian. For this reason, Howard Berman (1981) urged that the family not be called Algonquian-Ritwan because "Ritwan" would seem to suggest a closer connection between Wiyot and Yurok than had been established. Shortly afterward, however, he proposed certain innovations shared by Wiyot and Yurok which he took as suggesting "that they had a period of common development after the end of Algonquian-Ritwan unity" (1982:412), which show them to be closer to each other than to Algonquian proper (1990a). For this reason, he calls the family Algonquian-Ritwan. An attempt has been made by Proulx (1984) to reconstruct Proto-Algic phonology, but whether other specialists will accept it or portions thereof remains to be seen. Berman's work has had a better reception.

Goddard (1994c) presents Algonquian as a west-to-east cline, not of genetic subgroups but

Algic (Algonquian-Ritwan)

Ritwan
    †Wiyot [131] *California*
    Yurok [132] (Weitspekan) [moribund] *California*
Algonquian (Algonkian) [133]
    Blackfoot *Montana, Alberta*
    Cheyenne *Wyoming*
    Arapaho (Group)
        Arapaho *Wyoming, Oklahoma*
        Atsina [moribund] *Montana*
        Besawunena
        Nawathinehena
    Menominee (Menomini) [134] *Wisconsin*
    Ojibwa-Potawatomi(-Ottawa) [135] *Michigan, Ontario;* Algonquin (Algonkin) [136], Salteaux *Ontario,*
        Quebec
    Fox
        Fox *Iowa, Oklahoma, Kansas*
        Sauk [137]
        Kickapoo *Kansas, Oklahoma, Texas, Coahuila (Mexico)*
        †Mascouten
    Shawnee [138] *Oklahoma*
    Miami-Illinois [obsolescent] *Oklahoma*
    Cree-Montagnais(-Naskapi) [139] *eastern Canada*
    Eastern Algonquian
        Micmac *Nova Scotia, New Brunswick, Quebec, Newfoundland*
        Abenaki(-Penobscot) [140] *Quebec, Maine*
            Eastern Abenaki [moribund] *Quebec*
            Western Abenaki [moribund] *New England*
        Narragansett
        Powhatan
        Delaware (Munsee, Unami) [141] [moribund] *Oklahoma*
        †Massachusett [142] *Massachusetts*
        Maliseet(-Passamaquoddy) [143] *Maine, New Brunswick*
        †Nanticoke-Conoy
        †Etchemin *Maine*
        †"Loup B" *New England*
        †Christanna Algonquian *Virginia, North Carolina*

Goddard 1972, 1979a, 1994c.

of chronological layers, with the greatest time depth found in the west and the shallowest in the east. That is, each layer, in his view, is distinguished from those to the west by innovations and from those to the east by archaic retentions, where each wave of innovations is farther to the east, giving the characteristic clinal configuration that reflects the general west-to-east movement of the family. Blackfoot (in the West) is the most divergent; Arapaho-Atsina and Cree-Montagnais are the second oldest layer. The next oldest includes Arapaho-Atsina, Cree-Montagnais, Cheyenne, and Menominee; next is

Core Central Algonquian languages; the final layer is Eastern Algonquian (the only grouping or layer that constitutes a valid subgroup). These "dialect" layers represent innovations shared through diffusion, but this nongenetic shared history in this instance helps to determine the historical location of these languages and the relative age when they were in contact.

Siebert (1967) postulated that the original homeland of Proto-Algonquian people [144] must have been in the region between Lake Huron and Georgian Bay and the middle course of the Ottawa River, bounded on the north by Lake

Nipissing and the Mattawa River and on the south by the northern shore of Lake Ontario. In Siebert's analysis, the various Algonquian groups extended from this area to the various geographical locations where their speakers were first encountered by Europeans. Snow (1976) reexamined the question and concluded that an area considerably larger than that postulated by Siebert was the best candidate for the Proto-Algonquian homeland, but one nevertheless still bounded on the west by Niagara Falls (to accommodate the word for 'harbor seal'). In more recent work, Goddard finds the terms Siebert reconstructed "consistent with the homeland of Proto-Algonquians being somewhere immediately west of Lake Superior," but he points out the circularity of the method—that words for 'harbor seal' would typically survive only in languages in areas where harbor seals are found, thus eliminating languages that lacked a cognate for this term. Goddard concluded that "the Algonquians came ultimately from the west" (1994c:207).

It is generally agreed that there is no firm basis for selecting a Proto-Algic (Proto-Algonquian-Ritwan) homeland, in spite of considerable conjecture on the topic. Berman agrees that the homeland is "unknown" but speculates that the similarity between the Proto-Algonquian-Ritwan vowel system, as he reconstructs it, and that of Proto-Salish, if it were the result of contact rather than coincidence, "would place the Proto-Algonquian-Ritwan homeland near the Proto-Salish homeland . . . probably somewhere in the northwest, to the north of the Ritwan languages and to the west of the Proto-Algonquian homeland" (1982:419). Berman's proposed Proto-Algonquian-Ritwan vowels are unmarked *i·, *a·, and *o·, and marked *e and *a; Proto-Salish is postulated to have had *i, *a, *u, and *ə (1982:414, cf. Thompson 1979:720, Kuipers 1981:323), though Kinkade (1993) has argued in favor of eliminating ə from the reconstruction of Proto-Salishan. The gross similarities between the two systems are not necessarily compelling evidence, however. There are several languages with only three vowels—all with just one back-rounded vowel—and a number of languages have o but no u (Maddieson 1984:125, 127). Moreover, vowel systems with three or four vowels are cited as an areal trait of the

Northwest Coast and Plateau linguistic areas (see Chapter 9); they are found in some northern Californian languages (Shasta, Hupa) and are not unknown elsewhere in North America (they are found in some Caddoan and Uto-Aztecan languages, for example; Sherzer 1976:85, 104). It is also not uncommon for languages to have one or two reduced (or overshort) vowels in opposition to the fuller (often "long") vowels (as in Athabaskan). As Maddieson shows, "the higher mid long vowels /e:/ and /o:/ are far more likely to appear in a language without corresponding short vowels of the same quality than any of the other vowels . . . in 19.6% of the languages with the vowel quality /o(:)/ the vowel only occurs long" (1984:130). A number of northern Californian languages have phonological processes that reduce vowels in a number of contexts (see, for example, Berman 1985:347). Thus, although it is somewhat suggestive, the similarity to the Proto-Salish vowel system seems insufficient as a basis for postulating a Proto-Algic homeland.

At a more tangible level, Berman argues that the Ritwan homeland must have been in northern California, since "their [Wiyot's and Yurok's] location adjacent to each other amid a horde of languages unrelated to them is too much a coincidence to be the result of chance" (1982:419). Whistler, however, argues on linguistic and archaeological grounds that these languages arrived in California in separate movements from the north—from the Columbia plateau, perhaps from the middle Columbia River area following the Deschutes River, in about A.D. 900 (Wiyot) and about A.D. 1100 (Yurok) (reported in Moratto 1984:540, 564). He points out the remarkable likeness of their archaeological assemblages to those found along the mid-Columbia River. The Wiyot and Yurok brought woodworking technology, riverine fishing specialization, wealth consciousness, and certain distinctive artifact types, which initiate the Gunther Pattern in late prehistoric northwestern California (Moratto 1984:546).

(58) †Beothuk
Newfoundland (MAP 26)

The Beothuks were among the first natives of the New World with whom Europeans had contact. On his first voyage in 1534, Cartier reported their custom of covering themselves in red ocher (a trait frequently noted by explorers and writers), and it has been speculated that this may be the source of the appellation of "Red Indians" for Native Americans commonly used later (Hewson 1978:3). The language is extinct and very poorly documented. Only three short vocabulary lists are known (with a combined total of about 325 items; photographic facsimiles of all of them appear in Hewson 1978).[145] A number of subsequent copies of these three originals are also extant. As John Hewson indicates, "the[se] vocabularies are full of errors of every kind." The vocabularies were written down in chaotic English spellings, and "none of the native informants knew sufficient English to communicate in any satisfactory manner, so that the only means of interpreting the meaning of Beothuk words was through mime, drawing and pointing" (1982:181). For example, Hewson cites a telling instance from Gatschet's work:

> Gatschet . . . reports a form *stiocena* "thumb".
> . . . This item had started life as *ifweena* "thigh"
> in the Leigh vocabulary. . . . When Leigh came
> to copy his vocabulary for John Peyton . . . he
> wrote the English *thumb* and then instead of copy-
> ing the Beothuk word *pooeth,* inadvertently wrote
> instead the Beothok word *ifweena* which happens

to be the next word down the page in the original Leigh vocabulary. . . . Consequently, in the so-called Peyton copy of Leigh, the entry appears as: *Itweena* "thumb". Another copy of this item was made by James P. Howley and sent to Sir William Dawson . . . who in turn copied it out by hand and sent a copy to the Reverend Dr. Silas Rand. . . . Mr. Rand in turn copied it out and sent a copy to Gatschet. By the time this item had gone through all these varying copyings, the original capital *i* had become an *s*, the following ambiguous *f* [the only example of an *f* in the corpus] had become a *t*, the *w* had become an *i* and an *o*, the double *e* had become *ce* and only the *na* had survived intact. (1982:181–2)

Of Beothuk prehistory, little can be said with certainty. The Beothuks had a folk tradition of crossing into Newfoundland over the Belle Isle Strait. Archaeological evidence suggests they arrived in Newfoundland in about A.D. 500; before that (from 500 B.C. to A.D. 500) Newfoundland was inhabited by Dorset Eskimos. Culturally, Beothuks were like Algonquians and unlike Eskimos and Iroquoians (Hewson 1982:184).

It has long been conjectured that Beothuk may be related to the Algonquian family, but the material available on the language is so scant and poorly recorded that evaluation of the proposed connection is difficult. The various proposals are considered in Chapter 8.

5

Languages of Middle America

> In the distant past, no one could speak, which is one reason that people were
> destroyed at the end of the First and Second Creations. Then, while the sun
> deity was still walking on the earth, people finally learned to speak (Span-
> ish), and all people everywhere understood each other. Later the nations and
> municipios were divided because they had begun to quarrel. Language was
> changed so that people would learn to live together peacefully in smaller
> groups.
>
> Tzotzil oral tradition, quoted in Gossen 1984:46–7

IN THIS CHAPTER THE LANGUAGES OF
Middle America and their history are surveyed.
Linguistically speaking, these geographical
boundaries are arbitrary: "Middle America, in
spite of its special cultural position, is distinctly
a part of the whole North American linguistic
complex and is connected with North America
by innumerable threads" (Sapir 1929a:140).[1]
Some Middle American language families extend geographically north of the Mexican border
and others reach into South America, so it is
difficult to discuss their classification in isolation.[2] Also, the history of Middle American
language studies is intimately connected with
that of North America, and to a lesser extent
also with that of South America; many of the
scholars who worked on Middle American languages were influential in the classification of
North American and South American languages
as well—for example, Franz Boas, Daniel Brinton, Joseph Greenberg, Alfred Kroeber, J. Alden

Mason, Paul Radin, Edward Sapir, Morris
Swadesh, John Swanton, Benjamin Whorf, and
others (see Chapter 2).

The term "Mesoamerica" refers to the geographical region extending from the Pánuco
River in northern Mexico to the Lempa River
in El Salvador, but also includes the Pacific
coast of Nicaragua and Costa Rica. The term
was first applied to a culture area, defined by a
large number of diagnostic cultural traits shared
by the indigenous groups of this geographical
region. The notion of a culturally defined area
which functioned somehow as a unit in Middle
America goes back to Edward Tylor (author of
the first textbook on anthropology); there were
also early formulations in Vivó (1935a, 1935b)
and Kroeber (1939), but Kirchhoff (1943) is
typically cited as the founder of Mesoamerica
as a culture area. This Mesoamerican culture
area coincides closely with Mesoamerica as a
linguistic area (see Chapter 9; also Campbell,

Kaufman, and Smith-Stark 1986). It is hypothe-sized that both the Mesoamerican culture area (co-tradition) and the Mesoamerican linguistic area were shaped by the same forces—in part at least by extensive influence from the Olmecs (the earliest highly successful civilization of the area), especially through extensive trading and linguistic contact dating from Olmec formative times (from about 1200 B.C.). Most Middle American languages fall within Mesoamerica, the focus of this chapter, though some languages to the north in Mexico and others to the south in lower Central America are also treated here. For all the languages discussed in this chapter, see map 12.

The number of individual languages in Mid-dle America is large. Norman McQuown (1955:544–7) listed 351 in Mexico and Central America; Robert Longacre's (1967) map has more than 200 in Mesoamerica alone. These languages also exhibit great typological diver-sity: "In one small portion of the area, in Mexico just north of the Isthmus of Tehuantepec, one finds a diversity of linguistic type hard to match on an entire continent in the Old World" (McQuown 1955:501).

The classification of Middle American lan-guages presented here is generally accepted and not considered very controversial. (See Chapter 8 for a discussion of the major proposals of distant genetic relationships and the controver-sies surrounding them.)[3]

(1) Otomanguean

See the classification list. The Otomanguean family is very large in terms of geographical extent, number of speakers, and number of lan-guages; it extends from the northern border of Mesoamerica to Mesoamerica's southern border. These languages have at times been considered to be different from other American Indian lan-guages. While variously overlapping, partially conflicting classifications regarding various sub-sets of Otomanguean languages had been pro-posed, the full extent of the Otomanguean family was established gradually, in the work of Orozco y Berra, Pimentel, Brinton, Lehmann, Weitlaner, Swadesh, Longacre, Rensch, Suárez, and others (see Rensch 1976:1–5). Earlier, there had been

a debate concerning whether Otomí might not be related genetically to Chinese; proponents of this view assumed that languages of the "mono-syllabic" type shared a common origin (see Chapter 2; also Brinton 1897). Greenberg (1960:791) considered Otomanguean a possible exception to the genetic unity he postulated for almost all other American Indian languages (though Otomanguean is no longer presented as such in Greenberg 1987). Some aspects of Otomanguean languages which give them their peculiar character are the following: (1) tone (all have from two to five level tones, and most have gliding tones as well); (2) phonemic vowel nasalization; (3) open syllables (most Otoman-guean languages have only *CV* syllables except for those syllables that are closed with a glottal stop [CVʔ]); (4) syllable-initial consonant clus-ters are limited, usually to sibilant-C, C-y or C-w, nasal-C, and C-h or C-ʔ, where C-ʔ pro-duces glottalized consonants in many Otoman-guean subfamilies but not in Zapotecan; (5) lack of labial consonants (bilabial stops are lacking from most, though some languages have devel-oped labials from *k^w;* see Rensch 1976).

Otomanguean is an old family, with eight subfamilies. Linguists of the Summer Institute of Linguistics (who are to be credited with much of the Otomanguean comparative work) feel that their reconstruction rivals that of Proto-Indo-European in its completeness and accuracy (Longacre 1968:333). Indeed, Rensch's work is extensive (1973, 1976, 1977, 1978; see also Longacre 1957, 1966, 1967, 1968). See the clas-sification list for Kaufman's recent classification of Otomanguean.

Rensch's (1977:68) inventory of Proto-Otomanguean sounds is: /t, k, k^w, ʔ, s, n, y, w, h; i, e, a, u; four tones/. Kaufman (in press) reexamined Otomanguean and postulates the fol-lowing revised phonemic inventory: /t, c, k, k^w, ʔ, [θ], s, x, x^w, h, l, r, m, n, w, y; i, e, a, o, u; combinations [ia], [ea], [ai], [au]; tones (not yet worked out)/.

Subtiaba and Tlapanec are closely related languages, though Subtiaba (now extinct) was spoken in Nicaragua and Tlapanec is spoken by about 55,000 people in Guerrero, Mexico. Weathers (1976) reported six distinct dialects of Tlapanec, all with at least a minimal level of mutual intelligibility. He came to the conclusion

Otomanguean

Western Otomanguean
    Oto-Pame-Chinantecan
        Oto-Pamean
            Otomí *Hidalgo, Estado de México, Guanajuato, Queretaro*
            Mazahua[4] *Michoacán, Estado de México*
            Matlatzinca-Ocuilteco
                Matlatzinca[5] (Pirinda) *Estado de México*
                Ocuilteco[6] (Tlahuica, Atzingo) [obsolescent] *Estado de México*
            Pame *Estado de México*
            Chichimeco[7] (Jonaz) *Guanajuato*
        Chinantecan[8] *Oaxaca*
            Ojitlán
            Usila
            Quiotepec
            Palantla
            Lalana
            Chiltepec
    Tlapanec-Manguean
        Tlapanec-Subtiaba
            †Subtiaba *Nicaragua*
            Tlapanec *Guerrero* (Dialects: Azoyú, Malinaltepec)
        Manguean
            †Chiapanec[9] *Chiapas*
            †Mangue (Dirian, Nagranda, Chorotega, Orotiña) *Nicaragua, Costa Rica*
Eastern Otomanguean
    Popolocan-Zapotecan
        Popolocan
            Mazatec[10] *Oaxaca, Puebla* (Several dialects)
            Ixcatec [extinct?] *Oaxaca*
            Chocho *Oaxaca*
            Popoloca[11]   Puebla, Oaxaca
        Zapotecan *Oaxaca*
            Zapotec[12] complex (includes Papabuco) (a number of mutually unintelligible languages; estimated to number between 6 and 55 distinct languages)
            Chatino
    Amuzgo-Mixtecan
        Amuzgo[13] (two varieties) *Oaxaca, Guerrero*
        Mixtecan
            Mixtec[14] *Guerrero, Puebla, Oaxaca*
            Cuicatec[15] *Oaxaca*
            Trique *Oaxaca*

Kaufmann in press; see also Rensch 1973, 1976, 1977, 1978.

that Subtiaba is more conservative than Tlapanec.

For the Chinantecan subfamily, Rensch (1989:3) reports fourteen "moderately differentiated," mutually unintelligible languages: Ojitlán, Usila, Tlacoatzintepec-Mayultianguis-Quetzalapa, Chiltepec, Sochiapan, Tepetotuntla, Tlatepusco, Palantla, Valle Nacional, Ozumacín, La Alicia–Río Chiquito–Teotalcingo–Lalana, Lealao, Quiotepec-Yolox, and Comaltepec. He reconstructs the following sounds for Proto-Chinantecan: /p, t, k, kʷ, ʔ, b, dz, g, gʷ, s, h, l, r, m, n, ŋ; i, e, ɨ, ə, a, u; vowel length; nasalization; tonal contrasts: High (H), Low (L), HL, LH, HLH/ . The voiced affricate *dz (symbolized with z in Rensch 1989) before *i (and *iV) changed to tʸ in Usila and Quiotepec, and to g in Yolox, Temextitlán, and Comaltepec. The *s is reflected by *θ* in Tlacoatzintepec and Zapotit-lán, by *c* in Tepetotutla and Palantla, and by *c* when before **i* (and **iV*) in Valle Nacional and Ozumacín (Rensch 1989:11–12).

Otomanguean linguistic prehistory has received attention, though opinions contrast (compare Amador Hernández and Casasa García 1979; Hopkins 1984; and Winter, Gaxiola, and Hernández 1984). Glottochronological counts (considered invalid by most linguists) place the split up of Proto-Otomanguean at about 4400 B.C.; Rensch's (1976) reconstructed vocabulary indicates Proto-Otomanguean had terms for 'maize', 'beans', 'squash', 'chile', 'avocado', 'cotton', 'tobacco', 'cacao', and an 'edible tuber' (sweet potato); their status as Proto-Otomanguean etyma, however, should be reexamined since a number of Rensch's cognate sets have been questioned (Kaufman in press). In any event, the presence of these cultigen terms in Rensch's reconstructions has given Otomanguean a prominent role in discussions of the origin and diffusion of agriculture in Mesoamerica and in the New World in general. Hopkins (1984), following Amador Hernández and Casasa García (1979), connects Proto-Otomanguean and its early diversification with the rise of agriculture in the region. His hypothesis is that the Proto-Otomanguean homeland was in the Tehuacán Valley, in Puebla, and probably also in sites outside the Tehuacán region which took part in the same cultural developments, representing the Coxcatlán Phase (5000–3400 B.C.); the plant and animal names in the reconstructed vocabulary corresponded to the plant and animal remains discovered in this archaeological phase. The "development of a new complex of plants as a subsistence base . . . made possible the population growth and expansion reflected in the diversification of the Otomanguean family into its . . . major branches" (Hopkins 1984:33). Winter, Gaxiola, and Hernández contest the emphasis on the Tehuacán Valley and the associations with the origin and spread of agriculture in discussions of Otomanguean linguistics, "since there is no archaeological evidence that the Tehuacán Valley was a key area in the process of transformation from subsistence based on appropriation [hunting and gathering] to subsistence based on production [agriculture]" (1984:66). Though the Tehuacán Valley is ar-chaeologically the best known and most intensively studied area in the central Mexican highlands, evidence of incipient agriculture comes from several regions, and the chronological order in which cultigens appear in the archaeological record is different in each of these different locations—that is, apparently there were multiple centers of plant domestication. For example, domesticated pumpkin comes from the Valley of Oaxaca (ca. 6500 B.C.), and beans from Ocampo, Tamaulipas (ca. 4000 B.C.) (Winter, Gaxiala, and Hernández 1984:67–8). So, argue Winter et al. (1984), there is no necessary connection between the Tehuacán Valley and early agriculture, evidence of which is found in other areas as well; and therefore, the association of Proto-Otomanguean with some place exhibiting the cultigens whose names are reconstructed by Rensch need not necessarily be with Tehuacán. Nevertheless, Hopkins and Winter et al. are in agreement that the Tehuacán tradition (5000–2300 B.C.) was borne by speakers of Proto-Otomanguean; however, this tradition extends from the Mexican states of Hidalgo and Querétaro in the north to Oaxaca in the south, so the pinpointing of an Otomanguean homeland is difficult (Hopkins 1984:33; Winter, Gaxiola, and Hernández 1984:72–3).

The inhabitants of the archaeological site of Monte Albán, in Oxaca, are considered to have always been speakers of Zapotecan. The Mangue migration from Chiapas, Mexico, to Nicaragua took place some time after A.D. 600, while the Subtiaba migration from Guerrero, Mexico, to Nicaragua was later, about A.D. 1200. Otomanguean prehistory is rich and deserves much more study.

The controversy over the postulated Hokan and Otomanguean affinities for Tlapanec-Subtiaba is considered in Chapter 8 (see also Chapter 2). In spite of Sapir's (1925a) famous Subtiaba-Hokan paper, Subtiaba-Tlapanec turns out to be Otomanguean.

(2) **Tequistlatecan** (Chontal of Oaxaca)

See the classification list. Tequistlatecan is composed of three closely related languages: Huamelultec (Lowland Chontal), Highland Chontal, and Tequistlatec (now probably extinct) (Waterhouse 1985). The names can be confusing; many

Tequistlatecan

Huamelultec (Lowland Chontal)
Highland Chontal
Tequistlatec proper [extinct?]

call the family "Chontal (of Oaxaca)," which is
often confused with Chontal of Tabasco (a
Mayan language). For that reason, many linguists prefer to use the name Tequistlatec(an).
Viola Waterhouse (1985), however, recommends
that Tequistlatec (Chontal) be used only to refer
to the language of Tequixistlan and that Oaxaca
Chontal be reserved for the family name. Whatever name is used, it is important to recognize
the third language, often neglected, which was
described briefly by De Angulo and Freeland
(1925) and by Waterhouse (1985).

Proto-Tequistlatecan phonology has been
considered by Paul Turner (1969) and refined
by Waterhouse (1969). It has the following inventory: /p, t, c, k, ?, b, d, g, f', tl', c', k', ɬ, s,
l, m, n, w, y, h, W, N; i, e, a, o, u; phonemic
stress. (Probably voiceless *W* and *N* should be
reanalyzed as clusters of *hw* and *hn,* respectively; see also Turner and Turner 1971).

Brinton (1891) suggested that Yuman, Seri,
and Tequistlatec were genetically related;
Kroeber (1915) accepted this proposal and included them in the Hokan hypothesis. This has
been the subject of controversy; Turner (1967,
1972) argued against the proposed Hokan relationship for Tequistlatecan, and Bright (1970)
argued against Turner's methods and thus im-
plicitly for the possibility of the Hokan connection (see Chapter 8). Campbell and Oltrogge
(1980) see promising prospects for a possible
genetic relationship between Tequistlatecan and
Jicaquean, though they believe the broader Hokan proposal for these two is not currently supported.

(3) Jicaquean (Tol)
Honduras

See the classification list. There are two Jicaquean languages. Jicaque of El Palmar (Western
Jicaque), now extinct, is known only from a
short vocabulary (published in Membreño
1897:195–6, 233–42; reprinted in Lehmann
1920:654–68). Eastern Jicaque, also called Tol,[16]

Jicaquean (Tol)

†Jicaque of El Palmar (Western Jicaque)
Eastern Jicaque (Tol)

is spoken by about 350 individuals in La Mon-
taña de Flor, near Orica, Honduras, and by a
very few old people in the department of Yoro,
Honduras.

Proto-Jicaque phonology, as reconstructed by
Campbell and Oltrogge (1980), has the following phonemic inventory: /p, t, c, k, pʰ, tʰ, cʰ,
kʰ, p', t', c', k', l, m, n, w, y, h; i, e, ɨ, a,
o, u/ .

The two Jicaquean languages are not especially closely related, perhaps on the order of
English and Swedish. Jicaque(an) is often placed
in Hokan (based on Greenberg and Swadesh
1953), though the evidence presented is scanty
and unpersuasive. Campbell and Oltrogge
(1980) present a few possible cognates and
sound correspondences which are suggestive of
a possible genetic relationship with Tequistlatecan. This hypothesis should be investigated
further. The possibility of a connection between
Jicaquean and Subtiaba (including also Tequistlatecan), put forward by Oltrogge (1977), now
seems to lack support (see Campbell 1979,
Campbell and Oltrogge 1980).

(4) Seri
Sonora

Seri is spoken along the coast of Sonora, Mexico
in two main villages, Punta Chueca and El
Desemboque, and also in a number of seasonal
camps; it was once also spoken on Tiburón
Island in the Gulf of California. Seri and Tequistlatecan (and Yuman) were grouped early (see
Brinton 1891), and they were placed in Hokan
soon after its formulation (Kroeber 1915),
though that hypothesis has not proven persuasive
to the many who doubt Hokan in general (see
Chapter 8). For the present, Seri is best considered an isolate.

(5) Huave
Oaxaca

Jorge Suárez (1975) reconstructed Proto-Huave
based on four dialects: San Francisco, San Dio-

nisio, San Mateo, and Santa María. His Proto-Huave phonemic inventory is: /p, t, c, k, kʷ, mb, nd, nc, ng, gʷ, s, l, ř, (w), (r), (y), h, (đ); i, e, a, ɨ, o, u, tonal contrast (high, low), vowel length/ . Segments in parentheses are problematical and will probably be eliminated on the basis of future work. The đ occurs in only two cognate sets. The o, with only seven examples, is also rare. Though Suárez reconstructs two r sounds, he suggests that there was probably only one in the proto language and that these were conditioned variants. The w and y, in Suárez's opinion, may be merely neutralizations of certain vowels. The tonal contrast also exists only in penultimate syllables and is preserved fully only in San Mateo, though some residue of it is reflected in final consonants of other dialects. Since Huave tone has a low functional load, its origin may ultimately be explained so that it can be eliminated from Proto-Huave. Finally, many of the words Suárez reconstructed as Proto-Huave are loans; of his 971 reconstructed lexical items, more than 50 are loans from other indigenous languages.

Huave is generally considered an isolate, though unsubstantiated hypotheses have attempted to link it with Mixe (Radin 1916), Zoque and Mayan (Radin 1924), Algonquian-Gulf (Suárez 1975), and other languages (see Arana Osnaya 1964; Swadesh 1960b, 1964b, 1967a:87; Longacre 1968:343). The Huave-Otomanguean hypothesis, proposed by Swadesh (1960d) and followed by Rensch (1976, 1977, 1978), has not born fruit (a good number of the proposed cognate sets turn out to involve Zapotecan loans); most scholars now consider the hypothesis to be unlikely. Huave should thus be considered an isolate.

(6) Totonacan

See the classification list. Totonacan is a family of two languages, Totonac and Tepehua. Little comparative work on the family has been done so far (see Arana Osnaya 1953). Arana Osnaya

Totonacan

Totonac *Puebla, Veracruz* (Several dialects)
Tepehua[17] *Veracruz, Hidalgo*

reconstructed Proto-Totonacan phonology on the basis of three Totonac dialects and one variety of Tepehua, with a list of only sixty-eight cognates. Her inventory of reconstructed sounds is: /p, t, tl, c, č, k, q, ɬ, š, x, l, m, n, w, y; i, a, u; vowel length/ . Though Tepehua has glottalized consonants, they correspond in most environments to Totonac forms with glottal stop in $CV?(C)$—that is, the so-called glottalized vowels. Totonacan has quite complicated word formation, and this has led to speculation concerning its possible broader relationships, but no definitive evidence has turned up yet. Ethnohistorical and loanword evidence suggests the Totonacs are the strongest candidates for the builders of Teotihuacán, the most influential Mesoamerican city in its day (A.D. 200–650), and this inference is supported by a small but significant number of Totonacan loanwords in Lowland Mayan languages, Nahuatl, and other Mesoamerican languages (Justeson et al. 1985). Teotihuacán was not built by Nahua speakers; the Nahua speakers' arrival coincides more closely with the fall of Teotihuacan than with its rise.

Totonacan has most often been placed with Mayan and Mixe-Zoquean in a grouping called Macro-Mayan (McQuown 1942, 1956). While some aspects of this hypothesis are attractive, it remains inconclusive and requires much more investigation (see Chapter 8).

(7) Mixe-Zoquean

See the classification list. The most recent and so far most accurate classification of Mixe-Zoquean is that of Wichmann.

The inventory of Proto-Mixe-Zoquean sounds is: /p, t, c, k, ?, s, m, n, w, y, h; i, e, a, ɨ, o, u; vowel length/ (Kaufman 1964c, Wichmann 1995). The languages of the Mixean branch have innovated by inserting h after original short vowels in monosyllabic forms that are not verbs. The Zoquean branch changed original syllable-final *w to ŋ and lost original vowel length. Zoquean s corresponds to Mixean š, making the choice between *s and *š for the Proto-Mixe-Zoquean reconstruction somewhat arbitrary.

The Mixe-Zoquean family has special importance in Mesoamerican prehistory, since a Mixe-Zoquean language appears to have been spoken by the Olmecs, the first great Mesoamerican

Mixe-Zoquean

Mixean[18]
    Oaxaca Mixean
        North Highland Mixe (Totontepec)
        South Highland Mixe
            Zempoaltepetl (Tlahuitoltepec, Ayutla, Tamazulapan)
            Non-Zempoaltepetl (Tepuxtepec, Tepantlali, Mixistlán)
        Midland Mixe
            North Midland Mixe (Jaltepec, Puxmetacan, Matamoros, Cotzocón)
            South Midland Mixe (Juquila, Cacalotepec)
        Lowland Mixe (Camotlán, San José El Paraíso / Coatlán, Mazatlán, Guichicovi)
    †Tapachultec[19] (see Kaufman 1964a)
    Sayula[20] Popoluca
    Oluta[21] Popoluca [obsolescent?]
Zoquean
    Gulf Zoquean
        Texistepec[22] Zoque [moribund?]
        Ayapa[23]
        Soteapan Zoque (Sierra Popoluca)
    Chimalapa (Oaxaca) Zoquean
        Santa María Chimalapa[24] Zoque
        San Miguel Chimalapa Zoque
    Chiapas Zoquean
        North Zoque (Magdalena / Francisco León)
        Northeast Zoque
            Northeast Zoque A (Tapalapa, Ocotepec, Pantepec, Rayón)
            Northeast Zoque B (Chapultenango, Oxolotán)
        Central Zoque (Copainalá, Tecpatán, Ostuacán)
        South Zoque (Tuxtla Gutiérrez, Ocozocuautla)

Wichmann 1995.

civilization (see Campbell and Kaufman 1976, Justeson et al. 1985). Some form of Mixe-Zoquean was also the language of the Izapan horizon culture, which had a strong influence on its neighbors, including several Mayan languages, and on Classic Mayan art and hieroglyphic writing (Justeson et al. 1985). The Mixe-Zoquean speakers were the inventors of the Mesoamerican calendar and hieroglyphic writing, and Mixe-Zoquean has recently been shown to be the language of the Epi-Olmec writing system associated with the La Mojarra stela (Justeson and Kaufman 1993). Campbell and Kaufman presented some reconstructed Mixe-Zoquean vocabulary, finding the cultural inventory reflected in it to be consistent with that revealed in the archaeology of that period, and they identified Mixe-Zoquean loanwords in many other Mesoamerican languages (see also Kaufman 1964d, Nordell 1962, Thomas 1974,

Longacre 1967:178, and Campbell and Kaufman 1976).

(8) Mayan
(MAP 13; see also MAP 12)

See the classification list. The Mayan family of languages, spoken principally in Guatemala, southern Mexico, and Belize, has received relatively more attention from linguists than most other Native American language groups. As a result, the languages are fairly well documented and their historical relationships are well understood. Also, many grammars, dictionaries, and texts were written soon after first contact with Europeans (more than 450 years ago), and these provide rich resources. See the classification list for the most generally accepted classification of the Mayan family.

Mayan

Huastecan
    Huastec [25] *Veracruz, San Luis Potosí*
    †Chicomuceltec [26] *Chiapas*
Yucatecan–Core Mayan
    Yucatecan
        Yucatec-Lacandon
            Yucatec [27] *Yucatán, Campeche, Kintana Roo, Belize; Petén, Guatemala*
            Lacandón *Chiapas*
        Mopán-Itzá
            Mopán *Petén, Guatemala; Belize*
            Itzá (Itza') [28] [obsolescent] *Petén, Guatemala*
    Core Mayan
        Cholan-Tzeltalan (Greater Tzeltalan, Greater Tzotzilan)
            Cholan
                Chol-Chontal
                    Chol [29] (Ch'ol) *Chiapas*
                    Chontal [30] *Tabasco*
                Chortí-Choltí [31]
                    Ch'orti' (Chortí) *Zacapa, Guatemala*
                    †Choltí *Guatemala*
            Tzeltalan (Tzotzilan)
                Tzeltal *Chiapas*
                Tzotzil [32] *Chiapas*
        Q'anjob'alan-Chujean (Greater Kanjobalan)
            Q'anjob'alan
                Q'anjob'al-Akateko-Jakalteko
                    Q'anjob'al (Kanjobal) *Guatemala*
                    Akateko (Acatec) [33] *Guatemala*
                    Jakalteko (Jacaltec) [34] *Guatemala*
                Motocintlec [35] (with Tuzantec [obsolescent])
            Chujean
                Chuj [36]*Guatemala*
                Tojolabal [37] *Chiapas*
        K'ichean-Mamean (Eastern Mayan)
            K'ichean (Quichean) *Guatemala*
                Q'eqchi' (Kekchí) [38]
                Uspanteko (Uspantec) [39]
                Poqom-K'ichean
                    Poqom
                        Poqomchi' (Pokomchí)
                        Poqomam (Pokomam)
                    Core K'ichean
                        K'iche' (Quiché) [40]
                        Kaqchikel-Tz'utujil
                            Kaqchikel (Cakchiquel) [41]
                            Tz'utujil (Tzutujil)
                        Sakapulteko (Sacapultec) [42]
                      Sipakapense (Sipacapa, Sipacapeño) [43]
            Mamean
                Teco-Mam
                    Teco (Tektiteko) *Chiapas, Guatemala*
                    Mam [44] *Guatemala, Chiapas*
                Awakateko-Ixil
                    Awakateko (Aguacatec) [45] *Guatemala*
                    Ixil *Guatemala*

Campbell and Kaufman 1985.

In the spelling of Mayan language names I have followed the orthography now officially recognized in Guatemala for languages spoken in Guatemala (for example, K'iche'), with the spellings by which they are more conventionally known in the literature given in parentheses (for example, Quiché). I have not used such spellings for languages spoken outside Guatemala, where such spellings are unknown (for example, I have retained the traditional Huastec and have avoided the Wasteko spelling recommended in Guatemala but unknown elsewhere).

According to the most commonly held view of Mayan differentiation, Huastecan branched off first, followed next by Yucatecan; then the remaining branches separated from one another and began to diversify. Some scholars believe that Cholan-Tzeltalan and Q'anjob'alan-Chujean belong more closely together in a subgroup called Western Mayan (Kaufman 1976, Campbell and Kaufman 1985).

Proto-Mayan has been reconstructed with the following inventory of sounds: /p, t, c, č, k, q, ʔ, b', t', c', č', k', q', m, n, ŋ, s, š, x, l, r, w, y, h; i, e, a, o, u; vowel length/ . The *b'* was imploded in Proto-Mayan (and still is in most Mayan languages), while the other glottalized sounds are ejective (Campbell 1977, Campbell and Kaufman 1985, Kaufman 1964b). Some of the notable sound changes that have taken place are:

1. *r > y in Huastecan, Yucatecan, and Cholan-Tzeltalan, and in Q'anjob'alan-Chujean languages except Motocintlec (where *r > č); *r is retained in K'ichean and changed to *t* in Mamean.
2. *ŋ > h in Q'eqchi' and x in the other K'ichean-Mamean languages.
3. *q and *q' (uvular stops) are retained in K'ichean-Mamean and the Q'anjob'alan languages, but for the most part became k and k', respectively, in the other languages.
4. In several languages (especially Cholan and some Yucatecan languages) short a became ɨ (except in certain restricted environments).
5. Tonal contrasts have developed independently in Yucatec and Uspantec, and in one dialect of Tzotzil, reflexes of vowel length and former h or ʔ.
6. In Mamean languages there was a chain shift in which *r > t, *t > č, *č > č, and *š > š; the changes which produced retroflex consonants

diffused further to nearby Q'anjob'alan languages (Campbell and Kaufman 1985, Kaufman 1969).

Proto-Mayan syntax has received more attention than the historical syntax of most Native American language families (Smith-Stark 1976; Norman and Campbell 1978; Robertson 1980, 1992). Proto-Mayan had VOS basic word order, although VSO was also possible when (1) the object was equal in animacy with the subject; (2) when it was complex (that is, was a coordinate Noun-Phrase or contained a relative clause); or (3) when it was definite (old or given discourse information) (Norman and Campbell 1978, England 1991). Today, fixed VOS basic order is found in Yucatecan, Tzotzil, and Tojolabal and in some dialects of other languages; fixed VSO is found in Mamean, Q'anjob'al, Jakalteko, and one Chuj dialect; only Ch'orti' has SVO basic word order. Both VOS and VSO occur in Huastec, Tzeltal, Chuj, Akateko, and Motocintlec and in most K'ichean languages, usually with VSO where the O[bject] plays a non-neutral role with respect to animacy, definiteness, or complexity (as specified above) (England 1991). Proto-Mayan was an ergative language, with ergativity signaled by cross-referencing pronominal markers on the verb. Split ergativity has developed in Cholan, Yucatecan, and some others, with ergative alignment in perfective forms and nominative-accusative alignment in the nonperfective verb forms (Larsen and Norman 1979). Proto-Mayan had an antipassive rule (and modern K'ichean languages contain two separate antipassive constructions—one with focus on the object, the other emphasizing the action of the verb—both playing down the role of the agent). Proto-Mayan had at least one passive construction, and modern K'ichean languages have two. Nominal possession was of the form, as in the Kaqchikel example, *ru-kye:x ri ačin* [his-horse the man] for 'the man's horse'. Proto-Mayan locatives were indicated by relational nouns, a construction composed of a possessive pronominal prefix and a noun root—for example, with the equivalent of *its-stomach* for 'in it', *your-head/hair* for 'on you'.

Several Mayan languages have rich written documentation beginning very shortly after the earliest Spanish contact, and philological study of these sources has revealed much about the history of the languages (see Campbell 1973b, 1974, 1978b, 1988a, 1990b; Robertson 1984, 1992; and sources in Campbell et al. 1978).

The Proto-Mayan homeland is postulated to have been in the Cuchumatanes Mountains of Guatemala, where Mayan was unified, according to glottochronological calculations (which most linguists do not accept), until about 2200 B.C. Proto-Mayan speakers exploited both highland and lowland ecological zones. The cultural inventory of reconstructed Proto-Mayan vocabulary shows that Proto-Mayan speakers were highly successful agriculturalists, with a full range of Mesoamerican cultigens (beans, squash, maize), with the maize complex highly developed and at the core of the culture. In the most common view of Proto-Mayan diversification, after the early departure of Huastecan, other Mayan groups began to diversify and some expanded down the Usumacinta River into the Petén region around 1000 B.C., where Yucatecan and Cholan-Tzeltalan are found. Later (in about A.D. 200) the Tzeltalan branch migrated to the Chiapas highlands, formerly occupied by speakers of Mixe-Zoquean languages. The principal bearers of Classic Lowland Maya culture (A.D. 300–900) were first Cholan (or Cholan-Tzeltalan) speakers, later joined by Yucatecans. The Lowland Maya linguistic area was formed during this period, contributing many loanwords both within the Mayan family and to neighboring non-Mayan languages (Justeson et al. 1985). K'ichean groups expanded into eastern and southern Guatemala quite late, after A.D. 1200. Poqomam was split off Western Poqomchi' by the intrusion of the Rabinal lineage of the K'iche' after A.D. 1250 and was pushed into former Xinca territory. Poqomam had nothing to do with Classic Chalchuapa or with Kaminaljuyú. K'ichean dialect boundaries correspond exactly to pre-European political units as reconstructed from ethnohistorical accounts (Kaufman 1976, Campbell 1978c).

Proposals for distant relatives of the Mayan family abound and include Araucanian, Yunga, Chipaya-Uru, Lenca, Huave, Mixe-Zoquean, Totonacan, Tarascan, Hokan, and Penutian, among others. However, the evidence presented thus far is insufficient to demonstrate a Mayan affiliation with any of these, while some proposals have been seriously discredited. The initially promising claim of kinship with Chipaya-Uru (of South America) has now been abandoned (see Campbell 1973a). The Macro-Mayan hypothesis, which would join Mayan, Mixe-Zoquean, and Totonacan, has received considerable attention, but the evidence presented to date is inadequate to support it, though sufficient to suggest that the proposal merits further investigation. Perhaps the main problem in this case is to distinguish possibly inherited similarities among these languages from diffused traits widespread in the Mesoamerican linguistic area (Campbell et al. 1986). In sum, the Mayan family has no known relatives other than the languages listed in the preceding classification (see Campbell and Kaufman 1980, 1983; Chapter 8).

Considerable progress has been made toward a full reading of Mayan hieroglyphic writing. Hieroglyphic texts on Classical monuments are largely historical in content, containing dynastic histories of the births, offices, marriages, deaths, and kinship of Mayan rulers, written in Cholan (or better said, in Cholan's ancestor, Pre-Cholan, and then later in Cholan); the codices, which are later, were written in Yucatec. Mayan writing is a mixed script. It began with strictly logographic signs (signaling whole morphemes). With the introduction of rebuses, Mayan phonology became involved, where something easier to depict was employed for homophonous morphemes that were more difficult to represent graphically (for example, a depiction of a torch, from Cholan *tah* 'pine, torch', to represent *ta* 'in, at'). Phonetic determiners arose from logograms used phonetically to distinguish the different semantic values of certain logograms. For example, the HOUSE logogram sometimes bears as the phonetic complement *TA,* originally a logogram for 'torch' (*tah* 'torch' in relevant Mayan languages), where HOUSE + phonetic determiner *TA* served to indicate that the Mayan word -*otot* 'house', with final *t* (shown by the phonetic determiner *TA*), was intended, rather than *nah,* the other word for 'house'. Later, the phonetic determiners were used in contexts independently of logograms solely for their phonetic value to spell words syllabically. Glyph grammar corresponds to Cholan grammar. Its word order is VOS; it exhibits split ergativity, verb classes (with distinct morphological patterns for transitive, intransitive, and positional verbs), and the paired couplets so typical of ritual discourse in Mayan languages and indeed in Mesoamerican languages generally (Justeson et al. 1985).

(9) **Tarascan**
Michoacán

Tarascan has several dialects (Friedrich 1971), but no known relatives. It is an isolate, and none of the external relationships that have been proposed for it has any support. They include Tarascan-Mayan, Tarascan-Quechua, Tarascan-Zuni, and Tarascan as a member of putative Chibchan-Paezan (see Chapter 8).

(10) **†Cuitlatec**
Guerrero

Cuitlatec,[46] also an isolate, has become extinct in recent years (Escalante 1962). None of the several genetic affinities proposed for Cuitlatec is convincing, and little substantive data has been presented in support of any of them. They include Uto-Aztecan (Sapir 1929a [said to be "a doubtful member of the stock"], Swadesh 1960b, Arana Osnaya 1958 [with an assumed forty-nine minimum centuries separation from Nahuatl]); Hokan, Otomanguean, and Tarascan (Weitlaner 1936–1939, 1948b); Mayan and Xinca (Hendrichs Pérez 1947); Tlapanec (Lehmann 1920); and Paya (Arana Osnaya 1958 [given forty-seven minimum centuries separation]; see Campbell 1979).

(11) **Xincan**
Guatemala

See the classification list. Xincan is a small family of at least four languages in Guatemala; it is not well known, and the languages are now either extinct or very moribund. Yupiltepeque, also once spoken in Jutiapa, is now extinct (Lehmann 1920:727–68). Toponyms with Xincan etymologies indicate that Xincan languages once had a much wider distribution in Guatemala and in the nearby territory of Honduras and El Salvador (Campbell 1978c). Xincan languages borrowed extensively from Mayan and

other indigenous languages. The fact that most Xincan terms for cultigens are loans from Mayan suggests that speakers of Xincan languages may not have been agriculturalists before their contacts with Mayan speakers (Campbell 1978c).

Xincan has not been systematically reconstructed, but a reasonable guess as to the likely inventory of proto phonemes, based on sounds shared by the four languages in apparent cognates, is: /p, t, k, ʔ, p', t', c', k', h, s, š, l, l', r, r̓, m, n, m̓, n̓, w, y, w̓, y̓; i, e, ɨ, a, o, u/. Serious reconstruction is required, however, to confirm (or revise) this inventory. Xincan languages are subject to a vowel harmony constraint where vowels within either of the two harmonic sets may co-occur with each other within a word, but vowels from one set cannot co-occur with vowels from the other. The high-vowel set is *i, ɨ, u;* the mid-vowel set is *e, o;* and *a* is a neutral vowel which can co-occur with either the high- or the mid-vowel harmonic sets. Most of these languages voice plain stops after nasals. There is a complicated rule which glottalizes stops and affricates when these are followed by a *V(n/y)ʔ*. In this rule the glottalized counterpart of *š* is *c'* (there is no *č* or *č'*).[47] In Xincan languages, stress falls on the vowel before the last consonant (that is, V → V́ / C(V)#).

As for proposed external relationships, the most often cited would connect Xincan with Lencan (Lehmann 1920), but this has been discredited. It has also been suggested that Xincan (and Lencan) might link up with Penutian (Sapir 1929a) or to Hokan (in a letter from Kroeber to Sapir 1924, cited in Golla 1984:409), but these proposals have not been followed up. Greenberg (1987) places Xincan in his Chibchan-Paezan group. None of these currently has much merit, and Xincan should therefore be considered an isolated small family.

Xincan

†Yupiltepeque (Dialects?: Jutiapa, Yupiltepeque)
Jumaytepeque[48] [moribund/extinct?]
Chiquimulilla [moribund/extinct?]
Guazacapan [moribund]

(12) Lencan

See the classification list. Lencan is a family of two languages, Honduran Lenca and Salvadoran Lenca (the latter is also called Chilanga after the name of the principal town in which it was spoken). They fall just outside the Mesoamerican linguistic area. Honduran Lenca is extinct or very nearly so; it was spoken with minor dialect differences in Intibuca, Opatoro, Guajiquiro, Similatón (modern Cabañas), and Santa Elena.[49] The two languages are not closely related; Swadesh (1967a:98–9) calculated thirty minimum centuries of divergence. Arguedas Cortés (1987) reconstructs Proto-Lencan with: /p, t, k, p', t', c', k', s, l, r, w, y; i, e, a, o, u/. The Lencan homeland was probably in central Honduras; Salvadoran Lenca reached El Salvador in about A.D. 1 and is responsible for the archaeological site of Classic Quelepa.

Hypotheses attempting to link Lencan with broader genetic groupings abound, but most were presented without supporting evidence, and none appears promising at present. As mentioned above, following Lehmann (1920:727), a genetic connection between Xincan and Lencan has usually been assumed, but most of the only twelve lexical comparisons given by Lehmann are invalid. For example, several involve loanwords (see Campbell 1978a, 1979:961–2). Penutian, Hokan, Macro-Chibchan, Macro-Mayan, and even Uto-Aztecan connections have all been proposed (see Mason 1940, Arguedas Cortés 1987:4), but with little or no supporting evidence. Andrews's (1970) proposed Mayan connection is rejected, since the data are not supportive (see Chapter 8). Greenberg (1960:793) put Lenca together with Misumalpan, Xincan, and Paya in a division of his Macro-Chibchan (these languages are in what he calls Chibchan-Paezan in Greenberg 1987), and Voegelin and Voegelin (1965:32) repeat this, including Lenca as one of seventeen divisions in their Macro-Chibchan phylum. There is no solid evidence for connecting Lencan with Chibchan (see Chapter 8).

(13) Misumalpan[50]
(Maps 12 and 14)

See the classification list. Miskito is the most divergent of the Misumalpan languages. Cacaopera and Matagalpa together have been called Matagalpan (Brinton 1895) and were frequently thought to be merely dialects of a single language, although they are clearly separate languages. Sumu has considerable dialect diversity; it includes varieties called Tawahka, Panamaka, Ulua, Bawihka, and Kukra, among others. Some have supposed Sumu diversity to be as great as that between German and Dutch. That the Misumalpan languages constitute a linguistic family has long been recognized, but little rigorous historical study had been done until recently (see Campbell 1975, 1976d; Constenla Umaña 1987). The branches of the family are not closely related; Swadesh (1959, 1967a:89) calculated, on the basis of glottochronology, forty-three minimum centuries of divergence. Adolfo Constenla Umaña (1987:135) reconstructs the following phonemes for Proto-Misumalpan: /p, t, k, b, d, s, l, m, n, ŋ, w, y, h; i, a, u/.

An unresolved question in Misumalpan prehistory is how Cacaopera, spoken in El Salvador, which is closely related to Matagalpa in Nicaragua, came to be so separated geographically from the other Misumalpan languages, whose center of gravity seems to be in northern Nicaragua.

The Misumalpan family is often grouped with Chibchan or included in some version of the Macro-Chibchan hypothesis; this is a possibility (see Constenla Umaña 1987, Craig and Hale 1992), though there is little firm evidence to support such a connection (see Chapter 8).

Misumalpan

Miskito (Mísquito) *Honduras, Nicaragua*
Sumu-Cacaopera-Matagalpa
   Sumu *Nicaragua, Honduras*
   Cacaopera-Matagalpa (Matagalpan)
      †Cacaopera[51] *El Salvador*
      †Matagalpa[52] *Nicaragua*

Lencan

†Honduran Lenca
†Salvadoran Lenca (Chilanga)

(14) †Naolan

Tamaulipas, Mexico

Naolan was spoken in Naolan, near Tula in southern Tamaulipas. It was all but extinct when Roberto Weitlaner collected the only known material, forty-three words and phrases (1948a). He compared it to Otopamean languages (Otomanguean family), to some so-called Hokan languages, and to some South American languages, finding that "the few correspondences are distributed almost equally among the three linguistic groups." Weitlaner concluded that the language belongs to the Uto-Aztecan group (Weitlaner 1948a:217–18). William Bright, on the other hand, thought that Naolan belonged to Hokan-Coahuiltecan, perhaps to be identified with Janambre or Tamaulipec (1955:285); Swadesh also placed it in the Hokan-Coahuiltecan group, but with closer connections with Tonkawan (1968). There is little to recommend any of these proposals. For now, the language should be considered unclassified. Indications in Weitlaner's discussion suggest equating Naolan with Mazcorros, or (less probably) with Pizones—groups whose names are known in this area from colonial reports. Of Weitlaner's forty-three words and phrases, six are loans from Spanish, five are certain loans from other indigenous languages, and another four are probably also loans (Campbell 1979:948–9). This leaves very little native material to work with, perhaps too little for any reliable proposal of kinship.

(15) †Maratino

Northeastern Mexico

Swanton (1940:122–4) published the scant material available on Maratino. Swadesh (1963a, 1968) called the language Tamaulipeco or Maratín and classified it with Uto-Aztecan, though there is little evidence to recommend this. Maratino *chiguat* [čiwat] 'woman' is a borrowing from Aztec *siwa:tl*, as is *peyot* 'peyote' (from Nahuatl *peyotl*),[53] and Swadesh's other twenty-odd comparisons show little to recommend a Uto-Aztecan connection. For the present, Maratino's classification is best considered unknown.

(16) †Guaicurian (Waikurian)

The Guaicurian languages of Baja California are extinct. The surviving documentation is extremely slight, only translations of the Lord's Prayer, the twelve articles of the Apostles' Creed, a verb paradigm, and a few additional words in Guaicuri itself (recorded by German missionary Johann Jakob Baegert 1952[1771]). The extant linguistic evidence (actually the lack thereof) provides next to no basis for establishing that the languages traditionally assigned to the Guaicurian family are actually related or how they might be subgrouped if they are related. Reasonable inferences have been made based on snatches of information in other historical reports about where these languages were spoken, who used them, and which were most similar. Buschmann (1859) analyzed Baegert's materials and concluded that Guaicuri was both independent of the Yuman languages of Baja California and was different from all the other languages of the region. Robert Latham (1862) held that all the languages of Baja California were Yuman, and Gatschet (1877b) followed Latham in this regard, but later Gatschet apparently reversed this conclusion, opting to treat Guaicurian as distinct from Yuman (though he erroneously confused Laymon [Yuman] as a division of Guaicuri). Brinton (1891) also followed Latham, joining Guaicuri with the Yuman family. Henshaw judged that Guaicuri belonged to another family (see Gursky 1966b:41); Thomas and Swanton reported that Hewitt had demonstrated that "there can be no question of the independent position of the two languages [Guaicuri(an) and Yuman]" (1911:3). Subsequently, many scholars entertained the idea that Guaicurian was indeed independent of Yuman but was still possibly related to the broader Hokan grouping (Gursky 1966b:42). Gursky assembled some fifty-three "possible cognates" involving Guaicuri and other putative Hokan languages. These lookalikes are suggestive but far from persuasive, given the many target languages among those of the putative Hokan stock from which selected similarities are sought, and the many methodological problems (see Chapter 7).

See the classification of Guacurian languages favored by Massey in the classification list. It is important to keep in mind that this tentative

Guacurian (Waikurian)
Guaicura
    †Guaicura (Waikuri)
    †Callejue
Huchiti
    †Cora (not to be confused with the
        Uto-Aztecan Cora)
    †Huchiti
    †Aripe
    †Periúe
Pericú
    †Pericú
    †Isleño

Massey 1949:303; see also Gursky 1966b,
León-Portilla 1976, Robles Uribe 1964.

classification is based almost entirely on judgments of similarity reported in colonial sources and not on actual linguistic data.

(17) †Alagüilac

Brinton's (1887) identification of Alagüilac (in central Guatemala) as Pipil (of the Nahua [Aztecan] subgroup of Uto-Aztecan) has been generally accepted, though wrongly so. Campbell (1972, 1985b) showed that Brinton's evidence was in fact from post–Spanish contact sources of Nahuatl, from a town identified in colonial sources as "Mejicano" (Nahua) in speech and not from the nearby town and sur-

rounding area which was reported as Alagüilac speaking. The sources clearly distinguish Alagüilac from both Nahua and Chortí (a Mayan language, also spoken in the region), leaving open the possibility that Alagüilac perhaps had Xincan connections (Xinca was reported spoken in colonial times in towns not far removed, and the geographical proximity of place names of Xincan origin lends support to this speculation) (see Campbell 1978c).

(18) Other Extinct and Unclassified Languages of Middle America

There is a rather large number (more than 100) of lesser known extinct (and unclassified) "languages" of Middle America, whose names are mentioned in historical sources but about which relatively little is known. It is possible that some of these names are simply alternate names for languages known by other appellations; some probably refer only to bands, towns, or subdivisions of languages identified by other names. They merit more investigation; limitations of space prevent their discussion here (see Campbell 1979, Harvey 1972, Longacre 1967, McQuown 1955, Sauer 1934, and Swadesh 1968; see also the list of extinct languages from northern Mexico identified as possibly Uto-Aztecan in Chapter 4).

6

Languages of South America

According to our thinking the language of these people [the natives of Tierra del Fuego] barely merits classification as an articulated language.

Charles Darwin, diary entry, December 17, 1832

THE LANGUAGES OF SOUTH AMERica are also not strictly confined geographically to South America. Members of the Chibchan family extend as far north as Honduras; Cariban languages reach far into the Caribbean, and Arawakan (Maipurean) languages are found throughout the Antilles and as far as Belize, Guatemala, Honduras, and Nicaragua. The classification of South American languages presents several difficulties. First, South America, to the extent that it is understood at present, exhibits considerably more linguistic diversity than North America and Middle America together: there are 118 distinct genetic units in South America (by Kaufman's count [1990a]) as opposed to some 58 in North America and 18 in Middle America. About 350 South American languages are still spoken, though it is estimated that about 1,500 different ones may have existed at the time of first European contact. Čestmír Loukotka (1968) lists a total of 1,492 languages (see also Wilbert 1968: 13–17, Migliazza and Campbell 1988:167). In Brazil alone, the number of languages still spoken is estimated to be either 170 (Rodrigues 1985a:403) or 201 (Grimes 1988). Second, significant historical linguistic research has been conducted on only a few of these families and isolates. Even basic descriptive accounts for many of these languages—a prerequisite for adequate historical linguistic investigation—are nonexistent or extremely limited. That is, much remains to be done to clarify the history of individual genetic units and their possible broader connections. Third, the dominant tendency has been to present broad, large-scale classifications of the South American languages, while historical research on individual language families has received much less attention. Jorge Suárez held that the classification of South American Indian languages had reached an "impasse," with "either overall classifications on the remotest level of relationship but without accompanying evidence or reconstructive work for languages obviously related" (1973:138). The picture is particularly murky, since these broad-scale classifications frequently conflict with one another in their treatment of different linguistic groups and are often based on little or no real evidence for some of the entities they attempt to classify. Unfortunately, Suárez's assessment is still accurate: "In spite of the magnitude and fundamental character of these contributions their technical quality was below the level of work in other parts of the world" (1974:105).[1] (For the earlier history of research on South American languages, see Chapter 2.) However, on the positive side, large strides have been made in the last few years, and considerably more is now known about the languages of South America. In this chapter I attempt to survey what is known (or believed) concerning the historical linguistics of South American languages, concentrating on the genetic classification. (For areal linguistic studies involving South American languages, see Chapter 9.)

Terrence Kaufman's (1990a, 1994) overall classification of South American languages is the most recent and is very useful. It reports the results of his detailed comparison of the various other overall classifications, coupled with his own observations and conclusions. Therefore, this chapter follows Kaufman's classification for the most part, departing from it only where more reliable information has become available. Like others, I do not utilize Kaufman's spellings for those language names which are better known by more conventional spellings (see Bright 1992, McQuown 1955, Klein and Stark 1985, Grimes 1988; see especially Derbyshire and Pullum 1991:3 on decisions concerning the spelling of these names). I utilize Kaufman's spellings when specifically discussing his claims and proposals concerning certain languages; in many cases, I provide Kaufman's names/spellings in brackets for purposes of clarity. While Kaufman concentrates only on genetic classification, other relevant historical linguistic information is also presented here when it is available. Information on numbers of speakers can be found in the works of Kaufman (1994) and Grimes (1988), as well as in many of the articles on specific languages cited in the bibliography to this volume.

The Known Genetic Units (Language Families and Isolates) of South America

Kaufman (1990a, 1994) based his South American classifications on agreements in the large-scale classifications of Loukotka (1968), Greenberg (1987), Suárez (1974), and Swadesh (1959).[2] His goal was to harmonize, to the extent possible, these classifications which he compared. He reviewed the main proposals to link together genetic units that have been made since 1955 (Kaufman 1990a), and he believes that his comparison of these serves to identify the hypotheses that most deserve to be tested. Kaufman (1990a) classifies the languages of South America into 118 genetic units (ranging from large "stocks" to isolates), of which 70 are isolates and 48 are groups consisting of at least two languages that are unquestionably genetically related. He believes there are probably genetic relationships which combine some of these 118 isolates and families into larger groupings (some of these possibilities are pointed out in Kaufman 1990a and are proposed more vigorously in Kaufman 1994). He does not, however, present specific information supporting his classification, so it is not possible to determine the nature or strength of the evidence on which he bases his conclusions. Kaufman speaks of "clusters" (which he designates, perhaps misleadingly, as "Macro") when two of the four main classifications he has compared agree on associating two or more genetic groups. These clusters are indicated in the classification of South American languages that follow. Kaufman considers the classification which resulted from his comparison of others' large-scale treatments of South American languages to be conservative: "Every genetic group recognized here is either obvious on inspection or has been demonstrated by standard procedures. This classification can be simplified by the merging of separately numbered groups once cross-group genetic connexions [sic] are established by the comparative method" (1990a:37).[3]

In the following classification, alternative names by which the languages are known are enclosed in parentheses (not always an exhaustive list). The numbers of the groups discussed here are those of Kaufman 1990a and have been included for ease of cross-reference and comparison. In this earlier work, however, Kaufman entertained several broader, more inclusive proposals that he considered plausible (and these are listed with little qualification in Kaufman 1994); he presented his numbers out of numerical sequence in the 1994 study in order to allow the languages in these tentative groupings to be considered together. The 118 baseline groups are presented here but are sometimes grouped together out of numerical sequence, as in Kaufman's (1994 and sometimes also 1990a) order of presentation. Most of these groupings are definitely not to be taken as anything more than hypotheses for further testing.

(1) †Yurumanguí (Yurimangi)
Colombia

Yurumanguí is an isolate. The language is extinct, known only from a short list of words recorded by Father Christoval Romero, which was included in Captain Sebastián Lanchas de Estrada's account of his travels in 1768 (Rivet 1942). Rivet (1942) and Harrington (1943a) both proposed a Hokan affiliation, which Greenberg (1987) has accepted, though other scholars have found the purported evidence for this to be of extremely poor quality and unconvincing (see Poser 1992). Swadesh (1963b) relates Yurumanguí to Opaye (Ofayé) and Chamicura (Chamicuro; see the section on Maipurean below) (cf. Langdon 1974:49). It is best considered unclassified for the present.

(2) Timotean
Venezuela (see MAP 14, nos. 2–3)

See the classification list. Timote and Cuica are dialects of the same language. Timote is apparently extinct but may survive as Mutú [Loco], thus far an unstudied language; Migli-

azza and Campbell (1988:313) consider Mutú unclassified. Mucuchí and Maripú are dialects of the same language.

(3) Jirajaran
Venezuela (see MAP 14, nos. 4–6)

See the classification list.

(4) Chocoan (Choco/Chokó family)
Panama, Colombia (see MAP 14, nos. 7–10)

See the classification list. Adolfo Constenla Umaña and Enrique Margery Peña calculate the breakup of Proto-Chocoan at 2,100 years ago (1991:137). The phonological inventory of Proto-Chocoan includes /p, t, č, k, b, ß, s, h, ř, ř̃, m, n; i, e, a, ɨ, o, u, nasalized vowels/ (Constenla Umaña and Margery Peña 1991:161, 166).

Gunn classified the Chocoan languages into two branches: (1) Waunana, with variants called San Juan (Colombia), Quebrada (Colombia, Panama), and Costeño (or Coastal) (Colombia); and (2) the Emberá branch (all spoken in Colombia), with two divisions—Northern dialects (Catío, Chimila, Tucura, and Emberá) and Southern dialects (Saixa-Baudo, Citara, Tado, and Chamí) (1980:14–15). In his classification, Gunn considered Chocoan languages to be a branch of Cariban; Tovar and Suárez were of the same opinion. However, Constenla and Margery (1991) presented some preliminary evidence that indicates a possible genetic connection between Chibchan and the Chocoan families. Chocoan includes for them Waunana (Huaunana, Noa-

---

Jirajaran

    †Jirajara
    †Ayomán (Ayaman)
    †Gayón

Chocoan

Noanamá (Waunana, Huaunana) *Colombia, Panama*
Emberá Group (Chocó) *Colombia*
    Southern Emberá
    Northern Emberá
†Sinúfana *Colombia*
†Quimbaya (Kimbaya)

Timotean

†Timote-Cuica (Miguri, Cuica) [Timote-Kuika language]
†Mucuchí-Maripú (Mocochí; Mirripú) [Mukuchí-Maripú language]

namá) and Emberá (with several dialects, including Catío [Dabeiba], Saija, Chamí, and Sambú).

(99 + 100 + 5 + 6 + 7 + 98 + 112) **Macro-Paesan** cluster

Kaufman groups together his families/genetic units 99 (Cunza), 100 (Kapixaná) (he also raises the possibility that 99 and 100 have a closer connection among themselves), 5 (Betoi), 6 (Paezan [sub]stock), 7 (Barbacoan family) (he favors a possible connection between 6 and 7), 98 (Itonama), and 112 (Warao), in what he calls the Macro-Paesan cluster. Kaufman explains that "the macro-Paesan cluster is . . . supported from many quarters [is favored by others], though the work needed for developing the arguments in favour of this hypothesis remains to be done" (1994:53). Until that work is done, the decision on this broader grouping needs to be held in abeyance.

Since I follow the numbers in Kaufman 1990a but the order of presentation in Kaufman 1994, some of the groups are presented here out of numerical sequence.

Macro-Páesan cluster

Kunsa-Kapishaná stock
    Kunsa language
    Kapishaná language
Betoi language
Paes-Barbakóan stock
    Páesan (sub)stock
    Barbakóan family
Itonama language
Warao language

Kaufman 1994:53.

(99 + 100) **Cunza-Kapixanan** proposal [Kunsa-Kapishaná stock]

Swadesh grouped these together with a fairly low time depth, and Kaufman finds that the lexical evidence looks promising; Greenberg does not agree.

(99) **†Cunza** (Atacama, Atakama, Atacameño, Lipe) [Kunsa language]
Chile, Bolivia, Argentina (see MAP 16; see also MAP 21, no. 11)

Adelaar (1991:53–4) lists Atacameño as another extinct language of the highland-Andean region, which has only scarce documentation, but which offers the opportunity for investigation.

(100) **Kapixaná** (Kanoé) [Kapishaná] [obsolescent] *Rondônia, Brazil*

Price (1978) thinks this might be related to Nambiquara [104].

(5) **†Betoi** (Betoy, Jirara)
Colombia (see MAP 14, no. 13)

(6 + 7) **Paezan-Barbacoan** proposal [Páes-Barbakóa stock]

There is general agreement (among the classifications surveyed by Kaufman) that these two families form a larger grouping, and Kaufman also mentions what he takes to be clear lexical similarities, though he does not present them.

(6) **Paezan** [Páesan (sub)stock]
(MAPS 14 and 15, nos. 14–19)

See the classification list. There is no consensus upon Paezan, and opinions vary greatly. Paez is

---

Paezan

†Andaqui (Andakí) *Colombia*
Paezan
    Paez (Paisa) [Paes] *Colombia* (Dialects: Pitayo, Paniquita)
    †Panzaleo (Latacunga, Quito) [Pansaleo] *Ecuador*
Coconuco (Cauca) [obsolescent] *Colombia*
    Coconuco [Kokonuko] [obsolescent]
    †Totoró
    Guambiano-Moguez [Wambiano-Mogés]   (Dialects: Guambiano, Moguez)

customarily placed with Paniquitá [Colombia] and extinct Panzaleo; however, because there are scarcely any data on Panzaleo, the classification has no real linguistic basis (Loukotka 1968:245, Constenla Umaña 1991). No significant comparative studies have been done on Paez and its possible relatives, though glottochronological studies exist. For claims of broader affinity, see the discussions of Chibchan and Barbacoan below.

(7) Barbacoan [Barbakóan]
Colombia, Ecuador (see MAPS 14 and 15, nos. 20–25)

See the classification list. Louisa Stark reports that Proto-Barbacoan split into the Cayapa-Colorado and Coaiquer branches in about 50 B.C. and that Cayapa and Colorado remained a single language until they separated in about A.D. 1000. Before the arrival of the Incas in Ecuador, the Barbacoa language extended from the Guaytara River in Colombia to Tungurahua province in Ecuador and spread down the central cordillera almost to Quito (1985:158–9).

The Barbacoan family is generally considered a probable relative of Paezan, though at best a very distant one (Constenla Umaña 1981:9). Mary Key (1979:38) presents the following reconstruction of "Proto-Colorado-Cayapa" sounds: /p, t, t^y, k, ʔ, b, d, d^y, c, č, s, š, h, m, n, ñ, l, l^y, r, w, y; i, e, a, o, u/ . Key also classifies Colorado and Cayapa with Paezan, but includes Guambiano as Barbacoan (considered Paezan by Kaufman).

(98) Itonama (Saramo, Machoto)
Bolivia (see MAP 16, no. 26)

(112) Warao (Guarao) [Warao language]
Guyana, Surinam, Venezuela (see MAP 14, no. 27)

The mutually intelligible dialects of Warao include Warao, Cocuina (Mánamo), Hoanarau, Araguao (Mariusa), and Guasay (Warrau).

(8) Chibchan [Chibchan (sub)stock]
(see MAP 17; see also MAP 14, nos. 28–47)

The Chibchan family was first postulated by Max Uhle (1890[1888]); he included the following as its members: Chibcha, Chimila, Cuna, the Aruako [Arwako, Arhuaco] group (with Ika [Bíntucua], Guamaca [Wamaka], and Cogui [Cágaba, Kogi]), the Guaymi [Waimi] group (Mobe [Movere], and Bocotá), and the Talamanka group (Boruca, Bribri, Cabécar, and Teribe [Tiribí]). Brinton (1891) added Tunebo and Duit (though without seeing that Duit goes with Chibcha proper), and Cyrus Thomas (1902) further included Guatuso. The most accurate and reliable classification to date is that of Constenla Umaña, followed here—see the classification list.

Also to be considered are the extinct languages: †Huetar (formerly spoken in Costa Rica, perhaps more closely connected with Guatuso), †Old Catío and †Nutabe (dialects of a single language of Colombia), and †Tairona (Colombia).[4] There is good evidence of the Chibchan affiliation for these languages (less secure for Tairona), though the evidence is insufficient to subgroup them within Chibchan. Other extinct languages which have been proposed as belonging to Chibchan, but for which the meager evidence does not warrant such a conclusion, include Malibú, Mocana, and Cueva (this last is perhaps closer to Chocoan than to Chibchan, Constenla Umaña 1990). Finally, Paya has been

---

Barbacoan [Barbakoan]

Northern group
  Coaiquer (Cuaiquer, Awa) *Colombia, Ecuador* (Dialects: Coaiquer, Telembí)
  †Muellama [Muelyama] *Colombia*
  †Pasto *Ecuador, Colombia*
Southern group
  Cayapa (Chachi) *Ecuador*
  Colorado (Colima, Campaz) [Tsáfiki] (two subgroups: Yumbos, Tsachila) *Ecuador*
  †Caranqui [Kara] *Ecuador*

Chibchan

Chibchan A
  Tiribí (Tirub) (Dialects: Teribe Panama; Térraba [moribund] Costa Rica)
  Viceitic branch *Costa Rica*
      Bribri (Viceíta)
      Cabécar (Chirripó, Tucurrique, Estrella)
          (Tiribí, Bribri, and Cabécar are sometimes grouped together in a subbranch called Tala-
              mancan.)
  Boruca (Brunca) [moribund] *Costa Rica*
  Guaymíic branch
      Movere (Move [Mobe], Guaymí, Penonomeño, Ngawbere/Ngäbere) *Panama*
      Bocotá (Murire, Muoy, Sabanero) *Panama*
Chibchan B
  Paya (Pech) *Honduras*
  Votic branch
      Rama (Melchora, Voto, Boto) [moribund?] *Nicaragua*
      Guatuso [Watuso] *Costa Rica*
  Dorasque branch
      †Dorasque, †Chánguena (Chumulu, Gualaca) *Panama*
  Eastern Chibchan
      Cuna (Cueva, Paya-Pocuro, Kuna) *Panama, Colombia* (Dialects: Cueva/Coiba, Chuana, Chuncu-
          naque, Maje, Paya-Pucuro, Caimán)
      Colombian subgroup
          Northern Colombian group
              Chimila (Chamila)
              Arhuacan [Arwako group]
                  Cágaba (Cogui, Kogi)
                  Southern and Eastern Arhuacan
                      Bíntucua (Ica, Ika, Arhuaco)
                      Guamaca-Atanque
                          Guamaca (Sancá, Marocacero, Arsario, Malayo, Huihua, Damana)
                          †Atanque (Cancuama)
          Southern Colombian group
              Barí (Motilón, Dobocubí)
              Cundicocuyese
                  Tunebo (Tame, Sínsiga, Tegría, Pedraza)
                  Muisca-Duit
                      †Muisca (Mosca, Chibcha)
                      †Duit

Constenla Umaña 1981, 1990, 1991; see Gunn 1980:16–17 for
an earlier, less well founded classification.

demonstrated indisputably to be a member of the Chibchan family (see Holt 1986); it is the northernmost member of the family, still spoken by about 300 persons in Honduras.

Kaufman (1990a:51) computes the breakup of Proto-Chibchan at fifty-six centuries ago; Constenla Umaña (1990:122) calculates that the breakup took place sometime after 3000 B.C. (For other counts, see Weisshaar 1987 and Kaufman 1994.) Proto-Chibchan is reconstructed with the following sounds: /p, t, k, ʔ, b, d, g, c, s, h, r, l; i, e, a, o, u; vowel nasalization; three tones (high, medium, low)/ . There is some doubt about the status of *c, *r, and *l (Constenla Umaña 1991). Proto-Chibchan grammar has not been extensively investigated, though it has been postulated to have perfective and imperfective aspect suffixes, an intransitivizing or antipassive prefix, and a suffix indicating nonfinite or participle verb forms. Proto-

Chibchan word order was SOV, Noun-Adjective, Noun-Postposition, and Noun-Numeral. Nouns were not inflected, though there perhaps were noun classifiers. Several of the languages appear to share reflexes of an enclitic which marks ergative case at the end of noun phrases, but its status in the proto language is uncertain (see Constenla Umaña 1991).

The cultural inventory reflected in the reconstructed vocabulary indicates that the Proto-Chibchan speakers were agriculturalists, since they had terms for 'to plant/sow', 'cassava (sweet manioc)', 'squash' species, 'maize', and 'tobacco'. They manufactured boats, pottery, and maracas (rattles). The Proto-Chibchan homeland is postulated to have been in southeastern Costa Rica and western Panama (Constenla Umaña 1990, 1991). With regard to borrowing, some researchers have expected Chibchan influence on neighboring languages, particularly in the area where Muisca was spoken, given its association with pre-Columbian civilizations of the Lower Central American–Colombian culture area; others see linguistic contact which they believe shows evidence of Arawakan influence on coastal Chibchan languages (Weisshaar 1987:8, see Constenla Umaña 1991:139).

Chibchan is often seen as both a linguistic and cultural bridge between South America and Central America, and this has sometimes led to proposals of broader linguistic and cultural connections for the Chibchan languages and their speakers. Many scholars have proposed a broader definition of the Chibchan family, either to include additional languages within the family per se or to relate the Chibchan family as a whole to others in larger proposed groupings, but these proposals remain controversial and unconfirmed. In several of them, the Chibchan family proper (as defined above) is considered the core of some broader genetic grouping. Such unsubstantiated proposals have postulated Chibchan relationships far and wide—for example, with Cunza [Atacama] (Chile), Allentiac (Argentina), Tarascan (Mexico), Timucua (Florida), Hokan-Siouan (itself very controversial), Mayan, Misumalpan, Xincan, Lencan, Cariban, Arawakan, Uto-Aztecan, and Pano-Tacanan. Some students of the topic have even postulated connections beyond the Americas, with Uralic,

Austronesian, Southeast Asian, and Caucasian language groups (Weisshaar 1987). The Beuchat and Rivet article (1910) may be seen as the initial stage in what others would call "Macro-Chibchan." They grouped the Barbacoan languages and Paezan languages, both non-Chibchan groups, with members of the Chibchan family (Talamanca, Guatuso, Cuna, Guaymí, Chimila, and Rama). Rivet (1924) goes even farther, adding also non-Chibchan Betoi, Jirajara, Andaqui, and others to this larger grouping. Greenberg's version (1960, 1987; see 1962) is the most inclusive of the Macro-Chibchan proposals, often cited in the literature, though it is discounted by specialists. In his survey of broader proposals, Kaufman (1990a) found that two or more agreed in proposing connections between Chibchan and the following: Tanoan, Uto-Aztecan, Cuitlatec, Misumalpan, and Tucanoan. Kaufman (1990a) cautions that none of these proposals has been substantiated (though he finds the Chibchan-Misumalpan proposal attractive, whereas Campbell and Migliazza 1988:183 consider it doubtful). (Concerning these proposals, see Campbell and Migliazza 1988; Constenla Umaña 1981, 1991; Holt 1986; Greenberg 1987; Rivet 1924; Swadesh 1959; and Suárez 1974.) As mentioned earlier, Constenla Umaña and Margery Peña (1991) presented preliminary evidence indicative of a genetic connection between Chibchan and Chocoan. The term "Chibchan-Paezan" is sometimes repeated in the literature; it follows Swadesh's and Greenberg's very broad proposals which lump together a number of groups not demonstrated to be related. Greenberg's (1987) controversial proposal, for example, links Chibchan with so-called Paezan and with Tarascan, Timucua, Warao, Barbacoan, Chimu, Chocó, Cuitlatec, Itonama, Jirajira, Misumalpan, Mura, Xinca, and Yanomama. On the Paezan side, Greenberg places such wide-ranging languages as Allentiac, Andaqui, Atacama (Cunza), Barbacoa, Betoi, Chimu (Yunga), Chocó, Itoname, Jirajira, Mura, Paez, Timucua, and Warao, where Andaqui, Barbacoa, Chocó, and Paez form his nuclear Paezan. Because of the scant and flawed evidence presented by Greenberg, however, his groupings are not accepted by most specialists.

(9) **Misumalpan**
(see Maps 12 and 14, nos. 48–50)

Kaufman groups his [8] (Chibchan) and [9] (Misumalpan) into what he calls the Chibcha-Misumalpan stock (1994:54). I do not find the evidence assembled thus far to be supportive (see Middle America, Chapter 5, where the Misumalpan family is discussed).

(10) **Camsá** (Sibundoy, Coche) [Kamsá]
Colombia (see Map 14, no. 51)

(11) **Tiniguan** [Tiníwan family]
Colombia (see Map 14, nos. 52–53)

See the classification list.

(18 + 12 + 106) **Macro-Otomákoan** cluster

See the classification list. Kaufman indicates that, although this cluster represents the intersection of some opinions about genetic grouping, "no systematic effort has yet been made to validate this particular grouping" (Kaufman 1994:56). The three are best treated as independent for the present, and are so discussed here, as follows.

(18) **Harákmbut** language area (Tuyoneri)
Peru (see Maps 16 and 18, no. 54)

See the classification list. Scholars have been confused by the many names given these languages.

Tiniguan
†Tinigua (Timigua) [Tiniwa]
†Pamigua [Pamiwa]

Macro-Otomákoan cluster
Tuyoneri language area (called Harákmbut
        language area in Kaufman 1990a)
Otomákoan family
Trumai language

Migliazza places this with Macro-Arawakan (Migliazza and Campbell 1988:212, 395).

(12) **Otomacoan** [Otomákoan]
Venezuela (see Map 14, nos. 55–56)

See the classification list.

(106) **Trumai**
Xingu, Mato Grosso, Brazil (see Map 20, no. 57)

(13) **†Guamo** [Wamo]
Venezuela (see Map 14, no. 58)

Guamo had two dialects, that of Santa Rosa and that of San José (Barinas). Kaufman (1994:56) includes this language in his Wamo-Chapakúran stock.

(14) **Chapacuran** (Txapakúran) [Chapakúran]
Brazil, Bolivia (see Maps 16 and 18, nos. 59–67)

See the classification list on page 178. Kaufman (1994:57) combines this family with Guamo [13] in his Wamo-Chapakúran [13 + 14] stock.

(13 + 14) **Guamo-Chapacuran** proposal [Wamo-Chapakúra stock]

Guamo and Chapacuran are placed in the same low-level group by Greenberg. Kaufman mentions lexical similarities he has found (but does not present) that support this inclusion (1994:56).

Harákmbut
Huachipaeri (Tuyoneri, Toyoneri, Wachipayri)
        (Dialects: Toyoneri, Toyeri; Sapiteri, Arasairi)
Amaracaeri [Amarakaéri] (Dialect: Quisambaeri)

Otomacoan
†Otomaco
†Taparita

Chapacuran

Itene or Central Chapakúran group
  Wanham [Wanyam language] [few] *Rondônia, Brazil*
  Kumana (Torá, Toraz, Cumana) [Abitana-Kumaná language] [moribund/obsolescent] *Amazonas, Rondônia, Brazil*
  Kabixí (Cabishi, Habaishi, Parecís, Nambikuara) [Kabishi language] *Mato Grosso, Brazil*
  Itene (Iteneo, Itenez, More) [moribund] *Bolivia*
Wari or Southern Chapakúran group
  †Quitemo (Quitemoca) [Kitemo-Nape] *Bolivia* (Dialects: Quitemo, Nape)
  †Chapacura (Huachi, Wachi) [Chapakura] *Bolivia*
  Urupá-Jarú (Txapakura; Yaru, Jaru) *Rondônia, Brazil* (Dialects: Urapú, Jarú)
  Orowari (Pakaás-novos, Pacasnovas, Pacaha-novo, Uariwayo, Uomo, Jaru, Oro Wari) *Rondônia, Brazil*
Northern Chapakúran
  Torá *Amazonas, Brazil*

(15 + 16 + 17 + 30) **Macro-Arawakan** cluster

See the classification list. Kaufman includes his groups 15, 16, 17, and 30 (1990a) in a Macro-Arawakan cluster; however, since there is no real evidence that these are related (see Kaufman 1994:57), this should not be interpreted as an established (or even likely, for that matter) genetic grouping.

David Payne (1991) and Desmond Derbyshire (1992:103) tentatively group Maipurean, Arauan, and Guajiboan, as does Kaufman (though they do not include Candoshi), but they add Puquina and Harákmbet to their tentative Arawakan proposal.

(15) **Guajiboan** [Wahívoan family]
Colombia, Venezuela (see MAP 14, nos. 68–71)

See the classification list. Efforts to reconstruct the phonemic system were published by Chris-

---

Macro-Arawakan cluster
Guajiboan [Wahívoan family]
Arawakan stock and Maipurean substock
Arawán family (Arauan)
Candoshi [Kandoshi language]

Guajiboan
Guajibo (Wahibo, Guaybo) *Colombia, Venezuela*
Cuiva *Colombia, Venezuela*
Guayabero *Colombia*
†Churuya *Venezuela*

---

tian and Matteson (1972), based on Guajibo, Cuiva, and Guayabero: /p, t, k, b, d, Y, s, x, l, r, m, n, N, w, y, h; i, e, ɨ, a, o, u/ . Their *N is based on the correspondence of $l : l : n$, as opposed to *n with $n : n : n$ and *l with essentially $l : l : l$. The *Y is reflected by Guayabero *č*, and by Cuiva and Guajibo *y/i/Ø*.

Kaufman reports that "virtually all major 'lumpers' and classifiers group Wahivoan [Guajiboan] with Arawakan. The hypothesis deserves to be tested or looked into, but I have so far seen no evidence to convince me of the connection" (1994:57).

(16) **Maipurean (Maipuran)** or **Arawakan**
[Maipúrean (sub)stock, Arawakan stock][5]
(see MAP 19; see also MAPS 14, 15, 16, 18, 20, and 21, nos. 75–124)

See the classification list. The Maipurean or Arawakan family is the biggest in the New World—and it has considerable internal branching. It covers the widest geographical area of any group in Latin America, with languages spoken from Central America and the Caribbean islands to the Gran Chaco, from Belize to Paraguay, and from the Andes to the mouth of the Amazon River. Representatives of this family are spoken in all South American countries except Uruguay and Chile. It is also large in terms of number of languages, with approximately sixty-five, of which thirty-one, unfortunately, are now extinct. With respect to the name of this large family, David Payne points out:

The general trend in recent comparative work is to use the term "Maipuran" [or Maipurean] . . . to refer to the main group of unquestionably related languages, and to elevate the term "Arawakan" to denote the language stock or phylum which potentially relates these Maipuran languages to other more distantly related languages. . . . "Arawakan" would be the preferred family name to include, for example, Arauán, Guahiboan, Harakmbet, and Puquina, if these are, as some have suggested, related to the Maipuran languages. (1991:363)

As Kaufman indicates, "Maipurean used to be thought to be a major subgroup of Arawakan, but all the *living* Arawakan languages, at least, seem to need to be subgrouped with languages already found within Maipurean as commonly defined" (1994:57).

Several earlier comparative studies of Maipurean/Arawakan were based on real data (as opposed to the broad-scale classifications that present none of the evidence; see, for example, Matteson 1972, Noble 1965, and others discussed by David Payne 1991). Payne's appears quite solid, based on reasonably extensive cognate material (203 sets) from twenty-four of the languages. He presents two classifications; the first is based on earlier classifications and on his assessment of the data and the literature (1991:489). His second classification, posited as a "working hypothesis," is based primarily on calculations of lexical retentions in the twenty-four languages, but it is also supported in part by "shared phonological characteristics" and, for some of the subgroups, by grammatical data as well (1991:488). In the second, he attempts to establish some more inclusive, higher-order subgroups. Although several other linguists classify Piro-Apurinã and Campa together in a subgroup called Pre-Andine (see Wise 1986:568, for example), Payne finds no evidence that these are closer to each other than they are to other subgroups of the family. He also adduces persuasive evidence from the scant fifteen words recorded in extinct Shebayo (Shebaye) of Trinidad to show that it belongs with the Caribbean group (for example, it appears to have *da-* 'my', and these languages are the only ones which have an alveolar stop and not a nasal for 'first person singular') (1991:366–7).

I present Kaufman's (1994) classification of Maipurean in the list given here (here maintaining many of his spellings of the names), since it includes the languages not considered in Payne's study. Kaufman also ventures some hypotheses about more inclusive subgroupings.

The phonemes tentatively postulated for Proto-Maipurean by David Payne are: /p, t, k, p^h, t^h, c, č, k^h, b, d, s, š, h, m, n, l, r, w, y; i, e, ɨ, a, o, u/. The only syllable-final consonants are *n and *h; the only consonant clusters consist either of a nasal plus homorganic obstruent or of *h before a syllable-final consonant (Payne 1991:389–90).[7]

The proto language probably had SOV order. SVO word order is found today in most of the family, with frequent VS for intransitive verbs. VSO basic word order occurs in Amuesha, in Campa languages, and possibly in Garífuna. Baure and Terêna have VOS, Apuriña has OSV (probably), and Piro has SOV order (Derbyshire 1986:558, 1992).

Arawakan [Arawakan stock] (Arahuacan) is the name traditionally applied to what here is called Maipur(e)an, which used to be thought to be but one subgroup of Arawakan. Now, however, the languages which can clearly be established as belonging to the family (whatever its name) seem all to fall together with those languages already known to belong together in the so-called Maipurean subgroup. Kaufman suggests that the sorting out of the labels Maipurean and Arawakan will have to await a more sophisticated classification of the languages in question than is possible given the present state of comparative studies (see also Derbyshire 1992). However, Arawakan is also the name associated with various more inclusive proposals. For example, Greenberg (1987:83) would group the Otomaco, Tinigua, Katembri, and Guahibo (Guajibo) with Arawakan as a division of his Equatorial grouping. Rivet and de Wavrin (1951) argued that Resígaro (spoken by ten individuals in 1975 in the Colombia-Peru border area) belongs to Arawakan, though a competing classification of Resígaro as a Huitotoan [Witotoan] language has also been proposed (discussed in Payne 1985). Allin (1976, 1979) claims that Resígaro is related to Huitoto, Ocaina, and Bora, and that this group is connected to the Arawakan family. However, in a reassessment of Allin's

Maipurean

Northern division
    Upper Amazon branch
        Western Nawiki subbranch
            †Wainumá group
                †Wainumá (Waima, Wainumi, Waiwana, Waipi, Yanuma) *Amazonas, Brazil*
                †Mariaté *Amazonas, Brazil*
            †Anauyá *Venezuela*
            Piapoko group
                Achagua [Achawa] [obsolescent] *Colombia, Venezuela*
                Piapoco [Piapoko]
                †Amarizana *Colombia*
            Caviyari [Kaviyarí] [obsolescent] *Colombia*
            Warekena group
                Guarequena [Warekena, Guarenquena] *Venezuela, Colombia, Brazil*
                Mandahuaca [Mandawaka] *Venezuela, Brazil*
            Río Negro group *Amazonas, Brazil*
                †Jumana
                †Pasé
                †Cawishana (Kawishana, Kayuwishana) [Kaiwishana]
            Yucuna [Jukuna] language area *Colombia*
                Yucuna (Chucuna, Matapí) [Jukuna]
                †Garú (Guarú)
        Eastern Nawiki subbranch
            Tariana [few] *Brazil, Colombia*
            Karu language (area)
                Ipeka-Kurripako dialect group *Brazil, Colombia, Venezuela*
                Karútiana-Baniwa (Baniva) dialect group *Brazil, Venezuela*
                Katapolítani-Moriwene-Mapanai dialect? *Brazil*
        Resígaro [moribund] *Peru, Colombia*
        Central Upper Amazon subbranch
            Baré group
                †Marawá *Brazil*
                Baré (Ibini) *Venezuela, Brazil*
                †Guinao [Ginao] *Venezuela*
            Yavitero group *Venezuela*
                †Yavitero (Yavitano)
                Baniva
            †Maipure *Colombia, Venezuela*
        Manao group
            †Manao *Amazonas, Brazil*
            †Kariaí *Roraima, Brazil*
    Maritime branch
        †Aruán (Aruá) *Marajó, Brazil*
        Wapixana [Wapishana language (area)] *Guyana, Brazil*
        Ta-Maipurean subbranch
            †Taíno *Caribbean*
            Guajiro [Wahiro] group
                Guajiro (Goahiro) [Wahiro] *Colombia, Venezuela*
                Paraujano [Parauhano] [obsolescent] *Venezuela*

(Continued)

Maipurean (*Continued*)
          Arawak (Locono, Lokono, Arwuak, Arowak) *Guyana, Surinam, French Guiana, Venezuela*
          Iñeri (Igneri) [Inyeri] language area
              †Kalhíphona (Island Carib) *Dominica, Saint Vincent*
              Garífuna[6] (Black Carib) *Honduras, Guatemala, Belize, Nicaragua*
   Eastern branch
      Palikur language area
         Palikur *Brazil, French Guiana*
         †Marawán-Karipurá *Amapá, Brazil*
Southern division
   Western branch *Peru*
      Amuesha (Amoesha, Amuexa)
      Chamicuro [Chamikuro]
   Central branch
      Paresí group
         Paresí (Parecís, Paretí) *Mato Grosso, Brazil*
         †Saraveca (Sarave) *Bolivia, Brazil*
      Waurá group
         Waurá-Meinaku (Uara, Mahinacu) *Xingu, Mato Grosso, Brazil*
         Yawalpití *Xingu, Mato Grosso, Brazil*
         †Custenau [Kustenau] *Brazil, Paraguay, Argentina*
   Southern Outlier branch
      Terena (Tereno) *Bolivia, Brazil, Paraguay, Argentina* (Dialects: Kinikinao, Terena, Guaná, Chané)
      Mojo [Moho] group *Bolivia*
         Mojo [Moho] language (area)
            Ignaciano
            Trinitario (Dialects: Loretano, Javierano)
         Baure
         †Paunaca [Pauna-Paikone]
      Piro group
         Piro *Brazil, Peru* (Dialects: Chontaquiro, Maniteneri, Mashineri)
         †Inapari *Peru, Bolivia, Brazil*
         †Kanamaré (Canamari) *Acre, Brazil*
         Apuriná *Amazonas and Acre, Brazil*
   Campa [Kampa] branch—Campa [Kampa] language area *Peru*
      Ashéninga (Asheninca) (Dialects: Ucayali, Upper Perené, Pichis, Apurucayali)
      Asháninga (Ashaninca)
      Machiguenga [Matsigenga] (Dialects: Caquinte, Machiguenga)

NOTE: The following languages belong to the Upper Amazon branch, but there is not enough data to determine how they are to be classified with respect to the various groups in that branch:
   †Waraikú *Amazonas, Brazil*
   †Yabaána *Roraira, Brazil*
   †Wiriná *Roraira, Brazil*
   Shiriana *Roraira, Brazil*
The following are non-Maipurean Arawakan languages or are too scantily known to classify:
   †Shebaya (Shebaye) *?Trinidad* (but see Payne 1991:366–7)
   †Lapachu *Bolivia*
   †Morique [Morike] *Peru, Brazil*
Rodrigues (1986:72) also lists Salumã (Brazil) as an Arawakan language (see Kaufman 1994:59).

Kaufman 1994:57–8; for a different classification, see Migliazza and
Campbell 1988:223; for a similar one, see Derbyshire 1992.

evidence and claims, Payne (1985) finds the 375 items which Allin compared with Bora and other Witotoan (Huitotoan) languages unpersuasive, due to "the paucity of body parts, pronouns, and verbs in this list, and the plethora of animal names and 'culture-specific' items (for example, drum, rattle, mask, coca, Banisterium), [which] make these apparent similarities highly suspect of being loans" (Payne 1985:223). He argues plausibly that Resígaro belongs to the Northern Maipurean / Arawakan languages and that the putative connection between Arawakan and Witotoan is not sufficiently supported (1985, 1991). (The Witotoan/Huitotoan family is discussed later in this chapter.)

(17) **Arauan** (Arahuan) [Arawán family]
Brazil, Peru (see MAP 18, nos. 127–31)

See the classification list. It should be noted that "no one has yet offered an explicit classification of this family" (Kaufman 1994:60; see also Rodrigues 1986:72). It is also widely believed that Arauan constitutes a subgroup of a larger Arawakan genetic grouping, but this has by no means yet been demonstrated.

(30) **Candoshi** (Maina) [Kandoshi]
Peru (see MAP 15, no. 132)

The classification of Candoshi is uncertain; Zaparoan and Jivaroan are the main candidates for a genetic grouping to which it may belong. In fact, in some proposals, the Murato dialect has been classified as Zaparoan and the Shapra dialect has been grouped with Jivaroan (Wise 1985a:216). David Payne (in unpublished work cited by Wise 1985a:216) has attempted to demonstrate systematic phonological correspondences between Candoshi and the Jivaroan languages. Kaufman (1994:60) lists Candoshi after Arauan, apparently in response to unpublished evidence from David Payne linking Candoshi with Maipurean (Arawakan).

(19 + 20 + 115 + 116 + 117) **Macro-Puinávean** cluster

See the classification list. Kaufman (1994:60) considers the possibility that his numbers 19, 20, 115, 116, and 117 may be members of a Macro-Puinávean cluster. These groups are discussed in the following paragraphs.

(19) **Puinavean** (Makú stock) [Puinávean stock]
Brazil, Colombia, Venezuela (see MAPS 14 and 18, nos. 133–8)

See the classification list.

(20) **Katukinan** (Catuquinan)
Brazil (see MAP 18, nos. 140–2; see also MAPS 15 and 16)

See the classification list.

(115 + 116 + 117) **Kalianan** [Kaliánan stock]

Greenberg links these three, and Kaufman (1990a:50) finds the proposal "promising."

Arauan

†Arauan (Madi, Arawa) [Arawá] *Amazonas, Brazil*
Culina (Curina, Kulina, Korina) [Kulina] *Brazil, Peru*
Dení (Dani) *Amazonas, Brazil*
Jamamadí language area
    Jamamadí (Yamamadi, Madi, Yamadi) *Amazonas, Brazil* (Dialects: Bom Futuro, Juruá, Pauiní, Mamoría, Cuchucdu, Tukurina?)
    Kanamantí *Mato Grosso, Brazil*
    Jarawara (Jaruara) *Amazonas, Brazil*
    Banawá (Banavá) [obsolescent] *Amazonas, Brazil*
Paumarí (Pamari, Kurukuru, Purupuru) *Brazil* (Dialects: Paumarí, Kurukurú, Wayai)

Macro-Puinávean cluster

Puinávean stock (cf. 19)
Katukínan family (cf. 20)
Kaliánan stock
    Awaké-Kaliana family
        Awaké (cf. 115)
        Kaliana (cf. 116)
        Maku (cf. 117)

Puinavean

†Kuri-Dou *Amazonas, Brazil* (Dialects: Kurikuriaí, Dou)

Hupda *Brazil, Colombia* (Dialects: Tikié, Hupda, Yahup, Papurí)

Kaburí language area

    Nadöb (Nadëb) *Amazonas, Brazil*

    Kamán [obsolescent] *Amazonas, Brazil*

Guariba (Wariwa) [Wariva] [obsolescent] *Amazonas, Brazil*

Cacua [Kakua] *Colombia, Brazil*

Puinave (Guaipunavi) *Colombia, Venezuela*

Waviare (Makusa) *Colombia*

Katukinan

Katukina (Catuquina) [very moribund] *Acre, Brazil* (also known as Katukina do Jutaí—different from Katukina in Amazonas, which is a Panoan language—, Pidá-Djapá)

Southern Katukinan language (area)—Dyapá *Amazonas, Brazil* (Dialects: Kanamarí/Canamarí); Tshom-Djapá [obsolescent] (also known as Txunhuã-Djapá; perhaps the same as Tucundiapa [Tucano Dyapa, Hondiapa/Hon-Dyapá])

Katawixi [Katawishí] [moribund] *Amazonas, Brazil*

Compare Rodrigues 1986:79, 81.

(115 + 116) **Ahuaque-Kalianan** proposal [Awaké-Kaliana family]

Both Greenberg and Swadesh group these two, and Loukotka listed them side by side. Kaufman (1990a:50) mentions that there is lexical evidence to support this possible genetic relationship.

(115) **Ahuaqué** (Auaké, Uruak) [Awaké]

[moribund/obsolescent] *Venezuela, Brazil* (see MAP 14, no. 143)

(116) **Kaliana** (Caliana, Cariana, Sapé, Chirichano)

[moribund] *Venezuela* (see MAP 14, no. 144)

See Migliazza 1985[1982]:51.

(117) **Maku** (Macu)

[extinct?] *Brazil, Venezuela* (see MAP 14, no. 145)

Two speakers of Maku were reported in 1986 (other recent estimates vary from extinct to 400 speakers), formerly located between the Padamo and Cunucunuma rivers, Venezuela (Rodrigues 1986:95, 97–8). Greenberg (1960) classified Maku with his Macro-Tucanoan, based on some lexical similarities, but Migliazza (1985[1982]: 46, 52–4) notes that it also shares similarities with Arawakan languages and with Warao.

(21) **†Tequiraca** (Avishiri) [Tekiraka]

Peru (see MAPS 14 and 15, no. 146)

(22) **Canichana** (Canesi) [Kanichana]

[obsolescent] *Bolivia* (see MAP 16, no. 147)

(21 + 22) **Macro-Tekiraka-Kanichana** cluster (or stock)

Tequiraca and Canichana were listed as being independent by Kaufman (1990a), but he later grouped them together (1994:61).

(23) **Tucanoan** [Tukánoan stock]

(see MAPS 14, 15, and 18, nos. 148–61)

See the classification list. Waltz and Wheeler's (1972:129) reconstruction of Proto-Tucanoan phonemes is: /p, t, č, k, kʷ, ʔ, b, d, j, g, gʷ, s, S, z, Y, r, m, n, w, y, h; i, e, ɨ, a, o, u; vowel nasalization; phonemic stress/ . One may well raise questions about some of the sounds they postulate. For example, *S, *j, and *Y are unclear. The reflexes for *z and *j are the same— that is, not distinct—in all the daughter languages except for Siona, which has s' and y, respectively. The sounds *k and *kʷ are both reflected by k in all the daughter languages except Siona, which has k and kʷ, respectively. Similarly, reflexes of *g and *gʷ contrast only in Siona, and the reflexes of *s and *č also appear to be the same in all except Siona.

Tucanoan

Western Tucanoan
   Coreguaje (Coreguaje, Caquetá) [Korewahe] *Colombia*
   †Macaguaje (Kakawahe) [Piohé] *Ecuador, Peru* (Dialects: Macaguaje, Siona-Piojé, Angutero/Ango-
      tero, Secoya)
   Tetetó (Eteteguaje) [extinct?[8]] *Ecuador, Colombia*
   Orejón (Coto, Payoguaje, Payaguá) [Koto] *Peru*
   Yauna [Jaúna] *Colombia*
Central Tucanoan
   Cubeo (Cuveo, Kobeua) [Kubewa] *Colombia, Brazil*
Eastern Tucanoan
   Macuna (Buhagana, Wahana) [Makuna-Erulia] *Colombia, Brazil* (Dialects: Paneroa/Palanoa, Eduri/Eru-
      lia/Paboa, Bahágana)
   †Yupuá-Durina *Colombia*
   †Cueretú [Kueretú] *Amazonas, Brazil*
   Desano-Siriano *Colombia, Brazil* (Dialects: Sirianó/Siriana/Chiranga, Desano/Desana)
   Bará-Tuyuka (Pocanga, Pakang, Tejuca, Teyuka) *Colombia, Brazil* (Dialects: Barasano/Barasana,
      Southern Barasano, Waimaja / Bará / Northern Barasano)
   Carapano (Carapana, Karapana) *Colombia, Brazil* (Dialects: Papiwa, Tatuyo/Tatu-tapuya) Tucano (Tu-
      kana, Dasea) [Tukano] *Brazil, Colombia* (Several dialects, such as Yurutí/Juruti)
   Guanano (Wanana, Kotedia) [Wanana-Pirá] *Brazil, Colombia* (Dialects: Guanano, Pirá)
   Piratapuyo (Waikina, Uiquina) *Brazil*

Compare Migliazza and Campbell 1988, Waltz and Wheeler 1972. Sorensen's (1973)
classification of Eastern Tucanoan is different in some respects.

(24 + 25) **Yuri-Ticunan** [Jurí-Tikuna stock]

Greenberg and Swadesh group these, and Kaufman (1994:62) finds that there is lexical evidence in support of such a grouping.

(24) **Ticuna** (Tukuna, Tucuna) [Tikuna]
Colombia, Peru, Brazil (see MAP 18, no. 162)

(25) **†Yuri** (Jurí)
Colombia, Brazil (see MAP 18, no. 163)

(26) **Munichi (Muniche)**
[moribund/obsolescent] *Peru* (see MAP 15, no. 164)

(27 + 28) **Esmeralda-Yaruroan**
[Ezmeralda-Jaruro stock (Kaufman 1990a); Takame-Jarúroan (Kaufman 1994:62)]

All the broad classifiers of South American languages except Swadesh group these together. Kaufman (1994) reports that there are "possible" lexical similarities. The proposal merits study.

(27) **†Esmeralda** [Takame]
Ecuador (see MAP 14, no. 165)

Kaufman (1994:62) now calls this language Takame, though it is better known by its traditional name, Esmeralda (Ezmeralda in Kaufman's 1990a listing). He groups it with Yaruro.

(28) **Yaruro** [Jaruro]
Venezuela (see MAP 14, no. 166)

(29) **Cofán** [Kofán]
Colombia, Ecuador (see MAP 14, no. 167)

Cofán has borrowed from neighboring Chibchan languages (Wheeler 1972:95); it remains unclassified, not known to have any broader affiliation.

(31 + 32 + 37 + 60) **Macro-Andean** cluster

See the classification list. Kaufman (1994:62) groups together numbers 31, 32, 37, and 60 in what he calls the Macro-Andean cluster. The components of this cluster are discussed in the following paragraphs.

Macro-Andean cluster

Hívaro-Kawapánan stock (cf. 31 + 32)
    Hívaro (cf. 31)
    Kawapánan (cf. 32)
Urarina (cf. 37)
Puelche (cf. 60)

(31 + 32) Jivaroan-Cahuapanan
proposal [Hívaro-Kawapana stock]

Kaufman (1990a:42) finds that this proposal seems to be supported by some lexical data. Greenberg's (1987) Jibaro-Candoshi grouping is very poorly supported by the data cited in his book (see Kaufman's [1990a:62] criticism of Greenberg's lexical comparisons).

(31) Jivaroan [Hívaro language area]
Ecuador, Peru (see MAP 15, no. 168)

See the classification list. Many scholars also include Candoshi in or with the Jivaroan family (see Stark 1985, Wise 1985a:217). Loukotka thought Palta belongs with Jívaro; Palta is poorly documented, but even so there is very little resemblance between the two (Kaufman 1994:62).

(32) Cahuapanan (Jebero) [Kawapánan family]
Peru (see MAP 15, nos. 169–70)

See the classification list.

(37) Urarina (Shimacu, Itukale)
Peru (see MAP 15, no. 171)

(60) †Puelche (Guenaken, Gennaken, Pampa, Pehuenche, Ranquelche)
Argentina (see MAP 21, no. 172)

(33 + 34) Zaparoan-Yaguan proposal
[Sáparo-Yawan stock]

Doris Payne (1985) argues for this grouping, based primarily on a shared morphological trait, that of -*ta*, marking both transitivity and 'instrument/comitative'. The proposal requires further investigation.

(33) Zaparoan [Sáparoan family]
(see MAP 15, nos. 173–5)

See the classification list. Stark (1985:184–6) also lists †Aushiri (Auxira) and †Omurano

---

Jivaroan

Jívaro (Shuar; Achuar-Shiwiar [Achuar, Achuall, Achuara, Achuale, Jívaro, Maina]; Huambisa; Jívaro, Xivaro, Jibaro, Chiwaro, Shuara) [Hívaro] *Peru, Ecuador*
Aguaruna [Awaruna] *Peru*

Cahuapanan

Chayahuita (Chawi, Chayhuita, Chayabita, Shayabit, Balsopuertino, Paranapura, Cahuapa) [Chayawita]
Jebero (Xebero, Chebero, Xihuila) [Hevero]

Zaparoan

Záparo group
    Záparo-Conambo (Zápara, Kayapwe) *Ecuador, Peru*
    Arabela-Andoa *Peru* (Dialects: Andoa [Shimigae, Semigae, Gae, Gaye], Arabela [Chiripuno, Chiripunu])
    Iquito-Cahuarano *Peru* (Dialects: Cahuarano, Iquito [Iquita, Amacacore, Hamacore, Quiturran, Puca-Uma])

(Humurana, Roamaina, Numurana, Umurano, Mayna), both in Peru, as Zaparoan languages. Taushiro is included by Kaufman with Zaparoan, perhaps wrongly so (see the following discussion). Stark hypothesizes that the Proto-Zaparoan homeland was in the Cahuarano-Iquito area—along the Nanay River in Peru (1985:185).

(34) **Yaguan** [Yáwan family] (also known as Peban or the Peba-Yaguan family)
Peru (see MAPS 14, 15, and 18, nos. 176–8)

See the classification list.

(35a) **Taushiro** (Pinchi, Pinche)
[obsolescent] *Peru*

This language was unknown to most of the classifiers except Tovar (1961; though this is not repeated in the Tovar and Larrucea de Tovar 1984 edition), who placed it with Omurano. Kaufman notes certain lexical resemblances "that tend to support Tovar's claim" (1994:63). Pinche is grouped with Candoshi by Loukotka (1968) and Tovar and Larrucea de Tovar (1984), but Taushiro is classified under Zaparoan (see Kaufman 1994:63). Kaufman also reports Taushiro lexical similarities with Candoshi and with Omurano (no. 35) and he therefore assigns to the language the number 35a to indicate that it has been claimed to be related to Zaparoan but may have the other connections mentioned. Thus he presents "a tentative new macro-group *Kandoshi-Omurano-Taushiro*" (1994:63). He gives a table of sixteen lexical comparisons for the three languages, which, he believes, suggest "that Taushiro might be related to both Omurano

and Kandoshi, and more closely to the former." However, he adds that "the test of the suggested relationship will have to be the establishment of plausible lexical etymologies, recurrent sound correspondences and peculiar grammatical analogies" (1994:63). His table suggests two plausible sound correspondences: (1) Candoshi c : Omurano t : Taushiro t; and (2) $c : \theta : \check{c}$.[9]

(35) **†Omurano** (Humurana, Numurana; Mayna, Maina, Rimachu)
Peru (see MAP 15, no. 180)

The name Maina is ambiguous, applied also sometimes to Candoshi and Jivaroan. (See above for discussion of possible connections with Candoshi and Taushiro.)

(36) **Sabela** language (Auca, Huaorani)[10]
Ecuador, Peru (Dialects: Tiguacuna, Tuei, Shiripuno)

(38 + 39 + 40) **Witotoan** (Huitotoan) [Bora-Witótoan stock]
(see MAPS 14 and 15, nos. 182–90; see also MAP 18)

Kaufman lists Boran and Witotoan as distinct families which, together with Andoque, perhaps make up what he calls a Boran-Witotoan stock (38 + 39 + 40). Both Greenberg and Swadesh

---

Yaguan

Yagua
†Peba
†Yameo (Masamae)

Proto-Witotoan

Proto-Bora-Muinane
    Bora (Boro, Meamuyna; Miriña [Miranha] is a Bora dialect) *Peru, Brazil, Colombia*
    Muinane (Muinane Bora, Muinani, Muename) *Colombia*
Proto-Huitoto-Ocaina
    Ocaina [Okaina] *Peru*
    Early Huitoto
        Nipode (Witoto Muinane) [obsolescent] *Peru*
        Proto-Mɨnɨca-Murai
            Mɨnɨca (Witoto Meneca) [Meneka] *Colombia*
            Murui (Witoto Murui, Murai, Búe) *Colombia, Peru*

See Aschmann 1993

grouped 38, 39, and 40 together; Loukotka gave the languages consecutive numbers; Suárez grouped 38 and 39. Because of the general consensus concerning the grouping and the low glottochronological figure (fifty-four minimum centuries), Kaufman tentatively recognizes this group. Here, I follow the classification of Aschmann (1993), who shows that indeed "Boran" and "Witotoan" belong to the same family, which he calls "Witotoan." See the classification list for his classification.

Kaufman (1994:64) includes in his Witótoan also †Andoquero, †Coeruna (Brazil), Nonuya, and †Koihoma (Coixoma, Coto, Orejón, spoken in Peru).

Aschmann (1993:96) reconstructs the following Proto-Witotoan phonemes: /p, t, k, ʔ, b, d[r], dz, g, x, ß, m, n; i, e, a, o, ɨ; nasalized vowels; two tones/. Some of the more notable sound changes are that Proto-Witotoan *t split into *t and *c in Proto-Bora-Muinane after *i and *ɨ; the same split occurred in Ocaina, but only after what Aschmann reconstructs as *i·. Proto-Witotoan "preglottalized voiceless stops" (that is, ʔC sequences) produced the geminate series *pp, *tt, *cc, *čč, *kk in Proto-Bora-Muinane (preaspirated in Bora) (Aschmann 1993:96–7). As in many other Amazonian languages, voiced stops b and d become nasals m and n in the environment of nasalized vowels, with distinct reflexes in the different subgroups. See the classification list on p. 186.

(40) **Andoque** [Andoke]

[obsolescent] *Colombia, Peru*

(41) **Chimuan**

(see MAPS 15 and 16, nos. 192–4)

See the classification list.

(42 + 43) **Macro-Kulyi-Cholónan** cluster

Kaufman reports that both Swadesh and Greenberg regard these languages as related in a "fairly low-level genetic grouping" but that "the hypothesis has not been systematically tested" (1994:64).

(42) **Cholonan**

Peru (see MAP 15, nos. 195–6)

See the classification list.

(43) **Culle** (Culli, Linga) [Kulyi]

[extinct?] *Peru* (see MAP 15, no. 197)

Culle may be related to Cholonan. It is very poorly documented and is now probably extinct (Adelaar 1990). Given that the total corpus does not exceed 100 poorly recorded words, determination of its genetic affinity may prove very difficult.

(44 + 45 + 46) **Macro-Lekoan** cluster

See the classification list. Kaufman presents this grouping as possible. However, he adds that "the hypothesis has not been systematically tested, and all the constituent languages are dead and poorly documented" (Kaufman 1994:64). In 1990 he had given as possibly grouped only the 44 and 45 *Sechura-Catacaoan* proposal [Sechura-Katakao stock]. Greenberg had grouped these two, and Loukotka placed them side by side; Kaufman (1990a:43) mentions that there is supporting lexical evidence for grouping these two.

(44) **†Sechura** (Atalan, Sec)

Peru (see MAP 15, no. 198)

Chimuan

†Yunga (Yunca, Chimú, Mochica, Muchic) *Peru*
Ecuador branch
    †Cañari
    †Puruhá

Cholonan

†Cholón
†Híbito (Hibito, Xibito)

Macro-Lekoan cluster (44 + 45 + 46)

Sechura-Katakáoan stock (44 + 45)
    Sechura
    Katakáoan family
Leko

(45) **Catacaoan**
Peru (see MAP 15, nos. 199–200)

See the classification list.

(46) **†Leco** (Lapalapa) [Leko]
Bolivia (see MAP 16, no. 201)

(47 + 48) **Quechumaran** [Kechumaran stock]

The broad-scale classifiers have generally agreed in supposing that Quechuan and Aymaran are genetically related, though this is denied and argued against by most specialists today (see Adelaar 1992). Aymaran (Jaqi) and Quechuan share about 25% of their vocabulary and many structural similarities in their phonological and morphological systems, which to many scholars suggests a genetic relationship. But many of the lexical similarities are so close that they suggest borrowing, and some portions of the lexicon seem to exhibit few similarities (but see Chapter 8 and Campbell 1995, where additional supportive evidence is considered that suggests a genetic relationship but is not sufficient to demonstrate the postulated linguistic kinship).

(47) **Quechuan**
Colombia, Ecuador, Peru, Bolivia, Argentina (see MAPS 15 and 16, no. 204)

See the classification list. The Quechuan family (called a "language complex" by Kaufman 1990a) is divided into two main groups: Central Quechua (also called Quechua I, Quechua B, or Waywash, covering Central Peru's departments of Ancash, Huánuco, Junín, and Pasco, as well as parts of Lima and a few other locations), and Peripheral Quechua (also called Quechua II, Quechua A, and sometimes Wampu), which includes all the dialects not included in Central Quechua. With respect to numbers of speakers, Quechuan is the largest American family, with approximately 8.5 million speakers (more than half of them in Peru).

Gary Parker calculated the glottochronological date for the split of Proto-Quechua into its two branches to be approximately A.D. 850, finding that intelligibility for the speakers is not possible because Central Quechua (his Quechua B) and Peripheral Quechua (his Quechua A) share an overlap of only about 50% in inflectional morphology and about 70% in basic vocabulary (1969a:69).

Catacaoan

†Catacao [Katakao]
†Colán [Kolán]

Quechuan

Central Quechua (Huaihuash [Waywash] / Quechua I)
    Pacaraos
    Central Quechua
        "Waylay" (Huailay, North)
            Huaylas (Ancash)
            Conchucos
        Ap-am-ah
            Alto Pativilca
            Alto Marañón
            Alto Huallaga (Huánuco)
        "Wankay" (Huancay, South)
            Yaru (Tarma, Junín)
            Jauja-Huanca
            Huangascar-Topará
Peripheral Quechua (Huampuy / Quechua II)
    "Yungay" (Quechua IIA)
        Central
            Laraos
            Lincha
            Apurí
            Chocos
            Madeán
        Northern
            Cañaris-Incahuasi
            Cajamarca
    "Chinchay" (Quechua IIB–C)
        Northern
            Chachapoyas (Amazonas)
            San Martín
            Loreto
            Ecuador
            Colombia
        Southern
            Southern Peruvian Quechua
                Ayacucho-Chanka
                Cuzco-Collao
            Argentina
            Bolivia

Cerrón-Palomino 1987:247, Mannheim 1991:11, 114.

Proto-Quechuan's inventory of reconstructed sounds is: /p, t, č, ç̌, k, q, s, š (ṧ), h, m, n, nʸ, r, lʸ, w, y; i, a, u/ (Cerrón-Palomino 1987:128). Some linguists also reconstruct a series of glottalized and aspirated stops and affricates, though many today believe these were acquired through intensive contact with Aymaran (Jaqi) languages. Their reasoning is based in part on the fact that the Quechua varieties geographically close to Aymara exhibit these contrasts most fully, whereas others lack one or both of them. Arguments against this diffusional view of the origin of the glottalized and aspirated stops in Southern Quechua are presented in Chapter 8 and in detail in Campbell 1995. Quechuan languages have SOV order (see Cerrón-Palomino 1987; Mannheim 1985, 1991; Torero 1983).

There are several hypotheses for a Proto-Quechuan homeland. Perhaps the hypothesis that places the homeland on the coast, or on the coast and in the central highlands, of Peru has gained the greatest following (see Cerrón-Palomino 1987:324–49). The most extensive linguistic diversity is found in the territory of the Central Quechua branch; much of the wide geographical distribution of Quechuan is attributed to late expansion of the Southern Quechua (Cuzco-type) branch through the agency of the Inca state. Within this branch, Ecuadoran dialects (of Peripheral Quechua [Quechua II]) differ the most phonologically and morphologically.

(48) **Aymaran** (Jaqi, Aru)[11]
Bolivia, Peru, Chile, Argentina (see MAP 16, no. 209)

See the classification list.

(49) **Chipaya-Uru** [Uru-Chipaya language area]
Bolivia (see MAP 16, no. 210)

See the classification list. Chipaya and Uru have frequently been misidentified as Puquina, which is a different language (see Chapter 7). Greenberg connects Chipaya to Arawakan; Ronald Olson (1964, 1965) tried to connect it to Mayan; Suárez accepts both these connections; Swadesh had different ideas, placing Chipaya in his Macro-Quechuachón grouping; Migliazza thought it might be Macro-Arawakan. Stark

Aymaran
Aymara *Bolivia, Peru, Chile, Argentina*
Tupe branch
    Jaqaru (also known as Haqearu, Haqaru, Haq'aru) *Yauyos Province, Peru*
    Kawki [obsolescent] *Cachuy, Tupe district, Yauyos province, Peru*[12]

        Hardman de Bautista 1975, 1978a, 1978b.

Chipaya-Uru
Chipaya
Uru [obsolescent]

(1972b) accepted the Uru-Chipaya-Mayan connection (proposed by Olson 1964, 1965) and added Yunga to it. While the Mayan connection has largely been abandoned (see Campbell 1973a; however, compare Suárez 1977, who maintained some sympathy toward the proposal), the possible connection between Chipaya-Uru and Yunga deserves to be investigated more fully.

(50) **†Puquina** (Pukina)
Bolivia (see MAP 16, no. 211)

Puquina was an Andean language of high prestige in early colonial times, and attestations of it exist from a number of areas where Quechua later came to be spoken (see Mannheim 1991); nevertheless, Puquina has not been studied in any detail. The grouping of Puquina with Chipaya-Uru is a frequent mistaken identity; Chipaya and Uru were often called "Puquina" in their local area and by outsiders, although Puquina is a totally distinct language which has almost nothing in common with Chipaya and Uru.[13] The mistaken identity is an old and persistent one, found in Hervás y Panduro and taken from him by Adelung and Vater and subsequently by de la Grasserie, Brinton, Rivet (cf. Crequi-Montfort and Rivet 1925–1926), Swadesh, and Greenberg. That these are distinct languages, however, is hardly news, as demonstrated by Chamberlain (1910) and Ibarra Grasso (1958:10, 1964:37–43) (see Adelaar 1989:252 and Olson 1964:314); therefore, it is difficult to understand why the mistake should continue to be made.

(51) Callahuaya (Machaj-Juyai, Collahuaya, Pohena)
Bolivia

Callahuaya is a jargon used by Quechua speakers who (apparently) used to speak Puquina. Both Greenberg and Loukotka identified it as Puquina. Kaufman (1990a) allows for the possibility of a genetic grouping which he gives as "50 + 51 Pukina-Kolyawaya family(?)." He says that such a group would be recognized if Callahuaya were shown to descend from a sister of Puquina rather than from Puquina itself. Callahuaya is a jargonized (or mixed) language based predominantly on lexical items from Puquina and morphology from Quechua; today it is used by male curers who live in a few villages in the provinces of Muñecas and Bautista Saavedra, Department of La Paz, Bolivia, but who travel widely throughout this part of South America to practice their profession (Büttner 1983:23, Muysken 1994a, Oblitas Poblete 1968, Stark 1972a; see the appendix to Chapter 1 for more detail).

(52) Yuracare
Bolivia (see Map 16, no. 212)

(53 + 54 + 55 + 56) Macro-Pánoan
cluster

See the classification list. Kaufman (1994:65) groups 53, 54, 55, and 56 together as a hypothesis that "seems promising," based on intersecting portions of Swadesh's Quechuachón, Suárez's Macro-Panoan, and Greenberg's Macro-Panoan.

(53 + 54) Pano-Tacanan proposal
[Pano-Takana stock]

There is general agreement among the broad-scale classifiers that these two families belong

---

Macro-Pánoan cluster

Pano-Takánan stock (53 + 54)
    Pánoan family (cf. 53)
    Takánan family (cf. 54)
Mosetén-Chonan stock (55 + 56)
    Mosetén language area (cf. 55)
    Chon family (cf. 56)

---

together. Key (1968), Girard (1971a:145–71), and Loos (1973) have assembled evidence to support this proposal (cf. Suárez 1969, 1973, 1977). Thus, the Pano-Takanan relationship is now quite generally accepted.

(53) Panoan
Peru, Brazil, Bolivia (see Maps 15, 16, and 18, nos. 213–37)

See the classification list. Some other names that are sometimes listed with Panoan languages, whose classification is not clear at present, are: Panavarro, Purus, Arazaire, Cujareno (Peru), Katukina Pano (Yawanawa?) (Brazil), Maya (Brazil), Mayo (Peru?), Morunahua (Morunawa) (obsolescent, Peru), Nukuini (Brazil), †Pisabo (Peru), and Uru-eu (Brazil) (see Shell 1975:14, Migliazza and Campbell 1988:189–90, Rodrigues 1986:77–81).

Olive Shell's reconstruction of Proto-Panoan phonemes is: /p, t, c, č, k, k^w, ʔ, ß, s, š, ş, (h), r, m, n, w, y; i, +, a, o; nasalized vowels/ (1965, 1975:53; cf. Girard 1971b:146, Migliazza and Campbell 1988:196). The $*k^w$ is reflected as k^w only in Cashibo; it merged with k in the other languages (Shell 1975:56, 59).

(54) Tacanan [Takánan]
Bolivia, Peru (see Maps 15, 16, and 18, nos. 238–43)

See the classification list. Some scholars also list †Chirigua (from the mission of San Buenaventura, El Beni department, Bolivia) as a Tacanan language (see also Girard 1971b:41–2).

Girard's reconstruction of Proto-Tacanan phonemes is: /p, t, k, k^w, (ʔ), b, d, j, s, z, r, ř, m, n, w, y; i, a, +, o/ . This differs in certain important respects from Key's (1968) reconstruction. Girard eliminates Key's proposed $*č$ and $*š$ since virtually all the forms exhibiting the č correspondence set and most of those with the š correspondence set are borrowed from Quechua and Aymara (1971b:24). Where Key posited $*x$ and $*k$, Girard reconstructs $*k$ and $*k^w$, respectively. The Key $*x$ / Girard $*k$ is based on the correspondence set which has Tacana h / Ø : Cavineño k : Ese'ejja h / x, while Key $*k$ / Girard $*k^w$ is based on Tacana k^w/k :

Panoan

Kaxararí [Kashararí] *Brazil*
†Kulino (Culino) *Amazonas, Brazil*
Mainline branch
    Cashibo group
        †Nocamán (Nokamán) *Peru*
        Cashibo (Cacataibo) [Kashibo] [obsolescent] *Peru* (Dialect: Cacataibo)
    Pano language area
        †Pánobo (Panobo) *Peru*
        †Huariapano (Waripano, Pano)
    Shipibo group
        Shipibo (Shipibo-Conibo) *Peru* (Dialects: Conibo, Shetebo, Pisquibo, Shipibo)
        Capanahua [Kapanawa] *Peru, Brazil*
        Marubo (Marobo) *Amazonas, Brazil* (Dialects: Nehanawa, Paconawa)
        Waninnawa *Brazil*
        †Remo (Sakuya, Kukuini) *Brazil, Peru*
    †Tushinawa (Tuxinawa) *Acre, Brazil*
    Tri-State group (Amawak-Jaminawa group)
        Amawaka language (area)
            Amawaka (Amahuaca) *Acre, Brazil*
            Isconahua (Iskonawa, Iscobakebo) [Iskonawa] [obsolescent]   *Peru*
        Cashinahua (Kashinawa Kaxinawa, Tuxinawa) *Peru, Brazil*
        Sharanawa (Marinahua, Mastanahua, Parquenahua) *Peru, Brazil*
        Yaminawa (Yaminahua) *Brazil, Peru, Bolivia*
    †Atsahuaca (Yamiaca) [Atsawaka-Yamiaka language] *Peru*
    †Parannawa *Acre, Brazil*
    Puinaua [Poyanawa] *Acre, Brazil*
    †Shipinawa (Xipinahua) *Brazil, Bolivia*
Bolivian branch
    Karipuna (Karipuná) [extinct/obsolescent?] *Rondônia, Brazil*
    Pacahuara (Pacaguara, Pakaguara) [Pakawara] [moribund] *Bolivia*
    Chákobo (Chácobo) *Bolivia, Brazil* (Dialect: Shinabo)
Shaninawa (Xaninaua) [extinct?] *Acre, Brazil*
†Sensi *Peru*
Mayoruna-Matsés ([Majoruna], Matse, Matis) *Peru, Brazil*

Tacanan

Tacana group
    Tacana (Tupamasa) [Takana] *Bolivia*
    Reyesano (San Borjano, Maropa) *Bolivia*
    Araona (Carina, sometimes called Cavina) [obsolescent] *Bolivia*
Cavineña [Kavinenya] *Bolivia*
Chama group
    Ese'ejja (Ese'eha, Tiatinagua, Chama, Huarayo, Guacanawa, Chuncho)[Eseʔexa] *Bolivia, Peru*
    †Toromona *Bolivia*

Cavineño k^w : Ese'ejja k^w. Girard's $*j$ is based on Tacana $ř$: Cavineño h : Ese'ejja $š$. His $*z$ is for the correspondence set Tacana $đ$: Cavineño s : Ese'ejj $s/t/č$, for which Key had postulated $*s$; this contrasts with Girard's $*s$ (Key's $*ś$) for Tacana s : Cavineño h : Ese'ejja h/x (Girard 1971b:22–23). Girard's $*ř$ (Key's $*r$) is reflected by r in all the languages except for $Ø/y$ in Ese'ejja and $Ø$ in Huarayo and Araona, while the $*r$ (Key's $*ṙ$) is reflected by $Ø$ in all the languages except Cavineño, where it is r (Girard 1971b:43).

(55 + 56) **Mosetén-Chonan** [Mosetén-Chon stock]

Suárez and Swadesh both group these together, and Suárez (1969, 1973, 1974, 1977) has presented evidence for it. Kaufman (1994) is sympathetic to this proposal. Greenberg (1987), however, places Mosetén with Pano-Takana, but he includes Chon (his Patagon) in his Andean grouping.

(55) **Mosetenan** [Mosetén language area]
Bolivia (see MAP 16, no. 244)

See the classification list. Chimane and Mosetén have been thought to be related languages (and the only languages) of a small, isolated family, though recent research suggests that, rather than a family consisting of two separate languages, this is a single language separated only recently by the consequences of cultural contact (Martín and Pérez Diez 1990:574). Suárez argues, on the basis of similarities in the Swadesh 100-word list, that Mosetén, Pano-Tacanan, Arawakan, Yuracare, and Chon are genetically related (1977; compare Suárez 1969). These similarities, though suggestive, are very few in number and susceptible to other possible explanations.

Mosetenan

Chimane (Tsimane, Chumano)
Mosetén (Rache, Muchan, Tucupi)

(56) **Chon** [Chon family] (Patagonian)[14]
Argentina, Chile (see MAP 21, nos. 245–6)

See the classification list. Other scholars also group †Teushen (Patagonia, Argentina) with these languages.

(57) **Yagan** (Yahgan, Yaghan, Yamana) [Yámana] [extinct?] *Chile* (see MAP 21, no. 247)

In the early 1970s, there were different reports of two to twelve speakers. Five dialects of the language are sometimes mentioned (see Klein 1985:714).

(58) **Kaweskar** (Alacaluf, Alakaluf, Kawaskar,Kawesqar, Qawasqar, Qawashqar, Halakwalip) [obsolescent] *Chile* (see MAP 21, no. 248)

Kaufman (1994:67) posits a Kaweskar language area which consists of two emergent languages,[15] Aksaná and Hekaine (Alakaluf). Loukotka presented his Aksanás stock with the two languages, Chono (Caucau) and Kaueskar (Aksanás), neither of which was connected with his Alacaluf, which he classified as an "isolated language" (Loukotka 1968:43–4). I have eliminated Aksaná(s) on the assumption that Clairis (1985:756; see also 1978:32) is correct in showing that Aksaná(s) does not really exist but rather is traceable to Hammerly Dupuy's (1947a, 1947b, 1952) misidentification of a variety of Kaweskar (Alacaluf) as distinct based on his poor comparison of material recorded from 1698 (see Chapter 1 for details).[16] Kaufman gives Hekaine as the other Kawéskar language (presumably Kawéskar [Alacaluf] proper; see Loukotka 1968:43), in addition to Aksanás. Others also list †Chono (Caucau, Kakauhua [Kaukaue]) of Chile, Loukotka's other putative Aksanás language, as related to or a variety of Kaweskar (Alacaluf). On this Clairis reports that "people have discussed the Chono language—and still do so today—even though there is not a single linguistic fact available about this putative language. Whether or not the Chono existed as an ethnic entity may be an historic and/or ethnological problem; but to posit the existence of a

Chon

Tehuelche (Aoniken, Gununa-Kena [Gününa Küne], Inaquean, Tsoneka) [obsolescent] *Patagonia, Argentina*[17]

Island Chon branch / group / language area
    †Ona (Selknam, Selk'nam, Shelknam, Aona) *Tierra del Fuego, Argentina, Chile*[18]
    †Haush (Manekenken) *Tierra del Fuego, Argentina, Chile*

---

language for which there is no data is almost a logical contraction"[19] (1985:754).

(59) **Mapudungu** (Araucano, Mapuche) (Araucanian) [Mapudungu language (area)]
Chile, Argentina (see MAP 21, no. 249)

Huilliche, also called Veliche, is a variety of Mapudungu in Argentina.[20]

(61 + 96 + 97) **Macro-Warpean** cluster

See the classification list. Kaufman groups 61, 96, and 9. With regard to his proposal, Kaufman says that "no systematic study of this specific connection has so far been made" (1994:67), and for that reason it is best for now to consider these as independent groups.

(61) **Huarpe** [Warpe language area]
Argentina (see MAP 21, no. 250)

See the classification list. Swadesh and Suárez both related Huarpe to what Kaufman calls Hívaro-Kawapana. The possible connection should be investigated.

(96 + 97) **Mura-Matanawían** proposal [Mura-Matanawí family]

Except for Loukotka, the other broad-scale classifiers agree in grouping these languages to-

gether as a family; Kaufman (1994:67) includes Huarpe (his Warpe) with these languages in an even larger grouping.

(96) **Muran**
Amazonas, Brazil[21] (see MAPS 18 and 20, nos. 251–4)

See the classification list.

(97) **†Matanawí**
Amazonas, Brazil (see MAPS 16 and 18, no. 255)

(62 + 63 + 64 + 67) **Macro-Waikurúan** cluster

See the classification list. Again, Kaufman presents as possibly related several families. Kaufman says this "higher grouping . . . deserves to be explored and tested" (1994:67), but for the present it should not be accepted as anything more than a possibility.

(62) **Matacoan** (Mataguayan) [Matákoan family]
Argentina, Bolivia, Paraguay (see MAP 21, nos. 256–9)

Macro-Warpean cluster

Warpe language area (cf. 61)
Mura-Matanawian stock/family (96 + 97)
    Muran family (cf. 96)
    Matanawí (cf. 97)

Huarpe

†Huarpe (Allentiac)
†Millcayac

Muran

†Mura
Pirahã (Pirahá) [Pirahán] (cf. Rodrigues 1986:81)
†Bohurá
†Yahahí

Macro-Waikurúan cluster

Matákoan family (cf. 62)
Waikurúan family (cf. 63)
Charrúan family (cf. 64)
Maskóian family (cf. 67)

Matacoan (Mataguayan)

Chorote (Chorotí, Yofúaha) *Argentina, Bolivia, Paraguay*
　Chulupí (Churupi, Chulupe) *Paraguay, Argentina*
Ajlujlay (Nivaclé, Niwaklé) *Argentina*
Macá (Towolhi, Toothle, Nynaka, Mak'á, Enimaca, Enimaga) [Maká] *Paraguay*
Mataco (Wichí, Matahuayo) [Matako] *Argentina, Bolivia*

See the classification list. The classification of Matacoan followed here is that of Harriet Klein (1978:10) and Elena Najlis (1984). The sounds of the proto language, according to Najlis (1984:8, 15), are: /p, t, c, ç, k, q, p', t', c', ç', k', p^h, t^h, c^h, s, hs, l, hl, m, n, hm, hn, w, y, hw; i, e, ɛ, æ, a, ɔ, o, u/ .[22]

(63) Guaykuruan [Waikurúan family]
Paraguay, Brazil, Argentina, Bolivia (see Map 21, nos. 260–6)

See the classification list. Many are in agreement with the classification of Caduvéo as Guaykuruan (for example, Rodrigues 1986:23–6, 73–4), although Klein (1985:694), on the basis of her fieldwork with this and the other Guaykuruan languages, argues against this assumption.

(64) Charruan
Uruguay, Argentina, Brazil (see Map 21, nos. 267–8)

See the classification list.

Charruan

†Charrúa (Güenoa) *Uruguay, Argentina, Brazil*
†Chaná *Uruguay*

(65 + 66) Lule-Vilelan [Lule-Vilélan stock]

There is general agreement among those classifications which Kaufman compared, with the exception of Loukotka, that this is a genetic group. Kaufman (1990a:46) reports that there is lexical evidence to support such a conclusion.

(65) †Lule (Tonocoté)
Northern Argentina (see Map 21, no. 273)

Lule was reported in 1981 (albeit an unconfirmed account) as still spoken by five families in Resistencia, east central Chaco Province, Argentina.

(66) Vilela [Vilela language]
[obsolescent] *Argentina* (see Map 21, no. 274)

(67) Mascoyan [Maskóian family]
Paraguay (see Maps 16, 20, and 21, no. 272)

See the classification list.

(68) Zamucoan
Bolivia, Paraguay (see Maps 16 and 20, nos. 275–6)

See the classification list.

Guaykuruan

Guaykurú [Waikurú] branch
　†Caduveo (Mbayá-Guaycuru, Guaicurú, Ediu-Adig) [Kadiwéu] *Argentina, Brazil, Paraguay*
Southern branch
　Pilagá (Pilacá) *Argentina*
　Toba (Chaco Sur, Qom, Namqom) *Argentina, Paraguay* (different from Toba-Maskoy, a Mascoyan language)
　Mocoví (Mbocobí) [Mokoví] *Argentina*
　†Abipón (Callaga) *Argentina, Paraguay*
Eastern branch
　†Guachí [Wachí] *Mato Grosso, Brazil*
　†Payaguá [Payawá] *Paraguay*

For early work, see Adam 1899; cf. Klein 1985:694–578, Migliazza and Campbell 1988:292.

Mascoyan

Guaná (Kashika, Kashiha) [Kaskihá]
Sanapaná (Quiativs, Quilyacmoc, Lanapsua,
    Saapa, Kasnatan) (Dialects: Sanapaná,
    Lanapsua, Enenlhit)
Lengua (Vowak)   (Dialects: Angaité [Angate, En-
    lit, Coyavitis, Northern])
Mascoy (Emok, Toba-Emok, Toba) [Maskoi][23]

Zamucoan

Ayoreo (Ayoré, Moro; Zamuco) [Ayoréo] *Bolivia,
    Paraguay*
Chamacoco (Bahía Negra, Ebidoso, Tumarahá)
    [Chamakoko] [obsolescent] *Paraguay* (Dia-
    lects: Bahía Negra, Bravo)

(69) †Gorgotoqui
Bolivia

Loukotka (1968:61) lists Gorgotoqui as an "isolated language." Kaufman (1990a) suggests that
perhaps it should not be listed, since it is perhaps
completely undocumented, and indeed, the language is absent from Kaufman 1994.

(70 + 71 + 72 + 73 + 74 + 75 + 76 + 77 + 78 + 79 + 80 + 81 + 82) **Macro-Je** cluster

See the classification list. Kaufman (1990a,
1994:68–70) grouped several genetic units as
probably related in what he calls the "Macro-Je
cluster." He considers Macro-Je to be the best
supported of all South American "clusters" (proposals of remote but unsubstantiated genetic
relationship) (1994:68). Irvine Davis (1968) presented evidence that 72 and 74–81 are related.
Loukotka also presented evidence relating 72,
74–78, and 81. Rodrigues (1986) presents evidence that suggests 71–82 are related. Greenberg and Swadesh agree that 70 and 71 are connected. There is reason to believe that all of
these units are related, and research should be
undertaken to determine whether this is in fact
the case. Davis also pointed to possible connections between Macro-Je and Tupian. Kaufman's
grouping is discussed in the following paragraphs.

Macro-Je cluster (70–82)

Chikitano-Boróroan stock (70 + 71)
    Chikitano (cf. 70)
    Boróroan family (cf. 71)
Aimoré (cf. 72)
Rikbaktsá (cf. 73)
Je stock (cf. 74)
Jeikó (cf. 75)
Kamakánan family (cf. 76)
Mashakalían family (cf. 77)
Purían family (cf. 78)
Fulnió (cf. 79)
Karajá language area (cf. 80)
Ofayé (cf. 81)
Guató (cf. 82)

(70) **Chiquitano** (Chiquito, Tarapecosi, Tao)
Bolivia (Several dialects) (MAPS 16 and 18, no.
277)

(71) **Bororoan** [Boróroan family]
Brazil, Bolivia (see MAPS 16 and 20, nos. 278–80)

See the classification list.

(72) **Botocudoan** [Aimoré language complex]
Brazil (see MAP 20, nos. 281–3)

See the classification list. Krenak is the only
language of this family which is still spoken,
and it is nearing extinction (there are perhaps
fewer than twenty individuals who still know
the language) (Seki 1985).

Bororoan

Borôro (proper) (Boe) *Mato Grosso, Brazil*
Umotina (Umutina, Barbados) *Mato Grosso, Brazil*
†Otuké (Otuqué, Otuqui, Louxiru) *Brazil, Bolivia*

Botocudoan

Krenak (Botocudo) [obsolescent] *São Paulo, Mato
    Grosso, Pará*
†Nakrehé *Minas Gerais*
†Guêren (Borun) *Bahia*

(73) **Rikbaktsá** (Aripaktsá, Eribatsa, Eripatsa, Canoeiro; distinct from Ava-Canoiero and Kanoe [Canoe])
Mato Grosso, Rondônia, Brazil

(74) **Jean** (Gêan, Jêan) (Ye, Ge, Je family) [Je stock]
Brazil (see MAPS 20 and 21, nos. 285–96)

See the classification list. Davis's (1966:13) reconstruction of the Proto-Jê phonemic system is: /p, t, c, k, r, m, n, nʸ, ŋ, w, z; i, e, ε, a, ə, ɨ, ɔ, o, u; nasalized vowels (though no nasalized counterparts of ε, a, ɔ)/. Stress was probably predictable; the status of vowel length in the proto language is not clear.

(75) **†Jeikó** (Jeicó, Jaiko)
Brazil (see MAP 20, no. 297)

Davis (1968) groups this language with Macro-Jê.

(76) **Kamakanan** [Kamakánan family]
Brazil (see MAP 20, nos. 298–300)

See the classification list. Davis (1968) classifies this family with Macro-Jê.

(77) **Maxakalían** [Mashakalían family]
Brazil (see MAP 20, nos. 301–3)

See the classification list. Davis (1968) presents evidence suggesting that Maxakalían is related to Proto-Jê.

Jean

Northern (or Northeastern) branch
    Timbira *Maranhão, Pará, Goiás* (Dialects: Canela [Kanela], Apániekra, Rankokamekra(n), Kri(n)katí, Krenjé [Crenge, Bacabal, Kremye], Krahó [Crao], Pukobyé [Piokob, Bocobu])
    Ipewí (Kren-Akarore, Creen-Acarore) [obsolescent] *Xingu*
    Apinayé (Apinaye, Apinajé) *Goiás*
    Kayapó (Cayapó) *Xingu, Pará, Mato Grosso* (Several dialects)[24]
    Suyá [obsolescent] *Xingu* (Tapayuna is a dialect of Suyá)
Central (or Akwen) branch
    Xavante (Shavante, Chavante, Akuen) *Mato Grosso*
    †Akroá (Acroa, Coroa) *Bahia*
    Xerente (Sherente, Xerenti) [Sherente] *Goiás*
    †Xakriabá (Chicriaba) [Shakriabá] *Minas Gerais*
Southern branch
    Kaingang *Paraná, Rio Grande do Sul, São Paulo*
    Xokleng (Shocleng) *Santa Catarina, Paraná*
    †Wayaná (Guayaná) *Rio Grande do Sul*

Migliazza and Campbell 1988:288.

Kamakanan

Kamakán language area or complex
    †Kamakan (Camacán, Ezeshio) *Bahia*
    †Mangaló *Bahia, Minas Gerais*
    †Kutaxó (Catashó, Totoxó, Catathóy) [Kutashó] *Bahia, Minas Gerais*
†Menien (Manyã) [Menyén] *Bahia, Minas Gerais*
†Masakará (Masacara) *Bahia*

Maxakalían

†Malalí *Minas Gerais*
†Pataxó (Patashó) *Minas Gerais, Espírito Santo* (Dialects: Pataxó, Hãhãhãe [Hanhanhain])
Maxakalí (Caposho, Cumanasho, Macuni, Momaxo, Monocho) [Mashakalí] *Minas Gerais*

(78) **Purian** [Purían family] (Puri-Coroada)
Brazil (see Maps 20 and 21, nos. 304–5)

See the classification list. Davis (1968:45) also includes Coroado in Purian and groups the family with Macro-Jê.

(79) **Fulnió** (Furniô, Carnijó, Yaté)
Pernambuco, Brazil (see Map 20, no. 306)

(80) **Karajá** (Caraja) [Karajá language area]
Brazil (see Map 20, no. 307)

See the classification list. According to Davis, these "languages" may be dialects of a single language (1968:45). He argues that Karajá and Proto-Jê are related and presents suggestive evidence.

(81) **Ofayé** (Opaié-Shavante, Ofaié-Xavante, Opaye-Chavante, Guachi)
[obsolescent] *Mato Grosso, Brazil*
(see Maps 20 and 21, no. 308)

Davis (1968) groups Ofayé with Macro-Jê.

(82) **Guató**
Mato Grosso, Brazil (see Map 20, no. 309)

(83) **†Otí**
São Paulo, Brazil (see Map 21, no. 310)

Kaufman says that of the large-scale classifiers, "only Greenberg dares to link this language to anything else" (1994:70).

(84) **†Baenan** (Baenã)
Brazil

Kaufman comments that "this language is too poorly known for even Gr[eenberg] to dare classifying it" (1994:70).

(85) **†Kukurá** (Cucura, Kokura
Mato Grosso, Brazil

(86 + 113) **Macro-Katembrí-Taruma** cluster

See the classification list. Kaufman (1994:70) groups 86 and 113.

(86) **†Katembrí** (Mirandela)
Bahia, Brazil (see Map 20, no. 313)

(113) **†Taruma** (Taruamá)
Brazil, Guyana (see Maps 14 and 18, no. 314)

(87) **†Karirí** (Carirí, Kirirí, Quirirí)
Paraíba, Pernambuco, Ceará, Brazil (see Map 20, no. 315)

For earlier work, see Adam 1897.

(88) **†Tuxá** [Tushá] *Bahía, Pernambuco, Brazil*
(see Map 20, no. 316)

Macro-Katembrí-Taruma cluster

Katembrí (cf. 86)
Taruma (cf. 113)

Purian

†Coropó (Coropa, Koropo) [Koropó] *Minas Gerais, Rio de Janeiro*
†Puri (Colorado) *Espírito Santo, Minas Gerais*

Karajá

Karajá-Xambioá (Chamboa, Ynã) [Karajá-Shambioá] *Goiás* (Dialects: Karajá, Xambioá) (The men and women speak different varieties)
Javaé (Javaje, Javae) *Goiás*

(89) **†Pankararú** (Pancararu, Brancararu)
Pernambuco, Brazil (see MAP 20, no. 317)

(90) **†Natú**
Pernambuco, Brazil (see MAP 20, no. 318)

Kaufman says, "only Gr[eenberg] dares to classify this language" (1994:70).

(91) **†Xukurú** (Ichikile) [Shukurú]
Pernambuco, Paraíba, Brazil (see MAP 20, no. 319)

Kaufman says also of Xukurú that "only Gr[eenberg] dares to classify this language" (1994:70).

(92) **†Gamela** (Barbados, Curinsi)
Maranhão, Brazil (see MAP 20, no. 320)

As in the case of 90 and 91, Kaufman says, "only Gr[eenberg] dares to classify this language" (1994:70).

(93) **†Huamoé** (Huamoi, Uame, Umã; Araticum [Aticum], Atikum) [Wamoé language]
Pernambuco, Brazil (see MAP 20, no. 321)

As in the case of the three preceding languages, Kaufman tells us that "only Gr[eenberg] dares to classify this language" (1994:70, compare Migliazza and Campbell 1988:311–16).

(94) **†Tarairiú**
Rio Grande do Norte, Brazil

Kaufman remarks that "not even Gr[eenberg] dares classify this language" (Kaufman 1994:70).

(95) **†Xokó** (Choco, Shoco) [Shokó]
Alagoas, Pernambuco, Brazil (see MAP 20, no. 323)

(101) **Jabutian**
Rondônia, Brazil (see MAPS 16 and 18, nos. 324–5)

See the classification list. Swadesh groups this family with Kunsa-Kapishaná (99 + 100), with

Jabutian

Jabuti (Yabuti, Kipiu, Quipiu)[obsolescent]
Arikapú [obsolescent]
†Mashubí

a time depth of only forty-nine minimum centuries, but the available lexical material does not look promising for such a conclusion.

(102) **†Koayá** (Koaiá, Arara)
[extinct/moribund?] *Rondônia, Brazil*

(103) **Aikaná** (Aikanã, Huarí, Warí, Masaká, Tubarão, Kasupá, Mundé, Corumbiara)
Rondônia, Brazil (see MAPS 16 and 18, no. 328)

(104) **Nambiquaran**
Mato Grosso, Brazil (see MAPS 16, 18, and 20, nos. 329–31)

See the classification list. David Price (1978) postulates the following as Proto-Nambiquaran phonemes: /p, t, c, k, ʔ, s, h, l, m, n, w, y; i, e, a ə, ɨ, o, u; nasalized vowels; three tones; laryngealized vowels/ .

(105) **Irantxe** (Iranxe, Mynky, Münkü) [Iranshe]
Mato Grosso, Brazil (see MAP 20, no. 332)

(107) **Movima** (Mobima)
Bolivia (see MAP 16, no. 333)

(108) **Cayuvava** (Cayuwaba, Cayubaba) [Kayuvava]
[obsolescent] *Bolivia* (see MAPS 16 and 18, no. 334)

Greenberg and Suárez connect this language with Tupian.

(109 + 110) **Macro-Tupí-Karibe** cluster

Kaufman (1994:71) groups Tupian and Cariban, based on evidence from Rodrigues (1985a) and others. This proposal requires further investigation.

Nambiquaran

Kithãulhú (Northern Nambiquara)   (Dialects: Tawandé, Lakonde, Mamaindé, Nagaroté)
Mamaindê (Southern Nambiquara)
    Nambiquara (Nambiwara)   (Dialects: Campo, Manduka, Galera, Guaporé)
    Sararé
    Kabishi [obsolescent]
Sabané [obsolescent]

---

(109) **Tupian** [Tupían stock]
(see Map 22; see also Maps 14, 15, 16, 18, 20, and 21, nos. 335–80)

See the classification list for Kaufman's (1994:71) classification.

Rodrigues (1986:39) lists additional Tupí-Guaraní languages of Brazil along with numbers of speakers. Several of them are not included in, or are not classified as in, the preceding classification; one worth special mention is Lingua Geral Amazonica (Nheengatú, Tupi Moderno). (See the appendix to Chapter 1 for more detail; see also Lemle 1971:128 and Dietrich 1990 on Tupí-Guaraní and Rodrigues 1984–1985, 1986 on the Tupian family in general.)

Miriam Lemle's (1971) reconstruction of the phonemes of Proto-Tupí-Guaranian is: /p, t, c, k, kʷ, ʔ, ɓ, r, m, n, ŋ, w, y; i, e, ɨ, a, o, u; vowel nasalization /. The Tupí-Guaraní branch is characterized by two sound changes: *py > c and *c > Ø (see Migliazza and Campbell 1988:247).

Moore and Galucio (1994) reconstruct Proto-Tuparí with the following sounds: /p, t, c, k, kw, ʔ, b, (D), g, gw, m, n, (n)dz, ŋ, (mb), (nd), ỹ/ (ñ), (ŋg), (ŋgw), ß, r, h, w, y; i, e, a, ɨ, u(o); vowel nasalization/ . They consider *D a variant of *r; *D has the reflexes (n)d, s, and h in these languages and occurs mostly before i.

The Guaranian subfamily of the Tupí-Guaraní branch of the Tupian family is important because of its rich history, the attention it has received, and its large number of speakers (see map 22). Paraguayan Guaraní, with more than 3 million speakers, is the best known language of this subfamily; 95% of the population of Paraguay speaks Guaraní (only 50% speaks Spanish). Guaranian is composed of nine other languages spoken in Paraguay and in adjacent portions of Argentina, Bolivia, and Brazil. The Proto-Guaranian phonological inventory is reconstructed as follows: /p, t, k, kʷ, m, n, nʸ, ŋ, ɓ, r, č/s, ǰ/y; i, e, ɨ, a, o, u/ (see Lemle 1971; Dietrich 1990; and Rodrigues 1984–1985, 1986). Guaranian word order is SOV in dependent clauses, but tends toward VO in main clauses. SVO is reported from Paraguayan Guaraní, Mbyá, and Ñandeva; VSO is reported for Kaiwá. No direct descendant of Old Guaraní (Ruiz de Montoya 1640, Restivo 1724) is known (Dooley 1992). It has been argued that the Tupian family also originally had (S)OV basic word order (Moore 1991). Other Tupian family-wide traits include postpositions; genitive-noun order; prefixed person markers (on both nouns and verbs), with other inflectional morphemes being suffixed; possessive and object markers being the same; a distinction between inclusive and exclusive first person forms; and predominantly ergative alignment (Moore 1990). Many languages of the Tupian family are tonal, though those of the Tupí-Guaraní, Mawé, and Aweti groups are not (Moore 1992).

Ernest Migliazza finds the maximum diversification for the Tupian language family in the region of the Jiparana River, a tributary on the right side of the Madeira River (Migliazza and Campbell 1988:390). Six of the eight subfamilies have representatives here, and a seventh (Mundurukú) is near, to the northeast. He postulates that the Proto-Tupian homeland was located between the Jiparana and the Aripuana Rivers (tributaries of the upper Madeira River); the family expanded within a contiguous area limited by the headwaters of the Madeira to the northeast, the Guaporé to the south, and the headwaters of the Xingu to the east. The Proto-Puruboran speakers (on the Jiparana River) began to migrate southward toward the Guaporé River. Proto-Monde developed on the headwaters of the Jiparana, and Proto-Ramarama emerged on the lower part of this river. Later, Proto-Tupari and Proto-Arikém began to diverge

Tupían stock

Tupí-Guaraní family
- Guaraní group
  - Guaraní language (area)
    - Kaingwá *Brazil, Paraguay* (Dialects: Kaiwá/Kayová, Pãi/Pany, Tavüterán)
    - Bolivian Guaraní *Bolivia, Paraguay*
    - Paraguayan Guaraní (Avanye'e) *Paraguay*
    - Chiripá-Nyandeva *Paraguay, Brazil* (Dialects: Chiripá, Ñandeva/Nhandev) (Rodrigues [1986:39] lists for this: Guaraní [Kaiwá/Kayová], Mbiá [Mbya Guaraní], Nhandeva [Txiripá Guaraní])
    - Chiriguano *Paraguay, Bolivia, Argentina* (Dialects: Tapieté, Izoceño, Chiriguano, Chané, Nyanaigua)
    - Mbü'a (Mbü'a Guaraní) *Brazil, Argentina*
  - Xetá [Shetá] [moribund/obsolescent?] *Paraná, Brazil*
  - Guajaki (Aché) *Paraguay*
- Guarayú group
  - Guarayú (Ñañañe) *Bolivia, Paraguay*
  - Pauserna [extinct/moribund?] *Bolivia*
  - Sirionó *Bolivia* (Dialects: Sirionó, Yuqui, Jorá)
- Tupí group
  - Tupí language area
    - †Tupinamba (Colonial/Classical Tupí) *northern and central coast of Brazil*
    - †Southern Tupí (Lingua Geral Paulista, Tupí Austral) *Brazil*
    - Jeral *Brazil, Colombia, Venezuela*
    - †Potiguara *Paraíba, Brazil*
  - Cocama [Kokama subgroup]
    - Cocama-Cocamilla [Kokama-Kokamilya] *Peru, Brazil, Colombia* (Dialects: Cocama, Cocamilla) (Rodrigues [1986:39] lists Kokama as extinct)
    - Omagua-Campeva [Omawa-Kampeva] [obsolescent] *Peru* (Dialects: Omagua, Campeva) (Rodrigues [1986:39] gives Omagua (Kamibeba) as extinct[?])
- Araweté *Paraná, Brazil*
- Tenetehara group
  - Tapirapé *Mato Grosso, Brazil*
  - Akwawa [Akuawa] *Paraná, Brazil* (Dialects: Parakaná, Akuawa, Asurí, Mudjetire, Suru do Tocantins) (Rodrigues [1986:39] lists Akwawa with subvarieties Asuriní doTocantins, Suruí do Tocantins [Mudjetire], Parakanã)
  - Avá (Canoeiro) [obsolescent] *Goiás, Brazil*
  - Tenetehara *Maranhão, Brazil* (Dialects: Guajajara, Tembé)
- Wayampí group
  - Amanayé language (area) *Paraná, Brazil* (Dialects: Amanayé, Anambé, Guajá, Urubú) (Rodrigues [1986:39] lists Amanayé as extinct and Anambé [Turiwara] as obsolescent—sixty-one speakers)
  - Wayampí language (area) *French Guiana, Brazil* (Dialects: Oyampí/Wayampí, Emérillon, Karipuna)
  - †Takunyapé *Pará, Brazil?*
- Kayabí group
  - Kayabí *Xingu, Mato Grosso, Brazil*
  - Asuriní (do Xingú) (Asuriní do Coatinema, Awaeté) *Paraná, Brazil*
- Kawahib group
  - Parintintín *Alto Maranhão, Rondônia, Brazil* (Dialects: Parintintín/Tenharín/Juma, Kawahib/Paranawat/Pawaté-Wirafed, Tukumanfed, Diahoi)
  - Uruewauwau? *Rondônia, Brazil* (May be a variant of Parintintín-Tenharín)

(Continued)

Tupían stock (*Continued*)

   †Makirí? *Mato Grosso, Brazil* (May be a variant of Kawahib)
   Apiaká [moribund] *Mato Grosso, Brazil* (cf. Rodrigues 1986:39)
Kamayurá *Mato Grosso, Brazil*
Jo'é *Pará, Brazil* (Kaufman reports this as the language of a newly contacted group [in 1989], which is
      Tupí-Guaraní, "but its precise classification within the family is not yet worked out" [1994:72].)
Awetí [obsolescent] *Mato Grosso, Brazil*
Mawé-Sateré *Paraná, Alto Maranhão, Brazil* (Dialects: Mawé, Sateré)
Mundurukú branch
   Mundurukú *Paraná, Alto Maranhão, Brazil*
   Kuruaya [obsolescent] *Paraná, Brazil*
Juruna branch
   Juruna [obsolescent] *Mato Grosso, Brazil*
   †Xipaya [Shipaya] *Xingu River, Brazil*
   †Manitsawá *Xingu, Mato Grosso, Brazil*
Arikem branch
   †Arikem *Mato Grosso, Brazil*
   Karitiana *Rondônia, Brazil*
   Kabixiana [Kabishiana] [obsolescent] *Rondônia, Brazil*
Tuparí branch
   Tuparí [obsolescent] *Rondônia, Brazil*
   Mekens (Mekém, Mequens, Meké) [Amniapé] [obsolescent] *Rondônia, Brazil*
   Ayurú (Wayoró, Ajuru, Wayru) [Wayoró] [few/extinct?] *Rondônia, Brazil* (Dialects: Ajurú, Apichum)
   Makurap *Rondônia, Brazil*
   Kepkiriwat [extinct?] *Brazil*
Ramarama branch
   †Ramarama-Urumí *Mato Grosso, Brazil* (Dialects: Ramarama, Urumí)
   Arara-Urukú (Karo) *Rondônia, Brazil*
   Itogapuk [obsolescent] *Rondônia, Brazil*
Mondé branch
   Mondé-Sanamai [obsolescent] (Dialects: Mondé, Sanamai(kã)/Salamai)
   Suruí *Rondônia, Mato Grosso Brazil*
   Aruá *Rondônia, Brazil* (Dialects: Aruá/Aruashi, Cinta Larga, Gavião, Zoró)
Puruborá [obsolescent] *Rondônia, Brazil*

For historical antecedents, see Adam 1896.

from the rest of the family, with Proto-Tupari moving to the upper Jiparana and Proto-Arikém moving to the upper Madeira (where Makurap later separated off). Then Proto-Yuruma expanded eastward toward the upper Xingu River (it later split into Manitsawá and Shipaya). The last subgroup to develop was Proto-Mundurukú, which migrated to the north, to an extensive region between the lower Madeira and the Tapajós Rivers, and later extended to the east (where Kuruaya separated off). Finally, Proto-Tupí-Guaraní migrated a considerable distance from the center of the Proto-Tupian homeland. First Mawe went to the banks of the Amazon River near the mouth of the Tapajoz. Then Proto-

Kokama moved to the mouth of the Madeira, upriver along the Amazon all the way to the Ucayali River in Peru. Proto-Kawahiban was in the center of the original homeland; some speakers moved to the south (splitting into Proto-Pauserna and Proto-Sirionó); others moved to the headwaters of the Tapajoz. At the same time, Guaraní migrated to the southeast and later to the northeast along the coast of Brazil to the mouth of the Amazon and the Xingu Rivers.

The hypotheses of more remote genetic relationships involving Tupian, those that have been proposed but have little or no supporting evidence, are not discussed here. Rodrigues (1985a) finds some lexical evidence along with possible

sound correspondences linking Tupian and Cariban. Davis (1985[1968]:299–300]) sees lexical and general structural similarities between Tupian and Jean (Gêan) languages (see also Rodrigues 1985a:418). Both these proposals need to be tested.

(110) Cariban

(see Map; see also Maps 14, 16, 18, and 20, nos. 381–421)

See the classification list. Cariban is "a large family, with a large number of subgroups that do not seem to group together into major divisions" (Kaufman 1990a:49). The first references to Cariban speakers are in Columbus's journal, where he mentions that the Arawakan peoples he first encountered in the New World spoke of the fierce *Caniba* or *Canima,* whence the term *cannibal* 'people-eater' in English and equivalents in other European languages (Cummins 1992:170, Morison 1962:263, 275, 283). Columbus equated *Caniba* and *Carib* (as mentioned in Chapter 2). This is the origin of the *Carib* in 'Caribbean', the term used to designate a whole geographical area, and of 'Carib', referring to the native population of this region and of parts of Central and South America. *Carib* is apparently derived from a form which harks back to Proto-Cariban *karípona* 'Indian' (Kaufman 1994:74).[25]

There are a number of distinct classifications

of the Cariban family, which coincide only partially: Girard (1971a), Durbin (1977), Migliazza (1982, Migliazza and Campbell 1988), Kaufman (1994), and Villalón (1991). Girard's (1971a) seems now to be superseded. It included fifteen subgroups covering sixty-one languages; he was able to show that many of the language names sometimes associated with Cariban are only variant spellings of each other. Durbin's (1977: 35 [1985:358–60]) classification contains sixty languages, but only forty-seven of them agree with names given by Girard; Girard did not list the other thirteen. Villalón's is based on a lexicostatistical study of only fourteen of the many Cariban languages and is not as complete as the others. Durbin's is the best known and most frequently repeated Cariban classification; however, his scheme is not without problems; Kaufman asserts flatly that "Durbin's rationale for classifying the Kariban languages is fatally flawed. It makes use of a trivial phonological change or lack thereof (whether *p* remains or shifts to [f], [h], [w] or Ø) as criterial for subdividing the family into two branches" (1990b:168). Migliazza's classification differs in a number of respects from Durbin's (see Migliazza and Campbell 1988:382). Migliazza was able to reduce the number of Cariban languages usually listed by showing that a good number had been given multiple names; for example, he reduced twenty-eight names in one branch to six actual languages. Kaufman's classification,

---

Cariban

Opón-Carare [Opón-Karare] [extinct?] *Colombia* (Dialects: Opón, Carare)
Yukpa group
    Yucpa-Yaprería (Motilón) [Yukpa-Japrería] *Colombia, Venezuela* (Dialects: Yukpa, Shaparu, Chake,
        Yaprería, Sabril)
    †Coyaima (Tupe) [Koyaima] *Colombia*
Cariña (Carib, Caribe, Galibí) [Karínya][26] *Venezuela, Surinam, French Guiana, Guyana, Brazil*
Tiriyó group
    Tiriyó subgroup
        Akuriyo (Tiriyometesem, Triometesen) [obsolescent] *Surinam*
        Tirió (Trio, Pianakoto) [Tiriyó] *Surinam, Brazil*
    Karihona subgroup
        Jianácoto (Umawa) [Hianákoto] *Colombia*
        Carijona [Karihona][27] *Colombia*
    Salumá *Pará, Brazil*

(Continued)

Cariban (*Continued*)

Kashuyana group
    Kashuyana-Warikyana (Pauxi) *Pará, Brazil* (Dialects: Kashuyana, Warikyana)
    Shikuyana [few] *Brazil, Guyana, Venezuela*
Waiwai group
    Waiwai (Katawiana, Parukotó) *Brazil, Guyana*
    Hixkaryana (Waiboi) [Hishkariana] *Alto Maranhão, Brazil*
North Amazonian branch
    Yawaperí (Jawaparí) group
        †Boanarí (Bonari) *Amazonas, Brazil*
        Yawaperí (Atroarí/Atroahí, Waimirí, Krishaná) *Amazonas, Roraima, Alto Maranhão, Brazil*
    Paravilyana group
        Sapará [extinct?] *Roraima, Brazil*
        Paravilyana subgroup
            Pawixiana [Pawishiana, Pauxiana] [extinct?] *Roraima, Brazil*
            †Paravilhana [Paravilyana] *Roraima, Brazil*
    Pemón [Pemong] group[28]
        Pemón [Pemong] proper subgroup
            Makuxí (Macuxí, Teweya) [Makushí] *Brazil, Guyana, Venezuela*
            Pemón (Taurepan, Taulipang) [Pemong] *Venezuela, Brazil, Guyana* (Dialects: Taurepan, Kamarakotó, Jarekuna/Arekuna, Pemón)
            Kapong (Capón) *Guyana, Brazil, Venezuela* (Dialects: Akawayo, Ingaricó, Patamona)
            ?Purukotó [extinct?] *Venezuela, Brazil*
Central branch
    †Cumaná (Cumanagoto, Chaima) [Kumaná] *Venezuela*
    Yao group
        †Tivericoto [Tiverikoto] *Venezuela*
        †Yao *Trinidad, French Guiana*
    Wayana group
        Wayana (Urukuyana, Upuruí, Ouayana) *Surinam, French Guiana, Brazil*
        †Arakajú
    Apalaí *Pará, Brazil*
    Mapoyo-Yavarana (Tamanaco, Curasicana) [obsolescent?] *Venezuela* (Dialects: Mapoyo, Yavarana/Yabarana/Yauarana, others)
    Makiritare group
        Makiritare (Maquiritare) *Venezuela, Brazil*
        Wajumará (Wayumará) [extinct?] *Roraima, Brazil*
South Amazonian branch
    Bakairí group
        Bakairí (Kura) *Mato Grosso, Brazil*
        Amonap (Upper Xingu Cariban) *Mato Grosso, Brazil* (Dialects: Matipú, Kuikuro, Kalapalo, Nahukuá)
    Arara group
        Arara-Parirí [obsolescent?] *Pará, Brazil*
        †Apiaká-Apingi *Pará, Brazil*
        †Juma *Rondônia, Brazil*
        †Yarumá *Mato Grosso, Brazil*
        Txikão [Chikaon] *Mato Grosso, Brazil*
    †Palmela *Rondônia, Brazil*
    †Pimenteira *Piauí, Brazil*
    Panare *Venezuela*

Kaufman 1990b, 1994; see Gildea 1992:8.

which is like Migliazza's in that it reduces the number of language names, appears to be the best informed.

There have been a number of different proposals concerning the place of Panare in the family; they are discussed by Kaufman (1994:74), who leaves Panare as an independent branch. The numbers of speakers of most Cariban groups are not known, with the exception of the languages known to be extinct; some population figures, which do not correspond directly to number of speakers, are given by Basso (1977). Extinct languages of Guiana Carib, on which little linguistic material is known, include Wama (Akuriyó), Urukuyana, Triometesen, Kumayena, Pianakoto, Salumá, Chikena, Sapará, Yawaperí, Waimirí (Atroarí), Pauxiana, and Parukoto. Other extinct, undescribed Guiana Carib languages include Arakajú, Pauxi, Paravilhana, Bonari (Boanarí), and Arinagoto (Derbyshire and Pullum 1979, Migliazza 1985[1982]:67–8). Kaufman says of this classification: "While I do not believe any unjustified groupings have been made here, I specifically do not want to claim confidence in any grouping more inclusive than what is labelled by the capital letters A–T [that is, Kaufman's entire Cariban classification presented above]; any higher level groupings indicated here are hypotheses to be tested" (1994:74). None of the classifications of Cariban should be considered definitive, since so little historical linguistic work has been done on the family and so much remains to be done on Cariban subgrouping.

Opinions seem to abound concerning the Cariban homeland (see Villalón 1991:59–60); postulated locations range from the southern United States to Brazil. The Upper Xingu was favored by von den Steinen (1892) and by Rivet and Loukotka (Villalón 1991:59). Durbin (1977:35) locates the center of dispersal in the Guiana area of Venezuela, Surinam, or French Guiana, excluding Brazilian Guiana as unlikely. Migliazza postulates that the Proto-Cariban homeland was probably in the Northern Cariban area, where greater internal diversification is found than in the Southern Cariban area (Migliazza and Campbell 1988:393). Villalón's opinion is the most specific; she locates the center of dispersal "somewhere in the Venezuelan Guiana," explaining that "within this general area, the

slopes which give birth to the Caura, Cuchivero, and Ventuari watersheds, north of the junction of the sierras Parima and Pacaraima, seem the most likely site of the ancestral home of the Cariban speakers" (1991:87).

Opinions about possible remote genetic relationships involving Cariban have also been quite diverse; they include (1) Cariban with Arawakan, (2) Cariban, Arawakan, Chibchan, and Mayan (see Schuller 1919–1920), (3) Cariban and Tupian (Rodrigues 1985a), (4) Cariban, Tupian, and Arawakan (see de Goeje 1909), (5) Greenberg's (1960, 1987) Ge-Pano-Carib grouping, and (6) Landar's (1968) belief that Karankawa represents Cariban incursions into Texas, with Cariban and Hokan being connected—a view fully rejected by other scholars. None of these proposals is supported at present.

(111) **Yanomaman**
(see MAP 14, nos. 422–4)

See the classification list. This classification is from Migliazza (1985[1982], Migliazza and Campbell 1988). The phonemic inventory of Proto-Yanomaman, as reconstructed by Migliazza, is: /p, t, č, k, t^h, φ, š, h, r, m, n, w, y; i, e, a, ɨ, ə, o, u; vowel nasalization/ (Migliazza and Campbell 1988:197, 202–3). The reconstructions of *ɨ and *ə are uncertain. The *t^h had two allophones, with unchanged reflects in the daughter languages; one was *[s] before vowels, the other was *[t^h] in all other positions. The reflex of *č is y in two of the four languages, with the ñ variant of y before nasalized vowels in three of the languages. The word order was SOV, with OVS whenever the object was emphasized; the ergative agent suffix and the instrumental were the same in form (Migliazza and Campbell 1988:203).

As for more distant genetic connections, most broad classifications leave Yanomaman as independent, though Greenberg (1960, 1987) considers it to be a member of Chibchan (as he defines it), and a few other classifications have followed him. Migliazza presents lexical evidence with regular sound correspondences in support of a Yanomaman connection with Panoan languages, but also with possible Chibchan connections, and he urges that a possible Panoan-Chibchan relationship be investigated

Yanomaman

Yanam (Nimam, Xirianá, Shiriana Casapare, Kasrapai, Jawaperi, Crichana, Jawari; distinct from Xiriâna [Arawakan]) *Roraima, Brazil; southern Venezuela*

Sanumá (San+ma, Tsanuma, Sanema, Guaika, Samatari, Samatali, Xamatari) *Roraima, Brazil; southern Venezuela*

Yanomámi (Waiká, Yanoam, Yanomam, Yanomaé, Surara, Xurima, Parahuri; distinct from but related to Yanomamö) *Amazonas and Roraima, Brazil*

Yanomamö (Yanomam+, Yamomame, Guaicá, Guaharibo; different from but related to Yanomámi of Brazil) *Venezuela, Brazil*

(see Migliazza 1985[1982]:29; Migliazza and Campbell 1988:204–6).

(114) **Sálivan**

Colombia, Venezuela (see MAP 14, nos. 425–6)

See the classification list.

(118) **Jotí** (Joti, Waruwaru) [Hotí language]

Venezuela (see MAP 14, no. 427)

This language is not found in any of the major South American classifications; Migliazza (1985[1982]:46) lists it as an independent (unclassified) language.

(119) **Additional Language Considerations**

Not Given Prominence in Kaufman's Classification

In addition to the languages classified by Kaufman, Migliazza lists the following as unclassified South American languages: †Aguano (Awano, Ahuano), Peru; Kaimbe (Caimbe), Brazil; Carabayo, Colombia; †Muzo, Colombia; †Pakarara (Pacarará), Brazil; †Panche, Colombia; †Pantagora (Palenque), Colombia; †Patagón (not to be confused with the Patagón synonym

Sálivan

Sáliva (Sáliba)

Piaroa-Maco (Kuakua, Guagua, Quaqua; Ature/ Adole?)[Piaroa-Mako]

See Migliazza 1985[1982];41–3.

for Chon), Peru; Pijao (Piajao, Pixao, Pinao), Colombia; †Wakona, Wacona, Acona), Alagoas, state of Brazil (Migliazza and Campbell 1988:311–16). Migliazza also lists some twenty other names of languages (also unclassified) which are in some way uncertain or unconfirmed but that appear in some lists of South American languages.

Larger Groupings

The more widely known proposals concerning distant genetic relationship among South American families and isolates are reflected throughout Kaufman's classification, in the so-called clusters and names preceded by "Macro-". It should be emphasized that at present most of these hypotheses have not been investigated in any detail and most lack much support; therefore, they should be considered only as guidelines for the direction that future research should take, not as accepted or even probable genetic relationships.

7

Distant Genetic Relationships: The Methods

It is a truism of linguistic research that, given large enough vocabularies to compare, and making allowances for all possible changes in the form of a word or stem, as well as in its meaning, a number of apparent similarities, convincing to the uncritical, can be found between any two languages.

J. Alden Mason (1950:162)

The difficulty of the task of trying to make every language fit into a genetic classification has led certain eminent linguists to deprive the principle of such classification of its precision and its rigor or to apply it in an imprecise manner.

Antoine Meillet (1948[1914]:78)[1]

THE CLASSIFICATIONS OF FAMILIES and isolates presented in Chapters 4, 5, and 6 are relatively straightforward and for the most part not controversial. However, proposals abound for more inclusive, broader family groupings, hypotheses of distant genetic relationships. The purpose of this chapter is to assess the methods for determining family relationships, particularly distant genetic affinities. In Chapter 8, the principal proposals for various broader groupings of Native American languages are evaluated using the methods surveyed in this chapter. The criteria and methodological considerations utilized in distant-genetic research which are discussed here include basic vocabulary, sound correspondences, borrowing, semantic equivalence, grammatical evidence, morphological analyses, the principle that only comparisons involving both sound and meaning are reliable, onomatopoeia, erroneous reconstruction, sound symbolism, spurious forms, philological

and scribal problems, and the avoidance of chance.

It will be helpful to begin with an understanding of how many of these proposals of remote relationships came into being. The history of American Indian linguistic classification is characterized by historical accidents and the influence of powerful personalities (see Chapter 2; Campbell and Mithun 1979b:29–30). In view of the large number of distinct Native American languages, scholars set out early to reduce this vast linguistic diversity to manageable genetic schemes, and a large segment of the history of American Indian linguistics is comprised of rough-and-ready hypotheses of possible family connections, proposals which lumped languages into ever larger groups with the intent of reducing the ultimate number of independent genetic units in the Americas. Often these hypotheses were offered initially as very preliminary proposals (some were little more than hunches) to be tested in subsequent work, but unfortunately many of them came to be accepted uncritically and were repeated in the literature so frequently that they became entrenched; many scholars believed they had been established through valid procedures. This acceptance of the far-flung yet undemonstrated hypotheses of distant genetic relationships was abetted by the faith American anthropologists and linguists had in the intellectual abilities of such influential scholars as Edward Sapir and Alfred Kroeber who were engaged in large-scale classifications (see Campbell and Mithun 1979a, Darnell 1990, Golla 1984). Over time, more and more languages came to be proposed as relatives of languages already included in familiar proposals of larger groupings and distant relationships, such as Hokan and Penutian (see Chapter 8). The methods for investigating remote relationships have long been debated; particularly intense is the debate surrounding the separability of similarities that are shared due to genetic relationship (inherited from a common ancestor) from those that are due to diffusion.

It is often by sheer chance that attention is turned to certain languages and not to others as being possible relatives of one another. For example, the Maya-Araucanian hypothesis came about because Louisa Stark directed Karen Dakin, who was then a graduate student in one of her courses (Stark 1970:57), to look into a possible Mayan affinity with Arawakan (suggested by Noble [1965:26] in a footnote), but Dakin understood her to mean Araucanian (rather than Arawakan) and compared Mayan and Araucanian (Mapudungu) instead—and, presto, Maya-Araucanian![2] Some hypotheses of long-range relationships owe their origin to the tendency to see similarities among the languages with which one is familiar, especially when one becomes acquainted with a little-known new language, particularly a so-called exotic tongue. For example, Ronald Olson's (1964, 1965) Maya-Chipaya hypothesis (which proposes a link between Mayan and Uru-Chipaya, spoken in Bolivia—see Chapter 8) owes its inception to the fact that Frances Olson (Ronald Olson's wife), who as the daughter of missionaries in Chiapas, Mexico, had learned Tzeltal (a Mayan language) and saw similarities between it and the Chipaya spoken where she and her husband

worked (as members of the Summer Institute of Linguistics). Similarly, Gerdel and Slocum supported a Maya-Paezan proposal because they had spent several years working on Tzeltal under the auspices of the Summer Institute of Linguistics before investigating Paez in Colombia—or, as Key put it, "another fortuitous event furthers the piecing together of history" (1979:35; see also Wheeler 1972:96). Unfortunately, none of these proposals—neither Maya-Araucanian, nor Maya-Chipaya, nor Maya-Paezan—has proven defensible or productive (see Campbell 1973a, 1979). In short, in many such hypothesized distant genetic relationships, the evidence does not reach a level of plausibility sufficient even to encourage further investigation. This is not to say, however, that at times seemingly strange motivations for comparing unlikely languages cannot pay off with positive results, contrary to normal expectations (see Hamp 1979:1005).

In practice, the methods for establishing distant genetic relationships have not been different from the method used to establish any family relationship, regardless of how closely or distantly the languages might be related—namely, the comparative method. In fact, in North America the individuals who contributed to historical linguistic research at the (demonstrable) family level very often were also involved in proposals of more distant possible relationships. They applied the comparative method, and their criteria in both cases were vocabulary (especially basic vocabulary), grammatical agreements, and sound correspondences wherever the available data permitted. Benjamin Whorf, for example, who was the first to use the term "phylum" (now usually understood as referring to a proposed but unconfirmed distant genetic relationship), used presumed lexical cognates (more accurately called "matchings") and sound correspondences in formulating his distant genetic proposals (see, for example, Whorf and Trager 1937, Whorf 1943:7–8). Similarly, Edward Sapir (as discussed in Chapter 2) used this method in both his successful proposals (Uto-Aztecan, Ritwan-Algonquian; see Sapir 1913, 1913–1919) and his more disputed ones (for example, Na-Dene, Subtiaba-Hokan; Sapir 1915c, 1920, 1925a). In fact, the Subtiaba-Hokan paper (Sapir 1925a) is considered by many to be a statement of major importance with regard to methods for investigating remote relationships, though today we know the proposal was erroneous since Subtiaba has been shown to belong to Otomanguean and not to Hokan. The issue of whether methods for family-level and phylum-level research are radically distinct (as asserted, for example, by Voegelin 1942, Voegelin and Voegelin 1965; see also Voegelin and Voegelin 1985) arises only in the case of preliminary or pioneering proposals, offered as hypotheses for further testing, but which are not yet considered established. Sapir's (1929a) six super-stocks were based on gross morphological and typological similarities. He believed, however, that rigorous comparison and lexical evidence would increasingly support these preliminary proposals (1990[1921a]:93, 1925a:526; see Kroeber 1940a:465–6).

In actual practice, the standard comparative method has always been the basic tool for establishing genetic relationships, whether distant or not. The fact that the methods for establishing less remote families and those for investigating possible distant genetic relationships have not in practice been different may be a principal reason that devising the ultimate linguistic classification for the Americas has been so perplexing. Because the methods have not been different, the result is a continuum from established and noncontroversial relationships (Uto-Aztecan, Algonquian, Athabaskan), to more distant but still solidly supported relationships (Algonquian-Ritwan, Eskimo-Aleut, Siouan-Catawban, Otomanguean), to plausible but inconclusive proposals (Aztec-Tanoan, Penutian, Hokan), to doubtful but not implausible proposals (Yuchi-Siouan, Zuni-Penutian, Mexican Penutian), to implausible proposals (Yuchi-Yukian, Tarascan-Quechua, Maya-Chipayan), to virtually impossible proposals (Algonquian-Old Norse, Altaic-Mayan, Uto-Aztecan-Austronesian). It is difficult to segment this continuum so that plausible proposals based on legitimate procedures and reasonable supporting evidence are clearly distinguished from obviously unlikely hypotheses. The evidence is often not significantly better for proposals which would initially seem possible for geographical or other reasons than for highly unlikely suggestions such as Quechua-Turkish, Miwok-Uralic, and other marginal proposals.

Related to this continuum from established relationships to highy improbable proposals are the different practices that distinguish the initial setting up of a hypothesis, of a potential relationship to be checked out, from the later testing of such hypotheses to see whether they hold up. As Jacobsen (1990) points out, the way to approach such distant comparisons is not by making exclusions but rather by casting one's net broadly and then evaluating the comparisons that turn up. The quality of the evidence presented in support of proposals of distant genetic relationships typically varies in accordance with the proposer's intent. When the intention is to call attention to a possible connection that is as yet unelaborated or untested, a wide net is cast in order to haul in as much potential evidence as possible. When the intention is to test a proposal, forms admitted initially as possible evidence are submitted to more careful scrutiny. Of course, many researchers do not bother to distinguish the setting-up type hypotheses, with their more wide-eyed (liberal) view of possible evidence, from the hypothesis-testing type, where a steady-eyed (strict) scrutiny of potential evidence dominates. Both orientations are perfectly valid.[3] Also, it is important to keep in mind that "questioning evidence for a proposed genetic relationship is not the same as denying that relationship" (Callaghan 1991a:54) and that no proposal which has not been carefully evaulated can legitimately be shifted toward the "established" end of the continuum.

Methodology is indeed worthy of our concern if we cannot easily distinguish the fringe proposals from the more plausible ones. However, since methods for investigating potential distant genetic relationships are not radically different from those employed in research on more closely related languages, we can expect little else, and we do well to remain skeptical and to demand careful evaluation of evidence. In a historical survey of the methods and criteria which have been advocated or used for supporting genealogical relationships among languages not yet known to be related, it was clear that some methods are more successful than others—and that even the successful ones can be applied inappropriately (Poser and Campbell 1992). I now turn to an appraisal of these recommendations for appropriate methodological procedures for investigating possible distant genetic relationships.

Lexical Comparison

Throughout history, words have been employed as evidence of family relationship, but most scholars have insisted also on items from basic vocabulary, and convincing results were seldom achieved without additional support from other criteria, such as sound correspondences and compelling morphological parallels. The use of lexical material as the only (or primary) source of evidence has often resulted in invalid proposals, and therefore the practice has been controversial (Meillet 1948[1914]:92–3, 1925:36–7; Haas 1969b; Goddard 1975:254–5; Campbell and Mithun 1979a; Campbell 1988b). Morris Swadesh accurately observed the pivotal methodological problem attending lexical comparisons: "Given a small collection of likely-looking cognates, how can one definitely determine whether they are really the residue of common origin and not the workings of pure chance or some other factor? This is a crucial problem of long-range comparative linguistics" (1954b: 312). The importance of basic vocabulary and approaches that are largely lexically based is discussed in the next two sections.

Basic Vocabulary

From the beginning of the study of linguistic relationships, basic vocabulary (*Kernwortschatz, vocabulaire de base, charakteristische Wörter,* "noncultural" vocabulary) has been advocated as an important criterion or source of supporting evidence (see Chapter 2). Technically, if basic vocabulary is to play a significant role in the methodology of determining distant genetic relationship, the notion of what constitutes basic vocabulary ought to be carefully and explicitly defined. Nevertheless, scholars have always had a more or less intuitive common understanding of what constitutes basic vocabulary—terms for human body parts, close kin, commonly encountered aspects of the natural world (meteorological, geographical), low numbers, and so on. In his attempts to define core vocabulary, Swadesh arrived at progressively smaller lists, of 500,

205, 200, and finally 100 words. His lists may be considered useful compilations of basic vocabulary, though they are not exhaustive. Terrence Kaufman (1973b) prepared a list of the 500 meanings that recur most frequently in reconstructed vocabularies of proto languages. In effect, this constitutes a more precise definition of basic vocabulary, since these are in some sense the most stable glosses found in the language families investigated so far. In this book, I follow traditional practice, speaking of basic vocabulary as though it were somehow clearly and strictly defined, but I assume that most linguists have a fairly clear intuitive sense of what kinds of words are to be considered basic vocabulary.

It has generally been recognized that lexical matchings involving basic vocabulary can help control for the effects of borrowing, since in general basic vocabulary items are borrowed much less frequently than are other vocabulary items. Of course, basic vocabulary items can be borrowed, though this is much less common, so that this role of basic vocabulary as a buffer against borrowing is by no means foolproof (see below). Similarly, while basic vocabulary is indeed on the whole more resistant to replacement than lexical items from other sectors of the vocabularly, such basic words are in fact also often replaced, so that even in clearly related languages, not all basic vocabulary reflects true cognates—this is one of the valid insights of Swadesh's glottochronology, generally discredited as a method of dating, but nevertheless based on the valid observation that even basic vocabulary can be and is replaced over time (though probably not at the constant rate asserted by glottochronology; for criticisms, see Arndt 1959 and Bergsland and Vogt 1962, among others).

Lexically Based Approaches

Two approaches which rely principally on word comparisons are glottochronology and the comparison of inspectional resemblances, which Kroeber called "the simple frontal attack by inspection" (1940a:464); the latter is the approach utilized by Powell, by Dixon and Kroeber, and, more recently, by Greenberg, among others (see Chapter 2). Both approaches

are inadequate. Glottochronology has been rejected by most linguists since all of its basic
assumptions have been challenged (see Callaghan 1991c, Campbell 1977:63–5). In any
case, it does not find or test relationships; rather,
it assumes that the languages being compared
are related and proceeds to attach a date based
on the number of lexical similarities between
the languages that are checked off.[4]

A prime example of the inspectional resemblances approach is the method that Greenberg
calls "multilateral (or mass) comparison." It is
based on lexical look-alikes determined by visual inspection—"looking at . . . many languages across a few words" rather than "at a
few languages across many words" (1987:23),
where the lexical similarity shared "across many
languages" alone is taken as evidence of genetic
relationship, with no other methodological considerations deemed relevant. As has been pointed
out repeatedly, this procedure is only a starting
point (see Campbell 1988b; Goodman 1970;
Hock 1993; Peter 1993; Rankin 1992; Ringe
1992, 1993; Watkins 1990). The inspectional
resemblances detected in mass comparison must
still be investigated to determine whether they
are due to inheritance from a common ancestor
or whether they result from borrowing, accident,
onomatopoeia, sound symbolism, or nursery
formations (see Hymes 1959:55). Since Greenberg's application of his method does not take
this necessary next step, the results frequently
have proven erroneous or at best highly controversial.[5] In addition, this method, like glottochronology, essentially presupposes that if an
unspecified number of inspectional similarities
are discovered, a genetic relationship exists
among the languages being compared—it does
not test rigorously to determine whether such a
relationship holds or whether the similarities
dectected are due to factors other than genetic affinity (Mithun 1990:321). Moreover,
Greenberg did not in fact apply his much-
proclaimed method in establishing most of his
Amerind classification (see Greenberg 1949,
1953, 1960; Campbell 1988b, Campbell in press
a; see also Chapter 2). Rather, he had already
drawn his conclusions about most of the classification (repeating classifications by Sapir and
Rivet, see below) and later began filling in his
notebooks (which are not published but which

are available from the Stanford University library) upon which his classification is purported
to rely. The classification reflected by the arrangement of the languages in these notebooks
has not changed appreciably since his 1953 and
1956 studies (Greenberg 1953, 1960, 1962),
though most of the supporting data were assembled after the 1953 and 1956 work (see
Greenberg 1990a:6). As is clear from the arrangement of languages in these notebooks, they
were ordered according to this preconceived
classification, and "multilateral comparison"
was not used to arrive at the grouping.
Greenberg himself confirmed that he did not
apply his method to establish his classification
and that he had decided on most of it before he
assembled the data for his notebooks:

> Even cursory investigation of the celebrated "dis-
> puted" cases, such as Athabaskan-Tlingit-Haida
> and Algonkin-Wiyot-Yurok, indicate that these re-
> lationships are not very distant ones and, indeed,
> are evident on inspection. Even the much larger
> Macro-Penutian grouping seems *well within the
> bounds of what can be accepted without more
> elaborate investigation and marshaling of support-
> ing evidence.* (Emphasis added; Greenberg
> 1953:283)[6]

As a result of the prejudgments in this classification, some language groupings in Greenberg
1987 (which follows extensively earlier proposals by Edward Sapir [1929a] for North America[7]
and Paul Rivet [1924; Rivet and Loukotka 1952]
for South America) are now known to be indisputably wrong, and there is no way these parts of
Greenberg's classification could have followed
from an application of multilateral comparison
(or any other method) to the data. To illustrate,
I cite one erroneous classification from each of
the two scholars whose ideas Greenberg incorporated into his classification. Following Rivet
(see Crequi-Montfort and Rivet 1925–1926),
Greenberg classified Uru-Chipaya and Puquina
as closely related languages, although they have
almost nothing in common. This error is based
on the old misunderstanding that derives from
the fact that Uru-Chipaya is often called Puquina
in the Andes region (Adelaar 1989:252, Olson
1964:314; the error was pointed out, and the
differences between Puquina and Uru clearly
shown, by Chamberlain 1910 and Ibarra Grasso

1958:10, 1964:37–3—see Chapter 6). Following Sapir, Greenberg placed Subtiaba-Tlapanec with Hokan, although Subtiaba-Tlapanec is now known to be a clear and undisputed branch of Otomanguean (Campbell 1988b; Suárez 1979, 1983, 1986). The data in no way lead to Greenberg's classifications of these languages.

It is important to point out that Greenberg's methods, in particular his conception of multilateral (or mass) comparison, have undergone telling mutations since he first discussed them. Indeed, Greenberg 1957 was strikingly mainstream in his statement of how to approach distant genetic relationship. As he said, "the methods outlined here do not conflict in any fashion with the traditional comparative method" (1957:44). He advocated the same procedures advocated by other scholars; for example, "semantic plausibility, breadth of distribution in the various subgroups of the family, length [of compared forms], participation in irregular alternations, and the occurrence of sound correspondences" (1957:45; these criteria are discussed later in this chapter). Still, his emphasis—for pragmatic reasons, he suggests—was on vocabulary: "All available grammatical information should be systematically examined, but vocabulary leads most swiftly to the correct hypotheses as a general rule" (1957:42).

A major change, however, appears to be that in 1957 he viewed mass comparison as subordinate and auxiliary to the standard comparative method, whereas in 1987 he sees it as superior to and replacing the standard procedures. In 1957 (but not in 1987), mass comparison concentrated on cases in which the family relationships of most of the languages compared were known, and these groups were compared with one another to arrive at higher-level groups:

> Instead of comparing a few or even just two languages chosen at random and for linguistically extraneous reasons, we proceed systematically by first comparing closely related languages to form groups with recurrent significant resemblances and then compare these groups with other similarly constituted groups. Thus it is far easier to see that the Germanic languages are related to the Indo-Aryan languages than that English is related to Hindustani. In effect, we have gained historic depth by comparing each group as a group, considering only those forms as possessing likelihood of

being original which are distributed in more than one branch of the group and considering only those etymologies as favoring the hypothesis of relationship in which tentative reconstruction brings the forms closer together. Having noted the relationship of the Germanic and Indo-Aryan languages, we bring in other groups of languages, e.g. Slavonic and Italic. In this process we determine with ever increasing definiteness the basic lexical and grammatical morphemes in regard to both phonetic form and meaning. On the other hand, we also see more easily that the Semitic languages and Basque do not belong to this aggregation of languages. Confronted by some isolated language without near congeners, we compare it with this general Indo-European rather than at random with single languages. (1957:40–1)

Clearly, multilateral comparison as employed by Greenberg in 1987 is not the gradual build-up sort that it was in 1957, when Greenberg based the method on the comparison of an as yet unclassified language with a number of languages previously demonstrated to be related. (See Welmers 1956:558 for a clear exposition of Greenberg's earlier method of mass comparison and its reliance on languages already known to be related.) An array of cognate forms in languages known to be related might reveal similarities with a form compared from some language whose genetic relationships we are attempting to determine, where comparison with only a single language from the related group might not, given the possibilities of lexical replacement such that the language may or may not have retained the cognate form still seen in some of its sisters. However, this is equivalent, in essence, to the recommendation that we should do the historical linguistic research to reconstruct lower-level, accessible families—where proto forms can be reconstructed on the basis of the cognate sets, although not every language in the family will contain a witness/ reflex for some sets because some individual languages will have lost or replaced the cognate word—before we proceed to higher-level, more inclusive families. That is, a validly reconstructed form from the proto language is very much like applying the "multilateral comparison" to the various cognates from across the family upon which the reconstruction of that form is based. For attempts to establish more remote genetic affiliations, comparison utilizing either the reconstructed proto form or the languagewide cognate set are roughly equivalent. This is, however, not different from the business-as-usual approach advocated today by Greenberg's critics; for example, Callaghan advocates "climbing a low[er] mountain" (working out the historical linguistics of lower-level family relationships) before one can effectively proceed to loftier heights (more distant relationships) (1991a).

A question which is sometimes raised with regard to the use of lexical evidence to support long-range relationships has to do with the gradual loss or replacement of vocabulary over time. It is commonly believed that "comparable lexemes must inevitably diminish to near the vanishing point the deeper one goes in comparing remotely related languages" (Bengtson 1989: 30). Bengtson calls this "the law of dimishing returns." One may well ask, can related languages separated by many centuries undergo so much vocabulary replacement that there will simply not be sufficient shared original vocabulary remaining to enable detection of an ancient shared kinship? (See also Hock 1993.) While this possibility is sometimes brushed aside or ignored,[8] it does constitute a serious problem for those who believe that very deep relationships can be supported by lexical evidence alone. Realistically, we should be prepared to admit that after extremely long periods of separation, related languages may in fact have undergone so much vocabulary change that insufficient original lexical material may remain upon which a genetic relationship might plausibly be based.

Moreover, as has frequently been pointed out (see Hock 1993), it is surprising how the matched sounds in the languages involved in proposals of remote relationship are typically so very similar, often identical, while among the daughter languages of well-established noncontroversial families such identities in sound correspondences are not as frequent as they are in most of these more far-flung and controversial hypotheses. That is, while some sounds may remain relatively unchanged among related languages over long periods (see Campbell 1986b), many do undergo significant sound changes so that phonetically nonidentical sound correspondences are frequent. One wonders why corre-

spondences involving sounds that are not so similar are not more common in such proposals. The typical sound changes that lead to such nonidentical correspondences often change the form of cognate lexical items so that their cognacy is not immediately apparent from superficial visual inspection. These true but nonobvious cognates are missed by methods such as multilateral (mass) comparison which seek inspectional resemblances. For example, Hindi *cakkā* (compare Sanskrit *cakra-*) and *sīg* (compare Sanskrit *śṛṅga-*) are true cognates of English *wheel* and *horn,* respectively (Proto-Indo-European *$k^w ek^w lo$-* 'wheel' and *$\acute{k}er/\acute{k}\underset{.}{r}$-* 'horn') (Hock 1993), but such cognates would be missed in most investigations of distant genetic relationship. A method which scans only for phonetic resemblances (for example, Greenberg's multilateral comparison) misses such true cognates as those illustrated by Meillet's example of French *cinq* / Russian *$p^y at^y$* / Armenian *hing* / English *five,* which are not phonetically similar but are easily derived by straightforward changes from original Indo-European *$penk^w e$* 'five', or by French *boeuf* / English *cow* (both from Proto-Indo-European *$g^w ou$-*), or French /nu/ (spelled *nous*) 'we, us' / English *us* (from Proto-Indo-European *nes-*, French more immediately from Latin *nōs,* English from Germanic *uns* [from zero-grade *$\underset{.}{n}s$*]).

In short, no technique that relies on inspectional similarities among lexical items without additional support from other sources of evidence has proven adequate for determining distant genetic relationship.[9] Ives Goddard has aptly summarized the limitations of such approaches:

> It is widely believed that, when accompanied by lists of the corresponding sounds, a moderate number of lexical similarities is sufficient to demonstrate a linguistic relationship. . . . However, . . . the criteria which have usually been considered necessary for a good etymology are very strict, even though there may seem to be a high a priori probability of relationship when similar words in languages known to be related are compared. In the case of lexical comparisons it is necessary to account for the whole word in the descendant languages, not just an arbitrarily segmented "root," and the reconstructed ancestral form must be a complete word. . . . The greater

the number of descendant languages attesting a form, and the greater the number of comparable phonemes in it, the more likely it is that the etymology is a sound one and the resemblances not merely the result of chance. A lexical similarity between only two languages is generally considered insufficiently supported, unless the match is very exact both phonologically and semantically, and it is rare that a match of only one or two phonemes is persuasive. If the meanings of the forms compared differ, then there must be an explicit hypothesis about how the meaning has changed in the various cases. Now, if these strict criteria have been found necessary for etymologies within KNOWN linguistic families, it is obvious that much stricter criteria must be applied to word-comparisons between languages whose relationship is in question. (1975:254–5)

(See also Campbell 1973a, 1988b; Campbell and Mithun 1979b; Meillet 1948[1914]:92–3, 1925:36–7; Matisoff 1990; Rankin 1992; Ringe 1992; Watkins 1990.)

Sound Correspondences

Corresponding sounds have been a widely recognized criterion for showing genetic relationship throughout the history of linguistics (see Poser and Campbell 1992; Chapter 2). Evidence of recurring regular sound correspondences is considered by some scholars to be the strongest evidence of remote genetic affinity. It should be kept in mind that it is correspondences among related languages, not mere similarities, which are deemed crucial and that such correspondences do not necessarily involve similar sounds.

It is important to emphasize the value and utility of sound correspondences in the investigation of linguistic relationships. As valuable as they are, there are, nevertheless, a number of ways in which this criterion can be misapplied.

First, in general, recurrent sound correspondences (usually) indicate a historical connection, though in some instances it may not be easy to determine whether that connection is due to a common ancestor or to borrowing. As has repeatedly been shown, regularly corresponding sounds are sometimes also found in loaned vocabulary (see Hoijer 1941:5; Greenberg 1957; Pierce 1965:31; Rigsby 1966:370, 1969:72;

Goddard 1975; Campbell 1988b). Thus, for example, according to Grimm's law, real Spanish-English cognates should exhibit the correspondence $p : f$, as in *padre/father, pie/foot, por/for.* However, Spanish and English appear to exhibit also the correspondence $p : p$ in cases where English has borrowed from Latin or French, as in *paternal/paternal, pedestal/pedestal, por/per.*[10] Since English has many such loans, it is not difficult to find examples which illustrate this bogus $p : p$ sound correspondence. As Greenberg pointed out, "the presence of recurrent sound correspondences is not in itself sufficient to exclude borrowing as an explanation. Where loans are numerous, they often show such correspondences; thus French loanwords in English often show Fr. *š* = Eng. *č*, Fr. *ã* = Eng. *æn* (*šãs : čæns; šãt : čænt; šɛːz : čejr* [chance : chance; chant : chant; chaise : chair], etc.)" (1957:40). As Eric Hamp explains, "we all know that if we get perfect phonological correspondences and nothing else, we often have a beautiful illustration of some extremely old layer of loan words" (1976:83; see Hardman de Bautista 1978b:151 and Rigsby 1969:72 for other examples and discussion). In comparing languages which are not yet known to be related, caution should be exercised in interpreting sound correspondences to avoid the problems that may arise from undetected loans. Generally, correspondences in more basic vocabulary warrant greater confidence that the correspondence is not found only in loans, though basic vocabulary, too, can be borrowed (but such loans are rare). To take a simple but clear example, in Finnish the words *äiti* 'mother' and *tytär* 'daughter' are borrowed from Indo-European languages; if these were not recognized as loans, a regular sound correspondence of $t : d$ involving the medial consonant of *äiti* (Germanic **aidī*) and the initial consonant of *tytär* (Germanic **dohtēr*) might be suspected, based on these two basic vocabulary words.[11]

Second, nongenuine sound correspondences (that is, not due to genetic relationship) may also be fostered in other ways. For example, some lexical similarities among languages are totally accidental. For instance, Bancroft presented a rather long list of words "analogous both in signification and sound, selected from American, European, Asiatic, and other languages, between which it is now well established that no relationship exists" (1886:561); his examples included Latin *lingua* / Moqui [Hopi] *línga* [lengyi] 'tongue'; German *Kopf* / Cahita *coba* 'head'; Sanskrit *da* / Cora *ta* 'give'; and Sanskrit *mâ* / Tepehuan *mai* / Maya *ma* 'not/no'. Some personal favorites of mine of this sort are: Proto-Jean **niw* 'new' / English *new* (Davis 1968); Kaqchikel dialects *mes* 'mess, disorder, garbage' / English *mess;* Jaqaru *aska* 'ask' / English *ask;* Lake Miwok *hóllu* 'hollow' / English *hollow;* Lake Miwok *mé:na* 'to think', 'to guess' / Swedish *mena* 'to think', 'to guess', 'to mean' / English *mean* (comparisons with Miwok-Costanoan are from Catherine Callaghan, personal communication); Seri *ki?* / French *qui* (/ki/) 'who?'; Yana *t'inii-* 'small' (Haas 1964b:81) / English *tiny, teeny;* the famous examples Persian *bad* / English *bad,* and Malay *mata* 'eye' / Modern Greek *mati* 'eye' (the Greek form is derived in a straightforward manner from *ommation*) (see Bright 1984:7 for additional examples).

Examples of apparent but unreal sound correspondences may also turn up if promiscuous semantic latitude in proposed cognates is permitted, such that phonetically similar but semantically disparate forms are equated (see Ringe 1992 for a mathematical proof). Gilij (1965[1780–1784]:132–3) listed several examples: *ano* meaning 'day' in Tamanaco but 'anus' in Italian; *poeta* 'drunk' in Maipure, 'poet' in Italian; and *putta* 'head' in Otomaco, 'prostitute' in Italian. In such cases the phonetic correspondences are due to sheer accident, since it is always possible to find phonetically similar words among languages, if their meaning is ignored. The sanctioning of semantic liberty among compared forms can easily result in spurious sound correspondences such as the initial $p : p$ and medial $t : t$ of the Amazonian-Italian 'drunk-poet' and 'head-prostitute' forms pointed out by Gilij. Noninherited phonetic similarities may also crop up when onomatopoetic, sound-symbolic, and nursery forms are compared (for examples, see the next section). A set of proposed cognates involving the combination of loans, chance enhanced by semantic latitude, onomatopoeia, and sound symbolism may exhibit seemingly real but false sound correspondences. For this reason, some proposed remote

relationships whose propounders profess allegiance to regular sound correspondences in their methods nevertheless do not attain a level of plausibility sufficient to impress more discerning scholars (see Ringe 1992 for more detail).

The strongest proposals of distant genetic relationship present supporting evidence from both regularly recurring sound correspondences and grammatical agreements of the appropriate sort. However, in some cases either type of evidence alone may be sufficient to establish the plausibility of a given proposal. Most Americanists are happy—even eager—to have sound correspondences and consider them strong evidence, but they neither insist on them exclusively nor trust them fully in every case. However, they do insist on the application of the comparative method (see Watkins 1990). Although the comparative method is often associated with sound change, and hence with regularly recurring sound correspondences, this is not an essential feature of it. It should be recalled that Meillet (1967[1925]:13–14) introduced the comparative method, not with examples of phonological correspondences but with reference to comparative mythology. Thus, a comparison of patterned grammatical evidence also comes under the comparative method. Greenberg's treatment of lexical and grammatical examples (1987) is not persuasive precisely because he has not shown that the genetic hypotheses he proposes for these similarities are any stronger than other explanations such as chance, onomatopoeia, borrowing, sound symbolism, and nursery forms. Sound correspondences might help eliminate some of these possible competing explanations for some of Greenberg's forms, but he does not believe them to be necessary. In fact, as Catherine Callaghan points out, Greenberg "does not even state the parameters of what he considers to be valid [phonological] resemblance. He seems to think his masses of forms speak for themselves" (1991a:50). With no other means at his disposal for restricting the other potential explanations for the similarities he amasses, and with the demonstration (Campbell 1988b, in press a) that equally compelling chance similarities from other languages are easily assembled (to mention just one of the failings of his method), Greenberg's method cannot be successful.

Grammatical Evidence

Given that inspectional resemblances among lexical items are not sufficient to rule out chance and other possible explanations, and given that even seemingly real but spurious sound correspondences can be assembled if loans, onomatopoeia, accidentally similar forms, and the like are not taken out of the picture, many scholars feel that additional information is necessary, or at least helpful, to remedy this situation. Throughout linguistic history, the majority of scholars have held morphological evidence to be essential or at least of great importance for establishing family relationships among languages (Poser and Campbell 1992). Some have utilized as their principal grammatical evidence similarities in compared languages seen against the backdrop of a language's overall morphological game-plan (typology), while many have required idiosyncratic, peculiar, arbitrary morphological correspondences (Meillet's "shared aberrancy"; see the discussion that follows), those which are so distinctive they could not easily be explained as the result of borrowing or accident. Some have thought the arguments are stronger if the peculiar morphological matchings which they emphasize fit into a broader picture of the overall morphological or grammatical system. It is worthwhile to consider these different outlooks concerning grammatical evidence, and its importance in general.

Submerged Features

Sapir's classification of the native languages of North American into six super-stocks relied very heavily on morphological (typological) traits, and secondarily on lexical evidence.[12] His Subtiaba-Hokan article (1925a) is frequently cited as a model of how the study of distant genetic relationships should be approached, or at least of Sapir's method of doing so. In particular, the "submerged features" passage in this article has received much attention:

> When one passes from a language to another that is only remotely related to it, say from English to Irish or from Haida to Hupa or from Yana to Salinan, one is overwhelmed at first by the great and obvious differences of grammatical structure.

As one probes more deeply, however, significant resemblances are discovered which weigh far more in a genetic sense than the discrepancies that lie on the surface and that so often prove to be merely secondary dialectic developments which yield no very remote historical perspective. In the upshot it may appear, and frequently does appear, that the most important grammatical features of a given language and perhaps the bulk of what is conventionally called its grammar are of little value for the remoter comparison, which may rest largely on *submerged features* that are of only minor interest to a descriptive analysis. (Emphasis added; Sapir 1925a:491–2)

What Sapir meant by "submerged features" would seem to be illustrated in his example: "Thus, Choctaw *la^{n}sa* 'scar' / *mi^{n}sa* 'scarred' is curiously reminiscent of such alternations as Subtiaba *daša* 'grass' / *maša* 'to be green' and suggests an old nominal prefix *l*" (1925a:526). One interpretation is that Sapir's submerged features are like the specific, idiosyncratic facts often said to be what really counts in genetic comparison. This is essentially the interpretation of both Mary Haas (1941:41) and Harry Hoijer (1954:6), former students of Sapir's, and of Bright (1984:12), Campbell (1973a), Campbell and Mithun (1979a), Goddard (1975), Teeter (1964a), and Liedtke (1991:87–92), among others. As Krauss put it, "we often find our most valuable comparative evidence in certain irregularities in fundamental and frequent forms, like prize archaeological specimens poking out of the mud of contemporary regularity" (1969:54). A clear example of this view is Teeter's (1964a:1029) comparison of Proto-Central-Algonquian and Wiyot possessive formations; in Proto-Central-Algonquian a -*t*- is inserted between a possessive pronominal prefix and a vowel-initial root, whereas in Wiyot a -*t*- is inserted between possessive prefixes and a root beginning in *hV* (with the loss of the *h*-):

Proto-Central-Algonquian	Wiyot
*ne + *ehkw-	du- + híkw
= *netehkw- 'my louse'	= dutíkw 'my louse'

Sapir (1913) had proposed the Algonquian-Ritwan (now usually called Algic) relationship, which groups Wiyot and Yurok of California with Algonquian; this hypothesis was very controversial, but evidence such as Teeter's ultimately proved it to the satisfaction of everyone (see Haas 1958a, Goddard 1975; see Chapters 2 and 4).

This interpretation of Sapir's submerged features would seem to be confirmed by Sapir's own characterization of his method, where he referred to "peculiar details": "I have even unearthed some morphological resemblances of detail which are so peculiar as to defy all interpretation on any assumption but that of genetic relationship" (letter to Kroeber, December 23, 1912, cited in Golla 1984:71).

There is another interpretation of what Sapir meant. Sapir's use of typological information in setting up aspects of his more inclusive groupings has been taken as a claim that the overall morphological plan of compared languages may constitute evidence of their mutual relatedness. The underlying belief here seems to be that "languages which have been demonstrated as historically related almost invariably show a great many structural features in common. That is, their basic morphological patterns prove to be alike" (Kroeber 1940a:465). Kroeber interpreted Sapir's overall method as follows:

> It is this procedure which underlies a good part of Sapir's famous classification. Essentially what Sapir is doing when he connects Hokan and Siouan, or Chinook and Penutian, is to perceive structural resemblances which appear to him to work out into a coherent pattern beyond the scattered and random; and on the basis of this to predict that when sufficient analytical comparison of the content of these languages shall have been made, especially by the reconstructive method, it will turn out that genetic relationship will be demonstrable. (1940a:465–6.)

Thomas Smith-Stark (1992) has challenged the interpretation of Sapir's submerged features as being concerned primarily with idiosyncarcies and of Sapir's overall approach to distant genetic relationships; he reminds us that this interpretation of submerged features corresponds to the notions of Antoine Meillet's, but he doubts that that was Sapir's intent. Smith-Stark points out that in Sapir's view each language has a type or determining structural nucleus, which Sapir referred to in terms such as "basic plan," a "determined cut," a "general form," a "structural genius," a "great underlying ground-plan," and which he qualified with adjectives such as "internal," "basic," "fundamental," "deep," "profound," "general," "underlying," and (nota bene) "submerged."[13] Sapir contended that "languages are in constant process of change, but it is only reasonable to suppose that they tend to preserve longest what is most fundamental in their structure." He saw things in terms of gradual changes in morphological type: "Now if we take great groups of genetically related languages, we find that as we pass from one to another or trace the course of their development we frequently encounter a gradual change of morphological type. This is not surprising, for there is no reason why a language should remain permanently true to its original form" (Sapir 1949[1921c]:144–6). Sapir, nevertheless, held that the conceptual type, one of his typological classification scales, tended to persist longer (Sapir 1949[1921c]: 145), and Smith-Stark (1992:22) sees this as Sapir's program for the investigation of remote genetic relationships, typological and geographical at the same time, seeing Sapir as identifying what was most fundamental synchronically with what was most stable diachronically. Smith-Stark emphasizes Sapir's references to the weight of the aggregate of compared morphological features, although it is Sapir's mention of the importance of "specific resemblances" that is emphasized by others.

It appears that both interpretations of Sapir's methods are correct. We find in Sapir's work instances where he argues from the weight of the overall pattern of shared morphological similarities—that is, correspondences in basic morphological plans; however, we also find instances where he argues from the strength of individual or peculiar shared traits, such as those favored by Meillet and by many who have interpreted Sapir as emphasizing idiosyncratic agreements, including his own students. Bright's (1991, personal communication) interpretation of Sapir's procedures is that Sapir liked to use broad typological similarities to form hypotheses (such as the six super-stocks), but that by 1929 he had zeroed in on idiosyncratic, "submerged" traits as a way of moving beyond hypothesis to proof. Sapir was in methodological agreement, at least in part, with Antoine Meillet.

Antoine Meillet

Meillet, like many other scholars, employed the three standard sources of evidence—morphology, phonology, and vocabulary—and his discussions of them are well known. Although he favored morphological proofs (1967[1925]:36), his discussions of regular phonological correspondences and "phonetic laws" are also well known. Meillet's type of grammatical evidence, his "shared aberrancy," is often said to be illustrated by forms of the verb 'to be' in branches of Indo-European, as shown in Table 7-1, which indicates a suppletive agreement across the branches compared.

Meillet also occasionally referred to language "type" in terms suggestive of Sapir's type or basic plan; however, Meillet found the general type to be of little value for establishing genetic relationships:

Although the usage made of some type is often maintained for a very long time and leaves traces even when the type as a whole tends to be abolished, one may not make use of these general types at all to prove a "genetic relationship." For it often happens that with time the type tends to die out more or less completely, as appears from the history of the Indo-European languages. . . .

Common Indo-European presented in the most extreme way the type which is called "inflectional" . . . even the most conservative Indo-European languages have a type completely different from Common Indo-European. . . . Consequently, *it is not by its general structure that an Indo-European language is recognized.* . . .

Thus, it is not with such *general features of structure,* which are subject to change completely in the course of several centuries . . . that one can establish linguistic relationships. (Emphasis added; Meillet 1967[1925]:37–9)

Meillet, rather, favored "particular processes," "singular facts," "local morphological peculiari-

ties," "anomalous forms," and "arbitrary" associations (that is, "shared aberrancy"):

The more singular the facts are by which the agreement between two languages is established, the greater is the conclusive force of the agreement. *Anomalous forms* are thus those which are most suited to establish a "common language." (Emphasis added; Meillet 1967[1925]:41)

What conclusively establish the continuity between one "common language" and a later language are the particular processes of expression of morphology. (Emphasis added; Meillet 1967[1925]: 39)

Meillet's way of using grammatical evidence is now rather standard practice among Indo-Europeanists and historical linguists generally (see Paul Newman 1980:21).

Swadesh's Test of Grammatical Evidence

Morris Swadesh (1951:7), a student of Sapir's, attempted to test the ability of Sapir's method to distinguish between borrowed and inherited features (the basis of the disagreement between Sapir and Boas, see Chapter 2) by applying it to French and English. Swadesh here would appear to be responding, in a way, to the test Sapir had suggested: "It would be an instructive experiment in method to compare English grammar with that of the Indo-European language reconstructed by philologists. Whole departments of Indo-European grammar find no analogue in English, while a very large part of what English grammar there is is of such secondary growth as to have no relevance for Indo-European problems" (Sapir 1925a:492).

Swadesh listed several shared structural features, mostly of a rather general nature (for example, inflectional categories of singular and plural, past and present tenses) "which go back

TABLE 7-1 The Verb 'To Be' in Indo-European Languages

Language	Third Person Singular	Third Person Plural	First Person Singular
Latin	est	sunt	sum
Sanskrit	ásti	sánti	asmi
Greek	esti	eisi	eimi
Gothic	ist	sind	am

to their ancient common form, that is Indo-European," and a few "which reflect diffusional influences." Concerning his "residual common traits," he acknowledged that the "number is not so great" but was impressed that some "involve formational irregularities that could hardly come over with borrowed words" (1951:8). He speculated about what this might mean for more remote relationships:

> But what would happen after a much longer time [than 5,000 years]? Suppose twelve or twenty-four thousand years had elapsed since the common history of the two languages. Would not the structural similarities become less and less in number and more and more attenuated in form until they are reduced to perhaps only one recognizable but very vague similarity? In this case, would the situation be indistinguishable from one in which a single trait had been taken over by borrowing? Not necessarily. If the last vestigial similarity involved a *deep-seated coincidence in formation,* such as that between English *I-me* and French *je-moi,* then even one common feature would be strongly suggestive of common origin rather than borrowing. . . . However, it could also constitute a chance coincidence with no necessary historical relationship at all. (Emphasis added; 1951:8)

Having found this English-French comparison instructive, Swadesh proceeded to test "the case which Boas regarded as probably unresolvable, the relationship between Tlingit and Athabaskan" (1951:10) and listed Sapir's nine shared structural similarities. He concluded:

> The foregoing list of common structural features bears out Boas' statements that "There is not the slightest doubt that the morphology of the two groups shows the most far-reaching similarities" and further that "the inference is inevitable that these similarities must be due to historical causes" [Boas 1920:374]. However, in the light of our control case we no longer need have any doubts as to the kind of historical causes which gave rise to this array of structural similarities. It is clearly of the same general order as that shown by the residual similarities of English and French. In fact, Tlingit and Athabaskan show a distinctly closer structural affinity than English and French. (1951:11)

Here, Swadesh appears to rely on the aggregate of shared structural features, rather than the irregular and arbitrary correspondences of indi-

vidual "submerged" traits as in his English-French *I-me, je-moi* example.[14] In this regard, Swadesh's use of both individual striking grammatical correspondences and similarities shared in the overall morphological patterns seems to be consistent with Sapir's methods.

Greenberg's Use of Grammatical Evidence

Early in his career Greenberg had advocated the Meilletian approach for determining genetic relationships:

> The natural unit of interlingual comparison is the morpheme with its alternate morphs. The presence of similar morph alternants in similar environments is of very great significance as an indication of historical connection, normally genetic relationship. This is particularly so if the alternation is irregular, especially if suppletive, that is, entirely different. The English morpheme with alternants *gud-, bet-, be-,* with the morph alternant *bet-* occurring before *-ər,* "comparative," and the alternant *be-* before *-st,* "superlative," corresponds in form and conditions of alternation with German *gu:t-, bes-, be-,* with *bes-* occurring before *-ər,* "comparative," and *be-* before *-st,* "superlative." We have here not only the probability that a similar form is found in the meaning "good" but that it shows similar and highly arbitrary alternations before the representatives of the comparative and superlative morphemes. The likelihood that all this is the result of chance is truly infinitesimal. (1957:37–8.)

This being the case, it is puzzling that such arbitrary or irregular or suppletive alternations are not more significant in the evidence Greenberg (1987) presented in favor of his Amerind classification, though he did attempt to present similar arguments in regard to his Eurasiatic hypothesis (Greenberg 1991). The morphological comparisons in Greenberg 1987 are handled in essentially the same way as the lexical look-alikes which he assembled as his proposed Amerind "etymologies." What he there calls morphological or grammatical evidence is in fact simply phonetic resemblances observed among bound morphemes and includes almost no grammatical patterns or shared "peculiarities" of the sort sought by Meillet. In his methodological pronouncements in the 1987 book, Greenberg gave lip service to the type of grammatical evidence he had advocated in 1957, but he seems to go out of his way to play down its importance:

> Agreement in irregularities and evidence from survivals of grammatical markers that have become petrified are worthy of special attention and are used in the present work. An agreement like that between English 'good'/'better/'best' and German *gut/besser/best* is obviously of enormous probative value. However, subject as such agreements are to analogical pressure, their absence is not negative evidence, and their presence tells us that there is a relationship, but not at what level. They are psychologically reassuring in showing that we are on the right track and inherently interesting, *but not really necessary.* (Emphasis added; Greenberg 1987:30)

Greenberg continues to advocate Meillet's "agreements in irregularities," but counters that Meillet "never thought of the simple expedient of mass comparison" (1987:30). Although Greenberg says that such irregularities "are used in the present work [1987]," in fact there are none.[15]

Given that chance coincidences can sometimes result in morphological similarities, how should grammatical evidence be intererpreted, and how many and what kinds of examples are necessary to deny chance and borrowing as possible explanations of the similarities?

Considerations in the Interpretation of Shared Aberrancy and Submerged Features

The use of grammatical evidence in the investigation of distant genetic relationships is highly recommended—particularly the idiosyncratic sort advocated by Meillet and by Sapir. Such evidence is even stronger if it can be situated in the overall system and grammatical history of the languages being compared. In some instances such grammatical evidence alone may be sufficient to support the plausibility or even probability of a genetic relationship, but in general, proposed distant genetic relationships are more strongly supported when, in addition to such grammatical evidence, there is also support from basic vocabulary and sound correspondences. However, caution should be exercised in interpreting cases supported solely or primarily by such evidence. There are reasonably

strong instances of what appear to be the sort of idiosyncratic grammatical correspondences to which Meillet and Sapir have referred that in fact have nongenetic explanations, from accident or borrowing. Four examples follow.

Quechua and K'iche' (Mayan) share seemingly submerged or arbitrary and idiosyncratic features. Both languages have two different sets of pronominal affixes in distinct contexts, and their first person singular forms are strikingly similar: Quechua II (Peripheral Quechua) -*ni*- and -*wa*-, K'iche' *in*- and *w*- (Proto-Mayan **in*- and **w*-). Closer scrutiny, however, reveals that this striking idiosyncratic similarity is only a spurious correlation. The -*ni*- of Quechua II (the dominant languages in the Quechuan family) is derived historically from the empty morph -*ni*-, which is inserted between two morphemes when two consonants would otherwise come together. The first person singular morpheme was originally **-y* (Parker 1969b:150; ultimately **-ya* according to Cerrón-Palomino's [1987:141–2] reconstruction); it followed the empty morph -*ni*- when attached to consonant-final roots (for example, -*C*+*ni*+*y*), but ultimately the final -*y* was swallowed up as part of the *i* and the first person suffix attached to verbs was then reanalyzed as -*ni* (for example, -*ni*+*y* > -*ni*) (see Adelaar 1984:42, Cerrón-Palomino 1987:124–6, 139–42). Furthermore, the -*wa*- of Quechua II (Peripheral Quechua) comes from Proto-Quechua **ma*, as is evident in its cognates in Quechua I (Central Quechua) (Parker 1969b:193).[16] Thus, what seemed to be a striking idiosyncratic similarity for the first person (Quechua II *in/wa*, K'iche' *in/w*—recall Swadesh's *I-me, je-moi* example) is actually Quechua **y/*ma*, K'iche' *ni/w*, which are not very similar at all.

The second example of a shared seemingly submerged and striking idiosyncratic grammatical feature also comes from Quechua and K'iche'. It involves the phonetically similar discontinuous negation construction in the two languages: Quechua II *mana . . . ču*, K'iche' *man . . . tah*. This example, too, fails to withstand scrutiny. Proto-Mayan negation had only **ma*, and K'iche' acquired the discontinuous construction when the optative particle **tah* became obligatory in the context with negatives. The *man* negative apparently comes from *ma* 'negative' + *na* 'now, still, yet, later, first'. Thus the more accurate comparison would be with K'iche' *ma,* Quechua *mana . . . ču,* but this is not nearly as striking a similarity as it initially appeared to be. Moreover, the remaining phonetic similarity in the K'iche' and Quechua negatives is not very compelling, since there are many other languages with *ma* negatives (see chapter 8 for examples). Moreover, discontinuous (flanking) negative constructions are actually quite common in the world's languages (for example, French *ne . . . pas*), including some other American Indian languages (Allen [1931:192] cites Cherokee *ni . . . na,* Mohawk *ya' . . . de,* Tutelo *ki . . . na,* Biloxi *i . . . na;* and modern Muskogean languages have *ak- . . . -o* [Booker 1980:256]).

The third example is the seemingly idiosyncratic, arbitrary similarities between Quechua and Finnish shown in Table 7-2 (see Campbell 1973a). All of these grammatical morphemes seem to share the sound correspondence of *k : č,* which might suggest a quite plausible change of *k > č,* for example, and given that languages rarely contain all three of these morphemes as clitics or suffixes, this combination of facts might seem to argue for a historical connection. Presumably this configuration would be unlikely to occur by chance alone (though that is probably not outside the realm of possibility). Nevertheless, the explanation need not be a historical one. In many languages there is a morphosyntactic connection between negation and yes-no questions (for example, Mandarin, Somali, certain versions of formal logic; see Harris and Campbell 1995); therefore, languages that exhibit such a typological connection are not odd, and Finnish and Quechua can easily have similar question and negative markers whose similarity in the two languages does not require a historical explanation. The similarity between the imperative markers and the questions (and negatives)

in these two languages also has some internal motivation. In any case, such a correspondence certainly could be an accidental similarity. Thus, this seemingly "submerged" set of correspondences does not provide a persuasive example of linguistic affinity.[17]

In these examples, what at first seemed to be striking idiosyncratic morphosyntactic correspondences turned out to be merely accidental similarities. Such examples show why caution should be exercised in interpreting "submerged" or idiosyncratic morphological and grammatical features. The fourth example concerns a proposed relationship among some South American languages. David Payne presented an "intricate pattern whereby a set of recurring devices for marking possession also demarcates noun classes" in Proto-Maipurean [Arawakan], Proto-Cariban, Arauán, and Candoshi; he views this as "less likely to be accounted for by diffusion" and therefore as evidence for a probable genetic relationship (1990:80–85). The feature referred to is a set of possession markers on nouns (which at the same time mark noun classes) roughly of the following form: Possessive.Pronoun.Prefix-NOUN-Classificatory.Suffix. The suffixes vary according to noun class—for example, inalienably possessed nouns (kin terms and body parts). The forms of the suffixes are approximately *-nV, -tV, -rV,* vowel change, and Ø in some of the languages; Payne says "it may turn out to be the case that /-ri/, at least, is a widespread possessive suffix and nominalizer in Amazonian languages, and /*-ri/ is also the possessive suffix in Jivaroan languages on regular nouns. . . . No possessive suffix is required (i.e., zero) in the genitive construction for inalienable [*sic*] possessed nouns" (1990:85). Although this may be evidence for a genetic relationship, it is not impossible that such a similarity might be shared by accident. Many languages in the world have prefixed possessive pronominal markers, and it is also not uncommon (especially in the Americas) to find suffixes associated in various ways with possession. To cite an example, Pipil (a Uto-Aztecan language of El Salvador) has the possessive prefixes *nu-* 'my', *mu-* 'your', *i-* and 'his/her/its' and the possessive suffixes *-w* 'alienable possession' (after vowel-final roots), *-yu* 'inalienable possession,' *-wan* 'inalienable plural for kinship

TABLE 7-2 Correspondences between Quechua and Finnish

Gloss	Quechua	Finnish
Question morpheme	-ču	-ko/-kö
Negative morpheme	-ču	-ko/-kö, -ka/-kä
Imperative morpheme	-ču	-k, -ka/-kä

TABLE 7-3 Possessive Constructions in Apalaí and Pipil

Apalaí		Pipil	
i-pɨtɨ	'his wife'	i-siwa:-w	'his wife'
a-napɨ-rɨ	'your fruit'	mu-naka-w	'your meat' (alienable)
		mu-naka-yu	'your flesh' (inalienable)
ɨtapɨi-nɨ	'my house'	nu-manuh-wan	'my brothers'
ɨpɨre	'my gun'	nu-kal	'my house'

terms,' and Ø (after consonant-final roots) (Campbell 1985b:42–6). Pipil possessive constructions can thus be compared with those of Apalaí (Cariban), as shown in Table 7-3 (Payne 1990:82).

Although the suffixes are not particularly good phonological matches, this comparison illustrates that it is not difficult to find a combination of suffixes that are associated with possessive constructions and co-occur with possessive prefixes. Mayan languages provide a similar example, but the suffix comparisons reveal greater phonetic similarity. Possessed nouns in Mayan languages bear possessive pronominal prefixes, and certain classes of nouns bear suffixes of the shape either -il (-Vl) or Ø, depending on an arbitrary classification of nouns, which historically (at least in some of the languages) has been based on the distinction between alienable and inalienable possession. I take the -Ø class in Chol and Apalaí to be an exact match, while the Mayan suffixes with l are phonetically similar to those with r, n, and t in the Apalaí examples presented in Table 7–3 in the following Chol forms: (1) -Vl 'impersonal third person possession': i-tʸeʔ-el otʸot [its-wood-IMPERSONAL.POSS house] 'the wood of the house'; (2) -Ø 'personal third person possession': i-tʸeʔ tʸat [his-wood father] 'father's wood'; (3) -(i)lel 'personal possession' (for a limited class of nouns, mostly abstract): i-hun-ilel Mateo [his-paper-PERSONAL.POSS Matthew] 'Matthew's birth certificate'. Contrast the last with: i-hun Mateo [his-paper-Mathew] 'Matthew's paper' / 'Matthew's book' (Warkentin and Scott 1980).

Thus, although Payne's example might seem to reflect a submerged feature shared by the four language groups he cited, it is a chance similarity, and therefore additional evidence will be necessary before any firm conclusions can be reached concerning the proposed genetic relationship in this case.

Additional Considerations in Making Morphological Comparisons

The comparison of bound grammatical morphemes differs from the comparison of lexical material, and several cautions should be heeded in the interpretation of any similarities that are detected among bound morphemes. The first caution is that morphological affixes tend to utilize only a subset of all the consonants available within a particular language; typically this subset comprises the less marked phonological segments in the language (see below for details). Since the typically unmarked consonants involved in grammatical affixes are often those which recur with the greatest frequency across languages, numerous similarities that are purely accidental will likely be encountered in comparisons of such morphemes among languages, particularly since grammatical affixes are usually quite short (C, CV, or VC in shape; see Meillet 1958:89–90). The second caution is that bound morphemes in many languages often have more than one function; that is, a single affix of the form F_1 in language L_1 might have several grammatical meanings, $M_1, M_2, \ldots M_n$, that in another language L_2 may be signaled by several distinct markers, $F_1, F_2, \ldots F_n$, each of which has only one of the meanings, say, M_1, from the set of meanings F_1 has in L_1.[18] For example, in most modern Balkan languages the dative and genitive case function is merged into a single affix; if such a Balkan language (with a single morpheme which has multiple meanings, F_1-M_1/M_2) is compared with some other language in which the case endings for genitive and dative are formally distinct (that is, two case markers each with a single function, F_1-M_1

and F_2-M_2), the result would be multiple possible matchings for the single Balkan ending. This is a rather straightforward demonstration of the common one-to-many target ratio that can exist when a single marker (with multiple meanings/functions) of one language is compared with multiple markers of another language. This one-to-many target ratio increases the likelihood of accidental matchings. It is not uncommon for a single form to signal multiple functions.

The third caution is that many languages employ a number of different markers to signal the same function (that is, F_1/F_2/F_n-M_1); for example, German 'plural' markers *-ər, -n/-ən, -ə* (with or without umlaut). Since *r* and *n* are among the most common consonants, German offers several common targets for comparison with 'plural' markers from other languages. Not unexpectedly, good matches turn up in languages known not to be demonstrably related, for example: Nahuatl *-n* 'plural' (one of several), Uralic *-n* 'plural' (one of several; Laanest 1982:152–3), and Greenberg's *-l* or *-r* 'plural' of putative Macro-Panoan and Chibchan-Paezan (1987:294–5). The German *-r-* 'plural' finds a good match with the 'plural' and 'frequentative' *-l* that Sapir considered a "promising 'proto-American' feature" (letter to Kroeber, 1920; in Sapir 1990[1920]:81–3). Similarly, Arawak (Lokono) has the nominal plural suffixes (employed mostly with plural nouns with human referents) *-no, -be,* and *-kho* (D. R. Taylor 1976), and good matches are found to all of these: *-no* is comparable to the German *-n* 'plural'; Arawak *-be* can be matched with the Mayan *-Vb'* 'plural' (mostly limited to human referents, as in many American Indian and some other languages; see Campbell, Kaufman, and Smith-Stark 1986); and *-kho* matches Balto-Finnic **-k* 'plural' (Laanest 1982:152–5; note also Greenberg's [1987:293–4] Amerind plural *k*). If Arawak and Mayan each had more than one plural marker, all of which matched (as is the case with plural formations in Old English and German), or even if each language had only a single plural morpheme and this morpheme matched in the two languages, the agreement would carry considerably more weight than if there were several possible targets—several plural markers in each language—but only one of the several markers

in one language was similar to one of the several markers in the other language.[19]

Positional Analysis

Dell Hymes (1955, 1956) has argued that in languages with complex affix systems, the positional analysis of "cognate categories" (that is, the shared patterns of morphological structure where the phonological substance of the morphemes themselves is irrelevant) constitutes important evidence for genetic relationship. He illustrated this claim through examples from Athabaskan, from the Na-Dene hypothesis, and, to some extent, from Indo-European and Penutian. Hymes's method was applied to the Quechumaran (Quechuan-Aymaran) hypothesis by Yolanda Lastra de Suárez (1970; see Davidson 1977 for criticisms; see also Chapter 8). Sarah Thomason, referring to this as the "stable-morphology hypothesis," explains the rationale:

> If the morphology does change much more slowly than the rest of the language, and if it is not liable to be drastically restructured under the influence of other languages, then we should expect to find distantly related languages that share much morphology and little of anything else, in particular vocabulary. This in turn would mean that we should consider the use of shared morphological structure alone—not necessarily shared actual morphemes, but shared patterns even without cognate morphemes—as primary evidence for the establishment of a genetic relationship. (1980a:359)

However, as attractive as this method seemed initially to some scholars, it has been shown to have serious shortcomings and is therefore not valid for establishing genetic relationship. As Doris Bartholomew pointed out, in the Otopamean languages (with a time depth and diversity on the order of Romance languages) morphological changes resulted in the loss of grammatical categories, changes in the markers of some categories, and the introduction of new grammatical contrasts in several of the languages; this demonstrates that grammatical categories are not necessarily more resistant to change than vocabulary and phonology. She concluded that "without the correspondence of both form and function, there is no *proof* of common origin" (1967:78, emphasis in original). Thomason showed that "morphology is by no means so stable as to justify the assumption that lexical cognates may vanish almost entirely while the morphology holds firm" and that "the morphology may be restructured to a considerable degree through the influence of another language" (1980a:360; for additional examples, see Harris and Campbell 1985). For example, the assumptions of positional analysis are incapable of dealing with the attested developments in several branches of Indo-European from flexional toward isolating morphology (see Meillet 1967 [1925]:37–8). As Thomason points out, "all the evidence available from well-documented language families indicates that morphological diversification goes along with diversification elsewhere in the grammar" (1980a:368). Unrelated languages can acquire new morphological positions through grammaticalization which independently correspond to the pattern of these morphemes in other languages due to the typical directionality of many such changes and to general iconic/semantic constraints on the order of morphemes. For example, the following are some frequently occurring changes that can cause morphological categories independently to occupy parallel positions in different languages: case marker < postpositions; case marker < prepositions; case marker < definite article; case marker < pronoun; agreement markers < auxiliaries; agreement markers < personal pronouns / anaphoric pronouns; applicative affix < 'give'; preverb < auxiliary < main verb; causative affix < 'give'; causative affix < instrumental; classificatory verb affixes < noun-incorporation; comitative construction > possessive; comitative > instrumental; derivational morphemes < serial verbs; direct object markers < locatives; dative construction > accusative marker; durative aspect < 'remain', 'stay', 'keep', 'sit'; ergative case < adpositional (especially instrumental); evidential markers < cognition verbs ('say', 'guess', 'think', 'suppose'); future < 'want', 'have', 'go', 'come'; gender/class marker < definite article; genitive/possessive marker < ablative/locative; grammatical gender < noun (masculine < 'man', 'male', 'boy'; feminine < 'woman', 'female', 'girl'); incompletive < 'be at', 'be in'; locative > infinitive marker; noun classifier affixes < lexical nouns; past < adverbs ('yesterday', 'shortly afterward'); past < 'come', 'go'; perfect(ive) < 'finish', 'complete', 'have'; preverbal affixes < adpositions (for example, Noun-Postposition + Verb > Noun + Preverb-Verb); 'say' > quotative; switch reference markers < cases (same-subject < nominative; different-subject < accusative); tense–aspect–modality markers < main verbs. (For examples and discussion, see Harris and Campbell 1995; Givón 1984, 1990; Heine and Reh 1984; Heine, Claudi, and Hünnemeyer 1991; Hopper and Traugott 1993; and Mithun 1984a.)

When Hymes wrote about positional analysis, much less was known about typology, grammaticalization, and these paths of morphological change. Not only can nonrelated languages come independently to share positional categories through such morphological changes, related languages frequently come to have morphological categories whose positions do not match. Thomason shows that in some Finno-Ugric languages, the suffix order on nouns is 'case + possessive', whereas in others it is 'possessive + case' (1980a:362–3). She also presented similar examples from Salishan, to which can be added the example of a number of cognate morphemes which are now bound in different positions in various Mayan languages (prefixes in some branches, suffixes in others; see Robertson 1992). Such examples demonstrate that instances of cognate morphemes in different positions are not absent from Native American languages. Perhaps most damaging to Hymes's argument (which is based on morphological positions in Na-Dene languages) is the fact that even in these so-called Na-Dene languages there are significant positional differences; Krauss presented several examples of this: "We have noted here some horizontal mobility in the occurrence of certain prefixes themselves [among Eyak-Athabaskan and Tlingit] . . . a kind of irregular horizontal 'slippage' or erratic 'mutation' in the position and sometimes also function of an element" (1969:76).

Finally, Thomason also documents impressive convergences in morphological positions that are due to language contact and not to inheritance (see Thomason and Kaufman 1988 for other cases). She concludes that "the Na-Déné positional correspondences are too exact, in the absence of a comparable number of lexical correspondences, to be the only relic of a distant genetic relationship" (1980a:368), and indeed several of Hymes's categories are frequently cited as traits of the Northwest Coast Linguistic Area (see Chapter 9). In short, since nonrelated languages can develop impressive agreements in positional categories whereas frequently genetically related languages do not necessarily exhibit such agreements, the positional analysis approach to detecting genetic relationship proves not to be useful.

Elimination of Borrowing

Diffusion is a well-known source of nongenetic similarity among languages, and it may complicate the determination of remote genetic relationships. Many scholars who are well aware of this problem have nevertheless erred in not identifying and eliminating loans (see Campbell and Kaufman 1980, 1983; Campbell 1988b). I mention a few cases of undetected borrowing (which unfortunately is prevalent in many proposals) of remote genetic relationships. Greenberg (1987:108) cited among his "Chibchan-Paezan etymologies" forms from four languages in support of his proposed 'axe' etymology, including Cuitlatec *navaxo* 'knife' (this is a loan from Spanish *navajo* 'knife, razor') and Tunebo *baxi-ta* 'machete' (this is also a loan, from Spanish *machete*).[20] Thus, half of the forms cited in support of this so-called etymology are unrecognized loanwords. Swadesh's (1966) proposed connection between Tarascan and Mayan includes several loans: Tarascan *tu-pu* / Maya *tuch* 'navel' (the Maya form is a loan from Nahuatl **toš* 'navel'—borrowed by several other languages in the area as well); Tarascan *šan-tu* 'to make adobe' / Maya *šan* 'adobe' (both are from the Nahuatl form *-šan* 'adobe'). In grouping Tacanan, Panoan, Mosetén, Chon, and Fuegian languages, Key (1978) failed to eliminate a number of loans. For example, Mapudungu *čallwa* 'fish' is from Quechua *čaƚʼwa*; most of the forms for 'hen' (Mapudungu *ačawaƚʼ*; Mosetén *ataua, atavua*; Chama *waipa, waʔipa*; Reyesano *walípa*; Tacana *warípa*) are from Quechua *atawaƚʼpa, waƚʼpa* 'chicken', which was widely diffused, after the arrival of the Spanish, throughout adjoining regions of

South America (see Carpenter 1985); and the forms for 'pig' (Mapudungu *kuchi*, Cavineña *koči*, Chama *kweči*, Tacana *koči*) are all from Spanish *coche* 'pig'. Such examples could be greatly multiplied, but these suffice to demonstrate that undetected borrowings are indeed a serious problem in many proposals of distant genetic relationship.

It has been frequently suggested, as seen in Swadesh's statement, that "the borrowing factor can be held down to a very small percentage by sticking to non-cultural words" (1954b:313; see also Ruhlen 1994b:42)—that is, if it cannot be determined whether or not a particular word or phrase is a borrowing, more credit is due basic vocabulary, noncultural forms, because they are less likely to be loans.[21] Thus, for example, Jacobsen (1993) recommends setting aside from Sapir's (1915c) ninety-eight lexical comparisons the "tangible objects potentially subject to borrowing": 'crane', 'arrow[shaft]/harpoon', 'witches/grass', 'feather', 'dish / to put in a dish', 'mother-in-law', 'fir/spruce/cedar', and 'goose/mallard'. This is good practice, but, as mentioned earlier, even basic vocabulary and noncultural words can sometimes be borrowed. Finnish borrowed from its Baltic and Germanic neighbors various terms for basic kinship and body parts, including 'mother', 'daughter', 'sister', 'tooth', 'navel', 'neck', 'thigh', and 'fur' (Anttila 1989:155). Similar examples can be cited from Native American languages: Aleut *braata-X* 'brother' from Russian *brat* (Bergsland 1986:44) and Pipil *manu* 'brother' from Spanish *hermano* (Campbell 1985b). Pierce showed that approximately 15% of the 3,000 most common words in Turkish and Persian are Arabic in origin,[22] noting that "if Arabic, Persian and Turkish were separated now and studied 3,000 years hence by linguists having no historical records, lists of cognates could easily be found, sound correspondences established, and an erroneous genetic relationship postulated" (1965: 31). He sees this as instructive for how some proposals that would link Native American groups should be viewed:

> I would suggest that if Primitive Athapaskan, Tlingit and Haida had a long period of close contact prior to the expansion of the Athapaskan group, and we knew little or nothing about the grammars

of the three groups, it is highly probable that Sapir would get the picture that he did as a result of borrowing.

> In view of this evidence, all of Sapir's wider classifications and even some of the family connections need to be reexamined to be sure that the connections were not established on the basis of a number of cognates which could easily have been borrowed. If they have been postulated on the basis of insufficient data, then more work must be done before we can safely assume that his conclusions are correct. (Pierce 1965:31, 33)

English has borrowed from French or Latin *stomach, face, vein, artery,* and *intestine*; still in the realm of basic concepts, but not necessarily basic vocabulary, are the English loanwords *animal, anus, arrive, beautiful, defecate, excrement, female, finish, flower, forest, fruit, grand-* [of 'grandfather, grandmother'], *large, male, mosquito, mountain, navel, pain, penis, person, river, round, saliva, testicle, trunk* (of a tree), *urine, vagina,* and *vein,* to mention a few.[23]

Semantic Constraints

In proposals of remote genetic relationship, it is dangerous to assume that phonetically similar forms with different meanings can legitimately be compared because they may have undergone semantic shifts. Semantic shifts do indeed occur (for example, Albanian *motër* 'sister', cognate with forms for 'mother' in Indo-European), but in hypotheses of remote relationship the assumed shifts cannot be documented, and the problem is that the wider the semantic latitude permitted in compared forms, the easier it is to find phonetic similarity (as in Gilij's examples, earlier in this chapter). Thus, when the semantics of proposed cognates do not match closely, the possibility that mere accident accounts for the phonetic similarity is greatly increased. Donald Ringe has demonstrated this mathematically; he points out that "it is important to remember that admitting comparisons between non-synonyms cannot make it easier to demonstrate the relationship of two languages by the probablistic method; it can only make it more difficult to do so" (1992:67). For this reason, only semantically equivalent forms should be considered in the initial stages when attempting to make a plausible case for remote genetic relationship. Only after the hypothesis has been demonstrated to have some merit based on semantically equivalent forms should the possibility of semantic shifts be entertained, and it should be borne in mind that even etymology within families where the languages are known to be related requires an explicit and cogent account of how the changes came about.

To illustrate this problem, I mention some of the nonequivalent semantic pairings that Greenberg (1987) presents as evidence of his Amerind classification but to which others have objected: 'excrement/night/grass', 'ask/wish/seek/pleasure', 'bitter/to rot/sour/sweet/ripe/spleen/gall', 'body/belly/heart/skin/meat/ be greasy /fat/deer', 'child/copulate/son/girl/boy/tender/bear/small', 'deer/dog/animal/ silver fox /lynx', 'earth/sand/sweepings/mud/dirty', 'field/devil/bad/underneath/bottom', 'earth/island/forest/mud/village/town/dust/world/ground', 'feather/hair/wing/leaf', 'hole/mouth/ear/listen/chin/nose/smell/blow nose /sniff'. In a more extreme case (of which there are many), Swadesh (1966) included the following semantic alignments among the proposed cognates in his proposal for a Tarascan connection with Mayan: 'tooth/firewood', 'corner/nipple', 'dark/mole', 'to fall/hail', 'to dig/break up in pieces', 'callus/dry/bland', 'grease/liver', 'sharp/wasp', 'ripe, strong, old / man, male'. Wide semantic latitude in making comparisons is perhaps the single most common reason for unsuccessful or unaccepted proposals of distant genetic relationships. To attempt to avoid the problem of semantic latitude, Swadesh's advice (which, unfortunately, he often ignored) is helpful. It was to "count only exact equivalences" (1954b:314).

Onomatopoeia

Onomatopoetic forms in compared languages may be similar because the different languages have independently approximated the sounds of nature, not because they may share a common ancestor. Such forms, then, should be eliminated from proposals of distant genetic relationship. Swadesh's sensible proposal for doing this (which again he woefully violated in his own

TABLE 7-4 Onomatopoetic Forms in Tarascan and Mayan

Tarascan		Mayan	
pa-sa	'to applaud'	bax	'to beat'
thiwa-	'to spit'	tub	'to spit'
itsu-	'to nurse'	ts'ub	'to suck'
khau-	'to howl'	hau-tis-ncha-l (Huastec)	'to blow like a curer'

practice) was: "A simple way to reduce the sound-imitative factor to a negligible minimum is to omit from consideration all such words as 'blow', 'breathe', 'suck', 'laugh' and the like, that is, all words which are known to lean toward sound imitation" (1954b:313). Unfortunately, onomatopoetic forms are frequently included among proposed cognates in proposals of remoter kinship. For example, in support of his Amerind proposal, Greenberg (1987:196) listed forms such as *pui, puhi, phu-* 'blow', but such forms are widely known to be onomatopoetic (see Tylor 1871:229); this explains why similar forms are found in languages throughout the world (for example, Balto-Finnic *puhu-*, English *puff*). (For other examples and documentation of the difficulties that onomatopoeia and expressive or affective forms pose for historical linguists, see Mithun 1982; Campbell 1988b, in press c).

This problem is illustrated in Table 7-4, in a list of a few of the onomatopoetic forms that Swadesh (1966) offered as evidence for the failed relationship between Tarascan and Mayan.

The determination of which words reflect onomatopoetic formation is often subjective. In my investigations of proposals of remote relationships, I have discounted words as being possible onomatopes when the meaning plausibly lends itself to mimicking the sounds of nature and the words are frequently seen to have similar phonetic shapes in unrelated languages.[24]

Sound Symbolism

While sound change on the whole obeys standard Neogrammarian regularity, in some languages forms involving sound symbolism (ideophones, phonesthemes, expressive or descriptive formations) may exhibit irregular sound correspondences. By "sound symbolism" I mean just those cases which involve symbolic variation in a language's sounds which depend principally on size or shape, or both. Size-shape sound symbolism is related to expressive/iconic symbolism in general, and probably should be considered a subtype thereof, though sound symbolism can be more institutionalized as part of the structural resources of a language. For example, overly long vowel length may be used expressively to symbolize something big or intense, as it sometimes is in English ("it's soooo good", "it was a loooong time ago"), but the opposition between short and long vowels has no regular status in the grammar as a marker of bigger versus smaller things in English, as it may have in languages with a more institutionalized (or grammaticalized) sound symbolism. Productive or semiproductive sound symbolism is attested in a large number of Native American languages. Sound symbolism and sound-symbolic processes have been reported in many Native American languages (see Ballard 1985, Berman 1986, Broadbent and Pitkin 1964:33–4, Campbell in press c, DeLisle 1981, De Reuse 1986, Gamble 1975, Haas 1970, Langdon 1971, Nichols 1971, Whistler and Golla 1986, Mithun 1982, Rankin 1986a). Sound symbolism is reconstructible in Proto-Siouan and Proto-Yuman and is found in many languages of western North America (for example, Yokutsan, Miwokan, Wintun, Yana, Wiyot, Yurok, Karuk, Coos, Tillamook, Chinook, several Salishan languages, Quileute, Nootka, Kwakiutl, Sahaptian, Chumashan, Luiseño, Northern Paiute, Plains Cree, Zuni, and Navajo), and in Huave, Totonac, and others in Latin America—indeed, it is found in Selknam (Ona) at the far southern extreme of the Americas (Viegas Barros 1993).

It is not uncommon for otherwise regular

sound changes to appear to have exceptions in cases where sound symbolism is not recognized. For example, Mandan *s* corresponds (regularly) to the *š* of Dakota (and of other Mississippi Valley Siouan languages, of Chiwere-Winnebago, and of Dhegiha [Osage]), and Mandan *š* corresponds to Dakota *s*. There are exceptions to these, however, which are explained by sound symbolism. In these languages, sound-symbolic variants of the same root exist in many forms. For example, in Mandan, /s/ represents a smaller or less intense version of the basic meaning, /š/ represents a medium-sized or medium-intensity version, and /x/ represents a large or more intense version, as in Mandan *síre* 'yellow', *šíre* 'tawny', *xíre* 'brown', and in the Dakota cognates *zi* 'yellow', *ži* 'tawny', *γi* 'brown' (Hollow and Parks 1980:82, De Reuse 1986:62, Rankin 1986a). The problem for comparison is illustrated in the following cognate sets with sound-symbolic variants, where 'rattle' is a more intense version of the same root as 'tinkle':

Mandan	sró	'tinkle'	xró	'rattle'
Dakota	sná	'tinkle'	xná	'rattle'

The *s* of Mandan 'tinkle' normally corresponds not to the *s* of Dakota but to Dakota *š*. If the effects of sound symbolism were not recognized, the irregular correspondence would be unexplained and would be taken to be an exception to the regular sound changes (see Campbell 1976b, Ultan 1970).

Proto-Yokuts had been reconstructed with a series of both dental and alveopalatal affricates, but Whistler and Golla (1986:328–9; see also Gamble 1975) discovered that Proto-Yokuts had a sound-symbolic process that reflected "diminutivization" by the substitution of an affricate counterpart (*c, c', cʰ*) for the corresponding dental stop (*t, t', tʰ*); this affricate is palatalized in Nim-Yokuts (*č*, etc.). In other sets there is symbolic interaction between *n/ń* and the dental stop and affricate series (symbolized as N > T > C). An understanding of this sound-symbolic process (and of some minor, uncomplicated, conditioned changes such as the tendency in Yokutsan to affricate final aspirated dental and retroflexed stops) eliminates several sets of

sound correspondences and simplifies the overall reconstruction of Proto-Yokutsan because affricates now are located in only one place of articulation. Since undetected sound symbolism can complicate reconstruction in an otherwise straightforward language family such as Yokutsan, caution must be exercised to detect similarities among compared languages which are not yet known to be related which may stem from general tendencies in sound-symbolic representations rather than from possible common ancestry.

More specifically for our interests, the problem is known to complicate some long-range proposals (see Broadbent and Pitkin 1964:33, Gursky 1974:173–4, Rankin 1986a). For example, Berman pointed out sound-symbolic alternations in several putative California Penutian languages (Konkow, Nisenan, Mutsun, Wintu) and cautioned that "one must be careful not to attribute a vowel correspondence to regular sound change which may in fact be the result of . . . sound symbolism" (1989:4–5). Consonantal alternations involving size or intensity symbolic functions are also found in a number of putative Hokan languages. Karuk diminutives have *č, n, m*, whereas nondiminutives have *θ, r, v*, respectively; Yana has *n/l* in sound-symbolic alternations; various Yuman languages have a number of alternations, such as / *k/q, kʷ/qʷ, s/ʂ, l/r/n, lʸ/ l/r/nʸ* / (Langdon 1971, Kaufman 1988:58–9). Such alternations, with multiple and discrepant reflexes, have complicated many attempts to work out systematic sound correspondences among languages not yet demonstrated to be related; Gursky (1974:174) has complained of such difficulties in his research on putative Hokan relationships (also Kaufman 1990a:35).

Nursery Forms and Infant Vocalisms

It has been recognized for centuries that nursery formations, so-called *Lallwörter* (the mama-nana-papa-dada-caca sort of words), should be avoided in proposals of linguistic affinity, since they exhibit a high degree of similarity in languages throughout the world that is not due to common ancestry. Nevertheless, such forms are found in the evidence presented in support of perhaps most proposals of distant genetic relationship. The terms typically have glosses of 'mother', 'father', 'grandmother', 'grandfather', and often 'brother' 'sister' (especially elder siblings), 'aunt' and 'uncle'. D'Orbigny (1944 [1839]:112–5) assembled words for 'mother' and 'father' from some of the world's languages, especially those of South America; he believed that the similarity these forms frequently exhibited had to do with a child's first words being composed of his/her first sounds which, of necessity, are directed first to the mother "asking her instinctively for nourishment" and later to the father. Trombetti (1905:43) realized that around the world words for 'father' are characterized by a labial or dental stop, and those for 'mother' have a corresponding nasal; he noted that these traits are inverted in some languages (that is, nasal forms for 'father') and that the sounds are combined in others (*tama, tina*). George Murdock (1959) investigated "the tendency of unrelated languages 'to develop similar words for father and mother on the basis of nursery forms' "; his investigation included 531 terms for 'mother' and 541 terms for 'father' from the World Ethnographic Sample, and he concluded that the data " 'confirm the hypothesis under test'—a striking convergence in the structure of these parental kin terms throughout historically unrelated languages" (Jakobson 1962[1960]:538). Roman Jakobson explained conclusively the nongenetic similarity among the 'mama' and 'papa' terms cross-linguistically, an explanation that holds for many other so-called nursery forms as well. He said that such nursery forms can extend beyond nurseries "and build a specific infantile layer in standard vocabulary" that becomes part of common adult usage (1962[1960]:539). Jakobson observed from Murdock's forms that stops and nasals (consonants with complete oral closure) predominate, that labials and dentals are dominant over velars and palatals, and that the vowel *a* is preponderant. He reported also that reduplication of syllables (which typically lack consonant clusters) is "a favorite device in nursery forms" (1962[1960]:540, 542). Significantly, Murdock's data showed that nasals were dominant among the terms for 'mother', but were found in less than 15% of the terms denoting 'father'. Jakobson explained this in the following way:

Often the sucking activities of a child are accompanied by a slight nasal murmur, the only phonation which can be produced when the lips are pressed to mother's breast or to feeding bottle and the mouth is full. Later, this phonatory reaction to nursing is reproduced as an anticipatory signal at the mere sight of food and finally as a manifestation of a desire to eat, or more generally, as an expression of discontent and impatient longing for missing food or absent nurser, and any ungranted wish. . . . Since the mother is, in Grégoire's parlance, *la grande dispensatrice,* most of the infant's longings are addressed to her, and children . . . gradually turn the nasal interjection into a parental term, and adapt its expressive make-up to their regular phonemic pattern. (1962[1960]:542–3)

Jakobson (reporting also observations of others) finds a "transitional period when *papa* points to the parent present [mother or father], whereas *mama* signals a request for fulfillment of some need or for the absent fulfiller of childish needs, first and foremost but not necessarily the mother"; eventually, the nasal-mother, oral-father association becomes established. He also explained why "among familial terms the nursery forms are not confined to parental designations" and said it would be an interesting "task to attempt to trace how the different degrees of relationship correspond to the development of the child's language." He cited as examples Russian *baba* 'grandma', *d'ad'a* 'uncle', *d'ed* 'grandpa', *n'an'a* 'nanny' (1962[1960]:543–4).

Another explanation of infant vocalisms is the frequent (and often documented) spontaneous development of such terms for symbolic, affective reasons (compare *mother* inherited in English with *ma, mama, mamma, mammy, mommy, mom, mummy, mum,* and *father* with *pa, papa, pappy, pop, poppy, da, dad, dada, daddy*). The kin terms involved in nursery formations vary depending on cultural factors, but frequently they also include 'grandmother', 'grandfather', 'uncle', 'brother', and 'sister' (especially elder siblings). This is easily verified by the fact that similar forms, many of which conform to the traits Jakobson listed for the 'mother' and 'father' terms, recur in language after language which have no known common history (see the examples in Chapter 8).[25]

In sum, these nursery words do not provide reliable support for distant genetic proposals.

Short Forms and Unmatched Segments

The length of proposed cognates and the number of matched segments within them is an important consideration, since the greater the number of matched segments in a proposed cognate set, the less likely that accident accounts for the similarity (see Meillet 1958:89–90). Monosyllabic *CV* or *VC* forms may actually be true cognates, but they are so short that their similarity to forms in other languages could also easily be due to chance. Likewise, if only one or two segments of longer forms are matched, then chance remains a strong candidate for the explanation of the similarity. A match of only one or two segments in these longer forms will also not be persuasive; the whole word must be accounted for. (For discussion and examples, see Campbell 1973a, 1988b; for mathematical proof, see Ringe 1992.)

Avoidance of Chance Similarities

Much has already been said in this chapter about chance/accident as the possible explanation of various sorts of similarities, and additional advice to beware of forms which might owe their similarity to chance is hardly a very specific methodological consideration. Still, as Ringe points out:

> Resemblances between languages do not demonstrate a linguistic relationship of any kind unless it can be shown that they are probably not the result of chance. Since the burden of proof is always on those who claim to have demonstrated a previously undemonstrated linguistic relationship, it is very surprising that those who have recently tried to demonstrate connections between far-flung language families have not even addressed the question of chance resemblances. This omission calls their entire enterprise into question. (1992:81; in his response to Ringe, Greenberg [1993] seemed unable to answer this challenge)

Any insight as to what kind of similarities and what quantities thereof might legitimately be expected as a result of chance can be very helpful to the comparativist. Therefore, in this section I discuss several other considerations to

be weighed in dealing with chance agreements among languages.

Conventional wisdom holds that 5% to 6% of the vocabulary of any two compared languages may be accidentally similar. While much has been written about the mathematics of chance in linguistic comparisons,[26] probably the most telling is Ringe's careful mathematical demonstrations. Concerning chance and multilateral comparison, he concludes:

> The methodological consequences . . . should be clear. Because random chance gives rise to so many recurrent matchings involving so many lists in multilateral comparisons, overwhelming evidence would be required to demonstrate that the similarities between the languages in question were greater than could have arisen by chance alone. Indeed, it seems clear that the method of multilateral comparison could demonstrate that a set of languages are related only if that relationship were already obvious! Far from facilitating demonstrations of language relationship, multilateral comparison gratuitously introduces massive obstacles.

Because of the extravagant claims which Greenberg 1987 makes for a methodology of multilateral comparison, it is important to emphasize that most similarities found through multilateral comparison can easily be the result of chance. If Greenberg had published all the data on which his language classification is based, we could test his findings by the probablistic method outlined here to determine whether any of the interlinguistic similarities he has found are likely to be the results of nonrandom factors. In the absence of a full collection of data, we can only try to estimate the worth of his findings. But any reader who inspects his "Amerind Etymological Dictionary" (Greenberg 1987:181–270) will see at once that a large majority of his "etymologies" appear in no more than three or four of the eleven major groupings of languages which he compares; and unless the correspondences he has found are very exact and the sounds involved are relatively rare in the protolanguages of the eleven subgroups, it is clear that those similarities will not be distinguishable from chance resemblances. When we add to these considerations the fact that most of those eleven protolanguages have not even been reconstructed (so far as one can tell from Greenberg's book), and the fact that most of the first-order subgroups themselves were apparently posited on the basis of multilateral comparisons without careful mathematical verification, it is hard to escape the conclusion that the long-distance relationships posited in Greenberg 1987 rest on no solid foundation. (Ringe 1992:76)[27]

It is not necessary here to elaborate on Ringe's demonstrations, but it is helpful to keep in mind two of his points. First, phoneme frequency within a language plays a role in determining the number of possible chance matchings involving particular sounds that should be expected when that language is compared with other languages; for example, 13% to 17% of English basic vocabulary begins with s, whereas only 6% to 9% begins with w; thus, given the higher number of initial s forms in English, we can expect a higher number of possible chance matchings for s than for w when English is compared with other languages (see Ringe 1992:5). Second, the potential for accidental matching increases dramatically when one leaves the realm of basic vocabulary, when one increases the number of forms compared, and when one permits the semantics of compared forms to vary even slightly.[28] (Compare Ringe 1993; see also Hock 1993 and Matisoff 1990:110 for discussions of how the effects of erroneous equations and chance similarities are compounded rather than diminished in multilateral comparison.)[29]

Gerhard Doerfer (1973:69–72) discussed two ways in which languages may be accidentally similar. The first is by "statistical chance"; this has to do with what sorts of words and how many of them might be expected to be similar by chance. As an interesting example, consider the seventy-nine names of Latin American languages listed by Pottier (1983:191) which begin with na- (for example, Nahuatl, Naolan, Nambikwara, Naperu, Napeño; the list could be made much longer if North American language names were added—Navajo, Natchez, Nanticoke, Narragansett, Naskapi, Nass, Natick, and so on—see Chapters 4, 5, and 6 for other examples). Since for the most part there is no historical connection among the various forms of these names, the similarity in their first syllable is an example of statistical chance. The second way is by "dynamic chance": languages become more similar through convergence—for example, lexical parallels come about when sounds (known

originally to have been different) converge as a result of sound change. Cases of noncognate similar forms are well known in the handbooks of historical linguistics; for example, French feu 'fire' and German Feuer 'fire' (Meillet 1948[1914]:92–3) (French feu from Latin focus 'hearth, fireplace' [-k- > -g- > -Ø-; o > ö]; German Feuer from Proto-Indo-European *pūr [< *pwer-, compare Greek pūr] 'fire', via Proto-Germanic *fūr-i [compare Old English fy:r]); also Spanish día 'day' and English day (Spanish día from Latin dies [Vulgar Latin dia 'day', Proto-Indo-European *dyē, < earlier *dyeə-, a variant of *deiw- 'to shine, sky, heaven'], English day from Proto-Germanic *dagaz 'day', from Proto-Indo-European *agh- 'day').[30] It is known in both cases that these cannot be genuine cognates, since in the first example, French and Latin f comes from Proto-Indo-European *bh whereas German and Germanic f comes from Proto-Indo-European *p; in the second example, Spanish and Latin d comes from Proto-Indo-European *d, whereas English and Germanic d comes from Proto-Indo-European *t (as prescribed by Grimm's law). The resemblance between these phonetically similar forms for basic vocabulary nouns can be traced to convergence as a result of sound change and sheer chance, not inheritance from a common ancestral form.[31] That originally quite distinct forms in different languages can become similar through convergence resulting from sound changes should not be surprising since even within a single language originally distinct forms frequently converge. European languages are replete with examples, often involving basic vocabulary:

English son/sun (Germanic *sunuz 'son', Proto-Indo-European *sewə- 'to give birth', *su(ə)-nu- 'son'; Germanic *sunnōn, Proto-Indo-European *sāwel-/*swen-/*sun- 'sun')

English eye/I (Germanic *augōn 'eye', Proto-Indo-European *okʷ- 'to see'; Germanic *ek 'I', Proto-Indo-European *egō 'I')

English lie/lie (Germanic *ligjan 'to lie, lay', Proto-Indo-European *legh-; Germanic *leugan 'to tell a lie', Proto-Indo-European *leugh-)

French neuf 'new' / neuf 'nine' (Latin novus 'new', Proto-Indo-European *newo- / *nu-; Latin novem 'nine', Proto-Indo-European *newn̥)

Callaghan (1980, 1991a:51) presented an example of the dynamic-chance sort when she showed striking resemblances between Proto-Eastern-Miwok's declarative paradigm and Indo-European secondary endings; however, when longer forms and more comprehensive Miwokan and Miwok-Costanoan evidence are brought into the picture, the forms are not similar. (The forms are cited later in this chapter, in Table 7-8; see Callaghan 1988b:72.)

Goodman (1970:121) also pointed out a second way (similar to statistical chance) in which multilateral comparison increases the likelihood that accidental phonetic similarities will be included in putative cognate sets. Greenberg's presentations, an array of compared forms, are typically a chain of comparisons rather than a set where all forms are equally similar to all others. As an example, assume that three forms (say, F_1, F_2, and F_3) are compared from languages L_1, L_2, and L_3, respectively; in Greenberg's comparisons, each neighboring pair in the comparison (say, F_1 with F_2, and F_2 with F_3) usually exhibits certain similarities, but forms at the extremities of the chain (for example, F_1 compared with F_3) may exhibit little or no direct resemblance. To illustrate, Goodman cites the forms from number 34 of Greenberg's Niger-Congo list: *nyeŋ, nyã, nyo, nu, nwa, mu, mwa,* where adjacent pairs are reasonably similar phonetically, but those at the ends (*nyeŋ* and *mwa*) are not. He concludes: "The more forms which are cited, the further apart may be the two most dissimilar ones, and the further apart these are, the greater the likelihood that some additional form from another language will resemble [by sheer accident] one of them" (Goodman 1970:121). When the languages are not known to be related, the increase in nonsimilar (or less similar) forms in the sets of compared items permitted by multilateral comparison almost guarantees that many such forms will be the result of mere accident. Many of the putative cognate sets presented as Amerind etymologies by Greenberg (1987) are precisely of this sort, where several of the compared forms may actually be phonetically quite dissimilar, but within the chain of comparisons, similarities can be detected among cited forms that are immediately adjacent to one another. (While such divergent phonological shapes among related languages of

known families sometimes do diverge considerably, what distinguishes these forms is their known history and regular sound correspondences reflecting sound changes that have been worked out; this is not at all the case, however, in multilateral comparisons.)

To understand how easy it is to find what one is looking for if sufficient measures are not taken to guard against chance as the explanation of perceived similarities, one need but observe Greenberg and Ruhlen's example of what they assume to be the Proto-Amerind etymon *t'ana* 'child' (1992:96; also Ruhlen 1994b:183–206). They presumably consider this to be one of their best examples, judging from the way they refer to it in their writings. It is said to have "cognates" in all eleven of the branches they postulate for Amerind, but they cite forms from only thirty-nine American Indian languages. Clearly, we are not dealing here with any tight phonetic or semantic congruences. The semantics of the glosses encompass more than a dozen different meanings (for example, 'child,' 'brother [older and younger]', 'son', 'daughter', 'mother's sister', 'firstborn [child]', 'grandchild', 'male', 'boy', 'young man', 'niece', 'sister [older and younger]'). Many of the forms cited have a $t(')$-like sound + vowel + n; however, others they present do not have all these phonetic properties. For example, apparently the n is not necessary (as suggested by the inclusion of such forms as *tsuh-ki, u-tse-kwa*), and the $t(')$ can be represented by t', t, d, ts, s, or $č$. Let us symbolize these as the target template *TVN/TV.* Several of the kinship terms with t or n (or both) in their list would appear to be subject to Jakobson's (1962[1960]) explanations, discussed earlier in this chapter. Examples such as this reveal why many scholars object to Greenberg's methods; it is not difficult to find a form of the shape *TVN* or *TV* (or more precisely, from their forms: $t/d/ts/s/čV(w/y)(V)(n/ŋ)$) in virtually any language that has the meaning of some kinship term or some person (preferably young). For example, the following fit: English *son;* German *Tante* 'aunt'; Japanese *tyoonan* 'eldest son'; Malay *dayang* 'damsel'; Maori *teina* 'younger brother, younger sister'; Somali *dállàan* 'child', to mention just a few.[32] Moreover, if such forms can be easily found in other languages, why are only thirty-nine American Indian languages cited from among the several hundred that could have born witness if the form were a true "Amerind" cognate?[33] The few Amerind forms offered in support of the proposed "global etymology" *tik 'finger' is another example of this sort, which has even less to recommend it; see Salmons's (1992:213–14) criticism of it. While accidentally similar forms from additional languages are easily found in instances such as these global etymologies, the game becomes tricky, since any form that might be pointed to as a possible accidental similarity in some language not already compared might be accepted by proponents as further support for the "etymon," as part of some bigger genetic grouping, such as Proto-World, which both Greenberg and Ruhlen believe in.

In view of the stress that has been placed on pronouns in recent debate concerning the broader classification of American Indian languages (discussed later in this chapter), it perhaps should be pointed out that it is easy for dynamic chance to make pronominal markers similar or different (see Meillet 1958:89–90). Greenberg and Ruhlen believe steadfastly that there is a general *n/m* pronoun pattern in so-called Amerind languages (with *n* 'first person' and *m* 'second person'), which they contrast with their assumed *m/t* pronoun pattern for so-called Eurasiatic (which also includes Eskimo-Aleut and Uralic), and that this is strong proof of their Amerind proposal. But, for example, in Finnish (and closely related Balto-Finnic languages), Proto-Uralic final *-m* has changed to *-n,* and this had the consequence of changing *-m* 'first person singular' (as in Greenberg's putative Eurasiatic pattern) to *-n* (now equivalent to the asserted Amerind 'first person pronoun'). That is, an extremely common, garden-variety sound change (*-m > -n) has caused the Finnish 'first person' marker to shift from the putative Eurasiatic pattern to a match with the asserted Amerind form, by dynamic chance. Earlier in this chapter, it was shown that in Quechua II the empty morph -ni- (inserted to keep morphemes from coming together which would produce a consonant cluster) was reanalyzed as the marker of 'first person singular' in verbs, based on earlier cases with *C + ni + y,* where -y was the original marker of 'first per-

son'. Thus, Quechua II (but not Quechua I) now has a first person pronominal marker -ni, which fits Greenberg's putative Amerind pattern but only fortuitously, by dynamic chance. Moreover, Proto-Quechuan had (and Quechua I still has) a 'first person' object morpheme *-ma (which became -wa in Quechua II). Thus, by dynamic chance, Quechua II changed from a Eurasiatic-like language (with -ma in a 'first person' function) to an Amerind-like language with -ni 'first person'. (Quechua I is still Eurasiatic-like in this regard.)

Sound-Meaning Isomorphism

Meillet advocated permitting only comparisons that involve both sound and meaning, a principle also advocated by Greenberg (1957, 1963). By this criterion, positional analysis (as discussed earlier) would be eliminated. Its rationale is that similarities in sound alone (for example, where compared languages might share the presence of tonal contrasts) or in meaning alone (for example, where the languages under investigation might be similar by containing a category of grammatical gender)[34] are not reliable, since such similarities can be and often are independent of genetic relationship; they can be due to diffusion, accident, or typological tendencies. In Meillet's words: "Chinese and a language of Sudan or Dahomey such as Ewe . . . may both use short and generally monosyllabic words, make contrastive use of tone, and base their grammar on word order and the use of auxiliary words, but it does not follow from this that Chinese and Ewe are related, since the concrete detail of their forms does not coincide; *only coincidence of the material means of expression is probative*" (emphasis added; 1958:90, Johanna Nichols's [in press] translation).

McQuown's reasons for proposing Macro-Mayan, a relationship between Mayan, Totonacan, and Mixe-Zoquean, illustrate the sound-meaning isomorphism constraint (see Chapter 8): "The only other language family [besides Totonacan] of Mexico that has this glottalized series is Mayan, and this fact together with other significant details suggests to us the probable genetic relationship of Totonac-Tepehua with

Mayan; but the relatively small number of coincidences in vocabulary indicates to us that this kinship is quite distant"[35] (1942:37–8). The Macro-Mayan hypothesis had a shaky foundation if it relied heavily on the presence of glottalization, since it is now known that other languages of the region (for example, Tequistlatec, Jicaque, and some Oto-Pamean languages) also have glottalized consonants. Since glottalization can diffuse (as in the case of Armenian and Ossetic dialects, which have been influenced by other languages of the Caucasus which have glottalized consonants; see Bielmeier 1977) or can develop independently in a language, glottalization alone can hardly be strong evidence of genetic affiliation.

Many of the earlier proposals of remote relationship among languages in the Americas relied heavily on typological similarities (such as the canonical shape of stems, types of morphophonemic changes, and aspects of alignment—ergative, active, or nominative-accusative) because of "the lack of extensive detailed information on many, if not most, of the languages of the Americas," according to Voegelin and Voegelin (1985:608). However, this procedure conflicts with the correct principle of sound-meaning isomorphism. For example, as Hamp pointed out, "now that Na-Dene is perceived to require no reconstructed tones [see Krauss 1979, Cook and Rice 1989:7], the motivation for a relation to Sino-Tibetan [favored by Sapir and a few of his followers; see Golla 1984:316, 332] has largely vanished" (1979:1002–3).

Although this constraint on the types of similarities to be compared as possible evidence of affiliation is clearly valuable, some linguists maintain that certain matched grammatical parallels which may lack phonological matchings might support a genetic connection if they are pervasive enough in general, or if they function in appropriately intricate grammatical subsystems, or if they are idiosyncratic enough to defy chance and borrowing in the languages compared as potential explanations (see the earlier discussion of submerged features). This may be true in some instances, but skeptics will be happier with such proposals of remote linguistic kinship if they also present evidence from other sources.

Exclusion of Nonlinguistic Evidence

A valid principle, also advocated by Greenberg (1957, 1963), is to permit only linguistic information as evidence of genetic relationship among languages. Thus, shared cultural traits, mythology, folklore, and technologies must be eliminated from arguments in support of linguistic kinship. The wisdom of this principle is made clear by the many outlandish proposals of genetic relationship that have been based on nonlinguistic evidence, particularly those concerning languages of Africa and the Americas.[36] To cite one example, some had argued for a linguistic grouping which would join Mayan with Natchez and the "Chahta-Muskoki (Choctaw-Muskogee, that is, Muskogean) family" based on the assumed similarity between the "pyramids" of the Mayan area and mounds of the southeastern United States (Brinton 1867, 1869).[37]

This is not to discount nonlinguistic evidence as irrelevant in research on the history of the earliest Americans or in the resolution of other issues in prehistory. Because there are many possible scenarios for the peopling of the Americas that are consistent with the limited vision we can get currently from the linguistic record, archaeological and human biological information may prove to be far more revealing than linguistics in discovering the past of the earliest Americans (see Campbell in press a, Goddard and Campbell 1994, and Chapter 3). Such advances will not resolve questions of linguistic classification, however.[38]

Erroneous Morphological Analysis

For proposed cognates, it is necessary to account for the entire word that is being compared, not just for some arbitrarily segmented portion of it. Where such compared words are etymologized into assumed constituent morphemes, it is necessary to show that the segmented morphemes (roots and affixes) in fact exist in the grammatical system. Unfortunately, unjustified morphological segmentation is frequently found in proposals of remote relationship. Also, undetected morpheme divisions are a frequent problem.

Both can make the compared languages seem to have more in common than they actually do.

Several examples in Greenberg (1987) illustrate the problem of undetected morpheme divisions. He listed Rama *mukuik* 'hand' as cognate with froms from several other American Indian language families which exhibit shapes like *ma* or *makV* (1987:57), although 'hand' in Rama is *kwi:k;* the *mu-* is the 'second person possessive' prefix (Lehmann 1920:422, 426–7). However, *kwi:k* bears no real resemblance to Greenberg's (1987:57) postulated *ma-ki*. In another proposed cognate set labeled 'sky', Greenberg gave Kaqchikel *paruwiʔ* 'above', Tzotzil *bail* 'above', Huastec *ebal* 'above' (three Mayan languages), and Tunica *ʔaparu* 'heaven, cloud' (1987:158). However, the Mayan forms are not cognate and each reflects the problem of undetected morpheme boundaries. The Kaqchikel form is *pa-ru-wiʔ* [on-his/her/its-head/hair],[39] literally 'on, on top of him/her'; the Tzotzil is *ba-il* [top/first/head–adjective] 'top'; and the Huastec form is from *eb-al* 'up' (root + adjective derivational suffix). Greenberg's comparison of Tzeltal *jat* 'penis' and Tzotzil *jat* 'genitals' (two closely related Mayan languages) with Patwin *jot* 'penis' (1987:156) loses force because the Tzeltal and Tzotzil form is composed of two separate morphemes, *y-at* [his-penis].[40] Greenberg also compares Tzotzil *tiʔil* 'hole' with Lake Miwok *talokʰ* 'hole', Atakapa *tol* 'anus', Totonac *tan* 'buttocks', and Takelma *telkan* 'buttocks' (1987:152). The Tzotzil form is *tiʔ-il,* however, from *tiʔ* 'mouth' + *-il* 'possessive/adjectival suffix', meaning 'edge, rim, border, hem, outskirts, lips', but not 'hole'.[41] The appropriate comparison would be with *tiʔ*, but this bears no clear resemblance to the other forms listed.[42]

The other problem involving morphological errors is that the insertion of morpheme boundaries where none is justified. For example, Greenberg (1987:108) arbitrarily segmented Tunebo *baxi-ta* 'machete' (which is in fact a loan from Spanish *machete*), thus misleadingly and artificially making the form appear more similar to the other two forms cited with it as "cognates," Cabecar *bak* and Andaqui *boxo-(ka)* 'axe'. Greenberg's (1987) treatment of Yurumanguí (Yurimangui, an extinct unaffiliated language of Colombia, for which a Hokan affiliation has been proposed; see Poser 1992) also illustrates this problem. Greenberg (following Rivet 1942:40) analyzed Yurumanguí *joima* 'saliva' as containing two morphemes, *jo* 'mouth' and *ima* 'water', and included these two components as cognates under two separate entries, MOUTH and DRINK (1987:246, 214), respectively. But as Poser explains, "there is no evidence whatsoever that *joima* is morphologically complex. Neither of the putative component morphemes is independently attested" (1992:218). As Poser points out, Greenberg had assumed that the *ima* part is related *čuma* 'to drink', which he segmented as *č-uma,* though, "again, there is no language-interal evidence that *č* is a prefix" (1992:218). Clearly, the existence of a form *čuma* 'to drink', for which there is no evidence of morphological complexity, is not sufficient reason to segment *joima* 'saliva' into two parts and then to compare each independently to forms in a variety of other languages. Poser (1992) discusses a number of other forms in Salinan and Yurumanguí which have specious morphological analyses in Greenberg's (1987) treatment (eleven unjustified segmentations out of a total of twenty-six forms cited). Berman also finds that "there is not a single Tualatin [Kalapuya] word in which Greenberg [1987] segments any of these prefixes correctly. In almost every instance . . . where a form is misanalyzed, Greenberg compares the wrong elements" (1992:232).

In another instance, Greenberg (1987:150) compared Natchez *hak* 'afire' with Mixe-Zoquean terms for 'fire' (Texistepec *hugut,* Sierra Popoluca *huktə,* Zoque *hukətək*); however, the Natchez form is a misanalysis of *leˑ-hakiʔiš* 'to burn', with no sense of 'afire', and the assumed *hak* is only part of the 'intransitive auxiliary'–*hakiʔiš* (Kimball 1992:459). Greenberg (1987:159) also gave Atakapa *tˢom* (*com*) 'stick', but this is found only in the compound *neštsomš* 'cane', where *neš* means 'tree, wood, stick' and *tsom* (*com*) appears to be a shortened form of *hitsom* (*hicom*) 'little' (Kimball 1992:459). Poser aptly summarizes the problem of erroneous morphological segmentation: "Where languages are not known to be related[,] comparisons in which the morphological analysis itself depends on the relationship carry considerably less weight than those in which the segmentation is clearly established, for the simple reason that the additional degrees of freedom increase the probability with which similarities may be due to chance" (1992:219).

Noncognates and Neglect of Known History

Another problem to be avoided is the frequent practice of comparing noncognate forms within one family with forms from some other (as in the case of some of Greenberg's Mayan-Tunica comparisons in the set labeled 'sky' cited above). Unrelated forms from languages within one family are frequently joined together in the belief that they are cognates and then are compared with forms from other language families where they are then presented as evidence of more distant connections. Clearly, however, if the forms are not even cognates within their own family, any reconstruction based upon them is inaccurate. A further comparison of such inaccurate reconstructions with forms from other languages in hypotheses where the languages compared are not known to be related are of questionable value.[43] Many proposals of remote relationship present such noncognate forms within a particular language family as part of the evidence for postulated more distant relationships. Olson's Chipaya-Mayan hypothesis provides several examples of this (1964, 1965:30–31). He includes Tzotzil *ay(in)* 'to be born' (from Proto-Mayan *ar-* 'there is/are', Proto-Tzotzilan *ay-an* 'to live, to be born'; Kaufman 1972:95), which is not cognate with the *ya?* (read *yah*) 'pain' (from Proto-Mayan *yah* 'pain, hurt', Kaufman and Norman 1984:137) of the other Mayan languages listed, though the inclusion in this set of this noncognate Tzotzil form makes the Mayan comparisons seem more like the Chipaya *ay(in)* 'to hurt' with which it is compared. Olson also compares Yucatec Maya *čal(tun)* 'extended (rock)' to *č'en* 'rock, cave' in some other Mayan languages, but these are not cognates; Yucatec *č'e?en* 'well' (and 'cave of water') is the true cognate (all from Proto-Mayan *k'e?n* 'rock, cave' (Kaufman and Nor-

man 1984:119). Yucatec *čal-tun* means 'cistern, deposit of water, porous cliff where there is water' and is composed of *čal* 'sweat, rinse, liquid' and *tun* 'stone' (ultimately a loan from Cholan *tun;* compare Proto-Mayan *to:n* 'stone'). Again, the Yucatec noncognate form suggests greater phonetic similarity to the Chipaya *čara* 'rock (flat, long)' with which it is compared than is true of the set as a whole. Kaqchikel *ts'ilob'* (given as *(ts'i)lob*) 'to stain' and Tzeltal *bolob* 'to stain' (not attested) are not cognates, nor are they related to Tzotzil *bon* 'to paint'; the Kaqchikel form is composed of *ts'il* 'dirty' + *-ob'* 'derivational affix', and the Tzeltal form (if it exists) is from *b'ol* 'stupid' (compare Proto-Tzeltal-Tzotzilan *b'ohl* 'stupid'; Kaufman 1972:96) + *-ob'* 'derivational affix' (different from *b'on* 'paint'; compare Proto-Mayan *b'on;* Kaufman and Norman 1984:117). (See Campbell 1973a for several other examples.)

Comparisons with Forms of Limited Scope

Related to this last point is the frequent practice in research on distant genetic relationships of comparing a word from one language (or a few languages) of one family with a word thought to be similar in one language (or a few languages) in another family. Forms that have clearly established etymologies in their own families by virtue of having cognates in a number of sister languages stand a better chance of having more remote cognate associations with languages that may be even more remotely related than does an isolated form in one language that has no known cognates elsewhere within its family and for which there is thus no prima facie evidence of possible older age. Meillet's view on this can be taken as a heuristic principle to follow in order to reduce the likelihood that chance will account for similarities among words in different languages that have no known cognates in sister languages of their own language families: "When an initial 'proto language' is to be reconstructed, the number of witnesses which a word has should be taken into account. An agreement of two languages, if it is not total, risks being fortuitous. But, if the agreement extends to three, four or five very distinct languages, chance becomes less proba-ble"[44] (1925:38; also Rankin 1992:331).

Apropos of this, Greenberg's "Amerind" has been frequently criticized because the "etymolo-gies" he proposes are typically represented by only three or four of his eleven subgroups (Ringe 1992, Jacobsen 1994). Morever, the forms within these subgroups themselves are very of-ten limited to a very few languages, even though none of these putative groups is generally recog-nized by other scholars. In short, inspectionally resemblant lexical sets that are limited in this way are not very convincing.

Neglect of Known History

Another related problem is that seen in cases where an isolated form in a daughter language may superficially appear to be very similar to one with which it is compared in another lan-guage as a possible cognate in a remote relation-ship, but when the known history of that lan-guage or language family is brought into the picture, the similarity is shown to be fortuitous or at least less striking. For example, under the set labeled 'dance', Greenberg (1987:148) compared Koasati (Muskogean) *bit* 'dance' with forms from several Mayan languages for 'dance' or 'sing' (for example, K'iche' *bis* [should be *b'i:š*], Huastec *bišom*); however, Koasati *b* comes from Proto-Muskogean $*k^w$ (Haas 1947, Booker 1993) and the root was $*k^w it$- 'to press down'; the cognates in other Muskogean lan-guages do not mean 'dance', which is a semantic shift in Koasati alone, probably applied first to stomp dances (Kimball 1992:456). Because he neglected the known history of the Koasati form, Greenberg found similarities in both sound and meaning that are known to have arisen only later. When the known history of the Koasati word is taken into account, its phonological shape turns out to be less similar to the forms with which Greenberg compared it, as does its meaning.[45] It is not uncommon in proposals of distant genetic relationship to encounter forms from one language which exhibit similarities to forms in another language where the similarity is known to be due to changes in the individual history of one or the other of the languages. The listing of noncognates under the same "etymol-ogy" and the failure to detect morphological boundaries within the forms compared are also instances of neglect of known history. For exam-ple, Greenberg (1987:178) gave Seneca *ænn*-and Mohawk *oniete* under his "etymology" la-beled 'sweet' and asserted that they are related to Proto-Keresan *$*?an'e:za$ 'be tasty', but the known history of Iroquoian reveals that the Sen-eca form (really -*æn*) is from Proto-Northern-Iroquoian *-*ran*- (see Chafe 1959), while the Mohawk word has the morphological analysis *o*-'neuter prefix' + -*nyeht*- and means 'snow' (Mithun 1990:323).

False Reconstructions

Another related problem occurs when false re-constructions enter into more remote compari-sons. For valid cognates in one family an errone-ous reconstruction is sometimes made and then compared further in remote comparisons. Such erroneous reconstructions frequently err in a direction that favors some proposed remote rela-tionship which the scholar is defending. Some reconstructions misleadingly make the form ap-pear to be more similar to forms compared from other language groups than would be the case if accurate reconstructions had been compared. To illustrate this point, I mention a few examples from Brown and Witkowski's attempt to defend a Mayan-Mixe-Zoquean connection (though similar examples can be found in other proposals of distant genetic relationships). For example, though the forms they present from Mixe-Zoquean languages clearly reflect *$*ciku$ 'co-atimundi' with two syllables, Brown and Wit-kowski (1979:44) nevertheless present as its proto form *$*ci\cdot k$, apparently to make it seem more similar to the Mayan form which they give as *$*či\cdot q$ (or *$*či\cdot k$ or *$*ki\cdot q$)—Mayan roots are typically monosyllabic. There is no such Proto-Mayan form; the Yucatecan *či?ik* and Choltí <chiic>, the only Mayan languages with such words, are borrowings from Mixe-Zoquean (Justeson et al. 1985:23–4). A number of other clearly disyllabic Mixe-Zoquean cognate sets are presented in their treatment as mono-syllabic, which misleadingly makes them ap-proximate the Mayan forms with which they are paired.

Spurious Forms

A careful check of the forms offered in support of various hypothesized distant genetic relationships frequently reveals nonexistent "data." When scholars are dealing with languages they do not know well or with extensive data, it is not uncommon for 'bookkeeping' errors to enter the picture, so that spurious or erroneous forms become the basis of comparison. Rankin pointed out a very serious example of this, where "none of the entries listed as Quapaw [in Greenberg 1987] is from that language" (1992:342); rather, they are from either Biloxi or Ofo (other Siouan languages, not particularly closely related). Another example is the *ita(-asa)* 'wife' given by Greenberg (1987:142) for Yurumanguí; no such form (or even anything similar) exists in the only extant Yurumanguí data (Poser 1992:218). One source of spurious forms (as in the Quapaw case just mentioned) is the misattribution of forms from one language to another language. Poser shows that of the forms Greenberg claimed to be Salinan, four are actually Chumash and a total of eight of the other Salinan entries are spurious. Poser correctly observes that such forms "are of no comparative value, no matter what methodology one may favor" (1992:224). The form Greenberg (1987:157) cited as Apalachee *ani* 'I' is actually Creek; the Apalachee corpus contains no such word (Kimball 1992:448). Greenberg's Alabama *ni* 'say' is a recopying from Tunica *ni;* no such Alabama form exists (Kimball 1992:469). Another example is Greenberg's (1987:186) citation under the set labeled 'ashes' of Hitchiti *po:k* 'pulverize' and Choctaw *muki* 'smoke, dust'; no such word as Choctaw *muki* exists, and the Hitchiti form is actually *bok-*, derived from Proto-Muskogean *k^wokli* 'to beat' (which has no connection to 'ashes', 'dust', or 'smoke') (Kimball 1992:477). Greenberg's (1987:197) Chitimacha form *lahi* 'burn', given under the set labeled 'boil', also does not exist (Chitimacha has no phonemic *l*). He compared this to Choctaw *luak,* Atakapa *łok,* and Natchez *luk;* however, the Choctaw form is actually *lowa-k* 'fire', a nominalization of *lowa* 'to burn', and Greenberg's failure to see the morphological analysis erroneously makes the *k* of this suffix

seem to match the *k* of the roots in the other forms cited (Kimball 1992:478). (See Campbell 1988b:606 for other examples from Greenberg 1987.) As some of these examples show, both spurious glosses and spurious phonetic forms can result from a misreading of the sources. For example, Brown and Witkowski (1979:41) compared some Mixe-Zoquean forms meaning 'shell' with K'iche' *sak',* which they said means 'lobster' but which actually means 'grasshopper'—a mistranslation of Spanish *langosta,* which in Highland Guatemala means 'grasshopper'.

The problem of spurious forms is best dealt with by having accurate data (not always possible, of course, with languages that are poorly attested) and analyzing it carefully. Many spurious forms that cropped up in fieldwork situations have been the source of erroneous comparisons that were corrected later on the basis of more accurate data. For example, in his vocabulary list of Nambiquara, Albuquerque (1910) gives as the term for the straw that Nambiquara men wear through their upper lips a form which means 'mouth'; his entry for "egg" actually means 'the chicken over there.' As Price (1985:306) explains, the abundance of such spurious forms in the various Nambiquara vocabularies makes the dialects seem more divergent than they actually are. Another example is that of Aruá and Gavião, now known to be mutually intelligible dialects of a single language (see Chapter 6). These were classified by Loukotka (1968:124), on the basis of short lists of words, as separate languages of his Mondé family in the Tupi stock, where "grotesque errors in transcription and glosses [in the data available at the time] obscured this close relationship [as dialects of a single language]" (Moore 1990:3). As pointed out in Chapter 1, spurious fieldwork forms have sometimes led to more serious misunderstandings, as in the case of the fictive language *Aksansas*. Daniel Hammerly Dupuy (1952; see also 1947a, 1947b) reported a new language distinct from Alakaluf based on his comparison of words from the pirate Jean de la Guilbaudière's 1698 vocabulary with his own recording of Alakaluf. This mistaken identity, however, can be attributed to la Guilbaudière's elicitation technique; he gave *arret* for 'water'—

different from Hammerly Dupuy's *čafalai*—but what la Guilbaudière had actually recorded was *aret* meaning 'container of liquid,' apparently because he showed his informants a bucket of water in his attempt to elicit this form. Unfortunately, Loukotka (1968:45–6) accepted Hammerly Dupuy's "new language" and classified Aksanas as a language isolate distinct from Alakaluf, and Kaufman (1994:67) also appears to have been influenced by this classification (see Clairis 1985:757).

Several other spurious forms, some attributable to scribal errors, some to misunderstandings of the glosses, are also found in Greenberg (1987). He gave Chitimacha *tux* 'to spit', a misreading of *ša·pš tuhte,* literally 'to throw down spittle' (Greenberg 1987:157), where he erroneously took *tuhte* 'to throw down' as 'to spit' (Kimball 1992:468). He gave Atakapa *lam* as 'spider', an error based on *tamhewš hilam* 'venomous spider', literally 'spider that gives pain', where *tamhewš* is the real word for 'spider' (Kimball 1992:470). Greenberg's (1987:162) Huchnom *kua* 'like' involves a double scribal error, in both the phonetic form and its gloss, for *k'aw* 'light' (Kimball 1992:475). Greenberg (1987:150) compared Natchez *kus* with Koasati *kus* under the set labeled 'give', but neither form actually exists. The correct Natchez form for 'to give' is *hakušiʔiš;* the Koasati form given is a scribal error which recopies the (assumed) Natchez form (Kimball 1992:460).

Semispurious Forms and Glosses

What might be called partially spurious forms sometimes occur in hypotheses of distant genetic relationship—forms not totally different from those in the sources from which they are taken, but nevertheless changed enough so that when the actual form or meaning is considered, the equation seems less likely. For example, under a set labeled 'call' and following a form meaning 'call by name' Greenberg gave Atakapa *eng* (actually /e:ŋ/). However, this Atakapa word means neither 'call' nor 'call by name' but only 'name' (Kimball 1992:479). Although the difference between 'name' and 'call by name' is perhaps not remarkably great, the semantic difference between the 'call' of the main gloss and

the 'name' of this example is much greater; with the correct, not (semi-)spurious gloss, these no longer exhibit the similarity suggested by the inaccurate gloss. In another instance, Greenberg (1987:230) cited Tonkawa *mam* 'bring' in his forms in support of the Amerind etymology for 'hand', where his source has *mama* 'to carry a burden, to pack (it)'. The semantic discrepancy is not great, but the meaning suggests action performed more by the back than with the hand, making the connection with other forms meaning 'hand' less likely (Manaster Ramer 1993). Greenberg (1987:139) also listed Tonkawa *kala* 'mouth' as Hokan with Karuk *-kara* 'in the mouth', but he gave Tonkawa *kalan* as 'curser' in the Amerind list and equated it with Karuk *ka:rim* 'bad'. However in Greenberg's source, the later Tonkawa form is glossed as 'one who continually curses, a foul-mouthed person', showing the two Tonkawa words to be related and therefore not possibly separate cognates in the two distinct sets, in spite of the glosses Greenberg extracted (Manaster Ramer 1993). Greenberg (1987:146) also gave Natchez *onoxk* (/ʔo:nohk/), said by him to mean 'thorn' but really meaning 'blackberry', and hence not appropriate in a set labeled 'arrow' (Kimball 1992:453); he inappropriately listed Atakapa *uk* 'boil, ulcer' with the set 'boil (cook by boiling)' (1987:147; compare Kimball 1992:454); under 'live' Greenberg (1987:464) gave Atakapa *nun* as 'sit', but it is correctly *nuŋ,* defined as 'town' (Kimball 1992:464–5); under 'open' Greenberg (1987:156) had Chitimacha *hakin,* but this is *haki,* which actually means 'to peel' (Kimball 1992:467); Greenberg's (1987:161) citation of Natchez *pa* 'plant' under the set labeled 'tree' is misleading, since Natchez *pa·-helu·iš* (whence Greenberg's form) means 'to plant a garden', not a 'plant' (Kimball 1992:474).

Philological Slipups

Forms that are spurious or skewed due to scribal errors and mishandling of philological aspects of the sources utilized enter the data base for particular proposals. For example, Greenberg (1987) systematically mistranscribed the <v> and <e> of his Creek source as *u* and *e,* respectively, although they symbolize /a/ and /i/, respectively. Thus the source's <vne> 'I' was given by Greenberg (1987:53) as *une* when in fact the Creek word is *ani* (Kimball 1992:448). Under the set labeled 'kill' Greenberg (1987:153) listed Choctaw *ile* 'do' along with Hitchiti *ili* 'kill' (both Muskogean languages), but the 'do' of the Choctaw gloss is an error for this reflex of Proto-Muskogean **illi* 'kill'; Kimball (1992:463) holds that the erroneous 'do' gloss is apparently a misreading of the abbreviation for "ditto" used by Greenberg's source. Greenberg listed Chitimacha *nakš* under 'near' (1987:155), but it means 'war'— Greenberg's 'near' is a copying error for 'war' (Kimball 1992:466). Under 'go' Greenberg (1987:226) gave Wappo *mi,* but this is an error for *mí?* 'you', extracted from the phrase *?ikhá? mì? čó·si?* 'how are you going' (*čó-* is the root for 'to go') (Kimball 1992:483–4). Clearly, such philological mistakes can distort the comparisons.

A Single Etymon as Evidence for Multiple Cognates

A common error in proposals of distant genetic relationship is that of presenting a single form from one language as evidence for more than one proposed cognate set. A single form in one language cannot simultaneously be cognate with multiple forms in another language (except when the cognates are etymologically related, which in effect signifies that only one cognation set is involved). For example, Greenberg (1987:150, 162) cited the same Choctaw form *ałi* in two separate forms; he gave *łi* 'wing', actually *ałi* 'edge, end, boundary, margin, a border, a wing (as of a building)', under the cognate set labeled 'feather', and then gave *əłi* (misrecorded for *ałi*) under the set labeled 'wing'. In this case the Choctaw form cannot be cognate with either one (and it is logically impossible for it to be cognate with both) since, as Kimball (1992:458, 475) points out, the meaning 'wing' can enter the picture only if a wing of a building is intended. (Some other examples were mentioned in the preceding discussion.)

Closely related to this kind of mistake is the error of putting different but related forms which are known to be cognates under different presumed cognate sets. For example, under MAN₁ Greenberg listed Central Pomo *ča[:]č[']*, but he placed the Eastern Pomo cognate *ka:kʰ* under an entirely different "etymology," MAN₂ (1987:242; see Mithun 1990:323–4).

Word Families and Oblique Cognates

A methodological strategy that is employed, more often in Indo-European and South Asian linguistics, is that of seeking lexical doublets or even whole "families" of lexically related forms which are then presented as possible cognates or whole sets of interconnected cognates in the languages compared. Morris Swadesh (1967a) called for "oblique cognates," by which he meant resemblant forms among compared languages which represent different morphophonemic variants of the same root, especially consonant alternations. Other scholars have likewise assumed that when comparable interrelated lexical sets are found across the languages compared, the likelihood that chance accounts for their occurrence is reduced (see, for example, Pinnow 1985). DeLancey, Genetti, and Rude say:

> Another pattern [in addition to phonemic correspondences] among resemblant sets which reduces the plausibility of chance as an explanation is their apparent organization into word family sets. (1988:205)

> In such a set [the FIRE family, below] correspondences extend in two dimensions, i.e. across languages for the same meaning, and across related or easily relatable meanings within each language. Some of these resemblances are demonstrably not random. (1988:205–6)

They demonstrate the strategy with comparisons among Sahaptian, Klamath, and Tsimshian of what they call "the FIRE family," which involves the glosses 'fire', 'make fire', 'burn', 'wood', 'sun/sky', 'cook/dry', and 'warm' (not all their forms are reproduced here) (see table 7-5).

This is potentially a useful technique in that when whole sets of seemingly interrelated lexical items appear independently in compared languages, we feel more sympathy toward them as possibly genuine cognates than we might in the case of individual isolated lexical resemblances that might be compared. Nevertheless, the evidence yielded by this strategy is not as compel-

TABLE 7-5 The FIRE Word Family

	fire	make fire	burn	wood		sun, sky	warm
Nez Perce		ʔaalik				hawlaxhawlax	luʔuq-'ic
Sahaptin	ilkw-S	ilkw	ilkw-as				
Klamath	loloG-S	s-likw-				Galo:	loqwa
Coast Tsimshian	læk	sɨ-ləks	gwælək	læk/ʔołg		laxa	
Nass-Gitksan	lakw			*kwælkw (Proto-Tsimshian)		łoq-s	

Compare also Proto-Tsimshian *kwVlkw 'dry', Coast Tsimshian dziiə + lg [sic] 'melt', Nass-Gitksan ci + lks 'melt', lunks 'dry'; DeLancey, Genetti, and Rude 1988:205–6.

ling as it may seem at first, and DeLancey et al. (1988:206) do not pretend that the strategy will eliminate random resemblances, only that it is more effective in this regard than individual lexical comparisons. If two unrelated languages had an accidentally similar form (or, for that matter, one that was similar for any nongenetic reason, such as borrowing or onomatopoeia), it is conceivable that, as a result of normal derivation and word-formation processes, the two languages could each end up independently containing a battery of internally related forms that would still constitute a single entity for purposes of comparison in seeking genetic relationships. For example, if English *light* (note the similarity to DeLancey et al.'s FIRE family; compare Proto-Indo-European *leuk-*, Proto-Germanic from suffixed *leuk-to-*) is considered basically a noun, then the verb *to light* (as in 'to ignite, make a fire, start to burn') is an independent derivation and does not constitute two points of contact (rather than one) with the FIRE family forms.[46] Finnish has similar forms and meanings: *liekki* 'flame, small fire', *liekehtiä* 'to burn', *liekehdintä* 'blazing' (like 'warm'?), *lieska* 'flame (fire)', *liesi* 'fireplace', and *leisku-* 'to blaze'. However, this Finnish FIRE family does not indicate a genetic connection with Sahaption, Klamath, and Tsimshian; rather, it reflects a single accidental (or perhaps symbolic) similarity, a root with several derivations. We assume the involvement of expressive symbolism (as in English *shine, shimmer, sheen*, or *sleek, slick, slide, slime, slink, slither, slip*); it is not difficult to imagine how accidentally similar, seemingly comparable "word families" could crop up independently in different languages.[47]

It is also possible that the strategy could lead to comparisons of forms assumed to constitute such a word family but that in fact have no etymological connection. Pinnow (1985:31) presents the comparison, which he sees as a particularly impressive example, of Tlingit *t'àaw* 'feather' and Alaskan Haida *t'áaw* 'copper shield' under the assumption that an associated word family shows a compelling connection between them. He abstracts from the word family a basic *T'AA* 'to warm, cover', which is said to be combined with *-w* 'instrumental suffix' in the forms cited and thus is comparable with Eyak *t'ahł* 'feather', which is said to contain *ł* 'instrumental suffix'; all three forms are interpreted as reflections of the basic concept 'device for covering' *(Bedeckungsmittel)*. In view of the shortness of the assumed stem and the semantic latitude involved in the forms, as well as questions of morphological derivation, this example might not seem so convincing to some scholars. That is, the problems that plague proposed lexical cognates of the ordinary sort also complicate the determinination of whether a real word family exists and whether it is comparable to a word family of another language. Therefore, although it is sometimes helpful, the word family or "oblique cognate" strategy should be used with considerable caution.

The Pronoun Argument

Several claims about the distribution of pronominal markers in American Indian languages for purposes of classification have already been mentioned.[48] Because of the emphasis pronouns have received, it is important to assess these claims in order to set the record straight and to put the matter in perspective. Briefly stated, it is claimed that in American Indian languages there is a widespread pronominal pattern, with *n* for 'first person' and *m* for 'second person', and that this is evidence in support of Greenberg's (1987) Amerind classification. The *n/m* pronoun pattern has been referred to as "the most telling datum favoring the Amerind phylum" (Ruhlen 1994b:123); proponents of Greenberg's classification believe the pronoun argument to be totally convincing:

> The enormously widespread *n* first person and *m* second person in the Americas as against *m* first person and *t* second person in Europe and Northern Asia is powerful evidence. (Greenberg 1990c:19)

> It [the *n/m* pattern] also serves to distinguish the Amerind family from the world's other language families. In a recent study of personal pronouns in the world's languages (Ruhlen [1994b:252–60]) I found that the Amerind pattern (*n*- 'I' vs. *m*- 'thou') is virtually nonexistent elsewhere in the world. (Ruhlen 1994a:178; see also Ruhlen 1994b:21, 41, 271–2; Fleming 1987:196)

Greenberg and Ruhlen forget the 'first-person' *m* which they find in several "Amerind" groups (Greenberg 1987:276; Ruhlen 1994b:141, 228–9, 258), and they do not acknowledge the widespread **ta/tu* 'thou' suggested by Swadesh (1960c:909) as Proto-American. But if the *n/m* pattern distinguishes Amerind from languages of Europe and Northern Asia, with their alleged *m/t* pattern, then why do several Amerind groups exhibit pronoun forms *m* 'first person' or *t* 'second person' that Greenberg attributes to Eurasiatic? Moreover, in spite of the supposed clear distinction between Amerind and other languages of the world in pronouns, Ruhlen could nevertheless equate several putative Amerind pronouns with supposed Nostratic counterparts—specifically, Amerind **na* 'I, we' with Nostratic **na* 'we'; Amerind **ma* 'we' (and 'I') with Nostratic **mä* 'we inclusive' (and 'I'); and Amerind **na* 'we, I' with Nostratic **ni* 'we exclusive' (1994b:228–9, 231). This makes the pronoun argument less compelling. As will be seen later in this section, the claim has been overstated (see Goddard and Campbell 1994). A brief review of the history of claims about these pronoun patterns, together with the var-

ied explanations proposed to account for them, follows.

Historical Background

The observation that there are pronoun similarities among many American Indian (and other) languages is by no means new. In the late eighteenth century, Jonathan Edwards had observed similarities between Mohegan and Hebrew prefixes and suffixes, which included first person and second person pronouns suggestive of forms which Greenberg (1987) claims are particularly strong evidence for his Amerind hypothesis (Edwards 1787:18). Gilij was aware of widespread pronominal similarities; he cited examples from a variety of languages (1965[1780–1784]:274). Brinton (1859:12), citing Gallatin before him, reported that "in American philology it is a rule almost without exception that personal pronouns and pronominal adjectives are identical in their consonants"; he specifically mentioned first person and second person pronoun forms and cited comparisons with *n* 'first person' in some Native American languages. By 1874, the widespread *n* of 'first person' in various American Indian languages was well known, as indicated by Sayce's comment: "[There] is the phenomenon which meets us in several of the North American dialects [languages], where the pronoun *na, ni,* or *nu,* 'my,' has become an inseparable and meaningless affix of numberless words, just as in the Continental *milord*" (1874:216). Tolmie and Dawson (1884:128–9), in an appendix entitled "Comparisons of a few words in various Indian languages of North America," listed forms for 'I', all of which exhibit *n*, in twenty-seven different languages. In 1890 Brinton added to his earlier statement, indicating his awareness at the time of how common the *n* 'first person' forms were in American Indian languages and in languages in general:

> The N sound expresses the notion of the *ego*, of myself-ness, in a great many tongues, far apart geographically and linguistically. It is found at the basis of the personal pronoun of the first person and of the words for *man* in numerous dialects of North and South America. Again, the K sound is almost as widely associated with the ideas of *otherness,* and is at the base of the personal

pronoun of the second person singular. (1890 [1888]:396)[49]

Boas (1917:5) knew the American Indian pronoun facts, but thought they would submit to "psychological explanations" (and in this he is cited also by Haas 1966:102; see Ruhlen 1987a:222, 1994b:24, 41, 253). Boas cited Gatschet, who had been aware of the widespread phonetic similarities among the pronouns in American Indian languages before Boas; Gatschet, like Boas, did not attribute them necessarily to genetic inheritance (Haas 1966:102). Kroeber, too, was well aware of the American distribution of the n/m pronominal markers (having stated early in his career that the pronoun pattern was a well-known example), but he realized that a genetic explanation was not necessarily required; he favored diffusion/language contact as the probable explanation:

> Throughout the field of linguistic structure in the whole continent, there are abundant examples of the operation of the principle of territorial continuity of characteristics, and of the underlying one that even the most diverse languages affect each other, and tend to assimilate in form, if only contact between them is intimate and prolonged. Such are the exceedingly common occurence [sic] of n and m to designate the first and second person pronouns. (1913:399)

The alleged n/m pronoun pattern was also noted by Trombetti (1905) and it became very well known as a result of the Sapir-Michelson debates (Michelson 1914, 1915; Sapir 1915a, 1915b) and of Sapir's (1918) review of a book on Mosetén in the first volume of the *International Journal of American Linguistics*. In 1920 Sapir listed "persistence of n- 'I' [and] m- 'thou'" as "Proto-American possibilities" (1990[1920]:86; Golla 1984:452; see also Sapir 1918:184).[50] Widespread n for 'first person' was talked about widely: "Getting down to brass tacks, how in the Hell are you going to explain general American n- 'I' except genetically? It's disturbing to know but (more) non-committal conservatism is only dodging after all, isn't it?" (letter from Sapir to Speck in 1918, cited in Darnell 1990:122; see also Sapir's letter to Kroeber, October 1920, cited in Golla 1984: 316).

Jorge Bertolazo Stella (1929[1928]:98–109) discussed at length "o typo n- do pronombre da primeira pessoa" (the n- type of first person pronoun) and "o typo m- do pronombre da segunda pessoa" (the m- type of second person pronoun) and included citations from many American Indian languages; his analysis was similar to Greenberg's (1987) presentation.

As these citations show, these observations about pronoun similarities are not new arguments for Greenberg's classification (as some people mistakenly take them to be); rather they are the subject of old controversies (see Ruhlen 1987a:222, 1994b:253; Sapir 1918:184). The following statement by Mason shows just how widely recognized the pronoun pattern was and that, in spite of this, it was not generally assumed that a common genetic heritage was necessarily the explanation: "Many American Indian languages, North as well as South, show resemblance in the pronominal system, often n for the first person, m or p for second person. Whether this is the result of common origin, chance, or borrowing has never been proved, but the resemblance should not be used as evidence of genetic connection between any two languages" (1950:163). In fact, Greenberg's claim sounds very much like Swadesh's before him:

> At least two short elements, n for the first person pronoun and m for the second . . . are so numerous as to virtually eliminate the chance factor despite their brevity. In fact, even if one disregarded the cases which have one or the other and included only the languages which have both n and m for first and second person respectively, and if one holds to the restriction that both forms must belong to the same functional type [a restriction not imposed by Greenberg]—whether independent pronoun or subject, object or possessive affixes—the list of language groups would still be fairly impressive. It would include families of the Penutian and Hokan-Coahuiltecan phyla, Aztecanoan, Chibchan, and Mapuche. (Swadesh 1954b: 311–12)

Others had also noticed similarities like these among the pronouns in diverse languages throughout the world, but denied the genetic explanation (see Wundt [1900:33] and Trombetti [1905:44]).

Proposed Explanations of the Pronoun Pattern

Since Greenberg and Ruhlen view the pronoun pattern assumed to exist in American Indian languages as compelling evidence for Greenberg's classification, it is important to assess their claims. Greenberg asserted: "That a highly improbable event should have recurred more than a hundred times exceeds the bounds of credibility. . . . [It] cannot be explained plausibly except as the result of genetic inheritance" (1989:113). However, the assumption of genetic inheritance is by no means necessary, nor is it the only explanation available (as was pointed out by the scholars just cited). There are strong reasons for believing that other factors are involved in explaining the sounds found in these pronouns. Boas asked whether the pronoun pattern could be "due to obscure psychological causes rather than to genetic relationship" (1917:5). Following are some explanations that have been proposed which may make Boas's "psychological causes" less "obscure."

1. Certain sounds, especially nasals, are to be *expected in grammatical morphemes,* particularly in pronoun markers. As pointed out by Goddard and Campbell:

> The repeated appearance in different languages of the same consonants in grammatical functions is a real phenomenon of human language and as such requires an explanation. One contributing factor is the well-known general linguistic trait that a single language typically uses only a fraction of its full complement of consonants to form its primary grammatical morphemes and hence must use the same consonants over and over in different functions (Floyd 1981). The consonants that are used tend to be the ones that are least marked. . . . Specifically, the least marked consonants of the languages of the world include *m, n, t, k,* and *s* (cf. Ruhlen 1987a:11). As a result of this economy and, so to speak, lack of originality in the use of consonants, there is a much greater than chance agreement among the languages of the world on what consonants are used in grammatical elements. It is thus to be expected a priori that these consonants will show up again and again in different languages and language groups marking, say, first or second person, and many languages will therefore come to have similar

pronominal systems by this factor alone. (1994: 196–7)

German inflectional endings are constrained so that the only vowel that occurs is schwa, the only consonants /d, m, n, r, s t/. Of Latin's fifteen or more consonants, only /b, d, m, n, r, s, t, w/ occur in inflectional endings; Hebrew permits only eight of twenty-two; and English has similar limits. Of the fifteen consonants in Ancient Greek, only /t, tʰ, k, m, n, r, s/ occur in inflectional morphemes (Floyd 1981). Even Trombetti had realized something of the limited sounds encountered in pronominal forms in the world's languages: "In all these old pronominal forms only the vowels *a, i, u,* the stop consonants *k, t* and the nasals *n, m* are found. These are certainly primordial sounds" (1905:89).[51]

The most cogent statement on the likelihood of finding nonsignificant phonological matchings in pronominal markers is perhaps that of Meillet:

> It goes without saying that in order to establish genetic relatedness of languages one must disregard everything that can be explained by general conditions common to all languages. For instance, pronouns must be short words, clearly composed of easily pronounced sounds, generally without consonant clusters. The consequence is that *pronouns are similar in almost all languages,* though this does not imply a common origin. On the other hand, pronouns often show little resemblance in languages that are otherwise quite similar. . . . Even forms that descend from the same protoform, like French *nous* and English *us,* may no longer have a single element in common (the French *s* is purely graphic). *Therefore, pronouns must be used with caution in establishing relatedness of languages.* (Emphasis added; Johanna Nichols's [in press] translation; see also Matisoff 1990:9)[52]

These limitations mean that consonants from the same small set recur frequently in grammatical affixes of the world's languages, and therefore the probability of an accidental agreement in compared grammatical morphemes is very high and is frequently attested.

2. Nasals in particular are found in grammatical morphemes precisely because they are the most *perceptually salient* of all consonants (Maddieson 1984:70). "The more distinctive speech sounds . . . achieve the most successful transmission of a message." Nasals "are rarely subject to confusion with other types of consonants," and "there is value in incorporating such sounds [nasals] into any language" (Maddieson 1984:70).[53] The dental/alveolar nasal *(n)* is most common, and the bilabial *(m)* is also common; most languages have both (Maddieson 1984:60, 69). These findings would seem to explain why nasals, especially *n* and *m*, show up so frequently in markers of pronouns in languages throughout the world.[54] This is borne out in Ruhlen's (1994b:252–60) survey of first person and second person pronouns in the world's languages. He assembled examples of such pronouns for thirty-four distinct genetic groupings. Examples were given for fifty-two units, but some were united under a single grouping—for example, thirteen were grouped under Amerind; even some of the fifty-two are very long-range and controversial proposals. For 'I', twenty-six of the thirty-four have a nasal as the sole or primary consonant of one of the pronoun forms given; three others also have a nasal but not as the main consonant; only six of the thirty-four have no nasal. For 'thou' ('you singular'), sixteen of the thirty-four have a nasal as the sole or primary consonant; three others also have nasal consonants, and only thirteen have no nasal (for some, for example, Etruscan and Sumerian, no forms are given). In some instances, subordinate groups from among the fifty-two have nasals whereas the general form offered to represent the unit containing them does not; for example, Na-Dene, represented by **wī* 'thou', contains Athabaskan, which has *nani/nine/niŋ/nì*; Ruhlen's Caucasian pronoun forms lack nasals, but its constituent East Caucasian is represented by *mi(n)/me(n)*. More specifically, for 'I', eleven of the thirty-four exhibit the nasal *n*, as claimed for Amerind. (The other consonants exhibited in the non-nasal cases for 'I' are predominantly *t, s,* and *k*—also highly unmarked sounds. For 'thou', among those lacking nasals, the predominant consonants are *t, s, c,* and *w.*) For 'thou', eight of the thirty-four have *m;* two more can be added if 'you' ('you plural') forms are included, as Greenberg does in his treatment of Amerind pronouns. Finally, and most significantly, eight (in addition to Amerind) of the thirty-four have both *n* among the first person forms ('I' or 'we') and *m* among the second

person forms ('thou' or 'you plural'), counted in accordance with Greenberg's (1987) treatment of Amerind pronominal forms. Clearly, there is nothing remarkably unique about the assumed *n/m* pattern among American Indian languages, in spite of Ruhlen's claims to the contrary, as shown by his own data. Moreover, these recurrent sounds in the world's pronoun systems are not accidental but are predictable based on the perceptual saliency of the sounds employed (see explanation 1).

3. Johanna Nichols calls attention to the prevalence of nasals in pronominal markers which she explains as due to their deictic functions and their *roles in paradigmatically arranged morphological subsystems:*

> The problem with personal pronouns is that the forms of first and second persons, and of singular and plural numbers, are not independent; that is, in a personal pronoun system the relation of paradigmaticity to coding phonological form is nonarbitrary. These words tend to use consonant symbolism which shows their paradigmatic relationships and their deictic semantics . . . so that the presence of a nasal in one of the personal pronoun forms is to be expected and the presence of a labial in one of the forms makes it quite likely that the other person or number (or both) will contain a dental. . . . Cross-linguistically, nasals have a high frequency of occurrence in closed sets of paradigmatically organized morphemes (such as case endings, deictic roots, and nuclear-family kin terms). (in press)

4. Some linguists consider the possibility of *areal diffusion,* including diffusion of pronouns, among the various early groups which came to the Americas; they may have borrowed from one another before they crossed the Bering Strait, or after, or both (Bright 1984:15–16, 25; Milewski 1960, 1967:13–14; Kroeber 1913:399). Diffusion of pronouns in such a situation is not as unusual as some scholars might think (for examples, see Matisoff 1990:113; Newman 1977:306–9, 1979a:218–23, 1979b:305–7, 1980: 156; Rhodes 1977:9; Thomason and Kaufman 1988:219–20, 223–8, 235; see also Everett in press[55]). Even Ruhlen (1994b:257) concedes the possibility that Nahali borrowed 'you singular' from Dravidian. It is well known that English *they, their,* and *them* are borrowed from Scandinavian (replacing Old English *hie, hiera, him,* respectively; see Baugh 1957:120, 194). Surely we cannot deny the borrowing of pronouns elsewhere, when we English speakers have clear examples in our own linguistic backyard.[56]

Perhaps more to the point, there are many cases of borrowed pronouns documented in Native American languages. Several examples have already been mentioned and others follow. Miskito borrowed its independent personal pronouns from Northern Sumu relatively recently: Miskito *yaŋ* 'I' (compare Sumu *yaŋ*), *man* 'you' (compare Sumu *man*).[57] Another example of pronominal diffusion is particularly revealing because it concerns a Native American language, Mednyj Aleut (Copper Island), which has borrowed its verb morphology, including pronominal endings, from Russian. The pronominal verbal paradigm, in part, is shown in Table 7-6.

Not only is the Russian pronominal system (as represented in the table) borrowed pretty much lock, stock, and barrel, but even these borrowed Indo-European pronominal affixes have parallels with forms postulated by Greenberg as representative of American Indian languages. Mednyj Aleut's *-iš* 'second person singular' can be compared with Greenberg's (1987:278–9) *-s* 'second person' marker (with different shapes in a number of different languages). The *-im* 'first person plural' apparently fits Greenberg's (1987:276) *-m* 'first person', since he cites Miwokan *-m, me* 'first person plural subject of verbs' and Takelma *-am* 'first person plural object marker', among others, as evidence. The Mednyj Aleut 'first person singular' forms with *-ju* and *ja* appear to match Greenberg's (1987:273) 'first person' *i*, which he finds to be widespread in South American

languages, citing as related such forms as Payagua *ja-* 'my', *j(-am)* 'I', Mataco *ji-* 'my', and Moseten *je* 'I'. Mednyj Aleut's *-it* 'third person singular' has parallels to Greenberg's (1987:279) third person elements in South American languages; for example, he says that *i-* and *t-* alternate in several of his language groups. There are matchings of both the *i* and the *t* in the Mednyj Aleut third person form. Since these morphemes are clearly borrowed into Mednyj Aleut from Russian (and therefore cannot have any direct historical connection to other New World languages), the fact that they parallel forms postulated by Greenberg as being widespread among American Indian languages indicates how feeble Greenberg's pronominal argument is in general, and how weak his postulated grammatical evidence is on the whole. They show how easy it is to find accidentally similar forms that are as persuasive as those he listed. Most significant, however, is that the Mednyj Aleut forms demonstrate that borrowing cannot be ruled out as an explanation for some of the similarities among pronouns that Greenberg asserts are evidence for his Amerind classification. Moreover, since Mednyj Aleut pronominal affixes also fit "Amerind" forms, by definition, Russian pronominal affixes also fit them, since the Mednyj Aleut forms were taken directly from Russian.

That pronoun borrowing, as in the Mednyj Aleut case, does not require European colonialism is proven by such examples as Alsea (Oregon). Dale Kinkade (1978) found that although Alsea has no discernible genetic relationship with Salishan,[58] it appears to have borrowed a whole set of Salishan pronominal suffixes

TABLE 7-6 Pronomial Verbal Paradigm of Mednyj Aleut

Mednyj Aleut	Russian	Bering Aleut	Gloss
uŋuči-ju	ja sižu	u uči-ku-q	'I sit'
uŋuči-iš	ty sidiš	u uči-ku-Xt	'you sit'
uŋuči-it	on sidit	u uči-ku-X	'he sits'
uŋuči-im	my sidim	u uči-ku-s	'we sit'
uŋuči-iti	vy sidite	u uči-ku-Xt-xičix	'you (pl.) sit'
uŋuči-jat	oni sidjat	u uči-ku-s	'they sit'
ja uŋuči-il	ja sidel (masc.)	u uči-na-q	'I sat'

See Thomason and Kaufman 1988:234–5 (compare Comrie 1989:87); Golovko 1994; data from Menov-ščikov 1968, 1969.

TABLE 7-7 Pronomial Suffixes in Alsea and
Proto-Salishan

Gloss	Alsea	Proto-Salishan
'first person singular'	-an	-n
'second person singular'	-ax	-x^w
'third person singular'	-Ø	-Ø
'first person plural'	-ał	-ł
'second person plural'	-ap	-p
'third person plural'	-ałx	(lx)

See Kincade 1978.

(though Kinkade also allows for the possibility of chance convergence). Some of the suffixes given by Kinkade (1978) are in Table 7-7. Since, as Kinkade explains, these markers "are virtually identical to those in Salish" (personal communication), I take borrowing to be the explanation and regard chance as unlikely (though not an impossibility).[59]

5. Another explanation that has been offered involves child language in a complex way. In this view, child-language expressions around the world abound in self-directed and other-directed words containing nasal consonants. The ultimate reason for this is the universal physical fact that a gesture equivalent to that used to articulate the sound *n* is the single most important voluntary muscular activity of a nursing infant. As Ives Goddard (1986:202) points out, this factor and the tendency for primary grammatical morphemes to consist of a single, unmarked (phonetically commonplace) segment may account for the widespread appearance of *n*- in first person pronouns. Incidentally, in many societies, particularly among hunting and gathering groups, infants may continue to nurse until the age of five, and sometimes longer—well into and beyond the age of language acquisition (Goddard and Campbell 1994).[60]

6. More to the point, the claim of first person *n* and particularly second-person *m* in "Amerind" is grossly overstated. Many American Indian languages lack first person *n* or second person *m*, or both. Furthermore, many non-American Indian languages have one or both of them. The second person *m* is not as common among American language groups as is asserted by Greenberg and Ruhlen. In spite of the generality of first person *n* and second person *m*

claimed by Greenberg (1989:113), he finds that South American languages are typified by *i* 'first person', *a* 'second person', and *i* 'third person' (1979; 1987:44–9, 273–5, 277–81; see Swadesh 1954b:312)—a totally distinct pattern, with second person *m* totally absent. If the *i/a/i* pattern is the hallmark of South American languages, then the *n/m* pattern is not as diagnostic for Amerind as a whole, as claimed (Greenberg 1979 notwithstanding).[61] Moreover, as previously mentioned, Greenberg (1987:276) includes among the grammatical cases he presents in support of Amerind a first person *m* that he believes is representative of several Amerind groups—but recall that first person *m* is what Greenberg and Ruhlen expect of Eurasiatic; at the same time, several of Greenberg's other Amerind groups exemplify widespread second person *ka* or *s,* not the expected "Amerind" *m* (Greenberg 1987:278; see Ruhlen 1994b:252–60). In brief, the distribution of pronouns in American Indian languages has been exaggerated.

It is important to bear in mind that first person *n* is widespread in languages outside the Americas, and it is not difficult to find non-American languages with both first person *n* and second person *m*—for example, Paul Rivet (1957[1960]:127) compared Malayo-Polynesian *inya* / Hokan *inyau, nyaa* 'I', and *ma, mu, me, mo* / *maa, ma, mo', me, mi, mu* 'you', in his attempt to relate Malayo-Polynesian and Hokan. That is, it has been known for at least fifty years that the pattern with first person *n* and second person *m* also exists outside the Americas. I did not undertake a systematic search but cited a number of languages spoken outside the Americas which have first person *n* and second person *m* pronouns. They include Mbugu (Cushitic), several Munda languages, Dravidian, Gilbertese, Wagay (Australian), and others—that is, languages spoken in nearly all quarters of the globe (see Campbell 1994c;[62] for other examples and discussion, see Trombetti 1905:80–90, Benjamin 1976, and Matisoff 1990).

Perhaps most convincing of all, Matthew Dryer (in unpublished work, personal communication) found in his worldwide sample of 333 languages that 7% of the non-Amerind languages—that is, 17 out of the remaining 252 languages—had both an *n* in first person and an *m* in second person, either with both as singular or both as plural. These include (in addition to some languages mentioned above) Enga, Chuave (Papuan); Chrau (Mon-Khmer); Akan (Niger-Congo); seven Bantu languages; Tamazight (Berber); and Hebrew, Arabic, and Tigrinya (Semitic). In Dryer's sample, only 17% of the languages from Greenberg's Amerind (14 out of 81 languages) had this pattern.[63]

It is sobering to recall Callaghan's (1980:337) presentation of the accidental coincidences in Miwokan and Indo-European pronominal affixes, shown in Table 7-8. If it is conceded that Proto-Eastern Miwok and Indo-European can accidentally share so many coincidences in the paradigm of pronominal affixes, where the sounds involved are from a set of highly unmarked consonants, then what is to prevent such coincidence from arising in other languages, including different American Indian languages?[64] Moreover, as Ringe demonstrates mathematically, even without taking into account the typical presence of unmarked consonants in pronominal markers, "the two or three pronouns invoked by Greenberg . . . are obviously inadequate as a mathematical basis for anything" (1993:103).

In this context, it is interesting to recall Ruhlen's claims about the purported Amerind *n/m* pattern: "I collected the first- and second-person pronouns for all the world's major linguistic families [Ruhlen 1994b:252–60]. . . . I did not find a single family anywhere else in the world that shares the Amerind pattern, which turns out not only to *define* the Amerind family, but at the same time to *differentiate* it from the world's other language families" (1994b:24). Perhaps this illustrates how easy it is to find what one is

looking for, since there are abundant examples of the *n/m* pattern in languages outside the Americas.

Greenberg's argument is also not helped by languages which behave in ways that contradict his claims, for example, Amerind cases with *n* 'second person'—for example, Cayuse -*n*, Cherokee *nihi*, Atakapa *na*, Tonkawa *na·-*,[65] Siuslaw -*nx*, Cheyenne *ne-*,[66] Proto-Guajiboan *ni-hi*, Guambiano *ni*, Tupinamba *ené*, and Proto-Tupi-Guarani *ne* (see also the many cases with *m* 'first person'), and by languages whose behavior is the reverse of expectations, with *n* 'second person' / *m* 'first person', as in Lakota *miye* 'first person singular', *niye* 'second person singular'; compare *iye* 'third person singular') (Matthew Dryer, personal communication; Matteson 1972:65, 89).[67] Greenberg's claim is also not helped by "Amerind" languages which have neither *n* nor *m* in first person or second person pronoun forms; for example, Chumash, Zuni, Kuikuro (Amonap), and Muskogean. Proto-Muskogean had *a* 'I', *č* 'you' (and *p* or *l* 'we') (Booker 1980:26–7);[68] Proto-Chumashan had *k* 'first person with nominal forms', *m-* 'first person with verbal forms', and *p* 'second person (with both nominal and verbal forms)' (Klar 1980:92). There are many others.[69]

Whatever the correct explanation for the frequency of first person *n* and for the recurrence of second person *m*, it will not do to look only at American languages which contain them, but ignore the fact that many American languages lack them and that their presence in non-American languages is amply attested. The *n* 'first person' / *m* 'second person' is by no means unique to, diagnostic of, or ubiquitous in American Indian languages. Several nongenetic explanations have been offered. In short, the evidence in support of the pronoun argument has been misleadingly simplified and overstated.[70]

Nichols and Peterson in general come to essentially the same conclusions as given here and in Campbell (1994a): that the frequency of nasals in pronominal forms in general around the world is great and that the *n/m* pattern "includes only some of the Amerind language families, and it includes some languages . . . that are not Amerind" (Nichols and Peterson 1996:367).[71] They see this pattern's distribution as limited essentially to certain western Ameri-

TABLE 7-8 Miwokan and Indo-European Pronominal Affixes

Gloss	Proto-Eastern Miwok Declarative Suffixes	Late Common Indo-European Secondary Affixes (Active)
'first person singular'	*-m	*-m
'second person singular'	*-ṣ	*-s
'third person singular'	*-Ø	*-t <**Ø
'first person plural'	*-maṣ	*-me(s)/-mo(s)
'second person plural'	*-to-k	*-te

can Indian languages and to Austronesian languages of northern New Guinea and offshore islands, based on "a moderately large sample of the world's languages," largely copied from Nichols (1992). They argue that this distribution is no accident, but rather is "a single historical development . . . though we cannot determine the exact nature of the shared history (common descent? areal affinity?, etc.), it can be given a chronology and a geography and tied in a bigger picture of circumpacific migration" (Nichols and Peterson 1996:337). The interpretation of this single historical development, however, is obscured by the discussion.

Their view toward geographical distribution and ancient migration is somehow taken as an explanation of the single historical development which they postulate. They assert that it is "possible to identify the broader notion of historical connection, and . . . patterns of pronominal root consonantism can serve to identify deep historical connections among groups of language families for which orthodox genetic relatedness [by the comparative method] cannot be established" (Nichols and Peterson 1996:359). They argue that "the *n:m* paradigm cannot be proven to be a genetic marker," that "the languages involved in this shared history are a geographically coherent subpart of Amerind, but to our knowledge they do not correspond to any proposed deep subgroup of Amerind." They also acknowledge, seemingly, that their "17 American languages with strict [*n:m*] paradigms" crosscut almost as many families or stocks, but also allow for the possibility that "perhaps the language families with the *n:m* paradigm . . . are ancient sisters . . . beyond the range that the comparative method can reach." They also imagine something that "appears to be a relatively recent phase in colonization" which "suggests that immigrants retained their coastal orientation long after entry" (1996:367–9).

But how could the distribution they see in their sample of languages come about unless by accident, genetic inheritance, diffusion, mistaken interpretation, or some combination of these? The geographical distribution itself is not an explanation, but something to be explained, and if the pronouns were carried by migration, then it would have to be either by migration of

the linguistic forms themselves across space—through borrowing from neighboring languages which had the pronouns—or by migration of peoples speaking genetically related languages who retained the pronoun pattern as they moved, diversified, and settled in the different regions exhibiting the pronoun pattern. But these two possible accounts are not mysterious geographical explanations that happen to be seated in the far distant past; rather, they are mundane mainstream pathways of linguistic change.

However, from their discussion, it is clear that Nichols and Peterson have even fewer options for explaining the distribution. First, they deny sheer accident as a possibility since they assert their finding is the result of a single historical development. Second, they deny borrowing as a possible account; they assert that "pronouns are almost always inherited" (1996:337). They cite the instance of Mednyj (Copper Island) Aleut cited in Campbell (1994c, presented above in this section), but claim it is not due to normal language transmission, but to language mixture, and that in situations of normal transmission, pronouns are not borrowed. This is factually wrong, however. There are many documented cases of the borrowing of pronouns, whole pronominal systems; several are cited in this section, and the English pronouns borrowed from Scandinavian (mentioned above) show that we need not look very far afield to find instances. In fact, the pronouns of at least two of the languages in their sample are borrowed, Pirahã (from Nheengatú) and Miskito (from Sumu), as mentioned above. In denying borrowing of pronoun patterns, they in effect rule out "areal affinity" [diffusion] and thus limit, perhaps unwittingly, the possible interpretation of their "single historical development" to only one possible explanation: inheritance from a common ancestor. The only other option is mistaken interpretation, but even this possibility would seem to be ruled out by their insistence that the distribution is the result of a single historical development.[72]

The results depend crucially upon Nichols and Peterson's "moderately large sample" (1996:337) of "173 languages covering the world," the design of which is "largely copied" from Nichols 1992 (1996:342). However, there are serious problems with Nichols's sample (for details, see Poser and Campbell in preparation). The results depend upon the correct definition of the kinds of units compared—linguistic areas, families, and "stocks." These are specified in detail in Nichols (1992), but the basis of the sample in Nichols and Peterson (1996) is not made explicit—it differs in some regards from Nichols's. Nichols (1992) depends on comparing units at the same level. However, many of Nichols's "stocks" are actually on very different levels, though they are treated as though they were comparable; the same is true of her families—not all are correctly defined or are comparable in time depth. For example, among North American "stocks," "Hokan" and "California Penutian" (disputed proposals with insufficient support) are in no way commensurate with or on the same level as, for example, Uto-Aztecan or Salishan, both of which are fully established families whose histories have been successfully reconstructed to a high degree. Among "families," Chumashan (with very little internal diversity, perhaps no more than 1,000 years; see Klar 1977:10) is not on a comparable level of internal diversity/time depth with Algic or Siouan, both now established genetic relationships, but each involving distantly related languages whose affinity was worked out only with considerable effort. Misumalpan is by no means a "stock" but, rather, is on the "family" level by the criteria of the sample, with internal diversity on the order of Germanic. Muskogean, with internal diversity comparable to Germanic, is a "stock" for Nichols, where Siouan with the much more distant internal relationship among its languages attains only "family" level. Muskogean is placed on the same level as the controversial California Penutian and Hokan, even above the level of Nichols's "families" Ritwan and Siouan, both of which, however, are in actuality characterized by vastly older internal diversity than the Muskogean "stock." With respect to the definition and sampling of linguistic areas, Nichols's Mesoamerican linguistic area depends on a sample of ten languages; of these, two (Chichimec to the North and Miskito to the South) do not belong, but fall outside of the Mesoamerican area, both geographically and in terms of the linguistic traits they exhibit (see Campbell,

Kaufman, and Smith-Stark 1986). Other linguistic areas have similar problems.

While Nichols and Peterson do not list precisely which languages are found in their sample, I assume that many of these problems carry over here, and several questions are raised by what they do present. For one, it is not clear why the sample should not include representatives of all or most of at least the American Indian families. If the New World contains about 150 independent genetic units, how can a sample of 173 languages adequately represent both the Americas and the rest of the world? Their sample has 71 languages from Native America, inadequate to represent the approximately 150 as-yet unrelated language families, but, nevertheless, their sample is highly skewed toward America, with 71 of the 173 (41% of the total). If there are unrelated examples of the controversial pronoun pattern to be found in the world, then surely the chances are stronger for it to show up among these American languages by sheer accident than in other regions of the world, each represented by far fewer total languages. The Pacific has 47 of the 173 (27%), and it appears that more than 109 (63%) qualify as "Pacific Rim languages" (the 15 of Northern Asia, 8 of South and Southeast Asia, 28 of New Guinea, 19 of Australia, 29 of Western North America, 13 of Mesoamerica, and some portion of the 19 South American languages which I have not included in this figure); yet there are only 64 non–Pacific Rim languages in the sample. Does not such a sample create a greater pool of target languages from which to find some linguistic trait in the Pacific Rim region, while the much smaller pool of non–Pacific Rim languages affords fewer opportunities for the same trait to be found?

In particular, the South American languages are woefully underrepresented in this sample; while Kaufman (1990a) lists 118 genetic units, Nichols and Peterson's sample contains only 19 for South America. Moreover, the American statistics are skewed in another way. While each language of the sample is to represent a separate family,[73] the western American sample is skewed toward a greater percentage of conforming languages by having three Uto-Aztecan languages (Luiseño, Southern Paiute, and Pipil).

Since areal affiliation is important to Nichols's (1992) scheme, the choice of Pipil—a Uto-Aztecan language—in Mesoamerica makes the pronoun pattern seem to have a greater geographical spread than would be the case if the number of languages from the same family were constrained more tightly. Guaymí, on the other hand, seems to be treated differently. It is spoken in Central America, but since it is a Chibchan language, it is taken to represent South America. This is understandable, since they deal with only the broad areas, South America and Mesoamerica. However, if true geographical distribution is a significant factor, as the location of Pipil in Mesoamerica would seem to suggest, then Guaymí might as well be influenced by its Central American neighbors as by its Chibchan ancestry, split between northern South America and lower Central America. If one accepts Sapir's Northern Hokan, California Penutian, and Uto-Aztecan as genetic units, as they apparently do (Nichols 1992 accepts these), the representatives of their "western North America" group of languages are exhausted, and this makes the distribution seem not so interesting.[74] Since the languages of these three groups (the first two highly disputed) are neighbors, one might easily suspect that diffusion accounts for their pronoun patterns.

With respect to the *n/m* pattern, Nichols and Peterson conclude from their sample that "there is clearly a delimited portion of Amerind that is historically connected and a clearly delimited portion of Amerind that does not participate in the same historical connection" (1996:359). They see the pattern as a "historical marker," something that disfavors chance resemblance, is persistent in language families, not implied by typological universals, and so on. Logically, this assumption of continuity over time and within language families is a precarious position for them to take (and in any case, their proscription against borrowing should be recalled). Consider, for example, the very frequent change of final -*m* to -*n*; in the Balto-Finnic languages, this sound change converted first person singular -*m* (of the Old World pattern, Nichols and Peterson 1996:360) to -*n* (closer to the Pacific Rim pattern). That is, while other pronominal forms in the Balto-Finnic case might still suggest a first-person *m,* this change nevertheless illustrates

how a very low-level, perfectly natural sound change could render major shifts in a language's or even a whole language family's position in their scheme, looked at in this fashion.

Nichols and Peterson's actual claim about distribution is that the *n/m* "paradigm" is found "chiefly in western North American, Mesoamerica, and western South America" ("a western American phenomenon"), and "marginally in northern coastal New Guinea"—that is, "the Pacific Rim distribution"—though some instances show up in Africa and Asia. Of course, some non-western instances show up in the Americas even in their limited sample based on "strict paradigms"—for example, in Gününa Küne [Gununa-Kena] in eastern South America, and in Kiowa and Tunica. They classify the latter two among their thirteen languages of "eastern North America"—that is, 15.4% of these supposedly nonconforming languages still exhibit the pronoun pattern.[75] Moreover, as they point out, *n* is very frequent in first and second person pronouns in general, and as first person in Africa, New Guinea, and the New World; *m* is less represented overall, but occurs frequently in most areas in pronouns; as first person in Africa, South, and Southeast Asia, New Guinea, and Europe; and in both second person (singular) and first person (plural) in New Guinea (Nichols and Peterson 1996:357–67).

Bluntly put, we might conclude from this that if *n* first person is very frequent and *m* in pronouns in general is quite frequent, then the statistical likelihood of one of the very frequent *n* first person languages also having the frequent *m* show up in its second person pronominal form is reasonably high. I believe that such a convergent but independent development is exactly what explains the occurrence of the *n/m* pattern in New Guinea and in the Americas and also probably among several otherwise unconnected groups in the Americas. As for the distribution Nichols and Peterson find, it is limited to nasal-initial pronoun forms under "strict paradigm" conditions (1996:tables 14 and 18, pp. 353, 357–8, 361, and later based only on independent pronominal forms, table 19), as represented in their sample. In this constrained search, they find the *n:m* paradigm "occurs in only 18 languages" (still 10.4% of the total). When not looked at in this restricted way, the *n/m* convergence is seen in several other languages around the world, including some not so western American Indian languages (as discussed above). Even Nichols and Peterson find "there are 31 languages that have n in some first person and m in some second person form" (1996:361)—in 18% of their sample languages. However, even with their narrow strictures, appropriate for assaying proposals of remote linguistic connections, chance congruence with parts of New Guinea and parts of America is a much more plausible account than that there is a mysterious historical connection between just these two regions, which defies both time and space and is beyond standard notions of linguistic change associated with the comparative method, which is known to have upper limits (Nichols 1992).

They attempt to show that the New Guinea–New World pronoun connection they see is not sheer accident by arguing that "tones, numeral classifiers, and second person m must surely be structurally independent of each other, and the fact that all three characterize the same Pacific Rim population makes it quite clear that this population is not a random assemblage but has internal historical connection," to which they add mention of "the 9 base pair deletion in mitochondrial DNA Region V, a hallmark lineage of the New World and Oceania." These seemingly co-occurring features are not the support they imagine them to be. Tones, as they recognize, are found "also farther into New Guinea, farther north into British Columbia, farther into eastern North America," and "farther into South America . . . and throughout Southeast Asia, and "are also very frequent in Africa" (Nichols and Peterson 1996:366). In fact, there seems to be little correlation, since languages with tonal contrasts are found far and wide, even in Europe (Scandinavian, Latvian, Serbo-Croatian), and both develop and are lost fairly easily in languages. Many of the n/m American languages lack tone; for example, it is precisely the languages of the Andean region in South America which lack tones but have n/m, while those with tones for the most part lack the pronoun pattern. Similarly, while Athabaskan, Tlingit, and Haida (putative Na-Dene languages) are some of the best known tonal languages of the Americas, and are on the Pacific Rim, they are notorious for lacking the pronoun pattern, presumably a main reason why Greenberg left them out of his "Amerind." By the same token, there are many American Indian tonal languages that have no Pacific Rim connection—for example, Siouan, Keresan, Tanoan, one dialect of Hopi, Northern Tepehuan, Chibchan, one dialect of Tzotzil, Witotoan, Sabané, many Tupian languages, and many other languages in Amazonia. More important, there is nothing particularly stable about tones; neither Proto-Athabaskan nor Proto-Sino-Tibetan had tonal contrasts, in spite of their Pacific Rim locations; tones develop easily in languages fully isolated from other tonal languages, as seen in the histories of, for example, Yucatec Maya, Swedish, Latvian, Serbo-Croation, and others.

The same is true of numeral classifiers; they are usually a rather superficial part of the grammar of languages that have them, not tightly woven into the fabric of the grammar. Thus, they are not particularly stable, but can develop and be lost fairly easily; they diffuse easily as an areal feature. They also do not correlate well with the n/m pattern, but are found, for example, in several Algonquian languages, throughout Amazonia, and they are widespread in Asia (including Indo-Aryan and some Iranian languages); they are by no means restricted to Pacific Rim languages.

The geographical distributions of these traits would not correlate well with that of the n/m pronoun pattern even if its distribution were as claimed. Rather, it seems more likely that the seemingly shared pronoun pattern is just accidental, perhaps aided by diffusion in some cases. As for the human genetic trait, its relevance is questionable, since even if a biological genetic unity could be demonstrated involving Native Americans and Austronesians of New Guinea, no necessary historical conclusions for language history follow—as in the case of biological genetic traits known to be shared among Native American and northeast Asian groups (see Chapter 3). Even given the shared biological trait, nothing deterministic about Oceanic and New World language similarities follows from it. They could share linguistic similarities in spite of different genes or they could exhibit only linguistic differences while sharing some genetic elements—cases representing both these circumstances are known among peoples of the Pacific Rim. In any case, this biological trait does not correlate well, since it includes speakers of many languages who do not share the pronoun pattern.

In short, these proposed additional correlations do little to bolster the claims concerning the pronoun pattern.

Since the groups in their sample with the *n/m* pronoun pattern are widely separated, are typologically quite different, and exhibit no other reliable linguistic evidence which might suggest they are to be grouped together at the exclusion of the others, the conclusion that there is a "single historical development" lying behind this pattern does not appear sustainable on the evidence presented. That a genetic explanation must be intended would appear to be the only option left, given that the authors deny both chance and borrowing, the only logical alternatives, as the possible explanation for the distribution of the pattern. With Melanesia brought into the picture, surely coincidence (given the confirmed tendency for pronouns to exhibit nasals) is a far more likely candidate than the leap of faith into abstract time and space that the historical connection hypothesis requires.

I conclude this section on pronouns by agreeing with Meillet that "pronouns must be used [only] with caution in establishing relatedness of languages" (1958:89–90).

The Binary Comparison Red Herring

One of the inaccurate characterizations of the methodological principles and practices employed in research on American Indian languages is that Americanists rely exclusively on binary (pairwise) comparison. It is often maintained that "traditionalists" insist on "comparing languages two at a time" and that "those who compare languages two by two are simply ignoring much relevant evidence" (Greenberg and Ruhlen 1992:94; see also Fleming 1987:210–11). However, absolutely no one insists exclusively on a pairwise or binary comparison. Greenberg and Ruhlen repeat this characterization, asserting that the procedure is flawed, apparently in order to contrast it with their own approach and to emphasize their assertion that

only the multilateral comparisons they champion are legitimate. It is difficult to understand the basis of their claim, unless it is comes somehow from the articles in Bright (1964). The closest examples one might find in American Indian linguistic literature to this portrayal of practice are the few small-scale Hokan and Penutian studies that appeared in Bright (1964), which appear to utilize binary comparisons of two principal entities in Hokan or in Penutian (in some cases the compared entities are whole families; in others they are isolates). Each of these studies compares numerous forms from other putative Hokan or Penutian languages with those of the two entities in focus. Thus, they are not actually binary comparisons but rather investigations which involve the many other languages also proposed to be related in the Hokan or Penutian hypotheses. These make it clear that there was no methodological commitment to comparing only two languages at a time—the procedure was simply "adopted for convenience" (Broadbent and Pitkin 1964:19). Even the researchers who said they were doing pairwise comparisons consistently compared numerous forms from other languages at the same time (as seen in Haas 1964a, McLendon 1964, Silver 1964, and Broadbent and Pitkin 1964, discussed in Chapter 8). In fact, in these studies of alleged binary comparisons, a view nearly identical to Greenberg's concerning numbers of languages that ought to be compared was expressed:

> Since the cognates for any pair of languages are few, the relationships become clear only when a larger number of languages are compared; therefore, elaboration of the relationships within the Northern Hokan languages waits on a group comparison that will establish the conditions governing these reductive processes [reduction of forms through aphaeresis, syncope, and assimilation]. (McLendon 1964:144)

These "two-by-two" comparisons of Hokan and Penutian languages and Greenberg's multilateral comparisons have much in common, which makes them all inconclusive: they both catalogue a number of look-alikes, but they do not take the necessary additional steps of analysis to determine which forms are not supportive because other factors (diffusion, onomatopoeia, chance) may explain them better. Thus, the issue of the number of languages compared is in a sense merely a red herring; the real issue is the deployment of methodological considerations aimed at giving possible true cognates a chance by removing those forms which are clearly not cognate and disregarding those for which testimony is ambiguous at best.

Of course, some linguists from Boas's day to the present have preferred to work from the bottom up. They recommend that historical linguistic research be done first at more manageable family levels and then when these were solidly established, higher-level comparisons could be attempted which would depend on and benefit from the previously established lower-level foundation. For them, climbing a low mountain is a necessary first stage for being able to ascend the higher peaks beyond (Callaghan 1991a). This preference for where efforts should be cast, however, has nothing to do with comparing only two languages at a time, even when the ultimate goal is to get to the higher peaks. Despite the insistence of these scholars on a necessary first stage, most would not deny that on an odd occasion, one might be lucky enough to hit upon reasonably good evidence for higher-level relationships without the reconstruction of the individual families being compared. They hold that in many language families, the evidence of broader relationship will not be sufficiently clear until the historical linguistic work on the component language families is done first.

Greenberg's Methods and the American Indian Language Classification Controversy

As mentioned in the discussions of methodological considerations (in the preceding section, as well as in other sections of this book), Greenberg's methods, claims, and overall classification have received a negative evaluation. Greenberg's claims and methods are extremely controversial (see Chapters 2 and 3). They have been weighed fairly and rejected by virtually all specialists, yet they continue to receive much attention in the media and by scholars in other fields. In this section, I examine some other

problems with Greenberg's work and attempt to explain why it has been rejected by specialists, thus (I would hope) clarifying the controversy.

Data and the Reception of Greenberg's Claims

The "evidence" cited by Greenberg (1987) has been harshly criticized by other linguists because of the many problems surrounding it and the errors it contains. Nearly every specialist finds extensive distortions and inaccuracies in Greenberg's data: "the number of erroneous forms probably exceeds that of the correct forms" (Adelaar 1989:253); "nearly every form [cited for Yurok and Kalapuya] required some sort of emendation" (Berman 1992:230); "it [Greenberg 1987] is marred by errors in both methodology and data, which make it essentially useless for its intended purpose" (Kimball 1993:447). (For other criticisms, see Campbell 1988b, Chafe 1987, Goddard 1987b, Golla 1988, Kaufman 1990a, Matisoff 1990, Mithun 1990, Poser 1992, and Rankin 1992.[76]) Greenberg assembles forms which are similar from among the languages he compares and declares them to be evidence of common heritage.[77] Where he stops (after having assembled the similarities) is where other linguists start: "The real work of the linguistic scholar begins where the provisional labors of the word-collector end. . . . Surface collation without genetic analysis . . . is but a travesty of the methods of comparative philology" (Trumbull 1869:58–9). Similarities can be due to a number of factors (as discussed in this chapter), but Greenberg makes no attempt to eliminate other possible explanations. The similarities he has amassed appear to many scholars to be due mostly to accident and combinations of the factors discussed in this chapter. That is, the reason specialists reject his claims is that Greenberg has not presented a convincing case that the similarities he assembled are due to inheritance from a common ancestor and not to a combination of the other factors discussed here.

Given that his evidence is so deficient and his method has repeatedly been proven inadequate, how do we account for the favorable reception Greenberg's classification has received outside of linguistics? Dell Hymes raised a simi-

lar question about the reception of Greenberg
1960, which can also be addressed to Greenberg
1987:

> It is historically revealing to compare the reception
> of the classification of South American languages
> by the two men [Greenberg and Swadesh]. The
> two classifications agree on the essential unity of
> the languages of the New World, differing on
> various internal groupings. Greenberg's classifica-
> tion was obtained with a list of 30 to 40 glosses,
> Swadesh's with a list of 100 glosses. . . .
> Greenberg published the result without supporting
> data, backed essentially only by personal authority.
> Swadesh presented an explicit account of his pro-
> cedures, endeavored to make the data available,
> and regularly revised his findings in the light of
> new evidence and research. The classification
> based on authority without supporting evidence
> has been reprinted often in anthropological text-
> books and journals; the work presented as an
> explicit, continuing scientific enterprise has not.
> (1971:264)

Swadesh's work was similar to Greenberg's in
many ways, in its conclusions, its data, and the
general methods employed. In fact, Swadesh
himself pointed this out in his comments on
Greenberg's (1960) classification and "the
method of mass comparison": "I have been
applying a method of this type [mass compari-
son] to American languages for a number of
years. Some of my findings . . . agree with
Greenberg's; others do not" (1963b:317). Why,
then, was the work of Swadesh, who was extremely erudite and had firsthand knowledge of
many American Indian languages, rejected or
ignored, whereas Greenberg's classification is
frequently mentioned with approval in the media
and by scholars in other fields, although its
validity is denied almost totally by American
Indian linguists? The answer has nothing to do
with the quality of Greenberg's evidence or
his methods, since it is precisely these which
specialists find unconvincing (as they did also
in the case of Swadesh's work). That is, factors
other than the scientific legitimacy of the case
presented explain the favorable reception of
Greenberg's classification by nonlinguists.[78]

One of the most telling aspects of the debate
over the classification of Native American languages is that most American Indian linguistic

scholars are not opposed to distant genetic relationships, but in fact Greenberg shares their
research objective of attempting to establish
more family relationships among American Indian languages in order to reduce the ultimate
number of linguistic groupings. Most American
Indian linguists believe it possible (perhaps even
probable) that most (perhaps all) American Indian languages are genetically related. The main
difference is that they find Greenberg's methods
and evidence inadequate. In short, when scholars
who are predisposed to accept the possibility
that the languages are related, and have the
objective of reducing linguistic diversity in the
Americas, have trouble accepting Greenberg's
attempted reduction, there is probably good reason for their hesitation.

The African Fallacy

Greenberg has asserted repeatedly that his success in classifying African languages (Greenberg
1955, 1963) makes it likely that his American
Indian classification is correct: "There should be
some assumption that methods successful in one
area will also be successful when applied elsewhere" (Greenberg 1989:107). Since this claim
has been repeated so often, an attempt should
be made to clarify it, to analyze the basis for it,
and to explain why it is incorrect.[79]

The several indisputable and absolute errors
in Greenberg's classification of American Indian
languages, as documented throughout this book
and especially later in this chapter, clearly show
the futility of calling on the African classification
experience in the American linguistic arena. As
has been pointed out frequently, much of
Greenberg's African classification simply repeats the correct classifications of earlier scholars (see Greenberg 1963, Gregersen 1977, Kaufman 1990a:64, Thomason in press, Welmers
1973). Likewise, much of his American Indian
classification repeats the proposals of earlier
scholars, especially Sapir for North America and
Rivet for South America.[80] One big difference,
however, is that many of these repeated American Indian proposals, unlike their African counterparts, have not received acceptance and remain controversial, while some others have been
shown to be completely wrong (see Adelaar

1989:252). Thus, the part of Greenberg's strategy that helped to secure a measure of success for his African classification—the repetition of earlier classifications—has, ironically, contributed to the lack of success (that is, nonacceptance) of his American proposals.

Greenberg presupposes that his African classification is a success. However, the African classification is a more qualified (more limited) success than Greenberg says it is, and some measure of success in classifying closely related languages is possible even without valid methods. For example, Powell's (1891a) relatively successful classification of North American Indian languages was based on methods much like Greenberg's (see Chapter 2). Since Powell grouped mostly only obviously related languages, his inspection of short lexical lists was sufficient for the detection of many family groupings that have stood the test of time. But today no one applauds Powell's methods, which failed in several instances (see Chapter 2). This ease of recognizing close relationships is consistent with Greenberg's claim: "If I have a group like the Western Romance languages (Italian, French, Spanish, Portuguese), there is an enormous difference between adding Rumanian and adding Basque. If I add Rumanian many new three-way resemblances become four-way, and a fair number of new etymologies appear. If I add Basque almost nothing happens" (1989:112).

Notice, however, that new matchings (Greenberg's so-called etymologies) appear in the closely related Western Romance languages, just as within families in Powell's classification of American Indian languages; but this teaches us nothing in the case of a putative distant relationship. We must assess the similarities in a potential case of possibly distantly related languages also against the possibility that they may be due to nongenetic factors (such as chance, borrowing, onomatopoeia, and universals). Success depends on the nature of the languages to be classified—many African languages are simply more clearly related than many American Indian languages (Thomason in press). Some of Greenberg's other African hypotheses assume so much time depth and internal diversity that they remain unproven and perhaps can never be demonstrated (Bender 1987, Welmers 1973:16–19; see Hymes 1959:53, Kaufman 1990a:64, Thomason in press). In the final analysis, "invalid methods do not *necessarily* give wrong results; rather, one cannot tell whether their results are right or wrong without testing them by a cogent method" (Ringe 1993:104).

This raises the question, just how successful is Greenberg's African classification? We should not lose sight of the fact that Greenberg's methods were heavily criticized when applied in his African classification (see Tucker 1957; Winston 1966; Fodor 1966, 1968). It is important in this context to consider those aspects of Greenberg's African alignments which are considered mistaken and others where the proposals are as yet undetermined (undemonstrable?). I concur with Bernd Heine that "Greenberg's findings [in the African field] . . . now require considerable refinement, both in specific points of the classification, and in the underlying conceptual scheme" (1972:7; see also Winston 1966:160, Heine 1972:32).

Ringe urges a reexamination of this classification: "I would suggest that parts of Greenberg's famous classification of African languages, which was posited on the basis of multilateral comparison and more or less achieved the status of orthodoxy . . . , urgently need to be reinvestigated by reliable methods" (1993:104). Indeed, a comparison of Greenberg's Amerind with his African classification seems to call for a reassessment of the African proposals. When Ruhlen (1994b:123–4) confides that "the evidence that Greenberg adduces for the Amerind phylum is . . . considerably stronger than the evidence Greenberg presented for his African classification," there can hardly be room for doubt that some circumspection concerning the African classification is in order, since the extensive flaws in Greenberg's Amerind have been frequently reported and the classification has been almost universally rejected by specialists.

Harold Fleming's description of Greenberg's African procedures and his assessment of the outcome is telling in this regard, particularly since Fleming is a recognized Africanist and a well-known enthusiast of proposals of distant genetic relationships:

It [Nilo-Saharan] has also been called "Green-berg's waste basket," hence a collection of hard-to-classify languages and a very unreliable en-tity as a phylum. Vis-à-vis AA [Afro-Asiatic] or N-K [Niger-Kordofanian], N-S [Nilo-Saharan] is widely viewed as the more shaky of the three, but it no longer gets the kind of stubborn opposition that Khoisan receives in South Africa and Britain. When Greenberg finished his first classificatory sweep of Africa, he ended up with fourteen phyla. Of those, one was AA. One was N-C [Niger-Congo], which then had Kordofanian joined to it. The fourth was Khoisan. All the rest, or 10 phyla of the first classification, were put together as Nilo-Saharan. It represents far far less consensus, far less agreement on sub-grouping, and very little progress on reconstruction. (1987:168–9; see also Bender 1991, 1993)

As Fleming (basically a strong supporter of Greenberg) indicates, two of Greenberg's four African groups, Khoisan and Nilo-Saharan, are widely contested. While Fleming is in favor of Nilo-Saharan, even he recognizes that "Khoisan is the one African phylum where strong and continuing opposition exists" (1987:171).

M. Lionel Bender, who is also sympathetic to Greenberg's African classification and is also a well-known specialist in African languages, renders a similar judgment: "Controversies re-main in the case of all four phyla established by Greenberg" (1989:1). Bender's recent assess-ment of Greenberg's African classification (per-sonal communication, August 1993), although essentially positive in tone, shows that even Greenberg's supporters (as in the case of Flem-ing) can speak of serious problems with the African classification. With respect to Khoisan, Bender observes that "it may well be two or three phyla rather than a single one. . . . The evidence is minimal and maybe insufficient to answer this." Concerning Afrasian (Afro-Asiatic), he asks: "Are Cushitic and Omotic (Greenberg's West Cushitic) really part of the same family? . . . Is Cushitic really five sepa-rate families (Beja, Agew, etc.)?; Is there a special genetic grouping of Egyptian, Berber, and Semitic (or some other such arrangement . . .)?" He views Niger-Kordofanian as "a vast phylum for which there are problems about sub-grouping, some marginal members which seem to be possible overlaps with Nilo-Saharan or something else, plus a major problem of the

status of the Mande family." Regarding Nilo-Saharan (sometimes called Nilo-Sahelian), on which Bender has worked extensively, he be-lieves the evidence is indicative of "a genetic unity of the classical kind," though he suggests some major modifications in the membership proposed by Greenberg.

With respect to Greenberg's methods, Bender no longer supports multilateral (or mass) com-parsion, which he views as amounting to "a sanctioning of uncontrolled 'accumulation of re-semblances', the very method used by the 'world etymologists'. . . . A second criticism is that of the extremely careless documentation (forms wrongly cited in many ways)."

Without resurrecting the more usual and fre-quent methodological criticisms raised in the Africanist literature in regard to Greenberg's African hypotheses, I should point out that areal linguistics has not played a significant role in African historical linguistics, though clearly sev-eral indeterminacies remain precisely because of the difficulty of sorting out inheritances from diffused similarities (Heine 1972:7, Dalby 1971, Ferguson 1976, Sasse 1986). Similarly, Green-berg makes no attempt to deal with areal phe-nomena in the Americas, either, in spite of their demonstrated relevance to long-range compari-son (Bright 1984; Campbell, Kaufman, and Smith-Stark 1986; Campbell and Kaufman 1980, 1983; Derbyshire 1986; Kaufman 1990a; David Payne 1990; and Doris Payne 1990—see Chapter 9).

In short, acknowledging Greenberg's African success—realistically—does not deny his falli-bility in classifying American Indian lan-guages.[81] It is now possible to focus again on the African classification's methodological shortcomings due to its reliance on superficial lexical similarities:

Although Greenberg's work represents consider-able progress over that of previous writers, it leaves a number of questions open. His approach is largely inadequate for the proof of genetic rela-tionship; it can do little more than offer initial hypotheses, to be substantiated by more reliable techniques like the comparative method. In a num-ber of instances, languages or language groups have been placed in a given family solely on the basis of a handful of "look-alikes," i.e. morphemes of similar sound shape and meaning. The Nilo-

Saharan family, in particular, must be regarded as a tentative grouping, the genetic unity of which remains to be established. (Heine 1992:31–6)

Moreover, as Dalby points out, being too uncritical can mislead nonlinguists: "Unqualified acceptance of it [Greenberg's African classification] has lent a certain 'respectability' to his classificational units. This acceptance is potentially misleading to non-linguists, especially historians, and has helped to obscure the fact that many of these classificational units have never been scientifically established" (1971:17).

If Greenberg is going to call upon his African inning as indicative of probable success for his American Indian classification, then he can tally his batting average only after all his times at bat have been factored in. Since his Indo-Pacific hypothesis (which would lump "the bulk of the non-Austronesian languages of Oceania" from the Andaman Islands [Bay of Bengal] to Tasmania; 1971:807) has no supporters among specialists,[82] since the success of his African classification has to be qualified, and since there are, regardless of the outcome of other disputes, a number of absolute and uncontestable errors in his classification of a number of American Indian languages, Greenberg's previous batting average does not constitute a strong argument in favor of his American Indian classification. Whether any aspect of that classification holds up is totally independent of his work in Africa and elsewhere, irrespective of its accuracy or lack thereof. This is an empirical issue; therefore, posturing for the American Indian classification on the basis of an African classification platform is irrelevant.

So-called Pan-Americanisms

In the methodological debate concerning more inclusive classifications of American Indian languages that have been proposed, the issue of so-called pan-Americanisms has been misunderstood. In this section an attempt is made to clarify the matter. (For specific examples of pan-Americanisms, see Chapter 8.)[83]

Greenberg (1989:113) attributes the formulation of a "doctrine of Pan-Americanisms," which he takes to mean "genetically related forms," to

Campbell and Kaufman (1980), and some others have assumed that a similar interpretation was intended (for example, David Payne 1990:75). However, we referred only to "widespread forms (so-called pan-Americanisms)" (Campbell and Kaufman 1980:853), which are not (necessarily) genetically related forms but may be due to such factors as onomatopoeia, sound symbolism, borrowing, nursery formations, universals, and accident (as explained in Campbell 1991b, Campbell and Kaufman 1983). In explorations of possible distant genetic relationships, it must be shown that widespread pan-Americanisms (if they are to be used as evidence in support of remote relationships), cannot be easily explained by one of these other factors, thus leaving genetic inheritance from a common ancestor a stronger candidate for the explanation of the similarity.[84]

Greenberg (1989) criticized the recommendation (made in Campbell and Kaufman 1980) that pan-Americanisms should be eliminated from proposals of genetic relationship aimed at grouping certain American Indian language families. He equated this to the exclusion of proposed etymologies from an etymological dictionary, "contrary to normal practice"—specifically, the exclusion from a Germanic etymological dictionary of "English *two* and German *zwei* because this is an Indo-European etymon" (Greenberg 1989:113). However, he misses the point.

There are two different issues to be considered here. One is the problem of demonstrating that a widespread form (pan-Americanism) is indeed a cognate at some level. As mentioned, because several of these forms have other possible explanations, it is impossible to determine whether they are due to common ancestry or to some other factor. The other issue is the relevance of pan-Americanisms for establishing a closer relationship among some of the compared languages at a narrower level. It is to this situation that our recommendation applies.

The example of forms for 'hand' illustrates this point (Greenberg 1987:58; see also Swadesh 1954:309). A form phonetically approximating *ma* and meaning 'hand' or something similar is found in Greenberg's proposed Macro-Ge, Chibchan-Paezan, Equatorial, Central Amerind, Penutian, and Hokan groups. Clearly, such forms as Timote *ma* 'bring' (listed among the 'hand' forms; Greenberg 1987:58) cannot be used to argue for a closer grouping of Timote with other Equatorial languages if it is not yet known whether Timote has affinities with putative Equatorial languages or whether it is perhaps more closely related to one of the other groups that also exhibit the form. If the affinity of Timote is unknown[85] and evidence is still being sought to determine its closer relatives, a finding that many other American Indian languages (from various other of Greenberg's putative groups) also exhibit this widespread (pan-American) *ma* cannot be the sole basis for determining to which of these language groups Timote may be more closely related. Other evidence, not shared widely with Greenberg's non-Equatorial languages, would be required to support the proposed narrower (though still remote and undemonstrated) grouping of Timote with Equatorial languages.

This point, that widespread forms provide no useful evidence for less inclusive groupings, has been made previously, in fact with reference to the 'hand' example. In commenting on Harrington's (1943) attempt to link Quechua with Hokan, Swadesh observed:

> They [word comparisons] may simply represent the kind of agreements . . . possibly harking back to the earliest linguistic connections in the New World. Typical of Harrington's list are cases like Quechua *maki* 'hand', Pomo *ma-* 'with the hand', Salinan *meen* 'hand', and Yana *moo-* 'reach'. . . . One can do much better, as it happens, outside of Hokan, e.g. Totonac *makan,* Caxinaua *mikin* 'hand', Utaztecan **mahka* 'give', **mawi* 'hand'. (1954b:327)

In short, shared retentions are not valid evidence for subgrouping; only shared innovations provide support (as correctly shown by, among others, Greenberg 1957; also Campbell 1977:62–9). A shared pan-Americanism, if it could be shown to be a cognate within some broader grouping of languages, would be a shared retention and would therefore not be reliable evidence of a closer kinship at a less inclusive level.

The analog for the example of English *two* and German *zwei* with respect to the first issue would be a situation in which it is not yet known whether these two languages are related. These two somewhat similar forms might constitute evidence of a genetic affinity (assuming that a competing nongenetic explanation of the resemblance did not prove to be more attractive). At this level, however, this evidence does not tell us whether these two languages are more closely related to each other than to other languages exhibiting similar forms. Indeed, on the basis of initial visual inspection (which is how Greenberg makes determinations concerning what he calls "etymologies"), English *two* /tu/ might appear to be more closely related to Lithuanian *dù* or Latin *duo* than to German *zwei* /tsvai/. The analog with respect to the second issue, which is what Campbell and Kaufman (1980) addressed, would be a situation in which several languages known to be related exhibit an array of similar forms. Proof of a closer connection between English and German than to other languages that also exhibit similar forms would then require evidence of shared innovations uniting these two languages—*two* and *zwei* work for the subgrouping precisely because we understand the Germanic sound shift of **d > t,* an innovation shared by English and German as Germanic languages (German later *t > ts* [spelled *z*]), but not shared by Lithuanian, Latin, and other Indo-European languages.[86]

However, in a case such as the *ma* of Timote and many other Indian languages, we have no evidence of shared innovation to suggest that we should group Timote more closely with one group than with other groups—since they all share the similarity, such a form does not prompt us to select one possible grouping rather than other possible groupings that also have *ma*. For that reason, pan-Americanisms are not helpful in efforts to establish a closer connection between some American Indian languages when others also have the similarity.

The point about the inappropriateness of widespread forms (pan-Americanisms) could just as easily have been made through reference to Greenberg's claims about *n/m* pronoun forms (see the preceding section). If Greenberg's Amerind languages are assumed to be related and to exhibit widespread evidence of first person *n* and second person *m*, then these forms alone cannot be employed to argue that a closer relationship exists among certain putative Amerind languages—for example, among Wiyot, Yurok, and Algonquian (Sapir's [1913, 1915a, 1915b] Algonquian-Ritwan hypothesis of distant genetic relationship, now proven)—than among other putative Amerind languages that also have these widespread forms. Edward Sapir did, however, offer the presence of *n-* 'I' and *m-* 'you' as evidence for his Algonquian-Ritwan proposal. Truman Michelson (1914, 1915), who opposed Sapir's hypothesis, countered that the *n/m* pronouns were found in a number of North American languages in addition to Yurok, Wiyot, and Algonquian. Michelson thus had correctly perceived the problem faced when attempting to use forms that are widespread in languages outside the scope of the immediate comparison as evidence in support of proposals of distant genetic relationships among American Indian languages.[87] (See Goddard 1986 for a detailed examination of Sapir's evidence.) Because Sapir's pronoun examples were found in languages outside his proposed Algonquian-Ritwan group, they could not, by themselves, serve to demonstrate a connection among only the languages he compared.

Two points about so-called pan-Americanisms should be emphasized. First, these widespread forms are not necessarily traceable to inheritance from a common ancestor; second, these widespread forms are not valid indicators of narrower proposed genetic groupings if the forms are prevalent in languages not included in the comparison. Finally, the possibility must be entertained that some of these widespread forms may actually reflect wider historical connections than are recognized at present. However, if this is the case, detailed investigation far beyond that of Greenberg (1987) will be required to determine their real history.

No attempt will be made to list pan-Americanisms here; examples are readily seen in the lists of forms given in Greenberg (1987), Ruhlen (1994b), Radin (1919), and Swadesh (1954b,

1956, 1967a), and in various other proposals of long-range relationship that are evaluated in Chapter 8. Many of these forms do appear to have nongenetic explanations. For example, onomatopoeia or expressive symbolism is frequently evident in comparison sets glossed as 'baby/infant/child', 'beat/hit/pound', 'blow/wind/lungs', 'boil/bubble/foam', 'break/cut/chop/split', 'breast/nurse/suck/kiss', 'burst/bloom', 'cold', 'cough', 'cricket', 'cry/shout', 'drink/water', 'fly/flap/butterfly', 'frog/toad', 'goose', 'round/ball', 'spit', 'swell/blister/boil', 'tongue', 'urine/urinate', 'wide/flat', as well as in many bird names. Jakobson's (1960) explanation (discussed earlier in this chapter) is valid for many similarities among kinship terms. Some terms are apparently explained by diffusion (for example, 'beans', 'buffalo', 'dog(?)', 'tobacco').

Summary

Because of the confusion that certain proposals of distant genetic relationship and large-scale classification hypotheses have engendered, it has been important to consider carefully the methodological principles and procedures utilized in the investigation of possible remote linguistic relationships—that is, in how family relationships are determined. Principal among these are reliance on regular sound correspondences in basic vocabulary and patterned grammatical evidence involving submerged features or shared aberrancy, with careful attention to eliminating other possible explanations for compared material (for example, borrowing, onomatopoeia, accident, and others.). The methodological considerations of this chapter are applied in the following chapter to evaluate the major proposals of remote linguistic kinship involving Native American language groups.

8

Distant Genetic Relationships: The Proposals

To attempt to make an exact and complete classification of all languages in rigorously defined families is to prove that one has not understood the principles of the genetic classification of languages.

Antoine Meillet and Marcel Cohen (1924:10), cited from
J. Alden Mason's (1950:167) translation

THE METHODS FOR INVESTIGATING (and attempting to establish) possible distant genetic relationships were discussed and evaluated in Chapter 7. In this chapter I survey most of the better known distant genetic proposals involving Native American languages and attempt to assess their accuracy. In such an assessment, it is good to bear in mind that (1) "questioning evidence for a proposed genetic relationship is not the same as denying that relationship" (Callaghan 1991a:54) and (2) inadequate evidence cannot serve to establish such relationships.

Because of the large number of proposals, languages, and linguistic groups involved, I consider in some depth only three prominent and controversial proposals—Macro-Siouan, Aztec-Tanoan, and Quechumaran. These three will serve to illustrate the criteria, methods, and major concerns in dealing with hypotheses of remote kinship among Native American lan-

guages. After the evaluation of these three, the other proposals are considered, but in less detail. (A number of proposals of remote kinship among South American languages that were mentioned in Chapter 6 are not discussed further here.)

In the linguistic literature one often encounters an either-or, all-or-nothing view of proposals of remote genetic affinity—the assumption is that a hypothesis is either proven and the languages involved are therefore unquestionably related genetically, or it is unproven and therefore the languages are unrelated. Although ultimately we would like to establish definitively whether languages are related or not, a more realistic and revealing way to approach such postulated remote relationships is to consider the strength of the hypotheses and the level of confidence warranted. It is more accurate to view unconfirmed proposals of family relationships as falling somewhere along a continuum ranging from the highly probable to the very unlikely. A proposal may present evidence that is sufficient to attain a certain level of plausibility but not sufficient to eliminate all doubt. It is not appropriate in such instances to view the proposal in terms of a dichotomy of established/unestablished or related/unrelated.

Therefore, for each of the proposals considered here, I report my estimation of the strength of the hypothesis (the probability that there actually is a genetic relationship) and the level of confidence I feel is warranted in making this judgment. Percentages are given for both *probability* and *confidence*. For example, the hypothesis that the Germanic languages are related would be assigned a probability of +100% and a confidence of 100%; the hypothesis that Turkish and Quechua are related would have a probability −95% and confidence 95%. The plus sign (+) indicates that the languages are more likely to be related than unrelated (or not demonstrable) (the larger the plus percentage, the greater the probability of relationship); the minus sign (−) indicates that it is more likely that no relationship exists than that one does exist (the larger the minus percentage, the less likely the relationship). However, there is a danger in interpreting the pluses and minuses too literally; the difference between, say, a +5% probability and a −5% probability is not large, for both are on the borderline, where one cannot determine if it is more likely that the languages are related or unrelated (or, put differently, that any relationship that may exist has not been and perhaps cannot be shown). The difference is so slight that it would be misleading to present one language as related and the other as unrelated. A probability of 0% means totally uncertain—that is, the languages are equally as likely to be related as to be unrelated. I have included also the level of confidence figure (where higher percentages mean that more confidence in the probability judgment is warranted), since it is useful to know not only the estimation of how likely the relationship is and how strongly the evidence supports it, but also how secure that judgment is. For example, in the case of a family relationship among the Mayan languages, the amount of evidence available and my own experience working with them would lead me to give a +100% probability and 99% confidence—

virtually total certainty. But a proposal that would join Uto-Aztecan and Keresan would be given a −10% probability (the proposal is slightly more likely not to prove defensible than that these languages are related) and a 40% confidence—that is, I am not very confident about this assessment due in part on the limited amount of evidence upon which to base an opinion and in particular on my own lack of experience with Keresan. Clearly, the percentages I assign to these judgments are not determined in a rigorous manner but are merely impressionistic. Other scholars would no doubt have different judgments and might assign radically different percentages in many of the cases discussed here.

Far-Fetched Proposals

Before turning to the more seriously entertained proposals, I provide a small selection, in list form, of the many proposals which would link languages of the Americas with languages from elsewhere in the world. Although some of these proposals have been expounded in more detail than others, none reaches a level of plausibility that makes it worthy of additional attention. Each is near the −100% probability that the languages are unrelated (or if a relationship ever existed, it is impossible to demonstrate); the confidence ratings in these instances also approach 100%.

American Indian languages–Basque (Trombetti 1928[1926]:173)

American Indian languages–Asian languages (and Aztec-Sanskrit) (Milewski 1960)

American Indian languages–Altaic (Ferrario 1933, 1938)

American Indian languages–Polynesian (Key 1984)

Na-Dene with Mongol, Turkish, Chinese, Northeast Tibetan, Tokharian, and Italo-Celtic (Stewart 1991)

Hokan-Malayo-Polynesian, Hokan-Melanesian (Rivet 1957[1943])

Uto-Aztecan with Chukchi (Bouda 1952)

Nahuatl-Greek and Indo-European (Denison 1913)

Uto-Aztecan-Polynesian (postulated as "intimate borrowing or creolization" by Kelley 1957)

Mixe-Zoquean-Totonacan-Otomí with Caucasian languages (Bouda 1963)

Huave-Uralic (Bouda 1964, 1965)

Mayan-Altaic (Wikander 1967, 1970, 1970–71)

Mayan-Turkic (Frankle 1984a, 1984b)

South American–East Asian languages (Koppelmann 1929)

South American–Japanese (Gancedo 1922, Zeballos 1922)

Quechua-Oceania (Imbelloni 1926, 1928)

Quechua-Maori (Dangel 1930, Palavecino 1926)

Peruvian languages–Polynesian (Christian 1932)

Quechua-Turkish (Dumézil 1954, 1955, see also Hymes 1961b)

Quechua-Tungus (Bouda 1960, 1963; see also Hymes 1961b)[1]

Australian connections, such as Chon-Australian and Malayo-Polynesian (Rivet 1925a, 1957 [1943]); South American–Australian (Trombetti 1928)

As discussed in Chapter 2, several scholars in earlier times had imagined linguistic connections between languages of the Old World and the languages of the Americas (see Brinton 1869:5).

The Three Case Studies

Macro-Siouan (Siouan-Iroquoian-Caddoan[-Yuchi])
−20% probability, 75% confidence

There are several versions of the Macro-Siouan hypothesis. Earlier, some scholars hypothesized connections between Iroquoian and Siouan, to which Caddoan and Yuchi were eventually added (see Allen 1931; Haas 1951, 1952, 1969d:90–92; Latham 1845; Morgan 1871; see Chapter 2). The most extensive and informative formulation is that of Wallace Chafe (1964, 1973, 1976). Rudes (1974) and Carter (1980:180–82) provide additional considerations.[2] Chafe does not claim to have proven Macro-Siouan, Siouan-Caddoan, Iroquoian-

Caddoan, or Iroquoian-Siouan.[3] Still, many believe in some form of this hypothesis, primarily on the basis of Chafe's formulation (see Mithun 1990:324, 1991).[4] In view of the initial plausibility of the evidence presented so far and the mixed reception that the hypothesis has received among specialists, the evidence should be assessed carefully.

Chafe (1976) presents pairwise comparisons of the three families—Caddoan, Siouan, and Iroquoian. I discuss his evidence for each comparison in turn in the remainder of this section.

Caddoan-Siouan Comparisons

Chafe describes as "tantalizing, if inconclusive" (1976:1190) the five lexical resemblances shared by Caddo (Caddoan) and by two Siouan languages, Winnebago and Dakota. They are given in Table 8-1; I have taken the liberty of adding Proto-Siouan reconstructions (from Robert Rankin, personal communication) to the comparisons.

Chafe posits no sound correspondences, and the extremely small number of compared lexical items is a problem. Robert Rankin shows that some of these are of little value for defending a possible genetic relationship. In the comparison of Caddo *banit* and Winnebago *wanik* 'bird', the *-nik* in the Winnebago form is from Proto-Siouan *yįka* 'small'; the *wa-* referred to game birds generally, and the names of all smaller birds bear the diminutive suffix in this branch of Siouan (Rankin 1981:174).[5] As Rankin points out, "If the Caddo form cannot be similarly decomposed [analyzed morphologically] and a diminutive meaning assigned *-nit*, one is left with the much less convincing *CV* set" (1981:174). Rankin also doubts the comparison of Caddo *wit* 'self' with Dakota *wičhá* 'man',

TABLE 8-1 Chafe's Caddoan-Siouan Comparisons

Gloss	Caddo	Winnebago	Dakota	Proto-Siouan
'bird'	banit	wanik		
'blood'	bahʔuh	waʔih	wé	*waʔí·
'arrow'	baʔ	má'	wą-(híkpe)	*wą́·he ('chert'?)
'earth'	wádat	mą'	mą-(khá)	*awá·
'man' / 'self'/ Pawnee pita 'man'	wit		wičhá	*wą́·ke

since Dakota *čh* comes from earlier *kh*—Dakotan *wičhá* "is isolated to that language and, in fact, may be borrowed from Caddoan" (Rankin, personal communication). I would mention also the problem of the nonequivalent semantic associations ('self' and 'man'; see Chapter 7). Rankin also finds that the number of languages from each family compared here (one from Caddoan, two from Siouan) is a problem and that a comparison of reconstructed Proto-Siouan and Proto-Caddoan lexical items ought instead to be undertaken. We may add to these objections considerations of other problems. For example, in the 'earth' forms, the matching portion (presumably *wá* : *ma*') is very short,[6] and no explanation is given for the leftover portion *-dat* of the Caddo form. The possibility is greater that accident explains the similarity than would be the case if the forms were longer or if more segments matched. Similar forms for 'earth' are found in a good number of other Native American languages (and languages elsewhere in the world).[7] The forms for 'arrow' suffer the same objection, being short forms, and as a culturally salient item, 'arrow' is conceivably a diffused form. In any case, the Siouan stem *wá·he* is found in various other words for flaked implements and probably originally meant 'chert'; the bow was not introduced into the Mississippi Valley until about A.D. 400–600 (Rankin 1993). In short, without a larger number of such potential cognates, regularly corresponding sounds, and some evidence that the compared forms may not be explained by other factors, the Caddoan-Siouan relationship cannot be found to be persuasive.

Since Chafe presents few lexical look-alikes and no systematic sound correspondences, the grammatical features he discusses constitute his strongest evidence for a Caddoan-Siouan connection. Siouan languages have a series of about ten verbal prefixes that indicate instrument, such as *raka-* 'by striking', *ra-* 'by mouth', *ru-* 'by hand' (Rankin 1981:174 and personal communication), which Chafe compares to Caddo preverbs (see also Allen 1931:192): "These Caddo preverbs . . . must be accepted as simply arbitrary appendages to the verb roots"; the number of these in Caddo is about equal to the number of instrumental prefixes in Siouan, but "it is usually problematic whether they can be

associated with any consistent semantic feature" (Chafe 1973:1190–91). However, Rankin (1981) raises serious doubts about these preverbs as well. The strongest comparison is that between Proto-Siouan *aRá·-* 'by heat' (Rankin, personal communication) and the Caddo preverb *ta-/na-* derived from incorporated *nak-* 'fire'. Nevertheless, several methodological considerations should be taken into account regarding these preverbs. First, the preverb forms bear a phonetic resemblance, but there is no clear semantic matching; this violates the sound-meaning isomorphism requirement (see Chapter 7), which specifies that similarity of sound alone or of meaning/function alone is insufficient. Chafe believes that the prefixes in both languages may be from incorporated noun roots. In this case, however, as Rankin points out, there is reason to believe that the meaning/functions were actually different in origin in the two families, since "the only Siouan evidence for the origin of the instrumental prefixes points to a verbal rather than a nominal source" (1981:174), whereas the Caddoan preverbs, according to Chafe, are derived from nouns. This suggests an independent origin for the two phenomena in the two language families. Evidence that the Siouan instrumental prefixes were once verbs is presented by Siebert (1945), who points out that the Siouan instrumental preverbs are cognates to Catawban distinct verb roots. That is, in Proto-Siouan-Catawban they were, in effect, serial verb constructions; in both Siouan and Catawban it is the instrumental prefixes that usually receive the person-number marking for actor.[8] This makes it seem difficult to relate these Siouan instrumental prefixes to Caddoan forms, which are nominal in origin. Interesting additional evidence is seen in the fact that most Siouan subgroups underwent a change which deleted the vowel of initial syllables, and this applied to person-number prefixes, the absolutive *wa-*, and demonstratives (all of the form #CV-), but not to instrumental prefixes (or patient-object prefixes). It appears that the instrumental and patient morphemes were proclitic particles in Proto-Siouan, not prefixes, and this explains why they failed to undergo the rule of vowel loss. If this interpretation is correct, then the fact that these forms became prefixes in Siouan only more recently makes them even less similar to the Caddoan prefixes

(Rankin, personal communication). Second, the compared instrumental prefixes and preverbs are short forms, leaving chance a strong candidate for explaining the similarities. Third, the development of instrumental verbal affixes as a result of the grammaticalization of originally separate lexical pieces is widespread in the Americas (pointed out, for example, by Kroeber 1913:399) and can easily take place through independent innovation (see Givón 1984:128–9) and through areal diffusion (see Chapter 9).

Chafe also compares the use of the positional verbs 'sit', 'stand', and 'lie' as auxiliaries in Siouan (where they are suffixed to the verb root) and Caddoan (where they are prefixed to the verb root). As Rankin explains:

> The problem is that only the categories match; the PS [Proto-Siouan] forms themselves bear no resemblance to the Caddoan forms Chafe cites. Furthermore, the positional auxiliary category is found not only in Siouan and Caddoan but in nearly every language family in eastern North America. . . . These same auxiliaries [are found] in Muskogean, Yuchi, Tunica, Atakapa, and Chitimacha, all southeastern languages spoken in the areas just to the east of what is commonly assumed to have been the Caddoan homeland. The positionals also have special status in Iroquoian . . . and in Algonquian, and are not uncommon on a worldwide basis. (1981:175; see Haas 1956:71–2 for Muskogean and Natchez forms; see also Chapter 9)

Chafe gives the following "possible reconstructions" in Siouan: *-wáki 'lying' (Rankin, personal communication, reconstructs Proto-Siouan *wų·ke 'be lying'), *-ráki 'sitting' (Rankin's *rá·ke 'be sitting'), and *-haki 'standing' (Rankin's *hą́ke 'be standing [animate]'). Chafe notes that "there is probably a morpheme boundary between the syllables (some of the languages show reflexes of the first syllable only)" (1973:1193). Chafe's opinion that "the most suggestively similar shape [in Caddo] is ʔaniki- 'standing' " seems to be based on his belief that the other forms, ʔini- 'lying' and ʔawi- 'sitting', make it "appear that" in ʔaniki- the Caddo -ki- portion "was at one time a separate element" (see Allen 1931:188). This seems a very slim reason for analyzing the -ki- as a separate element in earlier times, and otherwise the forms

in the two language groups are otherwise not phonetically similar.[9]

In any case, the fact that the compared elements are prefixed in one family and suffixed in the other strongly suggests that even if there is a historical connection between the families, it would come from a time when the elements were still separate lexical items, before their grammaticalization as auxiliary affixes. Since such grammaticalization of auxiliaries is not uncommon in the world's languages, what seems to be at stake here is the comparison merely of the independent positional roots; but since these have little phonetic similarity, the existence of positional roots, which eventually become grammaticalized, is not strong evidence of a genetic relationship.[10]

Chafe also compares Caddo 'dual' -wiht- (piht- initially) with the Siouan *-pi 'plural' suffix (1973:1196). Rankin (personal communication) reconstructs this as *ape 'plural' in Proto-Siouan. Chafe's comparison involves a short form, prefixed in one language and suffixed in the other. If the comparison is valid, this suggests that some independent lexical element was independently grammaticalized in each of the languages and was in a different position in its host word. The fact that accidental similarities to Siouan *pi- 'plural' occur in a number of languages is not an encouraging sign for a historical connection between the Caddo and Siouan forms (see Greenberg's [1987:295] Macro-Panoan -bo 'plural' and Hokan w- 'plural'; Greenberg's [1987:291] "widespread reciprocal p in PENUTIAN"; and even the English prefix via Greek bi-).

With regard to the Siouan-Caddoan comparison in general, Rankin concludes that "it is unquestionable that Siouan and Caddoan are typologically rather similar, but there is little yet to indicate genetic relationship by the usual criteria" (1981:175).

Concerning the often mentioned Yuchi-Siouan hypothesis, Rankin is of the opinion that Yuchi and Proto-Siouan vocabulary are mostly "utterly alien to one another" and that the few word comparisons, which are nearly identical, are probably loans, which is to be expected, since Yuchi and at least some subgroups of Siouan are members of the Southeastern Linguistic Area (see Chapter 9). The presence of aspirated stops in the sound systems of both Siouan and Yuchi has also been mentioned as possible evidence of relationship (Haas 1969d:90–92), but internal evidence shows that they developed late in Pre-Proto-Siouan (minus Catawban), and they are not shared by clearly related but more distant Catawban (Rankin, personal communication).

Caddoan-Iroquoian Comparisons

In his Caddoan-Iroquoian comparisons (Table 8-2), Chafe again presented a few lexical resemblances—only four—and no recurrent sound correspondences.

For these resemblances to be more persuasive, the material in parentheses would need to be explained—and a much greater number would be needed, with sound correspondences. In some of these the matched portion is very short.[11] Conceivably, the forms for 'to pound corn'[12] are onomatopoetic (for example, English *thud* and forms for 'pounding' in other languages, especially those lacking labials, as Iroquoian languages do). The forms for 'feces' are short and are possibly affective/symbolic/nursery words;[13] similar forms are not hard to find (compare Proto-Mayan *tʸaꞏʔ).

Chafe compares the structure of verbs in Seneca and Caddo and notes the following similarities (1973:1194). In both languages, the verb consists of essentially four major parts: (1) various prefixes meaning tense, aspect, subordination, location, relation, and negation; (2) pronominal prefixes that relate to subject and object; (3) a verb base; and (4) a small set of suffixes for aspect or tense (or location in Caddo). However, Rankin observes that "the similarities are so broadly defined that one could easily accommo-

date Muskogean and Siouan in the same framework" (1981:175).

Rankin (1981) finds the comparison of Caddo and Seneca pronominal paradigms to be the strongest of Chafe's Caddoan-Iroquoian evidence (Table 8-3). (Allen also found "the most striking morphological parallel" between Iroquoian and Siouan in pronominal forms [1931:191].) In his 1964 article Chafe points out some pronoun similarities of Caddo and Seneca also with Siouan (see below), noting in particular two "resemblances of a more specific nature" (1964:861). One is the "form for the combination of first person subject with second person object," cited twice. Chafe gives the form once in the comparison of Seneca *(k)-ǫ* 'I (subject)– you (object)' / Proto-Siouan *ų (> Dakota *ų* 'inclusive person') (1931:856). However, as Rankin observes, the Dakota 'inclusive person marker' is *ūk-*, not *ų*, and comes from Proto-Siouan *wą́ꞏk- (there are clear cognates in languages of various branches of the family). He believes it is derived from the Proto-Siouan word for 'man, human being', *wą́ꞏke—the probable source of the Siouan 'inclusive person' (personal communication).[14] Chafe gives the form for the first person subject with second person object again in his comparison of Dakota *čhi-* / Seneca *kǫ-* (1973:861). The Dakota 'I–you' fused pronominal marker, however, is clearly derived from *wa + *yi, even in Mississippi Valley Siouan; the Dhegiha cognate, *wi*, is an indication of this. Presumably Chafe intended something like a *č : k* correspondence in his comparison, but when the known history of the pronominal marker is taken into account, this ceases to be a possibility. The other resemblance is "the occurrence of a labial consonant (Iroquoian *w*, Siouan *w* or *p*), although not in the same position, in forms which pluralize the meaning of the personal prefix." (The Caddoan-Siouan parallel is discussed in the preceding section.)

There are interesting similarities here (which may indeed be the result of a remote genetic relationship), but the following considerations should be kept in mind. These are short forms (*CV*), and hence the possibility of chance similarity is increased. These are also pronominal/ deictic forms and involve some of the least

TABLE 8-2 Caddo's Caddoan-Iroquoian Comparisons

Gloss	Caddo	Seneca
'to pound corn' (verb root)	(na)-dáʔ	-theʔt
'to make' (verb root)	(ʔa)-ʔnih	-ōni-
'to dye' (verb root)	(nača)-súʔ	-(ah)-so-
'feces' (noun or noun root)	ʔidah	-iʔta-

TABLE 8-3 Chafe's Caddo and Seneca Pronominial Paradigms

| | Caddo | | Seneca | |
Gloss	Subject	Object	Subject	Object
'first person'	ci-	ku-	k(e)-	wak(e)-
'second person'	yah?-	si-	s(e)-	sa-
'indefinite' (Caddo) 'feminine-indefinite' (Seneca)	yi-	yu-	ye-	(ya)ko-
'neuter'			ka-	yo-
'masculine'			ha-	ho-

marked, most salient sounds (k, s), which occur with greater-than-chance frequency in grammatical morphemes, especially deictic forms, in languages in general (see Chapter 7). The forms for all three persons are similar to those in a number of other American Indian languages; that is, they are so-called pan-Americanisms and thus are not particularly strong evidence that these two languages may be related to each other more closely than either or both may be to any of the other languages that have similar forms. For example, the first person forms with *kV-* are consistent with the list of languages in which Greenberg (1987:287–8) finds evidence of an Amerind k- for first person forms. (The forms Greenberg lists include *k-, -ki, kiki, ka-, -ko, -ku, kii, kua, -yku, kax-, -uk, koa, kwa, -ke, kakh, kɔ, gɔ, hka, ge-, kis, kak,* and *-gi*.) The second person forms with *sV-* in Caddo and Seneca would appear to be consistent with the batch of languages for which Greenberg (1987:278–9) finds a second person form with *s* (*-s, -s-, is, -səq, -ns, so:wa, -su, -is, -(a)so, -(a)s, (hi-)ṣu*) (see also Allen 1931:191, 192). Here we can recall the accidental coincidences in second person affixes between Eastern Miwokan *-ṣ* and Indo-European *-s* (Callaghan 1980:337). The third person forms with *yV-* in Caddo and Seneca would appear to match the third person forms with *i-* cited by Greenberg in American Indian languages (especially in South America), but similarities also occur in several others—compare Proto-Muskogean *i-* (to keep the Southeastern Linguistic Area in the picture), Proto-Mixe-Zoquean *y-*, and the *y-* of the non–K'ichean-Mamean Mayan subgroups, as well as Greenberg's (1987:279–81) claim that there is a general *i*-like third person marker throughout South America, among others.

Chafe (1973:1195) further points out that in both Caddo and Seneca, 'plural' number for the pronominal subject or object of the verb is signaled by *-wa-* (Siouan parallels have already been mentioned; see also Chafe 1964:861). Greenberg (1987:295) finds a 'plural' w- in many languages (which he classifies as Hokan, with the forms *w-, -wa, -u, -w, -wi, -wa-, -wa?, we-,* and *-wes*'). This marker is also similar to the Amerind *m* 'plural' that Greenberg (1987:293) sees in many languages; the associations of *m* with *w* in lexical forms compared by Chafe should be noted in this regard, as well as the fact that Iroquoian languages lack labials, making *w* a close phonetic approximation to missing *m* in these languages.

Another resemblance Chafe notes is that of Caddo *-t-* 'dative' and Seneca *-at-* 'reflexive' (or 'middle voice'); both elements occur as the leftmost constituent of verb bases and both affect transitivity, though in opposite ways. (The Caddo 'dative' "sometimes transitivizes bases otherwise intransitive, while the Seneca element sometimes has the opposite effect" [Chafe 1973:1197]; see also Allen 1931:190, 191.) Again in this instance, the compared forms are short and hence are possibly accidentally similar; the shared *t* is unmarked and is found very frequently in grammatical morphemes. Similar forms in other languages are easy to find. For example, if the *-tu-/-tü-* 'reflexive/middle voice' suffix of Finnish is similar only by coincidence, then the Caddo and Seneca forms might also be accidentally similar. Of relevance here are (1) Greenberg's lists of American Indian languages that exhibit "a reflexive *t*" (with forms *ta-, tu-, -t-, -ti, di-, d-, -ta,* and *-to* and with functions meaning 'reflexive possessive', 'reflexive', 'reflexive object', and 'reflexive marker on the verb') (1987:290); (2) Greenberg's postulated *-tV* 'locative' or 'instrumental' (locatives and datives are about as interchangeable as these are with reflexives and middle voice forms) (1987:303); and (3) Greenberg's 'derivational voice formation' (with the forms *-tu-, -tə, -te, -at, -et, -ət, -t, -d, -ʔnt, -tU, -ʔt,* and *-st* and with functions meaning 'transitivizer', 'denominative', 'causative reversive', 'transitivizer after local suffixes', 'causative', and 'actions made out of statives') (1987:313). I hasten to point out that, in making comparisons with Greenberg's lists, or with pan-Americanisms, or even with non-American languages, I mean only to show how easy it is for such similar forms to show up due to reasons other than genetic ones. In the case of the pan-Americanisms, it is possible that some of these similarities actually reflect some old genetic relationship (though this is by no means the only possible interpretation in most instances), but as pointed out in Chapter 7, this is not evidence of a closer relationship between any of the languages being compared than with any other language that also shares the form but was left out of the comparison.

Chafe (1973:1196–7) presents one case of similarity that might be considered to be of the "submerged features" sort discussed in Chapter 7. In Caddo, *ʔi-* occurs before some noun and verb roots to prevent the root from occurring initially or after a pronominal prefix. In Seneca, *ʔi-* occurs at the beginning of some verbs to prevent the occurrence of verbs containing only one vowel (see also Allen 1931:192). That is, both languages use *ʔi-* as a protection device to prevent certain phonological forms from occurring on the surface. Although this feature might be inherited, the use of inserted or epenthetic (prothetic) phonological material to "protect" against occurrence of certain phonological shapes is not unusual in languages in general and use of this device in other American Indian languages is well known. Moreover, epenthesis of *i, e,* or *a* is particularly common. For example, Spanish epenthetic *e* is used to prevent initial consonant clusters beginning with *s,* as in *escribir* 'to write', but compare *inscribir* 'to inscribe, register'. In Nahuatl, *i* is used before initial consonant clusters, as in *ikši-* 'foot', from /-kši/, but compare *no-kši* 'my foot'. It seems quite possible that such a process

could easily arise independently in the two languages.

Siouan-Iroquoian Comparisons

Chafe (1964) presents sixty-seven lexical comparisons between Siouan and Iroquoian languages as "suggested cognates" (repeating several of Allen's [1931] examples). More than half are comparisons of very short forms (most with *CV* only). In many of these sixty-seven, large portions are placed in parentheses and are left out of the comparison with no explanation as to the morphological status of the parenthetical material, though clearly in some cases the non-compared parenthetical portions are not established morphemes, as indicated for example by Chafe's statement concerning the example for 'near', which compares Seneca *(to)sk(ę)* with Proto-Siouan **(a)šk(a):* "Forms in parentheses [are] plausible as prefixes and suffixes" (1964:856). Some of the sixty-seven forms are onomatopoetic (for example, 'cough' Seneca *-(a)hsaʔk-* / Proto-Siouan **hoxp*; compare Mayan **oxob',* Quechua *uhu-,* English [kɔf] 'cough'; see also 'voice/sing'). Some are prevalent forms or pan-Americanisms—for example, 'earth' Pre-Seneca **-(ǫh)wę(j)* / Proto-Siouan **mą* (**awá·* above); 'feces' Seneca *-iʔta* / Proto-Siouan **įre* (see above); 'first person object' Seneca *wa-(k)* / Proto-Siouan **wa-* (Siouan forms with *ma-* and *wa-*);[15] 'second person' Seneca *s-* / Proto-Siouan **š-* (see above);[16] 'us' Seneca *-ǫk-* / Proto-Siouan **wąk.* Several others, although they are possible cognates, have the sort of cultural content and close phonetic similarity that makes them plausible loans: 'tobacco' Seneca *-yęʔ(kw)-/* Proto-Siouan **yą(ni);*[17] 'dish'; Seneca *-ksa-* / Proto-Siouan **kši* (there was considerable ceramic trade among some Plains groups before European contact); 'name' Seneca *-yas-* / Proto-Siouan **yaš;*[18] Pre-Seneca **-nęh(r)-* 'community' / Proto-Siouan **thą* 'town'; Choctaw (Muskogean) *tamaha, tomaha* 'town'; Mobilian *tamaha* 'town'; and various noncognate versions in various Siouan languages. Rankin (personal communication) makes clear that the term for 'town' in Siouan is diffused and is not reconstructible to Proto-Siouan; it is also found in various non-Siouan languages along the Mississippi River. Chafe's compared forms are in general semantically quite reasonable, but a few are not very equivalent, such as Seneca 'bile' / Siouan 'yellow', Seneca 'I (subject)–'you' (object) / Proto-Siouan 'inclusive person', 'know/heart', 'lineage/ dwell', and 'set down / sleep'.

In sum, there is reason to exercise caution about the majority of the sixty-seven forms as possible cognates, and those which are not questioned are so few in number that a clear case cannot be made for genetic relationship.

Chafe also mentions "some general similarities between Siouan and Iroquoian grammatical patterns." Some of these are very general, however, and would fit other Native North American languages (for example, "sentences in both families contain particles and more complex words that are based on roots inflected in a great variety of ways"). A more specific similarity is that "both families have a group of reflexive, reciprocal, or 'middle voice' prefixes which occur between the personal prefixes and the root," but it is not uncommon in general for such morphemes to be closer to the verb stem, and since Chafe admits that "for the most part . . . they do not appear to be cognate in shape" (1964:860–61), they are subject to the restriction that only forms similar in both sound and meaning can legitimately be compared (see Chapter 7). (Some other pronominal similarities were discussed above.)

Other Comparisons

Carter (1980:180–82) presents some additional evidence. He gave thirteen sets of lexical resemblances in Siouan, Iroquoian, Caddoan, and Yuchi which he believes reflect a Proto-Macro-Siouan *y, presenting the assumed sound correspondence set for this sound. Four of these sets involve considerable semantic latitude (for example, 'tree/firewood/stick/wood'); in seven sets short forms are compared; the forms in two sets are possibly diffused ('beaver', 'tobacco'); and 'water' is a pan-Americanism.[19] Carter admits that "the weakest link" (1980:181) is the Caddoan family (with only a single lexical set illustrating the supposed correspondences), but he adds three further comparisons between Caddoan and "Eastern Siouan" (that is, Catawban) (one overlaps Chafe's 'earth' set, see above),

which are presumed to evidence a correspondence of wa or ma- in Woccon and Catawba with hu- in Proto-North-Caddoan. Carter also compares eight lexical items from Woccon with forms from the other putative Macro-Siouan languages (but suggests no sound correspondences): four of these eight sets compare short forms and two are suggestive of diffusion ('arrow/awl', 'string/belt'); some overlap sets given by Chafe. In sum, Carter's added evidence is too sparse and too problematic, and subject to other possible explanation, to lend any real support to the Macro-Siouan hypothesis.

Rudes (1974) sees Macro-Siouan as having split first into Proto-Siouan-Yuchi and Proto-Iroquois-Caddoan, based on assumed sound change for which he presents no data (for example, loss of /ʔ/ in Vʔ in Siouan-Yuchi, loss of /ʔ/ in Cʔ in Iroquois-Caddoan, and rhotacism [s > r] in Siouan-Yuchi). However, since he gives essentially no data in this article, Rudes's claims lend no additional support to the hypothesis.[20]

Several scholars have expressed reservations concerning Macro-Siouan or some version thereof. After evaluating Chafe's evidence, Rankin expresses his overall conclusion concerning Macro-Siouan: "Speaking only as a Siouanist and a comparativist, it is difficult for me to regard the hypothesis as better established than, say, Penutian or Hokan" (1981:176), both of which are widely questioned (discussed later in this chapter). Concerning general similarities in the phonemic inventories of Siouan, Caddoan, and Iroquoian, they are also similar to Proto-Muskogean, Proto-Algonquian, and most of the languages of eastern North America.[21] Ballard's opinion of the Macro-Siouan evidence is instructive:

This is not the place for a critique of these suggestions [previous attempts to relate Yuchi to various other languages]; I only wish to express my doubt that most, if any, of the suggestions will turn out to be valid in the sense of demonstrating genetic relationships. It is possible, however, that various of these groups have borrowed features at various levels from each other. I wish to suggest in this regard that the i/e versus o distinction [of object pronouns in Yuchi] . . . may be related to an e/o alternation . . . that Chafe [1973:1194] suggests may have been common to Iroquoian and Caddoan. The consonantism of so [second person object] and perhaps yo [indefinite object] is also suggestive in comparison with Yuchi, but any other consonantal parallels seem rather farfetched. (1978:112)

Hollow and Parks, specialists in Siouan and Caddoan, respectively, concluded with respect to Chafe's evidence that "it must be viewed as no more than suggestive. We have worked with Siouan and Caddoan and have tried to find additional data to support a relationship between these two families; but beyond several additional lexical similarities, we have found no compelling evidence. . . . It seems that nothing more than various similarities can be pointed out" (1980:81).

My overall conclusion concerning Macro-Siouan agrees with that of the specialists in these languages just mentioned—that the evidence presented thus far is far from persuasive. For the present, I recommend that the language families included in the Macro-Siouan proposal be classified as unrelated.

Aztec-Tanoan
0% probability, 50% confidence

The Aztec-Tanoan hypothesis, which attempts to link Uto-Aztecan and Kiowa-Tanoan in a remote genetic relationship, has been widely accepted and is frequently repeated in the literature as though it were unproblematical, although a number of specialists have persistently expressed their doubts (Davis 1979, Hale and Harris 1979, Hoijer and Dozier 1949, Newman 1954; see also Miller 1959, Campbell 1979:964). Given this state of affairs, it is appropriate to assess the evidence which has been offered in support of this proposal.

Sapir (1921a, 1929a) grouped Kiowa-Tanoan together with Uto-Aztecan under the name Aztec-Tanoan in his overall classification of North American languages, but on the basis of what evidence we are not told. The first significant evidence (and still the primary evidence) in support of the proposal was presented by Whorf and Trager (1937); they recommended the name Aztec-Tanoan, but Sapir's version of the name has prevailed. The assessment by Hale and Harris of Whorf and Trager's evidence is incisive:

A careful review of this material [Whorf and Trager 1937], in an effort to arrive at a firm judgement concerning the Aztec-Tanoan relationship, leads to the conclusion that, while the case looks considerably more convincing than the comparison of randomly selected language families not believed to be related (like Uto-Aztecan and Pama-Nyungan of Australia), a cautious view must leave the question open. If Uto-Aztecan and Kiowa-Tanoan are related, then the time-depth is extremely great. (1979:170–71)

As for the two families involved, Uto-Aztecan (UA) has been demonstrated beyond doubt at least since Sapir's (1913–1919) study, though proof of the Kiowa-Tanoan family relationship came considerably later. Harrington (1910b, 1928) had suggested that Kiowa-Tanoan constituted a family, but it was not until the work of Miller (1959) and Trager and Trager (1959) that it was solidly supported, and Hale (1962, 1967) provided the conclusive evidence. When Whorf and Trager (1937) wrote their "Azteco-Tanoan" article, they equivocated about the position of Kiowa, on whether it should be seen as closer to Tanoan or as related in some other fashion more directly to Uto-Aztecan, and for this reason they left Kiowa out of their considerations.[22]

Since publication of the Whorf and Trager article, more extensive and reliable information has become available on a number of the languages in the two families, and this is reflected in the more recent reassessments by Davis (1989) and Shaul (1985), who nevertheless still largely address the examples originally presented by Whorf and Trager. The evidence for the Aztec-Tanoan hypothesis is based almost exclusively on lexical comparisons (sixty-seven in Whorf and Trager for which proposed cognates are presented, plus another forty for which just their Azteco-Tanoan "reconstruction" is presented to "indicate some other words common to the two stocks" [Whorf and Trager 1937:619]; and 107 in Davis [1989]), as well as putative phonological correspondences. All subsequent scholars cited here have expressed doubts about Whorf and Trager's reconstructions and about aspects of the data they present. In this section I assess the evidence for the Aztec-Tanoan hypothesis in terms of the considerations discussed in Chapter 7. In the examples, I refer to the

Whorf and Trager (WT) numbers and to Davis's (D) more accurate Uto-Aztecan (UA) forms and Kiowa-Tanoan (KT) forms, where available; PT is Whorf and Trager's Proto-Tanoan.

Davis (1989:377–8) presented solid reasons for rejecting seven of the Whorf and Trager sets (7, 13, 17, 36, 61, 81, 82). In WT7 Whorf and Trager compared UA *tuḷa, tuˣ-, taḷa* 'dark darkness' with their PT *dak'u*; however, their Tanoan forms are morphologically complex and should be compared only with the PT stem *k^hu* 'dark'. There are also problems on the UA side, since Whorf and Trager compared forms from two separate etyma, **tuka* 'night' (Miller 1987:204) and **tuhu* 'charcoal' (Miller 1987:204, see also Campbell and Langacker 1978:271). Davis objected that WT13 is "stretching the semantics," since the UA forms are glossed as 'open, hole, be stuck through', whereas the PT form means 'arroyo'. With regard to WT17, Davis found that the PT form is suspect, since Whorf and Trager's Taos form 'to plant' is not cognate with the Tewa word for 'leaf', and "neither is a likely cognate with the UA term" meaning 'tree, wood'. In UA, their Aztec form *$k^wa\cdot wi$-* 'tree, wood' is not related to their Aztec form *kili* 'plant'. Davis noted that in WT36, the Tanoan words meaning 'return, turn back' are not likely cognates with UA words meaning 'twist, spin'. As he pointed out concerning WT61 (WT's *yaˣ-, yaxpewi* 'sleep'), there is no justification for the initial **y*; the evidence rather points to something approximating **piwi* (Miller 1987:145). In WT81, *musa* 'cat, feline animal' is a Spanish loanword that has its own literature (see references cited by Davis 1987:377); and in WT82 *paguyu* 'fish' matches KT **pë* 'fish' with forms in some UA languages where the first syllable *pa-* is apparently the morpheme **pa·-* 'water'.

Still, Davis accepted fifty-two of Whorf and Trager's proposed cognate sets as "having a good possibility" (1989:377). In nine other cases, Davis accepted either their UA or their PT side of the equation but compared it to different forms in the other language family (WT5, 49, 52, 53, 24, 30, 34, 46, and 54; see D8, 33, 36, 48, 69, 70, 78, 84). He still had some doubt concerning five of the accepted sets (WT9, 28, 40, 63, 64). If we consider the 52 accepted WT forms and the 107 presented by

Davis, and accept Davis's objections to the others, we find that most still fall far short when judged by the criteria discussed in Chapter 7.

Probably the most significant problem is that most data presented as evidence in support of the Aztec-Tanoan hypothesis does not defy chance as a possible explanation. As discussed in Chapter 7, matchings of only *CV, VC,* or *V* in shape do not eliminate accidental similarity as a possible explanation (for the mathematical proof of this, see Ringe 1992, 1993). Davis readily admitted this problem: "Our comparisons involve, on the most part, matching of single syllables and are thus liable to some unavoidable chance convergences" (1987:378). This problem is especially troublesome in languages such as Uto-Aztecan, which, with its phonological inventory, is limited to unmarked consonants and vowels and with the canonical shape of a large portion of its morphemes being *CVCV*. In a situation such as this, it is very easy to find accidental similarities; this is what is behind the striking examples of coincidences cited as evidence in a number of far-fetched proposals which attempt to link Uto-Aztecan languages with, for example, Polynesian and Turkish, and other languages with similar phonological structure.

In fact, this problem is truly grievous in this case, since at least 41 of the 57 Whorf and Traeger comparisons involve such short *CV* or *V* matchings, and at least 74 of Davis's 107 sets of comparisons have short matchings. The situation is worse than these numbers indicate, however, since in a significant number of the remaining comparisons, although the forms may be longer than *CV*, the parts that match and are compared are frequently no longer than *CV* in length. For example, in WT1 Whorf and Trager suggested for '(finger)nail' the UA forms *su-, suta, sutuⁿ* (based on Hopi *suta* [also given is Hopi *so·ki*], Luiseño *-šla* [properly /šula-/; William Bright, personal communication], Cahuilla *šite,*[23] and Aztec *iste-*). More recent reconstructions based on a full range of cognates and an understanding of the sound changes in the various subgroups give PUA **suti* 'fingernail, claw' (see Campbell and Langacker 1978:272, Miller 1987:172–3; compare D67). This is compared with PT *-ci-, -ce-* (based on Taos *-ce-,* Isleta *-ci-,* and Jemez *-sǫ*; compare PKT **-cę,*

*-dzẹ, *-cẹl). Even in UA as understood at the time Whorf and Trager wrote, it was clear that '(finger)nail' had two syllables, although in the WT comparison the -tV syllable of UA is not paired with anything in KT. In WT2 (UA se^x-, se^xpa 'cold, ice' [see Miller 1987:168]—PT *ciya), presumably it is only the first syllable that is matched, with no explanation given for the other material in the word. Some other examples which appear also to suffer from this shortcoming are: WT1, 2, 7, 9, 11, 13, 18, 19, 20, 23, 25, 32, 40, 47, 49, 51, 52, 53, 59, 60, 61, 65. Shaul, who examined only forms with *l* or *r*, also found that "there is nothing in the KT data directly comparable to the UA data" (1985:584) in eight sets; he found similar problems in a number of other sets.

The onomatopoetic and expressive/affective symbolic forms are as follows:

WT45, D12 UA *puca 'blow'; KT *p^huce, *p^hud
D61 Proto-Numic *hahk^wa 'blow (wind)'; KT *g^wọ 'wind'
WT15, D93 UA *hi 'breathe'; KT *họ 'breath, breathe'
D4 UA *pon 'drum'; KT *pụ 'drum, bell, sound'
WT62, D74 UA ya 'sing'; KT *dzo (WT PT yo)
WT67, D107 UA ʔowaa (WT UA ʔu-, hu-) 'child'; KT *ʔu 'small, child' (WT PT u(u)-)
D65 UA *cun 'suck'; KT *cụ, *cẹ 'nurse'.

Also, nearly all the bird terms cited by Whorf and Trager involve the problem of onomatopoeia:

WT5, WT46, WT55, D70 UA *cutu 'bird' (Hopi 'bluebird'); PT *c^hu(l) 'bluebird'
WT5 UA ciru, cucu 'bird'; PT ciyw
WT46 UA saʔa 'jay'; PT se 'bluejay'
WT55 UA curu 'bluebird'; PT sule (D70 corrects some of the confused overlapping etymological comparisons of WT)
D87 PU *muhu 'owl'; KT *mọhụ
WT54 UA cu^x-, cuya, cu^xta 'to drip'
Probably also WT23 UA k^wa-, ko- 'wolf, coyote'; PT ko-l 'wolf'

Some possibly diffused items are:

WT8, D38 UA *totoli 'chicken' (WT UA toḷi, tuḷi 'hen'; compare 'turkey'); KT *delu 'chicken, fowl' (WT PT dilu)—The UA forms on which WT8 is based (Whorf and Trager gave Aztec [Nahuatl] totol-in, Papago čučuli [< tutuli], Tarahumara toli) are internally diffused among

Southern Uto-Aztecan languages, and very similar terms are so widely diffused among Mesoamerican languages that it is impossible to determine in most cases their origin or direction of diffusion (see examples in Chapter 1).

WT81 musa 'cat, feline animal'—This is a well-known loan from Spanish (see Davis 1987:377; see also above).

WT16, D43 Proto-Numic *ku(h)cuN 'buffalo'; KT *kon—Terms for 'buffalo' are widely diffused in the Plains languages and other languages (see examples in Chapter 1), and terms similar to these strongly suggest borrowing is involved here as well (compare Atapaka cokoñ; see A. R. Taylor 1976).

D17 UA *paci 'corn (ear)'; KT *p'ëa 'fresh corn'—The UA form has a disputed etymology; it certainly does not extend across the whole family, and it appears to fall into the large array of Mesoamerican and other Mexican languages which appear to have borrowed similar forms very widely.[24] In any case, terms for 'corn' might easily be borrowed.

D11 UA *pipa 'tobacco'; KT *p^hi 'smoke (verb)'—Similar forms for 'tobacco' appear to be diffused among several languages of North America[25] (see Miller 1987:138).

WT47, D22 UA *ti- 'deer'; KT *të 'elk' (WT UA teke 'deer'; PT tə(x) 'elk')—Even Whorf and Trager identified some of the forms cited as possible loans (1937:622). The UA forms are limited to Northern UA languages (Miller 1987:194–5).

WT50, D35 UA *tɨpa 'pine nut'; KT *t'ou (WT UA teva^x-; PT t'ow—The UA forms again are found only in Northern UA languages (Miller 1987:195).

Shaul (1985:586) viewed the matchings involving *l* and *r* as evidence of probable diffusion, rather than as support for the Azteco-Tanoan **l and **r Whorf and Trager had proposed, since the UA forms WT cite with *l* (or *r*), compared to KT forms with *l* or *r*, in fact reflect PUA *n (Southern Uto-Aztecan *l/r corresponds to Northern UA *n), not PUA *l or *r, as Whorf and Trager thought (see Chapter 4), but their matchings are not in forms reflecting UA *n compared with KT *l* or *r*.

Wide semantic latitude in the comparison between the two families is involved in the following sets: WT4 'shut a sack, wrap, wind, pressing together' / 'gather'; WT10 'twist, ball' / 'circle'; WT17 'tree, wood (stick, plant)' / 'leaf, inflorescence'; WT22 'oak (compress, leather)' / 'metal, iron, hard'; WT28 'speak'/'mouth'; WT35 'walk, run' / 'come'; WT36 'twist (curl, fire drill, turn [by twisting])' / 'return'; WT54 'drip'/'drink'; WT63 'run, stray, rush' / 'come'. (For semantic differences that are not so unlikely as these, see WT3, 5, 18, 25, 26, 32, 34, 48, and 57.)

Nursery words (of the mama, papa, nana, tata/dada, caca sort) are seen in the following sets:

> WT89, D24 UA *ta, *tata 'father; KT *ta, *tata
> WT38, D1 UA *pa 'older brother'; KT *pa-, *po-
> D19 UA *pa 'aunt', *paci 'older sister'; KT *p'a 'sister'—The UA form *paci, which Davis glossed as 'older sister', should be eliminated from this equation because it means 'older brother' in all the branches of the family except Numic (see Miller 1987:127, 132). It is quite possible that the two sets, D1 'older brother' and D19 'aunt, older sister', are not two separate etyma but belong to the same cognate set.
> D42 UA *ka 'grandmother'; KT *ka, *ko 'mother, aunt'—In the majority of UA languages, this cognate means 'grandparent (grandfather and grandmother)'; in most it is two syllables long, approximating kakV.

In a number of the Whorf and Trager sets, the UA forms include noncognates, leaving their reconstruction inaccurate or highly suspect. Two examples were already mentioned: WT7 UA 'dark, black' and WT17 UA 'tree, wood, stick, plant'. WT21 UA 'corn', / Aztec ka·- 'roasted corn' cannot be cognate with the others—Hopi ka?ö 'corn'; Southern Paiute ka?o (the similarity between the latter two suggests diffusion); Opata käwotü 'pluck corn'—since Aztec l corresponds to n in these other languages (which is not present in these forms). Borrowing is also suggested for these (see D47). WT22 UA Aztec kʷe[:]čoa 'compress' (actually 'to grind') and kʷetlaš- 'leather' (Proto-Nahua *kʷətla-) are in no way related etymologically, and neither is cognate with Luiseño kʷi·la 'oak' or Southern Paiute kwiya- 'scrub oak' cited by Whorf and Trager. In WT26 UA 'tail, drag, limp, lame', the forms meaning 'tail' reflect PUA *kʷasi (Miller 1987:84–5) and are not related to Tübatulabal wə·gi·n- 'drag', Opata gʷito 'limp', Aztec kʷin- 'lame', or Cora kʷanaše 'be tired'. In fact, the

Aztec term is spurious; it is chopped out of tenkwinoa 'to limp, be lame' but no such root exists.[26] WT40 UA 'flower' is based solely on Tübatulabal ibi·- 'flower', ibi·?- 'to bloom' and Aztec <ic-molini> [(i)tsmoli:ni] 'to bud', which are in no way related. There is no evidence in Nahuatl that the portion its- is an identifiable morpheme; the only thing close would be its- 'obsidian, obsidian blade', which is an unlikely incorporation in such a word, which in any case would not be cognate with the Tübatulabal 'flower / to bloom' form.

A few forms are morphologically complex, but are not recognized as such in the comparison. The example of WT7 'dark, black' (discussed above) involved a complex KT form for which Whorf and Trager had failed to recognize the root; WT56 UA waˣki 'dry, thin' and PT wok'i 'thin' appears to be another example. Whorf and Trager cast doubt on their own form; in PT they found it represented only in Taos wok'i 'thin', about which they said: "But if this is merely wo not + k'imã thick, then the AT [Azteco-Tanoan] reconstruction must be discarded" (1937:623). Davis (1987:373) did not accept this form and found a UA *w : KT *w correspondence supported by only one proposed cognate, WT58/ D90, a monosyllabic form meaning 'two'. For WT13 'open, hole, be stuck through', Shaul (1985:584) identified the UA forms as morphologically complex, bearing the suffix *-la 'causative'. I am not sufficiently familiar with KT languages to make a well-informed determination, but I suspect from the forms and glosses cited in a number of the WT sets that a number of similar noncognates and forms whose morphological analysis has not been recognized are joined on that side of the equation as well.

A few sets that are questionable because of the problem of pan-Americanisms are: WT2 'cold',[27] WT33 'hand',[28] WT37/D89 'I', WT66/ D101 'you', WT20/D45 'foot',[29] WT71/D63 'dog',[30] D19 'aunt, older sister',[31] WT79/D88 'to give'.[32] (Compare also WT9 'foot', WT13 'hole', WT87/D14 'tie', WT20/D45, WT18/D52 'lie, sit, be', WT35 'come', D21 'go', and D81 'excrement'.)

A number of the comparisons involve not a full cognate set from each of the language families but an isolated form from a single language in the family. As discussed in Chapter 7, such comparisons are far less persuasive than comparisons in which the forms can be demonstrated to have a legitimate etymology within their own language family. WT6 'squirrel' illustrates this; in UA this set has only Tübatulabal *ca·wane^n-*, and in PT it has only Taos *c'uwala-*.

If we eliminate all the examples with problems which are discussed in this section (or if we at least relegate them to a secondary status, that of less persuasive forms), in order to determine what could form the basis of a solid hypothesis, we find that the following WT forms remain:

WT12 'stand', UA *wine/wene/wi^n-*; PT *g^{w}ine*

WT31/D85, UA *siwa·-* 'woman'; PT *łiw-* (D KT *siu)

WT39 'three', UA *pahi*; PT *poyuwo* (D2 UA *pahi/*pahayu*; KT *podzu(a)/*pocua)

Perhaps D3 (see WT84) Proto-Numic *pi(h)wɨ, *pi(h)yɨ* 'heart'; KT *pia(D)

D14 (see WT87) UA *pu:la* 'tie'; KT *p^{h}ę, *p^{h}ęlę* 'wrap, tie' (Similar forms are known from a number of other Native American language families.)

This is not a very impressive list. Even if we throw in for good measure some of the more attention-getting short forms, such as WT41/D16 'water' (UA *pa[:]-*; KT *p'o); WT58/D90 'two' (UA *wa, *wo; KT *wi), the situation is not substantially improved. My general conclusion concerning the Aztec-Tanoan hypothesis is that the evidence presented in its favor so far falls far short of what would be necessary to warrant a positive feeling toward the hypothesis. In particular, in the absence of morphosyntactic evidence, the hypothesis comes across as very weak. Although the evidence offers very little to convince skeptics, there is enough to suggest that the hypothesis should not be rejected outright. It needs more study.

The Quechumaran Proposal
+50% probability, 50% confidence

The hypothesis that Quechua and Aymara (or, better said, that the Quechuan and Aymaran language families)[33] are related is old, persistent, and very controversial.[34] The name *Kechu-maran* for this proposed distant genetic relationship was coined by Mason (1950); the spelling used today is *Quechumaran* (after Orr and Longacre 1968). Since Quechumaran is examined in detail and new evidence is considered in Campbell (1995), here I do not repeat the evidence but rather limit the following discussion to some of the methodological issues involved. As will be seen, the arguments against the Quechumaran proposal are mostly without foundation. The additional evidence that has been presented in Campbell (1995) is suggestive of a genetic relationship but unfortunately is inconclusive. Therefore, the question of whether these two families are genetically related needs to be left open.

It will be good to keep Southern Quechua and its submember, Southern Peruvian Quechua, in mind for the following discussion, since much of the debate involves these varieties. (For the internal classification of these two families, see Chapter 6.)

Background of the Debate

The supposition that the Quechuan and Aymaran language families are genetically related was accepted by most scholars, though there had been little attempt to demonstrate it, until Orr and Longacre (1968) presented their evidence in support of the relationship.[35] Since then, Andeanists seem to have succumbed to a diffusionist bandwagonism; in article after article they have criticized Orr and Longacre, arguing both that language contact explains the similarities between the two families and that the families have no demonstrable genetic relationship (see Adelaar 1986, 1987; Büttner 1983; Cerrón-Palomino 1986, 1987; Hardman de Bautista 1985; Mannheim 1985, 1991; Parker 1969a; and Stark 1975[1970]). Since 1970 those favoring the genetic proposal and those supporting the contact hypothesis have been pitted against each other; most of the papers on the subject have repeated the same objections to the proposal. It is instructive to review this opposition.

Many scholars imply that acceptance of the diffusion hypothesis means denial of the possibility of a genetic relationship, but this is not necessarily so. In a number of well-known linguistic areas *(Sprachbünde),* clearly identified diffused features define the area and yet some members of the area are genetically related to other languages also found within the linguistic area. That is, the existence of extensive areal borrowing and change due to language contact in no way precludes a genetic relationship among some (and sometimes all) of the languages involved. It is the task of linguists to determine, as far as possible, the true linguistic history of such languages—whether it involve contact or common inheritance (or both). The possibilities in this case are (1) an all-or-nothing diffusionist explanation (witness Bruce Mannheim's statement that "there is good linguistic evidence which actually precludes the genetic hypothesis" [1985:646]) and (2) an explanation involving a combination of genetic relationship and diffusion. The other logical possibility, that all similarities may be due to genetic inheritance, cannot be the case, since clearly some similarities between Quechuan and Aymaran are demonstrably due to borrowing (see below).[36]

It is easy to see why many have thought the two language families might be genetically related. They are neighbors, and Quechuan and Aymaran share numerous similarities in vocabulary, phonology, morphology, and syntax. For example, approximately 20% of the vocabulary of Aymara and Cuzco Quechua is claimed to be identical or very similar (see Mannheim 1985:647, 1991:40). The two families are typologically very similar; both have internally consistent SOV word order and suffixing, and both are agglutinative.[37] At issue is whether, or to what extent, these shared traits and vocabulary are due to borrowing or to inheritance from a common ancestor. Parker argues in support of the former: "When a 200-item basic vocabulary list is used for a lexico-statistical comparison of Cuzco and Bolivian Quechua lexemes with their Aymara and Jaqaru counterparts, the items are found to be either virtually identical or obviously not related—a situation which in itself suggests borrowing"[38] (1969a:84). The main debate has centered on two interrelated issues: (1) which language varieties should be compared and (2) the origin of glottalized and aspirated consonants. I take these up in turn, and then address briefly other arguments against the proposal, as well as some for it.

The Varieties Compared

Most of the linguists who have favored the genetic relationship have unfortunately presented evidence for it only from Southern Quechua varieties (Cuzco-like dialects of Southern Peru and Bolivia), which they compare with some dialect of Aymara, totally neglecting the other branches of the two families. The diffusionists object, with good reason, that protagonists of the genetic hypothesis have not taken into account the internal diversity of the two families, particularly within Quechuan. Only since the 1970s or so has the diversity within Quechuan come to be appreciated (see, for example, Adelaar 1986, 1987; Cerrón-Palomino 1987). Thus, Orr and Longacre's (1968) reconstruction of Proto-Quechua has been criticized because it is based on nine different Quechua varieties, only one of which is from the very divergent Central Quechua branch of the family; their other eight dialects are associated with Southern Quechua (Mannheim 1985:647). Orr and Longacre concentrated on lexical items found in all nine of these varieties, an emphasis that critics assert has skewed the results in favor of "the vocabulary strata associated with the political hegemony" of the Cuzco-based Inca empire (Mannheim 1985:647). Given the linguistic impact of the Inca state and the extensive lexical borrowing that resulted, the focus of Orr and Longacre on dialects closely related to the Cuzco variety (eight of their nine) and their requirement that all nine should have a particular item does constitute a serious problem for their reconstruction. Thus, Orr and Longacre, like most others, drew their Quechuan evidence primarily from Southern Quechua dialects—precisely those varieties most heavily influenced by close contact with Aymaran languages, especially Aymara. They compared their reconstructed Proto-Quechua only with Aymara for arriving at their Proto-Quechumaran conclusions, neglecting Jaqaru and Kawki, the other Aymaran languages held to be structurally more distinct from Quechuan than Aymara (Mannheim 1985:647).

Mannheim (1985:649–57, 1991:43–53) argues against Quechumaran based on the history of the social context of the Quechuan varieties involved in comparisons. He presented historical documentation which demonstrates extensive language contact and multilingualism at the time of European contact in the Southern Quechua area of Peru and Bolivia, where both Puquina and Aymara were much more widely used then than now. It is easy to agree with Mannheim and concede that Southern Peruvian had heavy contact with Aymara (and other languages), but this simply means that some of the similarities shared by the two families are probably areal in nature. As neighbors, they could have been in contact and could have influenced each other regardless of whether they were ever members of a more remote family. The question remains: Are any of the similarities due to genetic inheritance, or are they all a result of contact (and other nongenetic factors)?

Suffice it to say that the fact that comparisons such as Longacre and Orr's rely largely on examples drawn mostly from Southern Quechua dialects does not demonstrate that the hypothesis is wrong. Since these Southern Quechua varieties putatively involve so much borrowing from Aymara, if a more persuasive case is to be made, it is necessary to include evidence also from Central Quechua and other non–Southern Quechua varieties (as in Campbell 1995).

The Issue of Glottalized and Aspirated Consonants

Most Southern Quechua varieties have a clear three-way contrast between plain, glottalized, and aspirated consonants, as in the following: *tanta* 'collect' / *t'anta* 'bread' / *tʰanta* 'old man'; *kanka* 'roast' / *k'anka* 'rooster' / *kʰanka* 'dirty'. As Hardman de Bautista tells us, "the major point of debate [about the Quechumaran proposal] is, and always has been, the question of aspiration and glottalization of the occlusive consonants" (1985:621). Central in this dispute have been claims concerning the origin of the aspirated and glottalized stops and affricates in Quechuan (henceforth *C'* and *Cʰ*, respectively). The views concerning these sounds are of no mean importance, since some Andeanist treatments contradict fundamental concepts of historical-comparative linguistics. Most of those in favor of the diffusionist explanation argue vigorously that these sounds are borrowed into Southern Quechua from Aymara.[39] A number of

observations are cited in support of this diffusion claim (and repeated in nearly all the recent papers touching on the proposal; see Adelaar 1986:386–7 for general discussion). They are discussed in the remainder of this section.

Distribution within Quechuan   It has been claimed that there are no known reflexes of either *C'* or *Cʰ* in the Central Quechua languages; *C'* and *Cʰ* are restricted to those Southern Quechua varieties which have been in contact with Aymaran languages (Mannheim 1985:649, 118). This is taken to indicate that *C'* and *Cʰ* are borrowed into these varieties of Quechua and are not original. Adelaar (1986: 386) goes so far as to assert that if *C'* and *Cʰ* had been in Proto-Quechuan, they would be reflected in some way in the many dialects that make up the Quechua I (Central) and Quechua IIA (a branch of Peripheral Quechua). But why? Why would there necessarily be distinct reflexes of contrasting sounds which totally merged in these dialects and languages? To cite just one example, there are no distinct reflexes in local varieties of Latin American Spanish in their pronunciation of such former contrasts as /lʸ/ with /y/ or /ṣ/ with /s/, now merged to just *y* and *s,* respectively, in most of Latin America. Total merger is a fact of linguistic life; therefore, that possibility here cannot be denied. In any case, the claim that there are no reflexes in Central Quechua is not actually true. Proulx (1974) reported some ten Quechuan cognates which demonstrate the prior existence of aspiration in Central Quechua; he pointed out the correspondence of Central Quechuan *CV:* to the *CʰV* of the Southern Quechuan varieties (for example, Central *pa:ri-*, Southern *pʰala-*, and Proto-Quechuan *pʰarV-* 'to fly').[40]

Moreover, there is evidence that the Ayacucho-Chanka branch of Southern Quechua, which does not now have glottalization, once had it and that therefore glottalization is reconstructible at least for Proto-Southern Quechua. Where the Cuzco-Collao varieties have an initial *h* which was added to vowel-initial forms containing a *C'* (a general process in these dialects), Ayacucho-Chanka has a corresponding *h,* though the glottalization which caused the *h* to be added is no longer present. These correspond to Ø (that is, vowel-initial forms) in Central Quechua.

TABLE 8-4 Comparison of Quechua Glottalization

Gloss	Cuzco-Collao	Ayacucho-Chanka	Ancash
'roasted grain'	hank'a	hamka	ankay
'toad'	hamp'atu	hampatu	ampatuy
'how much'	hayk'a	hayka	ayka

From Mannheim 1991:119; see Cerrón-Palomino 1987:185.

Table 8-4 provides a few examples; for Central Quechua, the Ancash variety is representative, since it preserves the etymological *h* from Proto-Quechua that most other varieties have lost.[41]

Some of the Ayacucho-Chanka dialects do have aspiration, though they lack glottalization (Cerrón-Palomino 1987:183). Southern Ecuadoran varieties (of the Southern Quechua branch) also have aspiration but not glottalization; Parker (1969b:154) and Cerrón-Palomino (1987:183) believe that both *C'* and *C^h* were present but that the glottalized consonants lost their glottalization because of influence from neighboring languages, while some other linguists have assumed that these sounds never existed in Ecuadoran dialects. Ecuadoran dialects also have a series of voiced stops that are found primarily in terms for local flora and fauna, rather than in cognate lexical items, which suggests that language contact is their historical explanation (Cerrón-Palomino 1987:186).

There is an instructive response to the assumption that the presence of *C'* and *C^h* primarily in dialects geographically closest to Aymara suggests they are borrowed. Language contact can not only cause foreign phonological material to be incorporated into a language, it can result in the reinforcement and preservation of native phonological and grammatical features. An example is the preservation of *ʎ* in Andean Spanish (Spanish *ʎ* has merged with *y* in nearly all other Latin American dialects and many Peninsular dialects), attributed to contact with Quechuan and Aymaran, languages that also have /ʎ/. This contact explains the maintenance of this contrast precisely and almost exclusively in the area where the majority of the population consists of Native Americans who speak languages that also have *ʎ* (see Campbell 1985).[42]

This has bearing on the case at hand. The fact that the branch of Quechuan which is geographically closest to the Aymaran languages has *C'* and *C^h*, whereas there is little evidence of them in the other major branch, has been taken by the diffusionists as strong circumstantial evidence that these features in those Quechua dialects are probably borrowed. However, this could well be an instance of preservation of older contrasts due to language contact, just as in the Andean preservation of Spanish *ʎ*. Since glottalization and aspiration are highly marked features, it is not at all implausible that they might merge with their less marked counterparts and be lost in some branches of the family, yet be maintained in varieties that are in contact with other languages that also have these sounds.

Constraints on C' and C^h in Southern Quechua   Glottalization and aspiration in Southern Quechua are subject to rigid distributional restrictions in words. As Hardman de Bautista puts it, "there are . . . extreme phonological limitations in terms of permitted environments" (1985:622). They include the following:

1. *C'* and *C^h* occur on only the first stop or affricate of the word (that is, no stop can be aspirated or glottalized within a word after the first *C'* or *C^h*).
2. *C'* or *C^h* can occur only once in a word; glottalization and aspiration do not occur together within the same word.
3. *C'* and *C^h* occur only syllable-initially, never syllable-finally.
4. A prothetic *h* is added at the beginning of words which contain a *C'* which otherwise would begin with a vowel ($\emptyset \rightarrow$ h / #__V . . . C').[43]
5. *C'* and *C^h* do not occur in bound grammatical morphemes.

(For more detail, see Stark 1979[1975] and Mannheim 1991:204–7; also Hardman de Bautista 1985:622.)

The existence of these constraints on the distribution of *C'* and *C^h* within a word in Southern Quechua, with the corresponding absence of such constraints in Aymaran languages, has been taken to mean that these features are borrowed from Aymaran into Southern Quechua. This is the most frequent argument of those asserting that *C'* and *C^h* were not original in Quechuan. Supporters of the genetic hypothesis, however, see no reason why these features could not have been present in the ancestral language and then have become restricted in their privilege of occurrence in some daughter languages (for example, Southern Quechua); in others, such restrictions could have been lost (as in Aymaran) or with these phonetic features might even have disappeared altogether (as in other branches of Quechuan) (Cerrón-Palomino 1987:358). For example, while Proto-Salishan and most other Salishan languages have no such distributional restrictions on their glottalized consonants, Shuswap innovated, deglottalizing all but the last glottalized obstruent in a root (Kinkade et al. in press).

There is a methodologically revealing response to this claim as well. It has been hypothesized as a general principle that in areal borrowing, segments tend not to be subject to the distributional restrictions that hold in the donor languages (Campbell 1976:83, 191–2). If this principle is valid, one would expect fewer, not more, distributional restrictions on the occurrence of *C'* and *C^h* in Southern Quechua words if these were borrowed sounds, and this would cast doubt on the diffusionist interpretation of the origin of these features in Quechuan.[44]

Differential Similarity to Aymaran of C'/C^h *Roots and Non-*C'/C^h *Roots* It has been claimed that Southern Quechua lexical stems with *C'* and *C^h* are disproportionately more similar to Aymara in sound and meaning (67%) than are lexical stems with neither of these features (only 20% similar):

> Given that the features ejectivity [glottalization] and aspiration have a far more restricted distribution [within words] in the Quechua varieties which use those features than in the Jaqi [Aymaran] languages, in very many cases the direction of the loan process—from the Jaqi languages to the Quechua—is fairly clear. . . . A claim of the op-

posite loan direction forces the analyst to claim that subsequent ejective or aspirated stops in the Jaqi stem in question are acquired entirely arbitrarily whereas from the Quechua side there is an independently motivated explanation for the loss of ejectivity and aspiration from stops which follow the first stop in the word. (Mannheim 1985:658; see also Mannheim 1991:53–4, Stark 1979[1975]).

This might be true if we could be absolutely certain that all instances of *C'* and *C^h* in Quechua were borrowed; but if they are inherited in the two language families, then Quechuan could have easily innovated the distributional restrictions on the features' occurrence in roots later (along the lines of Grassmann's law, which eliminates sequences of voiced aspirates [in the traditional reconstruction of Indo-European] by regressively dissimilating the first voiced aspirate in a word in Greek and Sanskrit). Moreover, just as Quechua varieties have propagated these features farther in the lexicon into nonetymological environments as a result of onomatopoeia and symbolic/affective formations (see below), some portion of the Aymara lexical items with multiple instances of *C'* and/or *C^h* may have undergone similar change. More importantly, the number of such Aymara (or Aymaran) loans in varieties of Quechuan or the presence or absence of *C'* and *C^h* in Proto-Quechua cease to be so weighty if other evidence of genetic relationship is found. Moreover, if some instances of these sounds are due to borrowing and others to symbolic expansion in Aymara (as is argued at least for Quechuan, see below, see also Mannheim 1985:659–70), this could hamper our ability to detect true cognates containing these features, if there is a genetic relationship. That the task is complicated, however, does not rule out the possibility of a genetic explanation for at least some of the words sharing these features in the two language families.

Instances of Nonoriginal C' *and* C^h *in Southern Quechua* A group of arguments against Quechumaran involves the citation of instances of *C'* or *C^h* for which there is reason to think that they were not original in Quechua, but rather have some secondary, nonetymological origin, with the fallacious implication that if any examples of *C'/C^h* prove not to be original, then none are original, implying further that Quechuan and Aymaran are therefore not genetically related. These conclusions do not follow, however, as will be seen in the following examination of three such arguments: those pointing to variation within Quechuan dialects, Spanish loans containing these sounds, and the utilization of these sounds for functional symbolic purposes.

Stark (1979[1975]) argued that the presence of C' and C^h in the Quechua of Cuzco, Cochabamba, and Sucre (closely related dialects of Southern Peru and Bolivia) varies so much in cognate material that reconstruction of the two features is problematic "even at the lowest taxonomic node in Quechua subgroupings" (Mannheim 1985:659; see also Mannheim 1991:53, 54). There are also cases of variation within the same Quechua dialect, even in the speech of the same individual, and doublets of related lexical items exist in which one has the glottalization or aspiration and the other does not (for example, in Cuzco Quechua $al^ypa/hal^yp'a$ 'ground', $haqay/haq^hay$ 'that [one]', $č^haqay/čaqay$ 'that [one over yonder] ') (Mannheim 1985:659, 1991:54; Stark 1979[1975]). It is, of course, not unknown for languages to have lexical doublets as a result of the different reactions of lexical items to sound changes, often involving mixture of social or regional dialects. (Some examples are English *curse/cuss, arse/ass, vermin/varmint, university/varsity*; compare forms reflecting the initial voicing of fricatives in some Southern English dialects but not in others, such as *vixen* and *fox*; and Spanish forms with and without loss of earlier initial /h/, such as *jalar* [xalár], /x/ < /h/, and *halar* [alár], with initial O (< /h/), both meaning 'to pull'.) Such variation does not preclude a genetic relationship, in spite of the apparent insinuation of diffusionists to this effect. Methodologically, it makes sense to avoid placing weight on forms that vary in this way and to rely instead on other, less problematic, evidence. However, it is a fallacy to assume that because some forms exhibit variation in C' and C^h (and hence may not be original), all instances of C' and C^h (including those which do not vary) must also be secondary in origin.

There is evidence that a number of Quechua words recently acquired aspiration and glottalization for expressive reasons (Mannheim 1986:

415–16, 1991:53). Mannheim argued that C' and C^h have diffused within Southern Quechua through certain semantic domains "by means of associative lexical influence" (1991:54; this was called "metaphoric iconicity" in Mannheim 1986), in most cases for symbolic/affective purposes—which Mannheim 1986 calls "imageal iconic" (for example, in forms meaning 'narrow space' $k'iski$, $t'iqi$, $q'iqi$, 'narrow object' $k'ikl^yu$, $p'iti$, and 'foam' p^husuqu, p^huqpu, p^hul^ypu) (see Parker 1969a:85, Mannheim 1985:659–70; see also Cerrón-Palomino 1987:253). Mannheim says of these that "the words for 'narrow' . . . are examples of both associative lexical influence and sound symbolism; they are sound symbolic in that the ejective feature reflects 'narrowness', as does the preponderance of high, front (narrow) vowels in the set" (1991:55). Aspiration in the demonstrative deictics was also imported for emphatic expressive purposes, giving the doublets kay/k^hay 'this', $čay/č^hay$ 'that', and $haqay/haq^hay$ 'that (yonder)' (Cerrón-Palomino 1987:358). Stark reported that "of the 33% of the Quechua words [with C' or C^h] which did not have similar forms in Aymará, 66% were later judged by Cuzco and Bolivian Quechua speakers to be either onomatopoetic or ideophonic" (1979[1975]:212). Hardman de Bautista asserted the figure that "22 percent of those [words] with aspiration and glottalization were judged by native speakers to be onomatopoetic, but only two percent of those without were so judged" (1985:624). This claim is difficult to assess, since we are not told the details of how the native speakers were instructed to identify onomatopoeia, what forms they examined, or even how many subjects were involved in the experiment. Linguists may be better judges of onomatopoeia, unlike in other domains of the vocabulary, in some languages than are the native speakers unless there is something in the speakers' folk linguistics that formally identifies onomatopoetic formations.

The sound-symbolic and affective deployment of such features as glottalization and aspiration has been observed with some frequency in other languages (Campbell in press c), where these features come to be employed for symbolic/iconic reasons in words where they do not etymologically belong. While this can make it difficult to determine whether individual lexical items have inherited the feature or whether they acquired it later for symbolic/affective reasons, the deployment of a phonological attribute for such purposes in and of itself does not tell us whether the feature entered that language through inheritance or through borrowing. In the case of Quechua C' and C^h, either is possible, and it is the task of the linguist to try to see beyond any later symbolic/affective motivation for spread of the features within the language in order to determine their real origins.

If the claim that these features are deployed for sound-symbolic reasons is accurate, it means methodologically only that in some instances the glottalized consonants are reflexes of formerly nonglottalized sounds. That some current glottalized and aspirated sounds are not original does not support the inference that all instances of such sounds must have a secondary origin. For example, some Sanskrit d's do not hark back to Proto-Indo-European $*d$ (in traditional reconstruction) but rather to $*dh$ in forms affected by Grassmann's law (according to which some $*dh$'s were dissimilated to d), but this does not imply that *none* of the Sanskrit d's can go back to Proto-Into-European $*d$, which in fact the majority of Sanskrit d's do reflect.

C' and C^h are also found in a few Spanish loanwords, perhaps due to the spread of these features for symbolic/affective reasons (Mannheim 1985:659–60). Some examples are: $k^huči$ 'pig' (Spanish *coche*), p^hustul^yu 'blister' (Spanish *pústula*), $hač'a$ 'axe' (Spanish *hacha* [$hač'a$ is Cuzco Quechua; compare *hača* Cochabamba Quechua]), $hasut'i$ 'whip' (Spanish *azote*), $limp^hiyu$ 'clean' (Spanish *limpio* [$limp^hu$ in Cochabamba Quechua])[45] (Stark 1979[1975]:212, Mannheim 1985:659–60, Cerrón-Palomino 1987:357). Again, the fact that the C' and C^h of some words may not descend directly from the proto language does not preclude the possibility that these features in other words were so inherited, if these languages prove to be related.

It has been observed that "many (though not all) of the words that had apical affricates and sibilants in proto-Quechua have ejectives in Southern Peruvian Quechua, though not necessarily in the same place in the word" (Mannheim 1991:55); the affricate itself was glottalized when it was word-initial and the initial stop of the word was glottalized when this affricate was

not in initial position (Mannheim 1985:660). Again, if this proves to be an accurate interpretation, it means only that some instances of C' are not reflexes of original glottalized sounds, just as they were not in the cases where C' and C^h were added for symbolic-affective purposes and in the Spanish loans. That some current glottalized and aspirated sounds do not descend from sounds which originally had these features is already known and does not support the inference that C' or C^h cannot be original in other words that have them.

Functional Load   Mannheim argues that the information-bearing ability of Southern Peruvian Quechua syllables (described as highly influenced by recent changes in the varieties which "acquired" glottalization and aspiration) indicates a more recent addition of C' and C^h to these dialects, though he admits that "this argument is more speculative than the others" (1991:55). In the Cuzco-like dialects which have the three-way contrast between plain, glottalized, and aspirated stops, the contrast occurs only syllable-initially, while syllable-final stops and affricates have undergone reductions, mostly becoming corresponding fricatives. In the Ayacucho-type dialects, there is no such three-way contrast and syllable-final obstruents have maintained their integrity. Mannheim calculates that "almost twice as much information is carried in the selection of a consonant-vowel combination in Cuzco as in Ayacucho"; however, the syllable-final consonant of Ayacucho, not having undergone the lenitions and mergers that the Cuzco variety did, carries a greater informational load, such that "the CV(C) combination in Ayacucho has a mean frequency of .00216 and in Cuzco of .00222"—that is, roughly equivalent when *CVC* rather than just *CV* is taken into account (1985:662). Mannheim explains: "In other words, in a Cuzco-Collao Quechua dialect that has undergone the weakenings and mergers of consonants at the ends of syllables, the information carried by the canonical syllable is of the same scale as the canonical syllable of Ayacucho-Chanka Quechua *without the ejectives and aspirates, and without the consonant weakenings and mergers*" (1991:56). Mannheim's conclusion from this is "it appears that the erosion of syllable-finals in the Cuzco variety represents a kind of compensation for the addition of glottalization and aspiration to the phonological system, an informational readjustment in the sound pattern relative to a fairly constant morpho-semantic system" (1985:662).

Since it is clear from historical attestations and internal evidence that the Cuzco-type dialects formerly had both the syllable-initial *C'* and *Cʰ,* and the nonmerged, nonlenited syllable-final stops and affricates simultaneously (Cerrón-Palomino 1987, 1990), Mannheim's argument is indeed curious. Clearly there are other languages with such features that have not "readjusted" their syllable-final stops and affricates, and it is apparent from historical attestations that colonial Quechua had not done so yet, either, at least not to the degree evident today. Therefore, it would be more accurate to say that the presence of *C'* and *Cʰ permitted* the erosion of syllable-finals in the Cuzco variety, given the built in redundancy and the high informational load that such noneroded syllables bore. To say, as Mannheim does, that the syllable-final erosion in Cuzco "represents a kind of compensation for the addition of glottalization and aspiration" is to suggest a causal relationship and to imply that *C'* and *Cʰ* must have been added late, since otherwise the erosions would have been necessary earlier with the earlier existence of these features, a situation belied by the colonial attestation of noneroded syllable-final stops and affricates. However, the presence of *C'* and *Cʰ* in no way required the erosions but perhaps merely allowed them, since the information-bearing content of the syllables with *C'* and *Cʰ* was robust enough to carry the appropriate word-discriminating signals even without the information that the noneroded syllable-finals could contribute. Since there is no reason to think that the erosion of the syllable-finals is in any way necessary (it is merely possible), this argument has no force.

Ironically, a different argument attributes the exact opposite significance to the functional weight of *C'* and *Cʰ*. It is claimed that since "even within Cuzco Quechua the functional load of aspiration and glottalization is very light" (Hardman de Bautista 1985:622), by implication these features may well be present due to borrowing, given that they are not very responsible for information bearing in Southern Peruvian

Quechua. Of course, it is typical for marked phonological features (where borrowing is not at issue) to be considerably less frequent than their unmarked counterparts—that is, for their functional load to be less.

Related to these notions of information-bearing capacity and functional load is Stark's (1979[1975]) count in a running text of 1,000 words from both Bolivian Quechua (Cochabamba) and Aymara, where she found that only 16.5% of the words in the Quechua text contained glottalized or aspirated sounds, whereas 33% of the words in the Aymara text had them. Such a difference is hardly surprising, however, since some common grammatical suffixes in Aymara contain these features but Quechua suffixes do not; in any case, sounds do exhibit different frequencies of occurrence from language to language, regardless of whether or not they are native sounds. Such a difference need not relate at all to whether or not these sounds might be borrowed.

Although it is possible that the diffusionists are right, that *C'* and *Cʰ* in Quechuan might owe their origin to contact with Aymaran languages, certain considerations should be taken into account that tend to weaken their arguments and thus strengthen the possibility that glottalization and aspiration are inherited features found already in Proto-Quechuan.

Problems with the Orr and Longacre Reconstruction   It is now generally conceded that Orr and Longacre (1968) failed to distinguish between "hechos de convergencia y otras semejanzas de orden más fundamental" (matters of convergence and other similarities of a more fundamental order) (Adelaar 1986:380). However, some scholars seem to have assumed that by pointing out the many problems with the evidence for Quechumaran presented by Orr and Longacre, they were demonstrating that the genetic hypothesis could not possibly be correct. According to Hardman de Bautista, 25% (63) of Orr and Longacre's 253 proposed cognates "must be eliminated from consideration because they are either non-existent forms, incorrectly stated forms, or complex forms poorly analyzed." Of the 190 remaining forms, "46% have a phonological structure that points to borrowing from Jaqi into Quechua rather than historical correspondence"; 26% "are pan-Andean words" that "do not really serve to prove anything one way or the other at this point, but could be used as evidence of widespread trade"; 20% "are terms shared only by Cuzco Quechua and Aymara, that is, they are characteristic of the Southern Andes, rather than of the respective language families"; and 5% "are clearly borrowings from Quechua to Aymara, mostly recent ones." . . . We have a remainder of only two percent, that is, four items, which could indeed be put forth as 'proof' of the common genetic origin of Quechua and Aymara" (1985:620–21). One problem is that since Hardman de Bautista did not tell us which of Orr and Longacre's lexical sets fall into which of these categories, we cannot check her judgment in these matters.[46] This notwithstanding, her criticism has been taken as having effectively demolished Orr and Longacre's proposal and by inference as making the genetic hypothesis in general extremely unlikely, particularly since Orr and Longacre's study is the only detailed favorable consideration of the hypothesis (see Cerrón-Palomino 1987:360).

A response to the claim that Orr and Longacre's (1968) failure to demonstrate the relationship signifies that there is no relationship is that Orr and Longacre failed only to present a convincing case, not that such a case could never be made. Additional research may help resolve this matter.

Adelaar's Basic Vocabulary Argument

Adelaar (1986:382) claimed that genetic kinship, if one existed, ought to be visible in such basic lexical items as shown in Table 8-5. I have added Spanish and English equivalents for comparison.

Adelaar does not say that lexical comparisons of this sort preclude the possibility of a genetic relationship, but he and others cast doubt on that possibility by citing lexical differences such as these and contrasting them to lexical similarities interpreted as probable loans. However, the presentation of a few dissimilar forms—an argument from negative evidence—is never a convincing argument against a possible genetic relationship, given what is known about lexical replacement and change. Even languages known to be related can exhibit considerable differences in precisely the vocabulary that no longer clearly reveals cognates. Thus, the comparison of the equivalent forms above in Spanish and English, languages known to be related, scarcely fares better than Adelaar's Quechua-Aymara comparisons, though many other Spanish-English cognates are known (many of the basic body parts, for example).

Other Positive Considerations

Standard Application of the Comparative Method Diffusionists typically assume that C' and C^h are present in Quechua only as a result of borrowing from Aymara, and therefore they simply ignore these features in their comparative reconstructions. However, these features are present in many of the Southern Quechua forms they presume to be cognate with forms from elsewhere in the Quechuan family which lack these features. The standard application of the comparative method dictates that if a correspondence cannot be explained away by some other means, then it must be assumed to have been present in the proto language. This would be similar, for example, to the case of the three-way Proto-Indo-European contrast in stops, represented here by the alveolar series $*t/$ $*d$ / $*d^h$, merging to t in Tocharian.[47] It is not the mergers in Tocharian which determine the

TABLE 8-5 Basic Lexical Items

Quechua	Aymara	Jaqaru	Spanish	English
wata-	činu-		amarrar (atar)	'to tie'
puñu-	iki-	iki-	dormir	'to sleep'
wasi	uta	uta	casa	'house'
alʸqu	anu		perro	'dog'
yaku	uma	uma	agua	'water'
suk/huk	maya	maya	uno	'one'
sinqa	nasa	nasa	nariz	'nose'

reconstruction of the Indo-European stop series but rather the overall comparative evidence. Just so, the resolution of the question of the origin of C' and C^h in Quechuan will have to depend on something other than just their presence or absence in Quechua dialects and the geographical distribution of the features in the Quechua-speaking region.

Since correspondence sets with C' and C^h are distinct from those without these features, they are to be treated differently in the reconstruction unless the C' and C^h can be explained as being derived in some way from the plain C that diffusionists assume these reflect in the proto language. It is one thing to know that some words containing these features are borrowed and that some others are of secondary origin, and it is quite another thing to assume that a large number of native etyma have come to contain these features in a rather arbitrary manner due to language contact. Although this could be the case (see Campbell 1976b), it will not do merely to assume it. In the context of this debate, it should perhaps be mentioned that Eastern Armenian, dialects of Ossetic, and some other Indo-European languages of the area have acquired glottalization through contact with their non-Indo-European neighbors of the Caucasus (Trubetzkoy 1931:233, Vogt 1954:371). Bielmeier (1977:43) shows that, just as in Quechua, the foreign glottalization comes to be used more widely in native Ossetic words for "expressive" and "onomatopoetic" purposes. Glottalization in these Indo-European languages, which has been discussed in a number of different contexts, has not caused problems for determining their genetic affiliation. We can simply ignore the forms with C' and still be assured of a more than adequate corpus attesting the Indo-European relationship of these two languages. I suspect the same ought to be true with regard to the problem of the origin of C' and C^h in Quechuan.

The Liabilities of Positional Analysis   The only other recent argument in favor of the Quechumaran propsosal is that of Lastra de Suárez (1970), whose support for the genetic hypothesis was based on a comparison of the positional classes of morphemes and grammatical categories in Aymara and Ayacucho-Chanka Quechua,

following the lead of Hymes (1955, 1956). She observed that although the suffixes have different phonological shapes (see also Mannheim 1991:41), they have similar meanings and occupy the same positions in the same relative order in the two languages. This argument fails to be convincing, just as it failed in the cases considered by Hymes (see Chapter 7), for several reasons. First, it violates the principle that only similarities involving both sound and meaning are valid comparisons (Chapter 7). Second, as Mannheim points out, "languages in contact frequently converge to the point that the relative order of grammatical elements matches" (1991: 41; compare Gumperz and Wilson 1971, Nadkarni 1975, and Thomason and Kaufman 1988). Third, there are typological and semantic iconic reasons for why the affixes are ordered as they are, and the categories are general enough and sufficiently vague "as to constitute virtual analytic universals" (Mannheim 1985:648–9), or, as Cerrón-Palomino puts it, taking these universal and iconic tendencies into account, "bien pueden encontrarse paralelismos sorprendentes entre el quechua y el turco" (surprising parallels between Quechua and Turkish can be found) (1987:362). Fourth, Davidson in a later study similar to that of Lastra de Suárez, concluded that "a detailed analysis of the suffix inventories has revealed no evidence of a decisive nature that would prove descent from a common source" (1977; cited in Mannheim 1985:671). Davidson compared 110 suffixes from Quechua and 151 from Aymara. His main doubts concerning evidence from the affixes for a possible genetic relationship have to do with (1) the lack of significant correspondence in the ordering of semantic features after the root and (2) the diversity of features peculiar to each language. He found some marked similarities in the combinability of classes of morphemes, roots, and themes in the two languages, as Lastra de Suárez had—for example, in both languages the order of nominal suffixes is essentially person + number + case. However, Davidson also found many differences; some categories existed in one language but not the other—for example, the rich system of verbal directionals and locatives in Aymaran languages—and the slots in the strings of affixes occupied by functionally equivalent morphemes frequently did not correspond.

While Davidson's arguments should be taken seriously, the number of morphological differences in two closely related languages can be considerable, and it is only the systematic correspondences or lack thereof that tell us whether they are genetically related. For example, Finnish and Estonian are closely related, on the order of the relationship between Spanish and Portuguese; however, they are like Quechua and Aymara in that they are suffixing, but with Finnish rather more agglutinative, like Quechua (that is, the suffixes and their boundaries are relatively easily identified), while Estonian is more like Aymara, where due to several phonological reductions the suffixes are somewhat more difficult to determine at first glance. Moreover, though closely related, the two languages have a considerable number of morphological and grammatical differences, such as those in the nominal case system, that are comparable with Davidson's differences in verbal directionals and locatives in Aymara and Quechua. For example, the Finnish 'comitative' case -ine-, based on the 'instrumental', is totally distinct from the Estonian 'comitative' case -ka (orthographic -ga), which is from a recent grammaticalization of the postposition -kan(ssa-) 'with'. In Estonian, the 'terminative' case (meaning 'up to, until') is a recent formation which does not exist in Finnish. (On these and other differences, see Laanest 1982:157–76.) It is not difficult to imagine that, in time, the morphologial differences between Finnish and Estonian may become as marked as those between Finnish and Hungarian and even between Finnish and Samoyed. Also, as the attested histories of a number of agglutinative languages (such as the Uralic languages just referred to) show, related languages can undergo different grammaticalizations whereby independent lexical material ultimately becomes attached as grammatical affixes. If these grammaticalizations take place after the breakup of genetically related languages, they can exhibit differences in their morphology, both in terms of what categories they have and the order in which the categories appear. A significant number of such differences have already been found between Central Quechua and Peripheral Quechua, two clearly related languages (Cerrón-Palomino 1987). A comparison of modern English and Russian using Davidson's procedure would surely fail to show little evidence of a genetic relationship.

Some Conclusions

I suspect that the Quechuan and Aymaran families are related, but it should be noted that the evidence is insufficient to support such a conclusion. A conclusion that is warranted, however, is that most of the arguments that have been presented against this genetic proposal have proven irrelevant, insufficient, or wrong, and there are important methodological lessons to be gained from the recognition of their shortcomings. The arguments for the language-contact explanation do demonstrate similarities which are due to borrowing or areal convergence, but since contact-induced change is not in dispute, these arguments are largely beside the point. The issue is whether, after we take into account the effects of language contact, there is any solid evidence of genetic relationship that cannot easily be attributed to diffusion or explained otherwise. I have presented fresh lexical and morphological evidence that is quite suggestive but unfortunately is still inconclusive (Campbell 1995). It is to be hoped that future research will make greater progress towards confirming or disconfirming the hypothesis.

These more detailed evaluations of the Macro-Siouan, Aztec-Tanoan, and Quechumaran hypotheses illustrate both the difficulties and the potential of research on distant genetic relationships, and they show how the methodological considerations discussed in Chapter 7 can be applied in actual case studies. I turn now to the evaluation of the better known of the many other proposals of distant genetic relationship among Native American languages, discussing these in much less detail.

Other Major Proposals

Eskimo-Aleut, Chukotan (American–Arctic–Paleo-Siberian Phylum, Luoravetlan), and Beyond
−25% probability, 20% confidence

The proposal of a genetic relationship between Eskimo-Aleut and so-called Chukotan in northeast Asia (Chukchi-Koryak and Kamchadal) is seen as promising by some reasonable scholars, but little direct research has been undertaken and at present there is not sufficient supporting evidence for it to be embraced uncritically (see Fortescue 1994:11, Hamp 1976, Krauss 1973a, Swadesh 1962, Voegelin and Voegelin 1967:575).[48] The initial attraction to the possibility of a relationship involving languages of northeast Asia and (some) Native American languages appears to have been certain typological similarities, which were commented on by scholars at least as far back as Duponceau (see Chapter 2). Reliance on such typological evidence alone would violate the sound-meaning isomorphism requirement of Chapter 7—that only compared items which involve both sound and meaning are persuasive, which was strongly advocated by Meillet (1958:90) and promoted by Greenberg (1957, 1963). This hypothesized connection is based on the notion that the Eskimo-Aleut's forebears, assumed to be the last Native American group to enter the New World, may have left discernible linguistic relatives behind them in northeastern Siberia.[49]

The notion that a connection may exist between Eskimo and either Uralic or Indo-European (or both) has a tradition going back at least as far as Rasmus Rask, and arguments have been presented both for and against (see, for example, Bergsland 1959; Bonnerjea 1975, 1978; Fortescue 1981, 1988, 1994; Hammerich 1951; Sauvageot 1924, 1953; Thalbitzer 1928, 1945, 1952). Greenberg's Eurasiatic classification is in this tradition and would group these languages and more: it places Eskimo-Aleut together with Indo-European, Uralic, Yukaghir, Altaic (Turkic, Mongolian, Tungusic), Ainu, Korean, Japanese, Nivkh (Gilyak), and Chukotian (1987:331–2, 1990d, 1991; see also Ruhlen 1994a:178–9). The evidence presented for this grouping is unconvincing. Greenberg (1990d) goes further; he finds his Eurasiatic to be basically compatible with the Nostratic hypothesis—where at one time or another some Nostraticist has proposed as a member of Nostratic each of the groups which Greenberg assigns to Eurasiatic. Though Greenberg does not see any immediate Eurasiatic affiliation for Afroasiatic, Dravidian, and Kartvelian, which many scholars assign to Nostratic, he believes they are all related, but that "these relationships are more

remote" (1990d:88). Ruhlen goes even further, arguing that Amerind and Eurasiatic are connected in a very far-flung classification which includes elements of the Nostratic proposal and others (1994b:207–41; see also Ruhlen 1994a). If Eurasiatic cannot be sustained on the basis of legitimate methods and the evidence available, it is out of the question to entertain even more far-flung connections between it and units that other linguists place in one version or another of Nostratic.

In this context it can also be mentioned that Mudrak and Nikolaev (1989) attempt, on the basis of unpersuasive evidence, to relate Gilyak and Chukchi-Kamchatkan to "Almosan-Keresiouan" languages (see Shevoroshkin 1990:8 for expressions of doubt).

The Na-Dene Proposal
0% probability, 25% confidence

Although there are some antecedents (see Chapters 2 and 4), the Na-Dene hypothesis is usually attributed to Sapir (1915c), who proposed a relationship between Haida, Tlingit, and Athabaskan. (Eyak was rediscovered by American linguists in the 1930s.)[50] Earlier, Adelung and Vater (1816) had discussed the similarities observed between Eyak, Tlingit, and Tanaina (Athabaskan), but they interpreted the vocabulary resemblances as the result of borrowing. Radloff's (1857–1858) findings were made more widely known as a result of Krause's (1885) discussion (see Krauss 1964:128). Boas (1894), too, had noted similarities and a possible relationship among these languages, but Horatio Hale's response to his claims was to urge caution: "You say—'It is likely that the Haida are allied to the Tlinget.' I can find no resemblance in the vocabularies, except in the word for *elk,* which is evidently borrowed. It will be well to be cautious in suggesting such relationships, unless there is clear grammatical evidence to confirm the suggestions" (letter to Boas, April 21–22, 1888; quoted in Gruber 1967:28). Swanton (1908b, 1911a:209, 1911b:164) had also suggested a relationship between Haida, Tlingit, and Athabaskan (in letters to Kroeber written in 1904 and 1905; see Golla 1986:27). In his Na-Dene work, Sapir appears to have been following up these suggestions by Boas and Swanton.

While Levine (1979) has frequently been cited recently as the principal source of doubt concerning the Na-Dene proposal, it has, nevertheless, been controversial from the beginning (see Pinnow 1958). After careful assessment of the phonological evidence, Krauss concluded that the question of the Na-Dene hypothesis is "more open than ever" (1964:128; see also Krauss 1965, Pinnow 1964b). As pointed out by Pinnow:

> The chief argument of the advocates of the Na-Dene theory is that the morphological systems of Tlingit, Eyak, and the Athapaskan languages, and to a lesser extent also of Haida, show conspicuous morphological similarities and common features which justify the assumption that they belong to a larger unit. . . . There is, however, a powerful argument against the genetic relationship. . . . These four groups have very few words in common. A glance at their so-called basic vocabularies—the most important words of everyday speech—and at the morphemes in their grammatical systems shows enormous differences which seem to preclude any possibility of genetic relationship. . . . On the other hand . . . their morphological systems also reveal close similarities which cannot possibly be the work of chance. The only way out of this dilemma has been to suppose that borrowing from one language to another took place. (1964b:155)[51]

Those who question the Na-Dene proposal suspect that many of these resemblances are the result of diffusion, accident, and poorly analyzed data. (For an attempt to sort out lexical borrowings, especially those of terms referring to fauna and flora, see Pinnow 1968, 1985.) Jacobsen (1990) reevaluated the lexical evidence; where Levine (1979) thought that only thirty-one sets comparing Haida with the other languages were not otherwise disqualified, Jacobsen opted to save fifty-seven. However, in evaluating these fifty-seven, he found that none of the Haida-Athabaskan pairs fell in the list of most stable meanings and that the compared forms were no more similar than would be expected to occur by chance.

That Haida is related to the other languages is now denied or at least seriously questioned by most specialists (Jacobsen 1993, Krauss 1979, Krauss and Golla 1981:67, Lawrence and Leer 1977, Leer 1991:162, Levine 1979, Pinnow

1964b:156; however, see support from Pinnow 1985, 1990; Greenberg 1987:321–30; and Ruhlen 1994b:91–110).[52] Therefore, it seems best to avoid the potentially misleading term "Na-Dene." Jacobsen's terminology is useful; he refers to the hypothesis of Na-Dene *sensu lato* (that is, essentially as Sapir proposed it, with Haida included—what Levine [1979:157] calls the "classical" Na-Dene hypothesis) and Na-Dene *sensu stricto* (that is, Tlingit and Athabaskan[+ Eyak], but excluding Haida). For now it is best to consider the genetic affiliation of Haida unknown. Levine showed that most of the structural similarities that had been presented as evidence for Haida's connection with other Na-Dene *sensu stricto* languages were due to Swanton's (1911a) misanalysis of Haida data; others involve areal features (see Chapter 9). The lexical evidence has proved especially unconvincing (see especially Levine 1979, Jacobsen 1993).

While most scholars reject this proposal, it has some supporters (see Pinnow 1985, 1990). Greenberg (1987:321–30) and Ruhlen (1994b:91–110) both have a chapter defending it. However, Greenberg's chapter is about disagreements he has with Levine's (1979) methods and presents no new data in support of the hypothesis. Ruhlen's (1994b:91–110) presents in print the Na-Dene "evidence" in Greenberg's unpublished notebook (located in Stanford University Library), listing 324 proposed "etymologies," only about 25 of which overlap with Sapir's (1915c) lexical sets. Of these, 119 lack Haida forms; and since the dispute is largely about whether or not Haida is related to the others, the strength of Ruhlen's argument must rest on the remaining 205 forms, many of which compare only two of the four entities (where Eyak is compared separately from Athabaskan). These forms are replete with problems of the sort discussed in Chapter 7. For example, under the gloss TREE (no. 288), Ruhlen gives Haida *qíit, qēt* 'spruce', Tlingit *k'ɛ* 'log'; this includes short forms and semantic nonequivalences, and only two languages are compared. It is not an atypical example. Of the forms which have Haida comparisons, thirty-nine reflect considerable semantic latitude (for example, no. 20 'blood / be bright / be white'; no. 115 'guts/brains'); ninety-one include short forms; eleven are onomatopoetic (for

example, no. 21 Haida *ux,* Tlingit *'úx* 'blow'—
note that these languages lack labials); nine
appear to be diffused (for example, no. 12 Haida
xúuts 'brown bear', Tlingit *xúts* 'brown bear',
Tsetsaut [Athabaskan] *xɔ* 'grizzly bear',[53] Proto-
Chumash **qus* [phonetically *xus* in most of the
Chumash languages; see Klar 1977:68–9]; the
forms for 'elk' were already identified as loans
by Hale in 1888 [see Gruber 1967:28]); in five
the Haida forms do not have sufficient phonetic
similarity (for example, no. 22 Haida *ʃu-łał*
'blue', Tlingit *khałłeh* 'blue', Eyak *khatl*
'green'); and five are nursery forms (see, for
example, no. 111. Haida *nān* 'grandmother',
and forms *ná, né, nan, -an* 'mother' in several
Athabaskan languages). It is safe to say that
whether a relationship exists between Haida,
Tlingit, and Eyak-Athabaskan cannot be determined on the basis of evidence Ruhlen has
presented.

Pinnow's (1985) evidence is the most extensive to date. He presents many grammatical
similarities, especially involving verbs, but since
the debate is partly about the recognized grammatical similarities, one wonders whether his
body of comparisons really answers the question
of whether borrowing and areal influence account for these similarities. He has a large number of lexical comparisons, about which I would
offer the following cautions. First, he relies
heavily on "word family" comparisons (reservations are expressed concerning them in Chapter
7). Second, although he believes in sound correspondences, he thinks it is too early, in view of
the present state of the research, to attempt to
work them out (1985:33). Third, a majority of
the forms compared are monosyllabic and many
involve considerable semantic latitude. His evidence is suggestive, but it is not conclusive. I
would conclude that the Na-Dene hypothesis, or
more specifically, the genetic affinity of Haida,
is still an open question; Haida might be related
to a Tlingit-Eyak-Athabaskan grouping, but
there is still too much uncertainty.

Tlingit-Eyak-Athabaskan

+75% probability, 40% confidence

Tlingit is usually assumed to be related to Eyak-
Athabaskan, and the two together are sometimes

called Na-Dene (Jacobsen's *sensu stricto*). However, as mentioned, Sapir's (1915c) original Na-
Dene proposal included also Haida, and since
this relationship is now seriously questioned
by most specialists it seems best to avoid the
potentially misleading term "Na-Dene" when
Haida is not part of the proposal. Tlingit, as
Krauss and Golla explain, "bears a close resemblance to Athapaskan-Eyak in phonology and
grammatical structure but shows little regular
correspondence in vocabulary"; therefore, "the
nature of the relationship between Athabaskan-
Eyak and Tlingit remains an open question"
(1981:67). (For "provisional" Tlingit + Eyak-
Athabaskan evidence, see Krauss and Leer 1981,
Leer 1991:162.)[54]

Beyond Na-Dene

The more extreme proposals of distant lin-
guistic kinship involving so-called Na-Dene
languages—such proposed groupings as
Athabaskan - Sino - Tibetan, Na - Dene–Basque
(–North-Caucasian), and Athabaskan-Tlingit-
Yuchi-Siouan—should be discounted, given the
extremely poor quality of current evidence.
Sapir was convinced that Na-Dene and Sino-
Tibetan were connected: "If the morphological
and lexical accord which I find on every hand
between Nadene and Indo-Chinese [Sino-
Tibetan] is 'accidental,' then every analogy on
God's earth is an accident" (letter to Kroeber,
October 1, 1921; quoted in Golla 1984:374; see
Sapir 1925b). Sapir did not pursue this publicly
and most scholars, even in Sapir's lifetime, were
reluctant to accept the notion (but see Tokarev
and Zolotarevskaja 1955). Nevertheless, we
know something today about the "accord" to
which he referred and indeed the "analogies" he
had in mind were in no way outrageous, though
from today's perspective they have nongenetic
explanations. Sapir referred to the "old quasi-
isolating feel" and "tone" of Na-Dene and said
it was similar to "Indo-Chinese," adding that he
found in Tibetan "pretty much the kind of base
from which a generalized Na-dene could have
developed" and citing "some very tempting material points of resemblance":

> Tibetan postpositions *ma* "in" and *du* "to, at", both
> of which, precisely as in Athabaskan and Tlingit,

are used also to subordinate verbs; in both Tlingit and Tibetan the tr[ansitive] verb as such is *clearly* passive [involves ergative constructions]; causative or tr[ansitive] verbs have *s-* prefixed in Tibetan, *si-* and *łi-* in Tlingit, *ł-* in Ath[abaskan]; Tibetan verb ablaut is staggeringly like Déné-Tlingit (e.g. present *byed* "make", pret[erite] *byas,* fut[ure] *bya,* imperative *byos*); and so on. Am I dreaming? At least I know that Déné's a long shot nearer Tibetan than to Siouan. (Letter to Kroeber, October 4, 1920; quoted in Golla 1984:350)

Such evidence would have seemed more striking in the 1920s than it does today, since now we know that there is nothing particularly unusual about "quasi-isolating" typology in languages of the world or the Americas (see, for example, Otomanguean languages, some of which were also suspected of having affinities with Chinese [or Sino-Tibetan]; see Chapter 2). The tones of Athabaskan languages are now known to be secondary, not reconstructible to Proto-Athabaskan, and to have arisen in normal sound changes from segmental phonology (see Chapter 4; similarly, the tonal contrasts in Sino-Tibetan languages are now known to have developed along normal paths of tonogenesis and were not a feature of the proto language). This diminishes considerably the initial attractiveness of a possible Sino-Tibetan connection with Athabaskan. Postpositions with relational/locative senses that became grammaticalized as markers of subordination are also unremarkable for they are found frequently in other languages, specifically in those with SOV order, including various Native American families (see Craig and Hale 1992). The passive nature of transitive verbs in Tlingit and Tibetan reflects the ergativity which is characteristic of these languages, but this is typologically common; some scholars have thought (erroneously) that ergativity derives from an earlier passive construction in all ergative languages. This is certainly true for some languages, but it is not the source of ergativity for all of them (see Harris and Campbell 1995:243–8, 419). The ablaut and causative prefixes (signaled by short forms with unmarked consonants) could easily be accidental. For example, Jicaque has very similar ablauted forms. Thus, although Sapir had legitimate reasons for entertaining the possibility

of such a relationship, the sort of evidence he had in mind is far from compelling today.

Shafer (1952, 1969) followed up on Sapir's Na-Dene–Sino-Tibetan hypothesis with evidence that was not very persuasive, and this prompted Swadesh to report his recollections of Sapir's discussion of the topic in lectures at Yale, together with his own examination of the hypothesis. Swadesh repeats that there were broad structural similarities, particularly in the tendency for prefixing and noted "old formative suffixes," as well as a body of Sapir's "cognates with regular phonetic correspondences" (Swadesh 1952:178). Shafer had compared Sino-Tibetan only with Athabaskan, and Swadesh said he had "found Tlingit and Haida parallels for about one fourth of Shafer's comparisons," which he presented (1952:179–80), along with eight new lexical comparisons of his own. All in all, this is not a very persuasive case.[55]

More recently, a number of mostly Russian scholars—Starostin (1989, 1991) in particular—who are sympathetic to the Nostratic hypothesis and other very far-flung proposals of genetic relationship, have collectively advanced the hypothesis that Na-Dene belongs in a grouping they call variously "Sino-Caucasian" and "Dene-Sino-Caucasian," which purportedly includes Basque, Sino-Tibetan, Yenisei, and North Caucasian, as well as Na-Dene (see Bengtson 1991, Nikolaev 1991, and Shevoroshkin 1991; compare Ruhlen 1994a, 1994b:24–8).[56] Shevoroshkin (1990:8–11) extends this much further and groups Nostratic, Sino-Caucasian, and "Amerind," which was first suggested by Starostin. In the same, somewhat ambiguous passage, Shevoroshkin seems to accuse Greenberg's Almosan-Keresiouan of "unamerind" behavior and lumped it together with these other groupings from the Old World. Shevoroshkin examined a list of twenty-six problematic look-alikes involving Salish and concluded:

This means that Salishan—apparently along with Wakashan, Algic and other Almosan-Keresiouan languages—belongs to Sino-Caucasian languages (= Dene-Caucasian) phylum [*sic*]. Nikolaev has demonstrated that the Na Dene (Athapascan) languages belong to this phylum as well (but they seem to be less archaic than Salishan—and Wakashan). So we have to "withdraw" the Almosan-

Keresiouan phylum from Amerind and "add" it to Sino-Caucasian (or Dene-Caucasian; this latter term seems better). (1990:10)

However, since not even Na-Dene has been satisfactorily demonstrated and is seriously challenged by specialists, to conjecture that broader connections might be established between it and Old World languages is out of the question. It is conceivable that some languages from the putative Na-Dene grouping could prove to be related to some of the others in this vast grouping, but the evidence presented thus far fails to make a plausible case for such relationships. Nikolaev (1991) presents 197 sets of look-alikes involving various Athabaskan languages, Eyak, and Haida, compared with Proto-North-Caucasian, Proto-Nakh, and some others, also including putative sound correspondences between "Proto-Eyak-Athapascan" and Proto-North-Caucasian. A large proportion of these lexical sets exhibits the problems discussed in Chapter 7, and the proposal is not at all convincing.[57] The same is true of Ruhlen's (1994b:26–7) thirty-three comparisons between Basque, North Caucasian, Burushaski, Sumerian, Nahali, Sino-Tibetan, Yeniseian, Haida, Tlingit, Eyak, and Athabaskan. There are several gaps in this list (for example, twenty are missing from Haida); there are three sets in which forms glossed 'thou' recur and two sets in which 'who' recurs; many forms are short, semantically divergent, phonetically not particularly similar, and onomatopoetic (for example, 'frog'). In short, the list is insufficient to constitute a plausible case of potential relationship.

The Mosan Proposal
−60% probability, 65% confidence

The Mosan hypothesis proposes a connection between Salish, Wakashan, and Chimakuan. Boas and Frachtenberg had independently noted structural similarities and some lexical look-alikes among these languages before 1920 (see Chapter 2). The name Mosan is from Frachtenberg (1920:295), based on forms approximating *mōs* or *bōs* 'four' found in languages of the three families. Sapir (1929a) accepted Mosan as a genetic grouping (he made it part of his more

inclusive Algonkian-Mosan group), and Swadesh (1953a, 1953b) attempted to provide supporting lexical evidence. Swadesh (1953a:29–30) also listed sixteen shared structural similarities, but they are unimpressive today, since most are Northwest Coast areal traits (see Chapter 9). Some of these sixteen are not independent of one another (for example, there is extensive use of suffixes and nearly complete absence of prefixes).

Subsequent research has called this classification into question and it is now largely abandoned. For example, not even Swadesh continued to maintain the Mosan hypothesis, since later he was grouping Wakashan (but not the other putative Mosan groups) with Eskimo-Aleut (and some Old World languages) (see Swadesh 1962). The similarities (particularly the structural resemblances) which these languages share suggest areal diffusion (Jacobsen 1979a, Thompson 1979). The proposed Mosan grouping has no current support among American Indian linguists.[58] Related hypotheses are taken up in the remainder of this section.

Wakashan and Chimakuan
0% probability, 25% confidence

Some linguists have thought that Wakashan and Chimakuan might be related (regardless of the ultimate status of Mosan or of possible broader connections with Salishan). The first to hold this view was apparently Bancroft (1882:564), followed by Andrade and Swadesh (see Andrade 1953; Swadesh 1953a, 1953b; also Powell 1993:451–2). These languages have considerable structural similarity, as well as lexical matchings, but much of this may be due to diffusion within the linguistic area (see Chapter 9). Current opinion on this proposed grouping appears to be mixed. Reasons for doubt are summarized by Jacobsen (1979a); Powell presents fresh evidence (mostly lexical, with suggestive sound correspondences and a few affixes) which to him indicate that "the case for relating Wakashan and Chimakuan [is] intriguing," though he makes no effort to "distinguish areal issues or loanwords" (1993:453). I would conclude that Powell's evidence is certainly sufficient to suggest that the question be left open for further investigation, though the impact of linguistic diffusion deserves careful attention.

Almosan and Beyond
−75% probability, 50% confidence

Sapir (1929a) combined Algic (Algonquian-Ritwan), Kutenai, and his Mosan (Chimakuan, Wakashan, and Salish) (see Gursky 1966a:412). Greenberg (1987) accepts Sapir's Almosan and combines it further with what he calls Keresiouan to form his Almosan-Keresiouan grouping. All these broad classifications involving Mosan are controversial at present and have not been accepted by specialists in the field.

Other Proposed Connections for Kutenai

Kutenai is now generally held to be clearly an isolate, but since many scholars view isolates as personal challenges begging to be related to something (as in the case of Zuni—see below), proposals for grouping Kutenai with other languages abound. Chamberlain (1892) gave Kutenai an independent status but spoke of some similarities with "Shoshonean" (1982, 1907), Siouan (1982), and Algonquian (1907). Later, however, he wrote against the possible Shoshonean (that is, Uto-Aztecan) connection he had favored earlier (Chamberlain 1909). Radin's controversial article (1919) in which he grouped all the North American languages suggested a possible Kutenai-Algonquian relationship (perhaps gotten from Sapir; see Haas 1965:81); the joining of Kutenai and Algonquian is presented in Sapir's "super-six" classification (1921a, 1929a), as part of his Algonkin-Wakashan stock. None of these proposals is thought to have much merit today. Some scholars have proposed a possible Salish-Kutenai connection (Thompson 1979). This is not implausible, but a thorough study has not been attempted.

Beothuk Proposals

It has often been thought that Beothuk must be related in some way to Algonquian; other possible connections for Beothuk have also been proposed. Latham asserted that "the language . . . was akin to those of the ordinary American

Indians rather than to the Eskimo" (as had sometimes been supposed) (1850:300) and that of these, "it was Algonkin rather than aught else" (1862:453). He listed twenty-two Beothuk words with what he took to be cognates in Algonquian languages (Hewson 1982:182). Brinton (1891:68) considered Beothuk to be Eskimoan in type. Gatschet (1885–1890), however, had declared that Beothuk was "totally unrelated to any other language on the North American continent!" (Hewson 1982:182). John Campbell (1892) defended Latham and attacked Gatschet, presenting another list of assumed Algonquian cognates. (Campbell was the author of several notoriously bad works on language and languages.) Howley reported that William Dawson was of the opinion that Beothuk was "of Tinné or Chippewan stock" (that is, Athabaskan) (1915:301), but was himself inclined to go along with Gatschet. Sapir (1929a) placed Beothuk in his Macro-Algonquian phylum with a question mark as being possibly "a very divergent member" of Algonquian. With regard to the sixteen words he compared, Gursky asserted that "diese Vergleiche sprechen dafür, daß die Beothuk-Sprache zum Algonkin-Ritwan-Sprachstamm gehört" (these comparisons suggest the conclusion that the Beothuk language belongs to the Algonkin-Ritwan language family) (1964a:4). He qualified this conclusion later when he compared seven Beothuk forms with quite similar Proto-Central-Algonquian roots: "Naturally these similarities are not sufficient for proof of a relationship. They could also represent cases of borrowing, although this is not particularly probable, since words from basic vocabulary are involved"[59] (Gursky 1966a:410–11). Hewson, a specialist in Algonquian languages, attempted to trace reflexes of Proto-Algonquian consonants in about sixty Beothuk vocabulary items (1971) and argued that the Beothuk verb forms could be interpreted as "common Algonkian inflexions" of the conjunct order, where parallels to Algonquian with transitive animate and intransitive animate endings were detectable (1978:140–41). His conclusion was: "There is evidence, therefore, that Beothuk, in spite of the distortions and errors of the vocabularies, can be interpreted as a language of the Algonkian type and should probably be considered related to the Algonkian family of languages" (1982:184). Goddard, however, advised caution:

> The long-conjectured relationship with the extinct and poorly documented Beothuk language of Newfoundland (Hewson 1968, 1971) must continue to be regarded with serious reservations as long as the phonology and morphology of the language remain so completely unkown as to make impossible an objective evaluation of the forms recorded. Ad hoc interpretations of Beothuk words based on proposed comparisons with Algonquian forms cannot in principle form a convincing basis for an understanding of the language, and without some systematic knowledge of its structure there is simply no Beothuk language to compare. One example of the pitfalls involved will suffice. Beothuk *gathet* 'one' (Leigh vocabulary) has been compared to PA [Proto-Algonquian] **kot-* (correctly **nekwetw-*), and Beothuk *yazeek* 'one' (Cormack vocabulary) has been compared to PA **pe·šikwi* (correctly **pe·šekw-*) (Hewson 1968:90). But other words show *th z* and *-k t: nunyetheek* (King vocabulary) *ninezeek* (Cormack) 'five'; *godawik* (Leigh) *hadowadet* (King) 'shovel' (Hewson 1968:89–90, 1971:247). Hence it is very likely that *gathet* and *yazeek* are attempts to render the same Beothuk word, presumably something like /ɣaži?/. If so, the cumulative error of the poor recordings, lack of systematic interpretation of the Beothuk sound system, and generous criteria of similarity have resulted in one and the same Beothuk word being compared to both PA **nekwetw-* and PA **pe·šekw-*. The only conclusion possible is that the comparisons between Beothuk and Algonquian are not yet on firm ground. (1979a:106)

In sum, two views concerning Beothuk's genetic relationships are prevalent today: one holds that the evidence is too sparse and imperfect to determine such relationships; the other argues (guardedly) for an Algonquian relationship. Indeed, the cultural and geographical evidence predisposes one to think that an Algonquian linguistic relationship would not be surprising (but linguistic inferences based on such information are always dangerous and frequently wrong; see Chapter 7). Moreover, the linguistic evidence presented by Hewson (the potential cognates, possible sound correspondences, and morphological agreements), although not conclusive, suggests that Beothuk has an Algonquian kinship. Although we may suspect, on the basis of intuition and circumstances, that Beothuk is

related to Algonquian, we cannot at present confirm such a relationship (see Hewson 1968, 1971, 1978, 1982; Goddard l979a; Proulx 1983). The exact nature of this relationship, if it exists, will probably never be determined.

Hokan and Related Proposals

Hokan is one of the most inclusive and most influential of the proposals of distant genetic relationships. It is still highly disputed today. The Hokan hypothesis has been aptly described by Jacobsen: "Several linguists have detected diffuse but strikingly similar characteristics in the structure of these [putatively Hokan] languages that give them reason to think that there may be a genuine, albeit distant, genetic relationship among at least several of these groups. . . . It is important to emphasize that potential relationships among the Hokan branches remains controversial" (1986:107). A thorough understanding of the Hokan hypothesis requires a knowledge of its history; therefore, major works on Hokan are surveyed here roughly in chronological order.

Hokan had the shakiest of origins. In two 1913 articles, Dixon and Kroeber framed, tentatively, the original Hokan hypothesis, which for them included "*certainly* Shasta [Shastan, including Shasta and Palaihnihan], Chimariko, and Pomo, *probably* Karok, and *possibly* Yana" (1913b; cited by Haas 1964b:73, her emphasis); to these they added Esselen and Yuman (1913a). This hypothesis was based on inspectional resemblances involving only five words in these languages: 'tongue', 'eye', 'stone', 'water', and 'sleep'. It was in these articles that Hokan, Penutian, Ritwan, and Iskoman were first proposed; the last was included within Hokan in their 1919 work. Kroeber (1915) argued that Seri and Tequistlatecan (Chontal of Oaxaca) were related to Yuman (see Brinton 1891), and hence by inference were also Hokan languages.[60] Following Harrington's claim, Dixon and Kroeber (1919) also added Washo to Hokan, thus completing the list of core Hokan languages. Harrington (1913) had also asserted, in an announcement, that Chumash was related to some of the proposed Hokan languages, and he is often given credit for the hypothesis linking Iskoman with Hokan (see Olmsted 1964:2).

Olmsted's reading of the history of Hokan studies beginning with Harrington's 1913 announcement is very perceptive: "Thus began an unfortunate tradition in Hokan studies, that of adding to, or subtracting from the group by assertion, without publishing much evidence. . . . Collection and publication of the data were thereby relegated to a subordinate place for a long period" (1964:2). As Haas observed, after Dixon and Kroeber's (1919) reduction of Californian languages into a few large families,

> there were no further serious attempts to reduce the number of stocks in California [and] the excitement attending the discovery of new genetic affiliations died down for lack of new fuel and very little was done even to substantiate earlier conclusions for almost forty years. [Indeed,] the consequence of this state of affairs is that the Dixon-Kroeber classification has been accepted without question by most anthropologists. Usually it is not even realized how little proof was, after all, adduced for their two most daring amalgamations, Hokan and Penutian. (Haas 1964b:74; see also Haas 1954:57)

Olmsted noted that until 1964, Sapir's three Hokan articles (1917a, 1920, 1925a) were considered the "chief [if not the only] substantive contributions to Hokan classification," and although "these papers were based on what were in most cases poorly recorded and inadequately analyzed data, they were, and remain, the principal demonstration of the support for the Hokan hypothesis" (Olmsted 1964:2, referring to Hoijer 1946a). He pointed out that Sapir (1929a) "speculated boldly" and that these views "appealed more to nonspecialists than his sober handling of the detailed evidence in the three earlier papers [Sapir 1917a, 1920, 1925a]" (Olmsted 1964:2).

In view of such dubious beginnings, one might wonder how Hokan was conceptualized by its framers and supporters. In this regard, an examination of the Iskoman proposal's development and fate is revealing and offers some perspective on the Hokan hypothesis in general (see Klar 1977 for more details). As early as 1903, Dixon and Kroeber had been of the opinion that Chumash and Salinan were somehow closely connected (Dixon and Kroeber 1903); in their 1913 articles, they grouped Chumash and Salinan together in a stock they called "Iskoman,"

mentioning that "an apparent structural similarity of Chumash and Salinan was long ago noted by the authors, but . . . lexical resemblances, while occurring, are to date not conspicuous" (1913a:652). They speculated then on further possible genetic connections between Iskoman and Hokan, but added this caution: "It is however idle to discuss further a possible relationship between Iskoman and Hokan, when the genetic connections between the members of Iskoman [Chumash and Salinan] is scarcely yet a matter of demonstrable proof, probable though it may seem" (Dixon and Kroeber 1913a:653). Kroeber (1904) had compared eight Chumash and Salinan forms, five of which were repeated in the list with a grand total of twelve Chumash-Salinan comparisons presented in Kroeber and Dixon (1913a). The twelve forms included 'dog' (now recognized as probably diffused); numerals two and four, ten, and sixteen (see Klar 1977:171–3 for a discussion of areal diffusion of Chumash numbers); short forms ('water', 'arm'); and semantically nonequivalent forms ('water'/'ocean'). As Klar says, "all in all none of these forms seems very convincing evidence for positing a genetic relationship between Chumash and Salinan" (1977:145).[61]

Dixon and Kroeber failed to heed their own earlier caution and flatly asserted that the Iskoman languages belong to Hokan:

> From the first it was apparent that Chumash and Salinan possessed more numerous similarities with each other than either possessed with any other language. In their second preliminary notice [Kroeber and Dixon 1913a] the authors accordingly set up an "Iskoman" group or family. Some of the data seemed to "lend themselves to the hypothesis of a connection between Hokan and Iskoman," although discussion of such a possible relationship appeared premature then.
>
> Subsequently, however, Mr. J. P. Harrington [1913] expressed his conviction of the kinship of Chumash and Yuman, and thereby implicitly of Iskoman and Hokan, if these groups were valid. And in his Yana paper Dr. Sapir [1917a] treats Chumash and Salinan outright as if they were Hokan, and with results substantially equal to his results from the other languages of the group.
>
> The tentative Iskoman group may therefore be regarded as superseded and merged into Hokan. (1919:104)

Sapir had reported Chumash and Salinan as "at present of more doubtful inclusion [in Hokan]" (1917a:1), however, and indeed he gave Chumash parallels for only 16 of his 141 sets of mostly lexical resemblances among Hokan languages. Klar observed that "to this day nothing comparable [in number of Chumashan forms assembled and compared with putative Hokan languages] has been done, except by Sapir himself" (1977:150). She carefully considered the evidence for a possible Chumash-Salinan relationship and for the inclusion of Chumash within Hokan; she showed similarities between Proto-Pomoan and Chumashan in nine instrumental prefixes and one lexical set, listing apparent "systematic correspondences (1977:154–5). Nevertheless, she found this evidence unpersuasive and suggested in her conclusion that "the Chumash family be considered an isolate family and not . . . grouped closely with any other particular family or language" (1977:156). Since in the most recent studies (Kaufman 1988; see also Klar 1977:156), Chumashan is generally eliminated from the Hokan hypothesis while Salinan is still maintained, the history of Iskoman and of the Chumash-Hokan association illustrates very clearly the problematic nature of Hokan and how truly flimsy the original evidence upon which the Hokan hypothesis was based was, and it shows how those who framed it thought.

In none of his works did Sapir present a reconstructed phonemic inventory for Hokan or a list of sound correspondences, but he did offer a number of reconstructed lexical items and occasionally made reference to individual sound correspondences involving particular languages. Margaret Langdon found that "from the items for which tentative reconstructions are provided, it is possible to extract a picture of the phonetic inventory which Sapir envisaged for Proto-Hokan . . . a well-developed series of plan stops *p t tc[č] k ?* and the skeleton of corresponding aspirated and glottalized series *p' k' [sic] t' tc'[č'] k'*; a series of spirants *s x x̣ h*; and the voiced resonants *m n (ŋ?) w l y*. Vowels are *i a u*" (1974:43). Langdon (1986:129) presented a chart of Sapir's reconstructed Hokan sounds (quite similar to the sounds given here) extracted from his various studies, together with the number of forms Sapir presented which contain

them. Kaufman (1988:51) extricated the following somewhat different phonemic inventory of Proto-Hokan and canonical forms from Sapir's (1917a, 1920, 1925a) studies, containing "over 100 suggested proto-Hokan reconstructions": /p, t, c, kʷ, ?, p', t', c', k', pʰ, kʰ, kʷʰ, s, xʸ, X, Xʷ˙ h, m, n, l, w, y/ . The canonical shapes of morphemes were: /CV, CVCV, VCV, CVhCV, VhCV, CV?CV, V?CV, CVCVCV, VCVCV/.

In his famous Hokan-Subtiaba article, Sapir (1925a) also proposed reconstructions of some Proto-Hokan morphemes, of which the nominal and verbal prefixes were the best known: Proto-Hokan *t- 'nominal, absolutive' (Subtiaba d-), *m- 'adjectival' (Subtiaba m-), *k- 'intransitive' (Subtiaba g-), and *p- 'transitive' (Subtiaba ?) (compare Langdon 1974:45). Langdon finds "the Subtiaba evidence for the synchronic existence of these elements . . . full and convincing" (1974:45) and pointed out also a Diegueño verbal prefix m- that translates English adjectives, for which no information was available to Sapir in 1925. I have considerable doubt concerning Sapir's assumed Subtiaba prefixes and I have not been able to convince myself that several of the segments Sapir considers to be Subtiaba prefixes are not just accidentally segmented portions of the roots that have no grammatical (or etymological) status on their own. That is, Sapir's assumed m- 'adjective prefix' (m- is chosen arbitrarily to represent any of Sapir's segmented morphemes d-, r-, s-/c-, p-, k-, and so on, for which the evidence is not compelling) could be some fused and now nonproductive old adjectival marker or some such thing, as suggested by Sapir in his juxtaposition of *ma·ša* (his <m-a·ca>) 'blue, green' with *d-aša-lu·* (<d-aca-lu·>'grass' (see below). However, since this assumed m- 'adjective prefix' has no general occurrence in the language in other relevant forms, it might be a mistakenly segmented part of the root, akin to assuming, for example, that a listing of English *thatch, thane, theft/thief, thigh, thimble, thistle,* and so on shows evidence of a frozen morpheme *th*, abetted by the article *the* and the demonstratives with *th* (*this, that, these, those*).[62] The fact that Subtiaba-Tlapanec has clearly been demonstrated to belong to the Otomanguean family (Chapter 5), not to Hokan, shows just how speculative Sapir's Hokan morphology was.

In spite of widespread acceptance of Sapir's work and of the Dixon-Kroeber Hokan hypothesis, there were other scholars with sober reservations. They have commented that Sapir's Hokan articles had stalled subsequent research and they raised objections to the quality of Sapir's evidence (Hoijer 1946a, 1954). Bright indicated that "proof of any of the relationships within the Northern Hokan group [of Sapir's] is still lacking" (1954:63) and referred to both the limited number of lexical and morphological similarities and the inadequacy of the recorded data. He compared about 250 words in the five so-called Northern Hokan languages (Karuk, Chimariko, Shasta, Achomawi, and Atsugewi); he found about 100 possible cognate sets and attempted to establish sound correspondences based on them, but he encountered the difficulty that "a given etymon can often be found in only two or three of the languages," with "some of the sets of cognates . . . very doubtful" (1954:64). Bright's conclusion was that "the results obtained are promising but not conclusive"; at the same time, however, he cast doubt on Dixon's Shasta-Achumawi grouping, since Dixon's "results make Shasta seem no closer to Achumawi-Atsugewi than to Karuk or to Chimariko" (1954:67; see Olmsted 1956, 1957, 1959). Haas (a student of Sapir's) reassessed the situation in 1964 and found that much of the material Sapir (1917a) had cited as supporting evidence was very poorly recorded, and that "further material of the same or better quality was not forthcoming either from Sapir or anyone else" (1964b:75).

Important in Hokan studies were the number of small comparisons among certain of the putative Hokan languages. Jacobsen (1958) compared lexical (and some morphological) resemblances in Washo and Karuk, though he noted similarities also with other Hokan languages and he attempted to establish sound correspondences. Some of his 121 sets are quite suggestive (and could be true cognates), but many suffer from the limitations warned about in Chapter 7. For example, eleven sets involve onomatopoetic forms (such as the forms for 'blow', 'cry', 'lungs', 'magpie', 'shoot', and 'suck'; for example, Washo *šú·* 'breast, chest' / Karuk *ʔú·čič* 'teat, woman's breast'). The shape and semantic content of seven suggests possible borrowing; for example, forms similar to Washo *pat'sá·gaʔ*

'flint, i.e., obsidian' / Karuk *sá·k* 'flint, i.e., obsidian, arrowhead, bullet' found in other languages of the area make the probability of borrowing seem very high (compare Coos *-cakʷkʷ* 'to spear', Takelma *saakʷ* 'shoot [arrow]'; Siuslaw *čaq-* 'to spear', Saclan *sagu* 'rock', and Salinan *asak'a* 'flint').[63] Eight are semantically quite distinct (for example, 'stretch out' / 'finger'; Washo *á·ša* 'urine, to urinate' / Karuk *ʔá·s* 'water, juice' is semantically nonequivalent and short, and it involves two different pan-American forms).[64] Four are nursery forms ('father', 'mother'); 13 include pan-Americanisms ('I', 'you', 'land'); and 118 involve forms that are short, have only one or two matching segments, or are phonetically very different (with little that corresponds). In short, the evidence is not persuasive.

Three such small comparative Hokan studies (Haas 1964b, McLendon 1964, and Silver 1964) were included in Bright's (1964) collection of studies on Californian languages. The three are similar in structure and viewpoint. The authors all comment on the more accurate materials on some of the languages that had then recently become available, and they employ them in their comparisons. All three studies appear to be binary comparisons of two principal Hokan members (in some cases the compared entities are whole families; in others they are isolates), but each also compares numerous forms from other putative Hokan languages with the two in focus. That is, in reality they are not merely binary comparisons but studies which involve the many languages included in the Hokan hypothesis (see Chapter 7). Each author presents a list of possible cognates plus putative sound correspondences. They mention the difficulties of doing comparative work within the Hokan hypothesis assumed to stem from "the confusing reduction of forms resulting from aphaeresis, syncope, and assimilation" (McLendon 1964:144). Only one of the studies (Haas 1964b) is assessed here, since the results of the three are strikingly similar to those of Jacobsen (1958) just presented.

Haas (1964b) compared ninety-two Yana and Karuk forms, and also frequently compared other forms occurring in Hokan languages. She attempted to establish regular sound correspondences between the two in focus. Many of her forms are questionable, thus leaving the sound correspondences in doubt. For example, of the ninety-two look-alikes compared, thirteen are onomatopoetic (for example, Yana *pu-*, Karuk *fum-* 'to blow'), twenty-six are short forms (Yana *ni-* 'one male goes', Karuk *in-* 'to go [rare]'), ten forms reflect semantic latitude (for example, 'snow':'to rain'), twenty-three are widespread or pan-American forms, fifteen have little phonetic similarity; 'digging stick' and 'manzanita berry' are suggestive of diffusion (there are similar forms in a number of northern Californian Indian languages); and 'father' is a nursery form. Needless to say, when so many forms are in doubt, a number of the proposed sound correspondences cease to be viable. For example, *p* : *f* is illustrated by only two proposed cognate sets ('blow' is clearly onomatopoetic and 'excrement' is a pan-Americanism); *b* : *f* is exhibited only by 'frog' (onomatopoetic) and 'manzanita [berry]' (probably borrowed). Of the other sound correspondences, three are illustrated by only one single putative cognate set (one example never constitutes a legitimate recurring correspondence), and ten are illustrated by only two such sets. Haas's evidence does not suffice to show a genetic relationship between Yana and Karuk.[65]

McLendon (1964), following the same general format as Haas (1964b), compared Eastern Pomo and Yana and also cited frequent forms compared with other putative Hokan languages. Silver's (1964) comparison was between Shasta and Karuk, and it also included forms from other putative Hokan languages. Neither succeeded in demonstrating a relationship either between the languages in focus or between them and other Hokan possibilities.

With respect to studies with broader scope, Haas proposed nine Proto-Hokan reconstructions based on phonologically similar lexical sets from many putative Hokan languages, all of which were based on the assumption that "certain long vowels in Shasta have resulted from the contraction of a Proto-Hokan . . . *VmV* . . . P[roto-]H[okan] *ama > Sh[asta] /a·/ and . . . *ima or *ami > Sh[asta] /e·/" (1963b:42). While her charts for these nine reconstructions show many similarities, they also leave considerable room for doubt. In the absence of a more fully developed proposal for

the historical phonological developments, one might suspect, for example in the case of 'ear', that Karuk *t*<*i·*v (< means that the sound is assumed to have undergone a change of assimilation), Chimariko *-sam*, and Chumash *tuʔ* may not really be cognate forms in genetically related languages and that they may not derive from Haas's proposed proto form **išamaruk'a/*iša-mak'aru* (1963b:46); similarly, Achomawi *owè·* > 'liver' is a stretch from the assumed Proto-Hokan **č-imapasi/*imačipasi* (1963b:47); and Chumash *top'o*, Achomawi *alu*, and Washo *í* > *ʔb* 'navel' are a far leap from each other and from the proposed Proto-Hokan **imarak'ʷi/* **imak'ʷari*. Her other sets exhibit similar problems. The number of forms (nine) is too small to constitute the basis for a convincing genetic hypothesis; some of them are pan-American-isms, and similar forms occur beyond just putative Hokan languages (for example, 'nose', 'tongue'[66]); and the alternative reconstructions and reliance on metathesis provide too much leeway in the matchable phonetic space of the compared items so that the possibility of accident is greatly increased.[67] In short, Haas's nine forms are suggestive, but they do not constitute compelling evidence of the relationship.

In their summary of the 1964 conference on classification, Voegelin and Voegelin (1965:141–2) presented the consensus classification from that time, but no supporting evidence; they listed the following as members of what they called the Hokan Phylum (the closer internal connections that they postulated appear here in parentheses): Yuman language family (interfamily connections with Pomo); Seri language isolate (affiliation with Yuman family, perhaps analogous to the relatively close affiliation of the Catawba isolate to the Siouan family); Pomo language family (interfamily connections with Yuman); Palaihnihan language family; Shastan language family (interfamily connection with Palaihnihan—minimized by Olmsted); Yanan language family; Chimariko language isolate; Salinan language family; Karuk language isolate; Chumashan language family (with reservations on phylum affiliations in Hokan); Comecrudan language family (with reservations on phylum affiliations in Hokan); Coahuiltecan language isolate (with reservations on phylum affiliations in Hokan); Esselen language isolate (strong reservations on evidence for phylum af-filiations of Esselen in Hokan); Jicaque language isolate; Tlapanecan (Subtiaba-Tlapanec) language family (interfamily connections with Tequistlatecan); and Tequistlatecan language family (interfamily connections with Yuman). They separated their Macro-Siouan Phylum from Hokan, thus dissolving Sapir's (1929a) Hokan-Siouan.

The most extensive lexical study of proposed Hokan languages to date is that of Gursky, who compared more than 700 forms among the Dixon and Kroeber original California Hokan languages (plus Seri and Tequistlatec). The similarities Gursky assembled are suggestive, but, as he pointed out, "research on the genetic relationship of the Hokan languages is found now still in a somewhat of a pioneering stage. The sound correspondences between the individual Hokan languages are—in spite of advances achieved in recent years—still only partially ascertained and even then not with any certainty"[68] (1974:173; see also 1988). Unfortunately, Gursky's lexical sets exhibit abundant problems of the type discussed in Chapter 7, and since there are no clear sound correspondences or compelling patterned grammatical agreements, they do not constitute compelling evidence of a relationship.

Langdon provided a historical overview of historical linguistic work involving putative Hokan languages. While she presented few direct arguments of her own (though occasionally filled in information relative to others' claims), her conclusion was that "while a full demonstration of the validity of the Hokan-Coahuiltecan hypothesis is not yet a reality, there is a growing sense of excitement as convergent results are reported" (1974:86). She reported that Tonkawa and Karankawa were unlikely to be members of Hokan-Coahuiltecan (see below) but that there may be a Chumash-Seri-Chontal (or Southern Hokan) subgroup. She concluded that according to "the convergent feelings of Hokanists,"

> Proto-Hokan probably had a rather simple sound system. . . . Contrasts involving plain *versus* aspirated and perhaps even glottalized consonants may well turn out to be accountable as independent developments; voiceless sonorants are already accounted for as innovations in Pomo, Yuman, and Washo. Vowels may not have been more than three with a probable length contrast. . . . In the few

available good cognate sets, the persisting elements appear to be essentially conservative. The great diversity of the daughter languages, it seems, must be accounted for by repeated processes of loss of vowels leading to subsequent loss and change of consonants (particularly in the laryngeal area), with resulting lexical items where little remains that is truly comparable. Typical Hokan morphemes must have been short (monosyllabic). (1974:87)

Although the Yuman family has not been demonstrated to be definitely related to any other languages, Langdon (1979) compared Yuman and Pomoan and indicated some suggestive lexical similarities, as well as what appear to be underlying phonological similarities in morpheme shapes and some broadly distributed grammatical traits. The case she presents is not convincing, but the evidence is sufficient to warrant more investigation. Of her fifty-two lexical comparisons between Proto-Pomoan and Proto-Yuman, I would question four that are onomatopoetic, eighteen that include short forms, two that reflect permissive semantic differences, three that are not phonetically plausible, and twelve that include pan-Americanisms. The thirteen remaining comparisons are suggestive, but there is a need for clearer sound correspondences and more supporting evidence. Langdon's 1990 article goes in the right direction, offering tentative proposals concerning "some patterns of verb system formation in Hokan languages" (1990b:57).

Given the reservations expressed here concerning the many Hokan studies, but also taking into account Langdon's more promising comparisons (and Kaufman's optimism—see the next subsection), I conclude that it is by no means clear or even likely that there was a proto language from which some or most of the putative Hokan languages diverged long ago, but that this hypothesis is fully worthy of continued research. Other hypotheses concerning Hokan languages, some of which link Hokan with other groups, are discussed in the remainder of this section.

Kaufman's Hokan

Throughout most of the 1980s, opinions varied concerning Hokan (in many guises), but, in general, doubt concerning its validity predominated. However, Terrence Kaufman (1988) took a more positive stance based on his reexamination of the evidence. He came out in favor of a rather wide Hokan stock (for which he suggests an age of about 8,000 years), though he eliminated some groups that had traditionally been included in Hokan. As "probable members" he gives: Pomoan, Chimariko, Yanan, Karok [Karuk], Shastan, Achumawi-Atsugewi (his "Achu" family), Washo, Esselen, Salina, Yuman, Cochimí, Seri, Coahuilteco, Comecrudan, Chontalan (Tequistlatecan), and Jicaquean. As "doubtful" he lists: Chumashan, Waikuri, Tonkawa, Karankawa, Cotoname, Quinigua, and Yurimangui. Kaufman's evidence is largely lexical, though unfortunately he did not present the forms on which his judgments were based; he provided only his phonological formulas representing tentative reconstructions. He postulates that Hokan lexemes were basically no longer than two syllables and that trisyllabic and longer morphemes are therefore somehow the results of secondary developments in the history of the languages which contain them. While Kaufman's proposals have stimulated some other linguists to accept more positive attitudes toward Hokan, they can be evaluated appropriately only after he presents the lexical evidence upon which they are based. Therefore, for the present, we are left with essentially the same uncertainty that has always attended the Hokan hypothesis—there certainly is enough there to make one sympathetic to the possibility of genetic relationship, and yet the evidence presented to date is not sufficient to confirm the hypothesis, regardless of which languages are included.

If Hokan is considered controversial, it is safe to say that Sapir's (1929a) broader Hokan-Siouan proposal has been completely abandoned (even by Greenberg [1987]). Sapir himself referred to it as his "wastepaper basket stock" (quoted in Haas 1973a:679).

Hokan-Subtiaba
−90% probability, 75% confidence

Given the importance in the history of Hokan in general of Sapir's (1925a) article, which proposes a Hokan affinity for Tlapanec-Subtiaba (see Chapters 2 and 7), it is important to consider it briefly here. Since Tlapanec-Subtiaba is now known to be a branch of the Otomanguean family, the question inevitably arises concerning the quality of the evidence Sapir presented in his attempt to link it with Hokan. In short, his evidence does not support the claim and fails many of the methodological tests in Chapter 7. The hypothesis originated with Walter Lehmann's comparison of Washo and Subtiaba. It appears to be the putative *d-* nominal prefix that Lehmann (1920:973–5) thought was shared by Subtiaba and Washo which drew Sapir's attention to the hypothesis, to which he added analogs from Salinan and Obispeño Chumash morphology (1925a:404). (Chumash is now not thought to be Hokan by some supporters of the Hokan hypothesis; see above.) Sapir accepted only four of Lehmann's seven lexical comparisons ('mouth', 'nape', 'sun/day', and 'frog'). I would eliminate two of these; the 'frog' form is probably onomatopoetic, and 'mouth' is a short form (comparing something approximating *au* in the languages considered). In spite of this less than propitious start, Sapir (1925a) set down 126 proposed cognate sets (103 lexical, 11 demonstratives, 7 "particles," and 7 "grammatical elements"), together with some suggested sound correspondences (of a fairly speculative nature). Most of these proposed cognate sets are problematic in one way or another, however, as shown by the following examples. Set (4) 'moon' compares *-ku·*, extracted from Subtiaba *d-uku·-lu*, *du·x̣ku·-lu·*, *d-uku* 'moon' and *imba-ku·* 'one month', with Ventureño Chumash *owai, awai, t-awa* 'moon'. The parts compared are short and are not phonetically similar, and the set involves only two languages, Subtiaba and Chumash. Set (37) 'flower, bloom' compares Subtiaba *di·i·* 'cortés, tree with beautiful white blossoms' with Chimariko *aṭe·i* 'flower'; this example involves short forms, semantic non-equivalents, and a comparison of only two languages (from the many targets among Sapir's supposed Hokan languages from which potential matchings could be sought). Set (21) 'wing' compares Subtiaba *t-ala·la* 'wing', *t-ala·la* 'bat' (and *t-alala* 'feather')—focusing on the "final reduplications, which is quite characteristic of Hokan—with Atsugewi *palala*, Washo *palolo*, Pomo *lila-wa*, all 'butterfly', and Salinan *ṭ-api-lale* 'bat'. But there is no real comparison in this example other than the reduplication; the 'butterfly' forms are widespread (pan-Americanisms);[69] the three Subtiaba forms apparently actually all have the same root, none of which matches 'butterfly' semantically. Set (58), glossed 'beseech', compares Subtiaba -waa 'to ask for' (Spanish pedir) with Yana -wa-, wa·- 'to weep', Chimariko -wo- 'to cry', Achomawi -wo 'to cry', Coahuilteco wa·yp 'to cry', and Karankawa owiya 'to cry'; the forms glossed 'weep/cry' in this set are onomatopoetic and similar ones are found in languages spoken all over the world. Moreover, short forms are compared, and there is too much semantic latitude between 'to ask for' and 'to cry/weep'. In general, 54 (more than half) of the 103 lexical sets (and nearly all of the demonstratives, particles, and grammatical elements) involve short forms; 19 involve comparisons with considerable semantic latitude—for example, set (36), 'wood'/'fire'; 9 include forms that are onomatopoetic or affective-symbolic; 18 involve forms with little phonetic similarity and with doubtful correspondence; 7 include pan-Americanisms; 3 include nursery forms; and at least one set, (48) 'axe'—perhaps also set (49) 'bow' and set (52) 'shirt'—appears to involve diffused forms. In 16 sets only two languages, Subtiaba and one other, are compared. At least 2 sets are not independent but actually include the same etymon repeated in separate proposed examples: set (88) Subtiaba <ma·ca> 'green, blue' and set (93) Subtiaba <ma·ca> 'raw'. ('Raw', 'unripe', and 'green' frequently have the same root in Mesoamerican languages.)

Coahuiltecan
−85% probability, 80% confidence

As Troike (1963:295) pointed out, the so-called Coahuiltecan languages played a pivotal role in the development of Sapir's (1929a) comprehensive six-stock classification of North American Indian languages (in which Coahuiltecan was a branch of Hokan-Siouan). This putative grouping has varied greatly in terms of the languages that have been proposed as composing it. The Coahuiltecan hypothesis began with Orozco y Berra (1864; see Chapter 2) and continued through differing interpretations to the present. The minimum grouping has assumed a relationship between only Comecrudo and Cotoname; the most common version of the hypothesis places Coahuilteco with these two; the maximum grouping has included these three plus Tonkawa, Karankawa, Atakapa, and Maratino with the presumption that Aranama and Solano were varieties of Coahuilteco. Swanton (1915) proposed a Coahuiltecan classification that included two divisions—Cotoname and Tonkawa on the one hand and Coahuilteco, Comecrudo, and Karankawa on the other. (He also pointed out resemblances between Karankawa and Atakapa.) The notion that some "Coahuiltecan" grouping existed came to be generally accepted in the literature largely as a result of the work of Swanton. Haas provided an apt assessment of the situation: "There is also a real mess concerning Coahuilteco, which goes back to Swanton, too. It is just a bunch of languages that he wants to forget about, and he insists on tying them up with something" (in her discussion published in Elmendorf 1965:106). Sapir (1920) included Atakapa with Coahuiltecan when he proposed the broader Hokan-Coahuiltecan. Sapir's 1929a version of the Hokan-Coahuiltecan stock is perhaps best known; here he grouped Tonkawa and Karankawa with Coahuilteco, Comecrudo, and Cotoname and proposed a relationship between these so-called Coahuiltecan languages and Hokan within his Hokan-Siouan super-stock, although he removed Atakapa and placed it with Chitimacha and Tunica in a separate branch of the grand Hokan-Siouan grouping. Swanton (1940) suggested that these individual languages be considered coordinate members of Coahuiltecan, but with Tonkawa excluded from the grouping. Similarly, in a glottochronological investigation, Bright found that the lexical counts provided no support for the proposed connection between Comecrudo and Tonkawa, but that Comecrudo "appears more closely related to Jicaque." He concluded that "Sapir's Coahuiltecan group must therefore be considered of doubtful validity." As for "Hokaltecan" (Hokan-Coahuiltecan), Bright concluded that the question of relationships "is not likely to be closed for a long time to come, until enough data and time are available to establish full sets of phonemic correspondences" (1956:48).[70]

Goddard's (1979b) reexamination of the proposals casts doubt on all of these Coahuiltecan hypotheses. He dismisses even the minimum grouping of Comecrudo and Cotoname. There is, however, support for a genetic relationship among Comecrudo, Garza, and Mamulique (Goddard 1979b). This new grouping might be called the "Comecrudan" family (see Goddard 1979b; Haas 1979; Swanton 1919, 1940; Gatschet and Swanton 1932; Troike 1963).

Most recently, Manaster Ramer (1996) has argued for genetic groupings which, in effect, would revive aspects of the Coahuiltecan proposal. He presents evidence he considers conclusive for his Pakawan family (Coahuilteco, Comecrudo, Garza, Mamulique, and Cotoname). He further believes the evidence for connecting Karankawa with this Pakawan is "quite strong," that for connecting Atakapa "is weaker but not to be dismissed" (1996:7). He accepts Goddard's Comecrudan family (Comecrudo, Garza, Mamulique), arguing that Cotoname is also related by comparing it to Comecrudo. This is a crucial link upon which he later attempts to build the inclusion also of Coahuilteco and ultimately others. From the scant Cotoname material available, he repeats ten Comecrudo-Cotoname look-alikes which Goddard (1979b) had dismissed (Manaster Ramer dismisses the form for 'woman'), adding to this others to make up a total of twenty-seven forms he sees as probable cognates and three others as possible. What gives this set of lexical matchings more credibility than those of many other proposals of remote linguistic kinship is the presence of some reasonable basic vocabulary items and the plausible sound correspondences Manaster Ramer discusses. Still, although it is plausible, perhaps even likely, this proposal, too, suffers when the forms offered in evidence are scrutinized more closely.

Manaster Ramer does not accurately represent Goddard's argument, which is based on his examination of the Berlandier manuscript vocabularies, which are in two parallel lists. From these lists, Goddard reasoned that if Comecrudo and Cotoname are related at the family level, there would be more similar forms, and in particular more partially similar forms, than can be found in the Berlandier lists, which show words that are either entirely different or very similar. He points out that this pattern points to borrowing as an explanation, especially given

the meanings of some of the similar items involved. From other materials Goddard mentioned a few additional matches that were inconsistent with Berlandier's forms, pointing out that this could be because Berlandier got it wrong or provided a different or more complex form. Manaster does not acknowledge Goddard's procedures, nor that he did not himself, apparently, examine the Berlandier lists.

Among the several that are loanwords or probable loanwords are 'bee', 'lion', 'horn', 'corn', 'reed/arrow', 'goose', 'crane', 'dog', and 'rabbit'. For example, in Manaster Ramer's lexical comparison with Comecrudo *tawelo* and Cotoname *tawalo* 'corn', both are from Nahuatl *tlao:l-li* 'maize, dried kernels of corn' (Proto-Nahua **tlayo:l,* from **tla-* 'unspecified object' + *o:ya* 'to shell corn'); see also Comecrudo *tawaló-hi* 'corncob', also Subtiaba *wiya* 'corncob' (from Pipil *ta-wiyal* 'maize', *wiya* 'to shell corn'). 'Bee' forms (given as Comecrudo *sepiahuek* [*sepiahouec* (*sepiaú* in another source)] : Cotoname *sapa*) are thought to be loans from Huastec (Mayan) *tsap(-tsam)* 'bee'; see Proto-Mayan **ka:b'* 'honey, bee', Cholan **čab'*; borrowed also from Mayan in Honduran Lenca *šapu* and Cacaopera *súpu* 'bee, wasp'. As for 'crane', it is widely borrowed in the area, seen in Coahuilteco *kol* 'crane, heron', Comecrudo *kol,* Cotoname *karakór,* Karankawa *kol*; see also Proto-Huave **tsólo,* Huave *tsol* 'crane', Tequistlatec *-tsolo* 'brown heron', Sierra Totonac *lo:ʔqoʔ,* Papantla Totonac *lo:qoʔ* 'crane'. Some of these forms may reflect onomatopoeia.[71] Since Coahuilteco was a lingua franca in the area (Troike 1967, Goddard 1979b), a number of borrowed similarities among the languages stemming from Coahuilteco are to be expected. Borrowing, then, is a serious problem for a number of these forms, but it is not addressed by Manaster Ramer. In view of the known loans among languages of the area, the Huastec and Nahuatl loans that have been identified in these languages (Campbell and Kaufman in preparation), borrowing must be given serious attention in the search for possible wider genetic links.

The forms for 'goose', Comecrudo *la-ak* : Cotoname *krak,* involve onomatopoeia and are widespread in North America, believed by some also to involve widespread borrowing (Haas 1969b:82, for examples). 'Uncle' (Comecrudo *kekiam* : Cotoname *kikaima* [actually *quiqua-ima*]) falls among the nursery forms and may also be borrowed. Several of the forms are questionable. For example, in 'lion' Comecrudo *kuepet (couepet)* : Cotoname *kuba-ajá (couba-ajâ),* the Comecrudo form is not clear; it is given as *xuepét, guepét, zuepet,* and *couepet,* meaning 'panther, wildcat' (Spanish *león* 'mountain lion', *tigre* 'jaguar, ocelot', *gato montés* 'wildcat, bob-cat') (Swanton 1940:79). 'Breast' (Cotoname *k(e)nam, caneam*) is likely to be onomato-poeic—forms for 'breast' with multiple nasals are found around the world, associated with sounds of nursing. Manaster Ramer compares Comecrudo *dom (knem)* : Cotoname *k(e)nam* 'breast'; since the Comecrudo form is connected with or derived from *kené* 'chest', *ken* found in various female kinship terms ('aunt, elder sister, younger sister'), and *yéye kenema* 'for the female', it appears that the *m* is not part of the root, but a suffix, perhaps possessive, judging from Swanton's (1940:71) examples. This makes association with the *m* of Comecrudo *dom* unlikely. Cotoname *kenám, knám* 'breasts', 'milk' is so similar to the Comecrudo form, it may illustrate the problem Goddard (1979b) mentioned of interference, since some of the Cotoname data are from a Comecrudo informant.

Some of the compared forms also involve considerable semantic latitude: 'straw/grass', 'tobacco', 'to smoke', 'hand/wings' (and those considered less certain 'vein/bow-string', 'orphan', 'small/little boy/girl', 'high', 'big/good').

Given the small amount of Cotoname lexical material available for comparison and the small number of lexical matchings proposed, it is crucial if the proposal is to be supported that the data in the sets said to exhibit sound correspondences be accurate. However, this is not the case, and therefore, the proposed sound correspondences become doubtful. For example, to illustrate the assumed change of *l* to *w* in Cotoname, three sets are presented in Table 8-6. But this proposed sound correspondence is not at all secure. In 'red', there is no *w* in the Cotoname form (since Berlandier has *pam-set* 'red' in Comecrudo, the *l* is not fully secure there, either; Swanton (1940:114) has *pamsól, pamsúl* 'black, brown, red' and *kuis* 'red'; see Goddard 1979b:378). Therefore this set does not illustrate the *l : w* correspondence. Moreover, it is not clear whether the Cotoname form is recorded accurately or whether it is perhaps morphologically complex, since it looks suspiciously similar to *mesó-* 'white' (note that forms with unstressed *e* generally vary with zero). The 'straw' : 'grass, tobacco, to smoke' form is questionable on semantic grounds, and otherwise has little phonetic similarity unless the proposed sound correspondence can be defended from other more secure cases. The Comecrudo *sel* 'straw' form was given by a second informant as *umsel* (Swanton 1940:94); the Spanish gloss of Cotoname *su(-)á-u* is *zacate, yerbas, tabaco,* 'grass', 'herb / small plants', 'tobacco'—that is, 'vegetation'; it is similar enough in both its semantics and phonetic shape to suggest possible borrowing involving Uto-Aztecan languages, see Proto-Uto-Aztecan **siwi* 'vegetation, grass, green', where Nahuatl *šiwi-tl* was borrowed into Yucatec *ší:w* 'herb/plant, vegetation, leaf' and Totonac *šiwi:ʔt, šíwi:t* 'green corn'. If there is no such sound correspondence, *al : o/aau* 'sun' would have little to recommend it as a potential cognate, and the forms are too short to combat well the possibility that chance may account for imagined similarity. In short, the proposed *l : w* sound correspondence, resting only on these three lexical comparisons, is not secure.

Manaster Ramer's other proposed sound correspondence involves *k, kw > x, xw* in Cotoname and rests on four suggested cognate sets (Table 8-7). There are problems also with these data.

TABLE 8-6 The Proposed Comecrudo-Cotoname *l : w* Correspondence

Comecrudo		Cotoname	
al	'sun'	o / aau	'sun'
sel	'straw'	suau	'grass, tobacco, to smoke'
pa = msol, pa = msol	'red'	msa-e	'red'

Manaster Ramer 1996:21.

TABLE 8-7 Change from *k, kw* to *x, xw*

Comecrudo			Cotoname	
gnax (na)	'man'		xuainaxe	'man'
pe = kla	'to suck'		huäxle	'to suck'
[ax] pe = kewek	'low [water]'		xuaxe	'low (said of water)'
pa = kahuai, pa = kawai	'to write, to paint, paper'		thawe	'painted (on body, face)'

Manaster Ramer 1996:21.

1. For 'man', Comecrudo sources give *gnáx, gna^n, gnávx, na, Nã*, while Cotoname sources give *xuaináxe, keafuea* (Swanton 1940:65, Uhde 1861:185, Berlandier and Chowell 1828–9); it is not clear that these are cognate or, if they were, what segments should be compared. In particular, it is not clear that Comecrudo had a *k* or *kw* at all or that Cotoname ends up with *x* or *xw*—that is, there is just too much of the phonetic form left unaddressed to be persuaded of cognacy.

2. As for 'to suck', the Cotoname *huäxle* 'to suck', glossed also 'he sucks', is problematic. There is no other form with *l* in the cotoname data except the clearly borrowed *tawaló* 'corn', and therefore *huäxle* is almost certainly mistaken, but this destroys the similarity with the Comecrudo form, which relies on both languages having *l*. This *huäxle* 'he sucks' is suspiciously similar to *huwáxe, xuwáxi* 'infant'. Since we know nothing of Cotoname morphology, we cannot know what parts of this word, if any, go with 'suck' and what possibly with person, tense-aspect, and so on. Also, Comecrudo has *aináp, kené,* and *pékla* all glossed 'to suck' (Swanton 1996:116), meaning there are multiple targets for possible matchings. From the context, it is possible that *pékla* means only 'to smoke tobacco' (perhaps 'to suck tobacco'), glossed in Spanish *chupar,* with the example being *áx pékla* glossed *chupar tobaco* [sic], and with *áx pékle* 'cigarette' (*cigaro*), where *áx* is 'tobacco' (Swanton 1940:56, 91). In many languages of Middle America 'to smoke' is based on 'to suck', and this carries over into local varieties of Spanish. The *aináp* form appears to refer to the kind of sucking associated the curers (typical in Middle America, and in the shamanism of many North American and circumpolar peoples). Swanton's *kené* form, glossed 'to suck', would appear actually to be 'chest' (glossed as such on p. 71), found in the context *kném yesó, yesó kném*, where *kném* is a form of 'chest, breast' and it is *yesó* which

apparently means 'to suck, to nurse' (listed as such on p. 104). Finally, while there is good evidence for a *pa-* verbal prefix, there is no compelling reason to segment the *pé-* of *pékla* as Manaster Ramer does (his use of = is to indicate morpheme segmentations he believes in but which are not in the original forms).

3. Just so, the motivation for *pe-* in Manaster Ramer's Comecrudo *[ax] pe = kewek* 'low [water]' also has no strong motivation. Swanton's *áx pekewék* is given with a question mark and glossed with 'low water' (*áx* 'water') as a translation of Spanish *mar bajo* (p. 57), perhaps better 'low tide', and shows up again (p. 91) under *pekís,* glossed "clean, *and* flat(?.)." If these are related forms, the segmentation of *pe-* as a separate morpheme seems less likely– 'low tide' and 'flat' make some sense together. Swanton's Cotoname *xuáxe,* glossed 'low (said of water) / not deep', with Spanish *está bajo* (*el agua en el mar,* for example) (literally, 'it's low [the water in the sea]'). However, Cotoname *xuáxe* 'to drink' (*bebidas y para beber* 'drinks and for drinking') is so similar as to raise questions about the 'low water / low tide' form. It also is suggestively similar to the Cotoname *huäxle* 'to suck', permitting speculation about all these forms' possibly being derivationally related. This possibility is further supported, and the similarity confirmed, by another of Manaster Ramer's lexical sets, Comecrudo *xop* 'far, distant', Cotoname *huanpa, xuanpa* 'far'. While Swanton (1940:119) lists Cotoname *huánpa, xuánpa* with the English gloss 'far', the Spanish gives both *lejos* 'far', and apparently by way of explanation, *agua que se retira* 'water which recedes'. Judging from the forms above glossed as 'low water' and 'to drink' (and perhaps also 'to suck'), and from the gloss of 'water which recedes', it seems highly probable that this *huánpa, xuánpa* form is a derivation containing the same root. And in any case, the gloss 'far' seems an error for 'water which recedes', meaning the

Comecrudo and Cotoname forms are not semantically comparable.

4. The last set said to represent the *k, kw : x, xw* correspondence is Comecrudo *pa = kahuai, pa = kawai* 'to write, to paint, paper' : Cotoname *thawe* 'painted (on body, face)'. If these are similar (and Manaster Ramer has no real account of the initial *t* of the Cotoname form), given the cultural nature of the gloss, they may well represent borrowings. However, the gloss is not clear; Swanton (1996:120) lists Cotoname *tháwe* 'painted (on body, face)', but gives the Spanish gloss as *pinto,* saying it refers to *Indios Pintos*; *pinto* is a Spanish adjective referring to animals which have various colors, and the Pinto Indians were a band in the area. If the referent is Pinto Indians, there is no reason why the name would have to signal 'painted' necessarily, just because that was the name given to them in Spanish. It is a peculiar form in any event, since it is the only one in the Cotoname material with *th.* Comecrudo has *estók pakahwaíle* for 'Indio Pinto' (*estók* 'Indian'), but with the explanation that *se rajan con aguja* 'they split/tattoo themselves with a needle'. Swanton relates this to *kawi* 'to shave' (p. 85). If the name for Pinto Indians is involved, this could be a borrowing. Finally, the account does not specify why with only four sets, we seem to see *g : xu, k : hu/xu,* and *k : h.* This cannot legitimately be called a regular sound correspondence.

Manaster Ramer (1996:21) speculates about another possible correspondence, Comecrudo Ø to Cotoname final *-e,* based on the forms (above) for 'man' and 'low', comparing also Comecrudo *el-pau* 'to kneel down, sink, sit down' and Cotoname *pawe* 'to sit'. However, not only are the cognacy of the 'man' and 'low' forms in question (above), so is this further example. Since *pa-* is a verbal suffix commonly segmented off in other of Manaster Ramer's examples and also in many of Swanton's forms, it would appear the Cotoname comparison should be with the root *-we,* while the Comecrudo form, on the other hand, appears to be derived from or at least be related to *elpa* 'to come down', which Swanton even gives on occasion as *elpá-u.* (Note that *el-* is a prefix meaning 'down, bottom', Swanton 1940:61.) This, then, is not very convincing. Another set, Comecrudo *pamawau* 'to snarl or growl' (glossed as Spanish *regañar,* thus actually 'to scold') : Cotoname *pama* 'to cry' (Spanish

gritar—that is, 'to shout', glossed also 'they shout'), is called into question for the same reason; thus, the Cotoname root appears to be *-ma* 'to shout'. This is too short, possibly onomatopoeic, and semantically rather different, and thus it is quite doubtful. Thus, this correspondence also does not hold up.

In short, the forms listed in support of Manaster Ramer's sound correspondences are simply too uncertain or problematic and too few to support the proposed Cotoname-Comecrudan relationship.

The two sets involving pronouns (Comecrudo *na* : Cotoname *na* 'I'; *emnã, men* 'thou'), while superficially quite suggestive, have the problems of nasals and unmarked consonants being typical of pronouns, the pan-Americanism problem (where these are not shown to be more closely related if several other languages not being considered also share the same similarity); the 'I' forms are short. The most serious problem for these is that Cotoname *men* 'thou' does not exist as such in the scant data available, but rather is based on Manaster Ramer's interpretation of the single phrase, *titcháx mén* 'what do you want?', with no other evidence of a second person pronoun form in the data available. This, however, is by no means a secure interpretation; even if the two languages prove to be related, a phonetic similarity with the Comecrudo 'thou' form would still not be sufficient to confirm that the Cotoname piece *mén* would necessarily mean 'thou'. But, then, the interpretation of the Comecrudo 'thou' form is also unclear. Under Swanton's entry *emna[n]',* which has ten example sentences or phrases, four refer to 'I', four are 'reciprocals' (not with second person forms), two to *vosotros* ('second plural familiar'), and one to *tu* ('you singular familiar', or 'thou'). Under the entry for 'you' (p. 118), Swanton has *emna[n]', nána[n],* and *ye-inán,* but then under 'I' (p. 111) Swanton has the same *ye-inán,* and *na* and *yén.* As was the case of *emna[n]',* there is also confusion concerning the gloss in the examples under the entry for *nána[n]* (p. 83), with several referring to 'I', some to 'reciprocal', some to 'you'. The fact that *naní* 'he/she' is very similar also does not reassure us that these pronominal forms have been correctly understood.

The Cotoname phrase, *titcháx mén* 'what do you want?', was the source also of another of

Manaster Ramer's sets, Comecrudo *tete* 'how, what, why' : Cotoname *tit* 'what?'; however, just as with *men* 'thou', there is no other evidence in the scant data on Cotoname for segmenting off a form *tit* and interpreting it as meaning 'what'. The presence of highly unmarked *t* in demonstratives and interrogatives is very common in the world's languages, and there is no way to know whether the second *t* is orthographically connected with *ch*, a part of a root, part of an affix, or what its status might be.

The forms for 'water' (Comecrudo *aal/ ax* : Cotoname *ax*) are short and like terms for 'water' are widespread in the Americas and beyond, perhaps for onomatopoeic reasons having to do with drinking noises. The comparison of Comecrudo *wax* : Cotoname *kox* 'belly', without some indication that the *w* : *k* correspondence recurs, is more likely to be just accidental. The "tentative comparison" of Comecrudo *somi* 'there is nothing, which is outside, without' : Cotoname *sa* 'no' involves a short form with very different semantics—the examples under the Comecrudo entry (Swanton 1940:95) make it clear the gloss is not 'negative', but rather 'alone, outside'. The 'tentative' Comecrudo *ketuau* : Cotoname *kowá-u* 'dog' is not much help. Cotoname has *kowá-u, kewáwia* 'dog', suggestive of onomatopoeia (along with names for dog and for dogs' barking such as *haw, waw, kaw, kwa(w)* that are found frequently among the world's languages). The Comecrudo form, however, appears to be mistaken in that the Spanish gloss is *perrico,* translated as 'little dog', but given with "parakeet is also suggested" (Swanton 1940:71). While *perrico* would be 'little dog' in elevated Spanish, the word is virtually unknown in Mexico, where *perrito* is the common diminutive. Swanton's comment suggests that *perico* 'parakeet, small parrot' was the intended gloss ('dog' in Comecrudo is *klam*), and indeed similar forms for 'parrot, parakeet' are seen in a number of Mesoamerican languages, again probably onomatopoeic at least in part (see Campbell and Kaufman 1993). The other "tentative comparison," given by Manaster Ramer as Comecrudo *kiextuén* : Cotoname *kiáx̱nem* 'rabbit', actually involves Comecrudo *kiexuén, kíehuen* and Cotoname *kiáxhem* (Swanton 1940:72, 119), which are essentially identical in

form and thus almost certainly involve either loans or an error stemming from a Comecrudo informant as a source for some of the Cotoname forms. In the set Comecrudo *aui* [*aoui*] : Cotoname *aue* [*aoue*], the forms are so similar they suggest borrowing or interference in the bilingual informant.

Perhaps the most attractive of Manaster Ramer's lexical sets is Comecrudo *mapi* 'hand' : Cotoname *miapa* 'wing', where Swanton has no Cotoname form for 'hand' and the Comecrudo form for 'wing' is *xám mapi*, literally 'bird hand'. However, without regular sound correspondences and other supporting forms to back this up, it could have other explanations. For one, forms for 'hand' constitute the most notorious of the pan-Americanisms, held by Greenberg (1987:57–8) to be *ma* in Amerind in general. Since body parts and animal parts here are usually inalienably possessed, it is important to keep in mind that some portion of, say, Cotoname *miapa* ('wings' according to the Spanish gloss *alas*) might well not belong to the root for 'wing' but to a possessive affix. Only two other forms in the Cotoname data end in *pa* or *p*, and they are consistent with this being a separate morpheme (one is *huanpa* 'water recedes', mentioned above).

In short, there are problems of a methodological sort with all of Manaster Ramer's Comecrudo-Cotoname comparisons, serious problems with most. The hypothesis is by no means confirmed, though it is still attractive and deserves further investigation.

From this comparison of Cotoname with Comecrudan, Manaster Ramer proceeds to a broader comparison with Coahuilteco. He suggests two sound correspondences. One is Comecrudo *k* to Cotoname *h/x* to Coahuilteco *h* in the set Comecrudo *kam* 'to drink' : Cotoname *hahame, xaxame* 'to eat, food' : Coahuilteco *hām* 'to eat'. In this case, in Swanton's phrases and sentences under the Comecrudo form we have *kámi, ikámi, pakámle, paikám,* but we also have *painók* (*que va* [*a*] *beber,* '(he) is going to / will drink'). Most of Swanton's examples (p. 68) mean 'to drink', but one has 'eat' (*glám yen kámi* 'my dog is eating' [*glám* 'dog', *yen* 'my']), though this could be a mistake for 'drinking'); however, the Comecrudo *kam* form, or better said its morphology, is not at all clear. It is not certain that the *m* is in fact part of the root 'to drink'. The other examples to illustrate this correspondence set give no Cotoname forms. The set with Coahuilteco *xāi* 'to be extinguished (of fire), to come to an end' : Comecrudo *kai* 'to eat' do not match semantically—essentially 'to end' and 'to eat'. The set Coahuilteco *axām* 'not' : Comecrudo *kam* 'no' provides no explanation for the unmatched initial vowel of Coahuilteco, and the Coahuilteco forms *ox* 'no' and *mō* 'no more than' suggest that there is more than might initially meet the eye to the morphological (or etymological) story of *axām*. The example with Coahuilteco *xūm* 'to die' : Comecrudo *kamau* 'to kill' would be more believable if there were some account of why the vowels are so different; since Coahuilteco also has *tzam* 'to die', one wonders if there is not more to the story. Some have speculated that influence from Mayan (see Huastec *tsam-* 'to die', Proto-Mayan **kam*) might not be involved in both the Coahuilteco and Comecrudo forms. The forms Coahuilteco *xasāl* and Comecrudo *kayasel* 'heart' look superficially similar, but no explanation is offered for the extra syllable of the Comecrudo form. This appears to be morphologically complex when seen with *kayaú* 'sore, ache, sick', since the heart is the seat of emotions, sensations, and thoughts in many Middle American languages. The final case, Coahuilteco *malāux* 'male sexual organs' : Comecrudo *melkuai* 'female sexual organs', unlike the others, appears to compare a final *x* with a medial *k* or *kw,* with no explanation of why they should turn up in different location within the forms compared. Swanton (1940:82) gives both *melkuaí* and *mekwaí*, and since there are no other forms with an *lk* cluster in the language, apparently we are obliged to assume *mekwaí* to be more accurate. This makes the Coahuilteco form much less similar.

Manaster Ramer gives another "somewhat tenuous" correspondence set (p. 23), illustrated by two lexical comparisons, of Coahuilteco intervocalic *xw* to *p* in Comecrudan. The first compares the 'hand/wing' forms already seen (Comecrudo *mapi* 'hand, fingers, arm', Cotoname *miapa* 'wings') with Coahuilteco *māux* 'hand'. This is slightly problematic for not hav-

ing the *w* intervocalically after all. The same comments concerning the 'hand' with *ma* pan-Americanism apply here, as well, though this is one of the more suggestive sets. The other example is Coahuilteco *uxual'* 'heaven' : Comecrudo *apel* 'sky, heaven, clouds', which could benefit from some account—otherwise missing—of the vowel difference. Comecrudo *apél* is the entry for 'face' as well as 'sky, heaven, clouds', and is listed together with *mapél* 'rain' and *mepel* 'bed covers' (as 'that which is above') (Swanton 1940:59); *iapel* is 'head', and *pela* is 'hair' (Goddard 1979b:369). Thus, neither the form nor the basic meaning is clear. It is possible that Coahuilteco *uxual'* is morphologically complex, since *u-* is the 'third person subject pronoun' prefix; this is suggested further by the fact that only two other forms begin with *u* (*ūm* 'to tell' and *uspamū* 'distant [of relationship]'). Thus, it might be speculated that *uxual'* 'heaven' has some connection with *xuālax* 'to conceal', as in 'to cover', a sense implicated in the Comecrudo from. Without more and better examples, this proposed correspondence set cannot be considered reliable evidence.

Manaster Ramer (1996:24) finds "more interesting" the correspondence between Coahuilteco *kuV* and Comecrudo *kiV* he proposes, as illustrated by Coahuilteco *kuas* : Comecrudo *kial* 'blood'. Since *s* and *l* appear to vary sometimes in certain Comecrudo forms, this is more similar than it might at first seem. The correspondence is said to be illustrated further in Coahuilteco *kuan* 'to go' : Comecrudo *kio* 'to go' (and *kie* 'to come'), but these are short forms; there is no account for the vowels or for the final *n* of the Coahuilteco form; English *go* and *come* are nearly as persuasive as possible cognates. Again, more and better cases would be needed to support this proposed sound correspondence.

Manaster Ramer sees another set of "possible regular correspondences" (p. 24) in Coahuiltecan *ts* to Comecrudo *y,* with three lexical sets. For 'to hear', Coahuilteco *tšei* : Comecrudo *ye,* the Coahuilteco form is "hypothesized by Swanton as the singular corresponding to the attested and apparently plural *tšakēi*" (Manaster Ramer 1996:33; the hypothetical singular form is given with a question mark by Swanton 1940:39). So, given that the form is short, hypothetical, and questioned, and in any case does not involve *ts* but rather *č*, it is safe to say this form is unworthy of much faith as an example of the proposed correspondence set. The set with Coahuilteco *tzōtz* 'chest' : Comecrudo *yeso* 'to suck, to nurse' would need an account of the vowels and the *tz* and *s*, and the semantics may be in doubt, since Swanton (1996:38) says specifically of the Coahuilteco 'chest' form that it means 'breast (of man)'. In the last lexical set, Coahuilteco *tzin* may match Comecrudo *yen* 'I', but the nasal involves the pan-Americanism, and since Comecrudo has other pronouns with *ye-*, for example, *ye-iná* 'you', *yenáx* 'you plural', *ye-inán* 'we', it is unlikely this *y* is a direct match for the *tz* of the Coahuilteco 'I' form.

The other proposed sound correspondences involve greater abstraction and less regularity, with fewer examples, involving differences in the nonlabial stops. It is said that Coahuilteco *t* "seems to correspond to *d* or *l* in the other languages" (p. 25). To accept this, we would have to accept the proposed cognate sets in Table 8-8. In the first, the semantic difference is serious; there's no account for the vowel, for the extra syllable, or for why the *t* is initial in one language while the *l* is medial in the other. In the second case, presumably it is not *č* (Swanton's *tc* symbol) we are to see, but rather perhaps an initial *t* somehow corresponding with initial *l*. Since no other form seems to fit this, it is at best questionable. Finally, even if the 'breast' set were accurate, it would be just an isolated instance of *t* : *d*, not a recurring correspondence. As for the sets assumed to involve glottalized *t'*, a match of *t'* with Ø (for example, Coahuilteco *t'il* 'day' : Comecrudo *al* 'sun, day, today') and of *t'* with *t* (Coahuilteco *t'āhaka, t'axakan* 'what' : Comecrudo *tete* 'how, what, why' : Cotoname *tahikam* 'whose') are both proposed, but only a single example of each is given, so that it cannot be said to be regular since the proposed

correspondence does not recur. With regard to the first, this makes any vowel-initial word a potential target, greatly increasing the chances of accidental agreements. With respect to the second, the semantics diverge considerably, and no account is given of why Comecrudo should have those vowels and a second *t* not matched to anything else, though the forms in the other two languages are very long. Also, if there is a *tete* : *tit* cognate set (above), then there must be an explanation for why *tete* is paired with *tahikam* for this occasion—both cannot be cognate with *tete* unless ultimately both Cotoname forms derive from a single etymon.[72]

Finally, another ten or so lexical look-alikes for Coahuilteco and Comecrudo are listed, but most are suspicious for various reasons. For example, two involve first and second person pronouns, short and pan-American, already challenged above. Most of the others involve no more than a *CV* matching, though other nonmatching phonetic material is present.

In short, the forms presented for Coahuilteco and Comecrudan are also not sufficiently robust to support the hypothesis, though it does deserve further investigation. However, in view of the known loans among languages of the area and the role of Coahuilteco as a lingua franca, the role of borrowing must be given serious attention in such an investigation.

Guaicurian-Hokan
0% probability, 10% confidence

Guaicurian (Waikurian) of Baja California is poorly documented and its linguistic affinities are in dispute (see Chapters 4 and 5), though it is usually thought not to be demonstrably related to any broader grouping. Gursky (1966b) attempted to group Waikuri with Hokan, citing fifty-three sets of look-alikes involving Waikuri and other putative Hokan languages. These sets

TABLE 8-8 Proposed Cognates

Coahuilteco		Comecrudo or Cotoname	
t'il	'posterior, anus'	alal	'leg'
tšum	'night, evening'	lesum, lesom	'evening'
tām	'breast (of a women)'	dom (Cotoname)	'breast'

involve the common problems (as discussed in Chapter 7), and most are doubtful for one reason or another.

Quechua as Hokan
−85% probability, 80% confidence

J. P. Harrington argued that Quechua was a Hokan language: "Hokanity pervades the entire make-up of Quechua" (1943a:335). Although he presented a number of lexical and typological similarities, these exhibit the usual methodological problems; most do not hold up under scrutiny. Today no one takes this claim seriously. It is mentioned here only because it is occasionally referred to in works by culture historians, who should be warned about it.

"Gulf" and Associated Proposals

Although many languages of the southeastern United States are today considered isolates, they have been implicated in a variety of proposals, each of which had for a time attained a certain degree of acceptance. They are discussed here in roughly chronological order.

Tunican
0% probability, 20% confidence

Swanton (1919) believed that Tunica, Chitimacha, and Atakapa were related in a stock he called "Tunican." The evidence is not persuasive (see below). Sapir (1929a) incorporated Swanton's Tunican into his Hokan-Siouan super-stock.

Natchez-Muskogean
+ 40% probability, 20% confidence

Attempts to relate Natchez to other languages have been unpersuasive. Swanton (1924) believed it was related to Muskogean, a proposal that was supported by Haas (1956). Sapir (1929a) placed these in the Eastern division of his Hokan-Siouan super-stock. Haas grouped Swanton's Natchez-Muskogean and Tunican (Tunica, Atakapa, Chitimacha) together in her Gulf proposal (1951, 1952), though she seems later to have retreated from the idea of a closer connection between Natchez and Muskogean

within Gulf (1969d:62; see also 1979:318). Today none of these proposals is accepted uncritically. Natchez is considered an isolate, but some linguists are still sympathetic to the idea of a Natchez-Muskogean relationship (for example, Geoffrey Kimball personal communication, see Kimball 1994). This possibility needs to be investigated thoroughly (see Haas 1979; Swanton 1917, 1919, 1946).

Broader connections of Muskogean with other language groups of the Southeast have been proposed, but there is no solid evidence in support of them. Haas's (1951, 1952) Gulf classification is widely known but is no longer upheld (see below). Those attempting to find broader genetic affinities for these languages will need to also take into account the effects of diffusion within the Southeast linguistic area (see Chapter 9).

Atakapa-Chitimacha
−50% probability, 60% confidence

Swadesh (1946, 1947) listed 258 lexical comparisons between Atakapa and Chitimacha (the languages from Swanton's Tunican for which Swadesh had data) and, based on these, attempted to establish "phonologic formulas" (correspondences). Of the 240 sets in the 1946 article, only 153 constituted what he considered "a main list." It includes 33 in a section of sets with "special problems of form"—"involving assumed affixation, assimilation, etc." (1946: 113); others are also questionable in terms of phonology or morphological makeup. Another 32 are said to have "divergent meanings," and 16 have "inferred meanings"—all of these putative cognates are doubtful for semantic reasons. In a 1947 article, Swadesh presented an additional 18 comparisons. Eliminating sets 154–240, since Swadesh himself called them into question (and indeed they have more problems than the others), I find that the remaining sets, on the whole, exhibit greater problems with respect to the criteria of Chapter 7 than most of the other proposals discussed in this chapter. For example, 54 include forms that are semantically divergent; 19 have the sort of semantic content and phonetic near identity that together suggest diffusion (for example, Atakapa *uk* 'shell, oyster', Chitimacha *ʔukšču* 'oyster'); 17 are onomatopoetic (for example, Atakapa *cok* 'blackbird', Chitimacha *jekt* 'red-winged blackbird'[73]); 82 include short forms or longer forms with only one or two matching segments (such as Atakapa *šo* 'seed', Chitimacha *šokt* 'pecan nut'); 23 are so different phonetically as to be implausible as potential cognates (as, for example, Atakapa *wil*, Chitimacha *ʔaʔišt-* 'to rock'; Atakapa *oc, oci* 'up, top', Chitimacha *kap* 'up'); and in 13 pan-Americanisms are implicated. In sum, Swadesh's evidence does not support an Atakapa-Chitimacha genetic relationship.

"Gulf"
− 25% probability, 40% confidence

Haas's (1951, 1952, 1960) proposed Gulf classification would connect Muskogean, Natchez, Tunica, Atakapa, and Chitimacha (see also Haas 1958b, 1979, Swanton 1917). However, in her later publications Haas expressed some misgivings; she doubted the status of Atakapa and Chitimacha as "Gulf" languages, given in her diagram with dotted lines and question marks (Haas 1969d:63; see Booker 1980:3), and she expressed reservations concerning the Gulf proposal in general (Haas 1979 and personal communication). None of these Gulf proposals is upheld today. Even Kimball, who is sympathetic to the possibility, concludes that "good apparent cognate sets are not common, and when one has to apply the possibilities of borrowing, onomatopoeia and chance, the number of sets shrinks further. This is the real frustration of comparative 'Gulf': there is just enough to suggest the languages are related, but there is not enough to provide clear and unequivocal proof" (1994:34).

Munro has recently reopened the question of Haas's Gulf (and also of Gulf-Yukian; see below). She presents a large number of sets of lexical parallels and some grammatical similarities, incorporating some examples from earlier comparisons. Munro admits that her "analysis of this new body of data remains preliminary" (1994:149, also p. 143), yet asserts that her article "provides stronger lexical support for the Gulf group" (1994:149). There is a similar equivocation about her methodology. She reviews the difficulties that arise from sound symbolism, "sets whose consonants do not fully overlap," onomatopoeia, nursery words, bor-

rowing, and sets assumed to illustrate metathesis in the matchings, and she explicitly identifies several of the lexical sets she presents as examples which illustrate these difficulties. She says of these that "there is no reason not to include the word [a nursery word or an onomatopoetic form] in the list, but perhaps it should be given less weight in the final analysis" and that "such sets [suspected borrowings] should not be excluded from our materials for a lexicon of Proto-Gulf or Proto-Yuki-Gulf, but they should not be used to argue for a relationship" (1994:144). This equivocal attitude makes it more difficult to evaluate her argument, since she presents many problematic forms in her lists with no clear indication of which are to be taken as the stronger examples. Munro also considers some sound correspondences, but the eight for which she mentions examples are identical in all the languages compared and they are not at all convincing (1994:145). An examination of her first correspondence, *p*, in all the languages compared is revealing. She lists the following five lexical sets as exemplifying this correspondence. I point out some of the problems that make the proposed cognate sets, and thus also the correspondence sets, illegitimate.

BALL₁ : Chitimacha *paci*, Creek *pokko*, Chickasaw *ilbak pocokkoʔ* 'fist', Koasati *kapoci* 'stickball stick', Natchez *puhs*, Tunica *púna*—Problems: Stickball is an areal trait of the Southeast culture area and therefore 'stickball stick' and 'ball' could easily be borrowed; the semantics of the items do not match ('ball/fist/stickball stick'); and the only sound that seems to correspond across these sets is the *p*. There is little similarity among other sounds, and Munro provides no explanation of the nonmatched segments (for example, contrast *paci* and *púna*).

BED: Atakapa *pil*, Chitimacha *keʔe:p', ketpa* 'mattress, quilt', Choctaw *topah*, Alabama *patka*, Natchez *hapat(a)-* —Problems: These could be diffused items, given the semantics, and several of them have very little phonetic material that is actually similar (contrast *pil/topah/keʔe:p'*).

BLOW: Atakapa *puns*, Chitimacha *pu:hte-* 'blow through a tube', Creek *po:fk-*, Natchez *puuW-hooʔis*, Tunica *púska* 'swell, inflate'—Problems: These are onomatopoetic forms, and not all of them are semantically equivalent.

CUT₁ : Chitimacha *pokšt-* 'cut irregularly', Tunica *póhtu* and the Muskogean languages' Alabama *pitaffi* 'gut', Koasati *pitaffi* 'slice up the middle', Choctaw *pataffi* 'split, plow', Chickasaw *pataffi* 'rip, disembowel'—Problems: These have no clearly corresponding sounds other than the *p*, they vary semantically (though all involve 'cut'), and some scholars might assert that they are sound-symbolic/onomatopoetic.

FEATHER: Chitimacha *kahmpa* 'plume', Choctaw *hapokbo*, Tunica *húhpa* 'to gather, to feather (an arrow)'—Problems: It is not clear which sounds, other than the *p* of these forms, are intended to correspond; the forms are not semantically equivalent; and the feathering/fletching of arrows might easily be a diffused term.

In short, each of the five proposed cognate sets that supposedly illustrate the *p* correspondence set has such serious difficulties that we cannot, on the basis of them alone, accept this as a likely sound correspondence. The same is true of the other seven sets (see Munro 1994: 145).

In fact, in nearly every lexical set that Munro presents there are several forms that have very little phonetic similarity; some share only one similar sound, and some have two similar sounds but her liberal appeal to metathesis permits them to appear in a different linear order in the lexical items compared. The following sets are typical of her data in general, except that I have perhaps selected a larger proportion that have fewer forms in each set for ease of presentation.

ALLIGATOR₂: Natchez *ʔa:titi:*, Creek *halpata*—Problems: little phonetic similarity, only two languages compared, forms possibly diffused

BARK₂: Koasati *kawka* 'to bark (of a fox)', Natchez *kaWkup* 'fox'—Problems: onomatopoetic, only two languages compared, semantic nonequivalence

BITTER: Atakapa *he*, Choctaw *homi*—Problems: short forms, with several nonmatched segments unexplained; only two languages compared

BLOWGUN DART: Koasati *łohpo* 'blowgun dart, thistle', Natchez *loho* 'blowgun dart, thistle'—Problems: probably diffused forms, only two languages compared

BREAST₁: Natchez *šu*, Tunica *ʔúču*—Problems: onomatopoetic, short forms, only two languages compared

DANCE: Atakapa *puh* (sing.), *pum* (pl.), Koasati *hopani* 'play', Choctaw *hōpa* 'whoop', Creek *opan-ita* 'dance', Tunica *ʔápanhára* 'the name of an old dance' (*hára* 'to sing')—Problems:

short or phonetically noncorresponding forms compared; forms semantically nonequivalent, possibly onomatopoetic, possibly involving diffusion

DILUTE: Alabama *bila* 'melt', Tunica *lúwa* 'mix in a liquid with, dilute'—Problems: only two languages compared, forms semantically nonequivalent; requires the assumption of metathesis for phonetic similarity

FRIEND: Chitimacha *keta*, Koasati *ittinkano* 'compatible', Natchez *kitah*, Tunica *-éti*—Problems: Chitimacha and Natchez forms involve borrowing; others not clearly phonetically similar; 'compatible' not semantically equivalent to 'friend'

HEART: Atakapa *šo* 'heart, soul', Chitimacha *ših* 'belly', Chickasaw *conkaš*, Natchez *ʔiNc*—Problems: short forms (and nonmatching segments), semantic nonequivalence

LEG: Choctaw *iyyi* 'leg', Tunica *-éyu* 'arm'—Problems: semantic latitude, only two languages compared

LICK₂: Creek *la:s-ita* 'lick', Tunica *lísu* 'taste'—Problems: semantically nonequivalent forms, only two languages compared, symbolic/onomatopoetic

QUAIL₁: Alabama *kowwayki:*, Natchez *ʔooweh* 'guinea', *ʔooweeneh* 'little guinea'—Problems: not semantically equivalent, possibly involving diffusion, onomatopoetic (at least in the case of 'guinea'; guinea fowl are not native to the Americas), only two languages compared, not clear what corresponds phonetically

RABBIT₂: Atakapa *anhipon*, Chitimacha *pu:p*—Problems: only two languages compared; not phonetically similar, with many unexplained, nonmatching segments

SNAIL: Mikasuki *silbāhk-i*, Natchez *mo:lih*—Problems: no phonetic match, only two languages compared

SOFTEN: Atakapa *li* 'grind, soften', Creek *lisk-ita* 'worn out'—Problems: short forms, semantic latitude, only two languages compared

SQUIRREL: Alabama *ipło*, Natchez *hi*—Problems: no phonetic match, short forms, only two languages compared, a term susceptible to borrowing

STRAWBERRY: Alabama *biyyokha*, Natchez *kickotoM*—Problems: phonetically not similar, possibly diffused, only two languages compared

TELL: Natchez *ha:wici:š* 'tell', Tunica *wi* 'listen, hear'—Problems: semantically nonequivalent, short form (with no explanation of leftover segments of the Natchez form), only two languages compared

YUM: Koasati *namnam,* Natchez *namnam-hal ʔiš* 'sweeten the mouth (opossum talking)'—Problems: onomatopoetic/affective, semantically nonequivalent forms, possibly diffused (through local oral literature), only two languages compared

In general, Munro's data do nothing to bolster the already widely questioned Gulf proposal. She identifies several forms in her data as "unattested." As mentioned previously, there is a lack of phonetic similarity in nearly every one of her 574 sets. In the longer examples, the segments typically do not match and no explanation is offered for the nonmatching ones; many of the forms are short. Other scholars have identified borrowings in a number of these sets, as indicated by Munro; the semantics and phonetic form of other sets are highly suggestive of possible borrowing. There are 95 sets that involve known or suspected borrowing (for example, see BOX, BUFFALO, CATFISH, CLAM, CYPRESS, DOCTOR, EVERGREEN, FOX, MULBERRY, OYSTER, PEPPER, PINE, ROBIN, TEN, TOWN, WHIPPOORWILL). Some 96 sets reflect wide semantic latitude; 112 sets include forms that are onomatopoetic, symbolic, or expressive-affective (for example, BARK$_1$, BARK$_2$, BEAT, BLACKBIRD, BLOW, BREAST$_1$, BREAST$_2$, BREATHE, CHICKEN, CHOKE, COUGH, CRICKET, CROW$_2$, DRIP, GOBBLE, LICK, MAKE NOISE (WHOOP), POP (EXPLODE), RATTLE$_1$, RATTLE$_2$, SNEEZE, SNORE, SPLASH, SUCK, SWELL, WHINE); 116 sets compare only two languages (counting Muskogean languages as one unit, as Munro does); 34 sets include pan-Americanisms; and 6 include nursery forms. It is safe to say that the Gulf proposal remains in doubt.

Algonkian-Gulf
−50% probability, 50% confidence

Haas's Algonkian-Gulf proposal—that there is a relationship between Algic (Algonquian-Ritwan) and the putative Gulf languages—received considerable attention in the past (see, for example, Gursky 1966–1967, 1968), but today it is largely abandoned (see Haas 1979). Haas left open the possibility of "additional affinities" and claimed that Tonkawa was "another likely affiliate" (1958b:231, see also 1960:985–6), but she remained noncommittal concerning possible

connections with Algonkian-Mosan (Algonquian-Ritwan, Mosan, and Kutenai), Mosan (Chimakuan, Wakashan, and Salishan), Siouan,[74] Hokan, and Hokan-Siouan, all of which were implicated in broader proposals (many formulated by Sapir) that involved in some way the other languages of Haas's new proposal. She reported her own surprise at what her comparison of Algonquian and Muskogean had revealed, since she had "assumed for a long time that any resemblances noted to Algonkian were the result of borrowing" (1958b:235). Given the Southeastern linguistic area and broader connections within eastern North America, the possibility of borrowing must be kept in mind and appropriate precautions taken not to include such forms (see Chapter 9). Haas presented 132 sets of lexical resemblances, together with tentative sound correspondences, in support of the Algonquian-Gulf proposal. However, when we evaluate this evidence on the basis of the criteria of Chapter 7, we find that many of these sets should be eliminated. For example, several of these involve onomatopoeia (for example, 'beat', 'bee', 'blow', 'breathe', 'crow', 'cry/weep', 'hawk', 'ring [hum, roar]', 'shoot', 'to sound', 'spit', 'split', 'swallow','whistle'); some include nursery forms (for example, 'older brother', 'daughter [daughter/father/mother]', 'father [three terms]'); some involve liberal semantic associations, though Haas is generally careful in this regard (for example,'brain / hair of head', 'son/father/mother/daughter', 'defecate/stink/rotten', 'mouth/tongue'); 28 include short forms or longer forms that have only short corresponding portions; and some include expressive or sound-symbolic forms (for example,'bloom', 'squeeze out juice / milk cow', 'foam', 'swell'). Several of her sets involve comparisons between Algic forms and forms from only one other language rather than from a wider range of Gulf languages (for example, 'big', 'crawfish', 'dry', 'dust', 'ear', 'far', 'father[1]', 'father[2]', 'father-in-law', 'fear', 'foam', 'hair', 'head', 'hot', 'joined', 'liver', 'male', 'mouth', 'neck[2]', 'open', 'otter', 'third person pronoun', 'road', 'shake', 'shoot[2]', 'skin/hide', 'skin[verb]', 'snow', 'son', 'stone', 'swing', 'tapering at base / pear-shaped', 'ten', 'true/good', 'turn around', 'turtle', 'two'). Some pan-Americanisms show up in the list (for example, 'belly', 'bone', 'cover/spread/wide',[75] 'dog', 'dust',[76] 'foot', 'give', 'hand', 'first person pronoun', 'second person pronoun', 'leg', 'negative',[77] 'wet/wash'. Diffusion may be involved in 'skunk' (see Haas 1963a), 'crawfish', and 'buy'. The remaining forms do not provide sufficient support to sustain the hypothesis. Although some of them are suggestive, stronger evidence would be required to make the Algonquian-Gulf proposal acceptable.

Other Broad Proposals of Relationships among Languages of the Southeast

Crawford (1979) presented similarities shared by Yuchi, Tunica, and Atakapa, though he also thought it "promising that a genetic relationship can eventually be shown to exist between Yuchi and Siouan" (1973:173). The possibility of a Yuchi connection with either Tunica or Atakapa requires further investigation, but at present such a relationship seems doubtful. (On Yuchi-Siouan, see Macro-Siouan above.)

In earlier work Haas had explored and defended possible connections between Algonquian and "Gulf" languages and between Tonkawa and "Gulf" languages, and this led her to examine evidence for a possible Tonkawa-Algonquian connection (1959, 1960, 1967a). Her evidence is quite scanty (forty-three sets of lexical similarities in 1959 and nineteen additional ones in 1967), with attempts at deriving regular sound correspondences. Some of these sets are suggestive, but many of them exhibit the methodological problems discussed in Chapter 7. With regard to about half of them, Haas admits that she "finds resemblances between Tonkawa and other languages and proto-languages as well" (1967a:318).

Gursky (1963, 1965–1966, 1966–1967, 1968) presented a lengthy list of lexical and some morphological resemblance on the basis of which he argued for a connection between Hokan-Subtiaban-Jicaquean and Algonkian-Gulf. Needless to say, if such component units as Hokan and Gulf have not been established, a much more inclusive grouping such as this one has little chance of succeeding. Gursky's examples fall prey to many of the methodological problems discussed in Chapter 7, and he

himself cautions that the material "reicht qualitativ und quantitativ noch nicht aus, um Zufall und Entlehnungen als mögliche Erklärungen auszuschliessen" (is not yet sufficient to eliminate chance and borrowing as possible explanations).[78]

Penutian

Like Hokan, the Penutian grouping is broad and influential, and opinions vary considerably concerning its potential validity as a genetic unit. Both hypotheses were first framed by Dixon and Kroeber (1913a, 1913b, 1919). (For a review of earlier work and suggested connections involving putative Penutian languages, see Callaghan 1958.) Versions of Penutian proposals have included languages spoken from Alaska to Bolivia and even Chile (see Voegelin and Voegelin 1967:578). The name is based on words for 'two', approximating *pen* in Wintuan, Maiduan, and Yokutsan, and similar to *uti* in Miwokan and Costanoan, combined to form *Penutian*. I survey the history of research on these languages in order to assess the various claims involved.

Dixon and Kroeber proposed a genetic relationship among these five language families of central California. Their 1913 articles were primarily announcements (Dixon and Kroeber 1913a, 1913b); the evidence was not published until 1919. They presented a list of 171 lexical similarities (which they called "cognate stems") and grammatical similarities, along with "an attempt at what would be rather chaotic sound correspondences in the modern sense" (Silverstein 1979a:651), but they did not connect their proposed reconstructed sounds with individual correspondences (Callaghan 1958:192). For their Proto-Penutian they proposed voiceless, voiced, and glottalized stops; fricatives *s, š,* and *x; m, n, l, r;* five vowels; and a basic stem pattern of *CVCV(C)*. Dixon and Kroeber also characterized Penutian typologically:

> Penutian possesses an elaborate and delicate system of vowel gradations or mutations. Etymological composition is scantily developed. Prefixes of any sort are totally lacking. The noun is provided with seven, and probably never more than seven, true cases. The verb does not express instrumentality or location, as it does in so many other American languages, but is altered only to express cate-

gories which in the main are expressed also in Indo-Germanic conjugation: intransitiveness, inception, and similar ideas; voice, mode, and tense, and person. A true passive occurs. (1913a:650)

Although very influential, the Penutian proposal has been controversial from the beginning. As mentioned in Chapter 2, Dixon and Kroeber's methods left much to be desired, since they rely heavily on mere juxtaposition of short word lists for evidence. This prompted criticism of both the methods and the proposed hypothesis (see Frachtenberg 1918:176, Shafer 1947:205). Nevertheless, Sapir extended the Penutian hypothesis greatly; already in 1916 he spoke of evidence he had collected "to show that it [Penutian] extends into Oregon, embracing Takelma, Coos, and Lower Umpqua [Siuslaw], possibly certain other languages" (1949[1916]:453; see pp. 457, 459). With evidence relating Takelma and Kalapuya, and both of these to Chinookan (see Frachtenberg 1918), Sapir completed his Oregon Penutian and added Tsimshian as a northern outlier (1921a, 1921c; see also Sapir and Swadesh 1953). Later he added two branches, Plateau Penutian and Mexican Penutian (see below). Sapir's Plateau group reflects the "Shahapwailutan" proposed by Hewitt and Powell, which grouped Lutuamian (Klamath-Modoc), Waiilatpuan (Molala-Cayuse), and "Shahaptian" (Sahaptin-Nez Perce; Sapir 1929a; see Silverstein 1979a:653). Silverstein considers this proposal "very improbable" (1979a:679). Sapir's notes, included in an article by L. S. Freeland (1930), indicate that he accepted the grouping of Mixe with Penutian, and a footnote in Freeland's article explains that Dixon, in a letter to Sapir, had proposed a connection between Zoque and Penutian that led Sapir to accept Mixe-Zoque and Huave as Mexican Penutian languages (1929a; see also Radin 1916, 1924). Sapir also spoke of even wider extensions: "The Penutian languages, centered in Oregon and California, must early have extended far to the south, as they seem to be represented in Mexico and Central America by Mixe-Zoque, Huave, Xinca, and Lenca" (1949[1929a]:178). Sapir's final classification of Penutian (1929a) was as shown in the list here.

This has usually been taken as the point of departure in later work on aspects of the Penutian hypothesis.

As pointed out in Chapter 2, Sapir's evidence involved the standard criteria (that is, lexical and grammatical evidence, as well as sound correspondences), but in setting proposals of remote relationships for further testing he also at times relied heavily on typological traits. This is particularly true in the case of his extended Penutian. Here he echoes Dixon and Kroeber's view (1913a), quoted earlier:

The *Penutian* languages are far less cumbersome in structure than the preceding three [Eskimo-Aleut, Algonkin-Wakashan, Nadene] but are more tightly knit, presenting many analogies to the Indo-European languages; make use of suffixes of formal, rather than concrete, significance; show many types of inner stem change; and possess true nominal cases, for the most part. Chinook seems to have developed a secondary "polysynthesis" form on the basis of a broken down form of Penutian; while Tsimshian and Maidu have probably been considerably influenced by contact with Mosan and with Shoshonean and Hokan respectively. (Sapir 1990[1929a]:101)

Earlier, Sapir had been impressed with what he believed to be a "characteristic presence in the Penutian languages as a whole" of the stem

---

Sapir's Penutian Classification

California Penutian (see Dixon and Kroeber's original Penutian)
    Miwok-Costanoan
    Yokuts
    Maidu
    Wintun
Oregon Penutian
    Takelma
    Coast Oregon Penutian
        Coos
        Siuslaw
        Yakonan
    Kalapuya
Chinook
Tsimshian
Plateau Penutian
    Sahaptian
    Waiilatpuan (Molala-Cayuse)
    Lutuami (Klamath-Modoc)
Mexican Penutian
    Mixe-Zoque
    Huave

shape $CVC_1V(C_2)$, of "disyllabic stems with a repeated vowel" (editorial note in Sapir 1990 [1921c]:273).[79] However, he appears to have had second thoughts about this stem shape soon after writing this article, for he did not mention it in the 1929 characterization of Penutian (see editorial note in Sapir 1990[1929a]:273). As Silverstein (1979a:655) pointed out, Sapir's ideas concerning Penutian traits as expressed in the later article (1929a) were still highly influenced by "correspondences which were first dimly brought to my consciousness years ago by certain morphological resemblances between Takelma and Yokuts" (Sapir 1921b:58). Silverstein assessed the features that Sapir postulated for the Penutian archetype to determine their consistency with what is now known of the languages and concluded that "the investigation of Sapir's Penutian superstock cannot proceed except by refining the kinds of assumptions he made about morphosyntactic structure as they provide the basis for specific comparisons of lexical form" (1979a:658–72). Silverstein (1975, 1979b) attempted to do this (see below).

Sapir published no large-scale Penutian comparative work comparable to his Hokan articles; as Swadesh reported, it was generally known among Sapir's students and colleagues that "he was waiting for the appearance of ample source material on some of the languages of the [Penutian] complex" (1964a:182; see also Sapir and Swadesh 1953:292–3).[80] It is interesting that, in spite of Kroeber's role in launching the Penutian hypothesis and his early use of methods that were less than precise in attempts to reduce the number of independent language families in North America (see Chapter 2), he came to have serious reservations about Sapir's broader conception of Penutian and about the methods upon which it was based:

> As soon, however, as the closely contiguous California Penutian languages are left behind, and one compares them with, say Kus in Oregon, the inspectional method [for example, of Powell, Dixon, and Kroeber] begins to leave us in the lurch: we get some, but not too many, superficially apparent resemblances. A step farther to Chinook, which Sapir also unites, and inspectional resemblances have disappeared altogether, not to mention that the structural pattern also seems heavily different. Obviously, we shall not be very sure

> whether Kus belongs with California Penutian, and shall remain in complete doubt whether Chinook does, until an intensive study by the reconstructive [comparative] method has been made. (1940a:467–8)

Though it remained controversial, Sapir's Penutian was widely accepted. Since Sapir's work, more extensive descriptive materials on most of these languages have become available and much historical research has been undertaken. In the remainder of this section I discuss briefly some of the more significant historical work in Penutian studies.

Radin proposed a connection between Mixe-Zoque and Huave (1916; see also 1924), and these languages became part of Sapir's Mexican Penutian grouping. Frachtenberg (1918), Jacobs (1931), and Sapir (1926, Sapir and Swadesh 1953) all contributed significantly to aspects of Oregon and Plateau linguistics, although they were not directly concerned with the original core or "California" Penutian question (see also Pierce 1966). Freeland presented 108 comparisons of Mixe with various of the California and Oregon languages, along with other supporting material added by Sapir (included in Freeland's footnotes). Contrary to what more recent investigators have found, Freeland viewed Mixe structure as "rather bare and scanty"; she thought Mixe morphology had "worn thin"—that the "morphological sparseness of Mixe . . . precludes extensive morphological comparisons. The evidence for classing Mixe in the Penutian family must therefore necessarily be largely lexical." Nevertheless, she found some Mixe "morphological traits that have a strong Penutian flavour" (1930:28). A consideration of these follows.

1. *Internal modification of the radical.* From her examples, it appears that Freeland had in mind Mixe alternations that today are known to be due to regular, low-level phonological assimilations—for example, voicing of stops after nasals, some vowel frontings, and consonant palatalizations caused by the presence of the 'third person' marker *y-*. These feel very different from the $CVCV \sim CVCC$- root alternations that Sapir considered to be diagnostic of Penutian.
2. *Incorporated pronouns.* These are, however, acknowledged as lacking in Yokuts and Costanoan, and the Mixe forms do not bear much

formal similarity to the Maidu and Miwok forms presented. In any event, one of the two Mixe sets is prefixed, while the Maidu and Miwok pronouns are suffixed; if these affixes were cognate, it would suggest that some independent, nonincorporated pronominals were the original source of the system which then became incorporated in different ways—before the verb stem in some languages, after the verb stem in others.

3. *Verbal [instrumental] prefixes* (for example, *ka-* 'action with the hand'). These are generally acknowledged to be probably more the result of areal diffusion than of genetic inheritance among so-called Penutian languages.[81]

As for the lexical comparisons, most of the 108 would be eliminated if they were judged by the methodological criteria of Chapter 7. There are many short forms with divergent meanings or leftover unmatched segments, or both (Mixe *hon* 'bird', Maidu *hu* 'to fly'; Mixe *ak,* Maidu *mako* 'fish'); nursery words (Mixe *nana,* Maidu *na/ne* 'mother'; Mixe *tat,* Wintu *tata* 'father'); and onomatopoetic comparisons (Mixe *poh* 'wind', Miwok *puš* 'to blow', Wintu *pul-* 'whistle', Chinook *po* 'blow'). In short, Freeland's data are of insufficient quality and quantity to support a possible distant genetic relationship.

Even more far-flung Penutian connections than those of Sapir were proposed by Whorf (1935:608, 1943:7), whose Macro-Penutian included, in addition to the groups in Sapir's Penutian, also Uto-Aztecan, Kiowa(-Tanoan), Mayan, Mixe-Zoquean-Huave (with reservations), Totonacan, and reportedly (though not mentioned in Whorf's published works) several other groups (Mason 1940:58, 81–6 [citing personal communication from Whorf; Mason accepted this version of Macro-Penutian]; Johnson 1940:104–10). Similarly, Swadesh's (1954b, 1956) lexicostatistically based "Penutioid" phylum attempted to link many additional groups (twenty in all) with Penutian, including, in addition to most of Whorf's groups, Coconucan, Paez, Cholonan, Quechua-Aymara, Tarascan, and Zuni. Swadesh had amassed certain lexical look-alikes among these languages, but he was using them to test "certain methodological innovations" concerning lexicostatistics. Neither Whorf's nor Swadesh's proposals have attained any significant following and today both are

mostly abandoned. Hymes's view of the history of the Penutian hypothesis to 1957 is a convenient summary: "The hypothesis of a Penutian genetic relationship has had three stages of development. Dixon and Kroeber related certain native languages of California, Sapir added a number of other Pacific Coast languages; Freeland, Sapir, Whorf, Swadesh, and others have extended the concept to include various native languages of Latin America" (1957:69).

Shafer was one of the few scholars at that time to take a critical stance on the proposed extensions of Penutian: "Setting up such far-flung linguistic empires with little or nothing to hold them together except the authority of their builders has gone so far that one of the founders of the original Penutian group, A. L. Kroeber [1941:289], has protested" (1947:206). Shafer preferred to attempt to "establish such phonetic equations as one can for the [original] five languages," eliminating "the greater mass of phonetically unsound comparisons in the earlier work on Penutian" (1947:206). Nevertheless, many of the sixty-three lexical comparisons Shafer himself advocated fall away under the methodological criteria of Chapter 7. The problems include (1) onomatopoeia ('cry', 'bluejay', 'crane/heron', 'raven/crow', 'blackbird', 'small hawk', 'owl'); (2) many short forms; (3) probable borrowings ('bear', 'white willow', 'bow [two forms]', 'arrow', 'mortar basket / pestle', 'manzanita', 'grebe/mud-hen', 'deer-snare', 'salamander', 'potato/tuber'); (4) semantic latitude (generally Shafer is not too permissive in this category, though there are several examples such as 'jaw/face', 'mouth/nose', and so on).

As Shipley (1980:437) indicated, the Penutian research during the period from the mid-1950s to the mid-1970s was mainly concerned with working out the internal history of the various families associated with the Penutian hypothesis. Only the more inclusive historical work undertaken during that period is assessed here. In 1958 Pitkin and Shipley conducted the first extensive investigation of Penutian since Dixon and Kroeber's presentation (1919) of their limited evidence. However, Pitkin and Shipley's assessment of the Penutian work that had been done was fairly critical; it also included indirect reference apparently to Swadesh's lexicostatistical "experiments":

Penutian investigations have followed a pattern of supplying to the literature new and bold, but undemonstrated, hypotheses of wider and wider relationships, while those suggestions already in the literature have stood uninvestigated for the last half century. Mere speculation based on the use of imaginative techniques which are themselves open to question is of doubtful value. One cannot use a suspect technique to establish a relationship nor a hypothetical relationship to validate a technique. . . . No series of sound correspondences has been published either between or within the Penutian families. Neither phonological nor morphological cognates have been demonstrated. Further, the significant factor of diffusion has remained uninvestigated, even though the borrowing of linguistic material undoubtedly plays an important role in the development of the relationships to be examined here. (Pitkin and Shipley 1958:175)

Pitkin and Shipley attempted to establish sound correspondences among the five California families, reconstruct the sounds, and eliminate diffused material. However, Shipley's assessment (1980) of this article and of other Penutian work undertaken before 1980 makes clear that these goals were not met.[82]

Broadbent and Pitkin compared Miwokan with Wintuan, offering "265 resemblant sets showing similarities of form and meaning in the two families" (1964:20) and postulating sound correspondences and reconstructed phonemes. However, as has been pointed out with regard to similar work done at this time (see the earlier discussion of Jacobsen 1958 and Haas 1964b), many of these forms exhibit the problems discussed in Chapter 7. This collection of resemblant lexical forms is simply insufficient as evidence in support of a genetic relationship; many of the proposed sound correspondences dissolve when these problematic lexical sets are taken out of the picture.[83]

Shipley attempted to investigate the possible relationship between the California Penutian kernel and Klamath, "explor[ing] phonological and lexical evidence" (1966:489). He presented some "recurrent consonant correspondences" and "tentative reconstructions" (see Table 8-9), based on the "etymologies" that he discussed. If these were true sound correspondences, Table 8-9 would constitute strong evidence for genetic relationship both among the California Penutian

languages themselves and between these languages and Klamath. However, there are problems. First, these sound correspondences involve virtual identities; there are none of the phonetically rather different compared sounds typical of sound correspondences in established remote relationships—differences that characteristically develop in time as a result of normal sound changes (see Chapter 7). Second, these correspondences are based on only twenty-six "etymologies" (potential cognate sets). Several forms are onomatopoetic or symbolic ('slurp', 'frog', 'cry', 'small', 'breathe', 'lightning'). Several involve pan-Americanisms and hence do not provide particularly compelling evidence that these languages are more closely related than the many others that also contain similar forms (for example, 'person', 'nose/smell/mucus', 'you', 'I', 'mouth'[84]) (see Chapter 7). Some of the sets reveal considerable semantic latitude (for example, 'slurp / thin soup', 'person/woman', 'body louse/woodtick/flea', 'run/quick/swift/rabbit/lizard / lizard species', 'small/animal/nice', 'snow/icicle', 'mouth/like food', and 'breathe/windpipe/lungs'). Several sets involve very short forms, which are more likely to be only accidentally similar (as in *hi/ṭhi*/etc. 'house', *hín/tlu*/etc. 'egg', *ko·/kel(a)*/etc. 'snow', and the forms for 'you' and 'I'). In some sets, only a few of the many languages actually exhibit the forms compared (for example, 'rotten' and 'eye' in Klamath and in two other languages). Problems with the set for 'two' are discussed at length below. Shipley observed that the set for 'lightning' has a "scrambling of segments in the various languages" (1966:494). He also mentioned the problem of "the relative paucity of cognate forms in Miwokan" and the "striking absence of correspondences representing stops or affricates with points of articulation intermediate between labials and velars," which he attributed to consonant symbolism. 'Breathe' was included only as an illustration that "there is evidence (though scanty) for **h" (Shipley 1966:492, 496).

In short, the proposed cognates are too few and far too problematical for the postulated correspondence sets to be taken as very significant. Shipley also proposed a "tentative chart of Proto-Penutian consonants" (1966:497): /p, [t], [c]?, k, (kʷ), q, [ʔ], ph, [th], [ch]?, [kh], [kʷh],

TABLE 8-9 Sound Correspondences in California Penutian and Klamath

Proposed Proto-Penutian	Klamath	Maidu	Wintu	Patwin	Yokuts	Miwok	Costanoan
**p	p	} p	} p	p	p	} p	p
**ph	ph		ph	ph	ph		
**k	k	k	k	k	k	k	k
**q	q	} k	q	k	x	k	k
**qh	qh				(-k)		
**m	m	m	m	m	m	m	m
**n	n	n	n	n	n	n	n
(?)	w-	w-	w-	w-	w-	w-	w-
	-l-	-l-	-l- -l	-l- -l	-l-	-l-	-l- -r
#**r	s[C, L[V	h	tl, s	tl	t̲h	n	l, r
**-r-	d, l	d	(r?)	r	t̲h	(n?)	r
**-r	?	?	r	r	t̲h	n	r
(**s	s-	s-			s-	s-	)

Source: Shipley 1966:496; see also Callaghan 1967:226.

qh, m, n, (ł), (s), (h), r, (l)?, (w), [y]?/ . With respect to broader Penutian connections beyond California, Shipley judiciously cautioned that "testing the various possibilities [beyond the Penutian kernel] must wait until the interrelations within the present Penutian kernel have been more carefully analyzed and described— an intricate and tedious task but indispensable to real progress. . . . Outside of California, however, no investigations have been undertaken to establish the genetic unity of [Sapir's extended] Penutian" (1966:497).

Hymes in 1957 was concerned with one general type of morphological category in Penutian languages (essentially as conceived by Sapir): "Elements of the general phonemic shape nV, lV . . . which occur marking one or another of the set of meanings which have plurality as a common ingredient. There are three groups of such elements: (1) those marking the continuative aspect of verbs, (2) those marking the distributive aspect of verbs, and (3) those which seem to share the sense of plurality in the relations of persons" (1957:69). (A number of these

elements were considered again by Berman [1983, 1989] and are discussed later in this section.) Hymes summarized his conclusion as follows:

Evidence has been presented for the postulation of two proto-Penutian affixes. . . . Taking the shape CV as basic for the present, we can postulate *la "continuative" on the basis of Chinookan -l/-la/-lal, -l- and la-, Tsimshian l-, Takelman -(a)l, Sierra Miwok -l/-lala, Yokuts -le·, and Northern Sahaptin la-. We can postulate *ni "distributive" on the basis of Chinookan -ni, Northern Sahaptin -nin, Coos -ni-, -ne·, Sierra Miwok -ni·, Maidu -noye, and Takelma -n(i). We note that where the continuative is found with -n, two cases are as alternants of forms with -l (Chinookan, Sahaptin) and the other is possibly so (Klamath). Where -l is found in the distributive forms, it is only in an alternant of a from with -n (Kathlamet Chinook, Northern Sahaptin). There is less evidence for postulating a reciprocal/plural element *na and an indirective element *ni/*na. (1957:82)

Although investigation of morphological correspondences is important, Hymes's evidence unfortunately fails to be convincing, for several reasons. The forms compared are all short, made up of a consonant with or without an associated vowel either before or after it. The consonants, *n* and *l,* are the most common, are least marked of all, and occur frequently in grammatical morphemes in languages spoken all over the world. Several of Hymes's comparisons range over a large number of different meanings or functions—that is, they reflect considerable semantic or functional latitude. Many of the forms Hymes compared involve suffixes in some of the languages but prefixes in others (particularly in Tsimshian and sometimes in Chinook); although these could be cognate, such a difference in placement of affixes suggests that they could share a period of common history only if they began not as bound affixes but as relatively independent words or particles which only later were grammaticalized as bound prefixes in some of the languages and suffixes in others. This origin not as affixes, however, would seem to diminish their value as morphological evidence of a genetic relationship. In any case, for these forms to be compared it is necessary that their original status and the paths by which they changed be taken into account. Finally, because a single function has several forms that signal it, there can be several formal targets when comparisons are made among forms with similar meanings in other languages, as discussed in Chapter 7. Several of the languages Hymes compared exhibit this problem. In Yokuts, for example, there are "five [different] methods of marking the continuitive," *ʔ . . . a(·)*, *-le·*, *-me·wɔ·*, *-a·*, and "double final reduplication of certain biliteral proclitics" (Hymes 1957:71). All of Hymes's kinds of morphological evidence are consistent with accidental similarities among compared elements and do nothing to tip the balance against chance and in favor of possible genetic inheritance as an explanation of the similarities detected.

The aggregate of Hymes's evidence fares no better for comparisons among the Penutian languages than it does for comparisons of these with Finnish (see the discussion of Berman below). If Hymes's evidence for genetic relationship cannot surpass that from comparisons with Finnish (or any other language not assumed to be part of the Penutian group), then the hypothesis

cannot be supported on the basis of this evidence alone.

In 1964, Hymes attempted a detailed study of two Penutian etymologies, 'hail' and 'bead' (1964b), and he presented 182 lexical comparisons among the languages grouped as Penutian by Sapir (1929a), though only 93 sets met his criteria for comparison (forms must recur in at least three of the groups being compared, and be represented by at least three matching phonemes in each of the three or more groups). Another 28 did not meet these criteria but nevertheless seemed convincing to Hymes, and still another group of 61 were deemed suggestive only (Hymes 1964a). While some of the sets he presented may be legitimate cognates, even his preferred 93 lexical look-alikes are fraught with the usual problems, as discussed in Chapter 7. Some examples from a few categories are given here to demonstrate why the evidence presented has not proved convincing. The degree of semantic latitude permitted is wide. The glosses under BLADDER, CONTAINER include: 'fat bag of sea-lion intestine',' bladder', 'lungs', 'stomach', 'quiver', 'kidneys', 'gall', 'heart', 'liver'; CHEW, EAT; CHIN, JAW: 'to eat up', 'to bite', 'to chew'; 'lips', 'beak', 'mouth', 'chin', 'parting of the hair', 'chin', 'beard', 'jaw', 'cheek'; CRIPPLED, INFIRM, ILL: 'lame', 'crippled', 'slant-eyed', 'about to die', 'decrepit old woman', 'consumptive', 'lean'; DIVE, SINK, DOWN, FALL: 'to dive', 'down', 'to fall', 'to sink', 'to drown', 'dip net', 'to lower', 'to slip', 'to slide', 'to descend', 'to uproot (tree)', 'to swim (of fish)'; PRESS, PINCH, NARROW, CHOKE: 'to be narrow', 'to notch', 'to pinch', 'to snatch up', 'to blow one's nose', 'to crunch', 'to strangle', 'to choke by squeezing the neck', 'to scratch', 'to puncture'. Onomatopoeia is involved in his sets for SMALL BIRD; CRICKET; DRIP, DROP; JAW, CROW; KINGFISHER; SKUNK[85]; and WOODPECKER. Sets that appear to reflect borrowing or diffusion include BEADS, SHELLS; ROBIN (said by Hymes to be "wider spread in Western America than Pen[utian]" [1964a:235]); SKIN, HIDE, BLANKET; and CLOTHING.[86]

Silverstein's arguments in support of Penutian seemed the most fetching for the time, perhaps because he seemed to break with the common practice of presenting lists of lexical look-alikes as his principal evidence. Silverstein set up two criteria to be followed in research on Penutian: "reconstructing chunks of the protolanguage" and "tracing the grammatical [morphological?] developments of attested daughter forms" (1975:369). He argued that his treatment of two distinct roots meaning *two,* each of which occurs in at least three of the five putative California Penutian families, meets both criteria, and that this "effectively 'proves' California Penutian in the most rigorous sense" (1975:370; see also 1979a:675). Nevertheless, he acknowledged that "by the criteria of regular sound correspondences among languages and of the reconstruction of total proto-forms of words, Penutian in the sense used here [essentially that of Sapir 1929a] is not a proven genetic relationship" (1979a:650).

Silverstein's (1975, 1979b) treatment of the historical phonology and morphology of words associated with the *pen* and the *uti* forms for 'two' in the five Californian language families is a brilliant application of the techniques of historical etymology. He argued that it is possible, following regular phonological developments and morphological analysis, that lying behind Wintu *pale-t* is *pan-le-t*; that underlying Maidun is *pe·néy*; and that behind what looks like Yokuts *po·ŋy* may be *pan-w(i)y.* Similarly, he contended that Miwokan and Costanoan forms for 'two' hark back to *ʔoti-*, which he argued is characteristically a verbal lexeme, and thus he related it to derivational forms meaning 'twins' by postulating historical developments leading to the modern forms in Yokuts (*ʔati·-ya < *ʔoti·-ya,* where *-ya* is suggested as a collective noun stem), and Nisenan (Maiduan) (with *ʔó·ya < *ʔótya < **ʔoṭṭya*). Here he postulated a California Penutian CVC- root with ablaut alternants *ʔoṭ-/*ʔa·ṭ- 'cleave, break, split (in two)'.

Even if Silverstein's deployment of the evidence were convincing, his enthusiastic exposition fails to be conclusive because, in the final analysis, after the application of etymological techniques in each of the component families, we are left with a similarity of terms for the number 'two' involving *pan, pe·néy* (and its alternants), and *po·ŋy-* which plausibly but not necessarily reflects even older *pan-w(i)y.* Although these similarities are probably not due

to accident (though even that is not entirely ruled out; see Chapter 7), it is possible that they reflect old borrowings, and numeral systems—even those including numbers as low as one and two—are subject to borrowing (see Beeler and Klar 1977:238, Callaghan 1990b:123, Campbell 1976d, Girard 1971b:138–9, and Rankin 1985). Moreover, "there has been much borrowing and reformation at all levels within the Costanoan languages" (Callaghan 1990b:132). In the *uti* case, we have relatively secure Miwok-Costanoan *ʔo·ti-* 'two', which could be related to forms meaning 'twin' in two other language families, where the *a* rather than the *o* of Yokuts (specifically Yawelmani), though addressed, is not convincingly explained. Since the forms have very short roots, the similarity may be due to chance or to borrowing. Examples of the borrowing of terms for 'twins' are known from a number of languages. Nahuatl *(ko-)kowa(-tsin)* 'twin' (with or without reduplication of the first syllable and usually with either the diminutive *-tsin* or the absolutive noun suffix *-t(l)*) alone has been borrowed into the following: Otomí *go*; Colonial Otomí <go>, <quahtè> 'twin'; Cuicatec *kwa²či₁* 'twins' (perhaps via Spanish *cuate*); San Mateo del Mar Huave *kʷič* 'twins', and even Mexican Spanish *cuate* 'twin, buddy' (a loan from Nahuatl). Thus, although Silverstein's case is an interesting one and could even be valid, a conclusive demonstration will require more than an inconclusive mustering of the etymological resources to show similarities (albeit greater in number than perceived previously) involving the two forms for 'two'.

Other Penutian specialists have not been convinced by Silverstein's "proof" for California Penutian and have found serious problems with the two proposed etymologies involving words for 'two'.[87] These scholars cast doubt on Silverstein's case, which initially seemed so promising. Silverstein's discussion of forms for 'two' has not "proved" the California Penutian relationship as he asserted.[88]

Silverstein also offered opinions concerning several of the proposed branches of Penutian. His interpretation of California Penutian relationships was: "It is Wintun that stands alone as a remote congener, while within the two subgroups Miwok-Costanoan and Yokuts-

Maidun, Miwok and Yokuts show the greatest retention of late common California Penutian structure" (1975:371). He asserted that California Penutian "is established or at least virtually certain" (1979a:675). Whistler concluded just the opposite—that the "hypothesis of a California Penutian kernel is dead. . . . Penutian entry to California must have occurred in several stages and likely from different directions" (1977:172). With regard to Oregon Peutian, Silverstein reported for Oregon Penutian that "it is not clear that this is a unified and separate grouping," though "a relationship between Takelma and Kalapuya is virtually certain," and the relationship of Coos to Takelma "is highly probable." However, "any 'Coast Oregon Penutian' grouping is very problematic"; nevertheless, "any statement at a level comparable to Sapir's Oregon Penutian will have to take into account Molale as well." He viewed Plateau Penutian (the Shahapwailutan grouping) as being "very improbable" and abandoned the Molale-Cayuse (Waiilatpuan) grouping; he thought Molale was "probably more directly related to Kalapuya-Takelma and the other 'Oregon Penutian' languages" and that Klamath had "strong possibilities for relationship with California Penutian" (in spite of proposals that place it in Plateau Penutian; see Aoki 1963). He considered the affiliation of Chinookan with Penutian to be "probable," but Tsimshian was, "if related, more problematic" (1979a:679–80).

It is interesting to contrast Silverstein's enthusiasm for California Penutian with the vigor of William Shipley's reservations. In 1980, Shipley, who had labored long and had published some of the more important work on Penutian, announced essentially that Penutian was dead:

Although we have amassed a vastly greater and more accurate amount of lexical data since [Dixon and Kroeber], it is very important to point out that the fundamental characteristics of the sets one finds are much as they were for Dixon and Kroeber. There are many resemblant forms—I believe Pitkin and I accumulated over three hundred for our 1958 article (Pitkin and Shipley 1958) and there are lots more—but they are irritatingly unsatisfactory. Most of the consonant resemblances are identities, furthermore there is little

parallelism from one set to another. The vowels also are either identities or seemingly random. The Penutian area looks as if it had been subjected to a massive and prolonged process of lexical diffusion, layered in like sedimentary rock. That postulation has its difficulties, however, since many of the glosses are for body-parts and other simple, non-cultural things, the terms for which seem unlikely to be subject to replacement. It has been very puzzling, and has engendered a steady stream of cautionary statements from people familiar with the situation. (1980:437–8; see also Whistler 1977)

Shipley instead proposed the "working principle":

The term 'Penutian' has no genetic definition at all. The very use of the term prejudges the case and sets us off to working from a kind of axiomatic entity which we have not defined. . . . If we ever find real genetic connections somewhere among [any of] these languages, then the term Penutian might be all right to use again, although it is pretty shopworn. I think we should stop misleading everybody and drop the term out of our working vocabulary even though it might produce an identity crisis in some of us. It is not that I feel there *are* no genetic connections to be found—I just don't want to name something until I have something to name. (1980:440)

From my reading of Penutian linguistic publications, I would agree with Shipley and second his recommendations. There is certainly enough solid material to encourage an open-minded linguist to be sympathetic to the possibility of genetic relationship(s), but the evidence is excessively messy and at present is not convincing.

Howard Berman attempted to reconstruct some morphological elements of "Proto-California-Penutian (PCP)," which he took as evidence that "these languages are indeed related to each other" (1983:400; see also 1989). He considered sound correspondences, mostly for vowels but at a fairly remote level of abstraction. He also presented evidence of twenty morphological elements, which is more important because morphological evidence of the right sort might go a long way toward breaking the impasse that exists in lexical comparison studies (problems such as those raised by Shipley 1980). Therefore, Berman's examples deserve careful scrutiny. The majority of these forms are, as might be expected, quite short—*C, V, CV,* or *VC* in shape. Needless to say, many scholars would probably not find such a list of short forms to be probative unless they were patterned in the fabric of the grammar in such a way as to argue against chance as an equally plausible explanation for the similarities they exhibit among the languages compared. Unfortunately for Berman's examples, this is not the case. I assume that most linguists will agree that if equally plausible Finnish parallels can for found for Berman's reconstructions, the genetic explanation then fares no better than chance. This comparison does not include all possible Finnish parallels of Berman's reconstructions, but only those which appear to be stronger (Finnish examples are from Hakulinen 1968, Laanest 1982).

Berman (1983:402) reconstructed six case endings for his PCP, but these are attested for the most part only in Miwokan and Yokutsan. His PCP 'possessive' (or 'genitive') *-n* with vowel stems, *-ən* with consonant stems is closely matched by Finnish 'genitive' -n. Berman's *-ni* 'instrumental' (also 'comitative' and 'indirect objective' in some instances) matches Finnish 'instrumental' *-in,* 'comitative' *-ine-*.[89] Regarding his last locative case, Berman says "there seems to be no reconstruction which will account for the different forms" (1983:403)—that is, Wintu *-ti* 'at, in'; Maidu, Konkow, Nisenan *-di* 'locative'; Central Sierra Miwok *-t, -to-* 'definite locative'; and Bodega Miwok *-to* 'allative'. These are comparable to Finnish *-tse* 'prolative' ('to, through, by means of') and *-tal -tä* 'ablative'.

Berman's other reconstructions are less impressive; I list a few examples: (1) 'suffixes forming verbal nouns' PCP *-n* and zero'; compare Finnish *-na* 'nominalizing suffix, noun formant'; (2) 'imperative' PCP *koʔ* (also *-k', -k'a* in several varieties of Yokutsan; additional discussion in Berman 1989:14); compare Finnish *-koo-* 'third person imperative', *-kaa* 'second person plural imperative' ('second person singular imperative' *-k*); (3) 'suffix forming passive verbs' PCP *-hen*; compare Finnish *-anl-än* 'present passive' (historically derived from *hen*), *-ene-* 'inchoative'.[90]

In short, Berman's data do not confirm California Penutian since they are insufficient to eliminate the possiblity of chance (and perhaps diffusion) as the possible explanation of the similarities. Plausible Finnish parallels exist for most of his proposed PCP morphological elements. This is remarkable, because Finnish fares better on the whole in the comparisons than do the five California Penutian families when they are compared to one another, since equivalents from Finnish (a single language) can be found for the majority of these comparisons, whereas most Penutian sets contain examples from only two or three of the five Penutian families compared and no single Penutian family exhibits so many matchings in Berman's comparisons as Finnish does. This may not be an entirely fair assessment, since Berman attempted to match sound correspondences (though he deviated from this policy in several cases and he also equated elements whose functions were not at all clearly connected). On the basis of the forms presented here, Finnish appears to be more consistently "Penutian" than any of the California Penutian languages.

Recently, Berman (1996:27) has proposed a "family tree" for California and Plateau Penutian as shown here:

Berman's California and Plateau Penutian

California Penutian
    Wintuan (Wintu, Nomlaki, Patwin)
    Yokuts-Maiduan-Utian
        Yokuts
        Maiduan (Maidu, Konkow, Nisesan)
        Miwok-Costanoan

Plateau Penutian
    Klamath
    Molala
    Sahaptian (Nez Perce, Sahaptin)
    Cayuse?

Berman's evidence for a genetic relationship between Sahaptian, Klamath, and Molala is very persuasive, though he admits that the evidence for grouping Cayuse with these is poor. Cayuse grammar is "virtually unknown," and the proposed relationship between Molala and Cayuse is based on "twenty or so words" which are "almost identical" and may be loanwords, though some involve basic vocabulary which he thinks might be the basis of a genetic relationship (Berman 1996:23). Berman (1996:24–7) also takes up the question of a comparison between "Plateau Penutian" and "California Penutian," mentioning again the lexical similarities between Klamath and California Penutian that have been presented (Shipley 1966), which are not compelling. However, DeLancey's (1987b) parallels between Klamath and Wintu pronouns (repeated by Berman 1996) are striking. When the Molala forms (from Berman 1996:13, 24) are factored in, they are still similar, but less strikingly so (see Table 8-10).

These agreements do seem to defy chance and perhaps also borrowing, though as pointed out in Chapter 7, there are instances where whole sets of pronominal forms have been borrowed. The case for Klamath (or Sahaptian or Molala) with California languages would be stronger if it were supported by additional evidence. Berman attempts to present such evidence for Molala and "various California Penutian languages" based on "a few grammatical morphemes shared" (1996:25–7). These, however, are in no way so striking as the Wintu-Klamath pronominal comparisons. They are the following, where I just list some of the phonetic forms and then some of the glosses for the "California Penutian" languages which Berman compared in each set.

> *Demonstrative pronouns: n-, ne-, no-, nu·pi* 'this, that, here'—Molala *ni·wi* 'this', *nuwi* 'that'. Demonstratives of similar phonetic form are found in many languages (Finnish, Nahuatl, Xinca, and others), and thus these could be only accidentally similar.
>
> *Intransitive verbs:* Yokuts and Miwok-Costanoan

-in, -n, -ŋ- 'medio-passive'—Molala *-in, -yn* "suffix forms intransitive verbs meaning 'to make a certain sound' " (Berman 1996:25). These are short forms with the highly unmarked and salient *n* as their only consonant; they do not match in function/semantics, and similar forms are easily found by accident in other languages (for example, Finnish *-ne-* 'inchoative, medio-passive', *-Vn, -hen* passives and reflexives, *-ntu/-nty* 'medio-passive, reflexive verb'; see Hakulinen 1968:196, 229, 234; Laanest 1982:277).

Noun formants: -tin, -taw; 'nominalizer, instrumental, passive gerundial, nondirective gerundial, nominalizing suffix with a subordinating function'—"Plateau Penutian" *-s, -t* 'noun formants'. Again, these are not semantically or functionally equivalent; they are short and unmarked; and similarities are easily found in other languages (for example, Finnish has a number of suffixes in *s* or *t* which nominalize verbs, make passives, and so on).

Past tense: -sa,- ši, -š, -šiʔ, -š·e-; 'recent past, past, distant past, aorist'—Again, these are short, involve unmarked consonants, and are easily matched in many languages (for example, varieties of Finnish and Estonian have *-si* 'past tense').

Verbal noun: -ŋti, -inti; 'predicated gerundial, verbal noun in subordinate clauses'—Molala *-int, -int^h* "a rare noun-forming suffix," "in most examples the underlying stem is not attested elsewhere in Molala" (Berman 1996:26). This Molala form is compared to only one other group, Yokutsan. It is unpersuasive, given the difference in function and the easily found similarity to forms from other languages (for example, Finnish *-ntal-ntä* 'nominalizing verb suffix'; for example, *etsi-* 'to search for', *etsintä* 'a search/searching'; Laanest 1982:223).

TABLE 8-10 Comparison of Penutian Pronouns

Wintu	Klamath	Gloss	Molala
ni	ni	'first person singular'	-ʔin enclitic possessive,
niyo	no:	'first person singular contrastive'	(ʔina personal pronoun)
nis	nis	'first person singular objective'	ʔinc objective
nele-	na:l'-	'first person plural (*l*-stem)'	-qənc enclitic objective,
nite-	na:d-	'first person plural (*t*-stem)'	(-qən, -q^han enclitic possessive)
mi (subj.)	mi	'second person singular (genitive)'	-ʔim enclitic possessive
mis	mis	'second person singular objective'	ʔims objective
male-	ma:l'-	'second person plural (*l*-stem)'	qəms 2du, pl. objective,
mite-	ma:d-	'second person plural (*t*-stem)'	(-qəm, -q^ham enclitic possessive)
pi	bi	'third person singular (K. contrastive)'	pinc objective, -pin enclitic possessive
pite-	ba:d-	'third person plural. (K. contrastive)'	-qənc enclitic objective, -qən, -q^han enclitic possessive

Again, apart from the pronominal forms, this evidence in support of broader "Penutian" connections is not convincing.

Mexican Penutian
−40% probability, 60% confidence

Scholars have differed in the language families they have proposed as members of Mexican Penutian. Sapir (1929a) included Mixe-Zoquean and Huave. Greenberg proposed these two plus Mayan and Totonac (1960) and called this group "a well-defined subgroup of Penutian" [1987:143]. Whorf grouped all these and Uto-Aztecan (1935:608, 1943:7; see also Mason 1940:58, 81–6; Johnson 1940:104–10; Swadesh 1954b, 1956). Many, in repeating these proposals, mention Macro-Mayan, Aztec-Tanoan, and other putative Penutian languages (see Hymes 1964a, 1964b; Swadesh 1954b, 1967a; Whorf 1943). However, most of these components are tenuous classifications themselves; the evidence for Macro-Mayan (discussed later in this chapter) and Aztec-Tanoan (discussed earlier in this chapter) has been called into question. Thus, it is premature to project these questionable entities into even more far-flung classifications. Mexican Penutian should be abandoned.

Cayuse-Molala

Horatio Hale (1846) proposed that Cayuse and Molala were related, and Powell (1891a) accepted the relationship as the Waiilatpuan family. Subsequently, this grouping was repeated unquestioningly (it was part of Sapir's "Plateau Penutian" [1929a]), until Bruce Rigsby (1966, 1969) disproved it. His reexamination of the evidence showed that it does not support a genetic relationship between the two, but rather that Hale had apparently based his classification primarily on nonlinguistic considerations.[91] Namely, Marcus Whitman, the well-known Protestant missionary, had reported to Hale that the two languages were mutually intelligible, though this is not supported by the extant linguistic data. Rigsby speculated that Whitman (or some other "white man") may have observed a situation in which the Cayuse and Molala used some common language to communicate with each other and he "may have mistaken this for evidence of mutual intelligibility" (1966:370; see Berman 1981:249).

Sahaptian-Klamath(-Molala)
+75% probability, 50% confidence

In 1917 Frachtenberg wrote to Sapir that "there was no reasonable doubt that it [Lutuami, that is, Klamath-Modoc] linked up satisfactorily with Sahaptian and Molale" (quoted in Golla 1984:254). As DeLancey accurately observes, "the hypothesis of a genetic relationship between Klamath and the Sahaptian languages (Nez Perce and various Sahaptin dialects) is widely regarded as one of the more promising of the yet unproved groupings of North American languages" (1992:235). Aoki (1963) pointed out ninety-nine lexical resemblances between Klamath and Northern Sahaptin together with Nez Perce, noting possible sound correspondences. A number of these comparisons arouse suspicion when judged by the criteria discussed in Chapter 7 (and Rigsby 1965b has argued that some of them can be explained without the languages necessarily being genetically related); still, there is a significant number of close lexical similarities that suggest a possible genetic relationship. More convincing evidence, including several additional lexical sets (and word family comparisons), basic numbers, and some morphological comparisons, is presented by Rude (1987), DeLancey, Genetti, and Rude (1988), and DeLancey (1992). Therefore, it appears that Klamath and Sahaptian are probably genetically related.[92]

Berman (1996) has presented strong evidence, including numerous corresponding morphological forms, which show that it is very probable that Molala is related to Klamath and Sahaptian.

Sahaptian-Klamath-Tsimshian
+10% probability, 10% confidence

DeLancey, Genetti, and Rude (1988) present plausible evidence that Tsimshian may be related to Klamath or Sahaptian, or to both, although some Tsimshianists have (orally) expressed doubts about the Tsimshian data and its handling in recent comparisons. This should be investigated further.

Klamath–California Penutian

In addition to the proposed Sahaptian-Klamath-Molala(-Tsimshian) connections, a special connection between Klamath and various California Penutian languages has been proposed (Shipley 1966; DeLancey 1987a, 1987b, 1991; see also Berman 1996). Evidence has been adduced and arguments advanced for a special Klamath connection with Sahaptian and Molala (that is, traditional Plateau Penutian) and various California languages, and this constitutes a good reason for keeping the question open concerning the traditional groupings within Penutian (as defined by Sapir 1929a) and for persisting in further investigations of these various possibilities.

Takelman (Takelma-Kalapuyan)
+80% probability, 60% confidence

Sapir (1921b) (whose doctoral dissertation was on Takelma) reported that he had assembled 145 sets (published some thirty years later, in Sapir and Swadesh 1953) showing that Coos and Takelma were related. He later included Takelma, along with Coos, Siuslaw, Alsea, and Kalapuya, in his Oregon Penutian grouping (1929a). Except for the Takelma-Kalapuyan connection, these proposals are not favored by scholars today because of lack of significant support, but they warrant further investigation. More important is the Takelman grouping proposed by Swadesh (1956) and Shipley (1969), which places Takelma and Kalapuyan together. Shipley's evidence, some two dozen sound correspondences and a good number of lexical comparisons, is quite compelling, and the proposal is currently accepted by several specialists in the field. Some of his lexical sets are brought into question by the criteria of Chapter 7 (some are onomatopoetic, some are possibly diffused, and some are nursery forms), but on the whole the evidence appears to be strong and I am inclined to accept the classification, though it should be investigated more fully.

Zuni-Penutian
−80% probability, 50% confidence

Zuni is an isolate, although there have been many attempts to link it with some larger group (see Chapter 4). Zuni has frequently been linked with some version of the Penutian hypothesis. The most clearly articulated hypothesis is that of Stanley Newman (1964) in which he compares Zuni with the languages of Dixon and Kroeber's California Penutian. Newman compared 187 lexical items—123 as "primary cognates" and the rest as "problematic cognates." He attempted to establish phonological correspondences based on these compared forms, but these are not persuasive, for they exhibit most of the methodological problems of lexical comparisons discussed in Chapter 7. Some examples of such problems follow, taken primarily from the 123 primary cognates.

> *Onomatopoetic forms:* 'to blow' (two sets), 'bluejay', 'breast' (with nursing noises), 'to click', 'to cry', 'to groan', 'to kiss', 'hawk' (two forms), 'nose' (with 'to blow one's nose', 'to give a snort', 'to make a snorting noise'), 'to rattle', 'to ring', 'to shout', 'to snap', 'to spit', 'to tear', 'thunder', 'to breathe', 'crow' (two forms), 'drum'
> *Nursery forms:* 'father', 'grandfather', 'grandmother', 'maternal uncle'
> *Forms reflecting semantic latitude:* 'bad/garbage', 'feather / wing / to fly / goose', 'horse/hoof', 'jaw / lower lip / chin', 'to be sticking out / to bounce up'
> *Short forms (or longer forms with only* CV *matching):* forty forms
> *Diffused forms:* 'goose' (under 'feather'), 'tobacco'

In short, all considered, Newman's evidence for a Zuni connection with California Penutian fails to be convincing.

Current Penutian Perspectives

The prevailing attitude today, even among some Penutian specialists, is that the languages involved in the various versions of the Penutian hypothesis have not successfully been shown to be related; therefore, one should not put much faith in the original Penutian hypothesis and, by implication, certainly not in the broader Macro-Penutian proposals (see Shipley 1980, Whistler 1977). However, the evidence that at least some of these languages share broader genetic relationships is also mounting, and most scholars do not discount entirely the possibility (probability?) that the near future will see more successful demonstrations of these family relations.

Victor Golla shared his intuitions about Penutian (in personal communication, 1993). He believes in a Penutian hypothesis which includes Sapir's original Penutian languages with the exception of Huave, but where "California Penutian" or the "Penutian Kernel" (as originally defined by Dixon and Kroeber) is not a subgroup and has been a stumbling block in Penutian studies. He finds Utian (Miwok-Costanoan) to be established (as do nearly all other specialists) and believes that soon work will probably verify a grouping that includes Klamath-Sahaptian-Molala and Maiduan (Alsea is probably not connected within this group; compare Golla 1980). He thinks Wintuan goes together with the Oregon Coast languages, and that Yokutsan is not directly linked with any of these, but rather its closest connections seem to be with Takelma-Kalapuyan (which he says might be called "Central Penutian"). Golla believes that Penutian had case marking and was ergative/absolutive in alignment. In contrast to Golla, Catherine Callaghan (1991b) presents evidence for a Yokuts-Utian connection, which does not include Wintuan or Maiduan. Thus, "Penutian" as originally conceived, composed of the five Californian families (Wintuan, Maiduan, Yokutsan, and Miwok-Costanoan), appears to be abandoned, though different combinations of these and other languages of the Oregon and Plateau Penutian groups still hold some hope. Naturally these hypotheses and claims can be fully assessed only after the supporting evidence has been assembled and made available. The final determination of Penutian is yet to come. At present, these are but tantalizing possibilities, no version of which has been demonstrated.

Broader Yukian Relationships

For many years, following Sapir's classification (1929a), Yukian was officially considered a part of Hokan-Siouan. Shipley (1957) presented some lexical similarities between Yukian and so-called California Penutian languages, but he left the question concerning affinity open. Elmendorf (1963, 1964) took up again the possibility of Siouan connections that had been suggested by Radin and accommodated by Swadesh; however,

his ninety-five sets of lexical similarities, although suggestive, do not support a genetic relationship (neither one between Yukian-Siouan nor one between these two and other members of some more inclusive classification).

Yukian-Siouan
−60% probability, 75% confidence

Greenberg (1987) accepted the Yukian-Penutian connection, but he also postulated Yukian connections with putative Gulf. Munro, following Greenberg's proposal, assembled a large number of lexical resemblances between Yukian and the Gulf languages and concluded that Greenberg's proposal "is certainly worth pursuing" (1994:149). However, the data she presented connecting Yukian and the Gulf languages are less compelling than her Gulf lexical sets, which were critically evaluated above. Virtually all her Yukian-Gulf equations exhibit several of the problems discussed in Chapter 7.

Yukian-Gulf
−85% probability, 70% confidence

The evidence presented thus far is not promising with regard to broader Yukian connections.

Broader Keresan Relationships

Keresan has no demonstrable relatives. Sapir (1929a) had placed it with Hokan-Siouan, his default stock for most unaffiliated leftovers, but no supporting evidence has yet been put forward. Swadesh (1967b) suggested a connection between Keres and Caddo (actually Wichita), and Rood clarified many of the compared forms, suggesting tentatively that the evidence "should go a long way toward proof" of a Keres-Wichita relationship (1973:190). Greenberg (1987:163) accepted part of Sapir's proposal, lumping Keresan, Siouan, Yuchi, Caddoan, and Iroquoian in what he called Keresiouan, but as part of his more far-flung Almosan-Keresiouan—Almosan combines (following Sapir 1929a) Algic (Algonquian-Ritwan), Kutenai, and so-called Mosan (Chemakuan, Wakashan, and Salish). Needless to say, since the various constituent units of Greenberg's Almosan-Keresiouan are contested at present, there is little hope that this more inclusive classification will be accepted.

Keresan and Zuni
−40% probability, 40% confidence

Gursky (1966a:419–20) thought the possibility of a Zuni-Keres relationship was promising. (He was referring to an idea first proposed in 1856.) However, the twenty-five look-alikes that he presented have problems—for example, nursery words (*papa* 'older brother' / *baba* 'grandchild'); onomatopoetic forms ('to break', 'to blow'), semantic nonequivalent forms ('elder brother' / 'grandchild', 'green / wheat-grass', 'word/mention', 'cut/break', 'eye/to see', 'sit-stay/house', 'breathe/lung', 'bite/tooth', 'water / he drank'). Nine forms are short or have only a few matching segments ('meat' Zuni *ši* / Proto-Keres *iša·ni*). These data are too few and too problematic to support a possible Zuni-Keresan connection.

Keresan and Uto-Aztecan
0% probability, 60% confidence

Davis (1979:412) tentatively considered the possibility of a remote relationship between Keresan and Uto-Aztecan, based on seven possible cognate sets in which Uto-Aztecan *k* is matched with Keresan alveopalatals before front vowels and velars elsewhere. (Four of the sets compare Proto-Keresan forms; three compare Santa Ana only.) Three of these sets compare forms that are *CV* only in length, and two match only the *CV* portion of longer forms. In short, the hypothesis is not supported.[93]

Timucuan Proposals

Many broader relationships have been proposed for Timucua, but all have been unsuccessful. Adelung and Vater (1816:285) noted a resemblance to Illinois (an Algonquian language). Brinton saw resemblances with Yuchi, Cherokee, and Illinois resemblances but believed that Timucua would prove to be connected with Cariban languages: "These [resemblances to Yuchi, Cherokee, and Illinois] are trifling compared to the affinities to the Carib [no examples were presented], and I should not be astonished if a comparison of Pareja [1614a, Timucua grammar] with Gilü [*sic*; see Gilij 1780–1784] and D'Orbigny [1839] placed beyond doubt its rela-

tionship to this family of languages [Cariban]" (1859:137; see also Crawford 1979:330). Sapir (1929a) placed Timucua (though with a question mark) in his Hokan-Siouan phylum, for no apparent reason. Granberry (1970) claimed to have found a connection with Warao (an unaffiliated language of Venezuela and Guyana), but he also noted "cognates" with "Proto-Arawak, Proto-Gulf, Proto-Muskogean, and late Muskogean" (1970:607, quoted in Crawford 1988:157). Swadesh (1964b) compared Timucua with Arawakan. Crawford (1988) presented twenty-three lexical and morphological similarities shared by Muskogean and Timucua; he found eight of them to be probable borrowings and the rest to be possible cognates. His forms are suggestive but they are far from compelling.[94] Connections with Cherokee (Iroquoian) and Siouan have also been suggested. Greenberg (1987) included Timucua in his Chibchan-Paezan group (which also includes Tarascan, Warrau [Warao], and many other languages of northern South America and lower Central America). None of these proposals is persuasive. Timucua at present has no demonstrated affiliations (see Crawford 1979).

Proposals of Broader Mayan Relationships

Perhaps because of the romance associated with ancient Maya civilizations, hieroglyphic writing, and calendrics, many have been attracted to Mayan languages, and there have been many proposals of genetic relationships with other language families in the Americas and around the world as a result. I consider only some of the more reasonable ones here (assuming there is no need to debunk proposed connections with Natchez, Turkic, Hebrew, Atlantian, and Venusian).

Macro-Mayan
+30% probability, 25% confidence

Many scholars have written about Macro-Mayan, which includes Mayan, Totonacan, Mixe-Zoquean, and in some versions also Huave (see Chapter 5). However, the hypothesis is too weak to be embraced without reservations. The evidence presented thus far has been suggestive, but it is not persuasive. The major problem, besides those encountered in many proposals of remote linguistic kinship (as discussed in Chapter 7) is that of distinguishing borrowed material from potential cognates. These languages participate in the Mesoamerican linguistics area (see Campbell, Kaufman, and Smith-Stark 1986) and greatly influenced each other (as well as other languages of the area). Therefore, it is important to try to separate the effects of diffusion before attempting to reach conclusions regarding genetic relationship (see Chapter 9). I believe that ultimately Mayan and Mixe-Zoquean, and perhaps also Totonacan, will be shown to be genetically related (Huave should definitely be removed from the picture). However, this will require much more detailed and careful work than has been done to date, and it will probably necessitate evidence beyond the lexical comparisons that have been assembled and must include morphological correspondences of the sort advocated in Chapter 7 (see Brown and Witkowski 1979; Campbell 1973a; Campbell and Kaufman 1980, 1983; Kaufman 1964a; McQuown 1942, 1956; Radin 1924; Swadesh 1961, 1967a; Wonderly 1953).

Maya-Chipaya
−80% probability, 95% confidence

A connection between Mayan and Chipaya-Uru of Bolivia was first proposed by Olson (1964, 1965), and the hypothesis was initially received favorably by some scholars (see Stark 1972b, Hamp 1970, Voegelin and Voegelin 1965). Olson's evidence, which would seem suggestive, included a goodly number of proposed cognates and sound correspondences; close examination, however, revealed that the evidence evaporates, leaving abundant examples of the problems discussed in Chapter 7 (see Campbell 1973a). The Maya-Chipaya hypothesis is now abandoned.

Maya-Chipaya-Yunga
−90% probability, 95% confidence

The hypothesis joining Maya-Chipaya and Yunga of Peru was first presented by Louisa Stark (1972b) and was accepted by Eric Hamp (1967, 1970). Stark's evidence for a relationship between Chipaya-Uru and Yunga is quite suggestive, but with respect to the Mayan portion

of the proposal, it is even weaker than the evidence in support of the Maya-Chipaya hypothesis. The Maya-Chipaya-Yunga proposal should be abandoned.

Really Broad Proposals which Include Mayan

I do not discuss here the Mayan-Tarascan (Swadesh 1956), Maya-Arawakan (Noble 1965:26, Schuller 1919–1920), and Maya-Lenca (Andrews 1970) proposals; suffice it to say that none of these has a following today. Some scholars have entertained the possibility of including Mayan in one of the very large groupings that have been proposed. For example, Sapir (1929a) thought Mayan to be "apparently of Hokan-Siouan type" (see Golla 1984:316, 357, 409); several other scholars have sought to connect it with Penutian (following Whorf). Greenberg held that "Huave, Mayan, Mixe-Zoque, and Totonac-Tepehua form a well-defined subgroup of Penutian" (1987:143). These proposals are speculative at best and do not merit serious consideration.

Broader Otomanguean Relationships

Otomanguean-Huave
+25% probability, 25% confidence

Swadesh (1960b, 1964a, 1964b, and 1967a:96) consistently maintained that Huave has Otomanguean affinities, and Robert Longacre (1968:343) was inclined to accept this hypothesis. However, the only significant body of evidence presented in its favor thus far is that of Rensch (1973, 1976). Huave does appear to have some typological similarities with Otomanguean, which is not surprising, since Huave is surrounded by Otomanguean languages and Huave includes many Otomanguean loanwords. Nevertheless, the evidence for a genetic relationship is inconclusive. It is strong enough to warrant further research but too weak to be considered very persuasive.

Tlapanec-Subtiaba as Otomanguean
+95% probability, 90% confidence

Until recently, it was generally believed, following Sapir (1925a), that Tlapanec-Subtiaba was

Hokan. However, Rensch (1973 1977, 1978) argued that Tlapanec-Subtiaba belongs with Oto-manguean, and Jorge Suárez (1979, 1983, 1986) has demonstrated this grouping beyond any reasonable doubt (see also Kaufman in press). With the vastly more abundant Tlapanec data made available in Suárez's work (1983), it is now clear that Tlapanec-Subtiaba is just one more branch of Otomanguean. The material Sapir (1925a) employed to try to link it with Hokan has turned out to be unconvincing and fraught with the sorts of problems discussed in Chapter 7.

Jicaquean Broader Relationships

Jicaque-Subtiaba
−60% probability, 80% confidence

David Oltrogge (1977) proposed that Jicaque is related to both Tequistlatec and Subtiaba, and, following Rensch, has suggested an Otomanguean relationship for these languages, though he also acknowledges the possibility, following Sapir (1925a), of an exclusive Hokan affiliation or a broader Hokan-Otomanguean grouping. His evidence in support of a Jicaque-Tequistlatec relationship is quite good (see also Campbell and Oltrogge 1980), but the evidence for Jicaque-Subtiaba is weak and I recommend that this latter proposal be abandoned.

Jicaque-Tequistlatecan
+65% probability, 50% confidence

I have found Oltrogge's (1977) proposed connection between Jicaque, Tequistlatec, and Subtiaba to be unsupported, but I have defended a possible Jicaque-Tequistlatecan relationship (Campbell 1979:966–7, Campbell and Oltrogge 1980). I believe that these two will ultimately prove to be related, but the evidence I presented—a few look-alikes as possible cognates and some phonological matchings (possible sound correspondences)—is not conclusive.[95] However, it is sufficiently suggestive to warrant future research.

Jicaque-Hokan
−30% probability, 25% confidence

Greenberg and Swadesh (1953) proposed a Hokan affinity for Jicaque. They chose sixty-eight lexical forms from the two Jicaque languages but did not identify them as being different and compared them loosely to look-alikes in any of the many languages in Sapir's Hokan-Coahuiltecan grouping. These forms do not demonstrate a relationship. Although this proposal has been repeated uncritically in the literature, neither Jicaquean nor any other language or language group can be shown to be connected to "Hokan," unless further work on the Hokan hypothesis itself should bolster the proposed relationship among these languages.

Other Proposals

The Xinca-Lenca Proposal
0% probability, 50% confidence

Walter Lehmann (1920:767) first suggested a Xinca-Lenca relationship on the basis of only twelve proposed cognates.[96] The hypothesis had been widely accepted; however, six of the twelve forms presented as evidence are loanwords ('bean', 'corn', 'two', 'three', 'four', 'dog'), and six are short, phonetically not very similar (*ik'ał/ etta, ita* 'one'), onomatopoetic ('cough'), or semantically not equivalent ('winter/water'). In general, they exhibit the problems discussed in Chapter 7. The proposal should be abandoned until more convincing evidence may be assembled (see Campbell 1978a, 1979:961–3).

The Tarascan-Quechua Proposal
−90% probability, 80% confidence

Swadesh (1967a:92–3) proposed that Tarascan and Quechua are related, though the hypothesis has essentially been ignored by linguists (though see Liedtke 1991:74). It would not be significant enough to mention here except that the notion has been cited with some frequency in archaeological papers dealing with possible contacts involving metallurgy between the Andes and western Mexico. Swadesh listed only twenty-seven inspectional resemblances, but these amount mostly only to a good example of how not to convince others of a possible relationship—nearly all are questionable by the criteria of Chapter 7. Many forms are short or have few matching segments; several are pan-Americanisms ('no', 'cold'); some are onomato-

poetic ('teat'); and several are not really phonetically similar (Quechua *hu-c'u* / Tarascan *sapí*
'small'). In short, not even the forms in this list
appear to suggest much similarity between the
two languages, and a genetic relationship is
therefore out of the question.

The Misumalpan-Chibchan Proposal
+20% probability, 50% confidence

The Misumalpan languages of Central America
are often thought to be related to the Chibchan
family or are included in some version of Macro-
Chibchan. There is, however, little clear evidence for the proposal, though it deserves more
investigation (see Constenla 1987). As Craig and
Hale say of the hypothesis, "comparative work
in the lexical domain is unrewarding for the
most part" (1992:173). They compare a verbal
suffix of the shape *-i* in the Misumalpan languages and in Rama and Ika, two Chibchan
languages, as possible evidence for this hypothesis. Their evidence is suggestive but not persuasive. Because the suffix is short, involves a
relatively unmarked vowel, and has not yet been
fully demonstrated across a spectrum of Chibchan languages or shown likely to be inherited
from Proto-Chibchan, chance is a strong possible explanation. Moreover, the functions of the
suffix in these languages overlap only partially.
In Misumalpan its functions relate to clause-
chaining, complementation, and verb serial constructions; in Rama it is involved in complementation, but as a verb tense; in Ika the suffix
signals clause chaining. Although it is not expected that morphological functions should not
change in time, the different functions the suffix
performs in these different languages provides
additional room for chance. More evidence is
necessary.

Proposals of Broader South American Groupings

A number of larger, more inclusive genetic
groupings have been proposed within the various
broad-scale classifications of South American
languages. Since South American classification
is characterized largely by this sort of proposal,
these groupings were surveyed in Chapter 6 and
are not evaluated individually here.

Greenberg's Eleven Subgroups

While Joseph Greenberg (1987) classifies all
Native American languages into only three large
groups—Eskimo-Aleut (accepted), Na-Dene
(position of Haida disputed), and Amerind
(mostly rejected)—he considers his vast Amerind grouping to be composed of eleven "subgroups," each of which is a highly controversial
long-range proposal in its own right. To the
extent that these "subgroups" incorporate earlier
proposals, aspects of them have already been
discussed in this and in other chapters of this
book. None of the eleven has been demonstrated,
and specialists have severely criticized the methods and evidence upon which they are based
(see Chapters 2 and 7). Some of them may
provide a framework for future testing of
hypotheses of relationship, but the evidence marshaled thus far in their favor does not justify
these proposed groupings. They are presented in
the following list.

1. *Macro-Ge:* Greenberg's Macro-Ge essentially
   includes all the languages that have been proposed as being connected with Ge (Loukotka
   1968, Davis 1968), plus a few proposed by
   Greenberg (Chiquito, Oti, and Yabuti). He
   includes fifteen groups in this category: Bororo, Botocudo, Caraja, Chiquito, Erikbatsa,
   Fulnio, Ge, Guato, Kaingan, Kamakan, Mas-
   hakali, Opaie, Oti, Puri, and Yabuti (1987:65–
   6; see Chapter 6 for more accepted classifications).
2. *Macro-Panoan:* Greenberg explains that here
   he combines "Panoan, Tacanan, and Moseten
   on the one hand and Mataco, Guaicuru, Char-
   ruan, Lule, and Vilela on the other," plus
   Lengua (Mascoy) (1987:74).
3. *Macro-Carib:* Greenberg follows Loukotka
   (1968) and Rivet (1924) and includes in this
   category Cariban, Andoke, Bora (Miranya),
   Kukura, Uitoto, and Yagua (Peba).
4. *Equatorial:* In 1960 Greenberg had an
   Equatorial-Andean grouping, but in 1987 he
   broke this up into three separate groups: Equatorial, Macro-Tucanoan, and Andean. (On
   Macro-Tucanoan and Andean, see below.) In
   Equatorial he now places Arawa, Cayuvava,
   Chapacura, Coche, Cofan, Esmeralda, Guahibo, Guamo, Jibaro, Kandoshi, Kariri, Katembri, Maipuran, Otomaco, Piaroa, Taruma,
   Timote, Tinigua, Trumai, Tupi, Tusha, Uro,
   Yaruro, Yuracare, and Zamuco (combining

into a subgroup which he calls Jibaro-Kandoshi the language groups Cofan, Esmeralda, Jibaro, Kandoshi, and Yaruro) (1987:83; see Chapter 6).

5. *Macro-Tucanoan:* This grouping encompasses Auake, Auixiri, Canichana, Capixana, Catuquina, Gamella, Huari, Iranshe, Kaliana, Koaia, Maku, Mobima, Muniche, Nambikwara, Natu, Pankaruru, Puinave, Shukuru, Ticuna, Tucano, Uman, and Yuri (1987:93; see Chapter 6).

6. *Andean:* Greenberg includes here Alakaluf, Araucanian, Aymara, Catacao, Cholona, Culli, Gennaken (Pehuelche), Itucale (Simacu), Kahuapana, Leco, Mayna (Omurana), Patagon (Tehuelche), Quechua, Sabela (Auca), Sechura, Yamana (Yahgan), and Zaparo (1987:99; see Chapter 6). He distinguishes a "Northern subgroup" (Catacao, Cholona, Culli, Leco, and Sechura) and a "Southern Andean" (Alakaluf, Araucanian, Gennaken, Patagon, and Yamana).

7. *Chibchan-Paezan:* This large grouping for Greenberg "consists of the following families": Allentiac, Andaqui, Antioquia, Aruak, Atacama, Barbacoa, Betoi, Chibcha, Chimu, Choco, Cuitlatec, Cuna, Guaymi, Itonama, Jirajara, Lenca, Malibu, Misumalpan, Motilon, Mura, Paez, Paya, Rama, Talamanca, Tarascan, Timucua, Warrau, Xinca, and Yanomama (1987:106–7). It may seem surprising to find North American Timucua; Mexican Cuitlatec and Tarascan; Central American Lenca and Xinca; and remote South American Chimu, Warrau [Warao], and Yanomama included here with the Chibchan and Paezan languages as more conventionally understood.

8. *Central Amerind:* Greenberg distinguishes "three apparently coordinate branches" of Central Amerind: "Kiowa-Tanoan, Uto-Aztecan, and Oto-Mangue" (1987:123). It is interesting that Greenberg here groups Otomanguean with the Aztec-Tanoan (Kiowa-Tanoan + Uto-Aztecan) of other scholars (see above).

9. *Hokan:* Greenberg's version of Hokan is like Sapir's Hokan-Coahuiltecan, but it also includes most of the languages (except for Quechua) that have been proposed as members of Hokan since publication of Sapir's (1929a) classification: Achomawi (including Atsugewi), Chimariko, Chumash, Coahuilteco, Comecrudo, Cotoname, Esselen, Jicaque, Karankawa, Karuk, Maratino, Pomo, Quinigua, Salinan, Seri, Shasta (including Konomihu),

Subtiaba (including Tlapanec), Tequistlatec (Chontal of Oaxaca), Tonkawa, Waicuri, Washo, Yana, Yuman, and Yurumangui.

10. *Penutian:* Greenberg's view of Penutian includes all of Sapir's Penutian families plus several others subsequently proposed as Penutian after Sapir, as well as some startling combinations of his own: Yokuts, Maidu, Wintun, Miwok-Costanoan (considered a "valid grouping . . . called here California Penutian"); "Oregon and Plateau Penutian," as well as Chinook and Tsimshian; "Huave, Mayan, Mixe-Zoque, and Totonac-Tepehua . . . a well-defined subgroup"; Yukian (Yuki and Wappo); "Gulf" (composed of Atakapa, Chitimacha, Muskogean [and maybe Yukian]; and Zuni (1987:143–4). The grouping of Gulf with Penutian contradicts both Sapir's association of these languages with his Hokan-Siouan and Haas's Algonquian-Gulf proposals (see Chapter 2).

11. *Almosan-Keresiouan:* This proposal of Greenberg's combines his two groups, Keresiouan (composed of Caddoan [including Adai], Iroquoian, Keresan, and Siouan-Yuchi) and Almosan (the same as Sapir's Algonquian-Wakashan, combining Algic and Mosan [Wakashan, Chimakuan, and Salish], plus Kutenai) (1987:162–4).[97]

In general, considering Greenberg's claims about the power of his method of multilateral comparison, his assertion that "the validity of Amerind as a whole is more secure than that of any of its stocks" (1987:59) may raise some eyebrows, since his eleven member branches are themselves proposals of very distant relationship, none of which has any general acceptance. Moreover, it has been pointed out that the evidence he presents in support of individual groups could just as easily be interpreted as reflecting other combinations or regroupings that crosscut those which he asserts. For example, Ringe found this to be the case in his lexical comparisons of several Native American languages, following Greenberg's procedures:

The above numbers [of lexical matchings] seem to contradict not only Greenberg's subgrouping of "Amerind," but even his delimitation of that supposed superstock. Uto-Aztecan and Mixtec are supposed to belong to the same first-order subgroup, but the former seems to resemble Zoque (a "Penutian" language) and Karok (a "Hokan" language) more closely than it does Mixtec, while Mixtec appears to resemble Tzotzil (another "Penutian" language [Mayan]) about as much as it does Uto-Aztecan. Inuit [Eskimoan] is supposed to represent a superstock which is (at best) coordinate with "Amerind" as a whole, yet it seems to participate in about as many matchings as Mixtec and Algonquian. (Ringe 1994:11)

Greenberg's classification has been reviewed, mostly negatively, by many Americanists, and needs little further elaboration here. For discussion, see Adelaar 1989; Berman 1992; Bright 1988; Callaghan 1991a; Campbell 1988b; Chafe 1987; Everett in press; Goddard 1987b, 1990b; Goddard and Campbell 1994; Golla 1988; Hock 1993; Jacobsen 1993, 1994; Kaufman 1990a; Liedtke 1989, 1991; Matisoff 1990; Poser 1992; Rankin 1992; Ringe 1992, 1993; and Watkins 1990, among others. Moreover, there is some reason to believe that not even Greenberg and Ruhlen have strong faith in the validity of these eleven groupings, since they repeatedly mentioned their belief that the overall Amerind construct "is really more robust than some [of these eleven] lower-level branches of Amerind" (Ruhlen 1994b:15; see Greenberg 1987:59).

All-Inclusive Classifications of Native American Languages

As mentioned in Chapters 2 and 3, throughout the history of American Indian linguistics, some scholars have been sympathetic to the idea that Native American languages might eventually prove to belong to only one (or alternatively to two, or to only three) large-scale families. For the most part it has not proven possible to combine the families discussed in Chapters 3, 4, and 5 into demonstrable groupings which are more inclusive (despite numerous hypotheses, some more promising than others). For that reason, I mention only some of the widely encompassing views here. Sapir had mentioned on various occasions the possibility that there are only three (and even just two) families (see Chapter 2). Radin (1919) had proposed that all American Indian languages belong to a single large family. Haas seemed to agree: "Recent investigations (while they still fall short of complete agreement) are nevertheless propelling us nearer and nearer to his [Radin's 1919] point of

view [that all the languages of North America except Eskimoan are related]." She also pointed out that "hints of a possible relationship between Hokan and Penutian (in the broad sense of that term) have also been alluded to from time to time in the literature" (1960:989); these two large-scale classifications encompass a large proportion of North American families. Swadesh observed that "recent research seems to show that the great bulk of American languages form a single genetic phylum going far back in time" (1960c:896). Indeed, Swadesh exceeded even Greenberg (1960, 1987) in his lumpings, saying that in "the conception of ultimate relatedness of all the [American] languages . . . I would now go farther and include Na-Dene and Eskimoan, and also languages of the Old World" (1963b:318; see also 1962). Greenberg's (1987; see also 1960) Amerind is the best known of the all-inclusive classifications. As pointed out earlier in this book, scholars have carefully weighed this proposal and found it without merit. In short, although the notion that most American Indian languages ultimately are probably genetically related may be attractive, the firm reality is that at present this cannot be demonstrated.

Nostratic-Amerind
−90% probability, 75% confidence

I end this review of distant genetic proposals by reporting that Vitaly Shevoroshkin (1989c:6–7) finds that I contributed evidence (unwittingly he admits) of an Amerind-Nostratic genetic relationship when I compared Finnish (and hence Uralic, and, for Shevoroshkin, therefore also Nostratic) forms with Greenberg's Amerind forms to show that Greenberg's methods were incapable of distinguishing Amerind from other languages chosen at random (see Campbell 1988b). Shevoroshkin compares fifty-seven forms from individual Salishan languages (said to be "archaic Amerind languages") with Nostratic in an attempt to support this claim further. Ruhlen (1989, 1994a:183–7, 1994b:207–41) also compares Nostratic and Amerind. Not surprisingly, these comparisons contain many forms which are onomatopoetic, short, and semantically different; in general, they exhibit many examples of the problems discussed in Chapter

7. Therefore, these arguments constitute no real support for this claim.

Summary

In this chapter I have reviewed attempts—successful, provisional, and unsuccessful—to classify Native American languages into larger groupings. I am impressed both by the sheer amount of success that has been achieved—indeed, we do know a great deal about Native American languages and their relationships—and by the amount of research still necessary to resolve the disagreements and resolve competing proposals involving many groups, especially higher-order combinations of groups. I agree with Shipley that "we may remain calm even though many languages are not now (and may never be) genetically identified. Presumably the goal of research is to find the truth where we can, not to tuck everything in somehow somewhere" (1966:498). Nevertheless, it is encouraging to know that this work is continuing. I feel justified in asserting that significant developments should be expected only to the extent that the methodological considerations discussed in Chapter 7 are significantly involved.

9

Linguistic Areas of the Americas

It is by now well-accepted that languages of the same geographical area may come to resemble each other in a variety of ways and hence it is clear that it is just as important to delineate areal resemblances as it is to depict genetic resemblances.

Mary R. Haas (1976:347)

THE GOAL OF THIS CHAPTER IS TO survey the linguistic areas of the Americas, to the extent that they have been identified. Areal linguistics is very important to the study of Native American languages, for the primary goal of historical linguistic investigations should be to find out what really happened—to determine the real history, be it genetic or contact, that explains traits shared by different languages (Bright 1976). Areal linguistics is concerned with the diffusion of structural features across language boundaries: "The term 'linguistic area' generally refers to a geographical area in which, due to borrowing, languages of different genetic origins have come to share certain borrowed features—not only vocabulary . . . but also elements of phonological, grammatical, or syntactic structure" (Bright and Sherzer 1978:228). Linguistic areas are also referred to at times by the terms "convergence area," "diffusion area", "Sprachbund", and "adstratum." The defining

characteristic of a linguistic area is the existence of structural similarities among the languages of a particular geographical area (some of which are genetically unrelated or at least not close relatives), where "languages belonging to more than one family show traits in common which do not belong to the other members of one of the families" (Emeneau 1980[1965]:127).

These resemblant traits shared among the languages of the linguistic area are normally assumed to be the result of extensive contact, convergence, and diffusion among the languages. Unfortunately, most students of American Indian linguistics after Franz Boas were so interested in reducing the linguistic diversity of the Americas that they often either ignored diffusion within linguistic areas or assumed the structural similarities to be evidence of possible genetic relationships.[1]

The studies of Native American linguistic areas that have been undertaken are of two kinds. The more common approach, which I have called the "circumstantialist" approach (Campbell 1985a, Campbell et al. 1986), merely catalogues similarities found in the languages of a geographical area, allowing the list to suggest diffusion—that it is not necessary to demonstrate the actual borrowing among neighboring languages. This approach has been sharply criticized because such lists do nothing to eliminate chance, universals, and possibly undetected genetic relationships as alternate explanations for shared traits. The other approach, which I have called the "historicist" approach, is to determine actual borrowing, insofar as possible, using documentary or comparative evidence. This more rigorous approach (which, of course, is more revealing historically) is generally preferred, although the lack of historical evidence (or the lack of investigation of existing data) often makes it necessary to be more tolerant of the less reliable circumstantialist approach.

The concepts of linguistic areas and culture areas (see Driver and Massey 1957, Kroeber 1939) are similar and to some extent have a common history. But areal linguistics enjoys renewed vigor among linguists, while culture areas are currently held to be of little interest among anthropologists. Joel Sherzer's work on the linguistic areas of North America (1973, 1976; see also Sherzer and Bauman 1972, Bright and Sherzer 1976) is important. It combines aspects of both linguistic areas and culture areas, and for that reason three considerations should be borne in mind. First, Sherzer equated the linguistic diffusion areas of North America directly with the previously defined culture areas (1973, 1976). However, it is not the case that the anthropological culture areas will a priori coincide with linguistic areas. Linguistic areas form much more slowly than culture areas because change in linguistic structure in general is considerably slower than change that leads to the sharing of culture traits which define the culture areas. In a number of cases, the languages spoken by people in recently formed culture areas do not provide any real evidence that a corresponding linguistic area is being formed. Second, Sherzer employed Sapir's (1929a) now largely rejected and highly controversial genetic classification of American Indian languages as the basis for distinguishing between traits that might be shared due to family relationships and areally diffused traits. Third, Sherzer's method of investigating linguistic areas was limited to surveying the languages of a given culture area to ascertain whether they exhibited the traits in a predetermined checklist. This means that he would miss any areally shared features which were not included in his list. As discussed later in this chapter, these considerations have frequently created difficulties in the study of the linguistic areas of North America.

Some of the larger families have languages in more than one linguistic area. For example, the Athabaskan family has members in the Northwest Coast, Plateau, Northern California, and Pueblo linguistic areas. Uto-Aztecan has languages in the Great Basin, Southern California–Western Arizona, the Pueblo area, the Plains, and Mesoamerica. Algic languages are found in Northern California, the Plains, the Southeast, and the Northeast.

Some linguistic areas in the Americas that are discussed here are fairly well established (the Northwest Coast, Mesoamerica, the Southeast); others are merely the subjects of preliminary hypotheses in need of extensive research; still others are clearly defined but little is known concerning them.

North American Linguistic Areas

Several important linguistic areas have been identified (at least tentatively) in North America. These are surveyed in this section.

Northern Northwest Coast Area
(MAPS 1, 2, and 3)

A linguistic area in the extreme northwest of the Northwest Coast was recently proposed by Leer (1991). It has long been suspected that lack of labial stops in Aleut is due to influence from Athabaskan or so-called Na-Dene languages (see Bergland 1958:625, though this is doubted by Hamp 1976:89). Leer (1991) adduced several additional shared traits which support the existence of a Northern Northwest Coast linguistic area. It is perhaps a subarea of the larger Northwest Coast Linguistic Area (see below). In the

Northern Northwest Coast area, Haida and Eyak were in close contact, forming with Aleut a looser contact group; Tlingit was allied with them, but peripherally to Haida and Eyak, constituting something of a bridge between Haida-Eyak and Athabaskan; the area was ultimately broken up by the intrusion of Tlingit and Alutiiq (Eskimoan). Leer considers the strong (diagnostic) traits of the Northern Northwest Coast area to be: (1) the lack of labial obstruents (in Aleut, Eyak, Tlingit, and Proto-Athabaskan, and marginally in Haida; labials are present in other Northwest Coast languages); (2) promiscuous number marking (in Aleut, Eyak, Haida, and Tlingit) (for example, in Tlingit the proclitic *has* signals plural of animate third person pronouns; as a proclitic to a transitive verb with animate third person subject and object, *has* may "promiscuously" pluralize either one, or both; in Haida, Eyak, and Aleut, the promiscuous number marking can associate semantically with any pronoun within the clause); and (3) periphrastic possessive construction (in Eyak and Haida) of the form 'money me-on he.stole-he', meaning ambiguously 'he stole my money' or 'he stole money from me'.

Among the weaker areal traits are the following. The Northern Northwest Coast languages and Eskimo have strict head-final (XSOV) syntax and a clear focus-position at the beginning of the sentence (several other Northwest Coast languages are VSO). In Northern Northwest Coast and Athabaskan languages, inalienable possession and postpositions are the same construction. Haida and Tlingit share active/stative alignment. In Haida, Tlingit, and Eyak, there is a distinction between nonhuman and human (or inanimate and animate) third person pronouns, and 'plural' is distinguished only for human (or animate) third persons. Finally, there is the shared presence of syllable-initial glottalized sonorants (in Eyak, Haida, but also in other families of the Northwest Coast Linguistic Area). Thompson and Kinkade (1990:44) mention the additional trait of noun-classificatory systems shared by Eyak, Athabaskan, and Tlingit, and Haida has a similar system marked by shape-prefixes.

Northwest Coast Area

(MAP 3; see also Maps 2 and 4)

As traditionally viewed, the Northwest Coast Linguistic Area includes: Eyak, Tlingit, Athapaskan languages of the region, Haida, Tsimshian, Wakashan, Chimakuan, Salishan, Alsea, Coosan, Kalapuyan, Takelma, and Lower Chinook. It also includes most of the languages Leer places in the Northern Northwest Coast area, with the exception of Aleut. The Northwest Coast is probably the best known of the North American linguistic areas. It is known for the linguistic complexity, both phonological and morphological, exhibited by its languages. It also has more linguistic diversity than any other well-defined linguistic area in North America, and representatives of twelve of Powell's (1891a) fifty-eight language families are found here.

The languages of the Northwest Coast are characterized by elaborate systems of consonants, which typically include: series of glottalized stops and affricates, labiovelars, multiple laterals *(l, ł, tl, tl')* (all have *ł*; most have *tl'*, though some lack a voiced *l*, and some do not have a plain nonglottalized *tl*), *s/š* opposition, *c/č* opposition, *q,* one fricative series (voiceless), and velar fricatives. A series of "resonants" structure together, in which nasals, lateral resonants, *w,* and *y* function as a single series, often in morphophonemic alternation with obstruent counterparts. The labial consonant series typically contains far fewer consonants than those for points of articulation further back in the mouth (labials are completely lacking in Tlingit and Tillamook, and are quite limited in Eyak and in most Athabaskan languages); in contrast, the uvular series is especially rich in most of these languages. The vowel systems, however, are limited; there are only three positions in several languages and usually no more than four, though a vowel-length contrast is common. Other well-known shared phonological traits which have a more limited distribution among these languages are pharyngeals, glottalized resonants, and glottalized continuants. Typical shared morphological traits are: the well-known reduplication processes (often of several kinds in one language, signaling various grammatical functions, such as iteration, continuative, progressive, plural, and collective); numeral classifiers; alienable/inalienable oppositions in nouns; pronominal plural; nominal plural; verbal reduplication signifying distribution, repetition, and so on; suffixation of tense-aspect markers in verbs; verbal evidential markers; and locative-directional markers in the verb; masculine/feminine gender; visibility/invisibility opposition in demonstratives; and nominal and verbal reduplication signaling the diminutive. Aspect is generally relatively more important than tense. All the languages but Tlingit have passive-like constructions. The negative appears as the first element in a clause regardless of the usual word order. Northwest Coast languages also have lexically paired singular and plural verb stems (Leer 1991:161; Sherzer 1973:766–71, 1976:56–83; Thompson and Kinkade 1990:42–4).

Some other traits shared by a smaller number of Northwest Coast languages include the following:

1. A widely diffused sound change of *k > č affected Wakashan, as well as Salishan, Chimakuan, and other Northwest Coast languages (Sapir 1926, Swadesh 1949:166, Jacobsen 1979b)
2. Tonal (or pitch-accent) contrasts are found in Tlingit, Haida, Bella Bella (a dialect of Keiltsuk), Upriver Halkomelem, Quileute, Kalapuyan, and Takelma
3. Interdental θ and θ', which developed in Halkomelem, in Saanich (a dialect of Northern Straits), and in dialects of Comox; one or both of these sounds exist in Pentlatch and in a Chasta Costa dialect
4. Also, w became k^w and y became č in Northern Straits, Clallam, Makah, and Chemakum
5. Several languages have ergative alignment, at least in part: Tlingit, Haida, Tsimshian, some Salishan languages (such as Comox; Interior Salishan is partly ergative), Taitnapam (Sahaptin), Chinookan, and Coosan (Thompson and Kinkade 1990:44).

"Lexical suffixes" are found at least in Wakashan and Salishan languages. They designate such familiar objects (normally signaled with full lexical roots in most other languages) as body parts, geographical features, cultural artifacts, and some abstract notions. Wakashan, for example,

has some 300 lexical suffixes (Thompson and Kinkade 1990:40, Kinkade et al. in press). The grammar of these languages has a severely limited role (some linguists assert that the contrast is totally lacking for some of the languages) for the contrast between nouns and verbs as distinct categories (see Thompson and Kinkade 1990:33, Kinkade et al. in press). (For more discussion and some other traits, see Thompson and Kinkade 1990.)

Some scholars have thought that Wakashan, Chimakuan, and Salishan are genetically related as proposed in the Mosan hypothesis (see Chapter 8; see also Powell 1993). These languages have considerable structural similarity, but much of it may be due to areal diffusion. In any case, the proposed Mosan grouping has little support today (Jacobsen l979a, 1979b; Thompson 1979; see also Swadesh 1949). Several of the traits associated with the Northwest Coast Linguistic Area extend beyond to the languages of the Plateau and Northern California areas, and to the Eskimo-Aleut languages, while others have a more limited distribution within the Northwest Coast, not found in all the languages of the area (Thompson and Kinkade 1990:42).

The subarea of the Northwest which lacks primary nasals includes Twana and Lushootseed (Salishan), Quileute (Chimakuan), and Nitinat and Makah (Nootkan, of the broader Wakashan family) (see Haas 1969c, Kinkade 1985, Thompson and Thompson 1972; see also Bancroft 1886[1882]:609). The last two, for example, have changed their original *m, *m̓ to b, and *n, *n̓ to d, due to areal pressure, but closely related Nootka has retained the original nasals.[2] Comox (Salishan) has been described as having b and d as optional variants of m and n, respectively, and a similar situation has been observed in Sechelt and Clallam and in two dialects of Halkomelem (all three are Salishan, Kinkade 1985:479). Boas observed that there was much confusion regarding "surds and sonants" in Lower Chinook pronunciation on account of "semiclosure of the nose," and older records of several of the other languages reveal a similar situation (Kinkade 1985:478–9). Kinkade reports that "in virtually every littoral language [at least twelve of them] of the Northwest from the 46th to the 50th parallel nasals were sometimes pronounced without full closure of the velum," and that in recent time many of the languages which had these sounds intermediate between nasals and voiced stops have settled in favor of one or the other of the sounds, eliminating the intermediate variant (1985:480).

Several individual languages of the Salishan and Wakashan families, and arguably also the Athabaskan family, in the Northwest Coast Linguistic Area have pharyngeal segments. Since pharyngeals are among the rarest speech sounds in the world (they also occur only in Afro-Asiatic [Semitic and Cushitic] and in Caucasian families), it is quite possible that those shared among languages of the Northwest Coast are the product of areal diffusion (Colarusso 1985).[3]

Melville Jacobs (1954) pointed out several shared features. He reported that Boas's finding of "anterior palatals" such as g^y, k^y, k'^y, and x^y was indicative of two subdistricts in the Northwest—in the adjacent languages Coos, Alsea, Tillamook (Coast Salish), and Lower Chinook (with a k^y allophone of k in Upper Chehalis [Coast Salish]), and separately again in Kwakiutl and Tsimshian in northern British Columbia. Jacobs found that in Tillamook anterior palatals were used only to express the diminutive, derived from the phonemes G, q, q', and X (1954:48; Thompson and Kinkade [1990:44] add Nitinaht, Sechelt, Lushootseed, and probably Nootka). Jacobs also reported that Molala and Kalapuya, neighbors on either side of the northern Oregon Cascade Mountains, share "bilabial continuants" (written f and f^w [presumably ϕ and ϕ^w]). Moreover, "Alsea, Molale, and Kalapuya, contiguous to one another, lack the contrast of s and š of many Northwest languages and use only a retracted s that may be transcribed ş. . . . Takelma, a little south of them, also has it" (1954:52–3; see also Haas 1969d:84–8.) Several of the traits associated with the Plateau and Northern California linguistic areas are also found in the Northwest Coast area (see Sherzer 1976:127).

Plateau Area
(MAP 24)

The languages commonly thought to make up the Plateau Linguistic Area are: the Sahaptian

family (Nez Perce and Sahaptin), Upper Chinook (Kiksht), Nicola (Athabaskan), Cayuse, Molala, Klamath, Kutenai, and Interior Salishan (a subgroup of the Salishan family with several members; see Chapter 4). The Plateau is a relatively clearly defined culture area, but whether it constitutes a legitimate linguistic area or whether it should be included in the Northwest Coast area (since most of the traits of its languages are also found in the Northwest Coast area) is an open question. Kinkade et al. are of the opinion that "there is no outstanding set of language traits that sets off the Plateau as a major linguistic diffusion area distinct from other regions; rather it is part of a larger area that includes the Northwest Coast culture area" (in press; see also Latham 1856:71). Further investigation is called for to decide this matter.

The Plateau area languages are characterized by glottalized stops, contrasting velar and uvular obstruent series (for example, k contrasted with q), and laterals (l, $ɫ$, tl, tl'; but tl' is lacking from Kutenai, Coeur d'Alene, Nez Perce, Cayuse, Molala, and Klamath). Other shared traits, thought less salient, include labiovelars, one fricative series, velar (and uvular) fricatives, a series of glottalized resonants (sonorants) contrasting with plain resonants (except in Sahaptin, Cayuse, Molala, and Kiksht), consonant clusters (in medial or final position in words) of four or more consonants (except in Kiksht, and uncertain in Cayuse and Molala), vowel systems of only three or four vowel positions (Nez Perce, with five, is the only exception), a vowel-length contrast, size-shape-affective sound symbolism involving consonantal interchanges, pronominal plural, nominal plural, prefixation of subject person markers of verbs, suffixation of tense-aspect markers in verbs (aspect as basic and tense secondary, except that tense is basic and aspect is secondary in Kiksht, Sahaptin, and Nez Perce), several kinds of reduplication (except in Nicola), numeral classifiers (shared by Salishan and Sahaptian languages), locative-directional markers in verbs, and different roots for the singular and the plural for various actions (for example, 'sit', 'stand', 'take'—except in Kutenai and Lillooet and uncertain in Cayuse and Molala) (Sherzer 1976:84–102, Kinkade et al. in press).

Haruo Aoki presented "a preliminary cross-genetic linguistic study of the eastern Plateau area" that included Nez Perce and eastern members of Interior Salish. He found that the "quinary-decimal" numerical system "is a diffused feature among the languages of Oregon, Washington, and Idaho" and that the bifurcate collateral kinship system shared by Sahaptian and Interior Salish "is probably convergent and brought about by diffusion." The phonology of the Interior Salish languages and Nez Perce also have "some interesting traits, probably attributable to diffusion" (Aoki 1975:187–8). One of these is labiovelars, which are found in most of the languages, including underlyingly in Nez Perce. Nez Perce (Sahaptian) and Coeur d'Alene (Salish) share a rule that a consonant (other than sibilants) and a glottal stop combine, resulting in a glottalized consonant (Nez Perce *ʔilp-ʔilp → ʔilp'ilp* 'red' [reduplicated]). Nez Perce has *a/i* alternations in pairs of related words, which also existed in Proto-Sahaptian; in some instances Coast Salish *a* corresponds to Interior Salish *i*; in others its *i* corresponds to Interior *a;* Aoki therefore suspects that the Sahaptian rule must have operated "across the Salishan-Sahaptian border" (1975:190).[4] The two groups also share a number of lexical borrowings and similarities in the formation of neologisms. Nez Perce and Coeur d'Alene share linguistic features in the various "abnormal types of speech"; for example, Coyote in folktales changes *s* to *š*. In fact, there are similarities in the genre of "abnormal speech" (also sometimes called "animal talk" or "baby talk") of a number of Northwest Coast and Plateau languages, including at least Nootka, Kwakiutl, Quileute, Takelma, Nez Perce, and Coeur d'Alene.

Sherzer (1973:760, 772–3) dealt with the Northwest Coast and Plateau areas independently, but he also combined them into a larger linguistic area, whose common traits are a glottalized stop series, pharyngeals, glottalized continuants, nominal and verbal reduplication, and numeral classifiers, plus others. Other researchers would additionally include Northern California in this larger area. There is also some overlap with the Great Basin, which raises questions about the definition of the Great Basin as a linguistic area. For example, Cayuse and Molala of the Plateau area have a voiceless bilabial

fricative (ϕ) and a velar nasal (η)—two traits they have in common with neighboring Northern Paiute, a member of the Great Basin area, but also with some languages of the Northern California and Greater South Coast Range areas, and with nearby Kalapuyan languages of the Northwest Coast linguistic area. Chinookan is particularly interesting in this regard, since it has representatives in both the Northwest Coast and Plateau areas, and these different varieties exhibit a number of traits in common with the other languages in their respective linguistic areas. While Lower Chinookan is characterized by aspects rather than tenses, Upper Chinookan (Kiksht) has developed complex tense categories as a result of the influence from other Plateau languages. For example it has a tense distinction between "recent" past and "remote" past, as do Nez Perce and Molala (Silverstein 1974). The Wasco and Wishram varieties of Upper Chinookan have borrowed possessive, instrumental, and locative case endings from Sahaptin, and they may also have borrowed the Molala allative suffix. Chinookan has ergative syntax, but these borrowed case endings and a borrowed derivational suffix display a rather different nominative-accusative syntax. Upper Chinookan also shares the directional categories of "cislocative" and "translocative" with Nez Perce, Sahaptin, and Columbian (Salishan) (Cayuse and Molala apparently also have the cislocative) (Silverstein 1974, Kinkade et al. in press).

Northern California Area
(MAP 5)

Languages of the Northern California Linguistic Area also have several traits in common with the languages of the Northwest Coast and the Plateau areas. The Northern California area includes: Algic (distantly related Yurok and Wiyot); Athabaskan (Hupa, Mattole, and Kato); Yukian (Yuki and Wappo); Miwokan (Lake Miwok and Southern Sierra Miwok); Wintuan; Maiduan; Klamath-Modoc; Pomo; Chimariko; Achomawi, Atsugewi; Karuk; Shasta; Yana; and for some scholars also Washo (though Washo is usually assigned to the Great Basin). (See Dixon and Kroeber's [1903] Northwestern California structural-geographical type, with Yurok as typical, contrasted with their Central Californian type, typified by Maidu.) Mary Haas, in her investigation of the languages of northern California to ascertain possible areal traits, noted the spotty occurrence in this area of back velar consonants (uvulars such as *q*) in Klamath, Wintu, Chimariko, and Pomoan; she observed that they are "highly characteristic of the Northwest Coast area, though rare in Athabaskan languages" (1976:352). She also pointed out that the voiceless laterals, *ł* and the less frequent *tl'*, of the Northwest Coast area and all Athabaskan languages are also found in this area in Yurok and Wiyot (both with *ł*), Patwin and Lake Miwok (with *ł* and *tl'*), and Wintu (in which *tl* is an allophone of *ł*). She found retroflexed stops shared by several languages of this area, including Chimariko, Kashaya Pomo, Wappo, Lake Miwok, and Sierra Miwok. In each language there is a retroflexed stop in all the stop series (three—plain, aspirated, and glottalized—in Chimariko, Kashaya Pomo, and Lake Miwok; two—plain and glottalized—in Wappo, and only one—plain—in Southern Sierra Miwok). This retroflexion is also shared by Yokuts, farther to the south. A few of the languages of this area have both *l* and *r*: Yurok and Wiyot, Wintu-Patwin, Lake Miwok, and perhaps Yana. (In Yurok and Wiyot, alternations in *r* and *l* are associated with consonant symbolism.) A distinct series of voiced stops is rare but is found in the east-west strip of languages that includes Kashaya Pomo, Wintu-Patwin, and Maidu (though with implosion in Maidu) (Haas 1976:353). Haas also described the areal trait of consonant sound symbolism that is found in Yurok, Wiyot, Hupa, Tolowa, Karuk, and Yana (1976:354–5) and the shared formal aspects of the numeral systems.[5] (See also Sherzer 1976:127–8, Jacobs 1954.)

It is important to point out that Washo, which is usually assigned to the Great Basin area, also shares a number of traits with Northern California languages. They include the pronominal dual; a quinary/decimal numeral system (similar to one in Maidu); the absence of vowel-initial syllables; and free stress (like that of Maiduan) (Jacobsen 1986:109–11). This calls into question the existence of, or at least the definition of, the Great Basin as a linguistic area.

Clear Lake Area
(MAP 5)

The languages of the Clear Lake Linguistic Area are: Lake Miwok, Patwin, Eastern Pomo, Southeastern Pomo, and Wappo. This is a very clear linguistic area, centered around Clear Lake, ca. 80 miles northeast of the San Francisco Bay. These languages share, among other things, retroflexed dentals, voiceless *l* (*ł*), and glottalized glides (see Callaghan 1964, Sherzer 1976:129). Lake Miwok, for example, has three series of stops (plain, aspirated, and glottalized), whereas its sister languages have only one; it also has *r*, *ł*, and the affricates *ts'*, *č*, *č'*, *tl'*, and word-final *š* which the others lack. These are clearly borrowed from neighboring languages—mostly imported with loanwords that contained them, after which they spread to some native Miwok words (Callaghan 1964:47, 1987, 1991a:52; Berman 1973).

South Coast Range Area
(MAP 5)

Leanne Hinton (1991) reports work which establishes a South Coast Range Linguistic Area, which contains Chumash, Esselen, and Salinan. The South Coast Range area is also part of a larger area that I refer to as the Greater South Coast Range Linguistic Area, which includes, in addition to the languages of the South Coast Range, Yokutsan and Northern-Uto-Aztecan languages. Dixon and Kroeber's (1903:8) Southern Phonetic Group, which included Chumashan, Yokuts, Salinan, Southern California Uto-Aztecan, and Yuman languages, may perhaps be seen as a precursor of this more recently recognized linguistic area (compare Dixon and Kroeber's [1903] Southwestern California structural-geographical type, typified by Chumash). Sherzer (1976:129) had pointed out that languages of what he called the Yokuts-Salinan-Chumash region share traits: three series of stops, retroflexed sounds, glottalized resonants, and prefixation of verbal subject markers. These traits are not unique to this region, however, and some overlap with the traits of other areas—for example, the retroflexed sounds and three series of stops in the languages of the Clear Lake area. The areal traits of the Greater South Coast Range area include h, i, c, and $ŋ$, shared widely in the area, but not all these traits are found in every language (for details, see Hinton 1991:139–40).

Langdon and Silver discuss the distribution of the /t/–/ṭ/ contrast in California languages, which includes several of these Greater South Coast Range area languages (but not all) and is found in others as well: "We find that their territory encompasses about half the state [of California], including a large continuous area extending north and south of San Francisco Bay, with one lone northern outlier (Chimariko) and a set of southern outliers (all Yuman)" (1984:141). Specifically, the languages involved which have this contrast are Salinan, Esselen, Yokutsan (but not all varieties; it is absent in Chukchansi Yokuts, for example), Miwok-Costanoan, Yukian, Pomoan, Chimariko, and Yuman (Diegueño, Cocopa, Yuma, Mojave—not all Yuman languages have a phonemic contrast, though Proto-Yuman is believed to have had the two sounds allophonically, Langdon and Silver 1984:144). With the recognition that /ṭ/ is actually realized as an affricate in some of these languages, we can add Kitanemuk-Serrano (Uto-Aztecan) and Tolowa (Athabaskan, in the extreme northern corner of California) to the list (Langdon and Silver 1984:149; see also Hinton 1991). Langdon and Silver observe that "the distribution of this contrast suggests that we are dealing with a classical case of areal diffusion" (1984:142). They conclude that there are two distinct subareas: the northern subarea (Yuki, Wappo, Pomoan, and Miwokan) is defined by languages in which there is a contrast between two stops; the southern subarea (Costanoan, Esselen, Salinan, Yokuts, and Kitanemuk-Serrano) consists of languages in which the contrast is between a stop and a retroflexed affricate (1984:155).

Southern California–Western Arizona Area
(MAPS 5 and 8)

Hinton has demonstrated that extensive areal linguistic change has affected the Yuman languages and Cupan, and less extensively the Takic languages (the Uto-Aztecan subgroup which includes Cupan) in general. Some of the more broadly distributed traits within Southern California include a distinction between k and q

and the presence of k^w, $č$, x. Traits shared more specifically between Yuman and Cupan include k^w/q^w contrast, s/$ṣ$ contrast,[6] x^w, $ñ$, $ľ$, r/l contrast, a small vowel inventory, and sound symbolism (see Hinton 1991:144–7 for details). Several of these characteristics are listed also by Sherzer as "regional areal traits of southern California" (1976:128). They reflect the strong influence from Yuman on Cupan languages, for each trait shows a divergence from common Takic (or Northern-Uto-Aztecan) in the direction of convergence with features known to have been present in Proto-Yuman (Hinton 1991:152–4). In addition, several Yuman and Takic languages share v, e, and more marginally $š$, though these are not in the proto language of either group. Though the first is not known in the South Coast Range area, the latter two are established there; they may have existed earlier in the South Coast Range and later spread to the Yuman-Takic area. It is the River subgroup of Yuman that shares the most traits in common with Cupan; the specific traits they share are mostly allophonic in one or the other and suggest very recent contact. Elliott (1994), however, argues that Cupan has been influenced more directly by Diegueño (Yuman) in that Cupan borrowed (1) the indefinite marker m- and (2) the concept of affixation of definite and indefinite prefixes onto verbs that mean 'to be', which results in words for 'thus' and 'how', respectively.

Shaul and Andresen's (1989) Southwestern Arizona ("Hohokam") area is surely related to that defined by Hinton. They believe that a linguistic area developed in southwestern Arizona through the interaction of Piman (Uto-Aztecan) and Yuman speakers as part of the Hohokam archaeological culture. They define this area based on a single shared feature: "The linguistic trait we have found important in defining a prehistoric linguistic area in southwestern Arizona is phonological, i.e., a retroflex stop shared by Pimans [/ḍ/, development from *r] and some Yuman speakers [/ṭ/]" (1989:109; see also Sherzer 1976:151). Although they make a plausible case that this trait was spread by areal diffusion, it would of course be stronger if other shared traits could be found that would support the linguistic area interpretation.

Oswalt (1976b:298) attributes the presence of switch reference in languages of the south-

western United States (in Southern Paiute, Tübatulabal, Hopi, Papago, and Zuni, as well as in
the Yuman languages) to diffusion. However,
Jacobsen shows that the trait is found in many
more languages, though its history is not yet
fully understood:

> The history of the development of the device of
> switch-reference in these languages is not under-
> stood in a detailed way. . . . A consideration of
> the geographical distribution of switch-reference
> in North America reveals a striking clustering of
> the languages in a largely continuous area center-
> ing on the Southwest and Great Basin culture
> areas. . . . It forms a solid area in the western half
> of the Southwest. . . . It also extends westward to
> a string of languages in the Plateau and California
> areas which border on these Great Basin lan-
> guages: from north to south, Klamath, Maidu,
> Yokuts, and Tübatulabal. Then there is a separate
> area in coastal northern California constituted by
> Pomo and Yuki. Outliers are Huichol farther south
> on the west coast, Tonkawa farther east in the
> southern Plains, and Muskogean in the Southeast.
> This Southwestern areal spread . . . has become
> even more salient with the . . . additions . . . of
> . . . Yuman-Cochimí and Seri, and it stands out
> by contrast with the larger northern and eastern
> areas of the continent from which this device
> seems to be lacking.
>   One naturally thinks of the likelihood of diffu-
> sion in at least some cases within this area.
> (1983:172–3)

Great Basin Area
(MAP 7)

As defined by Sherzer (1973, 1976), the languages of the Great Basin Linguistic Area are
those of the Numic branch of Uto-Aztecan and
Washo. He lists as particularly characteristic of
the Great Basin the shared traits: voiceless vowels, nasals, and semivowels; k/k^w contrast; bilabial fricatives; x^w; η; and an overtly marked
nominal case system (1976:165). The languages
also share an inclusive/exclusive pronominal
distinction and i is present in all of them (Jacobsen 1980).

However, there is some reason to doubt that
the Great Basin is a legitimately defined linguistic area. The common traits in Washo and Numic
are also found in languages of adjacent areas, as
well. As Jacobsen points out:

> This approach [Sherzer's] of starting out from
> culture areas seems to introduce some distortions
> as applied to Washoe, in that it minimizes the
> comparably great similarities to the California
> stocks (some of which Sherzer 1976:128, 164,
> 167, 238–239, 246 indeed notes). For example,
> . . . the two striking points of agreement, presence
> of i and η, are also shared with groups to the west,
> while the other features of Washoe—presence of
> glottalized stops, $\dagger$, and a $s/\check{s}$ contrast, and absence
> of k^w—separate it from Numic and unite it with
> one or more of its western neighbors. (1986:110)

Jacobsen (1986:110) mentions other features that
are common to Great Basin (Numic) and California languages. For example, similarities between Washoe and Northern Paiute systems of
kinship terminology are shared as well by Miwok and Yokuts; the Washo reduplication pattern
is similar to that of Numic but also to that of
Maiduan and less so also to that of Sierra Miwok. Instrumental verb prefixes are shared by
Washo and Numic (where they are unique
among Uto-Aztecan languages) and are also
found in Maiduan, Shasta, and Achumawi. The
pronominal inclusive/exclusive distinction, innovative in both Washo and Numic, is found
also in Miwokan. Jacobsen (1980) argues that
this distinction diffused in a number of more
or less contiguous languages of north-central
California, the Great Basin, and their neighbors—in Numic (Uto-Aztecan), Washo (an isolate), Tübatulabal (Uto-Aztecan), Yuki (Yukian),
Palaihnihan (primarily in Achumawi), Wintu
(Wintuan), Sahaptin (Sahapatian, in the Plateau
area, bordering Northern Paiute of Numic), and
Shuswap (Interior Salish), Kwakiutl (Wakashan), and languages of the east: Algonquian,
Siouan, Iroquoian, Kiowa, Pawnee, and Yuchi.
Both the inclusive/exclusive contrast and switch-
reference are also widely found in contiguous
languages extending across a large area (Jacobsen 1986:110). Whistler and Golla suggest that
"the presence of $*i$ in the phonemic inventories
of the Penutian languages of the Sierra Nevada
region [Maiduan, Utian, and Yokutsan] is the
result of early diffusion" (1986:352–3). The
presence of this sound is sometimes attributed
to Numic contact, but the sound is also found
in several of the putataive Hokan languages
(particularly in Washo and Chumashan; compare
the epenthetic ∂ in Atsugewi and Pit River) (see

also Jacobsen 1980). Oswalt (1976) showed that switch reference exists also in several of the languages of the Northern California area, including Washo, several Uto-Aztecan languages, Pomoan, and Maiduan.

Perhaps, then, the whole concept of a Great Basin linguistic area needs rethinking; perhaps it is merely an extension of the Northern California Linguistic Area. In any case, it demonstrates the difficulties that can be created by assuming, as Sherzer (1973, 1976) does, that culture areas and linguistic areas will coincide.

Pueblo Area
(MAP 8)

The languages of the Pueblo Linguistic Area are Keresan, Tanoan, Zuni, and Hopi, with intrusive Apachean. The Pueblo region is a recognized culture area, characterized by the kachina cult and medicine societies, among other things, and several of these traits (such as loom weaving, agriculture, and moiety systems) have diffused into neighboring Apachean. Though little studied, this culture area also corresponds to a linguistic area. Catherine Bereznak (1995) discussed twenty-eight shared linguistic traits and concluded that four were strong areal indicators, since they occur throughout the area but do not extend into neighboring languages (for example, Yuman and other Uto-Aztecan languages). They are: (1) glottalized consonants (with the exception of Hopi), (2) tones (absent only in Zuni; present in the Third Mesa dialect of Hopi), (3) final devoicing of vowels and sonorants, and (4) dual number distinction. Other supportive areal features which do not have the same distribution (throughout the area but not beyond) include: (5) k^w (Sherzer suggests that the development of this in Navajo "is perhaps due to contact with neighboring Pueblo languages" [1976:137]), (6) ɬi (innovative in Tiwa; Sherzer 1976:140), (7) aspirated consonants (perhaps diffused into Zuni), and (8) ceremonial vocabulary, among others.

Acoma (Keresan) and Navajo (Apachean branch of Athabaskan) share glottalized nasals and glides; Sherzer (1976:141, 142) suggested that Navajo acquired these traits as a result of contact with Keresan. Shaul (1982) interpreted the partial series of glottalized consonants with

low functional yield in Zuni as an areal feature acquired through contact with Keresan and Tanoan languages, which have a fully integrated glottalic series. There are other shared features, such as SOV word order, which are not strong areal indicators, since they are inherited in Apachean from Proto-Athabaskan and in Hopi from Proto(-Northern)-Uto-Aztecan, and are frequent in neighboring languages, as well as in languages spoken elsewhere in the Americas. Sherzer (1976:151–2) also suggests that the development of a 2–2–1 vowel system (i, e, a, o, u) in some Tanoan languages may be due to contact with Zuni and Keresan; that Santa Clara Tewa retroflexed sounds may be the result of contact with Keresan; that the Santa Clara c/č contrast may be the result of influence from neighboring languages; that the Navajo k/k^w contrast is perhaps the result of contact with its neighbors; that Navajo h^w is perhaps due to Tanoan contact; that Navajo's glottalized nasals and semivowels may be explained by contact with Keresan; and that the development of r in dialects of Tewa and Tiwa (I would add Hopi r to these) may be due to Keresan contact.[7]

Paul Kroskrity (1982, 1985, 1993:60–6) argues that some traits diffused from Apachean into Tewa. He finds the Tewa passive which is signaled by prefixes to be like the passive of Apachean and unlike the passives of other Tanoan languages (in which passives are simply verbs inflected for intransitivity which permit an "agent" argument). This construction includes the semantic foregrounding of patient subjects and a requirement that in certain conditions the subject must be animate (as in Navajo, where animate objects are obligatorily raised to subject when the logical subject is inanimate; in Southern Tiwa animate goals are obligatorily raised to subject when the logical subject is inanimate). Tewa and Navajo also exhibit similarities in their relative clause constructions; they are the only two languages in the southwest "with a recognizable anaphor as a relativizer" (Kroskrity 1982:65). There are similarities in the classificatory verbs of Tewa and Navajo. Kroskrity (1982:66, 1985, 1993:60–66) also finds that Tewa borrowed its possessive morpheme -bí from Apachean languages' third person possessive bi-; although it is a suffix in the former and a prefix in the latter, the positions of these morphemes match in nominal possession constructions—for example, Arizona Tewa *sen-bí kʰaw* [man-POSS song] '(a) man's song', Navajo *bisóódi bi-tsi* [pig POSS-flesh] 'the pig's flesh'. Moreover, this matching possessive morpheme is also used in postpositional constructions in both Tewa and Apachean. Other Kiowa-Tanoan languages lack this possessive construction entirely (instead they share a construction with a dative-like prefix on a relativized stative or existential verb, as in Taos Tiwa *'an-'u-k'o-'i* [1ST.SG.POSS-son-have/lie-REL] 'my son'), nor do they have such a postpositional construction (see also Bancroft 1886:673–4). Evidence of interethnic contacts between Tewa and Apachean which could lead to the sharing of these linguistic traits includes the stable trade networks between the two and the traditional winter settlement of Apachean peoples just outside the boundaries of various pueblos. Finally, the Arizona Tewa (Hano) *-tí* passive construction appears to have converged with the corresponding Hopi construction; Tewa maintained a native construction but borrowed the Hopi passive suffix (Kroskrity 1993:64, 74–5).

Some of these traits and others not mentioned here were considered by Sherzer (1973:784, 1976:132–52) in his areal survey of languages in the Southwest, though he concludes that the Southwest as a whole does not constitute a significant linguistic area.

Plains Area
(MAP 25)

Sherzer's Plains area illustrates well the problems caused by assuming that culture areas and linguistic areas will coincide. The languages spoken in the Plains Culture Area include representatives of Athabaskan (Sarsi, Kiowa Apache, Lipan Apache), Algonquian (Arapaho, Blackfoot, Cheyenne, and dialects of Cree and Ojibwa), Siouan (Crow, Dakota, Dhegiha, Hidatsa, Iowa-Oto, Mandan), Kiowa-Tanoan (Kiowa), Uto-Aztecan (Comanche and Wind River Shoshone), and Tonkawa (an isolate). Hollow and Parks (1980:68) count thirty-three languages (or distinct dialects) that are known to have been spoken in the Plains in historic times. However, these languages share extremely few linguistic traits that are indicative of mutual influence and

borrowing, and the traits that they do have in common are also found widely in languages outside the area. The Plains area is the "most recently constituted of the culture areas of North America (late eighteenth and nineteenth century)" (Sherzer 1973:773); thus, as would be expected, strong linguistic indicators of longterm mutual influence are not abundant here. Sherzer (1973:773–5) listed the following as area traits: prefixation of possessive pronouns of nouns, prefixation of subject person markers in verbs, and pronominal plural. However, these are very common among languages of North America. Frequent traits in the Plains, but not shared by all the Plains languages, include: one stop series, *x*, alienable/inalienable opposition in nouns, nominal plural suffix, inclusive/exclusive opposition in first person plural of pronouns, nominal diminutive suffix, animate/inanimate gender, and evidential markers in verbs. These are all found frequently outside the Plains. Plains languages, other than Comanche and the languages of the Southern Plains subregion, lack labiovelars. This is an indication of why the definition of a linguistic area's constituency should not be just assumed based on the existence of a culture area, for Comanche is known to be a recent arrival in the area, closely related to its Numic sisters in the Great Basin; the Comanches crossed into the Plains after having acquired horses, which the Spanish had introduced to the New World. Sherzer points to ð as a regional areal trait of the eastern Plains, and he lists phonemic pitch, *kʷ*, voiced/voiceless fricatives, and *r* as regional areal traits of the Southern Plains (Sherzer 1976:185–6).[8]

Hollow and Parks (1980:82) list a few other Plains areal features (though most of them are of limited distribution within the area) and point out that they were missed by Sherzer because of his dependence on his predetermined and limited checklist of traits for which he sought examples from all the North American areas. They argue persuasively that Arikara (Caddoan) acquired its sound-symbolic consonant alternations involving fricatives from Siouan languages, since this trait is unknown in other Caddoan languages, but it is reconstructible for Proto-Siouan. For example, in Arikara word-final *x* and *š* are replaced by *s* to indicate 'diminutive': *kunahúx* 'old man', but *kunahús* 'little old man'; and *wi:náxtš* 'boy', but *wi:náxts* 'little boy'. This can be compared with sets that illustrate sound-symbolic alternations in Dakota (*zi* 'yellow', *ži* 'tawny', *γi* 'brown') and in Mandan (*síre* 'yellow', *šíre* 'tawny', *xíre* 'brown'). (This is also an areal trait of the Southeast linguistic area.) Other examples are vowel devoicing shared by Arikara (Caddoan), Cheyenne (Algonquian), Comanche (Uto-Aztecan), and Fort Belknap Assiniboin (Siouan); sex differentiation (either according to the speaker's sex, as in Dakota and Arikara, or according to the addressee's sex, as in Mandan—also a putative feature of the Southeast linguistic area); contrasting kinship terms for siblings depending on the sex of ego (Siouan and Caddoan); and relatively restricted consonantal inventories (Caddoan has few consonants; Mandan, Hidatsa, and Crow have fewer than do their Siouan relatives).[9] Goddard pointed out that "the phoneme inventory of Proto-Arapaho-Atsina [Algonquian] is almost identical to that of Wichita [Caddoan]" (1974b:110), perhaps quite significant, since Arapaho-Atsina phonology has undergone very far-reaching changes from Proto-Algonquian.

I conclude that there is evidence of borrowing and of an incipient linguistic area in the Plains but that it is not well developed, and in any case it requires more study.

Northeast Area
(Map 26)

The Northeast Linguistic Area as defined by Sherzer (1976:188–201) includes the following languages: Winnebago (Siouan), Northern Iroquoian, and a number of Eastern Algonquian languages (Abenaki, Delaware, Fox, Malecite-Passamaquoddy, Menomini, Miami, Potawatomi, and Shawnee, plus dialects of Ojibwa and Cree). Sherzer proposes as central areal traits of the Northeast a single series of stops, a single series of fricatives, *h,* nominal plural, and noun incorporation. However, he finds that only the first (a single series of stops) is especially characteristic of the Northeast. That is, the Northeast is not a very well defined area. Indeed, Sherzer admits that "the Northeast can be characterized more for traits which are totally absent in the area than for traits which are present" (1976:201). Regional areal traits of New En-

gland are a vowel system with *i, e, o, a;* nasalized vowels; and a pronominal dual. Sherzer argues that the nasalized vowels and pronominal dual of New England Algonquian languages are the result of contact with Iroquoian languages. The nasalized vowels shared by Iroquoian and Eastern Algonquian languages is the best known Northeast areal feature (see Goddard 1965, 1971, Sherzer 1972). Proto-Eastern-Algonquian **a·* became a nasalized vowel in Eastern Algonquian due to influence from neighboring Northern Iroquoian languages, which have two nasalized vowels, reconstructed as **ɛ* and **ǫ* (Mithun 1979). In some respects it is difficult to draw a boundary between the Northeast and the Southeast linguistic areas, since some traits seem to extend over territory belonging to both.

Southeast Area
(Map 27)

The central constituents of the Southeast Linguistic Area are the Muskogean family; Chitimacha, Atakapa, Tunica, Natchez, and Yuchi (which are isolates); and Ofo and Biloxi (two Siouan languages). Less centrally the area includes also Timucua (an isolate); Tutelo and Catawban (both Siouan); Tuscarora and Cherokee (both Iroquoian); Quapaw (and Dhegiha Siouan generally); and Shawnee (Algonquian).[10] Several other languages that were spoken in this linguistic area became extinct before they were recorded (for example, Cusabo and Yamasee); evidence of this is the many attested tribal and town names in the Southeast, for which at present no linguistic affiliation is known, and historical references to a number of other languages formerly spoken in the area (see Rankin 1988, Haas 1969d:90–92, Haas 1973b). Muskogean subgrouping is made difficult by areal diffusion (see Chapter 4; see also Nicklas 1994). The Southeast Linguistic Area correlates well with the Southeast Culture Area, which is bounded by the Potomac and Ohio Rivers on the north, the Atlantic on the east, the Gulf of Mexico to the south, and by a line running parallel to the Mississippi River about 200 miles west of it (Crawford 1975:1, Booker 1980:1).[11]

The areal traits of the Southeast can be summarized as follows.

1. Bilabial or labial fricatives (ϕ, sometimes f) (Haas 1969d:90) are the only trait Sherzer (1976:217) found to be especially characteristic of the Southeast area. This shows the limitations of the method he used. By checking only for specific traits from the same preset list for all of his linguistic areas, he missed many of the traits that are most relevant in the Southeast Linguistic Area; they were discovered by others.

2. The lateral spirant $ł$ (Haas 1969d:90), according to Sherzer (1976:217), is a trait of the Muskogean-Timucuan region. Nicklas (1994) lists Atakapa, Proto-Muskogean, Yuchi, and Cherokee as languages with this sound.

3. There is extensive positional classification of nouns and noun phrases, for example, distinct articles such as those in Quapaw (shared by Quapaw and Dhegiha in general). Inanimate articles include k^he 'long horizontal objects', t^he 'long upright objects', na 'round or squat objects', $nike$ 'round or squat objects', and ke 'scattered objects, cloth'. Animate articles include ni 'animate singular moving', $(a)pa$ 'animate plural moving', nik^he 'animate singular sitting', nik^ha 'animate plural sitting', t^ha 'animate singular standing' (Rankin 1988:639–40).

4. 'Positional' classifiers of verbs (sitting, standing, lying objects) are salient in languages throughout the Southeast, including all Muskogean languages, Tunica, Natchez, Atakapa, Chitimacha, Yuchi, Biloxi, and Dhegiha. The trait is also present, though less salient, in Iroquoian and Algonquian (Rankin 1988:642).

5. Auxiliaries that are still related to their lexical source main verbs and other auxiliaries that are now derivational suffixes are found in Proto-Muskogean, Proto-Siouan, Natchez, and perhaps previously in Catawba (Nicklas 1994:17).

   The positional verbs also occur as continuative auxiliaries in Muskogean and in Siouan generally, and the evidence seems to indicate that the phenomenon has diffused from Siouan (where the auxiliaries are reconstructible) across Muskogean (where the suppletive auxiliaries are often not cognate from one language to another) (Rankin 1988:642–3; see also Booker 1980:75).[12] Auxiliaries based on verbs of location ('to be there') that have become inflectional suffixes mark 'priority in time' in Tunica and Yuchi (Nicklas 1994:14).

6. Southeast area languages typically have suppletive forms of positional verb stems based on number, as in Choctaw 'to sit': *hinili* 'singular', *hikiya* 'dual', *hinohmaaya* 'plural'. Biloxi has such suppletively related verb-stem forms for at least 'to sit', 'to stand', 'to lie', and 'to be around', though such suppletion for number is unknown elsewhere in Siouan (Rankin 1986b:82–3; Booker 1980:75, 79–82).

7. In both Biloxi (Siouan) and Choctaw (Muskogean), possessive constructions are composed of positional verbs (for example, 'to sit/move/ be located': 'my dog sits' and 'three children to us sit' are the equivalent of 'I have a dog' and 'we have three children', respectively) (Rankin 1986b:81–2).

8. Timucua and Natchez share the trait that for a plural possessor, a circumlocution with a copula of the form, for example, 'he who is father to us' is used for 'our father' (Nicklas 1994:9).

9. It is claimed that Dhegiha, Algonquian, and some Muskogean languages have preaspirated voiceless stops.[13] In Muskogean they are hC clusters; in Dhegiha they are best thought of as surface phonemes (not clusters);[14] in other Siouan languages they are (post-)aspirated (for example, Dhegiha /hp, ht, hc, hk/ correspond to Dakota, Tutelo, etc. /pʰ, tʰ, cʰ, kʰ/) (Rankin 1988:642). The aspirated stops shared by Siouan and Yuchi may enter the picture here, since Siouan evidence shows that they developed late in Pre-Proto-Siouan (minus Catawban); the rule (concerning a development in the second syllable of words) is not shared by more distantly related Catawban (Robert Rankin, personal communication). That is, since aspirated stops are secondary in Siouan, but are shared by Siouan, Yuchi, and to some extent also by some of the Muskogean languages, the preaspirated consonants are a good candidate for a possible areal feature.

10. Retroflexed sibilants (for example, Quapaw [š] and [ẓ]) are found in Creek (dialects), Hitchiti, Mikasuki, Alabama (allophonically in the last two), Mobilian Jargon, Natchez, Tunica, and Quapaw. Rankin says that "sibilant retroflexion is unquestionably a *bona fide* southeastern areal feature" (1988:644; see also Rankin 1984, Nicklas 1994:18).

11. Muskogean, Dhegiha, and Algonquian share a quinary counting system which contrasts with the system of more northern Siouan and neighboring Caddoan languages. Dhegiha has clearly adopted something foreign, though whether it was borrowed from Muskogean

or from Algonquian is not clear (Rankin 1988:642).

12. Koasati (Muskogean) appears to have borrowed its -na:nan 'marker of distributive of numerals' from Quapaw -nānā (same meaning), whereas the Choctaw-Chickasaw apparently borrowed a marker of ordinals for 'second' and 'third', formed with the prefix hi- (not the common Muskogean a-), which matches Quapaw hi- (same meaning). Both of these Quapaw forms have solid Siouan cognates (Rankin 1988:644). This is more a local borrowing than an areawide trait, though it may contribute to the aggregate of borrowing within the linguistic area.

13. A discontinuous (flanking) negative construction is shared by some languages of the area. For example, Allen (1931:192) cites Cherokee ni . . . na (compare also Mohawk ya' . . . de), Tutelo ki . . . na, and Biloxi i . . . na; modern Muskogean languages have ak- . . . -o (Booker 1980:256). This requires further investigation as a Southeast areal trait.

14. Crawford reports that the Hitchiti -ti 'negative suffix to verbs', which he says occurs in no other Muskogean language (except possibly Alabama), "undoubtedly was borrowed by Hitchiti from Timucua" (1988:159). (Timucua has the same suffix with the same meaning.) This also is a local borrowing, though it may contribute to the overall picture of borrowing within the linguistic area.

15. A trait found in many Siouan and Muskogean languages is the use of separate markers, usually postverbal, to distinguish between male and female speech in declarative or imperative categories (Rankin 1988).[15] Nicklas (1994:14) reports that nouns (both inanimate and animate) are marked for gender and number in Tunica, Yuchi, and Quapaw (most other Southeast languages mark plural only on human nouns). Such a difference is also reported as a trait of the Plains Linguistic Area.

16. Rankin (1986a) points out that "fricative ablaut" (essentially sound-symbolic alternations among fricatives involving size and intensity) is a possible Southeast area trait. It is shared by Muskogean and Siouan languages—for example, Dakota zi 'yellow' / ži 'brown' / γi 'dark brown', Winnebago -sox 'frying sound' / -šox 'bubbling sound' / -xox 'breaking sound'; Choctaw fopa 'bellow, murmur' / chopa 'roar (as water)' / hompa 'whoop, bang', fąma 'strike, beat' / samak 'sound of a bell' / chamak 'clink, to clink' / hąma 'to stroke'. (This

trait is also attributed to the Plains Linguistic Area.)

17. Rankin (personal communication) notes that a very prevalent structural feature in Southeastern languages is that a large number of verbs are not themselves directly inflected, but rather an accompanying postposed auxiliary bears the inflectional morphology. This trait is found at least in Muskogean, Natchez, and Catawba, and probably in other languages of the area.

18. Sonorants (m, n, l, r, w, and y) are devoiced word-finally and before a voiceless consonant in Tunica, Natchez, and Chitimacha. (In Chitimacha these voiceless sonorants further changed to h. On this and the remaining traits in this summary, see Nicklas (1994:7, 11–19).

19. Verbs are inflected with nominative-accusative marking in Natchez, Tunica, Atakapa, and Chitimacha (rather than the active-inactive alignment of Yuchi and Siouan languages). Nicklas (1994:14) argues that Tunica has changed from nominative-accusative (his "subject-object") to active-inactive (his "actor-patient") type inflection.

20. Nicklas (1994:18) finds that Choctaw changed from the agentive ("actor") suffixes of Proto-Muskogean to agentive prefixes. It did this by generalizing the pattern of a minority class of Proto-Muskogean verbs which had prefixes, thus coming in line with Siouan, Catawba, Yuchi, and Cherokee.

21. A different pronominal series is used to mark alienable and inalienable possession. In Iroquoian, Cherokee, Catawba, Yuchi, and Biloxi, the inalienable prefix series is identical to the agentive-subject prefixes; in other Siouan languages and Muskogean, it is identical to the nonagentive-object prefixes. (In Natchez and Timucua, the possessive markers are suffixed; Nicklas 1994:11, 13).

22. An inclusive first person category is shared by Proto-Muskogean, Proto-Siouan, and Caddo; it is based at least in part on indefinite third person elements (Nicklas 1994:17).

23. In Choctaw, Catawba, and Siouan, the demonstrative follows the nouns, but it precedes the nouns in all other Southeast area languages (Nicklas 1994:19). This suggests that Choctaw has been influenced by the Siouan pattern. (See Nicklas for additional information and other proposed examples.)

One difficulty in dealing with the Southeast Linguistic Area is that some features are shared not only across the Southeast but also generally throughout eastern North America (particularly in Algonquian and Iroquoian, and also in the Siouan languages) and in the Plains area. The possibility of a broader linguistic area, which might include the Southeast Linguistic Area as a subarea, merits investigation. Another consideration is the proposed Gulf distant genetic relationship which would group several of these southeastern languages (Natchez-Muskogean, Atakapa, Chitimacha, and Tunica, see Chapter 8). Doubts have been raised about this classification, and the grammatical features shared by these languages—though sometimes presented as inherited traits—may very well be areal features as well. These include the following: SOV basic word order (including postpositions), active and stative verbs, stative verbs inflected by patient affixes and stative verbs inflected by dative affixes (Natchez, Muskogean), nominal alignment markers (active-stative cases), locative cases (Natchez, Chitimacha, Muskogean), independent inflected verbs and auxiliary inflected verbs (Tunica, Muskogean, Natchez, Chitimacha), reference tracking devices (switch-reference [-t/-k/-n] and focus [-o-] in Muskogean, reference tracking [-k] and focus [-o·k] in Natchez, reference tracking [-man] in Tunica, and focus in Chitimacha [-š] and Atakapa [-š]), and possessive suffixes (Tunica, Muskogean, Natchez) (Kimball 1994). This possibility should also be investigated.[16]

Mesoamerican Linguistic Area

(MAP 12)

The existence of Mesoamerica as a linguistic area has been confirmed only in recent years, and it is now one of the best established linguistic areas in the Americas (see Campbell 1977, 1978a; Campbell et al. 1986; Kaufman 1973a, 1974a). The Mesoamerican Linguistic Area coincides closely with the Mesoamerican Culture Area (see Kirchhoff 1943). The two were probably formed simultaneously as a result of contact and exchange during the Mesoamerican Preclassic period (ca. 1500 B.C.–A.D. 100), perhaps with significant influence from Olmec culture (1100–400 B.C.) (Campbell 1979, Campbell et

al. 1986). The constituents of this linguistic area are: Aztecan (the Nahua branch of Uto-Aztecan), Mixe-Zoquean, Mayan, Xincan, Otomanguean (except Chichimeco-Jonaz and some varieties of Pame north of the Mesoamerican boundary), Totonacan, Tarascan, Cuitlatec, Tequistlatecan, and Huave. Because they lack traits diagnostic of Mesoamerican languages, some neighboring languages to the north and south (Cora, Huichol, Lenca, Jicaquean, and Misumalpan), which were formerly thought to be members of the area, have been excluded.

Five areal traits are common to nearly all Mesoamerican languages, and are particularly diagnostic of this linguistic area; they are not found in other languages outside the area:

1. Nominal possession of the type illustrated by the Pipil (Aztecan) construction: *i-pe:lu ne ta:kat,* literally 'his-dog the man', to mean 'the man's dog'.
2. Relational expressions composed of a noun root and possessive pronominal affixes, as in Tz'utujil (Mayan): *(č-)r-i:x* 'behind it, in back of it', composed of *č-* 'at, in', *r-* 'his/her/its' and *i:x* 'back' (compare *č-w-i:x* [at-my-back] 'behind me').
3. Vigesimal numeral systems, such as that of Chol, composed of combinations of twenty: *hun-k'al* '20' (1 *k'al*), *čaʔ-k'al* '40' = 2 × 20, *uš-k'al* '60' = 3 × 20, *hoʔ-k'al* '100' = 5 × 20, *hun-bahk'* '400' (1 *bahk'*), *čaʔ-bahk'* '800' = 2 × 400.
4. Word order that is not verb-final (that is, not SOV). Although Mesoamerica is surrounded on both the north and south by languages with SOV word order, all languages within this linguistic area have VOS, VSO, or SVO order.
5. Mesoamerican languages have many shared semantic loan translations (calques). They include examples such as 'boa' = 'deer-snake', 'egg' = 'bird-stone/bone', 'lime' = '(stone-)ash', 'knee' = 'leg-head', and 'wrist' = 'hand-neck'.

A sixth feature trait of Mesoamerican languages is the absence of switch-reference constructions. While switch-reference is found in the languages on both borders of Mesoamerica—in Jicaquean, Coahuilteco, Seri, and Yuman—it is entirely absent from Mesoamerica. However, this probably reflects the near universal that switch-reference is found almost exclusively in SOV languages, so the absence of switch-reference from Mesoamerican languages is probably just a concomitant of the absence of SOV word order.

Also, while lexical borrowings are not usually seen as the sort of diffusion that is the foundation of linguistic areas, the languages of the Meso-american area exhibit extensive loanwords. Some are quite widespread and the content of several suggest items that are diagnostic of the Mesoamerican Culture Area (Campbell et al. 1986, Justeson et al. 1985).

Many other traits are common to several Mesoamerican languages, but not to all of them. Other traits of Mesoamerican languages extend beyond the area's borders. Among features of these two kinds, some widely distributed phono-logical phenomena involving Mesoamerican lan-guages are the following:

1. Devoicing of final sonorant consonants *(l, r, w, y)*, occurs in K'ichean, Nahuatl, Pipil, Xincan, Totonac, Tepehua, Tarascan, and Sierra Popo-luca—as well as in Sumu and Cacaopera (for example, Nahuatl /no-mi:l/ [no-mi:ɬ] 'my cornfield').

2. Voicing of obstruents after nasals is found in most Otomanguean languages, Tarascan, Mixe-Zoquean, Huave, and Xincan—as well as in Jicaquean and Lencan (for example, Copainalá Zoque /n-tik/ [ndik] 'my house').

3. Vowel harmony (limited, often involving only subsets of suffixes) exists in Mayan, some varieties of Zoque, Mazahua, Xincan, and Huave—as well as in Lencan and Jicaquean.

4. Most Mesoamerican languages have predict-able stress. (Contrastive stress is very rare but is known to occur in Tequistlatecan and Cuitlatec.) Some languages share the specific stress rule which places the accent on the vowel before the last (right-most) consonant of the word (V → V́ / __C(V)#). They include Oluta Popoluca, Totontepec Mixe, Xincan, and many Mayan languages (by default; stress falls on final syllables but roots do not end in vowels)—as well as Lencan and Jicaquean.

5. There are many general similarities in phone-mic inventories: (a) *Contrasting voiced stops (and affricates)* are almost totally absent; they are present in a few Otomangueuan languages, Cuitlatec, and Tequistlatec (where they can be explained historically). (b) A *lateral affricate* is generally lacking but is found in some Nahua dialects, Totonac, and Tequistlatec. (In Tequistlatec, the sound in question is a /tl'/,

the glottalized counterpart of /l/; Tequistlatec has no plain *tl.*) (c) *Uvular stops (q)* are found only in Totonacan and Mayan languages. (d) *Contrastive voiced fricatives* are lacking, with the exception of the Zapotec lenis/nongemi-nate series. (e) *Aspirated stops and affricates* are rare but occur in Tarascan and some Oto-manguean languages; Jicaquean also has them. (f) *Glottalized consonants* occur in Te-pehua, Tequistlatecan, Otopamean, Mayan, and Xincan—as well as in Lencan, Jicaquean, and Coahuilteco. (g) *Tonal contrasts* are found in all Otomanguean languages, Huave, Cuitla-tec, and some Mayan languages (Yucatec, Us-pantec, and the San Bartolo dialect of Tzotzil). Several languages spoken just outside Meso-america (Northern Tepehuan, Cora-Huichol, Paya, Guaymí, and Bribri) have tone or pitch accent contrasts. (h) *Retroflexed fricatives (and affricates)* occur in Mamean, Q'anjob'al, Jakalteko, and Akateko (Mayan); Guazacapán and Chiquimulilla (Xincan); some Mixean languages; and Chocho, Popoloca, Mazatec, Trique, Yatzachi and Guelavia Zapotec (Oto-manguean); they occur allophonically in Tara-scan. (i) A *central vowel /ɨ/* (*or sometimes /ə/*) is found in Mixe-Zoquean, several Oto-manguean languages, Huave, Xincan, Proto-Aztecan, and some Mayan languages (Proto-Yucatecan, Cholan, dialects of Kaqchikel and K'iche', and allophonically in Mam), and allo-phonically also in Tarascan. This vowel is also found in Jicaquean and Northern-Uto-Aztecan languages (and in languages spoken in some areas of California).

6. Inalienable (or intimate) possession of body parts and kinship terms is characteristic of almost all Mesoamerican languages and of many languages spoken throughout the Amer-icas.

7. Numeral classifiers are found in many Mayan languages, Tarascan, Totonac, and Nahuatl—for example, Tzeltal *oš lehč teʔ* [three flat-thing wood] 'three plants', *oš tehk teʔ* [three plant-thing wood] 'three trees', *oš k'as siʔ* [three broken-thing firewood] 'three chunks of firewood'.

8. Absolutive noun affixes (a suffix on unpos-sessed and otherwise affixally isolated nouns) occur in Uto-Aztecan and Mayan and also in Paya and Misumalpan—for example, K'iche' *xolom-a:x* [head-Absolutive] 'head', but *a-xolo:m* [your-head] 'your head'.

9. Noun-incorporation, a construction in which a general nominal object becomes part of

the verb, is found in some Mayan languages (Yucatec, Mam), Nahua, and Totonac. An example is Yucatec (Mayan) *č'ak-čeʔ-n-ah-en* [cut-wood-Intransitive-Aspect-I] 'I cut wood' (compare the unincorporated version: *t-in-č'ak-ah čeʔ* [Aspect-I-cut-Aspect wood] 'I cut wood'). Noun incorporation is found widely in languages elsewhere in the Americas (see Mithun 1984a). Body-part incorporation occurs in Nahuatl, Totonac, Tarascan, Mixe-Zoquean, Tlapanec, and Tarascan. It is a type of noun-incorporation in which specific forms for body parts are incorporated into the verb, usually as instrumentals, though sometimes also as direct objects, as in Pipil: *tan-kwa* [tooth-eat] 'to bite', *ikši-ahsi* [foot-arrive] 'to reach, overtake', *mu-yaka-pitsa* [Reflexive-nose-blow] 'to blow one's nose'. This type of construction is found also widely in languages elsewhere in the Americas.

10. Directional morphemes (indicating, for example, away from or toward) are incorporated into the verb in Mayan, Nahua, Tequistlatec, Tarascan, some Otomanguean languages, and Totonac—for example, Kaqchikel *y-e-b'e-n-kamisax* [Aspect-3.Plural.Absolutive-thither-1.Singular.Ergative-kill] 'I'm going there to kill them'.

11. Locatives derived from body parts are found in most Mesoamerican languages (though they are found in many other languages as well); an example is Mixtec *čihi* 'stomach, in(side), under', *ini* 'heart, in, inside', *nuu* 'face, to, at, from'.

12. Noun plurals (as affixes) are absent or are largely limited to human referents (in most Mesoamerican languages); this is also typical of many languages throughout the Americas and the world.

13. Positional (or stative) verbs differ in form (morphological class) from intransitives and transitives in Mayan and Otomanguean.

14. There is an inclusive-exclusive contrast in the pronoun system of Chol, Mam, Akateko, Jakalteko, Chocho, Popoloca, Ixcatec, Otomí, Mixtec, Trique, Chatino, Yatzachi Zapotec, Tlapanec, Huave, and several Mixe-Zoquean languages—for example, Chol *honon la* 'we (inclusive)', *honon lohon* 'we (exclusive)'.

15. An overt copula is lacking from equational constructions in most Mesoamerican languages—for example, K'iche' *saq le: xa:h* [white the house] 'the house is white'. This feature is also found widely elsewhere in the

Americas. Pronominal copular construction occurs in Mayan, Nahua, Chocho, Chinantec, Mazatec, Otomí, and several Mixe-Zoquean languages. Copular sentences with pronominal subjects are formed with pronominal affixes attached to the complement—for example, Q'eqchi *išq-at* [woman-2.Singular.Absolutive] 'you are a woman', *winq-in* [man-1.Singular.Absolutive] 'I am a man'; and Pipil *ni-ta:kat* [I-man] 'I am a man', *ti-siwa:t* [you-woman] 'you are a woman'. This trait is found elsewhere as well; for example, several Northwest Coast languages have it.

16. Possessive construction and lack of a verb 'to have' are characteristic of Mayan (excluding Huastec), Mixe-Zoquean, Tequistlatecan, Xincan, Chinantec, Mazatec, and Trique, among others. The most common construction for 'to have' in Mesoamerican languages is equivalent to 'is' or 'there is' or 'there exists' plus a possessed noun, as in Kaqchikel *k'o xun nu-c'i:ʔ* [(there.)is one my-dog] 'I have a dog'.

17. Some "Sprechbund" traits (aspects of ethnography of communication) are also fairly widespread among Mesoamerican languages. For example, some form of whistle speech is found in Amuzgo, Mazatec, Otomí, several Zapotec groups, Mopán, Chol, Totonac, Tepehua, and some Nahua dialects—as well as in Mexican Kickapoo. A stylized form of ritual language and oral literature with shared conventional forms involving, among other things, paired couplets of semantic associations is very widespread and occurs in remarkably similar form in K'iche', Tzeltal, Tzotzil, Yucatec, Nahuatl, Ocuiltec, Amuzgo, Popoloca, Totonac, and others. This is called *Huēhuētlaʔtōlli* in Nahuatl, *Ts'ono:x* in K'iche'. (For details, see Campbell et al. 1986; see also the discussion in Constenla 1991.)

South American Linguistic Areas

Considerable structural diffusion and various areal phenomena have been identified in the languages of South America, but its linguistic areas have, for the most part, not been the subject of concentrated investigation and hence are not clearly defined. As Kaufman says, "There is much to be done here" (1990a:21–2). In this section, I review the literature on South American linguistic areas. Some of these studies overlap and conflict, making it clear that areal linguistic investigation in South America is only in its initial stages and requires extensive attention.

Colombian–Central American Area
(MAPS 14 and 17)

Holt and Bright (1976) attempted to distinguish two linguistic areas on the Mesoamerican frontier. What they called the Mayan Linguistic Area includes the Mayan, Xincan, Lencan, and Jicaquean languages; it is characterized by the presence of glottalized consonants and alveolar affricates and by the absence of voiced obstruents and labiovelar stops. Their Central American Linguistic Area includes the Chibchan, Misumalpan, Mangue, and Subtiaba languages; its features include the presence of voiced obstruents and labiovelar stops, as well as the absence of glottalized consonants and alveolar affricates. These beginnings have been refined in subsequent work by Adolfo Constenla (1991, 1992).

Constenla (1991) defined three distinct linguistic areas in lower Central America and northern South America on the basis of shared linguistic traits which involve Chibchan languages and other languages sometimes thought to be related to Chibchan. What he called the Colombian–Central American area is composed of Chibchan languages primarily, but it also includes Lencan, Jicaquean, Misumalpan, Chocoan, and Betoi (1992:103). Constenla listed the following traits shared within this area: voicing opposition in stops and fricatives, exclusive SOV order, postpositions, mostly Genitive-Noun order, Noun-Adjective order, Noun-Numeral order, clause-initial question words, suffixation or postposed particle for negative in most of the languages, absence of gender opposition in pronouns and inflection, absence of accusative case marking in most of the languages, absence of possessed/nonpossessed and alienable/inalienable possession oppositions, and "morpholexical economy"—that is, the presence of lexical compounds rather than independent roots, like the calques found in Mesoamerica but with a more limited number of compounding elements, as in Guatuso; there is one compounding element for liquid substances (*li:ka*, for example, *ko:ři li:ka*

'milk', compare *ko:ři* 'breast'), one for pointed extremities (*tai:ki*, for example, *ko:ři tai:ki* 'nipple'), one for flat surfaces, and so on (Constenla 1991:126–9, 1992:104).[17]

As Constenla (1991) has shown, these areal isoglosses do not coincide with the Intermediate Culture Area (of lower Central America, from Honduras to a part of northern South America) that has been defined for this region based on shared cultural traits (Haberland 1957, Willey 1971:277–8, Constenla 1991:4–12). This is one more indication that Sherzer's approach, which presupposes that the culture areas and linguistic areas will coincide, is misguided.

Venezuelan-Antillean Area
(MAP 14)

This area includes several Arawakan (Maipurean) languages (for example, Taino, Island Carib, Caquetío [see Loukotka 1968:128] , Locono [Lokono]), various Cariban languages (for example, Cumanagoto [Cumaná], Chaima [Cumaná], Tamanaco, and Cariña), and several languages of uncertain affiliation (Guamo, Otomaco [Otomacoan], Yaruro, and Warao). The traits common to the languages in this area are: exclusively VO order (absence of SOV), absence of voicing opposition in obstruents, Numeral-Noun order, Noun-Genitive order, and prepositions (Constenla 1991:125–6). Constenla (1991:136) believes that this area could be extended to the south to include the western part of the Amazon Culture Area (Amazonia), where Arawakan languages with VO order predominate.

Andean Area
(MAPS 15 and 16)

The central highland Andean region is recognized as a linguistic area by many, though little effort has been made to define it. Büttner (1983:179) includes Quechuan, Aymaran, Callahuaya, and Chipaya in the phonological area he defines. These languages share such traits as glottalized stops and affricates (not found in all varieties of Quechuan), aspirated stops and affricates (not found in Chipaya), uvular stops, *ñ*, *ľ*, *s/š* contrast, retroflexed affricates (*ṣ̌*, *č̣*) (more limited in distribution), absence of glottal stop, and limited vowel systems *(i, a, u)* (not true of Chipaya) (Büttner 1983:168–9). The extensive diffusion and convergence between Quechuan and Aymaran (Jaqi, Aru) is well known (see Chapter 8 for discussion of the significance of this contact for genetic hypotheses). They both have SOV basic word order, are suffixing, and bear considerable congruence in their morphological structure. Puquina, which was an important language in this area (it is now extinct), seems not to share these phonological traits. The extent to which unrelated languages spoken in adjacent regions of South America share any of these traits needs to be investigated carefully. For example, some languages of Chile exhibit several of the phonological traits that are typical of Andean languages.

Constenla (1991:123–4) has defined a broader Andean area, which includes his Ecuadoran-Colombian subarea, containing the languages of highland Colombia, Ecuador, Peru, and Bolivia (see below). These languages share the following traits: absence of the high-mid opposition in back vowels, absence of the opposition of voiced/voiceless affricates, voiceless alveolar affricate, voiceless prepalatal fricative, palatal lateral, palatal nasal, retroflexed fricatives or affricates, Adjective-Noun order, clause-initial interrogative words, accusative case, genitive case, and passive construction. Constenla (1991:136) believes that some languages spoken in the region east of the Andes could be incorporated into the Andean Linguistic Area; for example, those with Adjective-Noun order and with the absence of the high-mid opposition in front vowels.

Ecuadoran-Colombian Subarea
(Maps 14 and 15)

The Ecuadoran-Colombian subarea of the Andean Linguistic Area, as Constenla (1991) defines it, includes Páez, Guambiano (Paezan); Cuaiquer, Cayapa, Colorado (Barbacoan); Camsá; Cofán; Esmeralda; and Ecuadoran Quichua (Quechuan). These languages, for the most part, share the following traits: high-mid opposition in front vowels, absence of glottalized consonants, glottal stop, absence of uvular stops, voiceless labial fricative, rounding opposition in non-front vowels, lack of person inflexion in

nouns, and prefixes to express tenses or aspects (Constenla 1991:123–5).

Orinoco-Amazon Linguistic Area
(Maps 14, 16, 18, 19, 20, 22, and 23)

Migliazza (1985[1982]) identifies the Northern Amazon Culture Area as also constituting a linguistic area. The languages participating in this area today are as follows:

> Yanomaman family: Yanam, Yanomam, Yanomamɨ
> Sálivan: Piaroa
> Arawakan (Maipurean): Baniwa (Karútiana-Baniwa), Wapixana, Baré, Mandahuaca, Warekena, Baniva (Yavitero)
> Cariban: Panare, Yabarana (Mapoyo-Yavarana), Mapoyo, Yekuana (compare the Makiritare Group, Loukotka 1968:214), Pemón, Kapong, Makuxi, Waiwai, Waimirí, Hixkaryana, Warikyana
> unaffiliated: Jotí, Uruak (Ahuaqué), Sapé [Kaliana), Maku.

More than thirty other languages that existed in this area in about 1800 are now extinct. Some common typological traits of the area include a shared pattern of discourse redundancy (as defined in Derbyshire 1977), ergative alignment (except in a few Arawakan languages), O-before-V (SOV or OVS) order (except in a few Arawakan languages), lack of active-passive distinction, and relative clauses formed by apposition and nominalization. Diffusion from west to east of nasalization, aspiration, and glottalization has also been suggested (Migliazza 1985[1982]:20, 118).

Amazon Linguistic Area (Amazonia)
(Maps 14, 15, 16, 18, 19, 20, 22, and 23)

Derbyshire and Pullum find "area-wide typological tendencies" across the 4 million square miles of Amazonia, but they caution that "the amount of information available to us has clearly not been sufficient to permit any certainty in stating that the . . . characteristics identify an areal Amazonian linguistic type" (1986:16, 20). That is, "a lot more research needs to be done before much can be said about whether common traits are due to genetic ties or geographic contact" (Derbyshire 1987:311). The language families included in this area are: Arawakan (Maipurean), Arauan (Arawan), Cariban, Chapacuran, Ge(an) (Jean), Panoan, Puinavean, Tacanan, Tucanoan, and Tupian (Derbyshire and Pullum 1991:3). Derbyshire and Pullum mention the tendency of these languages to have O-before-S orders (VOS: Terena, Baure [Maipurean]; Kaiwa [compare Chiripá-Nyandeva] [Tupí-Guaraní]; OVS: Arecuna [compare Pemón], Hianacoto [Jianácoto], Hixkaryana, Apalaí [Cariban]; Asurini [Tupí-Guaraní]; Barasanos [Tucanoan]; Teribe [Tiribí] [Chibchan]; Urarina; OSV: Apuriña [Apuriná] [Maipurean]; Hupda [Puinavean]). They also observe that some Amazonian languages are undergoing change toward O-initial basic order (1986:17). Derbyshire (1987:313) notes that in many of the OVS and OSV languages the word order tends to be flexible, with lots of word order variations in clauses, making it difficult to decide which order is basic.

Other widely shared Amazonian traits are: verb agreement with both subject and object (plus null realization of subject and object nominals or free pronouns, which means that sentences frequently lack full noun-phrase subjects or objects); predictability of when subjects and objects will be full noun-phrases or when they will be signaled by verbal affixes (depending on whether they represent "new" or "given" information); use of nominalizations for relative clauses and other subordinate clauses (in many cases, there are no true subordinate clauses at all); nominal modifiers following their head nouns (the orders Noun-Adjective, Genitive-Noun, and Noun-postposition, which are inconsistent types in view of Greenberg's 1966[1963] most expected orders, Derbyshire 1987:314); no agentive passive construction (Palikur is an exception); indirect speech forms are nonexistent in most languages and rare in the languages that have them (hence, a reliance on direct speech constructions); absence of coordinating conjunctions (use of juxtaposition to express coordination); extensive use of right-dislocated paratactic constructions (sequences of noun phrases, adverbials, or postpositional phrases, in which the whole sequence bears only one grammatical relation in the sentence); extensive use of particles that are phrasal subconstituents syntactically and phonologically but are sentence operators or modifiers semantically; ten-

dency toward ergative subject marking; very complex morphology (Derbyshire 1986:560–61, Derbyshire and Pullum 1986:16–19).

Derbyshire and Payne (1990) add noun classifier systems to the traits widely shared among Amazonian languages. Their three basic types of classifier systems are *numeral* (lexico-syntactic forms, which are often obligatory in expressions of quantity and normally are separate words); *concordial* (a closed grammatical system, consisting of morphological affixes or clitics and expressing class agreement with some head noun [but they may occur on nouns or verbs]); and *verb incorporation* (lexical items are incorporated into the verb stem, signaling some classifying entity of the associated noun phrase). Some languages exhibit combinations of these basic types. In Amazonian languages they are as follows: numeral (in Yanomaman, Tupí), concordial (in Arauan, some Maipurean [Arawakan] languages), verb incorporation (Pirahã [Muran], Maipurean [Arawakan] languages), numeral + concordial (Peba-Yaguan, Tucanoan, Zaparoan, Huitotan, Saliban), numeral + verb incorporation (Waorani, Cahuapanan), concordial + verb incorporation (Harakmbet, some Maipurean [Arawakan] languages), and numeral + concordial + verb incorporation (Tupí, some Maipurean [Arawakan] languages). These classificatory systems merit further study because they might yield information that is useful in determining areal diffusion and possible broader genetic relationships. With regard to the case-marking and agreement systems of Amazonian languages, Derbyshire (1987:316) notes that (1) they tend to have ergatively organized systems (in whole or in part); (2) there is evidence of historical drift from ergative to accusative marking; and (3) certain types of split systems are prevalent. The languages that exhibit ergativity (at least to some degree) in both nominal case marking and verb agreement include: Arauan (Paumarí), Cariban (Apalaí, Hixkaryana, Kalapalo [Amonap], Kuikuru [Amonap], Makuxí, and Waiwai) and Jean (Canela-Krahô, Kaingang, Xokleng, and Xavante). Ergativity is expressed only by nominal case markers in Capanahua (Panoan), Cavineña (Tacanan), and Sanuma (Yanomaman). Ergativity signaled by verb agreement patterns is found in all the Tupian languages. There is no evidence of ergativity in Urubú (Tupian), most of the Arawakan languages, or Pirahã (Muran). Active or active-like alignment is found in Guajajara, Guaraní, Mundurukú (Tupían), and the Campa languages (Arawakan/Maipurean) (Derbyshire 1987:319).

Finally, it is also worth remembering that Mason (1950:163) found that many languages of central and eastern Brazil were characterized by the fact that words end in vowels and stress falls on the final syllable.

Lowland South America

Constenla (1991:135) raises doubts about some of these traits and about the overall definition of Amazonia as a linguistic area. He finds the following traits to be rather common also in the bordering linguistic areas: the absence of a passive construction (shared also by the languages of the three linguistic areas he assumed to be within the Intermediate Culture area: the Colombian–Central American area, the Venezuelan-Antillean area, and the Ecuadoran-Colombian subarea); agreement of transitive verb with subject and object and the correlated null realization of full noun phrases in cases of "given" information (common in the languages of the Carib, Intermediate, and Peruvian Culture Areas); and the predominance of the orders Noun-Adjective, Genitive-Noun, and postpositions (in the Colombian–Central American Lnguistic Area). He also senses that the use of nominalizations for subordinate clauses is common in the languages of the Peruvian Culture Area and that the absence of direct-indirect speech indicators predominates in the languages of the Intermediate Culture Area. For these reasons, Constenla believes that Amazonia should not be considered a single large linguistic area, and he would, instead, place some of its languages in neighboring linguistic areas (see also Klein 1992:33–4).

In contrast to Constenla's more particular findings, Doris Payne's (1990) investigation of possible areal traits pertaining to verb morphology in all of Lowland South American languages is even broader than Amazonia. She defines two broad typological groups. The western group, which forms what might be roughly described as a crescent extending toward the eastern border of the Andes, includes languages from the

following families: Pano-Tacanan, Maipurean (Arawakan), Tucanoan, Saliban (Sálivan), Zaparoan, Yaguan, Huitotoan (Witotoan), and Cahuapanan. This group is characterized by a high degree of polysynthesis, directionals in the verb (which may have tense-aspect-modality functions), noun classification systems (missing in Pano-Tacanan and some Maipurean languages), and verb-initial and postpositional orders (found in some Maipurean and Zaparoan languages, and in Taushiro and Yagua). The eastern group includes languages belonging to the Jê-Bororo (see Bororoan), Tupian, Cariban, and Makú families. These share a more isolating typology and minimal (or no) directionals in verbal morphology; they lack noun classification. Payne points out that since some linguists have thought these languages to be genetically connected, their typological similarities may conceivably be due to a genetic relationship.

David Payne (1990) has also pointed out some very widely shared traits among South American languages, and he believes they indicate either diffusion or an undocumented deep genetic relationship. They include: (1) a *negative morpheme* of the approximate shape /ma/ (Quechua, Mapudungu [Araucanian], Maipurean [Arawakan], Proto-Panoan, Proto-Tacanan, Apinayé [Ge], Tucano, Proto-Tupi, Pirahã [Muran], Amarakaeri [Harakmbet], Madija-Culina [Arauan], Nadëb [Puinavean], Yanomama [Yanomaman], Yagua [Yaguan], and Hixkaryana [Cariban]); (2) a *causative affix* of the approximate shape /mV/ (Mapudungu; Campa [Arawakan]; Proto-Panoan; Tacana [Tacanan]; Tupinamba Trumai [Tupian]; Apalaí, Hixkaryana [Cariban]; Aguaruna [Jivaroan]; Yuracare; Ona, Tehuelche [Chon]; Pirahã [Muran]; Nadëb [Puinavean]; and Yanomama [Yanomaman]); (3) a *causative verbal prefix,* usually a single back vowel in form (Achagua, Guajiro, Lokono, Garífuna, Palikur, Waurá, Amuesha [Maipurean]; Aguaruna [Jivaroan]; Amarakaeri [Harakmbet]; and Madija-Culina [Arauan]); (4) a *directional verb suffix* (often of the shape /pV/ or /Vp/) (Quechua, Mapudungu [Araucanian], several Maipurean languages, and Yagua); and (5) an auxiliary 'to have', 'to do', or 'to be', usually containing /ka/, often coinciding in the same language with the lexical verb 'to say, to work' and often with a valence-changing verbal affix of the same or a similar shape (Maipurean languages; Quechua; Aymara, Jaqaru [Aymaran]; Amarakaeri [Harakmbet]; Hixkaryana, Apalaí [Cariban]; Pirahã [Muran]; Nadëb [Puinavean]; and Arauan).

Although it is possible that Payne's features reflect diffusion or wider genetic affinities, it is also quite possible that some of them are due purely to chance or other factors. First, these forms are all short *(CV or VC)* and involve very common, unmarked consonants; therefore, the possibility of accidental similarity is great (see Chapter 7 for details). Second, there is internal evidence, at least in some of the languages, that the forms have arisen through independent innovation and have no direct historical connection with the other languages (for example, the several Quechua suffixes with *-ka* vary in form and meaning from dialect to dialect and are recent developments involving different grammaticalizations of the verb root *ka-* 'to be'). In the case of the negative morpheme approximating /*ma*/, the frequent occurrence of *ma*-like negatives in languages all over the world (for example, Indo-European, Afro-Asiatic, Sino-Tibetan, Old Japanese, North Caucasian, and Mayan; see examples in Chapter 8) make other possible explanations at least as plausible. As noted in Chapter 7, affixes and short grammatical morphemes whose meanings are most salient tend worldwide to be signaled by unmarked, perceptually highly salient consonants; since nasals are the most perceptually salient consonants of all (Maddieson 1984), it is not surprising that they tend to be found in negatives. In short, Payne's list of shared features deserves much more study, but they do not appear to support any firm areal or genetic conclusions concerning the languages involved.

David Payne (1990:80–85) presents a similarity shared among Proto-Maipurean [Arawakan], Proto-Cariban, Arauan, and Candoshi that he calls an "intricate pattern": a set of possession markers on nouns that also delineate noun classes (roughly of the form Possessive. Pronoun . Prefix - NOUN - Classificatory . Suffix). The suffixes vary according to noun class; there are forms approximating *-nV, -tV, -rV,* vowel change, and Ø in some of the languages. Payne observes that "it may turn out to be the case that /-ri/, at least, is a widespread possessive

suffix and nominalizer in Amazonian languages. . . . /*-ri/ is also the possessive suffix in Jivaroan languages on regular nouns. . . . No possessive suffix is required (i.e. zero) in the genitive construction for inalienable [*sic*] possessed nouns." He believes this pattern to be "less likely to be accounted for by diffusion" and leaves open the possibility of a genetic relationship between Cariban and Arawakan languages (Payne 1990:85).

Harriet Klein notes many of these same shared features in Lowland South American languages, which she says "seem to derive from diffusion or contact" (1992:33–4); they include a common pattern of discourse redundancy, ergativity for most of the languages, OV word order (SOV or OVS), and lack of a formal distinction between active and passive, among others.

There are in the literature also occasional discussions of local diffusion in individual languages that is suggestive of possible areal phenomena. For example, Ruth Wise (1985a:215) mentions phonological change in Amuesha, which is the result of numerous Quechua loans.

Southern Cone Area
(MAP 21)

Klein (1992:35) notes several traits common to the languages of the Southern Cone (represented strongly in languages of Argentina and Chile, such as Mapudungu [Araucanian], Guaycuruan, and Chon). They include semantic notions of position signaled morphologically by means of "many devices to situate the visual location of the noun subject or object relative to the speaker; tense, aspect, and number are expressed as part of the morphology of location, direction, and motion" (1992:25). Palatalization is a common phonological feature; there are more back consonants than front ones; and SVO is the basic word order.

Summary

Many of the linguistic areas discussed in this chapter require further study to determine whether or to what extent they are legitimate, to refine the real ones, and to trace the true history of the features they share. The continued investigation of areal linguistics in the Americas is essential, for in many instances proposals of remote genetic relationship will remain inconclusive until we can distinguish between traits that have been diffused and traits that may be inherited. Areal linguistics is currently receiving a great deal of attention, but in the case of most of the areas considered here, much remains to be done.

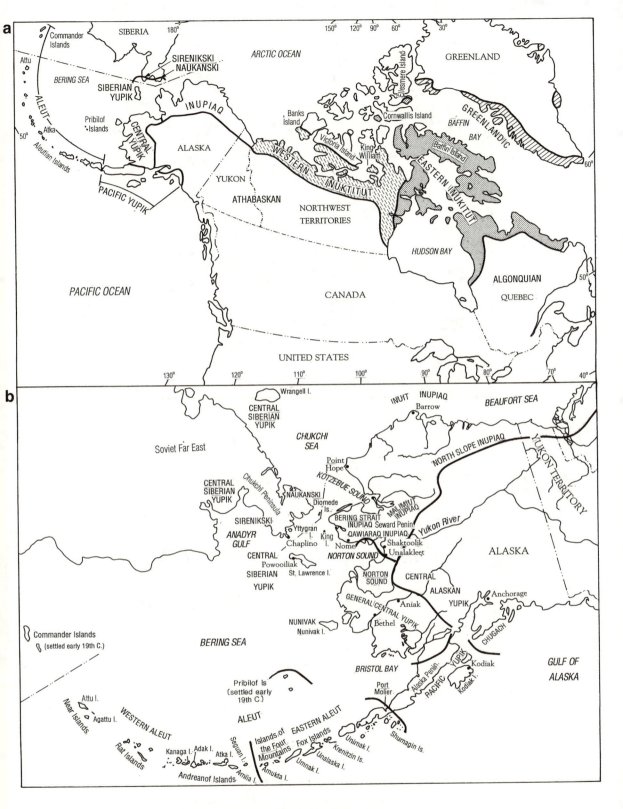

MAP 1 **Eskimo-Aleut Languages**
(a) Eskimo-Aleut Languages
(redrawn after *International Encyclopedia of Linguistics,* vol. 1, p. 416)
(b) Eskimo-Aleut Languages of Northeast Asia and Alaska
(redrawn after *Handbook of North American Indians,* vol. 5, p. 50, fig. 1)

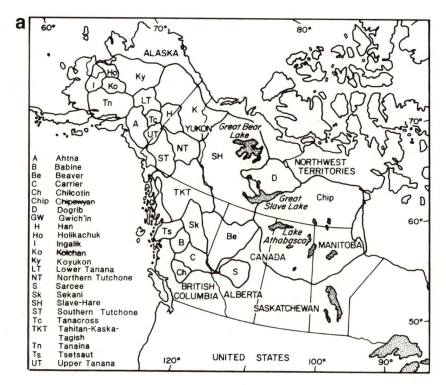

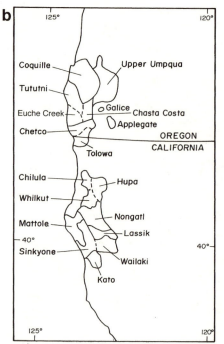

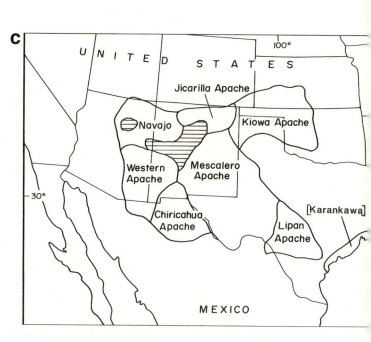

Key to map (a):

A — Ahtna
B — Babine
Be — Beaver
C — Carrier
Ch — Chilcotin
Chip — Chipewyan
D — Dogrib
GW — Gwich'in
H — Han
Ho — Holikachuk
I — Ingalik
Ko — Kolchan
Ky — Koyukon
LT — Lower Tanana
NT — Northern Tutchone
S — Sarcee
Sk — Sekani
SH — Slave-Hare
ST — Southern Tutchone
Tc — Tanacross
TKT — Tahitan-Kaska-Tagish
Tn — Tanaina
Ts — Tsetsaut
UT — Upper Tanana

MAP 2 **Athabaskan Languages**
(a) Northern Athabaskan Languages
(b) Pacific Coast Athabaskan Languages
(c) Apachean Languages
(redrawn after *International Encyclopedia of Linguistics,* vol. 1, pp. 123, 125, 126)

354

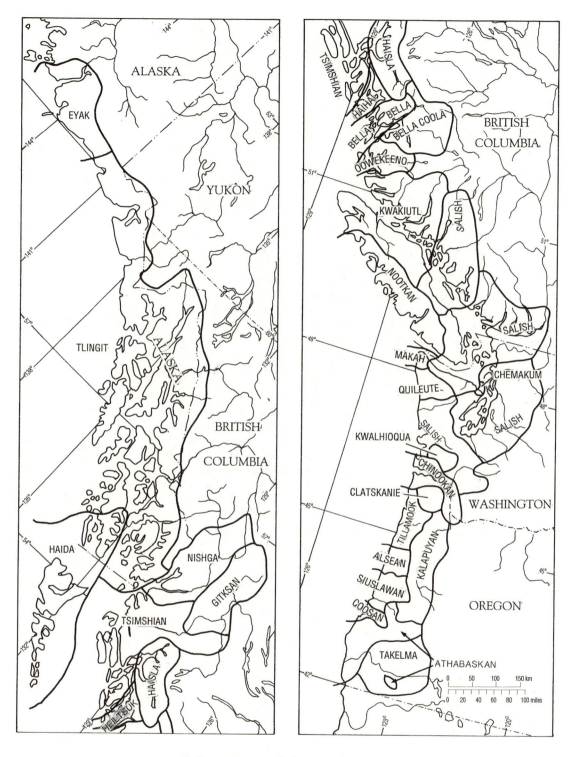

MAP 3 **Languages of the Northwest Coast**
(redrawn after *Handbook of North American Indians,* vol. 7, p. ix)

355

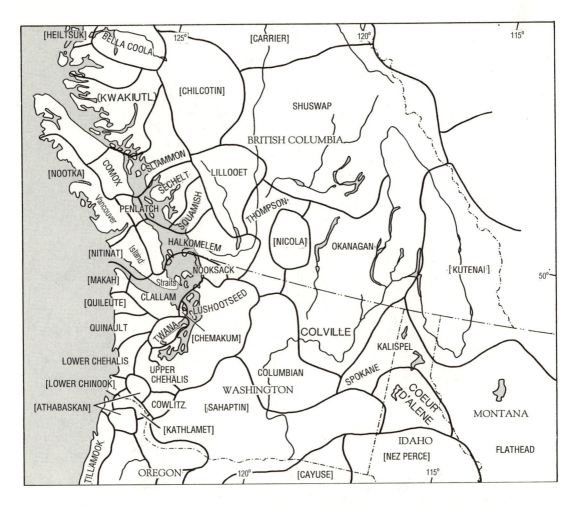

MAP 4 **Salishan Languages**
(redrawn after *International Encyclopedia of Linguistics,* vol. 3, p. 361)

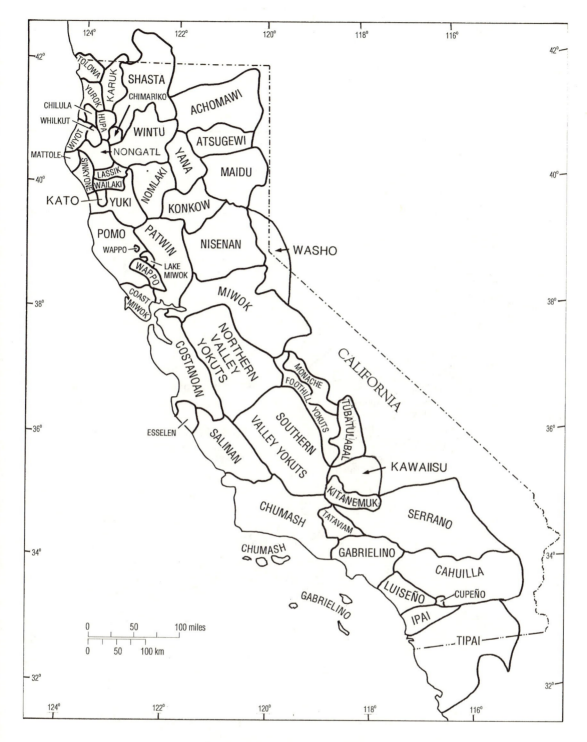

MAP 5 **Languages of California**
(redrawn after *Handbook of North American Indians,* vol. 8, p. ix)

MAP 6 Uto-Aztecan Languages
(redrawn after *Handbook of North American Indians,* vol. 10, p. 114)

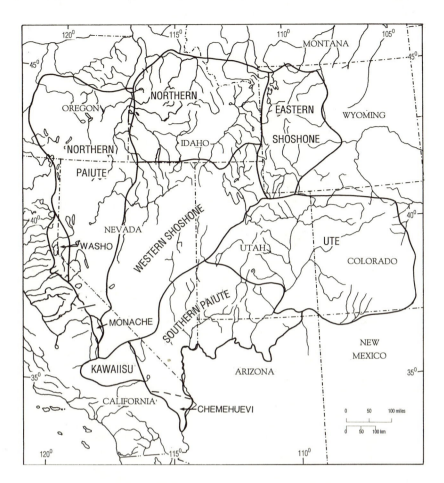

MAP 7 **Languages of the Great Basin**
(redrawn after *Handbook of North American Indians,* vol. 11, p. ix)

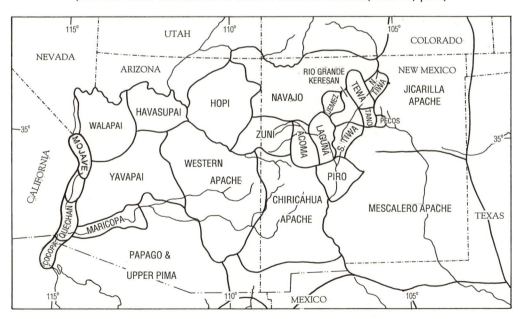

MAP 8 **Languages of the Pueblo Area and the Southwest**
(adapted from *Handbook of North American Indians,* vol. 9, p. ix)

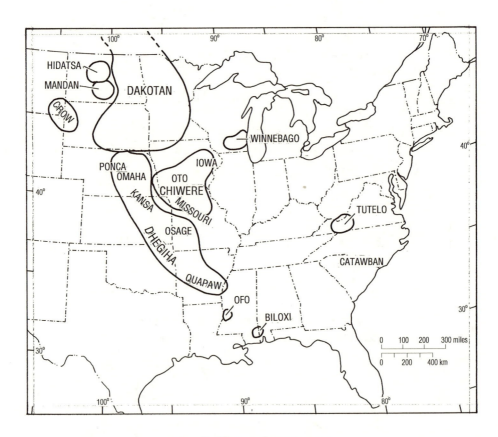

MAP 9 **Siouan Languages**
(adapted from *International Encyclopedia of Linguistics,* vol. 3, p. 450
and information supplied by Robert Rankin, personal communication)

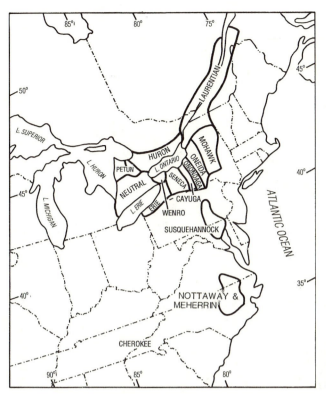

MAP 10 **Iroquoian Languages**
(adapted from *Handbook of North American Indians,* vol. 15, p. ix)

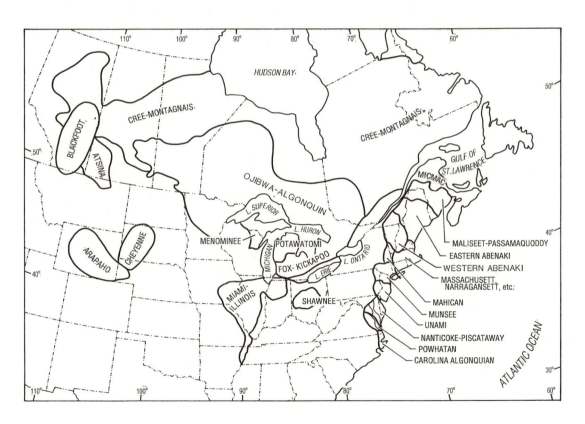

MAP 11 **Algonquian Languages**
(adapted from *International Encyclopedia of Linguistics,* vol. 1, p. 45)

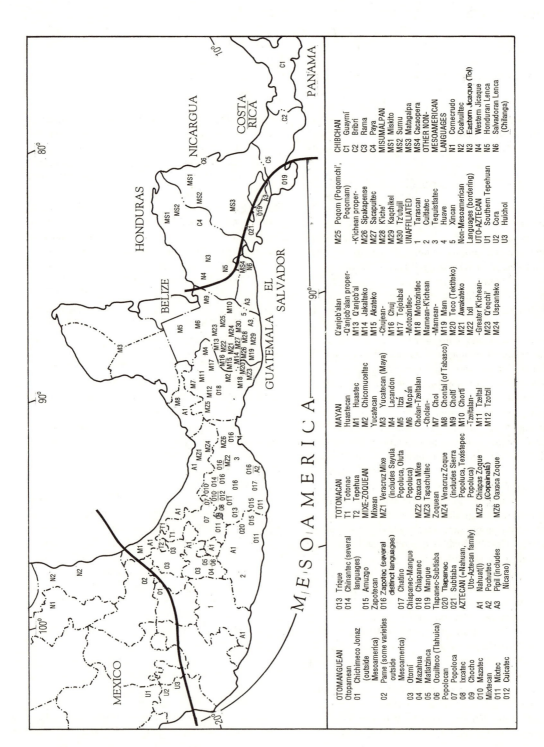

MAP 12 Mesoamerican Languages and Their Neighbors
(redrawn after Campbell et al. 1986, pp. 538–42)

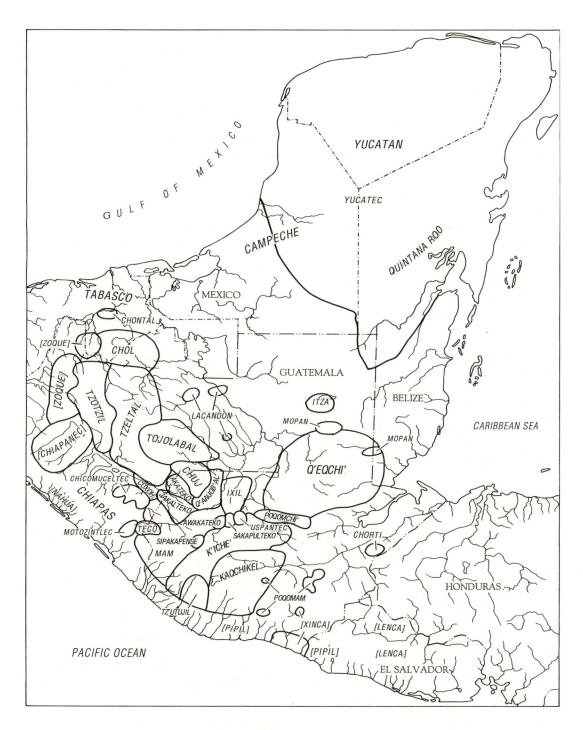

MAP 13 **Mayan Languages**
(redrawn after Campbell 1988b insert, map of Mayan languages)

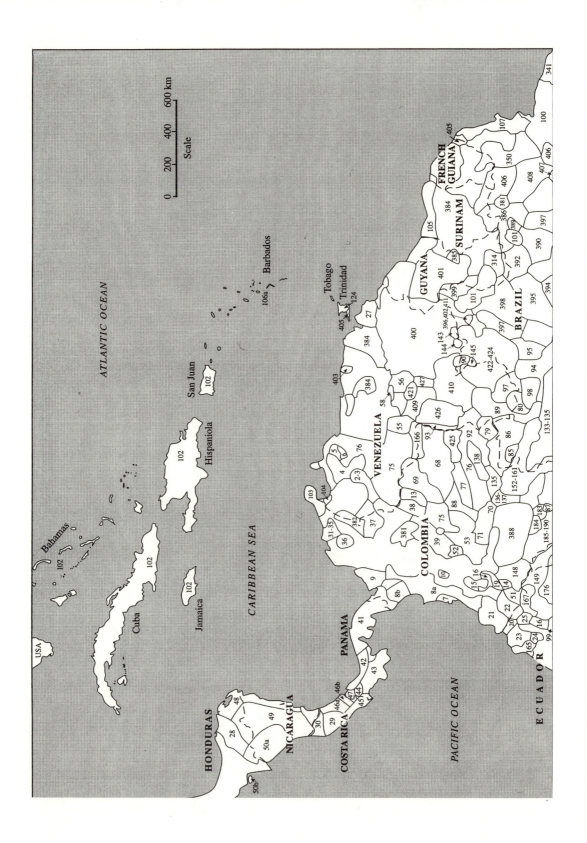

Key

2 Timote-Cuica	35 Ika	85 Tariano	146 Tequiraca	384 Cariña
3 Mucuchí-Maripú	36 Chimila	86 Karu	148 Correguaje	385 Akuriyo
4 Jirajara	37 Barí	87 Resígaro	149 Macaguaje	386 Tiriyó
5 Ayomán	38 Tunebo	88 Marawá	152 Yauna	388 Karihona
6 Gayón	41 Cuna	89 Baré	153 Cubeo	389 Salumá
7 Noanamá	42 Movere	90 Guinao	154 Macuna	390 Kashuyana-Warikyuna
8a Southern Emberá	43 Bocotá	92 Baniva	155 Yupuá-Durina	392 Waiwai
8b Northern Emberá	44 Dorasque	93 Maipure	156 Cueretá	394 Boanarí
9 Sinúfana	45 Boruca	94 Manao	157 Desano-Sirpiano	395 Yawaperí
10 Quimbaya	46a Cabécar	95 Kariaí	158 Bará-Tuyuka	396 Sapará
13 Betoi	46b Bribri	97 Yabaána	159 Carapano	397 Pawixiana
14 Andaqui	47 Tiribí	98 Wiriná	160 Tucano	398 Pararilhana
15 Páez	48 Mísquito	99 Shiriana	161 Guanano	399 Makuxí
16 Panzaleo	49 Sumu	100 Aruán	165 Esmeralda	400 Pemón
17 Coconuco	50a Matagalpa	101 Wapixana	166 Yaruro	401 Kapon
18 Totoró	50b Cacaopero	102 Taíno	167 Cofán	402 Purukotó
19 Guambiano-Moguez	51 Camsá	103 Guajiro	176 Yagua	403 Cumaná
20 Coaiquer	52 Tinigua	104 Paraujano	182 Bora	405 Yao
21 Muellama	53 Pamigua	105 Arawak	183 Muinane	406 Wayana
22 Pasto	55 Otomaco	106a Kalhiphona	184 Andoquero	407 Arakajú
23 Cayapa	56 Taparita	107 Palikur	185 Coeruna	408 Apalaí
24 Colorado	58 Guamo	124 Shebaye	186 Ocaina	409 Mapoyo-Yavarana
25 Caranqui	68 Guajibo	133 Kuri-Dou	187 Nonuya	410 Makiritare
27 Warao	69 Cuiva	134 Hupda	188 Murui	411 Wajumará
28 Paya	70 Guayabero	135 Kaburí	189 Koihoma	421 Panare
29 Guatuso	71 Churuya	136 Guariba	190 Minica	422 Yanomamö
30 Rama	75 Achagua	137 Cacua	314 Taruma	423 Yanam
31 Tairona	76 Piapoco	138 Puinave	341 Tupi	424 Sanumá
32 Cágaba	77 Amarizana	143 Ahuaque	350 Wayampí	425 Sáliva
33 Guamaca	79 Guerenquena	144 Kaliana	381 Opón-Cárare	426 Piaroa-Maco
34 Atanque	80 Mandahuaca	145 Maku	382 Yucpa-Yaprería	427 Jotí

MAP 14 **Languages of the Caribbean and Northern South America**
(redrawn after Kaufman 1994, map 20)

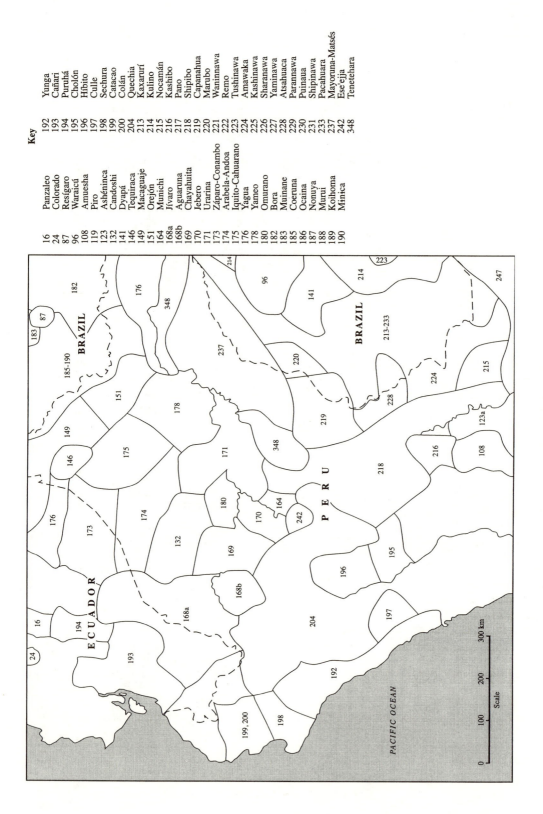

Key

16	Panzaleo		192	Yunga
24	Colorado		193	Cañari
87	Resígaro		194	Puruhá
96	Waraicú		195	Cholón
108	Amuesha		196	Híbito
119	Piro		197	Culle
123	Ashéninca		198	Sechura
132	Candoshi		199	Catacao
141	Dyapá		200	Colán
146	Tequiraca		204	Quechia
149	Macaguaje		213	Kaxarurí
151	Orejón		214	Kulino
164	Munichi		215	Nocamán
168a	Jívaro		216	Kashibo
168b	Aguaruna		217	Pano
169	Chayahuita		218	Shipibo
170	Jebero		219	Capanahua
171	Urarina		220	Marubo
173	Záparo-Conambo		221	Waninnawa
174	Arabela-Andoa		222	Remo
175	Iquito-Cahuarano		223	Tushinawa
176	Yagua		224	Amawaka
178	Yameo		225	Kashinawa
180	Omurano		226	Sharanawa
182	Bora		227	Yaminawa
183	Muinane		228	Atsahuaca
185	Coeruna		229	Parannawa
186	Ocaina		230	Puinaua
187	Nonuya		231	Shipinawa
188	Murui		233	Pacahuara
189	Koihoma		237	Mayoruna-Matsés
190	Mínica		242	Ese'ejja
			348	Tenetehara

MAP 15 **Languages of the Northern Pacific Coast of South America**
(redrawn after Kaufman 1994, map 21)

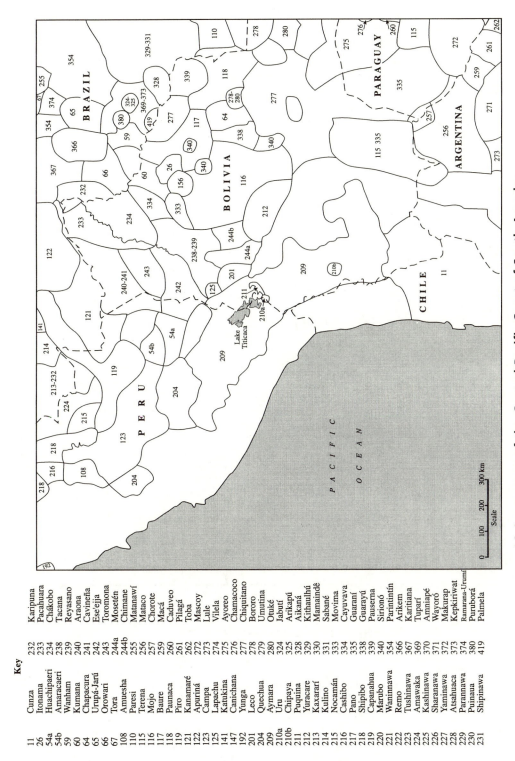

Key

11	Cunza		232	Karipuna
26	Itonama		233	Pacahuara
54a	Huachipaeri		234	Chákobo
54b	Amaracaeri		238	Tacana
59	Wanham		239	Reyasano
60	Kumana		240	Araona
64	Chapacura		241	Cavineña
65	Urupá-Jarú		242	Ese'ejja
66	Orowari		243	Toromona
67	Tora		244a	Mosetén
108	Amuesha		244b	Chimane
110	Paresi		255	Matanawí
115	Terena		256	Mataco
116	Mojo		257	Chorote
117	Baure		259	Macá
118	Paunaca		260	Caduveo
119	Piro		261	Pilagá
121	Kanamaré		262	Toba
122	Apuriná		272	Mascoy
123	Campa		273	Lule
125	Lapachu		274	Vilela
141	Katukina		275	Ayoreo
147	Canichana		276	Chamacoco
192	Yunga		277	Chiquitano
201	Leco		278	Bororo
204	Quechua		279	Umutina
209	Aymara		280	Oruké
210a	Uru		324	Jabutí
210b	Chipaya		325	Arikapú
211	Puquina		328	Aikaná
212	Yuracare		329	Kithaulhú
213	Kaxararí		330	Mamaindê
214	Kulino		331	Sabané
215	Nocamán		333	Movima
216	Cashibo		334	Cayuvava
217	Pano		335	Guaraní
218	Shipibo		338	Guarayú
219	Capanahua		339	Pauserna
220	Marubo		340	Sirionó
221	Waninnawa		354	Parintintín
222	Remo		366	Arikem
223	Tushinawa		367	Karitiana
224	Amawaka		369	Tuparí
225	Kashinawa		370	Amniapé
226	Sharanawa		371	Wayoró
227	Yaminawa		372	Makurap
228	Atsahuaca		373	Kepkiriwat
229	Parannawa		374	Ramarana-Urumí
230	Puinaua		380	Puruborá
231	Shipinawa		419	Palmela

MAP 16 Languages of the Central Pacific Coast of South America
(redrawn after Kaufman 1994, map 24)

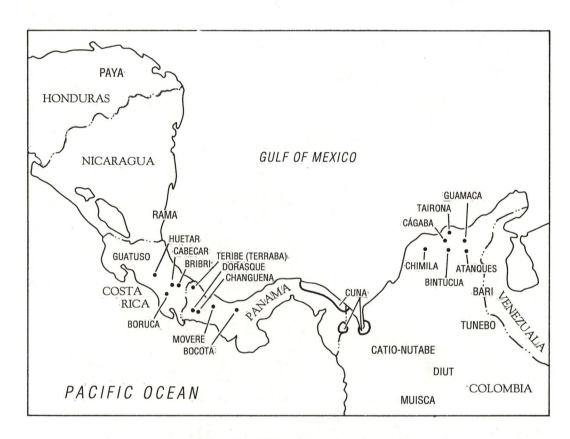

MAP 17 **Chibchan Languages**
(redrawn after Constenla 1991, p. 32)

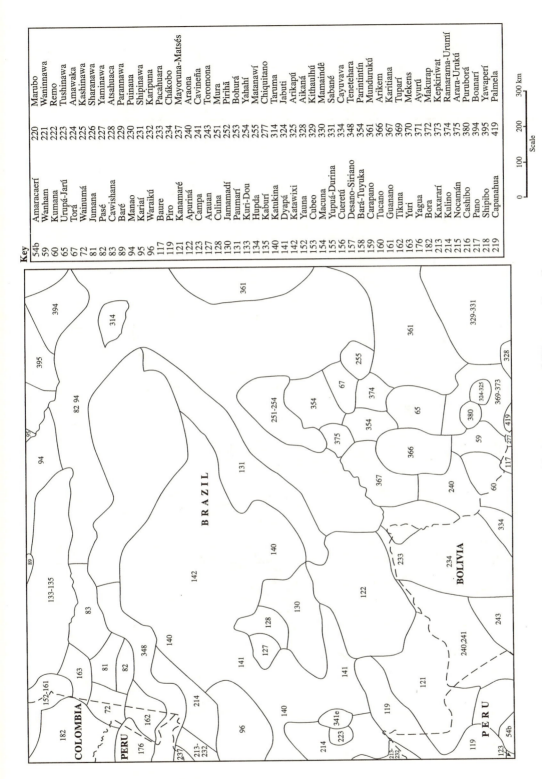

0   100   200   300 km

Scale

MAP 18 Languages of Western Brazil
(redrawn after Kaufman 1994, map 22)

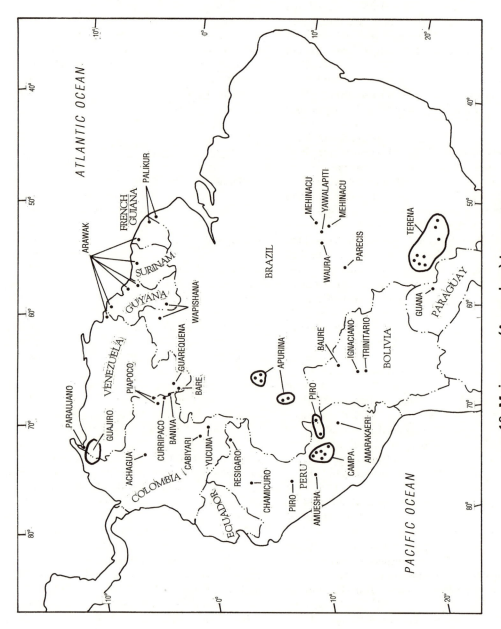

MAP 19 **Maipurean (Arawakan) Languages**
(redrawn after *International Encyclopedia of Linguistics*, vol. 1, p. 104)

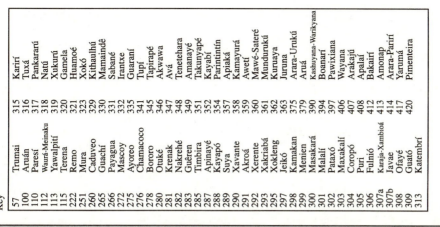

Key

57	Trumai
100	Aruán
110	Paresí
112	Waurá-Meinaku
113	Yawalpití
115	Terena
222	Remo
251	Mura
260	Caduveo
265	Guachí
266	Payagua
272	Mascoy
275	Ayoreo
276	Chamacoco
278	Bororo
280	Otuké
281	Krenak
282	Nakrehé
283	Guéren
285	Timbira
287	Apinayé
288	Kayapó
289	Suya
290	Xavante
291	Akroá
292	Xerente
293	Xakriabá
295	Xokleng
297	Jeikó
298	Kamakan
299	Menien
300	Masakará
301	Malalí
302	Pataxó
303	Maxakalí
304	Coropó
305	Puri
306	Fulnió
307a	Karaja-Xambioá
307b	Javae
308	Ofayé
309	Guató
313	Katembrí
315	Karirí
316	Tuxá
317	Pankararú
318	Natú
319	Xukurú
320	Gamela
321	Huamoé
323	Xokó
329	Kithaulhú
330	Mamaindé
331	Sabanê
332	Irantxe
335	Guaraní
341	Tupí
345	Tapirapé
346	Akwawa
347	Tenetehara
348	Amanayé
349	Takunyapé
351	Kayabí
352	Parintintín
354	Apiaká
357	Kamayurá
358	Awetí
359	Mawé-Sateré
360	Munduruki
361	Kuruaya
362	Juruna
363	Arara-Urukú
375	Aruá
379	Kashuyana-Warikyana
390	Boanari
394	Pawixiana
397	Wayana
406	Arakajú
407	Apalaí
408	Bakairí
412	Amonap
413	Arara-Parirí
414	Yarumá
417	Pimenteira
420	

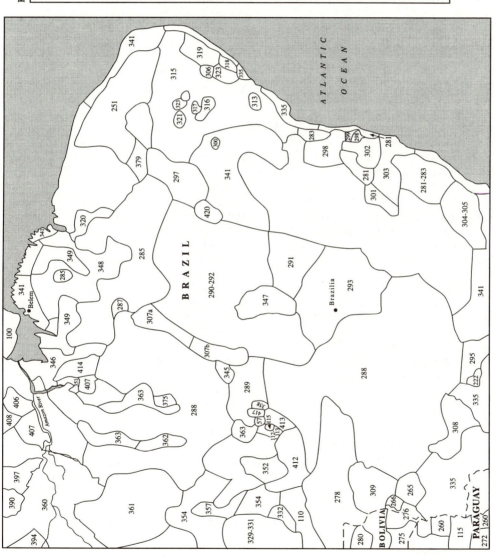

MAP 20 **Languages of the Brazilian Atlantic Coast**
(redrawn after Kaufman 1994, map 23)

371

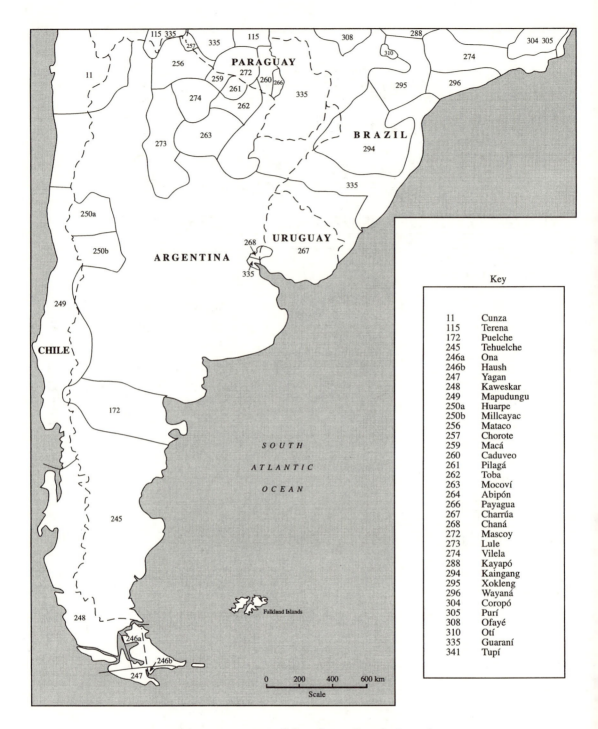

MAP 21 **Languages of Southern South America**
(redrawn after Kaufman 1994, map 25)

Key

11	Cunza
115	Terena
172	Puelche
245	Tehuelche
246a	Ona
246b	Haush
247	Yagan
248	Kaweskar
249	Mapudungu
250a	Huarpe
250b	Millcayac
256	Mataco
257	Chorote
259	Macá
260	Caduveo
261	Pilagá
262	Toba
263	Mocoví
264	Abipón
266	Payagua
267	Charrúa
268	Chaná
272	Mascoy
273	Lule
274	Vilela
288	Kayapó
294	Kaingang
295	Xokleng
296	Wayaná
304	Coropó
305	Purí
308	Ofayé
310	Otí
335	Guaraní
341	Tupí

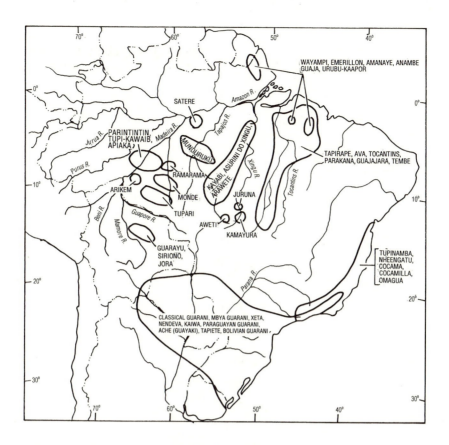

MAP 22 **Tupian Languages**
(redrawn after *International Encyclopedia of Linguistics,* vol. 4, p. 183)

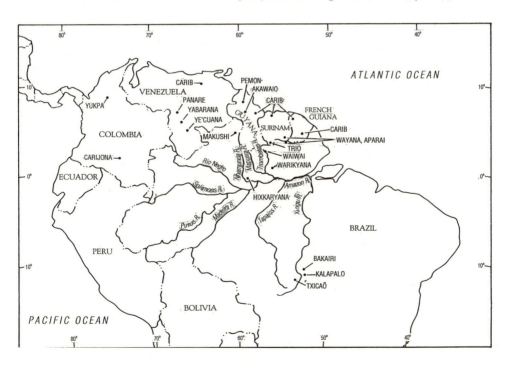

MAP 23 **Cariban Languages**
(redrawn after *International Encyclopedia of Linguistics,* vol. 1, p. 214)

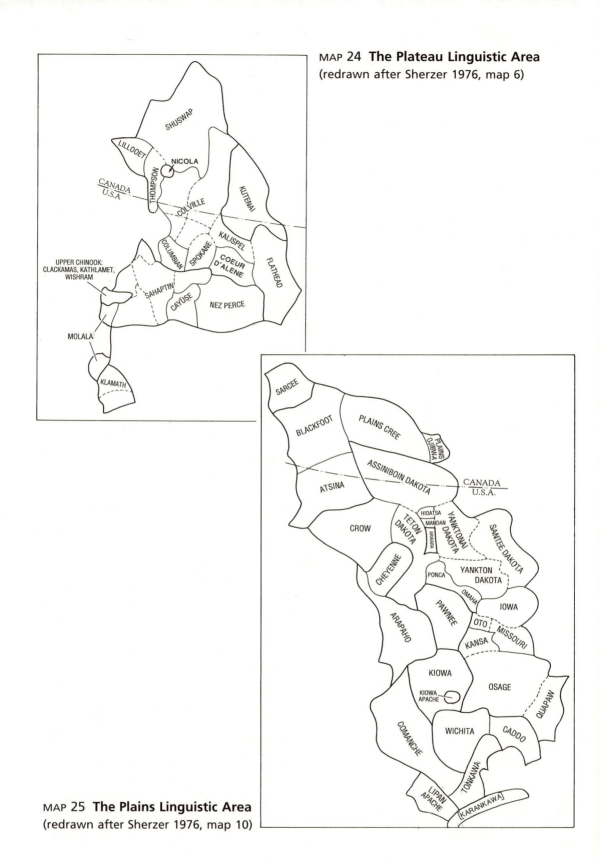

MAP 24 **The Plateau Linguistic Area**
(redrawn after Sherzer 1976, map 6)

MAP 25 **The Plains Linguistic Area**
(redrawn after Sherzer 1976, map 10)

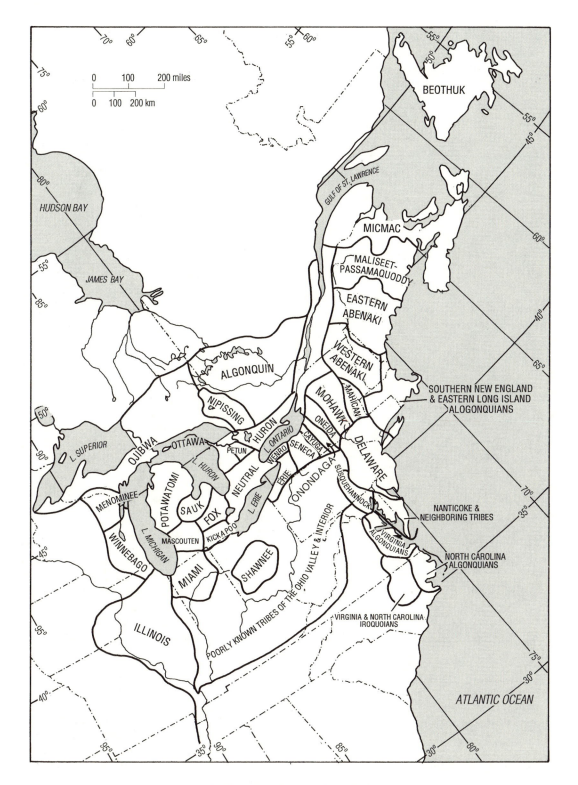

MAP 26 **The Northeast Linguistic Area**
(redrawn after *Handbook of North American Indian,* vol. 15, p. ix)

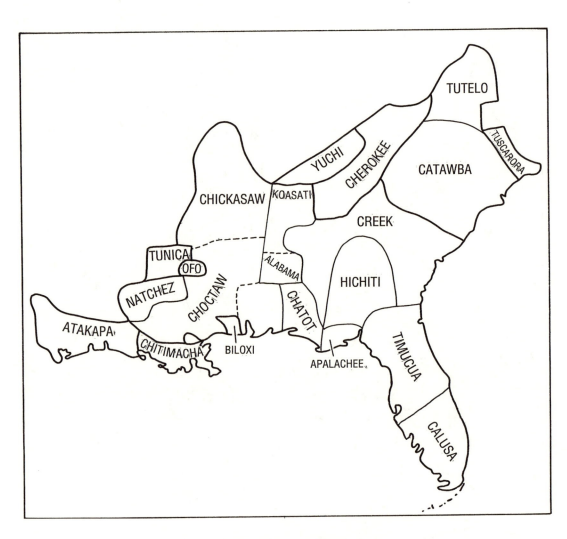

MAP 27 **The Southeast Linguistic Area**
(redrawn after Sherzer 1976, map 12)

376

NOTES

Chapter 1   Introduction

1. Swadesh (1960b:145) counted approximately 2,000 languages of which he said 1,200 still exist. Brazil alone is credited with 201 languages still spoken today (Grimes 1988). Gursky (1966a:401) counted about 300 in North America north of Mexico, 181 of which are still spoken. Foster (1982) lists 53 indigenous languages still spoken in Canada. Loukotka (1968) registered 1,492 languages for South America alone (see also Wilbert 1968:13, 15–17; Migliazza and Campbell 1988).

2. Isolates are in essence families that are composed of only a single language—that is, they are isolated languages that have (as yet) no demonstrated genetic affinity with any other languages. Elmendorf (1965:95) calls these "single-member units." The term is also frequently used to refer to single-language families that are assigned (rightly or wrongly) to larger groupings; it might be said, for example, that some stock or phylum has some members that are families and others that are isolates. Occasionally, the term "isolate" is also used to refer to very small and otherwise unaffiliated families: Chimakuan might be called an isolate, even though it has Chemakum and Quileute as constituent languages. My usage of the term, however, is restricted to the first definition—for unaffiliated single-language families.

3. For example, Bancroft, although he favored the notion that all American Indian languages were genetically related—that is, that there was a single original American family—reported that some "find, on the Pacific side of the northern continent alone, over six hundred languages which thus far refuse to affiliate" (1886[1882]:557). In North America, Pow-

ell's (1891a) "half-hundred" and Sapir's "half-dozen" (see Voegelin and Voegelin 1967:573) genetic groupings are often held up as the extremes, and compromise proposals of about two dozen are also bandied about, with little motivation other than to avoid the extremes (see Lamb 1959 and Pinnow 1964a; Bancroft 1886[1882]:557; see also Chapter 2).

4. By no means does the usage of "dialect" here refer to so-called exotic or little-known languages, though some have used the term in this sense, particularly in the past.

5. Philology has been defined in a number of ways. Some scholars hold that it is the study of some classical language, no more and no less. Some think philology is just historical linguistics as practiced in the nineteenth century. A more common definition is that philology is the study of written attestations of languages in order to obtain systematic linguistic information concerning the languages of the texts (Goddard 1973; see Campbell 1982). A branch of philology that is less practiced in American Indian linguistics attempts to obtain historical and cultural information from the interpretation of written documents. The more common view, presented here, is that written attestations should be subjected to linguistic examination and interpretation with the goal of obtaining information about the history of the language(s) in which the documents are written.

6. Cook recognized in 1778 that Eskimo and Aleut were related, based on a brief comparative vocabulary (Goddard in press).

7. Sequoya (also known as George Guess), the son of a German trader and a mixed-blood Cherokee mother, was brought up as an Indian and never learned

English. After being involved in a crippling accident, he spent years perfecting a Cherokee syllabary, which was enthusiastically received and widely used. In 1828 the weekly newspaper *The Cherokee Phoenix* was first published in the Cherokee syllabary.

8. The missionary Christian Le Clerq, who is traditionally assumed to have originated the notion of Micmac hieroglyphics, relates in his 1677 diary that the idea was inspired by native tradition: "Our Lord inspired me with the idea of [characters] the second year of my mission, when being much embarrassed as to the method by which I should teach the Micmac Indians to pray to God, I noticed some children were making marks with charcoal upon birchbark, and were counting these with the fingers very accurately at each word of prayers which they pronounced. This made me believe that by giving them some formulary, which would aid their memory by definite characters, I should advance much more quickly than by teaching them through the method of making them repeat a number of times that which I said to them" (cited in Battiste 1985:10). Father Pierre Antoine Maillard (who started a mission among the Micmacs of Cape Breton Island in 1735) expanded hieroglyphic literacy and helped in the transition to roman script (Battiste 1985:11). I thank Ives Goddard (personal communication) for some of the information on writing systems presented here.

9. Bergsland (1986:44) reports that there are "at least 600 Russian loanwords" in the Aleut dialects of Alaska, and 190 in Yupik Eskimo.

10. Specifically, *Mexico* is from the stem *me:ši?-*, of unknown meaning, + *-ko* 'in' (compare *me:ši?-ka* 'tribal name'); *Guatemala* comes from *kʷaw-* 'tree' + *te:mal* 'bunch' + *tla:n* 'place of', and appears to be the Nahuatl translation of *k'i:?-če:?* 'K'iche' (Quiché), literally 'many' + 'trees', i.e., 'forest'.

11. I thank M. Dale Kinkade for pointing these out to me.

12. I thank Adolfo Constenla for this information.

13. Barring the unanticipated but hoped for success of language revitalization programs, of which a number currently exist (see Hinton 1994, Jeanne 1992, Watahomigie and Yamamoto 1992), these languages will become extinct.

14. For more precise figures on numbers of speakers, see Foster 1982, Hinton 1994, Kaufman 1994, Kinkade 1991a, Muntzel and Pérez González 1987, and Chafe 1962.

Chapter 2   The History of American Indian (Historical) Linguistics

1. Unless otherwise specified, translations of quotations from languages other than English are my own, both in this chapter and throughout the book.

2. *Geisteswissenschaft* was earlier often translated as 'moral science,' *Naturwissenschaft* as 'physical science.' Schleicher was not the first to view linguistics as a natural science rather than as a "sentimental," "ideologic" intellectual pursuit *(Geisteswissenschaft)*. The close analogy of linguistics with biology had been insisted upon by Schlegel (1808); Rask held that language is an "objet de la nature" that "resemble à l'histoire naturelle" (Hjelmslev 1966[1950–1951]: 185); several others shared this outlook.

3. Certainly Jones, Hervás y Panduro, Leibniz, Adelung, and others believed they were working out the history of races and nations rather than that of mere languages in their linguistic works. As Rasmus Rask put it: "The human races about which I think I have a clear idea from their languages are: (a) Caucasian (ours), (b) Scythian (Greenlandic [or Polar]), (c) Malayan (Australian), (d) the Chinese (Seric). . . . To this may be added with relative certainty (e) the Negritic, (f) the American; but it is quite possible that there may be more" (in a letter written in 1818, cited and translated by Benediktsson 1980:21). This view is articulated clearly by Gatschet: "To establish distinct families of languages is tantamount not only to establishing the ancient state of nationalities, but of racial discrepancies among tribes" (1882:261).

4. Specifically, Darnell says that "techniques developed in Europe to deal with the history of Indo-European languages were not applied to American Indian languages because they were unwritten. . . . There were no European trained scholars specializing in American languages. The result, of course, was that the study of the languages and their genetic relationships proceeded outside the developing framework of European linguistics and depended heavily on observation of obvious lexical cognates. The purposes of such classifications were practical more than philosophical" (1971a:74–5).

5. Brinton, in his assessment of the "present status of American [Indian] linguistics," referred to a number of European scholars contributing to or specializing in "American languages" (1894b:337–8; see also those mentioned in P. E. Goddard's [1914] overview). Darnell, in spite of her statement, appears to be aware of this, since she mentions Brinton and several earlier scholars who were familiar with European developments as exceptions (1988:125–6). Andresen's reading of this history, more restrictive than mine, is that "up until the 1840s, American researchers—linguists and ethnologists—were self-defining, relying on their own resources and determining their own theoretical directions. They were not, however, isolated from European language-discussions, but fully participated

in discussing the general issues of the day. The period after the 1840s shows a return to a dependence on Europe" (1990:113). I would point to the mutual relationship and interaction apparent throughout this history, though European ideas were clearly more dominant (see the discussion later in this chapter). It is true that Powell's (1891a) classification had strong practical, anthropological motivations; "problems of ethnological classification (ultimately of reservation policy and Congressional approval) were more salient than complexities of historical linguistics" (Darnell 1971a:85). Sturtevant, too, saw Powell as stressing "the accumulation of data, rather than any problems of comparative linguistics" (1959:196). However, Brinton's classification also had these motives, to provide a practical means of classifying the peoples of the New World for anthropological interests far beyond purely linguistic ones. Nevertheless, Brinton insisted that he was following "the precepts and examples of students of the Aryan and Semitic stocks" (1891:x).

6. It may be that American Indian linguistics' mettle is finally being acknowledged by the broader linguistic community today, as suggested by such evidence as, to cite just one example, the fact that the principles, practices, and findings in American Indian linguistics are now at times openly used to justify arguments concerning aspects of Indo-European studies (see, for example, Mallory 1989:64, 153, 164–5, 168, 277; see also Watkins 1990:294–5).

7. The Hebrew origin hypothesis had an extremely long life; it was held by Saint Jerome (died in 394), Saint John Chrysostom (345–407), and Saint Augustine (Droixhe 1978:35). It was also applied early and frequently to American Indian languages.

8. Gallatin reported that "there is nothing I can perceive, in the number of the American languages and in the great differences between them, inconsistent with the Mosaic chronology" (1836:5).

9. Edwards began his essay with the following account of his knowledge of and association with Mohegan:

> When I was but six years of age, my father [the famous theologian and missionary Jonathan Edwards] removed with his family to *Stockbridge* [Massachusetts], which, at that time, was inhabited by Indians almost solely; as there were in the town but twelve families of white or Anglo-Americans, and perhaps one hundred and fifty families of Indians. The Indians being the nearest neighbours, I constantly associated with them; their boys were my daily school-mates and play-fellows. Out of my father's house, I seldom heard any language spoken, beside the Indian. By these means I acquired the knowledge of that language, and a great

facility in speaking it. It became more familiar to me than my mother tongue. . . . This skill in their language I have in a good measure retained to this day.

> After I had drawn up these observations, lest there should be some mistakes in them, I carried them to Stockbridge, and read them to Capt. *Yōghun,* a principal Indian of the tribe, who is well versed in his own language, and tolerably informed concerning the English; and I availed myself of his remarks and corrections. . . .

> When I was in my tenth year, my father sent me among the six nations [Iroquoian], with a design that I should learn their language, and thus become qualified to be a missionary among them. But on account of the war with France, which then existed, I continued among them but about six months. Therefore the knowledge which I acquired of that language was but imperfect. (1788:6–7)

10. Jones admitted as much: "I am sensible that you must give me credit for many assertions which, on this occasion, it is impossible to prove; for I should ill deserve your indulgent attention, if I were to abuse it by repeating a dry list of detached words, and presenting you with a vocabulary instead of a dissertation; but, since I have no system to maintain, and have not suffered imagination to delude my judgement; since I have habituated myself to form opinions of men and things from *evidence.* . . . I will assert nothing positively, which I am not able satisfactorily to demonstrate" (1799:49).

11. Perhaps it is not out of place to point out that Jones's hypotheses of relationship contained several blatant errors by today's standards. For example, he held that Hindi and Sanskrit are not genetically related but only that many loans were involved; that Chinese and Japanese are related to what are now called Indo-European languages; that Sanskrit and Austronesian languages belong to the same family; and even that "the language of Peru [Quechua]" is related to Sanskrit, with several other similar cases that seem shocking today (see Poser and Campbell 1992 for details).

12. For example, he seems to have had a rather clear vision of what today would be called the phoneme or underlying segment (though of this we may be reading too much of the present into the past he represents), as seen in the following discussion:

> Puede también decirse que los tamanacos no tienen la *b,* puesto que aunque algunas voces parece que la usen, no es naturalmente *b,* sino *p,* cambiada en *b* por costumbre de la lengua. . . . Es verdad que en conjunto las susodichas letras aparecen incidentalmente. Así por ejemplo se dice: *Uoto uorbaké tunaché ure,* he hecho el día pescando.

Pero la *b* que se usa aquí no es más que para hacer rápido el hablar y evitar el hiato. Originalmente la partícula postpuesta al verbo *uóri* no es *baké,* sino *paké.* (Gilij 1965[1784]:137)

(It can also be said that the Tamanacos do not have *b,* given that although some forms seem to use it, it is not naturally [underlyingly? organically?] *b,* but rather *p,* changed to *b* by the normal usage of the language. . . . It is true that the set of above mentioned letters [sounds] appear incidentally. For example, one says: *Uoto uorbaké tunaché ure* 'I have spent the day fishing.' But the *b* that is used here is only for speaking rapidly and avoiding a hiatus. Originally [underlyingly?] the particle postposed to the verb *uóri* is not *baké* but *paké.*)

13. También yo, con otros, la creo adoptada por las madres gracias a la facilidad que los niños tienen para pronunciarla [*mamma*].

14. Las letras juntas forman las sílabas. Las sílabas *sa, se, si,* etc., frecuentísimas en la lengua caribe, en la tamanaca, aunque su hija, no se hallan nunca, y todo lo que el caribe expresa por *sa,* etc., los tamanacos lo dicen con *chá.* Así por ejemplo, la escudilla que los caribes llaman *saréra* los tamanacos la llaman *charéra.* Es también dialecto de la lengua caribe el pareca. Pero estos indios, dejando a los tamanacos, y caribes, dicen suavemente, al modo francés, *sharéra* [⟨sh⟩ = /š/, spelling changed by Spanish translator]. Conjetúrese por esta palabra de las otras.

15. Gilij did not indicate precisely what he meant by *coherencia* and *correspondencia,* but it probably was not the meaning we understand by the technical term "sound correspondence," and his meaning may have been intended to refer to matchings of whole words, though his understanding clearly also involved the corresponding sounds.

16. El método y los medios que he tenido á la vista para formar la distinción, graduación y clasificación de las naciones que se nombran en la presente obra, y son casi todas las conocidas en el mundo, consisten principalmente en la observación de las palabras de sus respectivos lenguages, y principalmente del artificio gramatical de ellas. Este artificio ha sido en mi observación el principal medio de que me he valido para conocer la afinidad ó diferencia de las lenguages conocidas, y reducirlas a determinadas clases. . . . La atenta observación de las diversas pronunciaciones respectivas de las demas naciones del mundo bastaria para distinguirlas y clasificarlas.

17. Las cinco naciones *Iroquesas* usan cinco dialectos de la lengua *hurona,* casi tan diversos entre sí, como lo son las lenguas francesa, española é italiana.

18. Tienen pues afinidad las lenguas *maya, cakchi, poconchi, cakchiquil,* y *pocoman.*

19. Max Müller reported that Hervás y Panduro reduced "all the dialects of America to eleven families—four for the south, and seven for the north" (1866:63; see also Ibarra Grasso 1958:18), and Bancroft asserted that Hervás had classified all the American languages "under seven families" (1886[1882]: 557). Müller likened these families to Indo-European in their scope and suggested that Hervás could achieve this classification only because his methods were "the same careful and minute comparison which enables us to class the idioms spoken in Iceland and Ceylon as cognate dialects [Indo-European]." Müller, Bancroft, and Ibarra Grasso, however, failed to understand Hervás's use of terms. Hervás argued at length and very explicitly in his book (since he thought some of his readers would have trouble accepting the assertion) that there was great linguistic diversity in the Americas. Throughout, he spoke of many different *lenguas* and *lenguas matrices.* However, when he spoke of *naciones* 'nations', he apparently intended the term to apply only to those units which covered a considerable terrain and had been recognized as being of administrative importance. Thus he tells us:

> Aunque en América son grandes el número y la diversidad de idiomas, se podrá decir que las naciones de solas [*sic*] once lenguas diferentes ocupan la mayor parte de ella. Estas once lenguas son las siguientes: *araucana, guaraní, quichua, caribe, mexicana, tarahumara, pima, hurona, algonquina, apalachina,* y *groenlandica.* (Hervás y Panduro 1800:393)

(Although in America the number and diversity of languages are great, it will be possible to say that the nations of only eleven different languages occupy the greater part of them. These eleven languages are the following: Araucano, Guaraní, Carib, Mexican [Nahuatl], Tarahumara, Pima, Huron [Iroquoian], Algonquian, Apalachian [which includes a variety of Southeastern U.S. languages], and Greenlandic [Inuit].)

20. Guillaume Breton (1609–1679), the most famous contributor to the French colonial linguistic tradition outside of Canada, was born in Vitteaux (Côte d'Or), France. He entered the priesthood (after which he was called Frère Raymond) and left for America in 1635, arriving in "Gardeloupe." From 1641 to 1653 he lived in "Dominique," then retired in France, to the Convent of Beaune, where he composed his various influential works on Carib.

21. Roger Williams was born in the Smithfield district of London. He received a bachelor's degree from Cambridge University in 1623 and continued

toward an M.A. but left Cambridge in 1629, arriving in America in 1631. He established himself in Plymouth as a trader and friend to the Indians, and as an independent minister; he later founded the Providence settlement. In 1643 he returned to England to seek a charter for the Province Plantations, and it was on that voyage that he drafted his *Key into the Language of America.*

22. It is interesting to note that Barton's *New Views of the Origin of the Tribes and Nations of America* (1797) was dedicated to Thomas Jefferson, with whose opinion Barton disagreed (discussed later in this chapter).

23. Heckewelder was born in Bedford, England, to German-speaking Moravian parents who had emigrated to England seeking religious freedom; in 1754 he sailed to New York with his parents. On the day before his departure for America, he was asked if he could understand German, and he replied that he could understand it better than he could speak it. After settling in Pennsylvania, he found "slow advance in learning, on account of his limited knowledge of German, the only language spoken at Bethlehem" (Rondthaler 1847:33).

24. Jefferson explained the tragic fate of the vocabularies he had collected in a letter to Benjamin Barton (dated September 21, 1809):

An irreparable misfortune has deprived me of them [the Indian vocabularies he had collected]. I have now been thirty years availing myself of every possible opportunity of procuring Indian vocabularies to the same set of words: my opportunities were probably better than will ever occur again to any person having the same desire. I had collected about fifty, and had digested most of them in collateral columns, and meant to have printed them the last year of my stay in Washington. But not having yet digested Captain Lewis' collection [of the Lewis and Clark expedition, 1804–1806], nor having leisure then to do it, I put it off till I should return home. The whole, as well digests as originals, were packed in a trunk of stationary, and sent round by water . . . from Washington, and while ascending James river, this package, on account of its weight and presumed precious contents, was singled out and stolen. The thief being disappointed on opening it, threw into the river all its contents. . . . Among these were the whole of the vocabularies. . . . I am the more concerned at this accident, as of the two hundred and fifty words of my vocabularies, and the one hundred and thirty words of the great Russian vocabularies of the languages of the other quarters of the globe, seventy-three were common to both, and would have furnished materials for a comparison from which something might have resulted. (1984:1212–13; also 1984:1389)

25. From 1790 to 1792, Vater studied theology at the University of Jena (where theology and Oriental languages were closely connected) and in 1809 became a professor of theology and Oriental languages at the University of Königsberg.

26. Professor William Thalbitzer (1873–1958), of the University of Copenhagen, is another European who worked with Native American languages, though European involvement was denied or ignored by Kroeber and Darnell (see discussion at the beginning of this chapter). He was an associate editor of IJAL from its founding in 1917 until his death, and he published extensively, particularly works on Eskimo.

27. Duponceau, born in St.-Martin, on the Île de Ré, France, came to the United States in 1777, in the employ of Baron Friedrich von Steuben, who wanted a secretary who could speak and write English; Duponceau served throughout the revolutionary war as an aide to Steuben with the rank of major. Later he was, for a time, assistant foreign secretary in President Washington's administration. He became an attorney in Philadelphia in 1785 and was made an attorney of the Supreme Court in the following year. As a young man, he had intended to enter the army, but because he had become nearsighted in early adolescence, he was sent to theology school. This, however, was not to his liking, and so he ran away to Paris at age fifteen. There he was invited to become the private secretary of Antoine Court de Gébelin (1725–1784), who was also known for his scholarship on linguistic matters. For example, Court de Gébelin (1781) had assigned Island Carib (Galibí) a Cariban genetic affiliation based on a comparison of vocabulary, but Lucien Adam (1879), through a morpho-syntactic comparison of the verbal systems was able to correct this error and show that Island "Carib" is actually an Arawakan language (Auroux and Boes 1981:35, Auroux and Queixalos 1984; see also Smith 1983).

28. Aarsleff (1988) argues that Humboldt's typology owes much to the influence of Adam Smith and that both were influenced by Diderot and other French *idéologues* (Humboldt had spent the years 1797–1801 in Paris). Duponceau was also familiar with the work of the other French *Philosophes* (see also Leopold 1984:67).

29. The term comes from the field of mineralogy (Leopold 1984:68, Andresen 1990:104).

30. Le caractère général des langues américaines consiste en ce qu'elles réunissent un grand nombre d'idées sous la forme d'un seul mot; c'est ce qui leur a fait donner par les philologues américains le nom de *langues polysynthétiques*. Ce nom leur convient à toutes (au moins à celles que nous connaissons),

depuis le Groenland jusqu'au Chili, sans qu'il nous ait été possible d'y decouvrir une seule exception, de sort que nous nous croyons en droit de présumer qu'il n'en éxiste point.

31. Duponceau appears to have been so convinced that his polysynthetic structure was diagnostic of a family relationship uniting the American Indian languages that he also pronounced "Tschuktschi" (Chuckchi), in northeast Asia, to be an American tongue (though the reference is not entirely clear, since in the context of this pronouncement he spoke of it as an "Esquimaux" dialect, and he may have been referring not to the Chuckchi language proper but to Siberian Eskimo, spoken also on "the Peninsula called Tschukchikoi Noss" (1830; cited in Belyj 1975:44).

32. Duponceau (1838:68–73) discussed Nájera's (1837) claim that Otomí was different—essentially "monosyllabic" and not polysynthetic—and possibly connected with Chinese in some way. This view was to have reverberations for a long time in the literature on American Indian languages, for it gave rise to speculations about possible Chinese connections, although Duponceau himself insisted there was nothing to indicate that the Americas might have been populated by migrations from China (or to China from America) and used this work as an occasion to repeat his maxim, "il ne faut pas se hâter de généraliser" (1838:73). In several publications Brinton disputed the claim that Otomí might be different, arguing that it shared the incorporative properties he assumed, following Duponceau, to be characteristic of *all* Native American languages (see, for example, Brinton 1890[1885c]:366–74; 1891:136).

33. Ce rapport présente pour résultats les faits suivants:

  1° Que les langues américaines, en général, sont riches en mots et en formes grammaticales, et que dans leur structure complexe, on trouve le plus grand ordre et la méthode la plus régulière;
  2° Que ces formes compliquées, auxquelles j'ai donné le nom de *polysynthétiques,* paraissent exister dans toutes ces langues, depuis le Groenland jusqu'au cap Horn;
  3° Que ces mêmes formes paraissent différer essentiellement de celles des langues anciennes et modernes de l'autre hémisphère.

34. Duponceau's more complete language typology included: "Analytic, synthetic, monosyllabic, [and] polysyllabic languages, languages of inversion, languages in which the words follow in a more or less natural, governed order, languages of inflection, languages with particles, prefixes and suffixes" (Langues analytiques, synthétiques, monosyllabiques, polysyllabiques, langues à inversions, langues dans lesquelles les mots se suivent dans un ordre réglé plus ou moins naturel, langues à inflexions, langues à particules, à préfixes et suffixes) (1838:84; see Leopold 1984:67).

35. Ideas embodying such notions as "inner form" and "basic plan of thought" were by no means new contributions of Humboldt and Duponceau but had been part of the European linguistic heritage essentially since the classical period and in any event since the Modistae and the speculative (that is, logical, semantic-based) grammars of the Middle Ages. They were also found in universal grammar, in its various guises, from at least as early as Sanctius (1585/1587; see Breva-Claramonte 1983 and Campbell, in press b). Belyj argues that Duponceau's views "were to a great measure stimulated by the works of . . . P. Maupertuis" (1975:46), and also by those of Humboldt. Aarsleff mentions that "Maupertuis' plan of ideas corresponds to Humboldt's inner form" (1988:lxiv). Maupertuis in 1750 recommended the study of barbarous languages "because we may chance to find some that are formed on new plans of ideas" (quoted in Belyj 1975:46). Aarsleff reminds us that Humboldt's "judgements on the American-Indian languages . . . were familiar ones [that is, all these opinions belong to a tradition of European lore] long before he found them confirmed by his study of the influence of language-structure on the diverse mentalities of mankind" (1988:xxvi).

36. Duponceau refers to thirty languages, but a few were only slightly different dialects (Haas 1967b:819).

37. Pickering (born in Salem, Massachusetts) graduated from Harvard (in 1796), and though he was a lawyer like Duponceau, he became a very well-known Classics scholar. He was elected Hancock Professor of Hebrew at Harvard (in 1806) and was also offered the newly founded Eliot professorship of Greek literature (in 1812), but he turned down both positions (Andresen 1990:105, Edgerton 1943:27).

38. Andresen (1990:105) is of the opinion that while Duponceau received more attention, Pickering was a more important figure in the development of American linguistics. Hovelacque confirms the importance of both, with special praise for Pickering:

  In no part of the globe, says Frederic Müller, do so many languages exist as in America, whose resemblance is so striking, but whose constituent elements are so different. . . . Among the most instructive of these writings [on American Indian languages] may be mentioned John Pickering's "Remarks on the Indian Languages of North America," which has been long before the public; [and] Duponceau's "Système Grammatical des

Langues de quelques Nations de l'Amérique du Nord." . . . According to Fr. Müller, there would be in the whole continent, from Cape Horn to the regions of the Eskimos, twenty-six languages, or rather groups of different languages; a large number, when we remember that the native population bears no comparison with that of the Old World. (1877:123–4)

39. Wilhelm von Humboldt (1767–1835) was born in Berlin, two years before the birth of his brother, Alexander. Both were sent to the university at Frankfurt an der Oder and then to the influential University of Göttingen. Wilhelm completed his legal studies and held a government post for a short time in Berlin, but gave it up and dedicated himself to study for the next several years, including four years in Paris (1797–1801) and seven years in Rome (as Prussian resident minister accredited to the Vatican, 1801–1808). It was in Rome that he became interested in Native American languages, for his brother brought him many grammars from the Jesuit mission stations he had visited in Latin America. In 1808 Wilhelm returned to public service in Germany, as director of the education section of the Ministry of the Interior (1809–1810). In essence, he created the University of Berlin and subsequently had an enormous impact on the role and organization of academic institutions both in Germany and throughout the world. He was Prussian resident minister in Vienna, 1810, then ambassador to the Court of St. James, living in London from 1817 to 1818, but returned to private life in 1819 until his death in 1835 (Aarsleff 1988:vii–ix).

40. Leopold argues that Humboldt arrived at his notion of *Einverleibung* (incorporation) early in his career, before contact with Duponceau, and although it was exhibited by many American Indian languages, for Humboldt it was not a special type of language but was a construction that all "nations" could employ (Leopold 1984:69–70). In any case, it is clear that Humboldt was influenced significantly by Duponceau's views. Pott (1840:24, 1870:xvii) interpreted Duponceau's polysynthesis as equivalent to or a subdivision of the German term for incorporation, but reserved his use of the term "polysynthesis" basically for American Indian languages. In the works of Müller, Whitney, and others, incorporation and polysynthesis were synonymous (Leopold 1984:71). Lieber (1837) introduced the term "holophrasis," which some scholars employed later to include both incorporation and polysynthesis.

41. Andresen (1990:110–11) cites Haas (1969b) in support of the view that Gallatin started out in 1836, following Duponceau, basing his classification on structural properties, but by 1848 he was relying on "vocabularies alone."

42. On the expedition, Hale collected information on the languages of Patagonia, southern Africa, and Australia, and many languages of Polynesia and the Northwest Coast of America. During a stop in Rio de Janeiro, he collected vocabularies from recently arrived slaves, who spoke thirteen different southern African languages, with the goal of arriving at an "ethnographical map" of Africa south of the equator. He found they all belonged to a single family subdivided into two groups, "Congo-Makua" and "Caffrarian." He also traced origins and migrations of Polynesian groups based on comparative linguistics, coupled with information from mythology and royal genealogies (see Mackert 1994). While the Wilkes expedition was on the Northwest Coast, Hale collected extensive vocabularies and some grammar for fourteen Native American languages (including some from California, and elsewhere) (Kinkade 1990:99).

43. Although Barton (1797) had proposed that Cherokee was related to Iroquoian (as mentioned earlier in this chapter), his sparse evidence had not been convincing, and the affiliation was disputed until publication of Hale's (1883) proof.

44. Haas's discussion of Hale's attention to detail in grammatical comparisons suggests that Hale understood the value of shared idiosyncratic grammatical similarities as evidence for genetic relationship (discussed in the section on submerged features in Chapter 7): "When he [Hale] spoke of the similarity of grammatic structure between Cherokee and the other Iroquoian languages, he had in mind the same *niceties of detail* that had impressed Indo-Europeanists in their comparisons of Sanskrit with other Indo-European languages" (1978[1969b]:157).

45. Hale's reference to Müller is another indication of the cross-fertilization between European linguistics and American Indian language study. It also shows how influential Müller was. As mentioned earlier in this chapter, Gallatin's word list was recommended to Hale by Pickering and Duponceau.

46. Some have stressed the importance of Hale's influence on Boas's early fieldwork on Northwest Coast languages (Gruber 1967, Wolfart 1967:168, Hoijer 1973:662); however, Hymes (in a footnote to Hoijer's article [1973:663]) argues that such influence was "at best circumstantial."

47. By "linguistic prehistory" I mean the correlation of historical linguistic information with evidence from archaeology, ethnohistory, and ethnographic analogy to obtain a more comprehensive view of the prehistory of the groups being studied.

48. Whitney, born in Northampton, Massachusetts, was the son of a banker and younger brother of Josiah Dwight Whitney, the well-known geologist (after whom Mount Whitney, in California, is named).

William Dwight entered Williams College at age fifteen in 1842, graduated in 1845, worked three years in his father's bank, and entered Yale University in 1849 to study philology. (He had been stimulated by books on Sanskrit that his brother Josiah had brought back from Germany.) He then went to study in Berlin and Tübingen, in Germany, from 1850 to 1853, and upon his return he accepted a chair in Sanskrit at Yale.

49. Although Whitney was right in line with his predecessors in upholding a unilinear evolutionary scheme of "progress" from an original "radical [i.e., root] or monosyllabic stage" ultimately to inflectional languages (1867:290), nevertheless he argued against some of the more naive aspects of this evolutionism in the works of Max Müller, August Schleicher, and Heymann Steinthal (see Silverstein 1971:xxi).

50. El estar avecindados en los mismos terrenos y llevar las mismas costumbres, nos inducen á pensar que habia parentesco entre ambos pueblos y entre sus lenguas; si la opinión parece aventurada, no hay mas que desecharla.

51. A esta familia deben referirse todas las tribus que se encontraban al Este de las misiones de Parras y al Norte del Saltillo, hasta tocar con el río Grande; no olvidando que si todas hablaban el coahuilteco, se notaban en muchas algunas diferencias.

52. The comparative sections did not appear in the first edition (1862–1865) but were fully elaborated only in the 1874 edition.

53. . . . el primero que presenta una clasificación científica de lenguas mexicanas fundada en la filología comparativa.

54. Respecto á los principios en que fundo mis clasificaciones, método que sigo y conclusiones que deduzco diré dos palabras. Es sabido que los lingüistas se han dividido en dos escuelas por lo que toca al medio de clasificacion [sic], pues unos buscan la afinidad de las lenguas en sus voces y otros en la gramática. Yo creo que la gramática es lo mas consistente, lo mas estable en una lengua, donde se debe buscar el caracter primitivo de ella, mientras que el diccionario se altera con mas facilidad, se corrompe mas prontamente: un solo ejemplo servirá de confirmacion [sic]. Los Españoles durante ocho siglos no adoptaron ningun elemento esencial de la gramática del idioma árabe, mientras que si tomaron multitud de palabras de esa lengua. Sin embargo, no por esto me declaro partidario exclusivo de las comparaciones gramaticales: he observado que por mucho que se altere el diccionario de un pueblo quedan, por lo menos, algunas de esas palabras que se llaman primitivas, esto es, nombres que indican miembros del cuerpo, parentesco, fenómenos mas notables de la naturaleza, adjetivos numerales, verbos

mas usuales etc.: esta clase de palabras se consideran como esenciales á todo hombre en sociedad por imperfecta que sea. Esto supuesto diré que mi sistema consiste en comparar esas palabras llamadas primitivas, y al mismo tiempo la gramática, el sistema general de ella, así como las formas principales, especialmente el verbo.

55. Hasta ahora se está acostumbrado á considerar todas las lenguas americanas como vaciadas en un mismo molde; yo hago ver que en México existen cuatro órdenes de idiomas bajo el punto de vista morfológico.

56. Il est universellement admis que de simples concordances lexicologiques ne suffisent point pour établir scientifiquement la parenté originelle de deux ou plusieurs langues, et que les rapprochements de mots auxquels se complaisaient les etymologistes de l'ancienne école n'acquièrent de valeur qu'à la condition d'être corroborés par des concordances grammaticales.

57. Je suis donc autorisé à conclure qu'il faut tenir pour absolument fausse cette proposition devenue faute d'y avoir regardé de près une sort de cliché; que si les langues Américaines diffèrent entre elles par la lexique, elles possèdent néanmoins en commun une seule et même grammaire.

58. It should not be forgotten that sound correspondences were utilized as a criterion for determining family relatedness throughout the history of linguistics (Hoenigswald 1990:119–20, Metcalf 1974:251). As shown here and in Chapter 7, Greenberg's (1987, in press) insistence that, in general in the history of linguistics (specifically, in the Americas), sound correspondences were not utilized to establish genetic relationships is not consistent with the actual historical record (see also Campbell and Goddard 1990).

59. Passons maintenant au sous-groupe Yucatèque; il comprend, nous l'avons déjà dit, le Maya, le Tzendale et leurs dialects, ainsi que le Huastèque. . . . Les caractères du sous-groupe Yucatèque sont les suivants: l'absence de la lettre r généralement remplacée par i ou y.

60. Stoll (1849–1922), born in Frauenfeld, Switzerland, received a medical degree in 1873 from the University of Zurich. He went to Guatemala in 1878 to offer his services as a medical doctor, to collect zoological specimens, and later to study Guatemalan native languages. Stoll presented Zur Ethnographie der Republik Guatemala (1884[1958]) as his Habilitation thesis at the University of Zurich and continued an academic career as a professor of geography and ethnography. He published a number of long studies on Guatemalan Indian languages, but his interest gradually shifted to psychological matters.

61. Wenn es sich . . . darum handelt . . . auf deren Grund ich . . . die Zerfällung der Maya-Sprachfamilie vorgeschlagen habe . . . so kann hier . . . folgendes erwähnt werden: . . . Einer augenfälligsten Unterschiede zwischen den einzelnen Gruppen der Maya-Sprachen ist die *gesetzmässige Lautverschiebung* von einer Gruppe zur andern.

62. [C'est] la modification régulière de la même lettre radicale, en passant de telle langue à telle autre, suivant une véritable *Lautverschiebung,* ce qui écart l'hypothèse du hasard. Or, ces moyens de contrôle peuvent être appliqués avec succès aux sept langues que nous groupons.

63. Athabaskan linguistics had already been given a strong foundation by Emile Petitot's (1838–1916) dictionary (1876), which documented Loucheux (Kutchin), Hare, and Chipewyan. It included considerable lexical data on several other Northern Athabaskan languages of Canada, as well as its comparative grammatical introduction.

64. Dans l'intérieur d'une même famille, les rapprochements de mots sont légitimes et concluants, à la condition d'être opérés en conformité avec *les règles de la phonétique et de la dérivation, sans le respect desquelles l'etymologie n'est qu'un art puéril, indigne d'occuper l'attention des vrais savants.*

65. Die gegebenen Wortvergleiche erhalten aber hier schon eine wichtige Unterstützung durch Auffindung bestehender Lautgesetze, auf welche man für gewöhnlich bis jetzt bei Vergleichungen südamerikanischer Sprachen verzichtet hat. *Die Auffindung von Lautgesetzen unterstützt wissenschaftlich die Annahme tieferer Vervandtschaften der Völker.*

66. Dennoch sind alle jene Veränderungen nur gesetzmässige lautliche Differenzirungen von den alten, oft noch zu bestimmenden Formen der karaibischen Grundsprache.

In other areas of historical linguistics, Steinen proposed that the homeland of the Proto-Caribs was in the lower Xingu Basin, a proposal that many scholars still support. He also added several languages to the list of Cariban languages that Adam (1893) had compared (Durbin 1985[1977]:331; see Câmara 1965:145).

67. Uhlenbeck was a well-known Dutch specialist in Indo-European and American Indian languages. He worked on Eskimo and Blackfoot; he discussed the overall classification of Native American languages and included grammatical outlines of all the better known groups. Uhlenbeck was on the editorial board of the *International Journal of American Linguistics* from the time of its founding. He is representative of the interconnectedness of European and American Indian scholarship.

68. Greenberg (1987, 1991, in press; see Chapter 7) rejects any importance for sound correspondences as a criterion for distant genetic relationship. This conclusion is based on his assumption that sound correspondences were not accorded any important role in the establishment of Indo-European as a legitimate language family (this is clearly contradicted by the historical record; see Poser and Campbell 1992). He maintains that the Americanists of today are narrowly fixated on the criterion of sound correspondences. However, as discussed in this chapter and in Chapter 7, Americanists have not insisted on sound correspondences as the only criterion but have also considered the importance of certain sorts of grammatical evidence in determining genetic relationship. In sum, Greenberg has misread both the Indo-Europeanist and the Americanist literature, both of which have happily utilized sound correspondences but neither of which has relied on them exclusively in proposals of family relationship (see Chapter 7).

69. Eduard Seler (1849–1922) was born in Crossen an der Oder, Germany. He began his studies in natural history (botany) but shifted to linguistics; "Das Konjugationssystem der Maya-Sprachen" (1887) was his dissertation in linguistics at the University of Leipzig.

70. Brinton was trained as a physician and served as a surgeon and medical director of the U.S. Army during the Civil War. He studied in Europe (Paris, Heidelberg, and Vienna) beginning in 1861, the year after he received his medical degree. He was named professor of archaeology and linguistics at the University of Pennsylvania in 1886 (thus becoming the first to hold a chair in anthropology in the United States). Linguists and anthropologists have tended to forget that Brinton also had high standing in medicine; in addition to being a prominent surgeon during the Civil War, he was editor of the first journal to emphasize scientific medicine (Wissler 1942:194).

71. Here Brinton appears to be trying to emphasize the independence of his classifications from Powell's (1891a). However, the lack of access to Bureau of American Ethnology (BAE) materials is overstated. Brinton had a good relationship with James Pilling of Powell's staff, from whom he borrowed the BAE materials on Shawnee in 1885 and on Nez Perce in 1888 (Darnell 1988:57). He acknowledged Henry Henshaw's help with Northwest Coast materials (Brinton 1891:xii; cf. Darnell 1971a:95). Moreover, in a letter to Henshaw (dated November 15, 1890), Brinton acknowledged the BAE's offer to allow him to see their map, but he declined in order to be able to maintain his independence:

> I am much obliged to you for the courteous offer . . . about the map, etc. At first I was inclined to come on and look it over; but on second thoughts,

I think I had better not. The information I wish to gain could be made public soon in my lectures, and perhaps in printed reports from them, and this, I can readily see, might not be agreeable to the Bureau. It would, for this reason, be better for me not to see the map; as even if I confined my publication to matters already in my possession, some members of the Bureau might think I had learned them by the facilities you offer, and I had refrained from giving credit. There are, in fact, only a few points in the ethnology of the United States area about which I am much in doubt. (Quoted in Darnell 1971a:95)

72. The historical significance of Powell 1891b has been discussed by Ives Goddard (1994a), and I thank him for pointing this work out to me; its existence was (re)discovered by Patricia Afable, research assistant of the *Handbook of North American Indians,* Department of Anthropology, Smithsonian Institution. While the *Science* article does not appear with the map, Powell presented his famous map (companion of the 1891 classification) at the annual meeting of the American Association for the Advancement of Science in Washington, D.C., in August 1891.

73. In a similar vein, he opined: "The gradual development of grammar is strikingly illustrated in these [American Indian] languages. Their most prominent trait is what is called *incorporation.* Subject, verb, direct object, and remote object, are all expressed in one word. Some have claimed that there are American languages of which this is not true; but I think I have shown in an essay published some time ago [Brinton 1890(1885c):366–74], that this opinion arises from our insufficient knowledge of the alleged exceptions" (Brinton 1890[1888]:403).

74. In Brinton's classification the number is fifty-eight only when Maratino (in northeast Mexico) is included. Although he listed this language, most classifications do not mention it among the languages of North America north of Mexico.

75. Powell attended Illinois Institute (which later became Wheaton College), Illinois College, and Oberlin College, but he was largely self-taught in the sciences. He taught school in 1858 in Hennepin, Illinois, where he was made principal of public schools in 1860. Powell entered the army with the rank of private on April 14, 1861, and by November he had been promoted to captain. He lost one arm below the elbow at Shiloh but returned to service as an artillery officer. In 1865 he became a professor of geology at Illinois Wesleyan University; he subsequently taught at Illinois Normal University (Stegner 1962:15–17). Powell undertook many field trips to explore the West; in the famous expedition of 1869 he became the first to go through the Grand Canyon in a boat.

76. Powell is also credited with coining the term "Amerind" (Andresen 1990:191). It should be noted that the term "Amerind" is avoided by many specialists in American Indian linguistics. Originally the reasons for this avoidance were lack of familiarity to the general public and displeasure with purposefully created scientific neologisms, but it is avoided today in order to prevent confusion with Greenberg's (1987) extremely large proposed genetic grouping called "Amerind," which most specialists reject (see Chapter 7).

77. It is interesting that, in spite of the classification's importance and influence, the data on which it was based have never been published. A classification without the supporting evidence today would be strongly criticized and probably would not be accepted for publication in scholarly journals and monographs.

78. Jeremiah Curtin (1838–1906) did fieldwork for the BAE from 1883 to1890 in Oklahoma, Oregon, and especially in California. His chief interest was oral literature, and he collected many mythological texts and published works on North American creation myths (see, for example, Curtin 1898; Golla 1984:13). J. N. B. Hewitt (1859–1937), who was a good part Tuscarora, worked at the BAE from 1886 until he died. He concentrated mostly on Iroquoian, though Powell assigned him the task of investigating possible groupings of Sahaptian and "Lutuamian" (Klamath-Modoc), which he endorsed, and of Seri and Waikuri with Yuman, which he found doubtful (Golla 1984:98). James Owen Dorsey (1845–1895) was a missionary among the Ponca (Siouan) of Nebraska from 1871 to 1873. He had attended the Theological Seminary of Virginia and became a deacon in the Episcopal Church in 1871. He worked on a grammar and dictionary of Ponca and made comparisons between it and other Siouan languages (such as Dakota, for which he used Riggs's dictionary [1890]). He was a member of the Bureau of American Ethnology from its founding in 1879 until his death in 1895. In 1877 Powell commissioned him to develop a Ponca grammar and dictionary and in 1878 sent him to do fieldwork with the Omaha in Nebraska; when he returned two years later, the BAE hired him as an expert on Siouan languages and tribes (Hinsley 1981:172–4). Dorsey's report (1885) was the first comparative study of Siouan languages. Following standard BAE practice, he compared words and morphemes and presented 204 items in the four languages, arranged according to meanings. For the most part, sound correspondences were not dealt with directly in this practice, although Dorsey did present some specific correspondences (for example, Dakota *d-* corresponding with Dhegiha clusters of *š* + den-

tal). He also formulated a sound change, known now as Dorsey's law, which describes the change in which Proto-Siouan $*C_1C_2V_1$ regularly becomes $C_1V_1C_2V_1$ (in forms where C_1 = obstruent, C_2 = sonorant) in Winnebago. Even Boas was indirectly associated with the BAE, since Powell purchased the linguistic manuscripts that Boas prepared, which in the early years of his career was crucial to Boas's livelihood (see the section on Boas later in this chapter).

79. As Hinsley (1981:28) points out, the years of Morgan's career (1851–1881) saw a change in the primary concern of American anthropological thought, from the origins and early relationships of different peoples to the classification or ranking of human groups according to unilinear evolutionary stages of social, mental (and linguistic), or technological development. Morgan was the leading figure in American evolutionism—and, to be sure, his outlook was stimulated by linguistic models. He considered *Systems of Consanguinity and Affinity of the Human Family* (Morgan 1871) to be in the tradition of comparative philology, but he hoped that kinship would prove to be less changeable than language; language study had been used in Europe to ascertain historical relations among the various peoples of Europe and Asia. This classification of humans by language families inspired Morgan to use his kinship systems as a tool to apprroach the question of Indian origins. Mindful of the linguists' use of language as a gauge of universal stages of evolution, he hoped his approach might be "the most simple as well as the compendious method for the classification of nations upon the basis of affinity of blood" (1871:9; quoted in Hinsley 1981:28), a key to universal human history (Gruber 1967:8).

80. Kroeber credits Henshaw for the 1891 classification, saying it was "largely the results of the labors of H. W. Henshaw" (1913:390). P. E. Goddard (1914:559) attributed the classification to Dorsey and Gatschet, and Gatschet considered himself a co-author of it (Darnell 1971a:82). Kroeber also described a visit by Henshaw in 1904 or 1905 (see Hymes 1961a): "He [Henshaw] told me casually of his part in the fundamental classificatory paper [Powell 1891a]. . . . Naively, I was shocked at Powell having represented himself in print as responsible for work done much more by Henshaw and others. Not at all, said, Henshaw; it was understood and agreed upon beforehand, and Powell lived up to the agreement scrupulously. 'I was to help him,' he said, 'to do such and such things, and the results were to be published under Powell's name.' Henshaw certainly convinced me that he was satisfied, and that Powell had acted completely with justice and good faith" (1960:3).

81. Hinsley reports: "The linguistic map and clas-

sification of 1891, which fulfilled a vision shared by Jefferson, Gallatin, and Gibbs, proved to be the single most lasting and influential contribution of the early Bureau [of American Ethnology] to American anthropology. From the beginning, linguistics was the heart of Powell's 'New Ethnology,' his clearest window into the mind of primitive man. And yet his emphasis on language is initially puzzling, given his background in geology and natural history and his own mediocre linguistic abilities. . . . The inspiration behind his work probably came from Gibbs and William Dwight Whitney. Gibbs, as we have seen, envisioned a continental map and took important steps in that direction by collecting hundreds of vocabularies. Whitney's influence on Powell was subtler but perhaps stronger" (1981:158).

82. James Constantine Pilling was trained as a court reporter, but came to the fields of geology and ethnology out of devotion to Powell. He was Powell's amanuensis for years, and he had the background and temperament for the massive bibliographic research he undertook for the BAE (e.g., Pilling 1885). He was "dependable, tedious, stuffy" and he reminded Clarence King (whom Powell succeeded as director of the U.S. Geological Survey in 1881) "of George Hearst, who in Tucson was bitten on the privates by a scorpion, which fell dead" (Stegner 1962:263). King had said, "Do you want to do Powell a favor? Poison Pilling" (letter from Clarence King to G. F. Becker, April 4, 1882; quoted in Stegner 1962:264).

83. Henry Wetherbee Henshaw (1850–1930) was born in Cambridgeport, Massachusetts. Beginning in 1869 he was engaged in ornithological collection in Louisiana, Florida, Utah, and throughout the West; in 1872 he was a natural-history collector on the Wheeler Survey, which was absorbed by the U.S. Geological Survey in 1879. In 1880 Henshaw accepted Powell's invitation to work at the newly established Bureau of Ethnology (later renamed Bureau of American Ethnology). He spent many months collecting vocabularies for the bureau in Washington, California, and Nevada, during which he established Salinan as distinct, among other things. When the directorship of the U.S. Geological Survey became more demanding, Powell delegated much of the administration of the BAE to Henshaw. Henshaw was editor of the *American Anthropologist* from its second year (1889) to the publication of volume 9 (1896). Because of failing health, he resigned from the bureau in 1894 and lived in Hawaii for the next ten years (pursuing an interest in photography). He joined the Biological Survey in Washington, D.C. and became its chief from 1910 to 1916, when he retired (Hodge and Merriam 1931).

84. Hodge and Merriam state matter-of-factly that

the 1891 classification was published "under Powell's authorship but with credit to Henshaw" (1931:100). Hinsley agrees: "Powell looked to him [Henshaw] to establish a respectable scientific nomenclature. . . . Powell ambiguously credited Henshaw with the 'final form' of the classification, and his reliance may have been more general than appears" (1981:162; cf. Darnell 1971a:84, Hymes 1961b, Kroeber 1960).

85. Gatschet studied philology and theology in Bern and Berlin, then emigrated to New York in 1868. In 1872 Oscar Loew asked him to examine sixteen vocabularies of Indian languages obtained as part of the Wheeler Survey of the Southwest; Gatschet's analyses were published in the Wheeler Survey reports of 1875 and 1876 (also published in German; Gatschet 1876). Powell saw these publications and asked Gatschet to join his team as an ethnologist for the U.S. Geographical and Geological Survey of the Rocky Mountain Region. (It was at this time he began his Klamath research.) He became a regular BAE staff member when it was founded in 1879 and remained there until his retirement in 1905. His constant wish during his years at the BAE was to return to his long-cherished research with Klamath in Oregon, but Powell utlized his efforts instead in work with more than 100 languages as an observer and collector, and little else (Mooney 1907, Hinsley 1981:179). For example, Powell (1966 [1891a]:210) rejected Gatschet's separation of Siuslaw and Yakonan into two distinct units (see Chapter 4) on the basis of Dorsey's brief trip to Oregon (Darnell 1971a:83; Hinsley 1981:164). Moreover, Gatschet proposed the relationship of Catawba with Siouan and Powell accepted it only after Dorsey's reexamination of the evidence led him to the same conclusion (Powell 1966[1891a]:188; cf. Darnell 1971a:80). Nevertheless, in 1903 Boas judged Gatschet's Klamath work to be "at the present time by far the best grammar of an American language in existence" and asserted that Gatschet "has been by far the most eminent American philologist, away ahead of all of us" (quoted in Hinsley 1981:177, 180).

86. . . . die Lautverschiebung bei verwandten Sprachen unter sich, die als durchgreifendes Gesetz die consonantischen Laute auch der indogermanischen Sprachen beherrscht.

87. Indeed, P. E. Goddard attributed to Dorsey and Gatschet the inauguration of a new period of linguistic work, by scholars who were not intent on merely securing sufficient material for a classification, but who had a twofold interest: "A psychological interest in the languages themselves, a desire to know what ideas were expressed and what was the mental classification applied to these ideas by the particular people as evidenced by their language; and a historical interest

in the changes that had taken place in a single language or in the various languages belonging to one family" (1914:560).

88. That is, Humboldt (1822) maintained that all languages are "complete" (vollendet), but not all are "perfect" (vollkommen), and thus language is always in a state of becoming (ein Werdendes)—forever in a state of development.

89. Several scholars have asserted, erroneously, that no group put together by Powell subsequently had to be separated (see, for example, Kroeber 1940a:464).

90. In fact, Catawban's Siouan affiliation is still disputed by a few scholars (though without foundation) (see Chapter 4).

91. As Darnell correctly points out, the term "reduction," which has appeared frequently in writings after Powell, is misleading, since nothing was eliminated, but rather groups were merely "consolidated" into larger, more inclusive groupings (1969:323). In this book I will continue to speak of "reduction," but in the sense of consolidation, since the discussion often includes remarks by those involved at the time.

92. Franz Boas's (1858–1942) first anthropological and linguistic work was among the Eskimos of Baffin Island in 1883 and 1884. Immediately following this, he returned to his native Germany and later that year took advantage of the presence of some Indian visitors in Berlin to work on "Bilhoola" (Bella Coola, Salishan) (the results were published in Boas 1886). While still based in Germany, he attempted (unsuccessfully) to obtain research funds from both Germany and the United States for an extensive investigation of the Indians and Eskimos of the Northwest, because so little was known of them. Denied support, he carried out the research anyway in 1886 with minimum funds, covering his expenses in part through the sale of ethnographic specimens collected in the field (Gruber 1967:21). This field research was successful, and in 1887 Boas accepted the position of assistant editor of Science (Gruber 1967:24); during his tenure he published materials from his research in British Columbia. The research and publications made him highly qualified for the field agent position which he received from the British Association for the Advancement of Science. A committee was established for anthropological investigation of the natives of the Northwest Coast, and Horatio Hale (see the discussion earlier in this chapter), a leading member of this committee, became Boas's supervisor for the six years that Boas served on it. Hale apparently influenced Boas's thinking, but to what degree is a matter of dispute (Gruber 1967, Stocking 1974). There was some friction between the two—Boas perceived Hale's instructions as frequently unnecessary and domineering—but there are also commonalities in their points of view: language as the

basis of ethnology; disapproval of (often erroneous) preconceptions about native languages and cultures; especially opposition to the ethnocentric unilinear evolutionary stages that many assumed for societies and for languages; and the use of language to reconstruct prehistory. Boas later had associations with Powell and the BAE, though rather indirect ones, and some of Boas's early work is reflected in Powell's 1891 classification (for example, Powell 1966[1891a]:149, 179–80, 205). Boas received only piecemeal support from the bureau, which bought the vocabularies that he provided them. Nevertheless, in his early work Boas "operated largely within a Powellian framework" (Stocking 1974:456). His relationship with the bureau had deteriorated considerably by 1894, when he was pushed out of a post at the Field Museum. In 1889 Boas turned down the bureau's offer of a position in charge of its editorial work to accept a docentship in the department of psychology at Clark University (where the first American Ph.D. degree in anthropology was awarded, to Alexander F. Chamberlain in 1892; see later in this chapter). The following year, Boas moved to Columbia University, and thereafter the focus of American anthropology and linguistic studies shifted from the BAE to Columbia. From 1896 to 1911, from his position of authority at Columbia University, Boas had renewed relations with the bureau. In 1901 he was appointed the bureau's honorary philologist, thus becoming its chief linguistic adviser, and he prepared and edited the *Handbook of North American Indian Languages* (volume 1 appeared in 1911, volume 2 in 1922), published by the bureau (Hinsley 1981). A number of Boas's students, who also came to make significant contributions to the study of American Indian languages, received field experience through work performed for the bureau.

93. Boas argued against Brinton (without naming him), demonstrating the amount of syntax present in American Indian languages, in contrast to Brinton's (1890[1885d]:336) assertion that there was "no syntax"; for example, Boas showed many conjunctions in Chinook—countering Brinton's (1890[1885b]:404) declaration that there were no conjunctions in Indian languages.

94. In his review of Uhlenbeck 1916, Sapir repeated the same charge he had aimed at Boas; he reported that Uhlenbeck's intent had not been "a strictly philological one" and characterized it as "ethno-psychologic speculation" (1990[1917b]:86).

95. Dixon received his Ph.D. from Harvard University in 1900, having written a dissertation on Maidu grammar (see Dixon 1911). He had joined the Jesup North Pacific expedition led by Boas in 1898, working in British Columbia and Alaska, and began work in California in 1899, continuing fieldwork there until

about 1907. The American Museum had sponsored Dixon's early research in northern California, and later Kroeber supported his work on Chimariko. He became curator of ethnology at Harvard's Peabody Museum in 1912 and professor of anthropology there in 1915; he continued in that capacity until his death. Kroeber's first native language was German, though he grew up in Manhattan; his family was comfortably situated. He entered Columbia University in 1892 at age sixteen and completed both a B.A. and an M.A. in English literature. Kroeber enrolled in Boas's first course on American Indian languages at Columbia; as he put it, "I came from humanistic literature, [and] entered anthropology by the gate of linguistics" (quoted in Hymes 1966[1961a]:403; see also Kroeber 1970:144). He received his Ph.D. in anthropology from Columbia in 1901 (his dissertation was entitled "Decorative Symbolism of the Arapaho"); he was Boas's first student there. In 1900 Kroeber accepted a position as curator at the San Francisco Academy of Sciences, and in 1901 he accepted an instructorship in the department and Museum of Anthropology that was to be created at the University of California, Berkeley; he continued to teach at the university until his retirement (T. Kroeber 1970).

96. Though even in this largely typological study they did propose some genetic groupings; see the discussion later in this chapter.

97. This brings to mind Greenberg's notebooks (which are located in the Stanford University library), on which he claims to have based his 1987 book. (See Poser 1992 for discussion of Greenberg's inconsistent use of the data in his notebooks.)

98. Sapir was not fond of the name "Penutian": "I don't like 'Penutian.' In view of Cost[anoan] *ama*, Yokuts *mai*, Maidu *mai-*, Coos *mä*, I would suggest 'Mai' as stock name. Bother -an! Mai stock would be good enough" (Sapir to Kroeber, April 21, 1915; in Golla 1984:186; also p. 202).

99. The methods of Dixon and Kroeber (1913a, 1913b, 1919) have frequently been criticized (see Campbell and Mithun 1979a:23–5, and discussion of Frachtenberg later in this chapter). They based their classification largely on superficial lexical comparisons, but they were also influenced by morphological, structural, and typological information, as well. As Shipley noted: "How did they [Dixon and Kroeber] arrive at this classification [Penutian]? It is critical to take note that they did *not* do so by means of the application of the comparative method. The criteria were, in part, typological. A list of diagnostic features was compiled: noun cases, no prefixes, 'Indo-Germanic' type verbs with mode, tense, number, person, etc. and 'vowel gradation.' . . . The other criterion was lexical similarity" (1980:437).

100. Antoine Meillet (1866–1939), famous French Indo-Europeanist, had an indirect impact on American Indian linguistic study in that his doubts concerning the applicability of the comparative method to unwritten and exotic languages prompted strong reaction from scholars of American Indian languages (see discussion later in this chapter). His general comparative and historical linguistic methods, however, were influential (see Chapter 7).

101. Quand, dans son article de *Anthropos,* VIII (1913), p. 389 et suiv., intitulé *The Determination of Linguistic Relationship,* un américaniste éminent, M. Kroeber, a protesté contre l'emploi des concordances générales de structure morphologique pour établir des parentés de langues, il a eu entièrement raison. Seulement il n'est pas licite de conclure de là que les parentés doivent s'établir par la considération du vocabulaire, non par celle de la morphologie; si juste qu'elle soit, la critique de M. Kroeber ne justifie pas le procédé de certains américanistes qui fondent sur de pures concordances de vocabulaire leurs affirmations relatives à la parenté de telles langues entre elles. Les concordances grammaticales prouvent, et elles seules prouvent rigoureusement, mais à condition qu'on se serve du détail matériel des formes et qu'on établisse que certaines formes grammaticales particulières employées dans les langues considérées remontent à une origine commune. Les concordances de vocabulaire ne prouvent jamais d'une manière absolue, parce qu'on ne peut jamais affirmer qu'elles ne s'expliquent pas par emprunts.

102. Sapir (1884–1939) was born in Lauenberg, Pomerania (Prussia)—an area that today is Lębork, Poland); Yiddish was his first language. His family moved to England when he was four years old; to Richmond, Virginia, in 1890; and then to New York City. He entered Columbia University in 1901, graduated in 1904, and received an M.A. in Germanics in 1905. He completed his Ph.D. degree at Columbia University in 1909, a student of Boas; his dissertation was entitled "The Takelma Language of Southwestern Oregon" (Darnell 1990).

103. Truman Michelson (1879–1938) received his Ph.D. from Harvard University in 1904 in Indo-European philology, and studied in Berlin and Leipzig (1904–1905). He joined the BAE in 1910 and worked almost exclusively on Algonquian (Golla 1984:113).

104. Pliny Earle Goddard (1869–1928), a former lay missionary among the Hupa, received a Ph.D. in 1904 in Indo-European at the University of California at Berkeley. He studied with Benjamin Ide Wheeler, president of that university and well-known Indo-European philologist. Goddard took a position with the American Museum in 1909, where he continued his work on Athabaskan throughout his career, main-

taining a conservative and proprietorial attitude about this language family (Golla 1984:28).

105. As William Bright has reminded me (personal communication), in the case of Algonquian-Ritwan it appears that Sapir came to correct conclusions on the basis of evidence that was itself not particularly good. It was later work by Haas (and others), with new data from Wiyot and Yurok, that actually demonstrated the validity of the Algonquian-Ritwan relationship (see Goddard 1986; Haas 1958a).

106. In fact, in a letter to Lowie (May 23, 1921), Sapir in effect admitted that his disagreements with Boas had led him to the opposite extreme to such an extent that perhaps he had underestimated borrowing (cited in Darnell 1969:340).

107. Shipley refers to Sapir's super-stocks as "PR" (not Lamb's "probable relationship, but rather "possible" or "proposed" relationship)—"the type of formulation based on inspection carried only to the point of developing a hunch or an educated guess." Shipley believes that "activities leading to PR theories are obviously indispensable" but sees the danger that "the trap is sprung when these PR theories are in any way, thoughtfully or thoughtlessly, allowed to stand as goals in research. . . . PR theories are heuristic devices; especially tragic are those instances where one PR serves as a basis for postulating another PR, and so on" (1966:497–8).

108. Klar is speaking specifically about Hokan, but her statement fits the overall classification efforts as well.

109. Another perspective on the reductionist frenzy is that it represented Sapir's (and Kroeber's) revolt against papa Boas. In his later years, Sapir had little to say about more remote genetic classification. He published almost nothing new on the topic after 1925 and devoted his efforts largely to descriptive and ethnolinguistic work (William Bright, personal communication).

110. Frachtenberg, born in Austria, came to the United States in 1904 and enrolled as a graduate student at Columbia University in 1905 to study anthropology under Boas. He received a Ph.D. in 1910 with his Coos grammar as his dissertation. He was dismissed from the BAE in 1917 because of the anti-German sentiments prevalent in the United States during World War I (Golla 1984:41; Darnell 1969:411).

111. Radin, who was of German-Jewish background, received a Ph.D. in anthropology from Columbia University under Boas in 1910; his dissertation was on Winnebago Midewin (medicine society). He lost his position at the BAE (as did Frachtenberg) because of the shift of Bureau interests, according to Darnell (1969:408, 411). He worked on Zapotec and Huave for a year in Mexico; took a research post with Sapir in

Ottawa; taught in California from 1917 to 1920; went to England; taught at Fiske University in Nashville; returned to Mexico; then returned to Europe. He was teaching at Brandeis University at the time of his death. His interests were broad, his charm well known, and his "fecklessness legendary" (Golla 1984:47).

112. Kroeber wrote to Gifford that "Radin is the same old boy. He . . . finds that Siouan is Athabaskan. For 17 years we've all fiddled with California and in two weeks on Wappo he unites half the continent. Wappo may be Siouan; but you can't make Siouan Athabascan and Hokan on a jaunt to Healdsburg. It's the same old story: he goes to sell a dozen eggs and brings home a lame horse. This trick will only make him ridiculous in the profession" (letter dated June 18, 1918; quoted in Darnell 1969:371).

113. The earliest known version of this classification appears in a letter Sapir wrote to Kroeber in October 1920 (see Sapir 1990b[1920]). The six stocks were named (though constituent languages were not presented) in an undated abstract, "The Problems of Linguistic Relationship in America" (Sapir 1990a[n.d.]), and a fuller discussion and map are found in "Lecture Notes" (Sapir 1990c[n.d.]).

114. In the letter to Kroeber (October 1920), Sapir wrote that this six-stock classification was "of course . . . *exceedingly tentative*" (emphasis added; 1990b[1920]:82). In the 1921 *Science* article, Sapir stated that "any genetic reconstruction [classification of all the American languages] that can be offered now is necessarily an *exceedingly rough approximation to the truth at best*" (emphasis added; 1921a:408; also 1990[1921a]:93).

115. I thank William Bright for this observation (personal communication).

116. I thank Prof. Osahito Miyaoka for pointing this passage out to me.

117. Bloomfield, born in Chicago, entered Harvard College in 1903. At age nineteen he went to the University of Wisconsin as a graduate student and with a position as an assistant in German. Two years later Bloomfield enrolled at the University of Chicago and received a Ph.D. in 1909; his dissertation was entitled "A Semasiologic Differentiation in Germanic Secondary Ablaut." In 1913 and 1914, he studied at the Universities of Leipzig and Göttingen. He held positions at several universities, most notably at the University of Chicago and at Yale University, and during the summer of 1925 was even an assistant ethnologist at the Canadian Department of Mines, where Sapir was in charge of anthropological and linguistic matters.

118. When Swanton was a graduate student at Harvard University, he went to Columbia to learn linguistics under Boas and accompanied Boas on the Jesup North Pacific expedition. He wrote his dissertation on the morphology of the Chinook verb and received Harvard's first Ph.D. in anthropology.

119. Harrington, a native of southern California, majored in German and classics as an undergraduate at Stanford University (from which he graduated in 1905). He turned down a Rhodes scholarship in order to study (mainly phonetics) at the Universities of Leipzig and Berlin in 1905 and 1906. Harrington was generally known as an eccentric—that is, for his "unsurpassed brilliance and total unreliability" (Darnell 1969:314). It was said that "his skill as a phonetician was unsurpassed, but he lacked scholarly discipline, published little, and had few friends in academic circles" (Golla 1984:73). He was called an "angry god, perfectionist, paranoid worrier, culture hero, obsessed genius, thorn-in-the-side, doggerel poet, ruthless slavedriver, inattentive father, valued friend, skinflint, ascetic, academic outcast, great phonetician, indefatigable field worker, outrageous, laughable and endearing eccentric" (Hinton 1994:195; see also Laird 1975).

120. Diese Sprachen zeigen grosse Verschiedenheiten im Laut, keine im innern Bau.

121. Sie haben mit jenen Nordamerika's den polysynthetischen Carakter gemein, und ihre Grammatik lässt sich wahrscheinlich auf wenige allgemein durchgreifende Regeln zurückführen.

122. Chamberlain's was one of the first post-Powell classifications of American Indian languages; the 1903 version listed 133 total stocks in the Americas; 56 belonged to North America and 51 to South America.

123. Rivet, born in Wasigny (Ardennes), received a Diplôme de Docteur en Médecine at the University of Lille in 1897. In 1901, serving as the medical doctor, he went on a geodesic measuring mission to the equator, where he collected much information on the anthropology and archaeology of the region. In 1908 Rivet was appointed assistant director of the Laboratoire d'Anthropologie du Muséum National de Paris, and in 1926 he was designated secretary-general of the Institut d'Ethnologie de l'Université de Paris and was made professor of anthropology in the institute's museum in 1928. For many years thereafter he was the secretary-general of the Musée de l'Homme. He was involved in the resistance movement in World War II, and as a result found it necessary to go into exile in Colombia in 1941, where he founded the Institute of Ethnology of Bogotá. He returned to his previous position in France in 1944. Rivet published many works on South American Indian languages and their classification and was an associate editor of the *International Journal of American Linguistics* from publication of its first issue in 1917 until his death.

124. Mason, a native of Philadelphia, received his

B.A. from the University of Pennsylvania in 1907 and began graduate work there in anthropology, where he studied with Sapir. After Sapir left for Ottawa, Mason transferred to Berkeley, where in 1911 he received the second Ph.D. awarded by Kroeber's department of anthropology at the University of California; his dissertation was on Salinan ethnology (1912). He became a curator at the Field Museum in 1917, shifting to the American Museum of Natural History in 1924; he returned to the University of Pennsylvania Museum in 1926 (Golla 1984:42).

125. The discussion in this section parallels that in Campbell 1994b.

126. Jones was part Fox, raised as a native speaker by his grandmother. A student of Boas, his Ph.D. dissertation was on Algonquian morphology (1904). The BAE hired him as an Algonquian specialist. He was killed in the Philippines in 1909 while doing fieldwork (Golla 1984:23).

127. Goddard (1994b) shows that Bloomfield's *çk cluster is more accurately reconstructed as *rk.

128. I thank Ives Goddard for pointing out these facts to me.

Chapter 3 The Origin of American Indian Languages

1. A number of the points in this chapter are based on the discussion in Goddard and Campbell (1994); see also Campbell (in press a).

2. The name Anianus apparently is traceable to a Chinese province that Marco Polo called Ania. The Zalterus map of 1566 was the first to show the Strait of Anian. It was apparently a nonexistent body of water, a mythical strait extending from the Pacific through North America to the Atlantic. This myth, which is part of Spanish exploration lore, was often associated with the search for the Northwest Passage (Morison 1971:497, 514).

3. Gilij argued persuasively against this account of the vast number of languages in the Americas, on the assumption that the Indians would not accept linguistic changes against their will—not even from the Devil himself—and that change took place outside their awareness, resulting in the large number of languages; nevertheless, he added, "no negaré sin embargo que en las lenguas indias no haya sido alguna palabra introducida por el demonio" [I won't deny, nevertheless, that some words may have been introduced to the Indian languages by the devil] (1965[1782]:227–8).

4. Des savans moins enthousiastes, Vater, en Europe, et Barton, en Amérique, le premier dans la vue de rechercher, le second de prouver l'origine asiatique des aborigènes du Nouveau Monde (M. Jefferson veut, au contraire, que ce soit l'Amérique qui ait peuplé l'Asie) ont essayé de comparer entre elles les diverses langues des deux continens, et leurs laborieuses recherches n'ont produit aucun fruit. Comment est-il possible en effect de trouver de nombreuses affinités entre toutes ces langues, tandis qu'on n'en trouve point entre deux langue voisines, l'iroquois et l'algonquin, quoiqu'elles se ressemblent presque entièrement quant à la structure, ainsi que je le prouve dans le mémoire suivant par un vocabulaire comparatif de ces deux langues, où sur 250 mots on en trouve à peine un ou deux qu'on puisse rapporter à la même origine. Que sera-ce donc si on compare le groenlandais avec le péruvien, le huron ou le sioux avec la langue du Chili? *Selon moi, cette recherche est un jeu d'enfans et ne peut conduire à aucun résultat utile dans le but qu'on s'est jusqu'ici proposé avec des vues moins étendues.*

5. The notion of a single race of American Indians is by no means new or dependent on linguistic notions. The Spanish explorer Ulloa is reported to have said, "Visto un indio, de cualquier parte que sea, se han visto todos" [If you have seen an Indian from anywhere, you have seen them all] (quoted by Ibarra Grasso 1958:19).

6. Those interested in the historical record may wish to know that the origin of the "lumper-splitter" appellations in the context of Native American linguistic studies is unclear. I had always believed that I was the first to employ the terms "lumping" and "splitting" in this context, in the grant proposal submitted to the National Science Foundation, which many scholars saw, which provided the support for the conference that resulted in the book edited by Campbell and Mithun (1979a). However, Catherine Callaghan's recollection (personal communication) is that she was the first to use these terms in American Indian linguistics, having originally encountered them in a mystery novel. Margaret Langdon's recollection (personal communication) is that Mary Haas had used the terms previously. Therefore, the coiner of these terms, who should receive the dubious honor attendant thereto, remains uncertain.

7. Initially, following Sapir, I had intended to rename the lumper approach as the "intuitive" approach (what I call here the "inspectional" approach), intending it to be a neutral term. However, some think "intuitive" suggests lack of rigor or absence of scholarly standards, so I opted for "inspectional," hoping to avoid negative connotations.

8. In a letter to Boas in 1917, Michelson, a member of the conservative camp, said that he agreed with Sapir's characterization of Sapir's approach, though casting it in less favorable terms: "[Sapir has] fallen

victim to the deplorable tendency to consolidate linguistic stocks without adequate proof" (cited in Darnell 1990:116).

9. James Matisoff (1990) contrasts three main types of language classification: micro-, macro-, and megalocomparison; he considers Greenberg to be a major representative of the last type.

10. "Another [problem of Amerindian comparative linguistics] is the great linguistic diversity: there are probably far more than 1000 distinct Amerindian languages, and, if classified into groups comparable to the Germanic or Slavic, there would probably be 200 or more" (Swadesh 1954b:306; see also Bright 1974a:208, 209; Haas 1969a:99; Migliazza and Campbell 1988:15; Mason 1950:164; Pinnow 1964a:2; Sapir and Swadesh 1946:103).

11. In spite of recent advances, much remains unknown concerning South American language classification. Terrence Kaufman (1990a) lists 118 distinct groups as the smallest number of genetic units (families and isolates) that have definitely been demonstrated; the number is 98 when those he deems plausibly related are taken into account, though some of the groupings have not yet been demonstrated (see Chapter 6). He believes, however, that work based on reliable methods will probably reduce the total to approximately 80 distinct groupings, but probably not significantly fewer (personal communication; cf. Kaufman 1994). The ten genetic units of Middle America exclude those of North America and South America which lap over. Were these also counted, the total for Middle America would be fifteen genetic units.

12. Foster (1990) argues that Sapir's proposals concerning established families have had more influence in nonlinguistic aspects of American prehistory than his proposals for more remote families. This is true, but Sapir's broader claims also had considerable influence. For instance, Moratto (1984) made archaeological correlations with Hokan and Penutian correlations throughout the sequence of California prehistory. (For other examples and additional discussion of Sapir's influence, see Borhegyi 1965, Bray 1986, Hymes 1959, Swadesh 1961, and Williams et al. 1985.)

13. Sapir mentioned three groupings on several occasions, although his view of what the three were, and how they might be interrelated, varied somewhat from one occasion to the next. In the 1921 version of his six-stock classification scheme for North American Indian languages, Sapir mentioned the possibility of further reduction to just three (see Darnell 1990:123). In his 1920 paper, he had listed the three, though the constituents were slightly different from those of the three groupings implied in his 1916 work

(Golla 1984:452). In a letter to Kroeber in 1920, Sapir outlined his six super-stocks, but he made reference to only two migrations: "I do not feel that Na-dene belongs to the other American languages. I feel it as a great intrusive band that has perhaps ruptured an old Eskimo-Wakashan-Algonkin continuity. . . . I am seriously entertaining the notion of an old Indo-Chinese offshoot [Na-Dene] into N.W. America. . . . At least I know that Déné's a long shot nearer to Tibetan than to Siouan" (Sapir 1990b[1920]:83).

14. Perhaps by "grouping all" Sapir meant here a broad classification of the many genetic units rather than the assumption that all were genetically related. Still, on other occasions he came close to grouping most of them; for example, he wrote to Speck (October 9, 1920): "I feel now that all the linguistic groups in America from the Maya and Aztec north and including the Eskimo may be classified into six large divisions, each of which I feel to be a genetic unity. Even those six may not prove to be entirely unrelated. The most extensive is the one I tentatively know as Hokan-Siouan" (quoted in Darnell 1969:353).

15. William Bright points out (personal communication) that the notorious "pan-Americanisms" (see Chapter 7) might be explained plausibly by just such a hypothesis (perhaps coupled with recognition of the existence of "mixed languages," such as those mentioned in the appendix to Chapter 1).

16. To say there are no demonstrated cases of linguistic relationships between New World and Old World languages is not, however, to say that none has been postulated. In the history of American Indian linguistic study, several have been proposed, though the evidence for them is not convincing. They include Eskimo-Aleut and Finno-Ugric or Uralic (Bonnerjea 1975, 1978; Sauvageot 1924, 1953; Thalbitzer 1928; Bergsland 1959; Hamp 1976); Eskimo-Aleut and Indo-European (Thalbitzer 1945, 1952; Hammerich 1951); Eskimo-Aleut and Chukoto-Kamchatkan (or Luoravetlan) (Hamp 1976:81–92, Swadesh 1962); Na-Dene and Sino-Tibetan (Hymes 1959:53; Sapir 1925b; Shafer 1952, 1957; Swadesh 1952); and Hokan and Austronesian (Rivet 1926). (For discussion of such proposals, see Milewski 1960; Swadesh 1960a, 1960c; and Pinnow 1964a:29–30; see also Chapter 8.) Some linguists, moreover, currently believe in genetic relationships that span the Bering Strait. Several of them, moreover, do not stop with connecting some New World language groups with some Old World language groups but argue for more far-reaching connections between New World and Old World groups. For example, Greenberg would include Eskimo-Aleut in his proposed Eurasiatic family, with Amerind as a more distant relative, and would combine Na-Dene with Sino-Tibetan (1987:331–7); Ruh-

len goes further and combines Na-Dene with Sino-Tibetan, Basque, Nahali, Yeniseian, and North Caucasian in a vast phylum called Dene-Caucasian (1994b:3, 24–29, 70–92, 213–15; see Chapter 8). Several linguists even believe in the existence of something like Proto-World or Proto-Sapiens and argue that language groups throughout the world are related (see, for example, Bengtson and Ruhlen 1994; Greenberg 1987:62; Swadesh 1960c, 1960e; Ruhlen 1994b; Shevoroshkin 1989b).

17. For early claims involving the lost tribes of Israel, see Roger Williams 1643 and John Adair 1775. See Grotius 1552 for an early view involving Scandinavians. On such claims in general, see Goddard and Fitzhugh 1979; see also Alcina Franch 1985; Bieder 1986:10–11, 188–9; Huddleston 1967; Pinnow 1964a:29–31; and Rivet 1925a, 1925b, 1926, and 1957. A Viking presence has been documented at the archaeological site of L'Anse aux Meadows in Newfoundland, though there is no evidence of a significant Viking linguistic contribution to languages in the Americas.

18. Similar sentiments have been expressed with regard to archaeology by Dillehay and Meltzer: "We must learn to deal with ambiguity. . . . Some early records may never be clear, since not every human activity leaves a crisp and clean signature in the archaeological record, and nature does not cooperate to ensure full preservation and later accessibility and discovery. Even so, this is decidedly *not* a plea for relaxed standards of proof for earlier sites" (1991:292).

19. Greenberg asserted that "at the Boulder Conference [see Taylor, in press], the correlation [of Greenberg's classification] with the dental evidence held up completely" (1990a:11–12). Yet many of the serious reservations recounted in this section were also raised at the conference (as reported, for example, by Morell 1990:440–41). Since the dentition correlation is pivotal to the argument, the challenges expressed at the Boulder Conference reflect badly on the claimed mutual support and on the classification in general.

20. As for other attempts to correlate human genetic and linguistic histories on a global scale, which would also include Native Americans (Cavalli-Sforza et al. 1988, 1989), the interpretations are so flawed, both methodologically and substantively, that they command no serious attention. They certainly contribute no insight with regard to migrations to the New World, but rather those making the claims uncritically accept and utilize the three groups proposed by Greenberg in formulating their broad schemes. For criticism, see Bateman et al. (1990a, 1990b), Blount

(1990), Callaghan (1990a), Nichols (1990b), and Oswalt (1990).

21. Greenberg had said specifically of this proposed correlation: "When you find a convergence of results from linguistics, archaeology, and physical anthropology, you can't say that it doesn't strengthen the case for my classification: I think it does strengthen the case" (Newman 1991:457).

Chapter 4   Languages of North America

1. For numbers of speakers, I have relied on Kinkade (1991a) for Canadian languages and Dale Kinkade (personal communication) for languages of the Northwest Coast linguistic area. Figures for California languages are based on Hinton's (1994:27) conservative estimates, with additions from Victor Golla (personal communication). See also Chafe 1962 and Foster 1982.

2. The name *Eskimo* is often erroneously assumed to have come from an Algonquian language with a meaning of something like 'raw eaters'. However, early European attestations seem to indicate a Montagnais (Algonquian) source of *a·y-ask^{y}ime·w*, connected to the meaning 'snowshoe-netter' (Goddard 1984:6). The earliest uses of the name apparently refer to other Algonquian groups, notably Micmac, rather than to Eskimoan speakers (Ives Goddard, personal communication).

3. *Yupik* is from the Central Alaskan Yupik *yúppik* 'real, genuine person' (Goddard 1984:7).

4. *Inuit* is the self-designation, from *inuk* 'person, people'; *inuit* is the plural. *Inupiaq* is from *in^{y}upiaq* 'real, genuine person' (Goddard 1984:7). The name *Inuktitut* is widely used in Eastern Canada for this language.

5. For example, Swanton said that the "Ugalakmiut, or Ugalentz," of Kayak Island and the neighboring mainland "were formerly Eskimo and have now become thoroughly Tlingitized" (1911b:159).

6. The name *Eyak* is apparently derived from the Eyak's name for themselves (they called themselves "inhabitants of Eyak") and from the name of the Eyak village, *í·iyaq* (*ʔi·ya·G*), a borrowing from Chugach Eskimo *iɣa·q* 'outlet of a lake'. In the earlier literature, Eyak was often called *Ugalach(mute), Ugalents,* or something approximating this, known through the Russian name *Ugalyakhmyut,* itself from Chugach Eskimo *uŋala·ɣmiut* 'people of the southeast' (Birket-Smith and De Laguna 1938:338, De Laguna 1990a:196).

7. Four possible spellings of Athabaskan appear in the linguistic and anthropological literature: Atha-

paskan, Athapascan, Athabascan, and Athabaskan. I have opted for Athabaskan, both because it appears to be the currently most preferred spelling among specialists and among the Alaskan Native Americans themselves who represent these linguistic groups, and because it corresponds more closely to the dominant pronunciation of the name.

8. *Ahtna* comes through Russian from Ahtna *ʔ atnaʔ* meaning 'lower Copper River' (Goddard 1981:661–2).

9. *Tanaina* comes from the Tanaina self-designation, *dənaʔina* 'the people' (Goddard 1981: 638).

10. The name *Ingalik* comes through Russian to English, originally borrowed from Yupik Eskimo *iŋqiliq* 'Indian', literally meaning 'having many nits', in reference to the Athabaskans' "uncut hair style" (Goddard 1981:613).

11. The name *Koyukan* is related to the Inupiaq word *kuiyuk* 'river that flows', but the name is a created one, intended to suggest the names of the Koyukuk and Yukon Rivers (Goddard 1981:599).

12. *Han* is derived from the Kutchin name *han-g^{w}ič'in* 'people of the river' (*g^{w}ič'in* 'people') (Goddard 1981:512).

13. *Kutchin* is derived from the Kutchin word *g^{w}ič'in* 'people of, dwellers of'. The name *Loucheux* is a common name for the Eastern Kutchin in Canada; it is derived from French *loucheux* 'squinters', a translation of the Chipewyan name for the Kutchin, which means 'squint-eyed' (Goddard and Slobodin 1981:530).

14. The name *Tahltan* is from Tlingit *ta·ɬta·n,* "the name of a low flat at the mouth of the Tahltan River that was in important trading ground" (Goddard 1981:465).

15. The name *Chipewyan* came into English through Cree, apparently from *či·pwaya·n* '(those who have) pointed skins or hides', thought to be in reference to "their manner of cutting their hunting shirts or preparing beaver pelts, which the Cree ridiculed" (Goddard and Smith 1981:283).

16. It is assumed that *Slavey* (also *Slave,* from *Slavé*) results from placing the French ending *ais* (as in *anglais, français*) on the English word "slave" (Asch and Goddard 1981:347). The name is thought to be a translation of Cree *awahka·n* 'captive, slave', sometimes 'stranger'. It is reported that the Cree applied "slave" pejoratively to groups of Athabaskans they had driven out of the Lake Athabasca area in late precontact times (Asch and Goddard 1981:347–8). The name *Hare* is derived from these Indians' dependence on the hare for food and clothing.

17. The name *Dogrib* is presumed to come through Cree, who called these people the equivalent of 'dog side', possibly reflecting the widespread Northern Athabaskan creation story in which a woman mates with a dog (Helm 1981:303–4).

18. English *Carrier* is a translation of French *porteur,* which is itself from the translation of a Sekani form meaning 'carrier', apparently traceable to the custom of Carrier widows carrying the cremated remains of their husbands on their backs (Goddard 1981:430).

19. *Chilcotin* is from the Chilcotin name for themselves, given in phonemic orthography as *činɬqut'in* (phonetically [çə̣i̱ɬqot'in]) (Goddard 1981:412).

20. Nicola is attested only in very limited material of poor quality; it is sufficient to demonstrate clearly that Nicola is an Athabaskan language, but it is not adequate enough to determine its position in Athabaskan subgrouping. Nicola is often thought to be a branch of Chilcotin (Krauss 1973b:919, Kinkade et al. in press). The Nicola are named for their principal area of residence, the Upper Nicola Valley in British Columbia.

21. The names *Kwalhioqua* and *Clatskanie (Tlatskanai)* are from the names of these groups in Chinook, *tk^{w}lxiug^{w}áiks* and *iɬáck'ani,* respectively; the latter means literally 'those of the region of small oaks' (Krauss 1990:532).

22. *Tututni* reflects the self-designation, *dotodəni* (*doto* 'a village place-name' + *-dəni* 'people'). The Chasta Costa called themselves *šista q'^{w}ə́sta* (Miller and Seaburg 1990:586).

23. The name *Chilula* is related to Yurok *c'ulu-la* 'Redwood Creek people' (*-la* is the suffix or enclitic meaning 'people of') (Victor Golla, personal communication).

24. *Wailaki* is from a Wintu word meaning 'north language' (Hinton 1994:158).

25. *Navajo* comes via Spanish *Navajó,* which in the seventeenth century was the name of the territory in northwestern New Mexico inhabited by Navajos. There are early references to *Apaches de Nabajú* and *Apaches de Nauajó,* the last word said to mean 'large planted fields'. (Apaches and Navajos were not distinguished in the earliest sources.) The Spanish name *Navajó* appears to be a borrowing from Tewa *navahu·,* made up of *nava* 'field' and *hu·* 'wide arroyo, valley', denoting a large arroyo in which there are cultivated fields (Brugge, Goddard, and De Reuse 1983:496).

26. The name *Apache* comes through Spanish *Apache,* usually assumed to be from Zuni *ʔa·paču* 'Navajos' (De Reuse 1983:385).

27. *Tlingit* is a self-designation, from *ɬi·ngít,* meaning 'human being, person, Indian'. Powell

(1891b) called Tlingit *Koluschan*. The earlier name *Kolusch* (and varieties thereof) is said to come from Aleut *kalu·* 'wooden dish' in a form with the Russianized diminutive, *kalushka,* thought to refer to the wooden labrets worn by Tlingit women (De Laguna 1990b:226, Pinnow 1976:4).

28. The name *Haida* comes from the Northern Haida self-designation, Masset *hà·, ʰà·de·,* Alaskan *ha·dé·, hà·dá·y* 'the people'. This is a nominalization of the verb *hà·ta·, hà·da·* 'to be human, to be Haida' (Masset) (cf. Skidegate *Xà·ydəGa·,* the noun, and *Xà·ydəGa·y,* the verb) (Blackman 1990:258).

29. The name *Tsimshian* comes from *c'msyan* 'inside the Skeena River', the self-designation used by Coast Tsimshian and Southern Tsimshian speakers. Powell's (1891a) name for the group was *Chimmesyan,* a variant spelling. *Gitksan* is from the Gitksan speakers' name for themselves, *kitxsan* 'people of the Skeena River'. *Nishga* is from *nisqáʔa,* another self-designation, though with no clear etymology (Halpin and Seguin 1990:282).

30. The name *Wakashan* is thought to be from the Nootka word *wa·ka·š* 'bravo, good', which Captain James Cook heard at Nootka Sound and supposed to be the name of the local people. Gallatin used it for the name of the family, a practice that Powell followed (see Arima and Dewhirst 1990:410).

31. *Heiltsuk* is from *híldzaqʷ,* whose meaning is unclear. The name *Bella Bella* has an interesting history; it is from Heiltsuk *pálbálá,* a term referring to the site of Fort McLoughlin and the native village that developed around it (said to be based on a Heiltsuk pronunciation of *Milbanke*) that was then borrowed back into English as the name of the people (Hilton 1990:321).

32. Oowekyala (Oowekeeno) and Heiltsuk (with Bella Bella and Haihai) may be distinct languages (Hilton 1990:312).

33. The name *Haisla* is from *Xàʔisəla* '(those) living at the river mouth, (those) living downriver'. *Kitamat* is from Coast Tsimshian *kitama·t* 'people of the falling snow' (Hamori-Torok 1990:310).

34. *Nootka* is the name Captain James Cook gave to Nootka Sound, which came to be used to refer to the people of the area as well. Cook thought this was the native name; it is said to reflect perhaps Cook's misunderstanding of the verb *nu·tka·* 'circling around'. The name *Nuuchahnulth* is a recent creation for the Nootkan tribes, from *nuča·ṅuɬ* 'all along the mountains', referring to the mountains of Vancouver Island, which are common to all the Nootkan tribes (Arima and Dewhirst 1990:410).

35. *Makah* is based on Clallam *màg'áʔa,* the name of the Makah tribe (Renker and Gunther 1990:429). This explains why Makah, a language

which lacks primary nasals, can bear a name with a nasal in it.

36. The name *Quileute* comes from *kʷoʔlí·yot',* the name for the village at La push. *Chemakum* is the English version of a Salishan name for these people, variants of which are known from several Salishan languages, such as Twana *čə́bqəb* (note that Twana has no nasals) (Powell 1990b:437, Elmendorf 1990:440).

37. Comox is moribund, spoken on Vancouver Island; Sliammon is the mainland dialect, which still has a few hundred speakers (Dale Kinkade, personal communication). The name *Comox* is from Kwakiutl *q'ʷúmuxʷs,* based on *q'wm-* 'rich', applied to the Comox harbor area and later to the people who settled there. *Sliammon* comes from Comox *ɬáʔamin* (Kennedy and Bouchard 1990:450–51).

38. The name *Pentlatch* is from Sechelt and Comox *pə́ntl'əč* (Kennedy and Bouchard 1990:451).

39. *Sechelt* (sometimes spelled *Seshelt*) is from Comox *šíšáɬ,* for the part of a Seshelt reserve facing Trail Bay on Sechelt Peninsula (Kennedy and Bouchard 1990:452).

40. The name *Squamish* is from *sqXʷúʔmiš* and contains the suffix *-miš* 'people'; the root has no other identification (Suttles 1990:473).

41. *Halkomelem* is from *həlq'əmíyləm,* the Upriver Halkomelem version of the name of the language (Suttles 1990:473).

42. *Nooksack* is from *(nə)xʷséʔeq* 'place of bracken roots', the name of a village and prairie at the mouth of Anderson Creek (Suttles 1990:474).

43. *Lummi* is from *xʷlə́məẏ* or *xʷlə́miʔ,* said to be from *xʷláləməs* 'facing each other', the name of a large L-shaped house at Gooseberry Point (Suttles 1990:474).

44. The name *Clallam* "is probably from the Northern Straits or Halkomelem form *xʷstl'él'əm*" (Suttles 1990:474).

45. *Lushootseed* is from *dxʷ-lə́š-úcid* (composed of *ləš* 'Puget Sound region', flanked by *dxʷ- -úcid* 'language' (Suttles and Lane 1990:501).

46. The name *Twana* is from the self-designation, *tuwáduxq* (Twana now lacks nasals) (Suttles and Lane 1990:501).

47. The name *Quinault* comes from *kʷínayɬ,* the name of the largest Quinault village, near what is now Tahola (Hajda 1990:516).

48. *Chehalis* is from Lower Chehalis *c'Xíl'əs,* literally 'sand', the name of their principal village, at the site of Westport on Grays Harbor (Hajda 1990:516).

49. *Cowlitz* comes from *káwlic* 'Cowlitz River' and *kálicq* 'language/people of Cowlitz River' (Hajda 1990:516).

50. The claim that Salishan languages have no contrast between nouns and verbs is frequently asserted by some Salishanists and some syntacticians, though it is also disputed by others. It is clear, in any case, that the contrast, if it exists at all, is far less significant than in most other languages and that most lexical words can be used predicatively (in verblike function) or can be adapted for use as subjects, objects, and instruments.

51. *Kutenai* is the spelling preferred by linguists; *Kootenay* is the official Canadian spelling (Dale Kinkade, personal communication). Kutenai was the single member of Powell's (1891a) *Kitunahan* family.

52. For example, Chamberlain entertained the possiblity of a relationship with Uto-Aztecan. Radin (1919) first suggested the Kutenai-Algonquian connection, which some scholars have found plausible (see Haas 1960, Gursky 1966a:412–13).

53. The name *Chinook* began as the Lower Chehalis name *ts'inúk,* for the inhabitants of and a village on Baker Bay; it was applied later to all linguistically related people of the area (Silverstein 1990:544).

54. The name *Cathlamet* is from *gaɬámat,* referring to the people of the village at Cathlamet Head; *Clackamas* is from *gi(t)ɬáq'imaš* 'those of Clackamas River' (Silverstein 1990:544).

55. The name *Alsea* is from a name for the Alsea, seen as *alsí(·)* in Coosan and Marys River Kalapuyan and as *alsí·ya* in Tillamook. *Yaquina* is from *yaqú·na/yuqú·na,* the Alsea name for the Yaquina Bay and Yaquina River region (Zenk 1990a:570).

56. Upper Umpqua is an Athabaskan language and should not be confused with Siuslaw's Lower Umpqua. The name *Siuslaw* is from Siuslaw *šaʔyú·š-tl'a·,* the name of the Siuslaw River region (Zenk 1990c:578).

57. The origin of the name *Coos* is not clear, though in English it reflects the name of Coos Bay. It is said to be related to a form in Hanis meaning 'south' (e.g., *gusimídži·č* 'southward'), though a southwestern Oregon Athabaskan form *ku·s* 'bay' has also been mentioned. *Hanis* is from *há·nis,* the Hanis name for themselves; *Miluk* is the Miluk self-designation, *míluk,* related to a village name (Zenk 1990c:578–9).

58. *Takelma* is derived from *ta·kelmà·ʔn* 'person/people from Rogue River', from *ta·kelám* 'Rogue River' (*ta-* 'along, beside' + *kelám* 'river') (Kendall 1990:592).

59. The name *Kalapuya* comes from Chinookan (for example, Upriver Kiksht *igalapúyuiyukš,* Clackmas *itk'alapúyawaykš*), of unknown origin (Zenk 1990b:552).

60. *Nez Perce* is from French 'pierced nose'; some older Nez Perce remember the term of self-designation, *cú·pn̓itpel'u·* 'with a pointed object-pierce-people', which reflects their custom of piercing the nasal septum, presumably also the source of the French name (Kinkade et al. in press).

61. *Sahaptin* comes from a name for the Nez Perce Indians found in several Interior Salishan languages, compare Columbian *sḥáptənəxʷ* (Kinkade et al. in press).

62. The name *Klamath* is from Upper Chinookan *ɬamaɬ* 'their lake' (Kinkade et al. in press).

63. The Cayuse were called *wáylatpam* by the Sahaptins (*weyí·letpu* by the Nez Perce), and this is presumably the origin of the name of Hale's (1846) Waiilatpu family, which is the source of Powell's (1891a) Waiilatpuan stock name (for the family that was assumed to connect Cayuse and Molala; see Chapters 2 and 8, and the discussion later in this chapter).

64. *Karuk* (*Karok*) is from the Karok term *káruk* meaning 'upriver' (see Hinton 1994:157).

65. The name *Chimariko* comes from the Chimariko self-designation, *č'imarík'o* (based on *č'imar, č'imal* 'person') (Silver 1978a:210).

66. The name *Achomawi/Achumawi* is derived from their self-designation, *ajuma·wi* 'river people'; *Atsugewi* comes from *atsuke,* the native name for a place on Hat Creek in the middle of Atsuge territory (Garth 1978:243).

67. The names *Yana* and *Yahi* are native words meaning 'people' (*ya·na* and *ya·xi,* respectively).

68. The name *Pomo* appears to derive from a confusion of two different Northern Pomo forms, *pʰo:mo:* (*pʰo:* 'magnesite, red earth or clay' + *mo* 'hole' [with final vowel length it means 'at']), and *pʰoʔmaʔ* (*pʰó-* 'reside, live in a group'), which together mean something like 'those who live at red earth hole' (McLendon and Oswalt 1978:277).

69. The name is from the Washo word *wašiw* meaning approximately 'people from here' (Hinton 1994:158).

70. The name *Esselen* "is probably derived from the name of a major village, perhaps Exse'ein or the place called Eslenes, which was the site of the San Carlos mission" (Hester 1978a:499).

71. J. P. Harrington reportedly once thought Esselen to be Penutian (see Webb 1980:72), but this association has essentially been forgotten since Sapir (1917a) put Esselen in Hokan.

72. Records from both missions also refer to *playanos* ('beach people'), who may constitute a third group, but nothing is known of them (Hester 1978b:500).

73. The river name itself is from Spanish *salinas* 'salt source, salt flats'.

74. "The name Chumash was arbitrarily chosen

by Powell [1891a] from the word used by Coastal Chumash for Santa Cruz Island and its inhabitants, Mi-tcú-mac [*mičúmaš*], or Tcú-mac [*čúmaš*]. Each regional group had its own name for itself" (Grant 1978:507).

75. *Walapai/Hualapai* in English apparently reflects the Mojave *huwa·lʸapay* 'pine person'; the Walapai term is *hwa·la?pay* 'ponderosa pine people', originally the name of a single band that lived west of the Hualapai Mountains (McGuire and Goddard 1983:36). The name *Havasupai* is connected with the Havasupai self-designation, *havasúwə ?əpá* 'person/ people of the blue/green water', where *ha-* represents *?əha* 'water' and *vasúwə* 'blue/green color'. The name in English is probably from one of the related Yuman languages which have -*pai* (*pay*) 'person'; several of these languages have similar designations for Havasupai (Goddard 1983:23).

76. *Mojave* reflects *hàmakhá·v*, the Mojave name for themselves; the shortened form *makhá·v* is also used (Goddard 1983:69). *Quechan* is from *kʷacá·n*, the Quechan name for themselves, meaning literally 'those who descended', thought to refer to their traditional belief concerning their creation on a sacred mountain (Goddard 1983:97).

77. *Ipai* (*i·pay*) and *Tipai* (*ti·pay*) reflect cognate native terms, both meaning 'people, person, Indian'.

78. The name *Nomlaki* reflects the River Nomlaki name *nomlaka* 'west language', referring to the Hill Nomlaki on Thomes (Toomes) Creek (cf. *nom-* 'west') (Goldschmidt 1978:347).

79. *Nisenan* is from the self-designation, *nisena·n* 'from along us, of our side' (Wilson and Towne 1978:397).

80. *Miwok* is from Central Sierra Miwok *míw·ɨ·k* 'people, Indians'; compare Proto-Miwokan **miw·ɨ* (Callaghan 1988a).

81. *Costanoan* is derived somehow from Spanish *costeños* or *costanero*, terms for people living on the coast; there is, however, no Spanish *costaño* or *costano*, in spite of the fact that, in anthropological publications, such a form is often assumed to be the source of the English name.

82. "The word Yokuts is an English rendering of the general term for '(Indian) person' or 'people' in the westerly, or Valley dialects. The stem appears in Yawelmani, the best recorded dialect, as *yokʰoc*'" (Silverstein 1978:446).

83. *Nim-Yokuts* is Whistler and Golla's term for General Yokuts exclusive of Buena Vista; the term is based on *nim*, the first person possessive pronominal base in all these languages, but Whistler and Golla also intend it as a mnemonic device, "since Nim-Yokuts is also equivalent to the 'Newman-Yokuts'

covered in Newman's [1944] comparative grammar of Yokuts" (1986:321).

84. The bd-Yokuts dialects exhibit the sound change of **m* > *b*, **n* > *d*, hence their name.

85. "The name *Huchnom,* given to this group by the Yuki of Round Valley, means 'tribe outside (the valley)'" (Miller 1978:254).

86. According to tradition, the name is from the Spanish *guapo* 'brave' (also 'harsh, severe, daring', as well as 'handsome, showy'), which appropriately describes their resistance to the military adjuncts of the Franciscan missions.

87. Troike (1988:238) demonstrates that the four forms repeatedly identified as Suma-Jumano are actually from Amotomanco (once spoken along the Rio Grande) and argues that at least two of them ('corn', 'beans') are borrowed from Nahua, whereas the 'copper' term (*porba, payla*) is not comparable to anything known elsewhere, leaving *abad* 'water' (compare Proto-Uto-Aztecan **pa:*) as the only plausible cognate. Thus the question of Amotomanco's genetic affinity is open.

88. Miller says that "most commentators since Kroeber [1934] have assumed a Uto-Aztecan connection for Concho, but I do not think the evidence allows us to say more than maybe" (1983a:332; see also Troike 1988).

89. The name *Tübatulabal* 'pine-nut eaters' was applied to the Pahkanapil and Palagewan bands of Tübatulabal by their neighbors (Yokuts and Kawaiisu) and by themselves (Smith 1978:437).

90. The name *Hopi* is from *hópi,* the Hopi name for themselves; it also means 'good in every respect' in the Third Mesa dialect (comparable to *hóʰpi* 'is good, peaceful' and *hópi* 'is wise, knowing' in the Mishongnovi dialect). The older term Moki/Moqui is from the self-designation, *mó·kʷi,* but from Spanish spelling ⟨moqui⟩ this came to be Moki in English, a term that has been eliminated from official U.S. government usage because it resembles Hopi *móki* 'dies, is dead' (Schroeder and Goddard 1979:550–51).

91. "The Pima appear to have been named by the Spanish after their word for 'nothing', which was pimahaitu in the eighteenth century" (compare *Cahita* or Yaqui-Mayo, from *kaita* [*kaa hita*] 'nothing'). *Papago* is apparently derived from a form meaning 'bean Pimas', seen more clearly in an earlier Spanish version of the name *papabotas,* glossed 'pimas frijoleros' ('bean Pimas'); compare *bá·bawi-?ó?odham* 'bean Piman(s)' (*báwi* 'tepary bean') (Goddard 1983:134). O'odham, the preferred self-designation today, reflects this derivation.

92. *Cahita* is assumed to be from *kaita* [*kaa hita*] 'nothing', so named by the Spanish. Compare *Pima,*

said to be from *pimahaitu* 'nothing' in the eighteenth century (Goddard 1983:134).

93. *Pipil* is from Nahua *-pil* 'son, boy'; compare Pipil *pi·pil* 'boy'.

94. The name *Nahuatl* is from the Nahuatl root *na·wa-*, which enters in compounds and derivations with meanings 'divination, sorcery' and 'agreeable sound', 'understandable'.

95. Miller finds the evidence so "skimpy" for Suma and Jumano that "we cannot even say that the evidence is suggestive [of a Uto-Aztecan affinity]" (1983a:332), and Troike demonstrates that the four words (the only extant data except for proper names) usually identified as Suma-Jumano are actually from Amotomanco, leaving no basis for determining the genetic affinity of Suma-Jumano.

96. Sauer reported that the "Xamaca, by another name called Hueitzolme [Huichol], all . . . speak the Thequalme language, though they differ in some vowels" (1934:14).

97. The name *Al(l)iklik* is apparently based on the Purisimeño form *alik* 'northwest' (Beeler and Klar 1977:303).

98. Sydney Lamb held that, although Brinton was correct in relating Aztecan and Ute-Shoshonean, his evidence was not sufficiently convincing; therefore, "since Powell's work was on the whole more careful than Brinton's those who consulted only Powell and Brinton could hardly be blamed if they rejected the Uto-Aztecan stock" (1964a:120). In fairness to Brinton, however, it should be recalled that Powell published no evidence at all for his classifications.

99. The name *Keresan* was given by Powell (1891a); it is based on *Keres,* from *Queres,* the Spanish name for the same group. The etymology of the name is not known.

100. *Tanoan* comes from *Tañoan,* Powell's name for the family. The name *Tano* (Spanish *Taño*) appears to derive from Tewa *thanuge'in t'owa* 'southern people' (Kroskrity 1993:59). *Taño* had been a name for Southern Tiwa; the spellings *Tahano* and *Tagno* also occurred. The Rio Grande Tewa were called *Tano* in Spanish, with the form *táno* recorded (probably for *tʰáno*)—the Hopi-Tewa (or Arizona Tewa, the Tewa at Hano, living among the Hopi) call themselves *tʰá·nu té·wa* (borrowed as *há·no* in Third Mesa Hopi, hence the name '*Hano*') (see Goddard 1979c:234–5, 601).

101. *Taos* comes from a Spanish adaptation of Taos *tɔ̂otho* 'in the village', with the *-s* originally from Spanish *-s* 'plural' (Goddard 1979c:267).

102. *Tewa* is probably an anglicization of Spanish *Tegua,* from the Tewa self-designation, *téwa.* *Tiwa* was intended to replace Spanish *Tigua,* used primarily to designate the Southern Tiwa (Goddard 1979c:235).

103. *Towa* is based on what Harrington (1909:594) thought was Jemez (and Pecos) *tôwa* 'home'. Actually, the form is *tí·wa* 'at Jemez Pueblo [to the north]' (Goddard 1979c:235).

104. Alfredo Trombetti (1929–1937:922) claimed to have discovered the relationship between Kiowa and Tanoan independently. In the same encyclopedia article, he also claimed to have discovered, independently, the Ritwan-Algonquian connection.

105. The name *Zuni,* from the Spanish form *Zuñi* (which is also its earlier form in English), is from the Keresan name as exemplified by Acoma *sɨ́·ni* 'Zuni Indian(s), Zuni Pueblo', and Santa Ana *sɨ́·ni* 'Zuni Indian'. In Zuni, Zunis call themselves *šiwi* and call the Zuni Pueblo *šiwin?a* 'Zuni place' (Goddard 1979c:479–80). The latter form is somewhat similar phonetically to the Keresan names and invites speculation that they are connected in some way, though there is no real evidence to support this conclusion.

106. Information concerning numbers of speakers of Siouan languages was supplied by Robert Rankin, personal communication. Dorsey cites Trumbull in deriving the name *Sioux* (an alternate name for Dakota/Lakota, after whom the family is named) from the "French plural of the Ottawa *Nadowessi,* by which a Dakota was designated. The Ottawa plural is *Nadowessiwag* (or *-ak*); the French made it *Nadowessioux,* and the *Couriers de bois* reduced it to *Sioux*" (1885:919).

107. Dorsey said that *Çegiha* (his spelling of Dhegiha) means 'belonging to the people of the land' or 'those dwelling here', "i.e., the aborigines or home people" (1885:919).

108. *Winnebago* is from an Algonquian form, perhaps Potawatomi *winpyeko,* etymologically 'people of the dirty water', referring to "the muddy water of their river (the lower course of the Fox River of Wisconsin) plus Lake Winnebago" (Golla and Goddard 1978:706).

109. The first attempt to relate Woccon and Catawba was that of Adelung and Vater (1816:308; see also Carter 1980:171).

110. The older idea, that Mandan was related more closely to Crow and Hidatsa, is based on the fact that there has been lexical borrowing between Mandan and Missouri River Siouan. Some scholars might prefer to place Mandan with Mississippi Valley Siouan as the first to separate from that branch, though it is probably best left as an independent branch of the family, at least for the present (Robert Rankin, personal communication).

111. Saponi was essentially Tutelo or a dialectal variant thereof (Robert Rankin, personal communication). The Occaneechee (spelled variously) of southern Virginia and northern North Carolina were said

to have spoken basically the same language as the Tutelo and Saponi (Ives Goddard, personal communication); it may have been used as a lingua franca (see appendix to Chapter 1 and Goddard 1977).

112. Powell (1966[1891a]:121) derives the name from Caddo *hadai* 'brushwood'.

113. Even Swanton, who otherwise just assumed the Adai to have been a Caddoan "tribe," reported that "the vocabulary . . . shows that it [Adai] differed widely from the rest of the Caddo[an] dialects" (1946:84).

114. *Carrizo* is Spanish 'reed'.

115. *Comecrudo* is Spanish, literally 'eat-raw'.

116. *Garza* is Spanish 'crane, heron'.

117. The name *Seminole* is derived from a Creek word *simanó·li* 'wild, runaway, fugitive', from earlier Creek *simaló·ni,* which was borrowed from Spanish *cimarrón* 'wild, unruly' and 'runaway slave' (see *The Random House Dictionary of the English Language*).

118. Haas's original classification of Muskogean was similar, but different in some repects:

Muskogean
Western
    Choctaw
    Chickasaw
Eastern
    Alabama-Koasati
        Alabama (Alibamu)
        Koasati
        Apalachee
    Hitchiti-Mikasuki
        Hitchiti
        Mikasuki (Seminole)
    Creek-Seminole
        Creek (Muskogee)
        Seminole

    Haas 1941, 1979; see also Booker 1988, 1993
                         Kimball 1987a.

Haas (1947) implies a somewhat different internal division for the Eastern Muskogean branch:
Eastern Muskogean
    Alabama-Koasati-Hitchiti-Mikasuki
        Alabama-Koasati
        Hitchiti-Mikasuki
    Creek-Seminole

However, she abandoned this classification and returned to one essentially as presented in Haas (1941), accounting for the nonconforming sound changes in terms of areal diffusion (Haas 1979). Booker (1988, 1993), however, has suggested that the Haas 1947 classification has merit and is worthy of more thorough investigation.

119. Munro argues that her four Southwestern Muskogean languages share a number of traits which appear to be innovations; for example, the unusual assimilation rule affecting the *-li* auxiliary suffix, the

development of an *-l-* passive suffix, and the use of **ha* 'plural' in "first-person plural I" and "second-person plural II" affixes (1987a:5).

120. The question whether Tawasa is a Timucuan dialect or a sister language has not been resolved conclusively. Swanton (1929) showed that if the source from Lamhatty actually did represent Tawasa, then it does indeed belong to Timucuan.

121. The Tuscarora self-designation, *skarò·rə ʔ,* appears to be involved in the origin of the name; it is traditionally interpreted as 'those of the Indian hemp, *Apocynum cannabinum*', but the name for the Tuscarora in the other Iroquoian languages is longer and begins with *ta,* and while phonetically similar, it cannot be analyzed as involving 'Indian hemp' (Goddard 1978c:524).

122. The name *Nottaway* is from Algonquian. Terms derived from the Proto-Algonquian **na·to·we·wa* (which is connected with the Proto-Algonquian **-a·towe·-* 'speak a foreign language') are widespread among Algonquian languages as names referring to various Iroquoian tribes or groups (Goddard 1978c:320).

123. The name *Huron* was first used by Champlain, in July 1623; it is said to be from French *hure* 'boar's head, bristly head' since the haircut of these Indians resembled the erect bristles on the head of a boar, but it is also explained as possibly being from an Old French word meaning 'ruffian, knave, lout, unkempt person' (Heidenreich 1978:387).

124. *Wyandot* comes from the Huron and Wyandot self-designation, *wę́·ⁿdat,* probably a shortening of something corresponding to Mohawk *skaw·ę́nat* 'one language' or *tshaʔtekawę́·nat* 'the same language (word, speech)' (Goddard 1978c:405).

125. *Cayuga* reflects the Cayuga self-designation, *kayohkhó·nọʔ* 'people of Oiogouen'; the entymology of the town's name is unknown (Goddard 1978c:503).

126. *Onondaga* reflects the Onondaga name for themselves, *onọtáʔe·kàʔ* 'people of *onọtáʔke·kàʔ*', the chief Onondaga town, meaning literally 'on the hill' (Goddard 1978c:499).

127. The name *Susquehannock/Susquehanna* is held to be a French rendition of Iroquoian *skahenta-waneh* 'big grassy flat' (compare Mohawk *skahętó·-wanę* and Oneida *skahętowáňę* 'great field') (Jennings 1978:362).

128. *Mohawk* is an Algonquian name; of the various spellings that appeared in earlier sources, Roger Williams's ⟨Mohowawogs'⟩ was etymologically the most correct—with English *-s* 'plural' added to a Narragansett or Massachusett word for 'people-eaters' (compare the Unami Delaware cognate *mhuwé·yɔk* 'cannibal monsters') (Goddard 1978c:478).

129. *Oneida* reflects the Oneida name for themselves, *oneyoteʔa·kâ·* 'people of the erected stone' (compare *oneyóteʔ* 'erected stone'), after an Oneida village name that refers to a large syenite boulder, which, according to tradition, always appeared near the main Oneida settlement (Goddard 1978c:489).

130. Trombetti (1929–1937) claimed to have discovered this relationship independently of Sapir (see Trombetti's 1920–1921 short attempt to validate the relationship). In the same article, Trombetti claimed to have discovered, independently, the relationship between Kiowa and Tanoan.

131. *Wiyot* is from *wíyat,* the native name for the Eel River delta, which also referred to one of the three principal groups of Wiyots (Elsasser 1978:162).

132. *Yurok* is from Karuk *yúruk* meaning literally 'downriver'. The Yurok traditional name for themselves is *Puliklah* (Hinton 1994:157), from *pulik* 'downstream' + *-la* 'people of', thus equivalent in meaning to the Karuk name by which they came to be known in English (Victor Golla, personal communication).

133. The family is named for Algonquin (of the Ottawa River valley), the language of this family which the French studied intensively in their early contacts with native peoples. They recognized the closeness to Algonquin of other languages of the family with which they gained familiarity. The spelling *Algonquian* reflects this origin; some scholars have preferred *Algonkian* as the English spelling (both forms have the same pronunciation), but historical precedent is on the side of *Algonquian*.

134. The name *Menominee* is from Ojibwa *ma-no·mini·,* etymologically meaning 'wild rice people' (compare *mano·min* 'wild rice') (Spindler 1978:723).

135. *Ojibwa* is the most prevalent form of this name in linguistic literature; *Chippewa* is preferred by groups in the United States and southern Ontario, whereas *Ojibway* is a common spelling in the rest of Canada. The name Ojibwa/Chippewa reflects the self-designation, *očipwe·,* explained as meaning 'puckered up', reflecting the form of Ojibwa moccasins (Goddard 1978c:768–9).

Potawatomi is from Ojibwa *po·te·wa·tami·;* this matches the Potawatomi self-designation, *potewatmi,* a name whose etymology is unknown (Clifton 1978:741).

136. The name *Algonquin* is said to be from Maliseet *elakómkwik* 'they are our relatives (or allies)' (Day and Trigger 1978:792).

137. The Sauk (also spelled *Sac*) are known in French by the name *saki* (spelled variously). An Algonquian form of this name, such as the Ojibwa *osa·ki·,* perhaps without the *o-* prefix, was borrowed into English and then shortened. Other early spellings

reflect *asa·ki·waki* (*a-* is from earlier *o-*, and the form is plural), interpreted etymologically as 'people of the outlet', a reference to the mouth of the Saginaw River (Ojibwa *sa·ki·na·nk* '[at] the country of the Sauk') (Goddard 1978c:654).

138. The name *Shawnee* reflects their self-designation, *ša·wanwa* 'person of the south'; there are cognate names in several other Algonquian languages (Callender 1978:634).

139. *Cree,* from *kiristino·* in Old Algonkin (Ojibwa), can be traced to a little-known band from an area south of James Bay in the first half of the seventeenth century. The name was adopted by the French with the plural *-s* (with various spellings, ⟨Kiristinous, Kristinos, Christinaux⟩ and used to refer to all Cree-speaking groups. It was soon shortened to *Cris* (both singular and plural), sometimes *Cri* singular, which yields the English *Cree* (Pentland 1981:227–8). *Montagnais* is from French, meaning 'mountaineers', a reference to the mountains of their territory. *Naskapi* is reportedly a derogatory term signifying 'uncivilized people' or 'those who have no religion', but the etymology is unknown (Goddard 1981:185).

140. The name *Abenaki* comes from the Abenaki name for themselves, *wapánahki,* meaning 'dawn land people' (Snow 1978:137).

141. The name *Delaware* is derived from the name of the Delaware River, which was named for Sir Thomas West, Lord de la Warr, first governor of Virginia. The Unami self-designation is *lanápe·* (*lan-* 'ordinary, real, original' + *-a·pe·* 'person'), which is the source of *Lenape,* another common name for the Delaware in early publications. *Munsee* is from the Delaware term meaning 'person from Minisink' (Unami *mwáns·i,* Munsee *mán'si·w*). Unami (cf. Munsee *wəná·mi·w*) means 'person from downriver' (Goddard 1978a:235–7).

142. *Massachusett* "appears to mean 'at the great hill', presumably in reference to the Blue Hills in Milton southwest of Massachusetts Bay. . . . The Narragansett name was Massachusêuck" (Salwen 1978:174).

143. *Maliseet* is "from Micmac where it probably means 'lazy speakers' " (Erickson 1978:135). *Passamaquoddy* seems to be from their self-designation, *pestəmohkatíyək* ('singular' *pestámohkat*), which apparently originally meant 'those of the place where pollock are plentiful' (Erickson 1978:135).

144. Actually, as Kinkade (1991b:154) points out, this homeland was more properly only that of the central and eastern Algonquian groups, since Siebert included no data from Blackfoot, Arapaho, or Cheyenne, nor of course from Ritwan (Wiyot and Yurok). Nevertheless, this postulated homeland is still consid-

ered quite representative of the whole family, though with a more westerly orientation (Goddard 1994c).

145. All three word lists are from female speakers. The first (ca. 1791) is from Oubee, a little girl who was captured when her family was attacked by white settlers; she was adopted by Thomas Stone (who later became mayor of Poole, in Dorset, England) and taken to England, where she died (probably of tuberculosis). The second (about 200 words) is from Demasduit, also known as Mary March, who was taken prisoner in 1819. The third (ca. 1828) is from Shanawdidhit, who spent six years among the English.

Chapter 5 Languages of Middle America

1. The insignificance of political geographical boundaries for the concerns of this study is seen further when we take into consideration the fact that none of the eleven Native American language families of Canada is found exclusively within the political borders of Canada (Foster 1982:9).

2. Some of the North American and South American languages now spoken in Middle America are recent arrivals—for example, Apache, Garífuna (Black Carib), and Kickapoo. The Apachean bands are Athabaskan (see Chapter 4) and entered northern Mexico after 1500 (Krauss 1973b). Kickapoo, an Algonquian language closely related to Fox, spoken in Kansas and Oklahoma, is also spoken in La Rancheria Nacimiento (Colonia de los Kikapú), Coahuila, Mexico. The Mexican variety is considered conservative (see Voorhis 1971). In 1667 the Kickapoo were reported in Wisconsin. In 1775 they were granted land concessions in present-day Texas. They began going to Mexico in 1829, and in 1864 they petitioned for permission to stay and were granted the village of Nacimiento, which had been abandoned by Seminoles in 1861 (Gibson 1963). Garífuna (also called Black Carib, a variety of Island Carib, also known as Iñeri) is an Arawakan language spoken by about 30,000 people in Belize, Guatemala, Honduras, and small areas of Nicaragua. The forebears of Central American Black Caribs were deported from Saint Vincent, British West Indies, in 1797. Thus Central American Carib is a close offshoot of Island Carib women's speech of 300 years ago, and hence also of that spoken by the pre-Carib inhabitants of the Lesser Antilles, the so-called Iñeri (Igneri). These islands were invaded by Caribs who claimed descent from the Galibí, a Carib-speaking tribe of French Guiana and Brazil. However, they failed to establish their language, so the language remained basically that of the aboriginal Arawakan people, but with a men's

jargon in which Carib morphemes could be substituted for Arawakan equivalents (based probably on an old Carib pidgin; see the appendix to Chapter 1). The women's speech has not changed much in 300 years, but Garífuna (Central American Black Carib) has largely leveled out the men's forms. That is how Garífuna / "Black Carib" can be an Arawakan language but have a name that suggests a Carib affinity (see Taylor 1951, 1952, 1954, 1956, 1977a:24).

3. Information on numbers of speakers is taken from Muntzel and Pérez González (1987) and other sources, including Grimes 1988 and Kaufman 1994.

4. *Mazahua* is from Nahuatl *masa·-* 'deer' + *-wa?* 'pertaining to'.

5. *Matlatzinca* is from Nahuatl *ma·tla-* 'net, snare' + *-cin* 'diminutive' + *-ka-* 'inhabitant of'.

6. From Nahuatl *ok^wil-* 'worm' + *-la·n* (variant of *-tla·n*) 'place of'.

7. *Chichimeco* is a hispanicized form of Nahuatl *či·či·-me·-ka-* [dog?-plural-inhabitant.of]; it meant 'barbarous' in Classical Nahuatl and traditionally is derived from the root for 'dog', *čiči*, but the vowel-length differences suggest something more like *či·či(·)* 'breast, nurse/suckle'.

8. *Chinantec* is from Nahuatl *činami-* 'fense' (the term for a division in the social structure) + *-te·ka* 'resident of'.

9. From Nahuatl *čiya(n)* 'chia plant' + *-a·pan* 'river'.

10. From Nahuatl *masa·-* + *-te·ka* 'inhabitant of place of'.

11. From Nahuatl *popoloka* 'to babble, to speak a language badly'.

12. *Zapotec* is from Nahuatl *capo-* 'zapote fruit' + *-te·ka* 'inhabitant of place of'.

13. From Nahuatl *a·moš* 'moss' + *-ko* 'in'.

14. From Nahuatl *miš* 'cloud' + *-te·ka* 'inhabitant of place of'.

15. From Nahuatl *k^wi·ka* 'song' + *-te·ka* 'inhabitant of place of'.

16. *Tol* is the self-designation of Jicaque speakers.

17. From Nahuatl *te·-* 'human object' + *-pe·wa* 'capture', i.e., 'conquered'.

18. *Mixe,* as has sometimes been suggested, may be from Nahuatl *mi·ši·-* 'intoxicating herb (jimsomweed?)'.

19. From Nahuatl *tlapačo·l-* 'subject, someone ruled or governed' + *-te·ka* 'inhabitant of place of'. On the place of Tapachultec in the Mixe-Zoquean subgrouping, see Kaufman 1964d.

20. From Nahuatl *sa·yo·l-* 'fly' + *-la·n* 'place of'.

21. From Nahuatl *o·lo·-* 'corncob' + *-tla·n* 'place of'.

22. From Nahuatl *te·ksis-* 'shell (egg)' + *-tepe·* 'mountain' + *-k* 'in'.

23. From Nahuatl *a·ya·-* 'cloak or blanket of cotton or henequin' + *-pan* 'in, on'.

24. *Chimalapa* is from Nahuatl *či·mal-* 'shield' + *a·pan* 'river'.

25. *Huastec* is apparently from Nahuatl *wa·š-* 'gourd (tree)' + *-te·ka* 'inhabitant of place of'.

26. From Nahuatl *čiko·m(e)-* 'seven' + *o·se·lo·-* 'ocelot' + *-te·ka* 'inhabitant of place of'.

27. Apparently from Nahuatl *yo(ʔ)ka(·)-* 'richness, inheritance' + *-te·ka* 'inhabitant of place of'; compare *Yucatan*, from *yo(ʔ)ka(·)-* 'richness' + *-tla·n* 'place of'.

28. *Itzá* in the new orthography is *Itza'*, although it in fact has no final glottal stop; it is found in cognate forms reflecting **icah* in a number of Mayan languages. It relates to the Itza ethnic group (a powerful lineage that is so famous in the history of Yucatan and the Petén in Late Postclassic and early post-European contact times), and it probably relates to Proto-Mayan **i·c* 'sorcery'.

29. *Ch(')ol* is from *č'ol* 'Indian' in Cholan languages; it is often said to be related to *čol* 'cornfield', but the lack of glottalization makes this identification problematic.

30. *Chontal* is from Nahuatl *čontal-* 'foreigner', found also in the names of several other groups in Mexico and Central America (see Brinton 1892).

31. *Choltí* and *Chortí* are both from *č'ol* 'Indian' in Cholan languages + *-tiʔ* 'mouth, language'.

32. *Tzotzil* is from Tzotzil *soc'* 'bat' + *-il* 'nominal suffix', the name of a principal division of the Tzotzils; compare *Zinacantán*, the name of one of the major Tzotzil towns, which incorporates the Nahuatl equivalent: *cina·kan-* 'bat' + *-tla·n* 'place of'.

33. From Nahuatl *a·ka-* 'reed' + *-te·ka* 'inhabitant of place of'.

34. From Nahuatl *šaʔkal-* 'hut' + *-te·ka* 'inhabitant of place of'.

35. Apparently from Nahuatl *mo·to?-* 'squirrel' + *cin* 'diminutive' + *-tla?* 'place where are abundant' + *-e·ka* 'inhabitant of'.

36. *Chuj* is from *ču·x* 'steambath' in Mayan languages of the Huehuetenango district.

37. *Tojolabal* is from Tojolabal *toh-ol* 'straight, correct' + *ab'al* 'language'.

38. From the Q'eqchi *q'eq* 'black' + *-čiʔ* 'mouth, language'.

39. From Nahuatl *očpa·n-* (root for 'broom') + *-te·ka* 'inhabitant of place of'.

40. From K'iche' *k'i·(h)* 'many' + *če·ʔ* 'trees' (i.e., 'forest').

41. The name *Kaqchikel* includes the roots *kaq* 'red' (modern *kyaq*) + *-čiʔ* 'mouth, language'.

42. From Nahuatl *saka-* 'grass' + *-po·l* 'augmentative, derogatory' + *-te·ka* 'inhabitants of place of'.

43. This name is from Nahuatl *sipak* 'alligator, supernatural beast' + *a·pan* 'river'.

44. *Mam* is from the Mamean-K'ichean word *-ma·m* 'grandfather' (also 'grandson').

45. From Nahuatl *a·waka-* 'avocado' + *-te·ka* 'inhabitant of place of'.

46. *Cuitlatec(o)* is from Nahuatl *kʷitla-* 'excrement' + *-te·ka* 'inhabitants of the place of'.

47. One suspects the proto language had **ṣ̌* rather than **š* (though *š* is also a possible candidate for reconstructing this sound), since in three of the four languages this sound is clearly retroflexed (nonretroflexed in only one). It is possible that **š* will prove to be a better reconstruction (the retroflexion may represent a development diffused after the breakup of the proto language).

48. Jumaytepeque was unknown until I discovered it in the early 1970s; it is spoken near the top of the Jumaytepeque volcano (Campbell 1978c).

49. Most of the earlier extant materials on these two languages are reprinted in Lehmann (1920:700–19); for more recent work, see Arguedas Cortés 1987; Campbell 1976c, 1976d; Campbell, Chapman, and Dakin 1978; and del Río Urrutia 1985.

50. The name *Misumalpan* is an amalgam of small segments of the names of the component languages, Miskito, Sumu, and Matagalpan.

51. *Cacaopera* is frequently said to be from forms in Lenca approximating *kakaw* 'cacao' and *pera* 'jaguar'.

52. This name is from Nahuatl *maʔitlak* 'ten' + *-kal-* 'house' + *-pan* 'place of'.

53. The form *peyo-tl* in Nahuatl is apparently not native, since native nouns lost original *p* (Proto-Uto-Aztecan **p* > h > Ø in Nahua); most nouns with initial *p-* are clearly loans, although no donor language for 'peyote' has been identified (Campbell and Langacker 1978).

Chapter 6   Languages of South America

1. An additional limitation in this chapter is a personal one: I have much less direct experience with South American language groups on the whole than with those of North America and Mesoamerica. I am reasonably familiar with the relevant research on North American and Mesoamerican languages, where I have examined for myself the evidence that has been presented for most of the classifications that have been proposed. I have no such confidence in

South America, where my experience is restricted to work on Quechua (of Peru and Bolivia); to some fieldwork on certain Chibchan languages of Central America; to limited exposure to Aymara; and to some efforts to understand the historical linguistics of Chibchan, Uru-Chipaya, and Yunga.

2. Aspects of the work of Jijón y Caamaño (1943) were given serious consideration by some of the broad classifiers whose work Kaufman surveyed.

3. Concerning the classifications which he compared and his own conclusions regarding them, Kaufman indicates further (mentioned in Chapter 2) that "having sifted the data, I feel obliged to point out that Loukotka's 1968 classification is practically error-free as far as genetic groupings are concerned. The mistakes in Loukotka are easily summarized. He includes names of languages for which no data exist. . . . An occasional language has been assigned to the wrong genetic group, but these instances are few. The subgrouping claimed for the recognized groups is often faulty" (1990a:37). Kaufman also objects to Loukotka's inclusion in Chibchan of several groups which are proposed as being related (though undemonstrated), and his grouping of Wahivoan (Guajiboan) with Arawakan.

4. Tairona is perhaps still spoken, but as a secret language. It belongs to the Arhuacan subgroup. It is said to be used only in ceremonial songs which also have portions in Spanish and Latin, as well. Robert Jackson considers it a dead language, though it is still used by Cágaba [Kogi] shamans for liturgical purposes (see also Kaufman 1994:55). Jackson reports it as "an offshoot of the mother tongue, and a rather recent one at that. . . . according to . . . Damana informant[s], 'the ceremonial language that the Kogi still use . . . is an archaic form of Sanka [Damana] that was spoken in ancient times' " (1990:11).

5. The name Maipurean/Maipuran is from the Maipure language of Colombia and Venezuela, after which Gilij (1782) named the family, which he had recognized even then. *Arawakan* comes from the Arawak or Lokono language of Guyana and Surinam (see Payne 1991:363).

6. Garífuna is from the Proto-Cariban word *karípona* 'Indian' (Kaufman 1994:74).

7. A somewhat different view is obtained from the "core of segmental phonological units" of Maipurean reported by Derbyshire (1992:103), though these are not intended to be considered reconstructions: /p, t, č, k, s, h, m, n, l, r, w, y; i, e, ɨ, a, o, u/ .

8. In 1980 two speakers were reported in Ecuador; the language was extinct in Colombia.

9. Kaufman's sixteen comparisons are suggestive, but they fall far short of providing real support for the hypothesis. By the criteria of Chapter 7, several

of them would have to be eliminated or considered to be weaker evidence. For example, two monosyllabic forms are too short to eliminate the factor of chance (*-ta, -to*); 'pot' could be diffused, and several are not particularly similar phonetically (for example, *pochi/ yaleʔ/otintih* 'root'). Six compare forms in only two of the three languages.

10. *Auca* is from the Ecuadoran Quichua word meaning 'savage, enemy' (Stark 1985:171).

11. While the names *Jaqi* and *Aru* compete with one another and appear frequently in the literature, in recent usage the name *Aymaran* has been adopted for this family (Cerrón-Palomino 1993). The term *Aru* has its origin in Aymara *aru* 'language, word'.

12. Hardman de Bautista reports that, until about twenty-five years ago, a fourth Jaqi language was spoken in Huantan, Yauyos province, department of Lima, Peru (1978b:147).

13. In fact, there are many variant names for Uru: Uro, Huro, Ochomazo, Ochozuma, Uchumi, Kjotsuni, Bukina, Pukina, Puquina, Urocolla, Uroquilla, and Yuracare (not the Yuracare of eastern Bolivia). The third, fourth, and fifth names appear to be from *uchumi* 'we' in Uru-Chipaya (Olson 1964:314).

14. The term *Chon* for these languages was proposed by Lehmann-Nitsche (1913).

15. By "emergent languages" Kaufman means very closely related languages that are just "emerging" from a continuum of dialects and have progressed just beyond being mutually intelligible, as they formerly were and nearly still are.

16. *Aksanas* is the Kaweskar word meaning 'man' (as opposed to 'woman') (Clairis 1985:764).

17. Ethnic and linguistic names in Patagonia and Tierra del Fuego are complicated by the fact that the inhabitants have frequently been referred to by generic names such as *Tehuelches* or *Patagonians*. The terms *Aonikenke* 'people of the south' and *Peenkenke* 'people of the north' do not have exact referents. In an attempt to avoid some of the confusion, Clairis (1985:760–3) refers to:

> †Septentrional Boreal Tehuelche (SBT), disappeared in the middle of the last century without leaving a trace of the language
>
> Meridional Austral Tehuelche (MAT, Patagon, Aonikenke) [moribund] *Santa Cruz Province, Argentina*
>
> †Septentrional Austral Tehuelche (SAT, termed *Gününa Küne, Gennaken, Pampa*)
>
> †Meridional Boreal Tehuelche (MBT, called *Teushen, Tehues*)

The term *Tehuelche* is thus ambiguous, for it can mean either the language or the people of Patagonia, who spoke at least three different languages.

18. Elena Najlis (personal communication) ex-

presses her belief that Selknam (and the languages of its family) is related to languages of the Chaco—that is, Mataguayan, Guaycurian, and probably Ayoreo. She points to similarities in the system of demonstratives as evidence. This is an interesting hypothesis, but it will require much more investigation to ascertain whether sufficient support for it can be found.

19. Clairis adds the following in a footnote:
The only "evidence" for this language [Chono] consists of the three words collected by Fitz-Roy and the "chono or wayteka" vocabulary of 95 words, published by Samitier . . . which consists of an unspecified mixture of first-hand data gathered by him in a hospital . . . in 1937, from one—according to him—chon informant. This individual spoke the "wurk-wur-we"! language. Samitier added to these forms "a few rare words noted by former travelers, because it was not possible to find a chon vocabulary anywhere." . . . We simply can not take this seriously. (1985:763–4)

20. Both Mapuche and Mapudungu(n) are used as names of this language. Mapuche is from *mapu-* 'earth, land' + *-che* 'people'; Mapudungu(n) is from *mapu-* 'earth, land' + *-dungun* 'tongue, language' (Key 1978:280).

21. Some sources report as many as 1,300 speakers, though Kaufman lists Mura as extinct.

22. Najlis lists *hw, hl, hs, hm, hn* as "aspirated," parallel to the aspirated stop series, but she supplies no other details concerning their phonetic properties. I suspect they are clusters, since she speaks of the "porción aspirada" [aspirated portion] of *hl* becoming palatalized to *šl* in some dialect of Ajlujlay (1984:30). The ç and ç' are given as "palatal stops," though the cognate sets of some of the languages have č and č'.

23. It is not clear how the Toba-Maskoy (Toba of Paraguay, Quilyilhrayrom, Cabanatit, Machicui, Enenlhit, Mascoi) (Paraguay), which others list as Mascoyan, fits into Kaufman's classification.

24. †Southern Cayapo (not to be confused with Kayapó) is spoken in São Paulo, Brazil. It is a Gê language, but its classification within the family is unknown; Kaufman reports a personal communication from Aryon Rodrigues stating that Southern Kayapó "is not that different" from [Northern] Kayapó (1994:69; see also Migliazza and Campbell 1988:288).

25. D. R. Taylor (1977a:25) proposed that the name *Carib* was derived from the ancestral Arawakan *kaniriphuna,* composed of *kaniri* 'bitter manioc' + *-phu* 'morpheme which derives clan names from names of plants' + *-na* 'collectivizer/pluralizer'. This etymology seems less likely than the native Carib *karípona* 'Indian'.

26. These are all variants of names which derive

from Proto-Cariban *karípona* 'Indian' (Kaufman 1994:74).

27. Carijona [Karihona] is from Proto-Cariban *karípona* 'Indian' (Kaufman 1994:74).

28. Pemón is from [pemoŋ] 'person', a self-designation in Arekuna, Kamarakoto, and Taurepan (Migliazza 1985[1982]:79).

Chapter 7   Distant Genetic Relationships: The Methods

1. La difficulté de fait qu'on éprouve à faire entrer toutes les langues dans la classification généalogique a conduit certains linguistes éminents à ôter au principe de cette classification sa précision et sa rigueur ou à l'appliquer d'une manière inexacte. (The English translation is from Rankin 1992:324.)

2. The Maya-Araucanian hypothesis has been essentially abandoned, since the evidence presented on its behalf is mostly explicable by factors other than inheritance from a common ancestor (see Chapter 8).

3. Hymes described a somewhat different division of the "stages in genetic classification": "hypothesis, proof, and establishment" (1959:52).

4. Credit Eric Hamp for this observation, in personal communication several years ago.

5. Hock (1993) calls the noncognate similarities shared by languages "false friends" (an adaptation of a term frequently used in foreign language instruction); he cites a study in which Greenberg's method was applied to English, German, and Hindi; 65% of the forms that would be called "cognates" according to this method were in fact false friends (historically known not to be cognate).

6. Notice that if these relationships really were as obvious as Greenberg asserts, there would be no dispute; they would be accepted. However, the Athabaskan-Tlingit-Haida (or Na-Dene) classification is just as controversial today (perhaps more so)—precisely because it is not obvious, and methods such as that employed by Greenberg do not resolve the issue (see Chapter 8).

7. In fact, Greenberg's classification of North American languages differs from Sapir's only in grouping some parts of Sapir's Hokan-Siouan into three other groups.

8. Bengtson asserts that there are two countervailing forces to the "law of diminishing returns." One is that vocabulary replacement is seldom total but involves semantic shifts (and even chains of semantic shifts), where cognizance of such semantic variation makes "recovery of the most ancient vocabulary far more attainable"; the other is "the recovery power of *multilateral* comparison, as opposed to *bilateral*

comparison" (1989:31; the emphasis is Bengtson's). As discussed later in this chapter, neither of these "forces" has much countervailing efficacy—both are incapable of distinguishing accidental resemblances.

9. Concerning his empirical test, Ringe reports that "the method of multilateral comparison fails every test; its results are utterly unreliable. Multilateral comparison is worse than useless: it is positively misleading, since the patterns of 'evidence' that it adduces in support of proposed linguistic relationships are in many cases mathematically indistinguishable from random patterns of chance resemblances" (1994:28).

10. Spanish also has loans from Latin, some of which are evident in these examples.

11. Actually, *tytär* 'daughter' is usually considered to be a loan from Baltic (see Latvian *dukteř-*) rather than Germanic, but that does not affect the argument here, which concerns Indo-European (as a whole), not its individual branches.

12. I hasten to point out in this context that Sapir intended his six super-stock classification to be understood as only "suggestive but far from demonstrable in all its features" (1929a:137). In spite of its heavy morphological-typological leanings, Sapir felt that he also had both lexical and morphological evidence for the groupings and that in the future rigorous comparison of the traditional sort would increasingly support his preliminary proposals (1990[1921a]:93, 1925a:526; see also Campbell and Mithun 1979a:29).

13. Note the parallels to the notion of "inner form," the "genius of a language" that was so pervasive in nineteenth-century thinking on language (discussed in Chapter 2).

14. Swadesh's own methodological recommendations in this article did not stop with Sapir's shared structural features of morphology but (as tradition might lead us to expect) also included lexical and phonological evidence:

Highly dependable separate tests can be developed in the three areas of structure, basic vocabulary, and phonology. These three criteria, moreover, are mutually confirmatory. (1951:21)

Phonology, besides being a necessary concomitant of any effective study of vocabulary correspondences, constitutes an additional criterion for the differentiation of residual and cumulative similarities. If the phonologies of compared languages are such as to admit their being derived by realistic regular formulas of change from a realistic reconstructed prototype language, one cannot doubt the fact of common origin and residual relation. The interwoven fabric of a reconstructed speech-sound

pattern is too complex to be pulled out of thin air. (1951:20)

15. Greenberg presented no examples similar to those discussed by Meillet, Sapir, or Sapir's interpreters (see the discussion later in this chapter). His morphological comparisons are for the most part completely parallel to his vocabulary comparisons, though they involve shorter forms. He interpreted as a Meillet-like example the pattern of pronouns with *i-*, *a-*, *i(?)-* 'first, second, third person', respectively, which he argued is common to several South American language families (Greenberg 1987:44-6). He contended that this is an interesting example because the last (third person *i*), but not the first (first person *i*), does not palatalize following consonants and shows up as *e* in some languages. Greenberg sees this feature as evidence for a more inclusive Gê-Pano-Carib group. However, by his own admission, this example does not involve idiosyncratic alternations at all. Therefore, while it might constitute a small paradigm, it does not have anything like the force of an example such as, say, the *r/n* alternation exhibited by -*r* stem nouns in many Indo-European languages, as illustrated by words like Hittite *wâdar* 'water' (genitive singular), whose genitive is not (as might be expected) **wadaras,* but rather *wedenas*; this alternation is cognate with Greek *hudros* (nominative singular) / *hudatos* (< *hudṇtos*) (genitive singular)/. This is among the sort of facts which convinced the linguistic world that Hittite was indeed an Indo-European language. The South American *i/a/i* pattern is not like Swadesh's *I-me, je-moi.* In fact, a plausible alternative to Greenberg's interpretation is that the occurrence or nonoccurrence of palatalization is explained in strictly phonological terms; a possibility (hinted at in Greenberg's exposition) is that the proto forms are not *i/a/i?* but *i/a/e*, with palatalization restricted to *i*. This is not the sort of example Meillet (or Sapir) referred to.

Incidentally, Greenberg's discussion of general methods in his 1949 and 1957 articles was much more conventional (in agreement with principles discussed in this chapter) than his later work, particularly Greenberg 1987. As he said:

There is nothing recondite about the methods which I have employed. It is the common-sense recognition that certain resemblances between languages can only be explained on the hypothesis of genetic relationship. It is based on the type of conviction which moved Sir William Jones in 1786 to state that Sanskrit, Latin, and Greek "have sprung from a common source which, perhaps, no longer exists." . . . The membership of the Indo-European language family was accurately established decades before scientific workers began to insist on rigorous comparison. What impressed him [Jones] was, to state it in the technical terminology of present day linguistics, the presence of many morphemes in the three languages which resembled each other both in form and meaning. Such lexical resemblances, whether in root or inflectional morphemes are *sine qua non* for the establishment of all relations of a more obvious type. Only when these have been established may one use more subtle methods such as those employed by Sapir in North America. . . . But under no circumstances can we reject results attained from obvious lexical resemblances in fundamental vocabulary in favor of those based on vague structural traits. . . . Many languages have evolved case systems independently [Greenberg cites so-called Penutian languages as an example]. On the other hand, when faced with such correspondences as consonant stems; nominative Greek *s*, Sanskrit *s*; genitive Greek *os*, Sanskrit *as*; dative Greek *i*, Sanskrit *e*, we see that the possibility of this being the result of pure chance is infinitesimal.

Using this common-sense notion, I have given first place in setting up hypotheses of relationship to comparisons of vocabulary. I have then followed up such hypotheses with an examination of all available grammatical material. In not a single instance have I been forced to retract an initial thesis which seemed probable on the basis of lexical resemblances. This should not be surprising. Powell classified American Indian languages almost entirely in this manner. (1949:79-80)

Although this statement is seemingly reasonable, there are three things which led to his much criticized later practice. First, when he says that "lexical resemblances, whether in root or inflectional morphemes are *sine qua non* for the establishment of all relations," he seems to equate lexical comparisons with grammatical morpheme comparisons, as is apparent in his more recent procedures (as pointed out by Rankin 1992), though he attempts to portray the grammatical comparisons as somehow different in kind from his lexical equations. Second, it should be noticed that in 1949 and 1957 he relied on "correspondences" in sound in order to reduce the possibility that chance might account for the similarities; however, he now denies the relevance of sound correspondences. Third, his preference for lexical evidence is seen in his approbationary citation of Powell's lexically based method of classification of North American Indian languages; by 1987 raw lexical similarities had become nearly his only evidence, his lip service to grammatical evidence notwithstanding.

16. Whereas most Andeanists have been content with Parker's reconstruction of **ma* for the 'first person singular object' affix, Adelaar believed the *ma* of Central Quechua to be derived from **-mu-wa* > *-ma*, where *-mu* is a verbal directional 'hither', which he thought would explain why many (but not all) varieties of Central Quechua do not permit the sequence *-mu-ma* (cited in Cerrón-Palomino 1987:148–9). Cerrón-Palomino (1987:149), however, believed that Central Quechua *ma* derived from **-mu-ya*, the same directional plus his reconstruction for 'first person singular'. This is plausible as internal reconstruction, though there is no compelling evidence to support it.

17. I would include the Swadesh (1962) example, concerning Eskimo-Aleut and "Altaic," among those presented here. He noticed that Eskimo-Aleut and the so-called Altaic languages are essentially exclusively suffixing, with the exception of one seemingly shared prefix. The lone Eskimo-Aleut demonstrative prefix *ta(š)-* appears to correspond with the single prefix of the oldest Mongolian recoverable, the demonstrative *t-* (see Hamp 1976:81–2). I strongly suspect this is a case of sheer accident which apes submerged features. Given the typical tendency for demonstratives to exhibit unmarked consonants (where *t* has an extremely high frequency of occurrence among demonstratives in the world's languages), as well as the tendency for such grammatical markers to undergo stress reduction and become cliticized and then attached to more lexical constituents, this does not strike me as a particularly compelling example of the sort of grammatical evidence needed to argue successfully for a genetic relationship.

18. Actually, the various forms/affixes of L_2 could have one or more of the meanings of F_1 in L_1, but not all of them, in the situation described here.

19. Another way in which grammatical evidence has been presented in the study of remote linguistic relationships involves generative grammar. In early attempts to apply generative grammar to historical linguistics, it was sometimes claimed that its view of linguistic change as grammar change would provide particular insights into distant genetic relationship (see, for example, Teeter 1964a, King 1969:52–3, Rigsby 1969:72). Generative grammar, however, compares structural elements whose physical realizations remain the same regardless of what formal framework is included in the comparison. On the whole, this view turned out not to differ significantly from traditional ones—all require the application of the comparative method. Teeter's "depth hypothesis" appears to be nearly the same as Sapir's submerged features and Meillet's morphological peculiarities. Rigsby claimed that "the comparativist may formally

establish the genetic relationship of languages by demonstrating that they share grammatical rule-sets whose arbitrariness excludes chance convergence or universals and rules out borrowing" (1969:72). This is essentially the same method as that advocated by Sapir and Meillet, and presumably the same evidence is involved though it is dressed up in generative clothing.

20. Note that Tunebo [x] alternates freely with [š], that nasal consonants do not occur before oral vowels, and that the vowels of the Tunebo form are expectable substitutes for Spanish *e*.

21. Suárez has a valid point—"the danger of casual [chance] resemblance is as great in borrowing as it is in cognates" (1985:574). It is indeed true that the typical practice has been to raise "all the caveats" in assessing potential cognates, while loanwords have been treated less rigorously, almost as though they were "self-explanatory." Ultimately, equal care should be exercised in determining loans as in ascertaining cognates. Nevertheless, when the form under discussion is touted as potential evidence for an as yet undemonstrated distant genetic relationship, the very possibility of borrowing as the explanation should be taken very seriously. In a case where claims about loanwords were being tested, the reverse would be equally true—the possibility that similar forms were ancient cognates would have to be investigated carefully as potential counterevidence to the claim of borrowing.

22. Expressed in a different calculation: "In Turkish at least 20 of the 150 stems most frequently used by illiterate peasants are shared with some totally unrelated language [Arabic]" (Pierce 1965:27).

23. The several cases of undetected borrowing that complicate hypotheses of remote genetic relationships presented in this section (many others could also be presented) are sufficient to show the inaccuracy of Ruhlen's claim that "borrowing can in almost all cases be detected, and therefore does not constitute a serious impediment" (1994b:43). He believes that "only certain kinds of words are particularly susceptible to borrowing" and that "borrowing takes place only under special circumstances, almost always where the two languages in question are in intimate daily contact," and that these two factors "make borrowing only a modest impediment" (1994b:42). Of course, when it is not known whether compared languages are actually related, it is also not known whether they at one time borrowed from one another—that is, whether they were in the "special circumstances" that produce borrowing. Also, as discussed in this section, while certain vocabulary items are more likely than others to be borrowed, in fact there are clear cases which show that virtually any

sort of vocabulary can be borrowed, including pronouns, body parts, and the like.

24. Onomatopoeia has been recognized as a serious obstacle to the determination of family relationships throughout the history of linguistics, and even a cursory review of proposals of deep genetic relationships, as in Chapter 8, reveals. For this reason, it simply will not do to brush onomatopoeia off, as Ruhlen does: "Since such [onomatopoetic] words constitute a very small percentage of a language's vocabulary, and can only be a source of dispute, they may be safely ignored" (1994b:40).

25. Ruhlen seems to believe, mistakenly, that Jakobson's (1962[1960]) explanation of the *mama-papa* terms is based solely on "the order of acquisition of sounds in child language" (1994b:41). Ruhlen holds that these forms are legitimate evidence of remote relationships: "Were *mama* and *papa* the only such widespread kinship terms, one might be able to accept Jakobson's explanation [as misinterpreted by Ruhlen], but there are many others for which Jakobson's explanation seems far less viable, for example the kinship term based on the consonant [k] . . . where the meaning is typically 'older male relative, uncle, older brother'. . . . It is difficult to imagine that human society could be so finely organized that older brothers or uncles would show up at the baby's crib just when the child is learning velar consonants like [k]" (1994b:41). However, the existence of kin terms with *k* which exhibit a strong similarity in many unrelated languages is part and parcel of the same nursery formation phenomenon. Indeed, kin terms with *k* often do appear, and they frequently refer to some male kinsman, but *k* forms are also widely found that designate other kin as well. That is, most typically, the *mama/nana* type represents 'mother', secondarily 'grandmother', 'aunt', 'nanny', while the *papa/tata* (and *baba/dada*) forms more often refer to 'father' (or 'grandfather' secondarily). However, the picture is complete only when it is recognized that terms for 'mother' (as well as for elder female kin) are also often represented by *t*- and *p*-forms and terms for 'father' (as well as for other male kin) are represented by *m*- or *n*-forms, and that *k* is another sound frequently found in terms referring to close kin of both sexes (though the nasals predominate in terms for 'mother' for the reasons given by Jakobson).

26. For example, Greenberg (1953:270) argued that a 4% similarity due to chance is to be expected between unrelated languages, and this figure could go as high as 7% when the two languages are similar in morphophonemic structure (see Hymes 1959:56). Some others who have written on this topic include Bender (1969), Campbell (1973a), Collinder (1946–1948), and Justeson and Stephens (1980).

27. Ringe (1992:73–4) shows in one of his mathematical demonstrations that the probability of a "*t* : *t* matching" in the lists he compared was only 4 when only two language lists were compared, but that the number of chance matchings jumped to 420 when 15 such lists were compared. Clearly, then, the applications of multilateral comparisons will find it difficult to exceed the potential of chance to explain the similarities detected.

28. The commonly held opinion concerning basic vocabulary is that it is relatively resistant to change or replacement; however, we should also take into account Ringe's (1992) observation (see also Rankin 1992:332–3) that some of the most basic vocabulary (for example, 'hand', 'heart', 'head', 'eye', 'nose') tends to be used in extended metaphors in many languages, resulting in various sorts of semantic change involving even basic vocabulary. Thus, from 'nose' in known European languages one might find connections with 'smell, nostril, mucus, peninsula, insert, ask/inquire, small amount, prow, snort, direct/ direction, deceive/fool'. For 'hand' we find 'give, manual, handle (noun), handle (verb), collection, measurement, appreciation, slap/hit, help/assist, sell, understand'. Moreover, such extensions of items that are relatively basic in origin are more susceptible to being borrowed than is the actual basic vocabulary itself, as is evident in such English loans as *manual* (compare Latin *manus* 'hand'), *ocular* (Latin *oculus* 'eye'), and *nasal* (Latin *nāsus* 'nose'), which nevertheless incorporate references to basic concepts in their meanings.

29. Ruhlen's assertion that "we can recognize accidental similarities only *after* we have arrived at a classification of the languages involved" (1994b:40) misses the point. True, it is the detailed knowledge of the histories of the Indo-European languages which shows that Persian *bad* 'bad' and English *bad* are not cognates and are rather only accidentally similar. The existence of such accidental similarities among languages of the same family requires that caution be exercised in dealing with similarities among languages not yet known to be related. Without knowledge of linguistic history, of the sort that enabled detection of the English-Persian accidental similarity, it is impossible to eliminate the possibility that accident may account for the similarity among compared forms. Precisely for this reason, researchers studying hypotheses of distant genetic relationship should take all the available measures to limit chance as a possible explanation, to increase the likelihood that compared forms actually reflect a common ancestry.

30. Indo-European forms in this section are cited from Watkins 1985.

31. Swadesh made a similar point with respect to

similarities among sounds due to convergent developments in sound changes: "Cognates in English and Gaelic are generally far removed from each other because of the extensive phonological modifications which have taken place in each branch since the common Indo-European period. By contrast, Modern Greek and Spanish often agree perfectly in their consonants. In consequence of such variation in phonetic development, the only reliable approach is to seek evidence as to precisely what phonetic changes have taken place in the prehistory of each language and to judge word relationships insofar as possible in the light of known phonological correspondences" (1954b:314). This underscores the importance of correspondences over mere similarities in sound, and it highlights the role of phonological typology. That is, languages with relatively simple phonemic inventories and similar phonotactics will easily exhibit many accidentally similar words (which explains, for example, why Polynesian languages, with very simple phonemic inventories, have been proposed as the relatives of languages all over the world, including various Native American families; see Chapter 8). True cognates, however, are not necessarily phonetically similar, depending on what sorts of sound changes have taken place in the languages involved. Thus, it is good to keep Matisoff's (1990) example in mind: in a comparison of Mandarin Chinese *ér* with Armenian *erku* and Latin *duo*, all meaning 'two', it is the first two (which are unrelated) which have the greatest phonological similarity, but by sheer coincidence, while the second and third exhibit true sound correspondences which witness their genetic relationship.

32. Even English *daughter* (Old English *dohtor*, Proto-Indo-European **dhughəter*) appears to fit the set, in view of Greenberg and Ruhlen's inclusion of forms such as *tsuh-ki* and *u-tse-kwa*, which are rather far from the basic *TVN* template.

33. Greenberg and Ruhlen present another example, which they describe as "a single etymology [that] can illustrate both the unity of Amerind and its ties to the Eurasiatic/Nostratic constellation" (1992:98; see also Ruhlen 1994b:242–51)—their World etymology root *MALIQ'A*, said to mean 'swallow, throat'. In this case forms from only eighteen American Indian languages representing only eight of the assumed eleven branches of Amerind are compared with forms from Afro-Asiatic, Indo-European, Uralic, Dravidian, and Eskimo-Aleut. The range of glosses involved includes 'to suck, breast, udder, milk, to milk, chew, throat, cheek, swallow, neck, drink, nape of neck' (though the 'milk/breast/suck' glosses are fairly general in the languages presented, with the exception of Amerind). Phonetically, the Amerind languages seem

to fit the following patterns: $m(V)l/r/n(V)(k/g/q/X)$ or $m(V)k/g/q/X(V)(l/r/n)$, that is, they are composed of at least an m followed by either some resonant ($l/r/n$—let L represent the class) or some velar/uvular ($k/g/q/X$—let K represent the class). Often they include something from each set (for example, MLK or MKL, but sometimes only two of the consonant slots are represented (for example, ML or MK). Again, it is not difficult to find some form of the shape $MLK/MKL/ML/MK$ with a meaning that is consistent with the range of glosses involved here. Onomatopoeia and infant vocalism are surely factors in the development of some of these forms, increasing the likelihood that similarities will exceed those expected to result from chance alone (see Jakobson 1960; for a devastating criticism of the *maliq'a* example, see Hock 1993).

34. As Greenberg pointed out, several earlier proposed classifications of African languages lacked sound-meaning isomorphism in the purported supporting evidence; that is, Hottentot was classified as Hamitic because it has grammatical gender (Fleming 1987:207).

35. La única otra familia de lenguas de México, que posee esta serie glotalizada, es la mayance, y este hecho junto con otros detalles significativos, nos sugiere la probable relación genética del totonaco-tepehua con el mayance; pero el número relativamente pequeño de coincidencias de vocabulario nos indica que este parentesco es bastante lejano.

36. Some earlier classifications of African languages were notoriously bad violators of this principle; for example, proposals that Ari (Omotic) belongs to either Nilo-Saharan or Sudanic "because the Ari people are Negroes"; that Moru and Madi belong to Sudanic because they are located in central Africa; and that Peul/Fula is Hamitic because the Fulani herd cattle, are Moslems, and are tall and Caucasoid. As Fleming says of cases such as these, "lack of credible etymologies is bad news for a genetic hypothesis" (1987:207). Welmers found Greenberg "justifiably harsh and sometimes downright caustic on this subject" (1956:557), as when he lashes into Meinhof for using racial-cultural, nonlinguistic evidence: "I have little doubt that, on this basis, if a Negroid population had been found in Central Africa, speaking an Indo-European language, Meinhof would, without further ado, have classified it as Hamitic" (Greenberg 1955:44).

37. This can probably best be understood in historical context. Many scholars believed that Native Americans known to Europeans from the region in eastern North America where mounds were found were not sufficiently evolved socially to have the ability to construct such monumental earthworks themselves. For this reason, they assumed that either

Aztecs or Mayas, or Vikings, Welsh, or other Europeans, were the builders of the mounds. Of course, this was finally disproven. For example, Toomey grouped Natchez and Chitimacha linguistically, primarily on the basis of what he understood to be their "legends, customs and [social] organization" (1914:1).

38. In spite of the clear value of this principle, Greenberg himself, in his classification of American Indian languages, seems to set it aside when doing so suits his purposes. He says that he did not use findings from other fields to argue the correctness of his classification, but "when you find a convergence of results from linguistics, archaeology, and physical anthropology, you can't say that it doesn't strengthen the case for my classification: I think it does strengthen the case" (quoted in Newman 1991:457). Possible correlations with nonlinguistic evidence (dentition, human genetics, and archaeology) are ultimately irrelevant to issues of remote linguistic affinities, as required by Meillet and Greenberg's (1957, 1963) principle. As indicated by Newman, there is an irony in Greenberg's appeal to nonlinguistic evidence in support of his American Indian linguistic classification, since Greenberg (1963) demonstrated that external nonlinguistic evidence is irrelevant to linguistic classifications and is often misleading (Newman 1991:454; compare 459).

39. Note that the *pa-* 'in/on' of Kaqchikel, even without regard to the problem that it is short, is not a good match in this set, since it comes from *pam-* 'stomach'. Most Mayan prepositions and relational nouns are derived from body parts. This is hardly a convincing connection with Tunica *ʔaparu* meaning 'cloud, heaven'. Moreover, even if the Mayan forms had been cognate, this would not be an appropriate example of an "etymology" in this distant genetic proposal, since it would involve the comparison of only two language entities, Mayan and Tunica, which is a poor showing from among the hundreds of Native American languages when the possibility of accidental similarity has to be contended with. One might just as well throw in, say, Finnish *päälle* 'above, over, on' and argue that Finnish, too, is a Penutian language.

40. Because *-at* is so short and only two language entities (Mayan and Patwin) are compared, this set can hardly be considered outstanding evidence for the long-range grouping Greenberg is trying to defend here.

41. It is difficult to resist mentioning, just in case it was not immediately evident, that failure to take morpheme boundaries into account in this example results in a method which cannot tell its "anuses," so the saying goes, "from a hole in the ground."

42. Such examples show that Ruhlen's contention that "usually the portion of unanalyzed words being

compared is clear, even without the specification of morpheme boundaries" (1994b:95) is not valid. While Ruhlen is speaking specifically of the forms he presents which are taken from other linguists in connection with the Na-Dene hypothesis, this caution still applies.

43. It is, of course, possible that some of the noncognate forms within such proposed but errorneous cognate sets within a particular family may have a legitimate history of their own and therefore turn out to be cognate with forms compared from other languages where a distant genetic relationship is suspected. However, such forms do not warrant nearly as much confidence as do real cognate sets which have a demonstrable etymology within their own families and because of their attested age in that group, might be evidence of even more remote connections.

44. Quand on doit restituer une "langue commune" initial, il y a lieu de tenir compte du nombre de témoignages qu'on a pour un mot donné. Une concordance de deux langues, si elle n'est pas totale, risque d'être fortuite. Mais, si la concordance s'étend à trois, quatre ou cinq langues bien distinctes, un hasard devient moins vraisemblable.

45. In another instance, Greenberg (1987:159) compares Hitchiti (Muskogean) *hī:ɬi* 'squirrel' with forms such as Maidu *hilo* and Yakonan *xaɬt*; however, the word-initial *h* of Hitchiti is known to be epenthetic, while the *ɬ* is the reflex of what is reconstructed as *θ* in Proto-Muskogean. While Kimball (1993:449) presents this as markedly distinct, perhaps it is less so, given that the Proto-Muskogean *θ reconstruction, based on the reflexes *n : ɬ*, is not necessarily phonetically accurate. Greenberg also (1987:160) compared Atakapa *pax* and Choctaw *fahko* under the label 'thin'; however, the Choctaw word has no known cognates with other Muskogean languages, and in any case its *f* comes from Proto-Muskogean *x^w, making it much less similar to the Atakapa form.

46. While the FIRE family cannot, of course, be approximated entirely by words from English alone, we might stretch the point by also considering such terms as *lightning,* which is possibly the link with 'sky, sun' (as DeLancey , Genetti, and Rude [1988] link 'melt' with their 'cook, dry' category), and *lignum,* Latin for 'wood', found in tree names and other English derivatives (*lignite, lignin*), to get a match with the 'wood' forms of DeLancey et al.

47. In particular in this case, there may well be some proclivity in words for 'fire', 'light', and 'burn' toward expressive symbolism, as alleged in more fanciful accounts since the ancient Greeks and as the examples given here would seem to suggest.

48. A preliminary version of this section is published in Campbell 1994c; consequently, the discussion here is abbreviated.

49. Note also Greenberg's (1987:278) second person singular pronoun akin to Brinton's *K* forms, which he sees in a wide variety of American languages (with forms *ka, ikia, aki, ka-, -ke-, -ga,* and so on).

50. For example, here Sapir mentions "the curiously widespread American second person singular in *m-*" (1918:184).

51. In tutte queste antichissime forme pronominali si trovano soltanto le vocali *a, i, u,* le consonanti esplosive *k, t* e le nasali *n, m.* Questi sono certamente suoni primordiali.

52. Another source of new consonants in pronouns is reanalysis, where a consonant from another word or element that happens to be adjacent to the pronoun may be reinterpreted as part of the pronoun (Campbell 1988a:601–2). For example, in Swedish the old *i* 'second person plural pronoun' was replaced with *ni*; the added *n-* was from the second plural suffix *-en* of verbs, which preceded the pronoun in some constructions (Haugen 1976:375, 304). Incidentally, it is *n*, a nasal and a very salient consonant, that is the innovation marking the pronoun in this case. A parallel to the example just mentioned is the Quechua reanalysis: *-ni-*, the empty morpheme used to separate consonants that otherwise would come together over morpheme boundaries, was reanalyzed to mean 'first person singular pronoun', as described earlier in this chapter (see also Goddard and Campbell 1994).

53. This appears to explain such observations as "thus, word-initial nasal consonants such as *m-* and *n-* often remain intact for millennia" (Ruhlen 1990:76) and "the old *n* of proto-Indo-European [was] retained in English practically intact" (Swadesh 1960c:898).

54. I suspect that the perceptual salience of nasals and the importance in communication of being able to distinguish negative utterances from affirmative ones combine to help explain why negative markers in languages all over the world typically have *n* or *m,* and why *ma* and *nV* or something similar are so frequent (see the appendix in Chapter 1).

55. Everett claims that the entire pronominal system of the Pirahã language of Brazil was borrowed from Língua Geral (Nheengatú) (Everett in press).

56. These findings disprove the assertion that "pronominal affixes are among the most stable elements in language: they are almost never borrowed" (Greenberg and Ruhlen 1992:97). They also disprove the claim that "pronouns of the sort 'I', 'me', 'thou', 'thee' are not borrowed from language to language; they are inherited, and therefore the presence of *ni* 'I' and *mi* 'thou' in many American Indian languages certainly indicates that the languages in question are genetically related—be it only remotely" (Shevorosh-

kin 1989c:6). Moreover, it is well established that certain aspects of pronominal systems are easily influenced by contact from other languages—for example, the widespread diffusion of the inclusive/exclusive pronominal category in a number of languages of western North America (Jacobsen 1980), and the shift from independent plural pronimal affixes to pronoun markers composed structurally of the singular pronominal morpheme plus a plural affix (Robertson 1992). In particular, pronominal systems seem to be subject to analogical reformations, and many linguists believe that they are also dominated by tendencies towards iconic symbolization, as other deictic markers are (see Nichols in press).

57. Miskito *ba* 'third person, that (one)' appears to have been originally a demonstrative pronoun. Southern Sumu (Ulwa) pronouns differ, and in general Miskito owes much to diffusion from and convergence with Northern Sumu. (I owe these observations concerning Miskito and Sumu to Kenneth Hale, personal communication.)

58. Kinkade does not rule out entirely a possible genetic relationship between Alsea and Salish, but he notes that the conclusions of his investigation are negative; he adds further that at present it is not possible to answer the question, "how much of this Alsea pronominal system is originally Alsea and how much borrowed?" (1978:5–6).

59. Mary Haas concluded from her comparison of languages in northern California that the *n/m* pattern Greenberg regards as genetic evidence is widely borrowed: "There are clear *evidences of diffusion* in pronominal forms in northern California . . . belonging to a single diffusion area. . . . The most prominent feature is *n-* in the first person paired with *m-* in the second person. . . . But the total picture of *diffusion* of *n-* and *m-* in the first and second persons goes beyond the area being studied in this paper [Haas 1976] and so the problem really needs to be attacked on a larger scale" (emphasis added; 1976:358). Not all scholars today would agree that these forms are diffused in the way Haas described, but her report makes it clear that the pronoun pattern was well known before it became associated with Greenberg's claims and that the explanation for it was *not* automatically assumed to be a genetic one.

60. Greenberg's only response to the battery of negative evidence presented against his Amerind pronoun claims presented at the Boulder conference was to single out for ridicule this possible explanation of the nasal pronoun pattern that has been offered (a minor case, certainly not the one I favor most): "In a remark at the Boulder Conference Campbell attributed such a preponderance of nasals [in the pronouns] to the phonetic nature of infant sucking reflexes!"

(1990a:11) Ruhlen engages in the same seemingly purposeful neglect of the significant arguments, aping Greenberg's ridicule: "Greenberg's critics have offered even more fanciful explanation [than Boas's "obscure psychological causes"] for the American pattern, attributing the N and M pronouns to the sucking reflex of nursing babies. . . . One can only wonder why the infant sucking sounds of African and Australian children have not produced the same pronouns found in the Americas" (1994b:253). Greenberg has repeated this misrepresentation in a variety of interviews and publications; he implies that this is an unreasonable hypothesis without stating why. However, his "infant sucking reflexes" is not an accurate report of what was said. What Greenberg alludes to appears in a list of several explanations (some my own, plus many offered by other scholars) of the putative *n/m* pronoun pattern. It is Greenberg's garbled paraphrase, an explanation which comes originally from Ives Goddard (1986:202), in which the matter of nursing is only part of the story. Greenberg failed to mention the other, more relevant and damaging facts, which are discussed in this chapter.

61. Actually, Swadesh went even further than Greenberg, speculating on how he might derive the South American pattern from what he assumes to be the more general American *n/m* pattern:

"In parts of Aztectanoan and Chibchan, and in Arawakan, second person *m* gives way to *p* or *b,* and it is at least possible that the bilabial stop may be somehow derived from the nasal. In much of South America, first person *n* is replaced by *y;* in certain areas one finds *ñ.* The palatalized *b* may be a transition form, which could have easily arisen as the result of a preceding front vowel. That is, *ʔina* could give *ʔiña,* and the latter could have developed into *ʔiya.* In fact, forms approximating all stages of this transition can be attested, thus Sahaptin *ʔin,* Esselen *ʔene,* Yuman *ña,* Chontal *ʔiya.* If we can thus derive first person *y* from *n,* then the *n-m* pronominal set extends from Chinook (*naika* 'I', *maika* 'thou') in northwestern United States to ona (*ya* 'I', *ma* 'thou') on the Straits of Magellan. (1954b:312)

62. Some clear evidence of the nonuniqueness of *n* 'first person' and *m* 'second person' in "Amerind" comes from controversial sources, from the remote comparisons proposing very, very far-flung genetic relationships involving large segments of the world's languages which exhibit these forms. Moreover, the *m* 'first person' and *t* 'second person' pattern, which Greenberg and Ruhlen assert to be diagnostic of their Eurasiatic grouping, is also documented in "Amerind" by several of these comparisons. I mention four of them.

1. Swadesh (1960c:907–8) reconstructed *(ʔe)ne, often *(ʔi)ni 'I' for Proto–Ancient American, noting such "interhemisphere linguistic connections" as Malayan *i-na(w) 'I', Polynesian *na-ku 'I', Basque ni-k 'I', Hebrew ni 'I', and Somali-Galla ʔáni 'I'. For 'thou, thy' he reconstructed *ma/*mu and related it to such Old World forms as Melanesian *mu, Malay-Bugis mu, and Dayak ma. Swadesh (1960c:909) also presented a number of American Indian languages to illustrate his *ta/tu 'thou/thy', together with Old World comparisons (for example, Indo-European *te(w) 'thou', Hebrew ʔataa, Uralic *-t, and Avar dun, Kvarshi do).

2. Shevoroshkin presents the following as cognates of his Proto-proto-language **ni 'I': Nostratic *ni 'I', Nivkh ni 'I', Khoisan *ni 'I' (also *an 'I'; compare Dravidian *yan 'I', Austronesian *NV 'I', Indo-Pacific *n[i] 'I', Amerind *ni 'I'). These he relates to Nostratic *nAH 'we exclusive', Dene-(Sino-)Caucasian *nV 'we', and Amerind *naH 'we'. He presents similar evidence for a western group of this Proto-proto-language (including Amerind, Austric, and Indo-Pacific) for *m[i] 'thou' (also *kV 'thou') (Shevoroshkin 1989c:20). He also presents, however, evidence for Proto-proto-world **mi 'I', apparently *'I and you', in which he includes "Amerind": "cf. Nostratic *mi 'I', Dravidian *ma-/*m - 'we' (< Nostratic *mä 'we inclusive'), Khoisan *mi 'I' (also *me 'my'), Dene(-Sino)- Caucasian *mV 'I', Amerind *m 'I' (preserved as an archaism in different Amerind languages: see Greenberg 1987, Chapter 5)" (Shevoroshkin 1989b:19–20). Shevoroshkin also gives evidence of a widespread ** t 'you'.

3. Bengtson (1991:116) reconstructs for his Proto-Sino-Caucasian (a vast grouping that includes Na-Dene, Sino-Tibetan, North Caucasian, Yenisei, and Basque) 'first person' *nV-, *mV-, *SV-, and *tV- (not to mention a *nV- among his 'second person' forms). That is, we find here among the 'first person' forms the most basic, least marked consonants, including the n said by Ruhlen and Greenberg to be rare outside the Americas.

4. It should be pointed out that although both the m and t versions for 'second person' are widely attested in American Indian languages (and elswhere), a widespread k has also been proposed. For example, early in American Indian linguistic studies Michelson (1914) reported it in Wiyot k-, Yurok qe- 'thy', and Molala k·iʼⁱ. Greenberg (1987:277–8) cites for 'you' among his grammatical sets Kaliana ka(-be), Auake kai(-kiete), Proto-Ge *ka, Erikbatsa ikia, Bororo aki, Coroado ga, Allentiac and Millcayac ka, Xinca ka- 'second person singular pronoun'; Quechua kam, Gennaken kemu, Aymara huma, and Kahuapana kem, huma, koma 'second person singular independent pronoun'. Brinton (1890[1888]:396) also held that K was a widespread marker of the second person in Native American languages. One could easily associate these with Shevoroshkin's (1989b:19) forms for western Proto-proto-world *kV 'thou': Nostratic *k/gV 'thee', Dene(-Sino)-Caucasian *KV 'thou', Amerind *KV 'thou', Austronesian *kev/*keH 'thou', and Indo-Pacific *kV 'thou'.

63. Dryer found from pronoun data on 289 languages that 118 had more nasals in first person singular than in third person singular, 128 had the same number of nasals in both, and in only 47 were there more nasals in third person singular than in first person singular. He also found that 74 of these languages had more nasals in second person singular than in third person singular, while 48 had more nasals in third person singular than in second person singular. Dryer (personal communication) cautions that, although the numbers largely support his test hypotheses about nasals in pronouns, the nature of the sample precludes the use of statistics to test for significance. He is inclined to believe that the n/m pattern in American Indian languages may suggest genetic relationship, but he points out that if Hokan and Munda can share an n/m pattern as a result of chance, then Hokan and Penutian might share it by accident also.

64. It is interesting, in the context of accidental similarities, to note also that Atakapa has two Indo-European-like 'first person' pronominal markers: wi 'first person singular' independent pronoun, and -o 'first person singular' verbal ending (as in Spanish and Greek). (The K'iche'-Quechua pronominal forms which are accidentally similar were discussed earlier in this chapter.)

65. Manaster Ramer (1993) points out in this regard that Tonkawa, with sa·- 'I' and na·- 'you', is more similar to putative Na-Dene (compare Navajo shi/ni, Chipewyan si/nen) than putative Amerind.

66. Cheyenne, Siuslaw, and Miluk have n in both first person and second person pronouns. Cheyenne has na- 'I', ne- 'you' (from Proto-Algonquian *ne- and *ke-, respectively); Siuslaw has -n 'I', -nx 'you'; and Miluk has -enne'- 'first person singular subject', -ne- 'second person singular subject'. In Proto-Salish

we find *n- 'first person possessive', *ʔən- 'second person possessive' (Newman 1979a:211, Goddard 1988, Pierce 1965:383). Chimane has nasals in the pronouns for all three persons, both singular and plural (Martín and Pérez Diez 1990:576). Moreover, Greenberg's claim is not helped by Amerind languages (for example, Zuni and Kuikuro) that have neither n nor m in first person and second person pronoun forms.

67. Proto-Siouan had *w- and *r-, respectively, for these, reflected in Sioux as wa-/mā- 'I' and ya-/nị- 'you'. Note that Lakhota and Sioux are direct opposites of what Greenberg expects to find (Goddard 1988).

68. Greenberg (1987:53) misanalyzed specific Muskogean languages. He gave Creek une 'I', which is a misreading of the orthography for what should be ane, and Apalachee ani, a nonexisting form erroneously copied from Creek sources. However, Muskogean independent pronouns attach prefixes to -ni/-no bases (compare ani 'I', hasno 'you', pihno 'we'); it is a- that is 'I', not the n as supposed by Greenberg (Kimball 1993:448–9).

69. Nichols (in press) adds an another perspective; she criticizes the Amerind pronoun argument because it lacks the "paradigmaticity" found in "stock after stock and language after language," when 'first person' and 'second person' 'singular' and 'plural' are compared in the Nostratic hypothesis. That is, Nostraticists find in the various families that they believe make up Nostratic a recurring pronoun system with different but paradigmatically related forms for first person and second person, singular and plural, subject and object pronouns. This system is exemplified in Shevoroshkin's (1989c:3–4) Nostratic reconstructions of *mi 'I' / *minV 'oblique form of first person singular', *t'i 'thou' / *t'inV 'oblique form of second person singular'. There is no such paradigmatic pattern to the n/m of Greenberg's pronominal claim. DeLancey (in press) argues that paradigmatically related matching pronominal forms support the hypothesis of a genetic relationship between Klamath and Sahaptian and that there are similar patterns in some other languages from both North America and South America. However, a comparison of DeLancey's cases reveals a recurring pattern of n 'first person' and m 'second person', but no shared paradigmaticity among distinct 'first person' forms or differing 'second person' markers. DeLancey argues that the recurrence of such a pattern in different American Indian language groups is unlikely to be due to diffusion or chance. However, there are a number of explanations in addition to genetic inheritance. Given the frequency of first person pronouns with n in the world's languages, we cannot at present determine whether the frequent first person n in American Indian languages is genetically inherited. If we set aside n, we are left with recurrent m (which is not as general in American languages as Greenberg claims), and m by itself is not a paradigm (or a pattern). DeLancey's argument notwithstanding, the possibility of diffusion also cannot be ruled out (as argued earlier in this chapter).

70. Even in American Indian languages in which Greenberg finds the highly touted n/m pronoun pattern, it is clear that it is not always due to inheritance from an ancestor which had it. That is, even cases where the documentable history demonstrates that a currently existing 'first person' n- or 'second person' m- is derived from some other sound as the result of recent change are sometimes taken by Greenberg to be positive evidence for his claims (see Goddard and Campbell 1994 for additional discussion).

71. This article appeared after this book was in press, and is thus discussed only briefly here; there was no opportunity to integrate consideration of it more fully in the discussion here and elsewhere in the book.

72. On the other hand, they see as a "design fault" in papers by both sides of the "Amerind" pronoun issue, by Greenberg and Ruhlen, and by Campbell (1994a), that we, they claim, pursue only positive evidence supporting our separate claims (p. 337). However, Campbell (1994c) is a survey of the explanations for the n/m pattern which have been proposed, including also genetic relationship as a possibility. I did not look only for evidence supporting my claims; rather, I addressed the claims that n/m was general in America and absent elsewhere based on Ruhlen's survey (1994b), on Dryer's sample, and only cursorily on my own limited sampling. This claim about the distribution of n/m proves false even on Nichols and Peterson's own sample—thus it can hardly be said that I sought only "positive evidence" of my claims. In a strange sense, the claim of seeking only confirming evidence might be laid at Nichols and Peterson's feet, since they get their claimed distribution of n/m only by changing the rules of the game. That is, Greenberg and Ruhlen accept any language as a fit so long as it has any first person pronominal form with n and any second person with m, and these can be selected from among any first person or second person pronominal function (singular, dual, plural, inclusive, exclusive, subject, object, possessive, independent, clitic, affix, and so on) or any phonetic shape so long as n and m are among the principal consonants. Following this same procedure, Campbell (1994c) showed that a number of other languages in the world with the n/m pronoun pattern fit what was claimed to be all but absent outside the Americas. Nichols and Peterson, in considering criteria for

showing genetic relatedness, correctly point out that the procedure of seeking *n* and *m* from such a wide range of functions and shapes permits many targets and greatly increases the likelihood of finding a matching by accident; they recommend functional equivalence and stricter formal agreements (they permit only forms where the nasal is morpheme-initial); they seek paradigmatically arranged pronominal systems, with intersecting or cross-classifying patterns, since these defy chance as a possible explanation and can guarantee a historical connection. However, by imposing the conditions that the nasal be morpheme-initial and the compared forms have the same semantic function, they greatly limit the number of systems which constitute counter examples, by Greenberg and Ruhlen's own procedures, to the claims they make. While such restrictions in order to avoid chance are important, they would also lead us to miss connections, for example, where the dialects of a language with 'first person singular' *ni-* would form part of the search, but the dialects with *in-* would fall outside.

73. Nichols and Peterson do not specify this, but may be following Nichols (1992) in distinguishing "families" (at the level of Germanic) and "stocks" (up to the level of Afro-Asiatic). Apart from other difficulties with this division, clearly here the inclusion of several languages from a single genetic unit, known to be related of languages, whether at her "family" or "stock" level, increases the presence of certain traits in a way that the same number of representatives from unrelated languages would not.

74. I owe this observation to Ives Goddard, personal communication.

75. They have some doubt, that in Tunica the *m* may be part of a generic pronoun root.

76. This criticism of Greenberg is not new; his African classification was also castigated because of serious inaccuracies in the data cited (see, for example, Fodor 1966:79–82).

77. Ruhlen counts 2,003 "etymologies" (forms) cited in Greenberg (1987). However, these are divided into 281 proposed Amerind cognate sets, to which Ruhlen, by culling through Greenberg's 2,003 forms, has added another 167, making a total of 448 proposed Amerind cognate sets (1994b:157–79). This may seem to be a mass of evidence, but critics find the sets to be without merit as evidence of the far-flung genetic relationship Greenberg proposes.

78. This was also true in the case of his African classification; in Greenberg's own words: "At the beginning external [nonlinguistic] things had much to do with acceptance of the African classification. All in all, I think that these external factors have had a greater impact than the arguments about linguistic methodology" (quoted in Newman 1991:454).

79. It has not gone unnoticed by scholars that, rather than provide a "solid theoretical basis for his method," Greenberg has preferred to "seek support from past success [in Africa]" (Adelaar 1989:250) and has often cited favorable statements, sometimes by questionable authorities. Strangely, though "appeal to authority" is one of Greenberg's most frequent tactics (1987:1–3; 1989:107, 113; 1993; 1994), Ruhlen (1994b:122, 124) has charged Greenberg's detractors with making "appeals to authority." Furthermore, Adelaar (1989:250) points out that Greenberg's admission that "the validity of Amerind as a whole is more secure than any of its stocks" (Greenberg 1987:59) seems to be a confession of the weakness or inability of the method, which is aimed primarily at classification.

80. As Greenberg put it, "In general where other linguists had presented convincing evidence I adopted it" (1994:4).

81. As should be clear from this survey of the problems and limitations of Greenberg's African classification, Greenberg's statement, that "he [L. Campbell] still accepts my African results but cannot explain them except presumably on the strange assumption that I used the wrong method but got the right results" (1994:4), is quite inaccurate.

82. As Matt Gordon has pointed out to me, even Ruhlen (1987a), a strong supporter of Greenberg's other classifications, seems not to accept fully the Indo-Pacific hypothesis, since Ruhlen's subgroupings for these languages are closer to Wurm's (1982) than to Greenberg's. In fact, Gordon also pointed out that in several cases Greenberg classified what are now known to be dialects of the same language as distinct "languages" belonging to disparate subgroups within his broad Indo-Pacific classification.

83. The discussion in this section follows that in Campbell (1991b).

84. For the record, I did not invent this term but rather encountered it as a graduate student, though I have since been unable to find the source (perhaps it is somewhere in Swadesh's work). Because we do not yet know the full explanation of the few lexical items that seem to recur widely in different American Indian language groups, I would have preferred to avoid such a term, with its apparent suggestion of genetic relationship.

85. Indeed, the broader affinity of Timotean (two languages) is unknown (see Chapter 6).

86. I hasten to add that it is absolutely clear that by no means is Greenberg's (1987) an etymological dictionary in any real sense. Rather, it is a compilation of forms which he believes exhibit some shared similarities on the basis of which he would like to argue for genetic connections. Until such connections can

be successfullly demonstrated, it is premature to think of subgrouping, and it is out of the question to call it an etymological dictionary (see Goddard 1975, Watkins 1990).

87. Ruhlen failed to recognize this flaw: "Michelson was citing evidence that the Algonquian-Ritwan family was merely one component of an even larger genetic group, and it is this larger grouping, not just Algonquian-Ritwan, that is characterized by *n*-and *m*-, respectively, in the first- and second-person pronouns. Interpreted in this manner, Michelson's critique in no way affects Sapir's claim of genetic affinity between Algonquian, Wiyot, and Yurok" (1987a:222).

Chapter 8   Distant Genetic Relationships: The Proposals

1. It is surprising to find Hymes supporting a genetic connection between Quechua and the so-called Altaic languages; he is on record with the statement: "Clearly this attempt [Bouda 1960] . . . confirms the genealogical relationship of Quechua with Altaic, letting one recognize that still another ancient American Kultursprache stems from Asia" (1961c:362).

2. Allen (1931) compared a number of Siouan and Iroquoian "parallels," citing resemblant forms selected from various Siouan and Iroquoian languages, but "his data and methodology were rather disorganized" (Chafe 1964:852). In not a few of his cases, it is difficult to determine just what part of the words cited is being compared, and often the compared part is very short (*CV*). Since most of Allen's more plausible matchings are included in Chafe's work, which is clearer, Allen's forms are not addressed here directly (though reference is made to some individual cases).

3. It should be noted that in contrast to the more tentative and cautious claims he made in his articles, Chafe said of his then soon-to-appear article (1964) that he thought it would "show that Iroquoian and Siouan are related" and that "the relationship has been established" (Chafe's discussion published in Elmendorf 1965:104). However, when asked about the possible Iroquoian-Caddoan relationship, Chafe replied that he did not know why "everyone seems to have thought" the two related, "because there was no evidence"; but he added that "I don't know whether I should say this in public—I suspect that all three [Siouan, Caddoan, Iroquoian] are related. I hope I can prove this" (in Elmendorf 1965:104–5).

4. For example, Mithun (1991) does not argue for a genetic relationship between Siouan, Caddoan, and Iroquoian but rather asserts that there is one, citing Chafe and Allen. In her article, she explains that active

case alignment in Siouan and Caddoan is determined principally by agency, whereas in Iroquoian it is based on aspect. She argues that it is an easy step to shift from an active system based on agency to that of the Iroquoian languages where aspect is a determining factor. This may all be true, but even if we could show that all three language families were once characterized by an active system, the presence of active alignment in many other languages of the world (including some neighbors of these families in the Southeast linguistic area; see Nicklas 1994) would caution us that this typological trait could easily be shared without necessarily implying inheritance from a common ancestor. Moreover, it may be relatively straightforward for agency-oriented active marking to shift to a system where aspect (particularly perfective) dominates, but since both of these systems are perfectly normal and abundant in the world's languages, more evidence is required to show that such a historical shift actually took place in Iroquoian rather than merely that it could have. Since no convincing evidence of a genetic relationship between these languages has yet been presented, it is just as plausible that Iroquoian has always had the natural marking system exhibited by its daughter languages.

5. Alternatively, the *wa-* could be the nominalizing prefix on the stative verb root 'little' (Robert Rankin, personal communication).

6. All monosyllabic roots in Winnebago and other Mississippi Valley Siouan languages have long vowels, and the final glottal stops are not distinctive. The Winnebago forms for 'arrow' and 'earth' are homophonic, *ma·*, though in some Siouan languages these are not homophonic (Robert Rankin, personal communication).

7. The widespread distribution ("pan-Americanness") of words for 'land/earth/ground' in Native American languages is indicated by the following: Kutenai *ʔamak* (Haas 1965:85); Wappo *ʔomaⁱʔomi* (Elmendorf 1988); Chimariko *ʔámmá* (Crawford 1967:182); Shasta *má* (Webb 1974); Proto-Pomoan *ʔa(h)ma·*, *ʔahmáṭ/ʔamáṭ* (Langdon 1979:637); Proto-Yuman *ʔ-mat* (Langdon 1979:637); Tequistlatec *amac'* (Bright 1956); Salvadoran Lenca *omoŋ* (Río Urrutia 1985:57); Goajiro *uma* (Suárez 1977:247); Proto-Panoan *mai-* (Girard 1971b:166); Proto-Takanan *awa* 'land' (Girard 1971b:55), *meji* 'earth' (Girard 1971b:100); Mosetén *amañ* (Suárez 1977:247); Tupinambá *iβi*, Bakairí *iwi*, Apalaí *ipi-* (Rodrigues 1985:382); Mapudungu *mapu* (Key 1978:288). Of course, such similarities are not limited to Native American languages; compare Finnish *maa* 'land, earth, 'ground'; Sumerian *ma, mada* 'land', North Caucasian *měl-ǯǯV* 'earth, place' (Bengtson 1991:99).

Siouan-Catawban Comparisons

Siouan		Catawba	
*ru	'by hand'	du	'by hand', 'to take' (Siebert)
*raka	'by striking'	ka·ʔ	'to strike, hit' (Siebert)
*ra	'by mouth'	ną sing.,	'to eat' (Voorhis)
		wira pl.	
*rą	'by foot'	da·	
			'by foot', da·ʔ 'go' (Siebert)
*aRá·	'by heat'	wi·rá	'to burn', de 'blaze' (Shea) ?
*Wo	'by blowing/shoot'	pu·	'by blowing' (Siebert)

8. I thank Robert Rankin for bringing this information to my attention. He sent me the Siouan-Catawban comparisons shown in the table above. In Catawba, 'by foot' and 'go' differ slightly in conjugation.

9. Rankin agrees with Chafe that Chafe's -ki, Rankin's *-ke, in this and the other positional forms cited was a suffix; "-ke recurs with many other verbs and the roots themselves occur separately in some contexts." Also, there is a "competing and partially suppletive root ni- 'sit' found in Dhegiha, Chiwere, and a couple of Dakotan dialects; it is of uncertain age, but does resemble one of Chafe's Caddoan positionals, albeit both very short forms" (Rankin, personal communication).

10. Rankin (personal communication) points out further that the positionals seem to have had a continuative aspectual meaning when used as auxiliaries in all Siouan languages but apparently not in Catawban, which suggests, again, their later origin. Of course, Catawban could have once had the positional continuatives and later lost this category, but this seems unlikely, given that the positional continuatives are a prominent areal trait in the Southeastern linguistic area, to which Catawba belongs (see Chapter 9). Rankin describes these elements as postposed or in some cases postclitic to main verbs, and they often bear their own person-number inflection, so they cannot accurately be termed suffixes.

11. Rankin (personal communication) points out that Protozl-Siouan *ʔų́·-re 'make, do' (*-re is the so-called root extension, an empty morph) could be added to the Caddo-Seneca comparison.

12. Since 'maize' did not arrive in the Mississippi Valley until ca. 1 A.D. (Rankin 1993), it is highly unlikely that these forms could have originally meant 'to pound corn'; perhaps they meant just 'pound' (Rankin, personal communication).

13. Rankin (personal communication) notes the similarity between these and Proto-Siouan *é·-re or *é·-ye 'feces, defecate'. The matching part, however, is exceedingly short.

14. In the supporting evidence for this interpretation, Rankin mentions that "the inclusive is not incorporated into Siouan person-number morphology thoroughly: there are inalienable possessive prefixes for 1st and 2nd persons but not for inclusive. In addition, the inclusive prefix oddly occurs farthest to the left in verbs, preceding nearly every other prefix, thus giving the impression it was an add-on. This is reinforced by the fact that Crow and Hidatsa completely lack any trace of it. . . . The clearly reconstructible 'man' term, *wá·ke, has been replaced with secondary terms as inclusive person has spread: Dakotan wičhaša, Dhegiha níhka" (personal communication).

15. As Rankin points out (personal communication), these Siouan first person pronominal forms do not match up with even Catawban 'first person singular' forms and are apparently an innovation within core Siouan (Siouan minus Catawban). Catawban has 'first person singular' nV- ~ dV-. Since the Siouan *wa-/*ma- set is transparent and easily reconstructed, whereas the Catawba forms are fused to the verb roots in many cases and are hard to reconstruct, Rankin suspects the Catawban forms are probably older.

16. Rankin informs me (personal communication) that no such Proto-Siouan second person pronominal form exists. Rather, this is an obstruentized allomorph of the Proto-Siouan *ya- 'second person actor' prefix, which is cognate with Catawba ya-. The vowel-syncope sound change leaves y-, and this allomorph underwent spirantization (y > š, perhaps through y > ž > š, as in varieties of Argentine Spanish); Catawba also has an obstruentized allomorph, c-.

17. Rankin (personal communication) does not recognize this Siouan term for 'tobacco', but explains that Proto-Siouan has *ų·pa for 'tobacco, to smoke (tobacco or other plant, for example, sumac)' (compare Catawba ųpa·). However, phonetically similar terms for tobacco are fairly widespread in western North America. Also, the Tutelo and Mississippi Valley Siouan *ra·ni 'tobacco', similar to the Iroquoian term Chafe lists, contains several phonological irregularities and is a diffused term—in fact, probably a borrowing from Iroquoian itself.

18. Rankin (personal communication) indicates that the more current reconstruction is Proto-Siouan *i-rá·še 'name', where i- is 'third person inalienable possessor'. This is not as similar to the Iroquoian form, however.

19. Following are some examples of the 'water/drink' pan-Americanism that are similar to the forms cited by Carter: Hanis si 'drink' (Swadesh 1960c:918); Proto-Miwok *ʔuš·u- 'to drink' (Callaghan 1991c:228); Karuk ʔiš 'to drink' (Haas 1964b:77), ʔá·s 'water' (Bright 1957), sa- 'toward the river' (Haas 1954:59); Northern Yana sii- 'to drink' (Haas 1964b:77); Proto-Yuman *-isí- 'to drink' (Webb 1974); Tarascan icí 'water'; Tequistlatec iš 'to drink' (Webb 1974); Jicaque isí 'water'.

20. Rudes is concerned mostly with the 'second person singular pronominal prefix' (his Macro-Siouan *si-), which he interprets as having undergone rhotacism in Siouan-Yuchi, but he does not present the actual forms, mentioning only "irregular" verbs (for example, what he assumed to be Siouan-Yuchi *-re- 'to go'—the only one cited) which behave differently with respect to this postulated prefix.

21. Actually, considerable differences in these sound systems are pointed out by Chafe (1973:1197–8), but on the whole, each individual system is relatively simple.

22. What they said about Kiowa is ambiguous: "While Kiowa is related to Tanoan, the relationship is on a different plane from that of the Uto-Aztecan. In view of certain possibilities of relationship of our Azteco-Tanoan group to other groups in several directions from it. . . . We prefer to leave the question of the inclusion of Kiowa in the Azteco-Tanoan stock till another occasion" (Whorf and Trager 1937:609–10).

23. This Cahuilla form may be spurious; the correct shape is salu-, which is probably from *suta (William Bright, personal communication); hence it may not be cognate with the forms from the other languages cited.

24. Some examples are: Xinca pa:c'i 'to grind corn, corn dough'; Cholan-Tzeltalan *pac' 'tamale', compare Chol pac' 'tamale made of corn dough and immature beans', Tzotzil pača 'lowland corn', Choltí pa 'tortilla', peče 'to make tortillas'; Sayula Popoluca pac 'to make tortillas', Totontepec Mixe po:ca 'tamal de Todos Santos', Proto-Mixe-Zoquean *pici 'leached corn' (nixtamal); Tarascan píhtsi 'ear of corn'; Papantla Totonac, Xicotepec de Juárez Totonac paʔs(a) 'to shell corn'; Nahua pa:c- in compounds, for example, pa:c-ka 'to squeeze liquid out', pa[:]ca[:]wa 'to mash, grind, squeeze fruit or something similar' (Molina 1591:80) (some would relate the Nahua form to PUA *pa:- 'water, liquid'); Mazahua pɛɛčʔi, mbɛɛčʔi

'to make tortillas, applaud'; Tequistlatec -š-pac'áʔi 'corn tamale', -fuxtaʔ 'atole (made without lime)' (f < ph); Huave peac, Proto-Huave *pIca 'tortilla', pasol 'lime', *-pasa 'corn husk'; Poqom poč(-b'il) 'tamale'. (There may be an element of onomatopoeia in some of these forms—for example, the noise of "patting" tortillas—though certainly borrowing is also involved.)

25. Some examples of similarities (due either to accident or to diffusion) involving words for 'tobacco' are: Karuk ʔuhípih (Bright 1957); Chimariko h-óphat 'smoking' (Gursky 1974:209); Proto-Palaihnihan *o·xpi (Gursky 1974:209); Cocopa ú·p, Mojave ʔaʔú·v (Crawford 1976:187); Seri ʔapis 'tobacco'; Proto-Yuman *-pis 'suck, smoke'; Proto-Yokuts *pam'o·/*paʔom- 'to smoke (tobacco or pipe)' (Callaghan 1991b); Lake Miwok p'óm·a 'to puff, suck (pipe)' (Callaghan 1991c); Proto-Maiduan *pán (Ultan 1964:365).

26. I thank William Bright (personal communication) for this observation.

27. Some seemingly widespread similar words for 'cold', perhaps reflecting affective/expressive symbolism, are: Chimariko eso-ta 'cold', hači 'ice, frost' (Crawford 1967:182); Shasta ʔis·ík', Achomawi asjē·- (Gursky 1974:183); Wappo chach/cha-, Proto-Yuki *šat'/*šə- 'cold' (Elmendorf 1988); Proto-Uto-Aztecan *cɨ- (Miller 1987:39); Chitimacha č'aki (Swadesh 1946:127); Proto-Mayan *siʔk; Proto-Bora-Muinane *ciíko (Aschmann 1993:145); Chipaya sakiže (Polansky 1915:17); Aguaruna cekcék (Larson 1955–1957:8); Selknam čàrxi 'cold' (Najlis 1993:104). See also Greenberg (1987:69–70); for similar forms in languages spoken elsewhere in the world, see Ruhlen 1994b:26–7).

28. For examples of widespread similarities involving words for 'hand', see Swadesh 1954:309, Greenberg 1987:229–30.

29. The widespread similarities involving words for 'foot' and 'leg' are indicated by the following: Eyak q'aš/kuš 'foot' (Ruhlen 1994b:78); Yana gaadu 'leg', Isleño Chumash -kot 'leg' (Gursky 1974:195); Proto-Uto-Aztecan *kasi 'leg, foot'; Proto-Utian *kolo 'foot' (Callaghan 1991b); Proto-Yokuts *kalasa-ʔ 'leg, foot' (Callaghan 1991b); Proto-Central-Algonquian *-(x)ka·t- 'foot, leg' (Gursky 1963:18); Proto-Chibchan *kac 'foot', Proto-Chibchan *kisa 'foot, root' (Holt 1989); Proto-Panoan *kiši 'leg' (Holt 1989); Proto-Matacoan *qala, Selknam hàli (Najlis 1993:12, 92).

30. Examples of the pan-Americanism for 'dog' include: Proto-Sierra Miwok čuku-, Proto-Yokuts *c'i·sis (Callaghan 1991b); Karuk čiši·h (Bright 1957); Yana su:su (Sapir 1917a); Washo súkaʔ (Webb 1974); Blackfoot čúki, Quapaw šúke, Dakota šúka

(Wolff 1950:116); Tunica *sa* (Munro 1994:168); Nahuatl *čiči;* Totonac *čiči?* (Justeson et al. 1985:27);
Tequistlatec *čiki* (Webb 1974); Proto-Mayan **c'i?,*
Jicaque *cʰiyó,* Proto-Lencan **su* (Arguedas Cortés
1987:39); Proto-Chibchan **cul/*su* (Holt 1989); Mosetén *ačo,* Amuesha *o:ček* (Suárez 1977:244).

31. Examples of lexical similarities involving
words for 'aunt/elder sister', to which Jakobson's
(1960) explanation of similarities among kinship
terms probably applies (see Chapter 7), are: Northern
Sahaptin *paXɔ́X,* Nez Perce *pé:geX* (Aoki 1963:111);
Salinan *pé?* 'elder sister', *paš* 'aunt, female's elder
sister' (Turner 1980:67, 83); Tarascan *pípi* 'man's
elder sister', *pipe* 'woman's sister', Totonac *pi:pi?*
'man's elder sister', Nahuatl *-pi?* 'elder sister' (Justeson et al. 1985:27); Pipil *pi:pi* 'aunt, elder sister',
Francisco León Zoque *popo* 'aunt (mother's brother's
wife)', Salvadoran Lencan **peleh* 'older sister' (Arguedas Cortés 1987:36) (see Greenberg 1987:101,
125).

32. Similar forms for 'to give' are often included
in sets for 'hand', given earlier in this chapter.

33. While the family which includes Aymara, Jaqaru, and Kawki (Cauqui) is often known as the Jaqi
family (Hardman de Bautista 1975, 1978a, 1978b) or
the Aru family, more recently Andeanists have been
calling it the Aymaran family. Cerrón-Palomino's
(1993) reasons for adopting "Aymaran" as the name
of the family are persuasive, and therefore that is the
name I employ.

34. This discussion of the Quechumaran hypothesis follows that in Campbell 1995, which provides
additional information.

35. Max Uhle (1890) had reservations about the
genetic hypothesis; he was later joined by Ferrario,
Alfredo Torero, Parker, Hardman de Bautista, and
since 1970 by most other Andeanists (see Mannheim
1991:43).

36. It is perhaps appropriate to warn readers of my
predisposition (or bias?): I have always felt favorable
toward the possibility that these two families may
prove to be genetically related, though the tide of
recent opinion is in the opposite direction.

37. It is sometimes suggested that the two are
typologically somewhat different—that Quechua is
agglutinative but Aymara is "polysynthetic"—since
Quechua morphemes are quite clear and undergo little
morphophonemic variation, while some in Aymara
show the results of certain phonological reductions
and other changes; for example, Aymara *mamšqa*
'with our mother', composed of *mami* 'mother' +
-sa 'our' + *-wšqa* 'with' (see Cerrón-Palomino
1987:361). However, despite the impact of these eli-
sions (which is actually rather minor and for the most
part still leaves the variant forms clearly similar and

easily identified within Aymara), the two languages
are structurally remarkably similar.

38. Hardman de Bautista has gone so far as to
call Cuzco Quechua "una forma quechua acriollada
con el aymara" (a form of Quechua creolized with
Aymara) (1978a:14), though most other scholars do
not share this extreme view.

39. But Proulx (1987) argues that since *C'* and *Cʰ*
are found in so many American Indian languages,
they could be just a typological similarity and thus
might have nothing to do with either a genetic relationship or borrowing.

40. Cerrón-Palomino (personal communication)
finds Proulx's arguments in this matter to be convincing.

41. Mannheim (1991:119) admits, though reluc-
tantly, that this constitutes possible evidence for glottalization in Proto-Southern Peruvian Quechua
(though he believes borrowing from a variety with
glottalization is also a possibility).

42. Another example is the assibilated *r* of Guatemalan Spanish, found also in certain Peninsular Spanish dialects and present in the K'ichean (Mayan)
languages of Guatemala. The K'ichean pronunciation
and the Spanish dialect variant seem to have converged, thus preserving a pronunciation not found in
neighboring dialects of Spanish or indeed in the vast
majority of other Spanish dialects. A grammatical
example of preservation due to language contact is
the pleonastic possessive construction found in Mayan
languages and in Guatemalan, Chiapan, and Yucatecan Spanish and formerly in varieties of Peninsular
Spanish, for example, *tengo un mi caballo* 'I have a
horse' (literally 'I have one my horse')—compare
K'iche' *k'o xun nu-kye:x* (same meaning; literally
'exists one my-horse'). In this case, the retention of
the pleonastic possessive proves to be only in those
Spanish dialects which are in contact with Mayan
languages—that is, it is due to language contact. This
construction, once widely used in Peninsular Spanish,
is now no longer known there (see Martin 1978).

43. Mannheim interprets the prothetic *h* as pre-
venting the occurrence of a predictable glottal stop
before such vowel-initial words "which would violate
a constraint that prohibits the occurrence of two glottalized segments in a word" (1985:675).

44. However, as Mannheim (1985:664) points out,
even if this principle should prove to be well founded,
the presence of *C'* and *Cʰ* in both Quechuan and
Aymaran has little effect on the validity of the Quechumaran hypothesis, which can be demonstrated
only by means of systematic comparison. Mannheim
(1985:665) discusses a way of interpreting the role
of the distributional restrictions on *C'* and *Cʰ* in
Southern Quechua, not as involving more constraints

than those found in the assumed donor Aymaran languages, but as exhibiting fewer. In his view, structurally speaking, the distribution of *C'* and *C^h* in Southern Quechua is much more tightly constrained than in Aymara, but functionally, according to Mannheim, the opposite holds: glottalization (and perhaps also aspiration), with its limit of one occurrence per word, has a "culminative" role, signaling the word as a phonological unit. Mannheim reasons that "at the same time as ejectivity [glottalization] acquires a culminative function, its systematic integration from the sense-discriminative standpoint is weakened. . . . The 'once per word' restriction . . . is in a way a *generalization* of the sense-discriminative function of the feature to its most simple form: words are distinguished by the presence or absence of a feature (ejectivity, aspiration) whose position in the word is nearly predictable, and whose domain is the entire word" (1985:665). Mannheim sees the functional role of the structural distribution limitations as being more general in Quechua than in Aymaran, the assumed donor languages. Mannheim's view seems to suggest that *C'* and *C^h* may have come into Quechua with fewer structural distributional restrictions than they have today, and that these restrictions developed later to fill the function of word-discrimination. I concede that it is possible that these features may have entered Quechua through influence from Aymaran and only later acquired their restrictions, but this is by no mains the only or even most likely explanation. Mannheim, in taking this posture, seems to be abandoning the argument that the distributional restrictions are suggestive of borrowing. If the distributional restrictions are seen as evidence against borrowing as the explanation of the origin of *C'* and *C^h* in Quechuan (unless they were acquired after the borrowing), then the other possibilities are (1) the genetic hypothesis— that the two families share the features because they inherited them from their common ancestor and (2) accident—that the two families just happen independently to contain glottalized and aspirated consonants (see Proulx 1987).

45. Note that some forms formerly identified as loans from Spanish, such as *mut'u-y* 'to mutilate' (Spanish *mutilar*) and *hič'a-y* 'to throw' (Spanish *echar*), later turned out to be only accidentally similar to the Spanish forms and to have legitimate Quechuan etymologies (see Stark 1979[1975]:212, Cerrón-Palomino 1987, Mannheim 1985:660, 675). It is likely that *hasut'i* 'whip' has acquired glottalization for symbolic or affective reasons, the same as other words have acquired it, to reflect the sharp, stinging, popping attributes of whips. 'Axe' *hač'a* may have had the same motivation, though I suspect a combination of other factors may have been at work. It was probably

borrowed with the *h* of older Spanish (as it was in a number of other Latin American Indian languages), and was perhaps affected by the constraint that vowel-initial words with a glottalized consonant insert a prothetic *h*, so that initial *h* triggered the addition of glottalization to the affricate in this word. Also, a high proportion of stems in Southern Quechua that have an etymological **č* are now attested with glottalization: the affricate itself being glottalized when it is word-initial, and the initial stop of the word is glottalized when this affricate is not in initial position (Mannheim 1985:660). Since the Spanish loan contains an affricate (matching a principal reflex of **č*), conceivably this explains the loanword's acquisition of glottalization. Perhaps all these factors worked in concert to dispose this loan to acquire glottalization.

46. While Hardman de Bautista (1985) does not specify the forms she assigns to these categories, Cerrón-Palomino (1987:360) reports that what she meant was that (1) some of the forms do not exist in Aymara; (2) some Aymara forms are confused with others (for example, *q^hil^ya* 'ash' and *qil^ya* 'lazy'); and (3) some morphologically complex Aymara forms have been interpreted as roots (with a failure to identify and segment off from the roots such productive suffixes as *-t'a* 'participle' and *-iri* 'agentive').

47. Moreover, the three-way contrast merged to a two-way contrast in Hittite, Avestan, Old Irish, Lithuanian, Old Church Slavic, and Albanian.

48. In a letter to Kroeber (June 15, 1924), Sapir recommended that "the possibility of Chukchi-Kamchadal belonging to Eskimo-Aleut might well be hinted at" (cited in Golla 1984:413). Hamp (1976:85) includes Chukchi (Chukchee, also known as Luoravetlanskij), Koryak, Aliutor, Kerek, and Itel'men in his grouping of the languages.

49. Roman Jakobson is reported to have suggested that, conversely, some Paleosiberians may have returned to Asia after having migrated to North America in prehistoric times (Voegelin and Voegelin 1967:575–6).

50. The name Na-Dene is Sapir's creation, obtained by combining the Tlingit form *naa* 'tribe' and the Athabaskan form for 'person, people' (for example, Navajo *diné* 'person') (Pinnow 1985:25).

51. It should be pointed out that in spite of this preamble, Pinnow's purpose in this article is to argue that lexical comparisons support a genetic relationship between Tlingit, Eyak, and Athabaskan, though he says "the position of Haida is—at present—still uncertain" (1964b:156).

52. Hymes (1955, 1956) also argued in support of Na-Dene, but I take positional analysis on which Hymes based his conclusions to be thoroughly dis-

counted, and therefore I do not cover that ground here (see the discussion in Chapter 7).

53. I do not share Pinnow's (1968:208) doubts regarding diffusion in this example.

54. It is interesting that P. E. Goddard, in his criticism of Sapir's original Na-Dene hypothesis, made similar points concerning possible Tlingit-Athabaskan connections: "With this striking likeness in morphology [between Tlingit and Athabaskan languages], one would expect lexical similarity leading to the definite conclusion that the languages were originally one, or sprang from the same source. The comparisons made of the lexical content, however, do not justify this conclusion. The similarities are few, forming but a slight percentage of the whole. . . . Until some satisfactory explanations can be given for this mass of apparently unrelated material, a common genetic origin cannot be admitted" (1920:270). Krauss (1973b:953–63) suggests that Tlingit may be a "hybrid," a mix of Athabaskan-Eyak and some unrelated language (see also Krauss and Golla 1981:67). This opinion is not shared by most historical linguists. Leer (1990, 1991), however, also believes Tlingit is hybridized, but not in the way Krauss had imagined, but rather as composed of related varieties of pre-Tlingit (see Chapter 4).

55. Shafer's (1969) note adds a scant half dozen examples to the list of Chinese-Athabaskan comparisons.

56. Bengtson credits Trombetti (1926) with "first proposing special ties between Basque, Caucasian, 'Indochinese', 'Paleo-Asiatic' (including Yeniseian), and Western North America (i.e. Na-Dene), all in the context of his monogenetic global hierarchy" (1991:67). Other languages have been suggested as members of "Sino-Caucasian," such as Burushaski, Etruscan, Nahali, Gilyak, and, in the Americas, "Almosan-Keresiouan" (Shevoroshkin 1990, Bengtson 1991:67–8).

57. Nikolaev (1991) goes further and claims that Algonquian-Ritwan and Salishan are also connected with "Sino-Caucasian," and Shevoroshkin (1991) concurs. However, Nikolaev's forty lexical sets (comparing Sino-Caucasian with Algonquian and Salishan) and Shevoroshkin's (1991:7–8) thirteen sets (comparing mostly Salishan forms with words from the other languages) are hardly persuasive, for they exhibit the typical problems (onomatopoeia, short forms, semantic latitude, nursery forms, and so on).

58. Given the shakiness of the components of Mosan and other combinations such as Algonkin-Wakashan, I do not take up Swadesh's (1960e) "Vascodene" proposal, which covers much of Eurasia and in which Wakashan is considered part of Vascodene; Chimakuan and Salishan are no longer part of

Mosan but rather he includes them in his Macro-Hoka.

59. Natürlich genügen diese Ähnlichkeiten nicht für einen Verwandschaftsbeweis. Sie könnten ja auch Fälle von Entlehnungen darstellen, obwohl das nicht allzu wahrscheinlich ist, da es sich im allen Fällen um Wörter des Grundvokabulars handelt.

60. In the 1915 article, Kroeber compared a list of thirty-five words from Seri, Chontal (Tequistlatecan), and Mojave (the list is not complete in any of the three languages); he mentions sound correspondences, though many of those he presented are found in only one lexical set.

61. The 1904 list contained Chumash *talawaxa*, Salinan *talxual* 'work', which was later recognized as being derived from Spanish *trabajar* and eliminated from the 1913 list. The 1904 list also included forms for 'rabbit', 'jackrabbit', and 'ground squirrel', which are possible loans, and two kinship terms that were not repeated in the 1913 list.

62. For the purposes of this argument, I ignore the difference between the /θ/ of the nouns and the /ð/ of the demonstratives, since in a documented earlier stage of English there was no voicing contrast in these segments.

63. Ives Goddard has reminded me (personal communication) that some scholars would interpret words such as the one for Coos 'spear' as being expressive or onomatopoetic, like slam-crush-snap-bang-crack-hit words.

64. Some 'water' examples were presented earlier in this chapter. Some examples of 'urine/urinate', that may be explained by onomatopoeia or expressive symbolism, are: Proto-Nim-Yokuts *č'ulu·/*č'uyu·· 'to urinate', *č'ulon/*čuyon 'urine' (Callaghan 1991b); Konkow *c'úc'u*, Nisenan *ʔuc'u* (Ultan 1964:368); Washo *á·šaʔ* 'urine, to urinate' (Jacobsen 1958:204); Atsugewi *wisāq* 'urine' (Gursky 1974:210); Proto-Chumash *Sol'* 'to urinate' (Klar 1977:113); Proto-Uto-Aztecan *siʔ* 'urinate' (Miller 1967:62); Chitimacha *č'ište-* 'urinate' (Munro 1994:206); Proto-Tzeltal-Tzotzil *čuš*, Tojolabal *č'ul*, Chuj *-čul*, Yucatec *wì·š*; Jicaque *cúsi*; Proto-Lencan *waisa* 'to urinate' (Arguedas Cortés 1987:39); Proto-Misumalpan *usu* (Constenla 1987:156); Proto-Chibchan *h(ʷ)iši/a* (Holt 1989). (See Crawford 1976:187 for discussion of symbolic alternations; see Greenberg 1987:77, 121, 161 for other examples.)

65. Earlier, Haas (1954) had compared words for 'water' in the putative Hokan-Coahuiltecan languages; although these words appear to be similar, I discount them because: (1) a single form is never sufficient to demonstrate a genetic relationship; (2) many (most?) of these are short forms, often *ax* or *xa*; (3) 'water' is one of the most widespread so-

called pan-Americanisms; and (4) I suspect that the frequent similarity of terms for 'water' and 'to drink' in the world's languages is due at least in part to onomatopoeia—that is, imitative of the sound of drinking/pouring/running water. In any case, the relevant universe of discourse with regard to terms for 'water' and 'to drink' is not merely putative Hokan languages but the world's languages, including those of the Americas. Some examples are: Kutenai -ku (suffix) 'water' (Haas 1965:87); Proto-Costanoan *ʔukʷ·i 'to drink' (Callaghan 1991c:228); Proto-Utian *ki·k/*kik·i 'water' (Callaghan 1991c:230); Proto-Yokuts *ukun 'to drink' (Callaghan 1991c); Wappo ʔúk'-, Proto-Yuki *ʔuk' 'to drink, water' (Elmendorf 1988); Chimariko ʔaqha 'water' (Crawford 1976:187); Proto-Pomoan *ʔahqʰa 'water' (Langdon 1979:639); Proto-Yuman *ʔ-xa (Langdon 1979:639); Zuni k'a (Gursky 1966a:420); Tonkawa yakʷ-, yako- (Haas 1959:3); Chitimacha kuʔ 'water, liquid' (Swadesh 1946:124); Natchez kuN 'water' (Kimball 1993); Proto-Siouan *qʷaʔ/*qoʔ 'water' (Haas 1965:87); Proto-Central-Algonquian *akwa:- 'water' (Haas 1959:3); Timucua uku 'to drink' (Granberry 1993:172); Mapudungu ko (Stark 1970). (See Swadesh 1954:311.) Compare the proposed Proto-Nostratic *'Ek'u 'water, drink', Proto-Yeniseian *ag-'drink', Proto-North-Caucasian *-qV 'drink' (Starostin 1989:55); see Ruhlen (1994b:51) for similarities with putative Khoisan languages.

66. Examples of similar 'tongue' words (perhaps reflecting onomatopoeia or expressive symbolism) include: Kutenai walu·nak (Haas 1965:85); Nez Perce pe:ws (Aoki 1963:112); Klamath ba:wač (Aoki 1963:112); Southern Sierra Miwok neppit- (Broadbent and Pitkin 1964:45); Chitimacha wen (Swadesh 1946:129); Timucua bali (Granberry 1993:233); Nahuatl nenepil-; Salvadoran Lenca nepal (Río Urrutia 1985:41); Proto-Witotoan *-pe (Aschmann 1993:130) (see Greenberg 1987:141).

67. As William Bright (personal communication) points out, it is strange that 'ear', 'liver', and 'navel' should be four- and five-syllable words.

68. Die Erforschung der genetischen Zusammenhänge der Hoka-Sprachen befindet sich nun einmal immer noch in einem gewissen Pionierstadium. Die Lautentsprechungen zwischen den einzelnen Hoka-Sprachen sind—trotz der in den letzen Jahren erzielten Fortschritte—bisher nur teilweise und auch dann nicht mit letzter Sicherheit ermittelt.

69. Some examples of 'butterfly' (perhaps expressive or symbolic in origin) as a "pan-Americanism" are: Atsugewi palala, Achomawi walʔwāla, apōna (Gursky 1974:182); Washo paʔlóʔlo (Gursky 1974:182); Proto-Yuman *-ráp/*-ĺáp/*-náp (Gursky 1974:182); Yuki p'alp'ol (Gursky 1974:182); Lake

Miwok woló·lok (Gursky 1974:182); Proto-Wintuan *bolbolop (Whistler 1977:164); Wükchamni Yokuts walwal (Gursky 1974:182); Atakapa walwal (Gursky 1968:28); Nahuatl papalo-; Totonac špiʔpiʔle·qa; Proto-Mayan *pehpen; Cacaopera lapúlapú (Bertoglia Richards 1988:74); Proto-Panoan *pĭpĭšawa (Girard 1971a:168); Proto-Takanan *sapipi, *sababa, *sapuřa (Girard 1971b:168); Mapudungu nampe (Stark 1970). Compare Basque pinpirin/pinpilin (Bengtson 1991:105), putative North Caucasian *pɔrV/*pɔlV (Bengtson 1991:105), French papillon, Finnish perhonen, Maori purerehua, and other forms from languages spoken all over the world.

70. Landar's (1968) proposed affiliation of Karankawa with Cariban, and hence a connection between Cariban and Hokan, has not been found to be of merit.

71. Even 'nose', Comecrudo ia (yax), Cotoname iae (ya'ex), is sometimes thought to be a loan from Nahuatl yah- in compounds, yaka- otherwise.

72. Only one example is given for what Manaster Ramer takes to be *q' (Coahuilteco ānua : Comecrudo kan : Garza an 'moon', where this time it is Coahuilteco which lost the initial consonant and Comecrudo which kept a reflex, the opposite of the assumed *t'. The only instance for *k'w is Comecrudo wax, Cotoname kox 'belly', challenged above. The fact that additional examples of this proposed k : w set are not available casts further doubt on this set; no *k' was proposed.

73. Because of onomatopoeia, similar forms are found widely; an example is Proto-Mayan *č'ok 'grackle, blackbird'.

74. Nevertheless, Haas indicated that "it is my belief that the Siouan languages are at least distantly related to the Gulf languages" (1958b:233). She compared twenty-four lexical resemblances, offering some possible sound correspondences, involving Algonquian and Chimakuan languages that, she asserted, "greatly strengthen the case for a probable genetic affiliation between Algonkian and Chemakuan" (1960:983). These twenty-four forms exhibit many of the difficulties discussed in Chapter 7 and do not seem to constitute valid evidence of such a relationship.

75. Examples of the 'wide/flat' pan-Americanism include: Yana -dʔpal- 'flat' (Gursky 1974:188); Washo ílpil 'flat' (Gursky 1974:188); Wappo -paṭ-/-phaʔ 'flat, wide', Yuki pat/pat'/paʔat 'flat, wide' (Elmendorf 1988); Proto-Uto-Aztecan *pata- 'spread', Nahuatl patla(:wa)-k 'wide' (Miller 1967:410); Atakapa palpal 'flat, level', pahš 'flat, thin' (Munro 1994:172); Natchez pet 'spread' (Munro 1994:199); Tunica pélka 'flat' (Munro 1994:172); Chickasaw patali 'spread' (Munro 1994:190); Ofo ftétka 'flat' (Wolff

1950:172); Proto-Chibchan *pa(k) 'wide, flat, open' (Holt 1989) (see also Greenberg 1987:69, 102).

76. Some examples of similarities among words for 'ash/dust' are: Nez Perce puX-puX 'dust' (De-Lancey, Genetti, and Rude 1988:210); Wappo puṭʰ 'dust, ashes', Proto-Yuki *pot'(-il) 'dust, ashes' (El-mendorf 1988); Koasati pofotli 'dust' (Munro 1994:153); Timucua api 'ashes, dust' (Granberry 1993:184, 196); Tarascan hápu 'ashes', pú-rha 'dust'; Jicaque ipʰí 'ashes'; Proto-Chibchan *bur-/*burų́ 'ashes' (Constenla 1981:362), Teribe plun 'dust' (Gunn 1980:445); Proto-Maipurean *pʰa(ne)/*pʰe(ne) 'dust', *pališi 'ash' (Payne 1991:394, 401); Proto-Bora-Muinane *bái-giíxi 'ash, powder' (Aschmann 1993:133) (see Greenberg 1987:185–6).

77. There are two widespread negative "forms" that have been thought to be possible for pan-Americanisms—one based on m, the other on k; some examples of both are: Proto-Maiduan *-men (Ultan 1964:365); Shasta má· (Silver 1964:173); Proto-Yuman *(m)a·w (Langdon 1979:638); Seri m- 'nega-tive' (Bright 1956); Nahuatl amo; Tepehuan mai (Swadesh 1960b:169); Mixtec ma (Swadesh 1960b:169); Tequistlatec maa (Swadesh 1960b:169); Proto-Mayan *ma; Jicaque ma; Palikur, Island Carib, Guajiro (Arawakan) ma- 'negative possessor' (Taylor 1977b), Proto-Arawakan *ma- 'privative prefix [= 'without'] (David Payne 1990), Amuesha ama, Goajiro m-, Baniva ma/mo (Suárez 1977:244, 248); Quechua mana; Yanomama -ma (Migliazza and Campbell 1988:203); Proto-Takanan *-(a)ma 'nega-tive suffix' (Girard 1971b:53, 96), *-ma 'negative/privative suffix' (Girard 1971b:96); Proto-Panoan *-(ya)ma 'negative suffix (verbal)' (Girard 1971b:166); Mosetén am (Suárez 1977:244); Mapu-dungu mə (Stark 1970). David Payne (1990) shows that there is a negative morpheme approximately of the shape ma also in Quechua, Mapudungu [Arau-canian], Maipuran [Arawakan], Proto-Panoan, Proto-Tacanan, Apinaye [Ge], Tucano, Proto-Tupi, Pirahã, Amarakacri, Madija-Culina [Arauán], Nadëb, Yano-mama, Yagua, and Hiskaryana (see Swadesh 1954b:311 for other examples). Compare Sanskrit mâ, Modern Greek mi(n), putative Proto–North Caucasian *mV, Proto-Sino-Tibetan *ma (Starostin 1991:21), Proto-Nostratic *ma (Starostin 1989:64) (see also Ruhlen 1994a:83). Some examples of the other nega-tive (mentioned by Sapir as widespread) are: Tsim-shian k'aym, Proto-Sahaptin *ke, Klamath q'ay (De-Lancey, Genetti, and Rude 1988:215); Kutenai qa- (Haas 1965:85); Mutsun ʔekwe, Rumsen ku·welkuw·e, Chocheño ʔakwe (Callaghan 1991c:232); Chimariko k-, -k, -g, x-, -x- (Crawford 1967:183); Yana kuu- (Haas 1964b:80); Proto-Pomoan *kʰów/ʔAkʰ·ów (Langdon 1979:638); Salinan k-, ko- (Haas 1964a:80);

Proto-Uto-Aztecan *ka, *kai (Miller 1967:49); Proto-Central Algonquian *kaθ- (or *kan-), *kat- (Haas 1959:2); Coahuilteco -axaam (Gursky 1966:447); Comecrudo kam (Gursky 1966a:447); Chitimacha k'ay- (Munro 1994:187); Proto-Muskogean *k- 'nega-tive', *ki 'negative auxiliary' (Booker 1980:256); Proto-Mixe-Zoquean *ka:h (Wichmann 1975); Ma-taco ka (Swadesh 1954:331); Ona kanyer (Swadesh 1954b:331). It is not difficult to find similar forms in languages in other parts of the world; for example, the many ka-like forms Ruhlen (1994b:48, 59) lists as being representative of putative Khoisan lan-guages.

78. Later Gursky (1968:22) asserted that he had been careful to eliminate forms which chance and onomatopoeia might explain, and yet many of his forms do seem to reflect these two factors. Many are short (CV only), and thus chance is a possible explanation of any shared similarity; several are ono-matopoetic (such as 'blackbird', 'blow', 'breast' [two forms], and others).

79. Shafer said Sapir added the names of other Penutian languages to the California core "without citing any evidence except that the phonetic pattern of the stems of some languages was similar" (1947:206). Whistler and Golla offer views on California Penutian phonology as it relates to their reconstruction of Proto-Yokuts. They reconstruct for Proto-Yokuts a consonantal system resembling that of the Sierra Mi-wokan languages, with *ŋ, *s/*ṣ, *t/*ṭ, and a single series of affricates, though with a three-way manner distinction (plain/aspirated/glottalized), as opposed to a single series in Miwokan, but they "suspect that further investigation will show that a two-way manner contrast (plain/glottalized) lies behind both the Proto-Yokuts and Proto-Utian systems" (1986:352–3). They also find that their Proto-Yokuts reconstruction of certain morphological patterns parallels Miwokan (and Utian) patterns of stem formation, which involve an epenthetic and harmonizing *i. They conclude that "it seems likely that these archaic morphological patterns of harmonic high vowel epenthesis in stem formation are a shared retention from some earlier stage of Penutian historical development. In general, the relationship between Yokuts and Utian should continue to be an extremely fruitful area for historical research" (1986:353). However, since they believe that other aspects of their reconstruction participated in areal diffusion (for example, their *i and *ŋ, see Chapter 9), the question arises whether such morphophonemic patterns of stem alternation (involv-ing epenthesis or vowel harmony) could not similarly be explained by areal influences. Such alternations seem to have been a principal feature of Sapir's (1921b, 1929a) conception of Penutian; however, if

the languages cannot be demonstrated to be related, could not these shared patterns of stem alternation come about also through areal convergence among the languages? These questions merit investigation.

80. It might be said that Sapir's last contribution to Penutian was in 1953 and 1964, when Swadesh published (1) a manuscript left by Sapir in which Sapir compared forms from Coos, Takelma, and other languages he thought were Penutian (Sapir and Swadesh 1953; but see also Golla 1991a) and (2) a collection of the glosses on comparative Penutian that Sapir had written in the margins of several works on various so-called Penutian languages (Swadesh 1964a). The Coos-Takelma-Penutian article (Sapir and Swadesh 1953) essentially consists of a list of 151 comparisons, mostly of lexical forms, but also of some that are grammatical, in Takelma, Miluk, and Coos, together with equations from Siuslaw, Yokuts, Wintun, Chinook, Miwok, Maidu, and Costanoan (Mukne). There is no discussion of possible systematic correspondences, though it contains occasional notes about possible phonological developments. Many of these compared forms are problematic when judged by the criteria discussed in Chapter 7; Sapir himself indicated that ten of them are improbable. Several are good candidates for possible borrowings (for example, 'bow', 'knife', 'black bear [two sets]', 'arrow', '[brown] bear', and 'shell used for ornament'); twenty reflect wide semantic latitude (for example, 'to choke/squeeze'; 'to pound [acorns, seeds]' / 'to move with friction'); fifteen are onomatopoetic (for example, Takelman *phoophaw, phoow* 'to blow', Maidu *bö* 'to blow', Coos *puuX*ʷ- 'to spout'); fifty-nine are short (for example, Takelma *pʔii* 'fire', Wintun *po* 'fire'); seven have no real phonetic similarity (for example, Takelma *sŏm* 'mountain', Wintun *toλ, чoλ* 'mountain'); two are nursery forms; and thirteen involve pan-Americanisms. Many involve comparisons between only two languages (either Takelma or Coos and one other) or involve only three languages (both Takelma and Coos, with one other). All considered, the few forms that are not challenged here make a very small list of look-alikes; some are suggestive, but they are insufficient to show a relationship. Sapir's glosses, as published by Swadesh (1964a), amount to little more than raw lists of similarities and other observations, with no analysis or systematic correspondences. Many of the forms from the Coos-Takelma-Penutian manuscript (published in Sapir and Swadesh 1953) are repeated in this one— apparently both Sapir sources were written at the same time (ca. 1914) and in the same ink. Thus, from a Wintu grammar, twenty-two Wintu forms are given in scattered comparisons from Miwok, Coos, and Takelma. Many of these comparisons involve short

forms, and several of them are only one consonant in length; several involve semantically nonequivalent forms. From a Tsimshian source, forty such forms were found; these involve disparate comparisons among these same languages but also include forms compared from Lower Umpqua and Chinook. The largest source was Sapir's glosses in his copy of *Coos Texts* by Frachtenberg, with 195 comparisons, and his copy of Frachtenberg's *Coos Grammar* listed another 110 comparisons, mostly of Takelma forms, with some Chinook forms. There is considerable overlap, particularly of lexical items, in the two articles. Again, some of these compared forms are quite suggestive, but many are subject to doubt under the criteria of Chapter 7. There are a number of onomatopoetic and symbolic forms, short forms, pan-Americanisms, and nursery words. Some are suggestive of borrowing (for example, Coos -*cak*ʷ*k*ʷ, *ck*ʷ, 'to spear', Takelma *saak*ʷ 'shoot [arrow]'; compare Sapir's forms in a Siuslaw source: Siuslaw *čaq-* 'to spear', Takelma *sak*ʷ-). Some are clearly not intended as evidence of a genetic relationship (for example, Coos *laaʔma* 'drunk', said to be borrowed from '*rum*'). In short, these lists of Sapir's glosses give no idea of what he thought about the forms presented, and hence no clear idea of how the evidence might have been marshaled in support of the broader Penutian classification he believed in. The lists are suggestive, but a comparison showing the systematic correspondences and grammatical connections with each language is necessary before a case can be made that these languages are genetically related.

81. For example, Sapir had first entertained the idea that perhaps Yurok (and Wiyot) were related to Salishan because both had instrumental noun prefixes on verbs, but he abandoned this idea when it became clear that instrumental prefixes were widespread and probably involved areal diffusion (see Sapir's 1913 letters cited in Golla 1984:105–6, 108).

82. If we apply the criteria discussed in Chapter 7, a good number of the lexical matchings of Pitkin and Shipley (1958) would be set aside. For example, several sets are like the one that compares only Maidu *jîm*, Wintu *q'ede* 'arm', which are not phonetically similar, and none of the compared sounds fit the correspondences postulated in the article. As pointed out later by Shipley (1980), the very similar phonetics and cultural meanings of some of the compared forms strongly suggest diffusion (for example, the set with only Wintu *k'eni* and Lake Miwok *k'éni* 'basket'; compare 'arrow', 'goose', 'cocoon rattle', 'coyote', 'dice', 'earring', 'eel', 'puberty rites', 'shaman'). Several compared forms are onomatopoetic (for example, the sets for 'blackbird', 'blow', 'bluejay', 'breast', 'cough', 'crow', 'dove', 'kiss', 'owl'). Some are classic pan-

Americanisms (for example, 'hand', 'negative'). Several are nursery forms (for example, 'older brother', 'father', 'grandfather', 'mother'). Some involve liberal semantic associations (for example, 'chipmunk/lizard/mouse', 'leg/toe/dance', 'star/flower', 'stem of plant / flute / leg / kingsnake'). While Pitkin and Shipley's work is better than many of the more permissive and less cautious proposals, the data they presented still require careful sifting. That it is problematic is confirmed by the fact that Shipley (1980) later abandoned the Penutian hypothesis.

83. For example, sixteen sets have the sort of semantic content and very close phonetic similarity that are suggestive of borrowings (for example, Patwin *ʔuwas* and Southern Sierra Miwok *ʔuwas* 'grape' are from Spanish *uvas* 'grapes'; other probable loans are Hill and River Patwin *ʔe·ye,* Central Sierra Miwok *ʔey·e,* Southern Sierra Miwok *ʔe·ye* 'manzanita berry'; and Patwin *molok,* Central and Southern Sierra Miwok *mol·ok* 'condor'). Considerable semantic latitude is involved in thirty-six cases; forty-three are onomatopoetic; thirty-seven include short forms; forty have very little phonetic similarity (or have several nonmatching segments); and nine include pan-Americanisms.

84. A few examples of similar forms for words for 'mouth' in languages spoken throughout the Americas are: Kwakiutl *sms* (Swadesh 1954b:309); Klamath *som* (Shipley 1966:495); Proto-Maidun *sím* (Ultan 1964:366); Proto-Yokuts *sama?* (Shipley 1966:495); Nez Perce *him* (Swadesh 1954b:309); Molala *similk* (Swadesh 1954:309); Catawba *si-ma* (Swadesh 1954b:309); Proto-Quechuan *šimi* (Cerrón-Palomino 1987); Tehuelche *šam* (Swadesh 1954b:309); Selknam *sim* 'upper lip' (Najlis 1993:90).

85. 'Skunk' names would not perhaps be expected to be associated with onomatopoeia; however, Hymes commented on the similarity of the sound of the nighthawk's dive and the sounds of flatulence and mentioned that his Wasco teacher said that "the [Wasco] word 'sure sounds like skunk' " (1964a:236).

86. Hymes also presented an argument, which no one really followed up, that Tonkawa is perhaps affiliated with Penutian, based primarily on similarities in elements with deictic senses which have front-vowel vocalism for proximate. Hymes also recognized the possibility that there may be "a pervasive sound symbolism underlying the recurrence of elements with initial velar or dental stop as demonstratives, and the recurrence of front vowels in elements marking proximate as opposed to distal"; nevertheless, he felt that "based on certain similarities in morphophonemic patterning, and preliminary lexical comparisons, between Tonkawa and Chinookan . . . and Tonkawa and a portion of probable Penutian

cognate sets . . . a genetic connection will be proven" (1967:275). However, the opposition between front-vowel "proximate" and back-vowel "distal" is found in many languages and is probably due to an unremarkable sort of sound symbolism typical of deictic systems (as is discussed in many of Roman Jakobson's writings). For example, English, with *this/these* (proximate) and *those* (distal), is, after all, not a Penutian language.

87. Shipley and Smith (1979), in their careful exposition on vowel length and stress in Proto-Maiduan (on which Silverstein's analysis depends), show that the Maiduan data do not support Silverstein's analysis of the proto forms for 'two' and 'three' as containing reflexes of a 'verbal auxiliary formative' *-wèy/*-wy-* meaning 'say, do, make' as the second syllable. Moreover, the facts refute Silverstein's postulated Proto-Maiduan *pe·néy* 'two', particularly with regard to the stress placement, shape, and perhaps the whole existence of the second syllable; the *y* is actually part of a different morpheme (old distributive suffix). Therefore, Silverstein's *pe·néy* cannot reflect the postulated *pe(·)n + wéy,* which is assumed to be even more remote in time. Callaghan (1979) points out serious flaws in Silverstein's use of the Miwokan materials; she shows that his various forms all reduce to Proto-Miwok *ʔoṭi-* 'two' plus the suffix *-y(·)a* 'animate plural' or *-k(·)o* 'numeral suffix', and that there is no evidence of any such form as *ʔoṭí·yak·o,* which Silverstein attempts to associate with Yawelmani Yokuts *ʔaṭe·yasi* 'twin'. In fact, the Plains Miwok form *ʔoṭ·a* does not mean 'a couple' but rather 'friend(s)', and thus is not so indicative of the gloss 'twin' which Silverstein would need for the connection (though compare Mexican Spanish *cuate* 'twin, buddy'). Callaghan concludes: "The only reconstructible Proto-Miwok numeral for *two* is *ʔoṭi- ~ *ʔoṭ-.* Moreover, if Nisenan *ʔó·ja* [ʔó·ya] *twin* is a true cognate and not a loan from Plains or Northern Sierra Miwok, it is Proto-Miwok *ʔo·ja* [ʔo·ya] *twin, double* which should be used for comparison with the Maidun family" (1979:182). Marc Okrand (1979) raises similar objections to Silverstein's treatment of the Costanoan materials. Silverstein analyzed Costanoan numerals as being of two types—one based on a verb stem of the shape *CVCCV-* + a "medio-passive-adjectival" suffix *n,* the other based on a verbal root of the form *CVC(·)V-* + an "agentive nominalizer" suffix *s.* Okrand objects to these analyses, saying that "in none of these sources are the basic (cardinal) numerals analyzed, and in none are the notions of 'mediopassive' or 'agentive' ever specifically mentioned in regard to numerals or, with one exception, anything else" (1979:183). Okrand finds other suffixes with *n* and *s* more likely candidates,

one deriving adverbial numerals, the other distributives. He also objects to Silverstein's suggestion that in *ʔoṭxin the x reflects an old suffix related to k in Costanoan and Miwok; he demonstrates that Silverstein's attempt to show x alternating morphophonemically with k is erroneous, that "there is no example of such an alternation" and x must be considered original (1979:186).

88. Silverstein (1979b) has answered some of these objections, but unconvincingly in my opinion.

89. Berman's (1983:402) two proposed 'locative' suffixes, *-in and *-w, are not persuasive. Since Wintu and Patwin forms were not presented for the 'instrumental', it is not clear why Wintu -in 'locative-instrumental' should not be assumed to reflect the proposed 'instrumental'. Since locatives and instrumentals are typologically associated with one another, Patwin's archaic locative -in is not necessarily distinct from the proposed instrumental. Whether or not Central Sierra Miwok -win, -in, -n 'suffix-forming adverbs indicating place where or time when' is cognate is an open question, but this would need to be worked out in the history of Miwokan first before comparisons with other postulated California Penutian languages could be convincing. In any case, Finnish has close matches in the case of its -n, which is placed on adjectives to form adverbs. Berman's *-w locative seems particularly shaky. Besides Central Sierra Miwok -win as one locative variant, he cites Southern Sierra Miwok -wak, -ak 'from the direction' (said to be "another adverbial suffix which inserts -w- after nominal themes ending in a vowel" (1983:403–4) and frozen Central Sierra Miwok -wak 'a locative suffix occurring in a few expressions primarily referring to sides of the ceremonial house, but also used in other connections', along with Yokuts -w 'locative'. Berman (1989:6) suggests a possible additional cognate, Sierra Miwok 'indefinite locative' -m, -m(·)i(?) 'to, at, in, into' (m is thought to be from *w in certain environments). At best this evidence points to an unclear Miwokan and Yokuts -w.

90. Berman finds little to support PCP verb inflection. He indicates that he has found no cognate morphemes that express tense, that "the closest agreement appears to be an s- or š-element indicating the past tense . . . but there seems to be no reconstruction which will account for all of the attested forms" (1983:403). Finnish dialects and closely related sister languages have -si 'past' (see Laanest 1982:233–4), a close match. Berman has also found no person or number inflection on verbs, but he believes that "the Maidu verbal suffixes -s 'first person' and -n 'third person' are perhaps cognate with the Mutsun infixes -s- 'my' and -n- 'his', which indicate possession in kin terms" (1993:403). The -n

of 'his, third person' closely matches the -Vn/-nsA 'third person possessive' in Finnish.

91. Gursky (1966a:447) argued that the dissolution of Waiilatpuan as a family—the separation of Cayuse and Molala—was a mistake and that there was solid evidence for its validity. He presented twelve words between the two languages which showed virtual identities, based on forms taken from Buschmann. The forms from one or the other of these languages may have been incorrectly attributed to it, since other scholars now find no such similarity in the extant materials (see Rigsby 1966, 1969).

92. DeLancey, Genetti, and Rude (1988) also compare Tsimshian with Klamath and Sahaptian, achieving plausible results. They also present a few Chinookan comparisons, but these are far less convincing. In Liedtke's (1991:40) estimation, a relationship between Sahaptian, Klamath, and Tsimshian is "überzeugend dokumentiert" (convincingly documented) by DeLancey, Genetti, and Rude (1988). Liedtke (1991:134) adds eight word comparisons of his own between Tsimshian and various individual "Penutian" languages, which run the gamut from Zuni to Tojolabal Mayan. Needless to say, this splattering of isolated forms from here and there in languages from Alaska to Central America is not very compelling.

93. In an undated and unpublished paper called "Uto-Aztecan and Keresan," Irvine Davis gives 108 possible cognate sets with sound matchings as possible correspondences. I do not discuss this paper here, since it is unpublished and I am not sure what the author's intentions were with it. In brief, however, the sets have approximately the same number of difficulties as those dealt with in the Aztec-Tanoan hypothesis discussed earlier in this chapter: sixty-five compare short forms (CV in length, or longer but with only a CV portion matching), seventeen compare forms that appear to be onomatopoetic, sixteen compare semantically nonequivalent forms which include a considerable degree of latitude (I have not counted nonequivalent forms whose meanings are different but somewhat similar), and three involve probable loanwords.

94. Crawford does not identify several as loans, but borrowing might be suspected nevertheless in the cases of no. 9 'acorn / red oak / walnut/tree', no. 11 'slave/person/Negro / white man', and no. 12 'a beverage/roots from which they make bread/grass/leaf/tea / black drink'. No. 19 'first person pronoun' would have to be eliminated because the Timucua ni- is a pan-Americanism; such Muskogean forms as áno, áni 'I' are really based on a- plus a general pronominal base -no or -ni (see Kimball 1993), and hence are not visibly cognate with Timucua ni-, regardless of the pan-Americanism problem.

95. Liedtke has justifiably criticized this evidence, stating the evidence is "möglicherweise nicht überzeugender als viele, die im selben Band zurecht als zu wenig gesichert abgelehnt werden" (perhaps not more convincing than many in the same volume [Campbell and Mithun 1979a] that are rightly rejected as too slightly ensured) (1991:102, 137). The forms I presented are too few in number (twenty-two), and some are problematical when judged by the criteria of Chapter 7. For example, although most match *CVC* (or longer) forms, a few are shorter (for example, Proto-Jicaque *p^he : Tequistlatec *-fuh-* 'white'; *pe : -bik* 'stone'). Some are not basic vocabulary items (for example, 'iguana', 'coatimundi/agouti') and conceivably could involve borrowing. Since the two language families are not now, and are not known ever to have been, in contact with one another (Tequistlatecan in Oaxaca, Mexico, and Jicaquean in Honduras), borrowing from one another is perhaps not as likely as in the case of neighboring tongues. Nevertheless, we cannot rule out some past contact with concomitant borrowing if their history is unknown. Logically, borrowing among geographically remote languages is no more unlikely than genetic relationship is. That is, a genetic relationship, almost by definition, means that the distinct languages must have at one time been spoken in the same geographic location, if only before the proto language split up into these now geographically separated daughters. Thus the postulation of such an ancestor language and its subsequent split entails movement of the daughter languages from the linguistic homeland to their current locations. A hypothesis that adjacent languages borrowed from one another and later moved to their current locations is neither more nor less plausible.

96. In the literature it has usually been forgotten or ignored that Lehmann's hypothesis linking Xinca and Lenca was not limited to just these two but also included Mixe-Zoquean, Tequistlatec, and Chumash-Salinan.

97. It is interesting that Mudrak and Nikolaev (1989) relate Gilyak and Chukchi-Kamchatkan to "Almosan-Keresiouan" languages. Needless to say, their attempt falls short. Shevoroshkin finds their comparison "to be weak in many points" and prefers the grouping of Nostratic, Sino-Caucasian, and Amerind suggested by Starostin (see Shevoroshkin 1990:8; see also Ruhlen 1994b).

Chapter 9   Linguistic Areas of the Americas

1. As mentioned in Chapter 2, there was considerable disagreement among scholars before Sapir (1929a) about whether or to what extent similarities due to common inheritance could be separated from those due to diffusion. Boas was skeptical, but Sapir thought on the whole they could be determined and separated. Kroeber and Dixon's early work had a Boasian areal-typological cast to it, though they soon came to view similarities as indicators of possible remote family relationships. Thus we find Kroeber saying, in his paper on remote comparison methodology:

> Throughout the field of linguistic structure in the whole continent, there are abundant examples of the operation of the principle of territorial continuity of characteristics, and of the underlying one that even the most diverse languages affect each other, and tend to assimilate in form, if only contact between them is intimate and prolonged. Such are the exceedingly common occurrence of *n* and *m* to designate the first and second person pronouns; the geographical localization of families expressing sex gender; the prevailing tendency for pronominal elements, especially the possessive ones, and instrumental elements in verbs, to be prefixes rather than suffixes, as already mentioned for California. It is needless to multiply examples which are either familiar to the Americanist or readily compilable by him. (1913:399)

2. Nile Thompson's (1993) examination of historical records revealed that the denasalization change in Twana took place only about 100 years ago, after Europeans arrived.

3. Chilcotin (Athabaskan) has been said to have pharyngeals, but, as Dale Kinkade (personal communication) reports, Chilcotin has rather consonant retraction (which causes phonetic vowel retraction); this may have diffused from Salishan pharyngeals, but the trait is not pharyngealization in Chilcotin.

4. Kinkade (personal communication) points out that there are regular *a/i* diachronic changes in Salishan, as synchronic alternations. There may be *a/i* ablaut in Salishan, but full *V/ə* ablaut is more common (see Kinkade and Sloat 1972, Kinkade 1988).

5. Kroeber (1959) thought there was Athabaskan influence on Yuki, and later Yuki influence on Kato and Wailaki. His conclusion was based primarily on the shared structural traits of contrastive tones, the tendency toward monosyllabic morphemes, and the multiple forms taken by verb stems. Perhaps none of these would be seen today as particularly convincing evidence of language contact.

6. Bright has shown that a "retracted sibilant" ([ṣ]) is shared by many languages of California, as well as by a few languages in neighboring Oregon and Arizona. This feature appears to be areal, but "the very fact of its predominance in California and

adjacent areas makes it difficult for us to speculate about its origins" (1978b:56).

7. Trager (1967:342) had thought that much of the Tewa divergence from Tiwa was due to creolization of Tewa with Keresan, but Kroskrity (1993:59–60) dismisses this claim as lacking foundation.

8. Earlier Sherzer (1973:775–6) had distinguished a "Prairies" area, with Algonquian, Siouan, Caddoan, and Tonkawan representatives, though this area is included in the Plains area in his 1976 study. The Prairies area was described mostly in terms of features that were absent from the languages of the Prairies.

9. I suspect that this is not a significant areal trait, since the Siouan languages involved do have fairly rich consonantal systems, though some series may be merged in some of the sister languages.

10. Sherzer's (1976:202–18) discussion of the Southeast Linguistic Area is quite skewed because he accepts the Gulf hypothesis (see Chapter 8) and thus assumes that many traits shared by these languages that are not at present demonstrably related are family/genetic traits rather than the result of diffusion in the area.

11. Nicklas postulates a number of "linguistic provinces"—that is, "smaller areas included in the greater language area of the Southeast" (1994:2). Some of these provinces are supported by a number of reasonably strong shared traits, others less so; I do not discuss them here.

12. But they may not be original in Siouan, either. Robert Rankin (personal communication) points out that the positionals have a continuative aspectual meaning and are used as auxiliaries in all the core Siouan languages, but apparently not in Catawban. This suggests that they originated after Proto-Siouan-Catawban. It is possible that Catawban once had the category and lost it, but it seems unlikely that Ca-

tawba would have lost it while other languages in the Southeastern Linguistic Area developed the positional continuatives as a prominent areal trait.

13. Karen Booker states her reasons for doubting this claim, or at least some version of it, with regard to Muskogean languages: "Western Muskogean and Alabama-Koasati stops are (slightly) aspirated, Mikasuki, Creek and Seminole stops are very lenis and in many cases voiced throughout" (personal communication).

14. I thank Robert Rankin for this observation.

15. It should be noted that the men's versus women's speech in Koasati is the best known from Haas's (1944) much cited article, but that Kimball (1987b) has shown that the difference is not so much one of sex but of the social status of the speaker. This suggests that the notion of sex-marked distinctions as an areal marker should be carefully investigated.

16. Some "Sprechbund" areal features (shared ethnography of communication traits) include the following: (1) Southeast area clans are likely to be named after common animals, but Plains clans are not. Quapaw shares the Southeast pattern quite consistently, whereas other Dhegiha languages do so only partially. (2) In tales told in the Southeast, Rabbit plays the role of trickster; but in tales told outside the area, Coyote plays this part. Quapaw shares this Southeastern trait but Dhegiha, its close relative, does not (Rankin 1988:643).

17. Earlier Constenla (1991) had viewed the area as being composed mostly of branches of Chibchan; since the languages of this area were mostly Chibchan, it was difficult to determine which of the shared traits (if any) were diffused and which had been inherited from Proto-Chibchan. However, Constenla (1992) later included some non-Chibchan languages of Central America in this area.

REFERENCES

Abbreviations

AA	*American Anthropologist*	ILV	Instituto Lingüístico de Verano
AL	*Anthropological Linguistics*	INAH	Instituto Nacional de Antropología e His-
Am. Ant.	*American Antiquity*		toria
BLS	*Berkeley Linguistics Society*	SCOIL	Survey of California and Other Indian
CA	*Current Anthropology*		Languages
CLS	*Chicago Linguistic Society*	SIL	Summer Institute of Linguistics
CTL	*Current Trends in Linguistics*	*SJA*	*Southwestern Journal of Anthropology*
CWES	*The Collected Works of Edward Sapir*	*SWES*	*Selected Writings of Edward Sapir in*
HMAI	*Handbook of Middle American Indians*		*Language, Culture, and Personality*
HNAI	*Handbook of North American Indians*	UCPAAE	University of California Publications in
ICA	*International Congress of Americanists*		American Archaeology and Ethnology
IEL	*International Encyclopedia of Lin-*	UCPL	University of California Publications in
	guistics		Linguistics
IJAL	*International Journal of American Lin-*	UNAM	Universidad Nacional Autónoma de
	guistics		México

Aarsleff, Hans. 1988. Introduction to *On language: the diversity of human language-structure and its influence on the mental development of mankind* by Wilhelm von Humboldt, trans. Peter Heath, vii–lxv. Cambridge: Cambridge University Press.

Acosta, Joseph de. 1590. *Historia natural y moral de las Indias.* Seville: En Casa de Juan de León. [Republished several times.]

Adair, John. 1930[1775]. *The history of the American Indians,* ed. Samuel Cole Williams. Johnson City, TN: Watauga Press.

Adam, Lucien. 1878. *Examen grammatical comparé de seize langues américaines.* ICA 1878:161–244. Luxembourg.

———. 1879. Du parler des hommes et du parler des femmes dans la langue caribe. *Revue de Linguistique et de Philologie Comparée* 12:275–304.

———. 1882. *Les Classifications, l'objet, la méthode, les conclusions de la linguistique.* Paris: Maisonneuve.

———. 1885. *Le Taensa a-t-il été forgé de toutes pièces? Résponse à M. Daniel G. Brinton.* Paris: Maisonneuve.

———. 1890[1888]. *Trois familles linguistiques des bassins de l'Amazone et de l'Orénoque.* ICA 7:489–98. Berlin.

———. 1968[1893]. *Matériaux pour servir a l'établissement d'une grammaire comparée des dialectes de la famille caribe.* Nendeln, Liechtenstein: Kraus Reprint. [Original ed., Paris: Maisonneuve.]

———. 1968[1896]. *Matériaux pour servir à l'étab-*

lissement d'une grammaire comparée des dialectes de la famille Tupi. Nendeln, Liechtenstein: Kraus Reprint. [Original ed., Paris: Maisonneuve.]

———. 1968[1897]. *Matériaux pour servir à l'établissement d'une grammaire comparée des dialectes de la famille Karari.* Nendeln, Liechtenstein: Kraus Reprint. [Original ed., Paris: Maisonneuve.]

———. 1968[1899]. *Matériaux pour servir à l'établissement d'une grammaire comparée des dialectes de la famille Guaicuru.* Nendeln, Liechtenstein: Kraus Reprint. [Original ed., Paris: Maisonneuve.]

Adelaar, Willem F. H. 1984. Grammatical vowel length and the classification of Quechua dialects. *IJAL* 50:25–47.

———. 1986. La Relación quechua-aru: perspectivas para la separación del léxico. *Revista Andina* 4:379–426.

———. 1987. La Relación quechua-aru en debate. *Revista Andina* 5:83–91.

———. 1989. Review of *Language in the Americas* by Joseph H. Greenberg. *Lingua* 78:249–55.

———. 1990. En pos de la lengua culle. In *Temas de lingüística Amerindia,* ed. Rodolfo Cerrón-Palomino and Gustavo Solís Fonseca, 83–105. (Actas del Primer Congreso Nacional de Investigaciones Lingüístico-Filológicas.) Lima: Concytec/Deutsche Gesellschaft für Technische Zusammenarbeit.

———. 1991. Presente y futuro de la lingüística andina. *Revista Andina* 9:49–63.

———. 1992. Quechuan languages. *IEL,* ed. William Bright, 3:303–8. New York: Oxford University Press.

Adelung, Johann Christoph, and Johann Severin Vater. 1816. *Mithridates oder allgemeine Sprachenkunde mit dem Vater Unser als Sprachprobe in bei nahe fünfhundert Sprachen und Mundarten.* Vol. 3, Sec. 3 Berlin: Voss.

Albuquerque, Severiano Godofredo de. 1910. *Relatório dos serviços executados em Campos-Novos da Serra do Norte.* (Relatorios diversos; publicação no. 37 da Commissão de Linhas Telegraphicas Estrategicas de Matto Grosso ao Amazonas). App. 4:134–47. Rio de Janeiro: Papelaria Luiz Macedo.

Alcina Franch, José. 1985. *Los orígenes de América.* Madrid: Alhambra.

Allen, Louis. 1931. Siouan and Iroquoian. *IJAL* 6:185–93.

Allin, Trevor R. 1976. *A grammar of Resígaro.* Buckinghamshire, England: SIL.

———. 1979. Vocabulario Resígaro. (Working Paper no. 16.) Yarinacocha: ILV.

Alsoszatai-Petheo, John. 1986. An alternative paradigm for the study of Early Man in the New World. In *New evidence for the Pleistocene peopling of the Americas,* ed. Alan L. Bryan, 15–26. Orono: Center for the Study of Early Man, University of Maine.

Amador Hernández, Mariscela, and Patricia Casasa García. 1979. Un análisis cultural de juegos léxicos reconstruidos del proto-otomangue. In *Estudios lingüísticos en lenguas otomangues,* ed. Nicholas A. Hopkins and J. Kathryn Josserand, 13–19. (Colección Científica Lingüística no. 68.) Mexico: INAH.

Amoss, Pamela T. 1993. Hair of the dog: unraveling pre-contact Coast Salish social stratification. In *American Indian linguistics and ethnography in honor of Laurence C. Thompson,* ed. Anthony Mattina and Timothy Montler, 3–35. (Occasional Papers in Linguistics no. 10.) Missoula: University of Montana.

Anchieta, Joseph de. 1595. *Arte de grammatica da lingua mais usada na costa do Brasil.* Coimbra: Antonio Mariz.

Andrade, Manuel J. 1953. Relations between Nootka and Quileute. *IJAL* 19:138–40.

Andresen, Julie Tetel. 1984. Les Langues amérindiennes: le comparatisme et les études franco-américaines. *Amerindia* 6:107–44.

———. 1990. *Linguistics in America 1769–1924.* London: Routledge.

Andrews, E. Wyllys, V. 1979 [1970]. Correspondencias fonológicas entre el lenca y una lengua mayance. (Colección Antropología e Historia no. 15; Administración del Patrimonio Cultural.) San Salvador: Ministerio de Educación. [Original ed., in *Estudios de Cultura Maya* 8:341–87.]

Anttila, Raimo. 1989. *Historical and comparative linguistics.* (2d ed., Amsterdam: John Benjamins. 1st ed., New York: Macmillan, 1972.)

Aoki, Haruo. 1963. On Sahaptian-Klamath linguistic affiliations. *IJAL* 29:107–12.

———. 1966. Nez Perce vowel harmony and Proto-Sahaptian vowels. *Language* 42:759–67.

———. 1975. The East Plateau linguistic diffusion area. *IJAL* 41:183–99.

Arana Osnaya, Evagelina. 1953. Reconstrucción del proto-totonaco. In *Huastecos, Totonacos y sus vecinos,* ed. Ignacio Bernal and D. Dávalos Hurtado. *Revista Mexicana de Estudios Antropológicos* 13:123–30.

———. 1958. Afinidades lingüísticas del cuitlateco. *ICA* 33:560–72.

——. 1964. La posición lingüística del huave. *ICA* 35(2):471–5.

Arber, Edward, ed. 1885. *The first three books on America, being chiefly translations, compilations, &c., by Richard Eden.* Edinburgh: Turnbull and Spears.

Arguedas Cortés, Gilda Rosa. 1987. Los fonemas segmentales del protolenca: reconstrucción comparativa. Magister Litterarum thesis, Universidad de Costa Rica, San José.

Arima, Eugene, and John Dewhirst. 1990. Nootkans of Vancouver Island. In *Northwest Coast,* ed. Wayne Suttles. Vol. 7 of *HNAI,* ed. William C. Sturtevant, 391–411. Washington, D.C.: Smithsonian Institution.

Arndt, Walter W. 1959. The performance of glottochronology in Germanic. *Language* 35:180–92.

Arroyo de la Cuesta, Felipe. 1861a[1815?]. *Extracto de la grammatica mutsun, ó de la lengua de los naturales de la Mission San Juan Bautista: Grammar of the Mutsun language spoken at the Mission of San Juan Bautista, Alta California.* (Shea's Library of American Linguistics no. 4.) New York: Cramoisy Press.

——. 1861b[1815]. *A vocabulary or phrase book of the Mutsun language of Alta California.* (Shea's Library of American Linguistics no. 8.) New York: Cramoisy Press. [Original ed., *Jesus, Maria et Josp. Alphabˢ. Rivulus Obeundus, exprimationum causa horum Indorum Mutsun missionis sanct. Joann. Baptiste.*]

Asch, Michael I., and Ives Goddard. 1981. Synonymy. In *Subarctic,* ed. June Helm. Vol. 6 of *HNAI,* ed. William C. Sturtevant, 347–8. Washington, D.C.: Smithsonian Institution.

Aschmann, Richard P. 1993. *Proto Witotoan.* (Publications in Linguistics no. 114.) Arlington: SIL and the University of Texas at Arlington.

Auroux, Sylvain. 1984. L'Affaire de la langue Taensa. *Amerindia* 6:145–79.

——. 1990. Representation and place of linguistic change before comparative grammar. In *Leibniz, Humboldt, and the origins of comparativism,* ed. Tullio de Mauro and Lia Formigari, 213–38. Amsterdam: John Benjamins.

Auroux, Sylvain, and A. Boes [with the collaboration of Ch. Porset]. 1981. Court de Gébelin (1725–1784) et le comparatisme: deux textes inédits. *Histoire, Épistémologie, Langage* 3:21–67.

Auroux, Sylvain, and Francisco Queixalos. 1984. Le Caraïbe et la langue des femmes: théories et données en linguistique. In *Matériaux pour une histoire des théories linguistiques,* ed. Sylvain Auroux, Michel Glatighy, André Joly, Anne Nicolas, and Irène Rosier, 525–44. Lille: Université de Lille III.

Austerlitz, Robert. 1980. Language-family density in North America and Eurasia. *Ural-Altaische Jahrbücher* 52:1–10.

Baegert, Johann Jakob. 1952[1771]. *Observations in Lower California.* Trans. with introduction and notes by M. M. Brandenburg and Carl L. Baumann. Berkeley: University of California Press.

Bakker, Peter. 1987. A Basque nautical pidgin: a missing link in the history of *fu. Journal of Pidgin and Creole Languages* 2:1–30.

——. 1989a. The language of the coast tribes is half Basque: a Basque-Amerindian pidgin in use between Europeans and Native Americans in North America, ca. 1540–ca. 1640. *AL* 31:117–47.

——. 1989b. Two Basque loanwords in Micmac. *IJAL* 55:258–60.

——. 1994. Michif, the Cree-French mixed language of the Métis buffalo hunters in Canada. In *Mixed languages: fifteen case studies in language intertwining,* ed. Peter Bakker and Maarten Mous, 13–33. Amsterdam: Institute for Functional Research into Language and Language Use.

——. In press a. Broken Slavey and Jargon Loucheux: a first exploration. In *Language contact in the Arctic: northern Pidgins and contact languages,* ed. Ingvild Broch and Ernst Håkan Jahr. Berlin: Mouton de Gruyter.

——. In press b. Language contact and pidginization in Davis Strait and Hudson Strait (North East Canada). In *Language contact in the Arctic: northern Pidgins and contact languages,* ed. Ingvild Broch and Ernst Håkan Jahr. Berlin: Mouton de Gruyter.

——. In press c. A language of our own: the genesis of Michif, the mixed Cree-French language of the Canadian Métis. New York: Oxford University Press.

Bakker, Peter, and Anthony P. Grant. In press. Interethnic communication in Canada, Alaska, and adjacent areas. In *Atlas of languages of intercultural communication in the Pacific hemisphere,* ed. Stephen A. Wurm, Peter Mühlhäusler, and Darrell T. Tryon. Berlin: Mouton de Gruyter.

Balbi, Adriano. 1826. *Atlas ethnographique du globe, ou classification des peuples anciens et modernes d'après leurs langues précédé d'un discours, sur l'utilité et l'importance de l'étude des langues appliquée à plusieurs branches des connaissances humaines.* Paris: Rey et Gravier.

Ballard, William L. 1978. More on Yuchi pronouns. *IJAL* 44:103–12.

———. 1985. *sa/ša/la:* Southeastern shibboleth? *IJAL* 51:339–41.

Bancroft, Hubert Howe. 1874–1876. *The native races of the Pacific states of North America.* 5 vols. New York: Appleton.

———. 1886[1882]. *The native races,* vol. 3: Myths and languages. San Francisco: History Company.

Baraga, Frederic. 1878. *A theoretical and practical grammar of the Otchipwe language.* Montreal: Beauchemin and Valois.

———. 1879[1878]. *A dictionary of the Otchipwe language, Part 1:* English-Otchipwe. Montreal: Beauchemin and Valois.

———. 1881[1880]. *A dictionary of the Otchipwe language, Part 1:* English-Otchipwe. Montreal: Beauchemin and Valois.

Barker, M. A. R. 1963. *Klamath dictionary.* (UCPL, vol. 31.) Berkeley: University of California Press.

———. 1964. *Klamath grammar.* (UCPL, vol. 32.) Berkeley: University of California Press.

Bartholomew, Doris A. 1967. Review of *Studies in southwestern ethnolinguistics: meaning and history in the languages of the American Southwest,* ed. Dell H. Hymes and William E. Bittle. *Lingua* 23:66–86.

Barton, Benjamin Smith. 1797. *New views of the origin of the tribes and nations of America.* Philadelphia: B. S. Barton. 2nd ed., 1798.

Basso, Ellen B. 1977. Introduction: the status of Carib ethnology. In *Carib-speaking Indians: culture, society, and language,* ed. Ellen B. Basso, 9–22. Tucson: University of Arizona Press.

Bateman, Richard M., Ives Goddard, Richard O'Grady, V. A. Fund, Rich Mooi, W. John Kress, and Peter Cannell. 1990a. The feasibility of reconciling human phylogeny and the history of language. *CA* 31:1–24.

———. 1990b. On human phylogeny and linguistic history: reply to comments. *CA* 31:177–82.

Battiste, Marie. 1985. Micmac literacy and cognitive assimilation. In *Promoting native writing systems in Canada,* ed. Barbara Burnaby, 7–16. Toronto: Ontario Institute for Studies in Education.

Baugh, Albert C. 1957. *A history of the English language.* 2nd ed. New York: Appleton-Century-Crofts.

Beals, Ralph L. 1932. *The comparative ethnology of Northern Mexico before 1750.* (Ibero-Americana no. 2.) Berkeley: University of California Press.

Beeler, Madison S. 1961. Northern Costanoan. *IJAL* 27:191–7.

———. 1970. Sibilant harmony in Chumash. *IJAL* 36:14–17.

———. 1977. The sources for Esselen: a critical review. *BLS* 3:37–45.

Beeler, Madison S. and Kathryn A. Klar. 1977. Interior Chumash. *Journal of California Anthropology* 2:287–305.

Belyj, V. V. 1975. P. S. Du Ponceau—the father of American philology: his contribution to the development of Americanistics. *Zeitschrift für Phonetik, Sprachwissenschaft und Kommunikationsforschung* 18:41–9.

Bender, Marvin Lionel. 1969. Chance CVC correspondences in unrelated languages. *Language* 45:519–31.

———. 1976. Nilo-Saharan. In *Language in Ethiopia,* ed. M. L. Bender, J. D. Bowen, R. L. Cooper, and C. A. Ferguson, 53–62. London: Oxford University Press.

———. 1987. First steps towards Proto-Omotic. In vol. 4 of *Current approaches to African linguistics,* ed. David Odden, 21–35. Dordrecht: Foris Publications.

———. 1989. Nilo-Saharan pronouns and demonstratives. In *Topics in Nilo-Saharan linguistics,* ed. M. Lionel Bender, 1–34. (Nilo-Saharan: Linguistic Analyses and Documentation no. 3.) Hamburg: Buske.

———. 1991. Sub-classification of Nilo-Saharan. In *Proceedings of the fourth Nilo-Saharan linguistics colloquium,* ed. M. Lionel Bender, 1–35. (Nilo-Saharan: Linguistic Analyses and Documentation no. 7.) Hamburg: Buske.

———. 1993. Is Nilo-Saharan really a phylum? Paper presented at the Twenty-fourth African Linguistics Conference, July 23–25, Columbus, Ohio.

Benediktsson, Hreinn. 1980. Discussion: Rask's position in genetic and typological linguistics. In *Typology and genetics of language: proceedings of the Rask-Hjelmslev symposium,* ed. Torben Thrane, Vibeke Winge, Lachlan Mackenzie, Una Canger, and Niels Ege, 17–28. (Travaux du Cercle Linguistique de Copenhague no. 20.) Copenhagen: Linguistic Circle of Copenhagen.

Benfey, Theodor. 1869. *Geschichte der Sprachwissenschaft und orientalischen Philologie in Deutschland seit dem Anfange des 19. Jahrhunderts mit einem Rückblick auf die früheren Zeiten.* Munich: Gotta.

Bengtson, John. 1989. On the fallacy of "diminishing returns" in long-range lexical comparison. In *Reconstructing languages and cultures: materials from the first international interdisciplinary symposium on language and prehistory,* ed. Vitaly Shevoroshkin, 30–33. Bochum: Brock-meyer.

———. 1991. Notes on Sino-Caucasian. In *Dene-Sino-Caucasian languages: materials from the first international interdisciplinary symposium on language and prehistory,* ed. Vitaly Shevoroshkin, 67–157. Bochum: Brockmeyer.

Benjamin, Geoffrey. 1976. Austroasiatic subgrouping and prehistory in the Malay Peninsula. *Austroasiatic Studies, I,* ed. Philip Jenner, Laurence Thompson, and Stanley Starosta, 37–128. Honolulu: University of Hawaii Press.

Bereznak, Cathy. 1995. The Pueblo region as a linguistic area. Ph.d. diss., Louisiana State University, Baton Rouge.

Bergsland, Knut. 1951. Kleinschmidt centennial IV: Aleut demonstratives and the Aleut-Eskimo relationship. *IJAL* 17:167–79.

———. 1958. Aleut and Proto-Eskimo. *ICA* (Copenhagen) 32:624–31.

———. 1959. The Eskimo-Uralic hypothesis. *Journal de la Société Finno-ougrienne* 61:1–29.

———. 1986. Comparative Eskimo-Aleut phonology and lexicon. *Journal de la Société Finno-ougrienne* 80:63–75.

Bergsland, Knut, and Hans Vogt. 1962. On the validity of glottochronology. *CA* 3:115–53.

Berlandier, Jean Louis, and Rafael Chowell. 1828–1829. [Vocabularies of languages of South Texas and the Lower Rio Grande.] Additional manuscripts no. 38720, in the British Library, London. [Cited in Goddard 1979b.]

Berman, Howard. 1973. Review of *Lake Miwok dictionary* by Catherine A. Callaghan. *IJAL* 39:260–61.

———. 1981. Review of *The languages of Native America: historical and comparative assessment,* ed. Lyle Campbell and Marianne Mithun. *IJAL* 47:248–62.

———. 1982. Two phonological innovations in Ritwan. *IJAL* 48:412–20.

———. 1983. Some California Penutian morphological elements. *IJAL* 49:400–12.

———. 1984. Proto-Algonquian-Ritwan verbal roots. *IJAL* 50:335–42.

———. 1985. Consonant lengthening in Chimariko. *IJAL* 51:347–9.

———. 1986. A note on the Yurok diminutive. *IJAL* 52:419–21.

———. 1989. More California Penutian morphological elements. *Southwest Journal of Linguistics* 9:3–18.

———. 1990a. New Algonquian-Ritwan cognate sets. *IJAL* 56:431–4.

———. 1990b. An outline of Kalapuya historical phonology. *IJAL* 56:27–59.

———. 1992. A comment on the Yurok and Kalapuya data in Greenberg's *Language in the Americas. IJAL* 58:230–3.

———. 1996. The position of Molala in Plateau Penutian. *IJAL* 62:1–30.

Bertolazo Stella, Jorge. 1929[1928]. *As linguas indigenas da America.* São Paulo: Irmãos Ferraz. [Originally published in *Revista do Instituto Historico e Geographico de São Paulo* 26.]

Bessa Freire, José. 1983. Da "fala boa" ao português na amazônia brasileira. *Amerindia* 8:39–83.

Beuchat, Henri and Paul Rivet. 1910. Affinités des langues du sud de la Colombie et du nord de l'equateur. *Le Mouséon* (Louvain) 11:33–68, 141–98.

Bieder, Robert E. 1986. *Science encounters the Indian, 1820–1880: the early years of American ethnology.* Norman: University of Oklahoma Press.

Bielmeier, Roland. 1977. *Historische Untersuchung zum Erb- und Lehnwortschatzanteil im ossetischen Grundwortschatz.* (Europäische Hochschulschriften Series no. 27.) Frankfurt am Main: Peter Lang.

Birket-Smith, Kai, and Frederica De Laguna. 1938. *The Eyak Indians of the Copper River Delta, Alaska.* Copenhagen: Levin and Munksgaard.

Blackman, Margaret B. 1990. Haida: traditional culture. In *Northwest Coast,* ed. Wayne Suttles. Vol. 7 of *HNAI,* ed. William C. Sturtevant, 240–60. Washington, D.C.: Smithsonian Institution.

Bloomfield, Leonard. 1925. On the sound system of Central Algonquian. *Language* 1:130–56.

———. 1928. A note on sound-change. *Language* 4:99–100.

———. 1933. *Language.* New York: Holt, Rinehart and Winston.

———. 1946. Algonquian. In *Linguistic structures of Native America,* ed. Harry Hoijer, 85–129. (Publications in Anthropology no. 6.) New York: Viking Fund.

———. 1962. *The Menomini language.* New Haven, Conn.: Yale University Press.

Blount, Ben G. 1990. Comments on *Speaking of forked tongues: the feasibility of reconciling human phylogeny and the history of language. CA* 31:15.

Boas, Franz. 1886. *Mittheilungen über die Vilxûla-Indianer: Mittheilungen aus dem Kaiserlichen Museum für Völkerkunde* (Berlin), 177–82.

———. 1889a. The Indians of British Columbia. *Transactions of the Royal Society of Canada for 1888* (Montreal) 6(2):47–57.

———. 1889b. On alternating sounds. *AA*, o.s. 2:47–53.

———. 1894. Classification of the languages of the North Pacific Coast. In *Memoirs of the International Congress of Anthropology*, ed. C. Staniland Wake, 339–46. Chicago: Schulte.

———, ed. 1911a, 1922. *Handbook of American Indian languages*, Part 1, 1911; Part 2, 1922. (Bureau of American Ethnology Bulletin no. 40.) Washington, D.C.: Government Printing Office.

———. 1911b. Introduction to *Handbook of American Indian languages*, part 1, 5–83. (Bureau of American Ethnology Bulletin no. 40.) Washington, D.C.: Government Printing Office.

———. 1929. Classification of American Indian languages. *Language* 5:1–7.

———. 1930. Spanish elements in modern Nahuatl. Todd Memorial volume. *Philological Studies* 1:85–9. New York: Columbia University Press.

———. 1973[1933]. Relations between north-west America and north-east Asia. In *The American aborigines: their origin and antiquity*, ed. Diamond Jenness, 357–70. New York: Cooper Square Publishers.

———. 1974[1906]. Some philological aspects of anthropological research. In *The shaping of American anthropology 1883–1911: a Franz Boas reader*, ed. George Stocking, Jr., 183–8. New York: Basic Books. [Originally published in *Science* 23:641–5.]

———. 1982[1940, 1917]. Introduction. Chicago: University of Chicago Press. [Original ed., *IJAL* 1:1–8. Reprinted 1940 in *Race, language, and culture*, 199–210. New York: Free Press.]

———. 1982[1940, 1920]. The classification of American languages. Chicago: University of Chicago Press. [Original ed., *AA* 22:367–76. Reprinted 1940 in *Race, language, and culture*, 211–18. New York: Free Press.]

Bonnerjea, René. 1975. Some probable phonological connections between Ural-Altaic and Eskimo-Aleut. *Orbis* 24:251–75.

———. 1978. A comparison between Eskimo-Aleut and Uralo-Altaic demonstrative elements, numerals, and other related semantic problems. *IJAL* 44:40–55.

Booker, Karen M. 1980. Comparative Muskogean: aspects of Proto-Muskogean verb morphology. Ph.D. diss., University of Kansas.

———. 1988. The loss of preconsonantal *k* in Creek/Seminole. *IJAL* 54:371–86.

———. 1993. More on the development of Proto-Muskogean *k^w*. *IJAL* 59:405–15.

Booker, Karen M., Charles M. Hudson, and Robert L. Rankin. 1992. Place name identification and multilingualism in the sixteenth-century Southeast. *Ethnohistory* 39:399–451.

Borhegyi, Stephen. 1965. *Archaeological synthesis of the Guatemalan highlands*, ed. Gordon Willey. Vol. 2 of *HMAI*, ed. Robert Wauchope, 3–38. Austin: University of Texas Press.

Borst, Arno. 1959. *Der Turmbau von Babel*. Stuttgart: Hiersemann.

Bouda, Karl. 1952. Die Tschuktschische Gruppe und das Utoaztekische. *Die Verwandtschaftsverhältnisse der tschuktschischen Sprachgruppe* by Karl Bouda. *Acta Salmanticensia, Filosofía y Letras* (Salamanca) 5(6):69–78.

———. 1960. Tungusisch und Ketschua. *Zeitschrift der Deutschen Morgenländischen Gesellschaft* 110:99–113.

———. 1963. Zoque, ein mittelamerikanischer Brückpfeiler zwischen Westasien (Kaukasus) und Peru. *Zeitschrift der Deutschen Morgenländischen Gesellschaft* 113:144–67.

———. 1964. Huavestudien I: Uralisches im Huave. *Études Finno-ougriennes* 1:18–28.

———. 1965. Huavestudien II. *Études Finno-ougriennes* 2:167–75.

Bowlby, John. 1990. *Charles Darwin: a new life*. London: Norton.

Bray, Warwick. 1986. Finding the earliest Americans. *Nature* 321:726.

Breton, Raymond. 1892[1665]. *Dictionnaire caraïbe-françois*. Facsimile ed., ed. Jules Platzmann. Leipzig: Teubner. [Original ed., Auxerre: Gilles Bouquet.]

———. 1968[1877, 1667]. *Grammaire caraïbe*. Nendeln, Liectenstein: Kraus Reprint. [Original ed., 1667. New ed. 1877, Grammaire caraïbe suivie du catechisme caraïbe, ed. Lucien Adam and Claude-André LeClerc. Paris: Maisonneuve.]

Breva-Claramonte, Manuel. 1983. *Sanctius' theory of language: a contribution to the history of Renaissance linguistics*. (Studies in the History of Linguistics no. 27.) Amsterdam: John Benjamins.

Bright, William. 1954. Some Northern Hokan relationships: a preliminary report. In *Papers from the symposium on American Indian linguistics*, ed. Murray B. Emeneau, 57–62. (UCPL, vol. 10.) Berkeley: University of California Press.

———. 1955. A bibliography of the Hokan-Coahuiltecan languages. *IJAL* 21:276–85.

———. 1956. Glottochronologic counts of Hokaltecan materials. *Language* 32:42–8.

———. 1957. *The Karok language*. (UCPL, vol. 13.) Berkeley: University of California Press.

———. 1960. *Animals of acculturation in the Cali-*

fornia Indian languages. (UCPL, vol. 4, no. 4.) Berkeley: University of California Press.

———— (ed.) 1964. *Studies in Californian linguistics.* (UCPL, vol. 34.) Berkeley: University of California Press.

————. 1970. On linguistic unrelatedness. *IJAL* 36:288–90.

————. 1973. North American Indian language contact. In *Linguistics in North America,* ed. Thomas A. Sebeok. *CTL,* 10:713–26. The Hague: Mouton.

————. 1974a. North American Indian languages. In *Encyclopedia Britannica,* 15th ed. 13:208–13.

————. 1974b. Three extinct languages of Southern California. *American Philosophical Society Yearbook,* 573–4.

————. 1975. The Alliklik mystery. *Journal of California Anthropology* 2:228–30.

————. 1976. The first Hokan conference: conclusions. In *Hokan studies: papers from the First Conference on Hokan languages,* ed. Margaret Langdon and Shirley Silver, 361–3. The Hague: Mouton.

————. 1978a. Karok. In *California,* ed. Robert F. Heizer. Vol. 8 of *HNAI,* ed. William C. Sturtevant, 180–9. Washington, D.C.: Smithsonian Institution.

————. 1978b. Sibilants and naturalness in aboriginal California. *Journal of California Anthropology, Papers in Linguistics* 1:39–63.

————. 1979. Notes on Hispanisms. *IJAL* 45:267–88.

————. 1984. The classification of North American and Meso-American Indian languages. In *American Indian linguistics and literature* by William Bright, 3–29. Berlin: Mouton de Gruyter.

————. 1988. Review of *Language in the Americas* by Joseph H. Greenberg. *American Reference Books Annual* 19:440. Englewood, Colo.: Libraries Unlimited.

————. 1991. Sapir and distant linguistic relationship. *Edward Sapir Society of Japan Newsletter* (Tokyo) 5:19–25.

————, ed. 1992. *IEL.* 4 vols. New York: Oxford University Press.

————. 1993. The Aztec triangle: three-way language contact in New Spain. *BLS* 18:22–36.

Bright, William, and Joel Sherzer. 1976. Areal features in North American Indian languages. In *Variation and change in language,* essays by William Bright, 228–68. Stanford: Stanford University Press.

Brinton, Daniel G. 1859. *Notes on the Floridian Peninsula, its literary history, Indian tribes, and antiquities.* Philadelphia: Joseph Sabin.

————. 1867. The Natchez of Louisiana, an offshoot of the civilized nations of Central America. *Historical Magazine,* 2d. ser. 1:16–18.

————. 1868. *The myths of the New World: a treatise on the symbolism and mythology of the Red Race of America.* New York: Leypoldt and Holt.

————. 1869. Remarks on the nature of the Maya group of languages. *Proceedings of the American Philosophical Society* 11:4–6.

————. 1887. On the so-called Alagüilac language of Guatemala. *Proceedings of the American Philosophical Society* 24:366–77.

————. 1890[1885a]. American Indian languages and why we should study them. In *Essays of an Americanist* by Daniel G. Brinton, 308–27. Philadelphia: Porter and Coates. [Original ed., *Pennsylvania Magazine of History and Biography* 9:15–35.]

————. 1890[1885b/1888]. The earliest form of human speech, as revealed by American tongues. In *Essays of an Americanist* by Daniel G. Brinton, 390–409. Philadelphia: Porter and Coates. [The language of palæolithic man. Paper read before the American Philosophical Society. Original ed., *The language of palæolithic man.* Philadelphia: MacCalla.]

————. 1890[1885c]. Some characteristics of American languages. In *Essays of an Americanist* by Daniel G. Brinton, 349–89. [Original ed., On polysynthesis and incorporation as characteristics of American languages. *Proceedings of the American Philosophical Society* 23:48–86.]

————. 1890[1885d]. Wilhelm von Humboldt's researches in American languages. In *Essays of an Americanist* by Daniel G. Brinton, 328–48. Philadelphia: Porter and Coates.

————. 1890a. The curious hoax of the Taensa language. In *Essays of an Americanist* by Daniel G. Brinton, 452–67. Philadelphia: Porter and Coates. A compilation (with commentary) of (1) The Taensa grammar and dictionary: a deception exposed (*American Antiquarian,* March 1885) and (2) The Taensa grammar and dictionary (*American Antiquarian,* September 1885).

————. 1890b. A review of the data for the study of the prehistoric chronology of America. In *Essays of an Americanist* by Daniel G. Brinton, 20–47. Philadelphia: Porter and Coates.

————. 1891. *The American race.* New York: D. C. Hodges.

————. 1892. Chontales and Popolucas, a contribution to Mexican ethnography. *ICA* 8:556–64. Paris.

————. 1894a. On the various supposed relations between the American and Asian races. In *Mem-*

oirs of the International Congress of Anthropology, ed. C. Staniland Wake, 145–51. Chicago: Schulte.

———. 1894b. The present status of American Indian linguistics. In *Memoirs of the International Congress of Anthropology,* ed. C. Staniland Wake, 335–8. Chicago: Schulte.

———. 1895. The Matagalpan linguistic stock of Central America. *Proceedings of the American Philosophical Society* 34:403–15.

———. 1897[1894]. On the affinities of the Otomí language with Athabascan dialects. *ICA* 1894:151–62. Stockholm.

———. 1969[1883]. *The Güegüence: a comedy ballet in the Nahuatl-Spanish dialect of Nicaragua.* New York: AMS Press. [Original ed., Collections of the Philadelphia Free Museum of Science and Art Bulletin, vol. 2, Philadelphia.]

Broadbent, Sylvia M., and Harvey Pitkin. 1964. A comparison of Miwok and Wintun. In *Studies in Californian linguistics,* ed. William Bright, 19–45. (UCPL, vol. 34.) Berkeley: University of California Press.

Broadwell, George A. 1991. The Muskogean connection of the Guale and Yamasee. *IJAL* 57:267–70.

Brown, Cecil H., and Stanley R. Witkowski. 1979. Aspects of the phonological history of Mayan-Zoquean. *IJAL* 45:34–47.

Brugge, David M., Ives Goddard, and Willem J. De Reuse. 1983. Synonymy. In *Southwest,* ed. Alfonso Ortiz. Vol. 10 of *HNAI,* ed. William C. Sturtevant, 496–8. Washington, D.C.: Smithsonian Institution.

Buschmann, Johann Carl Eduard. 1856. Der athapaskische Sprachstamm. *Abhandlungen der Königlichen Akademie der Wissenschaften zu Berlin 1855,* 149–319.

———. 1857. Die Pima-Sprache und die Sprache der Koloschen. *Abhandlungen der Königlichen Akademie der Wissenschaften zu Berlin 1856,* 321–432.

———. 1858. Die Völker und Sprachen Neu-Mexikos und der Westseite des britischen Nordamerika's. *Abhandlungen der Königlichen Akademie der Wissenschaften zu Berlin.*

———. 1859. Die Spuren der aztekischen Sprache im nördlichen Mexico und höheren amerikanischen Norden. *Abhandlungen aus dem Jahre 1854 der Königlichen Akademie der Wissenschaften zu Berlin,* supplemental vol. 2.

Büttner, Thomas T. 1983. *Las lenguas de los Andes centrales: estudios sobre la clasificación genética, areal y tipológica.* Madrid: Magerit.

Callaghan, Catherine A. n.d. Resemblant forms—Miwok : Yukian. Unpublished paper.

———. 1958. California Penutian: history and bibliography. *IJAL* 24:189–94.

———. 1964. Phonemic borrowing in Lake Miwok. In *Studies in Californian linguistics,* ed. William Bright, 46–53. (UCPL, vol. 34.) Berkeley: University of California Press.

———. 1967. Miwok-Costanoan as a subfamily of Penutian. *IJAL* 33:224–7.

———. 1972. Proto-Miwok phonology. *General Linguistics* 12:1–31.

———. 1978. Lake Miwok. In *California,* ed. Robert F. Heizer. Vol. 8 of *HNAI,* ed. William C. Sturtevant, 264–73. Washington, D.C.: Smithsonian Institution.

———. 1979. The reconstruction of *two* and related words in Proto-Miwok. *IJAL* 45:176–81.

———. 1980. An 'Indo-European' type paradigm in Proto Eastern Miwok. In *American Indian and Indo-European studies: papers in honor of Madison S. Beeler,* ed. Kathryn Klar, Margaret Langdon, and Shirley Silver, 331–8. The Hague: Mouton.

———. 1982. Proto Utian derivational verb morphology. (Occasional Papers on Linguistics no. 11.) In *Proceedings of the 1982 conference on Far Western American Indian languages,* ed. James E. Redden, 23–31. Carbondale: Department of Linguistics, Southern Illinois University.

———. 1987. Lake Miwok naturalization of borrowed phonemes. In *A Festschrift for Ilse Lehiste,* ed. Brian D. Joseph and Arnold M. Zwicky, 84–93. (Working Papers in Linguistics no. 35.) Columbus: Department of Linguistics, Ohio State University.

———. 1988a. Karkin revisited. *IJAL* 54:436–52.

———. 1988b. Proto Utian stems. In *In honor of Mary Haas: from the Haas festival conference on Native American linguistics,* ed. William Shipley, 53–75. Berlin: Mouton de Gruyter.

———. 1990a. Comments on Speaking of forked tongues: the feasibility of reconciling human phylogeny and the history of language. *CA* 31:15–16.

———. 1990b. Proto-Costanoan numerals. *IJAL* 56:121–33.

———. 1991a. Climbing a low mountain. In *A Festschrift for William F. Shipley,* ed. Sandra Chung and Jorge Hankamer, 47–59. Santa Cruz: Syntax Research Center, University of California.

———. 1991b. Is there a Yok-Utian? Paper presented at the Hokan-Penutian Conference, University of Santa Cruz. Unpublished.

———. 1991c. Utian and the Swadesh list. (Occasional Papers on Linguistics no. 16.) In *Papers for the American Indian languages conference,* held at the University of California, Santa Cruz, July and August, 1991, ed. James E. Redden, 218–37. Carbondale: Department of Linguistics, Southern Illinois University.

Callender, Charles. 1978. Shawnee. In Northeast, ed. Bruce G. Trigger. Vol. 15 of HNAI, ed. by William C. Sturtevant, 622–35. Washington, D.C.: Smithsonian Institution.

Câmara, J. Mattoso, Jr. 1965. Introdução às línguas indígenas Brasileiras. 2nd ed. Rio de Janeiro: Livraria Académica.

Campanius, Johannes. 1937[1696]. Lutheri Catechismus Öfwersatt på American-Verginiske Språket. Stockholm: Almqvist and Wiksell. [Original ed., Stockholm: Burchardi.]

Campbell, John. 1892. Remarks on preceding vocabularies. Transactions of the Royal Society of Canada 10:26–32. [Cited in Hewson 1978.]

Campbell, Lyle. 1972a. A note on the so-called Alagüilac language. IJAL 38:203–7.

———. 1972b. Mayan loanwords in Xinca. IJAL 38:187–90.

———. 1973a. Distant genetic relationships and the Maya-Chipaya hypothesis. AL 15(3):113–35.

———. 1973b. The philological documentation of a variable rule in the history of Pokom and Kekchi. IJAL 39:133–4.

———. 1974. Quichean palatalized velars. IJAL 40:59–63.

———. 1975. El estado actual y la afinidad genética de la lengua indígena de Cacaopera. La Universidad (Revista de la Universidad de El Salvador), January–February, 45–54.

———. 1976a. Kekchi linguistic acculturation: a cognitive approach. In Mayan linguistics, ed. Marlys McClaran, 90–9. Los Angeles: American Indian Studies Center, University of California.

———. 1976b. Language contact and sound change. In Current progress in historical linguistics, ed. William Christie, 181–94. Amsterdam: North Holland.

———. 1976c. The last Lenca. IJAL 42:73–8.

———. 1976d. The linguistic prehistory of the southern Mesoamerican periphery. In Fronteras de Mesoamérica, 14a Mesa Redonda, vol. 1, 157–84. Mexico: Sociedad Mexicana de Antropología.

———. 1977. Quichean linguistic prehistory. (UCPL, vol. 81.) Berkeley: University of California Press.

———. 1978a. Distant genetic relationship and diffusion: a Mesoamerican perspective. ICA 52:595–605. Paris.

———. 1978b. Quichean linguistics and philology. In World anthropology: approaches to language, anthropological issues, ed. William McCormack and Stephen Wurm, 223–33. The Hague: Mouton.

———. 1978c. Quichean prehistory: linguistic contributions. In Papers in Mayan linguistics, ed. Nora C. England, 25–54. Columbia: Museum of Anthropology, University of Missouri.

———. 1979. Middle American languages. In The languages of Native America: historical and comparative assessment, ed. Lyle Campbell and Marianne Mithun, 902–1000. Austin: University of Texas Press.

———. 1982. Discussion [of philology]. In Papers from the fifth international conference on historical linguistics, ed. Anders Ahlqvist, 442–5. Amsterdam: John Benjamins.

———. 1984. The implications of Mayan historical linguistics for glyphic research. In Phoneticism in Mayan hieroglyphic writing, ed. John S. Justeson and Lyle Campbell, 1–16. (Institute for Mesoamerican Studies no. 9.) Albany: State University of New York.

———. 1985a. Areal linguistics and its implications for historical linguistic theory. In Proceedings of the sixth international conference on historical linguistics, ed. Jacek Fisiak, 25–56. Amsterdam: John Benjamins.

———. 1985b. The Pipil language of El Salvador. Berlin: Mouton de Gruyter.

———. 1986a. Cautions about loan words and sound correspondences. In Linguistic theory and historical linguistics, ed. Dieter Kastovsky and Aleksander Szwedek. Vol. 1 of Linguistics across historical and geographical boundaries: in honor of Jacek Fisiak on the occasion of his fiftieth birthday, 221–5. Berlin: Mouton de Gruyter.

———. 1986b. Comments on the settlement of the Americas: a comparison of the linguistic, dental, and genetic evidence. CA 27:488.

———. 1988a. The Linguistics of Southeast Chiapas. (Paper no. 51.) Provo, Utah: New World Archaeological Foundation.

———. 1988b. Review of Language in the Americas by Joseph H. Greenberg. Language 64:591–615.

———. 1990a. Mayan languages and linguistic change. In Linguistic change and reconstruction methodology, ed. Philip Baldi, 115–29. Berlin: Mouton de Gruyter. (Reprinted in: Patterns of change, change of patterns, ed. Philip Baldi, 71–86. Berlin: Mouton de Gruyter, 1991.)

———. 1990b. Philological studies and Mayan languages. In Historical linguistics and philology, ed. Jacek Fisiak, 87–105. Berlin: Mouton de Gruyter.

———. 1990c. Syntactic reconstruction and Finno-Ugric. In *Historical linguistics 1987,* ed. Henning Andersen and Konrad Koerner, 51–94. Amsterdam: John Benjamins.

———. 1991a. Los hispanismos y la historia fonética del español en América. In *El Español de América, Actas del tercer congreso internacional de el español de América,* ed. César Hernández, H. de Granda, C. Hoyos, V. Fernández, D. Dietrick, and Y. Carballera, 171–80. Valladolid: Junta de Castilla y León, Consejería de Cultura y Turismo.

———. 1991b. On so-called pan-Americanisms. *IJAL* 57:394–9.

———. 1994a. Language death. In *Encyclopedia of language and linguistics,* ed. R. E. Asher and J. M. Y. Simpson, vol. 4, 1960–68. London: Pergamon Press.

———. 1994b. Linguistic reconstruction and unwritten languages. In *Encyclopedia of language and linguistics,* ed. R. E. Asher and J. M. Y. Simpson, vol. 7, 3475–80. London: Pergamon.

———. 1994c. Problems with the pronouns in proposals of remote relationships among Native American languages. In *Proceedings of the meeting of the Society for the Study of the Indigenous Languages of the Americas and the Hokan-Penutian workshop,* ed. Margaret Langdon, 1–20. (SCOIL report no. 8.) Berkeley: Department of Linguistics, University of California.

———. 1995. The Quechumaran hypothesis and lessons for distant genetic comparison. *Diachronica* 12:157–200.

———. In press a. The classification of American Indian languages and its implications for the earliest peopling of the Americas. In *Language and prehistory in the Americas,* ed. Allan Taylor. Stanford: Stanford University Press.

———. In press b. Historical syntax in historical perspective. In *An international handbook of contemporary research, syntax handbook (Handbücher zur Sprach- und Kommunikationswissenschaft),* ed. Joachim Jacobs, Arnim von Stechow, Wolfgang Sternefeld, and Theo Vennemann. Berlin: Walter de Gruyter.

———. In press c. On sound change and challenges to regularity. In *The comparative method reviewed,* ed. Mark Durie. Oxford: Oxford University Press.

Campbell, Lyle, Anne Chapman, and Karen Dakin. 1978. Honduran Lenca. *IJAL* 44:330–2.

Campbell, Lyle, and Ives Goddard. 1990. American Indian languages and principles of language change. In *Linguistic change and reconstruction methodology,* ed. Philip Baldi, 17–32. Berlin: Mouton de Gruyter.

Campbell, Lyle, and Terrence Kaufman. 1976. A linguistic look at the Olmecs. Am. Ant. 41:80–9.

———. 1980. On Mesoamerican linguistics. *AA* 82:850–7.

———. 1983. Mesoamerican historical linguistics and distant genetic relationship: getting it straight. *AA* 85:362–72.

———. 1985. Mayan linguistics: where are we now? *Annual Review of Anthropology* 14:187–98.

———. 1993. Loanwords in Mesoamerican languages. Unpublished manuscript.

Campbell, Lyle, Terrence Kaufman, and Thomas Smith-Stark. 1986. Mesoamerica as a linguistic area. *Language* 62:530–70.

Campbell, Lyle, and Ronald Langacker. 1978. Proto-Aztecan vowels, parts 1, 2, and 3. *IJAL* 44(2):85–102; 44(3):197–210; 44(4):262–79.

Campbell, Lyle, and Marianne Mithun, eds. 1979a. *The languages of Native America: historical and comparative assessment.* Austin: University of Texas Press.

———. 1979b. North American Indian historical linguistics in current perspective. In *The languages of Native America: historical and comparative assessment,* ed. Lyle Campbell and Marianne Mithun, 3–69. Austin: University of Texas Press.

Campbell, Lyle, and Martha Muntzel. 1989. The structural consequences of language death. In *Investigating obsolescence: studies in language death,* ed. Nancy Dorian, 181–96. (Studies in the Social and Cultural Foundations of Language no. 7.) Cambridge: Cambridge University Press.

Campbell, Lyle, and David Oltrogge. 1980. Proto-Tol (Jicaque). *IJAL* 46:205–23.

Campbell, Lyle, Pierre Ventur, Russell Stewart, and Brant Gardner. 1978. *Bibliography of Mayan languages and linguistics.* (Institute for Mesoamerican Studies Publication no. 3.) Albany: State University of New York.

Campbell, T. N. 1983. Coahuiltecans and their neighbors. In *Southwest,* ed. Alfonso Ortiz. Vol. 10 of *HNAI,* ed. William C. Sturtevant, 343–58. Washington, D.C.: Smithsonian Institution.

Canfield, Delos Lincoln. 1934. *Spanish literature in Mexican languages as a source for the study of Spanish pronunciation.* New York: Instituto de las Españas en los Estados Unidos.

Carlson, Roy L. 1983. The far west. In *Early man in the New World,* ed. Richard Shutler, Jr., 73–96. Beverly Hills: Sage.

Carpenter, Lawrence K. 1985. How did the 'chicken' cross the Andes? *IJAL* 51:361–4.

Carreno, Alberto M. 1913. *Noticias de Nutka: diccionario de la lengua de los nutkeses y descripción del Volcán de Tuxtla por Joseph Mariano Moziño Suárez de Figueroa, precedidos de una noticia acerca del Br. Moziño y de la expedición científica del siglo XVIII.* Mexico: La Secretaría de Fomento.

Carter, Richard T. 1980. The Woccon language of North Carolina: its genetic affiliations and historical significance. *IJAL* 46:170–82.

Cavalli-Sforza, L. L., A. Piazza, P. Menozzi, and J. Mountain. 1988. Reconstruction of human evolution: bringing together genetic, archaeological, and linguistic data. *Proceedings of the National Academy of Sciences of the U.S.A.* 85:6002–6.

———. 1989. Genetic and linguistic evolution. *Science* 244:1128–9.

Cerrón-Palomino, Rodolfo. 1986. Comentario [sobre] Willem F. H. Adelaar, La relación quechua-aru: perspectiva para la separación del léxico. *Revista Andina* 4:403–8.

———. 1987. *Lingüística quechua.* (Biblioteca de la Tradición Oral Andina no. 8.) Cuzco: Centro de Estudios Rurales Andinos "Bartolomé de las Casas."

———. 1993. Quechuística y aimarística: una propuesta terminológica. *Alma Mater* (Universidad de San Marcos, Lima.) 5:41–60.

Chafe, Wallace L. 1959. Internal reconstruction in Seneca. *Language* 35:477–95.

———. 1962. Estimates regarding the present speakers of North American Indian languages. *IJAL* 28:162–71.

———. 1964. Another look at Siouan and Iroquoian. *AA* 66:852–62.

———. 1973. Siouan, Iroquoian, and Caddoan. In *Linguistics in North America,* ed. Thomas A. Sebeok. *CTL,* 10:1164–1209. The Hague: Mouton.

———. 1974. About language: a richness of words, a babel of tongues. In *The world of the American Indian,* ed. Jules B. Billard, 150–4. Washington, D.C.: National Geographic Society.

———. 1976. *The Caddoan, Iroquoian, and Siouan languages.* The Hague: Mouton.

———. 1979. Caddoan. In *The languages of Native America: historical and comparative assessment,* ed. Lyle Campbell and Marianne Mithun, 213–35. Austin: University of Texas Press.

———. 1987. Review of *Language in the Americas* by Joseph H. Greenberg. *CA* 28:652–3.

Chafe, Wallace L., and Michael K. Foster. 1981. Prehistoric divergences and recontacts between Cayuga, Seneca, and the other Northern Iroquoian languages. *IJAL* 47:121–42.

Chamberlain, Alexander Francis. 1888. *[The affinities of] the Catawba language.* Toronto: Imrie and Graham.

———. 1892. Report on the Kootenay Indians. *British Association for the Advancement of Science* 62:549–617.

———. 1903. Indians, American. In *Encyclopedia Americana* 9:1–16 (unpaged). New York: Americana Co.

———. 1907. *Linguistic families,* vol. 1, 766–8. (Bureau of American Ethnology Bulletin no. 30.) Washington, D.C.: Government Printing Office.

———. 1909. Kutenaian and Shoshonean. *AA* 11:535–6.

———. 1910. The Uran: a new South American linguistic stock. *AA* 12:417–24.

———. 1913. Linguistic stocks of South American Indians, with distribution map. *AA* 15:236–47.

Charencey, Charles Felix Hyacinthe, Le Comte de. 1870. *Notice sur quelques familles de langues du Mexique.* Le Havre: Imprimerie Lepellatier.

———. 1872. *Recherches sur les lois phonétique dans les idiomes de la famille mame-huastèque.* Paris: Maisonneuve.

———. 1883. *Mélanges de philologie et de paléographie américaines.* Paris: Ernest Leroux.

Christian, Dana R., and Esther Matteson. 1972. Proto Guahiban. In *Comparative studies in Amerindian languages,* ed. Esther Matteson, 150–9. (Janua Linguarum Series Practica no. 127.) The Hague: Mouton.

Christian, F. W. 1932. Polynesian and Oceanic elements in the Chimu and Inca languages. *Journal of the Polynesian Society* 41:144–56.

Clairis, Christos. 1978. La lengua qawasqar. *Vicus Cuadernos: Lingüística* 2:29–44.

———. 1985. Indigenous languages of Tierra del Fuego. In *South American Indian languages: retrospect and prospect,* ed. Harriet E. Manelis Klein and Louisa R. Stark, 753–83. Austin: University of Texas Press.

Clark, Lawrence E. 1977. Linguistic acculturation in Sayula Popoluca. *IJAL* 43:128–38.

Clifton, James E. 1978. Potawatomi. In *Northeast,* ed. Bruce G. Trigger. Vol. 15 of *HNAI,* ed. William C. Sturtevant, 724–42. Washington, D.C.: Smithsonian Institution.

Colarusso, John. 1985. Pharyngeals and pharyngealization in Salishan and Wakashan. *IJAL* 51:366–8.

Collinder, Björn. 1946–1948. La Parenté linguistique et le calcul des probabilités. (Språkvetenskapliga sällskapets i Uppsala Förhandlingar, 1946–1948.) *Uppsala Universitets årskrift 1948,* 13:1–24.

Collins, June M. 1949. Distribution of the Chemakum language. In *Indians of the urban Northwest,* ed. Marian W. Smith, 147–60. New York: Columbia University Press.

Comrie, Bernard. 1989. Genetic classification, contact, and variation. In *Georgetown University Round Table on Languages and Linguistics 1988,* ed. Thomas J. Walsh, 81–93. Washington, D.C.: Georgetown University Press.

Constenla Umaña, Adolfo. 1981. Comparative Chibchan phonology. Ph.D. diss., University of Pennsylvania.

———. 1987. Elementos de fonología comparada de las lenguas misumalpas. *Filología y Lingüística* (San José, Costa Rica) 13:129–61.

———. 1990. Una hipótesis sobre la localización del protochibcha y la dispersión de sus descendientes. *Filología y Lingüística* (San José, Costa Rica) 16:111–23.

———. 1991. *Las lenguas del área intermedia: introducción a su estudio areal.* San José: Editorial de la Universidad de Costa Rica.

———. 1992. Construcción posesiva y economía morfoléxica en las lenguas del área colombiano-centroamericano. *Lingüística Chibcha* (San José, Costa Rica) 11:101–14.

Constenla Umaña, Adolfo, and Enrique Margery Peña. 1991. Elementos de fonología comparada Chocó. *Filología y Lingüística* (San José, Costa Rica) 17:137–91.

Conzemius, Éduard. 1930. Une tribu inconnue de Costa-Rica: les indiens Rama du Rio Zapote. *L'Anthropologie* 40:93–108.

Cook, Eung-Do. 1981. Athapaskan linguistics: Proto-Athapaskan phonology. *Annual Review of Anthropology* 10:253–73.

Cook, Eung-Do, and Keren D. Rice. 1989. Introduction to *Athapaskan linguistics: current perspectives on a language family,* ed. Eung-Do Cook and Keren D. Rice, 1–61. Berlin: Mouton de Gruyter.

Court de Gébelin, Antoine. 1781. *Monde primitif analysé et comparé avec le monde moderne.* Paris: published by the author.

Craig, Colette, and Kenneth Hale. 1992. A possible Macro-Chibchan etymon. *AL* 34:173–201.

Crawford, James M. 1973. Yuchi phonology. *IJAL* 39:173–9.

———. 1975. Southeastern Indian languages. In *Studies in Southeastern Indian languages,* ed.

James M. Crawford, 1–120. Athens: University of Georgia Press.

———. 1976. A comparison of Chimariko and Yuman. In *Hokan studies: papers from the first conference on Hokan languages,* ed. Margaret Langdon and Shirley Silver, 177–91. The Hague: Mouton.

———. 1978. *The Mobilian trade language.* Knoxville: University of Tennessee Press.

———. 1979. Timucua and Yuchi: two language isolates of the Southeast. In *The languages of Native America: historical and comparative assessment,* ed. Lyle Campbell and Marianne Mithun, 327–54. Austin: University of Texas Press.

———. 1988. On the relationship of Timucua to Muskogean. In *In honor of Mary Haas: from the Haas festival conference on Native American linguistics,* ed. William Shipley, 157–64. Berlin: Mouton de Gruyter.

Créqui-Montfort, G. de, and Paul Rivet. 1925–1926. La Langue Uru ou Pukina. *Journal de la Société des Américanistes de Paris* 17:211–44; 18:111–39; 19:57–116.

Cummins, John. 1992. *The voyage of Christopher Columbus: Columbus' own journal of discovery; newly restored and translated.* New York: St. Martin's.

Cuoq, Jean-André. 1886. *Lexique de la langue algonquine.* Montreal: J. Chapleau.

Curtin, Jeremiah. 1898. *Creation myths of primitive America, in relation to the religious history and mental development of mankind.* Boston: Little, Brown.

Cutler, Charles L. 1994. *O brave new words! Native American loanwords in current English.* Norman: University of Oklahoma Press.

Dalby, David. 1971. A referential approach to the classification of African languages. In *Papers in African linguistics,* ed. Chin-Wu Kim and Herbert Stahlke, 17–32. Edmonton: Linguistic Research.

Dall, William H. 1870. *Alaska and its resources.* Boston: Lee and Shepard.

Dangel, Richard. 1930. Quechua and Maori. *Mitteilungen der Anthropologische Gesellschaft in Wien* 60:343–51.

Darnell, Regna. 1969. The development of American anthropology, 1879–1920: from the Bureau of American Ethnology to Franz Boas. Ph.D. diss., University of Pennsylvania.

———. 1971a. The Powell classification of American Indian languages. *Papers in Linguistics* 4:71–110.

———. 1971b. The revision of the Powell classification. *Papers in Linguistics* 4:233–57.

———. 1988. *Daniel Garrison Brinton: the "fearless critic" of Philadelphia.* (Publications in Anthropology no. 3.) Philadelphia: University of Pennsylvania.

———. 1990. *Edward Sapir: linguist, anthropologist, humanist.* Berkeley: University of California Press.

———. 1992. Anthropological linguistics: early history in North America. In *IEL,* ed. William Bright, 1:69–71. New York: Oxford University Press.

Darnell, Regna, and Joel Sherzer. 1971. Areal linguistic studies in North America: a historical perspective. *IJAL* 37:20–8.

Davidson, Joseph O., Jr. 1977. A contrastive study of the grammatical structures of Aymara and Cuzco Kechua. Ph.D. diss., University of California, Berkeley.

Davies, Anna Morpurgo. See Morpurgo Davies, A[nna].

Dávila Garibi, J. I. 1935. Recopilación de datos acerca del idioma coca y de su posible influencia en el lenguage folklórico de Jalisco. *Investigaciones Lingüísticas* 3:248–302.

———. 1942. Algunas afinidades de las lenguas coca y cahita. *El México Antiguo* 6:47–60.

Davis, Irvine. 1959. Linguistic clues to northern Rio Grande prehistory. *El Palacio* 66:73–84.

———. 1966. Comparative Jê phonology. *Estudos Lingüísticos* (São Paulo) 1(2):10–24.

———. 1979. The Kiowa-Tanoan, Keresan, and Zuni languages. In *The languages of Native America: historical and comparative assessment,* ed. Lyle Campbell and Marianne Mithun, 390–443. Austin: University of Texas Press.

———. 1985[1968]. Some Macro-Jê relationships. In *South American Indian languages: retrospect and prospect,* ed. Harriet E. Manelis Klein and Louisa R. Stark, 287–303. Austin: University of Texas Press. [Original ed., *IJAL* 34:42–7.]

———. 1989. A new look at Aztec-Tanoan. In *General and Amerindian ethnolinguistics: in remembrance of Stanley Newman,* ed. Mary Ritchie Key and Henry M. Hoenigswald, 365–790. Berlin: Mouton de Gruyter.

Day, Gordon M., and Bruce G. Trigger. 1978. Algonquin. In *Northeast,* ed. Bruce G. Trigger. Vol. 15 of *HNAI,* ed. William C. Sturtevant, 792–7. Washington, D.C.: Smithsonian Institution.

De Angulo, Jaime, and L. S. Freeland. 1925. The Chontal language (dialect of Tequixistlan). *Anthropos* 20:1032–52.

de Goeje, C. H. 1906. Handelsdialekt, tussen Aucaners en Indianen gebruikelijk (Handelsdialekt, ge-

bräuchlich zwischen Aucanern und Indianern). Bijdrage tot de ethnographie der surinaamsche Indianen. Supplement to *Internationales Archiv für Ethnographie* 17:109–11.

———. 1908. De "handelstaal" der Joeka's met de Trio's en de Ojana's. Appendix to *Verslag van Toemoekhoemak-expeditie,* 204–19. Leyden: E. J. Brill.

———. 1909. Études linguistiques Caraïbes, vol. 1. *Verhandelingen der Koninklijke Nederlandse Akademie van Wetenschappen te Amsterdam, Afdeeling Letterkunde,* n.s. 10(3).

———. 1946. Études linguistiques Caraïbes, vol. 2. *Verhandelingen der Koninklijke Nederlandse Akademie van Wetenschappen te Amsterdam, Afdeeling Letterkunde,* n.s. 40(2):101–2.

de Jong, J. P. B. de Josselin. 1966. In memoriam Christianus Cornelius Uhlenbeck. In *Portraits of linguists: a biographical source book for the history of Western linguistics,* 1746–1963, ed. Thomas A. Sebeok, 2:253–66. Bloomington: Indiana University Press.

de Laet, Joannes [Joanne de Laet Antverp]. 1640[1633, 1625]. *L'Histoire du nouveau monde ou description des Indes Occidentales.* Leiden: Elseviers. [1925 ed., *Nieuw Wereldt ofte Beschrijvinghe van West-Indien enz.* Leyden: I. Elzevier. 1633 ed., *Novus orbis, seu descriptionis Indiae Occidentalis.* Leyden: Elzevirios.]

De Laguna, Frederica. 1937. A preliminary sketch of the Eyak Indians, Copper River Delta, Alaska. (Publications of the Philadelphia Anthropological Society no. 1.) In *Twenty-fifth anniversary studies,* ed. D. S. Davidson. Philadelphia: University of Pennsylvania Press.

———. 1990a. Eyak. In *Northwest Coast,* ed. Wayne Suttles. Vol. 7 of *HNAI,* ed. William C. Sturtevant, 189–96. Washington, D.C.: Smithsonian Institution.

———. 1990b. Tlingit. In *Northwest Coast,* ed. Wayne Suttles. Vol. 7 of *HNAI,* ed. William C. Sturtevant, 203–28. Washington, D.C.: Smithsonian Institution.

DeLancey, Scott. 1987a. Klamath and Wintu pronouns. *IJAL* 53:461–4.

———. 1987b. Morphological parallels between Klamath and Wintu. (Occasional Papers on Linguistics no. 14.) In *Papers of the 1987 Hokan-Penutian languages workshop and Friends of Uto-Aztecan workshop,* ed. James E. Redden, 50–60. Carbondale: Department of Linguistics, Southern Illinois University.

———. 1991. Selected Klamath-Proto-Yokuts sets. Paper presented at the Hokan-Penutian Conference, University of Oregon, Eugene.

————. 1992. Klamath and Sahaptian numerals. *IJAL* 58:235–9.

DeLancey, Scott, Carol Genetti, and Noel Rude. 1988. Some Sahaptian-Klamath-Tsimshianic lexical sets. In *In honor of Mary Haas: from the Haas festival conference on Native American linguistics,* ed. William Shipley, 195–224. Berlin: Mouton de Gruyter.

del Hoyo, Eugenio. See Hoyo, Eugenio del.

Delbrück, Berthold. 1888. *Altindische Syntax.* (Syntaktische Forschungen no. 5.) Halle: Niemeyer.

————. 1893–1900. *Verglichende Syntax der Indogermanischen Sprachen.* Vol. 3 of *Grundriss der vergleichenden Grammatik der indogermanischen Sprachen,* ed. Karl Brugmann and Berthold Delbrück. Strassburg: K. J. Trübner.

DeLisle, Helga H. 1981. Consonantal symbolism in American Indian languages. *Journal of the Linguistic Association of the Southwest* 4:130–42.

Del Rey Fajardo, José. 1971. *Aportes jesuíticos a la filología colonial venezolana.* 2 vols. Caracas: Universidad Católica Andrés Bello, Instituto de Investigaciones Históricas, Seminario de Lenguas Indígenas.

Denison, T. S. 1913. *Mexican linguistics: including Nauatl or Mexican in Aryan phonology, the primitive Aryans of America, a Mexican-Aryan comparative vocabulary, morphology and the Mexican verb, and the Mexican-Aryan sibilants, with an appendix on comparative syntax.* Chicago: T. S. Denison.

Derbyshire, Desmond C. 1977. Word order universals and the existence of OVS languages. *Linguistic Inquiry* 8:590–9.

————. 1981. A diachronic explanation for the origin of OVS in some Carib languages. *Journal of Linguistics* 17:209–20.

————. 1985. *Hixkaryana and linguistic typology.* (Publications in Linguistics no. 76.) Arlington: SIL and University of Texas at Arlington Press.

————. 1986. Comparative survey of morphology and syntax in Brazilian Arawakan. In *Handbook of Amazonian languages,* ed. Desmond C. Derbyshire and Geoffrey K. Pullum, 1:469–566. Berlin: Mouton de Gruyter.

————. 1987. Morphosyntactic areal characteristics of Amazonian languages. *IJAL* 53:311–26.

————. 1992. Arawakan languages. *IEL,* ed. William Bright, 1:102–5. New York: Oxford University Press.

Derbyshire, Desmond C., and Doris L. Payne. 1990. Noun classification systems of Amazonian languages. In *Amazonian linguistics: studies in lowland South American languages,* ed. Doris L.

Payne, 243–71. Austin: University of Texas Press.

Derbyshire, Desmond C., and Geoffrey K. Pullum. 1979. A select bibliography of Guiana Carib languages. *IJAL* 45:271–6.

————. 1981. Object-initial languages. *IJAL* 47:192–214.

————. 1986. Introduction to *Handbook of Amazonian languages,* ed. Desmond C. Derbyshire and Geoffrey K. Pullum, 1:1–28. Berlin: Mouton de Gruyter.

————. 1991. Introduction to *Handbook of Amazonian languages,* ed. Desmond C. Derbyshire and Geoffrey K. Pullum, 3:3–18. Berlin: Mouton de Gruyter.

De Reuse, Willem J. 1983. Synonymy. In *Southwest,* ed. Alfonso Ortiz. Vol. 10 of *HNAI,* ed. William C. Sturtevant, 385–92. Washington, D.C.: Smithsonian Institution.

————. 1986. The lexicalization of sound symbolism in Santiago del Estero Quechua. *IJAL* 52:54–64.

Díaz-Fernández, Antonio Edmundo. 1993. Contactos entre el mapuzungun y dos lenguas del Perú antiguo: El quechua y el yunga. In *Actas: primeras jornadas de lingüística aborígen, 6 y 7 de octubre de 1992,* ed. J. Pedro Viegas Barros, 89–94. Buenos Aires: Facultad de Filosofía y Letras, Universidad de Buenos Aires.

Dibble, Charles E. 1966. The Aztec writing system. In *Readings in anthropology,* 2d ed., Ed. Jesse D. Jennings and E. Adamson Hoebel, 270–7. New York: McGraw-Hill.

Diderichsen, Paul. 1974. The foundation of comparative linguistics: revolution or continuation? In *Studies in the history of linguistics: traditions and paradigms,* ed. Dell Hymes, 277–306. Bloomington: Indiana University Press.

Dietrich, Wolf. 1990. *More evidence for an internal classification of Tupi-Guarani languages.* (Indiana, Supplement no. 12.) Berlin: Mann.

Dillehay, Tom D., and David J. Meltzer. 1991. Finale: processes and prospects. In *The first Americans: search and research,* ed. Tom D. Dillehay and David J. Meltzer, 287–94. Boca Raton: CRC Press.

Dixon, Roland. 1905. The Shasta-Achomawi: a new linguistic stock with four new dialects. *AA* 7:213–7.

————. 1907[1906]. Linguistic relationships within the Shasta-Achomawi stock. *ICA* (Quebec) 15(2):255–63.

————. 1910. *The Chimariko Indians and language,* 295–380. (UCPAAE no. 5.) Berkeley: University of California.

————. 1911. Maidu. In *Handbook of American In-*

dian languages, vol. 1, ed. Franz Boas, 679–734. (Bureau of American Ethnology Bulletin no. 40.) Washington, D.C.: U.S. Government Printing Office.

Dixon, Roland, and Alfred L. Kroeber. 1903. The native languages of California. *AA* 5:1–26.

———. 1913a. New linguistic families in California. *AA* 15:647–55.

———. 1913b. Relationship of the Indian languages of California. *Science* 37:225.

———. 1919. *Linguistic families of California,* 47–118. (UCPAAE no. 16.) Berkeley: University of California.

Doerfer, Gerhard. 1973. Lautgesetz und Zufall. In *Betrachtungen zum Omnikomparatismus.* Vol. 10 of *Innsbrucker Beiträge zur Sprachwissenschaft,* ed. Wolfgang Meid. Innsbruck: Institut für Vergleichende Sprachwissenschaft der Universität Innsbruck.

Dooley, Robert A. 1992. Guaranian languages. In *IEL,* ed. William Bright. 2:94–6. New York: Oxford University Press.

D'Orbigny, Alcide Dressalines. 1839. *L'Homme Américain (de l'Amérique Méridionale) considéré sous ses rapports physiologiques et moraux.* 2 vols. Paris: Pitois-Levrault. (Spanish translation 1944, *El hombre americano: considerado en sus aspectos fisiológicos y morales* [trans. Alfredo Cepeda]. Buenos Aires: Editorial Futuro.)

Dorsey, J. Owen. 1885. On the comparative phonology of four Siouan languages. In *Annual report of the Board of Regents of the Smithsonian Institution* [for 1883], 919–29. Washington, D.C.: Government Printing Office.

———. 1890. The Ꞓegiha language. In *Contributions to North American ethnology,* 6:1–794. U.S. Geographical and Geological Survey of the Rocky Mountain Region. Edited under the direction of J. W. Powell. Washington, D.C.: Department of the Interior.

Drechsel, Emanuel J. 1979. Mobilian Jargon: linguistic, sociocultural, and historical aspects of an American Indian lingua franca. Ph.D. diss., University of Wisconsin, Madison.

———. 1981. A preliminary sociolinguistic comparison of four indigenous pidgin languages of North America (with notes towards a sociolinguistic typology in American Indian linguistics). *AL* 23(3):93–112.

———. 1983a. The question of the lingua franca Creek. In *Proceedings of the 1982 Mid-America linguistics conference,* ed. Frances Ingemann, 388–400. Lawrence: University of Kansas.

———. 1983b. Towards an ethnohistory of speaking:

the case of Mobilian Jargon, an American Indian pidgin of the lower Mississippi Valley. *Ethnohistory* 30:165–76.

———. 1984. Structure and function in Mobilian Jargon: indications for the pre-European existence of an American Indian pidgin. *Journal of Historical Linguistics and Philology* 1(2):141–85.

———. 1987. On determining the role of Chickasaw in the history and origin of Mobilian Jargon. *IJAL* 53:21–9.

———. 1988. Wilhelm von Humboldt and Edward Sapir: analogies and homologies in their linguistic thoughts. In *In honor of Mary Haas: from the Haas festival conference on Native American linguistics,* ed. William Shipley, 225–63. Berlin: Mouton de Gruyter.

———. 1993. Basic word order in Mobilian jargon: underlying SOV or OSV? In *American Indian linguistics and ethnography in honor of Laurence C. Thompson,* ed. Anthony Mattina and Timothy Montler, 343–67. (Occasional Papers in Linguistics no. 10.) Missoula: University of Montana.

Driver, Harold E., and William C. Massey. 1957. Comparative studies of North American Indians. *Transactions of the American Philological Society* (Philadelphia) 47(2).

Droixhe, Daniel. 1978. *La Linguistique et l'appel de l'histoire 1600–1800: rationalisme et révolutions positives.* Geneva: Droz.

Dumézil, George. 1954. Remarques sur les six premiers noms du nombres de turc. *Studia Linguistica* 8:1–15.

———. 1955. Remarques complémentaires sur les six premiers noms du nombres de turc et du quechua. *Journal de la Société des Américanistes de Paris* 44:17–37.

Duponceau, Peter Stephen. 1819a. A correspondence between the Rev. John Heckewelder, of Bethlehem, and Peter S. Duponceau Esq., corresponding secretary of the Historical and Literary committee of the American Philosophical Society, respecting the languages of the American Indians. *Transactions of the Historical and Literary Committee of the American Philosophical Society* 1:351–465.

———. 1819b. Report of the corresponding secretary to the Committee, of his progress in the investigation committed to him of the general character and forms of the languages of the American Indians (read 12th January 1819). *Transactions of the Historical and Literary Committee of the American Philosophical Society* 1:xvii–xlvi.

———. 1830. The translator's preface. (A grammar of the language of the Lenni Lenape or Delaware

Indians. Translated from the German manuscript of the late Rev. David Zeisberger, for the American Philosophical Society, by Peter Stephen Duponceau. Presented to the Society, 2d December 1816.) *Transactions of the American Philosophical Society* 3:65–96.

———. 1838. *Mémoire sur le système grammatical des langues de quelques nations indiennes de l'Amérique du Nord; ouvrage qui, à la séance publique annuelle de l'Institut Royal de France, le 2 mai 1835, a remporté le prix fondé par M. le comte de Volney.* Paris: Pihan de la Forest.

Du Pratz, Antoine Simon Le Page. 1758. *Histoire de la Louisiane, contenant la découverte de ce vaste pays; sa description géographique; un voyage dans les terres; l'histoire naturelle; les mœurs, coûtumes & religion des naturels, avec leurs origines; deux voyages dans le nord du Nouveau Mexique, dont un jusqu'à la Mer du Sud; ornée de deux cartes & de 40 planches en taille douce.* Paris: De Bure, La Veuve Delaguette, Lambert. (English translation, 1947, *The history of Louisiana or of the western parts of Virginia and Carolina: containing a description of the countries that lie on both sides of the River Mississippi, with an account of the settlements, inhabitants, soil, climate, and products.* New Orleans: Pelican Press.)

Durbin, Marshall. 1985[1977]. A survey of the Carib language family. In *South American Indian languages: retrospect and prospect,* ed. Harriet E. Manelis Klein and Louisa R. Stark, 325–71. Austin: University of Texas Press. [Original ed., in *Carib-speaking Indians: culture, society and language,* ed. Ellen B. Basso, 23–38. Tucson: University of Arizona Press.]

Eden, Richard. 1885. *First three English books on America,* ed. Edward Arber. Birmingham.

Edgerton, Franklin. 1943. Notes on early American work in linguistics. *Proceedings of the American Philosophical Society* 87:25–34.

Edwards, Jonathan, Jr. 1823[1788, 1787]. *Observations on the language of the Muhhekaneew Indians; In which the extent of that language in North America is shewn; its genius is grammatically traced; some of its peculiarities, and some instances of analogy between that and the Hebrew are pointed out.* (Communicated to the Connecticut Society of Arts and Sciences, and published at the request of the Society.) With notes by John Pickering. Massachusetts Historical Society Collection, 2d ser., 10:81–160. Boston: Phelps and Farnham. [Original ed., 1787, New Haven: Josiah Meigs. Reprinted 1788, London: W. Justins, Shoemaker-Row, Blackfriars.]

Eliot, John. 1663. *The Holy Bible, containing the Old Testament and the New, translated into the Indian language and ordered to be printed by the commissioners of the United Colonies in New-England.* Cambridge, Mass.: Samuel Green and Marmaduke Johnson.

———. 1822[1666]. *A grammar of the Massachusetts Indian language,* ed. John Pickering. Boston: Phelps and Farnham. [Original ed., *The Indian grammar begun: a grammar of the Massachusetts Indian language.* Cambridge, Mass.: Samuel Green and Marmaduke Johnson.]

Elliott, Eric. 1994. 'How' and 'thus' in (Uto-Aztecan) Cupan and Yuman: a case of areal influence. In *Proceedings of the meeting of the Society for the Study of the Indigenous Languages of the Americas and the Hokan-Penutian workshop,* ed. Margaret Langdon, 145–169. (SCOIL Report no. 8.) Berkeley: Department of Linguistics, University of California.

Elmendorf, William W. 1963. Yukian-Siouan lexical similarities. *IJAL* 20:300–9.

———. 1964. Item and set comparison in Yuchi, Siouan, and Yukian. *IJAL* 30:328–40.

———. 1965. Some problems in the regrouping of Powell units. *Canadian Journal of Linguistics* 10:93–107.

———. 1968. Lexical and cultural change in Yukian. *AL* 10(7):1–41.

———. 1981. Features of Yukian pronominal structure. *Journal of California and Great Basin Anthropology, Papers in Linguistics* 3:3–16.

———. 1988. Wappo agreements with Northern Yukian—summary. Unpublished manuscript.

———. 1990. Chemakum. In *Northwest Coast,* ed. Wayne Suttles, Vol. 7 of *HNAI,* ed. William C. Sturtevant, 438–40. Washington, D.C.: Smithsonian Institution.

Elsasser, Albert B. 1978. Wiyot. In *California,* ed. Robert F. Heizer. Vol. 8 of *HNAI,* ed. William C. Sturtevant, 153–63. Washington, D.C.: Smithsonian Institution.

Emeneau, Murray B. 1956. India as a linguistic area. *Language* 32:3–16.

———. 1980 [1965]. India and linguistic areas. In *Language and linguistic area: essays by Murray B. Emeneau, selected and introduced by Anwar S. Dil,* 126–96. Stanford: Stanford University Press. [Original ed., in *India and historical grammar,* by Murray Emeneau, 25–75. (Department of Linguistics Publication no. 5.) Annamalai, India: Annamalai University.]

England, Nora C. 1991. Changes in basic word order in Mayan languages. *IJAL* 57:446–86.

Erickson, Vincent O. 1978. Maliseet-Passamaquoddy.

In *Northeast,* ed. Bruce G. Trigger. Vol. 15 of *HNAI,* ed. William C. Sturtevant, 123–36. Washington, D.C.: Smithsonian Institution.

Escalante Hernández, Roberto. 1962. *El Cuitlateco.* Mexico: INAH.

———. 1963. Material lingüístico del oriente de Sonora: Tonichi y Ponida. *Anales del INAH* (Mexico) 16:149–78.

Everett, Daniel L. In press. A structural comparison of Arawan and Chapacuran: any evidence for a genetic classification? In *Language and prehistory in the Americas,* ed. Allan Taylor. Stanford: Stanford University Press.

Ferguson, Charles A. 1976. The Ethiopian language area. In *Language in Ethiopia,* ed. M. L. Bender, J. D. Bowen, R. L. Cooper, and C. A. Ferguson, 63–76. London: Oxford University Press.

Ferrario, Benigno. 1933. La investigación lingüística y el parentesco extra-continental de la lengua "qhexwa". *Revista de la Sociedad "Amigos de la Arqueología"* (Montevideo, Uruguay) 7:89–120.

———. 1938. *Della possibile parentela fra le indue "altaiche" en alcune americaine.* Vol. 19 of *Congresso Internazionale degli Orientalisti,* 210–23. Rome: Tipographia della Reale Accademia dei Lincei del Dott.

Figueira, Luis. 1878[1621, 1687]. *Grammatica da lingua do Brasil.* Facsimile ed. Jules Platzmann. Leipzig: Teubner. [Original ed., 1621, Arte da lingua brasilica, Lisbon: Manoel da Silva. New ed., 1687, *Arte de grammatica da lingua brasilica,* ed. Miguel Deslandes.]

Fladmark, Knut. 1979. Routes: alternate migration corridors for early man in North America. *Am. Ant.* 44:55–69.

———. 1986. Getting one's Berings. *Natural History* 95(11):8–19.

Fleming, Harold C. 1987. Towards a definitive classification of the world's languages. (Review of *A guide to the world's languages* by Merritt Ruhlen.) *Diachronica* 4:159–223.

Floyd, E. D. 1981. Levels of phonological restriction in Greek affixes. In *Bono Homini donum: essays in historical linguistics in memory of J. Alexander Kerns,* ed. Yoel L. Arbeitman and A. R. Bomhard, 87–106. Amsterdam: John Benjamins.

Fodor, István. 1966. *The problems in the classification of the African languages: methodological and theoretical conclusions concerning the classification system of Joseph H. Greenberg.* Budapest: Center for Afro-Asian Research of the Hungarian Academy of Sciences.

———. 1968. La classification des langues négro-africaines et la théorie de J. H. Greenberg. *Cahiers d'Études Africaines* 8:617–31.

Fortescue, Michael. 1981. Endoactive-exoactive markers in Eskimo-Aleut, Tungus, and Japanese—an investigation into common origins. *Etudes Inuit* 5:3–41.

———. 1988. The Eskimo-Aleut-Yukagir relationship: an alternative to the genetic/contact dichotomy. *Acta Linguistica Hafniensia* (Copenhagen) 21:21–50.

———. 1994. The role of typology in the establishment of the genetic relationship between Eskimo and Aleut—and beyond. In *Languages of the north Pacific rim,* ed. Osahito Miyaoka, 9–36. (Publications in Linguistics no. 7.) Sapporo, Japan: Department of Linguistics, Hokkaido University.

Foster, Michael K. 1982. Canada's first languages. *Language and Society* 7:7–14.

———. 1990. The impact of Sapir's six-phylum linguistic scheme on speculation about North American Indian culture history: a bibliographic essay. *AL* 29(1):37–67.

Fowler, Catherine S. 1972. Some ecological clues to Proto-Numic homelands. In *Great Basin cultural ecology: a symposium,* ed. D. D. Fowler, 105–21. (Desert Research Institute Publications in the Social Sciences no. 8.) Reno: University of Nevada.

———. 1983. Some lexical clues to Uto-Aztecan prehistory. *IJAL* 49:224–57.

Fowler, William R., Jr. 1989. *The cultural evolution of ancient Nahua civilizations: the Pipil-Nicarao of Central America.* Norman: University of Oklahoma Press.

Fox, James Allan. 1978. Proto-Mayan accent, morpheme structure conditions, and velar innovations. Ph.D. diss., University of Chicago.

———. 1980. Review of *The Mobilian trade language* by James M. Crawford. *AA* 82:606–8.

Frachtenberg, Leo J. 1918. Comparative studies in Takelman, Kalapuyan, and Chinookan lexicography; a preliminary paper. *IJAL* 1:175–82.

———. 1920. Abnormal types of speech in Quileute. *IJAL* 1:295–9.

Frankle, Eleanor. 1984a. Los morfemas vocálicos para derivaciones verbales en los grupos mayance y túrquico. Investigaciones recientes en el área maya. *La 17a mesa redonda, Sociedad Mexicana de Antropología* 2:517–24.

———. 1984b. Las relaciones externas entre las lenguas mayances y altaicas. Investigaciones recientes en el área maya. *La 17a mesa redonda, Sociedad Mexicana de Antropología* 1:209–25.

Freeland, L. S. 1930. The relationship of Mixe to the Penutian family. *IJAL* 6:28–33.

Friederici, Georg. 1947. *Amerikanistisches Wörterbuch.* (2d ed., 1960.) Hamburg: Cram de Gruyter.

Friedrich, Paul. 1971. Dialectal variation in Tarascan phonology. *IJAL* 37:164–87.

Gallatin, Albert. 1973[1836]. *A synopsis of the Indian tribes within the United States east of the Rocky Mountains and in the British and Russian possessions in North America.* New York: AMS Press. [Original ed., Archaeologia Americana. In *Transactions and Collections of the American Antiquarian Society,* vol. 2.

———. 1848. Hale's Indians of Northwest America and vocabularies of North America, with an introduction. *Transactions of the American Ethnological Society* (New York) 2:xxiii–clxxx, 1–130.

Gamble, Geoffrey. 1975. Consonant symbolism in Yokuts. *IJAL* 41:306–9.

Gancedo, A. 1922. El idioma japonés y sus afinidades con lenguas americanas. *Revista de Derecho, Historia y Letras* (Buenos Aires) 73:114–22.

García, Bartholomé. 1760. *Manual para administrar los santos sacramentos . . . a los indios de las naciones: Pajalates, Orejones, Pacaos, Pacoas, Tilijayas, Alasapas, Pausanes, y otras muchas diferentes que se hallan en las misiones del Rio San Antonio, y Rio Grande.* Mexico.

García, Gregorio. 1729[1607]. *Origen de los indios de el nuevo mundo, e Indias occidentales,* ed. Andrés González de Barcia Carballido y Zúñiga. Madrid: Francisco Marínez Abad.

Garth, T. R. 1978. Atsugewi. In *California,* ed. Robert F. Heizer, Vol. 8 of *HNAI,* ed. William C. Sturtevant, 236–43. Washington, D.C.: Smithsonian Institution.

Garza Cuarón, Beatriz. 1990. Francisco Pimentel y la lingüística mexicana. In *Homenaje a Jorge A. Suárez: lingüística indoamericana e hispánica,* ed. Beatriz Garza Cuarón, 229–50. Mexico: El Colegio de México.

Gatschet, Albert S. 1876. *Zwölf Sprachen aus dem südwesten Nordamerikas (Pueblos- und Apache-Mundarten; Tonto, Tonkawa, Digger, Utah).* Weimar: Hermann Böhlau.

———. 1877a. Indian languages of the Pacific states and territories. In *The Indian miscellany,* ed. W. W. Beach, 416–51. Albany: Munsell. [Original ed., in *Magazine of American History* 1:145–71.]

———. 1877b. Der Yuma-Sprachstamm nach den neuesten handschriftlichen Quellen. *Zeitschrift für Ethnologie* 9:341–50, 366–418.

———. 1879. Classification into seven linguistic stocks of Western Indian dialects contained in forty vocabularies. Report upon United States Geographical Surveys West of the One Hundredth Meridian. *Archaeology* (Washington, D.C.) 7:403–85.

———. 1879–1880. The test of linguistic affinity. *American Antiquarian* 2:163–5.

———. 1882. Indian languages of the Pacific states and territories and of the Pueblos of New Mexico. *Magazine of American History with Notes and Queries* 8:254–63.

———. 1885–1890. The Beothuk Indians. *Proceedings of the American Philosophical Society* 22:408–424 (1885); 23:411–32 (1886); 27:1–16 (1890).

———. 1886. On the affinity of the Cheroki to the Iroquois dialects. *Transactions of the American Philological Association* 16:xl–xlv.

———. 1900a. Grammatical sketch of the Catawba language. *AA* 2:527–49.

———. 1900b. The Waikuru, Seri, and Yuman languages. *Science* 12:556–8.

Gatschet, Albert S., and John R. Swanton. 1932. *A dictionary of the Atakapa language: accompanied by text material.* (Smithsonian Institution Bureau of American Ethnology Bulletin no. 108.) Washington, D.C.: Government Printing Office.

Gibbs, George. 1863a. *Dictionary of the Chinook Jargon.* New York: Cramoisy Press.

———. 1863b. *Instructions for research relative to the ethnology and philology of America.* (Miscellaneous Collections no. 160.) Washington, D.C.: Smithsonian Institution.

———. 1877. *Tribes of Western Washington and Northwestern Oregon.* (Contributions to North American Ethnology no. 1.) Washington, D.C.

———. 1972[1853]. Vocabularies of Indian languages in northwest California. In *Historical and statistical information respecting the history, condition, and prospects of the Indian tribes of the United States,* ed. Henry R. Schoolcraft, 428–45. Berkeley: University of California Archaeological Research Facility. [Original ed., Philadelphia: Lippincott, Grambo.]

Gibson, Arrell M. 1963. *The Kickapoos: lords of the Middle border.* Norman: University of Oklahoma Press.

Gildea, Spike. 1992. Comparative Cariban morphosyntax: on the genesis of ergativity in independent clauses. Ph.D. diss., University of Oregon, Eugene.

Gilij, Filippo Salvatore. (1965[1782], *Ensayo de historia americana,* trans. Antonio Tovar. In *Fuentes para la historia colonial de Venezuela,* 3 vols. 71–73. Caracas: Biblioteca de la Academia

Nacional de la Historia.) [Original ed., 1780–1784. *Saggio di storia americana; o sia, storia naturale, civile e sacra de regni, e delle provincie spagnuole di Terra-Ferma nell' America Meridionale descritto dall' abate F. S. Gilij.* 4 vols. Rome: Perigio.]

Girard, Victor. 1971a. Proto-Carib phonology. Ph.D. diss., University of California, Berkeley.

———. 1971b. *Proto-Takanan phonology.* (UCPL, vol. 70.) Berkeley: University of California Press.

Givón, Talmy. 1984. *Syntax: a functional-typological introduction.* Vol. 1. Amsterdam: John Benjamins.

———. 1990. *Syntax: a functional-typological introduction.* Vol. 2. Amsterdam: John Benjamins.

Goddard, Ives. 1965. The Eastern Algonquian intrusive nasal. *IJAL* 31:206–30.

———. 1971. More on the nasalization of PA *aˑ in Eastern Algonquian. *IJAL* 37:139–45.

———. 1972. Three new Algonquian languages. *Algonquian Linguistics Newsletter* 1(2–3):5–6.

———. 1973. Philological approaches to the study of North American Indian languages: documents and documentations. In *Linguistics in North America,* ed. Thomas A. Sebeok, 727–45. (*CTL* vol. 10.) The Hague: Mouton.

———. 1974a. Dutch loanwords in Delaware. In *A Delaware Indian symposium,* ed. Herbert C. Kraft, 153–60. (Anthropological Series no. 4.) Harrisburg: Pennsylvania Historical and Museum Commission.

———. 1974b. An outline of the historical phonology of Arapaho and Atsina. *IJAL* 40:102–116.

———. 1975. Algonquian, Wiyot, and Yurok: proving a distant genetic relationship. In *Linguistics and anthropology in honor of C. F. Voegelin,* ed. M. Dale Kinkade, Kenneth L. Hale, and Oswald Werner, 249–62. Lisse: Peter de Ridder Press.

———. 1977. Some early examples of American Indian Pidgin English from New England. *IJAL* 43:37–41.

———. 1978a. Delaware. In *Northeast,* ed. Bruce G. Trigger. Vol. 15 of *HNAI,* ed. William C. Sturtevant, 213–39. Washington, D.C.: Smithsonian Institution.

———. 1978b. A further note on Pidgin English. *IJAL* 44:73.

———. 1978c. Synonymy. In *Northeast,* ed. Bruce G. Trigger. Vol. 15 of *HNAI,* ed. William C. Sturtevant, 320, 404–6, 478–9, 489–90, 499, 503, 524, 654–5, 768–70. Washington, D.C.: Smithsonian Institution.

———. 1979a. Comparative Algonquian. In *The languages of Native America: historical and comparative assessment,* ed. Lyle Campbell and Mar-ianne Mithun, 70–132. Austin: University of Texas Press.

———. 1979b. The languages of South Texas and the lower Rio Grande. In *The languages of Native America: historical and comparative assessment,* ed. Lyle Campbell and Marianne Mithun, 355–89. Austin: University of Texas Press.

———. 1979c. Synonymy. In *Southwest,* ed. Alfonso Ortiz. Vol. 9 of *HNAI,* ed. William C. Sturtevant, 234–5, 267, 479–81, 601. Washington, D.C.: Smithsonian Institution.

———. 1981. Synonymy. In *Subarctic,* ed. June Helm. Vol. 6 of *HNAI,* ed. William C. Sturtevant, 185–7, 412, 430, 465, 512, 599–600, 613–15, 638–9, 661–2. Washington, D.C.: Smithsonian Institution.

———. 1983. Synonymy. In *Southwest,* ed. Alfonso Ortiz. Vol. 10 of *HNAI,* ed. William C. Sturtevant, 23–4, 69, 97, 134–5. Washington, D.C.: Smithsonian Institution.

———. 1984. Synonymy. In *Arctic,* ed. David Damas. Vol. 5 of *HNAI,* ed. William C. Sturtevant, 5–7. Washington, D.C.: Smithsonian Institution.

———. 1986. Sapir's comparative method. In *New perspectives in language, culture, and personality: proceedings of the Edward Sapir Centenary Conference, Ottawa, October 1–3, 1984,* ed. William Cowan, Michael K. Foster, and Konrad Koerner, 191–214. (Studies in the History of the Language Sciences no. 41.) Amsterdam: John Benjamins.

———. 1987a. Leonard Bloomfield's descriptive and comparative studies of Algonquian. *Historiographia Linguistica* 14:179–217.

———. 1987b. Review of *Language in the Americas* by Joseph H. Greenberg. *CA* 28:656–7.

———. 1988. Pre-Cheyenne *y. In *In honor of Mary Haas: from the Haas festival conference on Native American linguistics,* ed. William Shipley, 345–60. Berlin: Mouton de Gruyter.

———. 1990a. Algonquian linguistic change and reconstruction. In *Linguistic change and reconstruction methodology,* ed. Philip Baldi, 99–114. Berlin: Mouton de Gruyter.

———. 1990b. Review of *Language in the Americas* by Joseph H. Greenberg. *Linguistics* 28:557–8.

———. 1994a. J. W. Powell's 1891 classification and map. Paper presented at the Annual Meeting of the American Anthropological Association, Atlanta, November 30.

———. 1994b. A new look for Algonquian. Paper presented at the Comparative Linguistics Workshop, University of Pittsburgh, April 9.

———. 1994c. The West-to-East cline in Algonquian

dialectology. In *Actes du vingt-cinquième congrès des algonquinistes,* ed. William Cowan, 187–211. Ottawa: Carleton University.

———. In press. The classification of the native languages of North America. In *Languages,* ed. Ives Goddard. Vol. 17 of *HNAI,* ed. William C. Sturtevant. Washington, D.C.: Smithsonian Institution. [Cited with permission.]

Goddard, Ives, and Lyle Campbell. 1994. The history and classification of American Indian languages: What are the implications for the peopling of the Americas. In *Method and theory for investigating the peopling of the Americas,* ed. Robson Bonnichsen and D. Gentry Steele, 189–207. Corvallis: Oregon State University, Center for the Study of the First Americans.

Goddard, Ives, and W. Fitzhugh. 1979. A statement concerning America B.C. *Man in the Northeast* 17:166–72. (Also in: *Biblical Archeologist* 41(1978):85–8.)

Goddard, Ives, and Richard Slobodin. 1981. Synonymy. In *Subarctic,* ed. June Helm. Vol. 6 of *HNAI,* ed. William C. Sturtevant, 530–2. Washington, D.C.: Smithsonian Institution.

Goddard, Ives, and James G. E. Smith. 1981. Synonymy. In *Subarctic,* ed. June Helm. Vol. 6 of *HNAI,* ed. William C. Sturtevant, 283. Washington, D.C.: Smithsonian Institution.

Goddard, Pliny Earle. 1914. The present condition of our knowledge of North American Indians. *AA* 16:555–601.

———. 1920. Has Tlingit a genetic relation to Athapascan? *IJAL* 1:266–79.

———. 1926. The antiquity of man in America. *Natural History* 26:257–60.

Goldschmidt, Walter. 1978. Nomlaki. In *California,* ed. Robert F. Heizer. Vol. 8 of *HNAI,* ed. William C. Sturtevant, 341–9. Washington, D.C.: Smithsonian Institution.

Golla, Susan, and Ives Goddard. 1978. Synonymy. In *Northeast,* ed. Bruce G. Trigger. Vol. 15 of *HNAI,* ed. William C. Sturtevant, 706. Washington, D.C.: Smithsonian Institution.

Golla, Victor. 1980. Some Yokuts-Maidun comparisons. In *American Indian and Indo-European studies: papers in honor of Madison S. Beeler,* ed. Kathryn Klar, Margaret Langdon, and Shirley Silver, 57–65. The Hague: Mouton.

———, ed. 1984. *The Sapir-Kroeber correspondence.* (SCOIL Report no. 6.) Berkeley: Department of Linguistics, University of California.

———. 1986. Sapir, Kroeber, and North American linguistic classification. In *New perspectives in language, culture, and personality: proceedings of the Edward Sapir Centenary conference, Ottawa, October 1–3, 1984,* ed. William Cowan, Michael K. Foster, and Konrad Koerner, 17–39. (Studies in the History of the Language Sciences no. 41.) Amsterdam: John Benjamins.

———. 1988. Review of *Language in the Americas* by Joseph H. Greenberg. *AA* 90:434–5.

———. 1991a. *Comparative Penutian glosses.* [Based on Comparative Penutian glosses of Sapir, by Morris Swadesh (1964)]. In *American Indian languages,* part 2, ed. Victor Golla. *CWES* 6:299–315. Berlin: Mouton de Gruyter.

———. 1991b. John P. Harrington and his legacy. *AL* 33:337–49.

Golovko, Evgenij. 1994. Mednyj Aleut or Copper Island Aleut: an Aleut-Russian mixed language. In *Mixed languages: fifteen case studies in language intertwining,* ed. Peter Bakker and Maarten Mous, 113–21. Amsterdam: Institute for Functional Research into Language and Language Use.

Goodman, Morris. 1970. Some questions on the classification of African languages. *IJAL* 36:117–22.

Gossen, Gary H. 1984. *Chamulas in the world of the sun: time and space in a Maya oral tradition.* Prospect Heights, Ill.: Waveland Press.

Granberry, Julian. 1970. [Abstract of Granberry's work on Timucua.] *American Philosophical Society Yearbook,* 606–7.

———. 1990. A grammatical sketch of Timucua. *IJAL* 56:60–101.

———. 1991. Amazonian origins and affiliations of the Timucua language. In *Language change in South American Indian languages,* ed. Mary Ritchie Key, 195–242. Philadelphia: University of Pennsylvania Press.

———. 1993[1984]. *A grammar and dictionary of the Timucua language.* 3d ed. (1st ed., 1984.) Tuscaloosa: University of Alabama Press.

Grant, Campbell. 1978. Chumash: introduction. In *California,* ed. Robert F. Heizer. Vol. 8 of *HNAI,* ed. William C. Sturtevant, 505–8. Washington, D.C.: Smithsonian Institution.

Grasserie, Raoul de la. 1890[1888]. De la famille linguistique Pano. *ICA* 7:438–49. Berlin.

Greenberg, Joseph H. 1949. Studies in African linguistic classification, part 1: The Niger-Congo family. *SJA* 5:79–100.

———. 1953. Historical linguistics and unwritten languages. In *Anthropology today,* ed. Alfred L. Kroeber, 265–86. Chicago: University of Chicago Press.

———. 1955. *Studies in African linguistic classification.* New Haven: Compass Publishing.

———. 1957. *Essays in linguistics.* Chicago: University of Chicago Press.

———. 1960. General classification of Central and South American languages. In *Men and cultures: fifth international congress of anthropological and ethnological sciences (1956),* ed. Anthony Wallace, 791–94. Philadelphia: University of Pennsylvania Press.

———. 1962. Provisional classification of aboriginal languages of Latin America [chart, unpaged]. In *Encyclopaedia Britannica,* vol. 12. Chicago: Encyclopaedia Britannica.

———. 1963. *Languages of Africa.* (Publications of the Research Center in Anthropology, Folklore, and Linguistics no. 25.) Bloomington: Indiana University.

———. 1966[1963]. Some universals of grammar with particular reference to the order of meaningful elements. In *Universals of language,* ed. Joseph H. Greenberg, 73–113. 2d ed., (1st ed., 1963.) Cambridge, Mass: MIT Press.

———. 1971. The Indo-Pacific hypothesis. In *Linguistics in Oceania,* ed. Thomas A. Sebeok, 807–71. (*CTL,* vol. 8.) The Hague: Mouton.

———. 1979. The classification of American Indian languages. In *Papers of the 1978 Mid-America linguistics conference,* ed. Ralph E. Cooley, 7–22. Norman: University of Oklahoma Press.

———. 1987. *Language in the Americas.* Stanford: Stanford University Press.

———. 1989. Classification of American Indian languages: a reply to Campbell. *Language* 65:107–14.

———. 1990a. The American Indian language controversy. *Review of Archaeology* 11:5–14.

———. 1990b. Comments on Speaking of forked tongues: the feasibility of reconciling human phylogeny and the history of language. *CA* 31:18–19.

———. 1990c. Correction to Matisoff: on megalocomparison. *Language* 66:660.

———. 1990d. The prehistory of the Indo-European vowel system in comparative and typological perspective. In *Proto-languages and proto-cultures: materials from the first international interdisciplinary symposium on language and prehistory,* ed. Vitaly Shevoroshkin, 77–136. Bochum: Brockmeyer.

———. 1991. Some problems of Indo-European in historical perspective. In *Sprung from some common source: investigations into the prehistory of languages,* ed. Sydney M. Lamb and E. Douglas Mitchell, 125–40. Stanford: Stanford University Press.

———. 1993. Observations concerning Ringe's *Calculating the factor of change in language comparison. Proceedings of the American Philosophical Society* 137:79–90.

———. 1994. On the Amerind affiliation of Zuni and Tonkawa. *California Linguistic Notes* 24:4–6.

———. In press. Indo-European practice and American Indianist theory in linguistic classification. In *The classification and prehistory of American Indian languages,* ed. Allan Taylor. Stanford, Calif.: Stanford University Press.

Greenberg, Joseph H., and Merritt Ruhlen. 1992. Linguistic origins of Native Americans. *Scientific American* 267(5):94–99.

Greenberg, Joseph H., and Morris Swadesh. 1953. Jicaque as a Hokan language. *IJAL* 19:216–22.

Greenberg, Joseph H., Christy G. Turner II, and Stephen L. Zegura. 1986. The settlement of the Americas: a comparison of the linguistic, dental, and genetic evidence. *CA* 27:477–97.

Greene, John C. 1960. Early scientific interest in the American Indian: comparative linguistics. *Proceedings of the American Philosophical Society* 104:511–17.

Gregersen, Edgar A. 1977. *Language in Africa: an introductory survey.* New York: Gordon and Breach.

Grimes, Barbara F., ed. 1988. *Ethnologue: languages of the world.* 11th ed. Dallas: SIL.

Grimm, Thaddeus C. 1987. A comparison of Catawba with Biloxi, Mandan, and Dakota. *IJAL* 53:175–82.

Grotius [de Groot], Hugo. 1884.[1552]. *On the origin of the native races of America,* trans. from the original Latin, and enriched with biographical notes and illustrations by Edmund Goldsmid. Edinburgh: Privately printed. [Original ed., *De origine gentium americanarum dissertatio.*]

Gruber, Jacob W. 1967. Horatio Hale and the development of American anthropology. *Proceedings of the American Philosophical Society* 111:5–45.

Gruhn, Ruth B. 1988. Linguistic evidence in support of the coastal route of earliest entry into the New World. *Man* 23:77–100.

Gumperz, John, and Robert Wilson. 1971. Convergence and creolization: a case from the Indo-Aryan/Dravidian border in India. In *Pidginization and creolization of languages,* ed. Dell Hymes, 151–67. Cambridge: Cambridge University Press.

Gunn, Robert D., ed. 1980. *Clasificación de los idiomas indígenas de Panamá, con un vocabulario comparativo de los mismos* (prepared by Michael

Kopesec). (Lenguas de Panamá no. 7.) Panama: Instituto Nacional de Cultura, ILV.

Gunnerson, James H. 1979. Southern Athapaskan archaeology. In *Southwest,* ed. Alonso Ortiz. Vol. 9 of *HNAI,* ed. William C. Sturtevant, 162–9. Washington, D.C.: Smithsonian Institution.

Gursky, Karl-Heinz. 1963. Algonkian and the languages of southern Texas. *AL* 5(9):17–21.

———. 1964a. *Bemerkungen zur Beothuk-Sprache.* (Abhandlungen no. 5.) Nortorf: Völkerkundliche Arbeitsgemeinschaft.

———. 1964b. The linguistic position of the Quinigua Indians. *IJAL* 30:325–7.

———. 1965–1966. Ein lexikalischer Vergleich der Algonkin-Golf- und Hoka-Subtiaba-Sprachen. *Orbis* 14:160–215.

———. 1966a. Der augenblickliche Stand der Erforschung der nordamerikanischen Sprachen. *Anthropos* 61:401–54.

———. 1966b. On the historical position of Waikuri. *IJAL* 32:41–5.

———. 1966–1967. Ein Vergleich der grammatischen Morpheme der Golf-Sprachen und der Hoka-Subtiaba-Sprachen. *Orbis* 15:511–37.

———. 1968. Gulf and Hokan-Subtiaban: new lexical parallels. *IJAL* 34:21–41.

———. 1974. Der Hoka-Sprachstamm: eine Bestandsaufnahme des lexikalischen Beweismaterials. *Orbis* 23:170–215.

———. 1988. *Der Hoka-Sprachstamm: Nachtrag I.* (Abhandlungen no. 58.) Nortorf: Völkerkundliche Arbeitsgemeinschaft.

Gyarmathi, Sámuel. 1983[1968, 1799]. *Grammatical proof of the affinity of the Hungarian language with languages of Fennic origin,* translated, annotated, and introduced by Victor E. Hanzeli. (Classics in Linguistics no. 15.) Amsterdam: John Benjamins. [Original ed., *Affinitas linguae Hungaricae cum linguis Fennicae originis grammatice demonstrata.* Göttingen: Joann. Christan Dietrich. Photolithic reproduction of 2d ed., 1968, ed. Thomas A. Sebeok (Ural and Altaic Series no. 95.) Bloomington: Indiana University; The Hague: Mouton.]

Haas, Mary R. 1941. The classification of the Muskgoean languages. In *Language, culture, and personality: essays in memory of Edward Sapir,* ed. Leslie Spier, A. Irving Hallowell, and Stanley S. Newman, 41–56. Menasha, Wisc.: Sapir Memorial Publication Fund.

———. 1944. Men's and women's speech in Koasati. *Language* 20:142–9.

———. 1946. A grammatical sketch of Tunica. In *Linguistic structures of Native America,* ed.

Harry Hoijer, 337–66. (Publications in Anthropology no. 6.) New York: Viking Fund.

———. 1947. The development of Proto-Muskogean **kʷ. IJAL* 13:135–37.

———. 1949. The position of Apalachee in the Muskogean family. *IJAL* 15:121–7.

———. 1950. *Tunica texts.* (UCPL, vol. 6, 1–174.) Berkeley: University of California Press.

———. 1951. The Proto-Gulf word for *water* (with notes on Siouan-Yuchi). *IJAL* 17:71–9.

———. 1952. The Proto-Gulf word for *land* (with a note on Siouan-Yuchi). *IJAL* 18:238–40.

———. 1953. *Tunica dictionary.* (UCPL, vol. 6, 175–332.) Berkeley: University of California Press.

———. 1954. The Proto-Hokan-Coahuiltecan word for 'water'. In *Papers from the symposium on American Indian linguistics,* ed. Murray B. Emeneau, 57–62. (UCPL, vol. 10.) Berkeley: University of California Press.

———. 1956. Natchez and Muskogean languages. *Language* 32:61–72.

———. 1958a. Algonkian-Ritwan: the end of a controversy. *IJAL* 24:159–73.

———. 1958b. A new linguistic relationship in North America: Algonkian and the Gulf languages. *SJA* 14:231–64.

———. 1959. Tonkawa and Algonkian. *AL* 1(2):1–6.

———. 1960. Some genetic affiliations of Algonkian. In *Culture in history: essays in honor of Paul Radin,* ed. Stanley Diamond, 977–92. New York: Columbia University Press.

———. 1963a. The Muskogean and Algonkian words for *skunk. IJAL* 29:65–6.

———. 1963b. Shasta and Proto-Hokan. *Language* 39:40–59.

———. 1964a. Athapaskan, Tlingit, Yuchi, and Siouan. *ICA* 35:495–500. Mexico.

———. 1964b. California Hokan. In *Studies in Californian linguistics,* ed. William Bright, 73–87. (UCPL, vol. 34.) Berkeley: University of California Press.

———. 1965. Is Kutenai related to Algonkian? *Canadian Journal of Linguistics* 10:77–92.

———. 1966. Wiyot-Yurok-Algonkian and problems of comparative Algonkian. *IJAL* 32:101–7.

———. 1967a. On the relations of Tonkawa. In *Studies in southwestern ethnolinguistics: meaning and history in the languages of the American Southwest,* ed. Dell H. Hymes and William E. Bittle, 310–20. (Studies in General Anthropology no. 3.) The Hague: Mouton.

———. 1967b. Roger Williams' sound shift: a study in Algonkian. In *To honor Roman Jakobson: essays on the occasion of his seventieth birthday,* vol. 1, 816–32. The Hague: Mouton.

———. 1969a. American Indian languages and historical linguistics. Appendix to *The prehistory of languages,* pp. 98–107. The Hague: Mouton.

———. 1969b. Grammar or lexicon? The American Indian side of the question from Duponceau to Powell. *IJAL* 35:239–55. (Reprinted 1978, The problem of classifying American Indian languages: from Duponceau to Powell. In *Language, culture, and history: essays by Mary R. Haas, selected and introduced by Anwar S. Dil,* 130–63. Stanford: Stanford University Press.)

———. 1969c. Internal reconstruction of the Nootka-Nitinat pronominal suffixes. *IJAL* 35:108–24.

———. 1969d. *The prehistory of languages.* The Hague: Mouton.

———. 1969e. Swanton and the Biloxi and Ofo dictionaries. *IJAL* 35:286–90.

———. 1970. Consonant symbolism in northwestern California: a problem in diffusion. In *Languages and cultures of Western North America: essays in honor of Sven S. Liljeblad,* ed. Earl H. Swanson, Jr., 86–96. Pocatello: Idaho State University Press.

———. 1973a. American Indian linguistic prehistory. In *Linguistics in North America,* ed. Thomas Sebeok, 677–712. (*CTL,* vol. 10.) The Hague: Mouton.

———. 1973b. The Southeast. In *Linguistics in North America,* ed. Thomas Sebeok, 1210–49. (*CTL,* vol. 10.) The Hague: Mouton.

———. 1976. The Northern California linguistic area. In *Hokan studies: papers from the first conference on Hokan languages,* ed. Margaret Langdon and Shirley Silver, 347–59. The Hague: Mouton.

———. 1979. Southeastern languages. In *The languages of Native America: historical and comparative assessment,* ed. Lyle Campbell and Marianne Mithun, 299–326. Austin: University of Texas Press.

Haberland, Wolfgang. 1957. Black-on-red painted ware and associated features in the Intermediate Area. *Ethnos* 22:148–61.

Hajda, Yvonne. 1990. Southwestern Coast Salish. In *Northwest Coast,* ed. Wayne Suttles. Vol. 7 of *HNAI,* ed. William C. Sturtevant, 503–17. Washington, D.C.: Smithsonian Institution.

Hakulinen, Lauri. 1968. *Suomen kielen rakenne ja kehitys* [The structure and history of the Finnish language]. Helsinki: Otava.

Hale, Horatio. 1846. *United States exploring expedition, during the years 1838, 1839, 1840, 1841, 1842, under the command of Charles Wilkes, U.S. Navy.* Vol. 6 of *Ethnography and Philology.* Philadelphia: Lea and Blanchard.

———. 1883. Indian migrations, as evidenced by language, part 1: The Huron-Cherokee stock. *American Antiquarian* 5:18–28.

———. 1884. The Tutelo tribe and language. *Proceedings of the American Philosophical Society* 21:1–47.

———. 1890a. *An international idiom: a manual of the Oregon Trade Language or Chinook Jargon.* London: Whittaker.

———. 1890b[1888]. Was America peopled from Polynesia? *ICA* (Berlin) 7:374–88.

Hale, Kenneth. 1958–1959. Internal diversity of Uto-Aztecan I and II. *IJAL* 24:101–7; 25:114–21.

———. 1962. Jemez and Kiowa correspondences in reference to Kiowa-Tanoan. *IJAL* 28:1–5.

———. 1964. The sub-grouping of Uto-Aztecan languages: lexical evidence for Sonoran. *ICA* (Mexico) 35(3):511–17.

———. 1967. Toward a reconstruction of Kiowa-Tanoan phonology. *IJAL* 33:112–20.

Hale, Kenneth, and David Harris. 1979. Historical linguistics and archaeology. In *Southwest,* ed. Alonso Ortiz. Vol. 9 of *HNAI,* ed. William C. Sturtevant, 170–7. Washington, D.C.: Smithsonian Institution.

Halpin, Margorie M., and Margaret Seguin. 1990. Tsimshian peoples: Southern Tsimshian, Coast Tsimshian, Nishga, and Gitksan. In *Northwest Coast,* ed. Wayne Suttles. Vol. 7 of *HNAI,* ed. William C. Sturtevant, 267–84. Washington, D.C.: Smithsonian Institution.

Hammerich, Louis L. 1951. Can Eskimo be related to Indo-European? *IJAL* 17:217–23.

Hammerly Dupuy, Daniel. 1947a. Clasificación del nuevo grupo lingüístico Aksánas de la Patagonia occidental. *Ciencia e Investigación* (Buenos Aires) 3(12):492–501.

———. 1947b. Redescubrimiento de una tribu de indios canoeros del sur de Chile. *Revista Geográfica Americana* (Buenos Aires) 28(168):117–22.

———. 1952. Los pueblos canoeros de Fuegopatagonia y los límites del habitat Alakalúf. *Runa* (Buenos Aires) 5(1–2):134–70.

Hamori-Torok, Charles. 1990. Haisla. In *Northwest Coast,* ed. Wayne Suttles. Vol. 7 of *HNAI,* ed. William C. Sturtevant, 306–11. Washington, D.C.: Smithsonian Institution.

Hamp, Eric P. 1964. 'Chicken' in Ecuadorian Quichua. *IJAL* 30:298–9.

———. 1967. On Maya-Chipayan. *IJAL* 33:74–6.

———. 1970. Maya-Chipaya and typology of labials. *CLS* 6:20–2.

———. 1971. On Mayan-Araucanian comparative phonology. *IJAL* 37:156–9.

———. 1976. On Eskimo-Aleut and Luoravetlan. In *Papers on Eskimo and Aleut linguistics,* ed. Eric Hamp, 81–92. Chicago: CLS.

———, ed. 1976. *Papers on Eskimo and Aleut linguistics.* Chicago: CLS.

———. 1979. A glance from here on. In *The languages of Native America: historical and comparative assessment,* ed. Lyle Campbell and Marianne Mithun, 1001–15. Austin: University of Texas Press.

Hancock, Ian F. 1980. Texan Gullah: the Creole English of the Brackettville Afro-Seminoles. In *Perspectives on American English,* ed. Joey L. Dillard, 305–33. The Hague: Mouton.

Hanzeli, Victor Egon. 1969. *Missionary linguistics in New France: a study of seventeenth- and eighteenth-century descriptions of American Indian languages.* The Hague: Mouton.

Hardman de Bautista, Martha J. 1975. Proto-Jaqi: reconstrucción del sistema de personas gramaticales. *Revista del Museo Nacional* 41:433–56.

———. 1978a. La familia lingüística andina jaqi: jaqaru, kauki, aymara. *Vicus Cuadernos: Lingüística* 2:5–28.

———. 1978b. Jaqi: the linguistic family. *IJAL* 44:146–53.

———. 1985. Quechua and Aymara: languages in contact. In *South American Indian languages: retrospect and prospect,* ed. Harriet E. Manelis Klein and Louisa R. Stark, 617–43. Austin: University of Texas Press.

Harrington, John Peabody. 1909. Notes on the Piro language. *AA* 11:563–94.

———. 1910a. Introductory paper on the Tiwa language, dialect of Taos, New Mexico. *AA* 12:11–48.

———. 19010b. On phonetic and lexic resemblances between Kiowa and Tanoan. *AA* 12:119–23.

———. 1913. [Announcement of the relationship of Yuman and Chumash.] *AA* 15:716.

———. 1917. [Announcement of the relationship of Washo and Chumash.] *AA* 19:154.

———. 1928. *Vocabulary of the Kiowa language.* (Bureau of American Ethnology Bulletin no. 84.) Washington, D.C.: Government Printing Office.

———. 1940. Southern peripheral Athapaskan origins, divisions, and migrations. In *Essays in historical anthropology of North America, in honor of John R. Swanton,* 503–32. (Miscellaneous Collections no. 100.) Washington, D.C.: Smithsonian Institution.

———. 1943a. Hokan discovered in South America. *Journal of the Washington Academy of Sciences* 33:334–44.

———. 1943b. Pacific Coast Athapascan discovered to be Chilcotin. *Journal of the Washington Academy of Sciences* 33:203–13.

———. 1974. Sibilants in Ventureño, ed. Madison S. Beeler and Mary R. Haas. *IJAL* 40:1–9.

Harris, Alice C., and Lyle Campbell. 1995. *Historical Syntax in cross-linguistic perspective.* Cambridge: Cambridge University Press.

Harvey, H. R. 1972. The relaciones geográficas, 1579–1586: native languages. In *Ethnohistorical sources,* ed. Howard Cline. Vol. 12 of *HMAI,* ed. Robert Waucope, 279–323. Austin: University of Texas Press.

Haugen, Einar. 1976. *The Scandinavian languages: an introduction to their history.* Cambridge, MA: Harvard University Press.

Haumonté, J.-D., J. Parisot, and L. Adam. 1882. *Grammaire et vocabulaire de la langue taensa avec texts traduits et commentés.* Paris: Maisonneuve.

Heath, Jeffrey. 1977. Uto-Aztecan morphophonemics. *IJAL* 43:27–36.

Heath, Shirley Brice. 1972. *Telling tongues: language policy in Mexico.* New York: Teachers College Press.

Heckewelder, John. 1876[1819]. *History, manners, and customs of the Indian nations who once inhabited Pennsylvania and the neighboring states.* (Memoirs no. 12.) Philadelphia: Historical Society of Pennsylvania.

Heidenreich, Conrad E. 1978. Huron. In *Northeast,* ed. Bruce G. Trigger. Vol. 15 of *HNAI,* ed. William C. Sturtevant, 368–88. Washington, D.C.: Smithsonian Institution.

Heine, Bernd. 1972. Historical linguistics and lexicostatistics in Africa. *Journal of African Languages* 2:7–20.

———. 1992. African languages. In *IEL,* ed. William Bright, 1:31–5. New York: Oxford University Press.

Heine, Bernd, and Mechtild Reh. 1984. *Grammaticalization and reanalysis in African languages.* Hamburg: Helmut Buske.

Heine, Bernd, Ulrike Claudi, and Friederike Hünnemeyer. 1991. *Grammaticalization: a conceptual framework.* Chicago: University of Chicago Press.

Helm, June. 1981. Dogrib. In *Subarctic,* ed. June Helm. Vol. 6 of *HNAI,* ed. William C. Sturtevant, 291–309. Washington, D.C.: Smithsonian Institution.

Hendrichs Pérez, Pedro R. 1947. Breve informe del idioma cuitlateco. *ICA* 27:289–95.

Henshaw, Henry W., and James Mooney. 1885. *Lin-*

guistic families of the Indian tribes north of Mexico. Washington, D.C.: Bureau of American Ethnology.

Hervás y Panduro, [Don] Lorenzo. 1784–1787. *Idea dell'universo: che contiene la storia della vita dell'uomo, elementi cosmografici, viaggio estatico al mondo planetario, e storia de la terra e delle lingue.* 6 vols. Cesena: Biasini.

———. 1800–1805. *Catálogo de las lenguas de las naciones conocidas y numeracion, division, y clases de estas segun la diversidad de sus idiomas y dialectos.* 4 vols. Vol. 1 (1800): *Lenguas y naciones Americanas.* Madrid: Administracion del Real Arbitrio de Beneficencia.

Hess, Thom. 1979. Central Coast Salish words for *deer:* their wavelike distribution. *IJAL* 45:5–16.

Hester, Thomas R. 1978a. Esselen. In *California,* ed. Robert F. Heizer. Vol. 8 of *HNAI,* ed. William C. Sturtevant, 496–9. Washington, D.C.: Smithsonian Institution.

———. 1978b. Salinan. In *California,* ed. Robert F. Heizer. Vol. 8 of *HNAI,* ed. William C. Sturtevant, 500–4. Washington, D.C.: Smithsonian Institution.

Hewson, John. 1968. Beothuk and Algonkian: evidence old and new. *IJAL* 34:85–93.

———. 1971. Beothuk consonant correspondences. *IJAL* 37:244–9.

———. 1978. *Beothuk vocabularies: a comparative study.* (Technical Papers of the Newfoundland Museum no. 2.) St. John's, Newfoundland: Department of Tourism, Historic Resources Division.

———. 1982. Beothuk and the Algonkian Northeast. In *Languages in Newfoundland and Labrador,* ed. Harrold J. Paddock, 176–87. St. John's, Newfoundland: Department of Linguistics, Memorial University.

Hilton, Susanne F. 1990. Haihais, Bella Bella, and Oowekeeno. In *Northwest Coast,* ed. Wayne Suttles. Vol. 7 of *HNAI,* ed. William C. Sturtevant, 312–22. Washington, D.C.: Smithsonian Institution.

Hinsley, Curtis M., Jr. 1981. *Savages and scientists: the Smithsonian Institution and the development of American anthropology, 1846–1910.* Washington, D.C.: Smithsonian Institution.

Hinton, Leanne. 1991. Takic and Yuman: a study in phonological convergence. *IJAL* 57:133–57.

———. 1994. *Flutes of fire: essays on California Indian languages.* Berkeley: Heyday Books.

Hjelmslev, Louis. 1966[1950–1951]. Commentaires sur la vie et l'œuvre de Rasmus Rask. In *Por-*

traits of linguists: a biographical source book for the history of Western linguistics, 1746–1963, ed. Thomas A. Sebeok, 1:179–99. Bloomington: Indiana University Press. [Original ed., Conferences de l'Institut de Linguistiques de l'Université de Paris 10:143–57.]

Hock, Hans Henrich. 1993. SWALLOTALES: Chance and the "world etymology" MALIQ'A 'swallow, throat'. *CLS* 29:215–238.

Hockett, Charles. 1966[1952]. Edward Sapir. In *Portraits of linguists: a biographical source book for the history of Western linguistics, 1746–1963,* ed. Thomas A. Sebeok, 2:489–92. Bloomington: Indiana University Press. [Original ed., *Word Study* 27:1–3.]

———, ed. 1970. *A Leonard Bloomfield anthology.* Bloomington: Indiana University Press.

———. 1970[1948]. Implications of Bloomfield's Algonquian studies. In *A Leonard Bloomfield anthology,* ed. Charles Hockett. Bloomington: Indiana University Press. [Original ed., *Language* 24:117–31.]

———. 1973. Yokuts as testing-ground for linguistic methods. *IJAL* 39:63–79.

Hodge, Frederick Webb, ed. 1907. *Handbook of American Indians north of Mexico.* 2 vols. (Smithsonian Institution Bureau of American Ethnology Bulletin no. 30.) Washington, D.C.: Government Printing Office.

Hodge, Frederick W., and C. Hart Merriam. 1931. Henry Wetherbee Henshaw. *AA* 33:98–105.

Hoenigswald, Henry. 1974. Fallacies in the history of linguistics: notes on the appraisal of the nineteenth century. In *Studies in the history of linguistics: traditions and paradigms,* ed. Dell Hymes, 346–58. Bloomington: Indiana University Press.

———. 1990. Descent, perfection, and the comparative method since Leibniz. In *Leibniz, Humboldt, and the origins of comparativism,* ed. Tullio de Mauro and Lia Formigari, 119–32. Amsterdam: John Benjamins.

Hoff, Berend J. 1994. Island Carib, an Arawakan language which incorporated a lexical register of Cariban, used to address men. In *Mixed languages: fifteen case studies in language intertwining,* ed. Peter Bakker and Maarten Mous, 161–8. Amsterdam: Institute for Functional Research into Language and Language Use.

Hoijer, Harry. 1933. Tonkawa: an Indian language of Texas. In *Handbook of American Indian languages,* ed. Franz Boas, vol. 3, i–x, 1–148. New York: Columbia University Press.

———. 1941. Methods in the classification of American Indian languages. In *Language, culture, and personality: essays in memory of Edward Sapir,* ed. Leslie Spier, A. Irving Hallowell, and Stanley S. Newman, 3–14. Menasha, Wisc.: Sapir Memorial Publication Fund.

———. 1946a. Introduction. In *Linguistic structures of Native America,* ed. Harry Hoijer, 9–98. (Publications in Anthropology no. 6.) New York: Viking Fund.

———. 1946b. Tonkawa. In *Linguistic structures of Native America,* ed. Harry Hoijer, 289–311. (Publications in Anthropology no. 6.) New York: Viking Fund.

———. 1949. *An analytical dictionary of the Tonkawa language.* (UCPL, vol. 5). Berkeley: University of California Press.

———. 1954. Some problems of American Indian linguistic research. In *Papers from the symposium on American Indian linguistics,* ed. Murray B. Emeneau, 3–12. (UCPL, vol. 10.) Berkeley: University of California Press.

———. 1956. The chronology of the Athapaskan languages. *IJAL* 22:219–32.

———. 1972. *Tonkawa texts.* (UCPL, vol. 73.) Berkeley: University of California Press.

———. 1973. History of American Indian linguistics. In *Linguistics in North America,* ed. Thomas Sebeok, 657–76. (*CTL,* vol. 10.) The Hague: Mouton.

Hoijer, Harry, and Edward Dozier. 1949. The phonemes of Tewa, Santa Clara dialect. *IJAL* 15:139–44.

Hollow, Robert C., and Douglas R. Parks. 1980. Studies in Plains linguistics: a review. In *Anthropology on the Great Plains,* ed. W. Raymond Wood and Margot Liberty, 68–97. Lincoln: University of Nebraska Press.

Holt, Dennis. 1986. History of the Paya sound system. Ph.D. diss., University of California at Los Angeles.

Holt, Dennis, and William Bright. 1976. La lengua paya y las fronteras lingüísticas de Mesoamérica. Las fronteras de Mesoamérica. *La 14a mesa redonda, Sociedad Mexicana de Antropología* 1:149–56.

Hopkins, Nicholas A. 1984. Otomanguean linguistic prehistory. In *Essays in Otomanguean culture history,* ed. J. Kathryn Josserand, Marcus Winter, and Nicholas Hopkins, 25–64. (Publications in Anthropology no. 31.) Nashville: Department of Anthropology, Vanderbilt University.

Hopper, Paul J., and Elizabeth Closs Traugott. 1993. *Grammaticalization.* Cambridge: Cambridge University Press.

Houston, Stephen D. 1989. *Maya glyphs.* Berkeley: University of California Press.

Hovelacque, Abel. 1877. *The science of languages: linguistics, philology, etymology.* London: Chapman and Hall; Philadelphia: J. B. Lippincott.

Howley, James P. 1915. *The Beothuk or Red Indians: the aboriginal inhabitants of Newfoundland.* Cambridge: Cambridge University Press.

Hoyo, Eugenio del. 1960. Vocabulos de la lengua quinigua de los Indios Borrados del noreste de México. *Humanitas* (Centro de Estudios Humanísticos, Universidad de Nuevo León) 1(1):489–515.

Huddleston, Lee E. 1967. *Origins of the American Indians: European concepts, 1492–1729.* Austin: University of Texas Press.

Humboldt, Alexander von. 1809–1814. *Versuch über den politischen Zustand des Königreichs Neu-Spanien.* 4 vols. Tübingen: Cotta. (French version, 1811, *Essai politique sur le royaume de la Nouvelle-Espagne,* vol. 2. Paris: Antoine-Augustin Renouard.)

Humboldt, [Friedrich] Wilhem [Christian Karl Ferdinand] von 1963[1822]. Über das Entstehen der grammatischen Formen, und ihren Einfluß auf die Ideenentwicklung. In *Wilhelm von Humboldt Werke in fünf Bänden,* ed. Andreas Flitner and Klaus Giel, 3:31–63. Stuttgart: Cotta. [Original ed., *Abhandlungen der Königlichen Akademie der Wissenschaften zu Berlin,* 401–30.]

———. 1988[1836]. *On language: the diversity of human language-structure and its influence on the mental development of mankind,* translated by Peter Heath, with an introduction by Hans Aarsleff. Cambridge: Cambridge University Press. [Original ed., Über die Verschiedenheit des menschlichen Sprachbaues und ihren Einfluß auf die geistige Entwicklung des Menschengeschlechts. Published as the introduction to *Über die Kawi-Sprache auf der Insel Java* (1836–1840) and issued separately (1836).]

Huttar, George L. 1982. *A Creole-Amerindian pidgin of Suriname.* (Society for Caribbean Linguistics Occasional Paper no. 15.) St. Augustine, Trinidad: School of Education, University of the West Indies.

Hymes, Dell H. 1955. Positional analysis of categories: a frame for reconstruction. *Word* 11:10–23.

———. 1956. Na-Déné and positional analysis of categories. *AA* 58:624–38.

———. 1957. Some Penutian elements and the Penutian hypothesis. *SJA* 13:69–87.

———. 1959. Genetic classification: retrospect and prospect. *AL* 1(2):50–66.

————. 1961a. Alfred Louis Kroeber. *Language* 37:1–28. (Reprinted, 1966, in *Portraits of linguists: a biographical source book for the history of Western linguistics, 1746–1963,* ed. Thomas A. Sebeok, 2:400–37. Bloomington: Indiana University Press.)

————. 1961b. Kroeber, Powell, and Henshaw. *AL* 3(6):15–16.

————. 1961c. Review of Tungusisch und Ketschua by Karl Bouda. *IJAL* 27:362–4.

————. 1963. Notes toward a history of linguistic anthropology. *AL* 5:59–103.

————. 1964a. Evidence for Penutian lexical sets with initial *C– and *S–. *IJAL* 30:213–42.

————. 1964b. 'Hail' and 'bead': two Penutian etymologies. In *Studies in Californian linguistics,* ed. William Bright, 94–8. (UCPL, vol. 34.) Berkeley: University of California Press.

————. 1965. The methods and tasks of anthropological philology (illustrated with Clackamas Chinook). *Romance Philology* 19:325–40.

————. 1967. Interpretation of a Tonkawa paradigm. In *Studies in southwestern ethnolinguistics: meaning and history in the languages of the American Southwest,* ed. Dell H. Hymes and William E. Bittle, 264–78. (Studies in General Anthropology no. 3.) The Hague: Mouton.

————. 1971. Morris Swadesh: from the first Yale school to world prehistory. Appendix to *The origin and diversification of language* by Morris Swadesh, ed. Joel Sherzer, 285–92. Chicago: Aldine.

————. 1980. Commentary on *Theoretical orientations in creole studies,* ed. Albert Valdman and Arnold Highfield, 389–424. New York: Academic Press.

Hymes, Dell H., and William E. Bittle, eds. 1967. *Studies in southwestern ethnolinguistics: meaning and history in the languages of the American Southwest.* (Studies in General Anthropology no. 3.) The Hague: Mouton.

Ibarra Grasso, Dick E. 1958. *Lenguas indígenas americanas.* Buenos Aires: Editorial Nova.

————. 1964. *Lenguas indígenas de Bolivia.* Cochabamba, Bolivia: Museo Arqueológico, Universidad Mayor de San Simón.

Imbelloni, José. 1926. *La esfinge indiana: antiguos y nuevos aspectos del problema de los orígenes americanos.* Buenos Aires: Museo Nacional de Historia Natural.

————. 1928[1926]. L'idioma Kichua nel sistema linguistico dell'Oceano Pacifico. *ICA* 22(2):495–509. Rome.

Jackson, Lawrence. 1990. Interior Paleoindian settlement strategies: a first approximation for the lower Great Lakes. Supplement to *Research in Economic Anthropology,* vol. 5, 95–142.

Jackson, Robert T. 1990. Comparative phonology and grammar of the Arhuacan languages: Sierra Nevada de Santa Marta. Unpublished paper.

Jacobs, Melville. 1931. *A sketch of Northern Sahaptin grammar.* (Publications in Anthropology no. 4.), 85–292. Seattle: University of Washington.

————. 1932. Notes on the structure of Chinook Jargon. *Language* 8:27–50.

————. 1954. The areal spread of sound features in the languages north of California. In *Papers from the symposium on American Indian linguistics,* ed. Murray B. Emeneau, 46–56. (UCPL, vol. 10.) Berkeley: University of California Press.

Jacobsen, William H., Jr. 1958. Washo and Karok: an approach to comparative Hokan. *IJAL* 24:195–212.

————. 1979a. Chimakuan comparative studies. In *The languages of Native America: historical and comparative assessment,* ed. Lyle Campbell and Marianne Mithun, 792–802. Austin: University of Texas Press.

————. 1979b. Wakashan comparative studies. In *The languages of Native America: historical and comparative assessment,* ed. Lyle Campbell and Marianne Mithun, 766–91. Austin: University of Texas Press.

————. 1980. Inclusive/exclusive: a diffused pronominal category in native western North America. In *Papers from the parasession on pronouns and anaphora,* ed. Jody Kreiman and Almerindo E. Ojeda, 204–27. Chicago: CLS.

————. 1983. Typology and genetic notes on switch-reference systems in North American Indian languages. In *Switch-reference and universal grammar,* ed. John Haiman and Pamela Munro, 151–83. Amsterdam: John Benjamins.

————. 1986. Washoe language. In *Great Basin,* ed. Warren L. D'Azevedo. Vol. 11 of *HNAI,* ed. William C. Sturtevant, 107–12. Washington, D.C.: Smithsonian Institution.

————. 1989. The Pacific orientation of western North American languages. Paper presented at the Circum-Pacific Prehistory Conference, Seattle.

————. 1990. Comments on *The feasibility of reconciling human phylogeny and the history of language* by Richard M. Bateman, Ives Goddard, Richard O'Grady, V. A. Fund, Rich Mooi, W. John Kress, and Peter Cannell (in *CA* 31:1–24). Unpublished manuscript. Reno, Nevada.

————. 1993. Another look at Sapir's evidence for inclusion of Haida in Na-Dene. Paper presented at the Annual Meeting of the Linguistic Society of America, January 8, Los Angeles.

———. 1994. Characterizing and evaluating evidence for distant genetic relationships. Paper presented at the Annual Meeting of the American Association for the Advancement of Science, San Francisco.

Jacobson, Steven A. 1984. *Yup'ik Eskimo dictionary.* Fairbanks: Alaska Native Language Center.

———. 1990. Comparison of Central Alaskan Yup'ik Eskimo and Central Siberian Yupik Eskimo. *IJAL* 56:264–86.

Jakobson, Roman. 1944. Franz Boas' approach to language. *IJAL* 10:188–95.

———. 1962[1960]. Why "mama" and "papa"? In *Roman Jakobson, Selected writings,* vol. 1: *Phonological studies,* 538–45. The Hague: Mouton. [Original ed., in *Perspectives in psychological theory,* ed. Bernard Kaplan and Seymour Wapner, 21–9. New York: International Universities Press.]

Jaquith, James R. 1970. *The present status of the Uto-Aztecan languages of Mexico.* (Occasional Publications in Anthropology, Linguistic Series no. 1.) Greeley: Museum of Anthropology, University of Northern Colorado.

Jeanne, La Verne Masayesva. 1992. An institutional response to language endangerment: a proposal for a Native American Language Center. *Language* 68:24–8.

Jefferson, Thomas. 1984. *Thomas Jefferson: writings.* Texts selected and notes by Merrill D. Peterson. New York: Library of America.

Jennings, Francis. 1978. Susquehannock. In *Northeast,* ed. Bruce G. Trigger. Vol. 15 of *HNAI,* ed. William C. Sturtevant, 362–7. Washington, D.C.: Smithsonian Institution.

Jijón y Caamaño, Jacinto. 1943. *Las lenguas del sur de Centro América y el norte y centro del oeste de Sud-América.* (El Ecuador Interandino y Occidental no. 3.), 390–661. Quito: Editorial Ecuatoriana.

Jiménez Moreno, Wigberto. 1943. Tribus e idiomas del norte de México. *Revista Mexicana de Estudios Antropológicos* 3:131–3.

Johnson, Frederick. 1940. The linguistic map of Mexico and Central America. In *The Maya and their neighbors: essays on Middle American anthropology and archaeology,* ed. Clarence L. Hay, Ralph L. Linton, Samuel K. Lothrop, Harry L. Shapiro, and George C. Vaillant, 88–113. New York: D. Appleton-Century. (Reissued, New York: Dover, 1970.)

Jones, William. 1798. The third anniversary discourse,

delivered 2 February, 1786. *Asiatick Researches* 1:415–31.

———. 1799. Sixth anniversary discourse: on the Persians. *Asiatick Researches* 2:43–66. (Delivered February 19, 1789).

Jones, William. 1904. Some principles of Algonquian word-formation. *AA* 6:369–411.

Justeson, John S., and Lyle Campbell, eds. 1979. Phoneticism in Mayan hieroglyphic writing. (Publication no. 9.) Albany: Institute for Mesoamerican Studies, State University of New York.

Justeson, John S., and Terrence Kaufman. 1993. Epi-Olmec writing. *Science* 259:1703–11.

Justeson, John S., William Norman, Lyle Campbell, and Terrence Kaufman. 1985. *The foreign impact on Lowland Mayan languages and script.* (Publication no. 53.) New Orleans: Middle American Research Institute, Tulane University.

Justeson, John S., and Laurence D. Stephens. 1980. Chance cognation: a probabilistic model and decision procedure for historical inference. In *Papers from the fourth international conference on historical linguistics,* ed. Elizabeth Closs Traugott, Rebecca LaBrum, and Susan Shepherd, 37–45. Amsterdam: John Benjamins.

Karttunen, Frances, and James Lockhart. 1976. *Nahuatl in the middle years: language contact phenomena in texts of the colonial period.* (UCPL, vol. 85.) Berkeley: University of California Press.

Kaufman, Terrence. 1964a. Evidence for the Macro-Mayan hypothesis. Unpublished paper.

———. 1964b. Materiales lingüísticos para el estudio de las relaciones internas y externas de la familia de idiomas Mayanos. In *Desarrollo cultural de los Mayas,* ed. Evon Vogt, 81–136. (Special publication of the Seminario de Cultura Maya.) Mexico: UNAM.

———. 1964c. Mixe-Zoquean diachronic studies. Unpublished manuscript.

———. 1964d. Mixe-Zoquean subgroups and the position of Tapachulteco. *ICA* 35:403–11. Mexico.

———. 1969. Teco—a new Mayan language. *IJAL* 35:154–74.

———. 1971. A report on Chinook Jargon. In *Pidginization and creolization of languages,* ed. Dell Hymes, 275–8. Cambridge: Cambridge University Press.

———. 1972. *El proto-tzeltal-tzotzil: fonología comparada y diccionario reconstruido.* (Centro de Estudios Mayas Cuaderno no. 5.) Mexico: UNAM.

———. 1973a. Areal linguistics and Middle America.

In *Diachronic, areal, and typological linguistics,* ed. Thomas Sebeok, 459–83. (*CTL,* vol. 11.) The Hague: Mouton.

———. 1973b. Kaufman's basic concept list on linguistic principles. Unpublished manuscript. Pittsburgh.

———. 1974a. *Idiomas de Mesoamérica.* (Publication no. 33.) Guatemala City: Seminario de Integración Social Guatemalteca.

———. 1974b. Middle American languages. In *Encyclopaedia Britannica,* 15th ed., 11:959–63.

———. 1976. Archaeological and linguistic correlations in Mayaland and associated areas of Meso-America. *World Archaeology* 8:101–118.

———. 1981. Comparative Uto-Aztecan phonology. Unpublished manuscript, University of Pittsburgh.

———. 1988. A research program for reconstructing Proto-Hokan: first gropings. Unpublished manuscript, University of Pittsburgh.

———. 1990a. Language history in South America: what we know and how to know more. In *Amazonian linguistics: studies in lowland South American languages,* ed. Doris L. Payne, 13–67. Austin: University of Texas Press.

———. 1990b. Review of *South American Indian languages: retrospect and prospect,* ed. Harriet E. Manelis Klein and Louisa R. Stark. *IJAL* 56:166–9.

———. 1994. The native languages of South America. In *Atlas of the world's languages,* ed. Christopher Moseley and R. E. Asher, 46–76. London: Routledge.

———. In press. Tlapaneko-Subtiaba, OtoMangue, and Hoka: where Greenberg went wrong. In *Language and prehistory in the Americas,* ed. Allan Taylor. Stanford: Stanford University Press.

Kaufman, Terrence, and William Norman. 1984. An outline of Proto-Cholan phonology, morphology, and vocabulary. In *Phoneticism in Mayan hieroglyphic writing,* ed. John S. Justeson and Lyle Campbell, 77–166. (Publication no. 9.) Albany: Institute for Mesoamerican Studies, State University of New York.

Kendall, Daythal L. 1990. Takelma. In *Northwest Coast,* ed. Wayne Suttles. Vol. 7 of *HNAI,* ed. William C. Sturtevant, 589–92. Washington, D.C.: Smithsonian Institution.

Kennedy, Dorothy I. D., and Randall T. Bouchard. 1990. Northern Coast Salish. In *Northwest Coast,* ed. Wayne Suttles. Vol. 7 of *HNAI.,* ed. William C. Sturtevant, 441–52. Washington, D.C.: Smithsonian Institution.

Kelly, David H. 1957. Our elder brother Coyote. Ph.D. diss., Harvard University. (Appendix: Uto-Aztecan lexemes with morphological functions having Rotuman or Polynesian parallels, 188–237.)

Key, Mary Ritchie. 1968. *The comparative Tacanan phonology.* The Hague: Mouton.

———. 1978. Araucanian genetic relationships. *IJAL* 44:280–93.

———. 1979. *The grouping of South American languages.* Tübingen: Narr.

———. 1984. *Polynesian and American linguistic connections.* (Edward Sapir Monograph Series in Language, Culture, and Cognition no. 12; supplement to *Forum Linguisticum* 8:3.) Lake Bluff, Ill.: Jupiter Press.

Kimball, Geoffrey. 1987a. A grammatical sketch of Apalachee. *IJAL* 53:136–74.

———. 1987b. Men's and women's speech in Koasati: a reappraisal. *IJAL* 53:30–8.

———. 1992. A critique of Muskogean, "Gulf," and Yukian material in *Language in the Americas. IJAL* 58:447–501.

———. 1994. Comparative difficulties of the "Gulf" languages. In *Proceedings of the meeting of the Society for the Study of the Indigenous Languages of the Americas, July 2–4, 1993, and the Hokan-Penutian workshop, July 3, 1993,* ed. Margaret Langdon, 31–9. (SCOIL, report no. 8.) Berkeley: Department of Linguistics, University of California.

King, Chester, and Thomas C. Blackburn. 1978. Tataviam. In *California,* ed. Robert F. Heizer. Vol. 8 of *HNAI,* ed. William C. Sturtevant, 535–7. Washington, D.C.: Smithsonian Institution.

King, Robert D. 1969. *Historical linguistics and generative grammar.* Englewood Cliffs, N.J.: Prentice-Hall.

Kinkade, M. Dale. 1978. Alsea pronouns. Paper presented at the Annual Meeting of the American Anthropological Association, Los Angeles.

———. 1985. More on nasal loss on the Northwest Coast. *IJAL* 51:478–80.

———. 1988. Proto-Salishan colors. In *In honor of Mary Haas: from the Haas festival conference on Native American linguistics,* ed. William Shipley, 443–66. Berlin: Mouton de Gruyter.

———. 1990. History of research in linguistics. In *Northwest Coast,* ed. Wayne Suttles. Vol. 7 of *HNAI,* ed. William C. Sturtevant, 98–106. Washington, D.C.: Smithsonian Institution.

———. 1991a. The decline of native languages in Canada. In *Endangered languages,* ed. Robert

H. Robins and Eugenius M. Uhlenbeck, 157–75. Oxford: Berg.

———. 1991b. *Prehistory of the native languages of the Northwest Coast.* Vol. 1: *The North Pacific to 1600,* 137–58. Portland: Oregon Historical Society Press.

———. 1993. The chimerical schwas of Salish. Paper presented at the Annual Meeting of the American Anthropological Association.

Kinkade, M. Dale, William W. Elmendorf, Bruce Rigsby, and Haruo Aoki. In press. Languages. In *Plateau,* ed. Edward E. Walker, Jr. Vol. 12 of *HNAI,* ed. William C. Sturtevant. Washington, D.C.: Smithsonian Institution. [Cited with permission.]

Kinkade, M. Dale, and J. V. Powell. 1976. Language and the prehistory of North America. *World Archaeology* 8:83–100.

Kinkade, M. Dale, and Clarence Sloat. 1972. Proto-Interior Salish vowels. *IJAL* 38:26–48.

Kinkade, M. Dale, and Laurence C. Thompson. 1974. Proto-Salish *r. *IJAL* 40:22–8.

Kirchhoff, Paul. 1943. Mesoamérica. *Acta Americana* 1:92–107.

Klar, Kathryn. 1977. Topics in historical Chumash grammar. Ph.D. diss., University of California, Berkeley.

———. 1980. Proto-Chumash person and number markers. In *Proceedings of the 1980 Hokan languages workshop,* ed. James E. Redden, 86–95. (Occasional Papers in Linguistics no. 9.) Carbondale: Department of Linguistics, Southern Illinois University.

Klein, Harriet E. Manelis. 1978. *Una gramática de la lengua toba: morfología verbal y nominal.* Montevideo: Universidad de la República.

———. 1985. Current status of Argentine indigenous languages. In *South American Indian languages: retrospect and prospect,* ed. Harriet E. Manelis Klein and Louisa R. Stark, 691–731. Austin: University of Texas Press.

———. 1992. South American languages. In *IEL,* ed. William Bright, 4:31–5. New York: Oxford University Press.

Klein, Harriet E. Manelis, and Louisa R. Stark, eds. 1985. *South American Indian languages: retrospect and prospect,* 691–731. Austin: University of Texas Press.

Koerner, Konrad. 1986. Preface. *Historiographia Linguistica* 13:i–iv.

Koppelmann, Heinrich L. 1929. Ostasiatische Zahlwörter in süd-amerikanischen Sprachen, 77–118. (Publication no. 30.) Leiden, Holland: International Archiv für Ethnographie.

Krause, Aurel. 1956[1885]. *The Tlingit Indians: re-* sults of a trip to the Northwest Coast of America and the Bering Straits, trans. Erna Gunther. Seattle: University of Washington Press. [Original ed., *Die Tlinkit-Indianer.* Jena: Constenoble.]

Krauss, Michael E. 1964. Proto-Athapaskan-Eyak and the problem of Na-Dene I: the phonology. *IJAL* 30:118–31.

———. 1965. Proto-Athapaskan-Eyak and the problem of Na-Dene II: morphology. *IJAL* 31:18–28.

———. 1969. On the classification in the Athapascan, Eyak, and Tlingit verb. Supplement to *IJAL,* vol. 35, no. 4, part 2. (Publications in Anthropology and Linguistics, Memoir no. 24.) Bloomington: Indiana University.

———. 1973a. Eskimo-Aleut. In *Linguistics in North America,* ed. Thomas A. Sebeok, 796–902. (*CTL,* vol. 10.) The Hague: Mouton.

———. 1973b. Na-Dene. In *Linguistics in North America,* ed. Thomas Sebeok, 903–78. (*CTL,* vol. 10.) The Hague: Mouton.

———. 1979. Na-Dene and Eskimo-Aleut. In *The Languages of Native America: historical and comparative assessment,* ed. Lyle Campbell and Marianne Mithun, 803–901. Austin: University of Texas Press.

———. 1980. *Alaska native languages: past, present, and future.* (Research Paper no. 5.) Fairbanks: Alaska Native Language Center, University of Alaska.

———. 1986. Edward Sapir and Athabaskan linguistics. In *New perspectives in language, culture, and personality: proceedings of the Edward Sapir centenary conference, Ottawa, October 1–3, 1984,* ed. William Cowan, Michael K. Foster, and Konrad Koerner, 147–90. (Studies in the History of the Language Sciences no. 41.) Amsterdam: John Benjamins.

———. 1990. Kwalhioqua and Clatskanie. In *Northwest Coast,* ed. Wayne Suttles. Vol. 7 of *HNAI,* ed. William C. Sturtevant, 530–2. Washington, D.C.: Smithsonian Institution.

———. 1992. The world's languages in crisis. *Language* 68:4–10.

Krauss, Michael E., and Victor K. Golla. 1981. Northern Athabaskan languages. In *Subarctic,* ed. June Helm. Vol. 6 of *HNAI,* ed. William C. Sturtevant, 67–85. Washington, D.C.: Smithsonian Institution.

Krauss, Michael E., and Jeff Leer. 1981. *Athabaskan, Eyak, and Tlingit sonorants.* (Research Paper no. 5.) Fairbanks: Alaska Native Language Center, University of Alaska.

Kroeber, Alfred L. 1904. The languages of the coast of California south of San Francisco, 29–80.

(UCPAAE, no. 2.) Berkeley: University of California Press.

———. 1906. The Yokuts and Yuki languages. In *Boas anniversary volume,* 64–79. New York: G. E. Stetchert.

———. 1907. *Shoshonean dialects of California,* 65–165. (UCPAAE, no. 38.) Berkeley: University of California Press.

———. 1910. *The Chumash and Costanoan languages,* 237–71. (UCPAAE, no. 9.) Berkeley: University of California Press.

———. 1913. The determination of linguistic relationship. *Anthropos* 8:389–401.

———. 1915. *Serian, Tequistlatecan, and Hokan,* 279–90. (UCPAAE no. 11.) Berkeley: University of California Press.

———. 1925. *Handbook of the Indians of California.* (Bureau of American Ethnology Bulletin no. 78.) Washington, D.C.: Government Printing Office.

———. 1934. *Uto-Aztecan languages of Mexico.* (Ibero-Americana no. 8.) Berkeley: University of California Press.

———. 1939. *Cultural and natural areas of native North America.* (UCPAAE, no. 38.) Berkeley: University of California Press.

———. 1940a. Conclusions: the present status of Americanistic problems. In *The Maya and their neighbors: essays on Middle American anthropology and archaeology,* ed. Clarence L. Hay, Ralph L. Linton, Samuel K. Lothrop, Harry L. Shapiro, and George C. Vaillant, 460–87. New York: D. Appleton-Century. (Reissued 1970, New York: Dover.)

———. 1940b. *The work of John R. Swanton.* (Miscellaneous Collections 100.) 1–9. Washington, D.C.: Smithsonian Institution.

———. 1941. Some relations of linguistics and ethnology. *Language* 17:287–91.

———. 1953. Concluding review (chap. 20). In *An appraisal of anthropology today,* ed. Sol Tax, 357–76. Chicago: University of Chicago Press.

———. 1959. Possible Athabascan influence on Yuki. *IJAL* 25:59.

———. 1960. Powell and Henshaw: An episode in the history of ethnolinguistics. *AL* 2(4):1–5.

Kroeber, Theodora. 1970. *Alfred Kroeber: a personal configuration.* Berkeley: University of California Press.

Kroskrity, Paul V. 1982. Language contact and linguistic diffusion: the Arizona Tewa speech community. In *Bilingualism and language contact: Spanish, English, and Native American languages,* ed. Florence Barkin, Elizabeth A. Brandt, and Jacob Ornstein-Galicia, 51–72. New York: Teacher's College Press.

———. 1985. Areal-historical influences on Tewa possession. *IJAL* 51:486–9.

———. 1993. *Language, history, and identity: ethnolinguistic studies of the Arizona Tewa.* Tucson: University of Arizona Press.

Kuipers, Aert H. 1981. On reconstructing the Proto-Salish sound system. *IJAL* 47:323–35.

Laanest, Arvo. 1982. *Einführung in die ostseefinnischen Sprachen.* Hamburg: Buske.

Laird, Carobeth. 1975. *Encounter with an angry god.* Banning, Calif.: Malki Museum Press.

Lamb, Sydney. 1958. Linguistic prehistory in the Great Basin. *IJAL* 24:95–100.

———. 1959. Some proposals for linguistic taxonomy. *AL* 1(2):33–49.

———. 1964a. The classification of Uto-Aztecan languages: a historical survey. In *Studies in Californian linguistics,* ed. William Bright, 106–25. (UCPL, vol. 34.) Berkeley: University of California Press.

———. 1964b. Linguistic diversification and extinction in North America. *ICA* 34(2):457–64. Mexico.

Landar, Herbert. 1968. The Karankawa invasion of Texas. *IJAL* 34:242–58.

———. 1973. The tribes and languages of North America: a checklist. In *Linguistics in North America,* ed. Thomas Sebeok, 1253–1441. (*CTL,* vol. 10.) The Hague: Mouton.

Langacker, Ronald W. 1970. The vowels of Proto-Uto-Aztecan. *IJAL* 36:169–80.

———. 1977. *An overview of Uto-Aztecan grammar.* (Studies in Uto-Aztecan Grammar, vol. 1: SIL Publications in Linguistics no. 56.) Arlington: SIL and University of Texas at Arlington Press.

Langdon, Margaret. 1971. Sound symbolism in Yuman languages. In *Studies in American Indian languages,* ed. Jesse Sawyer, 149–74. (UCPL, vol. 65.) Berkeley: University of California Press.

———. 1974. *Comparative Hokan-Coahuiltecan studies: a survey and appraisal.* (*Janua Linguarum* Series Critica no. 4.) The Hague: Mouton.

———. 1979. Some thoughts on Hokan with particular reference to Pomoan and Yuman. In *The languages of Native America: historical and comparative assessment,* ed. Lyle Campbell and Marianne Mithun, 592–649. Austin: University of Texas Press.

———. 1986. Hokan-Siouan revisited. In *New perspectives in language, culture and personality: proceedings of the Edward Sapir centenary conference, Ottawa, October 1–3, 1984,* ed. William

Cowan, Michael K. Foster, and Konrad Koerner, 111–46. Amsterdam: John Benjamins.

———. 1990a. Diegueño: how many languages? In *Proceedings of the 1990 Hokan-Penutian languages workshop,* ed. James E. Redden. (Occasional Papers on Linguistics no. 15.) 184–90. Carbondale: Linguistics Department, University of Southern Illinois.

———. 1990b. Morphosyntax and problems of reconstruction in Yuman and Hokan. In *Linguistic change and reconstruction methodology,* ed. Philip Baldi, 57–72. Berlin: Mouton de Gruyter.

Langdon, Margaret, and Pamela Munro. 1980. Yuman numerals. In *American Indian and Indo-European studies: papers in honor of Madison S. Beeler,* ed. Kathryn Klar, Margaret Langdon, and Shirley Silver, 121–35. The Hague: Mouton.

Langdon, Margaret, and Shirley Silver. 1984. California t/ṭ. *Journal of California and Great Basin Anthropology, Papers in Linguistics* 4:139–65.

Lapena, Frank R. 1978. Wintu. In *California,* ed. Robert F. Heizer. Vol. 8 of *HNAI,* ed. William C. Sturtevant, 324–40. Washington, D.C.: Smithsonian Institution.

Larsen, Thomas W., and William M. Norman. 1979. Correlates of ergativity in Mayan grammar. In *Ergativity: towards a theory of grammatical relations,* ed. Frans Plank, 347–70. London: Academic Press.

Larsson, Lars J. 1987. Who were the Konomihu? *IJAL* 53:232–5.

Lastra de Suárez, Yolanda. 1970. Categorías posicionales en quechua y aymara. *Anales de Antropología* (Mexico) 7:263–84.

———. 1986. *Las áreas dialectales del náhuatl moderno.* (Instituto de Investigaciones Antropológicas, Lingüística, Serie Antropológica no. 62.) Mexico: UNAM.

Latham, Robert G. 1845. Miscellaneous contributions to the ethnography of North America. *Transactions of the Philological Society* (London) 2:31–50.

———. 1850. *Natural history of the varieties of man.* London: J. Van Voorst.

———. 1856. On the languages of northern, western, and central America. *Transactions of the Philological Society* (London) 1856, 57–115.

———. 1860a. On the languages of the Oregon territory. (Paper read before the Ethnological Society on the 11th December 1844). In *Opuscula: essays, chiefly philological and ethnographical,* by Robert G. Latham, 249–65. London: Williams and Norgate; Leipzig: R. Hartmann.

———. 1860b. *Opuscula: essays, chiefly philological and ethnographical.* London: Williams and Norgate, Leipzig: Hartmann.

———. 1862. *Elements of comparative philology.* London: Walton and Maberly.

Laughlin, W. S. 1986. Comment on *The settlement of the Americas: a comparison of the linguistic, dental, and genetic evidence* by Joseph H. Greenberg, Christy G. Turner II, and Stephen L. Zegura. *CA* 27:489–90.

Lawrence, Erma, and Jeff Leer. 1977. *Haida dictionary.* Fairbanks: Alaska Native Language Center, University of Alaska.

Lawson, John. 1967[1708] *A new voyage to Carolina,* ed. Hugh Talmage Leffler. New ed. Chapel Hill: University of North Carolina Press.

Leap, William L. 1971. Who were the Piro? *AL* 13.(7):321–30.

Leechman, Douglas, and Robert A. Hall, Jr. 1955. American Indian Pidgin English: attestations and grammatical peculiarities. *American Speech* 30:163–71.

Leer, Jeff. 1979. *Proto-Athabaskan verb stem variation. Part one: Phonology.* (Research Paper no. 1.) Fairbanks: Alaska Native Language Center, University of Alaska.

———. 1990. Tlingit: a portmanteau language family? In *Linguistic change and reconstruction methodology,* ed. Philip Baldi, 73–98. Berlin: Mouton de Gruyter.

———. 1991. Evidence for a Northern Northwest Coast language area: promiscuous number marking and periphrastic possessive constructions in Haida, Eyak, and Aleut. *IJAL* 57:158–93.

Lehmann, Walter. 1920. *Zentral-Amerika.* Berlin: Museum für Völkerkunde.

Lehmann-Nitsche, Robert. 1913. El grupo lingüístico Tshon de los territorios magallánicos. *Revista del Museo de La Plata* 22:217–76.

Lemle, Miriam. 1971. Internal classification of the Tupi-Guarani linguistic family. In *Tupi studies 1,* ed. David Bendor-Samuel, 107–29. Norman, Ok.: SIL.

León-Portilla, Miguel. 1976. Sobre la lengua pericú de la Baja California. *Anales de Antropología* 12:87–101.

———. 1985. Ejemplos de la lengua califórnica, cochimí—reunidos por Franz B. Ducrue (1778–1779). *Tlalocan* 10:363–74.

Leopold, Joan. 1984. Duponceau, Humboldt, et Pott: la place structurale des concepts de "polysynthese" et d' "incorporation." *Amerindia* 6:65–77.

Levine, Robert D. 1979. Haida and Na-Dene: a new look at the evidence. *IJAL* 45:157–70.

Levy, Richard. 1978a. Costanoan. In *California,* ed. Robert F. Heizer. Vol. 8 of *HNAI,* ed. William C. Sturtevant, 485–95. Washington, D.C.: Smithsonian Institution.

———. 1978b. Eastern Miwok. In *California,* ed. Robert F. Heizer. Vol. 8 of *HNAI,* ed. William C. Sturtevant, 389–413. Washington, D.C.: Smithsonian Institution.

Lewin, Roger. 1988. American Indian language dispute. *Science* 242:1632–3.

Lieber, Francis. 1880. [1837]. On the study of foreign languages, especially of the Classic tongues: a letter to Hon. Albert Gallatin. In *Reminiscences, addresses, and essays by Francis Lieber, L.L.D., being volume 1 of his miscellaneous writings,* 499–534. Philadelphia: J. B. Lippincott. [Original ed., *Southern Literary Messenger* (March).]

Liedtke, Stefan. 1989. Review of *Language in the Americas* by Joseph H. Greenberg. *Anthropos* 84:283–5.

———. 1991. *Indianersprachen Vergleich und Klassifizierung: eine ethnolinguistische Einführung in die Grundlagen und Methoden.* Hamburg: Helmut Buske.

Lincoln, Neville J., and John C. Rath. 1980. *North Wakashan comparative root list.* (Canadian Ethnology Service Paper no. 68.) Ottawa: National Museum of Man, Mercury Series.

Lionnet, Jean. 1853. *Vocabulary of the Jargon or Trade Language of Oregon.* Washington, D.C.: Smithsonian Institution.

Lombardo, Natal. 1702[1641?]. *Arte de la lengua tegüima vulgarmente llamada ópata.* Mexico: Miguel de Ribera.

Longacre, Robert E. 1957. Proto-Mixtecan. *IJAL* 23, supplement. Bloomington, Indiana.

———. 1966. On the linguistic affinities of Amuzgo. *IJAL* 32:46–9.

———. 1967. Systemic comparison and reconstruction. In *Linguistics,* ed. Norman McQuown, vol. 5 of *HMAI,* ed. Robert Waucope, 117–60. Austin: University of Texas Press.

———. 1968. Comparative reconstruction of indigenous languages. In *Ibero-American and Caribbean Linguistics,* ed. Thomas Sebeok, 320–60. (*CTL,* vol. 4.) The Hague: Mouton.

Longacre, Robert, and Rene Millon. 1961. Proto-Mixtecan and Proto-Amuzgo-Mixtecan vocabularies. *AL* 3(4):1–39.

Loos, Eugene. 1973. Algunas implicaciones de la reconstrucción de un fragmento de la gramática del proto pano. In *Estudios Panos* 2, ed. Eugene Loos, 263–82. (Serie Lingüística Peruana no. 11.) Yarinacocha, Peru: ILV.

López de Gómara, Francisco. 1941[1552]. *Historia general de las Indias.* Madrid: Espasa-Calpe.

Loukotka, Čestmír. 1935. *Clasificación de las lenguas sudamericanas.* (Lingüística Sudamericana no. 1.) Prague: Published by the author.

———. 1942[1944]. Klassifikation der südamerikanischen Sprachen. *Zeitschrift für Ethnologie* 74:1–69.

———. 1968. *Classification of South American Indian languages.* Los Angeles: Latin American Studies Center, University of California.

Lounsbury, Floyd G. 1978. Iroquoian languages. In *Northeast,* ed. Bruce G. Trigger. Vol. 15 of *HNAI,* ed. William C. Sturtevant, 334–43. Washington, D.C.: Smithsonian Institution.

Ludewig, Hermann E. 1858. *The literature of American aboriginal languages.* London: Trübner.

Lynch, Thomas F. 1990. Glacial-age man in South America? A critical review. *Am. Ant.* 55:12–36.

Mackert, Michael. 1994. Horatio Hale and the great U.S. exploring expedition. *AL* 36:1–26.

Maddieson, Ian. 1984. *Patterns of sounds.* Cambridge: Cambridge University Press.

Mallory, James P. 1989. *In search of the Indo-Europeans: language, archaeology, and myth.* London: Thames and Hudson.

Manaster Ramer, Alexis. 1993. Is Tonkawa Na-Dene? A case study of the validity of the Greenbergian classification. *California Linguistic Notes* 24:21–5.

———. 1996. Sapir's classifications: Coahuiltecan. *AL* 38:1–38.

Mannheim, Bruce. 1985. Contact and Quechua-external genetic relationships. In *South American Indian languages: retrospect and prospect,* ed. Harriet E. Manelis Klein and Louisa R. Stark, 644–88. Austin: University of Texas Press.

———. 1986. [Comentario sobre] Willem Adelaar, "la relación quechua-aru: perspectivas para la separación del léxico." *Revista Andina* 4:413–18.

———. 1988. On the sibilants of colonial Southern Peruvian Quechua. *IJAL* 54:168–208.

———. 1991. *The language of the Inka since the European invasion.* Austin: University of Texas Press.

Marsh, Gordon H., and Morris Swadesh. 1951. Kleinschmidt centennial 5: Eskimo Aleut correspondences. *IJAL* 17:209–16.

Martín, Eusebia H., and Andrés A. Pérez Diez. 1990. Deixis pronominal en el chimane del oriente boliviana. *IJAL* 56:574–9.

Martin, Jack. 1994. Implications of plural reduplication, infixation, and subtraction for Muskogean languages. *AL* 36:27–55.

Martin, Laura. 1978. Mayan influence in Guatemalan Spanish: a research outline and test case. In *Papers in Mayan linguistics,* ed. Nora C. England, 106–26. Columbia: Museum of Anthropology, University of Missouri.

Martius, Carl Friedrich Philipp von. 1867. *Beiträge zur Ethnographie und Sprachenkunde Amerika's, zumal Brasiliens.* Vol. 1: *Zur Ethnographie Amerika's zumal Brasiliens, mit einem Kärtschen über die Verbreitung der Tupis und die Sprachgruppen.* Vol. 2: *Wörtersammlung brasilianischen Sprachen.* Leipzig: Friedrich Fleischer.

Mason, J. Alden. 1912. The ethnology of the Salinan Indians, 97–240. (UCPAAE no. 10.) Berkeley: University of California Press.

——. 1918. The language of the Salinan Indians, 1–154. (UCPAAE no. 14.) Berkeley: University of California Press.

——. 1936. The classification of the Sonoran languages. In *Essays in anthropology presented to A. L. Kroeber in celebration of his sixtieth birthday, June 11, 1936,* ed. Robert H. Howie, 183–98. Berkeley: University of California Press.

——. 1940. The native languages of Middle America. In *The Maya and their neighbors: essays on Middle American anthropology and archaeology,* ed. Clarence L. Hay, Ralph L. Linton, Samuel K. Lothrop, Harry L. Shapiro, and George C. Vaillant, 52–87. New York: D. Appleton-Century. (Reissued, New York: Dover, 1970.)

——. 1950. The languages of South America. In *Handbook of South American Indians,* ed. Julian Steward, 6:157–317. (Smithsonian Institution Bureau of American Ethnology Bulletin no. 143). Washington, D.C.: Government Printing Office.

Massey, William C. 1949. Tribes and languages of Baja California. *SJA* 5:272–307.

Matisoff, James A. 1990. On megalo-comparison: a discussion note. *Language* 66:106–20.

Matteson, Esther. 1972. Towards Proto Amerindian. In *Comparative studies in Amerindian languages,* ed. Esther Matteson, 21–89. (*Janua Linguarum* Series Practica no. 127.) The Hague: Mouton.

——, ed. 1972. *Comparative studies in Amerindian languages.* (*Janua Linguarum* Series Practica no. 127.) The Hague: Mouton.

McGuire, Thomas R. and Ives Goddard. 1983. Synonymy. In *Southwest,* ed. Alfonso Ortiz. Vol. 10 of *HNAI,* ed. William C. Sturtevant, 36. Washington, D.C.: Smithsonian Institution.

McLendon, Sally. 1964. Northern Hokan (B) and (C):

a comparison of Eastern Pomo and Yana. In *Studies in Californian linguistics,* ed. William Bright, 126–144. (UCPL, vol. 34.) Berkeley: University of California Press.

——. 1973. Proto Pomo. (UCPL, vol. 71.) Berkeley: University of California Press.

McLendon, Sally, and Robert L. Oswalt. 1978. Pomo: introduction. In *California,* ed. Robert F. Heizer. Vol. 8 of *HNAI,* ed. William C. Sturtevant, 274–88. Washington, D.C.: Smithsonian Institution.

McQuown, Norman A. 1942. Una posible síntesis lingüística macro-mayance. In *Mayas y Olmecas,* 37–8. (Reunión de Mesa Redonda sobre Problemas Antropológicos de México y Centro América.) Tuxtla Gutiérrez: Sociedad Mexicana de Antropología.

——. 1955. The indigenous languages of Latin America. *AA* 57:501–70.

——. 1956. Evidence for a synthetic trend in Totonacan. *Language* 32:78–80.

——. 1967. History of studies in Middle American linguistics. In *Linguistics,* ed. Norman A. McQuown. Vol. 5 of *HMAI,* ed. Robert Wauchope, 3–7. Austin: University of Texas Press.

Meillet, Antoine. 1948[1921, 1914]. Le problème de la parenté des langues. In *Linguistique historique et linguistique générale.* Paris: Champion. [Original ed., *Rivista di Scienza* 15(35):3.]

——. 1925. *La méthode comparative en linguistique historique.* Paris: Champion. (Trans., 1967, *The comparative method in historical linguistics.* Paris: Champion.)

——. 1958. *Linguistique historique et linguistique générale.* (Société Linguistique de Paris Collection Linguistique no. 8.) Paris: Champion.

Meillet, Antoine, and Marcel Cohen. 1924 *Les langues du monde.* Paris: Champion. (2d ed., 1952.)

Mejías, Hugo A. 1980. *Préstamos de lenguas indígenas en el español americano del siglo XVII.* (Publicaciones del Centro de Lingüística Hispánica no. 11, Instituto de Investigaciones Filológicas.) Mexico: UNAM.

Meltzer, David J. 1989. Why don't we know when the first people came to North America? *Am. Ant.* 54:471–90.

——. 1993a. Pleistocene peopling of the Americas. *Evolutionary Anthropology* 1:157–69.

——. 1993b. *Search for the first Americans.* Washington, D.C.: Smithsonian Books.

Membreño, Alberto. 1897. *Hondureñismos: vocabulario de los provincialismos de Honduras.* 2d ed. Tegucigalpa: Tipografía Nacional.

Mendizábal, Manuel Othon de, and Wigberto Jiménez Moreno. 1944. *Mapas lingüísticos de la Repúb-*

lica Mexicana. Mexico: Instituto Panamericano de Geografía e Historia.

Menovshchikov, Georgiy A. 1968. *Aleutskij jazyk. Jazyki narodov SSSR*. Series ed. V. V. Vinogradov et al. Vol. 5: *Mongol'skie, tunguso-man'czurskie i paleoaziatskie jazyki*, ed. Ja. Skorik. Leningrad: Nauka.

———. 1969. O nekotoryx social'nyx aspektax èvoljucii jazyka. In *Voprosy Social'noj*, 110–34. Leningrad: Nauka.

Metcalf, George J. 1974. The Indo-European hypothesis in the sixteenth and seventeenth centuries. In *Studies in the history of linguistics: traditions and paradigms*, ed. Dell Hymes, 233–57. Bloomington: Indiana University Press.

Michelson, Truman. 1914. Two alleged Algonquian languages of California. *AA* 16:361–7.

———. 1915. Rejoinder (to Edward Sapir). *AA* 17:4–8.

———. 1921. The classification of American Indian languages. *IJAL* 2:73.

Migliazza, Ernest C. 1985[1982]. Languages of the Orinoco-Amazon region: current status. In: *South American Indian languages: retrospect and prospect*, ed. Harriet E. Manelis Klein and Louisa R. Stark, 17–139. Austin: University of Texas Press. [Original ed., *Antropológica* 53:95–162.]

Migliazza, Ernest, and Lyle Campbell. 1988. *Panorama general de las lenguas indígenas en América*. (Historia General de América vol. 10.) Caracas: Instituto Panamericano de Geografía e Historia.

Milewski, Tadeusz. 1960. Similarities between the Asiatic and American Indian languages. *IJAL* 26:265–74.

———. 1967. Études typologiques sur les langues indigènes de l'amérique/Typological studies of the American Indian languages. (Prace Komisji Orientalistycznej no. 7.) Crakow: Polska Akademia Nauk—Oddzial w Krakowie.

Miller, Jay, and William R. Seaburg. 1990. Alseans. In *Northwest Coast*, ed. Wayne Suttles. Vol. 7 of *HNAI*, ed. William C. Sturtevant, 580–88. Washington, D.C.: Smithsonian Institution.

Miller, Mary Rita. 1967. Attestations of American Indian Pidgin English in fiction and nonfiction. *American Speech* 42:142–7.

Miller, Virginia. 1978. Yuki, Huchnom, and Coast Yuki. In *California*, ed. Robert F. Heizer. Vol. 8 of *HNAI*, ed. William C. Sturtevant, 249–55. Washington, D.C.: Smithsonian Institution.

Miller, Wick R. 1959. A note on Kiowa linguistic affiliations. *AA* 61:102–5.

———. 1961. Review of *The Sparkman grammar of Luiseño* by Alfred L. Kroeber and George W. Grace. *Language* 37:186–9.

———. 1964. The Shoshonean languages of Uto-Aztecan. In *Studies in Californian linguistics*, ed. William Bright, 145–8. (UCPL, vol. 34.) Berkeley: University of California Press.

———. 1967. *Uto-Aztecan cognate sets*. (UCPL, vol. 48.) Berkeley: University of California Press.

———. 1983a. A note on extinct languages of northwest Mexico of supposed Uto-Aztecan affiliation. *IJAL* 49:328–33.

———. 1983b. Uto-Aztecan languages. In *Southwest*, ed. Alonso Ortiz. Vol. 10 of *HNAI*, ed. William C. Sturtevant, 113–24. Washington, D.C.: Smithsonian Institution.

———. 1984. The classification of the Uto-Aztecan languages based on lexical evidence. *IJAL* 50:1–24.

———. 1987. Computerized data base for Uto-Aztecan cognate set. Unpublished manuscript. University of Utah, Salt Lake City.

Miller, Wick R., and Irvine Davis. 1963. Proto-Keresan phonology. *IJAL* 29:310–30.

Mills, Elaine L. 1988. *The papers of John Peabody Harrington in the Smithsonian Institution, 1907–1957*. Vol. 7: *A guide to the field notes: Native American history, language, and culture of Mexico, Central America, and South America*. White Plains, N.Y.: Kraus International.

Mills, Elaine L., and Ann J. Brickfield, eds. 1986. *The papers of John Peabody Harrington in the Smithsonian Institution, 1907–1957*. Vol. 4: *A guide to the field notes: Native American history, language, and culture of the Southwest*. White Plains, N.Y.: Kraus International.

Miner, Kenneth L. 1979. Through the years with a small language: more trouble with data in linguistic theory. *IJAL* 45:75–8.

Mithun, Marianne. 1979. Iroquoian. In *The languages of Native America: historical and comparative assessment*, ed. Lyle Campbell and Marianne Mithun, 133–212. Austin: University of Texas Press.

———. 1981. Stalking the Susquehannocks. *IJAL* 47:1–26.

———. 1982. The synchronic and diachronic behavior of plops, squeaks, croaks, sighs, and moans. *IJAL* 48:49–58.

———. 1984a. The evolution of noun incorporation. *Language* 60:847–94.

———. 1984b. The Proto-Iroquoians: cultural reconstruction from lexical materials. In *Extending the rafters: interdisciplinary approaches to Iroquoian studies*, ed. Michael K. Foster, Jack Campisi, and Marianne Mithun, 259–81. Albany: State University of New York Press.

———. 1990. Studies of North American Indian languages. *Annual Review of Anthropology* 9:309–30.

———. 1991. Active and agentive case marking and its motivations. *Language* 67:510–46.

Mixco, Mauricio J. 1978. *Cochimí and Proto-Yuman: lexical and syntactic evidence for a new language family in Lower California.* (Anthropological Papers no. 101.) Salt Lake City: University of Utah.

Molina, Alonso de. 1571. *Vocabulario en lengua castellana y mexicana.* Mexico: Antonio de Spinosa.

Mooney, James. 1907. Albert Samuel Gatschet. *AA* 9:561–70.

Moore, Denny. 1990. Languages of southern Rondonia, Brazil. Unpublished paper. Museu Emilio Goeldi, Belém, Pará, Brazil.

———. 1991. A few aspects of comparative Tupi syntax. Paper presented at the forty-seventh meeting of the ICA, New Orleans.

———. 1992. Gavião tonal system. Unpublished paper. Museu Emilio Goeldi, Belém, Pará, Brazil.

Moore, Denny, Sidney Facundes, and Nádia Pires. 1994. Nheengatu (Língua Geral Amazônica): its history and the effects of language contact. In *Proceedings of the meeting of the Society for the Study of the Indigenous Languages of the Americas, July 2–4, 1993, and the Hokan-Penutian workshop, July 3, 1993,* ed. Margaret Langdon, 93–118. (SCOIL report no. 8.) Berkeley: Department of Linguistics, University of California.

Moore, Denny, and Vilacy Galucio. 1994. Reconstruction of Proto-Tupari consonants and vowels. Unpublished paper. Museu Emilio Goeldi, Belém, Pará, Brazil.

Moratto, Michael J. 1984. *California archaeology.* New York: Academic Press.

Morell, Virginia. 1990. Confusion in earliest America. *Science* 244:439–41.

Morgan, Lewis Henry. 1870. Indian migrations. *North American Review* 110:33–82.

———. 1871. *Systems of consanguinity and affinity of the human family.* (Contributions to Knowledge no. 17.) Washington, D.C.: Smithsonian Institution.

———. 1877. *Ancient society.* New York: Holt.

Morice, Adrien Gabriel. 1891. The Déné languages, considered in themselves and in their relations to non-American idioms. *Transactions of the Canadian Institute* (Toronto) 1:170–212.

———. 1892. Déné roots. *Transactions of the Canadian Institute* (Toronto) 3:145–64.

———. 1904. Les langues dénées. *Année Linguistique* (Paris) 2:205–47.

———. 1907. The unity of speech among the Northern and Southern Déné. *AA* 9:721–37.

Morínigo, Marcos A. 1931. *Hispanismos en el guaraní.* (Instituto de Filología, Colección de Estudios Indigenistas no. 1.) Buenos Aires: Universidad de Buenos Aires.

Morison, Samuel Elliot. 1962. *Admiral of the ocean sea: a life of Christopher Columbus.* New York: Time, Inc.

———. 1971. *The European discovery of America: the northern voyages, A.D. 500–1600.* New York: Oxford University Press.

Morpurgo Davies, A[nna]. 1975. Language classification in the nineteenth century. In *Historiography of linguistics,* ed. Thomas A. Sebeok, 607–717. (*CTL,* vol. 13.) The Hague: Mouton.

Moshinsky, Julius. 1976. Historical Pomo phonology. In *Hokan studies:* ed. Margaret Langdon and Shirley Silver, 55–75. The Hague: Mouton.

Moziño Suárez de Figueroa, Joseph Mariano. 1793. *Noticias de Nutka, añadese un ensayo del diccionario de la lengua de los nutkeses.* Mexico City. [See Carreno 1913.]

Mudrak, Oleg, and Sergei Nikolaev. 1989. Gilyak and Chukchi-Kamchatkan as Almosan-Keresiouan languages: lexical evidence. In *Explorations in language macrofamilies: materials from the first international interdisciplinary symposium on language and prehistory,* ed. Vitaly Shevoroshkin, 67–87. Bochum: Brockmeyer.

Müller, Max. 1866[1861]. *Lectures on the science of language.* 2d ed. (1st ed., 1861; last revision, 1899.) New York: Scribner.

Müller-Vollmer, Kurt. 1974. Wilhelm von Humboldt und der Anfang der amerikanischen Sprachwissenschaft: Die Briefe an John Pickering. In *Universalismus und Wissenschaft im Werk und Wirken der Brüder Humboldt,* ed. Klaus Hammacher, 259–334. Frankfurt: Klostermann.

Muñoz, Nora Isabel. 1993. La influencia del español en el léxico del guaraní "yopará": un análisis cuantitativo. In *Actas: Primeras jornadas de lingüística aborígen, 6 y 7 de octubre de 1992,* ed. J. Pedro Viegas Barros, 201–9. Buenos Aires: Facultad de Filosofía y Letras, Universidad de Buenos Aires.

Munro, Pamela. 1984. On the Western Muskogean source for Mobilian. *IJAL* 50:438–50.

———. 1987a. Introduction: Muskogean studies at UCLA. In *Muskogean linguistics: a volume of papers begun at UCLA on comparative, historical, and synchronic Muskogean topics,* ed. Pamela Munro, 1–6. (Occasional Papers in Linguistics no. 6.) Los Angeles: Department of Linguistics, University of California.

———. 1987b. Some morphological differences between Chickasaw and Choctaw. In *Muskogean linguistics: a volume of papers begun at UCLA on comparative,* historical, and synchronic Muskogean topics, ed. Pamela Munro, 119–33, 179–85. (Occasional Papers in Linguistics no. 6.) Los Angeles: Department of Linguistics, University of California.

———. 1993. The Muskogean II prefixes and their significance for classification. *IJAL* 59:374–404.

———. 1994. Gulf and Yuki-Gulf. *AL* 36:125–222.

Muntzel, Martha, and Benjamín Pérez González. 1987. Panorama general de las lenguas indígenas. *América Indígena* 47:571–605.

Murdock, George P. 1959. Cross-language parallels in parental kin terms. *AL* 1(9):1–5.

Muysken, Pieter. 1977. *Syntactic developments in the verb phrase of Ecuadorian Quechua.* (Studies in Generative Grammar no. 2.) Lisse: Peter de Ridder.

———. 1980. Sources for the study of Amerindian contact vernaculars in Ecuador. In *Amsterdam Creole studies* 3, ed. Pieter Muysken and Norval Smith, 66–82. (Publikaties van het Instituut voor algemene Taalwetenschap no. 31.) Amsterdam: Universiteit van Amsterdam.

———. 1981. Halfway between Quechua and Spanish: the case for relexification. In *Historicity and variation in Creole studies,* ed. Arnold Highfield and Albert Valdman, 52–78. Ann Arbor: Karoma Publishers.

———. 1994a. Callahuaya. In *Mixed languages: fifteen case studies in language intertwining,* ed. Peter Bakker and Maarten Mous, 207–11. Amsterdam: Institute for Functional Research into Language and Language Use.

———. 1994b. Media Lengua. In *Mixed languages: fifteen case studies in language intertwining,* ed. Peter Bakker and Maarten Mous, 201–5. Amsterdam: Institute for Functional Research into Language and Language Use.

Nadkarni, Mangesh. 1975. Bilingualism and syntactic change in Konkani. *Language* 51:672–83.

Nájera, Manuel de San Juan Crisóstomo. 1837. De linguâ Othomitorum dissertatio. *Transactions of the American Philosophical Society* 5:249–96.

Najlis, Elena. 1984. *Fonología de la protolengua mataguaya.* Buenos Aires: Universidad de Buenos Aires.

Nebrija, Antonio de. [1492]. *Gramática de la lengua castellana,* ed. Antonio Quilis. New ed. Madrid: Editorial Nacional. [Original ed., Salamanca.]

Newcomb, W. W., Jr. 1983. Karankawa. In *Southwest,* ed. Alfonso Ortiz. Vol. 10 of *HNAI,* ed. William C. Sturtevant, 359–67. Washington, D.C.: Smithsonian Institution.

Newman, Paul. 1980. *The classification of Chadic within Afroasiatic.* Leiden: Universitaire Pers.

———. 1991. An interview with Joseph Greenberg. *CA* 32:453–67.

Newman, Stanley. 1944. *Yokuts language of California.* (Viking Fund Publications in Anthropology no. 2.) New York: Wenner-Gren Foundation for Anthropological Research.

———. 1954. American Indian linguistics in the Southwest. *AA* 56:626–44.

———. 1964. Comparison of Zuni and California Penutian. *IJAL* 30:1–13.

———. 1977. The Salish independent pronoun system. *IJAL* 43:302–14.

———. 1979a. A history of the Salish possessive and subject forms. *IJAL* 45:207–23.

———. 1979b. The Salish object forms. *IJAL* 45:299–308.

———. 1980. Functional changes in the Salish pronominal system. *IJAL* 46:155–67.

Nichols, Johanna. 1971. Diminutive consonant symbolism in Western North America. *Language* 47:826–48.

———. 1990a. Linguistic diversity and the first settlement of the New World. *Language* 66:475–521.

———. 1990b. More on human phylogeny and linguistic history. *CA* 31:313–14.

———. 1992. *Linguistic diversity in space and time.* Chicago: University of Chicago Press.

———. In press. The origin and prehistory of linguistic diversity: implications for the first settlement of the New World. In *Language and prehistory in the Americas,* ed. Allan Taylor. Stanford: Stanford University Press.

Nichols, Johanna, and David A. Peterson, 1996. The Amerind personal pronouns. *Language* 72:336–71.

Nichols, John D. 1992. "Broken Oghibbeway": an Algonquian trade language. Paper presented at the Twenty-fourth Algonquian Conference, Ottawa, October 23.

Nicklas, T. Dale. 1994. Linguistic provinces of the Southeast at the time of Columbus. In *Perspectives on the Southeast: linguistics, archaeology, and ethnohistory,* ed. Patricia B. Kwachka, 1–31. Athens: University of Georgia Press.

Nikolaev, Sergei. 1991. Sino-Caucasian languages in America. In *Dene-Sino-Caucasian languages: materials from the first international interdisciplinary symposium on language and prehistory,* ed. Vitaly Shevoroshkin, 42–66. Bochum: Brockmeyer.

Nimuendajú, Curt. 1926. *Die Palikur-Indianer und ihre Nachbarn.* (Göteborgs Kungliga Vetenskaps- och vitterhets-samhälles Handlingar, vol. 31, no. 2.)

Nimuendajú, Curt, and Rosário Farani Mansur Guérios. 1948. Cartas etno-lingüísticas. *Revista do Museu Paulista* (São Paulo) 2:207–41.

Noble, G. Kingsley. 1965. *Proto-Arawakan and its descendants.* Bloomington: Indiana University Press.

Nordell, Norman. 1962. On the status of Popoluca in Zoque-Mixe. *IJAL* 28:146–9.

Nordenskiöld, Erland. 1922. *Deductions suggested by the geographical distribution of some post-Columbian words used by the Indians of South America.* (Comparative Ethnographical Studies no. 5.) Göteborg: Elanders.

Norman, William, and Lyle Campbell. 1978. Toward a Proto-Mayan syntax: a comparative perspective on grammar. In *Papers in Mayan linguistics,* ed. Nora C. England, 136–56. Columbia: Museum of Anthropology, University of Missouri.

Oblitas Poblete, Enrique. 1968. *El idioma secreto de los Incas.* La Paz: Editorial "Los Amigos del Libro."

O'Grady, Richard T., Ives Goddard, Richard M. Bateman, William A. DiMichele, V. A. Funk, W. John Kress, Rich Mooi, and Peter F. Cannell. 1989. Genes and tongues. *Science* 243:1651.

Okrand, Marc. 1979. Costanoan philological practices: comments and criticism. *IJAL* 45:181–7.

Olmsted, David L. 1956. Palaihnihan and Shasta 1: Labial stops. *Language* 32:73–7.

———. 1957. Palaihnihan and Shasta 2: Apical stops. *Language* 33:136–8.

———. 1959. Palaihnihan and Shasta 3: Dorsal stops. *Language* 35:637–44.

———. 1964. *A history of Palaihnihan phonology.* (UCPL, vol. 35.) Berkeley: University of California Press.

———. 1984. *A lexicon of Atsugewi.* (SCOIL Report no. 5.) Berkeley: Department of Linguistics, University of California.

Olmsted, David L., and Omer C. Stewart. 1978. Atsugewi. In *California,* ed. Robert F. Heizer. Vol. 8 of *HNAI,* ed. William C. Sturtevant, 225–35. Washington, D.C.: Smithsonian Institution.

Olson, Ronald D. 1964. Mayan affinities with Chipaya of Bolivia 1: correspondences. *IJAL* 30:313–24.

———. 1965. Mayan affinities with Chipaya of Bolivia 2: cognates. *IJAL* 31:29–38.

Oltrogge, David F. 1977. Proto Jicaque-Subtiaba-Tequistlateco: a comparative reconstruction. In *Two studies in Middle American comparative linguistics,* 1–52. (SIL Publications in Linguistics no. 55.) Arlington: SIL and the University of Texas at Arlington.

Orbigny, Alcide Dressalines d'. See D'Orbigny, Alcide Dressalines.

Orozco y Berra, Manuel. 1864. *Geografía de las lenguas y carta etnográfica de México, precedidas de un ensayo de clasificación de las mismas lenguas y de apuntes para las inmigraciones de las tribus.* Mexico: J. M. Andrade and F. Escalante.

Orr, Carolyn and Robert Longacre. 1968. Proto-Quechumaran. *Language* 44:528–55.

Ortega Ricaurte, C. 1978. *Los estudios sobre lenguas indígenas de Colombia: notas históricas y bibliográficas.* Bogotá: Instituto Caro y Cuero.

Oswalt, Robert L. 1958. Russian loanwords in Southwestern Pomo. *IJAL* 24:245–47.

———. 1976a. Comparative verb morphology of Pomo. In *Hokan studies:* ed. Margaret Langdon and Shirley Silver, 13–28. The Hague: Mouton.

———. 1976b. Switch reference in Maiduan: an areal and typological contribution. *IJAL* 42:297–304.

———. 1990. Comments on Speaking of forked tongues: the feasibility of reconciling human phylogeny and the history of language. *CA* 31:21–22.

Palavecino, Enrique. 1926. Glosario comparado Kičua-Maori. *ICA* 22(2):517–25. Rome.

Pallas, Peter Simon. 1786–1789. *Linguarum totius orbis vocabularia comparativa.* St. Petersburg: Schnoor.

Pareja, Fray Francisco. 1614. *Arte y pronunciación en lengua timvquana y castellana.* Mexico: Emprenta de Ioan Ruyz.

Parisot, Jean. 1880. Notes sur la langue des Taensas. *Revue de Linguistique et de Philologie Comparée* 13:166–86.

———. 1882. Du genre dans la langue Hastri ou Taensa. *ICA* (Madrid) 4(2):310–35.

Parker, Gary J. 1969a. *Comparative Quechua phonology and grammar 1: classification,* 65–87. (Working Papers in Linguistics no. 1.) Honolulu: University of Hawaii.

———. 1969b. *Comparative Quechua phonology and grammar 4: the evolution of Quechua A,* 149–

204. (Working Papers in Linguistics no. 1.) Honolulu: University of Hawaii.

———. 1969c. *Comparative Quechua phonology and grammar 5: the evolution of Quechua B,* 1–109. (Working Papers in Linguistics no. 3.) Honolulu: University of Hawaii.

Parsons, James. 1968[1767]. *The remains of Japhet, being historical enquiries into the affinity and origins of the European languages.* Menston, Yorkshire: Scholar Press. [Original ed., London.]

Payne, David L. 1985. The genetic classification of Resigaro. *IJAL* 51:222–31.

———. 1990. Some widespread grammatical forms in South American languages. In *Amazonian linguistics: studies in lowland South American languages,* ed. Doris L. Payne, 75–87. Austin: University of Texas Press.

———. 1991. A classification of Maipuran (Arawakan) languages based on shared lexical retentions. In *Handbook of Amazonian languages,* vol. 3, ed. Desmond C. Derbyshire and Geoffrey K. Pullum, 355–499. Berlin: Mouton de Gruyter.

Payne, Doris L. 1985. *-ta* in Zaparoan and Peba-Yaguan. *IJAL* 51:529–31.

———. 1990. Morphological characteristics of lowland South American languages. In *Amazonian linguistics: studies in lowland South American languages,* ed. Doris L. Payne, 213–41. Austin: University of Texas Press.

Payne, Edward J. 1899. *History of the New World called America,* vol. 2. Oxford: Clarendon Press.

Pedersen, Holger. 1962[1931]. *The discovery of language: linguistic science in the nineteenth century.* Bloomington: Indiana University Press.

———. 1983[1916]. *A glance at the history of linguistics with particular regard to the historical study of phonology,* trans. (from Danish) Caroline C. Henriksen, ed. Konrad Koerner. Amsterdam: John Benjamins.

Pelleprat, Pierre. 1655. *Introduction à la langue des Galibis.* Paris: Cramoisy.

Pentland, David H. 1981. Synonymy. In *Subarctic,* ed. June Helm. Vol. 6 of *HNAI,* ed. William C. Sturtevant, 227–30. Washington, D.C.: Smithsonian Institution.

Peter, Stephen. 1993. All in the family? Greenberg's method of mass comparison and the genetic classification of languages. *CLS* 29:329–42.

Petitot, Émile. 1876. *Dictionaire de la langue Dènè-Dindjié.* Paris: Leroux.

———. 1889. *Quinze ans sous le cercle polaire: Mackenzie, Anderson, Youkon.* Paris: Dentu.

Pickering, John. 1819. Review of Heckewelder. *North American Review* 9:155–78.

———, ed. 1822. *The Indian grammar begun, or an essay to bring the Indian language into rules by John Eliot.* (Introductory observations [on the Massachusett language].) Collections of the Massachusetts Historical Society (Cambridge), 2d ser. 9:243–312. Boston: Massachusetts Historical Society.

———. 1830–1831. Indian languages of North America. In *Encyclopedia Americana* 6:569–75, 581–600. (German translation, 1834, *Über die indianischen Sprachen Amerikas, aus dem Englischen des Nordamerikaners Herrn John Pickering, übersetzt und mit Anmerkungen begleitet von Talvj.* Leipzig: Vogel.)

———, ed. 1833. A dictionary of the Abnaki language of North America by Sebastian Rasles [Sébastien Râle]. [with supplementary notes and observations on Father Rasles's Dictionary of the Abnaki language, by John Pickering]. *Memoirs of the American Academy of Arts and Science* 1:375–565.

Pickering, Mary Orne. 1887. *Life of John Pickering.* Boston: Printed privately.

Pierce, Joe E. 1965. The validity of genetic linguistics. *Linguistics* 13:25–33.

———. 1966. Genetic comparisons and Hanis, Miluk, Alsea, Siuslaw, and Takelma. *IJAL* 32:379–87.

Pilling, James Constantine. 1967[1885]. *Proof-sheets of a bibliography of the languages of the North American Indians.* Brooklyn: Central Book Co. [Original ed., Washington, D.C.: Government Printing Office.]

Pimentel, Francisco 1874[1862–1865]. *Cuadro descriptivo y comparativo de las lenguas indígenas de México.* Vol. 1, 1862; vol. 2, 1865. 2d ed., 3 vols., 1874. Mexico: Andrade y Escalante.

Pinnow, Heinz-Jürgen. 1958. Zwei Probleme der historischen Lautlehre der Na-Dene-Sprachen. *Zeitschrift für Phonetik und Allgemeine Sprachwissenschaft* 11:128–59.

———. 1964a. *Die nordamerikanischen Indianersprachen: ein Überblick über ihren Bau und ihre Besonderheiten.* Wiesbaden: Otto Harrassowitz.

———. 1964b. On the historical position of Tlingit. *IJAL* 30:155–64.

———. 1966. *Grundzüge einer historische Lautlehre des Tlingit: ein Versuch.* Wiesbaden: Harrassowitz.

———. 1968. Genetic relationship vs. borrowing in Na-Dene. *IJAL* 34:204–11.

———. 1976. *Geschichte der Na-Dene Forschung.* (Indiana, Supplement no. 5.) Berlin: Mann.

———. 1985. *Das Haida als Na-Dene-Sprache: Ma-

terialen zu den Wortfeldern und zur Komparation des Verbs. (Abhandlungen nos. 43, 44, 45, and 46.) Nortorf: Völkerkundliche Arbeitsgemeinschaft.

———. 1990. *Die Na-Dene-Sprachen in Lichte der Greenberg-Klassifikation.* (Abhandlung no. 64.) Nortorf: Völkerkundliche Arbeitsgemeinschaft.

Pitkin, Harvey. 1984. *Wintu grammar.* (UCPL, vol. 95.) Berkeley: University of California Press.

Pitkin, Harvey, and William Shipley. 1958. Comparative survey of California Penutian. *IJAL* 24:174–88.

Poser, William J. 1992. The Salinan and Yurumanguí data in *Language in the Americas. IJAL* 58:202–29.

Poser, William, and Lyle Campbell. 1992. Indo-European practice and historical methodology. *BLS* 18:214–36.

Pott, August F. 1840. Indogermanischer Sprachstamm. In *Allgemeine Encyklopädie der Wissenschaften und Künste,* sec. 2, part 18, 1–112.

———. 1870. *Etymologische Forschungen auf dem Gebiete der indogermanischen Sprachen, unter Berücksichtigung ihrer Hauptformen. Wurzeln mit consonantischem Ausgange.* 2d ed. Detmold: Meyer.

Pottier, Bernard. 1983. *América Latina en sus lenguas indígenas.* Caracas: Monte Avila Editores and UNESCO.

Powell, James V. 1990a. Chinook Jargon vocabulary and the lexicographers. *IJAL* 56:134–51.

———. 1990b. Quileute. In *Northwest Coast,* ed. Wayne Suttles. Vol. 7 of *HNAI,* ed. by William C. Sturtevant, 431–7. Washington, D.C.: Smithsonian Institution.

———. 1993. Chimakuan and Wakashan—the case for remote common origin: another look at suggestive sound correspondences. In *American Indian linguistics and ethnography in honor of Laurence C. Thompson,* ed. Anthony Mattina and Timothy Montler, 451–70. (Occasional Papers in Linguistics no. 10.) Missoula: University of Montana.

Powell, John Wesley. 1877. *Introduction to the study of American Indian languages.* Washington, D.C.: Government Printing Office.

———. 1880. *Introduction to the study of American Indian languages, with words, phrases, and sentences to be collected.* 2d ed., with charts. Washington, D.C.: Government Printing Office.

———. 1888. From barbarism to civilization. *AA* 1:97–123.

———. 1966[1891a.] Indian linguistic families of America north of Mexico. In *Introduction to Handbook of American Indian languages by*

Franz Boas and Indian linguistic families of America, north of Mexico, by J. W. Powell, ed. Preston Holder. Lincoln: University of Nebraska Press. [Original ed., Seventh annual report, Bureau of American Ethnology, 1–142. Washington, D.C.: Government Printing Office.]

———. 1891b. The Study of Indian languages. *Science* 17(418):71–74.

———. 1900. Philology, or the science of activities designed for expression. *AA* 2:603–37.

———. 1915. *[Map of] Linguistic families of American Indians north of Mexico by J. W. Powell, revised by members of the staff of the Bureau of American Ethnology.* (Bureau of American Ethnology Miscellaneous Publication no. 11.) Baltimore: Hoen.

Prem, Hans J. 1979. Aztecan writing considered as a paradigm for Mesoamerican scripts. In *Mesoamérica: homenaje al Doctor Paul Kirchhoff,* ed. Barbo Dahlgren, 104–18. Mexico: INAH.

Price, David P. 1978. The Nambiquara linguistic family. *AL* 20(1):14–39.

———. 1985. Nambiquara languages: linguistic and geographical distance between speech communities. In *South American Indian languages: retrospect and prospect,* ed. Harriet E. Manelis Klein and Louisa R. Stark, 304–24. Austin: University of Texas Press.

Prince, J. Dyneley. 1912. An ancient New Jersey Indian jargon. *AA* 14:508–24.

Proulx, Paul. 1974. Certain aspirated stops in Quechua. *IJAL* 40:257–62.

———. 1983. Review of *Beothuk vocabularies: a comparative study* by John Hewson. *IJAL* 49:217–19.

———. 1984. Proto-Algic I: phonological sketch. *IJAL* 50:165–207.

———. 1987. Quechua and Aymara. *Language Sciences* 9(1):91–102.

Radin, Paul. 1916. On the relationship of Huave and Mixe. *AA* 18:411–21. (Also *Journal de la Société des Américanistes de Paris* 11 [1919]:489–99.)

———. 1919. *The genetic relationship of the North American Indian languages,* 489–502. (UCPAAE, vol. 14.) Berkeley: University of California Press.

———. 1924. The relationship of Maya to Zoque-Huave. *Journal de la Société des Américanistes de Paris* 16:317–24.

Radlof[f] [Radlov], Leopold. 1859[1857–1858]. Einige Nachrichten über die Sprache der Kaiganen. *Mélanges tirés du Bulletin Historico-Philologique de l'Académie Impériale des Sciences de Saint Pétersbourg,* vol. 3. [Original ed., *Bulletin de la Classe des Sciences Historiques,*

Philologiques et Politiques de l'Académie Impériale des Sciences de Saint Pétersbourg 15(20–22):305–31.]

———. 1859[1858]. Über die Sprache der Ugalachmut. *Mélanges tirés du Bulletin Historico-Philologique de l'Académie Impériale des Sciences de Saint Pétersbourg,* vol. 3. [Original ed., *Bulletin de la Classe des Sciences Historiques, Philologiques et Politiques de l'Académie Impériale des Sciences de Saint Pétersbourg* 15(26–38):48–63, 126–39.]

Rankin, Robert L. 1981. Review of *The Caddoan, Iroquoian, and Siouan languages* by Wallace Chafe. *IJAL* 47:172–8.

———. 1984. Quapaw sibilant phonetics reconstructed from four nineteenth-century sources. Paper presented at the Comparative Siouan Workshop.

———. 1985. On some Ohio Valley Siouan and Illinois Algonquian words for 'eight'. *IJAL* 51:544–7.

———. 1986a. Fricative ablaut in Choctaw and Siouan. Paper presented at the Kentucky Foreign Language Conference, Louisville.

———. 1986b. Review of *A grammar of Biloxi* by Paula Einaudi. *IJAL* 52:77–85.

———. 1988. Quaqaw: genetic and areal affiliations. In *In honor of Mary Haas: from the Haas festival conference on Native American linguistics,* ed. William Shipley, 629–50. Berlin: Mouton de Gruyter.

———. 1992. Review of *Language in the Americas* by Joseph H. Greenberg. *IJAL* 58:324–51.

———. 1993. On Siouan chronology. Paper presented at the Annual Meeting of the American Anthropological Association, Washington, D.C.

Reeland [Relandus], Adriaan [Hadrianus]. 1706–1708. *De linguis Americanis,* vol. 3: *Dissertatio XII.* (Dissertationum Miscellanearum.) Rhenen: Gulielmi Broebelet.

Renker, Ann M., and Erna Gunther. 1990. Makah. In *Northwest Coast,* ed. Wayne Suttles. Vol. 7 of *HNAI,* ed. William C. Sturtevant, 422–30. Washington, D.C.: Smithsonian Institution.

Rensch, Calvin R. 1973. Otomanguean isoglosses. In *Diachronic, areal, and typological linguistics,* ed. Thomas Sebeok, 295–316. (*CTL,* vol. 11.) Mouton: The Hague.

———. 1976. *Comparative Otomanguean phonology.* (Language Science Monograph no. 14.) Bloomington: Indiana University Press.

———. 1977. Classification of the Otomanguean languages and the position of Tlapanec. In *Two studies in Middle American comparative linguistics,* 53–108. (SIL Publications in Linguistics no. 55.) Arlington: SIL and University of Texas at Arlington Press.

———. 1978. Typological and genetic considerations in the classification of the Otomanguean languages. *ICA* (Paris) 52:623–33.

———. 1989. An etymological dictionary of the Chinantec languages. (SIL Publications in Linguistics no. 57.) Arlington: SIL and University of Texas at Arlington Press.

Restivo, Paulo. 1892[1724]. *Arte de la lengua guaraní.* Stuttgart: Kohlhammer. [Original ed., Santa María la Mayor, Paraguay.]

Rezanov, Nikoai Petrovich. 1805. [Tanaina vocabulary.] Manuscript no. 118, Fond Adelunga, Academy of Sciences, Leningrad. [Not seen; cited by Krauss 1964:127–8.]

Rhodes, Richard. 1977. French Cree—a case of borrowing. In *Actes du huitième congrès des Algonquinistes,* ed. William Cowan, 6–25. Ottawa: Carleton University.

———. 1982. Algonquian trade languages. In *Papers of the thirteenth Algonquian conference,* ed. William Cowan, 1–10. Ottawa: Carleton University.

Riddell, Francis A. 1978. Maidu and Konkow. In *California,* ed. Robert F. Heizer. Vol. 8 of *HNAI,* ed. William C. Sturtevant, 370–86. Washington, D.C.: Smithsonian Institution.

Riggs, Stephen Return. 1890. *A Dakota-English dictionary,* ed. James Owen Dorsey. (Contributions to North American Ethnology no. 7; Department of Interior, U.S. Geographical and Geological Survey of the Rocky Mountain region, J. W. Powell in charge.) Washington, D.C.: Government Printing Office.

Rigsby, Bruce J. 1965a. Continuity and change in Sahaptian vowel systems. *IJAL* 31:306–11.

———. 1965b. Linguistic relations in the Southern Plateau. Ph.D. diss., University of Oregon, Eugene.

———. 1966. On Cayuse-Molala relatability. *IJAL* 32:369–78.

———. 1969. The Waiilatpuan problem: more on Cayuse-Molala relatability. *Northwest Anthropological Research Notes* 3:68–146.

Rigsby, Bruce, and Michael Silverstein. 1969. Nez Perce vowels and Proto-Sahaptian vowel harmony. *Language* 45:45–59.

Riley, Carroll L., J. Charles Kelley, Campbell W. Pennington, and Robert L. Rands. 1971. *Man across the sea: problems of pre-Columbian contacts.* Austin: University of Texas Press.

Ringe, Donald A., Jr. 1992. On calculating the factor of chance in language comparison. *Transactions of the American Philosophical Society* 82(1):1–110.

———. 1993. A reply to Professor Greenberg. *Proceedings of the American Philosophical Society* 137:91–109.

———. 1994. Multilateral comparison: an empirical test. Paper presented at the Annual Meeting of the American Association for the Advancement of Science, San Francisco.

Río Urrutia, María Ximena del. 1985. La lengua de Chilanga: fonología y léxico. Licenciatura thesis, University of Costa Rica, San José.

Rischel, Jørgen. 1985. Was there a fourth vowel in Old Greenlandic? *IJAL* 51:553–5.

Rivers, W[illiam] H. R. 1922. The unity of anthropology. *Journal of the Royal Anthropological Institute* 52:12–25.

Rivet, Paul. 1924. Langues américaines. In *Les Langues du monde,* ed. Antoine Meillet and Marcel Cohen, 597–712. (Collection Linguistique no. 16.) Paris: Champion.

———. 1925a. Les Australiens en Amérique. *Bulletin de la Société Linguistique de Paris* 26:23–63.

———. 1925b. Les mélanéso-polynésiens et les australiens en Amérique. *Anthropos* 20:51–4.

———. 1926. Les malayo-polynésiens en Amérique. *Journal de la Société des Américanistes de Paris* 18:141–278.

———. 1942. Un dialecte Hoka Colombien: le Yurumangí. *Journal de la Société des Américanistes de Paris* 34:1–59.

———. 1943. La influencia karib en Colombia. *Revista del Instituto Etnológico Nacional* (Bogotá) 1(1):55–93.

———. 1957[1943]. *Les Origines de l'homme Américain.* 8th ed. Paris: Gallimard. (Spanish translation, 1960[1943], *Los orígenes del hombre americano.* Mexico: Fondo de Cultura.)

Rivet, Paul, and Čestmír Loukotka. 1952. Langues de l'Amérique du Sud et des Antilles. In *Les Langues du monde,* 2d ed., ed. Antoine Meillet and Marcel Cohen, 1009–1160. (1st ed., 1924.) Paris: Champion.

Rivet, Paul, and Robert de Wavrin. 1951. Un nouveau dialecte arawak: le Resigaro. *Journal de la Société des Américanistes de Paris* 40:203–39.

Robertson, John S. 1980. *The structure of pronoun incorporation in the Mayan verbal complex.* New York: Garland Press.

———. 1984. Colonial evidence for a Pre-Quiche ergative 3sg *ru-. IJAL* 50:452–6.

———. 1992. *The history of tense/aspect/mood/voice in the Mayan verbal complex.* Austin: University of Texas Press.

Robins, Robert H. 1987. Duponceau and early nineteenth-century linguistics. In *Papers in the history of linguistics,* ed. Hans Aarsleff, Louis Kelly, and Jans-Joseph Niederehe, 435–46. Amsterdam: John Benjamins.

———. 1990. Leibniz and Wilhem von Humboldt and the history of comparative linguistics. In *Leibniz, Humboldt, and the origins of comparativism,* ed. Tullio de Mauro and Lia Formigari, 85–102. Amsterdam: John Benjamins.

Robles Uribe, Carlos. 1964. Investigación lingüística sobre los grupos indígenas del Estado de Baja California. *Anales del INAH* (Mexico) 17:275–301.

Rodrigues, Aryon. 1984–1985. Relações internas na família lingüística Tupi-Guarani. *Revista de Antropologia* (São Paulo) 27–28:33–53.

———. 1985a. Evidence for Tupi-Carib relationships. In *South American Indian languages: retrospect and prospect,* ed. Harriet E. Manelis Klein and Louisa R. Stark, 371–404. Austin: University of Texas Press.

———. 1985b. The present state of the study of Brazilian Indian languages. In *South American Indian languages: retrospect and prospect,* ed. Harriet E. Manelis Klein and Louisa R. Stark, 405–39. Austin: University of Texas Press.

———. 1986. *Linguas brasileiras: para o conhecimento das linguas indígenas.* São Paulo: Edições Loyola.

Rogers, Richard A. 1985. Glacial geography and native North American languages. *Quaternary Research* 23:130–7.

———. 1986. Language, human subspeciation, and Ice Age barriers in Northern Siberia. *Canadian Journal of Anthropology* 5:11–22.

———. 1987. Review of *Language in the Americas* by Joseph H. Greenberg. *CA* 28:652–3.

Rogers, Richard A., Larry D. Martin, and T. Dale Nicklas. 1990. Ice-Age geography and the distribution of native North American languages. *Journal of Biography* 17:131–43.

Rondthaler, Edward. 1847. *Life of John Heckewelder,* ed. B. H. Coates. Philadelphia: Townsend Ward.

Rood, David S. 1973. Swadesh's Keres-Caddo comparison. *IJAL* 39:189–90.

———. 1979. Siouan. In *The languages of Native America: historical and comparative assessment,* ed. Lyle Campbell and Marianne Mithun, 236–98. Austin: University of Texas Press.

———. 1992a. North American languages. In *IEL,* ed. William Bright, 3:110–15. New York: Oxford University Press.

———. 1992b. Siouan languages. In *IEL,* ed. William Bright, 3:449–51. New York: Oxford University Press.

Rowe, John Howland. 1954. Linguistic classification problems in South America. In *Papers from the symposium on American Indian linguistics,* ed. Murray B. Emeneau, 10–26. (UCPL, vol. 10.) Berkeley: University of California Press.

———. 1974. Sixteenth- and seventeenth-century grammars. In *Studies in the history of linguistics: traditions and paradigms,* ed. Dell Hymes, 361–79. Bloomington: Indiana University Press.

Rude, Noel. 1987. *Some Klamath-Sahaptian grammatical correspondences.* (Working Papers in Linguistics no. 12.) 67–83. Lawrence: University of Kansas.

Rudes, Blair A. 1974. Sound changes separating Siouan-Yuchi from Iroquois-Caddoan. *IJAL* 40:117–19.

Ruhlen, Merritt. 1987a. *A guide to the world's languages.* Vol. 1: *Classification.* Stanford: Stanford University Press.

———. 1987b. Voices from the past. *Natural History* 96(3):6–10.

———. 1989. Nostratic-Amerind cognates. In *Reconstructing languages and cultures: materials from the first international interdisciplinary symposium on language and prehistory,* ed. Vitaly Shevoroshkin, 75–83. Bochum: Brockmeyer.

———. 1990. Phylogenetic relations of Native American languages. *Prehistoric Mongoloid Dispersals* (Sapporo, Japan) 7:75–96.

———. 1994a. Linguistic evidence for the peopling of the Americas. In *Method and theory for investigating the peopling of the Americas,* ed. Robson Bonnichsen and D. Gentry Steele, 177–88. Corvallis: Center for the Study of the First Americans, Oregon State University.

———. 1994b. *On the origin of languages: studies in linguistic taxonomy.* Stanford, Calif.: Stanford University Press.

Ruiz de Montoya, Antonio. 1886[1640]. Arte y bocabulario de la lengua guaraní. In *Arte bocabulario tesoro y catecismo de la lengva gvarani,* 2 vols, ed. Jules Platzmann. Leipzig: Teubner. [Original ed., Madrid: Sánchez.]

Sajnovics, Joannis [János]. 1968[1770]. *Demonstratio idioma Ungarorum et Lapponum idem esse.* Photolithic reproduction of 2d ed., ed. Thomas A. Sebeok. (Ural and Altaic Series no. 91.) Bloomington: Indiana University Press; The Hague: Mouton.) (German translation, 1972, by M. Ehlers. Wiesbaden: Harassowitz.) [*Original ed.,* 1st ed., 1770, Copenhagen: Typis Collegi Societatis Iesu; 2d ed., 1770, Trnava (Tyrnau).]

Salmons, Joe. 1992. A look at the data for a global etymology: **tik* 'finger'. In *Explanation in historical linguistics,* ed. Garry W. Davis and Gregory K. Iverson, 207–28. (Current Issues in Linguistic Theory no. 84.) Amsterdam: John Benjamins.

Salwen, Bert. 1978. Indians of southern New England and Long Island: early period. In *Northeast,* ed. Bruce G. Trigger. Vol. 15 of *HNAI,* ed. William C. Sturtevant, 160–76. Washington, D.C.: Smithsonian Institution.

Samarin, William J. 1986. Chinook Jargon and pidgin historiography. *Canadian Journal of Anthropology* 5:23–34.

———. 1987. Demythologizing plains Indian sign language history. *IJAL* 53:63–73.

Sanctius (Brocensis), Franciscus [Francisco Sánchez (de las Brozas)]. 1585–1587. *Minerva seu de causis linguae latinae.* Salamanca: Ioannes and Andreas Renaut.

Sapir, Edward. 1984[1907–1908]. Herder's *Ursprung der Sprache. Historiographia Linguistica* 11:355–88. [Original ed., *Modern Philology* 5:109–42.]

———. 1909. The Takelma language of southern Oregon. Ph.D. diss., Columbia University.

———. 1910. *Yana texts,* 1–235. (UCPAAE no. 9.) Berkeley: University of California Press.

———. 1913. Wiyot and Yurok, Algonkin languages of California. *AA* 15:617–46.

———. 1913–1919. Southern Paiute and Nahuatl, a study in Uto-Aztecan. *Journal de la Société des Américanistes de Paris* 10:379–425; 11:443–88. (Also 1915 *AA* 17:98–120, 306–28.)

———. 1990[1915a]. Algonkin languages of California: a reply. In *American Indian languages,* part 1, ed. William Bright. *CWES* 5: 485–9. Berlin: Mouton de Gruyter. [Original ed., *AA* 17:188–94.]

———. 1915b. Epilogue [to Truman Michelson's rejoinder to Sapir 1915a]. *AA* 17:198.

———. 1915c. The Na-Dene languages, a preliminary report. *AA* 17:534–58.

———. 1949[1916]. Time perspective in aboriginal American culture: a study in method. In *SWES,* ed. David G. Mandelbaum, 389–467. Berkeley: University of California Press. [Original ed., (Canada, Department of Mines, Geological Survey, Memoir no. 90, Anthropological Series no. 13.) Ottawa: Government Printing Bureau.]

———. 1917a. The position of Yana in the Hokan stock. (UCPAAE, no. 13): 1–34. Berkeley: University of California Press.

———. 1990[1917b]. Review of *Het passieve karakter van het verbum transitivum of van het verbum actionis in talen van Noord-America* by C. C. Uhlenbeck. In *American Indian languages,* part 1, ed. William Bright, *CWES* 5: 83–4. Berlin: Mouton de Gruyter. [Original ed., *IJAL* 1:82–6.]

———. 1917c. The status of Washo. *AA* 19:449–50.

———. 1917d. Linguistic publications of the Bureau of American Ethnology, a general review. *IJAL* 1:280–90.

———. 1918. Review of *Moseteno vocabulary and treatises* by Benigno Bibolotti. *IJAL* 1:183–4.

———. 1920. The Hokan and Coahuiltecan languages. *IJAL* 1:280–90.

———. 1990[1921a]. A bird's-eye view of American languages north of Mexico. In *American Indian languages,* part 1, ed. William Bright, *CWES* 5:93–4. Berlin: Mouton de Gruyter. [Original ed., *Science* 54:408.]

———. 1949[1921b]. *Language: an introduction to the study of speech.* New York: Harcourt, Brace and World.

———. 1990[1921c]. A characteristic Penutian form of stem. In *American Indian languages,* part 2, ed. Victor Golla, *CWES* 6: 263–73. Berlin: Mouton de Gruyter. [Original ed., *IJAL* 2:58–67.]

———. 1922. *The fundamental element of Northern Yana,* 215–34. (UCPAAE no. 13.) Berkeley: University of California Press.

———. 1923. *Text analysis of three Yana dialects,* 1–235. (UCPAAE, no. 9.) Berkeley: University of California Press.

———. 1925a. The Hokan affinity of Subtiaba in Nicaragua. *AA* 27.402–35, 491–527.

———. 1925b. The similarity of Chinese and Indian languages. *Science* 62 (October 16):12

———. 1949[1926]. A Chinookan phonetic law. In *SWES,* ed. David G. Mandelbaum, 197–205. Berkeley: University of California Press. [Original ed., *IJAL* 4:105–110.]

———. 1949[1929a]. Central and North American languages. In *SWES,* ed. David G. Mandelbaum, 169–78. Berkeley: University of California Press; reprinted 1990 in *American Indian languages,* part 1, ed. William Bright, *CWES* 5:95–104. Berlin: Mouton de Gruyter. [Original ed., *Encyclopaedia Britannica,* 14th ed., 5:138–41.]

———. 1949[1929b]. Male and female forms of speech in yana. In *SWES,* ed. David G. Mandelbaum, 206–12. Berkeley: University of California Press. [Original ed., in *Donum Natalicium Schrijnen,* ed. W. J. Teeuwen, 79–85. Nijmegen-Utrecht: Dekker and van de Vegt.]

———. 1949[1929c]. The status of linguistics as a science. In *SWES,* ed. David G. Mandelbaum, 160–66. Berkeley: University of California Press. [Original ed., *Language* 5:207–14.]

———. 1930. Southern Paiute, a Shoshonean language, parts 1 and 2. *Proceedings of the American Academy of Arts and Sciences* 65(1):1–296, 65(2):297–536.

———. 1949[1931]. The concept of phonetic law as tested in primitive languages by Leonard Bloomfield. In *SWES,* ed. David G. Mandelbaum, 73–82. Berkeley: University of California Press. [Original ed., in *Methods in social science: a case book,* ed. Stuart Rice, 297–306. Chicago: University of Chicago Press.]

———. 1949[1933]. Language. In *SWES,* ed. David Mandelbaum, 3–82. Berkeley: University of California Press. [Original ed., in *Encyclopedia of the social sciences,* vol. 9, 155–69.]

———. 1936. Internal linguistic evidence suggestive of the Northern origin of the Navajo. *AA* 38:224–5.

———. 1990a[n.d.]. Abstract: The problems of linguistic relationship in America. In *American Indian languages,* part 1, ed. William Bright, *CWES* 5:83–4. Berlin: Mouton de Gruyter.

———. 1990b[1920]. Excerpt from a letter to Alfred L. Kroeber, October 1920. In *American Indian languages,* part 1, ed. William Bright, *CWES* 5:81–3. Berlin: Mouton de Gruyter. [Reprinted from Golla 1984.]

———. 1990c[n.d.]. Lecture notes (and map). In *American Indian languages,* part 1, ed. William Bright, *CWES* 5:84–91. Berlin: Mouton de Gruyter.

Sapir, Edward, and Morris Swadesh. 1946. American Indian grammatical categories. *Word* 2:103–12.

———. 1960. *Yana dictionary,* ed. Mary R. Haas. (UCPL, vol. 22.) Berkeley: University of California Press.

———. 1990[1953]. Coos-Takelma-Penutian comparisons. In *American Indian languages,* part 2, ed. Victor Golla, *CWES* 6:291–7. Berlin: Mouton de Gruyter. [Original ed., *IJAL* 19.132–7.]

Sapper, Karl Theodor. 1912. Über einige Sprachen von Sud-Chiapas. *ICA* (Mexico) 17(1):295–320.

Sasse, Hans-Jürgen. 1986. A southwest Ethiopian language area and its cultural background. In *The Fergusonian impact.* Vol. 1: *From phonology to society,* ed. Joshua A. Fishman, 327–42. Berlin: Mouton de Gruyter.

Sauer, Carl. 1934. *The distribution of aboriginal tribes and languages in northwest Mexico.* (Ibero-Americana no. 5.) Berkeley: University of California Press.

Sauvageot, Andrés. 1924. Eskimo et Ouralien. *Journal de la Société des Américanistes de Paris* 16:279–316.

———. 1953. Caractère ouraloïde du verbe eskimo. *Bulletin de la Société de Linguistique de Paris* 49:107–21.

Sawyer, Jesse O. 1978. Wappo. In *California,* ed. Robert F. Heizer. Vol. 8 of *HNAI,* ed. William

C. Sturtevant, 256–63. Washington, D.C.: Smithsonian Institution.

———. 1980. The nongenetic relationship of Wappo and Yuki. In *American Indian and Indo-European studies: papers in honor of Madison S. Beeler,* ed. Kathryn Klar, Margaret Langdon, and Shirley Silver, 209–19. The Hague: Mouton.

———. 1991. *Wappo studies,* ed. Alice Shepherd, with annotations by William W. Elmendorf. (SCOIL report no. 7.) Berkeley: Department of Linguistics, University of California.

Sayce, A. H. 1874. *The principles of comparative philology.* London: Trübner.

Schlegel, [Karl Wilhelm] Friedrich von. 1808. *Über die Sprache und Weisheit der Indier: ein Beitrag zur Begründung der Alterthumskunde.* Heidelberg: Mohr and Zimmer.

Schleicher, August. 1861–1862. *Compendium der vergleichenden Grammatik der indo-germanischen Sprachen: Kurzer abriß einer Laut- und Formenlehre der indogermanishcen Ursprache.* Weimar: Hermann Böhlau.

———. 1983[1863]. The Darwinian theory and the science of language. In *Linguistic and evolutionary theory: three essays by Auguŝt Schleicher, Ernst Haeckel, and Wilhelm Bleek,* ed. Konrad Koerner, 1–70. Amsterdam: John Benjamins.

Schoolcraft, Henry Rowe. 1975[1851]. *Personal memoirs of a residence of thirty years with the Indian tribes on the American frontiers.* New York: Arno Press.

———. 1860. *Archives of aboriginal knowledge, containing all the original papers laid before Congress respecting the history, antiquities, language, ethnology, pictography, rites, supersitions, and mythology of the Indian tribes of the United States.* 6 vols. Philadelphia: Lippincott.

Schroeder, Albert, and Ives Goddard. 1979. Synonymy. In *Southwest,* ed. Alfonso Ortiz. Vol. 9 of *HNAI,* ed. William C. Sturtevant, 550–3. Washington, D.C.: Smithsonian Institution.

Schuetz, Mardith K. 1987. Commenting on the Interrogations—ethnological data. In *Three primary documents: La Salle, the Mississippi, and the Gulf,* ed. Robert S. Weddle, 259–74. College Station: Texas A & M University Press.

Schuhmacher, W. W. 1977. Eskimo Trade Jargon: of Danish or German origin? *IJAL* 43:226–7.

Schuller, Rodolfo R. 1919–1920. Zur sprachlichen Verwandtschaft der Maya-Qu'itŝé mit der Carib-Aruác. *Anthropos* 14:465–91.

Seki, Lucy F. 1985. A note on the last Botocudo language. *IJAL* 51:581–3.

Seler, Eduard. 1960 [1902, 1887]. *Das Konjugations-system der Mayasprachen.* In *Eduard Seler, Gesammelte Abhandlungen zur Amerikanischen Sprach- und Altertumskunde* 1:65–126. Graz: Akademische Druck- und Verlagsanstalt. [Original ed., Berlin: Unger; reissued 1960, Berlin: Ascher.]

Shafer, Robert. 1947. Penutian. *IJAL* 13:205–19.

———. 1952. Athapaskan and Sino-Tibetan. *IJAL* 18:12–19.

———. 1957. Note on Athapaskan and Sino-Tibetan. *IJAL* 23:116–17.

———. 1969. A few more Athapaskan and Sino-Tibetan comparisons. *IJAL* 35:67.

Shaul, David L. 1982. Glottalized consonants in Zuni. *IJAL* 48:83–107.

———. 1985. Azteco-Tanoan ***-*l/r*-. *IJAL* 51:584–6.

———. 1988. Esselen: Utian onomastics. In *In honor of Mary Haas: from the Haas festival conference on Native America linguistics,* ed. William Shipley, 693–703. Berlin: Mouton de Gruyter.

Shaul, David L., and John M. Andresen. 1989. A case for Yuman participation in the Hohokam regional system. *Kiva* 54:105–26.

Shell, Olive A. 1965. Pano reconstruction. Ph.D. diss., University of Pennsylvania.

———. 1975. *Las lenguas pano y su reconstrucción.* (Serie Lingüística Peruana no. 12.) Yarinacocha, Peru: ILV.

Sherzer, Joel. 1972. Vowel nasalization in Eastern Algonquian: an areal-typological perspective on linguistic universals. *IJAL* 38:267–8.

———. 1973. Areal linguistics in North America. In *Linguistics in North America,* ed. Thomas A. Sebeok, 749–95. (*CTL,* vol. 10.) The Hague: Mouton.

———. 1976. *An areal-typological study of American Indian languages north of Mexico.* Amsterdam: North-Holland.

Sherzer, Joel, and Richard Bauman. 1972. Areal studies and culture history: language as a key to the historical study of culture contact. *SJA* 28:131–52.

Shevoroshkin, Vitaly. 1989a. Introductory remarks to *Explorations in language macrofamilies: materials from the first international interdisciplinary symposium on language and prehistory,* ed. Vitaly Shevoroshkin, 4–15. Bochum: Brockmeyer.

———. 1989b. Methods in interphyletic comparisons. *Ural-Altaische Jahrbücher* 61:1–26.

———. 1989c. A symposium on the deep reconstruction of languages and cultures. In *Reconstructing languages and cultures: materials from the first international interdisciplinary symposium on*

language and prehistory, ed. Vitaly Shevoroshkin, 6–8. Bochum: Brockmeyer.

——. 1990. Introduction to *Proto-languages and
proto-cultures: materials from the first international interdisciplinary symposium on language
and prehistory,* ed. Vitaly Shevoroshkin, 8–12.
Bochum: Brockmeyer.

——. 1991. Introduction to *Dene-Sino-Caucasian
languages: materials from the first international
interdisciplinary symposium on language and
prehistory.* Bochum: Brockmeyer.

Shipley, William. 1957. Some Yukian-Penutian lexical
resemblances. *IJAL* 23:269–74.

——. 1962. Hispanisms in indigenous California.
Romance Philology 16:1–21.

——. 1966. The relation of Klamath to California
Penutian. *Language* 42:489–98.

——. 1969. Proto-Takelman. *IJAL* 35:226–30.

——. 1970. Proto-Kalapuyan. In *Languages and
cultures of western North America: essays in
honor of Sven S. Liljeblad,* ed. Earl H. Swanson,
Jr., 97–106. Pocatello: Idaho State University
Press.

——. 1973. California. In *Linguistics in North
America,* ed. Thomas A. Sebeok, 1046–78. (*CTL,*
vol. 10.) The Hague: Mouton.

——. 1978. Native languages of California. In
California, ed. Robert F. Heizer. Vol. 8 of *HNAI,*
ed. William C. Sturtevant, 80–90. Washington,
D.C.: Smithsonian Institution.

——. 1980. Penutian among the ruins: a personal
assessment. *BLS* 6:437–41.

Shipley, William, and Richard Alan Smith. 1979.
Proto-Maidun stress and vowel length: the reconstruction of *one, two, three,* and *four. IJAL*
45:171–6.

——. 1982. Nouns and pronouns, Maidun and
otherwise. In *Proceedings of the 1981 Hokan
languages workshop and Penutian languages
conference,* ed. James Redden, 64–70. (Occasional Papers in Linguistics no. 10.) Carbondale:
Department of Linguistics, Southern Illinois University.

Sibley, John. 1832[ca. 1804]. *Historical sketches of
the several Indian tribes in Louisiana, south of
the Arkansas River, and between the Mississippi
and River Grande.* American State Papers, Class
II, Indian Affairs 1:721–31. Washington, D.C.

Siebert, Frank T., Jr. 1945. Linguistic classification of
Catawba, parts 1 and 2. *IJAL* 11:100–4, 211–18.

——. 1967. *The original home of the Proto-
Algonquian people. Contributions to Anthropology: Linguistics, part 1,* 13–47. (Bulletin no.
214.) Ottawa: National Museum of Canada.

——. 1975. Resurrecting Virginia Algonkian from
the dead. In *Studies in Southeastern Indian languages,* ed. James M. Crawford, 285–453. Athens: University of Georgia Press.

Silver, Shirley. 1964. Shasta and Karok: A binary
comparison. In *Studies in Californian linguistics,*
ed. William Bright, 170–81. (UCPL, vol. 34.)
Berkeley: University of California Press.

——. 1978a. Chimariko. In *California,* ed. Robert
F. Heizer. Vol. 8 of *HNAI,* ed. William C. Sturte-
vant, 205–10. Washington, D.C.: Smithsonian
Institution.

——. 1978b. Shastan peoples. In *California,* ed.
Robert F. Heizer. Vol. 8 of *HNAI,* ed. by William
C. Sturtevant, 211–24. Washington, D.C.: Smith-
sonian Institution.

Silverstein, Michael. 1971. [Introduction to] *Whitney
on language: selected writings of William
Dwight Whitney,* ed. Michael Silverstein, x–
xxxiii. Cambridge, Mass: MIT Press.

——. 1972. Chinook Jargon: Language contact and
the problem of multilevel generative systems.
Language 48:378–406, 596–625.

——. 1974. *Dialectal developments in Chinookan
tense-aspect systems: an areal-historical analysis.* (Publications in Anthropology and Linguistics, Memoir no. 29.) Bloomington: Indiana University.

——. 1975. On two California Penutian roots for
two. IJAL 41:369–80.

——. 1978. Yokuts: Introduction. In *California,*
ed. Robert F. Heizer. Vol. 8 of *HNAI,* ed. William
C. Sturtevant, 446–7. Washington, D.C.: Smithsonian Institution.

——. 1979a. Penutian: an assessment. In *The languages of Native America: historical and comparative assessment,* ed. Lyle Campbell and Marianne Mithun, 650–91. Austin: University of
Texas Press.

——. 1979b. *Two bis. IJAL* 45:187–205.

——. 1990. Chinookans of the lower Columbia. In
Northwest Coast, ed. Wayne Suttles. Vol. 7 of
HNAI, ed. William C. Sturtevant, 533–46. Wash-
ington, D.C.: Smithsonian Institution.

Smith, Charles R. 1978. Tubatulabal. In *California,*
ed. Robert F. Heizer. Vol. 8 of *HNAI,* ed. William
C. Sturtevant, 437–45. Washington, D.C.: Smithsonian Institution.

Smith, Murphy. 1983. Peter Stephen Duponceau and
his study of languages: a historical account. *Proceedings of the American Philosophical Society*
127:143–79.

Smith, Norval. 1995. An annotated list of creoles,
pidgins, and mixed languages. In *Creoles and*

pidgins: an introduction. ed. Jacques Arends, Pieter Muysken, and Norval Smith, 331–74. Amsterdam: John Benjamins.

Smith-Stark, Thomas C. 1976. Some hypotheses on syntactic and morphological aspects of Proto-Mayan (*PM). In *Mayan linguistics,* ed. Marlys McClaran, 44–66. Los Angeles: American Indian Studies Center, University of California.

———. 1992. El método de Sapir para establecer relaciones genéticas remotas. In *Reflexiones lingüísticas y literarias.* Vol. 1: *Lingüística,* ed. Rebeca Barriga Villanueva and Josefina García Fajardo, 17–42. (Centro de Estudios Lingüísticos y Literarios, Serie Estudios de Lingüística y Literatura no. 25.) Mexico: El Colegio de México.

Snow, Dean R. 1976. The archaeological implications of the Proto-Algonquian Urheimat. In *Papers of the seventh Algonquian conference,* ed. William Cowan, 339–46. Ottawa: Carleton University.

———. 1978. Eastern Abenaki. In *Northeast,* ed. Bruce G. Trigger. Vol. 15 of *HNAI,* ed. William C. Sturtevant, 137–47. Washington, D.C.: Smithsonian Institution.

Sorensen, Arthur P. 1967. Multilingualism in the northwest Amazon. *AA* 69:670–84.

———. 1973. South American Indian linguistics at the turn of the seventies. In *People and cultures of native South America,* ed. Daniel R. Gross, 312–41. New York: Doubleday.

———. 1985. An emerging Tukanoan linguistic regionality: policy pressures. In *South American Indian languages: retrospect and prospect,* ed. Harriet E. Manelis Klein and Louisa R. Stark, 140–56. Austin: University of Texas Press.

Spindler, Louis S. 1978. Menominee. In *Northeast,* ed. Bruce G. Trigger. Vol. 15 of *HNAI,* ed. William C. Sturtevant, 708–24. Washington, D.C.: Smithsonian Institution.

Spuhler, James N. 1979. Genetic distances, trees, and maps of North American Indians. In *The first Americans: origins, affinities, and adaptations,* ed. William S. Laughlin and Albert B. Harper, 135–83. Stuttgart: Gustav Fischer.

Stark, Louisa R. 1970. Mayan affinities with Araucanian. *CLS* 6:57–69.

———. 1972a. Machaj-Juyai: secret language of the Callahuayas. *Papers in Andean Linguistics* 2:199–227.

———. 1972b. Maya-Yunga-Chipayan: a new linguistic alignment. *IJAL* 38:119–35.

———. 1979. A reconsideration of Proto-Quechua phonology. *ICA* 39(5):209–19. Lima. (Also *Lin-*

güística e indigenismo en América. Lima: Instituto de Estudios Peruanos, 1975.)

———. 1985. Indigenous languages of lowland Ecuador: history and current status. In *South American Indian languages: retrospect and prospect,* ed. Harriet E. Manelis Klein and Louisa R. Stark, 157–193. Austin: University of Texas Press.

Starostin, Sergei A. 1989. Nostratic and Sino-Caucasian. In *Explorations in language macrofamilies: materials from the first international interdisciplinary symposium on language and prehistory,* ed. Vitaly Shevoroshkin, 42–65. Bochum: Brockmeyer.

———. 1991. On the hypothesis of a genetic connection between the Sino-Tibetan languages and the Yeniseian and North-Caucasian languages. In *Dene-Sino-Caucasian languages: materials from the first international interdisciplinary symposium on language and prehistory,* ed. Vitaly Shevoroshkin, 12–41. Bochum: Brockmeyer.

Stefánsson, Vilhjálmur. 1909. The Eskimo trade jargon of Herschel Island. *AA* 11:217–32.

———. 1922. *Hunters of the Great North.* New York: Harcourt, Brace.

Stegner, Wallace. 1962. *Beyond the hundredth meridian: John Wesley Powell and the second opening of the West.* Boston: Houghton Mifflin.

Steinen, Karl von den. 1892. *Die Bakaïri-Sprache.* Leipzig: Koehler.

Steinthal, Heymann. 1890[1888]. Das Verhältnis, das zwischen dem Ketschua und Aimará besteht. *ICA* (Berlin) 7:462–6.

Stewart, Ethel G. 1991. *The Dene and Na-Dene Indian migration—1233 A.D.: escape from Genghis Khan to America.* Columbus, Geor.: Institute for the Study of American Cultures.

Stipa, Günter Johannes. 1990. *Finnisch-ugrische Sprachforschung.* Helsinki: Suomalais-Ugrilainen Seura.

Stocking, George W. 1974. The Boas plan for the study of American Indian languages. In *Studies in the history of linguistics: traditions and paradigms,* ed. Dell Hymes, 454–84. Bloomington: Indiana University Press.

Stoll, Otto. 1884[1958]. *Zur Ethnographie der Republik Guatemala.* Zurich: Füssli. (Spanish translation, 1958, *Etnografía de Guatemala,* trans. Antonio Goubaud Carrera [Seminario de Integración Social Guatemalteca Publicación no. 8]. Guatemala: Ministerio de Educación Pública.)

———. 1885. Supplementary remarks to *The grammar of the Cakchiquel language,* ed. Daniel G. Brinton. *Proceedings of the American Philosophical Society* 22:255–68.

———. 1912–1913. Zur Psychologie der indianischen Hochlandsprachen von Guatemala. *Festschrift der Geographisch-ethnographischen Gesellschaft in Zürich* 1912–1913, 34–96.

Sturtevant, William C. 1958. Siouan languages in the East. *AA* 60:738–43.

———. 1959. The authorship of the Powell linguistic classification. *IJAL* 25:196–9.

———. 1994. The misconnection of Guale and Yamasee with Muskogean. *IJAL* 60:139–48.

Suárez, Jorge. 1969. Moseten and Pano-Tacanan. *AL* 11(9):255–66.

———. 1973. Macro-Pano-Tacana. *IJAL* 39:137–54.

———. 1974. South American Indian languages. In *Encyclopaedia Britannica,* 15th ed. 17:105–12.

———. 1975. *Estudios Huaves.* (Colección Científica, Lingüística no. 22). Mexico: Departamento de Lingüística, INAH.

———. 1977. La posición lingüística del pano-tacana y del arahuaco. *Anales de Antropología* 14:243–55.

———. 1979. Observaciones sobre la evolución fonológica del tlapaneco. *Anales de Antropología* 16:371–86.

———. 1983. *La lengua tlapaneca de Malinaltepec.* Mexico: UNAM.

———. 1985. Loan etymologies in historic method. *IJAL* 51:574–6.

———. 1986. Elementos gramaticales otomangues en tlapaneco. In *Language in global perspective: papers in honor of the fiftieth anniversary of the SIL, 1935–1985,* ed. Benjamin Elson, 267–84. Dallas: SIL.

Suárez, Victor M. 1945. *El español que se habla en Yucatán.* Mérida: Díaz Massa.

Suttles, Wayne. 1990. Central Coast Salish. In *Northwest Coast,* ed. Wayne Suttles. Vol. 7 of *HNAI,* ed. William C. Sturtevant, 453–75. Washington, D.C.: Smithsonian Institution.

Suttles, Wayne, and Barbara Lane. 1990. Southern Coast Salish. In *Northwest Coast,* ed. Wayne Suttles. Vol. 7 of *HNAI,* ed. William C. Sturtevant, 485–502. Washington, D.C.: Smithsonian Institution.

Swadesh, Morris [Mauricio]. 1946. Phonologic formulas for Chitimacha-Atakapa. *IJAL* 12:113–26.

———. 1947. Atakapa-Chitimacha *kʷ. IJAL* 13:120–21.

———. 1949. The linguistic approach to Salish prehistory. In *Indians of the urban Northwest,* ed. Marian W. Smith, 160–73. New York: Columbia University Press.

———. 1951. Diffusional cumulation and archaic residue as historical explanation. *SJA* 7:1–21.

———. 1952. [Review of] *Athapaskan and Sino-Tibetan* by Robert Shafer [1952]. *IJAL* 18:178–81.

———. 1953a. Mosan I: a problem of remote common origin. *IJAL* 19:26–44.

———. 1953b. Mosan II: comparative vocabulary. *IJAL* 19:223–36.

———. 1954a. On the Penutian vocabulary survey. *IJAL* 20:123–33.

———. 1954b. Perspectives and problems of Amerindian comparative linguistics. *Word* 10:306–32.

———. 1954c. Time depth of American linguistic groupings. *AA* 56:361–4.

———. 1955. Towards a satisfactory genetic classification of Amerindian languages. *ICA* (São Paulo) 31:1001.

———. 1956. Problems of long-range comparison in Penutian. *Language* 32:17–41.

———. 1959. *Mapas de clasificación lingüística de México y las Américas.* (Instituto de Historia Publicación no. 51.) Mexico: UNAM.

———. 1960a. Afinidades de las lenguas amerindias. *ICA* 34:729–38. Vienna.

———. 1960b. Estudios sobre lengua y cultura. *Acta Anthropologica* 22(2):145–90.

———. 1960c. On interhemisphere linguistic connections. In *Culture in history: essays in honor of Paul Radin,* ed. Stanley Diamond, 894–924. New York: Columbia University Press.

———. 1960d. The Oto-Manguean hypothesis and Macro-Mixtecan. *IJAL* 26:79–111.

———. 1960e. Tras la huella lingüística de la prehistoria. *Suplementos del Seminario de Problemas Científicos y Filosóficos* (Mexico) 26:97–145.

———. 1961. *The culture historic implications of Sapir's linguistic classification. A William Cameron Townsend en el vigésimoquinto aniversario del ILV,* 663–7. Cuernavaca: Tipográfica Indígena.

———. 1962. Linguistic relations across the Bering Strait. *AA* 64:1262–91.

———. 1963a. El tamaulipeco. *Revista Mexicana de Estudios Antropológicos* 19:93–104.

———. 1963b. [Comments on] On aboriginal languages of Latin America. *CA* 4:317–19.

———. 1964a. Comparative Penutian glosses of Sapir. In *Studies in Californian linguistics,* ed. William Bright, 182–91. (UCPL, vol. 34.) Berkeley: University of California Press.

———. 1964b. Linguistic overview. In *Prehistoric man in the New World,* ed. Jesse D. Jennings and Edward Norbeck, 527–56. Chicago: University of Chicago Press.

———. 1965. Kalapuya and Takelma. *IJAL* 31:237–40.

———. 1966. Porhé y Maya. *Anales de Antropología* 3:173–204. Mexico: UNAM.

———. 1967a. Lexicostatistic classification. In *Linguistics,* ed. Norman A. McQuown. Vol. 5 of *HMAI,* ed. Robert Wauchope, 79–115. Austin: University of Texas Press.

———. 1967b. Linguistic classification in the Southwest. In *Studies in Southwestern ethnolinguistics: meaning and history in the languages of the American Southwest,* ed. Dell H. Hymes and William E. Bittle, 281–309. (Studies in General Anthropology no. 3.) The Hague: Mouton.

———. 1968. Las lenguas indígenas del noroeste de México. *Anales de Antropología* 5:75–86. Mexico: UNAM.

Swanton, John R. 1907. Ethnological position of the Natchez Indians. *AA* 9:513–28.

———. 1908a. Haida texts and myths, Skidegate dialect. (Smithsonian Institution Bureau of American Ethnology Bulletin no. 29.) 1–448. Washington, D.C.: Government Printing Office.

———. 1908b. Social conditions, beliefs, and linguistic relationship of the Tlingit Indians. *Bureau of American Ethnology, annual report (1904–1905)* 26:391–486.

———. 1911a. Haida. In *Handbook of American Indian languages,* ed. Franz Boas, 1:205–82. (Smithsonian Institution, Bureau of American Ethnology Bulletin no. 40.) Washington, D.C.: Government Printing Office.

———. 1911b. Tlingit. In *Handbook of American Indian languages,* ed. Franz Boas, 1:159–204. (Smithsonian Institution, Bureau of American Ethnology Bulletin no. 40.) Washington, D.C.: Government Printing Office.

———. 1915. Linguistic position of the tribes of southern Texas and northeastern Mexico. *AA* 13:17–40.

———. 1917. Unclassified languages of the Southeast. *IJAL* 1:47–9.

———. 1919. *A structural and lexical comparison of the Tunica, Chitimacha, and Atakapa languages.* (Smithsonian Institution Bureau of American Ethnology Bulletin no. 68.) Washington, D.C.: Government Printing Office.

———. 1924. The Muskhogean connection of the Natchez language. *IJAL* 3:46–75.

———. 1929. The Tawasa language. *AA* 31:435–53.

———. 1940. *Linguistic material from the tribes of southern Texas and northeastern Mexico.* (Smithsonian Institution Bureau of American Ethnology Bulletin no. 127.) Washington, D.C.: Government Printing Office.

———. 1946. The Indians of the Southeastern United States. (Smithsonian Institution Bureau of American Ethnology Bulletin no. 137.) Washington, D.C.: Government Printing Office.

Swiggers, Pierre. 1984. Les langues amérindiennes à la Société de Linguistique de Paris (1863–1932). *Amerindia* 6:383–404.

———. 1985. Munsee borrowings from Dutch: some phonological remarks. *IJAL* 51:594–7.

Szathmary, Emöke J. 1986. Comment on The settlement of the Americas: a comparison of the linguistic, dental, and genetic evidence by Joseph H. Greenberg, Christy G. Turner II, and Stephen L. Zegura. *CA* 27:490–1.

———. 1994. Modeling ancient population relationships from modern population genetics. In *Method and theory for investigating the peopling of the Americas,* ed. Robson Bonnichsen and D. Gentry Steele, 117–30. Corvallis: Center for the Study of the First Americans, Oregon State University.

Taylor, Allan R. 1963a. The classification of the Caddoan languages. *Proceedings of the American Philosophical Society* 107:51–9.

———. 1963b. Comparative Caddoan. *IJAL* 29:113–31.

———. 1976. Words for *Buffalo*. *IJAL* 42:165–6.

———. 1978. Nonverbal communication in aboriginal North America: the Plains sign language. In *The Americas and Australia,* ed. D. Jean Umiker-Sebeok and Thomas A. Sebeok. Vol. 2 of *Aboriginal sign languages of the Americas and Australia,* 223–44. New York: Plenum Press.

———. ed. In press. *Language and prehistory in the Americas.* Stanford, Calif.: Stanford University Press.

Taylor, Douglas R. 1951. *The Black Carib of British Honduras.* (Viking Fund Publications in Anthropology no. 17.) New York: Wenner-Gren Foundation for Anthropological Research.

———. 1952. Sameness and difference in two Island Carib dialects. *IJAL* 18:223–30.

———. 1954. Diachronic note on the Carib contribution to Island Carib. *IJAL* 20:28–33.

———. 1956. Languages and ghost-languages of the West Indies. *IJAL* 22:180–3.

———. 1957. Spanish canoa and its congeners. *IJAL* 23:242–4.

———. 1976. The nominal plural in Arawak. *IJAL* 42:371–4.

———. 1977a. *Languages of the West Indies.* Baltimore: Johns Hopkins University Press.

———. 1977b. A note on Palikur and Northern Arawakan. *IJAL* 43:58–60.

Taylor, Douglas R., and Berend J. Hoff. 1980. The linguistic repertory of the Island Carib in the seventeenth century: the men's language—a Carib pidgin? *IJAL* 46:301–12.

Taylor, Gerald. 1985. Apontamentos sobre o nheengatu falado no Rio Negro, Brasil. *Amerindia* 10:5–23.

Taylor, R. E. 1991. Frameworks for dating the Late Pleistocene peopling of the Americas. In *The first Americans: search and research,* ed. Tom D. Dillehay and David J. Meltzer, 77–111. Boca Raton: CRC Press.

Teeter, Karl V. 1964a. Algonquian languages and genetic relationship. In *Proceedings of the ninth international congress of linguists,* 1026–33. The Hague: Mouton.

———. 1964b. *The Wiyot language.* (UCPL, vol. 37.) Berkeley: University of California Press.

Thalbitzer, William. 1922. The Aleutian languages compared with Greenlandic: a manuscript by Rasmus Rask, dating from 1820, now in the Royal Library at Copenhagen. *IJAL* 2:40–57.

———. 1928[1926]. Is there any connection between the Eskimo language and the Uralian? *ICA* (Rome) 22(2):551–67.

———. 1945[1944]. *Uhlenbeck's Eskimo-Indoeuropean hypothesis: a critical revision,* 66–96. (Travaux du Cercle Linguistique de Copenhague 1.) Copenhagen: Einar Munksgaard.

———. 1952. Possible contracts between Eskimo and Old World languages. In *Indian tribes of aboriginal America: selected papers of the twenty-ninth international congress of Americanists,* no. 3. Chicago: University of Chicago Press.

Thomas, Cyrus. 1902. Provisional list of linguistic families, languages, and dialects of Mexico and Central America. *AA* 4:207–16.

Thomas, Cyrus, and John R. Swanton. 1911. Indian languages of Mexico and Central America and their geographical distribution. (Smithsonian Institution Bureau of American Ethnology Bulletin no. 44.) Washington, D.C.: Government Printing Office.

Thomas, Norman D. 1974. *The linguistic, geographic, and demographic position of the Zoque of southern Mexico.* (Papers of the New World Archaeological Foundation no. 36.) Provo, Utah: Brigham Young University Press.

Thomason, Sarah Grey. 1980a. Morphological instability, with and without language contact. In *Historical morphology,* ed. Jacek Fisiak, 359–72. The Hague: Mouton.

———. 1980b. On interpreting "The Indian Interpreter." *Language in Society* 9:167–93.

———. 1983. Chinook Jargon in areal and historical context. *Language* 59:820–70.

———. In press. Hypothesis generation vs. hypothesis testing: a comparison between Greenberg's classification in Africa and in the Americas. In *Language and prehistory in the Americas,* ed. Allan Taylor. Stanford, Calif.: Stanford University Press.

Thomason Sarah G., and Terrence Kaufman. 1988. *Language contact, creolization, and genetic linguistics.* Berkeley: University of California Press.

Thompson, J. Eric S. 1943. *Pitfalls and stimuli in the interpretation of history through loan words.* (Philological and Documentary Studies no. 1: Middle American Research Institute publication no. 11.) New Orleans: Tulane University.

Thompson, Laurence C. 1973. The Northwest. In *Linguistics in North America,* ed. Thomas Sebeok, 979–1045. (*CTL,* vol. 10. The Hague: Mouton.

———. 1979. Salishan and the Northwest. In *The languages of Native America: historical and comparative assessment,* ed. Lyle Campbell and Marianne Mithun, 692–761. Austin: University of Texas Press.

Thompson, Laurence C., and M. Dale Kinkade. 1990. Languages. In *Northwest Coast,* ed. Wayne Suttles. Vol. 7 of *HNAI,* ed. William C. Sturtevant, 30–51. Washington, D.C.: Smithsonian Institution.

Thompson, Laurence C., and M. Terry Thompson. 1972. Language universals, nasals, and the Northwest coast. In *Studies in linguistics in honor of George L. Trager,* ed. M. Estellie Smith, 441–56. The Hague: Mouton.

Thompson, Nile Robert. 1993. An analysis of diachronic denasalization in Twana. In *American Indian linguistics and ethnography in honor of Laurence C. Thompson,* ed. Anthony Mattina and Timothy Montler, 303–16. (Occasional Papers in Linguistics no. 10.) Missoula: University of Montana.

Tokarev, S. A., and I. A. Zolotarevskaja, eds. 1955. *Indejcy Ameriki.* (Trudy Instituta Etnografii, n.s. 25.) Moscow: Akademija Nauk.

Tolmie, W. Fraser, and George M. Dawson. 1884. *Comparative vocabularies of the Indian tribes of British Columbia.* (Geological and Natural History Survey of Canada.) Montreal: Dawson Brothers.

Toomey, Noxon. 1914. *Relationships of the Chitimachan linguistic family.* (Bulletin no. 4.) St. Louis, Missouri: Hervas Laboratories of American Indian Linguistics.

Torero, Alfredo. 1983. La familia lingüística quechua. In *América Latina en sus linguas indígenas,* coordinated by Bernard Pottier, 61–92. Caracas: Monte Avila Editores and UNESCO.

Tovar, Antonio. 1961. *Catálogo de las lenguas de América del Sur: enumeración, con indicaciones tipológicas, bibliografía y mapas.* Buenos Aires: Editorial Sudamericana. [See Antonio Tovar and Larrucea de Tovar 1984.]

Tovar, Antonio, and Manfred Faust. 1976. Some questions regarding method in the genetic classification of South American Indian languages. *Indogermanische Forschungen* 81:240–8.

Tovar, Antonio, and Consuelo Larrucea de Tovar. 1984. *Catálogo de las lenguas de América del Sur.* 2d ed. Madrid: Gredos. [See Tovar 1961.]

Trager, George L. 1945. Review of *Map of North American Indian languages,* compiled and drawn by C. F. Voegelin and E. W. Voegelin. *IJAL* 11:186–9.

———. 1967. The Tanoan settlement of the Rio Grande area: a possible chronology. In *Studies in southwestern ethnolinguistics: meaning and history in the languages of the American Southwest,* ed. Dell H. Hymes and William E. Bittle, 335–49. (Studies in General Anthropology no. 3.) The Hague: Mouton.

Trager, George L., and F. E. Harben. 1958. *North American Indian languages: classification and maps.* (Studies in Linguistics Occasional Papers no. 5.) Buffalo: Department of Anthropology and Linguistics. University of Buffalo.

Trager, George L., and Edith Crowell Trager. 1959. Kiowa and Tanoan. *AA* 61:1078–83.

Troike, Rudolf C. 1963. A contribution to Coahuilteco lexicography. *IJAL* 29:295–99.

———. 1967. Review of *El cuadernillo de la lengua de los indios Pajalates* (1732), por Gabriel de Vergara, y *El confesonario de indios en lengua coahuilteca,* ed. Eugenio del Hoyo. *IJAL* 33:78–81.

———. 1978. The date and authorship of the Pajalate (Coahuilteco) *Cuadernillo. IJAL* 44:329–30.

———. 1987. Karankawa linguistics data. In *Three primary documents: La Salle, the Mississippi, and the Gulf,* ed. Robert S. Weddle, 288–301. College Station: Texas A & M University Press.

———. 1988. Amotomanco (Otomoaca) and Tanpachoa as Uto-Aztecan languages, and the Jumano problem once more. *IJAL* 54:235–41.

Trombetti, Alfredo. 1905. *L'unità d'origine del linguaggio.* Bologna: Libreria Treves di Luigi Beltrami.

———. 1920–1921. *Due lingue algonchine.* Rendiconti della R. Academia delle Scienze dell-Istituto di Bologna, c. di scienze morale, s 2ª V. [Not seen; cited by Gursky 1966a.]

———. 1928[1926]. Origine asiatica delle lingue e popolazioni americane. *ICA* 22(1):169–246. (Rome).

———. 1929–1937. America: lingue indigine. In *Enciclopedia Italiana* 2:921–9. Milano. [Not seen; cited by Gursky 1966a.]

Trubetzkoy, (Prince) N. S. 1931. *Phonologie und Sprachgeographie,* 228–34. (Travaux de Circle Linguistique de Prague no. 4.) (French translation 1950 [reissued 1970], *Phonologie et géographie linguistique.* Appendix to 1949 *Principes de Phonologie,* 343–50. Paris: Klincksieck.)

Trumbull, J. Hammond. 1869–1870. On the best method of studying the North American languages. *Transactions of the American Philological Association* 1:55–79.

———. 1876. Indian languages of America. *Johnson's New Universal Cyclopedia* 2:1155–61.

Tucker, A. N. 1957. Philology in Africa. *Bulletin of the School of Oriental and African Studies* 20:541–54.

Turner, Christy G. II. 1983. Dental evidence for the peopling of the Americas. In *Early man in the New World,* ed. Richard Shutler, Jr., 147–57. Beverly Hills: Sage.

———. 1985. The dental search for Native American origins. In *Out of Asia: peopling the Americas and the Pacific,* ed. by Robert L. Kirk and Emöke J. E. Szathmary, 31–78. Canberra: Australian National University.

Turner, Katherine. 1980. The reconstituted phonemes of Salinan. *Journal of California and Great Basin Anthropology, Papers in Linguistics* 2:53–92.

Turner, Paul R. 1967. Seri and Chontal (Tequistlatec). *IJAL* 33:235–9.

———. 1969. Proto-Chontal phonemes. *IJAL* 35:34–7.

———. 1972. On linguistic unrelatedness—a rejoinder. *IJAL* 38:146–7.

Turner, Paul, and Shirley Turner. 1971. *Chontal to Spanish-English, Spanish to Chontal dictionary.* Tucson: University of Arizona Press.

Turner, William W. 1852. [On Apachean connections.] *Literary World,* April 17. [Not seen; cited by Latham 1856:70.]

Tyler, David B. 1968. *The Wilkes expedition: the first United States exploring expedition (1838–1842).* Philadelphia: American Philosophical Society.

Tylor, Edward. 1871. *Primitive culture: researches into the development of mythology, philosophy, religion, language, area, and custom.* London: Murray.

———. 1881. *Anthropology: an introduction to the*

study of man and civilisation. London: Macmillan.

Uhde, Adolf. 1861. *Die Länder am untern Rio Bravo del Norte.* Heidelberg: Mohr.

Uhle, Max. 1890[1888]. Verwandtschaften und Wanderungen der Tschibtscha. *ICA* 7:466–88. Berlin.

Uhlenbeck, Christianus Cornelius. 1908. Die einheimischen Sprachen Nord-Amerikas bis zum Rio Grande. *Anthropos* 3:773–99.

———. 1916. Het passieve karakter van het verbum transitivum of ven het verbum actionis in talen van Noord-America. *Verslagen en mededeelingen der Koninklijke Adademie van Wetenschappen* (Amsterdam), afdeeling Letterkunde, 5th ser., 2:187–216.

Ultan, Russell. 1964. Proto-Maidun phonology. *IJAL* 30:355–70.

———. 1970. Size-sound symbolism. In *Working papers on language universals,* ed. Joseph H. Greenberg, 3:1–31. Stanford, Calif.: Department of Linguistics, Stanford University.

Urban, Greg. 1985. On Pataxó and Hãhãhãi. *IJAL* 51:605–8.

Valdivia, Luis de. 1887[1606]. *Arte y grammatica general de la lengua que corre en todo el Reyno de Chile, con un vocabulario y confesionario.* Facsimile ed., Leipzig: Teubner, [Original ed., Lima: Francisco del Canto.]

Vater, Johann Severin. 1810. *Untersuchungen über Amerikas Bevölkerung aus dem alten Kontinente.* Leipzig: Vogel.

Vázquez de Espinosa, Antonio. 1948[1630]. *Compendio y descripción de las Indias Occidentales,* ed. Charles U. Clark. (Miscellaneous Collection no. 108.) Washington, D.C.: Smithsonian Institution.

Viegas Barros, J. Pedro. 1993. La alternancia r/l en selknam: indicios de lexicalización de simbolismo fónico. In *Actas: primeras jornadas de lingüística aborígen, 6 y 7 de octubre de 1992,* ed. J. Pedro Viegas Barros, 271–8. Buenos Aires: Facultad de Filosofía y Letras, Universidad de Buenos Aires.

Villalón, María Eugenia. 1991. A spatial model of lexical relationships among fourteen Cariban varieties. In *Language change in South American Indian languages,* ed. Mary Ritchie Key, 54–94. Philadelphia: University of Pennsylvania Press.

Villiers du Terrage, Marc de, and Paul Rivet. 1919. Les indiens du Texas et les expéditions françaises de 1720 et 1721 à la "Baie Saint-Bernard." *Journal de la Société des Américanistes de Paris* 11:403–42.

Vinson, Julien. 1876[1875]. Basque et les langues Americaines. *ICA* 1875, 377. Paris.

Vivó, Jorge A. 1992[1935a]. Horizontes culturales de Mesoamérica. In *Una definición de Mesoamérica,* ed. Jaime Litvak King, 22–7. Mexico: UNAM, Instituto de Investigaciones Antropológicas. [Original ed., In *México prehispánico: culturas, deidades y monumentos.* Mexico: Editorial Emma Hurtado.]

———. 1992[1935b]. Rasgos fundamentales y correlaciones culturales de Mesoamérica. In: México prehispánico: culturas, deidades y monumentos. In *Una definición de Mesoamérica,* ed. Jaime Litvak King, 15–21. Mexico: UNAM, Instituto de Investigaciones Antropológicas. [Original ed., Mexico: Editorial Emma Hurtado.]

Voegelin, Charles F. 1939. Ofo-Biloxi sound correspondences. *Proceedings of the Indiana Academy of Sciences* 48:23–6.

———. 1941. North American Indian languages still spoken and their genetic relationships. In *Language, culture, and personality: essays in memory of Edward Sapir,* ed. Leslie Spier, A. Irving Hallowell, and Stanley S. Newman, 15–44. Menasha, Wisc.: Sapir Memorial Publication Fund.

———. 1942. Sapir: Insight and rigor. *AA* 44:322–3.

Voegelin, Carl F., and Florence M. Voegelin. 1965. Classification of American Indian languages. (*Languages of the world,* Native American fasc. 2, sec. 1.6.) *AL* 7(7):121–50.

———. 1966. *Map of North American Indian languages.* (Compiled for the American Ethnological Society.) New York: Rand-McNally.

———. 1967. Review of *Die nordamerikanischen Indianersprachen* by Heinz-Jürgen Pinnow. *Language* 43:573–83.

———. 1977. *Classification and index of the world's languages.* Amsterdam: Elsevier.

———. 1985. From comparative method to phylum linguistics and back again. *IJAL* 51:608–17.

Voegelin, Carl F., Florence M. Voegelin, and Kenneth L. Hale. 1962. *Typological and comparative grammar of Uto-Aztecan,* part 1: *Phonology.* (Publications in Anthropology and Linguistics, memoir no. 17.) Bloomington: Indiana University.

Vogt, Hans. 1954. Language contacts. *Word* 10:365–74.

von den Steinen, Karl. See Steinen, Karl von den.

Voorhis, Paul H. 1971. Notes on Kickapoo whistle speech. *IJAL* 37:238–43.

Waltz, Nathan E., and Alva Wheeler. 1972. Proto-Tucanoan. In *Comparative studies in Amerindian languages,* ed. Esther Matteson, 119–49. (*Janua Linguarum* Series Practica no. 127.) The Hague: Mouton.

Wares, Alan C. 1968. *A comparative study of Yuman*

consonantism. (*Janua Linguarum* Series Practica no. 57.) The Hague: Mouton.

Warkentin, Viola, and Ruby Scott. 1980. *Gramática ch'ol.* (Serie Gramáticas de Lenguas Indígenas de México no. 3.) Mexico: ILV.

Warner, George Frederick, ed. 1899. *The voyage of Robert Dudley, afterwards styled Earle of Warwick and Leicester and Duke of Northumberland, to the West Indies, 1594–1595, narrated by Capt. Wyatt, by himself, and by Abram Kendall, master.* London: Hakluyt Society.

Watahomigie, Lucille J., and Akira Y. Yamamoto. 1992. Local reactions to perceived language decline. *Language* 68:10–17.

Waterhouse, Viola. 1969. Oaxaca Chontal in reference to Proto-Chontal. *IJAL* 35:231–3.

———. 1985. True Tequistlateco. *IJAL* 51:612–14.

Watkins, Calvert. 1985. *The American Heritage dictionary of Indo-European roots.* Boston: Houghton Mifflin.

———. 1990. Etymologies, equations, and comparanda: types and values, and criteria for judgement. In *Linguistic change and reconstruction methodology,* ed. Philip Baldi, 289–303. Berlin: Mouton de Gruyter.

Watkins, Laurel. 1978. On **w* and **y* in Kiowa-Tanoan. *BLS* 4:477–84.

———. 1984. *A grammar of Kiowa.* Lincoln: University of Nebraska Press.

Weathers, Mark L. 1976. Tlapanec 1975. *IJAL* 42:367–71.

Webb, Nancy M. 1971. A statement of some phonological correspondences among the Pomo languages. (Supplement to *IJAL,* vol. 37, no. 3.)

———. 1980. Esselen-Hokan relationships. In *Proceedings of the 1979 Hokan languages workshop,* ed. James E. Redden, 72–80. (Occasional Papers in Linguistics no. 7.) Carbondale: Department of Linguistics, Southern Illinois University.

Weiss, Kenneth M., and Ellen Woolford. 1986. Comment on *The settlement of the Americas: a comparison of the linguistic, dental, and genetic evidence* by Joseph H. Greenberg, Christie G. Turner II, and Stephen L. Zegura. *CA* 27:491–2.

Weisshaar, Emmerich. 1987. Die Chibchan-Sprachen: geographische Ausbreitung. *Estudios de Lingüística Chibcha* (San José, Costa Rica) 6:7–70.

Weitlaner, Roberto J. 1936–1939. Notes on the Cuitlatec language. *El México Antiguo* 4:363–73.

———. 1948a. Un idioma desconocido del norte del México. *ICA* 28:205–27.

———. 1948b. Lingüística de Atoyac, Gro. *Tlalocan* 2:377–83.

Welmers, William E. 1956. Review of *Studies in African linguistic classification* by Joseph H. Greenberg. *Language* 32:556–63.

———. 1973. *African language structures.* Berkeley: University of California Press.

Werner, Oswald. 1963. A typological comparison of four Trader Navaho speakers. Ph.D. diss., Indiana University.

Wheeler, Alva L. 1972. Proto-Chibchan. In *Comparative studies in Amerindian languages,* ed. Esther Matteson, 93–108. (*Janua Linguarum* Series Practica no. 127.) The Hague: Mouton.

Whistler, Kenneth W. 1977. Wintun prehistory: an interpretation based on linguistic reconstruction of plant and animal nomenclature. *BLS* 3:157–74.

———. 1988. [1983–1984]. Pomo prehistory: a case for archaeological linguistics. In *Archaeology and linguistics,* 64–98 special issue of the *Journal of the Steward Anthropological Society,* vol. 15.

Whistler, Kenneth W., and Victor Golla. 1986. Proto-Yokuts reconsidered. *IJAL* 52:317–58.

Whitney, William Dwight. 1971[1901, 1867]. *Language and the study of language: twelve lectures on the principles of linguistic science.* New York: AMS Press. [Original ed., New York: Charles Scribner. 6th ed., 1901.]

Whorf, Benjamin L. 1935. The comparative linguistics of Uto-Aztecan. *AA* 37:600–8.

———. 1943. Loan-words in ancient Mexico. *Philological and Documentary Studies* 1:3–14. (Middle American Research Institute Publications no. 2.) New Orleans: Tulane University.

Whorf, Benjamin L., and George L. Trager. 1937. The relationship of Uto-Aztecan and Tanoan. *AA* 39:609–24.

Wichmann, Søren. 1995. *The relationship among the Mixe-Zoquean languages of Mexico.* Salt Lake City: University of Utah Press.

Wikander, Stig. 1967. Maya and Altaic: Is the Maya group of languages related to the Altaic family? *Ethnos* 32:141–8.

———. 1970. Maya and Altaic II. *Ethnos* 35:80–8.

———. 1970–1971. Maya and Altaic III. *Orientalia Suecana* 19–20:186–204.

Wilbert, Johannes. 1968. Loukotka's classification of South American Indian languages. Preface to *Classification of South American Indian languages* by Čestmír Loukotka, 7–23. Los Angeles: Latin American Center, University of California.

Willey, Gordon R. 1971. *An introduction to American archaeology,* vol. 2: *South America.* Englewood Cliffs, N.J.: Prentice-Hall.

Williams, Robert C., A. Steinberg, H. Gershowitz, P. Bennett, W. Knowler, D. Pettitt, W. Butler, R.

Baird, L. Dowda-Rea, T. Burch, H. Morse, and C. Smith. 1985. GM allotypes in Native Americans: evidence for three distinct migrations across the Bering land bridge. *American Journal of Physical Anthropology* 69:1–19.

Williams, Roger. 1973[1643]. *Key into the language of America.* Edited with a critical introduction by John J. Teunissen and Evelyn J. Hinz. Detroit: Wayne State University Press. [Original ed., London: Gregory Dexter.]

Wilson, Norman L., and Arlean H. Towne. 1978. Nisenan. In *California,* ed. Robert F. Heizer. Vol. 8 of *HNAI,* ed. William C. Sturtevant, 387–97. Washington, D.C.: Smithsonian Institution.

Winston, F. D. D. 1966. Greenberg's classification of African languages. *African Language Studies* 7:160–9.

Winter, Éduard, and Heinz Lemke, eds. 1984. *Johann Severin Vater—ein Wegbereiter der deutsch-slawischen Wechselseitigkeit.* Berlin: Akademie Verlag.

Winter, Marcus C., Margarita Gaxiola, and Gelberto Hernández. 1984. Archaeology of the Otomanguean area. In *Essays in Otomanguean culture history,* ed. J. Kathryn Josserand, Marcus Winter, and Nicholas Hopkins, 65–108. (Publications in Anthropology no. 31.) Nashville: Department of Anthropology, Vanderbilt University.

Wise, Mary Ruth. 1985a. Indigenous languages of lowland Peru: history and current status. In *South American Indian languages: retrospect and prospect,* ed. Harriet E. Manelis Klein and Louisa R. Stark, 194–223. Austin: University of Texas Press.

———. 1985b. Valence-changing affixes in Maipuran Arawakan languages. In *South American Indian languages: retrospect and prospect,* ed. Harriet E. Manelis Klein and Louisa R. Stark, 89–116. Austin: University of Texas Press.

———. 1986. Grammatical characteristics of Pre-andine Arawakan languages of Peru. In *Handbook of Amazonian languages,* ed. Desmond C. Derbyshire and Geoffrey K. Pullum, 1:567–642. Berlin: Mouton de Gruyter.

Wissler, Clark. 1942. The American Indian and the American Philosophical Society. *Proceedings of the American Philosophical Society* 86:189–204.

Wolfart, H. Christopher. 1967. Notes on the early history of American Indian linguistics. *Folia Linguistica* 1:153–71.

———. 1982. Historical linguistics and metaphilology. In *Papers from the fifth international conference on historical linguistics,* ed. Anders Ahlqvist, 395–403. Amsterdam: John Benjamins.

Wolff, Hans. 1950–1951. Comparative Siouan I, II, and III. *IJAL* 16:61–66, 113–21; 17:197–204.

Wonderly, William L. 1953. Sobre la propuesta filiación lingüística de la familia totonaca con las familias zoqueana y mayense. In *Huastecos, Totonacos y sus vecinos,* ed. Ignacio Bernal and D. Dávalos Hurtado. *Revista Mexicana de Estudios Antropológicos* 13:105–13.

Woodbury, Anthony C. 1984. Eskimo and Aleut languages. In *Arctic,* ed. David Damas. Vol. 5 of *HNAI,* ed. William C. Sturtevant, 49–63. Washington, D.C.: Smithsonian Institution.

Wrangell, Ferdinand von, and Karl Ernst von Baer. 1839. *Statistiche und ethnographische Nachrichten über die russischen Besitzungen an der Nordwestküste von Amerika.* St. Petersburg: Kaiserlichen Akademie der Wissenschaft.

Wundt, Wilhem. 1900. *Völkerpsychologie.* Vol. 1: *Die Sprache.* Leipzig: Alfred Kröner.

Wurm, Stephen. 1982. *Papuan languages of Oceania.* (Acta Linguistica no. 7.) Tübingen: Gunter Narr.

Wurtzburg, Susan J., and Lyle Campbell. 1995. North American Indian sign language: further evidence of its existence before European contact. *IJAL* 61:153–67.

Ximénez, Francisco. 1952. [ca. 1702]. *Arte de las tres lenguas cakchiquel, quiche y tzutuhil.* [University of Chicago Library. Microfilm collection of manuscripts on Middle American cultural anthropology, no. 26.]

Young, Robert W. 1983. Apachean languages. In *Southwest,* ed. Alonso Ortiz. Vol. 10 of *HNAI,* ed. William C. Sturtevant, 393–400. Washington, D.C.: Smithsonian Institution.

Zamora, Juan Clemente. 1982. Amerindian loanwords in general and local varieties of American Spanish. *Word* 33:159–71.

Zeballos, Estanislão S. 1922. Consultas: etimologías araucanas. *Revista de Derecho, Historia, y Letras* (Buenos Aires) 73:770–1.

Zegura, S. L. 1987. Blood test. *Natural History* 96:8–11.

Zenk, Henry B. 1990a. Alseans. In *Northwest Coast,* ed. Wayne Suttles. Vol. 7 of *HNAI,* ed. William C. Sturtevant, 568–71. Washington, D.C.: Smithsonian Institution.

———. 1990b. Kalapuyans. In *Northwest Coast,* ed. Wayne Suttles. Vol. 7 of *HNAI,* ed. William C. Sturtevant, 547–552. Washington, D.C.: Smithsonian Institution.

———. 1990c. Siuslawans and Coosans. In *Northwest Coast,* ed. Wayne Suttles. Vol. 7 of *HNAI,* ed. William C. Sturtevant, 572–9. Washington, D.C.: Smithsonian Institution.

INDEX OF LANGUAGES, LANGUAGE FAMILIES, AND PROPOSED GENETIC RELATIONSHIPS

Wintun. *See* Wintuan
Wiriná, 181
Wishoskan. *See* Wiyot
Wishram. *See* Kiksht
Witotoan, Witoto, 182, 186–187, 251, 326–327, 349–350
Wiyot, 68, 70, 72, 74, 79, 86, 88 n. 22, 152–154, 215, 225, 259, 335, 390 n. 105, 401 n. 130, 413 n. 62, 416 n. 87, 424 n. 81
Wiyot-Yurok. *See* Ritwan
Woccon, 43, 47, 88, 140–142, 268, 399 n. 109
Wökiare. *See* Uaiquire
Wyandot, 151, 400 n. 124

Xakriabá, 196
Xamatari. *See* Sanumá
Xambioá. *See* Karajá-Xambioá
Xaninaua. *See* Shaninawa
Xaranames. *See* Aranama-Tamique
Xavante, 196, 349
Xebero. *See* Jebero
Xerente, Xerenti, 196
Xetá, 200
Xibito. *See* Híbito
Xihuila. *See* Jebero
Xinca. *See* Xincan
Xinca-Lenca, 325
Xincan, 12, 14, 79, 165–167, 169, 176, 310, 319, 327, 344–347, 413 n. 62, 418 n. 24, 427 n. 96
Xipaya, 201
Xipinahua. *See* Shipinawa
Xirianá (Yanomaman). *See* Yanam
Xiriâna (Maipurean). See Shiriana (Maipurean)
Xivaro. *See* Jívaro
Xixime, 135
Xocó. *See* Xokó
Xokleng, 196, 349
Xokó, 6, 198
Xukurú, 198, 327
Xumana. *See* Jumano
Xurima. *See* Yanomámi

Yabaána, 181
Yabarana. *See* Mapoyo-Yavarana
Yabuti. *See* Jabuti
Yachikumne, 131
Yagan, 3, 192, 327
Yaghan. *See* Yagan
Yagua, 186, 326, 350, 423 n. 77
Yaguan, 186, 327, 349–350
Yahahí, 193
Yahgan. *See* Yagan
Yahi, 123, 397 n. 67. *See also* Yana
Yahup. *See* Hupda
Yakima. *See* Northwest Sahaptin
Yakon, 89 n. 30
Yakonan, 61, 73, 79, 87, 119, 310, 388 n. 85, 411 n. 45
Yamamadi. *See* Jamamadí
Yámana. *See* Yagan
Yamasee, 149, 341
Yamhill. *See* Northern Kalapuya

Yamiaca. *See* Atsahuaca
Yaminahua. *See* Yaminawa
Yaminawa, 191
Yamomame. *See* Yanomamö
Yana, 67, 87, 123, 214, 226–227, 258, 290–291, 293–294, 296–297, 327, 335–336, 397 n. 67, 418 n. 19, nn. 29–30, 422 n. 75, 423 n. 77
Yanam, 52, 205, 348
Yankton. *See* Dakota
Yanomaman, Yanomama, 13, 176, 204–205, 327, 348, 349, 423 n. 77, 423 n. 77
Yanomámi, 205, 348, 350
Yanomamɨ. *See* Yanomamö
Yanomamö, 205, 348
Yanuma. *See* Wainumá
Yao, 52, 203
Yaomais. *See* Yao
Yaprería. *See* Yucpa-Yaprería
Yaqui, 6, 89 n. 58, 134
Yaqui-Mayo-Cahita. *See* Cahitan
Yaquina, 119, 397 n. 55
Yaru. *See* Urupá-Jarú
Yaru Quechua, 188
Yarumá, 203
Yaruro, 33, 184, 326, 347
Yaté, Yathé. *See* Fulnió
Yauarana. *See* Mapoyo-Yavarana
Yauna, 184
Yavapai, 127
Yavarana. *See* Mapoyo-Yavarana
Yavitano. *See* Yavitero
Yavitero, 32, 180, 348
Yawalpití, 181
Yáwan. *See* Yaguan
Yawanawa. *See* Katukina Pano
Yawaperí, 203–204, 348
Yawdanchi. *See* Tule-Kaweah
Yawelmani. *See* Southern Valley Yokuts
Ye. *See* Jean
Yeniseian, 287–288, 394 n. 16, 413 n. 62, 421 n. 56
Yeral. *See* Nheengatú
Ynã. *See* Karajá-Xambioá
Yofúaha. *See* Chorote
Yokuts. *See* Yokutsan
Yokutsan, 15, 67, 86, 89 n. 27, 120–124, 128, 130–132, 226–227, 309–312, 317, 327, 336–338, 389 n. 98, 398 n. 82, n. 84, 422 n. 69, 424 n. 80, 426 n. 89
Yolox, 158
Yonkalla. *See* Southern Kalapuya
Yopará, 24
Yucatec Maya, 30, 33, 37, 52–53, 78, 102, 163–165, 214, 224, 235, 251, 345–346, 403 n. 27, 421 n. 64
Yucatecan, 12, 53, 163–165, 236
Yuchi, 79, 88, 138, 140, 150, 262, 264–265, 268–269, 309, 323, 327, 338, 341–343
Yuchi-Siouan, 76, 78–79, 88, 208, 264–265, 268, 327, 418 n. 20
Yucpa-Yaprería, 202, 327
Yucuna, 179

Yuit. *See* Siberian Yupik
Yuki, 76, 79, 87, 132–133, 327, 335, 337–338, 422 n. 69, 422 n. 75, 427 n. 5
Yukian, 87, 124, 132–133, 150, 322, 327, 335, 337
Yukian-Gulf, 322
Yukian-Penutian, 322
Yukian-Siouan, 322
Yukon-Kuskokwim. *See* Central Alaskan Yupik
Yukpa, 202
Yukpa-Japrería. *See* Yucpa-Yaprería
Yuma (Cochimí-Yuman). *See* Quechan
Yuma (Uto-Aztecan). *See* Jumano
Yuman, 6, 12, 57, 61, 67, 72, 74, 78, 87, 124, 127, 160, 227, 290–291, 294–296, 327, 336–338, 344, 386 n. 78, 412 n. 61
Yumbos. *See* Colorado
Yunca. *See* Yunga
Yunga, 30, 165, 176, 187, 189, 324, 327, 404 n. 1
Yungay, 188, 275
Yupik, 108–109, 378 n. 9, 394 n. 3
Yupiltepeque Xinca, 166
Yupuná-Durina, 184
Yuqui. *See* Sironó
Yuracare, 13, 190, 192, 326, 350
Yuracare (Chipaya-Uru). *See* Uru
Yuri, 184, 327
Yuri-Ticunan, 184
Yurimangui. *See* Yurumanguí
Yurok, 66, 68, 70, 72, 74, 79, 86, 122, 215, 226, 253, 259, 335–336, 390 n. 105, 401 n. 131, 413 n. 62, 416 n. 87, 424 n. 81
Yurumanguí, 172, 234, 237, 296, 327
Yurutí. *See* Tucano

Zacateco, Zacateca. *See* Zacateca, 133–135
Zamuco. *See* Ayoreo
Zamucoan, 194–195, 327
Záparo, 13, 24, 185
Záparo-Conambo, 185
Zaparoan, 185–186, 327, 349–350
Zaparoan-Yaguan, 185
Zapotec, 30, 51, 158, 345–346, 390 n. 111, 402 n. 12
Zapotecan, 157–159
Zapotitlan, 159
Zempoaltepetl, 162
Zia-Santa Ana, 138, 323
Zoe, 135
Zoque. *See* Zoquean
Zoquean, 30, 51, 161–162, 234, 314, 327, 345, 419 n. 30
Zuma. *See* Jumano
Zumana. *See* Jumano
Zuni, 73, 76, 78–79, 88, 103, 139, 226, 247, 312, 321, 323, 327, 338–339, 399 n. 105, 426 n. 92
Zuni-Penutian, 208, 321
Zuñi. *See* Zuni

AUTHOR INDEX

SUBJECT INDEX

accident, accidental similarity, accidental similarities, 31, 47, 68, 210, 213–215, 220, 229–232, 235, 240, 247, 248, 252, 408 n. 26, 409 n. 29, 410 n. 39, 413 nn.63–64
active alignment, 233, 416 n. 4
Amazon linguistic area, 348
American Philosophical Society, 35, 37–38
"Amerind," coining of the term, 386 n. 76
Anasazi culture, 137–139
Andean linguistic area, 347
Anianus, Strait of Anian, 91, 392 n. 2
archaeology, 90, 95, 97, 100–106, 112, 123–125, 127, 130, 132, 139, 154–155, 159, 165, 167, 410 n. 38, 383 n. 47, 394 n. 18
areal features. *See* areal traits
areal linguistics, 4, 31–32, 47, 63–64, 66–67, 72, 114–116, 244, 248–249, 256, 330–331, 352, 427 n. 1
areal traits, 61, 119, 132, 148, 154, 427 n. 6
areal-typological approach. *See* areal linguistics
assessment approach, 93–96, 99–100
Augustine Pattern, 128, 130, 132
Aztec hieroglyphics, 9

basic vocabulary, 51, 84, 206–207, 209, 230, 259, 409 n. 28
Berkeley Pattern, 130
binary comparison, 252–253
Borax Lake Pattern, 124
borrowing, 10–13, 19, 30–31, 61–64, 67–68, 72, 114–116, 118, 123, 125, 129, 132–3, 149, 161–162, 166–168, 176, 188, 190, 206, 209–210, 213, 215, 217, 224–225, 236, 244–245, 248, 259, 408 n. 22, 408 n. 23
branch, 7–8

Bureau of American Ethnology (BAE), 46, 54–55, 57–60, 73, 77–78, 140, 385 n. 71, 386 n. 78, 387 n. 81, n. 83, 388 n. 85, 389 n. 92, 390 n. 103, nn. 110–111, 392 n. 126
Bureau of Ethnology. *See* Bureau of American Ethnology (BAE)

Carib culture area, 350
Central American linguistic area, 347
Central Californian linguistic area, 66
Central Californian structural-geographical type, 66
chance. *See* accidental similarity
Cherokee syllabary, 9, 378 n. 7
The Cherokee Phoenix, 378 n. 7
Chipewyan syllabary, 9
Classic Lowland Maya culture, 165
Clear Lake linguistic area, 336
clusters, language, 171
coastal entry theory, 104–105
Cochise Desert Culture, 137
Colombian–Central American linguistic area, 347
comparative-historical approach. *See* etymologic approach
comparative method, 50, 56–57, 65, 77, 83–84, 112, 136, 207–208, 211, 214
comparative syntax 54, 84, 164
contact languages, 10, 18–24
correspondence set. *See* sound correspondence
Coxcatlán Phase, 159
Cree syllabary, 9
creoles, 20–21, 24, 114, 141, 149–50

dental clusters, 101–102
dental evidence, 100–102
depth hypothesis, 152, 215–216, 407 n. 19
descriptive forms, descriptive formations. *See* sound symbolism
dialect, definition of, 7, 377 n. 4

diffusion, 4, 10, 13, 21, 63–67, 71–72, 81, 94, 101, 111, 114–116, 127, 148, 153, 189, 207, 224, 232, 242, 244, 248, 250, 252, 427 n. 1
distant genetic relationship, 48, 68–76, 81, 138, 206–259
Dorsey's law, 386 n. 78
Duployer shorthand, 9
dynamic chance, 230–231

Ecuadoran-Colombian subarea, 348, 350
Einverleibung. See incorporation
endangered languages, 16–17, 25 n. 25, 107
Epi-Olmec, 9, 162
ergative, ergativity, 117, 164, 176, 233, 348, 349
erroneous morphological analysis, 233–235
Eskimo syllabary, 9
etymologic approach. *See* comparative-historical approach
expressive forms, expressive formations, expressive symbolism. *See* sound symbolism

fake languages, 13–15
false reconstructions, 236
Fox syllabary, 9
functional load, 279–280

Gallina culture, 139
Geisteswissenschaft, 27, 378 n. 2
genetic unit, 4, 7, 99, 171, 195, 415 n. 73
genetics, human, 90, 100–104, 106, 410 n. 38
global etymology, 232, 409 n. 33
glottochronology, 104, 112, 123, 129, 133, 136, 139, 143, 159, 165, 167, 202, 209–210